The Moneywise Guide to North America – 2000

This unique, traveller-centred guide first appeared in 1964 as the 'Guide to the New World', and contained just 64 pages! Since then, tens of thousands of users and contributors later, it has become the most sought-after guidebook for the budget traveller who wants to see and experience all that the North American continent has to offer and do it on a shoestring!

The *Moneywise Guide* continues to be the only guidebook covering all three countries of North America in one sensible-size volume, although the emphasis is on the USA and Canada. It remains the only guide which covers not only all the usual cities and tourist areas of North America, but also those lesser-known cities, towns and communities which form natural way-points on the major travel routes.

Ideal for the traveller just passing through or staying a while, the *Moneywise Guide* will inform you, entertain you and, above all, save you money.

Where to stay—budget accommodation tested, assessed and updated by the users, checked by the editors. Small downtown hostels, economy motels, YMCAs, youth hostels, bed and breakfasts, tourist homes and how to find them on the internet.

Where not to stay— 'no-go' areas, seedy spots, and places to avoid.

Where to eat—the latest in 'mean cuisine' for those who still buy their meals with cash, not plastic.

What to see—the sights you'll want to see, from Disneyland to national parks, the things you'll want to do, throughout the continent. Updated entrance fees. Hundreds of *free* attractions.

General information—the most comprehensive 'General' section of any guide to North America. How to get there to visit or to work, what to take, what to wear. Visas, insurance and other paperwork. Immigration, people and customs. Driving, hiking and other forms of low-budget travel. Where to get further information including access to the internet.

About the authors:
Anna Crew is British but lives in Connecticut from where she directs BUNAC'S camp counsellor programme, *Summer Camp USA*. A former journalist, she is a frequent traveller across the world. **Nicholas Ludlow** is also British and based in Washington DC. An inveterate traveller throughout North America and the world at large, Nick is a freelance writer and editor and specialist in the economics of developing countries.

Margarita Barritt, who revised the Mexico section of this edition, is a freelance writer and researcher based in Washington D.C. Born in Costa Rica, she majored in tourism management and promotion at the Universidad de Regiomontana in Monterrey, Mexico.

Juliet Eckford has a degree in American Studies from Leicester University and trained as a lawyer in London. She has worked in the travel industry for a number of years and has travelled extensively throughout North America. She is now a solicitor with a firm in Yorkshire specialising in travel law.

Rebecca Pawlowski holds a degree in Spanish and Linguistics from Georgetown University. Originally from Springfield, Missouri, she now lives in the Washington, D.C. area and works a freelance travel journalist and serves as travel marketing coordinator for Prince William County, Virginia.

Regina Van Horne is from Washington DC and is studying English and Spanish Literature at George Washington University. She has travelled extensively throughout the USA, South America and Europe and spent a semester at Queen Mary and Westfield College in London.

Acknowledgements The editors thank the following for their assistance, contributions, and suggestions – Sarah Eykyn, Sarah Frampton, Philippa Howe-Ivain, Lucinda Lambton, Joan Schwartz, Elisa Segrave, Carsten Simonsen, Jacqueline Sinclair, Peter Sinclair and Daniella Whittington.

Special thanks to Dr. Alvaro Rodriquez Tirado, Mexican Minister for Cultural Affairs, Washington DC.

Last and very far from least, the editors thank the many readers who sent in comments and contributions.

The Moneywise Guide to

NORTH AMERICA

THE USA
CANADA and selected MEXICO

Editors:
Anna Crew and
Nicholas Ludlow

Research and Revision:
Margarita Barritt, Juliet Eckford,
Rebecca Pawlowski, Regina Van Horne.

2000

THE MONEYWISE GUIDE TO NORTH AMERICA
31st Edition

© Copyright BUNAC 2000

Published by BUNAC Travel Services Ltd,
16 Bowling Green Lane, London EC1R 0QH

British Library Cataloguing in Publication Data
Moneywise Guide to North America: USA,
Canada, Mexico. – 30 Rev. ed
  I. Crew, Anna   II. Ludlow, Nicholas H.
  917.04
  ISBN 0–9526872–4–0

General Editors: Anna L. Crew and Nicholas H. Ludlow.

Research and Revision: Margarita Barritt, Juliet Eckford,
Rebecca Pawlowski, Regina Van Horne.

Cover design: Randak Design Consultants Limited, Glasgow, Scotland
Design and maps: Vera Brice; Randak Design Consultants Limited.

Printed and bound in Great Britain by The Bath Press, Lower Bristol Road,
Bath BA2 3BL.

Contents

THE FUTURE OF THIS GUIDE

Quoted comments throughout the *Guide* are genuine remarks made by users over the years. Comments from present readers, the more descriptive the better, are welcome for the next edition.

For brief comments and most importantly for correcting or adding information about accommodation, fares and so on, please use the **Correction and Addition** slips at the back of the *Guide*. Hotel brochures, local bus schedules, maps and similar tidbits are gratefully received. Also welcome are longer accounts, so feel free to send in letters about your travels and new places you may discover.

In all cases, please write only on one side of each sheet of paper. Thank you for your help.

☆ ☆ ☆

North America 2000

One of the most amazing things about travelling in North America is that it invariably turns out to be so different from what you expected. Everyone thinks they have a good idea of what it is like. American technology, politics, media and entertainments daily make their mark around the world. North America is the most publicised continent on earth.

But the projected image frequently hides, both from foreigners and North Americans themselves, a largely undiscovered continent. The polyglot of peoples out of which Canada, the United States and Mexico are each differently formed can make Europe, for example, look comparatively homogeneous. Just a ride on the New York City subway is enough to tell you that.

There are huge tracts of magnificent landscapes, unsettled and hardly explored: forests, glaciers, deserts and jungles; mountains, canyons, prairies, vast lakes and seashores; orchards in Oregon, farming valleys in Vermont, pre-Columbian Indian settlements, many of them unchanged and still inhabited, in Mexico and Arizona, totem poles in British Columbia, fishing villages in Nova Scotia.

Then there are the cities, the hubs of North American life and culture: Los Angeles, an exploding star in The Far West, San Francisco riding on a sea of hills, New York, a concrete canyon, Chicago scraping the sky with the longest fingers in the world, Houston, a port and rocket centre, New Orleans blowing jazz across the Mississippi, Québec only geographically in the New World, its soul still back across the Atlantic, Vancouver, Canada's golden gateway to the Pacific, and Mexico City a brilliant mosaic of Spanish and Aztec design. In between is the 'heartland', made up thousands of small communities each with its own distinctive character and way of life.

The reality, variety and complexity of it all are more than a lifetime of sitting in front of a television set, or searching on the internet could even remotely convey to you. There is the excitement and discovery too of the instant, of the future, for in North America you feel you are reaching ahead and in the running to be where it matters at the dawn of a new century.

☆ ☆ ☆

About The Moneywise Guide

This is a Guide to most of the usual and many of the unusual places in North America and should prove of service to anyone, but most of all the moneywise traveller. North America can be an expensive continent if you let it, but its great variety offers places to eat and sleep and different ways of moving about to suit every pocket. With the help of this guide it can be a real bargain. Anyone who is happy about spending more money will easily find a $90 hotel bed and a $40 meal, in which case this guide is content with showing you the way to the Statue of Liberty or the Grand Canyon. For people really on a budget, this is also a guide to thousands of inexpensive places to rest your head, eat cheaply and well *and* to get you to the Grand Canyon on a shoestring.

In separate sections this Guide covers the USA, Canada and parts of Mexico. General introductions precede the coverage of each country. Make a point of first reading these background chapters: here you will find general information on each country, facts about visas, currency, health and other things, money-saving tips on eating, accommodation and travel. *Note that much of the information found in the US Background section will also be of value for travel to Canada and Mexico.*

Each country is then divided into regions, e.g. The Midwest, and in the case of the USA and Canada, states and provinces within each region follow *alphabetically*. There is an index at the back of the *Guide*.

Hotel and restaurant listings are the result of the first-hand experience of the *Guide*'s authors and its thousands of readers since the preceding edition. Prices quoted are usually the lowest available. However, within the same month at the same hotel, one traveller might spend more on a room than another. This is usually because the rooms were of different standards, but never be afraid to question room rates or even to bargain over them. **You should also allow for inflation when budgeting for the trip. It is therefore probably advisable to allow more for the overall cost of accommodation than the rates printed here would indicate. Similarly it should be remembered that all travel/vacation costs tend to rise each year in North America and so it is quite possible that prices will change after the *Guide* has gone to print. Apologies if this happens to you.**

Please remember that the **maps in this *Guide* are only intended to give you a rough orientation**—an artist's impression—when first arriving in the city. They are not, nor are they intended to be, fully comprehensive. If staying anywhere for any length of time, buy a good street map, though first see if you can get one free from the local Chamber of Commerce or tourist office.

Accommodation Listings Abbreviations:
S = single; D = double; T = triple; Q = quad; XP = extra person in room; Bfast = breakfast; facs = facilities; ess = essential; rec = recommended; nec = necessary.

1. USA

BACKGROUND

BEFORE YOU GO
Unless you plan to enter the USA under the *Visa Waiver Program*, before departing you must obtain an entry visa (main categories listed below). Currently citizens of Australia, France, Germany, Ireland, Italy, Japan, The Netherlands, New Zealand, Sweden, Switzerland and the UK are eligible to participate in the Waiver Program under which visitors to the US for less than 90 days can apply for entry permission on arrival. Check with your airline or travel agent about this. If not applicable to you, you will have to obtain one of the following:

Visitors (B) Visa. This allows you to remain in the US for a maximum of six months, the period to be determined on arrival by immigration officials based on how long they think your money will hold out. When you first obtain your visa abroad it may be stamped 'valid indefinitely'. This means it may be used repeatedly; but each stay is limited to the six-month maximum. You may not work on a Visitors Visa.

In Transit (C) Visa. This allows you to go from A to B via the US and to stay in the US a maximum of 29 days. It can be issued for multiple entries.

Student (F) Visa. You must pursue a full-time course of study for one year minimum at a school that is identified and approved in advance. Sometimes you have to post a money bond before entering the US. It allows you to work, but only under certain, limited, circumstances.

Temporary Workers (H) Visa. Issued only if you offer specialised skills or qualifications, and requires a written offer from your prospective employer. It's very difficult to obtain.

Exchange (J) Visa. For non-immigrant exchange visitors, J-1 visas are obtainable only through an approved, sponsoring organisation. The terms are usually very specific. J-1 participants can work, study, train, research or lecture—depending on individual programme conditions—for a specified period of time.

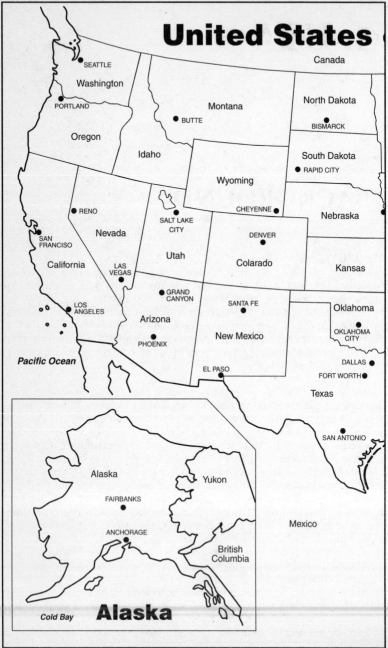

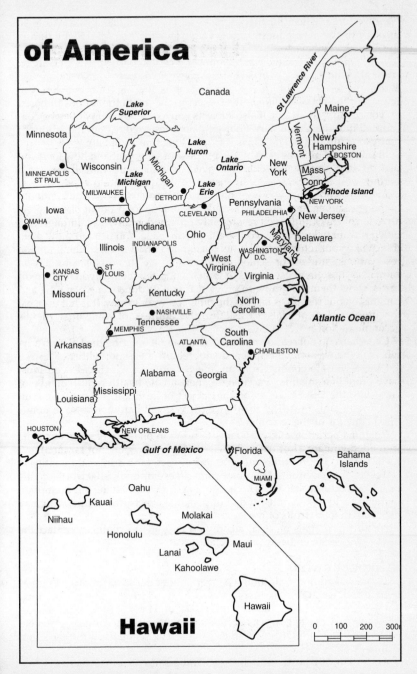

Fiancé (K) Visa. Given for the purpose of marrying a US citizen within 90 days. Unfortunately it doesn't allow you to look for 'Mr/Miss Right' during the first 89; you have to show a petition from the spouse-to-be.

(Q) Cultural Exchange Visa. A programme for certain participants who are on cultural exchanges, e.g. working at Disneyworld or Epcot Centre.

Permanent Resident Visa. (Green Card.) This is the Big One that lets you remain in the US *ad infinitum*. It's subject to the quota limitations imposed on your country of origin. It also subjects you to the possibility of being conscripted into the US military, an eventuality designed to cool the ardour of many a would-be (male) citizen. It takes a long time to obtain.

Immigration officials ask you the purpose of your visit and how long you plan to stay. You have probably arrived on a pleasure visit. If your visa permits you to work, say so. In answer to the question How long do you plan to stay? note that you need not possess X dollars per day or X amount of money. Rather, immigration officials are looking for proof of planning. As a reader of this Guide, you're probably on a budget anyway. Immigration officials want to know how you're going to manage. You need to show them things like your return ticket home; rail, air and bus passes; accommodation reservations; student or senior identification; etc. If you plan to stay in campsites, hostels, guest houses or with friends, tell them. If you have credit cards, show them. Anything to prove that you've done some planning and can make your resources last for the time you wish to stay. It is not unusual for immigration officials to ask for the address of your first night's accommodation.

Canadians do not require a visa (to visit), and if entering the US from anywhere in the western hemisphere do not require a passport either.

Unless you are coming from an infected area, in which case you must have proof of a smallpox vaccination, there are no **health requirements** for entry into the US. However, on the subject of health, it is most important that you organise medical **insurance** for yourself before you leave home. (See below for further comment.)

Customs permit foreign residents to bring in one litre of spirits or wine (provided you are 21 or over), 200 cigarettes or 50 cigars (not Havana) or 2 kg of tobacco or proportionate amounts of each (an additional quantity of 100 cigars may be brought in under your gift exemption), $100 worth of gifts provided you stay at least 72 hours and have not claimed the gift exemption in the previous six months, and your personal effects free of duty. You may not bring in food, fruits or meats.

For further details on visa, health and customs regulations, contact the nearest American embassy or consulate.

TEMPORARY WORK

This refers to summer vacation type work under the auspices of a J-1 visa as opposed to the more career-type of position in which one might work for a limited period of time in the USA under, say, an H visa. J programmes cover a great variety of categories: everything from hospital interns to counsellors working with children on summer camps. The regulations for each programme vary.

In Britain, BUNAC (the British Universities North America Club) organises educational work travel exchange programmes to the United States and Canada. The *Work America* programme is for full-time students studying at a British university or college, and provides the student with a work permit for the duration of the summer. Participants can take any job other than that of camp counselling. BUNAC also runs an 18-month J-I intern programme, *OPT USA* (Overseas Practical Training).

In Australia and New Zealand, contact International Exchange Programs, IEP, for their equivalent *Work USA* winter (northern hemisphere) programme.

If you are interested in working with children on an American summer camp, then the *Summer Camp USA* programme run by BUNAC may be for you. BUNAC will place you as a counsellor on a camp and loan you the round-trip fare across the Atlantic. All you pay to register on the programme is £59. You also have to pay for insurance once you get a definite place. You repay the loan for your airfare, etc. out of your salary and are still left with about $540-$600 pocket money at the end of camp. In Australia and New Zealand contact IEP for details on *Summer Camp USA*.

For details on these programmes contact: BUNAC, 16 Bowling Green Lane, London EC1R 0QH. Tel: (020) 7251 3472. IEP, 196 Albert Rd, South Melbourne, Victoria 3205. Tel:(03) 9690-5890. In New Zealand: IEP, PO Box 1786, Shortland St, Auckland. Tel: (09) 366-6255.

Doubtless many people do work in 'underground jobs' such as in casual labour, fruit harvesting, farm work, restaurant work etc., but if you are contemplating this you should be aware of the risks involved. The penalties you would be likely to incur include deportation, with the knowledge that you would have to face an extremely uphill task should you ever want to return to America again. You should also be aware that the terms of the recent Immigration Act mean that an employer hiring an illegal alien faces stiff penalties if caught. This of course acts as a deterrent should an employer be contemplating the possibility and lessens the chances of employment for someone without a work visa.

GETTING THERE

This Guide is used by readers all over the world, and the best and least expensive way to reach the United States will vary according to where you're starting out. Check advertisements, ask friends and travel agents— including the 'bucket shop' variety. Be alert. Fares are constantly changing.

For the budget traveller, the choices are basically: consolidated fares, charter, economy, APEX, inclusive package and, possibly, standby. If you are travelling to North America from Britain a consolidated or group charter fare will probably be cheapest. Watch the press for ads or ask a travel agent about such fares. Of the scheduled airlines Continental Airlines, flying from Gatwick, Manchester and Glasgow to Newark, NJ (New York), and Virgin Atlantic flying from Heathrow to JFK and Newark Airports, offer fares from about £250 to £700 return plus tax, depending on when you travel and when you book. Virgin also fly to Boston, Washington DC, Miami, Chicago and Orlando, FL, and to Los Angeles and San Francisco on the west coast. Continental can connect the traveller on to various US cities (and Mexico) through their domestic network from Newark.

However, don't overlook carriers like British Airways, United, US Airways, Delta and American Airlines. They will all sometimes have better deals and are worth investigating. Some also offer regional departures and it may also be less expensive to fly via Paris or Amsterdam (for example).

Economy fares are pretty expensive so if you're willing to accept a few restrictions you can save a lot of money on other types of fare.

Consolidated fares are offered by companies which buy seats in bulk from the airlines. However these fares often come with a lot of restrictions so check first!

APEX (Advance Purchase Excursion) tickets are sold by the scheduled airlines themselves and must be purchased at least 21 days before departure. At the time of purchase you must fix your date of departure and return; if you later decide to change either of these dates you'll have to pay a penalty charge.

Advanced Booking Charters (ABCs) have roughly the same restrictions as APEX tickets and you may find yourself either travelling on a plane wholly chartered by the travel operator or else on a scheduled airline from whom the operator will have bought a block of seats at a special charter rate. For the tourist or budget traveller this is probably the most popular method of getting to America. From Britain expect to pay about the same or a little less than the fares quoted above for Virgin and Continental.

It may be possible to get yourself hired as a *courier* for a one-off flight. Using this method you pay a reduced price on a scheduled flight and in return you carry with you and deliver a package at the other end. Check directly with the many courier operations that make their living shipping business packages back and forth across the Atlantic.

Inclusive packages abound, offering considerable flexibility. Some, however, treat America as a substitute for two weeks on the Costa del Sol— there was never much excuse for fish and chips at Torremolinos when there was all of Spain to see, and there is even less excuse for two weeks of fish and chips in Miami when an entire continent awaits you.

Fly-drive packages, including air fare, unlimited mileage car and accommodation vouchers are a good bet, especially if you're travelling as a family or with friends. Prices vary according to size of car, standard of accommodation and the number of people travelling together.

At the same time that you consider how to get to North America, you should be considering how to travel around once there. Certain discounts and travel passes may only be available to non-residents purchasing their tickets abroad. Also, when you buy your tickets outside the US you save the sales tax.

CLIMATE

Remember that you are not travelling over a country but across a vast continent and that the climate varies accordingly. Consider that the distance from New York to Miami is equivalent to that from London to Tangier, and that New York and Los Angeles are as distant from each other as London and Baghdad, and you get a good idea of what this can mean.

Indoors, these differences are minimised by central heating and air conditioning, but outside, winters can be very cold in Washington DC (for instance) and even further south, and summers extremely hot almost everywhere.

Temperatures approaching 90°F (32°C) day after day, sometimes accompanied by a suffocating humidity, are not unusual in the summer. New York, Washington DC, New Orleans and the Deep South can be particularly unpleasant. As early as September, however, nights can be cool everywhere, and freezing in mountainous areas.

Some generalisations on climatic regions:

New England, the Northeast, Mid-Atlantic and Midwest. Cold in the winter, often humid in the summer and as hot as anywhere else in America including Florida and southern California.

The Southwest. Warm to hot throughout the year, and nearly always dry.

The Pacific States. Washington, Oregon and northern California have moderate climates: not too cold in the winter—though often wet, not too hot in the summer. San Francisco is often bathed in summer afternoon fogs. Southern California is warm to hot the year round, and nearly always dry.

The South. Hot with thunderstorm activity in summer, mild in winter though agreeably warm in Florida. Summer is also the hurricane season in the Southeast.

The Mountains. In summer, days are warm but nights can be cold. Very cold throughout the winter.

The Deserts. Very hot and dry throughout the year, but can be cold at night.

WHAT TO TAKE AND HOW TO TAKE IT

Take as little as possible, choose clothes for their use in a variety of situations and when you have made your final selection, halve it!

It is always a nuisance to have too much, and anyway, if necessary, you can purchase what you need in America. The present exchange rate means that American stores offer many shopping bargains for visitors. In particular, items like jeans, shirts, T-shirts and casual clothes are good buys in the US. If you hunt around you can usually find something on sale.

Laundromats are often open 24 hours a day. The cost of a wash is usually $1.50 (in quarters); drying machines usually take 25¢—just keep feeding in the quarters, total per load is about $1.25.

Whatever luggage you take, make sure it's easy to handle. Getting on and off buses and trains, even just changing planes, can be an ordeal if your bags are too heavy or too many. The best solution is to take one hold-all, be it a suitcase or a backpack, and then a smaller bag which you can sling from your shoulder. When you have to check in your hold-all at the airport or bus station, you must keep all your documents, travellers' cheques and your paperback novel safely and conveniently by your side. It is also a good idea to keep a change of clothing in your shoulder bag in case your suitcase/backpack gets lost by an airline or bus company or your flight is delayed.

For extra security many travellers also wear a neck (or belt) wallet/pouch for passport, cash, travellers' cheques and other valuables. It is also a good idea to photocopy your passport and other important documents and keep the copies SEPARATE from the originals. Should you lose your passport you should immediately contact your nearest national consulate (British consulates are in Atlanta, Boston, Chicago, Houston, Los Angeles, New York, San Francisco, and Washington DC).

City temperatures (in Fahrenheit)		Jan-Feb	Mar-Apr	May-June	Jul-Aug	Sep-Oct	Nov-Dec
CHICAGO	Low	20°	35°	56°	67°	53°	28°
	High	34	51	74	83	69	42
	Average	27	43	65	75	61	35
DENVER	Low	18	29	58	43	43	22
	High	46	57	88	73	73	50
	Average	32	43	73	58	58	36
HONOLULU	Low	68	69	72	74	73	69
	High	74	75	80	84	83	79
	Average	71	72	76	79	78	74
HOUSTON	Low	48	58	71	75	67	50
	High	64	74	89	93	87	68
	Average	56	66	80	84	77	59
LAS VEGAS	Low	35	47	64	76	61	47
	High	57	73	84	102	87	61
	Average	46	60	79	89	74	54
LOS ANGELES	Low	46	50	57	62	59	49
	High	64	66	71	76	75	69
	Average	55	58	64	69	67	59
MIAMI	Low	59	64	72	75	73	61
	High	77	82	88	89	87	79
	Average	68	73	80	82	80	70
NEW ORLEANS	Low	49	59	71	76	68	52
	High	67	75	87	92	84	68
	Average	58	67	79	84	77	60
NEW YORK	Low	26	38	58	68	54	34
	High	40	54	76	84	72	44
	Average	33	46	67	76	63	39
SAN FRANCISCO	Low	43	46	51	54	52	45
	High	57	64	65	72	72	61
	Average	50	55	58	63	62	53
ST LOUIS	Low	24	38	58	67	52	30
	High	42	60	80	89	76	50
	Average	33	49	69	78	64	40
SEATTLE	Low	24	39	47	54	47	37
	High	46	55	69	76	65	49
	Average	35	47	58	65	56	43
WASHINGTON DC	Low	29	41	61	68	56	35
	High	45	61	79	86	74	51
	Average	37	51	70	77	65	43

Some tips: at bus stations in particular, make absolutely certain that your bag is going on your bus and that you get a check-in ticket for it. You would be amazed at the number of times bag and body go off in different directions. And if you're a backpacker just arrived in a big city, you can usually leave your pack at one of the museums for free and then skip off to look for a room or do a little sightseeing unencumbered.

TIME ZONES

The continental US is divided into four time zones, Eastern Standard Time, Central Standard Time, Mountain Standard Time and Pacific Standard Time. Exact zone boundaries are shown on most road maps.

Noon EST = 11 am CST = 10 am MST = 9 am PST. Standard time in Hawaii is two hours earlier than PST, i.e. 9 am PST = 7 am HST. Daylight Saving Time occurs widely though not universally throughout the United States; from the end of April to the end of October clocks are put forward one hour. Carefully check air, rail and bus schedules in advance.

THE AMERICAN PEOPLE

Keeping in mind the vastness of the United States and the knowledge that the area you are visiting covers an entire continent, it becomes a little easier to appreciate the diversity of the land and its people. America is an incredibly cosmopolitan society. Glance at the names in the telephone book of almost any town in America for evidence of this. Every nationality on earth, speaking scores of the world's languages, every creed, every race is represented here.

The only true native peoples of the USA, of course, are the Indians, who are thought to have arrived in America by way of the Bering Strait from Asia several thousands of years before the Pilgrim Fathers set foot in Massachusetts. Since the time of the European migration the lot of the 'Native American' has not been a happy one. Harried and hounded by the westward-moving white man, Native Americans were eventually pushed into reservations, inevitably on the poorest and most infertile land around. In more recent times the position of the Native American has improved a little but there is still a long, long way to go. Having Indian blood is a matter of fierce pride and many Indians still harbour great resentment towards the white man. Be aware of this should you visit a reservation and be respectful towards the people and their laws and customs.

America may be cosmopolitan, but it's not yet a full melting pot. National groups tend to stick together—you will see bumper stickers reading 'Irish-American', 'Proud to be Polish' for instance. At the top of the social heap are still the WASPS (White Anglo-Saxon Protestants) represented by the British, Germans and Scandinavians, and followed by the Irish and other European groups. Next come Asians, who are most visible in California, then Blacks and Hispanics, the fastest-growing group in America. It is estimated that Hispanics will soon outnumber the Black-American population and become the largest minority group. In fact, the Census Bureau has predicted that by 2050 whites will comprise only 50% of the population. As immigration continues and fortunes around the world turn this way or that, so will American society continue to evolve in order to cope with new national groupings and social trends.

Keeping up with the Presidential Election 2000

If you're travelling to the US in the summer of 2000, this is a prime opportunity for you to witness the American electoral process at work. In the months leading up to the November election the parties hold a primary or caucus in each state. Many states this year have moved the dates of their primaries forward in order to have greater influence on the choice of a nominee. So by the summer months both parties will probably already have a good idea of who will win the nomination at their conventions, but there will still be plenty of election action to witness. Alabama, New Jersey, South Dakota, Montana, and New Mexico will all hold their primaries in June, and both conventions will take place during the summer.

The Republican National Convention will be held in Philadelphia, from July 29-Aug 4, and the Democratic National Convention will take place in Los Angeles, from Aug 14-17.

Likely candidates for the Democratic nomination are Vice President Al Gore or NJ Senator Bill Bradley. For the Republican nomination Texas governor George W. Bush, magazine tycoon Steve Forbes, Arizona Senator John McCain, and political commentator Pat Buchanan have all thrown their hats in the ring. Property developer Donald Trump has also indicated his intention to run. For up-to-date election news, check out *www.2000Vote.com*.

This constantly changing society, the moving frontier, is perhaps one of the roots of the violence present in American society. Where a nation-wide sense of tradition is scarce, where the future is always being built anew, there is often a sense of rootlessness and self-doubt in which violence, crime, drug or alcohol dependency, and religious, political or social fads can easily flourish. There is a great deal of poverty in the land of opportunity, contrasting sharply with the material splendours of those who have in abundance.

That is the down side. On the brighter side, American people are hospitable, kind and generous. Even the newest immigrants take great pride in their new land. Everywhere there is a flag flying, on private homes as well as on public buildings; allegiance to America is constantly recited and renewed. The USA remains on the whole an optimistic land, still reaching towards the future, trying to stay ahead, and proud of its role in the world. Americans tend to be demanding, enthusiastic; living hard, playing hard; conforming, yet individualistic; still expecting the best of everything.

MEETING PEOPLE

Americans are naturally outgoing and hospitable, more so when they detect a foreign accent. Your novelty value is particularly enhanced outside of the big cities, where curiosity and interest is generated amongst locals as soon as you open your mouth. Don't be surprised if you are invited to dinner, taken places and shown round the local sights. Staying at a private bed and breakfast is a prime way to mingle with Americans—the services you get and the friendliness you'll receive go far beyond the monetary exchange.

State fairs and other such special events—rodeos, clambakes, New England autumn fairs, etc.—are an essential slice of the American pie and another way of meeting people informally.

If you want a more organised approach for meeting Americans, we suggest a number of organisations within our listings and also the following (most of which require making advance arrangements):

1. Contact the **National Council for International Visitors** (NCIV), 1420 K St NW, Suite 800, Washington DC 20005, (202) 842-1414. Ask for their *Membership Directory*, a complete rundown of local organisations willing to extend hospitality.
2. Enquire at the local **Chambers of Commerce** and Visitors Bureaux about their 'Visit a local family' programmes, if any. Some of them are very active in this area. Several also have volunteer language banks, if you're having difficulty communicating.
3. **Servas**. An organisation of approved hosts and travellers arranging homestays. Charges membership fee of $65 a year then requires a refundable deposit of $25 for 1-5 host lists. Guests then make their own contacts. US Servas, Inc., 11 John St, Rm 407, New York, NY 10038, (212) 267-0252.

HEALTH AND WELFARE
There is no free or subsidised national health service in the United States for anyone under retirement age. For most people, therefore, medical, dental and hospital services have to be paid for and they can be expensive. However, the emergency room of any public hospital provides medical care to anyone who walks in the door (and is prepared for a long wait), and will often only charge those who have insurance or are otherwise able to pay, the government reimbursing them for the rest.

The 'emergency' doesn't have to be a car crash or the like—it can be a high fever or stomach pains, anything of a reasonably acute nature or which you feel needs immediate attention. Teaching hospitals—medical and dental—are other possible sources of free, or cheaper, treatment. Women may find help through the local women's centre.

Nevertheless, it is essential to be insured (ask your travel agent), and it's a good idea to get a dental check-up before going. If you wear glasses or contact lenses take spares, or at least prescriptions.

MONEY
Dollars and cents are of course the basic units of American money. The back of all denominations of dollar bills are green (hence 'greenbacks'). The commonly used coins are: one cent (penny), five cents (nickel), 10 cents (dime), and 25 cents (quarter). 50¢ pieces (half dollars) are increasing in usage, while there has been talk of phasing out the penny—that's inflation for you. 'Always carry plenty of quarters when travelling. Very useful for phones, soda machines, laundry machines, etc.'

Bear in mind that since 1996 there are new, counterfeit-proof notes for $100, $50 and $20, though the old notes are still in circulation. The new dollar coin will enter circulation in 2000.

There is generally no problem using US dollars in Canada, albeit with a loss on the exchange rate; but this is never possible vice versa. It is difficult to change Canadian dollar travellers' cheques into American cash.

It's always useful to carry small change for things like exact-fare buses, but do not carry large sums of cash. Instead keep the bulk of your money in travellers' cheques which can be purchased both in the US and abroad and should be in US dollar denominations. The best known cheques are those of American Express, so you will have the least difficulty cashing these, even in out of the way places. (AMEX card holders may have mail sent to American Express offices—ask for a complete list on (800) 528-4800). Thomas Cook travellers' cheques are also acceptable, especially as lost ones can be reclaimed at some Hertz Car Rental desks. Dollar denomination cheques can be used like regular money. There's no need to cash them at a bank: use them instead to pay for meals, supermarket purchases or whatever. Ten or 20 dollar cheques are accepted like this almost always and you'll be given change just as though you'd presented the cashier with dollar bills. Be prepared to show ID when you cash your cheques.

Credit cards can be even more valuable than travellers' cheques as they are often used to guarantee room reservations over the phone and are accepted in lieu of a deposit when renting a car—indeed *without* a credit card you may be considered so untrustworthy that not only a deposit but your passport will be held as security too. Or, you may not be able to rent at all without a credit card. The major credit cards are VISA, MasterCard and Access (each with the other's symbol on the reverse), Diners Club and American Express. If you hold a bank card (e.g. VISA), it could well be worthwhile to increase your credit limit for travel purposes—you should ask your bank manager. If you have a Switch or Delta card you can use it to withdraw cash from ATMs (cashpoints). There is a small surcharge but convenience makes up for it - check with your bank to make sure your card will work abroad.

Banks. Bank hours are usually 9am—3pm, Mon-Fri, although some branches, especially in big cities, have a longer day. Many banks stay open until 6pm on Fridays and some are open limited hours on Saturdays.

If you ever receive a cheque, it is important to cash it in the same area— i.e. at a branch of the bank on which it is drawn. Without a bank account to pay into, it will be impossible to cash it elsewhere—the American banking system is not as integrated as elsewhere in the world. Some form of photo-identification (e.g. passport) is necessary when cashing a personal or company cheque.

Tax. There is usually a three to nine percent sales tax on most items over 20¢ and meals over $1. This is never included in the stated price and varies from place to place according to whether you are being charged state or city sales tax. There is also a 'bed tax' in most cities that ranges from five to ten percent on hotel rooms. 'Bed tax' does not generally apply to bed and breakfast places. *Note that unless stated, accommodation rates in this Guide do not include tax*.

Tipping. It is customary in the US to tip the following: taxi drivers, waiters, chamber maids, hotel bellboys, airport luggage porters. Ten to 15 percent is the accepted amount, although most waiters, especially in cities, will expect

15-20 percent. Some restaurants do include service in the menu price so make sure you don't tip them twice.

COMMUNICATIONS

Mail. Post offices are infrequent, but since the alternative is a commercial stamp machine that in the spirit of free enterprise sells stamps at a considerable profit, it is advisable to stock up at post offices when you can. As of going to press, first class letters within the US are 33¢; the air mail rate for post cards to Europe is 55¢, aerogrammes 60¢, air mail letters up to 0.5oz cost 60¢, up to 1 oz. cost $1.00.

Mail within the US travels at a snail's pace: allow a week coast to coast or to Canada, and four days for any distance more than around the corner. For two-day (no guarantees!) delivery use Priority Mail, $3.20. For guaranteed overnight delivery you have to use Express Mail which has a minimum rate of $11.75! You must always include the ZIP code on a US address. To mail a letter without a ZIP code is to invite considerable delay if not everlasting loss!

It is possible to have mail sent General Delivery (Poste Restante) for collection (also to American Express offices if you use their travellers' cheques). The post office will usually keep it for 10 days before returning it to sender.

American post offices deal *only* with mail.

Telephone. Phones in North America are easy to use. All numbers have an area code (3 digits), an exchange code (3 digits) and a number (4 digits). You do not dial the area code if you are within that dialling area (e.g. omit the 202 when calling Washington DC numbers from within Washington). For directory enquiries call 555-1212 wherever you are and that will get you through to information for that state; if you want a number in another state, use that state's area code before you dial. To call New York information from DC you would dial (212) 555-1212. For information on (800) numbers call 1 (800) 555-1212. A reverse charges call is called a collect call.

When calling from pay phones in most areas of North America, you dial the whole number preceded by 1 (if you have enough coins to pay for the call), or by 0 (zero, not the O in MNO) if you are making a collect call. Before dialling, you insert the minimum amount of money as instructed on the pay phone (e.g. 35¢). When you have dialled the complete number, the operator will come on the line and tell you how much to put in (if you dialled 1 first). If you dialled 0 first, a recorded message may ask you to 'please dial your card number or zero for an operator now'. Press 0, wait, and the operator will ask how he/she can help you. You then say: 'I'd like to make a collect call, please. My name is...'

Whenever the operator answers, your money is refunded to you. Don't forget to take it out of the machine! You may find that you are being spoken to by a recording which says something like 'Deposit 40 cents, please'. Obey the voice...

If calling at peak time, you may need to have ready up to $3.50 a minute in 25¢, 10¢ and 5¢ coins. The cheapest time to make a long distance call is between 11pm and 8am. Between 5pm and 11pm and at weekends is the next cheapest time; 8am-5pm is the most expensive time. Remember to allow for time zone differences when phoning.

If making calls from your hotel, remember that it is cheaper to use the phone in the hotel lobby rather than the one in your bedroom. It's always cheaper to dial direct and not through the operator. In many areas local calls are free from private phones. If you make a pay call from a private phone you can get the operator to tell you how much the call cost.

Look for pay phones in drug stores, gas stations, highway rest areas, in transport terminals and along the street. Phone cards are now more readily available in North America. However, the US-style phone cards work somewhat differently to those available, for example, in the UK. They use a more complicated electronic system and are generally offered initially in $10 or $20 units but with the ability to 'top up' the card once the initial investment runs out. BUNAC members get the special *Telekey Card* which also offers voice messaging. You will also encounter other phone cards, all offering slightly different packages.

ELECTRICITY

Voltage is 110-115V, 60 cycles AC. American plugs have two flat pins. Try to get an adapter before you go. Even if you have a dual voltage appliance you will still need an adapter. You will not be able to use your home hairdryer, shaver or whatever, unless it is dual voltage.

SHOPPING

Major stores in out of town malls often have long opening hours, e.g. from 9 am or 10 am to 9 pm or 10 pm—on one, several or even all days of the week. Smaller shops in cities are sometimes open all night: you should have no trouble getting a meal or a drink, or shopping for food and other basics, 24 hours a day—though you'll pay more for the privilege.

Large American supermarkets and department stores can make their foreign equivalents look like they're suffering from war-time rationing. The variety of goods on offer—and at relatively low prices—is amazing. The American consumer is a keen and well practised shopper with an eye for a bargain, seldom in fact, buying anything that's not on sale. Almost every town has at least one shopping mall on the outskirts where you can observe the credit card culture in action and browse to your heart's content from about 10 am to 9 pm.

Good buys in the US include cameras, CDs, electronic goods, sound equipment, denims, winter clothes, and casual clothes, in particular western gear. Just how good a bargain will of course depend upon the exchange rate at the time of your visit. Even if it is not in your favour, if you do as all Americans do and shop only when the item you want is on sale, you will still be able to net some bargains.

WEIGHTS AND MEASURES

The US still uses feet and miles, pounds and gallons, Fahrenheit instead of Centigrade/Celsius, and it appears as though it will for some time to come. The only things that have gone metric are liquor and wine bottles, some gasoline pumps and the National Park Service. A conversion table is to be found in the Appendix.

DRINKING

Although nation-wide Prohibition ended in the US in 1933, you will still find places in which you cannot get a drink at all, or where you cannot drink while standing, or must bring your own bottle—one anomaly after another. This is because each state decides whether it will be 'dry' or 'wet', and sometimes this is left to counties on an optional basis. You may notice some people on the street drinking out of paper bags. This is because in many cities it is illegal to *visibly* drink alcoholic beverages in public.

American beer (which as a legacy of Prohibition has a relatively low alcohol content) is of the lager variety—Knickerbocker, Miller, Schaeffer, Budweiser, Pabst. Be sure to ask for micro-brewery beers, now standard fare at most bars and restaurants, and tending to eclipse the old standards. There are now scores of interesting micro-brews from honey-brown ale to raspberry wheat.

America is the home of the cocktail. Spirit concoctions are excellent and a major part of American ingenuity is devoted to thinking up new ones—and extraordinary names for them! Bars never close before midnight and sometimes stay open till 4 am, or even 23 hours a day. Try to sample local wines. New York and California turn out the best although Washington State and Michigan also produce a few decent varieties. Visit a winery in these states too.

The minimum drinking age is now 21 in every state in the US. A strong anti-drink climate of opinion exists in the US at present and under-age drinking rules are strictly enforced. Someone under 21 may not be able to drink alcohol at all during their stay in the USA. You will need to carry photo ID when ordering a drink or buying liquor in a store just in case you are asked—even if you think you look much older than 21! Student cards etc. are generally not acceptable as ID and even a passport is sometimes not enough. You can, however, obtain a US ID with your photo on it from any DMV (Department of Motor Vehicles) office (where drivers licences are issued). Check *Yellow Pages* for location.

TOBACCO

Cigarettes are about $2.50 for a pack of 20, five big cigars for about the same price. Pipe tobacco is heavily flavoured—imported brands are better and not much more expensive. Unless you learnt to chew tobacco at the same time as you were breast-fed, forget it. Tobacco addicts should stock up on cartons at supermarkets for substantial savings.

Smoking is increasingly frowned upon and many restaurants (even McDonald's) and other public places now have 'non-smoking' sections. In New York City and California, the smoking in restaurants ban is total. Smoking is banned in all government buildings; post offices, libraries, subway stations, etc. and on all public transport, including Amtrak and Greyhound. Banks, cinemas and theatres also ban the weed and it is banned on all US internal flights except those of more than 6 hours duration.

DRUGS

A great deal has been written about the 'drug culture' of the US. Most of it is absolutely true. The best advice is the obvious— stay away from it. Reject all advances made to you on the street, in bus terminals, airports, wherever. It is illegal to possess or sell narcotics. Penalties can be severe.

PUBLIC HOLIDAYS
New Year's Day (1 January)
Martin Luther King Jr's Birthday (15 January)
Presidents Day (third Monday in February)
Memorial Day (last Monday in May)
Independence Day (4 July)
Labor Day (first Monday in September)
Columbus Day (second Monday in October)
Veterans' Day (11 November)
Thanksgiving (fourth Thursday in November)
Christmas (25 December)

Though many smaller shops and almost all businesses close on public holidays, many of the biggest stores and multiples will make a point of being open—often offering sales. Outside of cities, supermarkets are often open during at least part of a public holiday. On days of all primary and general elections all bars are closed. There are a few other public holidays that are not nation-wide, e.g. Patriots Day in Massachusetts and Maine. Jewish New Year brings New York to a standstill.

The summer tourism and recreational season extends from Memorial Day to Labor Day. After Labor Day you can expect some hours or days of opening to be reduced, or some attractions to be closed altogether. The same may apply to related transport services. Unless otherwise specified, times and days of openings in this guide refer to the summer season. Outside this period, you should phone in advance.

INFORMATION
A multitude of resources exists in the US both to make your stay more informed and enjoyable and to help you out if you encounter problems. Among the most useful:

1. *Libraries.* One in every town, often open late hours and on weekends, libraries and librarians are a traveller's best friend. Besides reference works, atlases, and local guidebooks, they offer transit schedules, local and other newspapers, magazines, free community newspapers, phone books, and brochures on helpful organisations. Librarians are unfailingly kind about answering questions and making phone enquiries for you. They also have toilets, comfy chairs and often a social calendar of free evening events.
2. *Traveler's Aid.* Their kiosks are found at bus, train and plane terminals across the country—invaluable for cheap lodging and other suggestions, helpful with free maps and brochures, and solid support if your trip runs into a snag (whether it's a medical, financial or practical problem).
3. *Chambers of Commerce and Visitors Bureaux.* Found almost everywhere, with lots of free materials, maps (although you usually have to purchase the really good maps) and advice. Big-city offices have multilingual staff, are open longer hours and sometimes weekends. Smaller places are open 9am-5pm, Monday to Friday; many have recorded events messages for local activities when they are closed. A major drawback is that they are

E-mail Access in North America

The Internet is making it easier and easier to communicate with people back home while you're abroad. If you have an e-mail account there are a couple of ways to check your mail from any computer with Internet access. Most computers have Telnet, which gives you access to your university e-mail account. If Telnet is not available or doesn't work with your e-mail address, *www.mailstart.com* works in basically the same way. Just enter your e-mail address and your password and it allows you to receive and send mail from your own account. Both Telnet and *www.mailstart.com* tend to be slow, but they're both faster than regular mail.

Another option is opening a web-based e-mail account. Several websites offer free e-mail services (paid for by advertising) and you can set up an account in a matter of seconds. Yahoo! has e-mail (go to *www.yahoo.com* and click on 'check e-mail.'), as does Hotmail (*www.hotmail.com*). You can also check your other e-mail accounts through Hotmail. The advantage to web-based e-mail is that you can check it anywhere you have access to the Internet, and it's not as slow (and frustrating!) as Telnet or *www.mailstart.com*.

Once you have your e-mail account set up you need a computer with Internet access. In most big cities in the US and Canada there are cybercafes where you can use the Internet for an hourly or per minute rate. We've listed cybercafes in all the major cities, but this is a new, volatile industry and many cybercafes are short-lived. When possible, call ahead to make sure the cybercafe is still in business. Two websites, *www.cyber-cafe.com* and *http://cybercaptive.com* list cybercafes throughout the world and are updated regularly. Many AYH youth hostels have computers available for their guests, but the rates tend to be high. Another place to consider is the public library. Most city libraries have computers available for Internet access. Some require you to have a library card, but many do not. In most libraries, there is a limited number of computers and users have a time limit, but access is free of charge. In cities that do not require you to have a library card, we list public library information under Internet Access.

primarily member organisations; few of them will even recognise much less recommend non-member hotels, restaurants, etc. That means that you won't hear much about low-budget places from them and some bureaux will even try to warn you off such places. Don't buy it. If driving, look out for state highway 'welcome stations'. They are a good source of free maps and local information and often provide free juice or coffee.

4. Many communities have a *volunteer clearinghouse phone service* designed to answer a variety of needs, from real emergencies to simple orientation. Usually listed in both the white and yellow pages of the phone book, and variously called Hotline, Helpline, Crisis Center, People's Switchboard, Community Switchboard, We Care, or some such. Their well-trained volunteers can steer you to the resources available in the community—free, cheap and not-so-cheap.

5. *Women's Centres and Senior Centres* provide the same kind of clearinghouse info and friendly support on a walk-in basis; you will find them in

nearly every US town, listed in the phone book. The centres also make excellent places to meet people, and often sponsor a range of free and interesting activities. You might also try the free clinics, which still exist in a number of big cities. Many of them operate hotlines, referral services, crash pad recommendations and other services besides free health care.

6. *Maps.* Besides the free ones from visitor centres, state tourism offices and so forth, you may be interested in speciality maps, such as Greyhound's excellent 'United States of Greyhound', a monster which shows all of the US and Canadian routes clearly marked, plus major parks and monuments. Free.

7. *The Internet.* There are two excellent Internet sites designed specifically for hostellers. *The Internet Guide To Hostelling* is an electronic magazine which offers a mountain of help to travellers. It has a world-wide hostel guide, tips and tales from other budget travellers, info on special events and discounts and the answers to the 'most frequently asked questions about hostelling'. The guide can be accessed at *www.hostels.com*. For information on how to access the guide using other methods contact The Editor, Pacific Tradewinds Hostel, 680 Sacramento St, San Francisco, CA 94111 (415) 433-7970. Email: hostelseditor@worldawaits.com.

A second useful site for budget travellers is the Hostelling International-American Youth Hostels web page, which features information on HI-AYH hostels throughout America and provides links to other helpful travel organisations. The address is *www.hiayh.org.*

Most states and cities have their own websites with helpful tourist information, as do many museums, parks, tour organisations, and bus and rail companies. We have listed helpful addresses throughout the book.

EMERGENCIES/SAFETY

Many towns and cities have '911' as the emergency telephone number—for police, fire, ambulance. Otherwise you would dial '0' for operator. The emergency number is always indicated on public telephones.

Yes, the USA can be a dangerous place, but then so can your own home town if you happen to be in the wrong place at the wrong time. In other words, chance or fate alone may determine what may or may not happen to you. This is not to say that you should not take reasonable, sensible, standard precautions to protect your safety.

Don't wander into parks or dark alleys alone or late at night; carry your valuables in a neck or waist pouch; don't leave your belongings unattended; stay in what you know to be safe areas of towns and cities—if it feels 'wrong', get out; don't hitchhike or drive alone; and stay alert to what is happening around you. Remember, although crime rates are high, most Americans *never* encounter crime in their daily lives.

Listed below are a few helplines and hotlines should you or anyone travelling with you run into difficulties. The first thing to remember is always consult your local telephone directory. Many states have their own 'information lines' or INR numbers (Info 'n' Referral). These lines may help you with anything from suicide prevention to health information, providing you with facts and referrals for counselling and support where needed.

The previously mentioned **Traveler's Aid** can be found at major bus and rail stations and airports and will help in emergency situations. Traveler's Aid can also be found nation-wide (check Yellow Pages) and specialise in helping people who are out-of-state get back to where they need to be.

National Aids Hotline, (800) 342-AIDS, 24hrs. Answers questions and gives out information as well as arranging counselling where needed. (See also 'Health Agencies' in Yellow Pages.)

(800) ALCOHOL, (800) 252-6465, 24 hrs. Provides referral in reference to drugs or alcohol.

National Drug Hotline, (800) 662-4357, daytime. Information on drug or alcohol abuse and related issues. Referrals to local drug treatment or counselling centres.

Pregnancy Hotline, (800) 848-5683, 24hrs. Information for pregnant (or suspecting) women, counselling etc. Or (800) 238-4269, free pregnancy testing and counselling.

THE GREAT OUTDOORS

One of the most exciting things about North America is the great tracts of unspoilt land. The most superlative examples have usually been specially preserved as national parks. There are 41 national parks in the United States, all of which offer the visitor beautiful scenery; everything from fantastic seascapes, deep canyons, spectacular volcanoes, to pure lakes and craggy mountains. Many parks are somewhat off the beaten track and although the roadways in all are excellent, the parks are best seen more slowly on foot, by bicycle, horse, or canoe. Most offer camping facilities (see Accommodation) and some offer cabin or hotel accommodation.

Some parks are free but in general the entrance fee will be $5-$10, and some of the most popular parks charge $20. Should you intend to use the National Park system extensively, purchase a Golden Eagle Passport on sale at all parks, or from the National Park Service, 1100 Ohio Drive, SW, Room 138, Washington DC 20242, (202) 208-4747. The pass costs $50 and gives you, and anyone accompanying you in a private vehicle, free entrance to all the parks for a year. Other activities such as camping, parking, or swimming, of course, cost extra. Also, visitors arriving before 7 am sometimes get in free. Reservations for camping are essential in peak season; apply in advance to be sure of a pitch. 1 (800) 365-2267 is the nation-wide number to reserve pitches—persevere, the line is always busy! For further information and much faster reservations, look up *http://reservations.nps.gov.*

There are also numerous national seashores, monuments and forests, and other federally-administered preserves which should not be overlooked. In addition there are thousands of state parks across America, many of which provide facilities for swimming, camping, hiking, etc, for a modest entry fee.

Almost all the national parks are included in this Guide. For more information write directly to the park, asking for details and brochures. A list of the major national parks in the US follows.

Acadia, Maine.	Kings Canyon, California.
Arches, Utah.	Lassen Volcanic, California.
Badlands, South Dakota.	Mammoth Cave, Kentucky.

Big Bend, Texas.
Bryce Canyon, Utah.
Canyonlands, Utah
Carlsbad Caverns, New Mexico.
Crater Lake, Oregon.
Denali, Alaska.
Everglades, Florida.
Glacier, Montana.
Grand Canyon, Arizona.
Grand Teton, Wyoming.
Great Basin, Nevada.
Great Smoky Mountains.
Tennessee/North Carolina.
Guadalupe Mountains, Texas.
Haleakala, Island of Maui, Hawaii.
Hawaii Volcanoes, Island of Hawaii,
   Hawaii.
Hot Springs, Arkansas.
Isle Royale, Michigan.

Mesa Verde, Colorado.
Mount Rainier, Washington.
National Reef, Utah.
North Cascades, Washington.
Olympic, Washington.
Petrified Forest, Arizona.
Platt, Oklahoma.
Redwood, California.
Rocky Mountain, Colorado.
Sequoia, California.
Shenandoah, Virginia.
Theodore Roosevelt, North Dakota.
Virgin Islands, St John, Virgin Islands.
Voyageurs, Minnesota.
Wind Cave, South Dakota.
Yellowstone, Wyoming/Montana/
   Idaho.
Yosemite, California.
Zion, Utah.

SPORT AND RECREATION

At times on your travels across America it may seem that every man, woman, child, and dog jogs, runs or otherwise 'keeps fit' at least four times a week. Certainly as a nation Americans tend towards the active, outdoors existence. After all they have the climate and the country to make it all possible.

In summer there's swimming, sailing, surfing, water skiing, fishing, diving and all the other water-based activities, plus tennis, baseball, camping, hiking, cycling ... the list is endless. Then just when you begin to get tired of all that, along comes the American football season, followed by basketball, and ice hockey. Then it snows and do Americans sit at home and watch it? Silly question. Now it's time for skiing (downhill or cross-country), skating, hunting, ice-fishing, more ice hockey and so on. In short if it exists as a sport you will find it somewhere in America—yes, even rugby and croquet.

On the professional scene the biggies are American football and baseball. The baseball season goes from April through October and football starts at the end of the summer and finishes in January when finally overtaken by the weather. Try to go to a professional game in either sport—it's a real slice of American pie (baseball can be very slow but it is as much about beer, hot dogs and tailgating as it is about the game). There is a major league team in almost every large city. Soccer is starting to catch on in a big way, although it doesn't cause the same sort of frenzy as it does in Europe. There is a national league but the real strength of the game is at grassroots level. Basketball, ice hockey, tennis, horse/motor racing and wrestling, are other major spectator sports.

One interesting point about the US sport scene is the attention given nationally to the often near-professional college/university teams. This is especially the case with basketball and football where the college teams are often followed with an enthusiasm equal to that given to the pros.

MEDIA AND ENTERTAINMENT

In these days of cable and satellite TV it is not unusual to be able to tune into more than 60 channels on your **television** set. Network television can be condescending, boring, total rubbish—an insult to the intelligence but also has excellent and interesting programmes. Best programmes feature old movies (squeezed in between commercials), news coverage, reruns of old sitcoms which always offer an interesting look at bygone America, and the public television channels which show British imports—*Absolutely Fabulous*, *Mr. Bean*, *Are You Being Served?*, *Lovejoy*, *EastEnders*, *One Foot In The Grave*, etc., and offer excellent current affairs, science and nature programmes as well as live theatre and music.

At whatever time of night or day there is always something to watch! The proliferation of cable has brought more specialist viewing to the small screen. Sport, religion, local events, movies, Spanish/Japanese/Cuban/whatever, and music videos (MTV) are just a few of the offerings. You will not be able to resist!

And there's even more **radio**. Here the overkill holds promise: in amongst the top 40 musical pop stations are first-rate classical, jazz, blues, bluegrass, country, gospel, R&B, progressive and regional music stations, as well as some solid all-news stations. Radio is also an excellent way of finding out about an area you're visiting or just driving through.

Every city with any claim to consequence will have **theatres** and its own **orchestra** and **opera company**, with performances often to a very high standard. In this respect, Americans arguably enjoy a greater access to culture than Europeans with their more distinguished but more centralised cultural traditions.

Hollywood still turns out more **movies** than anywhere else in the world except India, and with the decline of the studios there has been more freelancing, more opportunity for outsiders with new ideas to hit the big screen. In writing, directing and acting, America easily holds its own as one of the four or five great film-making nations.

Often movies are cheaper before 6 pm and some are just $2 at weekends. Free papers in every city are essential reading for entertainments/events etc. If you're interested in concerts, plays, etc, one easy solution is to look up **Ticketmaster** in the local phone book. They are nation-wide agents, but have information on what's on in the particular city you're in, though they take a percentage on any tickets you buy from them. There are half-priced ticket agencies in most major cities.

The *New York Times* is one of the most respected of American **newspapers** and in content comes closest to being the country's national newspaper. The mammoth Sunday edition of the *Times* should keep you going at least until Thursday. There is, of course, an actual coast-to-coast, national newspaper—*USA Today*. Published weekdays across America, and using full colour throughout, it manages to a large extent to overcome the problems of time zones, and the diversity of life in the US. In general people still buy their local papers and all towns and cities have at least one. Among the best of the rest are the *Los Angeles Times*, the *Washington Post* and the *Wall Street Journal*. The latter is a good read for the considerable insight it offers into a great variety of topics both inside and well beyond the world of finance.

Wherever you are, of course, the local paper (perhaps free) is your best resource for local events as well as adding to your picture of American life.

Magazines proliferate, covering every conceivable interest and point of view. Sample the offerings on hot rods, sex, flying saucers, sport, computers, snowmobiles, collectibles and so on if you want to appreciate the American appetite for every sort of information. There are also growing numbers of magazines for business women and the environmentally aware, plus large circulation African American publications. Some of the best writing is found in *The New Yorker*, *The Atlantic Monthly*—which grew out of the Transcendentalist and anti-slavery movements—and *Esquire*. *Rolling Stone* is still the voice of pop, *Ms.* is for politically correct women who have not yet graduated to reading the *Wall Street Journal*, and there's always *Time* and *Newsweek* to read on the loo.

Last but not least there are the **comics**, including that whole stable of Marvel heroes (Captain America, Spiderman, The Hulk) who express the variety of American neuroses, or those old standbys from a more innocent, confident age, principally Superman and Scrooge McDuck.

ON THE ROAD

ACCOMMODATION

Let's face facts: accommodation in North America is going to absorb at least one-third of your travel money. So how can you keep that figure to a minimum while enjoying your trip to the maximum? Here are eight pointers:

1. *Learn your accommodation options.* You'll constantly hear about the visible and well-advertised options: chain hotels and motels, lodgings close to freeways and tourist attractions, National Park accommodation and the conventional rock-bottom suggestions—YMCAs and youth hostels. But a wealth of inexpensive and almost invisible alternatives exist in North America. Examples: guest and tourist homes; bed and breakfast in private residences; farms and ranches; resorts and retreats; residence clubs, *casas de huespedes* and other pension-style lodgings; free campsites on Indian lands; non-hostel accommodations which honour hostel rates and philosophies; university-associated places to stay, many open to the general public; and self-catering digs, from apartments to rustic cabins to housekeeping/efficiency units in standard hotels/motels. (You will see lots of specific examples of these choices throughout this Guide.)
2. *Choose a lodging that also gives you a taste of North America.* Want to stay in a New York City brownstone, a San Francisco painted Victorian, a Maui condo, a solar-heated A-frame near a ski slope? How about spending a few days on a Mississippi River houseboat or riding through Kansas prairies with a covered wagon train? Maybe you'd rather tent-camp in a Sioux tepee, explore a Mennonite farm, visit a Southern plantation, sleep in a gold miner's cabin, gain a few pounds at a Basque boarding-house, beach-comb near a lighthouse hostel or stay in a 400-year-old Mexican

mansion. It's all here. And by integrating your sleeping (and sometimes eating) arrangements with an offbeat experience, you'll receive double value. In the process, you'll get acquainted with everyday Americans from many walks of life.

3. *Rent a room the way you shop for a car*. If tourism is down and vacancy rates are up, you'll have added leverage and bargaining power. Use it! Don't be afraid to haggle—hotel/motel rates in the US are extremely fluid and based on what the market will bear. (Unlike Mexico, where they are government regulated.) Rooms within a building are never identical—ask to see the cheapest. It may be small, viewless or noisy. It may also suit your needs very well. If you're willing to share a bath, sleep in a dorm, or take a room without air-conditioning or TV, *say so*. Most clerks (in the US anyway) will assume you require a private bath and colour TV to sustain life, and won't mention other accommodation. 'Ask for a room that is out of service and then offer a price for the night. You may be lucky.'

4. *Use impeccable timing*. Plan ahead to take advantage of special offers and slow times. Do your travelling on weekends so you arrive to catch the midweek (Sunday through Thursday) rates. Alternatively, look for higher-priced hotels at your destination that offer low-cost weekend or 'getaway' packages—often very good value. If you can possibly swing it, travel in May or September: best weather, fewer crowds and significantly lower off-season prices. Another timing tip: the later in the evening it gets, the more likelihood you have of a reduced rate on a room. You may be tired and worried about a place to lay your weary head but remember: the hotel/motel owner is even more worried about filling that room, which goes on costing him money whether empty or full. But beware: in resort areas and big cities at peak holiday times desirable accommodation fills by 4-5pm.

5. *Always ask about discounts and special rates*. You'd be amazed at the discount categories that exist in North America. A partial list: senior, student, youth hostel card-holder, bus/train/plane passholder, rental car user, member of AAA or other auto club, YMCA/YWCA member, Sierra Club or other environmental club members, military, family, group, foreign visitor, government employee, airline employee and corporate or commercial rates. Incidentally, hotels/motels sometimes grant 'commercial rates' as a face-saving way to fill rooms, so it pays to flash your company identification or business card and ask for them. Throughout this edition, you'll notice specific discount offers where known. 'Being a British student was worth a $2 discount to many motel owners'. Being a *Moneywise Guide* holder sometimes gets you a better deal too!

6. *Ask other travellers for accommodation leads*. When travelling in the US most Americans tend to stay with families/friends, at chain motels/hotels, or in campgrounds or RVs (recreational vehicles). Thus they are often oblivious to the unsung lodging opportunities around them.

7. *Double up. Better yet, triple up*. US lodging (with the exception of hostels, YMCAs and a few hotels/motels that give the lone traveller a break) has a Noah's Ark, two-by-two mentality. Your best bet is to travel with one or more companions. Relish your independence? Then split up and rendezvous with friends every couple of days—you'll still save money. 'Five

of us crammed into a $60 double room with owner's consent. Try any motel.'

8. *Learn about local variants and accommodation nomenclature.* Lodging traditions vary around North America. For instance, the best bargains in Hawaii are called hotel apartments—Honolulu is full of them. In Colorado, ski lodges with dorms (ask for 'hiker' or 'skier' rooms) are popular. San Francisco is a mecca for congenial residence clubs which offer superlative weekly rates for room and board. Parts of the South and New England are full of small guest houses. In Canada, low-priced B&B digs are called tourist homes. When you enter an area, ask the Visitors Centre or librarians, or look in the Yellow Pages; if there's a local variant, you should spot it. Second, learn what lodging descriptions really mean. In the US, the cheapest and simplest accommodation is variously described as 'economy', 'budget', 'no frills', 'rustic', 'basic' or 'European-style rooms'. The breakfast portion of bed and breakfast may vary from a continental roll-and-coffee to a full meal; ask. Unlike Europe, many US B&Bs offer (for a modest fee) other meals, transportation, tours and worthwhile goodies from free bike loans to use of libraries, saunas and tennis courts. Beware of lodging descriptions that include the words 'affordable', 'quaint', 'Old World charm' (evidently it costs a fortune to drag charm from the Old World to the New), and 'standard' or 'tourist class' (travel agenteese for mid-price range).

Hotels and motels. Thanks to the great success of the Motel 6 chain, the American travel industry has reluctantly concluded that no-frills lodging is not just a ploy for the pathologically frugal. Thus dozens of budget chain motels have emerged in the last decade. Except for Motel 6, however, they tend to be regional in scope and with prices that vary from unit to unit and season to season. To be fair: many of them offer more for your money (e.g. pool, larger rooms, bath, phones, TV, etc.). See the Appendix for a list of budget hotel chains in the US.

Budget motels work out cheapest with three or more people. Unfortunately, they are often difficult to reach without a car, but do call to ask about bus connections, if any. As a rule, cheapie motels (chain or non-chain) provide better, cleaner and safer accommodation for the money than do cheap downtown hotels.

Finding a hotel with the ideal mix of low price and reasonable quality is an art. Besides the suggestions in this Guide, you could try: (1) comparing notes with other travellers; (2) asking the Greyhound bus driver and at the terminal—but be careful with this; in small towns or out west maybe, but in New York, Detroit etc, forget it; and (3) check at the Travellers Aid kiosks in transit terminals. It's also wise to leave your luggage in a locker so you can check out your prospects. Ask to see rooms and don't settle for bad-news facilities (e.g. doors that don't lock or that have signs of forced entry, unclean linen, etc.). If you are a woman alone, we strongly advise you to arrive in big cities during daylight hours.

YMCAs and YWCAs. Most YMCAs offering accommodation are located in the often run-down heart of big city downtowns. Y lodgings have no membership or age restrictions and the use of rec facilities is often free. Two-thirds of them are co-ed; the rest, men only.

The economics of desperation bring in a mixed clientele; that, coupled with the grimy streets outside and steadily rising prices sometimes make the YMCA less and less of a bargain especially if there is more than one of you. For the single traveller the Y can still be the best bargain in town. You may do even better with prepaid reservations (valid at 124 YMCAs in the US, Canada and Mexico), and better still with an AYH card—many Ys give hostel rates. Contact the Y's Way, 224 E 47th St, New York NY 10017, (212) 308-2899.

The women-only YWCAs are concentrated in the Northeast, the Midwest and Texas. They tend to be smaller, more cheerful and better bargains than their YMCA counterparts—if you can get in.

Hostels. American Youth Hostels (AYH) has adopted the International Youth Hostel Federation blue triangle symbol and become Hostelling International—American Youth Hostels. Some 200 US hostels are already re-affiliated to the new HI-AYH, and members can now make reservations through the International Booking Network (IBN) for a $5 fee per hostel, (202) 783-6161 or through the free 800 number: 1-800-909-4776. Refer to HI-AYH *Handbook* for details on how this works. Most major USA gateway hostels are part of the network.

All in all, the hostel situation in the USA is pretty good and is especially bright in the Northeast states and in Ohio, Michigan, Minnesota, Colorado, Arizona, California, Oregon, Washington and Alaska (along the ferry route) but pretty thin elsewhere. There are hostels near Yellowstone and Yosemite, and in expensive cities like Chicago, Houston, Los Angeles, New York, San Francisco, Minneapolis, Miami Beach and Washington DC. Mexico has 20 hostels in Mexico City, Acapulco, Cancun and elsewhere. Canada has opened hostels in Montreal and Toronto and there are many others in major cities as well as in recreation areas.

If you belong to an overseas Youth Hostel Association, you're entitled to use HI-AYH and AAIH (see below) facilities. Annual fees in the US are $25 (age 18-54). Write to AYH, Membership Dept., 733 15th St NW, Suite 840, Washington DC 20005, or phone: (202) 783-6161. Overseas visitors who are not members in their own country must make use of the introductory pass most hostels offer so you can try it on a one-time basis. Get your pass stamped each time you use it, and after 6 times you become a 'guest member'—although you will not be entered onto the database, which may cause complications. It is recommended that if you plan to do a lot of hostelling you get the handbook published jointly by HI-AYH and the Canadian Hostelling Association which lists all hostels in both countries. In the US it comes free.

In addition to AYH-affiliated hostels there are a growing number of inde-pendently run hostels in the US and Canada. The American Association of Independent Hostels (AAIH) has hostels, or else provides hostel-type (i.e.. dorm.) accommodation within large hotels in several cities. Aimed primar-ily at the young, international traveller, they are generally located in down-town areas near the bus terminal. There are many other smaller independents which seem to spring up like mushrooms, mostly in the large cities such as Los Angeles (a prime hostel spot) and New Orleans. In some cases they last one season and then disappear! So be careful.

The accommodation provided by independent hostels can be a bit of a mixed bag. Some are very good, but others aim simply to cram in as many people as possible regardless of standards of cleanliness, safety or sanitation. If you are on a budget, of course, you may feel you don't really have a choice. The majority of the hostels listed in this book have been recommended by previous users.

One very useful association for travellers is Backpackers Hostels Canada run from Thunder Bay, Ontario by Lloyd Jones. Lloyd puts together listings of independent backpacker hostels for Canada, the USA and some other countries and their website listings are apparently updated daily. Check the website first if possible: *www.backpackers.ca*. Or write to: Backpackers Hostels Canada, RR 13, Box 10-1, Thunder Bay, Ont, Canada P7B 5E4, (807) 983-2042, or email: *candu@microage-tb.com*, for info on hostels and general advice on hostelling/travel-planning.

Another helpful resource is the *Hostel Handbook for the USA and Canada*, which provides information on both HI-AYH and independent hostels. To order a guide, send a cheque or money order for $4 ($5 from outside the US) to Jim Williams, The Hostel Handbook, 722 Saint Nicholas Ave, NY, NY 10031 (212) 926-7030. Email: *InfoHostel@aol.com*.

Pluses of North American hostelling: often in locales of great scenic beauty; a growing number are housed in buildings of historic or architectural interest (from decommissioned lighthouses to adobe haciendas); many offer special activities free or at low cost, from wilderness canoe or cycling trips to hot-tubbing. Reader comments show that US hostels are generally more relaxed and friendly than their European counterparts. 'I found youth hostels most convenient places to stay. Full of young people of all nationalities, the hostels were a nucleus of information and I met many travelling partners. Whilst not boasting of exceptional comforts, the hostels generally proved to be very good value and certainly took a lot out of the loneliness of travelling on one's own.'

Drawbacks? Uneven distribution make hiking or biking itineraries impractical, except for certain regions. Remote locales make it tough to use public transport to get to many of them. And hostel curfews and customs can cramp your style, particularly if you plan to do much urban or night-time sightseeing. 'Most US hostels insist on your having (or renting for 50¢) a sheet sleeping bag.' 'On the whole American hostels were very good indeed.'

University-associated lodging. Over 230 universities in the US and Canada offer on-campus housing in dorms and residence halls. Points to consider: usually available summer only (exceptions noted in listings); rates vary widely and definitely favour doubles and weekly stays; facilities often heavily booked; campuses can be far from city centres. It's always worth trying the local student union or campus housing office when in the vicinity. Many of these offerings are open to the general public.

You can also find off-campus residences, fraternity and sorority houses with summer space to rent, all of which tend to be looser, friendlier and cheaper than on-campus options. Fringe benefits: use of kitchen facilities (sometimes) and entree into the thirsty social life of local students, including the infamous TGs or kegger parties.

Camping. Camping provides the cheapest and one of the most enjoyable means of seeing the best parts of North America, the national and state parks and other preserves. Your choices are almost infinite—free campgrounds in the US alone total over 20,000! State park camping fees range from zero to $8 and are indicated with the state listings. National parks (same price range) are given considerable attention in this Guide; for further information, write to the National Park Service, 1849 C St, NW, Rm 1013, Washington DC 20240, or call (202) 208-4747. Other excellent sources for campground info are the AAA books, Rand McNally's *Campground and Trailer Park Guide* (17,000 US and Canada listings) and the tourism offices of each state.

You should be aware that the biggest drawback for the on-foot traveller is access. Ironic as it sounds, you really need a car to get to numerous campgrounds and trailheads to backcountry camping, especially those sites located on National Forest or Bureau of Land Management property. Once you have wheels it is possible to zigzag your way across America camping in some of the loneliest, loveliest spots in the world. It might even be worth investigating hiring a camper vehicle (the dreaded RV) for an extended trip. For a group of 3 or more it could be worth the extra expense.

Campground facilities vary from fully developed sites with electricity, bunk-equipped cabins and hot showers to primitive sites where you're expected to bury your wastes and pack out your rubbish. Tent campers are advised to avoid RV-oriented campgrounds. They may offer a pool, laundromat, store and other amenities but the noise, asphalt and vehicle fumes sadly dilute the 'wilderness' experience. More expensive, private campgrounds can be good. A number of readers have recommended KOA (Kampgrounds of America). In general, while their sites are not always the most scenic, their facilities are luxurious in camping terms. 'We used the KOA campgrounds the whole time—they have the best facilities available. Check out the KOA website for info on reservations and site locations: *www.koakampgrounds.com.* And get a KOA discount card; this allows a 10 percent reduction on the cost of a campsite, plus gives a "free" guide.' Sites cost $12-$20. For the hiking/biking camper, many state parks offer a few sites designated as 'hiker/biker' for 50¢-$1 per night on a first-come, first-served basis.

In the north, the camping season lasts from mid-May to mid-September or sooner, depending on weather. In the Rockies and other mountainous areas, temperatures drop dramatically in the evening, making warm clothing vital. In the warm dry Southwest, you probably won't have to put up a tent, although you might want to exclude any unwelcome wildlife! At Yellowstone and other Northern parks, you may encounter bears who roam the campground for food. Wear a bell! These bears are not interested in campers as nourishment and will not harm you as long as you leave them well alone. Do not leave food in the tent, in ice chests, on picnic tables or near your sleeping bag. Lock it in the trunk of your car, or use park-recommended 'bear cables'. Bring along a generous supply of insect repellent and calamine lotion to combat mosquito bites, chiggers (a maddening insect that burrows beneath your skin) and poison ivy/poison oak (glossy three-leafed plants).

Popular national and state parks get very crowded from Memorial Day through to Labor Day, making May and September the ideal months for visits. When possible, make advance reservations. To get the best site, try to arrive by 5 pm or earlier. Beware that some campgrounds keep the 'No Vacancy' sign up all summer so always ask. At the most popular parks queuing all night for space is not unheard of.

Native American campgrounds and other Indian-run lodging facilities are a first-rate way to get acquainted with North America's first people. Most sites are located on reservation land which, if you remember your history, has traditionally been located about a million miles from nowhere. Although the whites did their best to fob off nothing but marginal lands on the Indians, what they ended up with is often superbly scenic. A car is nearly imperative as you'll find little public transit to and from reservation land. Besides campgrounds, Native American owned facilities range from simple motels to sumptuous resorts. Some offer traditional dancing, crafts and native food.

Bed and breakfast. An old concept in Europe, B&B crossed the Atlantic a few years ago and has now hybridised in several directions. Most visible are the 'too cute to be true' B&B Inns, widely written about and gushed over and punitively expensive in most cases. Least visible but most moneywise are the private homes in the US, Canada and Mexico which only rent rooms through an agency intermediary. (This is partly for security reasons, partly because of US zoning laws.) Most agencies concentrate on a given city or state; you'll find their names and addresses under the appropriate listing. Their rates run from $35-$45 single and from $45-$90 double. (NB: higher rates are for incredibly lavish digs.) Booking procedures, type of breakfast, length of stay and other conditions vary from agency to agency. The common denominator is the need to book ahead. If in the US, this can often be handled with a phone call. Only rarely can you breeze into town and get same-day accommodation.

If you are planning to do a lot of B&Bing you should consider buying one of the many books on the market which list hundreds of guest houses or tourist homes on a national or regional basis. A good guide will also list the various reservation services, their rates and how they work.

Is the lack of flexibility worth it? Most people think so. Foreign visitors who want to meet locals, see American homes and eat home cooking are particularly enthusiastic. Private home B&Bs are an inexpensive, warm and caring environment for women travellers on their own, too. Bonuses: many B&Bs serve meals other than breakfast and a large number are willing to pick up and deliver guests (sometimes for a small fee). Hosts often speak other languages, so make your needs known at booking time. Canadian B&Bs are called hospitality homes. In Mexico, the B&B programme is known as Posada Mexico.

There are several B&B umbrella agencies which cover a number of states (and countries) and which cater to foreign and US travellers. They can book you into one B&B or work out a whole itinerary of B&Bs for you. Write for details and brochures. A few of the better known agencies:

1. B&B California, PO Box 2247, Saratoga, CA 95070-1247, call (800) 872-4500 or (650) 696-1690, *www.bbintl.com*. Outstanding host and guest match ups; fees from $75 for single or double; full breakfast; many homes throughout California and Nevada.
2. Pacific B&B, PO Box 46894, Seattle, WA 98146; (206) 784-0539 or (800) 684-2932. Rates from $44 single (shared bath), $49 for two. Homes in Washington and British Columbia.
3. B&B League Ltd, PO Box 9490, Washington DC 20016-9490. Phone: (202) 363-7767. Recommended primarily for travellers in pairs, since rates are $58-$125 single, $78-$145 double plus $10 booking fee. Continental breakfast. Makes rsvs for B&Bs in DC and area.

Like every other business in America, new organisations mushroom all the time. Some of them are very localised so it is always worth checking in the immediate vicinity (e.g. Yellow Pages) for local listings.

Other accommodation possibilities. If you're planning to bicycle around the US, it makes sense to contact Adventure Cycling, a national non-profit organisation, at PO Box 8308, Missoula, Montana 59807. Tel: (406) 721-1776. They provide books and maps to help you. Hostelling International offers special tours for cyclists and of course accommodation. Many individual hostels arrange their own bike rental and tours. Also recommended is a series published by Ballantine—*Cyclist's Guides to Overnight Stops*.

Should you decide to (or be reduced to) crash out, it is a good idea to ask locally whether or not your chosen spot is safe. The local police, or students, are probably the best people to ask but it's not a good idea to just crash out by the side of the road or on the beach without checking first. Some readers have suggested highway rest areas as good sleeping places but sometimes this is not allowed and you should only do this if other people are clearly doing so already—never alone.

If you're totally stranded and penniless then Traveler's Aid or the Salvation Army may be able to help.

FOOD

To eat cheaply and well in America is easy once you realise that menu prices have more to do with restaurant decor and labour costs than with food quality. Everyone will quickly develop his or her own game plan depending on available funds and taste. However you should plan to get at least some of your meals from non-restaurant sources: supermarkets, open-air farmers markets, roadside stands and farms.

When possible, avoid higher-priced outlets like 24-hour stores, bus station canteens, street vendors, beach stands, airport restaurants and liquor stores. 'Some supermarkets, especially 7-11s, have microwaves, so a hot stew can be eaten for the price of the can and if you are on the road this is generally also true of some gas stations.' In general the food you buy and prepare yourself will always be the cheapest. At least one meal a day should fall into this category.

Keep away from endless soft drinks; even at supermarkets, they're 75¢ and up, double that elsewhere. Accompany your dining-out meals with ice water or lower-priced multiple refills like coffee or tea.

If you can eat a good meal in the morning then you'd be wise to start with a big breakfast (best food bargain in the US) and/or to stay in bed and breakfasts, hotels, hostels and other lodgings which include it as part of the price. Everywhere you will find excellent breakfast 'specials' for as little as $1.25 for eggs, toast etc. At lunchtime, again look for daily 'specials'— usually the tastiest/freshest and cheapest choice available.

In the evening, plan to eat early (to take advantage of lower-priced 'sunset' or 'early bird' specials) or eat in a non-restaurant setting.

Wherever you are, check out the Happy Hour situation. States and cities with liberal liquor laws often honour a daily discount period (usually 4pm-7pm) with cheap drinks and free food, sometimes a stunning array of it. Fittingly, California is the Happy Hour paradise.

No matter where you are, ethnic restaurants are invariably the cheapest. Chinese, Mexican and Italian can be found in profusion. In larger areas, look for Vietnamese, Greek, German, Indian and other specialities. Cafeterias offer cheap if sometimes insipid food; besides downtown, look for them on campuses, around hospitals, in large museums, in department stores and at YMCAs. 'Anyone can eat in university cafeterias—all you want for the price of a burger, fries and soft drink at McDonalds.' The good old American diner, now unfortunately in decline, is another reasonably inexpensive option, usually with an amazing choice of dishes on the menu and enormous portions.

Regional and local specialities are usually wonderful, or at the very least a worthwhile cultural experience. As you work your way around the country sample Key Lime pie, Virginia ham and redeye gravy, Chicago-style deep-dish pizza, California guacamole dip, Texas chilli, Southern grits, Hawaiian poi and roast pig, Wisconsin bratwurst, Maryland crab cakes, Navajo tacos.

In the West, salads and salad bars are generally excellent. Large sandwiches (often with local nomenclature like grinder, submarine, po' boy, blimp, hero, hoagie, etc.) on rolls with meatballs, sausage, corned beef, you name it, are available everywhere for a couple of dollars.

Many readers have suggested the salad bars now available in some fast food chains or as sold by the pound in supermarkets and grocery stores. For about $3 you can eat as heartily as any well-to-do rabbit. Those on a budget will inevitably find themselves eating from time to time at McDonald's, Burger King, Boston Market, Pizza Hut, Kentucky Fried Chicken and the rest. At least you know what you're getting. Coast to coast it's always the same! The Taco Bell chain has been recommended for a good, filling, cheap vegetarian meal e.g. 89¢ for a bean burrito. And there's always pizza!

Americans are ice cream fanatics and eat it year-round in more flavours and combinations than you've ever dreamed of. Lots of the ice cream parlours will give you free samples until you hit on the one you want most.

Wherever you eat, portions are invariably enormous—you'll soon understand why Americans invented the doggie bag for leftovers! 'Forget doggie bags—nobody objected to our ordering one portion and two plates and sharing—portions still bigger than at home.'

'Nowhere have I found it difficult, and usually I've found it fun, hunting out a place to suit my quite small pocket. I do feel that discovering food, rather than following a map to it, is part of the holiday.'

TRAVEL

The means you choose to travel around North America will depend on your budget, your time, your adventurousness and a number of other factors. Since there are certain discounts available to travellers who buy their tickets outside North America, it is a good idea to give careful consideration to travel plans *before* you go. Also, when you buy your tickets outside the US, you save the eight percent sales tax. Basically, travel is like everything else in America—you have to shop around for the best buys. Never be afraid to ask for the cheapest fare. There are always variations and the clerk selling you a ticket is not necessarily about to offer you the cheapest one.

'Canada and the US cater for wheelchairs much better than the UK does. Theatres, museums, pavements, airports, bus stations, even buses are all usually equipped with either lifts or ramps.'

Bus. Travelling long distances cross-country by bus has become a part of American mythology and for natives and overseas visitors alike bus remains the most popular method of cheap travel in North America. Despite competition from comparatively inexpensive air fares which has resulted in the cutting back of bus routes and facilities in recent times, the major nation-wide company, Greyhound, and the many regional, smaller companies, survive and flourish and will no doubt still be the chief means of inter-city transportation for most budget travellers to North America for the foreseeable future. Greyhound International can be reached on: (01342) 317317 in the UK.

It is possible to travel comfortably all over North America whether it be on Greyhound or one of the many other bus lines. Bus terminals provide restaurants, ticket, baggage and parcel services, travel bureaux, restrooms and left-luggage lockers, although you should be aware that bus stations are often in the seediest areas of downtown and therefore not a place to actually plan on spending a lot of time. Periodic rest stops are made every three to four hours en route and if you are on a very tight budget you can save by travelling at nights and sleeping on the bus.

Currently, advance reservations on Greyhound are not accepted. It is advisable to turn up at the bus station at least an hour before departure on the day of travel, to allow time to purchase a ticket and get in the queue. Greyhound's central information number is (800) 231-2222.

When travelling by bus from point A to point B, always ask about the cheapest available fare. Fare reductions are made and usually depend on the time of travel, how long away, when returning etc. Available to overseas visitors, before leaving for the USA, are the various Greyhound **Ameripasses**. These are the 5-day Pass for £89; the 7-day Pass for £115; 15 days for £169; 30 days at £229 and 60 days at £315. You can no longer buy extra days while on the road. A 4-day Pass is also available for £75. It is non-refundable and valid for travel only on Monday to Thursday—i.e.. it is not possible to use the pass at weekends although you can interrupt usage and restart again after the weekend. The Ameripass is not valid for travel in Canada except for direct journeys from Seattle to Vancouver, Buffalo/Detroit to Toronto, and Boston or New York to Montreal. (*For further information on Greyhound fares in Canada, please see the Background Canada section of this book*.) It is also possible to buy the Ameripass from the Greyhound International office in New York City, Port Authority Bus Terminal. The 4-day pass costs $119, 5-day pass costs $139, 7-day pass $179, 15-day pass $269, 30 days, $369, and for 60 days of non-stop adventuring, a pass costs $499. Greyhound offer a 10% discount to ISIC holders and under 26 YHA card holders.

Time on all the passes starts ticking away when you start your journey. The passes offer unlimited travel on Greyhound routes (and those of participating carriers) and represent excellent value for the cross-country traveller. In addition, Greyhound has introduced regional passes so, for instance, a 21-day North East Regional Pass costs £189. You can also purchase a **Go Hostelling Pass** combining pre-paid hostel accommodation with bus travel. A 7 day/7 night pass, for example, is £225 (high season).

Some Tips. Whenever possible, take your bags on to the bus with you, otherwise get a check-in ticket, make sure they are labelled and watch them like a hawk—it is not uncommon for you and your bags to set off in different directions, and without the check-in ticket you may never get them back. If you have to put your bag underneath the bus it is recommended that at each stop en route to your destination you get off the bus and watch to make sure that your bag stays there and continues with you—on the same bus. 'If all lockers are taken, luggage can be stored for up to 24 hours at an approximate cost of $1.50 per piece, in the bus depot luggage store.'

'Bus pass coupons have to be validated each time for further travel. As ticket lines can be very long, it's good to have your ticket stamped for the next journey as soon as you arrive.'

If planning to sleep on the bus, get a cheap inflatable pillow. It can make all the difference to your comfort, though some readers say a sleeping bag is better 'and doesn't puncture'. Malleable wax ear plugs are also a good idea for lighter sleepers. Always have a sweatshirt or pullover with you. Bus drivers seem to be impervious to cold. 'Even at 3 am on a chill night the air conditioning is set to combat the climate of Death Valley.'

The bus passes often entitle you to discounts at station restaurants, nearby hotels and on various sightseeing tours. It's in fact cheaper to eat away from the stations, but you might not always have the time to do so.

Most bus routes are meant solely to get you from A to B; scenic considerations rarely come into it.

The Green Tortoise. A kind of alternative bus/tour combo designed to get the budget traveller across country cheaply, but in a fun, laid-back way. Time is not of the essence here. No effort is made to get there fast. The idea is to meander gently with the route changing at the request of the passengers. The coast to coast trips begin and end in either New York or Boston and San Francisco, depart weekly, last 11-14 days and at present cost between $349-$389. You will need extra money for meals en route. Other tours are available—to Yosemite, the Grand Canyon, Mexico, Alaska and New Orleans for Mardi Gras. Green Tortoise also provides a cheap way of travelling down the West Coast—Seattle to LA, $79; San Francisco to LA, $35, San Francisco-Seattle $59.

Buses accommodate 28 to 44 people and have most of their seats removed and replaced by wooden platforms covered with foam rubber padding. They also have stoves and refrigerators. Often cross-country tours are accompanied by a cook. Passengers can put about $9 or so a day into a kitty and get two full meals cooked on the bus but often eaten at some scenic place such as a Louisiana bayou or the banks of the Rio Grande. Smoking is banned on the buses.

'A wonderful trip. I made many new and lasting friends and saw many places I might otherwise have missed.' 'Don't do it if you're an insomniac, a loner, need a shower more than once every three days, or a moaner.'

Reservations should be made through Green Tortoise, 494 Broadway, San Francisco CA 94133. Or for information phone (800) TORTOIS (867-8647); when in the bay area call (415) 956-7500; when at your screen call up, *www.greentortoise.com.*

Car. The car overwhelmingly remains the most popular form of travel and the vast system of super-highways—'monuments to motion'—enables you to cover great distances at high average speeds. 'The National System of Interstate and Defence Highways is designed for maximum efficiency. For enjoyment, try state and country roads, even for a lengthy trip. The additional time spent will be more than compensated for by the increased intimacy with American culture and scenery.'

Buying a car. For a group of three or four it can be worthwhile buying a second-hand car. Try to buy and sell privately, utilising the notice boards of universities, and the local press.

Be sure to obtain a 'title' or, in states such as New York, a notarised bill of sale. If stopped by the police, proof of ownership will be required. (In some states it is illegal to drive without this.) Allow for a delay while the title comes through. If you buy from a dealer he can issue temporary licence plates on the spot.

You can have your car checked over at a gas station at a very low cost. If you have to buy new parts get them at one of the nation-wide stores like Montgomery Ward or Sears, or from major gas stations like Shell and Mobil. They will give you guarantees and have the advantage of being readily available all over the continent. Garages are efficient and friendly, and if you are from out-of-state, will usually do repairs, however major, on the spot.

Prices of second-hand cars vary widely from place to place and tend to be higher on the West Coast. Prices fall in September when the next year's new cars come on to the market. Leave several days for selling your car and if possible try not to do it in New York. Automatic cars are easier to sell.

'Two of us bought a large station wagon for $800 and drove it 12,000 miles in two months. We slept in it often, and sometimes ate in it too. We sold it back to the dealer we bought it from at half-price. Worst problems: two $50 repair bills and finding places to park.' 'We bought a car. It cost $400 among seven. I personally paid $50 and to travel 5000 miles it cost me $60 in gas. Well worth it and it gave us freedom to visit so many places.'

Insurance. You are strongly advised to take out at least third-party cover—and full comprehensive coverage is preferable—as insurance claims can be very high and inadequate insurance can lead to financial ruin. Expect to pay around $550 for three months' coverage.

Insurance premiums are generally high, particularly for males under 25. Women are considered better risks and their premiums are lower. Premiums are lower if you are resident outside large urban areas. Allow time for your policy to come through.

In states where insurance is compulsory it is necessary to have it before you can register your car. 'We bought a car in Colorado and had trouble insuring it with an International Drivers' License. So be prepared to take a test and get a state license!'

Licences. All states and provinces of the US and Canada now officially recognise all European licences and those of Japan, Australia and New Zealand among others. However, an International Driving Licence is recommended since it provides you with photographic ID. Also police are more familiar with them and this could save you time and embarrassment (but don't forget to bring your *original* licence too—you may not be able to hire a car or get a drive-away without it). In addition, your own licence can be validated by the AAA office in the USA. Although not a legal requirement, it's a good idea to have it done particularly if your licence is not in English. You won't encounter many multi-lingual patrolmen along the way. You must always have your insurance certificate, car registration certificate and driving licence with you in the car—there is no grace period; you will simply be fined for driving without the legally required documents.

Road Tips. Traffic regulations, including speed limits, vary from state to state, so familiarise yourself with them in each. Many readers recommend buying the Rand McNally *Interstate Road Atlas*, useful even for non-drivers. Maps from gas stations cost around $3.

'Most truck drivers have CBs. When driving, follow the example they set. If they adhere to the speed limit it means they've picked up the police lurking in the locality.'

If you have a breakdown, raising the hood is the recognised distress signal. Also switch on your flashing warning lights.

Never pass a stopped and flashing school bus (they are usually yellow) no matter which side of the road it is on: it is not only against the law, but could easily result in death or injury to young children.

AAA Membership. Benefits include: helping with car rental, hotel reservation, towing service, $5000 bail if arrested, excellent and free maps and regional guide books, and a comprehensive information and advisory service. For example, the AAA will plan your journey for you, giving the quickest or most scenic routes, and provide detailed maps of the towns you will pass through.

Touring membership varies depending on where you join. In New York for example it costs $55 for the first year and $45 thereafter. Apply to: AAA, 1000 AAA Drive, MS 75, Heathrow, FL 32746, (407) 444-8000, or to AAA, Broadway and 62nd St., in New York, 212-586-1166, or to the Club in whichever state you happen to be. Membership of your own national automobile association entitles you to AAA benefits. There are also a few other motor clubs with similar benefits. Allstate Motor Club, (800) 347-8880, $60, is one of the better known ones.

Gasoline. Depending on which part of the country you are in, expect to pay as much as $1.65 per gallon, or as little as about one dollar. (The American gallon is one-fifth smaller than the imperial gallon used in Britain and Canada and is equivalent to 3.8 litres.)

When driving in remote areas, always keep your tank topped up. Gas stations can be few and far between. Keep a reserve supply in a container for emergencies. Shop around and use self service pumps for cheapest gas.

Automobile Transporting Companies—Driveaways. Americans change homes more often than any other people, and may live for a few years in New York and then move off to California. When they do move they sometimes put their car (or one of them) into the hands of an automobile transporting company which does no more than find someone like you to drive the car from A to B.

Most movements are from east to west, major starting points being New York, Detroit and Toronto. 'East-west is the easiest route to get; otherwise New York-Florida or New York-Atlanta. The cheapest way to travel bar hitching'. Even on the popular routes you may have to wait a couple of days for a car, particularly in summer.

Conditions regarding age limitation, time schedules, routing, gas and oil expenses, deposit, insurance and medical fitness vary considerably and should always be carefully checked. And another thing: 'The car trunk may be full of the owner's belongings, leaving no room for yours.' A fair example would be for a driver 21 years or over, with character references, to be charged about $300 deposit, refundable on safe delivery. 'A superb and cheap way of travelling. I went with three others in a van and it only cost us $70 each in gas to get from New York to San Francisco via the Grand Canyon.' 'Beware. We had a series of bad experiences. Each office acts independently and sometimes against what the same company's office elsewhere tells you.' 'You have to take a reasonably direct route, but the time limit (after which you are reported to the FBI) allows a fair amount of sightseeing. I was given nine days for the coast-to-coast trip and made it in six. It's certainly a great way to see America.'

'I drove a new Cadillac with only two thousand miles on the clock. It was air conditioned, everything electric—really unbelievable, and we slept in it at night. Good places to sleep are truck-stops run by Texaco, Union 76, etc. They have 24 hr restaurants and free showers, and the truckers themselves, though rough-looking, are often interesting people to talk to.' 'Try and have more than one driver in the car.'

'When asking for your deposit back and before handing the keys over, hold out for cash. American cheques are a bugger to cash.' And a word of warning: 'It is essential to check the car thoroughly for dents and scratches before taking it. We lost $135 because the owner complained about scratches and we could not prove they were there before we took it.'

The names of companies can be found in the *Yellow Pages* under 'Automobile and Truck Transporting'. It is a good idea to shop around, go to the office in person, and make sure you do not sign away your insurance rights—i.e.. make sure you personally are covered and not just the vehicle. Try Auto Driveaway, 310 S Michigan Ave, Chicago, IL 60604, (800) 346-2277. The addresses of some other companies are listed under many towns and cities below or check the web at: *www.movecars.com.*

Car Rentals. The biggest national firms are Hertz, Avis, National, Budget, Thrifty and Dollar. The last two are generally cheaper, but even Hertz can offer some amazing deals. It's important to phone around. Always compare costs per day against costs per mile and other variations, such as unlimited mileage or so many miles free, within the context of your specific needs. Many rental companies offer discount rates to foreign visitors, though sometimes only when bookings are made abroad.

The renter must usually be 21 or over, sometimes over 25 (Sears has been mentioned as one hire company which may rent to someone under 21). If you don't have a credit card then a hefty cash deposit will be required, and for foreigners a passport may also have to be deposited as security. 'It's very difficult to rent a car without a major credit card, and in many cases it's not possible to leave a deposit.' 'Small companies generally ask drivers to be 25 or over; large companies usually accept drivers from 18 provided they have a major credit card.' 'Younger the driver, higher the surcharge'—in some cases as high as $45 per day!

Insurance is not usually included in the cost, or often it's only third-party. It's essential that you take out full coverage; the alternative may be a life-time of paying off someone's massive hospital bills.

Greyhound operates one of the cheapest rental companies, though it concentrates mostly on Florida and California. Alamo and Amerex are also recommended. Then there are the companies renting out older cars, e.g. Rent-a-Wreck, Rent-a-Heap, Rent-a-Junk and Ugly Duckling. But they are not always the cheapest or most flexible, e.g. in some instances you must stay within a 50- or 100-mile radius of the point of rental. Worth checking out, though. 'Phone the national company number as well as the local agent's number. One may well offer a better deal than the other.'

'Ask a travel agent for good deals; I found them to be in the know.' 'It's a good idea to check with the airline you're travelling on for special arrangements. Sometimes these can only be booked before the flight.' 'Don't entertain a firm that charges for mileage and drop-off; there are plenty that don't.' 'If you want unlimited mileage you must usually go to a large company.'

'We found car rental easiest, most convenient and, for groups of three or more, the cheapest way of getting to see National Parks and other areas where transport, other than tours, is minimal.'

Air. The vast distances of the North American continent have resulted in the popularity and relative cheapness of domestic air travel, and since government deregulation there has been a bewildering and ever-changing scramble to offer more for less. There are air travel bargains to be had but it is often hard to keep track of what is available. If you plan to fly check with a travel agent, phone around the airlines and keep an eye on newspaper and television advertising—and always ask for the cheapest available fare.

Some possibilities: night flights are sometimes cheaper than day flights; some airlines from time to time offer off-peak, cheaper, fares. Other airlines make discounts if you travel on a flight making stops en route and, if planning to travel great distances, it may pay to investigate the air passes (see below). There may be considerable price competition on major routes such as New York to Florida and New York to the West Coast. Once again, the clear message is shop around!

Additionally there are two Visit USA bargains available only to non-US residents and offering incredible value for cross-country travel. The terms and prices vary from airline to airline, but the principles are the same and the tickets have to be purchased BEFORE leaving for America.

Delta Airlines offer 'Discover America' coupons which can be bought in conjunction with Delta/British Airways/Sabena/Virgin Atlantic trans-Atlantic flights. For example, 3 coupons cost $377, 4 coupons are $482, and 10 coupons $1,049. 1 coupon equals 1 stopover. It is possible to buy coupons even if the transatlantic flight is on another airline. Not surprisingly it costs more: $479 for 3 coupons, $589 for 4 and $1,289 for 10 of them.

This fare offers a discount on all flights on the airline's system though the itinerary must be worked out and paid for prior to departure for the US. Reservations can be made at any time. This scheme may be preferable if you know in advance where you want to go and if you're not stopping at many places. Discounts are usually up to 40 percent.

Northwest Airlines have several pass-type options, but only in conjunction with a transatlantic flight on Northwest, KLM, BA or Virgin. Visit USA coupons are purchased with the transatlantic flight. There is a minimum of 3 coupons. 1 coupon represents 1 flight. Travelling from the UK, prices currently range from $359 for 3 coupons to $1249 for 10, depending on when you fly. Once you begin using your coupons there is a maximum stay of 60 days permitted. One of the advantages of travelling by air is that careful timing can get you free meals and night flights save on accommodation expenses. Air passes can be bought from most travel agents. Once in the USA, check the Sunday papers for special deals to the Caribbean, sometimes as low as $399 for four days.

Rail. The railroads played a major role in the history of the United States, but over recent decades they've declined in service, increased in price, lost money and seen much of their former business go to cars and airlines. Part of the reason for this may have been the great number of competing railways and the inability of the individual companies to undertake the new investment necessary to improve service and efficiency. But in 1971 Amtrak was established. All the major lines now operate under the one Amtrak board, and though the railways remain privately owned, losses on passenger services are made up for by government subsidy.

On long-haul Western routes, outdated equipment has been replaced by double-decker Superliners, variously fitted up as lounges, dining cars (restaurant upstairs, kitchen below), sleeping cars (with bedrooms) and open-plan coaches. On shorter routes and generally in the East, cylinder-shaped Amcoaches are used, their interiors like luxury airliners.

In the East, frequency, time-keeping and the large number of destinations served permit comparison with European railways. From Chicago west-wards it is the trans-Siberian railway that comes to mind. There are only four east-west routes, but all except one operate daily. Delays are common. But for the traveller that should not matter: the scenery is often spectacular, the service is better than on any railway in the world, the seats recline and have foot rests, you can eat and drink well and inexpensively, and the company is congenial. The Western railways are the last stronghold of graceful travel in America and many readers have written in to praise Amtrak and the standard of its services. 'Ideal for the student traveller going from city to city.' 'Very comfortable.' 'The best way to see a wide variety of scenery. On occasions we felt less worn from 20 hours on a train than four hours on a bus.' 'A wonderful window on to the USA.'

A rundown on some of the more interesting routes:

The Empire Builder runs between Chicago and Seattle via Milwaukee, Minneapolis/St Paul, Fargo in North Dakota, Glacier National Park and Spokane. Majestic scenery. Takes about 46 hours; operates daily.
The Coast Starlight, between Los Angeles and Seattle, offers superb coastal, forest and mountain scenery. 'Attracts many young people. A highly social train: spontaneous parties and lust.' Takes 33 hours; operates daily.
The California Zephyr, formerly operated by The Denver & Rio Grande Western Railroad, is now operated by Amtrak three times a week. The train starts in Chicago; the journey between Denver and Salt Lake City takes 14 hours, almost all in daylight, and climbs 9000 feet over the Rockies for what is considered the greatest railway ride in America. It then runs on to LA. Also special are the *Adirondack* between New York and Montréal, and the crack *Capitol Limited* between Washington and Chicago with the best onboard dining service.

Amtrak passes for 15/30 days unlimited travel are available to overseas visitors outside the US and are available in some cities at the Amtrak station. Check first however. Current high season rates (1 June-6th Sept) are: $425/$535 Nation-wide, $315/$395 Western Region, $250/$310 for the East, $240/$310 for the Far West Region. The Northeast Region pass is $200/$230. Discounted fares are available to ISIC card holders. Once you have bought the pass you can make reservations by phoning 1-800-USA-RAIL. 'Excellent value, great way to travel. Trains spacious and comfortable. Staff friendly and helpful.' 'Disadvantages—trains slow and often late.' 'It is essential to make reservations for the busy East Coast routes to Florida.' 'One drawback is the early morning (4 am!) arrival time at some mid-west stations.' 'Every time you phone, you get different information! Be pushy if need be.'

In Britain contact: Long Haul Leisurerail, PO Box 113, Peterborough PE1 1LE; 0733 51780. In the US call (800) 872-7245, Amtrak Vacations, (800) 321-8684, or look up some interesting routes on *www.amtrak.com.*

RIDING SCENIC RAIL

North America, especially the Rockies, is full of scenic narrow gauge railways, where restored steam locomotives backtrack to bygone days. These are some of the more interesting rides.

Blue Ridge Scenic Railway (800) 934-1898, in Blue Ridge, Georgia is a 26 mile trip along the Toccoa River. 3 hr r/t Fri-Mon, $22. **Cumbres & Toltec Scenic Railroad** in Antonito, CO, is North America's highest narrow-gauge steam railroad. Full-day, 64-mile tour, $52; (719) 376-5483. **Grand Canyon Railway** (800) THE-TRAIN, info@thetrain.com, 2 hr trip from Williams, AZ, through the northern Arizona countryside to Grand Canyon National Park. Includes strolling musicians and western characters recreating turn-of-the-century train travel. Coach, $49.95 r/t. **Great Smoky Mountain Railway**, Bryson City, NC (near Asheville). Trips through Nantahala Gorge and Fontana Lake, 9 am & 2 pm daily (subject to change); $21.95 for 4 hr r/t. To reserve call: (800) 872-4681. **Mt Washington (NH) Railway Co**, (800) 922-8825. Historic route with steep grade, highly scenic trip to highest point in Northeast; 3 hr trip, $44. **Royal Hudson Steam Train**, Vancouver, British Columbia, (604) 984-5246, follows the coast of Howe Sound to small mining town; $32.50 for full day. **Narrow Gauge Railroad**, Durango, CO, (970) 247-2733. Along Animas River Valley to Silverton. Old fashioned. $53 r/t, 4 trips daily. **Pikes Peak Cog Railway**, Manitou Springs, CO, (719) 685-5401. Several trips daily from Manitou Springs to Pikes Peak, the highest route in the US. $22.50 r/t. **Roaring Camp & Big Trees Narrow-Gauge Railroad,** Felton, California, (831) 335-4484. Winds through the Rincon Valley of giant redwood trees and down the San Lorenzo River Gorge to the beach at Monterey Bay. 1hr trip, 10.30 am and 2.30 pm daily, $15.00 r/t. **Skunk Train**, Ft Bragg, CA, (707) 964-6371. Half day $27, full day, $35. Scenic route through Redwoods. **Strasbourg Railroad**, Strasburg, PA, (717) 687-7522. 45 min route through Amish country 11am-4 pm on the hour, $8.25. America's oldest short-line steam locomotive.

Boats. 'If you want to take a longer trip on the Mississippi, you can try to get on a towing boat. But you'll have to work hard. Look in the *Yellow Pages* under "Towing—Marine".'

How about paddling your own canoe? The Appalachian Mountain Club publishes three books of interest to canoeists and kayakers including: *AMC River Guide Maine; AMC River Guide Massachusetts, Connecticut and Rhode Island; AMC River Guide New Hampshire and Vermont, Sea Kayaking in the Mid Atlantic;* and *Sea Kayaking in the New England Coast.* They're available by mail from AMC Books, 5 Joy Street, Boston MA 02108, or PO Box 298 Gorham, NH 03581, (800) 262-4455.

The Chicagoland Canoe Base Inc, 4019 N Narragansett Avenue, Chicago IL 60634, can provide you with all the information you need on canoes, kayaks, rafts, accessories, rentals, books and maps, (773) 777-1489.

Hitchhiking. Hitchhiking in the United States can vary from state to state, but generally it can be 'superb, simply due to the long rides'. However, we strongly recommend that women, or even men, do not hitch alone.

'A sure way of getting long rides in relative comfort and at speeds in excess of the general 55 mph limit is to ask for rides at truck stops. At Union 76 truck stops there will often be hundreds of trucks going to all parts of America. Just ask the drivers in the canteen. By using this method I managed to cover over 1000 miles from Mexico to New Orleans with only two rides.' 'Don't try truck stops unless on your own. Even then, due to new insurance regulations, it's difficult.' 'I had better luck at truck stops at night when drivers like passengers to keep them awake.' 'Truck stop directories can be obtained free at truck stops.'

Hitching is forbidden on freeways and interstates, so get your rides on the ramps, at rest areas, or at service areas. With regard to other roads, the laws vary from state to state, but even when hitching is technically illegal you can usually still get away with it if you are standing on the shoulder or side-walk, and sometimes even if you are walking with the traffic, regardless of the fact that you might be walking backwards. 'I had no problems except the usual ones. The police are okay, though they may ask to see your identi-fication.' 'Police in New York warned me, "Ten days in jail if we see you again". The next day I was given a ride by a policeman.'

Never carry any dope. Display your national flag. Always carry a sign saying where you want to go. 'We carried two signs: one stating our desti-nation, the other saying PLEASE. Fantastic results.' 'Female hitchhikers should not use destination signs; that way you have a chance to look over the driver before accepting.' Avoid getting off in cities if you don't want to stay there. 'People who gave us lifts often gave us meals and even a bed for the night.'

'Warning to female hitchhikers: don't hitch overnight trucks unless willing to satisfy the driver. No malice intended but "payment" is expected. At least that's what I found, and I was hitching with my boyfriend.' 'I often got rides with truckers and found them nice and helpful people. I slept in a cab of a truck three times without having to grant any favours, and I was a female alone. I'm not recommending overnight rides with truckers nor hitching alone for that matter, but I had no bad experiences.'

Holidays, especially Labor Day, are good times to travel as there are mil-lions of cars on the road. If you don't want to thumb, try radio stations or look in the local (especially the freaky) papers. 'For hitching long-distance, or if you're prepared to share the driving, try the ride boards at universi-ties—either advertise yourself or go to see what's offered. I got from Chicago to San Francisco this way in one car.'

'When crossing the US-Canadian border do not say you're a hitchhiker.' 'Beware the heat in the Southwest, i.e.. anywhere between LA and mid-Texas. In this area hitchers should carry a large container of water and some salt tablets. Hitchers have been found dead on the side of the road due to dehydration.' 'People are usually very congenial and offer accommodation and food.' 'I hitched from San Francisco to New York in four and a half days and could have done it in less. I experienced no more hassles than I have in Europe. The Southern states are populated by a different breed of people who are proud to be rebels and consider the Civil War to be still on, but they are still cool for hitching, especially if you are European. By the way, they call you Euro-penises.' 'I hitched 9500 miles with over 130 lifts and all but two were very friendly and helpful. I got beds, showers, endless meals, and made friends while hitching. Far more rewarding than bus travel.'

Hitching by air is another possibility. America is dotted with thousands of *small airfields* (i.e.. not JFK or LA International) located outside most towns from which people fly in *small aircraft* for pleasure or business. Those are the people you ask. 'Difficult across US/Canada border.' 'Air hitching is really difficult but saves so much time it's worth a try.' 'I walked into an air freight company office in San Francisco and got a free ride back to New York with the overnight packages.' Not a good idea to carry much luggage though— *small*, light, aircraft remember.

Bicycle. There's a 4450-mile TransAmerica Trail stretching from Virginia to Oregon, divided into five shorter routes. Five sectional booklets are available, with detailed maps and details of flora, fauna, campsites, eateries, bike shops and gradients en route. Free leaflet from Adventure Cycling, PO Box 8308, Missoula, Montana 59807, (406) 721-1776. Also, some hostels do bicycle tours; information is available from local regional offices and the hostels themselves.

A strong bicycle lock is advisable for security when parking in towns, plus a helmet (US drivers are not attuned to looking out for bikes). Bicycles are cheaper in the US than abroad. It's possible to ship a bike around the US with Amtrak or the bus companies provided it's dismantled and boxed. Bikes can sometimes be taken free on flights to and from the US as part of your baggage allowance and again must be boxed. The cost, if any, varies from airline to airline.

Walking. Yes it is done. Mostly by mad dogs and Englishmen. Like John Lees of Brighton, England, who in 1972 walked from City Hall, Los Angeles, to City Hall, New York, a distance of 2876 miles, in 53 days 12 hours 15 minutes, averaging 53.75 miles per day.

'When asking for directions, remember that most people think you are on wheels. I was directed to one place along a roadway that took me 15 minutes to negotiate in the boiling hot sun, an excursion I could have avoided by cutting—in one-third the time—through a leafy forest. Unfortunately, the guy I asked thought I was a Chevy, so I had to go the long way round.'

A list of more than 25 hiking clubs along the East Coast can be obtained by writing to the Appalachian Trail Conference, Box 807, Harpers Ferry WV 25425, (304) 535-6331. The Conference manages the 2000-mile Maine to Georgia Appalachian Trail in conjunction with the National Park Service. They'll send you information about the trail, membership, etc. Be sure to ask specifically for the list of clubs.

On the West Coast there's the Sierra Club. They can provide information about the Pacific Crest Trail, 2400 miles along the Pacific Coast from Canada to Mexico, but also offer backpack and camping advice as well as trips which last 6-10 days. 85 2nd St, 2nd floor, San Francisco CA 94105, (415) 977-5653.

Tours with a difference. If young and on your own and looking for fun and adventure, one of the proliferation of alternative tours or treks would be worth considering. Typically they either load up a van full of young people and tour chunks of the country or else they operate a roughly scheduled service allowing the traveller to get off and on when they please. One of the longest running companies (so to speak) is **TrekAmerica**. They run camping expeditions such as 25 days up the Alaska Highway, or six-week coast-to-coast journeys, stopping at the most interesting cities, towns and national parks en route. Trek America offers 57 different itineraries from 7 days to 9 weeks, covering virtually every area of North America. During July and August a 14-day tour costs approximately $770 plus $35 per week for food. They fill up quickly, so reserve early. There is a 15% discount for all BUNAC members. Extras such as horseback riding and rafting are available at additional cost.

In Britain, contact TrekAmerica, Worldwide Reservation, 4 Waterperry Court, Middleton Road, Banbury, Oxon, OX6 8QG. Tel: 01295-256777. In the USA: TrekAmerica, PO Box 189 Rockaway, NJ 07866. (973) 983-1144 or (800) 221-0596. Email: info@trekamerica.com. 'An excellent way to see America if you don't mind camping and long drives. For a girl travelling on her own who didn't want to Greyhound or hitch, it enabled me to see a terrific amount in three weeks.'

For exploring the western national parks north to Alaska, south to Baja California, you could consider **Adventurebus**. All trips depart from Los Angeles, San Diego or Las Vegas and, for example, the 16-day national parks trip costs $549 and $151 for food. Adventurebus offer a discount to BUNAC members. Call: 1-888-737-5263 for info and reservations, or check them on the web at: *www.adventurebus.com*.

See also a source book called *Adventure Travel North America* which lists all kinds of outdoor-type vacations including a wide range of 'Cowboy Vacations'. $16.95 plus $3 postage. The book is available from Adventure Guides Inc., 7550 E MacDonald Drive, Suite M, Scottsdale, Arizona 85250, (800) 252-7899. Adventure Guides Inc also arranges customised itineraries for travellers.

Urban Travel. City buses and subway systems generally offer good services throughout North America. Usually, a flat fare is used which can make short hops expensive but long rides very reasonable. Many cities have a transfer system allowing you to change from one bus line to another, or even from bus to subway, without paying extra. Robberies have meant that bus drivers will not carry any more money than is absolutely necessary, so you must always have the exact fare.

Taxis can be pretty expensive unless shared. The ubiquitous Gray Line company ensures that nearly every city has its bus tour, and some have boat tours as well.

For further details on all forms of urban travel, see city headings throughout the Guide.

FURTHER READING

Fiction

The Awakening, Kate Chopin
Bonfire of the Vanities, Tom Wolfe
Catcher in the Rye, J. D. Salinger
Changing Places, David Lodge
Ethan Frome, Edith Wharton
Gone with the Wind, Margaret Mitchell
Glitz, Elmore Leonard
The Grapes of Wrath, John Steinbeck
The Great Gatsby, F. Scott Fitzgerald
Huckleberry Finn, Mark Twain
Lake Wobegon Days, Garrison Keiller
Light in August, William Faulkner
The London Embassy, Paul Theroux
Main Street, Sinclair Lewis
A Month of Sundays, John Updike
Native Son, Richard Wright
Ninety-Two in the Shade, Thomas McGuane
On the Road, Jack Kerouac
O Pioneers!, Willa Cather
Outcasts of Poker Flat, Bret Harte
The Scarlet Letter, Nathaniel Hawthorne
Southern Discomfort, Rita Mae Brown
Stepping Westward, Malcolm Bradbury
To Kill a Mockingbird, Harper Lee
Trout Fishing in America, Richard Brautigan
USA, John Dos Passos

Other Works

Blue Highway: A Journey into America, William Least Halfmoon
Bury My Heart at Wounded Knee: an Indian History of the American West, Dee Brown
Democracy in America, Alexis De Toqueville
Fear and Loathing in Las Vegas, Hunter S. Thompson
New York Days, New York Nights, Stephen Brook
The Nine Nations of North America, Garreau
Old Glory, Johnathan Raban
The Lost Continent: Travels in Small Town America, Bill Bryson
Undaunted Courage, Stephen E. Ambrose
Vagabonding in America, Ed Buryn (if you can get hold of it)
Walk West, David Jenkins

NEW ENGLAND

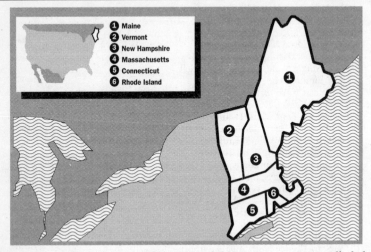

1. Maine
2. Vermont
3. New Hampshire
4. Massachusetts
5. Connecticut
6. Rhode Island

The upper north-east corner of the United States is sometimes called the nation's attic. One of the first areas in the New World to be colonised by Europeans, it is the old historical ties, more than any other, which bind these New England states together. It was here that American independence was born, embodied by such patriots as Paul Revere and Samuel Adams. The region's size does not match its great historical significance—its six states are together smaller than Oklahoma.

New England is a melting pot, spiced with a rich diversity gained from the British, Irish, Italians, French Canadians, Portuguese, Jews and many others who now make up the population. Cultural contrasts abound: contemporary, cosmopolitan Boston stands alongside peaceful country towns—revered reminders of early American society. To 'Southerners', however, New Englanders are still Yankees.

This compact region offers a great variety of scenery, from the rugged White Mountains of New Hampshire to the rolling green hills of Vermont, Massachusetts and Connecticut. The often spectacular coastline varies in its moods from state to state. Coastal roads stretch for miles weaving around jagged points and hidden inlets. Lush green countryside becomes weather-beaten and sun-bleached as it meets the Atlantic.

Politically, New England is important; the world's first written 'constitution'—the Mayflower Compact—was signed by the Pilgrim Fathers here in 1620. The American Revolution was hatched in Boston, and in modern times, ex-President Bush and the Kennedys hail from the area.

The seasons are distinct in New England: a long, cold, winter followed by a short blossom-filled spring, a hot, often humid summer, and best of all, a glorious autumn when the leaves turn the hillsides gold, scarlet and amber.

Hard-core hikers may like to tackle the 2000-mile long Appalachian Trail—the longest marked trail in the world. Beginning north of Bangor in Maine it winds more than 2000 miles from Baxter State Park to the mountains of Georgia.

CONNECTICUT *The Nutmeg State*

Connecticut has historically regarded itself as part of New England, although the area abutting New York State along Long Island Sound has far stronger ties with New York City than it has with Burlington, VT, or even Hartford, the state capital. Greenwich, Stamford and Bridgeport make up a significant commuter-belt and many people here look to the New York media for their news and entertainment.

Away from the coast, Connecticut is a state of broad rivers, farms, forests, rolling hills and placid colonial villages. In particular, the Litchfield Hills in the north-western part of the state offer pretty scenery and have several excellent state parks good for camping and walking.

Connecticut is the third smallest state in the Union and one of the most densely populated.

The submarine was invented here in 1776 and Connecticut is also the birthplace of the lollipop and the payphone. The insurance industry has its roots in Connecticut and the Constitution State is home to America's first law school. Some of the oldest university art collections are at **Yale University**, in New Haven. *www.yahoo.com/Regional/U_S_States/Connecticut* or *www.tourism.state.ct.us*
The telephone area code for the south-western corner of the state is 203, elsewhere it is 860.

HARTFORD The state capital is home to the nation's insurance industry, and thanks to the dark-suited image this presents, the city is not ordinarily known for its sparkling social scene. Recently, however efforts have been made to turn the city into a livelier regional attraction. The **Civic Center** and **State House Square** provide shopping, restaurants, and entertainment, and should be added to a list of more antique sights, such as **Mark Twain's House**, the pre-World War One carousel in **Bushnell Park**, and, in the nearby suburbs of Wethersfield and Farmington, some of the oldest colonial houses in the US.

While here, pick up the *Hartford Courant*, founded in 1764 and the newspaper with the oldest continuous name and circulation in the nation, possibly in the world. *www.enjoyhartford.com*

ACCOMMODATION
Most hotels downtown are $50 and up for doubles.
Days Inn, 207 Brainard Rd, 247-3297, D-$59, XP-$5. A bargain for four sharing!
Mark Twain Hostel, 131 Tremont St, 523-7255. Rambling Victorian house preserved in its natural state. $15 AYH, non-AYH $18, $1 linen. Private rooms $30-$38, rsvs required. Kitchen, dining room, picnic area, bike storage, laundry. Friendly, enthusiastic staff, open 24 hrs, 365 days a year. Tours available for Mark Twain House which is only a block away.

YMCA, 160 Jewel St, 522-4183. Private room $24/$161 weekly, dorm (men only) $19/$126 weekly. Close to Civic Center.

FOOD/ENTERTAINMENT
City Steam Brewery Cafe, 942 Main St, 525-1600. Lunch around $8, dinner around $12. Very popular with the locals. Live comedy on weekends, cover varies.
Russian Lady Cafe, 191 Ann St, 525-3003. In a wonderful old building topped with a statue of a royal Russian lady, hence the name. Live bands Tue-Sat. Drinks special offered every night. Check out the rooftop garden! Behind Civic Center.

OF INTEREST
Bushnell Park, adjacent State Capitol, 246-7739, has a 1914 carousel; you can ride one of its 48 horses or a chariot to the tunes of a Wurlitzer Band Organ for 50¢. Tue-Sun 11am-5pm.
Monday Night Jazz Series, Bushnell Park, Jul-Aug, free. 722-6231 for more info.
Hartford Festival of Jazz, Bushnell Park and Elizabeth Park, 722-6231. Last weekend in July, free.
Elizabeth Park Rose Garden, Prospect Ave. First municipal rose garden in the country. Nature walks, rock gardens, Pond House with auditorium. Open daily dawn-dusk.
Harriet Beecher Stowe House, Nook Farm, Farmington Ave at Forest St, 525-9317. This charming Victorian cottage was the home of HBS after the publication of *Uncle Tom's Cabin*, from 1873 to her death in 1896. Mon-Sat 10am-4pm, Sun noon-4pm, closed Mon in winter, tours $4.50.
Mark Twain House, 351 Farmington Ave, next door to Harriet Beecher Stowe House, 493-6411. Calling all lovers of American literature—MT, who was related on his mother's side to the Earl of Durham, lived here for almost 20 years, publishing *Huckleberry Finn* and other major works from this quirky Victorian-Gothic style mansion. Summer: Mon-Sat 9.30am-5pm, Sun 11am-5pm, last tour at 4pm. Closed Tue in winter; 1 hr tour $9. Bring a picnic to a free. 'Twain by Twilight' concert evening held in the grounds during July, includes free admission to first floor of house. Call for dates and details.
New England Air Museum, Bradley International Airport, Windsor Locks, 14 miles from Hartford, 623-3305. Two huge display hangars and more than 70 aircraft from all periods of aviation history. Daily 10am-5pm, $6.75.
Old State House, 800 Main St, 522-6766. Formerly the State Capitol, recently restored and refurbished back to its 1796 appearance. Information centre, Mon-Fri 10am-4pm, Sat 11am-4pm.
State Capitol, Capitol Ave and Trinity St, 240-0222, exit 48 off I-84. A dazzling Gothic monolith capped by a gold dome. Contains lots of Connecticut historical memorabilia. Be sure to see the dramatic Hall of Flags. Tours available hourly Mon-Fri, 9.15am-1.15pm, Sat 10.15am-2.15pm (Apr-Oct only), free.
The Trash Museum, 211 Murphy Rd, 247-4280. Tours and hands-on exhibits on solid waste management and recycling, including the 'Temple of Trash'. Summer hours: Wed-Sat 10am-4pm, free.
Wadsworth Athenaeum, 600 Main St, 278-2670. One of New England's best art collections with 45,000 works; it is the country's oldest public art gallery. Tue-Sun, 11 am-5pm; $7, $5 w/student ID. Free all day Thu, and Sat before noon.

INFORMATION
Convention and Visitors Bureau, Civic Center Plaza, 728-6789/(800) 446-7811. Mon-Fri, 9am-4.30pm.
Hartford Guides, 101 Pearl St, 522-0855. Goodwill ambassadors on duty throughout the town, ready to serve the lost and the curious. Easily recognisable in their red, white and khaki uniforms.

INTERNET ACCESS
Hartford Public Library, 500 Main St, 543-8628. Free use of computers for Internet.

TRAVEL
Greyhound, 1 Union Pl, 247-3524/(800) 231-2222. NYC ($18, 3 hrs), Boston ($22, 2 hrs).
Amtrak, 727-1776/(800) 872-7245, at Union Place. NYC ($25, 3 hrs, time restrictions apply).
Connecticut Transit Information Centre, behind old State House, btwn Main & Market Sts, 525-9181, has info on public transport within the city (basic fare $1) and a map of downtown area. Mon-Fri 7am-6pm.
NB. Only regular transport available from downtown to Bradley International Airport is via shuttle service from downtown hotels. Cost: about $1.

LITCHFIELD HILLS In the north-western corner of the state, this is an area of rolling hills, with woods, rivers, streams and lakes. The town of Litchfield is a movieman's epitome of New England, with its white wooden churches, fine colonial houses, and of course, picket fences. The town centre itself is a National Historic Site. Harriet Beecher Stowe and Ethan Allen were born here: the **Litchfield Historical Society**, 567-4501, has all the facts, with historical and art exhibits. Those of a judicial frame of mind may wish to stop at the **Tapping Reeve House**, 82 South St, 567-8919, America's first law school. Tue-Sat 11am-5pm, Sun 1pm-5pm. $5 to visit both, $3 w/student ID. **Haight Vineyard,** Chestnut Hill, 567-4045, Self-guided Vineyard Walk, as well as free tasting and guided tours Mon-Sat 10.30am-4pm, Sun noon-4pm. **Hopkins Vineyard**, 868-7954, in New Preston, is considered one of the most scenic vineyards in the east. Self-guided tours Mon-Fri, guided tours Sat-Sun 2pm, free.

Nearby is **Bantam Lake**, good for water sports, including ice yachting in winter. The **White Memorial Foundation**, a wildlife sanctuary and museum, takes up about half of the lake's shoreline, with 35 miles of trails for hiking.

Southwest of the lake via Rte 109 & Rte 47 is the village of **Washington**, another 'jewel of a colonial village', home to many artists and writers. The **American Indian Archaeological Institute**, 38 Curtis Rd, 868-0518, is also here. Take Rte 47 to Rte 199. The Institute is home to a replicated Algonquian village complete with wigwams and a traditional longhouse, a walking trail and museum. Mon-Sat 10am-5pm, Sun noon-5pm, $4.

Lime Rock Park, Lakeville, 435-5000, (800) RACE-LRP, for auto racing. Although 50 miles from Hartford, nestled in the scenic Berkshire Hills, the Park is a great day out if you can get there; you might even catch Paul Newman on the track! Bring a picnic and stay all day at one of the vintage car festivals, or take a look behind the scenes at a professional road race. Amateur races $12, from $50 for a full access weekend pass, with free on-site camping.

The Litchfield Hills are a good area for walking and camping. Three of the nicer state parks where you can do both are **Housatonic Meadows**, **Lake Waramaug** and **Macedonia Brook**, none of which are far from Kent. For more information on parks, historic sites, accommodation and restaurants in the area contact **Litchfield Hills Visitors Commission**, P.O Box 968, 499

Bantam Rd, Litchfield, CT 06759, 567-4506. For camping permits in the State Parks write to the **Bureau of State Parks and Forests**, 79 Elm St, Hartford, 06106, 424-3200. Mon-Fri 8am-4.30pm. *www.litchfieldhills.com*

BRISTOL   As you meander through picturesque landscapes and tiny hamlets on your way to New Haven, stop off in Bristol, the one time clock-making capital of the US. Arrive at the **American Clock and Watch Museum**, 100 Maple St, 583-6070, in time to hear the midday chimes! A horologist's delight, brimming over with 3,500 timepieces past and present, comic and stately, grand and miniature. March-Nov, 10am-5pm, $3.50.

Step back in time and visit the **New England Carousel Museum**, 95 Riverside Ave, Bristol, 585-5411, Mon-Sat 10am-5pm, Sun noon-5pm, $4.50. Some 300 carved horses, cats, elephants, chariots, etc., of intricate and occasionally bejewelled design. Guided tours include two hurdy gurdy organs, and a workshop restoring working carousel figures and parts. Magical.

Lake Compounce Theme Park, 822 Lake Ave, 583-3631, (exit 31 off I-84). Founded in 1846, this is the country's oldest running theme park. A beautifully hand-carved 1911 Carousel is the main attraction, but for a real boneshaking ride, try the 'Wildcat,' a wooden roller-coaster built in 1927. Other attractions include a water park, paddle boats, mini-golf. Mid-June-mid-Aug, daily 11am-8pm. $22 admission and rides all day, general admission $6, includes swimming and shows.

NEW HAVEN   The city grew up around its harbour and **Yale University** (boola, boola). This Ivy League university, one of the best and oldest in the United States, currently enjoys recognition for graduating President Bill Clinton, Hillary Rodham Clinton, *and* former president, George Bush.

Sadly, however, New Haven has failed to uphold its 19th-century reputation as one of America's most beautiful cities. While some areas are undergoing renovation, the nicest parts by far are still found on and around the **Green**. On the credit side, however, theatre and music thrive in New Haven, and there are numerous enjoyable bars, cafes, and restaurants patronised by the student population.

Going east along Long Island Sound, you come to New London, from where you can catch a ferry to Long Island and Block Island. Further still, there's Mystic, en route to Newport, RI and the Massachusetts seacoast. *www.cityofnewhaven.com*
The telephone area code for New Haven is 203.

ACCOMMODATION
Hotel Duncan, 1151 Chapel St, 787-1273. Downtown, right next to Yale, well-appointed for the price. S-$44, D-$60, XP-$15, TV.
Regal Inn, 1605 Whalley Ave, (Exit 59 off rte 15), 389-9504. S-$50, D-$60, TV.
Three Judges Motor Lodge, 1560 Whalley Ave, 389-2161. S-$41 king-size bed, D-$60, TV.

FOOD
The most popular restaurants in town are on Wooster St, in the attractive Italian district.
Archie Moore's, 188½ Willow St, ½ mile north of Peabody Museum, 773-9870.

Named 'best watering hole in state,' great buffalo wings, nachos, burgers, pasta, baseball on the tube, popular with grad students and locals. Moderately priced, $6.50-$12.

Atticus Bookstore, 1082 Chapel St, 776-4040. Relaxing coffee shop in the Yale Center for British Art. Daily 8am-midnight.

Clerks, 74 Whitney Ave, 777-2728. Grab fast food at great prices from this busy lunch-spot. Sandwiches from $2, deli sandwiches with fries $6, hot dogs $2.50,. Mon-Thu 7am-10pm, Fri-Sat 7am-11pm, Sun 9am-11pm.

Louie's Lunch, 263 Crown St, 562-5507. Enjoy breakfast cooked in a 250-year-old frying pan. Lunches are good, and worth the wait at this reputed birthplace of the hamburger, $3 and up. Unique, antique, friendly atmosphere.'

Pepe's Pizzeria, 157 Wooster St, 865-5762. Try their specials, clam and garlic, broccoli and sausage or invent your own! Small cheese and tomato $6.

Thai Taste, 1151 Chapel St, 776-9802. Appetisers from $4, entrees from $7.50. Pad Thai a speciality. Downstairs from Duncan Hotel. Evenings only. 'Extremely good.'

OF INTEREST

The Green, once a wild, swampy forest trodden by Indians, is now a shaded park. Despite encroaching modern buildings, the Green still retains much of its original flavour, flanked as it is on the north side by the impressive, ivy-clad halls of Yale.

In August, New Haven plays host to world tennis champions in the **International Tennis Tournament**, The Connecticut Tennis Center at Yale University, I-95, exit 44. Call 776-7331/(888) 997-4568 for details of this prestigious annual event when the world's top players, such as Agassi or Stich compete. If you missed Wimbledon, this is a must! Tickets $20; don't forget your strawberries!

Amistad Memorial, City Hall, 165 Church St. Statue depicting Senghe Pieh, leader of the Amistad revolt. Situated on the site of the jail where the captives were held.

East Rock Park, East Rock Road. Spectacular view of Long Island Sound and the harbour, nature trails, bird sanctuary, picnic facilities. Open daily dawn-dusk.

Peabody Museum of Natural History, 170 Whitney Ave, 432-5050. Dinosaurs and Connecticut flora and fauna. Mon-Sat 10am-5pm, Sun noon-5pm, $5.

Shore Line Trolley Museum, East Haven, 5 miles from New Haven, 467-6927. Summer: daily 10.30am-4.30pm. Admission and 3-mile ride, $5.

Yale Center for British Art, 1080 Chapel St, 432-2800. Hogarth, Constable, Turner, Pre-Raphaelites and contemporary art, including the work of Damien Hirst. Most comprehensive collection of British works outside Britain. Tue-Sat 10am-5pm, Sun noon-5pm, closed Mon; free. Provides a fascinating and informative tour through the permanent collections. *www.yale.edu/ycba*

Yale University, 432-2300. Free tours around the old spires and cobbled courtyards of the university, mostly built in the thirties, and meticulously designed to look effectively ancient, are available in summer, Mon-Fri 10.30am & 2pm, Sat & Sun 1.30pm, starting at Visitor's Center, 149 Elm St. Highlights include the Old Campus through **Phelps Gate** off College St, **Connecticut Hall** (the oldest building), the **Art of Architecture Building** designed by Paul Rudolph and the **Beinicke Rare Book Library**.

Yale University Art Gallery, 1111 Chapel St, 432-0600. Home to a good collection of French Impressionists, an excellent assortment of contemporary American paintings; Hopper, Aitkins and Homer, and Van Gogh's *Night Cafe*. Tue-Sat 10am-5pm, Sun 1pm-6pm, free.

ENTERTAINMENT

In summer try the *New Haven Advocate*, (Thu) a free arts and news weekly. *www.newhavenadvocate.com*

Anchor Bar, 272 College St, 865-1512. Authentic fifties bar with intimate booths, orange lighting, and good food at moderate prices.

Jazz Festival. Enjoy free outdoor concerts, R&B, Jazz and ethnic bluegrass, Latin, rock, folk and Cajun, in the Green, from mid-July—mid-Aug on Friday evenings at 6pm. Call the **Cultural Affairs Office**, 946-7821, for details.
Toad's Place, 300 York St, 624-8623. Dance club and concert venue. Box office 11am-6pm daily, tkts around $12.50. Wed night dance party, free w/college ID. *www.toadsplace.com*
Look for current productions at the **Long Wharf Theater**, 222 Sergent Dr, 787-4282. Season runs Oct-June. Closed Mon. Discount tkts available for students on day of performance. Pay what you can system first Thu after an opening, at the box office. The excellent **Yale Repertory Theater**, 222 York St, 432-1234, boasts Meryl Streep, Henry Winkler among others as alumni. Offers drama, comedy, classics Oct-May. $26-$34, half price day of tkts w/student ID.

INFORMATION
Maps and guides from the **University Information Office**, 149 Elm St, 432-2300. Mon-Fri 9am-4.45pm.
Traveler's Aid, 1 Long Wharf Dr, 495-7437. Mon-Fri 9am-5pm. Phone messages monitored at weekends for crisis situations.
New Haven Convention and Visitors Bureau, 59 Elm St, 777-8550/(800) 332-STAY. Mon-Fri 8.30am-5pm.

INTERNET ACCESS
New Haven Free Public Library, 133 Elm St, across from the Green, 946-8130. Free Internet access, half hour limit.

TRAVEL
Amtrak, Union Ave, (800) 872-7245. Newly renovated station but unsafe at night. NYC ($25), Boston ($36).
Connecticut Limousine Service, Sports Haven Complex, 600 Long Wharf Dr, (800) 472-5466. Frequent runs to JFK, Newark and La Guardia Airports. $38 to JFK and LGA, $41 to Newark. Also runs from other CT towns.
Greyhound, 45 George St, (800) 231-2222. NYC ($20), Boston ($28).
Metro-North Commuter Railroad, Union Station, (800) 638-7646/in NYC (212) 532-4900. Fares are cheaper to NYC than Amtrak, $11.50 off-peak, $15.25 rush-hour.

CONNECTICUT RIVER VALLEY The lower river valley, where river meets sea between New Haven and New London, is one of the state's loveliest, most unspoilt and peaceful areas. Once an important seafaring commercial centre, this is now an area for gentle sailing, pottering around the small towns, or watching the wildlife at **Selden Neck State Park** or on the salt marshes around Old Lyme. *Use area code 860.*

ACCOMMODATION
Unless you feel like treating yourself to a night at one of the expensive old inns here you will have to search out a motel or campground somewhere off I-95. Some worth trying are;
Heritage Motor Inn, 1500 Boston Post Rd, exit 66 off I-95, 388-3743. $65-$85 for two, free local calls, outdoor pool, 2 miles from downtown.
Liberty Inn, 55 Springbrook Rd, exit 67/68 off I-95, 388-1777. $68-$98 for two, bfast included, 1 mile from downtown Old Saybrook.

OF INTEREST
Essex: Main St is lined with white clapboard homes of colonial sea captains. America's first warship, *Oliver Cromwell*, was built here. At the **Ivoryton**

Playhouse, 103 N. Main St, Ivoryton, 767-8348, Katharine Hepburn 'found out what theatre was all about'. The **Valley Railroad Company,** 767-0103, runs scenic steam train and riverboat rides from Essex, $16.50.

Gillette Castle State Park, across the river from Essex, off Rte 82, 526-2336. Once the estate of actor William Gillette who made his name playing Sherlock Holmes. The castle was built and furnished like a Victorian stage-setting. 'Weird.' Closed for renovation, call ahead (the park will remain open throughout the renovation). Reached by the **Chester-Hadlyme ferry** 443-3856, which has been in service since 1769. The trip across the river costs $2.25 for a car and driver, XP-75¢.

Old Lyme, Rte 156. Summer artists' colony and home of the **Nut Museum**, 434-7636, dedicated to a greater awareness of nuts. Owner Elizabeth Tashjian, artist and visionary, collects art, music, and lore on the nut and has appeared with Johnny Carson and David Letterman and on MTV and *The Howard Stern Show* singing her 'nutty' songs. See a 35-lb coco-de-mer, the world's largest kind of nut. Admission by appointment only, $3 plus one nut (no, your friend doesn't qualify). 'Indescribably bizarre.'

A one-time boarding house and centre of the Old Lyme art colony is now the **Florence Griswold Museum**, 96 Lyme St, 434-5542. The bohemian antics of Miss Griswold and her fellow impressionists were considered somewhat shocking by the locals. You can see their work Tue-Sat 10am-5pm, Sun 1pm-5pm; Jan-Mar, Wed-Sun 1pm-5pm; $5, $4 w/student ID.

Valley Railroad, Exit 3 off Rte 9, 767-0103. Scenic 2½ hr combined train/boat ride along the Connecticut River past Gillette Castle and Goodspeed Opera House, $16. Train only, $10. Daily in summer, otherwise Wed-Sun, closed in winter except for special Xmas trains.

INFORMATION
Connecticut River Valley & Shoreline Visitors Council, 393 Main St, Middletown, 347-0028/(800) 486-3346. Mon-Fri 8.30am-4.30pm.

NEW LONDON   Off I-95, on the River Thames (pronounced as it looks), the town, once an important whaling port, had the distinction of being burnt to the ground by Benedict Arnold and his troops in 1781. Today it is the home of **Connecticut College** and the **US Coast Guard Academy**. There are some well-restored houses on Star Street and on Green Street is the **Dutch Tavern** once frequented by Eugene O'Neill. 'The best bar in the US; unique atmosphere.'

ACCOMMODATION
Motel 6, west of New London, in Niantic, exit 74 off I-95, 739-6991. S-$59-$65, D-$65-71, XP-$3.

FOOD
Bangkok City, 123 State St, 442-6970, Thai food at cheapish prices. Spice-rating allows you to go as hot as you dare.

For picnic table informality, the **Sea Swirl**, 536-3452, in Mystic, at the junction of Rtes 1 & 27, is an ice-cream stand much favoured locally for really good clam strips ($6.60) and clam bellies ($11.95). Daily 11am-10pm.

In **Groton** there is **Paul's Pasta**, 223 Thames, 445-5276. A favourite with students, it has churning pasta machines in the window and a view of the ships in New London harbour from the terrace. Offers classics such as lobster ravioli ($8.95) and spaghetti pie ($7.95).

OF INTEREST

The *Argia*, a replica of a 19th-century gaff-rigged schooner, will take you cruising to Fisher's Island on half-day adventures, full-day sailing odysseys or sunset cruises. Departs from Steamboat Wharf, 10am, 2pm, & 6pm. $32, $34 w/ends, refreshments included. **Voyager Cruises**, 73 Steamboat Wharf, 536-0416.

Connecticut College Arboretum, Williams St, 439-5020. 425 acres of hiking trails and ponds, open daily dawn 'til dusk. Call 439-2787 for details of 'Shakespeare in the Arboretum' during July and August, $10, $7 w/student ID.

Groton, across the Thames, on Rte 12. Investigate WW2 paraphernalia and climb aboard the world's first nuclear-powered sub launched from the Electric Boatyard here in 1954. **Historic Ship *Nautilus* & Submarine Force Museum**, 694-3174/(800) 343-0079, Wed-Mon 9am-5pm, Tue 1pm-5pm, free. *www.ussnautilus.org*

Lyman Allyn Art Museum, 625 William St, near the arboretum, 443-2545, specialising in furniture and silver, also includes outstanding collection of dolls and doll houses. Tue-Sat 10am-5pm, Sun 1pm-5pm. $4, $3 w/student ID, free on Sun.

Monte Cristo Cottage, 325 Pequot Ave, 443-0051, boyhood home of Eugene O'Neill, inspired sets for *Ah, Wilderness* and *Long Day's Journey Into Night*; named after the Count of Monte Cristo, his actor-father's most famous part, $4. Summer: Tue-Sat 10am-5pm, Sun 1pm-5pm. *www.eugeneoneill.org/mcc.htm*

Mystic Marinelife Aquarium, just off I95, 572-5955. Whales, sea lions, dolphins, seals. Daily 9am-6pm, gates close at 5pm, last mammal demo at 4.30pm, $15. Call the aquarium collect if you see a marine mammal stranded on the beach.

Mystic Seaport, 572-0711. A re-created mid-19th century coastal village and maritime museum on Rte 27. Some of the fastest clipper ships were built in Mystic and the last of the wooden whaling ships, the *Charles W. Morgan* (which celebrated its 150th anniversary in 1991) awaits inspection. Daily 9am-6pm in summer; $16 (ticket valid for two days). Seasonal events include a lobster festival over Memorial Day weekend, and an October Chowderfest.

Ocean Beach Park, foot of Ocean Ave, 447-3031. Recreation area offering swimming in Olympic size pool, triple water-slide, mini-golf, food concessions. Summer: Daily 9am-midnight, gates close 10pm. $5 admission (includes parking) weekdays, $8 w/ends. Rides cost extra.

U.S. Coast Guard Band Concert Series, 701-6826, Leamy Hall Auditorium, 15 Mohegan Ave. Free concerts throughout the year.

MAINE *Pine Tree State*

As big as the other five New England states combined, Maine has a modest population similar to that of Rhode Island. In some areas the wildlife outnumbers the human inhabitants which means it is the perfect place to get away from it all. Maine offers a variety of spectacular environments and unspoiled natural wonders, from rugged coastline to mountains, clear lakes and breathtaking white water.

Especially recommended is the drive 'down east' (north-east) along the rocky coastline. On a straight line, the coast of Maine is 250 miles long, but all the bays, harbours and peninsulas lengthen the shoreline to some 2400 miles. Inland are acres of unexplored, moose-filled forests and huge lakes, remote and seldom visited, 2,500 in all. While here, look out for blueberry festivals, clambakes, and lobster picnics—the state annually harvests millions of pounds of fish and shellfish, and fertile farmlands mean Maine is also among the top spud producers in the US.

In addition to hiking, boating, and swimming, Maine offers great opportunities for biking and white water rafting. Thousands of miles of peaceful, scenic secondary roads—good for biking—wind through the interior and along the coast. Bike rentals are widely available, and two guidebooks list scenic routes and travel tips: *25 Bicycle Tours in Maine*, by Howard Stone (Back Country Publications, PO Box 175, Woodstock, VT 05091), and *Bicycling*, by DeLorme Publishing Company.

White Water Rafting in Maine is an adventure not to be missed. You'll find both water and outfitters to be plentiful at **The Forks** (named for the confluence of the **Dead** and **Kennebec** Rivers in the upper Kennebec Valley) and the West Branch of the **Penobscot** between Moosehead Lake and Baxter State Park in the Katahdin/Moosehead Region. Several outfitters throughout the state organise kayaking tours; try: Loon Bay Kayaking, (888) 786-0676, *www.cyberway.com/cafe/kayaks*; Maine Sport Outfitters, (800) 722-0826, *www.mainesport.com*; World Within Sea Kayaking, (207) 646-0455, *www.worldwithin.com*; Maine Island Kayak Co., (800) 796-2373, *www.maineislandkayak.com*.

For more information on camping and access rules write to the **Bureau of Parks and Lands**, Maine Department of Conservation, 22 State House Station, Augusta, 04333-0022, or call on (207) 287-3821. Camping fees are about $15 per site, $2 rsvs fee.

If all that exercise is not for you, then Maine has one other main attraction: **factory outlet stores** 'headquartered' in the Kittery area, one hour north of Boston, and south of Portland, exit 3 off I-95, call 1-888-KITTERY. There are real bargains to be found with products often having 20%-75% off. *www.yahoo.com/Regional/U_S__States/Maine* or *www.visitmaine.com*
The telephone area code for Maine is 207.

SOUTH COAST If you're in a hurry to head 'down east', hop on I-95, but if you have the time to meander try coastal Rte 1. This winding road, which can be busy during the summer, provides easy access to a variety of seaside towns and attractions.

Though actually beginning further south, the Maine section of Rte 1 begins in **Kittery**. Known historically for its shipbuilders, this town is buzzing with bargain hunters at the factory outlets mentioned above. If relaxing on a long, sandy beach is more appealing, head for **Ogunquit** about 10 miles north. Centuries after the Indians named this 'beautiful place by the sea,' it is still an attractive and popular resort. You'll find a quieter spot a few miles off Rte 1 on Rte 9 at the **Rachel Carson National Wildlife Refuge** in **Wells**, 646-9226. Here, solitude and rare birds among 1600 acres of shady wetlands combine to delight ornithologist and picnicker alike.

Continuing up Rte 9 brings you to **Kennebunkport**, vacation residence of former president George Bush. Though beautifully maintained, this one-time ship-building village is sadly falling victim to 'quaint disease'. Avoid downtown at rush hour.

Try **Dixon's Campground**, 2 miles south of Ogunquit on **Cape Neddick**, 363-2131, free shuttle to beach 5 times daily. Sites for two, $28 with hook-up, XP-$7.50, rsvs recommended.

PORTLAND   The gateway to north-east Maine, Portland is the largest city (pop. 64,000) in a state where cities and towns are few and far between. Here the coast changes from long sections of beach to a hodgepodge of islands, bays and inlets. Portland had an early history of Indian massacres and British burnings. The city has recently been revitalised and restored and is now a commercial and cultural centre, as well as being home to the **University of Southern Maine**.

Take a ferry to one of the hundreds of islands in **Casco Bay**. Inland there is vast **Sebago Lake** for summer swimming, sailing, waterskiing and sunning. *www.visitportland.com*

ACCOMMODATION

Oak Leaf Inn, 51A Oak St, 773-7882. S-$65, D-$85. Off-season rates lower. 'Clean and only 5 minute walk from scenic Old Port area.'

Portland Summer Hostel, 645 Congress St, 874-3281 (in season) (617) 731-8096 (off season). Downtown, close to Greyhound station, Portland Hall in Southern Maine University. $16 AYH, $19 non-AYH, bfast and linen included. Kitchen, TV, laundry and storage facilities. Check-in 5pm. Rsvs recommended.

Inn at St. John, 939 Congress St, 773-6481. S-$54-64, D-$64-99, shared bath, bfast included. 20 min walk from downtown. 'Excellent location opposite Greyhound.' 'Exceptionally clean and pleasant.'

YMCA, 70 Forest Ave, 874-1105. S-$36.25 first night, $26.25 additional nights, $99.75 week. Single rooms, men only. Turn up at 11am for the best chance of a room.

YWCA, 87 Spring St, 874-1130. $12.84 per person, 2 beds in each room. Women only. Free use of pool in morning. 'A clean, friendly place, very handy for Old Portland.' Rsvs recommended in summer.

FOOD

Great Lost Bear, 540 Forest Ave, 772-0300. Choose from over 100 items on the menu and 54 varieties of draft and bottled beer! Burgers and veggie specials $6-$9. Mon-Sat 11.30am-11.30pm, Sun noon-11.30pm. Best place to drink in Maine.'

Silly's, 40 Washington Ave, 772-0360. Burgers, pizza, seafood, home-made ice-cream shakes. Try their famous Jamaican jerk chicken $6.50, or their creative roll-up sandwiches,' $2.25 upwards. Mon-Thu 11am-9.30pm, Fri 11am-10pm, Sat noon-10pm, closed Sundays.

Three Dollar Dewey's, 241 Commercial St, 772-3310. Pub-style eatery. 36 beers on tap, 50-plus bottle beers, three alarm chilli, lots of seafood and ethnic veggie dishes. Nothing on menu over $9.50.

OF INTEREST

For memorable boat trips and best views of the rugged coastline try **Casco Bay Lines** (America's oldest ferry service), CBITD Ferry Terminal, Commercial & Franklin Sts, 774-7871. Year round service to Peaks, Chebeague, Long, Great and Little Diamond and Cliff Islands. $8.50-$14.50, or take the Mailboat for $9.75.

Farmers Market: sells local produce; some organic food. Mon-Sat 9am-7pm, Sun 10am-5pm, one block from Monument Square behind the library.

Henry Wadsworth Longfellow House, 485 Congress St, 772-1807. Was the poet's childhood home. June-Oct, Tue-Sun 10am-4pm, $5, includes tour.

Old Orchard Beach, south of Portland. 'Maine's answer to Blackpool. Large water slides, good beach. Lots of French Canadians frequent this place.' Biddeford/Saco Shuttle Bus, 282-5408, leaves Portland for Old Orchard Beach six times daily, from corner of Elm & Congress on Monument Sq, $3 o/w.

Higgins, **Crescent** and **Scarborough** beaches are also good, and **Prout's Neck** is where artist Winslow Homer did much of his painting.

Old Port Exchange, on the waterfront. Reconstructed in Victorian style with cobblestone streets, gas lamps, boutiques and restaurants. Favourite haunt for locals as well as visitors.

Portland Head Coastguard Station and Lighthouse, 799-2661, follow road to Cape Elizabeth south from Portland, off US 1. Commissioned by George Washington and built in 1791, Portland Head is Maine's oldest lighthouse. Small museum and picnic facilities, $2. 'Great views.'

Portland Museum of Art, 7 Congress St, 773-ARTS. Painting, sculpture and decorative arts, including works by Homer and Wyeth. July-Oct, Tue, Wed, Sat and Sun 10am-5pm, Thu & Fri 'til 9pm, $6, $5 w/student ID.

INFORMATION
Greater Portland Convention and Visitors Bureau, 305 Commercial St, 772-5800. Sells maps for self-guided walking tours; $1. Daily 8am-6pm, w/ends 10am-6pm.

INTERNET ACCESS
JavaNet Cafe, 37 Exchange St, 773-2469. $6/hr. *www.javanet.com/cafe*
Portland Main Library, 5 Monument Sq, 871-1700. Free Internet use, half hour time limit.

TRAVEL
Concord Trailways, 100 Sewall St, (800) 639-3317. Boston ($16.50, 2 hrs), Bangor ($31, 2 hrs).
Greyhound, St John & Congress Sts, 772-6587/(800) 231-2222. Be careful at night. Boston $13.
Prince of Fundy car ferry to Yarmouth, Nova Scotia, 775-5616, (800) 341-7540. Runs nightly May-Oct, 11 hr trip. Call for prices and schedule.

Continuing on up the coast will bring you to **Freeport**, a haven for over 100 factory outlets, chief of which is *THE* sporting and outdoor goods store, L.L. Bean. Open 365 days, 24 hrs, Bean's is a Mecca to middle America, and the pilgrims come here at all hours. 'It was really strange to be shopping at 3am.' *www.freeportusa.com* has info about the town's outlets. In case you're feeling overly verdant, there's relief just around the corner at the **Desert of Maine**, Desert Rd, Freeport, exit 19 off I-95, 865-6962. A natural phenomenon, $6.75 includes guided tour (daily 9am-6pm) and tram rides (9am-4pm) through the dunes. Watch the unusual art of sand-sculpting with the 100 different shades of sand in the desert. Acres and acres of sandy glacial remains create dunes up to 80 feet high. You have to feel it to believe it. If you don't have transportation from Freeport, call ahead and ask if the Desert of Maine Shuttle is coming into town.

MID-COAST **Brunswick** is home to small, but lovely **Bowdoin College**, alma mater of writers Hawthorne and Longfellow and explorers Peary and MacMillan among others. The college hosts **Bowdoin Summer Music Festival** featuring nationally renowned artists and low-priced concerts, call 725-3322 for details. Also on campus: the **Peary-MacMillan Arctic Museum** in Hubbard Hall, 725-3416. Polar exploration, ecology and Inuit culture, Tue-Sat 10am-5pm, Sun 2pm-5pm; and the **Museum of Art** in the Walker Art Building, 725-3275, featuring Baskins as well as old masters and Greek and Roman artefacts. Hours as above.

You can camp among the tall pines at **Thomas Point Beach** (*www.thomas-*

pointbeach.com), off Rte 24, Cook's Corner, Brunswick, 5 miles from downtown, 725-6009. Sites $17 for two, $21 w/hook up. The park is the site of an annual **Bluegrass Festival** on Labor Day weekend, and in August it hosts the **Maine Highland Games** and the **Maine Arts Festival**, which features folk arts, workshops and local foods, tkts $12. **Brunswick Chamber of Commerce**, 725-8797, *www.midcoastmaine.com*.

Dipping off Rte 1 onto Rte 27 takes you into **Boothbay Harbor**, a bit touristy but a good taking off point for quiet, isolated **Monhegan Island** where cars are prohibited and artists take refuge. This is not an island for wild nights (no bars or discos in town), but if you're in the mood for rocky cliffs, ocean spray, and hiking amid 600 varieties of wildflowers it's worth the 1½ hr ferry ride into Muscongus Bay. Daily from Pier 8, 63 Commercial St, 633-2284, $29 r/t, rsvs recommended.

Getting back onto Rte 1 and continuing north you hit **Rockland**, which hosts an annual **Maine Lobster Festival** in early August, call 596-0376 for details. Generations of artists have found this coast an inspiration; Andrew Wyeth spent much of his life in nearby **Cushing**, and the **William A. Farnsworth Museum and Library** in Rockland, 596-6457, $9, has a large collection of paintings by the Wyeth family. Just north of Rockland is **Camden**. Picturesquely situated with a busy little harbour, the town has a Cornish-like charm despite the tourists. Even though the trash-trend emporia fast encroach, there are still genuine and attractive local craft shops. If it's not foggy, the observatory atop **Mount Battie** affords a spectacular view of Camden harbour, the sea and the surrounding hills. It's an enjoyable two-mile hike from the town. Try camping at **Camden Hills State Park**, 1½ miles north of town on Rte 1, 236-3109. Rsvs recommended, apply to the Park Bureau in Augusta, 287-3824, 14 days in advance (but arrive btwn 10am & 4pm and you'll probably get a pitch). Hot showers, stone fireplace and picnic table at each site, take-out store within walking distance.

If you have your own transport, spend a few relaxing days at the beautiful wooded **Megunticook Campground By-The-Sea** between Camden and Rockland at Rockport on Rte 1, 594-2428. Sites $30 w/hook up, rsvs recommended in summer. Tents can be hired ($10) but call first. Small store, bathrooms and free showers, laundry and heated outdoor pool. Rent kayaks ($15-$50) and bikes ($5 per day), on site or nearby.

Feeling adventurous? Contact **Maine Sport**, Rte 1 between Rockport and Camden, 236-7120; ask about their guided kayaking trips. The Camden harbour trip ($30) takes 2 hrs. The Megunticook Lake day-trip ($45) takes 4 hrs—try navigating a keowee! Equipment provided, no experience necessary, rsvs required. For energetic landlubbers, bikes are available to rent; $25 full-day, includes helmet and lock, cheaper weekly rates available.

For tourist info on Rockport and Lincoln, contact **Camden Chamber of Commerce**, PO Box 919, Camden, Maine 04843, 236-4404.

Take a detour off Rte 1, following State Road 166 to the charming town of **Castine**. This is where Paul Revere, of 'Midnight Ride' fame, ended his undistinguished military career in the ill-fated naval battle against British troops in the **Penobscot Bay** in 1779, the second worst US naval disaster after Pearl Harbor. Revere was arrested for disobeying orders and abandoning the expedition—a court martial later acquitted him and he got by with just a censure. The **Castine Historical Society,** on the town commons, has exhibits about local history, 326-4118.

Continue on your way to **Bar Harbor** via the coastal route, or else head inland where thousands of lakes make this a popular area for canoeists. **Moosehead Lake**, 40 miles long and 10 miles wide, is the largest.

ACADIA NATIONAL PARK/BAR HARBOR   The park encompasses a magnificent wild, rocky stretch of coast and its hinterland. Its granite hills sweep down into the Atlantic where the ocean has carved out numerous inlets, cliffs and caves. At every twist and turn of the roads around the coast a new and spectacular view of the sea becomes visible.

For the best view of all, it's an easy walk or drive to the summit of **Cadillac Mountain** (1530 ft), the highest place on the Atlantic coast north of Rio. Beneath the 'mountain' lie lakes, cranberry bogs, quiet spruce forests, and the Atlantic itself. The dramatic Loop Road, cars $10 per week, $5 pp, from the Park Visitor Center takes about 1½-3 hrs (depending on the number of stops you make) and offers incredible views. A stop right on the Loop, not to be missed, is tea and popovers ($6) at **Jordan Pond House**, 276-3610. The House is an easy drive from Seal or Bar Harbor and accessible by several hiking trails.

Bar Harbor is the most popular resort on the **Mount Desert Island** part of Acadia National Park. This was a town of fashionable summer homes owned by the wealthy until 1947 when a great fire destroyed most of them. More recently, chic boutiques and restaurants have moved in, forcing prices up. Come and enjoy the **Bar Harbor Music Festival** in July and August or take in a whalewatching tour or an excursion on a working lobster boat. The *Bluenose Ferry*, 288-3397, leaves from here on its way to Nova Scotia. The less-frequented **Isle au Haut** is the other half of Acadia; a good place for walking, it can be reached by ferry from Stonington on the southern tip of Deer Isle.

Further inland lies **Bangor**, a good stopping off point before heading into the interior. With a name said to be derived from an old hymn tune, the town is socially about that exciting. The best time to be there is during the **Bangor Fair**, one of the oldest in the country, held annually the first week in August, 947-5555. In early summer **harness racing** is held at Bass Park on Main St, 941-0872, free.

ACCOMMODATION
Bass Cottage in the Field, off Main St, downtown Bar Harbor, 288-3705. From $60 for two. Rsvs required in summer.
Bar Harbor Youth Hostel, 27 Kennebec St, 288-5587. Summer only, $12 AYH, $15 non-AYH, rsvs recommended.
YWCA, 36 Mt Desert St, 288-5008. Women only. Dorm $20/$65 weekly, S-$30/$90 weekly, D-$25 pp/$75 pp weekly. Rsvs recommended.
Camping. Within the park there are sites at Black Woods, 288-3338, and Seawall, 244-3600. Both areas can be reached by car, Black Woods costs $18/night, Seawall $18/night with car, walk-ins $12. Seawall operates on a first-come, first-served basis, but rsvs are essential at Black Woods in peak season, apply two months in advance to be sure of a pitch. (800) 365-2267 is the number to reserve pitches in parks nation-wide—persevere, the line is always busy! There are also more expensive private campgrounds near the park.

OF INTEREST
Bike rentals are available from **Bar Harbor Bicycle Shop**, 141 Cottage St, 288-3886, $10 half-day, $15 full-day. **Acadia Bike and Canoe**, 48 Cottage St, 288-5483, bikes $12 half-day, $17 full-day, and organise kayaking trips $34 2½hrs, $45 half-day, $69 full day.
Whale Watcher, Frenchman Bay Co, 1 West St, Harbor Place, 288-3322, (800) 508-1499. A 3½hr cruise costs $35, 3 hr tour costs $32, rsvs recommended. *www.atlantiswhale.com* gives detailed information and photos of various cruises offered.

INFORMATION
Acadia Outdoors, 45 Main St, 288-2422. Sells camping gear.
Chamber of Commerce, 93 Cottage St (in basement), 288-5103. 'Extremely helpful.' *www.barharbormaine.com*
Park Visitors Center, 288-3338, just off Rte 3 at Hulls Cove. Short film about the park shown every hour, offers audio cassette tours and all the information you'll need. Daily 8am-4.30pm. *www.nps.gov/acad*

TRAVEL
Bay Ferry to Yarmouth, Nova Scotia, (888) 249-7245. 6 hr crossing, leaves daily at 8am, June-Oct. $46 pp, $60 car.
Greyhound/Vermont Transit run a shuttle to Ellsworth, 20 miles away, ($5.50). Leaves every day at 8am, in front of Post Office. **Concord Trailways** runs a shuttle to Ellsworth 4 times daily, $7.50, rsvs. required. Leaves from Kennebec and Cottage Sts. Call 288-3366 for info on either shuttle.

THE APPALACHIAN TRAIL/BAXTER STATE PARK   About 100 miles north of Bangor is **Baxter State Park**, where **Mount Katahdin** (5267 ft) marks the northern starting point of the Appalachian Trail. This is wild, remote country where moose out-number humans. (Best time to see a moose: early morning/late afternoon, late spring to early summer. Best place: near bogs and ponds, keep yourself unobtrusive.) The park can be reached via **Millinocket** on Rte 11 off I-95, or **Greenville**, a small lumber town, on Rte 15, at the southern end of Moosehead Lake. There are ten campgrounds in the park, $6 pp per night (min $12), only two of which are inaccessible by car. For all information on camping and for detailed area maps call in or write to the **Baxter State Park Headquarters**, 64 Balsam Drive, Millinocket, 04462. Tel: 723-5140.

Just to the north of Baxter lies the **Allagash Wilderness Waterway**. This is a canoeist's paradise, a 100-mile-long stretch of lakes and rivers preserved in their primitive state to provide white-water and backwoods experience for the modern canoeist.

For the bargain price of $23/day, **Allagash Wilderness Outfitters** in Greenville, (May-Nov) radio contact (207) 695-2821, will provide complete equipment for your adventures (right down to an axe!) including two-person tent and canoe. For a few days, a week or longer, explore the lakes or accept the challenge of the thundering rapids, fish for your salmon-supper then camp ($5 pp) under the stars with moose and deer as your companions. For around $23 you might prefer a log cabin on the shores of Frost Pond in Maine's North Woods. Call 695-2821 for details.

If you are staying near Greenville, contact **Folsom's Air Service**, Greenville (207) 695-2821, about their Floatplane adventures; it costs $30 to take in the local sights and the vast Moosehead Lake.

INFORMATION
Write to the **Appalachian Trail Conference**, P.O Box 807, Harper's Ferry, WV 25425, (304) 535-6331; or the **Appalachian Mountain Club**, 5 Joy St, Boston, MA 02108, (617) 523-0636.
Moosehead Lake Chamber of Commerce, Route 15, 695-2702. Summer: daily 9am-5pm, otherwise Mon-Fri only.

MASSACHUSETTS   *The Bay State*

The Bay State is rivalled only by Virginia in the richness of its history. Massachusetts was the colony where the loudest and most open protests were raised against the British prior to 1777. After the initial skirmishes, the war moved to the other colonies, but Massachusetts contributed the largest number of troops.

Presidents John Adams, John Quincy Adams, John F. Kennedy and George Bush all came from Massachusetts, as did Daniel Webster; in the field of literature, Robert Frost, John Whittier, Emily Dickinson, Louisa May Alcott, Nathaniel Hawthorne (read *The Scarlet Letter* for a look into Massachusetts' Puritan past), Henry David Thoreau, e.e. cummings, Eugene O'Neill, John Updike, Robert Parker, James Carroll and Ralph Waldo Emerson were either born or came to live here. Just to show that there is a lighter side to the Bay state, Massachusetts is also the birthplace of sewing machines, plastic pink flamingos, frozen food and roller skates.

Massachusetts takes its name from the Massachuset Indians who occupied the Bay Territory, including Boston, in the early 17th century. An annual Indian pow-wow is still held at Mashpee in July.
www.mass-vacation.com
The telephone area code for the eastern part of the State is 617, for mid-Massachusetts and the Cape it's 508, and in the west it's 413.

BOSTON   Capital of Massachusetts and, undeniably, of New England, Boston is a proud Yankee city and seaport thick with reminders of its past. Bostonians are fiercely loyal, regarding their city as the hub of New England and revelling in its Colonial past. Boston was the spiritual heart of the Revolution, the birthplace of American commerce and industry, and leader of the new nation in the arts and education. These days, the original WASPs (White Anglo-Saxon Protestants) have been joined by successive generations of Blacks, Irish, Poles and Italians, and the city has developed a more cosmopolitan feel. The city has always had its own unique character; for a glimpse into local culture watch Oscar-winning *Good Will Hunting,* a fairly adequate introduction to the 'real Boston'; or brush up on your Boston English ('pahk the cah in Hahvahd Yahd') at *www.boston-online.com/glossary*. George V. Higgins' *The Friends of Eddie Coyle* follows a crook through the Boston Underworld, and for classics-lovers, there's always Henry James' *The Bostonians*.

Known as 'America's Walking City', Boston has a cosier feel to it than most major US cities, and also something of a European flavour. Within a comparatively small area you can stroll through 18th century cobbled

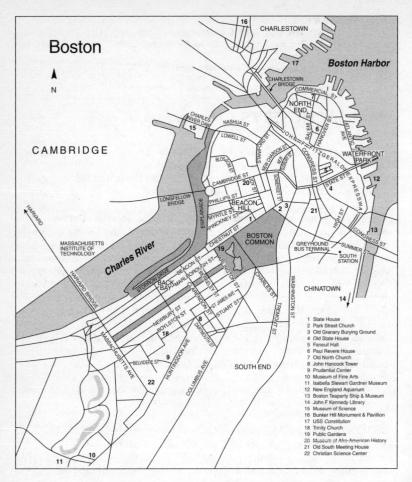

1 State House
2 Park Street Church
3 Old Granary Burying Ground
4 Old State House
5 Faneuil Hall
6 Paul Revere House
7 Old North Church
8 John Hancock Tower
9 Prudential Center
10 Museum of Fine Arts
11 Isabella Stewart Gardner Museum
12 New England Aquarium
13 Boston Teaparty Ship & Museum
14 John F Kennedy Library
15 Museum of Science
16 Bunker Hill Monument & Pavillion
17 USS Constitution
18 Trinity Church
19 Public Gardens
20 Museum of Afro-American History
21 Old South Meeting House
22 Christian Science Center

streets, on the **Common** where the colonists grazed their cattle, down by the harbour or river, or around such fine examples of modern architecture as in the **Back Bay** or the impressive **Government Center**.

For all its historical associations, Boston is a city of youth and vitality. In addition to prestigious **Harvard** and **MIT**, there are 70 accredited colleges in Greater Boston, and many of the city's businesses and amenities cater to the young and diverse population.

Boston acquired its nickname, 'the Athens of America', by the 19th century and continues to earn it as a centre for music, literature and the arts. At any time it is possible to see good theatre and modern dance or hear classical, jazz, folk and pop music. Sport too has its place. In summer, when the Boston Red Sox baseball team is battling it out in the race for the American League title, the only place to be is at **Fenway Park**, eating Fenway franks, shelling peanuts, and drinking cold beer. In winter the mania transfers itself to basketball with the Celtics, football with the New England Patriots and ice hockey with the Boston Bruins.

One of the nation's finest examples of creative urban renewal is **Faneuil Hall Marketplace**. Once a rundown building on the blighted waterfront, its revitalisation became Boston's bicentennial gift to itself. It now houses over 150 shops, boutiques and food stalls along with 23 restaurants.

Boston is particularly convenient for visits to nearby Cambridge, Concord, Lexington, Salem and Gloucester. Further afield, the Berkshire Hills and sun-drenched Cape Cod are unforgettable destinations for an expedition. *www.boston-online.com*
The telephone area code for Boston and Cambridge is 617.

ACCOMMODATION
The Information Center at the Tremont St side of the Boston Common provides a list of low-cost accommodation. Budget chain hotels can be expensive in summer, but call for details of special offers; see appendix for details.
Boston International Youth Hostel, 12 Hemenway St, 536-9455, in Back Bay. 24 hrs, check-in 8am. Dorm $20 AYH, $23 non-AYH, private room $60 AYH, $66 non-AYH. Rsvs recommended, credit card required. Individual lockers in room, will rent locks. E-mail facilities, $.20/min. Must have photo ID for security records. 'Superb kitchen facilities. Very friendly staff.' 'Excellent hostel, launderette, clean, good value, maximum stay 5 nights, take subway to Hynes Convention Center then 2 blocks.' 'Good for meeting people. Go early to reserve a bed.'
Brookline Manor Inn, Coolidge Corner, 32 Centre St, Brookline, 232-0003/(800) 201-9676. S-$99, D-$109 sleeps three, up to six sharing, XP-$20. TV, phone. 'Beautiful room, clean and close to centre. Lovely staff. Should ring in advance.' 'Well worth it.'
Farrington Inn, 23 Farrington Ave, Allston, (800) 767-5337, UK toll free (0800) 896-040. Beds $25, private room $85, bfast, free local calls. Rsvs recommended for private rooms, dorm is first-come, first-served. 20 min. subway ride from downtown. 'Good part of town, old-fashioned but very friendly.'
Greater Boston YMCA, 316 Huntington Ave, 536-7800. Co-ed, S-$41, D-$61, plus $5 cash key deposit; includes breakfast, free use of pool and well equipped gym. Mixed reviews. 'Clean, friendly, safe.' 'Unpleasant clientele, be careful, seems to have a bad atmosphere.'
Irish Embassy Hostel, 232 Friend St, 973-4841. Dorm $15, kitchen, free bands and BBQs, 24 hrs. Rsvs recommended. 'Very friendly, safe, clean and great location.'
Longwood Inn, 123 Longwood Ave, Brookline, 566-8615. Green Line subway, downtown 10 mins. S-$79-$99, D-$89-$109, XP-$10. Kitchen, parking, TV and laundry. 'Clean and safe.' 'Old-fashioned style guest house.'
Nolan House B&B, 10 G St, So. Boston, 269-1550. D-$75-$85. No credit cards. 'Full breakfast and large, comfortable room.' Rsvs required.
YWCA, Berkeley Residence Club, 40 Berkeley St, 482-8850. Women only. S-$51, D-$78, T-$90, XP-$10 plus $2 temp. membership. 'Very safe, clean, canteen, laundrette and roof-deck. Access to pool and gym $3, dinner $6.50, bfast $2.50. 'Absolute bargain despite women in their night attire!'

HOUSING INFORMATION
Meegan Services, 569-3800, located in Logan Airport, has listings of hotels, guest houses, etc. Daily 9am-midnight. Free.
Roommate Connection Referral Agency, 24 hr info 262-4679/(800) APT-SHARE or *www.dwellingsma.com/roommateco/trc.html*. If you're staying for the summer it might be cheaper and safer to pay the $75 fee rather than advertise. 'Shared

accommodation, short/long term Boston & suburbs. From $500/month depending on location. By appointment. 'Very helpful.'

FOOD

In addition to clam-bakes and seafood, Boston is home to many diverse restaurants. Small family owned eating places occupy every corner of the North End. Thai, Vietnamese and Polynesian foods are available in Chinatown, while the South End offers American Southwestern fare and cafes. Other nearby neighbourhoods tempt the hungry and the curious with Indian, Japanese, Mexican, Hungarian and Greek delights.

Bull & Finch, 84 Beacon St, 227-9605, by the Public Garden. An English pub; burgers, sandwiches, etc from $6. Only the exterior has anything to do with *Cheers* (the series was filmed in LA), but at least you can imagine that Sam or Diane is going to walk in the door. 'Great wings!' 'Very disappointing.'

Charlie's Sandwich Shoppe, 429 Columbus Avenue (between Dartmouth and West Newton Streets), 536-7669. Strangers share tables at this old-time diner. Lunch for around $7.

Country Life, 200 High St. (Financial dist., across from Rowes Wharf, Aquarium subway), 951-2462. 'Supreme veggie food.' All you can eat lunch $6 (10% off before noon), dinner $7, (Sun, Tue, Weds, Thu) Sunday brunch $8.

Dixie Kitchen, 182 Massachusetts Avenue (Near Boylston Street), 536-3068. Blues and zydeco music along with classic Cajun creations like gumbo, jambalaya, and even fried alligator tail. Lunch for around $8, dinner $12.

Durgin Park, 390 Faneuil Hall in Quincy Market, 227-2038. Known for its good food, great prices, long bar, and wisecracking waitresses: 'They throw food in front of you, spill water on your head and insult you. Hilarious. An excellent act.' An *act*? Family-style eating. Ribs, seafood; famous for its prime rib and great chowder. Go for lunch for the best buys. Daily 11.30am-10pm.

No-Name Restaurant, 15½ Fish Pier, near south-east end of Northern Ave, 338-7539. In old warehouse. Seafood from $10. Expect queues. 'Vibrant atmosphere.' 'Hard to find; a bit of a walk, but the best seafood for the price in Boston.' 'A shouting match and a shovelling session, but great.'

The Purple Shamrock, 1 Union St, 227-2060. A favourite among sports fans, it has long been Boston's place to warm up and cool down for Boston Garden events. TV, live bands cover $3-$5 Thu-Sat, supreme chowder from $4 and large beers.

Quincy Market, complete with street performers and hordes of tourists, has plenty of food stalls of great variety: Chinese, Italian, Greek, health foods and of course, the requisite pizzas, burgers, doughnuts etc. It also claims to sell more lobster items than anywhere else in the world.

Haymarket, just around the corner from Quincy Market. Fruits and vegetables hawked by loud vendors trying to draw in customers, cheap prices. Some worry that it may be heading for extinction: the 'Big Dig', a giant project to put the freeway underground, will eventually take away the land where the market now meets. Outdoors, Fri-Sat.

OF INTEREST

If you plan on being in Boston for more than a few days consider buying the **City Pass**, $27.50. The pass is valid for nine days from start of use and includes admission at the JFK Library and Museum, the John Hancock Observatory, the Museum of Fine Arts, the Museum of Science, the New England Aquarium and the Gardner Museum. It can be purchased at any of the museums or at the **Visitor Information Center** on Boston Common.

Back Bay, south-west of the common, is a lively, beautiful 19th century development project built on land reclaimed from the Charles River. In this area is **Trinity Church**, Copley Square, 536-0944. Daily 8am-6pm. Designed in 1877 by HH

Richardson, this church is French Romanesque style on the outside. Inside its highly decorated walls and flamboyant mosaics give it more the feel and look of Greek Orthodox. The IM Pei designed **John Hancock Tower**, 572-6429, stands behind the church. This is the tallest building in New England; the observatory on the 60th floor offers unparalleled views of Boston and beyond. Daily 9am-10pm; $5. 'A must. Sets you up for the whole city.' 'There are two interesting audio-visual presentations in the observatory on the city and its history.' There is one small problem with the building—hundreds of the 10,344 panes of tempered glass have fallen out onto the street below. Pei has had to replace them all, costing millions of dollars. The problem has never been solved but fortunately up to now no one has been hurt.

Boston Common. Boston is the only large American city still to have its common, but the flower-filled **Public Gardens** have more to offer; enjoy gliding around the lagoon on the world-famous **swan boats** in summer. This is where Louis the silent cygnet serenaded passengers in E.B. White's *Trumpet of the Swan*. Both areas are unsafe at night.

Beacon Hill, especially Louisburg Square, is Boston's old residential section to which every visitor must make a pilgrimage. Louisa May Alcott, William Dean Howels, the Brahmin Literary Set and many other famous Bostonians lived here. *www.beaconhillonline.com*

Black Heritage Trail, a guided walking tour that explores the history of 19th century Boston's African American community. Tour starts at **Robert Gould Shaw and 54th Regiment Memorial**, Beacon and Park Sts, and ends up at the **Museum of Afro-American History** (*www.afroammuseum.org*), 138 Mountfort St, 739-1200. Highlights include the **Abiel Smith School** and the **African Meeting House**. Daily at 10am, noon, and 2pm, Free.

Christian Science Center, 175 Huntington Ave, 450-2000, world HQ of the Christian Science religion, is a conglomerate of stunning buildings including the Mother Church; the Publishing Society, which produces among other literature the highly respected *Christian Science Monitor*; and the **Mapparium**, a beautiful 40-foot stained glass, walk-thru globe with unusual acoustics. 'You walk *into* the world! Tremendous visual and sensory delight.' Closed for renovation; scheduled to re-open in mid-2000.

Faneuil Hall, Merchants Row, Faneuil Hall Sq, 242-5642. Built in 1742 and given to the city of Boston by Peter Faneuil. Known as the 'Cradle of Liberty', the hall was the scene of mass meetings during the pre-revolutionary period. Daily 9am-5pm. Don't leave without catching a glimpse of the weathervane in the form of a grasshopper that sits atop Faneuil Hall, placed there at the request of Peter Faneuil himself. 'Grasshopper' was the symbol of the Boston port; during the War of 1812 it was the password used to weed out spies: if you couldn't identify it as the symbol of Boston, you were in trouble.

The Freedom Trail is a walking tour through the heart of old Boston, beginning in Boston Common at the Visitors Center. On it you can visit nearly all Boston's associations with the American Revolution. The Trail is clearly marked by a path of red bricks set in the sidewalk; few visitors to Boston escape it. The Trail tends to be a tad dull, and unless you have a passionate interest in American revolutionary history, forget it.

Institute of Contemporary Art, 955 Boylston St, 266-5152. Weds-Sun 11am-5pm, Thu 'til 9pm, tours on Thu at 3.30pm, 4.30pm, and 5.30pm. $6, $4 w/student ID, free after 5pm on Thu.

Isabella Stewart Gardner Museum, 280 Fenway, 566-1401. Italianate villa built by the eccentric Mrs Gardner to house her art collection in 1903. It lost many fine works in a 1989 robbery but still has a lot to see, including the house itself. Retreat to the cool sanctuary of the Venetian courtyard. Tue-Sun, 11am-5pm, $10 weekdays, $11 w/ends, $5 w/student ID ($3 on Weds). 'Excellent.' *www.boston.com/gardner*

Literary Trail. *The Literary Trail, a Guide to Greater Boston's Newest Trail* suggests self-guided tours of sites relating to Boston writers, including the homes of Nathaniel Hawthorne, Henry Wadsworth Longfellow, Louisa May Alcott, and Henry David Thoreau. $4.95, available at area book stores or from the Boston History Collaborative, 175 Berkely St, 3E, 574-5950. The Boston History Collaborative also offers guided Literary Trail tours, $35. Call for rsvs.

Museum of Bad Art, 580 High St, Dedham, just south of Boston, 325-8224. Proudly displays 'art too bad to be ignored' in its permanent collection in the basement of the Dedham Community Theater, (781) 326-1463. Mon-Fri 6.30-10pm, Sat-Sun 1.30-10pm, free. MOBA also produces several public events in Boston throughout the year. Call or check out *www.glyphs.com/moba* for more info.

Museum of Fine Arts, 465 Huntington Ave, 267-9300. One of the finest art collections in the US, with outstanding Asiatic and 'marvellous Egyptian' sections. Also some fine American water colours, wonderful Gaugins and Degas and the largest collection of Monets outside of France. Mon-Tue 10am-4.45pm, Wed 10am-9.45pm, Thu-Fri 10am-4.45pm (West Wing remains open 'til 9.45pm), Sat-Sun 10am-5.45pm. $12, $10 w/student ID. Wed 4pm-9.45pm voluntary contribution, Thu-Fri 4.45pm-9.45pm all admission fees reduced $2. 'Well worth the money; allow at least a whole day.' 'Inexpensive cafeteria.'

Old Granary Burying Ground, in the location of a 17th century granary. An interesting graveyard with many 18th century heroes including Paul Revere, Sam Adams and John Hancock. A grave marked 'Mary Goose' is supposedly the final resting place of Mother Goose.

Old North Church, Salem St, in the north end. Built 1723, gave Revere the signal to ride. 'Perhaps the most historic church in the USA.'

Old South Meeting House, School & Washington Sts, 482-6439, built 1729, was where Samuel Adams gave the signal that launched the Boston Tea Party in 1773. Open daily 9.30am-5pm, $3, $2.50 w/student ID.

Old State House, Washington & State Sts, 720-3290. Built 1713 as the seat of British colonial government; the Declaration of Independence was read from the East Balcony in 1776. Has an important display of Americana. Daily 9am-5pm, $3, $2.50 w/student ID.

Old Town Trolley shuttle bus, 269-7010, goes everywhere of historical note; you get on and off and on again when you like (9am-last re-board at 4.30pm), tkts $23. The Trolley Tours also operate a 3 hr jaunt around Boston providing an 'insiders' look at the city and its favourite son—JFK ($27), Sun 9am. Info and tkts for both tours available from the Trolley Stop Store at Charles and Boylston Sts, 422-0105. National Park Service tours leave from **Visitors Center,** 242-5642, at 15 State St, 90 mins; 10am-3pm—Old South Meeting House, Old State House, Paul Revere's house, and Old North Church, free.

Park St Church, 523-3383, at Brimstone Corner, built 1809. Where *America* was first sung, in 1832. Tue-Sat 9am-3pm.

Paul Revere House, in the North End on the Freedom Trail, 523-1676. Paul Revere lived here from 1770 to 1780 and set out from here on his famous ride to inform the nation the British were about to attack. Probably the oldest wooden structure in Boston; built 1670s. Daily in summer 9.30am-5.15pm, otherwise 9.30am-4.15pm; $2.50, $2 w/student ID.

Prudential Center, 859-0648. A daring, $150 million urban renewal project of the 1960s, with apartments, offices, and countless shops. On the 50th floor is an observatory, **SkyWalk**, which has a 360 degree viewing deck. Daily 10am-10pm, $4.

State House, 727-3676, with its large gold dome, is the seat of the Massachusetts State Government. Charles Bulfinch, greatest American architect of the late 18th century, designed the central part of the building. Look for the Sacred Cod over the entrance to the House of Representatives, pointing to the party in power. In 1933, a group of Harvard students stole the fish and the State House was thrown into turmoil—reps refused to conduct any business until the fish was found, four days later. Free guided tours Mon-Sat 10am-3.30pm. Enter on Beacon St.

On the waterfront:

Bay State Cruise Co, 748-1428, runs Summer Entertainment Cruises, with concerts and dances on board, Fri-Sat from Commonwealth Pier. Leaves at 8.30pm, returns 11.30pm. Rsvs required, must be over 21. $16-$20.

Boston Harbour Cruises, leaving from Long Wharf, 723-7800. Runs ferries to **Boston Harbor Islands State Park**, 30 islands with colourful names such as Grape, Bumpkin, and Gallops. 90 min sightseeing historical tour, $15. 'Go in the morning, stop off at Georges Island and get picked up later.' Cruise to the *USS Constitution*, $8. Sunset cruises, at 7pm last 90 mins, $15. Take warm clothing.

Boston Tea Party Ship & Museum, Congress St Bridge, 338-1773. *Beaver II*, replica of ship whose dumped cargo brewed rebellion in 1773. Daily 9am-6pm. $8, $7 w/student ID or Old Town Trolley tkt. 'A rip-off. Makes you feel proud to be British.'

John F Kennedy Library and Museum, Columbia Point, overlooking harbour, 929-4523. Another IM Pei building, it houses mementoes and memorials to not only JFK but also his brother Robert. Daily 9am-5pm; $8, $6 w/student ID. Take T to U Mass then take free shuttle bus (runs every 20 mins).

Museum of Science, on the Charles River Dam in Science Park, 723-2500. The $10 million large-screen theatre is worth a visit—so big it can project a life-size image of a whale. 'Could spend 2 days here and still not see it all.'. **The Computer Museum and the Museum of Science** (*www.tcm.org*) is a recent addition—test drive the information super-highway! 'Hands-on.' 'Hats off.' Accept the robot challenge, and through interactive screens, control a robot over the Internet. Daily 9am-7pm, Fri til 9pm; combo tkts to theatre, planetarium and museum $20, $10 for museum only. *www.mos.org*

New England Aquarium, Central Wharf, off Atlantic Ave, 973-5200. World's largest collection of sharks and 2000 other specimens in a 187,000 gallon tank. Dolphin and sea lion shows daily. 'Excellent! Could spend the whole day there.' Summer hours: Mon, Tue, Fri 9am-6pm, Wed-Thu 9am-8pm, Sat-Sun 9am-7pm. Admission: weekdays $12, w/ends $13.50, Wed-Thu after 4pm take $1 off admission, on w/ends if you're in line by 9 you get half-off the ticket price. *www.neaq.org* is great for landlubbers who want to try virtual whale-watching!

USS Constitution, a frigate from the war of 1812, preserved in Charleston Navy Yard, 242-0543. Daily 9am-6pm, free. Interesting tours conducted by members of Navy. Nearby is the **Bunker Hill Monument** commemorating the first set battle of the Revolution. The battle was actually fought on a different hill, but all the good stuff is here; **Bunker Hill Pavilion**, 241-7575; $3, $2 w/student ID: An audio-visual programme, *The Whites of Their Eyes*, gives the background to the battle with dramatic effects (every ¹/₂ hour from 9.30am-5pm).

Whale-watching trips, 973-5281, organised by the Aquarium April-Oct, $26, $21 w/student ID. Also qualifies for half price entrance to Aquarium. Rsvs recommended.

ENTERTAINMENT

For who, what, where and when read the *Boston Phoenix* (*www.bostonphoenix.com/standard/listings_index.html*) or check the Thuday edition of the *Boston Globe 's* Calendar section. Theater Mirror (*www.theatermirror.com*) has play reviews and listings along with links to area theatres. The **Bostix** booth in Faneuil Hall has half-price tickets on day of performance. Look for free jazz concerts in Copley Square, lunch-time in summer.

Axis, 13 Lansdowne St, near Fenway Park, 262-2437. Techno, House, Funk & Soul. British bands and videos. Cover $15. Sun is gay night. Over 21s only.

Sevens, 77 Charles St, 523-9074, 'Authentic British pub atmosphere; serves both local and imported beer. Friendly.' Most expensive item on the menu is $5.50!

Symphony Hall, 301 Massachusetts Ave, 266-1492. Discount available Fri 9am, Tue & Thu at 5pm for evening performances in the fall/winter. Home of the Boston Symphony and the Boston Pops. During the first week in July, the Pops, who were for many years led by John Williams of *Star Wars* music fame play at the **Hatch Memorial Shell** by the Charles River. The free outdoor concerts, including Jazz, start at 8pm, so get there early if you want to get good places. 'Take a picnic, lots of fun.'

Wang Center for the Performing Arts, 270 Tremont St, 482-9393. If you don't manage to 'catch a show' at this old vaudeville theatre make a visit anyway, the building is an historic landmark and the architecture is more than worth it; the lobby was used as the interior of Jack Nicholson's mansion in *The Witches of Eastwick*. See the world-renowned **Boston Ballet** here. Occasionally 'student rush' discounted tickets are available, call 695-6950 for more info.

Friday Flicks at the Hatch Shell at sunset, Jul-Aug. Check the Metropolitan District Commission's web page for movie listings and other park events: *www.magnet.state.ma.us/mdc/home99.htm.*

Tune into **WGBH**, the city's non-commercial TV channel and reputed to be one of the best in America. *www.wgbh.org*

SPORT

Boston's four professional sports teams inspire devotion in the city and in fans nation-wide. In summer the **Boston Red Sox** play at historic **Fenway Park**, 267-1700, one of the most beautiful ball parks in the States. In fall and winter the **New England Patriots** play American football at **Foxborough**, (800) 543-1776, an easy train ride from South Station. 'A fantastic day out.' The **Boston Garden** is the home of both the **Celtics** for basketball, 523-3030, and the **Bruins** for ice-hockey, 624-1050. Call TicketMaster, 931-2000, to purchase tickets.

Beaches: Closest beach is **Revere**. 'Scruffy but only 85¢ (to Airport Station) on the Blue Line.' Further afield is **Ipswich**, only a short train ride away for a splash in the sea; orange line to North Station, then commuter rail, $3.50, for schedules and info call 722-3200.

Biking: A 14 mile loop follows both banks of the Charles River, from the museum of Science to Watertown, and may be entered at any point on the Cambridge or Watertown sides. Or explore Boston's hidden places in Beacon Hill and along quaint side-streets in the North End and the Waterfront. Call **Back Bay Bikes and Boards,** 336 Newbury St, 247-2336. Rent a bike for $20 all day, $10 half-day.

Canoeing: Charles River Canoe & Kayak, 965-5110, kiosk located on the bank of the river across Soldier's Field Rd from Harvard Stadium (head upstream from Elliot Bridge), open Fri afternoons and w/ends. Canoes $9 p/hr, $36 p/day, double kayaks $12 p/hr, $48 p/day.

Inline skating: 'Paths along both banks of the Charles River are good for novice rollerblading'. Start from Memorial Dr at Harvard. Rent skates from Blades, Board & Skate, 349 Newbury St, 437-6300. $15/day.

SHOPPING

The **Newbury Street** area in Back Bay is good for books, records and lively evenings.

INFORMATION

Boston Common Visitors Center, the Common on Tremont St, 536-4100, daily

9am-5pm; and **Greater Boston Convention and Tourist Bureau**, west side of Prudential Plaza, 867-8389, daily 10am-6pm. For $2.10 you can purchase the *Official Guidebook to Boston*, 100-plus pages with numerous maps of city and discount coupons. *www.bostonusa.com*;

Massachusetts Office of Travel and Tourism, 10 Park Plaza, Suite 4510, 727-3201. Mon-Fri 9am-5pm.

National Park Service Visitor Center, 15 State St, 242-5642, centrally located. Has short slide show of Freedom Trail, books, pamphlets and brochures on Boston and surrounding areas. Free guided tours of the trail in the summer, hourly, 10am-3pm. Office open daily 9am-6pm.

INTERNET ACCESS
Designs for Living, 52 Queensberry St, 536-6150. Internet access, $8/hr. *www.mynet.com/main.html*

TRAVEL
Auto Driveaways, Co. 1170 Commonwealth Ave, Allston, 731-1261. Four miles south-west of Boston. Over 21s, cash deposit $300-$350.

Amtrak, (800) 872-7245, South Station (Red Line, main station) and Back Bay Station (Green Line, Copley; Orange line, Back Bay). NYC ($47, 5 hrs).

Bonanza Bus Lines, South Station, (800) 556-3815, buses to New York, Portsmouth, Newport ($15).

Green Tortoise, (800) 227-4766. Camper bus touring company which offers interesting, economical 1-4 week trips all over North America. (Leave from Boston to west coast but no travel between east coast cities—see New York section for more details.)

Greyhound, South Station, (800) 231-2222. NYC ($37, 5 hrs).

Logan Airport is across the bay only 3 miles from downtown: Blue Line T to Airport station (85¢) from where there's a free shuttle bus to the terminals. Taxis from airport to downtown cost $10-$18.

You can take the **water shuttle**, (800) 235-6426, from Logan, across the harbour, to Rowe's Wharf for $10. Leaves every 15/30 mins Mon-Thu 6am-8pm, Fri 6am-11pm, Sat 10am-11pm, Sun 10am-8pm. 'A great way to see the city.'

Massachusetts Bay Transit Authority (MBTA), 722-3200, runs buses, trains and trolleys throughout Boston and surrounding towns. Flat fare subway 85¢, bus 60¢, no transfers. The **subway** is referred to as the 'T' and comprises four intersecting lines: the Blue, Green, Orange and Red. The stations can be identified by a black T on a white circular sign. Maps are posted in stations, you can pick up a free colour-coded pocket version at any station or visitors centre, where you can also buy the **Boston Passport** which provides unlimited travel on bus, trolley and subway lines: 1 day ($5), 3 days ($9) or 7 days ($18). Bus and subway services shut down around 12.30am. MBTA also run a commuter rail system to Rockport and Salem.

Peter Pan Bus Line, South Station, (800) 237-8747, serves Massachusetts, New Hampshire, and Connecticut. For Maine/New Hampshire, try **Concord Trailways**, South Station, (800) 639-3317.

Plymouth & Brockton Bus Lines, South Station, 773-9401, to Plymouth ($8), Hyannis ($12) and Provincetown ($21).

CAMBRIDGE Just across the river, Cambridge is often referred to as 'Boston's Left Bank'. Teeming with an eclectic collection of cafes, bookstores and boutiques, and nestled in the shadows of two of the world's premier educational institutions, **Harvard** and **Massachusetts Institute of Technology (MIT),** the lively streets and bustling squares are home to a young, diverse population. The lifestyle of the students here sets the pace for both sides of the Charles River, and **Harvard Square** is where it all happens. You will be amazed at the range of entertainment and activity to be found in such a small area. Over one hundred restaurants and cafes will satisfy any craving and on warm summer evenings street entertainers fill the air with music. For a cosier atmosphere head to one of the many blues bars and jazz clubs. For those interested in history there are some outstanding 19th century mansions.

You can take the T to Harvard Square from Boston, but it's better to walk across **Harvard Bridge**, taking in the cityscapes, and the sailors, windsurfers and rowers on the Charles River below.

www.cambridge.ma.us provides informative introduction to the city.

ACCOMMODATION
Cambridge is a 10 min T-ride from the heart of Boston where accommodation is more readily available.

ABC Accommodations, 335 Pearl St, (800) 253-5542. Comfortable B&B accommodation in family homes, from $80. Rsvs essential.

Bed & Breakfast in Cambridge & Greater Boston, PO Box 1344 Cambridge, MA, 02238, (800) 888-0178. Rooms from $75 in Cambridge, Boston, and Lexington.

Budget Chain Hotels: Before you call, check out the discounts available at the information booths off I-90, make rsvs from phones there to take advantage of the best deals.

Cambridge YWCA, 7 Temple St, Center Sq, 491-6050. Advance rsvs only; $35 pp for members, $40 non-members.

The Irving House at Harvard, 24 Irving Street, 547-4600. Two blocks from Harvard Yard and T, D-$115 w/shared bath. Bfast included.

FOOD
An array of ethnic restaurants and sidewalk cafes will tempt even the most adventurous palate. Pick up the free *Square Deal* newspaper for special offers at local eateries.

Border Cafe, 32 Church St, 864-6100. Super tasty Tex-Mex and Cajun cooking at this ever popular hot spot. Fabby fajita dinners for $9, Mexican specials $8-$10. Open late. 'Good, authentic food.'

Brookline Lunch, 109 Brookline St, 354-2983. Huge portions at super cheap prices, French toast $3, scrumptious veggie omelette with toast and special home fries, $4. Meaty dinner dishes $5. Daily 8am-5pm.

Cafe of India, 52A Brattle St, Harvard Sq, 661-0683. Good, hearty Indian food. Lunch $5-$8, dinner $10-$18.

Hong Kong, 1236 Mass Ave, 864-5311. Chinese. Lunch from $5, dinner from $6. Share a 'Scorpion Bowl,' a potent mix of fruit juices and secret ingredients sucked through long straws. 'Excellent drinking establishment (lounge upstairs). A Harvard/Tufts hangout.'

Pizzeria Uno, 22 Harvard Sq, 497-1530. Pizzas $5-$13, try their special Spinniccoli! 'Lively Italian restaurant. Good value.'

OF INTEREST
Old Town Trolley Tours, 269-7010, Mon-Fri 9am-4pm, Sat-Sun 9am-5pm. Nonstop tours of Boston and Cambridge last 1 hr 20 mins, otherwise get off and on again when you like, $24.

Harvard University, founded 1636, is the oldest university in North America. Massachusetts Hall (1720) is the oldest building still standing. The **Harvard University Visitors Information Center** is at 1350 Mass. Ave, 495-1573 (in the Holyoke Center). Guided walking tours, Mon-Sat at 10am, 11.15am, 2pm, and 3.15pm, Sun at 1.30pm and 3pm, free. Walk from Harvard Square up Brattle St past

Radcliffe, previously a women's college, now fully merged with Harvard, to **Longfellow's house**, 876-4491, where the poet lived between 1837 and 1882. The house is furnished with Longfellow's furniture and books. In earlier times George Washington used this house as his HQ. Scheduled to re-open in 2000 after major rehabilitation, call for hours and admission. Also in the campus area is the **Fogg Art Museum**, Quincy & Broadway Sts, 495-9400; which has the largest collection of Ingres outside of France, and works by Rembrandt, Monet, Renoir, Picasso and Rothko. Mon-Sat 10am-5pm, Sun 1pm-5pm, $5, $3 w/student ID, free all day Wed and Sat morning.

Le Corbusier's Carpenter Center of the Visual Arts and **Houghton Library** (housing the Keats collection), 495-3251, are opposite **Memorial Church**; the **Harvard Museums of Natural History**, contained in one building with entrances at 11 Divinity & 26 Oxford St include: **Peabody Museum of Archeology and Ethnology**, **Museum of Comparative Zoology**, **Botanical Museum** and **Mineralogical and Geological Museum**. 'It takes all day to see most of it. There's a spectacular collection of glass flowers in the Botanical Museum.' For info on all Harvard museums: 495-3045. All museums (except Fogg) open Mon-Sat 9am-5pm, Sun 1pm-5pm; $5, $4 w/student ID, free Sat 9am-noon.

MIT tours, 253-4795, include a look at the lovely chapel designed by Eero Saarinen. Student conducted tours Mon-Fri begin at 10am & 2pm at the information centre, 77 Massachusetts Ave. 'It's probably just as worthwhile to get a map and wander around yourself.'

MIT Museum, 265 Massachusetts Avenue at Front Street (Building N52), 253-4444. Science and technology, architecture, and nautical exhibitions, plus the 'Hall of Hacks' documenting MIT students' pranks. Come here to learn about the weather balloon that exploded in a cloud of talcum powder on the playing field of the 1982 Harvard-Yale football game. Tue-Fri 10am-5pm, Sat-Sun noon-5pm, $5, $2 w/student ID. *http://web.mit.edu/museum/home*

Mt Auburn Cemetery on Mt Auburn St, contains the graves of Longfellow, James Lowell, Oliver Wendell Holmes and Mary Baker Eddy, founder of Christian Science. Both a cemetery and a park, with ponds, hills, footpaths, arboretum. 'Quiet relaxing place, great for bird watching in spring.'

Walking tours, pick up a self-guided tour map ($2) from the info booth in Harvard Sq and discover the historic sites of Cambridge and Harvard Yard for yourself.

Book Stores: It's not surprising, perhaps, that America's academic capital plays host to one of the world's largest concentrations of book stores. A few of the more intriguing shops:

Grolier Poetry Bookshop, 6 Plympton St, 547-4648, oldest continuously operating poetry book shop in US, more than 14,000 titles. Tue-Sat noon-6.30pm.

Harvard Co-op, 1400 Mass Ave, 499-2000, books, posters, music, and more.

Revolution Books, 1156 Mass. Ave, 492-5443, anything you could want by Marx, Lenin, Stalin, Mao, etc.

Words Worth, 30 Brattle St, 354-5201, over 100,000 titles in 110 categories. Mon-Sat 9am-11.15pm, Sun 10am-10.15pm.

ENTERTAINMENT

Watch the *Boston Phoenix* for details of concerts and lectures. *The Harvard Gazette*, *Crimson* and *Independent* are also good, though the latter is not published in summer. The active music scene is closely tied to Harvard and MIT; summer is therefore quieter.

Cantab Lounge, 738 Mass. Ave, Central Sq, 354-2685. Packed out with locals enjoying Little Joe Cook and his Blues band. Cover $5-$8.

John Harvard's Brew House, 33 Dunster St, 868-3585. Brewery restaurant serving good home-made ales, lagers and seasonal beers. Try a brewery sampler, five tasters for $4.95. Daily 11.30am-10pm. Mon nights, free bands.

Ryles Jazz Club, 212 Hampshire St, Inman Sq, 876-9330, Cover $7-$12, Sun Brunch 10am-3pm. Not cheap, but good jazz. *www.rylesjazz.com*
TT The Bear's Place, 10 Brookline St, Central Square, 492-0082, hard rock, beer. Live 'n loud!

LEXINGTON/CONCORD   Lexington and Concord are ideally situated for day trips from Boston, and are easily accessible by public transport or pedal power (you can bike up the **Minute Man Commuter Bike Trail** from Arlington). Known as the 'Birthplace of American Liberty', the towns share the distinction of being the site of the first skirmish in the American Revolution. Near Concord's **Old North Bridge** on 19 April 1775, local farmers took aim at advancing British redcoats and fired the 'shot heard round the world'.

The bridge is part of the **Minute Man National Historic Park**, (978) 369-6993; park rangers give excellent historical talks here on request. Battle re-enactments are staged throughout both towns in April to mark Patriot's Day (closest Monday to April 19), and a special 'Colonial Weekend' in early October.

Concord is also the home of the literary transcendentalist movement. Interestingly, all of the best-known transcendentalists—Ralph Waldo Emerson, Henry David Thoreau, Nathaniel Hawthorne, Amos Bronson Alcott and his daughter, Louisa May—at one point lived within blocks of each other in this tiny, pristine town. Also here is **Sleepy Hollow Cemetery**, (3 blocks from town) where some of them have been laid to rest. Not far away is Thoreau's **Walden Pond**.
The telephone area code for Concord is 978, Lexington is 781.

ACCOMMODATION
Accommodation here is limited and rather expensive. See Cambridge for local B&B options.
Col. Roger Brown House, 1694 Main St, Concord, 369-9119. D-$90.
Desiderata B&B, 189 Wood St, Lexington, 862-2824. D-$70, includes good bfast. No credit cards, rsvs recommended.
Red Cape B&B, 61 Williams Rd, Lexington, 862-4913. D-$70, XP-$10. Rsvs recommended.

FOOD
Bertucci's, 1777 Mass Ave, Lexington, 860-9000. Pizza, pasta, salads; $7-$15.
Brighams, 15 Main St, Concord, 369-9885. Famous ice-creams! Hot Fudge Sundae $3.20, burgers from $4.50, breakfast specials from $2.50.
Concord Tea Cakes, 59 Commonwealth Ave, 369-7644. Home-made cakes, muffins, cookies and tea-time treats.
Sally Ann Food Shop, 73 Main St, Concord, 369-4558. Soups, sandwiches and bakery takeouts at reasonable prices.

OF INTEREST
Hancock-Clarke House, 36 Hancock St, Lexington, 861-0928, is where Sam Adams and John Hancock were staying when Paul Revere came galloping by to warn them. Mid-April to Oct, Mon-Sat 10am-5pm, Sun 1pm-5pm (last tours 4.30pm). A $10 combo ticket gets you into the house and the Buckman and Monroe taverns nearby, otherwise $4 for each building. **Monroe Tavern**, 1332 Mass Ave, was headquarters and hospital for British troops. Call 862-1703, opening times as above.
Lexington Green, where it all happened two centuries ago, is lined with lovely

Colonial houses; on the east side, facing the road by which the British approached, is the famous Minute Man Statue. Over in the south-west corner of the Green is the Revolutionary Monument erected in 1799 to commemorate the eight minute men killed here. Near the Green is **Buckman Tavern**, the oldest of the local hostelries and gathering place of the minute men on drill nights.

INFORMATION/TRAVEL

Concord Chamber of Commerce, call 369-3120, or write 2 Lexington Rd, Concord, Mass 01742.

Lexington Information Centre, 862-1450, near Buckman Tavern at 1875 Mass Ave, has details and literature. Daily 9am-5pm. In summer guides give lectures on the Green.

To get there; take the commuter train ($3.25) from Boston's MBTA North Station, (617) 722-3200, to Concord, or the subway to Alewife in Cambridge, then the bus to Lexington.

THE NORTH SHORE Meandering north on Hwy 1 your first port of call should be **Salem**. The **Witch House**, 310 Essex St, 744-0180, has tours ($5) of the judges' quarters in what was the site of the famous witch trials in 1692 during which Puritan judges sent 19 suspected witches to the gallows and ordered a man to be crushed to death under millstones. ArThu Miller uses the whole horrific series of events in his play *The Crucible* as a metaphor for McCarthy's communist 'witch hunts' in the 1950s. The **Salem Witch Museum**, 19½ Washington Sq North, 744-1692, has an audio-visual programme with life-sized dioramas that tell the story of the witchcraft hysteria. Daily in summer 10am-7pm, $5. For a slightly more sensational rendition of history, visit the **Witch Dungeon**, 16 Lynde St, 744-9812. A witch trial is re-enacted for the audience's edification. Afterwards, visitors tour the lower dungeons. Daily 10am-5pm; $5. 'A rip-off. Lasts about 15 minutes and not very realistic.'

Nathaniel Hawthorne's birthplace—made famous in his novel—the *House of Seven Gables*, 54 Turner St, 744-0991, still stands complete with secret stairways, hidden compartments and beautiful period gardens. Daily in summer 10am-5pm; $7.

A prominent port in Colonial days, Salem is a veritable museum of American architecture of the 17th and 19th centuries. Chestnut Street is lined with the lovely homes of Salem Clipper captains and owners. The **Pioneer Village** off West Ave in Forest River Park just outside Salem's historic district, 745-0525, recreates typical homes of the Puritan community, *circa* 1630. Costumed guides take tours through the village, $5, Mon-Sat 10am-5pm, Sun noon-5pm. House of Seven Gables combo tkt $10.

On **Cape Ann**, about 30 miles north of Boston, lies **Gloucester,** a rugged port packed with fishing boats and seafood restaurants. Four miles north of Gloucester, off Rte 127A, is the typical fishing village of **Rockport**, now an artist colony and full of arty-crafty stores. 'Great for browsing and getting broke.'

On your way north from here to New Hampshire and Maine, there's the small town of **Newburyport**. The High Street is adorned with splendid early American mansions. 'While you're here, go whale watching; from Hilton's Fishing Dock, 462-8381. $25 for 4½hrs; money goes to finance research.' Daily 8.30am & 1.30pm.

The telephone area code for Salem and the North Shore is 978.

PLYMOUTH   South of Boston, Plymouth marks the spot where the Pilgrims landed in 1620; the first Thanksgiving celebrations were held here in 1621. A few 17th-century houses still stand, and on Leyden St markers indicate where the very first houses stood. Moored by the Rock is *Mayflower II*, a full-size replica of the original. 'Worth a quick visit, but it's really for Americans.'

Today Plymouth County is known as **Cranberry Country**. Harvest in September is a colourful ritual; the dazzling crimson of America's native berry covers over 12,000 acres and seems to reach to the horizon.

The telephone area code for Plymouth is 508.

ACCOMMODATION

Guest houses are the cheapest option, but they become more coveted and expensive every year. Try looking in the area behind the Tourist Information Center.

Blue Anchor Motel, 7 Lincoln St, 746-9551. Rooms S-$50, D-$56.

In-Town B&B, 23 Pleasant St, 746-7412. D-$65, $90 for three, full bfast. Good location. 'Lovely people.'

Camping: Indianhead Campground, 1929 State Rd, 12 miles south of Plymouth, 888-3688. Sites $20 for two w/hook up, XP-$10. Laundromat, showers, groceries; fishing, swimming and mini golf, boat rentals and amusement arcade.

Plymouth Rock KOA Kampground, Middleboro, 15 miles from Plymouth on Rte 105, just off US44, 947-6435. Laundromat, showers, pool, game room, food store. Sites $24.50 for two, $30 w/hook-up, $38 for a cabin, XP-$4. 'Friendly; great place.'

FOOD

There are many reasonably priced sub shops and good greasy spoons in Plymouth. Generally, the farther away from the water, the cheaper.

Cap'n Harry's Deli & Sandwich Shop, 170 Water St, 747-5699. Sandwiches $3.50-$5, try their Cajun turkey roll-ups. Mon-Fri 8am-3pm, Sat-Sun 7.30am-3pm.

Court Street Cafe, 39 Court St, 746-2057. Breakfast special $2.99 before 10am. Nothing over $6.25. Mon-Fri 7am-3pm, w/ends 7am-2.30pm.

OF INTEREST

Cranberry World Visitor Center, Water St near *Mayflower II*, 747-2350. See how cranberries are grown and harvested, then view the cranberry bogs that produce the tart fruit for which Massachusetts is famous. Daily 9.30am-5pm; free. 'Nice facility and tour.' 'More than you ever wanted to know about cranberries.' Free samples.

Pilgrim Hall Museum, 75 Court St, 746-1620. Personal possessions and records of the Pilgrims. Daily 9.30am-4.30pm, $5.

Plimouth Plantation. Rte 3 & Warren Ave, 746-1622. Re-creates the 1627 Plymouth community, 3 miles south of town square. Daily, 9am-5pm. Combo tkt: *Mayflower II* and Plimouth Plantation $19 valid for two days. Both staffed by American students dressed as Pilgrims speaking with 'English accents', pretending they are still in the 17th century. 'Less pro-American bias than elsewhere on the East Coast. Characters very knowledgeable.'

Plymouth Rock, on the harbour, supposedly the site of the pilgrims' arrival in the New World. Good for a chuckle, but don't make a special trip for it. Moored on the adjacent pier is *Mayflower II*, 746-1622. The replica of the original, built in England and sailed to America in 1957. $6.50 (but see above).

Whale Watching, Captain John's Boats, (800) 242-AHOY. Four trips daily in summer, $25.

INFORMATION

Plymouth Information Center, 130 Water St, 747-7525. General information on historical attractions. Daily in summer 9am-9pm.

TRAVEL
Plymouth & Brockton Bus Lines, 746-0378. Boston, $8.
Take the short cut to Provincetown with **Capt John Boats**, (800) 242-2469/746-2643, Town Wharf. Express ferry takes 1½hrs from Plymouth to the tip of Cape Cod, $25.

CAPE COD   A 65 mile-long hook jutting out into the Atlantic, the Cape is a narrow string of sand from where, atop a dune, you can gaze at the ocean on one side and Cape Cod Bay on the other. Known for its distinctive architectural style of gable-roofed houses, the Cape can be an icy cold and blustery spot out of season, but summers are warm and sunny with a refreshing tang of salt in the air.

The Cape, with no less than 77 beaches, is home to many scientists who come to study the ocean's mysteries. The **Woods Hole Oceanographic Institute**, at the southern point of the Cape, is the most famous research group here. Be sure to see the **National Marine Fisheries Service's Aquarium**, 495-2267, daily 10am-4pm, free, home to many rare New England species of sea life. At the other end of the Cape, near the north-east tip, is the **Wellfleet Bay Wildlife Sanctuary** in South Wellfleet, a 1000-acre area operated by the Massachusetts Audubon Society.

Although the Cape is an extremely popular summer resort, it is still possible to avoid the crowds and escape to deserted sand dunes or down beautiful, sandy New England lanes leading to the sea: simply avoid Hyannis and the coast south of Cape Cod National Seashore.

Hyannis and the surrounding area is the part of the Cape most exploited by tourism and free enterprise, but over in the lower Cape, small towns like Sandwich, Barnstaple, Catumet and Pocasset remain relatively quiet, even in the high season. After Labor Day you can have the whole Cape to yourself. (Well, sort of; Cape Codders let you know in no uncertain terms that it belongs to them. However, high unemployment in recent years means that the Cape's commercial community is depending on tourists more than ever for their livelihood.)

On the Cape you will come up against numerous private beaches, or public ones that extract heavy parking fees. The Chamber of Commerce booklet *Cape Cod Vacationer*, free and available everywhere, lists all beaches and their status and has other useful information. There is plenty of camping near Sandwich where there is also a free public beach. State run and private sites can also be found in Bourne, Brewster, and Truro. Near Brewster is Orleans—a favourite beach for surfers.

Aside from the tourist, the Cape's great source of revenue is the cranberry. Nearly three-quarters of the world's cranberry crop is produced here and in neighbouring Plymouth County.
The telephone area code for Cape Cod is 508.

ACCOMMODATION
Can be expensive, but there are several camping sites and also 3 youth hostels. For other listings, see Hyannis or Provincetown, or else consult *Yankee Magazine's Guide to New England* or the *Cape Cod Vacationer*.
Bed & Breakfast, Cape Cod, Box 341, West Hyannisport, MA 02672; 775-2772/ (800) 686-5252. Reservation service; in-season rooms from $75 incl. bfast, plus $10 one-time booking fee and 25% deposit.

Mid-Cape Hostel, 75 Goody Hallet Dr, Eastham, 255-2785. Mid-May to mid-Sept; 7.30am-10am and 5pm-10pm. $14 AYH, $17 non-AYH, linen $2. Summer rsvs essential. 20 miles from Truro, ideal if you're working your way up the Cape.' 'Very strict.'

Camping: Shawme Crowell State Forest at Sandwich, 888-0351, and the **Roland C Nickerson State Forest** at Brewster, 896-3491, are both recommended. Sites at each are $6 per night; but be warned: 'Campsites are often full right up to Labor Day and you may need to drive right out to North Truro to find a vacancy.' Plan your summer Cape Cod accommodation as early as possible.

TRAVEL
See also under Hyannis.
The **Cape Cod Automated Travel Service**, 771-6191, offers 24 hr comprehensive info on fares and schedules for transport to, from and within the area.
Bonanza Bus Lines, 59 Depot Ave (old train depot), Falmouth, 548-7588/(800) 556-3815. Boston $13.50, New York $45, and Bourne, $5.

HYANNIS   The metropolis of the Cape, Hyannis is the main supply centre for the area and a busy summer resort. Main Street is an example of the typical all-American strip; for charm you want the outlying areas like Hyannisport and Craigville with its excellent beach for swimming.

More upper crust than most of the other Cape Cod towns, Hyannis is the home of wealthy trendies and is bathed in the aura of the Kennedy family sequestered in their Hyannisport compound.

ACCOMMODATION
Cascade Motor Lodge, 201 Main St, 775-9717. D-$68-$78, very close to bus station. 'Had large, luxurious room with bathroom and double waterbed!'
Ocean Manor, 543 Ocean St, 771-2186. D-$74, private bath, comfortable rooms. Close to beaches, 1 mile from downtown. Summer rsvs recommended.
Sea Beach Inn, Inc, 388 Sea St, 775-4612. D-$60-$65, XP-$10. Bfast included.

FOOD
Hearth & Kettle, 412 Main St, 771-3737. Breakfast from $4, lunch from $5. Try a kettle of lobster chowder $4. 'Recommend the Early Bird Specials 12pm-6pm daily.'
Mooring, 230 Ocean St, on the harbour, 771-7177. Open into the wee hours, depending on the crowd. Lunch from $6, dinner from $10. 'Good food.'
Perry's, 546 Main St. 775-9711. Breakfast from $2, sandwiches from $3.50, stacked sandwiches with fries $5.50. Daily 5am-9pm.

INFORMATION
Cape Cod Chamber of Commerce, Rtes 6 & 132, 362-3225/(888) 332-2732. Offers accommodation and entertainment information for the entire Cape area. Ask for *The Vacationer* booklet, *Resort Directory*, and the *Current Events* booklet. A good place to start learning about the Cape highlights. Summer hours; Mon-Fri 8.30am-5pm, Sat 9am-5pm, Sun 10am-4pm. *www.capecodchamber.org*
Hyannis Area Chamber of Commerce, 1481 Rte 132, 775-2201. Mon-Sat 9am-5pm, Sun 10am-2pm.

TRAVEL
Cape Cod Central Railroad, (888) 797-7245, Hyannis to Sandwich, Tue-Sun, $11.75 r/t.
Ferries: During the summer, boats leave frequently from Hyannis South St Dock for Nantucket, r/t is $24, cars $230. R/t from Woods Hole to Martha's Vineyard is $10, cars $94. Contact **Steamship Authority**, 477-8600 for schedule.
Trips around the Hyannis Inner Harbour to gape at the Kennedy compound are also available for $10. Contact **Hy-Line Harbour Cruises**, on the Ocean St docks,

775-7185. Hy-Line give discounts with coupons available at any Cape or Island hostel.

Plymouth & Brockton Bus Lines, 17 Elm Ave, 746-0378. Provincetown $9, Boston $12.

PROVINCETOWN P-town, as it's known locally, is at the very tip of the Cape, thus giving it its other nickname: Land's End. The Pilgrim Fathers' first landfall in North America was actually here. They stayed for four or five weeks before moving on to Plymouth. The town has made its name on tourism and fishing.

Provincetown has been a haven for artists since the 1870s. In 1899 Charles Hawthorne opened Provincetown's Cape Cod School of Art. Modernists dominated the scene from the 30s to the 50s—Jackson Pollock and Mark Rothko both lived here.

In summer the town is still jam-packed with artists, playwrights and craftsmen (including a very large gay community), now out-numbered by the tourists and hangers-on who come to watch them. All in all, the off-season population of around 4,000 swells to nearly 50,000 people! P-town is an attractive spot with old clapboard houses, narrow streets and miles of sandy beaches. Commercial St, appropriately named, is the main drag, so to speak.

In the summer months, it's a perpetual street fair. For a special evening's entertainment, take a beach taxi ride over the sand dunes. 'Nightlife is very limited if you are looking for "straight" bars and there are very few college age students around.' *www.provincetown.net* or *www.provincetown.com*

ACCOMMODATION
Alice Dunham's Guest House, 3 Dyer St, 487-3330. Victorian sea captain's house. Bunk n' Brew—D-$53-$59 plus a cold beer! One night free for each week you stay; 20% discount Sept-June. 'Nicest place in town.' 'Very friendly, interesting proprietor.' Rsvs recommended.
HI-Truro, N Pamet Rd, 349-3889, 10 miles from Provincetown. $14 AYH, $17 non-AYH, linen $2, kitchen. Rsvs essential. Two minute walk to beach.
Joshua Paine Guest House, 15 Tremont St, in the west end (quiet, non-commercial part), 487-1551. June 15-Sept 15. S-$45, D-$50, XP-$10. 'Friendly; nice place.'
The Outermost Hostel, 28 Winslow St, 487-4378. $14.95 per night. Dorm-style cabins, kitchen facilities, May-Oct 8am-9.30am, 5.30pm-9.30pm. 'Good location.'

FOOD
Cafe Heaven, 109 Commercial St, 487-9639. Home-made muffins and granola for breakfast, over-stuffed sandwiches for $5-$7.
Clem and Ursie's Food Ghetto, 89 Shank Painter Rd, 487-2333. Inexpensive seafood, sea clam pot pie $6.50
Stormy Harbor, 277 Commercial St, 487-1680. Italian, Portuguese, and seafood. Bfast from $5, dinner from $12. Open April-Oct.
Surf Restaurant, 315 Commercial St on MacMillan Wharf, 487-1367. Eat on the deck overlooking the harbour. A drafthouse with jug band, washboard, and kazoos! Seafood menu $9-$27.

OF INTEREST
Art's Dune Tour, 487-1950, leaves from Commercial & Standish Sts. April-Oct. $12 for standard tour, $15 for sunset tour (need rsvs). From 10am throughout the day. Interesting ride out to the site of dune shacks once belonging to Tennessee Williams and Eugene O'Neill, then on to a cranberry bog before heading out to the ocean.
Fine Arts Work Center, 24 Pearle St, 487-9960. Conducts a summer workshop for

prominent writers and artists and offers weekly readings, lectures, slide shows, and exhibits. Gallery open Mon-Fri 9am-5pm. *www.capecodaccess.com/FineArtsWorkCenter*
Provincetown Art Association and Museum, 460 Commercial St, 487-1750. Daily noon-5pm and 8pm-10pm. Suggested donation $3.
Provincetown Museum, at the base of the Pilgrim Monument, 487-1310. 'The Treasures of the pirate ship, *Whydah*. Artefacts from the ship of the pirate Samuel (Black Sam) Bellamy sunk in 1717 and identified in 1984.' Daily 9am-7pm, last admission 6.15pm; shorter winter hours. $5 admission to monument, museum and exhibit.
Whale Watching from MacMillan Wharf, $19 for 3½hrs at sea (off season $18). Call Dolphin Fleet: (800) 826-9300, or Ranger Five: 487-3322 for savings on 8.30am trips. 'Good, interesting commentary on board; we saw several whales, including one that swam under and around the boat; incredible and not to be missed.'

INFORMATION
Province Land's Visitors Center in Cape Cod National Seashore, 487-1256, off Race Point Road. Tour information, maps of seashore. Daily in summer 9am-5pm.
Provincetown Chamber of Commerce, 307 Commercial St, 487-3424. Offers maps and accommodation listings. Daily 9am-5pm. *www.capecodaccess.com/provincetownchamber*
Summer Shuttle Bus, 432-3400, will take you from the town centre to the beach, daily in summer 10.30am-6.30pm every hour. The shuttle (a yellow school bus) may be hailed at intersections on Bradford St, or pick it up at the MacMillan Parking Lot behind the Chamber of Commerce. Buy tkts on board, $1.25 o/w.

NANTUCKET 'The Little Grey Lady of the Sea', as the island is known, provided inspiration for Melville's *Moby Dick*. You will find yourself in another world as you step off the ferry: thirty miles off Cape Cod, the island retains a certain charm with its weather-worn (though meticulously preserved) houses, cranberry bogs and salt marshes. Lobster boats crowd the small harbour in the evenings, when they sell their catch to restaurateurs and passers-by. On every side of the island there are miles of open sand beaches terrific for swimming, surfing, fishing and all-night bonfire parties. Rent a bike near the ferry port and follow the bike paths or explore the island on the narrow streets and winding lanes. The 10-mile scenic ride to the beaches at Siasconset on the east coast will whet your appetite for a dip in the ocean.

The cobblestoned Main Street of Nantucket town and fine Colonial homes testify to the past prosperity built on the blubber of hunted whales. Today the money flows in with the flood of 'off-islanders' in summer. It can be a crowded place then, but a lot of fun. For the pristine scene, come out of season when there's nobody there but the 'on-islanders', some of whom brag that they have never seen the mainland.
www.nantucket.com
The telephone area code for Nantucket is 508.

ACCOMMODATION
The island is generally a very expensive place to stay, and to maintain premium hotel rates any riffraff caught camping will be fined $50, i.e., what you would have paid for a bed. But all is not lost:
Nantucket Accommodations Bureau, P.O Box 217, Nantucket, MA 02554, 228-9559. Lists most of the island's guest houses and inns. Charges $15 for service. Call or write early for best bargains.

Nesbitt Inn, 21 Broad St, 228-2446 in centre of town. S-$75, D-$85; Bfast included. Rsvs required.

Robert B. Johnson Hostel, 31 Western Ave, Nantucket, MA 02554, 228-0433. 3 miles from ferry wharf. $14 AYH, $17 non-AYH, linen $2. Two mins to beach. April-Oct 7.30am-10am, 5pm-10pm, 11pm curfew. Rsvs essential in summer. admin_hienec@juno.com

FOOD
Captain Tobey's Chowder House, Straight Wharf, 228-0836. Winner of 'Best Chowder' award. Lunch from $9, dinner from $16, early bird special (5pm-6.30pm) $13, .'Good seafood.' Pricey but worth it. Daily 11am-10pm.
Henry's, on Steamboat Wharf, 228-0123, has the biggest, and some say the best, sandwiches on the island, $3-$6. Daily 9am-10pm.

OF INTEREST
Whaling Museum, Broad St, 228-1736. In the 18th and early 19th centuries, Nantucket was the best known whaling town in America. You can recapture something of the flavour of those times here. Has a good scrimshaw collection. Daily 10am-5pm; $5.
Whale Watching. Call 1-800-WHALING for details. About $79 for a day trip (9.30am-4.30pm), Tue and Fri only. Guarantee sighting or return visit. 'Saw more than 20 whales. Best part of our trip.' Rsvs. recommended.
Young's Bicycle Rental, 6 Broadstreet, 228-1151. $20 per 24 hrs, $16 if returned by 5pm.

ENTERTAINMENT
Gaslight Theatre, N Union St, 228-4435. Mainstream and art films, $7.
The Muse, 44 Surfside Rd (1 mile out of town), 228-6873. Best live entertainment on the island: rock 'n roll, reggae, blues, cover up to $10. Don't miss the lip-synching contest on Sundays! *www.museack.com*
Rose and Crown, S Water Street, 228-2595. Good pub-grub from $7. Live entertainment, karaoke, cover for bands around $5. 'Packed out but has a dance floor.'

INFORMATION
Chamber of Commerce, 48 Main St, 228-1700, maps, restaurant and accommodation information. Mon-Fri 9am-5pm. *www.nantucketchamber.org*
Hub Board, Main St. Very useful for ads of jobs and rooms. 'We found two rooms from it on the first day.'
See under Hyannis for travel information.

MARTHA'S VINEYARD Once you've experienced the 'Vineyard', as it is fondly called, you will never forget it. Just five miles off the Cape, New England's largest island boasts sandy beaches, pine forests, moorland, winding lanes and picturesque towns steeped in maritime history. It's a pleasure to visit at any time of year, although July and August are the most lively. In September, the island becomes a peaceful haven once again, basking in the warmth of Indian summers.

Surfing, swimming and sailing are the attractions, although ever-increasing prices exclude such sports to anyone other than the jet-set who take over the island in the summer. Bill and Hillary Clinton are currently among the island's most prominent visitors. Settle instead for a bicycle (rentals widely available) and pedal around Edgartown, the elegant yachting centre where you can admire the fine old houses of the whaling captains, or make the strenuous 20-mile-trip out to Gayhead to watch the setting sun do its light show against the dramatic coloured cliffs. In summer it is possible to take a tour bus from the ferry terminals in Vineyard Haven and Oak Bluffs for a fascinating visit 'up-Island' (and 'down-Island'). While in Oak Bluffs, take a ride on the **Flying Horses Carousel**, the country's oldest platform carousel. Circuit Ave, 693-9481, $1.

If you long to ditch people for the gentler company of swans, lesser terns and mergansers, pay a visit to one of the Vineyard's three wildlife refuges: **Cedar Tree Neck** on the North Shore, 693-7233; **Long Point** on the South Shore, or **Wasque Point** on Chappaquiddick, 627-7689. Massachusetts Audubon Society run natural history tours to bird haven **Monomoy Islands**. 3hr tour $30, rsvs required, 349-2615.

The island is dry (no alcohol sold) except for Edgartown and Oak Bluffs. *www.mvol.com*
The telephone area code for Martha's Vineyard is 508.

ACCOMMODATION
Manter Memorial AYH, Edgartown Rd, PO Box 3158, W Tisbury, MA 02575, 693-2665. 7.3 miles from ferry terminal. April-Nov 7am-10am, 5pm-10pm. $12 AYH, $15 non-AYH, linen $2. Rsvs essential for summer; include SAE with first night deposit for confirmation. 'A long way from anywhere.'
Camping: Martha's Vineyard Family Campground, Edgartown Rd, Vineyard Haven, 693-3772. Sites $30 w/hook up, XP-$10.

FOOD
The Black Dog Inn, Beach St, Vineyard Haven, 693-9223. Breakfast, lunch and dinner at moderate prices, very popular with both tourists and locals.
Linda Jean's Restaurant, Circuit Ave, Oak Bluffs, 693-4093. Home cooking, breakfast $5-$6, lunch and dinner $7-$15, daily specials. Daily 6am-8pm.
90 Main Street Deli, 90 Main St, 693-0041. Gourmet sandwiches $4.25-$8.95, salads and subs. Daily 6.30am-11pm.

INFORMATION/TRAVEL
Visitor Center, at Ferry terminal in Vineyard Haven, 693-0085. Accommodation lists, maps and employment information available. Daily 8am-8pm. *www.mvy.com*
See under Hyannis for travel information.

NEW BEDFORD / FALL RIVER   On Rte 6 on the way from the Cape to Providence, RI, **New Bedford** was once the whaling capital of the world. It has recently been transformed from a dismal, rundown place to a cross between Mystic Seaport and Nantucket. There is a fascinating **whaling museum**, well worth visiting and known for its exceptional collections of scrimshaw, 18 Johnny Cake Hill, 997-0046, daily 9am-5pm, Thu til 8pm, $4.50. Scrimshaw, perfected by New England sailors in the 19th century, involves carving and etching the surface of the teeth or jawbone of the whale.

Further west is the port town of **Fall River**, where the *Battleship Massachusetts*, 678-1100, veteran of WWII Pacific battles, is moored. Daily 9am-6pm in July & Aug, $9.
The telephone area code for New Bedford/Fall River is 508.

THE BERKSHIRE HILLS   Only about two and a half hours from NYC and Boston, Berkshire County is an ideal escape from the hustle of the city. The Green Mountains of Vermont in the north slope down to become the

Berkshire Hills, a sub-range of the Appalachians that sneaks south to leafy Connecticut along the western border of Massachusetts.

A great area to venture off the beaten track, explore picturesque villages such as **Lenox** and **Stockbridge**, or hike in idyllic countryside on the trails around Mt Greylock (at 3491 feet the highest peak in the state) or the 80 miles of the Appalachian Trail that winds through Massachusetts. Drive along The Mohawk Trail and feast your eyes on panoramic views of this green and pleasant land. Finish up in **Williamstown** (famous for its college), or make your stop in **Pittsfield,** the county seat of the Berkshires, and from here canoe the Housatonic, investigate the many theatrical and musical events on offer around Lenox, Lee and Stockbridge or simply soak up the local history. The free *Berkshire Eagle* will keep you abreast of current happenings.
The telephone area code for the area is 413.

ACCOMMODATION
Super 8, Massachusetts Turnpike, exit 2, on Rtes 7 & 20, 637-3560. Summer D-$75-$165. Bfast included. Rsvs recommended.
YMCA, 292 North St, Pittsfield, 499-7650. S-$28, $67 weekly plus $6 key deposit.

OF INTEREST
Pittsfield was the birthplace of writer Herman Melville of *Moby Dick* fame. The **Atheneum** has a room devoted to his effects, and you can visit his house, **Arrowhead**, at the edge of Pittsfield on Holmes Road 442-1793. Daily 9.30am-5pm, last tour at 4pm; $5, $3 w/student ID.
Hancock Shaker Village (5 miles West of Pittsfield), 443-0188. Earning their name from an early nickname 'Shaking Quakers', the Shakers originated in the late 18th century in Manchester, England and flourished for two centuries. Perhaps due to an avowal of celibacy, only one Shaker community remains, in Sabbathday Lake, Maine. Known for their simple yet exquisite architecture, furniture and handicrafts, the Hancock Shaker Village, founded in 1790, displays many fine examples of their craftsmanship. Alas the Shakers abandoned their village to the tourists in 1960. Daily in summer 9.30am-5pm, $13.50. 'Worth a visit.' *www.hancockshakervillage.org*
The Mount, Plunkett St, Lenox, 637-1899. Designed and built in 1901 by the writer Edith Wharton, author of *Ethan Frome, The Age of Innocence* and *The Buccaneers*. Wharton's opulent mansion was a source of inspiration for her writings. Summer: Daily 9am-2pm, $6.
Norman Rockwell Museum, Rte 183, Stockbridge, 298-4100. The museum houses a vast collection of original works and the studio of America's favourite illustrator. Daily 10am-5pm, $9.
The **Tanglewood Music Festival** held in Lenox late June-Labor Day, is the summer home to the Boston Symphony Orchestra. Sit out on the lawns with a blanket and picnic. Tkts from $10, for info call 637-1600. All kinds of music are performed, and many other fringe activities are available in the area.
Jacob's Pillow Dance Festival, 243-0745, with ballet, jazz and contemporary dance, held at the Ted Shawn Theater off US 20 east of Lee, late June-August. North of Lee is the **October State Forest**, with the Appalachian Trail running through it.

INFORMATION
Berkshire Visitors Bureau, 2 Berkshire Common, Pittsfield, 443-9186/(800) 237-5747. Mon-Fri 8am-5pm. *www.berkshires.org*
Mount Greylock Visitors Information Centre, Rockwell Rd, Lanesborough, 499-4262, have free maps of the trails. Daily 9am-5pm.
Pittsfield Information Booth on the Rotary Circle for further info.

Williamstown Information Booth at junction of Rte 2 & Rte 7, staffed 10am-6pm June-Sept, but open 24 hrs for info. Will help find accommodation in local **B&Bs**.

TRAVEL
Amtrak's *Lake Shore Limited*, Boston-Chicago, stops here: Depot St between North & Center. Call (800) 872-7245. Boston-Pittsfield $29, 4hrs, rsvs recommended.
Berkshires Regional Transit Association, 499-2782, covers the Berkshires from Great Barrington to Williamstown. Fares 75¢-$3.
Bike Rentals, from Arcadian Shop, 637-3010, Pittsfield Rd, Lenox. 4 hrs $25, 8 hrs $35.

NEW HAMPSHIRE *The Granite State*

Many people consider the Granite State the most scenic state east of the Mississippi. The only state named after an English county, New Hampshire has a short but sandy Atlantic coastline, hundreds of lakes (the biggest is 72-square-mile Lake Winnipesaukee), the impressive White Mountain range, more than 60 covered wooden bridges and a 90 percent tree cover. The countryside, warm and green in the summer, seems to catch fire when the leaves change colour in the Fall Foliage Show. The long, cold, snowy winters make the state a popular and fashionable skiing centre.

Notice the granite walls everywhere. Built by the early settlers to enclose their fields, the walls remain even though most of the fields are forest again.

New Hampshire was the first state to declare its independence and also the first to adopt its own constitution. Nowadays it is regarded as a political barometer, the results of its early primary elections strongly influencing the country's choice of candidates in the presidential elections.

The inhabitants are mostly genuine, laconic Yankees, and the state motto 'Live Free or Die' reflects the tough Yankee spirit behind the Revolutionary War. New Hampshire's passion for freedom extends to shopping—the state has no sales tax, so you may want to check out the outlets while you're here. *www.visitnh.gov*
The telephone area code for New Hampshire is 603.

PORTSMOUTH   Its situation at the mouth of the Piscataqua River has always made Portsmouth a significant port, and it was the state capital until 1808. The only seaport on the state's modest 18-mile coastline, the city has numerous old and well-preserved colonial homes. Nearby are several fine, sandy beaches, including those at Wallis Sands and Rye Harbor. *www.portcity.org*

ACCOMMODATION/FOOD
Accommodation in town is invariably expensive, a better bet would be to try areas off US-1 instead.
Comfort Inn at Yoken's, on US-1, 433-3338/(800) 552-8484. Rooms from $90, pool. Adjacent to Yoken's, 436-8224, a popular and inexpensive ribs restaurant.
Pine Haven Motel, 6½ miles south of town on US-1, 964-8187. Prices from: S-$69, D-$79, XP-$10.
Portsmouth Brewery, 225 Heritage Ave, 431-1115. New Hampshire's original brewpub, lagers and ales brewed on the premises. Pizza and sandwiches $5-$7,

dinner from $10. Brewery tours given on request. *www.portsmouthbrewery.com*
Muddy River Smokehouse, 21 Congress St, 430-9582, has live blues and good bar food.

OF INTEREST
Isles of Shoals, just off-shore, and the supposed haunt of Blackbeard the pirate. Boat trips are available from the harbour, call 431-5500.
John Paul Jones House, Middle & State Sts, 436-8420. Built 1758, house of the US Naval hero. Jones obtained the surrender of a British warship in 1779, as his own ship was sinking. Later, he became a Russian contra-admiral and died in Paris during the French Revolution. Mon-Sat 10am-4pm, Sun noon-4pm, $5.
Old Harbor Area, Bow & Ceres Sts, once the focus of the thriving seaport, is now an area of craft shops and eateries.
Portsmouth Farmer's Market. Fresh produce, arts and crafts. Every Sat at Parrot Ave parking lot, South Mill Pond, (207) 363-0557.
Strawberry Banke Museum, just off I-95 on the waterfront, 433-1100. From this settlement, starting in 1623, grew the town of Portsmouth. Tour historic homes and period gardens dating from 1695. Craft demonstrations and exhibits. Daily 10am-5pm, $12.

INFORMATION
Portsmouth Chamber of Commerce, 500 Market St, 436-1118. Mon-Wed 8.30am-5pm, Thu-Fri 8.30am-7pm, w/ends 10am-5pm.

CONCORD Situated on the banks of the Merrimack River, New Hampshire's financial and political centre is reputedly home to the fourth largest deliberative body in the world.

While much of the region's character is shaped by the state's three largest cities—Concord, Nashua and Manchester—the Merrimack Valley is surprisingly rural. If you're about to tour the state, this is a reasonably central place to start. Located on the main highway from Boston, it has long been the main thoroughfare to the lakes of central New Hampshire, the alpine-like White Mountains and further north still to Quebec, Canada.

ACCOMMODATION
Brick Tower Motor Inn, 414 S Main St, I-93 Exit 12S, 224-9565. S-$55, D-$64-$75. Large rooms, TV. Pool.
Dame Homestead, 203 Horse Corner Rd, Chichester, Rte 4 off 393E, 798-5446. $30 pp, shared bath.
Camping: Sandy Beach Campground, 677 Clement Hill Rd, Contoocook, 746-3591. Sites w/hook-up $25, XP-$4. Lake swimming.

FOOD
Durgin Lane Deli, 2 Capital Plaza, 228-2000. Sandwiches for about $5. Mon-Fri 7am-5pm.
Eagle's Nest Restaurant & Lounge, 1 Eagle Square, 228-6608. Standard American fare, seafood, dinners range from $7-$15.
Margarita's, 1 Bicentennial Sq, 224-2821. Eat Mexican food and massive Margaritas ($4.25), behind bars at this atmospheric watering hole in the old police station. Food $6-$15. Mon-Thu 4pm-11pm, Fri-Sun 3pm-11pm for food, bar open 'til 1am.

OF INTEREST
America's Stonehenge, Mystery Hill, N Salem, 893-8300. Daily 9am-7pm. One of the largest and possibly the oldest stone-constructed sites in the country. $8, $6 w/student ID.
Anheuser-Busch Brewery, 221 Daniel Webster Hwy, Merrimack, 595-1202. Free

tours of the world-famous Budweiser Brewery and Clydesdale Hamlet, complimentary beer samples with valid ID, sodas for those without! Tours daily 9.30am-4.45pm.

Christa McAuliffe Planetarium, I-93 exit 15E, then exit 1 off of I-393, 271-STAR. 'Take an expedition through space,' land on Mars or explore the constellations in the night sky. Shows (last 1 hr) 10am-5pm Tue-Sun, $7, $4 w/student ID, advance tkts recommended. *www.starhop.com*

Coach and Eagle Walking Trail, a self-guided tour of 17 historic sights including the **State House**, where the Hall of Flags is worth seeing. Free brochures available from Chamber of Commerce.

Franklin Pierce Homestead, meeting of Rtes 9 and 31, Hillsborough, 478-3165. Restored home of President Franklin Pierce. June-Sept, Mon-Sat 10am-4pm, Sun 1pm-4pm, $2.50.

Robert Frost Homestead, Rte 28, Derry (south on I-93 from Concord), 432-3091. Home of poet Robert Frost from 1901-1909. June-Sept, daily 11am-5pm, $2.50.

INFORMATION/TRAVEL

New Hampshire Office of Vacation Travel, 172 Pembroke St, 271-2666. Mon-Fri 8am-4pm.

Greater Concord Chamber of Commerce, 244 N Main St, 224-2508. Mon-Fri 8.30am-5pm.

Concord Trailways, 228-3300. From Boston $11.50, 1½hrs.

INTERNET ACCESS

The White Mountain Coffee Shop, 15 Pleasant St, 228-3317. Internet use $3 per half-hour. Mon-Fri 6am-10pm, Sat 7am-5pm.

Concord Public Library, 45 Green St, 225-8670. Free Internet access, half-hour limit.

THE WHITE MOUNTAINS A popular destination year-round with hikers in summer and skiers in winter, the range is dominated by **Mount Washington**—at 6288 ft the highest peak in the Northeast—where wind velocity has been recorded at 231 miles per hour! Climbing the mountain is quite a feat, but it can be done in summer and the view is well worth the effort. Be warned: the weather can be nasty, even in July and Aug; take warm clothing and seek local advice before setting off on a serious expedition. Most visitors ride the **Mt. Washington Cog Railway**, 278-5404/(800) 922-8825, to the top, from where six states and Canada are visible on a clear day. It's not cheap, though; the 3 hr round trip costs $44, discount available on 8am & 5pm trains. The auto (toll) road to the summit is almost as costly: $16 per car plus $6 pp. $20 pp for a tour, call 466-3988 for info.

Loon Mountain, 745-8111/(800) 229-LOON provides summer and winter activities, with scenic chair-lifts, mountain bike trails, rollerblading and horse riding. **Ski Bretton Woods**, 278-5000/(800) 232-2972, offers similar attractions. North Conway is the best area for equipment rentals. Bikes are available from **Loon Mountain Bike Center**, 745-8111, on Kancamagus Hwy, Lincoln; and **Joe Jones**, 356-9411, Main St, N Conway. While in N Conway take a ride on the **Conway Scenic Railroad**, 356-5251/(800) 232-5251. The ride to Crawford Notch carries you past some of the finest scenery on the east coast, 5 hrs, $31 r/t, rsvs strongly recommended, especially in fall. There are also shorter rides available.

At the base of Mt Washington, along Rte 302, is the resort of **Bretton Woods**, site of the 1944 conference that laid the groundwork for a post-war financial structure that created the World Bank and International Monetary Fund. Now it's a cosy ski resort. About 20 miles north of Bretton Woods on

Rte 2 is **Christie's Maple Farm**, (800) 788-2118, where you can visit the Maple Heritage Museum and an authentic working sugarhouse with the White Mountains and Presidential Mountains as a backdrop, daily 9am-5pm, free. *www.ChristiesMapleFarm.com*

Visit **Franconia Notch** and its 700-ft flume chasm with the **Old Man of the Mountain**, a natural stone profile rising at the north-west end. **Cannon Mountain** can be conquered by an aerial tramway. The **New England Ski Museum** is on Rte 3 in Franconia Notch State Park, 823-7177. Ancient skiing artefacts from New England and elsewhere. Daily noon-5pm, free. **The Frost Place**, Ridge Rd, Franconia, 823-5510, Robert Frost's farm is now a centre for poetry and the arts with a museum and a nature-poetry trail, Wed-Mon 1pm-5pm, $3.

Cranmore and **Wildcat Mountains** to the south-east of Mt Washington are more sheltered than most, and have the best skiing facilities in the White Mountains.

If you head further north, be sure to catch the **Moose Festival** in the towns of Colebrook and Pittsburg. The annual August event includes street fairs, live music, hot-air balloon rides, and of course, moose calling contests and moose sighting tours. Call the North Country Chamber of Commerce, 237-8939, for more info, or visit *www.northcountrychamber.org*.

ACCOMMODATION

Hikers might consider staying at one or several of the **Appalachian Mountain Club's 8 huts**, spaced a day's hike apart; from $62 pp, depending on amenities and meals provided. Rsvs and deposit required. Call 466-2727 or write for brochure and to make rsvs at AMC Pinkham Notch Camp, P.O Box 298, Gorham, NH 03581. 'Clean, friendly and helpful. Hearty meals.'

Crawford Notch Youth Hostel, Rte 302, 466-2727, run by AMC. $16 AMC members, $18 non-AMC. Open year round. 'We went midweek after Labor Day and the hostel was almost empty. Avoid Fridays and Saturdays.'

Hikers Paradise at the Colonial Comfort Inn, 370 Main St, Gorham, (800) 470-4224. Co-ed dorm, $12 pp. Private rooms at the inn start at D-$52.

Hostelling International-Conway, 36 Washington St, Conway, NH 03818, 447-1001. $18 members.

Camping: campers may pitch their tents, for free (with $5 admission to forest), anywhere below the tree line in the White Mountains National Forest, but there are strict rules for your safety; call the **U.S Forest Service**, 528-8721.

INFORMATION

White Mountains Attractions Center, exit 32 off I-93 in N Woodstock, 745-8720/(800) FIND-MTS, can provide maps and help find accommodation. *www.whitemtn.org*

White Mountain National Forest Information, 466-2713. Crawford Notch State Park, 374-2272. Trail & weather info 24 hrs, 466-2725. Franconia Notch State Park, 823-5563, visitor centre open daily 9am-5.30pm.

LAKE WINNIPESAUKEE is New Hampshire's largest body of water. Set against a backdrop of tree-covered hills and the White Mountains to the North, it is a popular summer spot. Come here for sunning, swimming and sailing. **Center Harbor**, **Laconia**, **Wolfeboro** and **Meredith** are the main centres for accommodation and sightseeing. There are several campgrounds around the lake.

Winnipesaukee Railroad, 279-5253, operates 1 hr ($7.50) & 2 hr ($8.50) scenic trips along the lake shore between Meredith and Weirs Beach, daily in summer. **Cruise Lake Winnipesaukee,** 366-5531/(800) THE-MOUNT, offers scenic tours of the lake leaving from Weirs Beach, 2 1/2 hrs, $16.

About 50 miles east of Laconia lies the small town of **Enfield**, where you can stay at **The Shaker Inn at the Great Stone Dwelling**, 632-7810/(888) 707-4257, centrepiece of the **Enfield Shaker Village**. Double rooms start from $105. There are no more Shakers in New Hampshire, but the village operates as a museum of Shaker history, $7. Nearby is **Canterbury Shaker Village**, 783-9511. $9.50 admission includes guided tour of original Shaker buildings. *www.theshakerinn.com* for more info.

RHODE ISLAND   *The Ocean State*

'Little Rhody' is the smallest state in the nation. With 400 miles of shoreline, it is dominated by the sea and Narragansett Bay, which cuts the state almost in half.

Founded by Roger Williams, who dissented from Massachusetts' Puritan theocracy, Rhode Island developed successfully by smuggling, slaving and whaling and for a while hesitated to sacrifice its post-Revolutionary War independence by joining the United States.

Little Rhode Island is home to some of America's biggest music events—the Newport Jazz and Folk Festivals.
www.visitrhodeisland.com
The area code for the entire state is 401.

PROVIDENCE   Founded by Roger Williams in 1636 and named for the act of God that he believed led him there. Rhode Island's state capital and New England's fourth largest city, Providence is enjoying a renaissance as a modern industrial city and port. A college town and home to the prestigious **Brown University**, it is fiercely proud of its success, its traditions and its historic past. Elegant Colonial homes and early nineteenth century commercial buildings survive on Benefit St, the 'mile of history'. Many of these are open to the public during the **Festival of Historic Houses** in May.

ACCOMMODATION
Days Inn Providence, 220 India Street, (800) 528-9931, rooms from D-$99. One mile from Brown University, many rooms overlook Providence Harbor.
International House, 8 Stimson Ave, 421-7181. $45 pp, $35 w/student ID, XP-$10, rate drops for stays of five nights or more. Kitchen facilities. Advance rsvs essential. 'Clean, friendly and cheap.'
Super 8 North Attleboro/Providence, 787 S. Washington, North Attleboro, MA, (508) 643-2900. 20 mins away from Providence, S-$55, D-$65.
Susse Chalet Inn, 341 Highland Ave, Seekonk, MA. (½ mile south on I-95, exit 1, 5 miles east of town), (508) 336-7900. From D-$66-$76, bfast included.

FOOD
Meeting St Cafe, 220 Meeting St, on College Hill, 273-1066. Pastries, soups, salads, sandwiches. Bfast $4-$7, lunch $7-$10.

Murphy's Delicatessen, 55 Union St (behind the Biltmore), 621-8467. 'Mountain High' sandwiches ($3-$5) are as big as Rhode Island. Daily 11am-midnight, w/ends 'til 1am.
South Street Cafe, 54 South St, 454-5360, sandwiches for around $5, Mon-Fri 11am-1am, Sat-Sun noon-1am.
Wes's Ribs, 38 Dike St, Olneyville Sq, 421-9090, ribs from $2.50, sandwiches, dinner special $4.95. Sun-Thu 'til 2am, 'til 4am Fri & Sat.

ENTERTAINMENT
The free weekly *Nice Paper* has complete entertainment listings.
Providence's nightlife is generally student-generated, though Thayer Street is always bustling and in summer the influx of tourists ensures a lively atmosphere.
Lupo's Heartbreak Hotel, 239 Westminster St, 272-5876. Blues Traveler, The Dave Matthews Band, Counting Crows and Joan Baez have all performed here. Dance party every Thu night. Tkts range from $8-$25. *www.lupos.com*
The Met Cafe, 130 Union St, 861-2142, The original home of the blues in Providence, established in 1969. Up-and-coming modern bands, national touring acts, and blues legends all perform here. Cover ranges from $6-$12. *www.lupos.com/Mcal.html*
Providence Performing Arts Center, 220 Weybosset Street, 421-ARTS, an architectural jewel in the heart of the city. Broadway shows and popular musical entertainment. *www.ppacri.org*
The Cable Car Cinema, 204 S Main St, 272-3970 and the **Avon Cinema**, at 260 Thayer St, 421-3315, show good independent and art films ($6.50).

OF INTEREST
Arcade, btwn Westminster & Weybosset Sts, a Greek Revival Building, the first enclosed shopping mall in America. Shops, fast food stalls, restaurants. 'Very small and expensive.'
Brown University, College Hill, 863-1000. A member of the Ivy League, here since 1764; interesting libraries and exhibitions (e.g. pre-16th century books and Renaissance through 20th century paintings in the **Annmary Brown Memorial**). For tours, stop by Admissions Office, 45 Prospect St, 863-2378, Mon-Fri.
Rhode Island School of Design, 224 Benefit St, contains a first-rate museum, 454-6500. 19th century French and modern Latin American painters, 18th century porcelains and oriental textiles, and classical art; also the **Pendleton House**, faithfully furnished replica of an early Providence house, scheduled to re-open in Sept of 2000 after renovation. Museum hrs: Wed-Sun 10am-5pm, Fri 'til 8pm, $5, $2 w/student ID. Third Thu of the month, 5pm-9pm, and last Sat of each month, free.
Providence Waterfront Festival, annual Sept event in Waterplace Park, features music, dancing, food and entertainment, as well as the one-day **Waterfront Jazz Festival** with performances by prominent jazz artists, admission $7. Call CapitolArts Providence, 621-1992, or check out *www.caparts.org*.
A Stroll Through Providence, a self-guided walking tour (brochure available from Visitors Centre) takes in all the sights including: the **Beneficent Congregational Church**, an early example of Classical Revival, the **First Baptist Church**, which dates from 1775 and stands where Roger Williams founded the first Baptist church in America in 1638, the **Providence Athenaeum** and the **State House**, which has the second largest unsupported marble dome in the world (St. Peter's in Rome has the largest). Inside is the 1663 charter granted by Charles II and a full-length Gilbert Stuart portrait of George Washington. Mon-Fri 8.30am-4.30pm.

INFORMATION/TRAVEL
Providence Preservation Society, 21 Meeting St, 831-7440. 1772 publishing house; plenty of info here on historical Providence, booklets ($2.50), free maps. Mon-Fri 9am-5pm.

Visitor Center, in the Convention Center Rotunda, 1 Sabin St, 751-1177. Mon-Sat 10am-4pm.
Visitor Information Center, 1 West Exchange St, 3rd floor, 274-1636, (800) 233-1636. 'Very helpful.' 9am-5pm Mon-Fri.
Amtrak, 100 Gaspee St, 727-7379/(800) 872-7245, Boston $15.
Bonanza Bus Lines, 1 Bonanza Way (off I-95), 751-8800/(888) 751-8800, Boston $8.75, 1 hr. Buses also pick passengers up downtown in Kennedy Plaza.
Greyhound, 102 Fountain St, 454-0790/(800) 231-2222. Boston $9, 1 hr.
Rhode Island Public Transit Authority (RIPTA), 265 Melrose, 781-9400. Fares throughout Rhode Island from $1.25.

INTERNET ACCESS
Channel's, 272 Thayer St (at Meeting St), 2nd fl, 276-0100. Internet use for $8/hr. *www.channelsinternet.com*

PAWTUCKET   If you're in the mood for a side trip of historic and contemporary dimensions, make the short (5-10 min) drive up I-95 to Pawtucket. **Slater Mill Historic Site**, Roosevelt Ave, 725-8638 features an 8-ton water wheel operating a 19th-century machine shop as well as exhibits of local history and fibre artists. Tours given Mon-Sat 10.30am,1pm, and 3pm; Sun 1pm and 3pm, $6.50.

Travelling east across town on Armistice Blvd takes you to **Slater Memorial Park**, a fine place for a picnic and a tour through **Daggett House**, the Colonel's home built in 1645, which has an impressive collection of 17th and 18th century memorabilia. Open summer-December w/ends only, 2pm-4pm, $2. The park has no less than 9 baseball fields, tennis courts and a merry-go-round. Daily 9am-dusk. Wind down your day as the pitchers wind up at **McCoy Stadium**. Eat hot dogs, drink beer and watch the **AAA Pawtucket Red Sox** play their hearts out to make the major leagues. 724-7300 for ticket and schedule info.

NEWPORT   Thirty miles from Providence on Narragansett Bay, Newport is a lively summer resort and home to such enchanting events as the Newport Bermuda Race—a tall ships regatta—and the famous Newport Folk and Jazz Festivals.

Although a rival of Boston and New York in Colonial times, Newport really came into its own only around the turn of the century when the town became the place for millionaires to build their summer 'cottages'. Many of these ridiculously ornate relics of the Gilded Age are now open to the public. Find them close to Newport's fabulous beach and on Bellevue Avenue.

The new Americas Cup Ave has changed the feel of the waterfront. Somewhat sanitised bars and boutiques have recently appeared, but the twinkling lights of the harbour still make for a beautiful setting to sit and watch the world go by on summer evenings. *www.visitnewport.com*

ACCOMMODATION
Hotels here are above average in price and fill up quickly, especially in summer, so make plans for Newport as early as possible.
Gateway Visitor Center, 23 Americas Cup Ave, (800) 976-5122. Has some helpful accommodation listings. Sun-Thu 9am-5pm, Fri & Sat 9am-6pm.
Anna's Victorian Connection, 5 Fowler Avenue, 849-2489/(800) 884-4288. State-

wide B & B reservation service, rooms in Newport w/shared bath from $75.

Bed and Breakfast Newport, (800) 800-8765. Accommodations in B & Bs through-out the area, starting from $90. *www.bbnewport.com*

Burbank Rose, 111 Memorial Blvd West, 849-9457/(888) 297-5800. Downtown loca-tion, private baths, hearty breakfast, $49-$159. *www.burbankrose.com*

Fort Getty Recreational Area, Fort Getty Road, Jamestown, 423-7264. 6 miles west of Newport on RI-138. Boat ramp, fishing dock, and beach, tent sites $20. Call 423-7211 for reservations.

Seaman's Church Institute, 18 Market Square, 847-4260. $100 per week, men only. First come, first served with preference to seafaring folk, but 'if you're here and there's a vacancy, we'll take you.' People start arriving in May for the summer.

FOOD

Anthony's Seafood, 963 Aquidneck Ave, Middletown, 848-5058, casual, family, picnic setting, inexpensive chicken and seafood with great view of Newport harbour, moderate prices from $6.95.

Dry Dock Seafood, 448 Thames St, 847-3974. Bring-your-own-booze. Inexpensive fish n' chips $6.95, lobster dinner $11.95. Sun-Thu 11am-10pm, Fri & Sat 11am-11pm.

OF INTEREST

Beaches: **Easton's Beach,** Memorial Blvd, 846-1398. Includes amusements and carousel, $8 Mon-Fri, $10 w/ends. **Fort Adams State Park,** Ocean Drive, 847-2400. Site of a 19th century fort, includes beach and fishing areas. Tours of the fort avail-able, free. **Beavertail State Park,** Jamestown on Rte 138. Beach, hiking trails, pic-nicking and fishing, free. Call 884-2010 for info.

Belcourt Castle, Bellevue Ave, 849-1566, has a staggering collection of antiques and treasures from all over the world. Daily 10am-4pm. Guided tours $8.50, $6.50 w/student ID, ghost tours $14, Thu 5pm.

Cliffwalk, designated a National Recreation Trail, meanders for 3.5 miles along the Atlantic Ocean and offers views of the sea and several mansions. Maps available in the Visitors Center, 849-8048.

Cruising by ship or sailboat around Narragansett Bay is a pleasant introduction. **Spirit of Newport**, departing Newport Harbor Hotel, 49americas Cup Ave, 849-3575, offers 1 hr narrated cruises of the Bay, $8; **Newport Sailing School & Cruises Ltd**, departing Goat Island, 848-2266, offer 1 hr ($18) & 2 hr ($30) cruises aboard 23' & 30' sloops. Pure sailing, no motors! Rsvs only. **Viking Boat Cruises**, depart Goat Island Marina, 847-6921, and offer 1 hr cruises, $8, as well as a 2$^{1}/_{2}$hr trip that stops and tours Hammersmith Farm, $15.

The Newport Preservation Society, 424 Bellevue Ave, 847-1000, maintains 7 of Newport's mansions: **The Breakers, Marble House, Rosecliff, Chateau-sur-Mer, Kingscote, Hunter House,** and **The Elms** plus **Green Animals**, a topiary garden. **The Breakers**, Cornelius Vanderbilt's villa, is unquestionably the most opulent. **Marble House** is thought to have been inspired by the Petit Trianon at Versailles. **Rosecliff** is where *The Great Gatsby* was filmed. The Breakers is $12; other houses are $9. Combo tkts available. Open daily in summer, 10am-5pm, The Breakers and Marblehead 'til 6pm on Fri & Sat. *www.newportmansions.org* Other privately owned mansions of interest: **Mrs Astor's Beechwood**, 589 Bellevue Ave, 846-3772, is the most enjoyable to visit, with actors playing Mrs Astor's servants and hangers-on leading you as her personal guest in a tongue-in-cheek tour of her home. (Most of the characters portrayed are British). Daily, 10am-5pm, $8.75. **Hammersmith Farm**, on Ocean Dr next to Ft Adams, 846-0420. This was the setting for Jack and Jackie's wedding reception, and the presidential hideaway during the early 60s. Kennedy memorabilia abounds. Daily in summer 10am-5pm, $8.50.

Theatre-by-the-Sea, 364 Card's Pond Rd, Matunuck, 782-8587, 25 miles from

Newport. Experience Broadway theatre in a picturesque barn only moments away from the beach. Open only in summer.

Newport Folk Festival. *The* folk festival of the sixties. Recently revived by Ben and Jerry of ice cream fame, it once again provides a forum for top talent. Held annually at Fort Adams State Park over two days in August, call 847-3700 for details.

Newport Jazz Festival. The oldest—and considered by many to be the finest—jazz festival in the world. Held outdoors in mid-August. For details write: Jazz Festival, PO Box 605, Newport, RI 02840, 847-3700, or ask at the Chamber of Commerce. 'Expensive but worth it.'

Block Island 12 miles south of the mainland, a peaceful summer resort with wonderful beaches first settled in 1661; classified by the Nature Conservancy as one of the '12 great places in the Western hemisphere'. Has two interesting restored lighthouses, one featuring a 19th century newspaper story that tallied the value of ships wrecked around the island as greater than that of the island itself. Ideal for biking (plenty of rentals from $15 p/day). Day trips recommended since food and lodging prices tend to gouge the unwary; although **Maple Leaf Cottage**, Beacon Hill Rd, 466-2065, a farmhouse in the remote interior of the island, is worth a try; D-$85-100, includes bfast. Rsvs essential in summer.

Try lobster rolls at **Smugglers Cove**; **Cappizanos** for pizza; and clam chowder at **Harborside**. Ferries run by Interstate Navigation/Nelseco, 783-4613, go to the island from New London ($15 one way), Newport ($8.25), Point Judith (Galilee) ($8.40) and Providence ($9.45). The 4 hr trip from Providence is recommended. 'Great getaway.' The **Block Island Chamber of Commerce** is helpful—466-2982/(800) 383-BIRI, or visit *www.blockislandinfo.com*.

INFORMATION/TRAVEL
Both the *Newport Life* and the monthly *Pineapple Post* have details of what's on in and around Newport.

Newport Chamber of Commerce, 45 Valley Rd, in Middletown, 5 min drive from Newport, 847-1600. Mon-Fri 8.30pm-5pm. Very helpful.

Bonanza Bus Lines, 23 Americas Cup Ave, 846-1820. Boston $15, 1 hr 40 mins. Visit the **Newport Visitors Center** here, 849-8048, Sun-Thu 9am-5pm, Fri-Sat 9am-6pm.

INTERNET ACCESS
Cybertower, 164 Broadway (across from Dunkin' Donuts), 846-5297. Internet use for $.15/minute.

Newport Public Library, 300 Spring St, 847-8720. Free Internet use, 1 hr limit—expect to wait for a computer.

VERMONT   *Green Mountain State*

Vermont has always been known for its fiercely independent people, from Colonial days when it asserted its own independence by forming a republic. The state remained that way for 14 years, operating its own post office and minting its own money. Vermonters have retained their independent spirit and protective sentiment for the state—their motto is 'Freedom and Unity'. They cherish the beauty of their Green Mountains, banning billboards and imposing the toughest anti-pollution laws in the US. The **Long Trail** runs 270 miles along the highest ridges of the Green Mountains. Contact the Green Mountain Club, Rte 100, Waterbury Center, 244-7037, for advice and books on hiking in Vermont.

Vermont is famous for maple syrup, Cheddar cheese and its magnificent autumn foliage and winter ski trails. The autumn colours are at their best toward the end of Sept; this is also the time for foliage festivals and get-togethers. March is the season for syrup festivals, but there are a number of museums open year-round devoted entirely to the history and manufacture of this state institution.

The state has many small, progressive schools and has always attracted artists, craftsmen and writers. The painter Norman Rockwell lived in Arlington and Rudyard Kipling wrote *The Jungle Book* in Dummerston. *www.vtguides.com*
The area code for the entire area is 802.

BURLINGTON This small city of approximately 45,000—a metropolis by Vermont standards—is set on the eastern shore of **Lake Champlain**, the beautiful 120-mile-long lake (the seventh largest in the US) which divides the New York Adirondacks from the Green Mountains of Vermont. Home of the **University of Vermont** and several other colleges, the city is crawling with young people. It became the first city in the US to elect a socialist mayor in 1981, and the town's economy boomed as a result. Burlington hosts a number of festivals each year, the craziest of which has to be the 'Fools-a-Float' challenge each September.

As an interesting sidebar, Lake Champlain has the distinction of being the shortest-lived 'Great Lake' in US history. On 5 March 1998 President Clinton signed the National Sea Grant Act to provide funding for environmental research on the Great Lakes. Determined not to lose out on precious grant money, Vermont Sen. Patrick Leahy (D) had added an amendment to the bill stating that 'the term "Great Lakes" includes Lake Champlain.' This one sentence automatically changed the status of Lake Champlain despite the fact that it measures just one fourteenth the size of the smallest Great Lake (Erie) and lies 130 miles away from the Great Lakes Basin. Incensed, the Great Lakes states complained that the newest 'Great Lake' would dilute funding for Lakes Studies programs already in place. Just weeks later, a new bill was signed revoking Lake Champlain's new status. Michigan Sen. Carl Levin (D), expressing the relief of all the Great Lake states, noted that 'Lake Champlain is a beautiful lake but it is not great'. *www.vermont.org*

ACCOMMODATION
Allenholm Orchards Bed and Breakfast, 150 South St, South Hero, 20 miles from Burlington on Rte 2, 372-5566. Stay on a working apple orchard on an island in Lake Champlain. Eat apple pie for breakfast! D-$85, rsvs recommended.
Midtown Motel, 230 Main St, 862-9686. S-$50 incl tax, D-$55 incl tax, XP-$5.
Mrs. Farrell's Home Hostel, 865-3730. Open April-Oct. $15 AYH, $18 non-AHY. Bicycles available for use. Office hours 4pm-6pm, call ahead for reservations.
Tetreault House, 251 Staniford Rd, 862-2781. 3 miles from downtown, located on lakefront near bicycle path. S-$40, D-$45.

FOOD
Ben & Jerry's, 36 Church St, 862-9620. 'Best ice cream in the world,' according to *Time* magazine. A Vermont original; destined to reach the far ends of the earth.
Carbur's Restaurant, 115 St Paul St, 862-4106. A downtown landmark, richly deco-rated in 'Vermontabilia.' Best known for 'Grandwich' combinations. Over 150

sandwich variations! Moderate prices. Sun-Thu 11.30am-10.30pm, Fri-Sat 11.30am-11.30pm.

Cheese Traders, 1186 Williston Rd, South Burlington, 863-0143/(800) 540-4261. Wide selection of Vermont cheeses and gourmet foods, free samples.

Daily Planet, 15 Center St, 862-9647. Good bar food, moderately priced. Bass and Guinness on tap ($4), student and yuppie hang out.

Five Spice Cafe, 175 Church St, 864-4045. Award-winning Asian food. Sumptuous feasts include Vietnamese Calamari, Evil Jungle Prince with chicken. Lunch $5-$8, dinner $9-15.

Gateway Cafe, 30 Main St, 862-4930. Standard American fare, waterfront location, meals from $5-$10.

Henry's, 155 Bank St, 862-9010. In the heart of Burlington, a local hangout serving Americana, burgers and 'blue-plate specials'. 'Cheap and cheerful.'

Kountry Kart Deli, 155 Main St, 864-4408. 'Famous' Philly cheese-steaks, inexpensive. Daily 7.30am-3am.

Vermont Pub & Brewery, 144 College St, 865-0500. Indulge in Dr Walter's Wonder Pilsner, bangers n' mash $6.95. Free live entertainment. 'Best pint I had all summer.'

OF INTEREST

Boat tours of Lake Champlain aboard *Spirit of Ethan Allen*, 862-8300. Replica of a vintage paddlewheeler. Four daily cruises around the lake, $8.25, sunset trips $9.50.

Champlain Valley Weekender, 463-3069, scenic train ride through beautiful Champlain Valley to Middlebury and back, 3 hours r/t, $12. You may also stay in Middlebury for a few hours and return on the afternoon train.

Church Street Marketplace, downtown. One of the most successful pedestrian malls in the country, a vibrant thoroughfare often compared to Boston's Faneuil Hall area. In summer the marketplace is crawling with street performers, musicians, and the Great Rondini, an escape artist.

Ethan Allen Homestead Trust, off Rte 127 N, 865-4556. Restored 1787 farmhouse home of Ethan Allen, Revolutionary War hero. 200-acre park with picnicking, fishing, canoeing. Mon-Sat 10am-5pm, Sun 1pm-5pm, $4.

Magic Hat Brewing Co, 5 Bartlett Bay Rd, South Burlington, 658-BREW. Free tours Wed-Fri 3.30pm-5pm, Sat 1pm-2.30pm. *www.MagicHat.net*

Robert Hull Fleming Museum, U of Vermont, Colchester Ave, 656-2090. European, decorative and Native American art. Tue-Fri noon-4pm (9am-4pm in winter), Sat-Sun 1pm-5pm, $3.

Shelburne Museum, 7 miles south on Hwy 7, 985-3344. Outdoor museum of early New England life. 45 acres of Americana, folk-art and architecture. Daily in summer, 10am-5pm, $17.50, $10.50 w/student ID, pass valid for two days. 'Worthwhile if you have a whole day.'

Vermont Wildflower Farm, Charlotte, 12 miles from Burlington on Rte 7 (on the way to Middlebury), 985-9455. Pathways through six acres of wildflowers, $3.

Waterfront Boat Rentals, Perkins Pier, 864-4858. Kayaks $10/hr, $25 half-day; canoes $15/hr, $30 half-day.

INTERNET ACCESS

Fletcher Free Library, 235 College St, 863-3403. Free Internet use, half-hour limit. Rsvs for time slot essential, no rsvs over the phone.

INFORMATION

Chamber of Commerce and Visitor Center, 60 Main St, 863-3489. Mon-Fri 8.30am-5pm, w/ends 11am-3pm.

MIDDLEBURY This small, beautiful New England town bordering on the Green Mountains has miles of hiking trails—including the Appalachian—with overnight shelters and various state parks for camping. One of Vermont's nicest state parks is not far from Middlebury, on beautiful **Lake Dunmore**.

The town is built around a village green and **Otter Creek**, flowing right through the middle of Middlebury. Picturesque, stone-built **Middlebury College**, founded in 1800, is famous for its excellent 'total-immersion' summer school of foreign languages, and gives a lively flavour to the town.

ACCOMMODATION
Accommodation in Middlebury itself is expensive but usually elegant and friendly. Call ahead as most have limited availability.

The Annex Bed and Breakfast, Rte. 125, East Middlebury, 5 miles from College, 388-3233. 1830 Greek Revival home, hearty breakfast. D-$70-$75.

Covered Bridge Home Hostel, 388-0401. Located close to the oldest covered bridge in the state. $13.50 AYH, $16.50 non-AYH. Call for rsvs and directions, 8pm-10pm.

Cream Hill Farm, near Shoreham, 20 mins south-west of Middlebury, 897-2101. 1100-acre sheep and cattle farm. Renovated 18th-century farmhouse, family atmosphere; S-$25, D-$45, XP-$10, incl bfast. Rsvs recommended.

Redemption Farm, 457 Coy Hill Rd, Middletown Springs, 45 miles from Middlebury, 235-2105. Small farm with 5 bedroom colonial home listed on the National Historic Register, w/end rental $200 for up to eight people. Rsvs required.

Camping: **Branbury State Park** on east side of Lake Dunmore, 10 miles south of Middlebury on Rte 53, 247-5925. Swimming, fishing, boating, bath house. Sites $13 for four, XP-$3, lean-to $17 for four, XP-$4. **Lake Dunmore Kampersville**, south of E Middlebury on Rte 53, 352-4501. Sites from $18. **Rivers Bend Inc Camping Area**, 3 miles north of Middlebury, 1 mile off Dog Team Rd, 388-9092. Sites $18, $22 on the riverbank, all w/hook up. Small store and great swimming hole.

FOOD
Fire and Ice, 26 Seymour St, 388-7166. Friendly. Seafood, steak, great salad bar. Locals, students, and travellers. Tue-Sat lunch 11.30am-4pm, dinner 4pm-9pm, Mon from 5pm, Sun 1pm-8.30pm. Sandwiches $7, Dinner entrees from $15.

Woody's Restaurant, 5 Bakery Lane, 388-4182. Outdoor dining. Seafood specials, steaks, pasta. Lunch $5-$8, dinner $10-$18, burgers, etc. 'til late, Sunday brunch.

OF INTEREST
UVM Morgan Horse Farm, 74 Battell Dr, Weybridge, off Rte 23N, 388-2011, where the first American breed of horse is bred and trained. Tours $4.

Vermont Folklife Center, 2 Court St, 388-4964. Oral and physical history exhibits, live demonstrations and performances. Summer gallery hours: Mon-Sat 11am-5pm, free.

Vermont State Craft Center at Frog Hollow, 1 Mill St, 388-3177. Craft gallery featuring the work of over 300 Vermont craftspeople, studios open to the public.

INFORMATION
Chamber of Commerce, 2 Court St, 388-7951. Mon-Fri 9am-5pm, Sat 11am-3pm.

MONTPELIER   This smallest capital in the nation (less than 9,000 people) is also surely one of the most beautiful. The granite industry built Montpelier and nearby Barre. Today the economy is based mainly on the state government and the insurance business, though a granite revival is afoot. The town also holds the dubious honour of being home to the largest number of lawyers per capita of any city in America.

Montpelier is a thriving centre for theatre, music, crafts and antiques, and boasts its own museum and Historical Society. If you want to get away from it all, wander the back roads and admire the scenery. 'Come here for a slice of 50s rural village community life!' *www.montpelier-vt.org*

ACCOMMODATION

Capitol Home Hostel, RD 1, Box 2750, 05602, 223-2104, $13 AYH, $16 non-AYH. Call for rsvs and directions.

Econolodge, 101 Northfield St, ½mile from downtown, 223-5258. S-$62, D-$68, XP-$5.

Emergo Farm Bed and Breakfast, 261 Webster Hill, Danville, 32 miles from Montpelier on US-2, (888) 383-1185. B&B on a working farm, rooms from $65 w/shared bath. Rsvs recommended. 'There is no extra charge for helping with the farm chores'!

Hollister Hill Farm Bed and Breakfast, 2193 Hollister Hill Rd, Marshfield, 15 miles from Montpelier on US-2, 454-7725. Working farm with walking and ski trails. Participation in farm activities welcome. Rooms $55-$85, rsvs required. *www.central-vt.com/web/hhfarmbb*

Montpelier Guest Home, 22 North St, 229-0878. $45-$55. Victorian house, 10 min walk to downtown, no smoking. 15% discount on second night for those with bikes. Spacious deck and lovely gardens. Free use of cross-country skis and snowshoes for those adventuring to nearby Hubbard Park in winter.

Vermonter Motel, Barre-Montpelier Rd, 3 miles from Montpelier and Barre, 476-8541. S-$42 incl tax, D-$49 incl tax, XP-$4.

FOOD

Montpelier is home to the **New England Culinary Institute**, so quality, low-priced restaurants abound.

Coffee Corner, 83 Main Street, 229-9060. Diner with good food at reasonable prices. Read the hand-lettered messages tacked up by customers while you wait for your food. Daily 6am-3pm.

Horn of the Moon Cafe, 8 Langdon St, 223-2895. All-natural, wholefood bakery and vegetarian food. Tue-Sun 7am-9pm, Sunday brunch from 9am, $5-$9.

Hunger Mountain Co-op, 626 Stonecutter's Way, 223-6910. 1½ miles from Montpelier. Natural foodstore, open daily. 'Fantastic selection at great prices. Good place to stock up on food.'

Julio's, 44 Main St, 229-9348. Good Tex Mex food, $4.50-$8.50. 'The cheapest eats in town.' Open late on Fri & Sat.

Thrush Tavern, 107 State St, 223-2030. Lunch, dinner, seafood, burgers, sandwiches. Mon-Fri 11am-11pm, Sat 4pm-midnight. Lunch $2-$6, dinner $7-$12.

OF INTEREST

Swimming/Boating at Groton and Elmore lakes nearby.

Ben & Jerry's Ice Cream Factory, Hwy 89 north to Waterbury, 1 mile north on Rte 100, 244-5641. The genesis of the ice cream made by two guys from Vermont. Taste for yourself during factory tours—ice cream cold off the dasher! Mon-Sat 9am-8pm, frequent tours, $2. Ask about their interesting management philosophy. 'The only flavour graveyard I've ever seen!'

Cold Hollow Cider Mill, Rte 100, Waterbury Center, 16 miles from Montpelier, 244-8771/(800) APPLES. Watch cider-making, drink free samples, and buy cider jelly in the store. Daily 8am-7pm, free. *www.coldhollow.com*

Farmers' Market, State and Elm Sts. Flowers, baked goods, and organic foods produced by local farmers. Sat 9am-2pm, May to October.

Hubbard Park, 200 acres of woodland with seven miles of hiking and skiing trails, picnic areas, a small pond, a sledding hill, and an observation tower.

Morse Farm, County Rd (3 miles from Montpelier; follow signs on Main St), 223-2740. Watch maple syrup being made here in March & April, and sample the end product! Daily 9am-5pm, 8am-8pm in summer.

Rock of Ages Quarry, Barre, 476-3119. Narrated shuttle tours of an active quarry, June-Oct, Mon-Fri 9.15am-3pm, $4.
State Capitol, 115 State St, 828-2228. Newly restored, topped with a gold-leaf dome and adorned with intricately carved wood trim. Free tours in summer and fall, Mon-Fri 10am-3.30pm, Sat 11am-2.30pm.

INFORMATION
Montpelier Chamber of Commerce, Stewart Rd & Paine Turnpike, 229-5711. Mon-Fri 9am-5pm.
Visitor's Center, 134 State St, 828-3237. Open daily 8am-8pm.

INTERNET ACCESS
Kellog-Hubbard Library, 135 Main St, 223-3338. Free Internet access, half-hour time limit. Call ahead to reserve time slot.

STOWE At the foot of Vermont's highest peak, Mt Mansfield (4393 ft), sits Stowe, one of New England's most popular resorts. Although predominately a skiing town, Stowe is gaining popularity in all seasons for its variety of outdoor activities—hiking, biking, canoeing and hang-gliding. It is also the home of the von Trapp Family, of *Sound of Music* fame, who operate a lodge and ski touring centre.

ACCOMMODATION
Anderson Lodge, 3430 Mountain Rd, 253-7336. Rooms from D-$78, including bfast.
Baas' Gastehaus B&B, 180 Edson Hill, 253-8376. D-$79 including bfast. Rsvs recommended.
Riverside Inn, 1965 Mountain Rd, 253-4217. Rooms from D-$45.
Mt. Mansfield Hostel, on Rte 108, 8 miles from the centre of Stowe, 253-4010. Independent winter hostel, $15-$24 pp. Bfast $5, dinner $7. Linens $4. 'The best in town.'

FOOD
Fox Fire, 1606 Pucker St, (Rte 100), 253-4887. Daily 5.30pm-9.30pm. Italian home-style cooking at moderate prices, $11-$18.
McCarthy's, Mountain Rd, ½ mile from centre of town, 253-8626. Sandwiches, grinders, soups, daily specials. 'Lots of home-made goodies.' Daily 6.30am-3pm.
Ye Olde England Inn/Mr Pickwick's Pub, Rte 108, 253-7558. English-style pub with pints of ale and darts. 'Great place.'

INFORMATION
Stowe Chamber of Commerce, Main St, 253-7321. Accommodation and travel info. Mon-Sat 9am-8pm, Sun 'til 5pm.

THE NORTHEAST

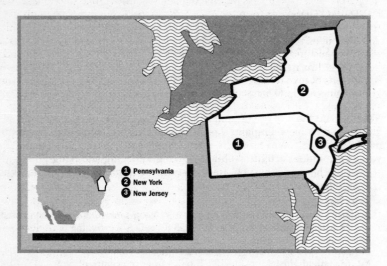

Through the North-eastern region runs most of the 400-mile strip of that megalopolis known as 'Boswash' (Boston to Washington). This rates as the USA's most crowded urban concentration, containing the nation's largest city, New York, and heaviest industry. The region has been called the head-quarters of Enterprise America for, from the time of the industrial revolution, much of the impetus for commercial and industrial expansion has stemmed from these states.

You would be cheating yourself if during your tour of the Northeast you did not veer away from the nasty highway, I-95, to visit the large tracts of unspoiled countryside within easy reach of the cities. Especially worth seeing are the mountainous Adirondacks in northern New York State and the rolling farmlands of western Pennsylvania; and there is greater variety still. In a region rich in historical and cultural associations, there is a wealth of places to visit and things to do. The climate varies as much as the geography. Winters are very cold and snow can be expected everywhere, while summers are marked by searing heat and sapping humidity.

NEW JERSEY   *The Garden State*

Sandwiched between industrial Pennsylvania and New York, New Jersey when first glimpsed after crossing the Hudson River from Manhattan seems an incredible wasteland, a lunar cesspool difficult to miss. The **New Jersey Turnpike** (toll road) dominates the landscape—people in New Jersey don't ask where you're from, they ask, "what exit?" Riding the turnpike between New York and Delaware and seeing mile after mile of refinery pipes, gasoline storage tanks and smelly smokestacks, you may well ask yourself what happened to America The Beautiful!

What is hard to believe is that there really is some truth to the state's label, the Garden State. West from the New York suburbs and interstate highways that bisect the state lies the bucolic **Delaware River Valley** in a corner of the Appalachian Mountains. To the east lies a virginal pine forest called the **Pine Barrens** and the **Jersey Shore** along the Atlantic, 150 miles of sandy beaches and boardwalks. From paved paths to muddy tracks, New Jersey has dozens of bike trails. *25 Bicycling Tours in New Jersey*, by Arline and Joel Zatz, is a useful book, available from Backcountry Publications, PO Box 748, Woodstock, VT 05091, (800) 245-4151.
www.state.nj.us
There are six telephone area codes for New Jersey: 201, 609, 908, 973, 732, and 856.

NEWARK   In truth, this is one of America's most unpleasant cities, with a history of physical decay, political corruption, racial tension and plain old ugliness. Manhattan's poorer cousin, Newark even *sounds* like a corruption of *New York*, but the city has recently been redeveloping as its airport draws more commerce to the region. The busy international airport has made Newark a frequent first and last stop in America for overseas travellers—and is as much as the traveller need ever see.

There is no reason to go into downtown Newark. Accommodation is available near the airport but it is on the expensive side. It's better to catch the Olympia Trails Airport Express ($10) for an exciting ride into Manhattan and stay there. (See New York City section for further accommodation and travel information.)

INFORMATION/TRAVEL
Travel and Tourism, Gateway Center, (973) 624-4462.
Greyhound, Penn Station & Market St, (800) 231-2222.

THE PALISADES   are a 15-mile long line of granite cliffs rising as high as 500ft above the Hudson. The most impressive view is from the George Washington Bridge when riding over from Manhattan, but on the New Jersey side you can enjoy the **Palisades Interstate Park** with its picnic grounds and beautiful woods.

West from Newark, in an area of dense suburbs, is the residence and laboratory of American inventor Thomas A. Edison, creator of the phonograph, incandescent light bulb and other harbingers of modernity. The site is closed now for restoration, but it will re-open in the spring of 2001. From the Garden State Pkwy (toll) take exit 145 to I-280 W, then exit 10, turn right at light, go through two more lights, left at second one on to Main St. Edison's home, Glenmont, is at the corner of Main St & Lakeside Ave., (973) 736-0550. Daily 9am-5pm, $2.

Just across the Hudson river from lower Manhattan is the gritty port town of **Hoboken**, famous as the place where *On The Waterfront* was filmed, and where Frank Sinatra was born. PATH commuter trains from New York will get you there, and as you pass through the station, marvel at its intricate marble construction. One of the better technological universities, **Stevens Institute**, also calls Hoboken home, as does an aromatic Maxwell House coffee plant.

Two fine universities lie just off the New Jersey Turnpike (toll) south-west of Newark. **New Brunswick** is the home of **Rutgers University**, and 30 miles further is **Princeton**, a beautiful New England town that ran away to New Jersey. Both Albert Einstein and Thomas Mann lived here, while F. Scott Fitzgerald and Eugene O'Neill are among the more luminous alumni of **Princeton University**. Free tours of the campus start at the yellow Maclean House, (609) 258-3603, Mon-Sat 10am-3.30pm, Sun 1.30pm & 3.30pm. Highlights include Nassau Hall, built in 1756, where the Continental Congress met in 1783, and which was used as barracks during the Revolution by both American and British soldiers.

FOOD IN PRINCETON
Chuck's Spring St Deli, 16 Spring St, 921-0027. Daily 11am-9.30pm.
Yoko's Kitchen, 354 Nassau St, 683-9666. Chinese, average price $4. Mon-Fri 11.30am-7pm.
Small World Cafe, 14 Witherspoon St, 924-4377. Pastries and desserts at reasonable prices, small lunch menu. Mon-Thu 6.30am-11pm, Fri and Sat 6.30am-midnight, Sun 7.30am-11pm.

Fifteen miles west from Princeton is the point where General Washington crossed the Delaware River on a bone-chilling Christmas night in 1776 to deliver a special Christmas present to the British troops at Trenton. Eight days later he stormed the garrison at Princeton.

THE JERSEY SHORE   begins south of Newark. Drive along the **Garden State Pkwy**, which follows the contour of the coast. Gritty **Asbury Park**, where it seems everyone works in a garage, is Bruce Springsteen country. Forty miles further south is the road to **Long Beach**. 'A great place to relax and enjoy sea, sun and sand. No usual boardwalk, but no usual commercialism.'

ATLANTIC CITY   'The playground of the world' was once the best loved seaside resort in America and the original model for the game of Monopoly, but Atlantic City saw its glamour wilt when better-off bathers made for hotter climes in the South and the West. The home of salt-water taffy (America's equivalent of Brighton Rock) and the Miss America contest, the town was revitalised in 1977 when casino gambling was legalised here.

With the arrival of the gambling resorts, a new game of monopoly has ensued (Donald Trump heading the list of players), with speculators razing entire city blocks in hopes of profit, and investors raising a dozen garish, neon-lit pleasure palaces. The result is an urban desert spotted with casinos and linked to the rest of the world by hundreds of buses bringing the hopeful from Philadelphia, New York and Washington. Special Amtrak trains, with connecting buses to the casinos, go there too.

To escape the crowds and gaudy joie de vivre of Atlantic City, go north to the 2700 acres of **Island Beach State Park**, (732) 793-0506.
The telephone area code for Atlantic City is 609.

ACCOMMODATION

Atlantic City is more expensive than the rest of the Jersey shore, especially during the summer season. If you're stranded and have to stay in town, try **AmeriRoom Reservations**, (800) 888-5825. Free reservation service for hotels, condos and casinos throughout the city; pricey, but efficient. Inexpensive, family run motels can be found on the Whitehorse Pike in Abescon, Rte 30.

Beachside Hotel, 162 St James Pl, 347-9085. D-$100-$130 p/week. Adjacent to the **Irish Pub**, S-$25, D-$55.

Camping: is the cheapest alternative. **Casino Campground**, Hwy 575 & Moss Mill Rd, 12 miles west of Atlantic City, 652-1577. Sites $24 for two XP-$2.

FOOD/ENTERTAINMENT

Baltimore Grill (Tony's to the locals), 2800 Iowa & Atlantic Ave., 345-5766. Cheap food in snug booths with your own personal juke-box. 'Pizzas are the best in city, especially topped with home-made sausage.' $5.50 up. Beer 95¢ a mug. Daily 24 hrs (kitchen open 11am-3pm).

White House Sub Shop & Deli, 2301 Arctic Ave., 345-1564. World famous since 1946. $6-$9, half-subs $3-$4.50.

Many of the casinos serve breakfast, lunch and dinner buffets. Eat as much as you want, $4-$10.

OF INTEREST

Convention Hall where the Atlantic City Expressway meets the train station, 348-7000, is the largest in the world, seating 70,000 in the main auditorium. It also has the world's largest pipe organ to match. Watch the Miss America Pageant here mid-Sept.

Lucy the Margate Elephant, 9200 Atlantic Ave., 823-6473. A building in the shape of an elephant, originally built of wood and tin in 1881. Tours $3, daily in summer, 10am-8pm Mon-Thu, 10am-5pm Fri-Sun.

Renault Winery, 16 miles from Atlantic City on Breman Ave., off Rte 30, 965-2111. Tours of working winery which was built in 1864. Guide will show you bottling process, museum and take you through a wine-tasting, $2. Grape stompin' Festival at harvest time in September. Mon-Sat 10 am-4pm, Sun noon-4pm.

INFORMATION/TRAVEL

Chamber of Commerce, 1125 Atlantic Ave., Suite 105, 345-5600. Mon-Fri 8.30am-4.30pm.

Convention and Visitors Bureau , 2314 Pacific Ave., 348-7111. Daily 9am-5pm.

Many of the casinos run free or low-priced buses to Atlantic City from New York and Philadelphia. Check the *Yellow Pages* under 'Casinos' for information or look for billboard advertisements.

Greyhound, Arctic & Arkansas Aves, 345-6617/(800) 231-2222. Also, **New Jersey Transit**, same location, (800) 582-5946 (in state only), (215) 569-3752.

www.nj.com/navigator/ provides comprehensive transport information for the whole state.

OCEAN CITY   8 miles south, tee-total cousin to hedonistic Atlantic City. Alcohol cannot be bought on the island but the summer workers who flock here every year can walk a sobering 2.3 miles across 9th St bridge to find importable drink on the mainland. Plenty of casual jobs in 'America's greatest family resort' make this a popular destination for BUNACers and others who share the long, crowded beaches and lively nightlife. There is a wide choice of cheap rooms in boarding houses and old resort hotels, if you get

there early enough (beginning of June if you're planning to stay.) Ocean City's 2.5 mile long boardwalk is known for its wacky contests and festivals, which reach a bizarre peak in July and August.
The telephone area code is 609.

ACCOMMODATION
Commodore Guesthouse, 701 Plymouth Place, 399-4761. D-$45-49, XP-$7.
Ocean City Guest House Association, P.O Box 356, Ocean City, NJ 08226, 399-8894. Rooms in private residences from D-$50. Brochure available.

OF INTEREST
Ocean City Boardwalk Art Show, over 500 artists, sculptors and photographers from the Northeast display work for sale and compete for prizes. First w/end in August.
Miss Crustacean Hermit Crab Beauty Pageant, the world's only beauty pageant for hermit crabs. 2nd Aug, 6th St beach , free.
Weird contest week, includes french-fry sculpting. Mid Aug, free.

INFORMATION
Ocean City Information Center, Rte 52, 9th St Causeway, btwn Somers Point & Ocean City, 399-2629/(800) BEACHNJ, has info on beaches, hotels, restaurants. Help and information also available at bus station. Summer Mon-Sat 9am-5pm, Sun 10am-2pm.

WILDWOOD   is a smaller, perhaps more wholesome, version of Atlantic City, practically at the tip of the southern peninsula of the state. The beach is 1000 ft wide in some places and there are 2 miles of boardwalk, six amusement parks, and plenty of wild nightlife. It's also a resort where families come for their traditional week by the sea. 'Lots of American students work here. Everyone works hard and plays hard. We had a fabulous time.' 'A fantastic place to spend the summer.'

ACCOMMODATION
'Accommodation easily found by walking around and asking. Wildwood Crest is the nicest area to live.'
Beachwood Hotel, 210 E Montgomery Ave., 729-0608. D-$65, pool, TV, refrigerators. 1 block from boardwalk and beach. 'Small, but friendly.'
Clearview Hotel, 317 E. Poplar Ave., 522-0985. $70 weekly rate. Also recommended: **Holly Beach Hotel**, 137 E. Spicer Ave., 522-9033.

FOOD/ENTERTAINMENT
Recommended for its 'good food and atmosphere,' is **Big Ernie's** on Atlantic Ave., 522-8288. Summer hours: Mon-Thu, 7.00 am-11.00 pm, Fri-Sun, 7.00 am-3.00 am. Other suggestions include **The Hot Spot**, Schellenger and Boardwalk and **Kelly's Cafe** on Pacific Ave.

CAPE MAY   Family-orientated Victorian beach resort where the 700-800 well-preserved houses date from the 1870-80s. The main attraction is the pristine beach where beach tags must be displayed if you plan to hit the sand, $4 from beach vendors or the Beach Tag Office, 884-9520. More secluded beaches and gentle dunes are located at Cape May Point, take Cape Ave. off Sunset Blvd. At Sunset Beach you can join the hunt for the famous and elusive Cape May diamonds, milky stones which, when polished, glitter like precious gems.

For spectacular views of the coast walk for about 30 mins from the town centre and climb the curling stairs of the old lighthouse, built in 1859, which stands just inside the entrance gates to Cape May State Park. $4. If you're heading south, you may want to take the **Cape May Ferry**, 886-1725, to Lewes, Delaware. Frequent daily sailings, $20 car and driver ($6.50 per car passenger), foot passengers $6.50 o/w, same-day r/t $12.50. Bikes $7.

OF INTEREST
The East Creek Trail 10 mile long cycle path in the **Belleplain State Forest**, Woodbine, which may be accessed from country Rte 550, call 861-2404 for details.
Cape May Ghost Tour, candlelight walking ghost tour through the historic district. Meets at Elaine's Dinner Theater every evening at 8pm, Apr-Nov, $10. Rsvs recommended. Call 88-GHOST for more info. *www.ghosttour.com/capemay*
Bikes may be rented at **Village Bike Rentals**, Lafayette and Elmira Sts, in the Acme parking lot, 884-8500, $4 p/hr, $10 day, $35 week. Daily 7am-6pm.

INFORMATION
Welcome Center, 405 Lafayette St, 884-9562, has info on restaurants, accommodation, tours, etc. Free phones for calling guest houses. Mon-Sat 9am-4pm.

OCEAN GROVE Founded in 1869 by a group of Methodist lay leaders, this seashore resort boasts the largest assemblage of Victorian architecture in the country, for which it was entered into the National Register of Historic Places in 1976. When you get sick of the beach, stroll along the boardwalk or Main Ave to browse in the gift and antique shops, or take in one of the many arts and crafts shows. Every year in June and September there are giant flea markets. Beach tags ($11 w/end, $27.50 for 7 days) are sold at the Beach Office, Ocean and Embury Aves, 988-5533. *www.oceangrovenj.com*
The telephone area code is 732.

ACCOMMODATION
Albatross Hotel, 34 Ocean Pathway, 775-2085. S-$35 D-$54, bfast incl on w/ends.
The Amherst, 14 Pitman Ave, 988-5297. S-$34-40 D-$44-50, bfast incl. If you check in on Mon and check out Fri, weekly rates are S-$120, D-$160.

OF INTEREST
Trolley Tours, 40 min drive-by tours of Ocean Grove's historic homes, buildings, gardens, and parks. Jul-Aug, Sats noon-5pm. $4, leaves from Auditorium park.

INFORMATION
Ocean Grove Tourist Information, 45 Pilgrim Pathway, 774-1391.

DELAWARE WATER GAP   Where the 'Garden State' comes into its own. Here the mountains diverge dramatically to make way for the Delaware River and a national recreation area which is a haven for outdoor enthusiasts, offering everything from swimming to rafting, canoeing to cross-country ski-ing, hiking to biking. For information call (570) 588-2451.

NEW YORK   *The Empire State*

Everything about New York State is big. It has the biggest industrial, commercial and population centre in the United States all rolled into one great metropolis, which together with the vast upstate area contributes mightily to the nation's manufacturing and agricultural output.

In Colonial times New York was one of the most sizeable chunks of land in North America, hence its nickname, the Empire State. Although New York State was technically discovered in 1524 by Giovanni da Verrazano sailing for France, Henry Hudson (an Englishman employed by the Dutch) sailed through the Lower Bay of New York in 1609, and on up the river which now bears his name. The river was later fought over by the British and the Dutch, whilst the Brits also wrested the Northern area from the French.

Peter Minuit founded the Dutch Colony of New Amsterdam (renamed New York City by its conquerors in 1664) after buying Manhattan from the Indians for $24 worth of trinkets. Yet it says something about the vastness of the state, much of it still wilderness even today, that as late as 1700 the most formidable empire in New York was that of the Iroquois Confederacy of the Five Nations based in Syracuse and controlling the water routes to the coast and therefore trade. Their power was broken only in the middle of that century when the British defeated the Indians and their French allies at Ticonderoga, Niagara and Montréal. The year 2000 will see another important battle unfolding in the state as First Lady, Hillary Rodham Clinton and New York City Mayor, Rudolph Giuliani, compete in the race for Senate in what promises to be the most watched local campaign in the country. *www.iloveny.state.ny.us*

NEW YORK CITY   'There are many apples on the tree, but when you pick New York City, you pick the Big Apple.' So said the jazz musicians of the roaring 20s, as fascinated by the lure and excitement of NYC as visitors are today.

More than 14 million people now live and work in New York, the USA's largest city, home to the United Nations and the business, entertainment and publishing capital of the nation. It isn't possible within this book to give more than the merest introduction to New York, so, if you plan to spend some time here, we recommend you buy one of the many available guides to NYC.

The city comprises five boroughs, Queens, Brooklyn, the Bronx, Staten Island and Manhattan, but the greater metropolitan area stretches out into New Jersey and Connecticut. You're really talking about Manhattan when you say New York: that long stretch of stone lying between the Hudson and East Rivers, the place where skyscrapers tower over an intense mangle of social extremes.

New York's explosive variety and its appeal to so many different types of people make it an exciting place to visit. Chances are that whatever you are looking for, you will find, and so much more besides. In the words of President John F Kennedy, 'Other cities are nouns. New York is a verb.' New York offers the finest in theatre, cinema, music, museums, shopping, restaurants and general tourist attractions, as well as a riveting study in social contrast. You'll see bag ladies huddle over steam grates across the street from a row of limousines, and homeless men slumped in the doorway of some gilded apartment building. Summers can be painfully hot and humid, and winters are bitterly cold and windy. It can be filthy, or dangerous, flashy, or funny, but it is always outrageous, alive, enthusiastic and, above all, resilient.

The Big Apple nearly went sour in the 1970s as it tottered on the brink of bankruptcy but it sprang back through the hot-shot 80s and is now going through a renaissance. Whilst facing drug problems, escalating homelessness, deteriorating schools and hospitals, and the increasing overcrowding common to any modern metropolis, crime rates in the city actually dropped 50% in the 90s. Controversial Republican Mayor, Rudolph Giuliani, promised a safer, cleaner city when he was elected in 1993, and he has delivered—especially in Manhattan where assaults have plummeted and the streets are no longer littered with trash. In an effort to combat New York's reputation as 'the capital of rude', Giuliani had recorded messages placed in NYC taxis politely reminding passengers to take all personal belongings and request a receipt, and recently ordered city cops to address citizens as 'sir' and 'madam'. Such moves do not impress Giuliani's critics, who say the mayor has overlooked issues of human rights with his 'zero tolerance' policy on crime. Nevertheless, in 1998 the FBI recognised New York as the safest big city in America. Crime is still a problem, but most NYC natives live there, travel by subway and move around safely. Visitors who use caution and common sense rarely have problems. Indeed, New York is one of the most vibrant, electric places in the country; the city's rebirth is perhaps most evident on a sunny Sunday afternoon in Central Park, when hoards of New Yorkers come out to stroll, jog, play ball or just relax. Whatever your approach to Manhattan, when you see the skyline, day or night, you will experience an unforgettable feeling of intimidation, enchantment and awe—this is New York! Welcome to the fastest-moving, most famous and fascinating city on earth.

The telephone area codes are 212 and 917 for Manhattan, 718 for the Bronx, Brooklyn, Queens and Staten Island. For the numbers in this guide, use 212 unless otherwise specified. *www.nycvisit.com*

NEIGHBOURHOODS
Brooklyn Heights: in Brooklyn, the birthplace of Mae West, Mary Tyler Moore, Woody Allen and Jerry Seinfeld. A neighbourhood of brick, brownstone and wooden houses, overlooking New York harbour. New York as it was 100 years ago. You can walk here across the **Brooklyn Bridge**, a 117-year-old suspension bridge, from South Street Seaport, for a fine view of lower Manhattan.

The Financial District: This is the oldest part of the city, a maze of narrow winding canyons that stand where Peter Stuyvesant once erected his wall to keep the Indians out. Hence *Wall* Street. The New York Stock Exchange is here on Broad St, and the American Stock Exchange is on Trinity Place. George Washington was inaugurated first President of the United States at Federal Hall, Wall and Nassau Sts, in 1789. From Battery Park you can take the ferry to Staten Island and the Statue of Liberty. Towering over everything are the second tallest buildings in the world—the 1350-ft twin towers of the World Trade Center, at West St.

Battery Park City: situated near Battery Park is literally a land-fill. Water was pumped out and the *roads dropped* to create this waterfront community. The district is a necropolis on Sundays, thus great for cycling or a picnic on the steps of City Hall. The thriving **South Street Seaport area** combines a museum, tall ships, a small shopping mall, and a cluster of seafood restaurants that collectively bear witness to New York's origins as a port.

Chinatown: The public telephones are housed in miniature pagodas, and the local grocery shops are great for snow peas or bok choy (Chinese lettuce). Restaurants are good, plentiful and cheap. Chinese New Year is celebrated with the explosion of firecrackers the first full moon after 21 January. Mott and Mulberry are the major streets.

Little Italy: Just north-west of Chinatown, in the area of Mulberry and Grand Sts. Good restaurants, bakeries and grocery shops, and a lively place in June with the Feast of St. Anthony, and again in September with the feast of San Gennaro, when you can ride ferris wheels in the middle of the street, eat lasagne and zeppoles, and buy large buttons that beckon, 'Kiss me, I'm Italian.'

SoHo: Formerly a warehouse and trading district, SoHo, the area south of Houston (pronounced HOW-ston) St and, increasingly, **Tribeca** (stands for triangle below canal), the area between Soho and the World Trade Center, is a haven for up-and-coming artists and musicians. Their artwork, music and theatre fill the old industrial lofts with avant-garde American culture. Chic (yet affordable) restaurants and designer stores are opening all the time, and excellent cheap clothing and electronic stores abound. Tribeca is also home to a wealth of nice restaurants (buy your coffees and brunches here) and, like Soho, there are many cast-iron buildings, dating from the turn of the century. Movie star Robert De Niro moved here in 1982 and opened his own film centre and grill restaurant (the TriBeCa Grill). Other celebrity residents include Dan Ackroyd and Bette Middler.

The Lower East Side: Orchard and Delancey Streets have attracted waves of immigrants: Eastern European Jews in the early part of this century, Puerto Ricans and Haitians today. Some older Jews still remain and Sunday is their big market day, a good time to swoop in for bargains. Note that many stores are closed on Saturdays—the Jewish Sabbath. The Lower East Side is slowly growing more fashionable, with poor immigrants being chased out by galleries and restaurants. Visit the **Lower East Side Tenement Museum**, 90 Orchard St at Broome St, 387-0341, to experience nineteenth century immigrant life, $8, students $6.

The East Village: St Mark's Place and 2nd Ave. took the overflow from increasingly pricey Greenwich Village to become the hang-out for struggling artists, writers and students. It's also home to some of the more wasted punks, drug-users and drop-outs, who can make this a dangerous and intimidating area late at night, so tread carefully. However, as with the Lower East Side, the East Village is experiencing something of a renaissance, with an increasing number of trendy new bars, cafes and clothing stores attracting a vibrant young community with a style all its own. A recent influx of galleries, theatres and music venues has meant the East Village is becoming a hang-out for the cultural style-setters of the 21st century. Former inhabitants of the East Village include WH Auden and James Fenimore Cooper.

Greenwich Village: New York's original bohemian quarter and one-time home of such figures as Edgar Allan Poe, e.e. cummings, Eugene O'Neill, Alan Ginsberg and Dylan Thomas, the Village is not what it used to be. Lots of expensive plastic cafes now cater to the tourists, but 10th, 11th and 12th Sts remain somewhat peaceful, lined with the brownstone homes of celebrities and the wealthy. New York University faces onto ever-lively Washington Square, with its version of the Arc de Triomphe. In the square listen to everything from casual guitar strumming to classical violin; watch the jugglers and break dancers, and compare strategy with the hustlers working the chess boards. During the summer, street fairs and markets are common up and down Village streets. The area centred around Christopher Street is also home to New York's large gay community.

Chelsea: Home to the garment district, where one-third of all the clothes worn in the US are made or handled, Chelsea is a vast stretch of warehouses and lofts that is starting to gentrify under pressure from Greenwich Village. The flower district is dug in around 27th St. To forget the grime of the city, walk along here among the ferns, tropical plants and examples of every imaginable flower in season. To the west lie the crumbling remains of the docks where the great steamships used to call. Better known as **Hell's Kitchen**, the hope is that the waterfront will revive now that the giant space-age Jacob K Javits Convention Center is complete. Further uptown, around Herald Square and 34th St, things are bustling around the large department stores like Macy's and A&S, as well as inside the nine-storey Herald Center shopping mall. Just a block away in either direction stand the Empire State Building and revamped Madison Square Garden. The Garden is where sports events, exhibitions and pop concerts happen; beneath it is **Penn Station** where you can catch commuter trains out to Long Island, or Amtrak to Boston, Washington or Chicago.

Midtown: The core of the Big Apple. East and West, btwn 42nd & 59th Sts, is the heart of the theatre, cinema, and shopping districts, and was once the centre of NYC's porn industry. Few vestiges of Midtown's former, seedier self remain, though, now that Giuliani's new zoning laws have advanced an invasion by Disney and other, tamer, businesses.

5th Ave. splits midtown down the middle, marking the border between the East side and the West side. The swankiest shops in the city elbow for space along this justifiably famous street. Rockefeller Center and St Patrick's Cathedral are here, and when Britain decides to pawn the crown jewels, they'll be on sale at Tiffany's, corner of 57th St. The impressive Trump Tower, ritziest building in New York, packs five floors of astonishingly expensive boutiques around a rose marble waterfall. 'You won't be able to afford anything, but definitely worth a look.' The brotherhood of mankind fulminates daily in the United Nations Building on 44th St, by the East River. **Grand Central Station**, with trains to upstate New York and Connecticut, dominates E 42 St.

Times Square, once home to pimps and tarts as well as Broadway theatres, dominates W 42nd St. Until recently attempts to clear the area of junkies, peep shows, porn cinemas and all manner of sleaze were in vain. However the Disney Corporation have acquired a massive block of real estate here and are forcing a sanitising transformation of the entire area, including Times Square itself. Renovation work is currently underway and several hotels and office buildings have sprung up: an indication that the area is gradually becoming more respectable. Well policed, it's not as dangerous as it seems, but be on your guard— the action here goes on all night. Pleasant places in which to picnic or relax are the 'pocket parks' hidden away in Midtown: 57th St east of 5th Ave., and 47th St btwn 2nd & 3rd Aves.

Central Park: A huge, rambling green oasis designed by Frederick Law Olmstead and Calvert Vaux. Stretching for miles through the heart of Manhattan, the park extends from 59th to 110th St with ponds, gardens, tennis courts and a zoo. On Sundays the streets are blocked off, and the park fills with New Yorkers rollerblading, walking, sailing, jogging, riding, cycling, skate boarding, playing baseball or reading the *Sunday Times*. Others contemplate Strawberry Fields, the international garden of peace named in memory of John Lennon. Nearby an imitation medieval castle, Belvedere, nestles in the park with climbable turrets and spires that offer an unusual view of the Manhattan skyline. Look for the Shakespeare Festival and free concerts, plays and opera in the summer; ice-skating in the winter. And don't forget to clear out at night; the park is unsafe after sundown.

The Upper East Side: The 60s, 70s and 80s in this area are among the most coveted addresses in New York. The vast Metropolitan Museum of Art and the spiralling Guggenheim anchor Museum Mile along 5th Ave. East 86th St is the heart of Yorkville, the German part of town, with beer and Gemutlichkeit on draught. Beginning at 96th St and running north to 145th is East Harlem, the largely Puerto Rican section called El Barrio. A sprinkling of Irish and Italian families remain, but Spanish dominates storefront signs.

The Upper West Side: At the intersection of Columbus and Broadway lies the cultural hub of Manhattan, The Lincoln Center, which includes the Metropolitan Opera House and the New York State Theatre. At night it's pretty crowded; by summer's day it's a pleasant place to sit and eat ice cream. Around 72nd St and on Columbus Ave. is a young, semi-posh and lively neighbourhood; on Central Park West is the impressive Victorian Dakota building where John Lennon lived and died. North on Central Park West is the Natural History Museum, and still further, in the Morningside Heights area, is **Columbia University** at Broadway & 116th St.

Harlem: This is the centre of New York's black community, stretching from the top end of Central Park up to 155th, and encompassing everything from miserable tenements to fashionable residential rows. A historic area in terms of religion and culture, Harlem is trying to get over its 'stay out' reputation and attract daytime visitors to its landmark churches and soul/gospel/jazz venues like The Cotton Club and the famous Apollo Theater. One of the best, if expensive, ways to see the district is by guided tour, (**Harlem Spirituals**, 757-0425, $35, Wed and Sun, or **Grayline Harlem Gospel Tour**, 397-2600, $33, Sun only). Head for a tour which includes Sunday brunch if possible because this is the place to try tongue-tingling Cajun cuisine. Away from the tours Harlem can be a rough area where money for drugs is in short supply, especially on 125th St, and the night visitor should be wary.

ACCOMMODATION

To find cheap accommodation try the classified ads in *The Village Voice* newspaper, published late Tuesday evening in Manhattan. Shops near **Columbia** are sometimes good for sub-lets. Also try the fraternity houses around **NYU** (NYU Loeb Student Center, Washington Sq, 998-4900) and Columbia (Columbia University Office of Student Activities, Alfred Lerner Hall, 2920 Broadway, 854-3611)

New York Habitat, 307 7th Ave., Suite 306, New York, NY 10001, 255-8018. Finds accommodation from 1 bedroom shares to apartment sublets in safe areas and according to budget. Fee: less than 30 days 35% of one month's rent, 30 days-3 months, 50%. Call in advance for the best deals. *www.nyhabitat.com*

'NY Information Center at Penn Station has price info on all hotels in New York. Very useful if you don't want to stay at a hostel.' Single accommodation can be astronomically expensive, but rates for doubles and triples are markedly less, so travel in herds where possible.

Big Apple Hostel, 119 W 45th St, 302-2603. $28 dorm, $75 (including tax) for small private room. 'Excellent location.' 'Absurdly hot in summer—no AC.' 'No advance res.'

Carlton Arms Hotel, 160 E 25th St (at 3rd Ave.), 679-0680. S-$57-$68, D-$73-$84, T-$90-$101, Q-$95-$106, depending on shared or private bath. Flamboyant artwork makes each room a shrine to downtown New York style. 'Check the room first!'

Chelsea International Hostel, 251 W 20th St, 647-0010. On a leafy street btwn 7th & 8th Aves, directly opposite a police station. dorm $23, private rooms $55, $10 key deposit. The linen, showers and toilets are clean, as are the single-sex dorms. Will lock-up bags until 6pm. Great location, within easy walking distance of the subway, Amtrak, Greenwich Village and midtown Broadway. Non-AYH if space allows. 'We made some great international friends here.' 'Good self-catering facilities.'—'Rooms cramped and hot.' 'Be there by 1.30pm.'

Chelsea Center, 313 W 29th St, 243-4922. $27 dorm style, bfast included. Kitchen, showers. $5 key deposit. German & French spoken. Check-in 8.30am-11pm.

Foreigners only, no curfew, rsvs required. 'Very cramped.' 'Safe, friendly, personal atmosphere.'

Gershwin Hotel, 7 E 27th St, 545-8000. Mixed dorms $27 incl. tax, private room with bath $99-$139 w/o tax.   Sundeck. Near Empire State Building. Check-in 3pm. 'Basic, but clean and good security.' 'Nice, friendly staff.' 'Slow check in and out.'

Habitat Hotel, 130 E 57th St, btwn Park and Lexington Aves, 753-8841. Excellent location, small rooms with shared bath from $75. Includes continental breakfast. 'Stylish modern hotel'.

International AYH-Hostel, 891 Amsterdam Ave., and 103rd, 932-2300. Take #1 or #9 subway to 103rd St and walk 1 block east. Largest hostel in the USA. Kitchen, garden, daily activities, travel services. 24 hrs, must be IYH/HIAYH member. Dorms $24-$29 depending on number of beds in dorm, singles with bath $120. Rsvs recommended. *www.hostelling.com* E-mail: *hostel@hostelling.com*.

International Student Center, 38 W 88th St, 787-7706. $15 dorm-style. Kitchen, linen provided. Foreigners only. Check-in 10.30am, 7 night max stay, 3 weeks in winter. 'Friendly place in heart of big city.' 'Good safe area but dirty rooms.'

International House, 500 Riverside Drive, 316-8400. Dorm, $40-$45. Summer only. Check-in after 1pm. Close to Columbia U and subway. 'Clean. Excellent and cheap canteen.' Rsvs recommended.

Jazz on the Park Hostel, 36 W 106 St, 932-1600. Dorm $27 incl. tax. Incl. light breakfast. Social activities. 'Groovy new hostel;' 'very cramped rooms'.

Madison Hotel, 21 E 27th St, 532-7373. D-$105, Q-$126. Check-in at mid-day. 'Good location, security and helpful staff.'

Martha Washington Hotel, 29 E. 29th St, 689-1900. Women only. Re-opens in August 1999 after refurbishment.   Rates unavailable.

On the Ave. Hotel, 2178 Broadway, 362-1100. 'Economy' hotel, conveniently situated. Fridge, TV, AC. Rooms with queen beds, ranging from $125-$165.

Quality Inn, 94th and Broadway, 866-6400. $130 quad. special rate.

Sugar Hill International Hostel, 722 St. Nicholas Ave., 926-7030. E-mail, *infohostel@aol.com*. Run by author of the *Hostel Handbook* (see background USA section) keen to pass on knowledge of hostelling and NYC. Clean, spacious dorms $20. 'Very friendly staff, safe hostel (opposite 145th St subway stop),' for those who don't mind being uptown in Harlem. Check in 9am-10pm, 24 hr access. Lock-up available. Kitchen. Take A, B, C, or D train to 145th St. Rsvs required.

Travel Inn Motor Hotel, 515 W 42nd St, 695-7171. Expensive, but Q-$185, bath, TV, pool, roof deck. Secure indoor parking is free—'very useful in the city!' 'Can be quite cheap if several share a room—the floors are comfortably carpeted.'

YMCA—McBurney, 206 W 24th St, btwn 7th & 8th Aves, 741-9226. Co-ed. S-$59, D-$71. $5 key deposit. 25 day max stay. Café, TV, gym, 24 hrs. 'Reasonable rooms, but mainly frequented by older people; handy for Washington Sq and Greenwich Village.' 'Didn't always feel safe.'

YMCA—Vanderbilt, 224 E 47th St, 756-9600. Co-ed. S-$68. $10 key deposit. TV in rooms. Three week advance rsvs required. Gym, pool. 'Great location—10 mins from Empire State.'

YMCA—West Side, 5 W 63rd St, 875-4100. Co-ed. S-$68-$95. D-$80-$110. Check-in 2pm. One week advance rsvs required.

FOOD

A spirit of adventure will keep you well-fed in Manhattan. With over 13,000 multi-ethnic eateries serving everything from bagels to Bratwurst, borscht to baklava, do not resist the temptation to try it all! Food can be expensive but for a budget alternative the all-American diner will provide endless coffee and pancakes drenched in maple syrup. Below you'll find two lists of places to try, one containing some tried-and-true favourites, the other, a list of neighbourhoods known to have a lot of cheap, good restaurants.

Abyssinia, 35 Grand St at Thompson St, SoHo, 226-5959. Delicious, spicy Ethiopian cuisine eaten off low wicker tables and stools. From $7.

Big Nick's, 77th and Broadway, 362-9238. Hamburgers, Greek food and pizza next door. Open 23 hrs, dinner from about $5; 'the best'.

Carnegie Deli, 7th Ave. at 55th St, 757-2245. Sandwiches large enough to feed two, from $10.50. Other Jewish specialities. This was the restaurant featured in Woody Allen's *Broadway Danny Rose*. Staggering cheesecake and their corned beef and pastrami are rated no.1 in the country.

Dallas BBQ, 21 University Place, 674-4450. Friendly, spacious student favourite, right across from NYU. Mobbed in the evenings. 'Great early bird specials.' ($7.95 for two, Mon-Fri 2pm-6.30pm, w/ends 2pm-5pm). Filling bowl of home-made chilli with corn-bread, $4. Veggie options. Mon-Fri 11am-midnight, Sat & Sun 'til 1am.

El Cantinero, 86 University Place, 255-9378. Authentic Mexican food. Fajitas a speciality. Lunch average $6.50, dinner average $10.50. Large garden. Mon-Thur 4pm-11pm, happy hour. Mon nights $9 all-you-can-eat, Tues nights 15% off bill. Fri & Sat 'til 1am, Sun 'til 10.30pm.

H&H Bagels, 2239 Broadway, W 80th St, 595-8000, and smaller store at 639 W 46th St. Traditional American bagels. Great bargain snacks to hold off mid-sightseeing starvation. Unadulterated plain or cinnamon raisin are best, 75¢ each. 24 hrs.

Harley Davidson Cafe, 1370 Ave. of the Americas, corner of SE 56th St & 6th, 245-6000. Yes, *another* Hollywood-style themed restaurant. But still a good place to sit back and lap up American culture amongst the gleaming Harleys and biker memorabilia. $8-$20, veggie options. Daily 11.30am-midnight.

Katz's Delicatessen, 205 E Houston St (at Ave. A), 254-2246, Lower East Side. You can sample the meat before deciding which sandwich, average price $10. A New York Jewish institution for more than 100 years. Sun, Mon, Tues 8am-10pm, Weds, Thur 'til 11pm, Fri & Sat 'til 3am.

Famous Ray's Pizza, 319 6th Ave., 645-8404, and 11th St & 6th Ave., 243-2253. Greenwich Village. One slice of pizza the size of Luxembourg costs less than $3 and is a filling meal. 'This is the best.' Regular cheese slice $1.70, six slices $9. 24 hrs.

West End Gate, 2911 Broadway, btwn 113th & 114th Sts, 662-8830. Bar/restaurant popular with CU students. Pasta and burgers from $7-$15. Occasional jazz nights. Daily 11am-11pm.

Orloff's Deli, 58 W 65th St, off Central Park. 799-4000. From donuts and muffins to full entrees.   All-day breakfast. Entrees run $5-$12.   Daily 6am-midnight.

Street vendors hawk salty wheel-shaped pretzels, hot-roasted chestnuts and the quintessential New York 'dog' with everything on.

For cheap, spicy **Indian** food, visit Madison Ave around 27th St, also E Sixth St btwn 1st & 2nd Aves and other nearby streets. The number of hole-in-the-wall restaurants here has exploded recently. Dinner for $6 isn't a fantasy, but bring your own booze if you want a drink with dinner. **Chinatown** justifies its reputation as a haven for good, inexpensive Chinese cooking. Walk along Mott, Bayard & Pell Sts, read menus, and look for the restaurant where the most Chinese people are eating. For oom-pah-pah bands and the wurst in **German** cooking, stroll through **Yorkville**, along E 86 St. **Little Italy**, next to Chinatown, has a number of good Italian restaurants, cafes and groceries, with waiters surlier than Rocky ready to push the pasta. Mulberry & Lafayette Sts, south of Houston, are especially fertile territory.

The Bowery, east of Chinatown, is more famous for its bums (that's American for derelict) than for places to eat. But if your budget is rock bottom, walk along Bowery St by day for some of the lowest food prices in the city. Be careful at night. Try **MacDougall's**, 89 MacDougall, 477-4021. General American $4-$17, 9am-4am daily.

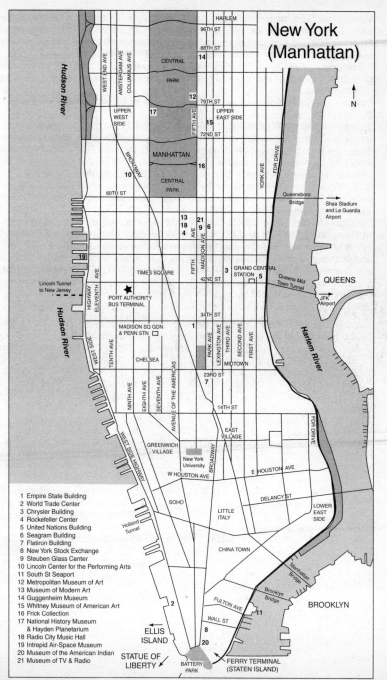

New York (Manhattan)

N

HARLEM
96TH ST
88TH ST
14
CENTRAL
PARK
12
79TH ST
17
UPPER EAST SIDE
15
72ND ST
UPPER WEST SIDE
MANHATTAN
16
CENTRAL PARK
10
60TH ST
Queensboro Bridge
Shea Stadium and La Guardia Airport
13 21 6
18 9
4
19
TIMES SQUARE
GRAND CENTRAL STATION
3 5
42ND ST
QUEENS
Queens Mid Town Tunnel
Lincoln Tunnel to New Jersey
PORT AUTHORITY BUS TERMINAL
JFK Airport
34TH ST
MADISON SQ GDN & PENN STN
1
Hudson River
CHELSEA
MIDTOWN
7
23RD ST
Harlem River
14TH ST
EAST VILLAGE
GREENWICH VILLAGE
New York University
W HOUSTON AVE
E HOUSTON AVE
SOHO
DELANCY ST
LOWER EAST SIDE
Holland Tunnel
LITTLE ITALY
CHINA TOWN
Manhattan Bridge
Brooklyn Bridge
FULTON AVE
BROOKLYN
2
WALL ST
11
8
ELLIS ISLAND
20
STATUE OF LIBERTY
BATTERY PARK
FERRY TERMINAL (STATEN ISLAND)

Avenues labelled: WEST END AVE, AMSTERDAM AVE, COLUMBUS AVE, BROADWAY, FIFTH AVE, YORK AVE, FDR DRIVE, HIGHWAY, ELEVENTH AVE, TENTH AVE, NINTH AVE, EIGHTH AVE, SEVENTH AVE, AVENUE OF THE AMERICAS, PARK AVE, LEXINGTON AVE, THIRD AVE, SECOND AVE, FIRST AVE, MADISON AVE, WEST SIDE HIGHWAY

1 Empire State Building
2 World Trade Center
3 Chrysler Building
4 Rockefeller Center
5 United Nations Building
6 Seagram Building
7 Flatiron Building
8 New York Stock Exchange
9 Steuben Glass Center
10 Lincoln Center for the Performing Arts
11 South St Seaport
12 Metropolitan Museum of Art
13 Museum of Modern Art
14 Guggenheim Museum
15 Whitney Museum of American Art
16 Frick Collection
17 National History Museum & Hayden Planetarium
18 Radio City Music Hall
19 Intrepid Air-Space Museum
20 Museum of the American Indian
21 Museum of TV & Radio

Upper West Side, btwn 60th & 90th Sts has an endless succession of trendy restaurants. Try **Victor's Cafe**, 236 W 52nd, 586-7714 for Cuban food. $15-$32, noon-11.30, Fri & Sat 'til 12.30. Lots of new, trendy cafe-type places open all the time, especially along Columbus & Amsterdam Aves.

SoHo, south of Houston to Canal, has a large number of interesting restaurants (although they can be expensive) squeezed between the galleries and second-hand clothing stores.

Veselka, 114 Second Ave at 10th St, 228-9682, a 24 hr Ukrainian café, has the best Borscht in the city.

Greenwich Village West and **East Village** are probably the most varied and exciting places to look for food. Walk btwn 14th St south of Houston, and west on 1st Ave to the river. Cheaper spots cluster around NYU, along 2nd Ave, and if you take a walk along Avenue A between E 11th & E 3rd, you will find an exciting array of temptations at very reasonable prices: including **The Flea Market**, 131 Ave A , 358-9282, **7A**, 109 Ave A, 475-9001, for 24 hr people watching, and breakfast specials $2.50, and **Two Boots To Go**, 42 Ave A, 505-5450, for festive Cajun pizza. St Mark's Place offers: **Stingey Lulu's**, 129 St Mark's Place, 674-3545, with drag queens to indulge your every whim, **Yaffa Café**, 97 St Mark's Place, 674-9302, for 24 hr kitsch, **St Dymphna's**, 118 St Mark's Place, 254-6636, for great Boston Scrod, and **Bel Air**, 110 St Mark's Place, 677-6563, for the best iced-coffee in the city! Also in this area, and definitely worth a visit; **Mission Burrito**, 91 E 7th St, 477-0773, for the very best burritos, **Mama's**, 200 E 3rd St, 777-4425, for home-cooked delights, **Miracle Grill**, 112 1st Ave, 254-2353, for bargain Cajun brunch at w/ends, and **Tea and Sympathy**, 108 Greenwich Ave, 807-8329, to satisfy any English food cravings.

OF INTEREST

Cathedral of St John the Divine, 112th St & Amsterdam Ave, 316-7540. The largest Gothic cathedral in the world, with an awe-inspiring vaulted roof that sweeps up as high as a 12-storey building. Otherwise known as St John the Unfinished. Work began in 1892, but was suspended in 1941 when America entered the war. Enthusiasm waned, funds dried up and Americans forgot how to build Gothic cathedrals. Magnificent, even with 100 years' work still to go. Now work is ongoing again. Tours Tue-Sat, 11am, Sun, 1pm, $3. 'Weird, wonderful, memorable.' Also, don't miss the **Peace Park** and its amazing fountain right next door.

Chrysler Building, 405 Lexington & 42nd St, 682-3070. An evocative landmark of the NYC night skyline, the famous Chrysler spire sits atop a building which typifies the art deco style inside and out. Built as a tribute to the great American automobile in the 1920s, some of its gargoyles are radiator caps. At 77 storeys, (1045 ft), it was the world's tallest building for one whole year until the Empire State Building snatched the record in 1931. No tours.

Chelsea Hotel, 222 W 23rd St, 243-3700. This hotel was once a haven for artists, writers and other fringe-elements in NYC. Expensive rates (D-$175) now mean it's better just to look at the landmark where Thomas Wolfe wrote, Dylan Thomas drank and Sid Vicious offered his honey.

Coney Island, (718) 372-0275, where generations of New Yorkers met, played, fell in love and screamed on the Cyclone roller-coaster (amusement park $13). Crowded beach. While here visit the **NY Aquarium**, (718) 265-3400/265-FISH. Daily 10am-6pm, last tkt 5pm, $8.75. See penguins, walrus, dolphins, sharks and Beluga whales. 'Fantastic.' Take F or D subway to W 8th St exit. Coney Island is directly opposite, a pedestrian bridge leads to the Aquarium. While there, take the boardwalk to amazing Brighton Beach where the Russians have really landed.

Ellis Island. Once the landing point for 15 million European immigrants entering the US between 1892 and 1924, and consequently a museum of enormous significance and poignancy for many Americans. The fortress-like building can only be reached by an excellent ferry ride from Manhattan's Battery Park or Liberty State

Park, NJ, (201) 435-9499. 'Highly recommended.' Mon-Fri 9.30am-5.30pm (extended summer hours). For info call 363-3200. For ferry info call **Circle Line**, 269-5755. Ferries leave Battery Park every 20 mins, 9.30am-3.30pm, $7 r/t.

Empire State Building, 5th Ave & 34th St, 736-3100. Not the tallest building any more, but the view, night and day, is still fantastic. If it's breezy, try the outdoor deck to really get the adrenaline buzzing. 'Go up at night, unforgettable views and less crowded.' Daily 9.30am-11.30pm, last tickets sold at 11pm, $9.

Flatiron Building, Madison Sq at 22nd St. The first iron-framed building and progenitor of New York's skyscrapers. An ornate wedge shaped building, it's still worth seeing.

Grand Central Station, 42nd St & Park Ave, itself a star of many movies. Take a look at the famously beautiful zodiac ceiling which depicts a Mediterranean winter sky with 2500 stars. Said to be backwards, it is actually seen from a point of view outside our solar system. A mammoth cleaning operation took place in 1997—using only soap and water!

Liberty Island. Info: 269-5755. Beware of hours of heated queuing with no shade: go to the dock early (arrive by 8am; first boat leaves for Ellis Island directly, 8.30am). Consider going by way of New Jersey (from Liberty State Park—75% of visitors leave from Manhattan.)

Lincoln Center for the Performing Arts, 62nd-65th Sts & Columbus Ave, 546-2656. Largest performing arts centre in the world, containing opera house, concert hall, theatre, museum, Juilliard School. 1 hr tour $8.25, $7 w/student ID, daily 10am-5pm. The **Metropolitan Opera House** has its own 90 min backstage tours, but closes early in the summer. Call 769-7020 for details and rsvs. Look for free concerts and other events during the summer.

NBC Television Studio Tours, 30 Rockefeller Plaza, btwn 49th & 50th Sts, off 6th Ave, 664-4444. 1 hr tour of studios, famous home to *Saturday Night Live* amongst other shows. Daily, 8am-7pm, every 15 minutes, $17.50. First come, first served at tour desk, 49th St entrance. 'Fantastic, definitely the best tour I went on. Free tkts for shows offered.'

New York Stock Exchange, 20 Broad St at Wall St, 656-3000. Free admission to the observation gallery and Visitors Center, Mon-Fri 9am-4.30pm. Arrive early to get a ticket.

Radio City Music Hall, 1260 Ave of the Americas (6th at 50th St), 632-4041. Newly-renovated art deco showtime palace, created by 30s impresario 'roxy' Rothafel. Home to the world's largest movie theatres, some two-ton chandeliers and 60 years of showbiz history. 1 hr tours every half hour, Mon-Sat 10am-5pm, Sun 11am-5pm, $14. See the Great Stage and meet a Rockette.

Seagram Building, 375 Park Ave, btwn 52nd & 53rd Sts, 572-7000. Designed by Mies Van Der Rohe and Phillip Johnson as first 'anti-bourgeois' modern building. Brief free tour, Tue, 3pm.

South Street Seaport, 748-8600, by Fulton St Fish Market. Historic waterfront district, just off Wall St, restored as it was 200 years ago. Now featuring a ship museum ($6, $4 w/student ID), and shopping mall with cheap fast-food outlets. Includes a craft centre and 19th century printing store. Several different tours and cruises offered daily. Summer hours, daily 10am-6pm, Thu 10am-8pm. *www.southstseaport.org*

Staten Island Ferry, (718) 815-BOAT (815-2628). Nobody should miss what is certainly the best travel bargain to be found anywhere. It costs just nothing!! Frequent departures from Battery Park, at the tip of Manhattan. Passes close to the Statue of Liberty. Superb view of the Manhattan skyline, many people's (among them poet Walt Whitman's) favourite view of New York.

Statue of Liberty National Monument, Liberty Island, 269-5755. After getting the world's largest facelift, Lady Liberty is again open to the public. Take Circle Line ferry ($7 r/t) from Battery Park, daily, 269-5755. 'Can queue for two hours to climb to the crown—not worth it, take the lift to mid-way.'

Steuben Glass Center, 5th Ave & 56th St. Too expensive to buy but always superb to look at.

United Nations Building, 1st Ave & 46th St, 963-4475. 45 min tours every 20 mins, 9am-4.45pm. $7.50, $4.50 w/student ID. Expect an hour-long wait. Call in advance as hours vary depending on meetings of the General Assembly.

Woodlawn Cemetery. In the Bronx, and the last stop on the subway. The last stop for much of New York's high society, too. 400 landscaped acres of opulent mausolea and monuments to men who started from nothing and worked their way to a spot of turf at Woodlawn. Cast includes Westinghouse, Bat Masterson, associate of Wyatt Earp, Fiorello La Guardia, FW Woolworth, JC Penney, and A Bulova, the watch tycoon.

World Financial Center, across from the World Trade Center, Battery Park City, Hudson River & West St. Take the subway #1 or #9 to Courtland St. A gathering place of shops, restaurants and entertainment. Particularly relaxing (and free!) on a hot day is the **Winter Garden**, one of the most beautiful indoor spaces around, and a popular venue for free performances and recitals. Tall, elegant palm trees and AC, a superb view of the harbour and a flowing monumental staircase. Info: 945-0505. *www.worldfinancialcenter.com*

World Trade Center, Church, Vesey, West & Liberty Sts, 323-2340. Miss this and you miss the best view anyone will ever get of New York. Make sure it's not foggy. Stomachs plummet in the elevators up to the glassed-in observation deck on the 107th floor, which offers a panoramic view of the city. Thrill-seekers can send their stomachs even deeper and venture outside onto the highest open-air observation platform in the world, at over a quarter mile high. Go just before sunset and the horizon will change colour as you walk round (it can take up to an hour) while night-time New York lights up before your eyes. Daily 9.30am-11.30pm, June-Aug, until 9.30pm the rest of the year. $12.50, $10.75 w/student ID. 'Breathtaking.'

MUSEUMS AND ART GALLERIES

American Museum of Natural History, Central Pk W btwn 77th & 81st Sts, 769-5000. Vast natural history collection from all continents and seas. Especially strong on Africa and North America. Meet Tyrannosaurus Rex and Velociraptor in the newly renovated dinosaur halls. Daily, Sun-Thur 10am-5.45pm, Fri & Sat 10am-8.45pm. Entry by donation, suggested $8, $4.50 w/student ID. In the same complex is the **Hayden Planetarium**, a new improved version will re-open in 2000.

The Cloisters, Fort Tryon Park, off Henry Hudson Pkwy, call 923-3700 for bus and subway info. A branch of the Metropolitan Museum of Art devoted to medieval European art and architecture. On top of a hill overlooking the Hudson, the museum gives the impression of a 12th-century monastery. One of the lesser known but more enjoyable galleries, it shelters magnificent medieval sculptures and the famed Unicorn Tapestries. Mar-Oct, Tue-Sun 9.30am-5.15pm; otherwise closes at 4.45pm. $10, $5 w/student ID (includes same-day admittance to Metropolitan Museum of Art).

The Frick Collection, 1 E 70th St at 5th Ave, 288-0700. Walk in to this Italianate villa, once Henry Frick's home, and there is a peaceful hush in the small courtyard. Walk round the rooms and see works by Titian, Velzquez, Whistler and a searing Rembrandt self-portrait; plus wonderful furniture and interiors. A small delight. Tues-Sat 10am-6pm, Sun 1pm-6pm; $7, $5 w/student ID. 'Unsuspected highlight of New York.'

Solomon R. Guggenheim Museum, 1071 5th Ave at 88th St, 423-3500. After restoration the fantastic building is finally as architect Frank Lloyd Wright wished it. A spiral winds down taking you past the contemporary art collection. Now with a new wing for more permanent displays. Sun-Weds 9am-6pm, Fri & Sat 'til 8pm,

$12, $7 w/student ID, Fri 6pm-8pm pay what you can. Second location downtown, with Impressionist, Surrealist and Minimalist collection, 575 Broadway at Prince St, $15, $5 w/student ID. Sun, Weds, Fri noon-6pm, Sat 11am-8pm.

Intrepid Sea-Air-Space Museum, W 46th St & 12th Ave, Pier 86, 245-2533. Restored aircraft carrier with planes, also space exhibit and submarine. Mon-Fri 10am-5pm (last admit 4pm), Sat-Sun 10am-6pm (last admit 5pm), $10, $7.50 w/student ID.

Metropolitan Museum of Art, Central Park, 5th Ave & 82nd St, 879-5500. One of the world's greatest collections and the largest of its kind in the Western Hemisphere. There are over 3 million works tracing the evolution of art from the 13th century to the present day, plus the largest Egyptian collection outside Egypt. Particularly restful on a blistering summer's day is **Astor Court**, the Ming scholar's retreat. Stone, flora and a miniature waterfall are arranged in a yin and yang relationship, installed by 27 Chinese engineers in 1980. Tue, Wed, Thu, Sun 9.30am-5.15pm, Fri-Sat 9.30am-8.45pm, closed Mon. Suggested donation, $10, $5 w/student ID.

Museum of Modern Art, 11 W 53rd St, btwn 5th & 6th Aves, 708-9480. Set up in 1929 because the Met refused to acknowledge the existence of modern art. This is the place to see Picasso, Monet, and just about any other modern painter you can care to think of, plus superb photography. Rest those weary feet in the tranquil and heavily stocked sculpture garden. Sat, Sun, Mon, Tue, Thu 10.30am-5.45pm, Fri 'til 8.15pm, $9.50, $6.50 w/student ID, pay what you can 4.30pm-8.15pm Fri. For evening jazz concerts call 708-9491. Films are shown daily except Weds, free tkts w/admission to museum available at 10.30am for afternoon shows and 1pm for evenings. *www.moma.org*

Museum of the American Indian, Smithsonian Institution, Alexander Hamilton US Customs House, 1 Bowling Green, near Battery Park, far southern end of Broadway, 668-6624. One of the finest collections of native American artefacts in the world. Forerunner to the Museum of the American Indian scheduled to open on the Mall in Washington DC by 2002, this is a museum where contemporary issues receive as much attention as past history. Daily 10am-5pm, Thur 'til 8pm, free. 'A treasure house.'

Museum of TV and Radio, 25 W 52 St, btwn 5th & 6th Aves, 621-6800. The computer library here holds over 40,000 TV and radio programs, commercials for listening and viewing. Popular, so reserve on arrival. Also special exhibits and screenings. Tue-Sun noon-6pm, Thurs noon-8pm. $6, $4 w/student ID.

Museum of the City of New York, 5th Ave at 103rd St, 534-1672. Fascinating story of city's growth from a small Dutch community. Free, although donations suggested, $5, $4 w/student ID. Wed-Sat 10am-5pm, Sun noon-5pm. *www.mcny.org*

Whitney Museum of American Art, 945 Madison Ave, at 75th St, 570-3676. Devoted exclusively to 20th-century American art. Tue-Wed 11am-6pm, Thur 1pm-8pm, Fri-Sun 11am-6pm; $12.50, $10.50 w/student ID, first Thu of every month 6pm-8pm, pay what you can. *www.whitney.org*

TOURS

Tours really worth taking include the boat trips around Manhattan and the guided bus/foot tours of Harlem. Other than these, one of the best and cheapest ways to explore New York is on foot.

Circle Line, Pier 83, 12th Ave & W 42nd St, 563-3200. 3 hr boat trips circumnavigate the island of Manhattan 10.30am-3pm, $22, 90 min $18. Bar onboard. Harbour Lights cruise at 7pm, $18. 'Make sure you sit on left side of boat.' 'Can get chilly.' 'Great value.' 'Breathtaking at night.'

Grayline Tours, 900 8th Ave btwn 53rd & 54th Sts, 397-2600. Offers twenty different tours (including Harlem and Manhattan) daily. From 2 hrs to all day ventures, from $22, departing from north wing of Port Authority bus terminal, W 42nd St & 8th

Ave. See leaflets in hotel lobbies and tourist centres. The Grayline tours are probably not worth taking unless you're only in New York for a brief time—a 'hop on and off' tour starts at 9am.

Harlem Your Way, 690-1687. Bus and walking tours of gospel churches and jazz venues, from $25

New York Apple Tours, several locations, 944-9200. Sightseeing and shopping aboard double-decker buses, $39. May-Oct daily 9am-10pm, otherwise 'til 6pm.

ENTERTAINMENT

No other American city can offer such a variety of amusements. Entertainment, however, can be expensive for the stranger who does not know his way around. Broadway theatres, most night clubs and some cinemas will put a strain on modest budgets. At the same time, free entertainment abounds. Read the *New Yorker*, *Village Voice*, *Where Magazine*, *Seven Days*, *New York Magazine*'s Cue section, or look for a free copy of *NY Talk*, for complete details of shows, jazz and cinemas. The New York Convention and Visitors Bureau, Times Square, 397-8222/(888) 692-2775, can also provide useful information regarding shows, events and entertainments. There are free orchestral, pop, operatic concerts, dance groups, and theatrical performances in **Central Park** throughout the summer. These are popular, so try to arrive at least 2 hrs before the performance to stake your claim. Also, look out for local street festivals.

Greenwich Village and **SoHo** are two of the most interesting entertainment areas. Good jazz and folk music, as well as eating places, can still be found among the many tourist traps in the Village, although SoHo is definitely where New Yorkers go now. Go to the better places, even if there is an admission charge; you will find the best music. Beware of places that do not advertise an admission or cover charge but extract large sums for a required drink and offer inferior entertainment.

Washington Square is infested with pseudo folksingers on w/end afternoons.

JAZZ

Check the *Village Voice*, *New York Magazine*'s Cue section and *Jazz Interactions* news sheet for all the gigs. Jazz remains one of New York City's biggest sounds and the action takes place all over town.

Apollo Theatre, 253 W 125th St, 749-5838, nearest subway stop: 125th St station on 8th Ave line. Historic 1930s jazz cabaret and theatre which featured Duke Ellington, Louis Armstrong and Ella Fitzgerald in its time. Now has shows from $30. Try the famous Wednesday Amateur nights, which gave so many their big break, for $13-$21. Book ahead at Ticketmaster, 307-7171. Look for some of the biggest names in contemporary music to play here. Remember to be careful in Harlem at night.

Cajun, 129 8th Ave at 16th St, 691-6174. Come here for the classic New Orleans sound. Jazz brunch on Sundays, $12, noon-4pm.

Blue Note, 131 W 3rd St, 475-8592. Serves food and hot jazz. 'Small, but attracts some big names.' 'Jazz capital of the world.' Cover charge varies depending on artist, $5 min drink (drinks from $4). *www.bluenote.net*

Greenwich Village Jazz Festival. In Washington Sq. Free. 'Great atmosphere and big names.'

Sweet Basil, 88 7th Ave S, 242-1785. Smallish room with nice atmosphere and pleasant food; attracts the best bands; a steep $17.50 cover, $10 min food & drink.

Village Vanguard, 178 7th Ave S, 255-4037. Sleazy, unkempt, chaotic and cramped; the perfect jazz club, always worth going to, whoever's playing. Sun-Thu $15, Fri-Sat $20, $10 drink min all nights. Mon is Big Band night.

BLUES

Dan Lynch's, 29 St. Mark's Pl. at 2nd Ave, 677-0911. A melting-pot of blues music in an atmospheric, faded dive.

Manny's Car Wash, 1558 3rd Ave at 87th St, 369-2583. Mostly local bands playing upbeat bluesrock. Interior is like *Budweiser* commercial; 45rpm singles, photos and beer signs adorn the walls.

Tramps, 51 W 21st St, 727-7788. The *New York Times* bills it 'the most comfortable and refined place in the city to hear genuine blues.'

ROCK, POP & INDIE

Acme Underground, 9 Great Jones Street, 420-1934. A new and increasingly popular venture, the Acme is the latest haunt of A & R scouts looking for the next big hit. Great bands and good acoustics. Cover $6.

Arlene Grocery, 95 Stanton St, 358-1633. Promotes an assortment of up-and-comers and established stars, always a good scene. No cover.

CBGB's, 315 Bowery at Bleecker, 473-7743. Starts new rock bands off on the route to fame and fortune. Blondie and Talking Heads both had their debuts here. Whilst still infamous, other clubs are now eclipsing its reputation. *www.cbgb.com*

CLUBS

Limelight, 660 6th at 20th St, 807-7850. Get hot and sweaty in a converted church. Popular, mainly techno. Closed Mon. Mon-Thur $15, Fri & Sat $20.

Midsummer Night's Swing, at the Lincoln Center, 546-2656. Take a 6.30pm lesson then dance the night away to the music of a live band, Tue-Sat. Learn to salsa, fox trot, swing or jitterbug, for a bargain $11 pp.

Spy, 101 Greene, 343-9000. More bar than club, Spy is a people-watcher's paradise. Dark, palatial and luxurious, not to mention intimidating—this is the place to see and be seen. Dress in your very best finery if you want to look like you belong! Depending on night, cover charge $10-$12, some nights free.

Webster Hall, 125 E 11th St, 353-1600. Mainstream mega-club with several floors spinning house, hip-hop, '80s and rock 'n' pop. Look out for stilt walkers and trapeze artists.

COUNTRY/WESTERN

Rodeo Bar/Albuquerque Eats, 375 3rd Ave at 27th St, 683-6500. Authentic Southwest cuisine with late night country & western entertainment.

COMEDY

In the past few years, the number of comedy clubs across America has exploded, led by New York City. Since these clubs are popular, call at least a day before to reserve a table and check out prices.

Caroline's, 1626 Broadway btwn 49th & 50th Sts, 956-0101, light snacks, cabaret, two drink minimum. 'The later the set the better the comedy.' *www.carolines.com*

New York Comedy Club, 241 E 24th St at 2nd Ave, 696-5233. Former stomping grounds of Chris Rock and Damon Wayans. Cover $5-$10, 2 drink minimum. Rsvs recommended. *http://members.aol.com/nycomclub*

For more information about comedy clubs in New York—*www.nycomedy.net/clubs*

THEATRE

Broadway prices are high, but tickets go on sale at 25% or 50% off ($2.50 service charge) on the day of performance at the **TKTS** booth, 47th St at Times Sq. 'Be prepared for very long queues.' Wed, Sat matinee sales 10am-2pm, Sun 11am-closing, Mon-Sat evening sales 3pm-8pm. Get there at least 1½ hrs in advance. Discounted same day tickets also available at 2 World Trade Center, where the lines are shorter. Matinee tickets are only sold the day before. (Mon-Fri 11am-5.30pm, Sat 11am-3.30pm) Cash and travellers' cheques are accepted at both booths; credit cards are not. There is also always something interesting happening 'Off-Broadway' and prices are lower. **La MaMa**, 74 E 4th St, 475-7710, and the **Brooklyn Academy of Music (BAM)**, (718) 636-4111, are always good for interesting and experimental theatre. Read the *Village Voice* or *Passport* (available in theatres) for 'Off-off-

Broadway' plays, discounts and the best theatre buys. Keep a look-out in hotels, drugstores, coffee shops, news-stands and Visitors Bureaux in Times Square for 'Two Fers' (two tkts for the price of one). If you hang around outside a show that is not sold out right before it begins you can bargain your way into very cheap theatre seats, but timing is critical. Standing room is often available at the most popular shows.

CINEMA

Movie houses around Times Square and along the Upper East Side start around $8. For both art house and mainstream movies, visit the **Sony Lincoln Square**, 1998 Broadway at 68th St, 336-5000, a lavishly decorated monster of a movie house with twelve screens, plus an eight-storey-high IMAX theatre. Also worth a visit is the enormous screen at the **Ziegfeld**, 141 W 54th St, 765-7600, but for independent films and a more intimate atmosphere, try the **Angelika**, 18 W Houston at Mercer St, 995-2000. There are many other smaller and cheaper neighbourhood cinemas, however. Look them up under 'Other Movies' in the *Village Voice*, or in *Time Out New York*. For a real New York summer experience catch a free Monday night movie at **Bryant Park**, W 42nd St east of 6th Ave, for info call 512-5700. Thousands take picnics and watch old classics under the stars. Pitch your site in the afternoon to be sure of a good view. 'A great atmosphere.' The Park is also a venue for music and dance throughout the summer, call 768-1818.

Info on tickets to TV shows being taped in Manhattan can often be obtained from the Convention and Visitors Bureau in Times Square. Or just call the TV stations.

SHOPPING

Department Stores: **Macy's**, 695-4400 (Broadway at 34th St). New York's biggest; **Bloomingdale's**, 705-2000 (Lexington Ave & 58th St), **Saks 5th Ave**, 753-4000, and **Lord and Taylor**, 391-3344, are the epitome of American style. Try **Century 21**, 227-9092 (22 Cortland St btwn Broadway & Church Sts, near the World Trade Center). Bargain-hunters in the know swing through the revolving doors of this enormous store to find discounts on everything from Armani jeans to Levi's and Chanel No 5. **F.A.O. Schwarz Fifth Ave**, 767 5th Ave at 58th St, 644-9400, opposite the Plaza Hotel. Magical toy store with several storeys of fantasy-fulfilling goods. Where actor Tom Hanks danced on a pavement-sized electric keyboard in *Big*. Worth a visit just to gawk at the amazing Lego and pedal-power Porsches that cost almost as much as the real thing.

Book Stores: **Strand Bookshop**, Broadway & 12th St, 473-1452. Huge second-hand bookstore. **Barnes and Noble**, 33 E 17th St, 253-0810, 675 6th Ave, 727-1227, and on Broadway at 82nd, 362-8835 (and other locations all over the city). The world's biggest book store with almost 13 miles of shelving and reductions on best sellers and others. **Science Fiction Bookshop**, 214 Sullivan St, 473-3010. Stocks virtually every SF book in print. **Rizzoli Books**, 57th St off 5th Ave, 759-2424, beautiful, coffee table books.

Records: **Downstairs Records**, 1026 6th Ave, 354-4684. A great place to look for that lost Deanna Durbin single. **J&R Music World**, 31 Park Row, 238-9000. Enormous stocks of records and tapes. **Venus Records**, at 13 St Mark's Place, 598-4459. 'Good for old records, collector's items. **Tower Records** at 66th St & Broadway, 799-2500, and 4th St and Broadway, 505-1500, and nearby **HMV Superstore** at 72nd & Broadway, 721-5900. The **Virgin Megastore** is at Times Square, 921-1020.

Clothing: **Canal Jean Co**, 226-1130, 504 Broadway at Spring St. Jeans, etc. **Orchard St Market**, Lower East Side, off Canal St, Sun mornings. 'Traditional Jewish street market, lots of bustle and colour.' For **vintage** classics visit **Screaming Mimi's**, 382 Lafayette St, btwn 4th & Great Jones Sts, 677-6464; or **Cheap Jacks**, 841 Broadway, 995-0403. If you yearn for a little designer number, take a look in the **Armani Exchange**, 568 Broadway near Prince St, 431-6000, for his 'diffusion collection'—labels at affordable prices.

Outlets: **Woodbury Commons**, Rte 32, Central Valley, junction of Rte 17 & I-87, Harriman exit. A mind-boggling massive collection of premium outlets, including Levi's, Timberland, Calvin Klein, Gap, J. Crew and every big name designer you can think of—spend a full exhausting day there and you still won't cover it all! For buses from Port Authority, call Shortline Bus Company, 736-4700, from $33 r/t .

Markets: The **Farmer's Market**, in Union Square every summer weekend is a not-to-be-missed experience. Fresh produce, pressed juices, homebaked pies, breads, fruit and flowers—wander amongst the bustling crowds, investigate the stalls and ask to taste, the stall holders are generally very willing. Listen out for interesting street musicians—jazz quartets frequently appear.

Flea Markets: **Annexe Antiques Fair & Flea Market**, 6th Ave, btwn 25th & 26th Sts, 243-5343. Sat & Sun only. For quintessential East Village style on the cheap, try the parking lot at Ave A & 12th St, also on Sat & Sun mornings.

OUT OF DOORS

The Bronx Zoo, properly the New York Zoological Park, Fordham Rd & Southern Blvd, (718) 367-1010. Take the #5 or #2 to E 180th St. Mon-Fri 10am-5pm, Sat-Sun 'til 5.30pm, $7.75, free all day Weds. Shorter hours in winter. New York's biggest zoo. All rides have additional fees. *www.wcs.org/zoos/bronxzoo*

Central Park Zoo, 830 5th Ave at 64th St, north of Plaza Hotel, 861-6030. A compact collection of 100 species, with exquisite rainforest, arctic and other exhibits. The Bronx Zoo has larger wildlife. Mon-Fri 10am-5pm, w/ends 10.30am-5.30pm, $3.50. *www.wcs.org/zoos/wildlifecenters/centralpark*

Central Park offers so much to the visitor and resident alike—a zoo, skating rinks, pools, playgrounds, horse paths, and even a maze garden—that it is impossible to conceive of life in New York without it. Visit the information centre at the **Dairy**, west of the zoo near 64th St, 794-6564, (Tue-Sun 10am-5pm in summer) for an excellent map and orientation to one of the world's great parks. **Belvedere Castle**, 79th St, mid-park, 772-0210, also has information and an unusual view of the park from the ramparts. May-Nov. 'Extremely helpful staff.' *www.centralpark.org*

Prospect Park in Brooklyn. Designed by Olmstead and Vaux, the architects of Central Park, and considered to be their masterpiece. The park features play-grounds, an ice rink, a carousel, and a boathouse along its 60-acre lake. Stand in the 90-acre Long Meadow in the centre of the park and you'll forget you're in New York—building restrictions in the surrounding neighbourhood prohibit tall build-ings. It's also worth taking a stroll around the neighbourhood outside, Park Slope, known for its beautiful brownstones. Take the 2 or 3 train to Grand Army Plaza, the F train to 7th Ave, or the D or Q trains to Prospect Park. *www.prospectpark.org*

Rockefeller Center, 48th & 50th St, btwn 5th & 6th Aves, 632-3975. At Christmas the Rockefeller Plaza has a gigantic, sparkling tree, gossamer angels and a cold bite rising off the ice-rink. In summer it's a place to sit and enjoy the free lunchtime con-certs. Skating from Oct, 332-7654. $7 plus $4 skate hire.

Beaches: Coney Island and **Brighton Beach**, Brooklyn, reached by D Subway—both have interesting Russian communities. **Jones Beach**, by Long Island Railroad from Penn Station to Freeport, then local bus to beach. $14 r/t.

SPORT

Chelsea Piers, W 23rd St on the Hudson River, 336-6666. Sports and entertainment complex incl in-line skating, basketball, roller hockey, soccer, golf range, ice-skating, wall-climbing, shopping, eating, etc. Built in converted historic piers.

Times Up! , 802-8222. Organises several free bicycle and skate tours of the city. Hordes assemble for their guided tour of Wall St area sights on summer evenings. *www.times-up.org*

Pro-Sports NY, 987 8th Ave, 397-6208. In-line skate rentals close to Central Park, $16 all day. Daily 9.30am-8pm.

Skating: Blades, Boards & Skate, 120 W 72nd St, 787-3911 (and other locations). In-line skates $16 all day.

Skate Patrol, 439-1234. In-line skating classes in Central Park, Blades West, 120 W 72nd St. First and third weekend of every month, except holiday weekends. $20 pp. rsvs recommended. *www.skatepatrol.org*

Wollman Ice Rink, Central Park, 396-1010. Oct-April, ice-skating all day $7.50, skate-hire $3.50. Open in the summer for in-line skating, $4, skate-hire $6. Ask about lessons.

Wollman Center and Rink, Prospect Park, Brooklyn (718) 287-6431. Nov-March, $4, skate-hire $3.50.

Roller-Hockey, St Catherine's Park, 68th St btwn 1st & 2nd Aves, all are welcome on weekend mornings, whether you want to watch or play in a pick-up game.

Spectator sports: Baseball in summer: the Mets at Shea Stadium in Queens, the Yankees at Yankee Stadium in the Bronx. **Basketball**: the Knicks at Madison Square Garden, the NJ Nets across the Hudson in the Meadowlands. The Islanders **ice hockey** team plays at the Coliseum, Uniondale on Long Island, and the Rangers skate in Madison Square Garden. For **tennis** devotees, the US Open takes place at Flushing Meadows in Queens in early September. The Jets and Giants **American football** teams play at the Meadowlands in New Jersey.

INFORMATION

New York City Convention and Visitors Bureau, btwn 52nd & 53rd Sts on 7th Ave, 484-1222. Mon-Fri 8.30am-6pm, w/ends 9am-5pm. Free maps, list of tourist attractions, pamphlets with walking tours of the city. *www.nycvisit.com*

Times Square Visitors Center, 768-1560, 1560 Broadway btwn 46th and 47th Sts. Daily 8am-8pm, free tours of Times Square at noon on Fridays. *www.timessquarebid.org.*

Traveler's Aid, (718) 656-4870, JFK Airport LAB Terminal 2nd floor.   Mon-Thu 9am-7pm, Fri 10am-6pm, Sat 11am-6pm, Sun noon-6pm.

Post Offices: there are dozens around the city but the major ones are, 8th Ave at 33rd St (24 hrs), 340 W 42nd St, Lexington Ave & E 45th St, in Macy's, Herald Square, beneath Rockefeller Center (enter at 620 or 610 5th Ave), and 62nd St & Broadway.

INTERNET ACCESS

Internet Cafe, 82 E 3rd St btwn 1st and 2nd Aves, 614-0747. $10/hr Internet access along w/live jazz and films. *www.bigmagic.com*

Mid-Manhattan Library, 455 5th Ave at 40th St, 340-0818. Free Internet use, half hour time limit.

TRANSPORTATION WITHIN MANHATTAN

Subways: One of the largest and most complex subway systems in the world—714 miles of track and 468 stations, the subway is one of the quickest, cheapest ways to get around NYC and contrary to popular belief, generally safe. The information/ticket booth in every station, distributes a useful leaflet called *Manhattan Transit*. It has maps, instructions on using the subway/buses and a guide on how to reach major tourist attractions. For travel info call Transit Authority at (718) 330-1234, 24 hrs daily. Basic fare: $1.50. Buy tokens or MetroCards (an automated fare card, allows free transfers to local buses) at the kiosk or vending machines near the turnstiles. MetroCards are also sold in many area stores. There are various options for unlimited travel on the subway and local buses, all of which include free transfers: The Fun Pass, $4, is good for one day; or you can buy the 7-Day MetroCard, $17, or 30-Day MetroCard, $63. You may also buy a pay-per-ride MetroCard, pay for 10 rides and get one free (pay $15 and the 10% bonus is automatically added). There are express and local trains; it is very important to know which you have to take to reach your destination. Since the whole system is very badly marked, alertness and a venturesome spirit are prerequisites. Women alone should avoid using the subway at night. 'Off-hour waiting areas,' visible to the clerks at all times, are marked by yellow signs which usually hang from the ceiling. There are information centres at Penn Station, Grand Central Station and Port Authority. **PATH** trains link several subway stops with points in New Jersey, fare $1.

Buses: (718) 330-1234. 4100 blue and white buses will take you to just about anywhere within the five boroughs. Fare: $1.50 in exact change (no bills or pennies), token or MetroCard. Free transfers available. Exit buses from rear doors only.

Taxis: Only ride in the bright yellow taxis, others are impostors. 'Insist that the meter is put on, "private deals" don't work.' Learn the meaning of fear, as your certified driver squeezes the cab between two buses at 45mph. Always tip the driver 15 percent, if you arrive alive. Expensive for one, but for three or four, economical over short distances.

ARRIVING IN/LEAVING MANHATTAN

Buses : All inter-city bus lines, including Greyhound, (800) 231-2222, use the Port Authority Bus Terminal, 8th Ave & 41st St. Arrive at least one hour early to purchase tickets. It's worth shopping around, cheaper and faster travel can sometimes be found with Peter Pan/Trailways, (800) 237-8747. Ask at information desk on street-level floor if confused about where to go—don't accept offers of help or directions from 'friendly' strangers who sidle up as you walk through the door unless you want hassle. Most will expect a tip for showing you the way and can be offensive if you say no. Though the building is new, the inhabitants late at night are a bit run down. Be careful.

Green Tortoise, (800) 227-4766. 14 day bus trips Westbound to SF, LA for $349-$389 plus $111-$121 for food. May-Oct. See p. 32 for more details. *www.greentortoise.com*

Trains: Penn Station, 33rd St & 8th Ave, under Madison Sq Garden. Amtrak service, (800) 872-7245, between Boston, Washington, Chicago and further south and west, as well as north towards Montréal and Toronto. Also Long Island Railroad, (718) 217-5477, and PATH, (800) 234-7284, which operates in Manhattan and New Jersey, fare $1. New Jersey Transit trains, (201) 7625100, can take you to Princeton and Philadelphia.

Grand Central Station, 42nd St & Park Ave. Handles Metro-North Commuter Railroad (532-4900) to NY suburbs and Connecticut

Car Rental: Difficult if you're under 25, or don't have a major credit card. Try bargaining and arguing. See *Yellow Pages* for companies. Thrifty, National and Rent-a-Wreck among the cheapest. 'Most companies want driver to have licence and credit card with a sufficiently large credit limit; they won't allow splitting the cost between several people. Cash is generally useless except at international airports in conjunction with a passport.'

Car Driveaways: Automobile transporting companies come and go quickly, check *Yellow Pages* for details. For **maps** try the Rand McNally Map Store, 150 E 52nd St btwn Lexington & 3rd Aves, 758-7488, or AAA, 1881 Broadway at 62nd St, 586-1166.

Car Rides. For rides with college students, check the bulletin boards at NYU, Loeb Center, Washington Sq, or at the Columbia University Bookshop, near Columbia U. Hitchhiking is illegal on major roads in New York State, discouraged by police and highly dangerous. Single men or women absolutely mustn't do it.

J. F. Kennedy Airport, (718) 244-4444. Allow at least 1½ hrs travel. The cheapest way: subway to Howard Beach, $1.50, then free shuttle bus to airport terminals. Otherwise: take the E/F subway trains to Union Turnpike/Kew Gardens, then catch the Q10 bus to JFK. Total cost $1.50 with MetroCard bus transfer, (718) 995-4700 for info. You can also take the Long Island Railroad train from Penn Station to Jamaica, $5.50, then the NY Airport Service bus (718) 706-9658, $5. Another quick, easy way: NY Airport Service bus $13, $6 w/student ID, o/w from

125 Park Ave near Grand Central Station and from Port Authority to JFK/La Guardia. For general info on transportation to New York airports: (800) AIR-RIDE. **LaGuardia Airport**, (718) 533-3400. Allow at least 1 hr travel. The cheapest way in and out: Q47 or Q33 bus to Roosevelt Ave/Jackson Heights subway station, then E train to Manhattan. Easier: NY Airport Service bus—$10, $6 w/student ID, to 125 Park Ave near Grand Central Station and Port Authority. Also, bus M60 from 116th St and Broadway or 125th St direct for $1.50.

Newark Airport, (973) 961-6000. Allow at least 1 hr travel. Olympia Airport Express to Penn Station, Grand Central Station, World Trade Center at West St, or Port Authority, $10. (212) 964-6233. Or, take the NJ Transit train from Penn Sta ($2.50) to Penn, Sta, Newark and from there catch the airport shuttle bus ($4).

LONG ISLAND 'The Island,' as New Yorkers call it, is a 150-mile-long glacial moraine, the terminal line of the last encroachment of the Ice Age. Extending eastwards from Manhattan, it includes the New York City boroughs Brooklyn and Queens, and the built-up suburban county of Nassau, though more than half its length is occupied by the more rural county of Suffolk.

Long Island Sound quietly laps against its North Shore where hills, headlands, fields and woods have been home to some of America's rich and famous. F. Scott Fitzgerald's Gatsby partied here, and **Sagamore Hill**, 922-4788, outside of Glen Cove, Nassau, was the home of President Theodore Roosevelt. You may take a tour of what Roosevelt described as "that nook of old-time America" for $5. In **Huntington**, further east, poet Walt Whitman spent his childhood (you can visit the house, 246 Old Walt Whitman Rd, 427-5240, hours vary, tours $3, $2 w/student ID) and, nearby, the Vanderbilts had an estate which they connected to New York City with their own private motorway.

The South Shore, protected by Fire Island, receives a surprisingly gentle Atlantic breeze. The beaches here are generally flat and sandy. Except right out at the **Hamptons** (Southampton and East Hampton), this shoreline has always been less exclusive than the North Shore. Its magnificent beaches stretch in a virtually unbroken line 100 miles out from the city, attracting throngs of tourists.

All areas of Long Island are easily accessible from Manhattan via the Long Island Railroad from Penn Station, or via the Northern State and Southern State Parkways, and the Long Island Expressway, which at the city end is so often jammed with traffic that it's known as 'the longest parking lot in the world.' Eventually, though, it sweeps beyond the pandemonium towards the remoteness of Montauk Point's majestic lighthouse.

Long Island is fraught with social experiments, and **Jones Beach** is one of the nicest of them. With millions unemployed during the Depression, President Franklin Roosevelt found work for many and fun for more by developing this four-mile stretch of the South Shore into an excellent sandy beach. On a hot summer's weekend, especially the 4th of July, up to half a million people and their cars join the seagulls for a good splash in the sun and water. Go there during the week if you want more of the beach to yourself. The Long Island Railroad, (718) 217-5477/(516) 822-LIRR, offers train/bus service between the beach, at Freeport Station, and Manhattan, $14 r/t.

Fire Island, on a long sandbar further east than Jones Beach, is nicer yet. Not so much developed as preserved for its natural beauty and bird life, the

AMERICA'S AMAZING THEME PARKS

America's incredible amusement parks have evolved from trolley company-sponsored carnivals, a ploy to attract passengers, to today's megaparks that entertain over 129 million visitors annually in hundreds of versions of derring-do, spine-tingling, and otherwise. The thrill rides you'll find here have an all-American spirit, though the concept of coasters themselves has its roots in eastern Europe. The first "coasters" were, in fact, ice-covered slides built for winter amusement in 15th century Russia. Coasters evolved, and eventually arrived in America, making quite an impact. If you're looking for modern-day thrills, try these:

THEME PARKS: Coney Island, New York City, (718) 372-0275. Indulge in nostalgia, of the sort featured in Woody Allen's *Radio Days* and countless other films. Ride the *Cyclone*— one of the most revered coasters of all time. **Hershey Park**, Hershey PA (717) 534-3900. Besides 7 roller coasters and 6 water rides, this park features a tour of Hershey's Chocolate World, along with free samples. **DisneyWorld**, Orlando, FL, (407) 824-4321. The largest and most visited in America features Epcot Center, Magic Kingdom, Animal Kingdom, Typhoon Lagoon and Blizzard Beach water parks and Pleasure Island night-club extravaganza. **MGM Studios** is nearby, (407) 824-4321, currently featuring the *Indiana Jones Epic Stunt Spectacular, Fantasmic!, Backstage Pass to 101 Dalmations*, and *Twilight Zone Tower of Terror*. **Disneyland**, Anaheim, CA, (714) 781-4000. The original Disney park and 2nd most visited, includes Space Mountain roller coaster and *Star Tours* ('a ride to the Moon of Endor'). **Universal Studios Florida** (407) 363-8000. The Orlando branch has 444 acres of rides, shows and attractions from the movie world. Virtual reality rides include *Back to the Future, ET* and *Kongfrontation*. There's also an *Alfred Hitchcock—the art of making movies* show. **Universal Studios Hollywood** (818) 622-3801, a smaller version of Universal Studios Florida.

ROLLER COASTER PARKS: The fastest, highest and biggest US roller coasters are in the flat Midwest. Among the most well-known: **Paramount's Kings Island**, Mason OH, (513) 754-5800 / (800) 288-0808. Eight banked turns and 70mph speeds make the wooden roller coaster *The Beast* the world's longest with 7400ft of tracks (lasting a death-defying 3mins 40secs). Their *King Cobra*, a stand-up looping coaster, is described as 'the ultimate elevator nightmare in forward motion.' The *Racer*, built in 1972, launched a renaissance of newer, taller, faster coasters. The park is sometimes hired out to private groups so call ahead to check if open. Even more terrifying, according to the *New York Times*, is the *Magnum XL-200* at **Cedar Point**, Sandusky OH, (419) 627-2350. This coaster climbs 20 storeys only to hurtle down a 60-degree drop with curves at 70mph. Cedar Point's most recent addition is *Snake River Falls*. With 80ft drops at 50 degree angles, this is the world's tallest, steepest and fastest water-ride. For true rush-junkies, there is also the horrifying 65mph *Meanstreak*. **Paramount's King's Dominion**, Richmond VA (804) 876-5000, is home to the *Anaconda*, the only looping roller coaster in the world that showcases an underwater tunnel, and the new *Volcano, the Black Coaster* ride, which shoots you straight out of a raging volcano. **Six Flags America**, Largo MD (301) 249-1500, a theme park and water park, features the *Mind Eraser*, 2 minutes of rollovers and spins, plus an intense corkscrew sequence following an inverted loop. **Six Flags Great America**, Gurnee IL (847) 249-1776, offers the double-track triple helix wooden *American Eagle* which reaches speeds of over 66 mph; *Batman*, a 2 min suspended outside looping thrill-of-a-lifetime; and the triple looping *Steel Shockwave*. **Six Flags over Mid-America**, St. Louis MO, (314) 938-5300 features the *Ninja*, which has spirals, drops, a sidewinder and 360 degree loop. **Worlds of Fun** (and Oceans of Fun water park next-door), Kansas City MO, (816) 454-4545, has two equally thrilling coasters. The *Timber Wolf* is faster but the *Orient Express* has twists and coils and even doubles back on itself. In the south, **Six Flags over Texas** in Arlington, (817) 530-6000, features *Flashback*, a sky coaster that zips you forward and backwards in corkscrew spirals. The *Shock Wave* boasts its ability to cause some riders to black out during its intense, double-loop filled segment. The *Texas Giant* drops 137 ft at 62 mph and is second in size only to the 166 ft drop *Rattler* at **Fiesta Texas**, San Antonio (210) 697-5050. At **Six Flags Houston**, TX, (713) 799-1234, try the *Texas Cyclone*, a long-time favourite, and the *Ultra Twister*, once compared to 'riding inside a giant slinky, with a 9-storey free-fall to start.' Their new *Serial Thriller* tears through seven inversions at up to 55 mph. At **Six Flags over Georgia** near Atlanta, (770) 739-3400, the *Free Fall* slowly climbs 10 storeys only then descends at 50 mph. Here also is North America's first triple-loop roller coaster, the *Mind Bender*. **Six Flags Magic Mountain**, Valencia, CA, (661) 255-4111, where the world's largest looping roller coaster, the *Viper*, reaches 70 mph and achieves 7 inversions. 'The initial drop is truly heart-stopping!' 'They even have cameras mounted on the cars.' Other rides include the latest addition, *Superman—the Escape*, the first coaster to reach 100mph, necessitating a drop of 41 storeys! Also try the *Colossus*, one of the largest double-track, wooden coasters in the world; and the *Revolution*, whose track threads through tunnels. 'A knee-wobbling experience.' For still more thrills *www.yahoo.com/Entertainment/Amusemgnt_and_Theme_Parks*.

WATER PARKS: Of growing popularity and ingenuity, especially in the warmer states, are America's 136 water parks. In Florida, **Typhoon Lagoon** in Orlando, (407) 560-4141 has the largest wave pool in the US; **Adventure Island**, Tampa, (813) 987-5660 is home of the *Tampa Typhoon*, a slide that shoots down from a height of seven storeys. **Waterworld's** *Thunder Bay*, in Denver CO, (303) 427-7873, releases mammoth waves. **Water Country USA**, Williamsburg VA, (800) 858-0844, boasts *The Rampage*, a nearly-vertical water slide of 75 ft. On the *Jet Scream* flume stay up to 25 mph as you round a curve—on your back. Or shoot through the *Malibu Pipeline*, a flume ride through a dark tunnel over 3 storeys high. **Wet 'n Wild** parks, located in Orlando FL, (407) 351-3200 and Las Vegas NV, (702) 734-0088, as well as **Six Flags Hurricane Harbor** in Dallas TX, (817) 265-3356 all feature fast, helical rides on water mats and sensational 7-storey free falls. Explore Wild Rivers Mountain, with 25 water rides, at **Wild Rivers**, Irvine CA, (949) 768-9453.

Check out *www.ultimaterollercoaster.com* for info on practically every roller coaster and theme park in the country.

area has been designated a National Seashore run by the National Park Service. This is an excellent place for swimming, surfing, sunbathing, fishing, cooking over an open grill and getting up to no good in the sand dunes. Take Long Island Railroad to Bay Shore, $19 r/t, then ferry, 665-3600 to Ocean Beach, $11.50 r/t.

Facing the calm waters of Gardiners Bay, **Sag Harbor**, once a whaling port, is now a pleasant town where John Steinbeck chose to end his days, and where those wealthy enough to own sailing boats moor them. The **Sag Harbor Whaling Museum**, 725-0770, is on Main St. Mon-Sat 10am-5pm, Sun 1pm-5pm, $3.

There are in fact several such salty and tranquil spots at the end of the island, as well as an Indian Reservation. A few days wandering is well worth it. For more info—*www.nps.gov/fiis*

Many of the place names on Long Island derive from the Indians who once lived here fishing, planting or hunting deer: the Wantaghs, Patchogues and Montauks were a few of the tribes. **Montauk Point** marks the eastern extremity of Long Island where a towering lighthouse, 668-2544, built in 1792 by order of George Washington, looks over three sides of water and offers magnificent views of the rising sun.

Curiously enough, the oldest cattle ranch in the United States is also located out here: Deep Hollow Ranch in Montauk, 668-2744, where visitors can go horseback riding. 'Birthplace of the American cowboy.'
The telephone area code is 516.

INFORMATION
Long Island Convention and Visitors Bureau, 951-3440/(800) 441-4601. Offer a comprehensive, free Long Island travel guide and have information centres on the Southern State Pkwy btwn exits 13 & 14 and on Long Island Expressway btwn exits 52 & 53.

ACCOMMODATION
Camping: There are vast campsites scattered around the State Parks in Long Island. All advise rsvs at w/ends during the summer, tent sites $13. **Wildwood State Park**, 929-4314. Campsite on Long Island Sound with path to the beach. Picnic area, baseball/volleyball courts. By train, take Long Island Railroad to River Head Station, catch a bus, 766-6722, to the campsite. Rsvs (800) 456-CAMP.

HUDSON RIVER VALLEY   Though not the key to the Northwest Passage that many early explorers hoped it would be, the Hudson has gouged a considerable valley from the mountains of upstate New York past the chalk cliffs of the Palisades to the granite slab of Manhattan, and onwards even from there, forming a great underwater trench several hundred miles long out to the edge of the continental shelf.

Much of the scenery along the valley is very beautiful and contains several historical towns such as **Tarrytown**, **West Point**, **Hyde Park** and **Ossining**, home of electrifying **Sing Sing State Prison**.

About 16 miles north of the George Washington Bridge on the eastern side of the Hudson, **Tarrytown** was the home of Rip Van Winkle creator Washington Irving and the model for his story *The Legend of Sleepy Hollow*. His books, manuscripts and furniture are still here, in his house, **Sunnyside**, on West Sunnyside Lane, (914) 591-8763. The creeper-covered, white brick cottage is open to visitors Apr-Dec, Wed-Mon 10am-5pm. Both Irving and Andrew Carnegie, the American Steel magnate, are buried in Sleepy Hollow Cemetery. Also worth a visit are two restored (with Rockefeller money) Dutch colonial manors, the **Philipsburg** and **Van Cortlandt Manors**. The Philipsburg Manor has a working gristmill. Entrance to Sunnyside and each of the manors is $8. For information call (914) 631-8200, or look up *www.hudsonvalley.org*.

If your feet can't take any more punishment then **NY Waterway**, (800) 533-3779, offer a 1 hr cruise along the Hudson River, departing from Tarrytown ferry dock on W Main St, May-Oct Sat-Sun at 10.30am, $15. They also offer all-day excursions to Sleepy Hollow from New York City.

West Point is the site of the US Military Academy, founded in 1802 to train military officers. The Academy is the alma mater of such architects of victory as Robert E Lee, General Custer and William (Sue the Media) Westmoreland. Visitor Center, 938-2638, Mon-Sat 10am-3.30pm, Sun 11am-3.30pm, 1 hr guided tours, $6.

If you like brass bands and cadets walking in straight lines, this is the place for you. Museum and grounds open daily. Parade schedules can be obtained by calling the information officer at 938-2638. Close by is the 5000-acre **Bear Mountain State Park**, good for camping and hiking. Park office, 446-4736, Beaver Pond Campground 947-2792, tent sites $13, $8 registration fee, rsvs recommended.

Hyde Park, a small village 80 miles north of New York City, lies on scenic Rte 9 overlooking the Hudson River. It was the home of President Franklin D Roosevelt and both he and Eleanor lie buried in the Rose Garden of the **FDR Library and Museum,** 229-8114. Nearby is the **Frederick W Vanderbilt Mansion**, a Beaux-Arts-style house set in 600 glorious acres, formerly country retreat of the industrialist/philanthropist Vanderbilt. See how the big-time millionaires lived, daily 9am-5pm, $8. For information call (914) 229-9115. **Hyde Park Trail**, 229-9115 is an 8.5 mile hiking trail which snakes along the banks of the Hudson River, linking historic sites such as the Roosevelt Home and the Vanderbilt Mansion.

About 18 miles to the west of Hyde Park lies the small town of **New Paltz**, an excellent starting point for a trip to **Minnewaska State Park,** 255-0752. The park offers two lakes for swimming and several hiking trails with excellent views of the Shawangunk Mountains.

Just a little further up the Hudson is the quaintish, stockade city of **Kingston**, founded as a Dutch trading post in 1614. In 1777 it became the first state capital and you can visit the restored **Senate House**, 338-2786, on Fair St, where the senators met before fleeing for their lives in the face of a British attack. April-Oct Wed-Sat 10am-5pm, Sun 1pm-5pm, $3. There are several Colonial buildings in the area, including the Old Dutch Church on Main St.

Woodstock, a magic name from the 1960s, is nearby off Rte 28. Many an ageing hippie can be seen making a nostalgic pilgrimage to the village which came to symbolise the Age of Aquarius youth movement after the rock concert to end all concerts in 1969. Imagine their surprise upon learning that the festival was actually held 57 miles south on Rte 17-B in the town of Bethel! Promoters intended to hold the festival in Woodstock but as its popularity grew they were forced to move it to a more spacious location. Today Woodstock is, as it has long been, an arts colony with lots of boutiques and summertime craft and theatrical festivals. Call the **Woodstock Chamber of Commerce,** 679-6234, for more info.

The **Catskill Mountains,** just to the west of Kingston, is an area of hills, streams, hiking paths and ski trails, and is reputedly the spot where Rip Van Winkle dozed off for 20 years. The Catskills used to be the place where wealthy New Yorkers took their holidays and there is just a touch of decay and nostalgia at the resorts, an air of having seen better days. The resorts still operate, catering to a more Eastern European Jewish clientele, hence the nickname for the area, the Borscht Belt. The area remains a marvellous retreat for walking and getting away from it all. **Catskills Regional Tourist Office,** (800) NYS-CATS.
The telephone area code is 914.

ALBANY   Capital of the State of New York and named after the Duke of York and Albany who later became James II of England. Not the greatest place for the casual visitor but downtown does have some interesting architecture in the shape of the **Rockefeller Empire State Plaza,** a massive shopping, office and cultural complex that cost a billion dollars to build.

Situated near the juncture of the Hudson and Mohawk Rivers, and on a line with the boundary between western Massachusetts and southern Vermont, the city is a convenient halting place before visiting these states, or before exploring the local New York attractions of Saratoga, Lake George and Ticonderoga, the Adirondacks and Ausable Chasm.
The telephone area code is 518.

ACCOMMODATION

The most inexpensive accommodation during the summer is likely to be at the residence halls of the **College of St Rose,** 454-5171. Call ahead to see if a room is available.

Ramada Inn, 300 Broadway, (800) 272-6232/(518) 434-4111. Prices vary by day, $62-$88, includes full bfast. Pool, TV. Conveniently located in downtown. 'Will pick up from Amtrak.' 'Quoted one price over the phone and a more expensive one when we got there.'

Pine Haven B&B, 531 Western Ave, 482-1574. Family run Victorian house in safe neighbourhood. S-$49, D-$64. Singles for $29 w/AYH card. 'Friendly; excellent breakfast!'

YMCA, 13 State St and Connecticut, 374-9136. Men only. $23.50, $60 weekly, plus $10 key deposit.

OF INTEREST

Albany Institute of History and Art, 125 Washington Ave, 463-4478. Oldest museum in the state, some say the country. Dutch period and Hudson River School landscape paintings, 18th and 19th century furniture, etc. The museum itself is closed for renovation until spring of 2001, but a smaller satellite site has been opened at 63 State St. Mon-Fri 11am-6pm, free.

Gov. Nelson A. Rockefeller Empire State Plaza, btwn Madison & State Sts, centre of town. 12-building complex housing 30 state agencies and cultural facilities. The most striking feature of this ultra-brute-modern affair is the 44-storey state office tower with **observation deck** up top, panoramas 10am-3.45pm, free.

New York State Museum, Empire State Plaza, 474-5877. Geology, history, Indians and natural history. In the New York Metropolis Hall is a vast display of the NYC urbanisation process, including a 1940 subway car, 1929 Yellow Cab, 1930 Chinatown import-export shop and mock-up of Sesame Street stage set. Daily 10am-5pm. Free. 'Superb.'

Schuyler Mansion State Historic Site, 32 Catherine St, 434-0834. Built in 1762, home of Gen. Philip Schuyler, revolutionary luminary. Gentleman Johnny Burgoyne was a prisoner and Schuyler's daughter Betsy married Alexander Hamilton here. Tours $3, April-Oct Wed-Sat 10am-5pm, Sun 1pm-5pm.

State Capitol, northern end of Empire State Plaza, 474-2418. Free 1 hr tours daily at 10am, noon, 2pm, and 3pm. Begun in 1867, the building includes the Million Dollar Staircase. The stone carvers of the staircase reproduced in stone not only the famous, but also their family and friends. Also Senate and Assembly Chamber. Free.

INFORMATION
Albany County Visitors Center, 25 Quackenbush Sq, (800) 258-3582/(518) 434-0405. Mon-Fri 9am-4pm, Sat-Sun 10am-4pm.

Visitors Assistance, #106 on the Concourse, Empire State Plaza, 474-2418, 8.30am-5.30pm daily. Has information of free events taking place in the plaza.

Chamber of Commerce, 107 Washington Ave, 434-1214. Mon-Fri 9am-5pm.

TRAVEL
Greyhound, 34 Hamilton St, 434-8095/(800) 231-2222.

Amtrak, Albany-Rensselaer station, East St, (800) 872-7245/462-5763. The scenic *Adirondack* train passes through btwn NYC & Montréal.

SARATOGA SPRINGS About 30 miles north of Albany, this favourite resort with its mineral springs bears a Mohawk name meaning 'place of swift water.' The waters, high in mineral content, are on tap at the Spa State Park. Abraham Lincoln's son, Bob, came here to celebrate his graduation from Harvard and found a town agog with its new racecourse. Now the nation's oldest thoroughbred racing track, the **Saratoga Race Course**, 584-6200, (called America's Ascot when it opened 100 years ago) runs races every August. The **National Museum of Racing**, 584-0400, is located in town on Union Ave and Ludlow St. During August, accommodation is therefore more expensive and less available than at other times of the year. However, the **Saratoga Downtowner**, 413 Broadway, 584-6160, is a good deal D-$79, $155 in summer, includes bfast. Pool. Read Damon Runyon's short stories before you go.

Saratoga Springs is also the summer home of the **New York City Ballet** in July, the **Philadelphia Orchestra** in August, and various transient rock and roll bands, all of which play at the outdoor **Saratoga Performing Arts Center**, 584-9330. Lawn seats cost $12-$30, depending on event. The Arts Center also hosts the **Saratoga Jazz Festival** in June. *www.spac.org*

Saratoga claims to have more restaurants per capita than any other American town, so finding good food won't be hard. Finding cheap food may be harder, so to savour the essence of Saratoga cuisine, buy a bag of crisps called *Saratoga Chips*, which were invented here 100 years ago.

Saratoga City Chamber of Commerce, (800) 526-8970, Mon-Fri 9am-5pm. *The telephone area code is 518.*

LAKE GEORGE Another 25 miles north of Saratoga Springs is the town of Lake George and the lake itself, running to Fort Ticonderoga where it constricts before opening out again as Lake Champlain.

Lake George is billed as the resort area with 'a million dollar beach,' but that refers less to the shore's quality and more to how much it probably costs to clean the place up after the tourist hordes have been by. Best to keep going through the area and on to the Adirondack Park.

Fort Ticonderoga at the other end of the lake is accessible by road or by boat from Lake George town, and is of interest to those who would know the methods by which the British Empire grew great. Constructed by the French in 1755, the British waited just long enough for it to be made comfortable before taking it over in 1756. Perhaps requiring some repairs to be made, the British then let rebel Ethan Allen grab it in 1775, and when suitable again for officers and gentlemen, Burgoyne took it back in 1777. The Yanks got the place in the end and now conduct guided tours for $10, $8 w/student ID. Includes the museum and displays inside the fort where 'non-stop action' is promised all summer. Call 585-2821 for information. Daily 9am-6pm mid-May to mid-Oct. There is a car ferry service from Ticonderoga to Vermont.

The telephone area code is 518.

THE ADIRONDACKS /This 108 year old state park encompasses the year round resort area of the Adirondack Mountains, an enormous expanse of mountains (including the state's highest peak, Mt. Marcy at 5344 ft), forests and lakes stretching thousands of square miles west of Lakes George and Champlain.

Lake Placid is the sporting centre of the area and hosted the original Winter Olympics in 1932. The games came back in 1980 and left behind an Olympic ski-jump platform which still offers the best view of the area. Call 523-2202, daily 9am-4pm, $8. The landscape, with cross-country and downhill ski trails, large lakes and chairlifts is equally suitable for summer and winter excursions. 'Worth it for the view alone.' **Lake Placid Visitor Center**, (800) 447-5224, Mon-Fri 10am-6pm, w/ends 10am-4pm. *www.lakeplacid.com*

Angling fanatics can obtain **fishing licences** for the river from the Town Hall on Main St (523-2162), or in local stores. $11 day pass $20 five days, $35 season pass. **Adirondacks Regional Information**, (800) 648-5239. Mon-Fri 8am-5pm.

The telephone area code is 518.

ACCOMMODATION
Lake Placid is generally expensive. These are the best deals:
Hotel St Moritz, 31 Saranac Ave, 523-9240. D-$39 mid-week, $50 w/end, XP-$10, includes bfast.
Northway Motel, 5 Wilmington Rd, across from junction of Rts 73 & 86, 523-3500. S-$50, D-$68-$80.

OF INTEREST
Ausable Chasm, 834-7454, on the western shores of Lake Champlain where the Ausable River has cut a vast canyon through the rock The tour by foot, raft and return bus costs $19. Available mid-May-mid-Oct, daily 9.30am-5pm. 'Not worth the effort. Big tourist trap full of little English grannies.'
Blue Mountain Lake, about 40 miles south-west of Lake Placid en route to Utica and Syracuse. Lake and mountain scenery, and the **Adirondack Museum**, 1 mile north, 352-7311. Shows life in the Adirondacks since colonial times, with 1890 private railroad car, log hotel, 1932 Winter Olympics memorabilia. May-Oct, daily

9.30am-5.30pm, $10. 'Allow 4 hrs to see it all.' 'Excellent.' Lake Placid: **John Brown Farm State Historic Site**, 2 miles out of town on Rte 73; 523-3900. This is where he lies a'mouldering in the grave (see Harper's Ferry, West Virginia). Summer: Wed-Sat 10am-5pm, Sun 1pm-5pm, free.

THE FINGER LAKES   These slender lakes splay like the fingers of an open hand across midwestern New York. Their names—Canandaigua, Seneca, Cayuga, Owasco and Skaneateles—still speak of the Indian legend that the lakes are the impress of the Great Spirit who here laid his hand upon the earth.

The region is the oldest wine-producing district in the East and offers plenty of opportunities to sample the local product. The **Cayuga Wine Trail** will take you on a tipsy tour through 8 vineyards which sit on the lake's edge. Call the **Finger Lakes Association**, (800) 548-4386, Mon-Fri 8am-4pm, for this and other tourist information.

En route be sure to pitch up to the **National Baseball Hall of Fame** in the pleasant summer resort of **Cooperstown**. The Hall of Fame is open May-Sept 9am-9pm, 9am-5pm the rest of the year. (607) 547-7200, $9.50. *www.cooperstown.net*

Syracuse, to the east of the Finger Lakes, was the site Chief Hiawatha chose about 1570 as the capital for the Iroquois Confederacy. Around the council fires of the longhouse met the Five Nations which for two centuries dominated north-eastern North America. Salt first brought the Indians and later the French and Americans to the shores of Lake Onondaga. Syracuse was founded in 1805 and for many years most of the salt used in America came from here. The New York State Fair is held annually in Syracuse from late August through Labor Day. Well-regarded **Syracuse University** was founded here in 1870. **Downing International Hostel, AYH**, 535 Oak St, (315) 472-5788. $12 AYH, $15 non-AYH, linen $1, towels $.50. Check-in Sun-Thur 5pm-10pm, Fri & Sat 'til 11pm. Rsvs recommended. 'Arrive early.'

ITHACA   As the bumper sticker saying goes 'Ithaca is gorges'. Situated at the southern end of **Cayuga Lake**, Ithaca has within its boundaries many deep river gorges and spectacular waterfalls as well as hills that rival those of San Francisco in their steepness.

Perched high atop a hill overlooking Cayuga Lake is Ivy-Leaguer **Cornell University** (on a campus considered by many to be the most beautiful in the US) and also in town is well-regarded liberal arts **Ithaca College**. This high concentration of students (24,000 or so) make the campus and town a fun, lively place to visit.
The telephone area code is 607.

ACCOMMODATION
Elmshade Guest House, 402 S Olbany St, 273-1707. S-$35, D-$45-$50. Includes bfast.
Hillside Inn, 518 Stewart Ave, 272-9507, S-$40-$45, D-$55-$65. AC, TV, continental bfast. Rsvs recommended.
Super 8 Motel, 400 S Meadow St, 273-8088. D-$60-$80.
Camping: Buttermilk Falls State Park, 273-5761, 1 mile south on Rte 13, $15.50 first night, $13 extra nights. Rsvs on (800) 456-2267.

FOOD/ENTERTAINMENT
Cornell is reputed to have the best campus food in the US. **The Ivy Room**, **Willard**

Straight Hall, is open to all, term-time only. Cornell also makes its own ice cream. The **Collegetown area** on the edge of campus is also good for eating and is the place to be when the sun goes down. Try **The Nines**, 311 College Ave, 272-1888, for live bands, beer and cheap pizza and **Collegetown Bagels**, 415 College Ave, 273-0982, for 'cheap, yummy bagels'. Big student hang-out.

Ithaca Commons downtown has various inexpensive eateries and student bars, recommended is **The Haunt**, 275-3447, with live music on Sat.

Hal's Delicatessen, 115 N Aurora St, 273-7765. Old fashioned, but cheap, filling sandwiches ($4) etc. 'Well fed for $5.'

Moosewood Restaurant, Seneca & Cayuga Sts, 273-9610. Famous vegetarian restaurant. The owners have written several very popular vegetarian cookbooks to be found on the kitchen shelf of every self-respecting college student. Lunch $5-$7.50, dinner $11-$15.

OF INTEREST

Hiking and biking are the ways to get around the area. There is a 30-mile hiking trail which loops around Ithaca and this may be a good way to start.

Cornell University: On the north-east side of town and can be reached by local bus from downtown. Take a guided tour (255-2000) or just wander. Climb the **McGraw Tower** (162 steps) for a glorious view of the lake and hills. Further vistas can be had from the **Herbert F. Johnson Museum of Art**, University and Central Aves, (255-6464). Designed by I M Pei and dubbed 'the sewing machine,' the museum also offers excellent collections of Asian, graphic and modern art. Tues-Sun 10am-5pm. Free.

Cornell Plantations: The campus covers some 4000 acres including the main campus buildings, experimental farms, nature trails, Beebe Lake and **Sapsucker Woods**, a bird sanctuary. The Plantations are one of the nicest things on campus and comprise an arboretum, specialised plant collections in the botanical gardens, and a network of forest trails. Nice to wander and picnic. Off Judd Falls Rd; tel 255-3020.

Taughannock Falls State Park, 8 miles N on Rt 89, 387-6739. A mile-long glen with 400 ft walls and 215 ft high falls (higher than Niagara).

Buttermilk Falls State Park, south on Rte 13, 273-5761. Waterfalls and quiet pools are the main features. Good for swimming, hiking and a picnic, $6.

INFORMATION/TRAVEL

Ithaca City Convention & Visitor Bureau, 904 East Shore Drive, (800) 284-8422/(607) 272-1313.

Local Ithaca Transit (T-CAT), 277-RIDE, covers Ithaca, Tompkins County and Cornell campus. Fares 75¢-$1.50.

Greyhound, W State & N Fulton Sts, 272-7930/(800) 231-2222.

Still within the Finger Lakes region is **Corning**, 50 miles south-west of Ithaca. Corningware and Steuben Glass originated here, and it's well worth spending several hours at the amazing **Corning Glass Center**, watching glass being cut, moulded, blown into any shape for every conceivable use. For information phone 974-8271. Daily 9am-5pm, 'til 8pm Jul-Aug. $10, $9 w/ student ID. Midway between Ithaca and Corning is **Elmira** where Mark Twain wrote *Huckleberry Finn*. He is buried here—in **Woodlawn Cemetery**.

North of Corning at the extremity of Seneca Lake is **Watkins Glen,** famous for a lovely park, motor racing and discount shopping. For info on international motor racing events phone 535-2481. Various car and go-kart meets are held throughout the summer. The small town of **Hammondsport**, at the southern end of Keuka Lake, has its own salute to another form of high speed travel—flying. This is the birthplace of pioneer aviator, **Glen H. Curtis** and you can visit the aviation museum named after him here, 569-2160.

Northeast of the Finger Lakes, on the shores of Lake Ontario, **Rochester** is a grimy, crowded city encircled by insipid flowery suburbs. But one mile east of downtown is the **George Eastman House**, (716) 271-3361, abode of the founder of Kodak and now the **International Museum of Photography**, 900 East Ave, sure to fascinate amateur and professional alike. Tue-Sat 10am-4.30pm, Sun 1pm-4.30pm. $6.50, $5 w/student ID.
The telephone area code for the whole region is 607.

NIAGARA FALLS A traditional destination for honeymoon couples in search of the awesome, including Marilyn Monroe in *Niagara*. Mere tourists also flock to Niagara to see one of the most outstanding spectacles on the continent.

On the US side are the American Falls and the Bridal Veil Falls with a drop of 190 ft and a combined breadth of 1060 ft in a fairly straight line; the Horseshoe Falls, belonging half to the US and half to Canada, describe a deep curve 2200 ft long though with a slightly lower drop of 185 ft. About 1,500,000 gallons of water would normally plummet over the three falls each second, but the use of the river's waters to generate electricity reduces that flow by half in the summer and by three-quarters in the winter.

The Canadian side offers the better view (see Niagara Falls, Ontario), but (or therefore) it's more commercialised.
The telephone area code is 716.

ACCOMMODATION
Coachman Motel, 523 3rd St, 285-2295. Rates vary, w/ends in summer are the most expensive times, S-$59, D-$69. 'Very good location near falls.' 'Clean and comfortable, but quite noisy, rough area of town.'
Frontier Youth Hostel (AYH), 1101 Ferry Ave, corner of Memorial Pkwy, 282-3700. $14 AYH, $17 non-AYH. Rsvs recommended. 'One of the friendliest and most helpful hostels in America; clean small dormitories; 20 mins from falls.' 'Very cramped.' Closed 9.30am-4pm. Check in 1pm-11.30pm. 11.30pm curfew.
Olde Niagara House, 610 4th St, 285-9408. D-$55, XP-$20, includes bfast. Check-in after 1 pm. 'Brilliant.'
Rainbow Guest House, 423 Rainbow Blvd S, 282-1135. D-$75-$110, includes 'wonderful breakfast.' Rsvs essential. Less than 10 mins from falls. 'Friendly and welcoming.'
Scottish Inn, 5919 Niagara Falls Blvd, 283-1100. Mon-Fri July-Aug, D-$69-139. Discount $5 if staying more than 1 night. TV, pool, rsvs advised. $45 tour of falls. Taxi from Falls $6. 'Clean, bright and friendly ... some rooms have waterbeds.' 'Free coffee and donuts.' 'Very cheap for a group of 4/5 people.'
YMCA, 1317 Portage Rd, (716) 285-8491. "mat room," (provide your own sleeping bag), co-ed, $15; mattress, private room $25 for men only, $10 key deposit sleeping hrs 10pm-6am. Exact change only for check-ins after 9pm.'Wonderful showers, incredible security.' 30 min walk to the falls.

FOOD
'Rainbow Blvd N, variety of quite cheap places to eat Chinese, Italian, American.'

OF INTEREST
Beware of tours offered by various information centres charging anything up to $60, the ones listed below see the same sights. If you plan on spending a lot of time here, consider buying the Master Pass, $21, which includes admission to the obser-

vation tower, the Cave of the Winds, **Festival Theater** in the Visitors Center, Maid of the Mist, and other attractions. The pass is sold in the Visitors Center or at any park attraction. Call 278-1770 for more info.

Aquarium, 701 Whirlpool St, 285-3575. World's first inland oceanarium, using synthetic seawater. Sea lions in summer, dolphins and sharks in winter; $6.50. Daily summer 9am-7pm, otherwise 'til 5pm.

Cave of the Winds Tour, 278-1730, on Goat Island is not really a cave. Don oilskins for a trip to the base of Bridal Veil Falls, $6. Daily 8am-8pm. 'A must see.'

Old Fort Niagara. About 6 miles north in Fort Niagara State Park, 745-7611. The fort saw service under three flags—British, French and American, and contains some pre-revolutionary buildings. Displays of drill, musket firing, etc. $6.75.

Prospect Point Observation Tower, 50¢. Deck overlooking falls adjacent to Maid of the Mist, daily 8am-11pm.

Seeing the Falls. Walk from the US to Canada via the **Rainbow Bridge**. Cost $.25 each way, and don't forget your passport. If you have a restricted visa, check in with the customs people on the US side to make sure you won't have any problems returning. On either side you can don oilskins for a trip on the **Maid of the Mist** boat, 284-8897, which will carry you within drenching distance of the Falls. Cost $9, mid-Apr-mid-Oct, 9.15am-8pm, 'til 7.30 after Aug. Boat leaves every 15 mins. 'Youth Hostel provides people staying there with a discount voucher.' 'Excellent.'

Niagara International Factory Outlets, 1900 Military Rd, (716) 297-2022. Huge 'fabulous' mall stocked to the roof with discounted name brands.

INFORMATION
Niagara Falls Convention and Visitors Information Line: 285-2400/(800) 421-5223. Mon-Fri 9am-5pm. Ask about the festival of lights in Nov.

Visitors Center at 4th & Niagara Sts, adjacent to bus station, 284-2000, daily 8.30am-7.30pm.

TRAVEL
Amtrak, twice daily, (800) 872-7245/683-8440. NB: station is two miles out of town.

Greyhound, 343 4th St, 282-1331, not actually a Greyhound stop, but you can get Greyhound tkts and a city bus to Buffalo Greyhound Station for $1.85 (in exact change).

From/to Buffalo Airport, 855-7211, #24 bus to downtown, $1.45, ask for zone 2 transfer. Get off at Eagle St and catch #40 at Main and Church Sts to Falls. $.25 to enter bus w/transfer, pay $.20 more when you get off the bus.

BUFFALO   is better known for its cold snowy winters than for its tourist attractions. This is not a city to dawdle in, but it is near enough to the Falls, and is an important travel centre. If fate should cast you into the city, be sure to enjoy one nice thing Buffalo is famous for—spicy chicken wings, $3 and up for 10 at many restaurants, especially along the Elmwood strip.
The telephone area code is 716.

ACCOMMODATION
Buffalo Hostel International, 667 Main St, 852-5222. Members: $19 p/night May-Aug, $17 the rest of the year, non-members add $3 per night. Starting in 2000, the hostel will close from Dec-Feb, except for group reservations. Kitchen, laundry. Check in 8am-10am and 5pm-11pm. 'Clean, well-equipped.' *hibuffalo@juno.com. www.hostelbuffalo.com*

Lord Amhurst, 5000 Main at Kensington Ave, (800) 544-2200. From D-$75, Q-$89 includes bfast. Pool, laundry, game room. Rsvs advised.

FOOD
Anchor Bar, Main & North Sts, 886-8920. Where the chicken wings originated. $5-$20.

Convention and Tourism Division of Greater Buffalo Chamber of Commerce, 617 Main St, 852-0511/(888) 228-3369. Will advise on accommodation. Mon-Fri 8am-5pm.
Amtrak, 75 Exchange St, (800) 872-7245. Also Depew Sta. with buses downtown and to Falls, w/transfer ($2.10).
Greyhound Station, 181 Ellicott St, (800) 231-2222/855-7531. Bus 40 to Falls, $1.75.
Buffalo Bus and Metro. Information: 855-7211. Basic fare $1.25.

PENNSYLVANIA   *The Keystone State*

The 'Keystone State' seemed at one time destined to become one of the most powerful states in the nation, bridging the gap between North and South. The Civil War, one of the worst armed conflicts America has known, was fought in the centre of the state. During the Industrial Revolution, Pennsylvania retained its prominence, with Pittsburgh as the steel-producing capital of the country. Today, as industry has migrated south, Pennsylvania's economy and population have shifted. Pittsburgh and Philadelphia, the two major cities, are enjoying a renaissance and renewed economic growth, and tourism in all parts of the state is now second only to health services in contribution to Pennsylvania's economy.

Pennsylvania is known for its lush scenery: rolling hills; rich, meticulously cultivated farmlands; and the Appalachian Mountains, which provide good hunting, hiking, and camping.

PHILADELPHIA   English Quaker William Penn founded Philadelphia in 1682, on New World land given to him by Charles II in payment for a debt. By the time of the American Revolution the city had become the second largest in the English-speaking world—it is currently the fourth largest city in the country. Both the Declaration of Independence and the Federal Constitution were signed here. For visitors interested in pursuing the Liberty Trail, Philadelphia rivals Boston in historical reminders.

In the early 1800s, when commercial and political power moved to New York City and Washington DC, Philadelphia's stature began to wane. The early 1900s were dreary for the city, which gained the nickname 'Filthy-delphia' and became the brunt of jokes by W C Fields, who quipped that he 'spent a month in Philadelphia one day.' Asked by *Vanity Fair* magazine what he would like to have on his tombstone, he replied, 'I'd rather be in Philadelphia.'

Today Philadelphians are having the last laugh. The city is once again an important manufacturing and cultural centre, and some glamour has returned, the result of a recent urban and riverside face lift. Although one of the country's oldest cities, Philadelphia has one of the youngest populations; 53% of which is aged between 18-54 years; in addition, there are numerous universities and colleges in the area, hence plenty of restaurants, bars, pubs and clubs; and the Italian Market and Chinatown provide a special ethnic flavour. The City of Brotherly Love lives up to its nickname— *Conde Nast Traveler* magazine has ranked Philadelphia the friendliest and most honest city in the country. Philadelphians refer to downtown as Center City.

Valley Forge and the Pennsylvania Dutch Country lie just to the west, and New York City is only an hour and a half away. *www.libertynet.org/phila-visitor, www.gophila.com*

The telephone area code for the Philadelphia area is 215.

ACCOMMODATION

Major hotels in the city centre are worth checking for special offers which allow three or four people to take a double room for around $110, (e.g. Holiday Inn, 923-8660, City Center Hotel, 568-8300, Clarion Suites, 922-1730, next to Greyhound).

Bank Street Hostel, 32 S Bank St, 922-0222. Dorm $16 AYH member, $19 non-member, $2 for sheet sleeping bag (must use one). AC, TV, laundry, kitchen. Closed 10am-4.30pm. 12.30 am curfew. Within walking distance of all major attractions. 'The perfect hostel.' No rsvs over the phone.

B&B Connection/B&B of Philadelphia, PO Box 21, Devon PA, 19333, (610) 687-3565 (in Philly) or (800) 448-3619 (out of Philly). email: bnb@bnbphiladelphia.com. Rooms in and around Philadelphia, some hosts fluent in European languages. From $45. Credit card required to make reservation. Some hosts require a two night stay. Be sure to ask about cancellation fees. *www.bnbphiladelphia.com*

Chamounix Mansion International Youth Hostel, W Fairmount Park at end of Chamounix Dr, 878-3676. $11 AYH member, $14 non-member, plus $5 deposit for groups and $2 sheet rental. 'Excellent, but out of the way.' 'I cannot speak highly enough of this place.' Take #38 bus from Market St. Get off at Ford & Cranston, continue on Ford, left at Chamounix to the end. 'Take food with you.'

Divine Tracy Hotel, 20 S 36th near U of Penn, 382-4310. Long list of rules: no smoking, no alcohol, no meals in rooms; women required to wear dresses or skirts w/stockings, and shorts are prohibited for either gender. But if the limitations don't bother you, the price is right: S-$33-$40, D-$23-$26 pp, shared bath, all rooms on single-sex floors. Cash or traveller's cheques only.

Several fraternity houses at the **University of Pennsylvania** offer summer housing to transient students. Call 898-5263 for information.

Camping: West Chester KOA, in **Embreville** on Rte 162 (just west of West Chester), 30 miles from Philadelphia, (610) 486-0447, laundry, showers, store, swimming, fishing, miniature golf, daily van trips into Philadelphia with minimum of 4 people. Tent site $22.50; camper cabin, $52 for two.

FOOD

The local specialities are 'hoagies,' cold subs of all kinds; 'Philly steaks,' thin slices of steak on an Italian roll with onions, catsup, mayo, green peppers, cheese ... and you name it; and soft pretzels, gigantic twists of dough freckled with salt crystals, zigzagged with mustard. All these and many more are sold everywhere on the street, especially in neighbourhoods filled with fast food stalls.

The Bourse, 111 S Independence Mall East, 625-0300, certainly the most convenient collection of eateries, in the heart of the historical area—opposite the Liberty Bell. A restored building full of interesting shops and a large variety of food stalls, including a good one for your mandatory Philly Cheesesteak. Closes at 6pm.

Famous 4th St Delicatessen, 700 S 4th St, (4th & Bainbridge), 922-3274. Traditional, Jewish delicatessen established in 1923. Award-winning chocolate-chip cookies.

Gold Standard Cafeteria, 3601 Locust Walk, 387-3463, on U Penn campus and near the International House. Good prices and a good place to meet people. Sept-May 8.30am-3pm.

Jim's Steaks, 400 South St, 928-1911. A local tradition, features mouth-watering Philly Cheesesteaks, $5, served cafeteria-style. Open into the small hours, daily.

Reading Terminal Market, 12th & Arch Sts, 922-2317. Huge Farmers Market where

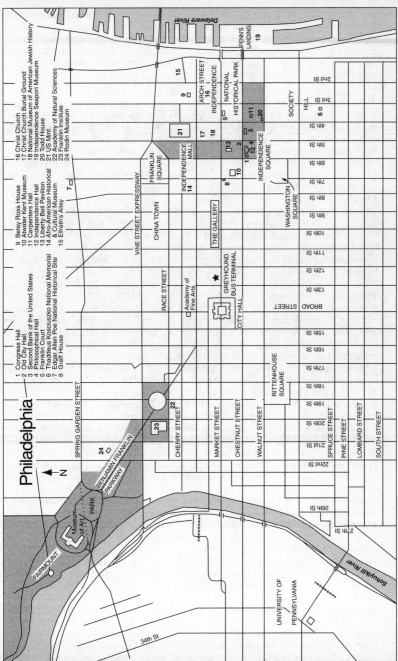

Philadelphia

1 Congress Hall
2 Old City Hall
3 Second Bank of the United States
4 Philosophical Hall
5 Franklin Court
6 Thaddeus Kosciuszko National Memorial
7 Edgar Allen Poe National Historical Site
8 Graff House

9 Betsy Ross House
10 Atwater Kent Museum
11 Carpenters Hall
12 Independence Hall
13 Liberty Bell Pavilion
14 Afro-American Historical & Cultural Museum
15 Elfreth's Alley

16 Christ Church
17 Christ Church Burial Ground
18 National Museum of American Jewish History
19 Independence Seaport Museum
20 Todd House
21 US Mint
22 Academy of Natural Sciences
23 Franklin Institute
24 Rodin Museum

Delaware River

PENN'S LANDING

ARCH STREET

INDEPENDENCE
NATIONAL
HISTORICAL PARK

SOCIETY
HILL

FRANKLIN
SQUARE

INDEPENDENCE
MALL

INDEPENDENCE
SQUARE

WASHINGTON
SQUARE

VINE STREET EXPRESSWAY

CHINA TOWN

THE GALLERY

RACE STREET

Academy of
Fine Arts

GREYHOUND
BUS TERMINAL

CITY HALL

BROAD STREET

RITTENHOUSE
SQUARE

SPRING GARDEN STREET

CHERRY STREET

MARKET STREET

CHESTNUT STREET

WALNUT STREET

SPRUCE STREET

PINE STREET

LOMBARD STREET

SOUTH STREET

BENJAMIN FRANKLIN PARKWAY

Museum of Art

FAIRMOUNT
PARK

Schuylkill River

UNIVERSITY OF
PENNSYLVANIA

N

2nd St
3rd St
4th St
5th St
6th St
7th St
8th St
9th St
10th St
11th St
12th St
13th St
15th St
16th St
17th St
18th St
19th St
20th St
21st St
22nd St
26th St
27th St
34th St

you can satisfy your heart's desire—from Pennsylvania Dutch breakfasts to Southern Soul Food. Try 'shoo-fly pie', a heavy, molasses-packed Pennsylvania Dutch concoction and 'the best blueberry pancakes ever!' Mon-Sat 8am-6pm.

Southeast China Restaurant, 1000 Arch St, 629-1888. In the centre of Chinatown. 'Good for vegetarians.' Lunch $5-$7, dinner $8-$11, Mon-Thur 11.30am-11pm, Fri & Sat til midnight, Sun noon-10pm.

OF INTEREST

The best way to begin a tour of Philadelphia is to go first to **Independence Hall National Historical Park,** the four-block area near the Delaware River known as the 'Most Historic Square Mile in America'. The park's **Visitors Center**, 3rd & Chestnut Sts, 597-8974, distributes the *Visitors' Guide Map of Philadelphia* and other free maps and literature on the city and surrounding area. Open daily in summer, 9am-6pm. The park includes: **Carpenters Hall**, home of the first Continental Congress; and **Independence Hall**, Chestnut St btwn 5th & 6th Sts, where the Declaration of Independence was signed. Here also is the **Liberty Bell Pavilion**, at Market St btwn 5th & 6th Sts. Independence Hall and Liberty Bell Pavilion are open daily in summer 9am-8pm; Carpenters Hall Tue-Sun 10am-4pm; the other buildings are open daily 9am-5pm. After Labor Day, all buildings are open daily 9am-5pm. Admission to Colonial buildings in the area is free.

Other historic sites within or close to the park include:

Afro-American Historical and Cultural Museum, 7th & Arch Sts, 574-0380. Mon-Sat 9am-5pm, Sun noon-5pm, $6, $4 w/student ID.

Atwater Kent Museum, 15 S 7th St btwn Market & Chestnut Sts, 922-3031. Depicts Philly's growth through the centuries. Weds-Mon 10am-5pm; $3.

Betsy Ross House, 239 Arch St, 627-5343. Betsy Ross is said to have put together the first American flag from strips of petticoats. Daily 10am-5pm, free. Near this house, off 2nd Ave is **Elfreth's Alley**, 574-0560. The oldest continuously occupied residential street in America, lined with Georgian homes. House No 126 is a museum, Tue-Sat 10am-4pm, Sun noon-4pm, $2.

Christ Church, on 2nd St above Market St, 922-1695, Mon-Sat 9am-5pm, Sun 1pm-5pm. Franklin and six other signatories to the Declaration of Independence are buried at **Christ Church Burial Ground**, 5th & Arch Sts.

Congress Hall, Chestnut & 6th Sts next door to Independence Hall, is where the legislature met when Philadelphia was the nation's capital.

Franklin Court, at Market btwn 3rd & 4th Sts, 592-1289. Interesting collection of buildings. A working print shop, showing Franklin's trade; a post office (daily 9am-5pm), where you can get your letters hand cancelled with a colonial style stamp; an underground museum which features a diorama of Franklin's life and inventions and a phone bank (you can call up Thomas Jefferson and find out what he thought of Ben).

Graff House, 7th & Market Sts, is a reconstruction of the house where Thomas Jefferson drafted the Declaration of Independence.

Haunted Philadelphia, 413-1997. Candlelit walking ghost tours of the Old City, 7.30pm every evening May-Oct. The tour meets at 5th and Chestnut Sts. $10, rsvs required. *www.ghosttour.com/phila.html*

Italian Market, 9th St btwn Wharton and Christian Sts, the world's largest outdoor market with 150 stores and street stalls. Lots of Italian and Vietnamese restaurants in the surrounding neighbourhood.

Mural Arts Program (MAP), 1515 Arch St, 683-3689. There are over 2000 wall murals throughout Philadelphia and MAP sells pamphlets w/self-guided tours of some of the more interesting ones, $5. A great way to see Philly's neighbourhoods. Call ahead to check office hours.

National Museum of American Jewish History, 55 N 5th St, 923-3811. Exhibits on the participation of American Jews in the social, cultural, economic and political life of the nation. Mon-Thu 10am-5pm, Fri 10am-3pm, Sun noon-5pm. $3, $2 w/student ID.

Penn's Landing, East of Columbus Blvd, btwn Market and South Sts, 923-8181. Re-vitalised waterfront area with restaurants and shops. Free concerts in summer. Also here; **Independence Seaport Museum**, 211 S Columbus Blvd & Walnut St. 925-5439. Museum telling the story of the city's port and maritime history. Daily 10am-5pm. $7.50, includes tours of historic ships and working boat-building shop, museum only $5.

Old City Hall, 5th & Chestnut, was the first home of the US Supreme Court. Daily 9am-5pm.

Philosophical Hall, 150 S Independence Mall East, the home of the American Philosophical Society, founded by Benjamin Franklin in 1743.

Second Bank of the United States, Chestnut btwn 4th & 5th Sts, a beautiful Greek Revival building looking somewhat out of place here, has an interesting portrait collection.

Society Hill, restored colonial town houses around Spruce & 4th Sts. The name comes from the Free Society of Stock Traders, a company formed here by William Penn.

South Street, between 11th and Front Sts, largely a Jewish neighbourhood in the 1800s, now the street is lined with clothing, book, music and antique stores, sidewalk cafes and restaurants. South's St's east end is known for its nightlife.

Thaddeus Kosciuszko National Memorial, 3rd & Pine Sts, where Mr K, helped the colonists win the revolution, stayed 1797-98.

Todd House, 4th & Walnut Sts. A house that figured prominently in Philadelphia society of the 1790s and the home of Dolley Pane, who later married James Madison. Sign up at the Visitors Center, 3rd St btwn Walnut & Chestnut Sts for a tour. Free.

United States Mint, 5th & Arch Sts, 408-0114. Small museum, self-guided tour along viewing balcony, free unless you want to mint your own souvenir coin for $2. Mon-Sat 9am-4.30pm, open daily Jul-Aug. No cameras.

Elsewhere in Philly: **Academy of Natural Sciences**, 19th St & Benjamin Franklin Pkwy, 299-1000, big dinosaur exhibit and tropical butterflies. Mon-Fri 10am-4.30pm, w/ends 10am-5pm, $8.50.

Edgar Allen Poe National Historic Site, 532 N 7th St, 597-8780, where Poe lived when his short stories *The Black Hat*, *Gold Bug*, and *The Telltale Heart* were published, 1843-1844. Daily 9am-5pm, free.

Fairmount Park, west along Benjamin Franklin Pkwy towards the Schuylkill (pronounced 'Skoo-kill') River. A beautiful riverside park of nearly 9000 acres. No less than 73 baseball diamonds, 115 all weather tennis courts, and 75 miles of walks, bike and bridle paths. Outdoor concerts, and a 90 min ride on a recreated turn-of-the century trolley to see it all. Within the park are several colonial mansions, and other attractions: (*www.libertynet.org/iha/districts/fairmountpark*)

Japanese House and Gardens the grounds of the Horticultural Center, 878-5097. Visitors required to wear socks and no shoes. May-Oct Tues-Sun 10am-4pm, $2.50, $2 w/student ID.

Rodin Museum, 22nd St & Benjamin Franklin Pkwy, 763-8100. Somehow, they prised *The Thinker* and *The Burghers of Calais* away from the French. Tue-Sun 10am-5pm. Suggested donation, $3. *www.rodinmuseum.org*

Philadelphia Museum of Art, in the centre of Fairmount Park, 763-8100, ranks as one of the world's greatest, with more than 500,000 works of art. (It's the third-largest museum in the US). See the arms & armour collection. Tue-Sun 10am-5pm, til 8.45pm Weds, $8, $5 w/student ID. Sun free until 1pm. 'Worth every penny.' While you're here, look for the plaque on the museum steps marking the site where the famous 'Rocky' scene was filmed. *www.philamuseum.org*

Philadelphia Zoo, 34th & Girard Sts, 243-1100, America's first, open daily 9.30am-

4.45pm (w/ends 'til 5.45pm), $10.50, treehouse $1 extra. *www.phillyzoo.org*—a whistle stop tour of the zoo and animal houses.

Fairmount Water Works, right next to the art museum, 236-5465. Free tours of the water works Sat-Sun 1pm-3pm.

Fairmount Park Commission, 685-0015, arranges group trolley tours of the park upon request.

Franklin Institute Science Museum and Fels Planetarium, 20th St & Benjamin Pkwy, 448-1200. Worth a visit. Daily 9.30am-5pm; planetarium show 2.15pm daily, $9.75. $12.75 combo tkt. The complex now includes the **Mandel Future Center** and the **Omnibus Theater**, one of the world's most modern cinemas with a 4-storey screen and 3D sound, $8. *www.fi.edu*

Germantown, 6 miles north-west of Center City and originally settled by German folk. Many old houses and fine mansions, some of distinctive German design. Among the best is **Cliveden**, 6401 Germantown Ave, 848-1777, dating back to 1763. Thur-Sun noon-4pm, $6, $4 w/student ID.

Mummers Museum, 2nd & Washington Aves, 336-3050. Wed-Sat 9.30am-4.30pm, Tue 9.30am-9pm, $2.50, $2 w/student ID. Hypnotic and hilarious, the Mummers—a Philly original—are hard to explain; you just have to *see*. Their New Years Day parade is legend. They also hold outdoor string band concerts Tue at 8pm.

Pennsylvania Academy of the Fine Arts, Broad & Cherry Sts, 972-7600. Nation's oldest art museum and school. Good collection of American art dating from 1750. Mon-Sat 10am-5pm, Wed 'til 8pm, Sun 11am-5pm. $8, $7 w/student ID, free 3pm-5pm Sun.

University Museum of Archaeology/Anthropology, University of Pennsylvania Campus, 33rd & Spruce Sts, 898-4000. Outstanding archaeological exhibits. Tue-Sat 10am-4.30pm, Sun 1pm-5pm, closed Sun during summer; $5, $2.50 w/student ID. *www.upenn.edu/museum*

ENTERTAINMENT

Check the *Weekend* section of the Friday *Philadelphia Inquirer*. Half price day of show tkts are available from **Upstages**, at Liberty Place, 16th & Chestnut Sts, 569-9700. Mon-Fri 10am-6pm, Sat 10am-5pm, Sun noon-5pm.

Shampoo, 417 N 8th St, 928-6455. Unique club, cutting-edge dance music until 2am, avant garde art and stylish jazz lounge. Cover $7-$20 depending on night.

South St, from Front to 7th and from South to Market, the old city area, is the funky end of town, with many restaurants, pubs and clubs. The area around Walnut and 38th Sts is also good for pubs.

INFORMATION

Visitors and Tourist Information Center, 16th St & JFK Blvd, 636-1666. Daily in summer 9am-6pm, otherwise 'til 5pm.

Philadelphia Convention and Visitors Bureau, 1515 Market St #2020, 636-3300. Mon-Fri 8am-5.30pm.

Independence Hall National Historical Park Visitors Center, 3rd & Chestnut, 597-8974. *www.libertynet.org*

Thomas Cook Currency Services, 1800 JFK Blvd, 563-7348/(800) 287-7362. Mon-Fri 9am-5pm.

Travelers Aid, 121 N Broad St, 523-7580. Mon-Fri 8.45am-4.45pm. At Greyhound terminal, 238-0999.

INTERNET ACCESS

Access Caffe, 1207 Race St, 988-1891. $.10/min. *www.access-caffe.com*

Central Library, 1901 Vine St, 686-5322. Free Internet use, half hour time limit.

TRAVEL

Amtrak, for intercity trains, 30th St Station, 824-1600/(800) 872-7245. To and from NYC, DC, Boston.

Greyhound, 10th & Market Sts, 931-4014/(800) 231-2222. To NYC, DC, $20 o/w.

PHLASH buses, 636-1666, are purple buses which run in a loop from Logan circle through center city, to waterfront, to South St and all major attractions. Bus stops are all along Benjamin Franklin Pkwy, Market St and Old City, marked by signs with PHLASH wings. $1.50 per ride or $3 all day pass. Buses run May-Sept 10am-midnight, Sept-May 10am-6pm.

SEPTA, 580-7800, operates trains to suburbs from Market East Station, buses and street cars in the city. Base fare, $1.60, additional suburban zones $.40, transfer $.40. Tourist-friendly DayPass, $5 for unlimited travel on all city transit vehicles, plus o/w on the airport line, available at 30th St, Market East, and Suburban Stations. Bus #76 goes via Society Hill/South St, along Market St, to Philadelphia Museum of Art, and the Zoo in Fairmont Park.

VALLEY FORGE/BRANDYWINE RIVER VALLEY Just south-east of

Philadelphia, this is a region steeped in history and art. **Valley Forge National Historical Park**, (610) 783-1077, one of the nation's most solemn memorial grounds, is 20 miles west of Philadelphia. (Inquire at Visitors Center about buses, tours.) General Washington hibernated here along with his half-starved troops through the bitter winter of 1777-78. Loaded with Americana, including Washington's headquarters, cabins modelled after those in which the troops were billeted, and a few museums. Dogwoods blooming in spring enhance the pastoral air. For those more interested in shopping, check out the huge **King of Prussia** mall. You can get there from Phillie by bus. Call (888) VISITVF for more info on the Valley Forge area, or check out *www.valleyforge.org*

South of Valley Forge, the **Brandywine River Valley** has inspired three generations of Wyeths—NC, Andrew and Jamie—to produce a uniquely American brand of art. The **Brandywine River Museum** in **Chadds Ford**, (610) 388-2700, holds the world's largest collection of Wyeth paintings. Daily 9.30am-4.30pm, $5, $2.50 w/student ID. 'Highly recommended.'

PENNSYLVANIA DUTCH COUNTRY While most of the original settlers

of Lancaster County have long since been absorbed into modern society, the Amish and Mennonites have retained their traditional identities in this stretch of country west of Philadelphia. Eschewing electricity and modern machinery, the 'plain people' still speak a form of Low German ('Dutch' is a derivation from 'Deutsch,' the German word for 'German'). The women in their long dresses and small caps and the bearded menfolk in sombre black suits and broad-brimmed hats continue to live as simply as they did centuries before in southern Germany.

The Pennsylvania Dutch have always fascinated visitors, and the 1984 award-winning film *Witness* only increased the interest. In order to really understand what you are seeing, try reading *Amish Life*, by John A. Hostetler, and *A Quiet Peaceable Life*, by John L. Ruth, which provide an excellent introduction to the area and its people; another highly informative book, recommended by the Amish people themselves, is *Twenty Most Asked Questions about the Amish and Mennonites*, by Merle Good, $6.95. All are available at the **Peoples Place**, Main Street, Intercourse, 768-7171. *Note*: Restrain your cameras; the people here consider photographs to be 'graven images'.

The area lies on Hwy 30, but to avoid an excess of tourists, take to the side roads. One good excursion is the 3 mile jaunt from **Paradise** to **Strasburg**, equally enjoyable on foot or via the old railroad. **Lancaster**, US capital-for-a-day (the day was 27 September, 1777), was a prominent city in the late 18th century; the well-preserved downtown reflects the town's colonial heritage. If you're looking for **Intercourse**, you'll find it signposted at the junction of Hwys 772 & 340 east of Lancaster.

Keep an eye out in late June and early July for the **Kutztown Folk Festival**: soap making, sauerkraut shredding, pewtering, square dancing and folklore sessions. 'The festival is a real hoe-down, straw-in-the-hair fun affair.' Call (800) 963-8824 for details.

The telephone area code is 717.

ACCOMMODATION

Accommodation is relatively inexpensive here, but in summer prices rise and the best deals go quickly. The best places to stay are the farm homes: they're cheaper, serve hearty breakfasts, and you'll learn more about your hosts. For the best information on accommodation, contact the **Mennonite Information Center**, (see below).

Benner's Home For Tourists, Bird-in-Hand, 299-2615. On main bus route from Lancaster, 2 miles from Intercourse. $22 per room (can squeeze 5 in) with private bathroom. Rsvs required.

Country Acres Family Campground, (717) 687-8014. 20 Leven Road, Godonville. Tent site $18, $21 w/hook-up. Cabins for $40, 2 night min. stay.

FOOD

Amish austerity does not extend to eating. Many restaurants in the area serve bountiful communal feasts of sausage, scrapple, pickles, beef, chow-chow, schnitz and knepp, noodles, homebaked bread, apple butter, funnel cakes and molasses shoo-fly pie.

Lancaster's **Central Market**, King & Queen Sts, 291-4723, sells produce and goodies; it's one of the best places to see what Pennsylvania Dutch food is all about. Tue & Fri 6am-4pm & Sat 6am-2pm.

OF INTEREST

Amish Village Inc., on Hwy 896, 7 miles south-east of Lancaster, 687-8511. See the Amish way of life, and tourists seeing the Amish way of life. Summer daily 9am-6pm, Nov 9am-4pm, otherwise 9am-5pm, $5.75.

Ephrata Cloister, 12 miles north of Lancaster on Hwy 272, 733-6600, was founded and later forsaken by a German community of Seventh Day Baptists. Living as sisters and brothers, they stooped through low doorways to learn humility and walked down narrow hallways to assure themselves of the straight and narrow path. Many of their original structures of unpainted wood, now gloomy-grey with time, still stand. Mon-Sat 9am-5pm, Sun noon-5pm (last tour at 4pm), $6. There are candlelit tours on Sat evenings, in July and August, from 6pm-8pm, $6.

Historical Lancaster Walking Tours, 100 S Queen St, 392-1776. Interesting walking tour of colonial Lancaster. 1½ hr tours daily at 1pm, Tues, Fri, Sat at 10am & 1pm, $7.

Pennsylvania Farm Museum, in Landis Valley on Hwy 272, 3 miles north of Lancaster, 569-0401. Museum village with the buildings, homes, trades and tools of three centuries. Mon-Sat 9am-5pm, Sun noon-5pm, $7.

People's Place, Main St, Intercourse, 768-7171. Mon-Sat 9.30am-8pm. The self-guided tour, 'Twenty Questions,' $4. Award-winning 25 min slide documentary, *Who are the Amish?*, shown every 30 mins, 9.30am-7.30pm. $4, $7 combo ticket for tour and slide show. 'Worth every penny.'

Railroad Museum of Pennsylvania, Rte 741 east of Strasburg, 687-8628. Historic locos and rolling stock. Mon-Sat 9am-5pm, Sun noon-5pm, closed Mon in winter, $6.

Strasburg Railroad, Rte 741 1 mile east of Lancaster on Rte 896 south, 687-7522. America's oldest short-line steam locomotive goes to and from Paradise, 45 mins. Summer daily 11am-6pm, $8.25.

INFORMATION/TRAVEL
Mennonite Information Center, 2209 Millstream Rd, 4½ miles east of Lancaster off Rte 30, 299-0954. Go here first. Very helpful and friendly staff who can assist you in finding accommodation, tours and background on Mennonites and Amish. Informative introductory film of the area and people. The center also has the most non-commercial tour of the area, which is a treat in this overly exploited area. Here you can hire a local Mennonite guide (2 hr min.) for a fascinating country tour of homes, barns, factories, $26. 'Not to be missed.'
Pennsylvania Dutch Convention and Visitors Bureau, 501 Greenfield Rd, Lancaster, 299-8901. Brochures and maps. Daily 8.30am-5pm.
Amtrak, McGovern Ave, 291-5080/(800) 872-7245.

READING 30 miles from Lancaster. With over 300 factory outlets Reading is known as the 'Outlet Capital of the World'. Besides deals on clothing, appliances, jewellery, and even chocolate, the town also boasts several antique and farmers' markets. From Lancaster take US 222 north. Call the **Reading and Berks County Visitors Bureau**, (610) 375-4085/(800) 443-6610, or check out *www.readingberkspa.com* for more information.

HARRISBURG The undistinguished capital of Pennsylvania has two outstanding features. Heading west, the landscape becomes beautiful, even dramatic, where the broad Susquehanna River cuts a gap through granite bluffs and green forests. The city itself is crowned with a stunning Italian Renaissance capitol dome modelled after St. Peter's in Rome (and built on graft; get the scandalous scoop from a local resident). **Rockville Bridge**, 4 miles west of Harrisburg, spanning the Susquehanna, is the longest and widest stone arch bridge in the world.

The Harrisburg area sprang to international attention in 1979 after the nuclear accident at nearby **Three Mile Island**, which brought into question the safety of nuclear reactors. The accident didn't scare away tourists, of course not. Tourism, in fact, increased fourfold in the area. The **TMI Visitors Center**, across from the plant near **Middletown** on Rte 441 south, 944-7621, has a fascinating description of what happened and what steps have been taken to keep it from happening again. Thurs-Sun 12pm-4.30pm.

Further north up the Susquehanna River lies the **Pine Creek Gorge**, otherwise called the Grand Canyon of Pennsylvania, and said to be one of the last and most extensive wilderness regions between New York and Chicago. This once industrial area has been reabsorbed into nature and, with its free-flowing river and creek-side track, is now a haven for hikers, bikers, canoeists and horseback riders alike. **Wellsboro** is the nearest town for the area and a good base for activities. Call Pine Creek Outfitters, (570) 724-3003, for more info.

East of Harrisburg, in **Hummeltown**, are the **Indian Echo Caves**, 566-8131, with impressive natural formations. Daily 9am-6pm; $9 for a 45 min guided tour. You can pan for gems at Gem Mill Junction, $5 a bag.
The telephone area code is 717.

HERSHEY A company town built in 1903 by a Mennonite candy bar magnate of the same name who came up with the inspired concept of milk chocolate. The air is thick with the aroma of chocolate and almonds; the two main streets are Chocolate and Cocoa Aves, and even the street lamps are shaped like Hershey's famous 'kisses.' A beautiful Spanish-style resort hotel, the Hotel Hershey, sits atop the town; luscious gardens surround it. **Hershey's Chocolate World** near the park entrance takes you on a 12 min ride from the cocoa bean to the candy shop (but not into the factory). May-Oct daily 9am-10pm, otherwise 9am-5pm. Free, plus sample, and you never leave without spending money on chocolate (there are worse fates). Call 534-4903 for more information.

Also here is **Hershey Park**, 534-3900, a theme park with 50 rides and enough entertainment to keep you occupied all day. Daily, 10am-10pm, $31 for the day. Call (800) 437-7439 for info about Hershey, or check out *www.hersheypa.com.*

GETTYSBURG The quiet peaceful town that Gettysburg is today belies its history as the site of 51,000 casualties in 3 days in the most significant battle of the worst war America has ever known, the Civil War. On 3 July, 1863, General Robert E Lee was defeated here, and the tide turned irrevocably against the South. Lincoln came later to give his famous Address at the dedication of the National Cemetery. The battlefield is now preserved as a national military park where visitors may follow the struggle of both sides on maps and displays.
The telephone area code is 717.

ACCOMMODATION
Gettysburg has many 'Ma and Pa' motel/guest house operations, so with a little bit of searching you can find good, central, and relatively inexpensive accommodation even in the summer, the peak season.
Budget Host, 205 Steinwehr Ave, 334-3168, Bus rt 15. D-$62. Pool, morning coffee, walk to all major attractions. For rsvs call (800) 729-6564.
North of Gettysburg: Ironmonger's Mansion Youth Hostel, on Rte 223 in Pine Grover Furnace State Park, 486-7575, $12 AYH members, $15 non-members, $2 sleeping sheet. Check-in 5pm-10pm; rsvs essential. Built in 1762, the building was an ironworks which manufactured cannonballs during the Revolutionary War. It was also part of the underground railway which sheltered escaped slaves.
Round Top Campground, south on Rte 134, 334-9565. Showers, laundry, pool and mini-golf. Tent site $16.50 for two, XP-$5, $25 w/hook-up.

OF INTEREST
Go directly to the **National Park Visitors Center**, on Business Rte 15, 334-1124, for complete introduction and information. Park staff are extremely knowledgeable and helpful. Here you can make arrangements for touring. You can hire a local licensed battlefield guide for $30 for 2 hrs (AutoTour cassettes, $12.72 for 2 hrs, are available from the **Wax Museum** in town, 334-6245). Here also you can see the **Electric Map**, showing troop movements during the battle; daily 8am-6pm, $3. The **Cyclorama**, next door to the Visitors Center, is probably the most dramatic rendition; view this dioramic painting of Pickett's charge, augmented by a sound-and-light show, daily from 9am-5pm, $3.
A. Lincoln's Place Theater, 213 Steinwehr Ave, 334-6049. Here James Getty, a Lincoln scholar and look-alike, gives an intimate talk in which he, as Lincoln, recounts memories, describes events and answers any question you could possibly have about the

man. Not to be missed. 'Unbelievable!' (As far as anyone knows, Getty is not related to J Gettys, the town's founder.) Summer shows Mon-Fri 8pm; $7.

Civil War Heritage Days, last w/end in June—1st week in July. When the town comes out to commemorate the Battle of Gettysburg with concerts, shows and fascinating battle re-enactments involving thousands of 'troops.'

Eisenhower National Historic Site (take shuttle bus from Visitors Center), 338-9114, is a farm where the President retired and died. Daily 8.30am-4pm; $5.25, includes shuttle, admission and tour.

National Tower, 334-6754. Daily 9am-6.30pm. $5.25. Let the high speed elevators whisk you up 300 ft to the top for a spectacular view of the area.

INFORMATION
National Park Visitors Center, Business Rte 15, 334-1124. Daily 8am-6pm.
Gettysburg Convention & Visitor Bureau, 35 Carlisle St, 334-6274. Mon-Fri 8.30am-6pm, Sat-Sun 8.30am-5pm. Very helpful; has accommodation information.

PITTSBURGH   When Rand McNally named Pittsburgh 'the nation's most liveable city' in 1985, everyone was surprised but the Pittsburghers, for they have always had fierce pride in their city. Famous for steel and home of much of the nation's industry, Pittsburgh coughed its way through the Industrial Revolution in a perpetual cloud of smoke. After World War II it began a clean-up campaign and in recent years has emerged, blinking, into the sunlight. And an amazing transformation it is: Pittsburgh's skyline of blast furnaces, open hearths, steel mills and primrose yellow bridges is imposing, and the city's air is reportedly now cleaner than that of any other American metropolis. There is some exciting architecture down at the Golden Triangle, where the Allegheny and Monongahela Rivers join to form the Ohio River. The dramatic view here was first seen in 1753 by George Washington, who was a British major at the time. Pittsburgh's terrain is an appealing mix of plateaux and hillsides, narrow valleys and rivers; with elevations ranging from 715 ft to 1240 ft; expect to do some climbing.

As a bizarre footnote, the former nation of Czechoslovakia was founded in Pittsburgh, of all places. In 1918, the leaders of the Czechs and the Slovaks met in the Moose Club (now the Elks Club) at Penn & Scott Place to hammer out the Pittsburgh Agreement uniting these peoples.
The telephone area code for Pittsburgh is 412.

ACCOMMODATION
Hotel and motel accommodation is expensive in the Pittsburgh area; if you have a car, you would do better to stay on the outskirts in the Monroeville and Green Tree areas. Wherever you stay in Pittsburgh reservations are advisable, particularly at the guest houses.
Days Inn, I-79 & Steubenville Pike, 922-0120. S-$41, D-$49, $5 extra on weekends.
Pittsburgh International Hostel—HI, 830 E Warrington Ave, 431-1267. New hostel in a renovated bank, 10 mins to downtown and South Side. $17 members, $20 non; also some family accom. available. Closed betw 10 am and 5 pm 'Best hostel I stayed in.'
Point Park College, 201 Wood St, 392-3824. $15, check-in 2pm-midnight, 5 day limit. Students only. Ring in advance.

FOOD
The local brew is Iron City Beer, available at any bar that knows it's in Pittsburgh.
Benkovitz Seafood, 23rd & Smallman Sts, 263-3016. A market and one-time truckers' joint in the wholesale district, now moved up several pegs but keeping down its prices. Sun-Fri 9am-5pm, Sat 8am-5pm.

Big Z Hamburgers, 961 Liberty Ave, 1¹/₂ blocks from Greyhound (turn right out of terminal), 566-2600. $2-$4.

Parmanti Brothers, 3 outlets in Pittsburgh on Cherry, Forbes & 18th Sts (24 hrs), 263-2142. Unique recipe grilled cheese sandwiches served with fries and coleslaw. $4-$5.50. Also soup and chilli.

OF INTEREST

Pittsburgh culture was once severely neglected by the city's big-money steel magnates, who couldn't wait to get out of town to the refined air of Europe and New York's 5th Ave. The cultural life has picked up considerably since then, and Pittsburgh now boasts several fine museums and universities as well as the world-class Pittsburgh Symphony Orchestra.

Carnegie Museums of Pittsburgh, 4400 Forbes Ave, Oakland, 622-3131, *www.clpgh.org*. Encompasses the main branch of the **Carnegie Library** (as seen in *Flashdance*) and two internationally-known museums: the **Museum of Art** includes masterpieces of the French Impressionists and contemporary works as well as decorative arts of the ancient world; and the **Carnegie Museum of Natural History** tells the story of the earth and man in hundreds of displays of arts, crafts and natural history, including minerals, gems and Egyptian mummies. An impressive herd of prehistoric monsters towers over strange skeleton birds. The museums are open Tue-Sat 10am-5pm, Sun 1pm-5pm; $6, $4 w/student ID. Open Mondays Jul-Aug. Plus there's the new **Andy Warhol Museum**, 117 Sandusky St, 237-8300, which is the biggest single-artist museum in the US. Wed & Sun 11am-6pm, Thurs-Sat 11am-8pm. $7, $4 w/student ID.

Carnegie Science Center, 1 Allegheny Ave, W of Three Rivers Stadium, 237-3400. This includes the former Buhl Science Center and Planetarium. Don't miss the Van de Graaf generator which spits indoor lightning several times a day (announced over loudspeakers). The new **Henry J. Buhl Jnr Planetarium** gives sky shows daily, and the **Omnimax Theater** with shows on the 79 ft domed ceiling drawing the audience into the action. $6.50, 40 mins. There are also tours around the WW2 *Requin* (meaning 'shark') submarine in front of the Center. Sun-Fri 10am-6pm, Sat 'til 9pm. $6.50-$12 depending on what you opt to see.

Duquesne Incline, 1220 Grandview Ave, 381-1665, a vertical trolley from 1877 carries you 400 ft into the air for a bird's eye view of the city and its three rivers, daily 'til 12.40am, $1 each way.

Fallingwater, south-east of Pittsburgh, (724) 329-8501. This futuristic home-over-a-waterfall is a paragon of Frank Lloyd Wright design. Take Hwy 51 South to Uniontown, Rte 40 East to Farmington, 381 North for 12 miles (through Ohio Pyle Park) to Fallingwater on left. Tours every half hour, Tue-Sun 10am-4pm, $8, w/ends $12. Rsvs essential.

Frick Museum, 7227 Reynolds St, Pt Breeze, 371-0600. French, Italian and Flemish Renaissance paintings. Tue-Sat 10am-5pm, Sun noon-6pm; free. Free jazz and chamber concerts Oct-April, offers free lectures on temporary exhibits. Also the recently-restored **Clayton House** (call 371-0606 for rsvs), $8, $6 w/student ID and **Clayton Greenhouse** and **Carriage Museum**.

Nationality Classrooms at University of Pittsburgh, in the Gothic masterpiece, the Cathedral of Learning, 624-6000. Impressive conglomeration of 23 classrooms designed in different international designs with authentic furnishings from all over the world. 'Worth a visit.' Mon-Sat 9.30am-3pm, Sun 11am-3pm. Classrooms are locked on w/ends, but tape-recorded tour includes key; during week they are empty and quiet in the afternoon. $2.

Pittsburgh Zoo, Hill Rd, Highland Park, 665-3640. 55 acres of natural habitat, animals that include 16 species of endangered primates. A new tropical rain forest exhibit covers 5 acres inside and 5 acres open air. 10am-6pm, last admittance 5pm, $6.50.

White-Water Rafting on the Youghiogheny River. Day trips last 5-6 hrs and cost $35-$65 during the week, more at the w/ends. Includes orientation, lunch and guide. Call **Laurel Highlands River Tours**, (724) 329-8531, or **White Water Adventurers Inc**, (724) 329-8850, for more info. 'A spectacular experience.'

ENTERTAINMENT

For students, **Oakland** is the place, although the **Shadyside** area still has its fair share of swing. Read *Rock Flash* and *In Pittsburgh* free from around town, to find out what's going on. Rock and pop concerts, ice shows, sports events at the **Civic Arena**, Center and Bedford Aves, downtown at Washington Plaza, 642-1800. The arena has a vast, retractable, dome-shaped roof.

Heinz Hall, 600 Penn Ave, downtown, 392-4900/642-2062 (info line). Elegant hall named after the ketchup king. Home to the Pittsburgh Symphony Orchestra.

Shakespeare in the Park. Three Rivers Shakespeare Festival offers free outdoor performances in city parks throughout the summer, call 624-0102/624-7529 for details.

Three Rivers Stadium is home turf for the Pirates (baseball) and the Steelers (football); 321-0650 for schedule info.

INFORMATION/TRAVEL

Convention and Visitors Bureau, 4 Gateway Center, Suite 1800, 281-7711, (800) 366-0093. Mon-Fri 9am-5pm.

Amtrak, Liberty Ave & Grant St, near bus terminal, 471-6170/(800) 872-7245.

Greyhound, 11th & Liberty Ave, 392-6500/(800) 231-2222.

INTERNET ACCESS

Carnegie Library, 4400 Forbes Ave, 622-3131. Free Internet use.

TITUSVILLE   The oil well business got off to a picturesque start out here in north-western Pennsylvania. In 1859, Col Edwin Drake, right here in Titusville, sank the first oil well in the world. The site is now **Drake Well Memorial Park**, with a working reconstruction of the original rig and a museum containing photos and artefacts of the early boom days, (814) 827-2797, Mon-Sat 9am-5pm, Sun 10am-5pm. $4. Park daily 9am-dusk.

THE MID-ATLANTIC

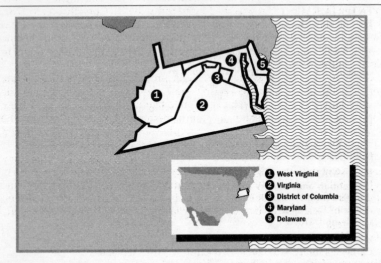

① West Virginia
② Virginia
③ District of Columbia
④ Maryland
⑤ Delaware

A visit to this region, where North meets South historically and climatically, reveals not only America's past but the shape of its future: decisions made here are the stuff from which history books are written. Centred around Washington DC, the area features politics, Colonial and Civil War history, legions of lawyers, and a growing amount of federal research. The nation's governmental heart has spawned technology, research and information industries in neighbouring Maryland and Virginia where there are such notable federal establishments as NASA's Goddard Spaceflight Center, the National Cancer Institute at Frederick, the Agricultural Department Research Center at Greenbelt, the National Security Agency at Fort Meade, the National Institute of Health in Bethesda, and the Smithsonian Institution in Washington. The I-270 'Technology Corridor' from Washington to Frederick now outpaces growth in California's 'Silicon Valley.'

The region has a varied climate (snowy in winter, almost monsoonal in July), brilliant springtime flora (azaleas, dogwoods, flowering cherries), and its natural resources offer recreation in all seasons. You can sail, swim and fish on the Chesapeake Bay or hike, raft and ski in the Appalachians of Virginia and West Virginia.

DELAWARE   *The First State*

This skinny triangle of a state should have been named, in all fairness, 'du Pont': it was built on the success of the du Pont empire. (The family traces its roots in Delaware back 200 years to when Pierre Samuel du Pont de

Nemours, a counsellor to Louis XVI at the time of the French Revolution, decided to visit his friend Thomas Jefferson and take an extended vacation in the US for his health.) The state is instead named for the British Lord de La Warr, who never set foot on his namesake's soil. Delawareans proudly call it the First State, as it was the first to ratify the US Constitution in 1787. A former slave-holding state, Delaware sided with the North in the Civil War, and was a throughway along the 'underground railway,' a clandestine escape route from house cellar to house cellar that brought 3000 blacks to Northern freedom.

If you're like most travellers, you will probably only pass through the northern tip of the triangle—across the Delaware Memorial Bridge (the world's largest twin span bridge) and on to Baltimore, Philadelphia, or New York City. Between the state's northern metropolis, Wilmington, and the southerly Fenwick Island lie miles of sandy coastline. Great beaches offer a variety of sporting activities and cheap camping.

Flat coastal plain covers 94 per cent of Delaware's three counties (New Castle, Kent and Sussex); there's even a cypress swamp, the most northerly in the US. Ponds and tidy farms are sprinkled across the wooden backbone of the peninsula, which levels out towards the Maryland border. There's no sales tax in Delaware so if you have any large purchases to make do it here. *www.state.de.us*
The telephone area code for the entire state is 302.

WILMINGTON   The 'Chemical Capital of the World,' and the lucky spot where Eleuthere du Pont decided to build his powder mill in 1802. Wealth, labs, factories and eyesores followed, though downtown renewal has restored the **Grand Opera House.** There are several other imposing or otherwise interesting historical relics to see before pushing on to Dover, 45 miles south.

ACCOMMODATION/FOOD
Washington St. Ale House, 1208 N Washington St, 658-2537. Burgers, Spanish, Mexican, sandwiches. Dinner from $10.
Red Rose Inn, 1515 N du Pont Hwy, New Castle, 328-3500. S-$45, D-$48.
Days Inn, 5209 Concord Pike, N Wilmington, (800) 445-0852. D-$65.

OF INTEREST
Brandywine Park, 571-7713. One of Delaware's 13 state parks. Along the river between Augustine and Market St Bridges. Zoo and landscaped gardens with 118 Japanese cherry trees.
Grand Opera House, 818 N Market St Mall, 652-5577. Built in 1871 with an ornate cast iron facade, it now houses the **Delaware Center for the Performing Arts.**
Hagley Museum, Barley Mill Rd & Brandywine Creek, 658-2401. 225-acre complex on the site of the original du Pont black powder works, with restored granite buildings amidst wooded hillsides and huge trees; pleasant walks along the Brandywine. Exhibits, demonstrations and museum. Daily 9.30am-4.30pm. $9.75; $7.50 w/student ID. 'Very interesting and worthwhile.'
Longwood Gardens, 12 miles north of Wilmington at US 1 & Rte 52 near Kennett Square, PA, (610) 388-1000. Yet another du Pont hangout, formerly the country estate of industrial magnate Pierre S du Pont. Spectacular gardens 9am-6pm, Tue, Thu & Sat 'til 10pm; conservatories 10am-6pm, Tue, Thu & Sat 'til 10pm. $12, Tue $8. Admission includes concerts and choreographed fountain displays. 'Beautiful.'

Nemours Mansion and Gardens, 3¹/₂ miles north-west on Rockland Rd, 651-6912. 102-room Louis XVI chateau look-alike with all the gear: furniture, tapestries, French gardens, built in 1910 by Alfred I du Pont. Tours Tue-Sun by appt., $10, May-Nov.

New Castle, 6 miles south of Wilmington on Rte 9, is a small town full of the atmosphere and architecture of the Colonial and early republic periods. Near Strand and Delaware Sts, William Penn entered his vast Colonial lands. Here, a round border separates the states of Pennsylvania and Delaware; the spire of the New Castle courthouse was used as the compass point to create this odd configuration.

The Rocks, waterfront park at the foot of 7th St, 1 block south of Church St. A monument marks the site of **Fort Christina**, built by the Swedish-Dutch expedition which landed here in 1638, making it the site of the first permanent settlement in the Delaware Valley.

Wilmington & Western Railroad, Greenbank Station, off Route 41, 998-1930. Ride through historic red clay valleys on this turn-of-the-century steam train. W/ends only, 1 hr trip $8.

Winterthur Museum, 6 miles north-west on Rte 52, 888-4600. Once the home of Henry Francis du Pont, Winterthur now houses one of the world's greatest antique collections—nearly 200 period rooms display American decorative arts from the 17th-19th centuries. General admission $8, tours cost an additional $5, $9, or $13. Mon-Sat 9am-5pm, Sun noon-5pm.

INFORMATION/TRAVEL
Visitors Bureau, 100 W 10th St, Suite 20, 652-4088.
Amtrak, Martin Luther King Jr Blvd & French St, 429-6529/(800) 872-7245.
Greyhound, Wilmington Bus Station, 101 N French St, 655-6111/(800) 231-2222. Open 24 hrs.

DOVER   One of the oldest state capitals in the nation, Dover was founded in 1683 when William Penn decided to build two key elements of civilised life - a prison and a courthouse - on the site.

ACCOMMODATION
Howard Johnson, 561 N du Pont Hwy, 678-8900. Pool, TV, laundry. D-$65-$75.
Super Lodge, 246 N du Pont Hwy, 678-0160. Pool, TV, laundry, fridge in room. S-$49, D-$59.

OF INTEREST
Museum of Archaeology and **Museum of Small Town Life**, 316 S Governors Ave, 739-4266. Three galleries house fascinating range of Americana. Tue-Sat 10am-4pm.
Legislative Hall, capitol building on Court St.
Old State House, the Green, 739-2466. Built in 1792, a fine example of American Georgian architecture with portraits of Delaware celebrities inside. Tue-Sat 10am-4pm, Sun 1.30pm-4pm. Go to visitor center for tickets.

INFORMATION/TRAVEL
Delaware Visitor Information, 99 King's Hwy, (800) 441-8846.
Dover Information Center, 406 Federal St, 739-4266. Information on accommodation, restaurants and museums. 'Very helpful.' Mon-Sat 8.30am-4.30pm, Sun 1.30pm-4.30pm.
Trailways, 650 Bay Court Plaza, 734-1417. Mon-Fri 9am-4pm, w/ends 11am-4pm.

THE DELAWARE COAST   Much of the coastline follows Delaware Bay out towards the Atlantic, but even the southern shore is protected from the open ocean by Fenwick Island. **Lewes** (pronounced 'Lewis') is one of the earliest European settlements in the New World. First inhabited by the Dutch, Lewes is now the traditional home of pilots who guide ships up Delaware Bay—and a charming town to explore by foot. Lewes is also the port for the ferry to Cape May, NJ, 645-6346. Further south near Delaware Seashore State Park, **Rehoboth Beach,** famous for its mile-long boardwalk, is popular with Washingtonians fleeing the capital's cruel summer heat. 'Rehoboth', Hebrew for 'enough room' will seem ironic to anyone visiting the body-blanketed beach on a hot weekend. Nearby **Dewey Beach** and **Bethany Beach** are nearly as popular.

ACCOMMODATION/INFORMATION
In **Rehoboth**, summer rates are very high. Try searching on foot away from the ocean or contact the **Chamber of Commerce**, 501 Rehoboth Ave, in the old train station, 227-2233, for room listings.

Joseph's Cottages, 506 Rehoboth Ave, 227-2222. Motel $50, cottages w/kitchens $350/week. No air conditioning, 5 blocks from beach.

Oak Grove Motel, Rehoboth Ave and Canal St, 227-7156. Pleasant, 6 blocks from beach. $85, $460 weekly.

Roope's Cottages and Motel, Grove and 6th Sts, 227-7858. Motel for $50/night, cottages w/kitchens $85, $300 weekly. 5 blocks from beach.

Camping: Near Lewes, **Cape Henlopen State Park** on Rte 9, 645-8983. Sites $20 for four, XP-$2. Between Dewey and Bethany Beaches,

Delaware Seashore State Park on Rte 1 at the Indian River inlet, 227-2800. Sites from $18 for four, XP-$2. 'Friendly proprietors.' **Big Oaks Family Campgrounds,** on Rte 1 2 1/2 miles north of Rehoboth, 645-6838. Pool, store, boating, fishing; sites for $27. Shuttle to beach, $2.

FOOD
Rehoboth Beach is paradise for junk-food junkies, e.g. pizza at **Nicola's** on 1st St, and french fries at **Thrasher's**, on Rehoboth Ave.

The Avenue Diner, 19 Rehoboth Ave, 226-0132. Pancakes, waffles, sandwiches, Italian food and seafood. Lunch for under $7, dinner under $15.

Dolly's Candyland, Boardwalk at Rehoboth Ave, 227-0757. Famous taffy, huge red sign is a Rehoboth boardwalk landmark.

Summer House Restaurant and Saloon, across from City Hall, 227-3895. Sandwiches, burgers, seafood. Sandwiches from $5, dinner from $11.

OF INTEREST
Bike rentals, Bob's Bike Rentals at 1st and Maryland Ave in Rehoboth Beach, 227-7966. $3-$3.50/hour, $10-$15/day. Note that in summer months biking is only allowed on the boardwalk from 5am-10am.

Boat rentals, Bayside Adventures on Collins St in Dewey, 226-2012. Rents skiffs that seat 4 people, $65/half-day.

Concerts, at the bandstand on Rehoboth Ave. Summer weekend evenings at 8pm. Call 227-6181 for more info.

Outlet Shopping, Rehoboth Outlets on Rte 1, 226-9223/(888) SHOP-333. 20%-70% discounts and no sales tax. More than 140 outlets including the GAP, J. Crew, Nike, and Polo Ralph Lauren.

Queen Anne's Railroad, 730 King's Highway, Lewes, 644-1720/(888) 456-TOOT. A live murder mystery is acted out between courses on a Royal Zephyr Dinner Train. Trains leave Lewes for a two hour round trip on Wed and Sat evenings. $60 includes dinner and entertainment. Rsvs required.

Surfing, Surf Sessions, 10 South Carolina Ave in Fenwick Island, 539-2126. Offers surfing lessons, $25 first half-day, $15 every half-day thereafter. Week-long surf camp programs also available.

Whale and Dolphin Watching, Fisherman's Wharf Cruises in Lewes, 645-8862. 2 hour dolphin cruise leaves at 9.30 am, $12. 4 hour dolphin and whale cruise leaves at 1pm, $21, 1 1/2 hour sunset cruises leave at 7pm, $10.

TRAVEL
Carolina Trailways/Greyhound, (800) 231-2222. Daily trips to DC ($32.75 o/w), Baltimore ($28.75), and Wilmington ($17). Flag the bus down on the corner of Rehoboth and Columbia Aves in Rehoboth Beach, buy tkts from the driver (cash only).
Jolly Trolley of Rehoboth, runs between Rehoboth and South Dewey with stops throughout the area every 30 minutes, 8am-2am. Catch the trolley at Rehoboth Ave at the Boardwalk. 227-1197 for more info.
Park 'n Ride Transit System, runs along Rte 1 between Lewes and Dewey Beach with various stops in Rehoboth Beach, including the outlets. $2 all day pass. 226-2001 for more info.

DISTRICT OF COLUMBIA

WASHINGTON DC When the framers of the Constitution chose a site for the new nation's capital they heeded Thomas Jefferson's advice that the seat of government should be free of regional interest. The location eventually chosen lay between North and South along the Potomac River. Congress entrusted the design to Frenchman Pierre L'Enfant, who began work on the city in 1791. L'Enfant envisioned a city that would rival the capitals of Europe while at the same time reflecting the bold qualities of the new America.

Washington today does indeed have a monumental quality, with its broad avenues, magnificent memorials, and great granite buildings in the Classical style. It is only in recent years, however, that Washington has overcome its backwater past, progressing steadily from the days when John F. Kennedy wryly described it as 'a city of Northern charm and Southern efficiency.'

Though still a fairly transient town, the city that once changed populations with every new presidential administration has become a highly desirable place to live. This is particularly evident in Georgetown, where quaint brick houses - some of which were once quarters for slaves, poor labourers and free blacks - now command million-dollar sums. Georgetown's Wisconsin and M Streets buzz with cosmopolitan restaurants, art galleries, and expensive boutiques. Its quiet townhouse-lined streets are best explored on foot, and its waterfront is the perfect spot for a stroll on warm evenings.

While Georgetown caters increasingly to well-heeled tourists and suburbanites, the Adams-Morgan neighbourhood attracts a more diverse, local crowd. 'Flavour' is the password to this vibrant international community just a few minutes' walk from Dupont Circle. From Cajun to Caribbean, Ethiopian to Hispanic, you name it and you're likely to find it (at bargain prices) along 18th St at Columbia Rd. Primarily a night-time neighbourhood, things change every September on Adams-Morgan Day when the streets explode with music, dance and ethnic food as thousands of Washingtonians exchange their pinstripes for T-shirts and let it all hang out.

Indeed, despite its bureaucratic image, DC is surprisingly youthful, due in part to a large student population (Georgetown, George Washington, American, Catholic, and Howard Universities are all located here). The city is home to an equally large international community that includes embassies, the 11,000-person World Bank, its sister the International Monetary Fund (IMF), the Inter-American Development Bank, and the Organization of American States (OAS), plus sizeable immigrant groups.

Fortunately for the traveller, crime is concentrated in residential areas that most tourists don't visit. The majority of attractions, accommodation, and restaurants are located in safe areas. Even so, it is always advisable to travel with caution, especially at night.

Washington is a pleasant city to visit. There is a tremendous amount to see (mostly free), and it's cleaner and greener than most US cities, with a subway system that's graffiti-proof, efficient and safe. The MCI Arena - a venue for sports and concerts - is slowly breathing new life into the city's once moribund downtown area. During the summer there is a constant stream of interesting events on the huge village green known as the Mall and at other locations, but beware the great heat and humidity. The most agreeable times to visit are spring, when daffodils, cherry trees, tulips, azaleas, and magnolias bloom; and autumn, when the air is crisp and clear and the museums are not overflowing with tourists. DC is divided into four quadrants - NW, NE, SW, and SE - branching out from the capitol building. It's possible for the same street address to exist in all four quadrants so be sure to pay attention to which section of the city an address is in.

www.washington.org
The telephone area code for Washington is 202.

ACCOMMODATION
Housing is more expensive than in other US cities and less abundant for the budget traveller. For longer, summer stays, be prepared to search long and hard as you will be competing with the hoards of interns that descend on the capital from May to September. The classified section of the free *City Paper*, out every Thursday evening, is packed with temporary/shared housing and summer sublets—move fast to get the one you want. Available from most convenience stores and street corner vending machines. It's also worth checking the Friday and weekend classifieds in the *Washington Post*.

Allen Lee Hotel, 2224 F St NW, 331-1224. Close to the Lincoln Memorial, State Department and Kennedy Center. D-$47 shared bath, $57 private bath. Rsvs recommended. Metro: Foggy Bottom.

Braxton Hotel, 1440 Rhode Island Ave NW, 232-7800/(800) 350-5759. D-$60-$70. TV, easy walk to White House, Metro: McPherson Sq. 'Good value for money.'

Connecticut Woodley Guest Home, 2647 Woodley Rd NW, 667-0218. S-$53 incl tax, D-$59 incl tax, shared bath. Metro: Woodley Park/Zoo-Adams Morgan.

Davis House, 1822 R St NW, near Dupont Circle, 232-3196. Run by Quakers, limited, bare accommodation, single $45, sharing with other $35. No smoking or drinking, international guests, peace and justice workers only.

George Washington University Off-Campus Housing Office, Marvin Center, 800 21st St NW, 994-7221. Advertises apartments and shared houses available for the summer period. *www.och.gwu.edu*

Georgetown University publishes a good weekly listing of summer accommodation for rent; contact the student housing office at 100 Harbin Hall on campus, 687-4560. You will have to go in person to get a copy of the list. In general, campus accommodation is only available to students taking summer courses at those universities—and these are usually full by the end of May. Try the notice boards at local cafes (**Chesapeake Bagel Bakery** and **Food for Thought**, both on Connecticut Ave, have boards brimming with ads), and at Union Station.

Hotel Harrington, 11th & E NW, 628-8140. Downtown, between Capitol and White House. $94 for up to 4. 'Crowded.' 'Clean, safe & central location, near all tourist attractions, self-service cafeteria downstairs.' 'Brilliant.'

International Guest House, 1441 Kennedy St NW, 726-5808. 4 miles from downtown. Shared room, shared bath $25 pp, includes breakfast and tea and cookies at 9pm. Rsvs, max 2-week stay. Half-hour bus ride to metro. 'Very kind people; you can meet travellers from all over the world here.'

Kalorama Guest House, 1854 Mintwood Pl NW, 667-6369. D-$50-$70, XP-$5 shared bath, rsvs required. 'We were very well looked after.' Metro: Woodley Park/Zoo-Adams Morgan.

Washington International AYH Hostel, 1009 11th St NW, 737-2333. $20 AYH, $23 non-AYH. Linens free, bring your own towel. Open all day; organises tours and outings. Rsvs. 'All the facilities you could need—the red jelly baby of the hostel world.' Metro: Metro Center

William Penn House, 515 E Capitol St, 543-5560. A Quaker Seminary Center open to travellers when there are no conferences. $35 p/night (students), dorm-style room, includes a hearty breakfast. 'Clean and friendly, no smoking or alcohol.' Metro: Capitol South.

Camping: **Greenbelt Park**, Greenbelt, MD, (301) 344-3944. 6 miles north of Washington along I-95, off at exit 23. Sites $13.

HOUSING INFO:
For B&B listings: **The Bed & Breakfast League/Sweet Dreams and Toast**, PO Box 9490, DC 20016-9490, 363-7767, S-$63-120, D-$78-140.

FOOD
NEAR THE MALL: Restaurants are scarce around the Mall, and the distance between them can be daunting to a hungry stomach-on-legs. Most museums have a (crowded, noisy) cafeteria with some awful, overpriced, plastic food. A few government cafeterias are open to the public during working hours: '**Dept of Commerce** building cafeteria—good food at reasonable prices.' Here are some inexpensive eating alternatives, but be aware that, in the summer, all the other visitors to the nation's capital are going to head for them, too.

Au Bon Pain, at locations all over DC. Choose from a variety of different breads and design your own sandwich at little cost, half sandwiches available. 'Good places for BUNACers.'

The Cascades Cafe, in the basement of the **National Gallery of Art** between the old and new wings. Mon-Sat 10am-4.30pm, Sun 11am-5.30pm. Buffet (right next to the cafe) Mon-Sat 10am-3pm, Sun 11am-4pm. 'Tourist food, tourist prices, but it's beside a fabulous waterfall—it's like being a part of a sculpture. Worth a cup of coffee.' (The gallery also contains two other decent cafeterias).

International Square, 19th & K Sts NW, 223-1850, French, Italian, Chinese, US, etc. Watch Washington bureaucrats eat lunch. Mon-Fri 8am-6pm, Sat 10am-5pm.

Library of Congress Cafeteria, top floor of the Madison Building of the L of C, 1st St and Independence Ave SE. Open only for lunch, standard cafeteria food at reasonable prices, but offers one of the best views of the city. Mon-Fri 12.30pm-2pm, open 'til 3.30 only for snacks.

Old Post Office Pavilion, 1100 Pennsylvania Ave NW. 'Large selection of reasonably priced places to eat—American, Greek, Indian, Chinese, etc,' plus entertainment. Summer hours: Mon-Sat 10am-9pm, Sun noon-7pm.

Reeve's Bakery, 1306 G St NW, 628-6350. Excellent bakery with simple restaurant in the basement, burgers and sandwiches for reasonable prices, hasn't yet been discovered by the tourists. Mon-Sat 7am-6pm.

Scholl's Colonial Cafeteria, 1990 K St NW in the Esplanade Mall, 296-3065, is *the* place to eat for those on a budget. Good, home-cooked food at unbelievably low prices. 'Try the rhubarb pie, in fact, any pie!' Mon-Sat 7am-8pm. Closed between meal times.

Shops at National Place, 14th St & Pennsylvania Ave NW, 662-1250. Plenty of inexpensive eateries. Mon-Sat 10am-7pm, Sun noon-5pm.

Union Station, 1st St & Massachusetts Ave NE, houses a wide variety of eating places, everything from bagels to rice bowls to gourmet frozen yoghurt. Easy access by metro.

US Senate Cafeteria, 224-4249, in the basement of the Dirkson Bldg, Capitol Hill. Famous for its Bean Soup. 'Try it—you'll know where they get their wind.' Open to public 7.30am-3pm. Noon-1.30pm is feeding time for congress people alone.

ETHNIC FOOD: DC excels at cheap, authentic ethnic restaurants. Generally speaking, look for **Vietnamese** food in the Vietnamese enclave in Arlington, VA (take the blue/orange metro line to the Clarendon stop); good **Ethiopian** and various types of **Hispanic** eateries in the Adams-Morgan 18th St & Columbia Ave NW area; and **seafood** at Market Lunch (in Eastern Market, 225 7th St SE) at the Eastern Market metro stop on the blue/orange line - try the excellent crab cakes; and on Maine Ave along the Potomac River in SW, Metro: Waterfront. If you're feeling spontaneous, go to Adams-Morgan and look around; it would be hard to go wrong, no matter which restaurant you stumble into. Unless otherwise noted, assume Georgetown restaurants are a rip-off. Some recommendations:

Burrito Brothers, 332-2308, 1718 Connecticut Ave NW. Carry-out your quesadillas, tacos, etc, a few southward steps to Dupont Circle for a Mexican picnic amid an ever-changing crowd of bike messengers, chess players, musicians, protesters. Delicious and filling for a good price. Sun-Thu 11am-10.30pm, Fri-Sat 'til 11pm. Metro: Dupont Circle

Cactus Cantina, 3300 Wisconsin Ave NW, 686-7222. The best value Mexican in DC, look for the big plastic cacti outside. Daily 11.30am-11pm 'til midnight on Fridays and Saturdays.

City Lights of China, 265-6688, 1731 Connecticut Ave NW. Absolutely the best Chinese food in Washington; even the fortune cookies are delicious! Try pan-fried dumplings and vegetable curl. $9-$12, 'moderately expensive and worth it.' Metro: Dupont Circle

El Tamarindo, 1785 Florida Ave NW, 328-3660. Salvadoran and Mexican dinners, from $9. By all accounts the cheapest and best in Adams-Morgan. Most potent margaritas in DC. Free tortillas and salsa; wash it all down with a Mexican beer.

Meskerem, 2343 18th St NW, 462-4100. Ethiopian restaurant renowned for quality cuisine and affordable prices. Eat upstairs sitting on floor cushions, and soak in the ambience. Be warned, though; you'll struggle to your feet after filling up on a plate of *injera* and *wats*! Friendly staff and bright decor. Appetisers $7-$11, dinner $9-$12. Worth it: 'You won't have to eat for a week!' Noon-midnight daily.

Thai Room, 5037 Connecticut Ave at Nebraska NW, 244-5933. Mingle with overlanders over real Thai food. Don't get this mixed up with the more expensive and not-as-good Thai restaurant down the street.

White Tiger, 301 Massachusetts Ave NE, 546-5900. Lunch buffet $9 Mon-Fri, $10 w/ends. Indian dishes varying from eggplant to chick-pea to lamb. Metro: Union Station.

PLAIN OLD AMERICAN: Plenty of these in DC, too.
Booeymonger's, 3265 Prospect St NW, 333-4810; or 5258 Wisconsin Ave NW, 686-5805. Great sandwiches, burgers $6-$8, daily lunch specials for $5.50.
The Brickskellar, 22nd St NW, btwn P & Q Sts, 293-1885. Over 600 different beers from all over the world. Good, cheap food includes buffalo. 'Tastes like beef.' Beers from US microbreweries more potent than US domestic beers—you have been warned! Mon-Thu 11.30am-2am, Fri 11.30am-3am, Sat 6pm-3am, Sun 6pm-2am. Metro: Dupont Circle
Lindy's, 2040 Pennsylvania Ave NW, near Tower Records, 452-0055. Perfect for lunch. Choose from the 22 different varieties of burgers, each with vegetarian equivalent, and lots of sandwiches, $2-$6. Tempting ice-cream store in the arcade next door. Metro: Foggy Bottom
Safeway Townhouse, 20th & S Sts, 483-3908. Small supermarket with 'good salad bar.' **Safeway,** 2000 Wisconsin Ave NW. Gigantic supermarket otherwise known as 'Social Safeway'; full of shoppers picking up ice-cream and each other.
Trios Restaurant, 17th & Q Sts NW, 232-6305. 'Very friendly little restaurant, serving good food. Frequented by locals. About $10 per head.' Metro: Dupont Circle
Waffle Shop, 522 10th St NW, 638-3430. Classic greasy spoon, great diner food, sandwiches at reasonable prices. Popular with locals, everyone eats at the counter. Metro: Metro Center
Coffee shops have sprung up all over DC in recent years. You'll find, **Starbucks**, **Dean & Deluca**, and **Foster Brothers**, to name but a few, at locations city-wide.

BREAKFAST: Chesapeake Bagel Bakery, 1636 Connecticut Ave NW, just above Dupont Circle; 215 Pennsylvania Ave SE, on Capitol Hill, and at several locations throughout DC. Great coffee and bran muffins, as well as 60¢ bagels (also open for lunch and supper).
The Florida Avenue Grill, 1100 Florida Ave NW, 265-1586. Taxi drivers originally frequented this small corner cafe near Howard University when it opened in the 1940s. Today it is visited by all walks of life. Breakfast is highly recommended; country ham, eggs, grits, sweet fried apples and hot biscuits. All meals under $13. Not safe at night. Metro: U St-Cardozo.
Jimmy T's, 501 E Capitol St SE, 546-3646. Breakfast all day long, also burgers and sandwiches, most meals under $6. Wed-Fri 6.30am-3pm, Sat-Sun 8am-3pm. Metro: Capitol South
Sherrill's Bakery, 233 Pennsylvania Ave SE, Capitol Hill, 544-2480, bee-hive coifed waitresses are pros at moving food and people. Don't cross them!

ATMOSPHERE: Au Pied de Cochon, 1335 Wisconsin Ave, NW, 337-6400, Georgetown. Site of real-life spy hi-jinx involving KGB defector (or not?) and flab-bergasted CIA agent. Ask a bartender for a commemorative 'Yurchenko shooter' and for the *true* tale behind the events of 4 Nov 1985. Open 24 hrs.
Food for Thought, 1738 Connecticut Ave NW, 797-1095. Vegetarian food; whole-earth music nightly. Bargain prices for substantial meals. Metro: Dupont Circle
Kramerbooks and Afterwords Cafe, 1517 Connecticut Ave NW, 387-1400. Bookshop and cafe with jazz, folk and bluegrass music; the place to book-browse or people-watch. Order margaritas and split the atomic nachos, or chill out with a smoothie (blended ice-cream, fruit and liqueur—delicious!) 24 hrs at weekends.

SWEET TOOTH: The best ice cream in DC is **Max's Best Ice Cream**, 2416 Wisconsin Ave NW. Featuring the best-seller Orange Chocolate Chip. Winners in the variety stakes are: **Ben & Jerry's**, in the Old Post Office Pavilion, 842-5882, M St & Wisconsin Ave in Georgetown, and 327 7th St SE on Capitol Hill. Flavours include environmentally-conscious *Rainforest Crunch*. A cool place to hang out.
Thomas Sweets, Wisconsin Ave & P St, Georgetown, 337-0616. Try their cinnamon ice cream if you like 'Cheerios'!

OF INTEREST
GOVERNMENT BUILDINGS:
Botanic Garden, 1st St & Independence Ave SW, btwn Air and Space Museum and Capitol, 225-7099. Tired feet will enjoy a respite as you lounge on benches amid 500 varieties of orchids and other tropical flora. Indoor conservatory closed for renovation until late 2000, but the landscaped gardens outside will remain open to the public until then. Free. Metro: Federal Center SW.
Bureau of Engraving and Printing, 14th & C Sts SW, 622-2000. Manufactures paper money, government bonds and stamps. Free guided tours Apr-Sep, Mon-Fri 9am-2pm. Get tickets for the tour at the ticket booth on Raoul Wallenberg Pl (formerly 15th St), the booth opens at 8am. 'No free samples.' Metro: Smithsonian.
Folger Shakespeare Library, 2nd & East Capitol Sts SE, behind the Library of Congress's Jefferson Building, 544-4600. Here you'll find America's finest Shakespeare collection, including 79 copies of the First Folio (the first published edition of Shakespeare's collected works)—more copies than anywhere else. At least one is always on display. Mon-Sat 10am-4pm. Metro: Capitol South.
J Edgar Hoover FBI Building, Pennsylvania Avé btwn 9th & 10th Sts NW, 324-3447, named after the man they couldn't get rid of because he had the goods on them all, even though, as it turns out, the Mafia had the goods on *him*. The only way to enter the building is to go on the free 1-hr guided tours starting from the E St entrance. See various FBI labs, a fire-arms demo and mildly impressive displays of riches recovered from bad guys. 'Ugliest building in DC.' 'Disappointing.' 'Hour-long queues.' Tours were suspended indefinitely in 1999, call ahead to check for availability. Metro: Metro Center.
Library of Congress, 1st St & Independence Ave SE, opposite Capitol, 707-5000. The largest library in the world is made up of three buildings, but the one you'll want to see is the astounding **Jefferson Building**: walls, ceilings and floors are covered with inspiring, allegorical scenes representing such popular subjects as 'Truth, Beauty'. The cumulative effect is overwhelming (west entrance on 1st St is open for viewings of the Great Hall, 10am-5.30pm, Mon-Sat. Tours available, 707-8000). Among the library's holdings are a perfect copy of the Gutenberg Bible (1450), the first book to be printed from moveable type; Jefferson's rough draft of the Declaration of Independence; Lincoln's drafts of the Gettysburg Address; a vast folk music collection you can listen to (by appt.); and a major portion of the books published in the US since the Civil War. Metro: Capitol South.
National Archives, 8th St & Constitution Ave NW, 501-5402. Daily from 8.45am, Mon & Weds 'til 5pm; Tue, Thu, Fri 'til 9pm, Sat 'til 4.45pm, free. Preserves and displays government records of enduring value, e.g. Declaration of Independence, Bill of Rights, Constitution and Watergate Tapes. Metro: Archives/Navy Memorial.
Supreme Court Building, 1st St, btwn Maryland Ave & E Capitol St NE, facing the Capitol, 479-3000. Where the country's highest judicial body holds its sessions. You can see the court in session by waiting in line, but the court is usually adjourned from the last part of June until October. Mon-Fri 9am-4pm, tours 9.30am-3.30pm. Metro: Capitol South.
The Capitol, 225-6827, on Capitol Hill, the central point of Washington, from which the city is divided into quadrants. The city's most familiar landmark, it holds the chambers of the Senate and the House of Representatives. Of particular note are the works of Brumidi in the Great Rotunda and corridors. Free guided tour covers only the Rotunda and the Crypt, then you're left to your own devices. 'Very interesting tour, certainly worthwhile.' 'Most interesting part is the Senate Chamber-much smaller than you'd expect.' Summer tour hours: Mon-Fri 9.30am-6pm, Sat 'til 3.30pm. Get tickets for the tour (guided or self-guided) outside, on the east side of the building near the fountains. When the Senate or House is in session, you need a pass to enter either chamber. Passes for the Senate Gallery can be obtained from the

Senate Appointment Desk; for the House apply to the House Appointment Desk. Passport or photo ID required. If Congress is in session after 6pm or on a Saturday, no pass is required. The underground train linking the Capitol and the Senate Office Buildings is available to all. Metro: Capitol South.

Voice of America, 330 Independence Ave SW, 619-4700. Watch and listen to live broadcasts. 'Fascinating; not just another radio station.' Tours Mon-Fri 10.30am and 2.30pm.

White House, 1600 Pennsylvania Ave NW, 456-7041. Although he chose the site, George Washington is the only president never to have slept here. The White House has been rebuilt or redesigned inside and out many times, most memorably in 1814, courtesy of the British Army who burnt it down. The structural integrity may have been most severely tested in 1829 during Andrew Jackson's inaugural carouse - the new president's backwoods buddies nearly destroyed the place. On a tour you'll be shuffled through a few of the well-proportioned rooms and furnishings supplied by successive Mrs. Presidents. Free tours Tue-Sat 10am-noon. 'Long, slow lines.' Tickets are only issued on the day of the tour, from the White House Visitor Center on 15th & E Sts. They start issuing them at 7.30am and you *must* get there early. Metro for the Visitor Center: Federal Triangle; for the White House: McPherson Sq.

MONUMENTS: The National Park Service, which runs all of DC's monuments and major parks, has an amazing web site, *www.nps.gov* Entrance to all the monuments is free.

The **Franklin D Roosevelt Memorial**, 426-6841, is situated near the cherry tree walk on the Tidal Basin, W Potomac Park. Each of FDR's four terms in office are represented by a landscape of four outdoor rooms with inscribed walls and sculpted figures, surrounded by a profusion of waterfalls, trees and plants. Metro: Foggy Bottom.

Jefferson Memorial, 426-6841, on Tidal Basin south of Mall. The dome, based on Jefferson's home at Monticello, and the quiet serenity of the ionic columns create an intimate monument. See it at night, floodlit, for best effect.

Korean War Memorial, adjacent to **Lincoln Memorial Reflecting Pool**, 426-6841. Built at a cost of $18m. A sculptured row of 19 foot soldiers ready for combat, and a 164 ft mural etched with over 2000 photographic images of service men and women, depicts in detail the hardship and tragedy of a war in which 54,000 Americans lost their lives. Daily 8am-midnight. Metro: Foggy Bottom.

Lincoln Memorial, 426-6841, at the foot of the Mall, open 8am-midnight. The large brooding figure flanked by two Lincoln addresses etched into the walls, is an impressive sight which no visitor to the city should miss. Rather than becoming an overgrown tombstone, this memorial has evolved into a living symbol of freedom and human dignity. The **Vietnam Veterans Memorial** is just next door, a sombre granite slab that lists the names of all 58,000 American dead and has a shockingly direct power. The faces of the visitors tell more than the memorial does. The **Vietnam Women's Memorial,** across from the Wall, depicts three service-women with a wounded soldier. Metro: Foggy Bottom.

Washington Monument, on the Mall at 15th St, 426-6841. A 555 ft obelisk, by law the tallest structure in DC. The view at the top is splendid, but the observation room is grungy, small and usually overcrowded. Get free tickets from the booth on 15th St - it's a good idea to go early. Don't believe anyone who tells you that the line about ¾ of the way up the side of the monument is the 'high water mark' from spring floods (it's the point at which construction was halted during the Civil War and later resumed with a different colour of stone). 'Closes during thunderstorms!' Summer: daily 8am-midnight, otherwise 9am-4.30pm. Walk down tours of inside at 10am and 2pm. Metro: Smithsonian.

SMITHSONIAN INSTITUTION. The world's largest collection of museums, begun by British scientist James Smithson, who left his entire fortune (105 bags of gold) to finance it. The Smithsonian comprises the National Zoo and 14 museums, most of which are on the Mall between the Capitol and the Washington Monument. There are millions of catalogued items ranging from Lindbergh's plane to Glenn's capsule, from fossils to the Hope Diamond, from moon rocks to the First Ladies' gowns. All museums are free (nominal charge for films). General hours 10am-5.30pm (some museums extend their hours in summer). 357-2020 for 24 hr info on new displays and museum events; for general info 357-2700. *www.si.edu* The **Arthur M. Sackler Gallery** and the **National Museum of African Art**, both 357-1300, 10th St & Independence Ave SW. Underground museums behind the Smithsonian Castle. The former houses a collection of Asian art and artefacts, while the latter is the only museum dedicated to African art in the US. The **Freer Gallery**, 12th St & Jefferson Dr SW, has a wonderful collection of Asian and Asian-inspired art, with an underground link to the Sackler. The **Smithsonian Castle**, the museum's original building, houses a Visitors Center with info on all there is to see and do.

The **Arts and Industries Building**, 9th St & Jefferson Dr, houses the Centennial collection from the World Exposition in 1876. Funky old place, full of old machinery, trains and stuffed stuff. The South Hall features changing exhibits from the **Anacostia Museum and Center for African American History**. Metro: Smithsonian.

Hirshhorn Museum and Sculpture Garden on the Mall at Independence Ave, has a modern art collection not to be missed. The upper floors of the controversial, donut-shaped Hirshhorn display a fine permanent collection of 20th century art (1930-1970ish); the lounge has a nice view of the Mall. But the changing exhibits in the basement are where the avant-garde action is. The theatre in the basement occasionally screens free cutting-edge films. Metro: L'Enfant Plaza.

Museum of Natural History, 10th St & Constitution Ave, is truly 'the nation's attic'— some 118 million artefacts—it even *smells* like mothballs and formaldehyde. Scattered throughout seemingly endless hallways are wildlife dioramas, dinosaur bones, the Hope Diamond, a scale model of a blue whale, a functioning coral reef, live insects, Indian skulls with partially-healed holes, a perfect crystal ball and the world's largest stuffed elephant. The museum's newest feature is a 3D IMAX movie theatre. Metro: Smithsonian.

National Air and Space Museum, next door to the Hirshhorn, is the world's most popular museum, with everything from space capsules to U2 photographs of Soviet missile sites, to the earliest planes. 'Best thing we did in Washington, take a tape-recorded tour for most benefit.' 'A must.' See the 'mind-blowing' films such as *To Fly* and *The Dream is Alive* on a 5-storey IMAX screen that gives you the impression you are riding through a forest in a coach, zooming over the desert in your fighter jet or hovering outside your space capsule above the earth. 'Highly recommended.' Check out the award-winning *Cosmic Voyage*, $5.50, $4.25 w/student ID. Call 357-1686 for listings. 'Good cafe.' The museum is currently undergoing a major renovation that is scheduled to be completed in 2001 - some exhibits will be closed throughout the renovation. Metro: L'Enfant Plaza.

National Gallery of Art, 737-4215, sprawls magnificently along Constitution Ave at the upper end of the Mall. The west wing houses one of the world's great collections of Western European painting and sculpture, from the 13th century to the present, and American art from Colonial times. Rembrandt, French Impressionists, and Flemish, Spanish, German and British artists are all represented, plus one proudly-displayed da Vinci, the sole work by that artist on the North American continent. Connected via an underground walkway, **IM Pei's east wing** is a work of art in itself. This modern structure, formed by unexpected juxtapositions of triangles, displays the gallery's modern art. Picasso, Mondrian, Rothko, Motherwell and O'Keeffe line the walls, and magnificent changing exhibitions keep things lively. Mon-Sat, 10am-5pm, Sun 11pm-6pm. Metro: Archives/Navy Memorial.

National Museum of American Art & National Portrait Gallery, in the Old Patent Office Bldg, bounded by 7th & 9th, G & F Sts NW. Greek Revival architecture with beautiful vaulted galleries. The permanent collections include 200 years of American art, plus portraits of famous Americans. Also displays important photography exhibits. Free jazz/blues concerts in the summer. Metro: Gallery Place/Chinatown. The museums will be closed for renovation starting in January 2000. The renovation is expected to take at least two years to complete, but in the meantime there will be periodic temporary displays on the Mall.

National Museum of American History, 357-1300, across the Mall at 12th St & Constitution Ave, has all sorts of Americana including Dorothy's ruby slippers, Fonzie's leather jacket, and Archie Bunker's chair. The original 'Star-Spangled Banner,' immortalised by Francis Scott Key, comes out to the blare of trumpets every hour on the half hour. 'A delve into the realms of American culture!' Don't miss the Information Technology exhibit. Metro: Smithsonian.

National Postal Museum, City Post Office Building, Massachusetts Ave & North Capitol St NE, 357-1300. The newest addition to the Smithsonian empire is a fascinating paean to not only the lowly stamp, but also the way the postal system has helped to define the country. Metro: Union Station.

MORE OF INTEREST

Capitol River Cruises, (301) 460-SHIP. Cruises along the historic DC waterfront start on the sweeping curve of the Potomac river at Washington Harbour Pier in Georgetown. Sun-Thu noon-8pm, Fri-Sat noon-9pm on the hour, from pier at 31st & K Sts, $10. Also contact **Spirit Cruises**, 554-8000, who provide an alternative way to view the city. Pleasant cruise to **Mount Vernon**, $26.50, departs at 9am (be there at 8.30am) from Pier 4, 6th at Water St. There are also lunch and dinner cruises, $30.85 and $59.70.

Corcoran Gallery of Art, 500 17th St btwn E St & New York Ave NW, 639-1700. Extensive collection of 18th-20th century American art; European paintings, sculpture, tapestries and pottery; changing exhibits of modern art and photography. Wed-Mon 10am-5pm, Thu 'til 9pm, suggested donation $6, $4 w/student ID. Metro: Farragut West or Farragut North.

Dumbarton Oaks, 31st St btwn R & S Sts, 339-6400. Hidden away above Georgetown sits a discreet wonder. The museum has a great collection of Byzantine and Mayan art, some of it in a Phillip Johnson-designed extension with truly bizarre acoustics. The gardens are simply heavenly, the design making every corner private, romantic and relaxing. 'The one real "must see" in DC.' Tue-Sun 2pm-5pm, gardens open daily 2pm-6pm, suggested donation $1.

Ford's Theatre, 511 10th St NW, 426-6924 (box office 347-4833). Where Lincoln was shot by John Wilkes Booth in 1865. Beautifully restored; call first to avoid rehearsals and performances if just looking. Daily 9am-5pm, free. Interesting talks on the half hour. Excellent museum in basement. Opposite is the house where Lincoln died the next day, open daily 10am-5pm, free. Metro: Metro Center.

Holocaust Memorial Museum, 100 Raoul Wallenberg Place SW (formerly 15th St, south of the Washington Monument), 488-0400. Intense, moving, thought-provoking record of the Holocaust and its victims between 1933 and 1945. Daily 10am-5.30pm, free (passes available from 10am at the 14th St entrance—get there early). 'Highly recommended.' 'Very moving, it will stay with you for the rest of your life.' Metro: Smithsonian.

John F Kennedy Center for the Performing Arts, at the bottom of New Hampshire Ave NW on the Potomac, 467-4600. The finest music, drama, dance and film from the US and abroad. Some student discounts. Many free events including tours,

Mon-Fri 10am-5pm, Sat-Sun 10am-1pm, and daily evening performances at Millennium Stage in the Grand Foyer, 6pm. Terrace views of the Mall, Georgetown and Rosslyn across the Potomac are gorgeous, especially at night. 'Excellent tours.' Metro: Foggy Bottom.

National Geographic Society, Explorer's Hall, 17th & M Sts NW, 857-7588. The world famous magazine displays some of its work with interesting exhibits showing some breathtaking photography. The world's largest free-standing globe brings geography to life. Mon-Sat 9am-5pm, Sun 10am-5pm, Free. 'Quality museum.' Metro: Farragut North.

National Museum of Women in the Arts, 1250 New York Ave NW, 783-5000. One of the few museums devoted entirely to art created by women, including Mary Cassat, Georgia O'Keeffe. Mon-Sat 10am-5pm, Sun noon-5pm. $3 donation. 'Worth seeing.' Metro: Metro Center

U.S Navy Memorial and Heritage Center, 701 Pennsylvania Ave, NW, 737-2300/(800) 723-3557. The outdoor memorial features an enormous, granite map of the world and its oceans, overlooked by the Lone Sailor. Free Navy band concerts Tuesday evenings in summer. The Heritage Center includes interactive exhibits and the breathtaking film, *At Sea*, shown Mon-Sat at 11am and 1pm, $4. Mon-Sat 9.30am-5pm, free. Metro: Archives-Navy Memorial.

Old Post Office Pavilion, 1100 Pennsylvania Ave NW, 606-8691, has a short tour that includes a free ride in an interior glass elevator to a tower overlooking the city. Not as high as the Washington Monument, but the lines are not as long and the breezy arches afford an equally good - if not better - view of the city. Daily in summer 8am-10.45pm. There's entertainment in the food court daily. Also free lunch-time concerts at **Freedom Plaza** across Penn. Ave. Metro: Federal Triangle.

Phillips Collection, 1600 21st NW at Q St, 387-2151. In a modest house and gallery extension sits a treasure house of art. While its centrepiece, Renoir's *Luncheon of the Boating Party*, attracts all the tourists the Cezannes, Picassos, Delacroixs, Goyas, and a room of Rothko are equally worth a look. Tue-Sat 10am-5pm, Sun noon-5pm. Suggested donation $6.50, $3.25 w/student ID. 'Beautifully designed; superb collection.' 'A wonderful surprise.' Metro: Dupont Circle.

Washington Cathedral (Cathedral Church of St Peter and St Paul), Wisconsin Ave and Woodley St NW (near the intersection of Wisconsin and Massachusetts Aves), 537-6200. Beautiful, despite being close to architectural pastiche. It dominates the skyline from wherever you are in DC, perched as it is on one of the city's highest points. Teddy Roosevelt laid the cornerstone in 1907 and it was finally completed in 1990. It has gargoyles of Washington lawyers and a moon rock embedded in one of its stained glass windows. Woodrow Wilson, Admiral Dewey, and Helen Keller are interred here. Carillon concerts every Sat, organ recitals every Wed and Sun; tours Mon-Sat 10am-3.15pm, Sun 12.30pm-2.45pm. Tower is open until 9pm Mon-Fri, 'til 4.30pm Sat, and 'til 5pm Sun in summer. Metro: Tenleytown-American University.

Nearby in Arlington, VA:

Arlington National Cemetery, (703) 692-0931, where more than 218,000 people are buried, including JFK and his brother Robert. Changing of the Guard Ceremony at the **Tomb of the Unknown Soldier** takes place every half hour May-Oct; otherwise once on the hour. 'Impressive!' 'Beautifully serene—hard to believe Washington could be this peaceful.' Apr-Sep 8am-7pm, Oct-May 'til 5pm. Metro: Arlington Cemetery.

Iwo Jima Memorial. A sculpture of 5 marines and a sailor hoisting an American flag on to Mt Surabachi on the island of Iwo Jima, modelled after a famous World War II photograph by Joe Rosenthal. 'Stunning, as is the view from here to Washington.' Right next door is the **Netherlands Carillon**, the perfect place for a picnic. Free concerts are given here May-Aug. Come on Saturdays at 6pm to hear the bells chime and take in one of the best views of Washington. Metro: Rosslyn.

The Pentagon, (703) 695-1776, nearby, gives desperately dull tours of its gargantuan facility. Foreigners require a passport for entry. Metro: Pentagon.

Alexandria, a few miles down the George Washington Memorial Parkway, is a mini-Georgetown, a delight with over 100 18th century buildings, including the church attended by George Washington and Winston Churchill. Follow King Street east toward the water to get to the heart of Old Town. Don't miss the unique **Torpedo Factory**, whose original purpose has been subverted by artists in search of studio space. Metro: Alexandria/King St.

Mount Vernon, 8 miles south of Alexandria via the George Washington Parkway, (703) 780-2000. Home of George Washington and a fine example of a Colonial plantation house, built 1740. Original furnishings, plus key to the Bastille, etc. George and Martha are buried here, too. Daily 8am-5pm 1 March-31 Oct, otherwise 9am-4pm; $8.

OUT OF DOORS

The **Chesapeake & Ohio Canal** passes through Georgetown, and the towpath makes for good cycling, walking or jogging. Summer barge trips from Georgetown, 653-5190, $7.50, 3 trips daily Wed-Sun. Upriver the **Great Falls of the Potomac**, (703) 285-2965, are worth a look from either the MD or VA side.

The Harbour Front in Georgetown, a collection of expensive restaurants and bars along the Potomac River, interesting for its architecture and for people watching. Especially lovely at night, when the orchestrated fountain gushes in a colourful symphonetta. Water taxis stop here.

Kennilworth Aquatic Gardens, Anacostia Ave and Douglass St NE, 426-6905. Amazing collection of water lilies, lotuses, and bamboo grown in ponds along the Anacostia River. Hard to get to without a car and located in one of the grittier areas of the city, it's still definitely worth the trip. Open daily 7am-4pm, free.

National Arboretum, 3501 New York Ave NE, 245-2726. A hidden treasure, this beautiful park is a jewel in the middle of a somewhat run-down area of the city. With more than 400 acres of trees, plants, picnic grounds, and a famous Bonsai collection, most visitors forget they're in a city altogether. Especially beautiful in autumn and spring. Daily 8am-5pm, free. It's best to drive, but you can take the metro to Stadium/Armory, then the B2 bus.

National Zoological Park in Rock Creek Park, entrances along the 3000 block of Connecticut Ave NW, 673-4800. A giant panda is the pride of the zoo, along with Golden Lions, Tamarinds, and a fabulous wetlands exhibit. Check out the Amazonia exhibit. Summer: 6am-8pm (animal houses 10am-6pm), winter 6am-6pm (animal houses 10am-4.30pm). Metro: Woodley Park/Zoo-Adams Morgan—and follow the trail of families pushing prams.

Rock Creek Park, 282-1063. Almost 1,800 acres of rustic woods surrounding Rock Creek. There's a network of trails, riding stables, tennis courts, picnic areas, and a nature centre. Daily 8am-dusk, free. The park occupies a large part of Washington's north-west section and can be entered at several points. By metro, the Woodley Park/Zoo-Adams Morgan, Cleveland Park, Foggy Bottom, and Silver Spring stations are all within walking distance. The park's **Carter Barron Amphitheatre,** 426-0486, hosts seasonal events, including an annual summer Shakespeare free-for-all.

Theodore Roosevelt Island, Potomac Park NW, (703) 289-2530. This peaceful isle is accessed by footbridge from the car park off the northbound lane of the George Washington Pkwy. The 17 ft bronze statue of Roosevelt, champion of nature and wildlife conservation, can be seen in the Statutory Garden. The island is also home to a wildlife refuge with over 2 miles of trails. Daily dawn-dusk. Metro: Rosslyn.

The Tidal Basin, is surrounded by a ring of cherry trees, a gift from Japan in the early 1900s. The Cherry Blossom Festival takes place the first two weeks in April. The Tidal Basin Boathouse, 479-2426, rents paddle boats Mon-Fri 10am-5.30pm, Sat-Sun 'til 7pm, spring and summer; $7 for two-seater, $14 for four-seater. Metro: Smithsonian.

SPORT

Evenings on the Mall are a treat for sports enthusiasts. 'Pick-up games of softball, hockey, football, volleyball, and ultimate frisbee,' are always on the go.

American Football: Redskins Stadium, in Landover, MD, (301) 276-6000 , is the home of the Washington Redskins, '88 and '92 Superbowl Champs, who play here August (pre-season) - January. Tkts are expensive and hard to come by, but it may be worth it to see 'Redskins Fever' in action. Call Top Centre Ticket Service, 452-9040, or Ticket City, 544-0919. Both have tickets starting from $100, but it's a good idea to call at least two weeks in advance. 'Skins fever hits the city in early August.' 'Fans are fiercely proud.' Metro: shuttle bus service from Addison Rd, Landover, and Cheverly stations.

Basketball/Hockey: MCI Center, Chinatown. The Washington Wizards (men's basketball) play here Nov-Apr, tkts from $20. The women's basketball league is only a few years old, but the Washington Mystics' fans are intensely loyal, and tickets are cheaper (from $8), June-Aug. The Capitals (hockey) play here Oct-Apr, tkts from $20. Call TicketMaster, 432-SEAT. Metro: Gallery Place/Chinatown.

Biking: DC and the surrounding area is home to hundreds of miles of trails for walking and biking. The Mall and the C&O Canal are great spots for a bike ride. Another scenic route is the Mt. Vernon Trail, from Memorial Bridge through Alexandria to Mt. Vernon. **Bike the Sites,** 966-8662, runs three-hour, 8 mile bicycle tours of Washington. The $35 price includes bicycle, helmet, water and snack. Call ahead for rsvs. *www.bikethesites.com* Rent bikes from **Big Wheel Bikes,** at 33rd and M Sts NW in Georgetown, 337-0254. $5/hour, $25/day, 3 hour minimum. **Fletcher's Boat House**, Reservoir and Canal Rds NW, 244-0461 rents bikes for $8/2 hours or $12/day. **Thompson's Boat House**, Virginia Ave and Rock Creek Pkwy NW, 333-4861, rents bikes for $4/hour or $15/day. Both boat houses are located along the C&O Canal.

Football: RFK Stadium, E Capitol St, 547-9077. Home of the DC United, a relatively new soccer team, winners of the '96 and '97 league championship. Tickets from $13, available at the RFK ticket booth or from TicketMaster, 432-SEAT. Metro: Stadium-Armory.

Golf: DC has two public golf courses. **The East Potomac Golf Course**, 554-7660, offers 18-hole and two 9-hole courses year round. **The Rock Creek Golf Course**, 882-7332, offers two 9-hole courses, may be played as 18-holes.

Ice Skating: the small **Sculpture Garden Ice Rink** on the Mall at Constitution Ave & 7th St NW, 371-5340, offers skating Dec-March, Mon-Fri 10am-11pm, Sat-Sun 9am-11pm. $5.50, skate rental $2.50. Metro: Archives/Navy Memorial. **Pershing Park Ice Rink,** Pennsylvania Ave & 14th St NW, 737-6938. Intimate rink in the foreground of the ornate Willard Hotel, Dec-March, $5.50, skate rental $2.50. Metro: Federal Triangle.

Swimming: Out of the 35 outdoor and 11 indoor free public pools in DC, the indoor **Capitol East Pool**, 724-4495, the **Marie Reed Pool**, 673-7771, and the **Georgetown Pool**, 282-2366, all come highly recommended.

Tennis: The city maintains more than 50 free public tennis courts. For info and a permit, call 673-7671. At Haines Point in East Potomac Park, there are indoor/outdoor courts available at low cost, 554-5962.

SHOPPING

Department Stores, **Hechts** at 12th & G Sts NW (Metro: Metro Center) and **Lord and Taylor** at 5255 Western Ave NW (Metro: Friendship Heights) are the two big stores—watch out for constant sales with huge savings. **Pentagon City**, a state of the art, multi-level mall easily accessible on the Metro. 'Worth it just to see the building—amazing.'

Georgetown is the place to be seen shopping. Levis, Timberland, Gap, Banana Republic and assorted more interesting stores (try Commander Salamander at 1420

Wisconsin Ave NW and Second Hand Rose at 1516 Wisconsin) are here on Wisconsin Ave but the real bargains will be elsewhere. The weekend flea markets on Wisconsin Ave, if you can stand the blistering heat, are like walking into an unexplored old attic full of **bargain** Levis, antique clothing, ethnic jewellery, Pentax cameras and even electric guitars. **Eastern Market,** 7th St SE on Capitol Hill, an open-air farmers' market on Saturdays and flea market on Sundays. On both days you'll find handicrafts, artwork, and used clothing on sale. The indoor section of the market is DC's last old-timey food market, open every day but Monday. (Metro: Eastern Market) There are insipid malls accessible by metro such as **Mazza Gallerie** (Friendship Heights) and **Ballston Commons** (Ballston).

Potomac Mills, 20 miles south of DC off I-95 near Woodbridge,1 (800)-VA-MILLS. An enormous shopping mall filled with outlet stores of all the major chains. Levi Strauss, Calvin Klein, Nike, Macy's, Nordstrom and others offering merchandise at warehouse prices. 'Levis 501's for $25.' Mon-Sat 10am-9.30pm, Sun 11pm-7pm. Shuttle bus from Dupont Circle metro, $12, (703) 551-1050.

TOURS

A tour is not really necessary; most Washington sights are easily reached on foot or metro, and Arlington is an easy walk across the Potomac.

DC Ducks, 966-3825. A land *and* water tour in a WW2 amphibious landing craft. Vessels depart regularly from Union Station, 10am-3pm every hour. 1½ tour $24.

Gray Line, (800) 862-1400. Specialises in sightseeing tours of DC and surrounding areas. Catch the bus from most major hotels and Union Station. 2 hr trolley tour $25. Union Station.

Old Town Trolley Tour, (301) 985 3020. A loop of DC taking in all the sites, you can hop off and on again later. $24. Non-stop tour lasts 2 hrs.

Tourmobile, 554-5100/554-7950 (24-hrs), offers Washington and Arlington Cemetery tours for $16. Passes are good for a day of unlimited re-boarding and you can begin at any sight. Look for Tourmobile Sightseeing Shuttle Bus Stop sign (main ones at Washington Monument, Lincoln Memorial); buses run every 20 min. 'Convenient and easy to use.' Also conducts trips to Mt Vernon in the spring and summer, $22.

ENTERTAINMENT

For the best, most comprehensive listings and reviews of what's going on in the area, pick up a free copy of the *City Paper* Thu (in shops and from street-corner boxes); the *Weekend* section of Friday's *Washington Post* and the NW neighbour-hood paper, *The InTowner*, a free monthly paper available around Dupont Circle and Adams-Morgan.

Festivals: The **Smithsonian Folklife Festival**, held before 4 July on the Mall; **Adams-Morgan Day** (mid-Sept) on 18th St. Ethnic music, dance and food plus blues and gospel sounds. **Taste of DC**, early Oct on Pennsylvania Ave, food dished up from area restaurants, free concerts and entertainment. **The Smithsonian Kite Festival**, late March on the grounds of the Washington Monument. Kite flying competitions and demonstrations fill the sky with some of the most elaborate kites in the world. **Cherry Blossom Festival,** late March to early April, throughout DC. Several events, including a race, sports tournaments, an arts and crafts show, and a parade.

The Mall is the grassy stage for all manner of summer entertainment. On July 4, fireworks and fun concerts are held there (for best viewing of fireworks get there early and take a blanket.) The Mall also plays host to sporting events every weekend, including polo.

Theme Parks: Six Flags America, in Largo, MD, (301) 249-1500, a theme park and newly expanded water park, features the *Mind Eraser*, 2 minutes of rollovers and spins, plus an intense corkscrew sequence following an inverted loop, along with

AMERICAN MUSIC—THE SOUND OF SURPRISE

BLUEGRASS: A uniquely American style of music, Bluegrass can be thought of as a mix of folk music, country and blues with a hint of jazz thrown in. Invented in the 1930s by Bill Monroe and his Blue Grass Boys, bluegrass is heard today throughout the Midwest, South and in larger cities, too. **The Birchmere** in **Alexandria, VA**, (703)549-7500, presents a premiere showcase of folk music, bluegrass and country. **The Station Inn, Nashville, TN**, (615) 255-3307, plays bluegrass six nights a week. Live bands most evenings. For progressive style, hear the *New Grass Revival*. Most bluegrass action happens at some 400+ festivals across the country. For a listing refer to *Bluegrass Unlimited*, Box 111, Broad Run, VA 22014, (540) 349-8181 or look online, *www.bluegrassmusic.com.*

BLUES: Legendary performer Memphis Slim described them best: 'The blues ain't nothin' but a botheration on your mind." There are good local blues bands all over the US, but those in **Chicago** reign supreme. Pick up a copy of *The Reader* for info. Don't miss **B.L.U.E.S**, (773) 528-1012, with low-down blues, fresh acts; hot, smoky, and cramped, or sister club **B.L.U.E.S etcetera**, (773)525-8989, for bigger names. Try also **Rosa's**, (773) 342-0452, small, not as well known, but great music. Don't miss the free **Blues Fest** in early June, (312) 744-3315. In **Washington, DC**, try **City Blues**, (202) 232-2300, for atmosphere or **Madam's Organ**, (202)667-5370. Raunchy live blues, jazz and eclectic clientele. Oakland, CA is also filled with blues bars.

COUNTRY: Branson, MO, has become the new center for country. With over 30 theatres featuring over 60 shows, Branson plays host to musical legends such as Andy Williams and the Osmond family, and also to a bounty of country stars. The **Grand Palace**, (800) 572-5223, has been host to big names like Johnny Cash and Kenny Rogers. You can catch performances on a regular basis by country greats such as **Mel Tillis**, (417) 335-6635, **Mickey Gilley**, (800)334-1936 and **Moe Bandy**, (888) 3-BANDY-4. The legendary **Broken Spoke, Austin, TX**, (512)442-6189, once frequented by Willie Nelson and Ray Price, is one of the last honky-tonks. Continues to showcase bands just on the verge of hitting big time. **Rodeo Bar**, (212) 683-6500, NYC, south-western food, country and western entertainment. **Crazy Horse, Santa Ana, CA**, (714) 549-1512, is billed as the top country and western entertainment spot; top names perform here. **Jimmy Driftwood Music Barn, Mountain View, Ark**, (870) 269-8042, hosts the best Ozark country bands. You never know what legend will turn up next at the **Grand Ole Opry**, (615) 889-6611, in **Nashville, TN**. Want more big names? **The Legends of Western Swing Festival**, Scurry County Coliseum, Snyder, TX, late June. For reading, try *Music City News*.

FOLK: Smithsonian Folklife Festival, Washington, late-June-early July, has authentic folk and ethnic music, dancing. Excellent performers grace the back room of this guitar shop at weekends: **McCabe's, Santa Monica, CA**, (310) 828-4497. Try the **New Orleans Heritage Fest**, (504) 522-4786, for an eclectic mix of gospel, zydeco, progressive rock, jazz and more. Held late Apr-May. The **Aspen Music Festival, Aspen, CO**, late June-Aug, 9 weeks, (303) 925-9042. As good as **Tanglewood Music Festival** in Lenox, MA, in terms of prestige and importance. Open rehearsals and other free events.

GOSPEL: Two million people fill the streets of **Harlem** during its massive week-long fest of gospel, rhythm & blues, and jazz. To hear gospel at its best, go to church in Detroit, Chicago or Harlem. In Washington DC, superb, uplifting gospel music can be heard each Sunday at **St Augustine's Catholic Church**, 15th & V Sts NW, 265-1470. For information on venues and on the gospel music industry itself, go to *www.gospelflava.com.*

JAZZ: There are good jazz clubs in most North American cities. **The Baked Potato** near Universal Studios in LA, (818) 980-1615, is the oldest major jazz club in the US and launching pad for many famous performers. **Preservation Hall**, hub of **New Orleans** jazz, hosts pioneers of Dixieland, (504) 523-8939. In **Washington, DC**, **Blues Alley**, (202) 337-4141, has attracted such greats as the late Dizzie Gillespie and Ahmad Jamal and recently Wynton Marsalis. There's no place like **New York City** for jazz: try **Blue Note**, (212) 475-0049; downstairs in the **Time Cafe**, is the **Fez Club**, (212)533-2680; **Sweet Basil's**, 242-1785, 'Village temple of jazz'; the venerable **Village Vanguard**, 255-4037. Don't miss **JVC Jazz Festival**, NYC, late June, (212) 397-8222. More than 40 events and 1000 performers at different locations including Lincoln Center and Carnegie Hall. All the best including Ella Fitzgerald, Ray Charles and many others. Other excellent festivals: **Chicago Jazz Fest** is exceptional, Labor Day weekend, (312) 744-3315; **Monterey, CA, Jazz Festival**, mid-September, (831) 373-3366; and **Montreux/Detroit Festival**,in Michigan, early Sept, (313)963-7622. More than 100 performers play their licks in **Burlington, VT**, in June, call DISCOVER JAZZ, (802) 863-7992. See magazines *Jazz Times* or *Downbeat* for the latest on the jazz scene nationwide.

RHYTHM & BLUES: The tradition rooted in Bo Diddly, Jerry Lee Lewis, Chuck Berry, Carl Perkins and others still survives at the **Rum Boogie Cafe, Memphis, TN**, (901) 528-0150, or catch blues legend B.B King at his own club, **B B King's Blues Club**, (901) 524-5464.

ALTERNATIVE: Lollapalooza. Originally conceived in 1991 by Perry Farrell as an alternative music and political travelling roadshow, the 27-odd shows are now as mainstream as Genesis. **House of Blues Smokin' Grooves Tour**. This recently established event has featured such artists as The Fugees, A Tribe Called Quest, The Pharcyde, and has been described as 'the most comprehensive sampling of the diversity of Hip-Hop culture in the 90s.' Touring North America Jun-Aug. **The Vans Warped Tour**, combines skateboarding and rock n' roll creating a global event that hits most major US cities throughout the summer. Info on all the above music genres, *www.excite.com/Entertainment/Music/Genres/*

Festival info, *www.yahoo.com/Entertainment/Music/Events/Concerts/Festivals/.*

several other roller coasters and eight water rides. Admission is $32, but there are usually promotional discounts available.

Nightlife: Much of it centres on drinking in dingy bars, although such establishments can be good places to meet people and sample the character of Washington. Many establishments in the Dupont Circle area cater to a gay crowd.

Childe Harold, 1610 20th NW, 483-6702, a centre of activity in Dupont Circle; **Sign of the Whale**, 1825 M St NW, 785-1110, drink specials every night, **The Big Hunt**, 1345 Connecticut Ave NW, 785-2333, pizza, beer and pool.

Eclectic music/spectacles abound:

Blues Alley, off Wisconsin between M & K NW, Georgetown, 337-4141, showcases best jazz artists in the country. Expensive and reservations necessary, but worth the entrance charge of $14-$40. Also serves Creole cuisine.

Dance Place, 3225 8th St NE (2 blocks from Brookland stop on the metro's red line), 269-1600. Innovative modern dance performances.

The Front Page, 19th St and New Hampshire Ave NW, near Dupont Circle, 296-6500. 'Popular bar for Happy Hour.' (Mon-Fri 4pm-7pm). Cheap beer and free food. 'Good atmosphere, especially on Fridays.' 'Full of interns and would-be politicians.'

The Improv Comedy Club and Restaurant, 1140 Connecticut Ave NW, 296-7008. Sun-Thu at 8:30pm, Fri-Sat at 8pm and 10.30pm, dinner served only at early show times. Tkts range from $12-$15. Metro: Farragut North.

Kelly's Irish Times, 14 F St NW, 543-5433. The place to go for those feeling homesick—full of Brits and Irish! A fair number of Americans too: fraternity boys ('sigma chi 'til I die!'), marines, fire-fighters . . . the world is here. Live music; place your requests and sing along—but keep your eye on the bill. Has downstairs pub theatre, ID needed. Also worth a visit—**The Dubliner** just down the road at 4 F St or enter through the Phoenix Park hotel. Metro: Union Station.

Mr. Smith's of Georgetown, 3104 M St NW, 333-3104. College crowd, heated garden that's quiet enough to have a conversation in. Come for the 'super happy hour,' with dollar beers and half-price appetisers. Dancing on weekends.

One Step Down, 2517 Pennsylvania Ave NW, 955-7141. Great jazz just over the bridge from G'town. No cover for jam sessions on weekend afternoons. Much cheaper than Blues Alley and more intimate, too. $5-$20 cover plus two drink minimum. Metro: Foggy Bottom.

The Tombs, 1226 36th St, NW, at Prospect in Georgetown, 337-6668. College bar—rowing blades on the wall—food under $10.

For dancing:

Babylon, 911 F St NW, 637-9723. Euro-techno, $10. Metro: Gallery Place/Metro Center.

Club Heaven & Hell, 2327 18th St NW, 667-HELL. In the heart of Adams-Morgan, this two tier club/bar is heaven upstairs, hell down. Infamous '80s retro night on Thursdays—packed with interns.

Kilimanjaro, 1724 California St NW. African dance music, calypso, reggae—with some rap thrown in. Live music at weekends; cover jumps to $10 or more. Strict dress code; no shorts, caps, etc. Closed in 1999 for renovation, call 986-1002 to check if open.

Lulu's, 2119 M St NW, 861-5858. Street lamps, rubber trees, and giant fireplaces add to the New Orleans decor. House downstairs, 70s and 80s music upstairs. Metro: Foggy Bottom or Dupont Circle.

9.30 Club, 815 V St NW, 3-930-930 (concert-line). It smells, it's dark, dingy and small but if indie's your thing, then this is it. Has great live music, SuperGrass, Blur, and The Charlatans have all played here, $10-$20. Metro: U St/Cardozo.

Tracks, 1111 First St SE, 488-3320. Great club, horrific area. Indie/Euro-dance. Thu-Sun, $10 cover. Sat-Sun the crowd is predominantly gay. Metro: Navy Yard (take a taxi!).

Theatre in Washington gets better and better. Look for the **Washington Theater Festival**, in July, 462-1073. Call **Ticketplace**, 1100 Pennsylvania Ave NW, 842-5387, for half price tkts on the day of a show, or on Sat for a Sun or Mon show. Cash only, 10% service charge. Metro: Federal Triangle

The Arena Stage, 6th & Maine Ave SW, 554-9066, has one of the finest repertory companies in the nation. Metro: Waterfront.

John F. Kennedy Center for the Performing Arts on the Potomac River south of Georgetown, 467-4600, has several theatres: the Opera House (ballet, plays, opera); the Eisenhower Theater (plays); the Terrace Theater; the Concert Hall, home of the world-class National Symphony; and the movie house of the American Film Institute (AFI). Students half-price for some performances. Daily evening performances at Millennium Stage in the Grand Foyer, 6pm, free. Metro: Foggy Bottom.

National Theater, 1321 E St NW, 628-6161, also has some of the best performances in the city, direct from—or heading for—Broadway. Metro: Metro Center.

Source Theatre Company, 1835 14th St NW, 462-1073, does some powerful productions on small stages. Prices are reasonable, but be careful in this area at night. See *Washington Post* for listings. In addition, **DC Arts Center**, 462-7833, **Church St Theatre**, 265-3748, **The Shakespeare Theatre**, 547-1122, and the **Studio Theatre**, 332-3300.

Wolf Trap Park, 1551 Trap Rd, Vienna, VA, (703) 255-1868, the only US national park devoted to the arts. You can sit on the lawn or in the open-air theatre for top-notch ballet, symphonies, opera or popular music. Lawn tickets are cheaper, and you can picnic during the performance, but come early and bring a blanket. Metro: orange line to West Falls Church and pick up a shuttle to Wolf Trap for $3.50. For info call **Ticketplace**, 12th & F Sts NW, 842-5387, to purchase discount tickets on the day of a show or on Sat for a Sun show, you must pay cash.

The **U.S. Marine Band,** 433-4011, a nationally-renowned group, gives free concerts in summer throughout the city. Wednesday at 8pm on the west steps of the Capitol, Sun at 7pm on the Ellipse at the Washington Monument, and Fri at 8.45pm at the Marine Barracks, 700 8th St SE (Metro: Eastern Market).

INFORMATION

For current information on events around the city, the following numbers are useful:

Dial-a-Museum, 357-2020, info on current exhibits at the Smithsonian.

Dial-a-Park, 619-PARK, info on activities at memorials and park areas. *www.nps.gov*

Travelers Aid, in Union Station, 371-1937. Also at National Airport, (703) 417-3975, and Dulles Airport, (703) 572-8296.

Washington DC Convention and Visitors Bureau, 13th St and Pennsylvania Ave NW in the Ronald Reagan Building, 789-7038. Distributes information by mail or in person. Metro: Federal Triangle.

White House Visitor Center, 15th & E Sts, 7.30am-3pm, 456-7041. Stop here for maps etc. Ask for leaflets on attractions other than the White House. Metro: Federal Triangle.

INTERNET ACCESS

Martin Luther King Library, 901 G St NW, 727-1126. Free Internet use, half hour time limit. Metro: Gallery Place/Chinatown or Metro Center.

cyberSTOPcafe, 1513 17th Street NW, 234-2470. $7/hour, $5/half-hour. Metro: Dupont Circle.

Kramerbooks & Afterwords Cafe, 1517 Connecticut Ave NW, 387-1400. One computer available for free Internet use. Metro: Dupont Circle.

TRAVEL

Confusion over the street layout here is forgivable. The same address may have four different locations, one in each quadrant. Just remember that NS streets are numbered, EW streets are lettered, and the Parisian-style diagonal avenues are named after US states, one of the focal points being the Capitol, another obvious one is the White House.

Metro, 637-7000, Washington's space-age subway system is an experience in itself. Never-ending escalators descend below ground to reveal cavernous, museum-like vaults—'something out of 2001.' It whisks you in minutes to museums, sights, and shopping. The system is clean, efficient and safe; platform walls are protected from graffiti by deep dry-moats and trains are carpeted (vacuumed daily). Cynics claim that everyone in DC could have been given a car for the money! Most places are within easy reach of a station, which are identified rather obscurely by brown posts marked with a white 'M.' Lines are denoted by colour and end-of-line destination. Farecards cost $1.10 (more during rush hour and for longer journeys) obtained from machines before you reach the platform. One-day passes are $5, good after 9.30 am Mon-Fri and all day w/ends. Dollar bills are accepted and change given. Transfers to buses are $.25 (paid on the bus), get them before you board the train. Trains run Mon-Fri 5.30am-midnight, Sat-Sun 8am-midnight.

Metrobus, 673-7000, is a complex but extensive system integrated with the Metro—practically every block in the city is reachable by bus. When stuck, ask any bus-driver for assistance, they are willing to help. All buses stop every couple of blocks on their route. #30, 32, 34 & 36 are very useful for Penn Ave, Georgetown and Wisconsin Ave. Exact fares are required—'carry a wad of $1 bills.' Flat fare is $1.10, an all-day pass is available for $2.50, bus-to-bus transfers are free.

Taxicabs are cheaper here than in most major cities, but the 'zone system' is often confusing for tourists. Instead of meters, the fare is based on your starting and ending zone. Almost the entire Mall and downtown area are covered by one zone (single non-rush hour fare $4). Visitors are vulnerable to the small minority of cabbies who may try to overcharge, but the lack of meters eliminates the incentive to take you out of your way. Before you get in the cab, ask the driver to tell you how much a ride will be. Fares shouldn't vary between cabs, so if you fear a quote may be too high, find another cab. There's a $1 surcharge during rush-hour (7am-9am and 4pm-6.30pm), $1.50 for each extra passenger, $.50 for each large bag, and a $1.50 charge for radio calls. If you take a taxi from DC to Maryland or Virginia the driver will use the odometer to determine the mileage and the fare. Cabs are plentiful in the downtown area but if you're in a quiet residential area you may want to call one. The biggest companies are **Yellow Cab**, 544-1212, and **Diamond Cab**, 387-6200.

Airports: **Baltimore Washington International Airport (BWI)**, (410) 859-7111, one hour north of Washington, is served by Amtrak, (800) 872-7245, $17 o/w, and MARC commuter trains, (410) 539-5000, $5 o/w.

National Airport, (703) 417-8000, is close to the city and easy to get to on the Metro's blue and yellow lines. A taxi from DC would be $12-$15. Domestic flights only.

Washington Dulles International Airport, (703) 572-2700, is located about 26 miles from downtown Washington. Flights are generally cheaper here. A taxi from DC would be about $45, but the cheapest way to get here is the Washington Flyer shuttle from the West Falls Church metro station on the orange line, $8. (703) 417-8471 for info.

Washington Flyer, (703) 417-8471, run airport shuttles from the Washington Convention Center at 11th St and New York Ave NW (Metro: Metro Center) to Dulles Airport. Buses run every half hour weekdays, 6.15am-9.15pm, w/ends 6.15am-1.15pm every hour, 1.45pm-9.15pm every half hour. $16 o/w, $26 r/t, cash only. Buy tkts from back of Convention Center.

Greyhound, 1005 1st NE, (800) 231-2222. Terminal behind Union Station. 24 hrs. Not an area to be alone in at night.

Union Station, 1st & Massachusetts NE, 484-7540, serves Amtrak, Maryland Rail Commuter (MARC), Virginia Railway Express (VRE) and metro. 8 mins from downtown. Day trips and overnights from here to Baltimore, Harpers Ferry, Fredericksburg. 24 hrs. Beautifully renovated, lots of eateries, shops and a multiplex cinema.

Car pooling: Look in the *Washington Post* for *shared expense rides*, especially late August/early Sept when students are returning to college.

MARYLAND   *Free State, Old Line State*

Locals boast that Maryland is 'America in miniature'. The Mason-Dixon Line, surveyed by English astronomers Charles Mason and Jeremiah Dixon in 1767, marks the border between Maryland and Pennsylvania, but it has also come to represent the unofficial border between North and South. Maryland shows northern influences in its western mountainous area settled heavily by British and Germans, and southern character along the eastern shoreline famous for old antebellum mansions and delicious Chesapeake Bay crabs and oysters.

The Chesapeake Bay dominates Maryland's cuisine and exerts a major influence on the state's economy, culture and politics. Don't leave without sampling Maryland's famous crabs and experiencing a sample of Bay culture. If you're here in September be sure to visit the small town of Crisfield for its annual Labor Day **Hard Crab Derby and Fair**. The three day event includes a crab race, parades, a beauty pageant, boat races, crab picking contests, and a carnival. If you have time, visit the tobacco auctions in Hughesville, La Plata, Upper Marlboro, Waldorf or Waysons Corner; the auctioneer's patter is riveting.
www.mdisfun.org
The telephone area code in the southern part of the state is 301, in the north and east it's 410.

BALTIMORE   One of the nation's major seaports and not long ago considered Washington DC's ugly step-sister, today Baltimore enjoys one of the most successful urban renewal programs in America. The city's **Inner Harbor**, the centrepiece of its rebirth, was designed by the same prolific company that re-galvanised Faneuil Hall in Boston and designed the entire city of Columbia, a pleasant stop-over near Baltimore.

On the sea-front, recently re-discovered (though trying hard not to be) **Fells Point** offers an unpretentious step back into the city's Colonial and sea-faring past. The country's oldest waterfront has for the most part avoided both development and tourism, resulting in a setting strikingly unchanged for some 200 years. But don't think this is an old-fashioned area; 'real' people live and work here, and in addition to history, the Point has a great food market, bars, restaurants and summer festivals.

The city is fiercely proud of its baseball team, the Orioles, and of its heroes, which include baseball star Babe Ruth, journalistic curmudgeon H. L. Mencken, and writer Edgar Allen Poe. While you're here, don't miss tasting fresh crab; and use correct pronunciation when referring to city or state: it's 'Balmer, Merlin'. *www.baltconvstr.com*

ACCOMMODATION
Travellers on a tight budget may find the **Baltimore Quick Guide** helpful. Available at tourist offices in the Inner Harbor.

Baltimore International Hostel, 17 W Mulberry St, 576-8880. $14 AYH, $17 non-AYH, free linen. 'Close to Inner Harbor area; 4 blocks from Greyhound. Clean; nice staff.' Check-in 10am-11am. baltimore.hostel@juno.com. The hostel schedules to re-open in summer of 2000 after a renovation; in the meantime the nearby **Mt. Vernon Hotel,** 24 W Franklin St, 727-2000, is offering a special rate of $59 per room for hostelers (up to four people in a room). Light rail: Centre. Subway: Lexington Market.

Abbey Hotel, 723 St Paul St at Madison, 332-0405. $29-$50. 'Rough but cheap.' Subway/Light rail: Lexington Market.

Wellington Hotel, 9th St & Baltimore Ave, 289-9189. Clean, bright, rooms, $89-$139. Close to boardwalk, amusement park and local attractions. 'Excellent location.'

FOOD
Crab, Baltimore's speciality, is available practically anywhere. The scrumptious crustaceans are served by the dozen hot from the pot, peppered with volcanic Old Bay seasoning. Your only implements will be a mallet and a newspaper. Soft shell crabs are delicious too. Also try **Phillip's** crab cakes at **Harbor Place**, a giant Inner Harbor pavilion with countless fast food stalls and a few restaurants. 'Beautiful view of harbour.' Subway: Shot Tower.

Bertha's Dining Room, 734 S Broadway, Fell's Point, 327-5795. The restaurant's catch-phrase is 'EAT BERTHA'S MUSSELS!' and you can for about $9. Wash it down with one of 90 different beers.

Ikaros, 4805 Eastern Ave, 633-3750. Greek, $8-$15. Closed Tue.

Jimmy's, 801 S Broadway, Fell's Point, 327-3273. Good, solid breakfasts and lunch at low prices, specials $4, a whole meal for $6. 'Usually crowded, especially Sun mornings.'

Lexington Market, Lexington & Eutaw, historic public market established in 1782. Endless displays of food of almost every type and description. It's worth it just to come and watch the vendors in action. Mon-Sat 8.30am-6pm. Light rail/Subway: Lexington Market.

Louie's Bookstore Cafe, 518 N Charles, 962-1225. Seafood and literature, live classical music every night, local art exhibits. Lunch $6-$7, dinner $10-$12. Light rail: Centre Street.

One World Cafe, 904 S Charles St, 234-0235. Friendly atmosphere; hot and cold sandwiches for $3-$7.

Ostrowski's Polish Sausage, 524 S Washington St, 327-8935. Excellent kielbasa. Closes early in the afternoon.

Pete's Grille, 3130 Greenmount Avenue, 467-7698. 'A real diner with good, cheap food and a great atmosphere.' Winner of local 'Best Breakfast' award, $1-$7. Mon-Sat 6am-2pm, Sun 7am-1pm.

OF INTEREST
Babe Ruth Birthplace and Maryland Baseball Hall of Fame, 216 Emory, 727-1539. Memorabilia of America's favourite slugger and other Maryland heroes. Daily in summer 10am-5pm (7pm when Orioles are playing), $6. Light rail: Camden Yards.

Baltimore Museum of Art, Charles & 31st Sts, 396-7100. Owes its wonderful Matisse collection to the shrewd purchases of the Cone sisters from the artist himself. Plus good Modernism section. Wed-Fri 10am-4pm; Sat-Sun 11am-6pm. $5.50, $3.50 w/student ID, free Thu.

Baltimore Streetcar Museum, 1901 Falls Rd, 547-0264. Streetcar rides, tours, and exhibits featuring a permanent collection of Baltimore streetcars from 1859-1944. Sun noon-5pm, Jun-Oct open Saturdays also, $5.

Edgar Allen Poe House, 203 N Amity, 396-7932. Winding staircase leads to the tiny garret where Poe wrote 1832-1835. Sporadic hours: Jun-July Fri-Sat noon-3.45pm, Aug-Sept Sat only noon-3.45pm, closed mid-Dec to March; $3. Phone to check. NB: Poe was never wealthy, and his former home is in a rundown area. Use caution.

Eubie Blake National Jazz Institute and Cultural Center, 847 Howard St, 625-3113. Features permanent exhibits on Baltimore jazz greats Billie Holliday and Cab Calloway, among others, $2. Light rail: Centre Street.

Flag House, Pratt & Albermarle Sts, 837-1793. The house where Mary Pickersgill sewed the flag that inspired Francis Scott Key to write the *Star Spangled Banner*. Tue-Sat 10am-4pm, $5, $3 w/student ID. Subway: Shot Tower. The **Maryland Historical Society**, 201 W Monument St, 685-3750, has the original manuscript of that poem which was later (1931) adopted as the national anthem, as well as the art collection of the former Peale Museum. Tue-Fri 10am-5pm, Sat 9am-5pm, Sun 1pm-5pm. $4, Sun free. Light rail: Centre Street.

Federal Hill, bordered by Hughes St and Key Highway to the north, Cross St to the south, and Key Highway and Hanover St to the east and west. A federal historic district of primarily brick late-19th century homes. To the north is Federal Hill Park, a Baltimore landmark with spectacular views of the Inner Harbor and downtown skyline. The Cross Street Market and the surrounding business district on Charles and Light Sts have a wide range of moderately priced restaurants and taverns.

Fell's Point, a revamped harbour area around Aliceanna, Lancaster, Ann and Thames Streets. Shops and good places to eat. Can be reached by the water taxi that ferries people around the harbour.

Fort McHenry, end of Fort Ave, 962-4290. Successful defence of the fort in the War of 1812 was the inspiration for Francis Scott Key to write the 'Star Spangled Banner.' When Key saw that the garrison flag had been raised the morning after the British attack, he knew that the fort had not fallen. Today, ancient cannons still cover the harbour. Daily 8am-7.45pm, $5. 'Catch the water taxi across to the fort, leaves every ½hour from Inner Harbor, $4.50 all-day pass allows you to get on and off at various points en route. Very worthwhile.' The **National Seaport Pass**, $15.75, includes unlimited water taxi rides for one day plus admittance to the Maritime Museum, the USS Constellation, the Museum of Industry, and Top of the World. Call (877) NHCPORT for more info.

Jewish Museum of Maryland, 15 Lloyd St, 732-6400. The country's largest Jewish museum, including two synagogues. Tue-Thu and Sun noon-4pm. Tours at 1pm and 2.30pm, $4.

Maryland Science Center and Davis Planetarium, 601 Light St on the harbour, 685-2370. Hands-on exhibits; computer games, Chesapeake Bay and Baltimore City displays. $10.50 admission includes entrance to planetarium and 5-storey IMAX theatre. Mon-Thu 9.30am-6pm, Fri-Sun 9.30am-8pm. 'Not worth it.'

B&O Railroad Museum, in the **Mount Clare Station**, Pratt and Poppleton Sts, 752-2490. The first railroad station in the US, erected 1830. Samuel Morse sent the first telegraph message, 'What hath God wrought', from here. Daily 10am-5pm, $6.50.

National Aquarium, Pier 3, E Pratt St, 576-3800. Take the elevator to the 4th floor, then the escalator to the rain forest where piranhas glower, sloths dangle, and free-flying birds practically land on your head. Then walk along a spiralling aquarium tank to the friendly, schmoo-like Beluga whales, who laugh at the crowds around their 1st-floor tank. 'Expensive, but worth it. Modern and interesting design; the shark tank is amazing.' Summer: Daily 9am-8pm, $14. Subway: Shot Tower.

Poe's Grave at Westminster Hall, Fayette & Green, 706-2072. The tombstone marking his grave is near the front gate. Take a fascinating tour -1st & 3rd Fri (at 6.30pm) & Sat (at 10am) in each month—of the church's catacombs and grounds for $4 (rsvs required). Cemetery open daylight only, free. On Halloween the local historical society hosts a weirdly funny party in the graveyard, during which 'Frank the Body-Snatcher' lectures on the perils of his profession. On the anniversary of Poe's death (Oct 7th), fans come from around the world for a midnight celebration that began in 1949, 100 years after his death. It continues to this day unchanged: a mysterious man clad in black appears after midnight to offer a toast of French cognac to Poe's memory; after the ceremony he leaves roses and the open bottle at the grave and vanishes into the night.

Top of the World at the top of the **World Trade Center**, 401 East Pratt St, Inner Harbor, 837-VIEW, the world's tallest pentagonal building, designed by I M Pei. Offers panoramic views of harbour and city and exhibits on Baltimore's history. $3.

U.S.S. Constellation, Pier 1, Inner Harbor, 539-1797. The only surviving Civil War era naval vessel and last tall-sail war ship built by the US Navy, open daily 10am-6pm, $6.

Walters Art Gallery, 600 N Charles St at Centre, 547-9000. One of the largest private collections in the world with something of everything from across the ages, including a floor housing Oriental decorative arts. Tue-Fri 10am-4pm, Sat-Sun 11am-5pm. $5, $3 w/student ID, free to all Sat 11am-1pm and the first Thu of every month, 5pm-8pm. Light rail: Centre Street.

Washington Monument, Charles St and Mt Vernon Pl. 178 ft high, the monument was built between 1815 and 1842, long before the one in DC.

ENTERTAINMENT

Harbor Place may seem the logical hot spot, especially the enormous factory here converted into an adult Disneyland with corresponding steep tariff, but it's best avoided. Instead head for **Fell's Point**, east of Harbor Place, where the real fun is. Around 9pm or 10pm, serious drinking and dancing get underway in the numerous little bars filled with local rowdies, yuppies, bohemians, unrepentant pirates and assorted lowlifes, all in good fun. Most places here charge a buck or two cover, if that, on weekends. Tourists invariably get lost trying to find it, not because it's difficult to find but because locals intentionally give them the wrong directions. Just take the trolley from Inner Harbor or follow Broadway toward the harbour till you run out of street.

Center Stage Theater, 700 N Calvert St, 332-0033. A nationally acclaimed professional theatre. Tickets from $10.

Lyric Opera House, 140 W Mt. Royal Ave, 685-5086. Home of the Baltimore Opera Company, and also the stage for musicals and other shows.

SPORT

Baltimore Orioles, Orioles Stadium, Camden Yards, 685-9800. 'Great baseball in an electric atmosphere. Highly recommend.' THE place to go for a good time. Watch out for 'Wild Bill' the beloved taxi driver/cheerleader. 'Tasty roast beef sandwiches made on outdoor grills.' Amtrak and MARC run trains from DC to Camden Yards, $10.25 r/t, from Union Station, 539-5000/(800) 325-7245. Return bus service is provided when the game ends after the last train leaves. 'Great value and a real Oriole atmosphere even before you reach the ground.'

INFORMATION
Baltimore Area Convention and Visitors Association, on the Inner Harbor, 837-4636, info on accommodation, restaurants, attractions.
Travelers Aid, at Baltimore-Washington International Airport, 859-7555.

INTERNET ACCESS
The Strand CyberCafe, 105 East Lombard Street, 625-8944. $.20/minute. Light rail: Convention Center.
Enoch Pratt Free Library, 400 Cathedral St, 396-5430. Free Internet access. Light rail: Centre St, Subway: Charles Center or Lexington Market.

TRAVEL
Amtrak, Penn Station, 1515 N Charles St, (800) 872-7245.
Baltimore/Washington International Airport, 10 miles south of Baltimore. Take the #17 Mass Transit bus, or light rail, from downtown.
Greyhound, 210 W Fayette and Howard Sts, 752-0908/(800) 231-2222.
Mass Transit, 539-5000, for bus, subway, and light rail schedules for downtown and suburbs; $1.35-$1.65.
Water Taxi service, Constellation Dock, Pratt St, (410) 563-3900. Calls at all major attractions around the harbour. $4.50 all-day unlimited use, 10am-11pm, 'til midnight Fri & Sat.

ANNAPOLIS
Situated on Chesapeake Bay, the city of Queen Anne is the capital of Maryland. At the State House, George Washington resigned his command of the Revolutionary Army after his victory over British forces. Clustered behind the 18th century waterfront is one of the most beautiful of America's colonial towns.

Annapolis is synonymous with sailing and the United States Naval Academy. Now co-ed, the academy is still 'where the boys are' and acts as a magnet for young women, especially on weekends. The bars on the wharf are good for a beer and overhearing the fishermen's stories of the Chesapeake Bay. Treat yourself to a basket of hot crab, delicious and cheap, and catch the Clam Festival in late August. A trip round the harbour is a must. The movie, *Patriot Games*, was shot here. *http://visit-annapolis.org*

ACCOMMODATION
Accommodation tends to be expensive in this trendy little town.
Annapolis Accommodations, 66 Maryland Ave, 280-0900/(800) 715-1000. B&B rsvs from $90.
Capital KOA Campground, 11 miles from Annapolis on Rte 3 north in Millersville, 923-2771. April-Nov; sites $26 for two, $31 w/hook-up, XP-$5, cabins available $44, rsvs required.

FOOD
Chick and Ruth's, 165 Main, 269-6737. Down the street from the state capitol, this 24 hr deli has politically-named specials, $4-$7, in a homey, memorabilia-crammed atmosphere.
Market House, Market Space, City Dock. Restoration of an 1858 building with tons of fresh seafood and various other foods. 'Best value, tastiest seafood in town!' 'Best oysters in the east!'
Historic Inns, Church Circle, 263-2641. Well-known early 18th century inn, houses the **King of France Tavern**, 'excellent jazz'. Thu-Sun, cover $10-$15.

OF INTEREST

A **Boat trip** round the harbour is the pleasantest way to experience the many facets of Annapolis; **Chesapeake Marine Tours**, Slip 20, City Dock, 268-7600, 40 min harbour cruises $6, 90 min Severn River cruises $13.

Maryland State House, State Circle, 974-3400. Oldest US State House in continuous legislative use. 9am-5pm daily, free tours at 11am and 3pm. 'Interesting tour.'

US Naval Academy, bordered by King George St & Severn River, 263-6933. Large, beautiful chapel has sarcophagus of John Paul Jones. Guided walking tours, $5.50, depart from Ricketts Hall. Free admission to grounds, Mon-Sat 9.30am-3.30pm. 'Excellent, interesting tour.'

Walking Tours: **The Museum Store**, 77 Main St, 268-5576, rents audio self-guided tours for $5. **Three Centuries Tours**, 263-5401, offers two walking tours daily. The 10.30am tour meets at the Visitors Center, 26 West St, and the 1.30pm tour meets at the information booth on the city dock, $9.

ASSATEAGUE ISLAND, a narrow, 37 mile long barrier island on the Atlantic coast of Maryland and Virginia, is home to the threatened peregrine falcon and piping plover as well as 275 other bird species. The Chincoteague ponies, herds of wild horses of uncertain origin, have been roaming the island since the 17th century. **Assateague State Park,** 641-2120, is a 2-mile stretch of beach and dunes directly across the bridge from the Maryland mainland. **Chincoteague National Wildlife Refuge,** (757) 336-6122, occupies most of the Virginia end of the island. The rest of the island is managed by **Assateague Island National Seashore**, 641-1443. Camping is available in the State Park and the National Seashore, $9-$20, rsvs recommended. Lots of opportunities for hiking, as well as for canoeing and kayaking in the back bays. 'Delightful area,' be sure to bring plenty of insect repellent.

OCEAN CITY   Maryland's only major ocean-side resort. The town has a lively boardwalk and a wide beach, but gets crowded in the summer. This is the place to go if you want a wild time. Plenty of boarding house accommodation and good for summer jobs. 'Packed with British and Irish students. Anticipate bumping into your enemies from home.'

ACCOMMODATION

Accommodation can be reasonable here during the off season, but in summer months even the tackiest dives can get away with outrageous rates. A rule of thumb is the farther away from the boardwalk, the better. Accommodation is available—you just have to walk around to find it, particularly around 5th St. 'Beware of those selling "cheap" accommodation at the bus terminal and realtors who are out to make money from summer employees.'

Jarman House, 105 Talbot St, 289-7678. 'Low weekly rates. Great for working students.' Apartments w/ kitchens, $400 per week. Linens not provided.

Ocean City Convention and Visitors Bureau, 4001 Coastal Highway, 289-8181, can provide accommodation information.

Periwinkle Apartments, 11 79th St, Nov-April (301) 649-4172, April-Oct (410) 524-6481. All units 3 bedrooms, kitchens, TV, 'ideal for international students.' $500/week.

Summer Place Youth Hostel, 104 Dorchester St, 289-4542. 'Cheapest place in town.' $25 per night, $80-$150 per week. Kitchen, BBQ, sun-deck and hot tub. Rsvs recommended.

Whispering Sands Apts, 45th St, 723-1874. Approx. $68 per night, weekly rates from $400. 'Reasonable; friendly.' 'Ace.'

FOOD/ENTERTAINMENT
Ocean City has a league of bars, clubs and eateries. Many restaurants close after Labor Day, but even so, you'll never starve here.
The Angler, 312 Talbot St, 289-7424. Lively bar and restaurant with drinks specials on Sundays, Tuesdays and Thursdays, $2-$5 cover, 50¢ drafts on Sundays. 'Excellent!'
Bull on the Beach, 12th St at Boardwalk, 289-3744. 'Excellent sandwiches.'
La Hacienda, 80th St at Coastal Hwy, 524-8080. 'Great Mexican food.' Most dishes under $10.
Seacrets, 542-4900, 49th St and the Bay. Huge complex of bars constructed on and around the Bay. 'Live reggae, great atmosphere.' Mon-Sat 11am-2am, Sun 2pm-2am, cover $3-$5.
Tavern-by-the-Sea, 16th St and Boardwalk, 289-8444. 'Very popular bar/restaurant, always packed!' Infamous 'Import Night' on Wed, $5 cover, $1 for imported beers. All-you-can-eat Crab, $13.

SMITH ISLAND/TANGIER ISLAND   Tiny Smith Island (population 450) is Maryland's only inhabited island accessible exclusively by boat. The residents here are said to be direct descendants of the original inhabitants who came here from England and Cornwall in 1657. The story goes that Capt. John Smith gave the island his name when he discovered it in 1608, and was so taken by the beauty of the place that he wrote in his log: 'Heaven and earth seemed never to have agreed better for man's commodious and delightful habitation.' The famously friendly people of Smith Island and nearby Tangier Island (population 850) derive their livelihood from the Bay, and their distinct dialect is often compared to Elizabethan English. Summer cruises to the islands run daily from Crisfield, call 425-2771 for Smith Island or 968-2338/(800) 863-2338 for Tangier Island. There is also a daily ferry year-round at 12.30pm, call 425-5931 for Smith Island or 968-1118 for Tangier Island. Accommodation is scarce; the Smith Island Motel, 425-3321, has rooms from $60, and the Inn of Silent Music, 425-3541, on Smith Island, has rooms from $75 incl. breakfast.

ANTIETAM BATTLEFIELD   An interesting side-trip from Baltimore heading west on Rte 70—the site of the Civil War's bloodiest battle which resulted in 23,000 casualties in 1862. The scene of the battle is now a national park with an excellent museum and diorama at its Visitors Center, (301) 432-5124, near Sharpsburg, off Rte 65 (Hagerstown Pike). Daily 8.30am-6pm, $2.

CHESAPEAKE & OHIO CANAL   Until the advent of the railways, America made use of a considerable system of canals throughout the Northeast and Midwest, one of these being the Chesapeake & Ohio, running along the Maryland border from Washington DC to Cumberland via Harpers Ferry, West Virginia. The canal is now a national historic park extending 185 miles, the longest of all national preserves. Mostly disused but leafy and beautiful, the banks of the canal are well worth a hike or bicycle ride (see DC section for bike rental info), (301) 739-4200.

VIRGINIA   *The Old Dominion, Mother of Presidents*

Virginia is famed for its Colonial heritage, its historic homes and estates, and its great battlefields on which the fate of the nation was decided in both the 18th and 19th centuries. Seven of the 15 pre-Civil War Presidents were born here.

Virginia is the least southern of the old Confederate states in both geographical and cultural terms. Northern Virginia is a mainly urban collection of Washington suburbs where a growing technology industry is fast converting the area into the Silicon Valley of the east. Away from the DC suburbs, though, Virginia retains its mostly rural southern character, and Virginians everywhere are fiercely proud of the state's long role in American history. Virginia has a great deal to offer from both a scenic and a historic perspective. In the east are sandy beaches and the amazing 17½ mile Chesapeake Bay Bridge Tunnel linking Virginia to Maryland; in the west, Skyline Drive and the Shenandoah National Park. Everywhere there are countless well-preserved links with the past.
www.virginia.org

RICHMOND   The capital of Virginia and of the old Confederacy, Richmond was largely destroyed by retreating southern troops. Today, old and new meld forming an attractive, bustling city with plenty of history and entertainment. Richmond also makes a good base for visiting nearby landmarks, but—'it's dead at weekends'.
The telephone area code is 804.

ACCOMMODATION
Days Inn North Motel, 1600 Robin Hood Rd, 353-1287. Downtown area. D-$54-$75. Pool and restaurant.
Radisson Hotel, 301 West Franklin St, 644-9871. D-$79.
Massad House Hotel, 11 N 4th St, 648-2893. S-$50.63 incl tax, D-$54 incl tax, Q-$61.88 incl tax. Recommended by YMCA, which does not have overnights. 'Good accommodation.'
Motel 6, 5704 Williamsburg Rd, 222-7600. Six miles east on Hwy 60, near airport. S-$34-$40, D-$34-$45. 'Good value for money.'
Pocahontas State Park, 10301 State Park Rd, 796-4255. 19 miles south of Richmond, Exit 61 off I-95 to Rte 10, take country road 655. Sites $18, showers, boating and biking. 'Nice place.'
Grand Plaza Hotel, 555 East Canal St, (five blocks from the Capitol), 788-0900. D-$109-$139, pool, jacuzzi, mini-gym.

FOOD
Aunt Sarah's Pancake House, 7927 Broad St, 747-8284, and other Virginia locations. Real old-time Virginny cooking. Daily 24 hrs.
Blue Marlin Seafood Kitchen, 7502 West Broad Street, 672-3838. A Southern country seafood restaurant, serving shrimp and grits, crab cakes, and fresh fish, entrees from $9-$16.
Farmer's Market, on 17th St in Richmond's old town Shockoe Bottom near Shockoe Slip, 780-8597. Oldest continuously operating farmer's market in the country. Mon-Sat 9am-5pm, Sun 9am-4pm. Mon-Wed there is only one vendor.
Mamma Zu, 501 South Pine St, 788-4205. Huge pasta dishes $7-$9, large pizza will

feed three for $9.

The Strawberry Street Cafe, 421 North Strawberry St, 353-6860. Boasts the 'best burger in town', $5.50. Famous for its bathtub salad bar, a cast-iron claw-foot tub stocked with salads, home-made soup and fresh fruit for $6.95.

3rd Street Diner, 3rd & Main Sts, 788-4750. Popular with locals, 'fantastic sandwiches', $4-$6, breakfast specials from $3.15. Daily 24 hrs.

OF INTEREST

Take a historic walk through Richmond, starting from the Court end. Many attractions —national landmarks, museums and other notable buildings - are located within 8 blocks. A discount block ticket, $15, covers admission to most museums, valid for 30 days. The ticket is really only worth it if you plan to visit at least three attractions that have admission fees.

City Hall Skydeck, 9th & Broad, 780-7000, for a view of the city. Mon-Thu 8am-8pm, Fri-Sun 8am-5pm, free.

Hollywood Cemetery, Albemarle and Cherry Sts, US Presidents James Monroe and John Tyler, and Confederate President Jefferson Davis, are buried here along with some 18,000 Confederate soldiers.

Monument Avenue, a beautiful tree-lined boulevard with statues commemorating, among others, Arthur Ashe, JEB Stuart, and scientist and oceanographer Matthew Fontaine Maury.

Science Museum of Virginia, 2500 W Broad St, 367-0000. Has 'hands-on' exhibits and the excellent Universe Space Theater, where films are shown on a large planetarium dome providing sight and sound from every direction. Mon-Thu 9.30am-5pm, Fri-Sat 9.30am-7pm, Sun 11.30am-5pm. Admission to museum $5, IMAX films $4, combo ticket $8.

St John's Church, 24th & Broad. Built 1741, this is where Patrick Henry made his famous 'Give me liberty or give me death' speech. Nearby is a '**Poe Museum** ' in a house Poe never lived in. You would be well advised to skip it. The museum's only attraction is that it is across the street from a cigarette company—Poe would have been amused.

The State Capitol, Capitol Square, 698-1788, neo-classical domed building designed by Thomas Jefferson. Daily 9am-5pm, free tours.

Steeplechase races, a Virginia tradition. In spring, private country estates throughout Virginia's Piedmont region open their doors to the public for steeplechase horse racing. Watching the ritual tailgate parties can be just as entertaining as the race. In Richmond, steeplechase races are held at the Strawberry Hill State Fairgrounds, 228-3238, generally in April, $16-$25.

Valentine Museum, 1015 E Clay St, 649-0711, on the life and history of Richmond. Mon-Sat 10am-5pm; Sun noon-5pm. $5.

Virginia Aviation Museum, 5701 Huntsman Rd, near the International Airport, 236-3622, houses an extensive collection of vintage flying machines. Daily 9.30am-5pm, $5.

Virginia Museum of Fine Arts, Boulevard and Grove Sts, 367-0844. A panorama of world art from ancient times to the present. Suggested donation $4. Tue-Sun 11am-5pm, Thu 'til 8pm.

White House and Museum of the Confederacy, 1201 E Clay St, 649-1861. Mon-Sat 10am-5pm, Sun noon-5pm, $9.

ENTERTAINMENT

King's Dominion, north on I-95 (20 miles north of Richmond), 876-5000, $34 all day. 'Great rides—don't miss the Anaconda—a looping roller-coaster featuring an underwater tunnel.'

Shockoe Slip, Carey St btwn 12th & 14th Sts, old warehouses now store galleries and eclectic craft shops, hip restaurants, bars, and nightclubs.

Sixth St Market, btwn Coliseum & Grace St, live music, beer and dancing Friday afternoons in summer.

SPORT
Biking and Hiking: There are over 200 miles of trails to explore in the Richmond-Petersburg area, many cut through surrounding battlefields. **Golf**: Several courses in the metropolitan area, check out **Glenwood**, 3100 Creighton Rd, 226-1793, $15 weekdays. Also **The Crossings**, 800 Virginia Center Pkwy, 266-2254, $35 before 11am, $45 11am-3pm, $29 after 3pm.
Whitewater Rafting: One of only a few 'urban' whitewater runs in the country rages right through the heart of historic Richmond. Contact, **Richmond Raft Company**, 4400 E Main St, 222-7238, with trips from $35-$50, or **James River Runners**, 286-2338, tubing excursions for $13, rafting excursions for $23. *www.jamesriver.com*

INFORMATION
Visitors Information Center, 1710 Robin Hood Rd, exit 78 off I-95, 358-5511. Has short video on Richmond and Virginia and info on accommodation, restaurants, travel, and attractions. Daily, summer 9am-7pm, winter 9am-5pm. Another **Visitors Center** is located at Sixth Street Marketplace, 782-2777.

INTERNET ACCESS
Cafe Communique, 2401 W Main St, 359-3238. $6/hour, $2.50/15 minutes.
Richmond Public Library, 101 E Franklin St, 780-4672. Free Internet use, 45 minute limit, good idea to call ahead and sign up for time.

TRAVEL
Amtrak, 7519 Staples Mill Rd, (800) 872-7245. About five miles from downtown, no buses available. Taxi fare $15. (Washington $24-$30, rsvs required).
Greyhound, 2910 N Blvd, 254-5904/(800) 231-2222. Then take GRTC bus to town. (Charlottesville $16, 1^1/₂hrs, Williamsburg $10, 1 hr).
Richmond International Airport, 226-3052. Buses to and from the airport are few and far between; call Grooms Transportation, 222-7222, for pick-up service to downtown Richmond, $14.25 one person, $18.50 for two, $22.75 for three, after that $7 a head. Prices depend on which zone in Richmond you are travelling to.

FREDERICKSBURG One hour north of Richmond off I-95, the place where four great Civil War battles were fought. You can tour the **Fredericksburg Battlefield** where Lee's army fought off wave after wave of charging Federals from Marye's Heights.

The town itself has several interesting old houses, among them the home of George Washington's mother Mary Washington; **Kenmore**, the home of George's sister Betty Washington Lewis; and the **Rising Sun Tavern**, owned by George's brother Charles. Antique shops selling overpriced Americana line the quaint streets, but there are some good, inexpensive, places to eat; **Goolrick's Pharmacy**, 901 Caroline St, 373-3411. Original soda fountain, milkshakes, soup and sandwiches will satisfy for under $5, or try **Sammy T's** 801 Caroline St, 371-2008, where delicious vegetarian fare costs around $6.50.
The telephone area code is 540.

INFORMATION
Fredericksburg Battlefield Visitors Center, Lafayette Blvd, 373-6122. Museum exhibits, guided walking tours (in summer), and slide show describe the four battles of Fredericksburg. Summer: Daily 8.30am-6.30pm, otherwise 9am-5pm, $3.

WILLIAMSBURG   As state capital between 1699 and 1780, Williamsburg played a significant role in the heady days leading up to the American Revolution. Nowadays there's **Colonial Williamsburg**, with hundreds of houses painstakingly restored to create the look of earlier times and actors dressed up to give an air of reality. They even address the subject of slavery with actors 'living' a slave's life. Even so this is, as one reader put it, 'a sort of Colonial Disneyland'. Major tourist area.
www.visitWilliamsburg.com
The telephone area code is 757.

ACCOMMODATION
Williamsburg is loaded with hotels, but even the modest ones charge high rates. The **Colonial Williamsburg Visitors Center**, 229-1000, has a list of guest houses from about $80.
Johnson's Guest Home, 101 Thomas Nelson Lane, 229-3909. Rooms from $28. Kind, friendly landlady will pick up from train or bus station. 'Excellent place.'
Mrs H J Carter Guest House, 903 Lafayette St, 229-1117. S-$25, D-$35, Q-$40. 1 mile from downtown. Further afield is **Sangraal By-The-Sea Hostel**, in **Wake** (south of Urbanna, VA), (804) 776-6500. Actually, it's by the Rappahannock River where it meets the Chesapeake Bay, but a lovely location all the same. Urbanna is almost due north of Williamsburg (30mi); take Hwy 17. Dorm $16, private room $21, add $4 for non-AYH, linen $3, meals available; rsvs rec.
Williamsburg Hotel/Motel Association, (800) 446-9244. Rooms from $60.
www.williamsburghotels.com
Camping: Fair Oaks Family Campground, 901 Lightfoot Rd (exit 234 off I-64), 565-2101. $16, $19.50 w/hook-up. Showers, 5 miles from Colonial Williamsburg, 10 miles from Busch Gardens.

FOOD
Authentically decorated taverns in Colonial Williamsburg offer 18th and 21st century fare at 21st century prices.
A Good Place to Eat, 410 Duke of Gloucester St, 229-4370. A wide variety of good food, complete meal for $6.50.
College Deli, opposite William and Mary College, 229-6627. 'Best sandwiches in North America.' Dinner $6-$10, 10am-2am daily.
Paul's Deli Restaurant and Pizza, 761 Scotland St, 229-8976. Popular student hangout. Huge subs, pasta, and seafood specials, $4-$10. Half price Happy Hours, Wed-Sat 7pm-9pm. Daily 10.30am-2am.
Sal's Pizza, 1242 Richmond Rd, in the commercial part of town, 220-2641. 'Best pizza in town.'

OF INTEREST
Busch Gardens, 3 miles east of Williamsburg on Hwy 60, (800) 772-8886. A fanciful re-creation of old world Europe and action packed theme park operated by the Anheuser Busch Brewing Company. Authentically-detailed European hamlets alongside wet, dry and mind-erasing rides with such fear-inducing names as 'Atomic Breakers' and 'Drachen Fire,' one of the fiercest roller-coasters in the world! Free beer samples await at the brewery, but have ID ready. Summer: open daily 10am-10pm, $35. A 3-day pass for admission to both Busch Gardens and Water Country USA is available for $55. 'Loads of fun. Don't miss the Big Bad Wolf.'
College of William and Mary. Founded 1693, the second oldest in the nation. The **Sir Christopher Wren Building** at the west end of Duke of Gloucester St, is purported to be the oldest academic building in continuous use in the US. Also part of the college, the **Muscarelle Museum of Art**, 221-2703. Permanent collections

feature old master paintings, contemporary works and Colonial Virginia portraits. Mon-Fri 10am-4.45pm, w/ends noon-4pm.

Colonial Williamsburg. Perhaps the best buildings are the Capitol, jail, Raleigh Tavern, Governor's palace, and various colonial craft shops. Tickets are priced according to the number of buildings and craft shops visited—basic admission, 12-bldgs, $27, a Patriot's Pass provides unlimited admission to all exhibits for $35. Buildings open daily 9am-5pm. Call 229-1000 for more info. You can also just wander for free without going into the houses at all. Start at Merchants Sq and continue in a rough counter-clockwise direction. Go first to the **Visitors Center**. You can see a documentary film here which may make the visit more meaningful.

James River Plantations, take Rte 5 along the river to visit several plantation homes of early American leaders; then Hwy 60 to **Carter's Grove** (also to Busch Gardens), often called 'the most beautiful Colonial home in America.'

Jamestown, first permanent English settlement in America. Not that much has been restored: the visitor must often be content with looking at foundations. Plagues, Indians, starvation and fires hindered its development, and when the peninsula finally became an island, Williamsburg and Yorktown prospered in its stead. The original settlement is about a mile from the more recent **Jamestown Settlement Park**, 229-1607. In the park are replicas of three ships, a re-creation of the first fort, an Indian village and a museum. Daily 9am-5pm, $10.25. 5 min from Williamsburg on Hwy 31 south.

Yorktown is the least restored of the James River historical areas, but the battlefield and 67 18th century structures remain. The surrender of the British at Yorktown ended the War of Independence, although the final peace treaty wasn't signed until two years later. **The Yorktown Victory Center**, in Yorktown on Rte 238, 887-1776, sits on a 21-acre tract overlooking the York River. Built for the Bicentennial, it is a permanent museum dramatising the military events of the Revolution. Daily 9am-5pm, $7.25.

Water Country USA, west of Williamsburg on I-64, (800) 772-8886. Sister park to Busch Gardens, focus on water rides. $27, 3-day pass for both Busch Gardens and Water Country USA is $55.

INFORMATION
Colonial Williamsburg Visitors Center, on State Hwy 132-Y, (800) HISTORY. Daily 9am-5pm. Runs shuttle bus (8.30am-10pm) to historic section, free with admission ticket.
Williamsburg Chamber of Commerce, 201 Penniman Rd, 229-6511. Mon-Fri 8.30am-5pm.

TRAVEL
Greyhound, 229-1460/(800) 231-2222; and **Amtrak**, 229-8750/(800) 872-7245, at Lafayette & N Boundary St.

VIRGINIA BEACH Continuing south-east from Williamsburg and past Norfolk, you come to this fast-growing resort with a 28-mile beach running from the landing dunes of America's first permanent colonists on Cape Henry to Virginia's Outer Banks. From here you can access the amazing **Chesapeake Bay Bridge Tunnel** for the northern drive up the Atlantic coastline, stopping off to visit Assateague National Seashore (see Maryland).
The telephone area code for Virginia Beach is 757.

ACCOMMODATION
All prices skyrocket from June to Labor Day. $59 for a double passes for 'economy' at the tackiest hotel or motel. It's cheaper to rent an 'efficiency apartment' and cram everyone you know into it. For starters, go to or call **Angie's Guest Cottage**, 302 24th St, 428-4690; $14.45 incl tax AYH, $17.75 incl tax non-AYH, linens $2, rates

drop $3 off season. B&B, D-$66-$84, XP-$10. Camping available when the hostel is full, $3 less than hostel prices. If they don't have space, they'll recommend others that might, although no one's prices come close to matching Angie's. *www.bbinternet.com/angies*

Coral Sand Motel, 23rd & Pacific Ave, 425-0872. Close to beach, rooms from $55 for two, includes small breakfast. (Predominantly gay resort.)

Sundial Motel, 308 21st St, 428-2922. D-$59-$99, close to beach.

Camping: Seashore State Park, 5 miles north of town on US 60 (about a mile from the resort area). (800) 933-7275. Pitch your tent ($18, up to 6 people) in the dunes or under a cypress tree, showers available; cabins for four $572/week.

FOOD

Junk food heaven! Fast food joints crowd the boardwalk which at night becomes loud and luminous!

Giovanni's Pizza Pasta Place, 2006 Atlantic Ave, 425-1575. Inexpensive Italian food. Lunch and dinner $5-$8. Daily noon-midnight.

The Jewish Mother, 3108 Pacific Ave, 422-5430. Burgers, sandwiches, etc. $8 average meal price. 'Friendly place, and while waiting you can crayon on the walls and menus!' At night a popular bar with live music.

OF INTEREST

Poe wasn't the only Edgar around these parts with a finger on the pulse of the para-normal: the work of Edgar Cayce, the 'best documented psychic of modern times' is explained in exhibits, lectures, movies and tours at his **A.R.E. Library and Conference Center**, 67th & Atlantic, 428-3588. You can learn about life after death and have your ESP tested too. Mon-Sat 9am-8pm, Sun 11am-8pm. Free.

The **Viva Elvis Festival**, (800) 446-8038, in early June has Elvis impersonators, Elvis films, Elvis food (fried peanut-butter-and-banana sandwiches) and a 'Flock of Elvi' skydiving to the beach (!) not to mention four days of Elvis karaoke contests, so if you've ever fancied yourself as a bit of a hound dog, here's your chance! Virginia Beach is amusement park paradise. If you're looking for thrills, try **Ocean Breeze,** a water park, 422-4444, **Fun Spot Action Park**, for go-carting, 422-1401, or **Atlantic Fun House**, 422-1742.

SPORT

Virginia Beach is host to a leg of the annual **Bud Surf Tour**, attracting pros world-wide. If you fancy your chances, **Wave Riding Vehicles**, 422-8823, provide local surf reports and info on main surf areas. You can also rent surfboards from their store at 19th and Cypress Sts. Cycling, jogging and skating are popular along the boardwalk, and there are a couple of fishing piers for those wishing to take things easy.

Skating: **Mount Trashmore Skatepark**, South Blvd & Edwin Dr, 473-5237.

INFORMATION

The Virginia Beach Visitor Information Center, 2100 Parks Ave, (800) VA-BEACH. Free publications full of useful info and accommodation directories. Daily 9am-8pm.

CHARLOTTESVILLE   Located in central Virginia and surrounded by beau-tiful dogwood-laden countryside and old estates, Charlottesville is one of the most interesting and charming places in the state. Several celebrities have moved here to enjoy the gentleman-farmer lifestyle, including Sissy Spacek, Sam Shepherd and Jessica Lange. Much of the architecture was either designed by Jefferson or influenced by his example. The elegant **University of Virginia** is testimony to his humanism and architectural genius.

The telephone area code is 804.

ACCOMMODATION

Budget Inn, 140 Emmet St, 293-5141. Near University and CSXT railway line. Rooms from D-$42-$50.

Econo Lodge, 2014 Holiday Dr, 295-3185, D-$46-$60, XP-$5, & 400 Emmett St, 296-2104, D-$55-$75, XP-$5.

Town and Country Motor Lodge, Rte 250E, 293-6191. S-$46 D-$48. 'Very friendly and clean.'

FOOD

Baja Bean Co, 1327 W Main St, 293-4507. California-style Mexican food washed down with a choice of 12 Mexican beers and 15 different Tequilas. 'Cheap and delicious.'

Big Jim's Barbeque, 2104 Angus Rd, 296-8283. Huge burgers that you can't finish, Cajun-style, $1.60-$4.50.

White Spot Restaurant, 1407 University Ave, 295-9899. Small, basic diner food. Try the 'Gus,' an egg-cheese-cholesterolburger, with fries and a soda for $3.50. 'Friendly, helpful staff.'

OF INTEREST

Ash Lawn, 2^{1}/₂ miles beyond Monticello on Rte 53, 293-9539, 535-acre estate of the 5th US president, James Monroe. The site was chosen by his close friend Thomas Jefferson. Daily 9am-6pm. $7.

Historic Court Square, E Jefferson St, self-guided tour info available free at Albermarle County Historical Society at 200 2nd St NE.

Michie Tavern, ¹/₂ mile from Monticello on Rt 53, 977-1234. Re-creates 18th-century tavern life. Story has it that Jefferson, Monroe, Madison and Lafayette met here. Converted log-house next door serves all-you-can-eat 18th-century southern-style lunch. 9am-5pm, $6 museum. With lunch the museum ticket is $1 off.

Monticello, 3 miles south-east of the town on Rte 53, 984-9800. The architectural masterpiece where Thomas Jefferson lived and experimented. Built from his own design, this Palladian villa has many ingenious extras such as the clock that sits over the front door. Daily 8am-5pm Mar-Oct, $9, frequent tours. 'Magnificent, with fine views of the surrounding countryside.'

Steeplechase racing, in April at the Foxfield Race Course, 293-9501, $15-$20.

ENTERTAINMENT

Durty Nelly's, 2200 Jefferson Park Ave, 295-1278. Bar/deli, choose from over 50 beers. Happy Hour specials, live music at weekends, cover $3-$4. Daily 11am-2am.

Friday After Five, on the mall, live entertainment, festive atmosphere, every Friday during summer.

Millers, 109 W Main St near the mall, 971-8511. Bar with live music Mon-Sat, $2-$4 cover. 'Cheap food.'

INFORMATION

Albemarle County Historical Society, 200 2nd St NE, 296-1492, brochure on historic sites, museum features law in Virginia and local history. Walking tours leave from here on Saturdays at 10am, suggested $3 donation.

Charlottesville Visitors Center, at intersection of Rte 20 and I-64 on the way to Monticello, 293-6789, has info on places to eat and stay, and things to do in Charlottesville; also has exhibit 'Thomas Jefferson at Monticello.' Daily 9am-5.30pm.

TRAVEL

Amtrak, 7th & W Main Sts, 296-4559/(800) 872-7245, for fare and schedule info.

Greyhound, 310 W Main St, 295-5131/(800) 231-2222. (Richmond $16, 1 hr 15 mins).

SHENANDOAH NATIONAL PARK Only 80 miles from Washington DC, the park is a lovely wilderness area. The 105-mile Skyline Drive runs along the crest of the Blue Ridge Mountains following the old Appalachian Trail, with an average elevation of over 3000 ft. The southern end of the drive meets the Blue Ridge Parkway which takes the traveller clear down to the Smokies.

The route affords a continuous series of magnificent views over steeply wooded ravines to the Piedmont Plateau on the east and across the fertile farmlands of the Shenandoah Valley to the west. Check the weather before doing the Skyline Drive. If it's bad, you'll just drive through clouds.

There are over 500 miles of foot trails for every type of hiker. Campgrounds, lodges and shelters can be found throughout the park (see below). Look out for pioneer dwellings and homesteads. **Skyline Drive Entrances**: (North to south) Front Royal off Hwy 340; Thornton Gap near Luray off Hwy 211; Swift Run Gap near Elkton off Hwy 33; Rockfish Gap near Waynesboro off Hwy 250 or I-64. $10 per vehicle.
The area code is 540.

ACCOMMODATION
Bear's Den AYH-Hostel, just off Rte 601 S, near Bluemont, 554-8708. A stone lodge that sits on the Appalachian Trail, overlooking the Shenandoah River. Office hours 5pm-10pm, front gate locked at 10pm. $12 AYH, $15 non-AYH, linen included. Rsvs recommended. Camping $6 pp.
Lodges: **Skyland Lodge** at milepost 41.7 or 42.5. Room with 2 D beds $84 weekdays, $97 w/end; **Big Meadows Lodge** at milepost 51, easy access to hiking trails and restaurants. Same rates as Skyland Lodge. Rsvs required (months in advance for fall), contact ARA Virginia Skyline Company Inc, 743-5108. All campgrounds and lodges have rangers-in-residence who provide info on trails, natural history, etc. Shelters for day hikers, and huts for backpackers with *3-night* or *Appalachian-Through-Trail-Permits* only are scattered throughout the park. Be sure to talk to rangers about location, availability and permits.
Campgrounds: **Mathews Arm** at Skyline Drive milepost 22.2 (no showers); **Big Meadows** at milepost 51; **Lewis Mountain** at milepost 57.5; **Loft Mountain** at milepost 79.5. Tent sites $14. All on first-come, first-served basis, except Big Meadows which requires reservations and charges $17—(800) 365-2267.

INFORMATION
Shenandoah National Park Visitors Centers: Byrd Center at Big Meadows (milepost 51), 999-2243 (has info on camping within the park); and Dickie Ridge Center (milepost 4.6), 635-3566.

OF INTEREST
Luray Caverns, on Rte 211, 743-6551, with stalactites and -mites, and eerie organ. Daily 9am-7pm, $14, 1hr tours. 'Excessive.' 'Worth every cent.'

LEXINGTON At the southern end of the Shenandoah Valley, a quaint picturesque town where both Stonewall Jackson and Robert E. Lee lived. Visit the **Stonewall Jackson House**, 8 E Washington St, 463-2552, for a guided tour and information on Jackson's younger years, $5. The **Lee Chapel and Museum** at Washington and Lee University, 463-8768, is where Lee and his beloved horse Traveler are buried, free. Nearby **Rockbridge Vineyard**, in Raphine, 377-6204, offers tours and tastings of its award-winning wines. North of town on Rte 39 is the **Goshen Pass**, a breathtaking mountain gorge with miles of whitewater rapids, the perfect spot for swimming, tubing, fishing, or hiking. The **Natural Bridge,** spanning 90 ft, is one of the seven natural wonders of the world and lies just 16 miles from Lexington off of Interstate 81. **The Natural Bridge Caverns**, 291-2121/(800) 533-1410, have stalagmites and stalactites along with hanging gardens and flowstone cascades, $8 for the bridge, $15 for both the bridge and caverns. Stay at **Overnight Guests**, 216 W. Washington St, 463-3075, massive rooms in a sprawling old clapboard house, shared bath, $10 pp. Camping is available at the **Campground at Natural Bridge**, 291-2727, tent sites $16-$18.

WEST VIRGINIA *Mountain State*

A common image people have of West Virginia is of a poor but proud population struggling to make a living from coal mining and enduring a hard life between business cycles as rocky as the Appalachian mountains that cover the state.

Though this image is partly accurate, 50 years of federal programmes, a growing tourist economy, and industries flourishing in other, less mountainous parts of the state have combined to alter the economic picture of West Virginia. The most striking (and most lucrative) aspect of the Mountain State, however, remains its natural beauty. Tree-covered mountains, raging rivers, caves, waterfalls and gorges offer the visitor a variety of scenic vistas and wilderness adventures.

The state was formed during the Civil War when people in the western part of Virginia refused to join the rebels and seceded from the Confederacy to stay with the Union. The mountain people, who still speak a form of Elizabethan English, are authentic hillbillies. Local bluegrass musicians can be heard in small town and big city alike.

www.westvirginia.com

The telephone area code for the entire state is 304.

CHARLESTON Not to be confused with Charleston, South Carolina. This is the state capital and an industrial town; not much to look at, but there are nice hills nearby, and the city is a good base for a more interesting visit to the countryside.

ACCOMMODATION
Dunbar Super 8 Motel, 911 Dunbar Ave, 768-6888. S-$45-$50, D-$52-$57.
Night's Inn, 6401 MacCorkle Ave, I-77 exit 95, 925-0451. S-$36, D-$43, XP-$5.
Red Roof Inn, 4006 MacCorkle Ave, I-64 exit 54, 744-1500. S-$45-$55, D-$50-$55, XP-$5.

FOOD
Charleston Town Center Picnic Place and Restaurants, Clendin, Court, Lee and Quarrier Sts, 345-9525. 160 stores and restaurants, one of the largest downtown enclosed malls in the US. Mon-Sat 10am-9pm, Sun 12.30pm-6pm.
Kanawha Mall, 57th St & MacCorkle Ave SE, 925-4921. Mall with food court and restaurants. Mon-Sat 10am-9pm, Sun 12.30pm-5pm.

OF INTEREST

Coonskin Park, 2000 Coonskin Dr, 341-8000. Swimming pool, golf course, paddle boat lake, and tennis courts.

Cultural Center, Greenbrier & Washington Sts, 558-0162. Free exhibits of West Virginia arts, crafts and history. Mon-Fri 9am-5pm, Sat & Sun 1pm-5pm.

East End Historic District, residential district bordered by Bradford, Quarrier, and Michigan Sts and Kanawha Blvd. Many fine examples of Colonial, Greek Revival, Late Victorian, and Georgian homes.

PA Denny Sternwheeler, 925-7899. Scenic cruises along the Kanawha River, starting from **Daniel Boone Park**, just east of Charleston on Rte 60. $6. Call for schedule info.

State Capitol, Main rotunda, Washington St E, 558-4839, free tours daily 9am-3.15pm.

Sunrise Museum, 746 Myrtle Rd, 344-8035. Cultural centre located in two historic mansions overlooking the city. Art galleries, science museum, planetarium and 16 acres of gardens and trails. Wed-Sat 11am-5pm, Sun noon-5pm, $3.50, $2.50 w/student ID.

INFORMATION/TRAVEL

Convention and Visitors Bureau, 200 Civic Center Dr, 344-5075.

Amtrak, 350 MacCorkle Ave SE, (800) 872-7245. Baltimore $49-$93, Washington DC $46-$87, rsvs required.

Greyhound, 300 Reynolds St, (800) 231-2222. Baltimore $58, Washington DC $58, Richmond $62.

INTERNET ACCESS

Kanawha Public Library, 123 Capitol St, 343-4646. Free Internet use on a first-come, first-served basis.

NEW RIVER GORGE

In the southernmost part of the state, the New and Gauley rivers churn some of the most exciting rapids anywhere. The Gauley, in fact, is billed as one of the top ten whitewater rivers in the world. The major city serving the region is **Beckley**, where accommodation and hiking equipment can be found. The area can be reached by following I-77, the West Virginia Turnpike (toll).

ACCOMMODATION

Budget Inn, 223 S Heber St, 253-8318. S/D-$36-$43. 'Convenient.'

Days Inn, off I-77 exit 44, 255-5291. D-$65-$67.

OF INTEREST

Cliffside Amphitheatre, in Grandview, near Beckley, 256-6800. Classic and modern drama by local repertory companies. June-Sept, Tue-Sun, 8.15pm. Every summer *Hatfields and McCoys* and *Honey in the Rock* are presented. Tkts $12.

Exhibition Coal Mine, New River Park in Beckley, 256-1747. Learn about coal mining by going down into a real coal pit. April-Nov, daily 10am-5.30pm, $8. 'Take a sweater.'

Fayetteville Ghost Tours, 20 miles north of Beckley on US-19, 256-TOUR. Tour meets at the Fayetteville County Courthouse Fri-Sat at 8.15pm, $7.

Fayetteville Walking Tours, 574-0890. Tour Civil War sites of the town. Begins at the Fayetteville County Courthouse, Fri-Sat 7pm.

New River Gorge, every Sunday, Wednesday, and Friday, the Amtrak *Cardinal* between Chicago and New York, offers a narrated trip through the gorge between White Sulphur Springs and Montgomery. 3 hours, $23-$44, rsvs required, (800) 872-7245.

New River Gorge Bridge, on US-19 past Fayetteville. The world's longest single-arch steel bridge spans the gorge at one of its most stunning points.

WHITEWATER

North America's wildly beautiful and spectacular rivers make it an ideal spot for white-water rafting: a mind-blowing experience you'll remember for years. These are some of the most fun whitewater rivers:

EAST: **Chattooga, Long Creek, SC**. 50 ft/mile drops through most inaccessible canyons in Southeast, site of movie *Deliverance*. Best tackled in spring or early summer Day trips $46-$99, call Wildwater Limited, (800) 451-9972. **Cheat, Albright, WV**. Try 'Big Nasty' and 'Coliseum' rapids, part of largest natural watershed in East; only rafted April-May. Day trips from $66; for more info call Mountain Streams, (800) 245-4090. **Gauley, Summerville, WV**. 2-day autumn trip rated 'the best;' don't try the Upper section unless you've got rafting experience (or a deathwish!). Day trips from $60, for more info call (800)879-7483. **James, Richmond, VA**. Raft past commuters in metropolitan Richmond. Day trips from $48 include nature refuge, or raft through evening rush hour from $35. Call Richmond Raft Co, (804) 222-7238 for details.

New, Beckley, WV, is the world's second oldest river after the Nile. Lower section is known as 'Grand Canyon of the East,' with spectacular view of the longest, highest single-span bridge on earth. Day trips from $90; for more info call Class VI River Runners (800) 252-7784. **Youghiogheny** (The 'Yough,' pronounced Yock'), **Ohiopyle State Park, PA**. Splendid, challenging rapids , prices depend on season and difficulty. Wilderness Voyageurs Inc, (800) 272-4141. **Upper Yough, Friendsville, MD**. Ranks among most challenging in world with rapid names including 'Meat Cleaver' and 'Double Pencil Sharpener' (!); an experienced rafter's dream, a beginner's night-mare.

Penobscot, Maine, through the steep-walled granite Ripogenus Gorge, one of the most scenic whitewater stretches in east US. But no time for the view if you ride the 'Exterminator' Class V rapid—'intense.' Call Northern Outdoors, (207) 663-4466, $79-$114, depends on day and season. USA Raft, (800) 624-8060, is the reservation company for several outfitters. They can help you choose from among 30 different outings, to suit all skill levels, on ten of the best whitewater rivers in the east. More info, check out the American White-Water Affiliation Homepage, *www.awa.org*.

WEST: **Colorado, Grand Canyon, AZ**. Over 150 world-class rapids between Badger Creek and Lava Falls, surrounded by canyon walls a mile high. Arizona Office of Tourism, (602)230-7733. **Middle Fork of Salmon, Boise, ID**. Whitewater of unforgettable intensity and beauty, natural hot springs and waterfalls. Idaho Outfitters and Guides Association (208)342-1438.

Snake, Boise, ID. Rafting through Hells Canyon, the deepest gorge in the world, on 'reorganizer' rapids and warm water. Idaho Outfitters and Guides Association (208) 342-1438. **CANADA: Kootenay, Windermere, BC**. The Kootenay tumbles through some of the most scenic passes of the Rocky Mtns. Contact Columbia Rafting Adventures, (250) 345-6155. Day-long excursions are $80. Also **Jasper National Park** provides amazing scenery and exhilarating runs. Contact Whitewater Rafting, Limited, (800)557-RAFT.

A beginning rafter should check out *The Complete Whitewater Rafter* by Jeff Bennett, McGraw-Hill, NY, NY, for historical background on the sport and tips for handling the wildest of rivers. For more information on whitewater routes, consult *Whitewater Rafting in North America* (2nd Edition) by Lloyd D Armstead, Pequot Press, Chester, CT. For extended trips on Western rivers, contact the *American Wilderness Experience*, Boulder, CO, (800)444-0099. Also check out *www.westernriver.com/* and *www.travelsource.com/rafting*.

Tips: Wherever you decide to go, bear in mind the following: look for an established outfitter that has been in business for a number of years and has a current licence. Decide what you want and know the level of ability required (Class IIII for first-timers, IV-VI more advanced, difficult rapids). Plan ahead—deposits may be required; w/ends are more expensive than weekdays; find out what the price includes (meals, equipment, etc). Finally, if you fall out of the raft, fold your arms across your chest and point your feet DOWNstream.

Whitewater Rafting. The Chamber of Commerce in Beckley, 245 North Kanawha St, 252-7328, has brochures of many organisations that run whitewater rafting tours along the New and Gauley Rivers at various prices. The Southern West Virginia Convention and Visitors Bureau, above the Exhibition Coal Mine, has a listing of all the whitewater rafting companies in the area, 252-2244. $80 could buy you the thrill of a lifetime, but prices start as low as $40.

New River Gorge is surrounded by numerous State Parks, including; **Babock**, **Bluestone**, **Carnifex Ferry**, **Hawks Nest**, and **Pipestream**. All offer exceptional recreational facilities and camping.

MONONGAHELA NATIONAL FOREST

Sounding like the name of a monster from a Japanese sci-fi flick, the Monongahela is actually a charming and beautiful forest covering much of eastern West Virginia. Unusual geological formations beneath the mountains have resulted in the creation of some of the largest caverns in the world, as well as warm mineral springs that bubble up in several valleys. There's coal under the mountains too, and many of the back roads are made bumpy by the giant coal trucks that roll in convoy all day and all night.

Within a few miles of the town of **White Sulphur Springs** are the **Lost World Caverns**, in Lewisburg, 645-6677, filled with amazing rock formations and bats. Self-guided tour $8, daily 9am-7pm. Also along Hwy 219 is the **Droop Mountain State Park**, site of a Civil War battle. Two hours northeast of White Sulphur Springs is **Cass Scenic Railroad**, 456-4300, where a coal-fired locomotive hauls visitors along old logging railways through the remote corners of the National Forest late May through early Oct. 1½ hr rides at 10.50am, 1pm, 3pm; $10; 5 hr trip at noon (except Mon), $14. All weekend trips are $2 extra.

Green Bank National Radio Astronomy Observatory, on Rte 28, 456-2011, is 10 miles away from the Cass Railroad. This is a major radio telescope which American scientists are using to map the universe and study its chemical composition. Free daily tours from mid-June-Sept between 9am-4pm.

ACCOMMODATION
Allstate Motel, Hwy 60, 1½ miles east of White Sulphur Springs, 536-1731. S-$55, D-$65.
Budget Inn, Hwy 60, 536-2121. Rooms from $40.
Camping: There are no camping restrictions in the forest, so if you have some of that pioneer spirit, just find a spot and camp down. State parks with campgrounds: **Greenbrier**, near White Sulphur Springs, 536-1944, has cabins suitable for groups; from $75 incl tax for four people, $88 incl tax on weekends. Tent sites are $11, $16 w/hook-up. **Watoga**, near Hillsboro, Rte 28, 799-4087. Tent sites $12 (no hook-up), cabin for four $75.

NORTHERN PANHANDLE

The section of the state that sticks up between Ohio and Pennsylvania has two things worth visiting: **Grave Creek Mounds**, at Moundsville, 843-4128, the largest pre-historic, conical Indian burial site in the US. Mon-Sat 10am-4.30pm, Sun 1pm-5pm, $3.
Prabhupada's Palace of Gold in Moundsville, south of Wheeling on Hwy 250, 843-1600. This glittering gold complex is a Hare Krishna tribute to their departed leader, and includes a temple and a spectacular rose garden.

Future plans include a theme park called 'City of God,' proving that it's not *all* spirituality, after all. Daily 10am-11.30am and 1pm-6pm, $6 donation.

HARPERS FERRY The National Park Service preserves this small, historic town where in 1859 John Brown raided the government arsenal, freed a few slaves and hoped to spark a general slave uprising. He was captured the following evening by Col Robert E. Lee and two months later was tried and publicly hanged in neighbouring Charles Town.

Highly recommended for Civil War buffs—Harpers Ferry changed hands 17 times during the war—the area also appeals to nature lovers for the view from Jefferson Rock, so named because Thomas Jefferson stood here after returning from Europe and said, 'This scene is worth a voyage across the Atlantic'. Park Service tours throughout the day, 11am-3pm in summer; in winter talks are few and far between, but exhibits and orientation films are open 8am-5pm. 535-6298 for more info. Pedestrian bridge connects into C&O Canal Towpath over the river.

Nearby **Shepherdstown**, the oldest town in West Virginia and home of Shepherd College, offers shops, higher priced accommodation and restaurants (**Old Pharmacy Cafe, Betty's Restaurant, Mecklenburg Inn**). Worth a visit is the **Shepherdstown Opera House**, a movie theatre in a restored early 1900s building.

Charles Town has a race track with nearby motels and cheap eats (**Stuck and Alger** on W. Washington St) as well as country fairs, carriage rides and charming old houses. The first rural postal delivery service in the US began here.

ACCOMMODATION
Bear's Den, 25 miles south of Harpers Ferry in Bluemont, VA, (540) 554-8708. $12 AYH, $15 non-AYH. Office hours 5pm-10pm. See also 'Virginia.'
Harpers Ferry AYH Hostel, on Sandy Hook Rd in Knoxville, MD, 2 miles from Harpers Ferry, (301) 834-7652, ferrylodge@aol.com. $13 AYH, $16 non-AYH; $3 AYH primitive camping, $4.50 non-AYH, $6 camping with access to showers and kitchen, $9 non-AYH, closed 9.30am-6pm. Overlooking the Potomac and Shenandoah Rivers, this is a great location for hiking and rafting. Taxi from the train station is about $5, call 725-3794 or (301) 834-7653.

OF INTEREST
Ghost tours, 725-8019. An exploration of Harpers Ferry's ghost-ridden past, March-Oct Fri-Sun at 8pm, $2. Meets in front of Hot Dog Haven on Potomac St. Rsvs required in October.
Whitewater Rafting on the Shenandoah, a tamer ride than the New River Gorge. Blue Ridge Outfitters, Hwy 340, 2 miles from the Harpers Ferry National Park, (304) 725-3444. Raft and canoe trips, Mar-Oct, $50 raft, $55 canoe. Rsvs recommended.

INFORMATION/TRAVEL
Harpers Ferry is readily accessible by car from Washington DC, Baltimore, and Harrisburg.
Amtrak, Pontiac St and Railroad Bridge, (800) 872-7245, from Washington's Union Station once a day, $9-$17 o/w, rsvs required.
MARC Line Trains, (800) 325-7245, also run from DC, Mon-Fri only, $7.25 o/w. You might also want to pass through here if you're on your way to the Skyline drive through Virginia's Shenandoah National Park.

THE MIDWEST

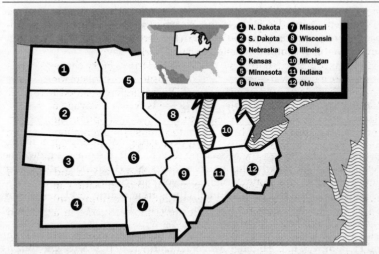

1. N. Dakota
2. S. Dakota
3. Nebraska
4. Kansas
5. Minnesota
6. Iowa
7. Missouri
8. Wisconsin
9. Illinois
10. Michigan
11. Indiana
12. Ohio

The Midwest (defined here as the 12 states from Ohio west to the Dakotas) is the rich, flat underbelly of the US whose glacier-scoured fertile lands yielding massive quantities of corn, soybeans, hay, wheat and livestock. It's also the manufacturing, transportation and industrial heart of America; the Chicago-Gary area alone once poured more steel than all of France. The region boasts the world's most powerful and fastest computer, CRAY-2 (in Minneapolis), the highest-energy particle accelerator (near Batavia, Illinois), and the largest manufacturer of farm equipment (in Moline, Illinois).

But the recession of the early 1980's hit the Midwest hard. From some it earned the nickname 'the rust belt' for its deteriorating and closed-down factories. Falling prices and excessive debts trapped many farmers in a downward spiral toward bankruptcy, causing unprecedented suicides that tore at the fabric of a settled life. However, industry has recently revived somewhat; farm prices and the value of land have also risen.

The essential quality of Midwestern life is its small-town character, and that's where you should seek it out. Take time to meet its friendly and generous people, to get to know the prairie villages and the slow drawl of fields between them. Listen to the charming Scandinavian brogue of the northern states. And try to find time to read the novels of Nobel Prize winner Sinclair Lewis (*Babbitt, Main Street, Elmer Gantry*), each of which was carefully mapped out by Lewis in quintessential Midwestern cities.

Mother Nature provides much of the drama here, from tornadoes in spring-summer to the fantastic electrical storm displays that light up summer evenings. The area is also seismically active: in 1811-1812, the biggest quakes in recorded history rolled through one million square miles, causing the Mississippi and Ohio Rivers to flow backwards.

The region's mighty rivers and Great Lakes serve as liquid highways for its products, just as they did in paddlewheeler days. They also create liquid disasters such the great flood of 1993 that caused over $10 billion in damage and left millions of people homeless and (ironically) without water. Itself once 'the West', the Midwest in turn became the staging area for pioneer trails like the Santa Fe, Oregon and Mormon. With the advent of the railroad, the region became the distribution link between cattle ranch and consumer— a role it continues to play today.

ILLINOIS *The Prairie State*

Illinois takes its nickname from the prairie, the original ground cover for the vast region lying east of the Mississippi River. On it, the grasses grew nine feet or more, which is why Illinois' corn shoots up so high today. Stand in an Illinois cornfield on a summer night and you can actually *hear* it grow! West of the Mississippi, the land gradually turns from prairie to plains; they're just as flat but receive less rain, more sun, and have thinner soil—prime wheat-growing land.

Illinois has a tradition of plain-spoken eloquence, from Lincoln, Sandburg and Hemingway to the Grange Movement farmers of the 1870s who took as their slogan: 'Raise less corn and more hell!' Its premier city, Chicago, is also the birthplace of the only truly American architecture and the earthy Chicago blues. In the countryside, you'll taste Midwestern hospitality at its best, as sweet and honest as an ear of young corn.
www.yahoo.com/Regional/U_S__States/Illinois/

CHICAGO   In the aftermath of the Great Fire of 1871, a Chicago realtor put up a sign that read: 'All gone but wife, children and energy!' That unquenchable spunk is still Chicago's trademark. The place hurls superlatives at you: tallest buildings, largest grain market, greatest distribution point, busiest airport and train terminal, biggest Polish populace outside Warsaw, highest concentration of practising psychics—the list is endless.

Chicago, where Ferris Bueller took his famous day off, has two popular nicknames, Second City and The Windy City. For decades it was the nation's second most populous region (after New York) but that title has since passed to Los Angeles. It's the politics, not the breeze sweeping in off Lake Michigan, that explains Chicago's other nickname.

Volatile is the word for Chicago's politics, particularly for the periods following the deaths of Mayor Richard Daley and more recently, of the much-admired black mayor, Harold Washington. The ruthless Mayor Daley ran one of the last great political machines in America for a generation after World War II. He made Chicago 'the city that works'. His son, Richard M Daley was elected in 1988. Having captured the affection and trust of Chicago's crazy quilt of ethnic and political groups, he leads the windy city into the next millennium.

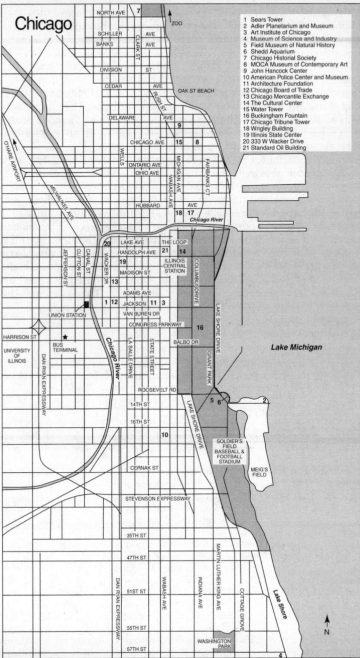

Chicago

1 Sears Tower
2 Adler Planetarium and Museum
3 Art Institute of Chicago
4 Museum of Science and Industry
5 Field Museum of Natural History
6 Shedd Aquarium
7 Chicago Historial Society
8 MOCA Museum of Contemporary Art
9 John Hancock Center
10 American Police Center and Museum
11 Architecture Foundation
12 Chicago Board of Trade
13 Chicago Mercantile Exchange
14 The Cultural Center
15 Water Tower
16 Buckingham Fountain
17 Chicago Tribune Tower
18 Wrigley Building
19 Illinois State Center
20 333 W Wacker Drive
21 Standard Oil Building

Lake Michigan

Although it was built on a swamp the Indians called 'place of the stinking wild onions', Chicago is the fount of architectural innovation in the United States as well as a vital communications and trading centre and hub for both industry and agriculture in the Midwest. Both the true skyscraper, in which the stress falls on the metal skeleton rather than the walls, and balloon framing, a cheap breakthrough in housing construction, were born here. At various times Chicago was the home of Louis Sullivan, Frank Lloyd Wright, Daniel Burnham, Helmut Jahn and Mies van der Rohe. The city possesses the finest architectural tradition in the country and had the good sense to preserve its lake shore as recreational land, giving it an extraordinary skyline along 27 miles of park lands and clean beaches.

Always pugnacious, Chicago in its gangland heyday (1920's-1940's) had wide-open criminal activity and hundreds of unsolved mob murders. The 1988 movie, *The Untouchables*, reveals the morbid underworld of infamous criminal Al Capone and his gang. One public official tried to divert attention from his Capone connections with an anti-British Empire campaign. He periodically offered to punch King George V 'in the snoot' if the monarch ever ventured near Chicago. Mob action may be gone, but the city still has an exceptionally high murder rate. As a natural corollary, Chicago also has more practising lawyers than all of England. With this in mind, visitors should remember that the Loop and lake shore areas are the safest. After dark, stay clear of parks and poorly-lit streets. These cautions hold particularly true for women. The South Side is very risky at night.

The telephone area code is 312 or 773.
www.chi.yahoo.com.

ACCOMMODATION

AAIH-Chicago International Hostel, 6318 N Winthrope Ave, (773) 262-1011. S-$15, $5 deposit, bike rental $8. Take Howard St train to Loyola Station, walk 3 blocks S on Sheridon Rd to Winthrop. Closed 10am-4pm, curfew 12am Mon-Fri. 'Sunny, safe location'. 'The best hostel we stayed in. Close to university and good, safe location. Sells basic food supplies.'

Arlington House Hostel, 616 W Arlington Pl, (773) 929-5380. $19.50 AYH, $23 non-AYH, $2 linen rental. Private room from $41. 'Excellent hostel, but dirty bathrooms.' Close to Chicago nightlife. 'Not worth it. Dingy and horrible.' Mixed reports.

Blackstone Hotel, 636 S Michigan Ave, across from Grant Park, (312) 427-4300. S/D-$89-$109 w/student ID on non-convention days (Fri, Sat & Sun). Near museums, State St shopping. 'Area can be dodgy.'

Cass Hotel, 640 N Wabash Ave, (312) 787-4030. S-$69, D-$74. 2 blocks off Michigan Ave. 'Excellent, clean rooms, recently refurbished.' 'Good breakfast café'. Popular with BUNACers. $5 off with ISIC.

HI-Chicago Summer Hostel, 731 S Plymouth Court (773) 327-5350. $19 AYH, $22 non-AYH (inc. shared suite and bath). Private room D-$69, $2 linen rental, $5 key deposit. Packed with students. Rooms sleep 4-6. Kitchen, laundry. Location may change.

Hotel Wacker, 111 W Huron, (312) 787-1386. Close to downtown, easy to find (look for the big green sign on the corner). 'Clean rooms,' TV, phone, 24hrs. S-$45, D-$50.

International House, 1414 E 59th, (312)753-2270. Take Illinois Central RR to 59th St, walk ½ block W. S-$37. Rsvs essential. Cheap in-house cafeteria. Near science museum. 'Good place'. 'Part of Uni of Chicago, neighbourhood can be dangerous.'

Ohio East Hotel, 15 E Ohio, (312) 644-8222. Month: S/D-$350 ($25 application fee takes 24 hrs to process, $50 deposit). 'No AC or TV but clean and with excellent views.' 'Full of weirdoes.'

Parkway Eleanor Club, 1550 N Dearborn Pkwy, (312) 664-8245. (For less than 28 days) S-$60, D-$95, $5 key deposit. If you plan to stay longer than 28 days you must go through an application process to join the club. Both include bfast and dinner. Women only. 'Full of American students, located by Lake Michigan.'

Three Arts Club of Chicago, 1300 N Dearborn Pkwy, (312) 944-6250. Check-in, noon-11pm, out, noon. Coed conference centre and summer hostel. Located on the 'Gold Coast', one of Chicago's most beautiful neighbourhoods. Bus and subway 1 block, close to 'Magnificent Mile' shopping district. Courtyard, art studio, pianos, TV lounges, laundry. $45 includes bfast and dinner. Also try **Northwestern Uni**, Accommodation Office, Goe McClellan Bldg, 850 Lakeside Dr, 908-8514. $16-$20, June-July only, call for application.

FOOD

Local specialities: Chicago-style deep-dish pizza, stuffed pizza, kosher all-beef hot dogs and el-cheapo hamburgers called sliders. Pick up *Chicago Magazine* from most tourist offices for an extensive, comprehensive guide to eating out.

Ann Sathers, 929 W Belmont, (773) 348-2378, take the El to Belmont. Bakery and Swedish diner. Home-made cinnamon rolls, pies and bread. Sun-Thur 7am-10pm, w/ends 'til 11pm. Bfast served all day.

Berghoff's, W of State at 17 W Adams, (312) 427-3170. German menu, a Chicago tradition, big helpings. Closed Sun. Open daily 11am-9pm, Fri 'til 9:30pm, Sat 'til 10pm.

Billy Goats, 430 N Michigan, (312) 222-1525. Cheap rib-eye steaks. 'Run by Greeks who holler your order across the Midwest: 'Cheezebooga, Cheezebooga, Pepsi, Pepsi! No fries, Cheeps!' Open Mon-Fri 6am- 2am, Sat 10am- 3am, Sun 11am-2am.

Cafe Ba-Ba-Reeba, 2024 N Halsted, (773)935-5000. It's the place to go for tapas. Open Mon-Thur noon-10pm, Fri-Sat 'til midnight, Sun 'til 10pm.

Ed Debevic's, 640 N Wells at Ontario, (312) 664-1707. 50s-style diner where the staff's deliberate rudeness gives you a break from Midwestern hospitality. 'Great American food. The most fun you can have eating out—you have to go in there just to read the outrageously rude messages posted around the restaurant'. Open Sun-Thur 11am- 10pm, Fri- Sat 'til 11:30pm.

Edwardo's, 8 locations including 1212 N Dearborn, (312) 337-4490, on the near North Side; 521 S Dearborn, (312) 939-3366, downtown; and 1321 E 57th St, (773) 241-7960, in Hyde Park. Pizza, pasta & salads. Hours depending on locations.

Frontera Grill, 445 N Clark St, (312)661-1434, excellent Mexican food. Open Tue-Sat, Sat brunch at 10:30am.

Gibsons Steakhouse, 1028 N Rush St, (312)266-8999. One of Chicago's best steak-houses. Open Mon-Sat 5pm-midnight, Sun from 4pm. **Gino's East**, 160 E Superior, (312) 943-1124. 'Most well-known pizza house in Chicago.'

Giordano's, 747 N Rush St, (312) 951-0747, and about thirty other locations. Voted best pizza by *Chicago Magazine*. 'The best pizza ever.' Open Sun-Thur, 11am- 11pm, w/ends 'til midnight.

Jacob's Deli, 185 N Wabash Ave, (312) 553-9053, inside the food-court at Wabash and Lake. Chicago hot-dogs for $1.25. Jacob's Bfast Special (4 eggs, bacon, ham, sausage, hash browns, toast, butter, jelly, coffee) $3. 'Amazing value.'

John Barleycorn Memorial Pub, 658 W Belden Ave at Lincoln Ave, (773) 348-8899. Free slide show set to classical music. An English-style pub with artsy intellectuals. Open daily 3pm-2am, Sat 'til 3am.

Hamilton's Bar, Broadway and Sheridan, (773) 764-8133; good cheap food. Open Sun-Thur 11am-2am, Fri-Sat 'til 3am.

Lou Malnati's Pizzeria, 439 N Wells St, (312)828-9800. The pizza is *buonissima!* Open daily at 11am, Sun 'til 10pm, Mon-Thur 'til 11:30pm, Fri-Sat 'til midnight.

Lou Mitchell's, 565 W Jackson, (312) 939-3111, 1 block from Union Station. A family operation since it opened in 1923, this venerable eatery gives free Milk Duds to the 'ladies', donut holes and a prune to all. Fresh-ground coffee, baked goods, Greek toast. 'Wonderful atmosphere.' Open daily 5:30am- 3pm, Sun from 7am.

For ice-cream lovers: try the luscious **'frango mint'** at Marshall Fields 3rd floor ice-cream parlour, State and Randolph.

Mitchell's Original, 101 W North at Clark, (312) 642-5246. Good filling bfasts for under $6. Opens daily at 6am.

Miller's Pub, 134 S Wabash Ave. (312) 645-5377, 'Good for breakfast, with friendly service, moderate prices and a good atmosphere.' Open daily, 11am- 3am.

Nookies Tree, 2114 N Holland, (773) 248-9888 . Run by a talkative Irish ex-pat, you can get 3 course meal with refill coffee for under $7. 'Very wide selection from quality burgers to gourmet.' Mon-Thur 7am- midnight, Fri-Sat open 24 hrs.

Oodles of Noodles, 2540 N Clarke, (773) 975-1090. Great choice of different types of noodles, $4-$9. 'Friendly.' Sun-Thur 11:30am-9:30pm, Fri-Sat noon-10pm.

Pegasus Restaurant and Taverna, 130 S Halsted St, (312) 226-3377. Exquisite Greek cuisine. Open daily at noon, Sun-Thur 'til 10pm, Fri-Sat 'til midnight.

Pete's Restaurant, 407 E Oakwood Blvd, (773) 538-4300. Bfast for under $6. 'Good value and filling—keeps you full to lunch.' Open daily 7am- 7pm.

Scoozi, 410 W Huron, (312)943-5900, Open for lunch Mon-Fri 11:30am-2pm, for dinner Mon-Thur 5pm-9:30pm, Fri-Sat 'til 10:30pm, Sun 4pm-9pm. As Italian as it sounds.

Shaw's Crab House, 21 E Hubbard, (312)527-2722. A fun place to go for seafood. Open Mon-Fri 11:30am-2pm for lunch, for dinner Mon-Thur 5:30-10pm, w/end 'til 11pm.

Thai Star, 660 N State, (312) 951-1196. Charming, inexpensive, one of the first of its kind in Chicago. Open Mon-Thur 11am- 10pm, Fri- Sat 'til 10:30.

White Castle, several locations around Chicago. Home of the slider, so called because its grease content helps it slide down the throat easily. Order 4 or more for a meal.

West Egg Cafe on Monroe, 525 W Monroe, (312) 454-9939. Wide variety, excellent. Open Mon-Sat 6am-3pm, Sun from 8am.

OF INTEREST

Adler Planetarium and Museum, 1300 S Lake Shore Dr, (312) 322-0329. $5 sky shows. Free on Tues. 'Good show, interesting photos.' 9am-6pm daily, 9pm Thur-Fri.

American Police Center and Museum, 1717 S State St, (312) 431-0005. All you've ever wanted to know about police and FBI work from forensics to an exhibition of death masks (including Dillinger's) to their authentic electric chair for visitors to try. Indulge your obsession with the macabre. Mon-Fri 9.30am-4.30pm; $4.

Architecture Foundation, 224 S Michigan, (312) 922-3432, offers tours of outstanding Chicago architecture. 2 hr walk around the Loop costs $10, Daily 10am Sat & Sun also at 1.30pm. 'Good way to see a variety of Chicago architecture. Wear comfortable shoes.' Bus tour departs Sat at 9.30am in spring, summer and fall, for 30 mile 4 hr tour including Frank Lloyd Wright's **Robie House**, $25. (Rsvs essential). For a panoramic view of the city you can ascend **Sears Tower**, (312) 875-9447, the tallest and one of the ugliest buildings in the world, at Wacker Drive and Adams. On a clear day you can see across the lake to Michigan—60 miles. Go at night for a truly spectacular view of the city but forget the audio-visual show beforehand, it's a waste of time. Open 9am-10.30pm, $8.50. Or take a **boat trip**—Chicago is at its best from the lake. 'Best thing I did in Chicago.' Mercury, (312) 332-1353, and Wendella, (312) 337-1446, boats leave from opposite sides of the Chicago River at Michigan and Wacker Dr: 1¹/₂hr trip, $14; 2hr trip $16. The longer the better as you sail further and proportionately less of your time is taken up with passing through the locks into Lake Michigan (which is 8 ft higher than the river). Best of all is the 2 hr night-time trip (7.30pm departure) for the dazzling lights. 'Boat stops in front of Buckingham Fountain—spectacular lights and colour show.'

Art Institute, Michigan & Adams St, (312) 443-3500. A magnificent collection of Impressionism, post-Impressionism—great Cezanne and Gaugin, modern American art and the Thorne Rooms: a series of minutely detailed period rooms—in miniature. Mon-Fri 10.30am-4.30pm, Tue 'til 8pm, Sat 10am-5pm, Sun 12pm-5pm. $8, $5 w/student ID, Tues. free. Good basement cafe. 'Wonderful, well worth six bucks.' 'Fantastic art collection. Give yourself a whole day if you want to see everything.'

Chicago Board of Trade, 141 W Jackson Blvd, (312) 435-3500. 'This is the commodities exchange, there is a free visitors' gallery with an audio-visual presentation.' An incredible $25 billion changes hands here each day, in grain contracts, treasury bonds and other commodities. Mon-Fri 9am-12.30pm. Free.

Chicago Historical Society, Clark St & North Ave, (312) 642-4600. An impressive collection of exhibits centred on Chicago and Illinois. Outstanding on Lincoln with notebooks, letters, fashions, photos, manuscripts, furnishings. Mon-Sat 9.30am-4.30pm, Sun noon-5pm; $5, $3 w/ student ID, free Mon. Library open Tue-Sat only.

Chicago Mercantile Exchange, 30 S Wacker Dr, (312) 930-1000. The largest financial futures exchange in the world handles over 400,000 contracts each day, including those of pork bellies and other livestock. From the visitors centre, you can observe the colourful, madcap behaviour on the floor below. Mon-Fri 8am-3.15pm, main floor; 8th floor for foreign currency, 7.15am-2pm.

The Cultural Center at Michigan and Randolph, is the best place to plan your sight-seeing. Before hitting the streets, wander around the changing exhibitions (modern art, photography, aspects of Chicago, etc.) situated on the ground floor. Everything is free.

Field Museum of Natural History, Roosevelt Rd & Lake Shore Dr, (312) 922-9410. Anthropology, botany, zoology, geology. In May 2000, the Field Museum unveils Sue, the largest T-Rex skeleton in the world. Daily 9am-5pm; $7, $4 w/student ID, free Wed. 'There are interesting exhibits on American Indians and Eskimos.'

Frank Lloyd Wright houses. There are 25 in the suburbs; the Art Institute book-shop has good guidebooks. You need a car to see many of them, but FLW's own house and studio at Chicago and Forest Aves in Oak Park is reachable by El—to Harlem. From here, some of the houses are within walking distance. **Visitors Centre**, 158 Forest Ave, (708) 848-1500, open daily 10am-5pm. Tours are $4-$14; call for times.

John Hancock Center, 875 N Michigan, (312) 751-3680. Tallest residential building in the world. Cocktail bar skywalk. Views of the city at night; $8.50, observation hall. Open 9am-midnight. Try the 95th floor restaurant, (312) 751-3680, for lunch buffet $10.

The Loop, a 5-by 7-block city core, is defined by the steel tracks of the elevated subway ('El'), a strangely loveable transit system with a voice like a giant trash compactor. Besides being fast and cheap, this dotted line of noise gives free rein to voyeurism, letting you virtuously peep at a thousand fleeting tableaux as you flash past. Within the Loop are theatres, smart hotels and shopping districts, including the once pre-eminent **Marshall Fields** department store (still has the best Christmas windows anywhere).

Marina City, 300 N State St, a prototype self-contained 'vertical city' of residences, offices and spiral car port; resembles two upended corncobs.

Michigan Ave, 20s and 30s facades, mortared with money, opulent restraint, shops for ogling only.

Museum of Contemporary Art, 220 E Chicago Ave (312) 280-2660. The MCA's new building, located near the historic **Water Tower**, holds exhibits of fine art dating from 1945, as well as permanent collections featuring the works of Kline, Magritte and Warhol. 'Good Café'. Tue 10am-8pm, Wed-Sun 10am-5pm. $7, $4.50 w/ student ID, free Tue.

Museum of Science and Industry, E 57th St & Lake Shore Dr, (773) 684-1414. Visit the Apollo 8 spacecraft, go for a simulated space shuttle ride, or see the latest Omnimax presentation. Open daily 9.30am-5.30pm. $7, plus extra for Omnimax Theatre. Free Thurs. 'Best I've ever been to—easily spend a whole day here.' 'Magnificent place.'

Shedd Aquarium, next to Field Museum, (312) 939-2426. One of the world's largest indoor aquariums. Over 6000 species of fish occupy 206 tanks. Daily 9am-6pm year-round (last entry at 5:15pm); $5, free Thur. Also an oceanarium with Beluga whales, dolphins, penguins, etc. $11 combo tkt. 'Very disappointing—save your money for the coastal aquariums in Boston and Baltimore.'

State Street, running north-south, and **Madison**, east-west, bisect within the Loop at what's called the world's busiest intersection. (At 1 S State, take a peep at the delicate ironwork, by Louis Sullivan, F L Wright's mentor.) All street numbers in Chicago begin here, each block representing increments of 100. One block east of the Loop is Michigan Ave; its most elegant stretch, the **Magnificent Mile**, gives a glittering, often windy view of Lake Michigan.

University of Chicago, 7 miles south of the Loop on the Midway. Dominating the Hyde Park neighbourhood is the beautiful campus of one of America's best universities. 'Wonderful examples of Gothic architecture', and the "Nuclear Energy" sculpture, marking the site of the first sustained nuclear chain reaction. Although patrolled by Uni police, surrounding areas are dangerous, especially at night.

Water Tower Pumping Station, 806 N Michigan Ave at Pearson St. This fanciful Gothic Revival station conceals a very utilitarian pump—it distributes over 72 million gallons of water each day. One of the few public buildings to survive the 1871 fire, consequently revered by Chicagoans. Mon-Thur 9.30am-5.00pm, 7pm Fri. **Visitors Center** with maps, discount coupons in booklet 'Chicago's Got It' in the lobby, 9.30am-5pm daily.

There is enough to see without having to spend a dime:

Beaches: 18 sandy miles of 'em—free! Try **Oak St** beach just NE of John Hancock Center. 'The best beach we found in America. Clean, safe and a nice place to relax after seeing the city.' Or **Lincoln Park** beaches. The area is pleasant and relatively safe, with bars, cafes, and restaurants. 'Makes Chicago seem like the seaside.' 'Quite pleasant walking along waterfront—a park all the way to Museum of Science.'

Buckingham Fountain: set in Grant Park along Chicago's lake front, the fountain is outlined against the skyscrapers of the Loop. At night a light show transforms the fountain into a dazzling, many-coloured sculpture.

Great Ape House, Lincoln Park Zoo, 2200 N Cannon Dr, (312) 742-2000. More than 2,000 exotic and endangered species, including special exhibits on big cats, primates and others. Daily 9am-5pm, free. Ingenious glass cylinder arrangement lets you see monkeyshines at close hand. NB: Keep out of park after sunset.

Outdoor Art

The skyscrapers in Chicago are amazing. **The Standard Oil Building**, 200 E Randolph St, the world's fourth tallest; the **Hancock Tower**; the **Chicago Tribune Tower** with its ornate faux-Gothic design, 435 N Michigan Dr, and the **Wrigley Building** opposite; the elliptical, mirrored offices that look out onto the river, 333 W Wacker Dr; the wedge-shaped **Illinois State Center**, 100 W Randolph St, with its light, airy atrium; and, of course, the black monolith that is **Sears Tower**.

Sculpture fills the city. Outside the State Center sits Alexander Calder's *Flamingo*, a huge set of pink interconnecting girders; *The Picasso*, Daley Center Plaza at Washington and Dearborn, is a 63 ft steel woman with typical abstraction; *Untitled Sounding Sculpture* by Bertoia outside Standard Oil; *Batcolumn*, Claes

Oldenburg's huge baseball bat in full erection at 600 W Madison; Miro's *Chicago*, a smaller homage to the city than most, Brunswick Plaza, 69 W Washington; and finally Marc Chagall's *Four Season*'s 70 ft mosaic wall that looks like graffiti, First National Bank Plaza.

Tomb-hopping. Al Capone has two graves, one at Mt Olivet ('qui riposa'), another at Mt Carmel ('My Jesus mercy').

The industrial Chicago suburb of **Des Plaines** is the birthplace of that most American of eateries, McDonald's. The original is now the **McDonald's Museum**, 400 Lee St, (847) 297-5022. Tues.-Sat, 10am-4pm. Lots of 50's McDonald's memorabilia—but you can't eat here! Go to the *operating* McDonald's across the street for your Big Mac instead. In Oak Brook, the nation's only **Hamburger University** trains McDonald's managers.

The Chicago Motor Coach Company, (312) 922-8919, provides tours of the downtown area. They depart every 20-30 mins; pick-up at **The** Riverboat cruises are a wonderful way to see the city. **Chicago from the Lake**, (312)527-2002, offers 90-min narrated cruises. Departs from North Pier Festival Market, $18. **Shoreline Sightseeing**, (312)222-9328, presents a condensed 30 min boat tour, $9.

Sears Tower and various locations. 1 hr narrated tours cover a 9-mile route stopping and picking up at the major sights. $15. Unlimited boarding. 'Plenty of seats but so noisy it's impossible to hear the commentary!' . 'Only for people with limited time and sore feet.'

ENTERTAINMENT

Chicago is the centre of the blues world, has one of the strongest folk scenes in America and boasts an impressive amount of jazz activity. Pick up a free copy of *The Reader*, published Fri and available at record shops, to find out where it's happening. Also check the listings in *Chicago Magazine* or buy Hargrove and Snooks' *500 Things to Do in Chicago for Free*. NB: Stick to Old Town, the Rush Street area, and the North Side at night, even if you are in an armoured car.

B.L.U.E.S., 2519 N Halsted, (773) 528-1012. 'The people—exhilarating. The blues—totally overpowering.' 'Crowded, small, hot.' A larger sister club, **B.L.U.E.S etcetera** is now in existence and is the place to go to see big names such as Bo Diddley, Albert King and Dr John. Cover for both $6-$9. 8pm-2.30 am.

Club 720, 720 N Wells St, (312) 397-0600. 4 levels, 14,000 sq ft. Live jazz main floor, DJ and dancing downstairs, cigars/billiards 2nd floor, Big Band upstairs. Mon-Fri 5pm- 2am, w/end 7pm- 4:30am.

Club 950, 950 Wrightwood, (773) 929-8955. Alternative and new wave. $4 cover after 10pm w/ends, ladies free on Fri. 'Lots of English music.' Experience 'slam' poetry at the **Green Mill Lounge**, 4802 N Broadway, (773) 878-5552. Every Sun at 7pm, local poets recite their work, one-on-one, for up to $50 in winnings at this 80-year-old mobster hangout.

Crobar, 1543 N Kingsbury Ct, (312) 587-8574. 'Futuristic industrial warehouse dance club'. 'Bladerunner meets Batman'. Boasts the largest dancefloor in the city. Wed-Sun 10pm-4am, $5 before midnight, $10after midnight.

Downtown Thursday Night, every Thursday 5pm-8pm from the river to Roosevelt Rd. Mingle with locals and take advantage of the many specials offered on downtown accommodations, dining, entertainment, services and shopping. 'Something for every taste and budget'.

Hot Tixx, 108 N State St, (312) 977-1755. 'Half-price tickets for same day performances—theatre, dance, the arts.' Mon-Sat, 10am-6pm, Sun 12 noon-5pm. Must buy tkts personally. Show up 15-20 mins before booth opens for your pick.

Jazz Andy's, 11 E Hubbard, (312) 642-6805. A great place to hear jazz, blues and Rock 'n' Roll. Free shows at noon Tue-Fri; daily shows at 5pm, w/end shows 6pm and 9pm. Cover $3-$10.

North Pier Chicago, a restored warehouse on the Chicago River with shops, restaurants and **Dick's Last Resort**, a large jazz bar. Close by is **Navy Pier**, stretching into Lake Michigan.

Second City Comedy Revue, 1616 N Wells, (312) 337-3992. 'The place to see great comedians with a twisted sense of humour.' John Belushi, Jim Belushi, Chris Farley and Bill Murray are among the egregious graduates of this wellspring of irreverent American comedy. Two sets of revues Fri & Sat, one show Tue, Wed, Thur & Sun. $15.

Sluggers World Class Sports Bar, Inc., 3540 N Clark, (773) 248-0055. Has acres of screens with all sports and a games room with an indoor baseball batting cage! Cheap beer too. 'A right laugh.'

Check out *www.barsonline.com/chicago.htm* for other suggestions.

Chicago Blues Festival (in early June) and **Chicago Jazz Festival** (in late August), Grant Park. Largest free blues and jazz festivals. To hear who's playing, call (312) 744-3315. Afterwards, there's more jamming at the clubs.

Two Chicago theatres are especially well-known, and have prices to match their fame. **The Steppenwolf Theater**, 1650 N Halsted, 335-1650, where Malkovich and Mamet grew up, and **The Goodman Theater**, 200 S Columbus Drive, 443-3800. Both provide consistently good original work. Tkts $20-$30. The monthly *Chicago* and the weekly *Chicago Reader* give thumbnail reviews of all major shows, with times and ticket prices. Also, the monthly edition of *Where Chicago* is available from the Visitor Center.

SPORT
Chicagoans are sports mad. The Chicago Bulls basketball team was the NBA powerhouse of 1990s, winning 6 championships in 8 years and drawing a huge following around the world. Although the Bulls have faltered since the departure of Michael Jordan, fans still flock to see their team play at the **United Center**, 1901 W Madison, (312) 455-4000, in the summer, tkts, $22-$85. The Blackhawks play ice-hockey there in the winter, (312) 455-4500. NFL action can be viewed at **Soldier Field**, McFetridge Dr and S Lake Shore Dr, (708) 651-2327. **Wrigley Field**, 1060 W Addison, (773) 404-2827, is the home of the Cubs and one of the most beautiful baseball parks in the country. Intimate and packed to the rafters with people and atmosphere, it was the last park in the leagues to introduce floodlights: night games didn't arrive until 1988. An ideal way to taste the most American thing this side of apple pie. The White Sox play at **Comiskey Park**, (312) 674-1000, and have equally fervent supporters. Tkts range from $8-$20. Tkts from Ticketmaster, Bulls and Blackhawks (312) 559-1212, White Sox (312) 831-1769, Cubs (312) 831-2827.

Cycling: Bike Chicago, locations at Oak St Beach, Navy Pier, Buckingham Fountain, Lincoln Park Zoo, (800) 915-2453. 'Great way to tour the city.' Service includes free bike route maps, free guided tours, free delivery to your hotel for daily rentals. 18 mile Lakefront Bike Tours depart Navy Pier, Mon-Fri 1.30pm. Bikes $8 hr, $30 daily. In-line skates also for hire $8 hr, $30 daily.

INFORMATION
Chicago Office of Tourism, (800) 226-6632.
Travelers Aid , 327 S LaSalle, (312) 629-4500; at **Greyhound**, (800) 231-2222; and airport, Terminal Two (773) 686-7562. Maps, brochures. 'Extremely helpful.'

INTERNET ACCESS
Screenz Digital Universe, 2717 N Clark St, (773) 348-9300 or 101 W Grand Ave, (312) 245-0900. Open Sun-Thur 9am-midnight, Fri-Sat 'til 1am. $9.60/hr. Rate drops Fri-Sat eves to $6.60/hr.

TRAVEL
Amtrak, Union Station, Canal & Adams Sts, (312) 655-2354/(800) 872-7245. Hub of

the Amtrak intercity system. Think *The Untouchables*. Think Kevin Costner standing atop of a set of steps, gun in hand. Think pram going down the steps between bullets. Now walk up the steps in the station and relive it.

Auto Driveaway, 310 S Michigan, (312) 341-1900. 'Friendly.' 'Very helpful.'

Greyhound, 630 W Harrison St, (312) 408-5883/(800) 231-2222. 'Public library nearby, with free art exhibits—good place to go if between buses.' Local bus CTA/RTA, 836-7000, for fare and schedule info..

O'Hare International Airport (312) 686-2200, the busiest airport in the world. The Northwest El line takes you directly to the airport for $1.50. There are buses, but congestion is horrific, it'll take forever.

SPRINGFIELD The pleasant state capital has one main attraction: Abraham Lincoln. At the age of 28, 'The Great Emancipator' arrived in the city to practice law and stayed for twenty years. See the only house he ever owned, 426 S 7th St, 789-2357 (Mon-Fri, 8am-6pm). Recently beautifully restored, it has a useful visitors bureau; you can also visit Lincoln's old law offices, 6th & Adams, 785-7289 (Mon-Fri 9am- 4:45pm); the **Lincoln Depot**, Monroe & 9th, 544-8695, (Mon-Fri 10am-4pm) where he boarded the train to go to DC for his inauguration; the **family tomb**, Oak Ridge Cemetery, 782-2717 (daily 9am-5pm); and the **Old State Capitol**, Capitol Plaza, 785-7960, (Mon-Fri 9am-5pm) where he was a member of the Illinois House of Representatives. There are other 'highlights' such as walking the same route as Abe did when he worked at the post office, the family pew in the church, and his bank ledger. Northeast of the city on Rte 97 is **New Salem Historic Site**, 632-4000, a reconstruction of the 1830's village where Lincoln lived as a young man (daily 9am-8pm). All this is free. The state's other adopted golden boy, Frank Lloyd Wright, is also on show in Springfield. The **Dana-Thomas House**, 301 E Lawrence, 782-6776, was built in 1903 for a local socialite. This prime example of the 'Prairie Style' that Wright pioneered also has furnishings by the man himself. Wed-Sun 9am-4pm, $3.
The telephone area code is 217.

ACCOMMODATION
All-Star 8 Inn, 2224 E Cook, 789-0361. S-$25.

Best Rest Inn, 700 N Dirksen Pkwy, 522-7966. Laundry, TV, fridge available. S-$28, D-$38.

Capitol City Motel, 1620 N 9th, 528-0462. Near the fairgrounds and with kitchenettes. S-$33, D-$38.

Mr Lincoln's Campground, 3045 Stanton Ave, 529-8206. 4 miles E of downtown, take bus #10. Free showers, tent space $14-$16pp. Cabins $25 for 2, XP $3.

Nights Inn, 3125 Widetrack Dr, 789-1063. S-$33, D-$42.

FOOD
Try around the Vinegar Hill Mall, 1st and Cook Sts, for cheap eats, there are lots of places to quell those hunger pangs. 12pm-1am. No food after 9pm. If you haven't had enough of Lincoln, try Abe's Tradin' Post, 2704 N. Peoria Rd, 753-2237, for quality country fare. Mon-Fri 10am-2pm, w/ ends 7am-2pm. Try the weekend breakfast buffet— all-you-can-eat for $5.25.

INFORMATION/TRAVEL
Springfield Convention and Visitors Bureau, 109 N 7th, 789-2360. Mon-Fri 8am-5pm.

Greyhound, (800) 231-2222, take the #10 bus into town from the nearby shopping centre. Ticket Office Mon-Fri 5am-2.30pm, w/ends 6am-10am.

GALENA   Once an opulent riverboat and lead-mining town in north-west Illinois, Galena is now a beautiful backwater of stately homes and small-town friendliness. Galena produced a clutch of Civil War generals, including Ulysses S Grant; each year, the townspeople re-enact a battle or two.

If you have a car, by all means take the Great River Road south from Galena, which follows the Mississippi all the way to New Orleans. A lovely drive.

METROPOLIS   It's a bird, it's a plane, it's Clark Kent's 'home town' in southern Illinois on the Ohio River. Giant mural of Superman in the park, free kryptonite from the Chamber of Commerce, and for entertainment and the comics—the *Daily Planet*. No, this isn't where Superman was invented, or even where he was supposed to have lived ('Metropolis' in the comic book was a big city; this Metropolis is a small town of a few thousand friendly souls). Nonetheless, locals hold a 'Superman Celebration' each year on the 2nd w/end of June, complete with bank robbery foiled by you-know-who; (618) 524-2714 for more info.

INDIANA   *The Hoosier State*

Indiana has a wholesome, almost cornball ingenuousness about it, so it's not surprising to learn that it's the home of Notre Dame, Johnny Appleseed, Orville Wright (Wilbur was born in neighbouring Ohio), Studebaker, Cole Porter, Amish villages of *Friendly Persuasion* fame and David Letterman of late-night TV show notoriety. The rural portions have most to offer: rustic landscapes of country roads, covered bridges (notably in Parke County west of Indianapolis), round barns (in Fulton County) and even a 'Steamboat' Gothic mansion (in Vevay on the Ohio River).

Indiana cranks out lots of steel and more band instruments than any place on earth. Most of the heavy industry is in the north-west corner of the state, near Chicago, so don't let the atrocity called Gary colour your opinion of the rest of the state. Another note to travellers: Indiana doesn't practice Daylight Savings Time. Check the local time before you set your watch.

Several rebels, with and without causes, are buried here: Eugene Debs in Terre Haute and James Dean in Fairmont (whose gravestone behind Friends Church is walking away in ghoulish bits and pieces). For a more mundane type of rebellion, check out Sunny Haven Recreation Park, a 20-acre nudist camp and site of sunbathing conventions.
www.yahoo.com/Regional/U_S__ States/Indiana/

INDIANAPOLIS   Foursquare in the centre of the state, Indianapolis is state capital, national headquarters for the American Legion, home of the Indy 500auto race and cross-roads of America, so-called because a dozen or so major routes meet here. The city is as exciting as mashed potatoes except during the month of May, when the '500' Festival, the Indy time trials and other pre-race madness stir things up a bit. It's almost impossible to get seats for the race itself on Memorial Day Sunday (you must write for them a year in advance), but standing room and scalpers' tkts are available closer to race day. Time trials and qualifying runs begin 2-3 weeks before the main event and provide nearly the same thrills and mayhem as the big race. Bring beer, lunch and make a day of it. At night, party with the racing fans along Georgetown Ave. Call 481-8500 for an application form, or write to: Tkts, Indianapolis Motor Speedway, PO Box 24152, Speedway, IN 46224.

During spring, summer and fall, folk festivals take place by and around the Monument Circle area downtown.

The telephone area code is 317.

ACCOMMODATION
Basic Inn, 5117 E 38th St, 547-1100. S-$33, D-$45.
Indianapolis Motor 8, 3731 Shadeland, 545-6051. S-$30, D-$36.
Motel 6 Inn, 5241 W Bradbury St at Lyndhurst, 248-1231. S-$33, D-$38.
Skyline Motel, 6617 E Washington St, 359-8201. S/D $42-$52.
YMCA, 860 W 10th St, 634-2478. S-$25, $77 weekly ($5 key deposit). Higher during 500 Festival. 'Raunchy area.' Take #13 or 6 bus to get there. Reserve 2 weeks ahead.
For the more adventurous (ie with strong legs and country hearts) there are numerous campgrounds throughout the state. Few rent tents/trailers so bring your own.
The Indianapolis State Fair Recreational Vehicle Campground, 1202 E 38th St, 927-7510. 6 miles from downtown. Can be reached by bus. Tent space-$10.50. All amenities.
Indianapolis KOA, 5896 W 200 North, Greenfield, 894-1397. 12 miles from downtown. Tent space-$18, $20 w/hook-up.

FOOD
The Aristocrat, 5212 N College Ave, 283-7388. American and pub-style food at reasonable prices. Open Mon-Thur 10am-11pm, Fri-Sat 'til 1am, Sun 'til 10pm.
Between Bread, 136 N Delaware, 638-4174. Great sandwiches. Mon-Fri, 10am-4pm.
Bravo's Italian Kitchen, 2658 Lake Circle Dr, 879-1444. Open Sun-Thur 11am-10pm, w/ ends 'til 11pm.
Broad Ripple Village, north of city centre at 62nd St, is a mall full of ethnic restaurants and quaint shops.
Fireside South, 522 E Raymond St, 788-4521. Enjoy sizzling steaks, German entrees, spirits and a wide selection of seafood. Heart-healthy menu available. 'Quality food in a comfortable, relaxed atmosphere.'
La Jolla, 921 Broad Ripple Ave, 253-5252. Home of the famous margarita.
Paco's Cantina, 737 Broad Ripple Ave, 251-6200. Tacos $1.25, burritos $3. Open 24 hrs.
Renee's French Restaurant, 839 E Westfield Blvd, 251-4142. 'Cheap, friendly with a really pleasant atmosphere.' 11am-11pm daily.
Shapiro's Deli, 808 S Meridian, 631-4041. Cheap and good cafeteria style food.
Some Guy's Pizza, 6235 Allisonville Rd, 257-1364. Open daily for lunch, 11:30am-2pm, dinner Mon-Thur 4pm-10pm, Fri-Sat 'til 11pm, Sun 'til 9pm.
Yorkshire Rose Pub and Deli, 1168 Keystone Way, 844-4766. Large selection of imported beers, soup, sandwiches, sides, salads and entrees, $3-$11. Daily 11am-midnight.

OF INTEREST
Benjamin Harrison House, 1230 N Delaware, 631-1898. Home of the 23rd President of the US. Mon-Sat 10am-3.30pm, Sun 12.30-3:30pm. $5.
Conner Prairie Pioneer Settlement, 6 miles N of Indianapolis, is a restoration of a 30-building pioneer village *circa* 1836. Visit typical homes and work-places of the era, eat frontier cooking, celebrate various festivals and meet inhabitants.

Allisonville Rd exit off I-465, 776-6000. Tue-Sat 9.30am-5pm, Sun 11am-5pm, $9.75.

Children's Museum, 3000 N Meridian, take 29th St exit off I-65, 924-5437. Daily 10am-5pm, Thur 'til 8pm, Sun noon-5pm; $8. Free Thur 5pm-8pm. World's largest kiddie museum: puppets, films, mummy, Tyrannosaurus Rex, huge toy and antique train layout.

Harrison Eiteljorg Museum, 500 W Washington, 636-9378. A private collection of American art, both Native and Western, in a lovely atmosphere. Mon-Sat 10am-5pm, Sun noon-5pm; $5, $2 w/student ID.

Indiana State Fair, Meridian St and Rte 37. Two weeks of Hoosier hoopla in mid-August, with an audience of almost a million. 'Huge, mad, big name groups.'

Indianapolis Motor Speedway, 4790 W 16th St, 481-8500. Tkts for the time trials are sold at the gates the day of the trials. Gates open at 7am the opening day; 9am other days. You can park in the infield. Tkts range from $30 to $150.

Museum of Art, 1200 W 38th St, 923-1331. Major permanent exhibitions include one of the largest collections of Turner prints outside Great Britain, and the W J Holliday collection of neo-impressionist. Mon-Tue, Fri-Sun 10am-5pm; Thur 'til 8:30pm, free.

Union Station, 200 S Illinois St. Built in 1888, one of the finest examples of Romanesque Revival architecture in the US. Galleries, restaurants, boutiques and passenger trains.

Speedway Museum, located in the infield of the Speedway, 481-8500, has a collection of Indy racers and memorabilia. Daily 9am-5pm, $5.

ENTERTAINMENT

BW Three's, 15 E. Maryland St, 577-2999. Open 'til 3am.

The Chatterbox, 435 Massachusetts Ave, 636-0584. Dicey bar but good jazz. Open 'til 3am.

Crackers Comedy Club, 6281 N. College, 846-2500. Sun, Tue-Fri, shows at 8pm, extra show Fri-Sat at 10.30pm.

Ike's and Jonesy's, 17 W Jackson, 632-4553. 50s and 60s music. Open until 3am, no cover. Closed Sun.

The Slippery Noodle, 372 N Meridian, 631-6974. Live blues 7 nights a week, 'til 3am.

The Vogue, 6259 N College, 259-7029. Music for the masses, $2-$7 cover. Wed, Fri-Sat 'til 3am. Check out their 80s night.

INFORMATION/TRAVEL

Amtrak, 350 S Illinois St, 263-0550/(800) 872-7245.

Chamber of Commerce: 464-2200.

Greyhound, Union Station, 1 block S of Pan Am Plaza, (800) 231-2222. Open 24 hrs.

Indianapolis International Airport, 7 miles NW of downtown; hop on the #8 'W Washington' bus to get there, basic fares apply.

Metro Bus, 36 N Delaware, 635-3344. Runs the city buses, $1.

Visitors Information: Indianapolis City Center at Pan Am Plaza, 201 S Capitol Ave, (800) 323-INDY or 237-5200 direct. Mon-Fri 10am-5.30pm, Sat 'til 5pm, Sun noon-5pm. Tourist information available online at *www.indianapolis.com.*

INTERNET ACCESS

Indianapolis Central Library, 40 E St Clair St, 269-1700. Free.

AMISH COUNTRY An hour north and east from Peru lands you in the counties of **LaGrange** and **Elkhart**— the heart of Amish country. The town of **Shipshewana**, SR 5 off US 20, is a centre of Amish culture, with an auction and flea market every Tuesday and Wednesday in the summertime (phone 768-4129 for info). **Yoder's Department store** also carries Amish crafts and goods for those who miss the market days. For info about Mennonite and Amish history visit **Menno-Hof** across from the flea market on SR 5, 768-4117. Open Mon-Sat, 10am-5pm, last tour starts at 4:30, $4. At the **Buggy Wheel Restaurant and Bakery,** 160 N. Morton St, 768-4444, try German sausage or roast pork and for dessert eat outrageous wet-bottom shoo-fly pie. Open Mon-Fri, 11am-7pm, Sat 7am-7pm.

In the town of **Nappanee** on US 6, **Amish Acres**, (800)800-4942, conducts tours of an Amish farm, complete with buggy rides. Nappanee also hosts the **Pletcher Art Festival** in early August and the **Apple Festival** in late September. Amish Acres is home to the **Round Barn Theater**, 1600 West Market, US 6 West, where you can see a live Broadway musical classic about Amish life and love in a 400-seat restored round barn theatre. Tues., Thur, Fri-8pm; Wed and Sat-3pm and 8pm, from $20. The **Essenhaus Restaurant** in Middlebury, at the intersection of SR 13 and US 20, serves up Amish cooking. NB: Watch out for slow-moving Amish buggies on back roads. For info: **Chamber of Commerce**: 773-7812.

The telephone area code is 219.

BLOOMINGTON is a pleasant college town, home of Indiana University, an hour's drive south-west from Indianapolis on Rte 37. The movie *Breaking Away* was filmed here and featured a bike race called the little 500. The race is an annual event in mid-April. Look too for the numerous abandoned stone quarries, also featured in the movie, which now serve as swimming holes on hot summer days.

An hour south-west from Bloomington takes you to the Wabash River town of **Vincennes**, site of **Grouseland**, 882-2096, the home of the shortest-lived US president—William Henry Harrison. At his inauguration, doubt-less ignoring his mother's advice, Harrison gave a 2 hr speech in freezing rain, contracted pneumonia and died 31 days later, never having made a major decision as president. His 32-day term lasted from 4 March-4 April, 1841. The mansion is open Mon-Sat 9am-5pm, Sun 11am-5pm. $3, $2 w/ student ID.

Seventy-five miles downstream from Vincennes lies the town of **New Harmony**, where two Utopian communities were set up in the early 19th century. In 1814 a grumpy Lutheran named George Rapp quit Germany to found New Harmony, where he awaited the coming of the Lord for 10 years. Being delayed for some reason, the Lord never appeared and Rapp departed. He left New Harmony to Welsh expatriate Robert Owen, who founded a community of equality based on education. Kindergarten, co-ed public education and other new ideas in education were first tried here, and what remains is a historic district of 20 buildings, including a dramatic 'roofless church' designed by Philip Johnson.

The telephone area code for the region is 812.

ACCOMMODATION
Lake Monroe Village Campground, 8107 S Fairfax Rd, 824-2267. 8 miles N of Bloomington. Free showers, pool. $21.50, w/hook-up $25, cabins available $45 for two, XP-$9.
Motel 6, 1800 N Walnut St, 332-0820, clean, spacious rooms and pool. S-$34, D-$40.

FOOD
The **Downtown Sq**, an abundance of restaurants within 2 blocks. Most found on
Kirkwood City Ave, near College and W Walnut St.
Nick's, 423 E Kirkwood Ave, 332-4040. Cheap hamburgers and beer.

TRAVEL/INFORMATION
Greyhound, 1490 W Bloomfield Rd, 332-1522/(800) 231-2222.
Chamber of Commerce: 400 W 7th St, 336-6381.

IOWA   *The Hawkeye State*

In the movie *Field of Dreams*, Kevin Costner stood face to face in a spectacular
baseball field with the ghost of his father. "Is this heaven?" asked the ghost, his
freshly-oiled leather baseball glove in hand. "No, it's Iowa," answered the son.
Given the verdant beauty of the land, it's easy to see how he could have been
confused. There is an ethereal quality to the state, whose recent history reads
like pages from the Bible. An agricultural mecca, Iowa is a veritable Eden that
produces unfathomable quantities of corn, soybeans and cattle and quarter of
the nation's porkers and generates over $10 billion annually from its agricul-
ture. This bounty was destroyed in 1993 when Iowa was hit by the worst flood
in history— a flood that turned the whole state into a National Disaster Area
and left hundreds of thousands of people homeless and without water.

The weather has always been famous here. A freak Iowa blizzard resulted
in the serendipitous development of the Golden Delicious apple, and the
powerful electrical storms are amazing celestial displays. A strong Quaker
community resides here whose most famous member was the 31st
President, Herbert Hoover. The Quakers played an integral role in the
success of the Underground Railroad— the pathway to freedom for thousands of slaves. It was to Iowa that black scientist and inventor George
Washington Carver fled to escape persecution. Every four years Iowans are
remembered by the rest of the country when they have first shot in the
choice of the next President in the mid-winter political caucuses.
www.yahoo.com/Regional/U_S__States/Iowa.

DES MOINES   Trisected by rivers, Iowa's capital (population 193,000,
excluding hogs) is a green and friendly place to catch your breath and take
advantage of good food and lodging. Like Minneapolis, the city has a carpeted skywalk connecting major downtown buildings. 'A really beautiful
city.' Worth seeing is the **Living Farms** complex, whose visitors have
included Nikita Krushchev and Pope John Paul II (the latter delivered
mass—shades of *Animal Farm*).
The telephone area code is 515.

ACCOMMODATION
A-1 Motel, 5404 SE 14th St, 287-5160. From S-$32, TV.
Iowa State Fairgrounds Campgrounds, E 30th St at Grand Ave. Site $10, $12
w/hook-up. Open mid May-mid Oct.
Motel 6, 4817 Fleur Dr, 287-6364. Close to airport. Newly renovated. S-$40, D-$46.
Village Inn, 1348 Euclid at 14th St E, 265-1674. 'Large, clean, comfortable rooms.'
S-$42, D-$47.

YMCA, 101 Locust, 288-0131. Men only. $25 ($5 key deposit).
YWCA, 717 Grand, 244-8961. Women only. Generous rooms. S-$8, $46 weekly.

FOOD

Big Daddy's Barbeque, 1000 E 14th St, 262-0352. The owner has an on-going contest. If you can eat a sandwich with his hottest sauce, you win five times the money you bet (in $100 increments). If you lose, the money goes to charity.
Drake Diner, 1111 25th St, 277-1111. Frequented by local students. Mon-Thur 7am-11pm, Fri-Sat 'til midnight, Sun 'til 10pm.
Iowa Beef Steakhouse, 1201 Euclid Ave, 262-1138. Quality steaks at reasonable prices. Open Sun-Thur 5pm-10pm, Fri-Sat 'til 11pm.
Manhattan Deli, 3705 Ingersoll Ave, 274-1208. Fabulous subs! Open Mon-Sat, 10am-3:30pm.
Mondo's, 4001 Westown Pkwy, 327-9000. Generous portions of tasty Italian cuisine. Open Sun-Thur 11am-10pm, Fri-Sat 'til 11pm.
Porky's Tenderloin, 4444 Douglas Ave, 270-6058. Iowa is famous for its pork. Try it here. Open Mon-Sat 6am-10pm.
Reed's, 2712 Beaver Ave, 255-8521. The place to go in Des Moines for breakfast. Open 7am-2pm, closed Mon.
Stella's Blue Sky Diner, 4th and Locust, 246-1953, with cheese frenchies and vintage rock n' roll. Order a milkshake— the servers put on a show. Open Mon-Fri 6:30am-6pm, Sat 8am-6pm.
The Tavern, 2058 5th St, 255-9827. 'The best pizza in town', with some of the most obscure toppings, $7-$15. Mon-Thur 11am-11pm, Fri-Sat 'til midnight, Sun 'til 10pm.
University Library Cafe, 3506 University Ave, 255-0433. Reputedly has the best buffalo wings in Des Moines. Open 11:30am-2pm, 5pm-10pm (dinner only on Mon).

OF INTEREST

Adventureland, east of city, 142A exit off I-80, 266-2121. Over 100 thrill rides, shows and attractions including the Tornado roller coaster and the Spaceshot. 'Lame'. Daily, Memorial Day-Labor Day, Fri-Sun 10am-10pm, Mon-Thur 10am-9pm; $22.
Iowa State Fair, 10 days in late Aug, one of the oldest and largest in the country attracting thousands of visitors. Top-notch. Camping at fairgrounds at Dean Ave, 262-3111. Huge, good amenities, wooded area;$8-$10 site. For more info call (800) 545-3247.
Living History Farms, I-35and I-80at Hickman Rd exit, 278-5286. Four operating farms: 1700's Indian, 1850's pioneer, 1900's farm and farm of the future; also 1870 town of Walnut Hill. Lots of special events, exhibits. May-Oct, daily 9am-5pm; $8.
Science Center of Iowa, 4500 Grand Ave, 274-6868. Home of the Digistar Planetarium, 'fabulous laser shows', and simulated shuttle flights. Mon-Sat 10am-5pm, Sun noon-5pm, $5.50.
White Water University Water Park, 5401 E University Ave, 265-4904. Enjoy the wave pool, tubing rides, water slides, The Lazy River and twin-engine go-carts on an over/under track. Open 11am-8pm. $14, $9.25 after 5pm.

INFORMATION/TRAVEL

Central Iowa Tourism, 832-4808/ (800) 285-5842.
Des Moines Convention and Visitors Bureau, (800) 451-2625.
Visitors Bureau, 309 Court Ave, 242-4705, in Saddlery Bldg, 2nd Floor, and at Des Moines International Airport, 286-4960.
MTA city bus, 283-8111. Serves downtown, the fairgrounds. $1. There is a bus service to the airport, but it is rather erratic and takes a tortuous route; take a cab to be sure, $10-$12.

INTERNET ACCESS
Des Moines Public Library, 100 Locust St, 283-4152, free. Call ahead to schedule time.

EFFIGY MOUNDS NATIONAL MONUMENT In north-east Iowa, the 1500 acre monument stretches alongside the Mississippi River. The prehistoric burial mounds dotted across the bluffs are shaped like birds and bears; some of them date back to 1000BC. In the north unit, 'Great Bear' stretches 120 ft from head to tail. Museum with artefacts, interpretative history 3 miles N of Marquette on Hwy 76, open daily 8am-7pm summers, 873-3491. 'The March of Bears' lies in the south unit, where ten bear mounds and three bird mounds are strung together in one line. Most impressive when outlined by snow; area has lovely autumn colours also. Greyhound goes no closer than Dubuque, IA or LaCrosse, WI, so car rental or hitching a must. 12 miles SW of Dubuque, the Trappist monastery of **New Melleray Abbey** allows free overnight stays ($30 offering encouraged) Sun-Thur, a nice counterpoint to mound exploration. Often full, call to make rsvs, 588-2319.
The telephone area code is 319.

MADISON COUNTY This rural county boasts an ironic Hollywood legacy. It became a household name when Robert James Waller's book about its bridges was adapted for the silver screen. The movie tradition, however, goes back even further. **Winterset**, the largest city in the county, was the childhood home of John Wayne. You can visit both John Wayne's birthplace, 216 S. Second St, (515) 462-1044, in Winterset, and Francesca's House (the house in which *The Bridges of Madison County* was filmed), in nearby **Cumming**, (515) 981-5268. Open 10am-6pm daily, $5. Also check out the splendid covered bridges— of the original 19 bridges that dotted this county, 6 are still intact. Madison County Farm and Country Tours, (515) 462-3515, arranges tours of the bridges, free.

AMANA Settled by German mystics in 1854, the Amana Colonies (7 villages located one hour apart by oxen) became the longest-lived commune in the US. Reorganised along corporate lines in 1932, Amana residents no longer practice communal living but instead produce microwave ovens and other appliances along with woollens, wine and other hand-crafted goods. You can walk past the houses, factories and workshops (built along traditional German lines) and visit museums but the main attraction is the solid food (heavy on pork and carbohydrates).
The telephone area code for Amana, Brooklyn, Dyersville, Iowa City and Williamsburg is 319.

DYERSVILLE "If you build it, he will come." That's what a mysterious voice told Kevin Costner in the 1989 hit movie, *Field of Dreams*. Universal Studios built the famous baseball park in Dyersville, and people do come to the *Field of Dreams* **Movie Site**, 1-888-875-8404, *www.fieldofdreamsmoviesite.com*. The 92 year-old Lansing family farm, 200 miles west of Chicago, draws movie lovers and baseball fans by the carload each summer. Dyersville sits on US-20, 175 miles from Des Moines. The farm and field are open April-Nov, 9am-6pm, free.

ACCOMMODATION/FOOD
Super 8 Inn, Rte 2, Box 179H, Williamsburg, 668-2800. Rooms from $39-$52.
Colony Inn, 741 47th Ave, Amana, 622-6270. 'Great breakfast—$7 for fruit salad, pancakes, eggs, sausage, hash browns and more.'! Open daily 7am-8pm.

OF INTEREST
Heritage Museum of Johnson County, 310 Fifth St, Coralville, 351-5738. Illustrating the culture and heritage of eastern Iowa and Johnson County. Wed-Sat 1pm-5pm, Sun 1pm-4pm. Free.
Museum of Natural History, on Clinton and Jefferson Sts, Iowa City, 335-0480. Exhibits include a wide variety of displays interpreting Iowa's geology, early Native American cultures and ecology. Mon-Sat 9.30-4.30pm, Sun 12.30-4.30. Free.
Tanger Factory Outlet Center, Exit 220 on I-80, 668-2811 or (800) 1-TANGER. More than 60 brand-name manufacturers and designer outlet stores. Save 30%-70% off regular retail prices. Mon-Sat 9am-9pm, Sun noon-6pm.

INFORMATION
Amana Convention and Visitors Bureau, 622-7622/ (800) 245-5465
Eastern Iowa Tourism, 472-5135/ (800) 891-3482.
Iowa City Area Convention and Visitors Bureau, 337-6592/ (800) 283-6592.

INTERNET ACCESS
Cyberbeans, 126 E Washington, Iowa City, 337-7243. Open 9am-10pm, $8/hr.

KANSAS   *The Sunflower State*

Kansas is America's heartland— the quintessential prairie state with all the home-sweet-homeyness you could want. But there's still a wildness in the air here: namely, the wind. For all its landlocked glory, Kansas is mysteriously powered by oceanic forces—full of wheat fields rippling under the caress of constant breezes.

This same, unceasing wind has played a hand in the state's history— kicking up deadly dust storms and twisters (one of which sucked up poor Dorothy in *The Wizard of Oz*), driving lonely pioneer women insane with its howling. The survivors, however, must have been of good stock, for Kansas boasts the first female US senator, Nancy Landon Kassebaum, the most famous aviatrix, Amelia Earhart, and the most fanatical and annoying prohibitionist, Carry Nation.

Carry began by singing hymns to saloon idlers, but soon found it more effective to turn saloons into kindling with a hatchet. Besides being anti-booze, Carry's vendetta targeted tobacco, corsets, barroom paintings and foreign foods. Her last 'hatchetation' ended in ignominy: she unwisely took on a female saloonkeeper, who thrashed her soundly. Carry's zeal kept prohibition alive in Kansas until 1948.

Kansas' bid for statehood was the fuse for the outbreak of the Civil War, and ferocious anti-and pro-slavery factions earned it the epithet 'Bleeding Kansas'. In the rip-roaring cattle and railroad era of mid/late 1800's, cowhands drove one million cattle a year to Abilene, and 'blew' their $1-a-day wages on cards, rotgut and fancy 'wimmin'. The cow capital eventually moved west from Abilene to Wichita and Dodge City. As the 'breadbasket to the world', Kansas sells much of its surplus wheat to needy Russia. Ironically, the original seeds for 'Turkey Red', a hard winter variety, were brought here from Russia in 1874 by Mennonite settlers.

'A remarkable state, well worth making an effort to discover.' 'At night, a magnificent and fulfilling stillness falls over the plains.' *www.yahoo.com/Regional/U_S__States/Kansas/*

ABILENE   Considering its associations with the Chisholm Trail and Wild Bill Hickok, Abilene's lack of westernness disappoints. Abilene is really Ike's Kansas—grain elevators, porch swings and funky little cafes and is the unlikely subject of the affectionate chorus, 'prettiest town I've ever seen'. The Eisenhower buildings are pompous but do stop for a look at Ike's simple boyhood home. Check out the Abilene City Guide at *http://history.cc.ukans.edu/heritage/abilene/city.htm*
The telephone area code is 785.

ACCOMMODATION
Best Western, 1709 and 2210 N Buckeye, off I-70, (1-800) 701-1000. Year-round, S-$45+, D-$59, $4 XP. Free continental bfast.
Diamond Motel, 1407 NW 3rd St, Abilene, 263-2360. Year-round S-$27-$31, D-$31-$37, XP-$4. Sml refrigerator in room.
Super 8, 2207 N Buckeye, 1 mile from downtown, 263-4545. S-$42, D-$47, $5 XP.

FOOD
Genny's Country Cupboard, 300 N Broadway. 263-4714, Open 7:30am-5pm Tues-Fri, 'til 4pm on Sat.
Mr. K's Farmhouse Restaurant, 407 S. Van Buren St, 263-7995, Open Tues-Sat 11am- 2pm and 5pm- 9pm, Sun 11-2 only.

OF INTEREST
CW Parker Carousel, 412 S Campbell. Go for a spin on a genuine turn of the century carousel. 263-2681, Mon-Sat 10am-8pm, Sun 1pm-4pm, $1.
Great Plains Theatre Festival, 263-4574. Kansas' premiere professional regional theatre.
Old Abilene Town and Museum, SE 6th at Buckeye. Recreation of historic Texas Street during the cowtown days. On the weekend, can-can girls perform and gunfights liven things up. Open daily 8am-5pm.
Seelye Mansion and Museum, 1104 N Buckeye, 263-1084. Tours of 1905 Georgian mansion and museum Mon-Sat 10am-3pm, Sun 1pm-3pm, $10
The Garden of Eden-yes, you read it here first-is in **Lucas**, 22 miles E of Paradise, west of Abilene on I-70, off Hwy 272. An eccentric by the name of SP Dinsmoor built this statue garden in the 1920s in his front yard, using 113 tons of concrete, among other things. A Civil War veteran, Dinsmoor held a cynical and rather prophetic view of the 20th century, particularly toward crooked bankers and lawyers. Daily 10am-5pm in the summer, 525-6395. $4. 12 miles from the geodetic centre of the US.

ATCHISON   The birthplace of Amelia Earhart and the Topeka, Atchison, and Santa Fe Railroad, Atchison sits alongside the Missouri River, a short trip north-west of Kansas City. Most of the town's attractions centre around its famous aviatrix daughter. *Area code is 913.*

OF INTEREST
Amelia Earhart Birthplace Museum, 223 N Terrace St, 367-4217. Earhart amassed a long list of break throughs for women: first to fly Atlantic as a passenger, first to fly solo across Atlantic and first to fly solo across US. She was out to become the first woman to fly around the world when she disappeared somewhere in the Pacific on July 2, 1937. Daily guided tours 9am-noon, 1pm-4pm from May thru Sept; open w/ends at other times. $2. Nearby Warnock Lake is home to the **International Forest of Friendship**, an expansive woodland area dedicated to aviation and aerospace endeavours. Located within the forest is a memorial to the 10 astronauts who have lost their lives in space exploration. A more recent addition to the forest is the **Earhart Earthwork**, a living portrait of Earhart, created in 1997 from stones and plantings to celebrate her 100th birthday.

FOOD/LODGING
Comfort Inn, 409 S 9th St, 367-7666. S-$44. D-$48, XP-$4.
Paolucci's Restaurant and Lounge, 113 South Third St, 367-6105. 'A casual, cosy restaurant and bar with panelled walls, where a hamburger, $2.25, and glass of Merlot, $2.25, hit the spot.'

WICHITA   Wichita has Kansas' most worthwhile cowboy mock-up in its Cow Town ('authentic, much better than Dodge City'), with five original and 32 replica buildings. Boeing, Cessna and Beech—three major aircraft producers—make Wichita the 'Air Capital of the World'. 'Great place to hitch-hike by air.'
The telephone area code is 316.

ACCOMMODATION
Inn at Willowbend, 3939 Comotara, 636-4032. W/end room special D-$59. Bfast included. Complimentary videos and cocktails.
Motel 6, 5736 W Kellogg St, 945-8440. S-$34, D-$40. Winter: S-$29, D-$35.
Red Barn, 6427 N Greenwich Road, 744-0866. Rooms from D-$65-$80. Privately owned house. Features the *Pioneer Room, Sunflower Room, Americana Room*, and the *Heritage Room*. Own bathroom. Shared hot tub. Bfast included. Rsvs req.
Super 8, 6075 Aircap Drive, 744-2071. S-$47, D-$57.
Town Manor Motel, 1112 N Broadway at 10th, 267-2878. From $30, Winter: from S-$28.

FOOD
La Galette Bakery, 1017 W Douglas Ave, 267-8541. Daily 8.30am-5pm.
Miller's Bar-B-Que, 4601 E 13th St, 684-8080. Plentiful ribs, brisket and baked beans.
New York Bagel Shop & Deli, 4618 E Central Ave, 683-3700. Bagel and sandwich shop serves bfast and lunch. Mon-Fri 6.30m-6pm, Sat 8am-3pm.
The Artichoke, 811 N Broadway, 263-9164. 'Cold beer on tap, great acoustic music at w/end and a Nancy's #8 on your plate! Exceptionally cool lunch stop.' Open 11am Mon-Thur, Fri 'til 11pm, Sat 'til 12am.
The Chinese Express Buffet, 123 E Douglas, 262-8882. 'All you can eat' Chinese Buffet (including salad bar), $4.75. 'All you can eat' salad bar, $2.85. 1 trip Chinese buffet, $3.85. Mon-Fri, 11:30am-2pm.

OF INTEREST
First National Black Historical Society of Kansas, 601 North Water, 262-7651. This museum and cultural centre was established to give recognition to black participation in early Wichita. Their contributions in the fields of sports, government,

entertainment, medicine, education and the military are depicted in the museum. Also exhibited are African artefacts, wood carvings, jewellery and dress. Tues.-Fri, 10am-5pm. Free.

Kansas Bike Trails: Shawnee Mission Park, Dornwood Park, The Levee, The Bowls and Clinton Park (from Kansas City, take K-10 which switches to 23rd St. Go west until you arrive at park. One of the largest trails in area. Lots of hills, rocks, and hikers to watch out for!)

Old Cowtown Museum, 1871 Sim Park Dr, 264-6398. A 'living' historic village. Daily 10am-5pm, Thur 'til 8pm; $7. Thur 5pm-8pm, $5.

There are several good (free!) art museums, including the **Ulrich Museum** at the Univ of Wichita, 689-3664, which has on its outside wall an exquisite Miro mosaic with over one million pieces of glass. Closed summers, Wed-Sun during school year. Kansas skyscrapers hold wheat, not people, and you'll find the tallest **grain elevators** in the world in **Hutchinson**, 45 miles NW on SR 96. They hold 20 million bushels of grain. Annual **Wichita Beerfest** is held at the beginning of June, at the **Kansas Coliseum Pavilion**, 1-5pm. Sample over 150 beers, try a selection of foods. Live bands, booths, exhibits and bagpipes! Meet the brewers personally! Must be 21yrs+ and present ID. Call (316) 687-2222.

INFORMATION
Chamber of Commerce, 265-7771.
Kansas B&B Assoc, 1-888-8-KS-INNS.
Kansas State Tourist Bureau, (785) 296-5403.
Visitors Bureau, 100 S Main, #100, 265-2800. Stop here first for map and information. Open Mon-Fri, 8am-5pm.
For more info on Kansas, try **Kansas Community Networks**: *http://history.ac.ukans.edu/heritage/towns/*

THE SANTA FE AND OTHER TRAILS   Because of its geographic position, Kansas was crosshatched with trails: the Santa Fe, Chisholm, Oregon and Smoky Hill, among others. Whether travelling across Kansas or settling it, pioneers needed grit and resilience. South of Colby (60 miles from Colorado), near I-70, you can examine an authentic sod house at the Prairie Museum. **Fort Larned** (6 miles from Larned off Hwy 154) and graffiti-covered **Pawnee Rock** (NE of Larned on 156) still stand as trail markers. Along US 50, 9 miles W of Dodge City, wagon ruts of the Santa Fe trail can be seen.

MICHIGAN   *The Wolverine State*

When you look at a map of Michigan, you'll be struck by its unique shape. It looks something like a hand— natives will eagerly indicate the part of the state they're from by pointing to it on their hands. The extended hand is indicative of a friendly people and a surprisingly friendly climate.

Michigan features 3000 miles of shoreline and more lighthouses than any other state, yet touches no ocean. Like its neighbouring state, Minnesota, it has more than 10,000 lakes.

A campers' and hikers' dream, Michigan has youth hostels, thousands of campsites (including the unspoiled northern pleasures of Isle Royale National Park) and a rich network of farm trails and roadside produce markets on its two peninsulas. The state produces a bounty of cherries,

blueberries and other fruits that beg to be sampled as you're passing through.
www.yahoo.com/Regional/U_S__States/Michigan/

DETROIT Detroit isn't just about car manufacturing, Motown and race riots. Auto assembly lines and good soul music are both disappearing, while crime is ever present. A bustling inland port, the city is working to revitalise a decaying downtown with flashy complexes like the Renaissance Center poised to snare lucrative convention gigs. Parts of downtown, however, still look like bomb sites. Homesick visitors may consider Detroit a desperately sad place to be, but natives are quick to defend Motown. Of course, they live out in the suburbs, primarily and that's probably (if you have to come here at all) where *you* should stay too!

The Motor City came by its name and fame quite by accident, largely because Henry Ford, Ransom Olds and other auto innovators happened to live and work in the area. The auto industry brought thousands of blacks to Detroit. One of them was Berry Gordy, founder in 1959 of the Motown sound (Smokey Robinson, the Supremes, the Temptations, etc), who used to make up songs on the Ford assembly line to relieve the monotony. *Meet Me In Detroit*, at *www.milner-hotels.com/dtravel.html* is a comprehensive city guide providing travellers with convenient hot links to airlines, car rental companies, dining and local attractions.
The telephone area code is 313.

ACCOMMODATION
Knights Inn, 10501 E Jefferson Ave, 822-3500. A short drive from downtown. S-$47 w/days ($57 w/ends). Dubious area.
Cabana Motel, 12291 Harper Ave, 371-1220. Located near Connor off I-94. S-$40 for two, D-$50, $5 key deposit.
Country Grandma's Home Hostel, 22330 Bell Rd, (734)753-4901. Located halfway between Detroit and Ann Arbor, surrounded by 3 parks. The hostel is 1hr from Toledo and 30 mins from Windsor, Ontario. $11 AYH, $14 non-AYH.
Falcon Inn Motel, 25125 Michigan Ave, Dearborn, near Telegraph on US 12, 278-6540. Convenient for the Henry Ford Museum and Greenfield Village. S-$45, D-$60.
Village Inn, 21725 Michigan Ave at Oakwood Blvd in Dearborn, off Southfield Fwy, 565-8511. Near the Henry Ford Museum and Greenfield Village. D-$55.
Wayne State University may be your best bet for summer lodging in a safe, eclectic neighbourhood near downtown. Apts with fully-equipped kitchens run D-$45-55. Call the housing office at 577-2116 for details.

FOOD
Strong ethnic communities here, so head for Greektown, Chinatown and the Polish community (called Hamtramck—actually an independent city within Detroit).
America's Pizza Cafe, 2239 Woodward, 964-3122, next to the Fox Theatre. Serves excellent little pizzas. Open Mon-Thur 11am-9pm, Fri-Sat 'til 1pm.
Bob's Big Boy, 400 Renaissance Center, 259-0606. Try the sandwiches and home-made desserts. Open Sun-Thur 7am-10pm, w/ end 'til 11.
Edmund Place, 69 Edmund Pl, 831-5757. Tues.-Thur 11:30am- 9pm, Fri 'til 11pm, Sat 4pm-11pm, Sun 1pm-9pm. 'Succulent fried chicken, luscious pork chops with mashed potatoes and corn bread. Pleasant African-American staff. A worthy destination for anyone seeking true urban American soul food.'
Jacoby's, 624 Brush St, 962-7067. Open 11am, kitchen closes 10pm. Near Greyhound, 2 blocks N of RenCen, has landmark status. **Mexicantown** is home to

many authentic Mexican restaurants and mercados. Try **Los Galanes**, 3366 Bagley St, 554-4444 for dinner— it often has dancing at night. Mon-Fri 9am-11pm, w/end 9am-3am.

Markets: **Hart Plaza** btwn the RenCen & Civic Center holds w/end ethnic festivals all summer long. **Eastern Market** on Russell St has produce bargains. Open year round.

Lafayette Coney Island, 118 W Lafayette Blvd, 964-8198. Open nearly round the clock, serves wieners smothered in chilli and raw onions with a cup of bean soup on the side.

Pizza Paplis Tavern, 553 Monroe in Greektown, 961-8020. Open 11am-1am. Deep-dish Chicago pizza, fresh pasta and large sandwiches.

Soup Kitchen Saloon, 1585 Franklin, 259-2643. Mon-Fri 11am-midnight, 5pm-2am w/ends. Known as 'Detroit's home of the blues'. Pasta, Creole and fresh fish specials. Cover $3-$7.

Traffic Jam, 511 W Canfield, 831-9470, on the Wayne State campus. The extensive menu, in-house brewery, fresh-baked bread, and decadent desserts make this restaurant a Detroit favourite. Mon 11am-3pm, Tues.-Wed 'til 9pm, Thur 'til 10:30, Fri 'til midnight. Sat 4pm-midnight.

OF INTEREST

Belle Isle, 852-4075, is an island park in the Detroit River (bridge at E Jefferson), has 5 sections: an aquarium (free), conservatory, a safari-like zoo, and the **Dossins** Great Lakes Museum, $2.

Detroit Grand Prix, Indy Cars World Championship race takes place in mid-June. The course follows the city streets by the RenCen.

Detroit Institute of Arts (DIA), 5200 Woodward Ave (off I-75, 1 miles W), 833-7900. Wed-Fri 11am-4pm, w/ends 11am-5pm. $4, $1 w/student ID. From fine primitives to Andy Warhol, plus Diego Rivera's famous and scathing mural on factory life. Also: has one of the best African art collections in the country, and *Quilting Time*, a mosaic by black modern artist Romare Beardon. Cafe in Renaissance decor.

Ford Montreux Detroit Jazz Festival, 963-7622. This is the US half of the Swiss Montreux International Jazz Festival, one of the most prestigious and widely recognised festivals. Most of the concerts are free. During the first weekend of Sept.

Gospel Music Hall of Fame and Museum, 1830 W McNichols, 592-0017. A far cry from Motown, this museum chronicles the history and development of Gospel Music. Opened in 1995. Call ahead for hours, donations encouraged.

Greenfield Village and adjacent **Henry Ford Museum** in **Dearborn**, W of Detroit. Greenfield Village is 240acres containing 100+ genuine historic buildings amassed by Henry Ford and set up in sometimes curious juxtaposition: Abe Lincoln's courthouse, Wright Brothers' cycle shop, Edison's lab (complete with vial said to contain Edison's dying breath). Almost everything runs or ticks or does something—a stunning microcosm of the roots of technological Americana. Fee rides for horse carriages, steam trains, Model-T Fords, steamboats, horse-drawn sleighs. The fantastic 12-acre Ford Museum has huge transportation collection, antique aircraft. Daily 9am-5pm; $12.50 to village and museum, 2-day pass to both for $22; 271-1620.

Graystone International Jazz Museum, 1249 Washington Blvd, 963-3813. Museum specialising in jazz memorabilia from 1920 to the present. The collection includes musical instruments from the Graystone Ballroom, as well as artefacts of such great jazz artists as Count Basie, Duke Ellington, and others. The museum also organises travelling exhibits. Open Tues.-Fri 11am-3:30pm, Sat by appointment only. The **K-Zoo Skate Zoo**, is Michigan's oldest indoor skatepark. Located at 1502 Ravine Rd, Kalamazoo, (616) 345-9550, it has the best spine ramp and a great street course with 6800 sq ft of skating area for all skateboarding, in-lining and BMX enthusiasts! Mon-Fri 3pm-9pm, Sat from noon, Sun noon-6pm. Also: **Airborne** is on the corner of Martin and Hayes Sts; 5½ spine ramp, fun box, launches, rails, quarter pipes, 2x11 ft half pipes.

Joe Louis Arena at **Cobo Hall**, 600 Civic Centre Dr, 983-6606, where sporting events, ice capades, concerts and the circus come to town.

Motown Museum, 2648 W Grand Blvd, 875-2264. It all began here, Hitsville USA, as Berry Gordy Jr. called it. Motown sound was introduced to the world in the 1960s from this small home. Offices and recording studios remained here until the company moved to LA, California in 1972. Museum filled with gold discs, rare photos, vintage clothing, memorabilia and artefacts recapturing the history of this seminal era in American music. Exhibits feature musicians, songwriters and black singing groups such as Diana Ross and the Supremes and The Temptations. Mon noon-5pm, Tues.-Sat 10am-5pm, Sun-Mon noon-5pm, last tour at 4.30pm; $6.

Renaissance Center, the 'RenCen' on the river, 568-8000, is a mirrored fortress of four 39-story towers protecting an 83-story hotel. The glass-fronted elevator ride is certainly worth it for the view ($3.50), if the costly drinks at the top are not. 'Fantastic views of Detroit, Windsor, the river.' 100+ shops, restaurants. Across the street is **Mariner's Church**, 1848 shrine for lake sailors, whose bells still toll each time a life is lost on the lake.

SPORT
On the professional scene, the Detroit Tigers play in the American Baseball League, the Pistons are the city basketball team, the Detroit Lions (American football) and the Redwings (ice hockey) keep everyone jumping in winter.

Winter sports: For info on events, sports and activities, call **Michigan Travel Bureau**, (800) 5432-YES. Skiing resorts around the Michigan state include Big Powderhorn Mountain, Bessemer (800) 222-3131and Blackjack, Bessemer (906) 229-5115. Boyne Highlands, Harbor Springs, and Boyne Mountain, Boyne Falls (800) GO-BOYNE. Crystal Mountain, Thompsonville (800) 968-7686, Indianhead Mountain Resort, Wakefield (800) 3-INDIAN, Shanty Creek, Bellaire (800) 678-4111.

Windsor, Canada: this city which gets mixed reviews is *south* of Detroit. It is reached via bridge or tunnel and recommended, but with a few warnings: 'I was given a difficult time because I was backpacking and had only $100 plus ticket home. Plenty of trucks outside immigration to ask for a ride though.' Once you get inside Canada, though, you'll find a bounty of good clubs and cheap eats, as well as beautiful parks. And unlike Detroit and the rest of the states, the drinking age in Windsor is only 19.

INFORMATION
Michigan Travel Bureau, (800) 543-2937.

Travelers Aid, at **Greyhound** and 211 W Congress, 962-6740; at **Metro Airport**, (734) 941-3943.

Visitors Bureau, 211 W Fort St, Suite #1000, 202-1800.

Visitor Hotline, 1-800-DETROIT.

Look online at *www.visitdetroit.com.*

INTERNET ACCESS
Detroit Public Library, 5201 Woodward Ave, 833-1000, free.

TRAVEL
Amtrak, 2601 Rose St, 336-5407/(800) 872-7245. Not the best station or area to be stuck in at night.

Greyhound, 1001 Howard St, 961-8011/(800) 231-2222.

Detroit Department of Transportation (DOT), 933-1300. Runs buses in the downtown area; $1.25.

Southeastern Michigan Area Regional Transit (SMART), 962-5515. For buses to the 'burbs.

Metropolitan Wayne County Airport, (734) 942-3550. Detroit's main airport, about 21 miles from downtown. To get there by bus, take a SMART bus #200 from Michigan Ave to Middlebelt, change there and take the #285 to the airport, takes about 90 mins-2 hrs, $1.60. Alternatively, Commuter Transportation, (734) 941-3252, runs a shuttle bus from major downtown hotels; rsvs req, $19 o/w. Taxi approx $30.

FLINT   Midway between Detroit and Lake Huron's Saginaw Bay has what Motor City lacks nowadays: **auto plant tours**. Buick City has hi-tech and robotics tours on Tue & Thur. You'll need to book tours far in advance during summer. Call the Flint Area Convention & Visitors Bureau, 400 N Saginaw St, (800) 288-8040, for more information. Flint's own homepage may be accessed at *www.flint.org/*
The telephone area code is 734.

ANN ARBOR   An hour's bus ride west of Detroit, Ann Arbor is thoroughly dominated by the University of Michigan and loves it. As a consequence, lots of good hangouts, live music including excellent bluegrass, cheap eats, support services, and events like the July Art Fair. For info on the **Ann Arbor 36th Film Festival**, held at the Michigan Theater annually every March, go to *www.citi.umich.edu/u/honey/aaff/*
The telephone area code is 734.

ACCOMMODATION
Ann Arbor YMCA, 350 S 5th Ave, 663-0536, downtown at William St. Clean dorm rooms for men and women, $90 weekly, $330 monthly, $10application fee + security deposit. Rsvs essential.
Lamp Post Motel, 2424 E Stadium Blvd, 971-8000. S-$49, D-$59. Friendly management.
U of M, Conference & Catering Services, 603 Madison, 764-5325. Summer dorm rooms; S-$36, D-$46. $59 w/ air conditioning. Rsvs required.

FOOD/ENTERTAINMENT
Afternoon Delight, 251 E Liberty St, 665-7513. This place has all-natural muffins and pita sandwiches. Try the yoghurt shakes. Open Mon-Tues. 8am-3:30, Wed-Fri 'til 8pm.
Rick's American Cafe, 611 Church St, 996-2747. Reggae and blues bands, $3-$6 cover, closed Sun. Serves burgers, burritos, nachos and more; dinner only. Best bar in Ann Arbor, according to the locals.
Zingerman's Deli, 422 Detroit St, 663-5282. Serves every kind of sandwich; the menu is a good hour's read. Also stocks a tremendous inventory of cheese, smoked fish, meats, breads, coffees etc.

OF INTEREST
Ann Arbor Summer Festival, in July. Offers a variety of performances and exhibits every day.
Gerald R Ford Presidential Library, 1000 Beal Ave, 741-2218. Mon-Fri 8.30am-5pm. Not a museum.
Museum of Art in Alumni Hall, S University, 525 State St, 764-0395. First-rate collection of Asian and Western art. Tue-Sat 10am-5pm, Thur 'til 9pm, Sun noon-5pm; $3 donation requested.
Nichols Arboretum and Gallup Park are next to the Huron River on the city's north-eastern edge. You can canoe, fish and swim. Daily 6am-10pm. Call the University of Michigan, 763-4033 or the Park and Recreation Dept, 994-2780.

INTERNET ACCESS
Web Chateau, 1220 University, Suite #2111, 995-5977. Open Mon-Fri 11am-1am, $5/hr.

INFORMATION/TRAVEL
Amtrak, 325 Depot St, 994-4906/(800) 872-7245. Services to Detroit and Chicago.
Ann Arbor Convention and Visitors Bureau, 120 W Huron, 995-7281.
Greyhound, 116 W Huron St, 662-5511/(800) 231-2222, at Ashley St, 1 block off Main St.

NATIONAL LAKESHORE/UPPER PENINSULA Michigan has two wilderness areas, the **Upper Peninsula** and the **Sleeping Bear Dunes National Lake Shore**. The Upper Peninsula is located just above Wisconsin. This multi-million acre forest is bordered by three of the Great Lakes. It provides a rare retreat into untouched wilderness; hiking, cross-country skiing, fishing and canoeing are available. For more information, contact the Upper Peninsula Travel and Recreational Association, PO Box 400, Iron Mountain, MI 49801, or 618 Stevenson Ave, Iron Mountain, 774-5480. Also, the US Forestry Service, Hiawatha National Forest, 2727 North Lincoln Rd, Escanaba, MI 49829, 786-4062, can supply you with guides and maps.

Sleeping Bear Dunes, 45 mins from **Traverse City**, is known for its magnificent sand dunes and polar-bear swimming (Lake Michigan never seems to warm up). 'Traverse City has excellent sugar-sand beaches on its two Lake Michigan bays—it feels like the sea-side!' In Traverse City, catch the **Bing Cherry Festival** in mid-July, an excellent festival. **Interlochen Center for the Arts,** SW of Traverse City, showcases some of the most well-known musical acts in their summer concert series, superbly staged in Kresge Auditorium, (616) 276-6230. 'Musical nirvana on a warm summer evening!'
The telephone area code for the Upper Peninsula is 906; for Sleeping Bear Dunes, 616.

ACCOMMODATION/FOOD
Northwestern Michigan Community College, East Hall, 1701 E Front St, Traverse City, (616) 922-1409. About 1 mile from the bus station. Accommodation provided on limited basis. S-$30, D-$40.
Dale's Donut Factory, 3687 South Lake Shore Dr, St Joseph, (616) 429-1033. The donut factory of donut fans' dreams! Mon-Fri, 5:30am-6pm, Sat 'til 5pm.

MACKINAC ISLAND When you set sail for Mackinac Island, leave your cares, worries and rental cars behind. No motor vehicles are permitted here— your transportation choices are horseback, bicycle, surrey or shank's mare. Tranquil, beautiful and Victorian in design, Mackinac (pronounced 'Mackinaw') is especially nice during the June Lilac Festival. Chocoholics Note: island speciality is homemade fudge. Boat runs every hour in summer.

Take a peek at the elegant 1880s Grand Hotel, featured in the movies *This Time for Keeps* and *Somewhere in Time*. It has a porch that never ends, the longest in the world. Check out the Mackinac Island pages, created on the island by the islanders themselves. Rich in pictures, info, news and stories, the web site is *www.mackinac.com/*
The telephone area code is 906.

ACCOMMODATION

Unfortunately, accommodation is rather expensive here and no camping is allowed on the island. Also, there are few lockers to be found here, or on the mainland at St Ignace and Mackinaw City, so you will be carrying your rucksack with you—'an exhausting bind if you go over to the island intent on walking'. The moral of this is: if you plan to go here, plan ahead. The Chamber of Commerce is helpful, 706 S Huron, 847-3783/6418.

Bogan Lane Inn, PO 482, Mackinac Island, ³⁄₄ mile E of the boat docks, (906) 847-3439. S or D-$70, T-$85, Q-$100. All include bfast. Rsvs req. Open year round. There are the usual motel chains along I-75; they are probably your best bet. **Camping:** camping isn't allowed on the island, but try nearby Mackinaw City. For campground information, call (616)436-5574.

TRAVEL/INFORMATION

Arnold Mackinac Island Ferry, Box 220, 847-3351. Departures from Mackinaw City and St. Ignace, every half hour, $13.50 r/t.

Mackinac Island Chamber of Commerce, 847-3783/6418.

Shepler's Mackinac Island Ferry, Box 250, Mackinaw City, MI 49701, (616) 436-5023. Serves Mackinaw City and St Ignace, also $13.50 r/t.

ISLE ROYALE NATIONAL PARK This is the roadless, wild and beautiful 'eye' in Lake Superior's wolfish head. Natives shun the pretentious name, calling it 'Isle Royal' instead. Free camping by permit only, including use of screened shelters around the island. 'Boil surface water at least 5 mins.' Carry salt along—inland lakes on the island have leeches. Island closed in winter.

MINNESOTA *Land of 10,000 Lakes*

Driving through Minnesota, you may well wonder if you took a wrong turn somewhere and wound up in Scandinavia. The Minnesota countryside almost duplicates the Nordic landscape, with fertile farmland in the south, dense pine forests in the north and 15,000 glacier-scoured lakes all around. Doubtless this is why so many immigrant Swedes and Norwegians moved here earlier this century; to them, the state looked like home.

Vikings may have learned of Minnesota's Nordic delights early on, if a Viking runestone dated from 1000AD proves authentic. Much of the population still appears Nordic, and the countryside and cities are among the cleanest and most well-preserved in the US.

The land also seems to attract giants, both literal and figurative. It's the birthplace of J Paul Getty, Bob Dylan, Charles Lindbergh, F Scott Fitzgerald, Sinclair Lewis and the Mississippi River, as well as the home of Paul Bunyon the woodsman and the Jolly Green Giant of canned pea fame. Minnesota also holds the dubious distinction of being the only state governed by a former professional wrestler; pop culture fanatics cheered and political purists jeered when Jesse 'the Body' Ventura was elected in 1998.

The state is especially lovely during Indian summer; highway markers often point out the most vivid colour displays. Free maps of the fall colour routes are obtainable from the Minnesota Tourism Bureau, 375 Jackson, Room 250, St Paul, MN 55101. Any time of year, **North Shore Drive** (US 61) along Lake Superior north to Canada is a top contender for the most beautiful camping and gawking route in America. Miles of well-kept biking paths criss-cross the state. **The Heartland Trail**, a 27 mile paved bike trail in north-central Minnesota, is one of the loveliest. Call (800) 657-3700 for more information. While here be sure to go canoeing—a peculiarly Minnesotan tradition passed down from Chippewa Indians and French-Canadian trappers to present day. You can disappear into the north country wilderness and not see another person for days on end. Given the number of lakes, it's not surprising that fishing is hugely popular here. Beware the land of 10,000 lakes in the summertime—Minnesotans joke that the official state bird is the mosquito.

www.yahoo.com/Regional/U_S__States/Minnesota/

MINNEAPOLIS/ST PAUL Minneapolis and St Paul are 'Twin Cities' only in geographic terms, laced together by the Mississippi River. It's said that Minneapolis was born of water, St Paul of whiskey.

Minneapolis is young, Scandinavian, modern and relaxed, a working-class city freckled with lakes and home base of a number of Fortune 500 companies, headed by the biggest names in engineering. As in San Diego and Seattle, residents here sensibly take advantage of their versatile setting; many spend their lunch hour sailing in summer. Minneapolis was and is Mary Tyler Moore territory, as bouncy and clean as the Pillsbury doughboy, another local product.

St Paul began as an outpost with the uncouth name of Pig's Eye, described in 1843 as 'populated by mosquitoes, snakes, Indians and about 12 white people'. Perhaps to compensate for these rough beginnings, St Paul has become a conservative capital city of Irish and German Catholics, doting on history and Eastern refinement. F Scott Fitzgerald is a St Paul native, as is Charles Shultz of 'Peanuts' fame, whose cartoons were rejected by his high school yearbook.

To the south is the younger sibling of **Bloomington**, where lurks the gigantic "Mall of America" (#7 bus). Out of the three metropolitan areas, Minneapolis offers most for the visitor: friendly, outgoing locals, a handsome downtown with mall, skyways, parks, a meandering waterfront and swimmable lakes. Stick to downtown, however: 'I am astonished—could other US downtowns be like this, given a chance? The rest of Minneapolis that I've seen is as ordinary and soulless as anywhere else in America.' Check out the Yahoo! Twin Cities Metro city guide at *www.minn.yahoo.com*
The telephone area code for Minneapolis and Bloomington is 612, for St. Paul it's 651.

ACCOMMODATION
City of Lakes International House, 2400 Stevens Ave, Mpls, 871-3210. Located in the historic mansion district. Living room with piano and fireplace, outdoor patio. Clean and relaxed. Close to major attractions, downtown, bus lines and lakes. No smoking, drinking, drugs. 'Not a party hostel.'! Bike hire $3 daily. Private room $34, dorm $16-17, $105/wk. 'Friendly, helpful staff!'
Fraternities in the 16-1700 block of University Ave can sometimes offer room to travellers. 'Very cheap and plenty of lovely half-naked men wandering around—just what you need after two months in camp.'

HI-Caecilian Hall, 2004 Randolph Ave, St. Paul, 690-6604. 1 June-14 August. S-$14/22, D-$28/34, T-$39. AYH members only.

Hillview Motel, Hwys 169 & 41, 445-7111. S-$49-69, D-$59-109.

Students Co-op, 1721 University Ave SE, 331-1078. $10, available only in summer. Kitchen, laundry, colour TV. 'Smashing place to live—full of friendly lunatics. Great social life.'

Super 8 Motel, 7800 S 2nd Ave, exit at Nicollet Ave off I-494, 888-8800. S-$75, D-$83. Close to airport, shops, and zoo. Several around the twin cities. Call 738-1600.

Camping: Lebanon Hills Regional Park Campground, 12100 Johnny Cake Ridge Rd, Apple Valley, (612) 454-9211. Tent site $11.

FOOD

Be sure to try Minnesota specialities: wild rice, walleyed pike, sweet corn and Fairbault blue cheese. St Paul's soul dish is *boya* , a Hungarian stew served on the slightest pretext. For cheap munchies try some of the downtown and college bars during happy hour.

Al's Breakfast, 413 14th Ave, SE, 331-9991. Mon-Sat 6am-1pm, Sun 9am-1pm. 'Best morning meal in town! Good things happen here; people's lives change. If you want a car, or an apartment, or a sweetheart, come in, have coffee, and chat a while.'

Big City Bagels, LaSalle Plaza, 825 Hennepin Ave, Mpls, 305-4880. 'Café-cum-bakery, serves a wide selection of bagels and spreads, sandwiches, bakery and cream cheeses at reasonable prices.' Open Mon-Fri 6am-6:30pm, Sat 8am-2pm.

Black Forest Cafe, 1 E 26th St, Mpls, 872-9435. Lovely German food! Open Mon-Sat 11am-11pm, Sun noon-10pm.

Brit's Pub, 1110 Nicollet Mall, Mpls, 332-3908. Very popular with locals. Open daily 11am-1am.

Cafe Latte, 850 Grand Ave, St Paul, 224-5687. Located in Victoria Crossing. Energetic urban cafeteria. 'Seductive sprawling triple-layer turtle cake.' Bring a friend so you can try more than one. Choice of four interesting soups every day. Open daily at 9am, Sun 'til 10am, Mon-Thur 'til 11pm, Fri-Sat 'til midnight.

Caravan Serai, 2175 Ford Pkwy, St Paul, 690-1935. Afghani, Middle Eastern, and Greek fusion. If restaurant is too pricey, try the **Deli and Take-out** next door. Restaurant open for dinner Mon-Thur 4:30-10pm, Fri-Sat 'til 11:30pm, Sun 'til 9pm. Deli open Tue-Fri 11am-9pm, Sat from noon.

Cossetta, 211 West Seventh St, St Paul, 222-3476. An Italian market and deli. Fresh meats, cheeses and salads are served cafeteria style. Lunch or dinner for two with wine is about $15. Open daily, 10:45am-10pm.

Emily's Lebanese Delicatessen, 641 University Ave NE, Mpls, 379-4069. Great lunch spot! Open Sun-Mon, Thur 11am-9pm, Fri-Sat 'til 10pm.

Famous Dave's BBQ, 4262 Upton Ave S, Mpls, 929-1200, Live blues and delicious barbecue. Open Sun-Wed 11am-9pm, Thur-Sat 11am-10pm.

Gasthof Zur Gemeutlichkeit, 2300 University Ave NE, Mpls, 781-3860. Fabulous German restaurant and bar that draws customers of all ages. Polka and live German music. Order the 'boot'— a mammoth-sized glass boot filled with beer, shared with a large group. Restaurant open Tue-Thur 5pm-10pm, Fri-Sat 4pm-11pm, Sun 10:30am-10pm. Bar stays open 'til 1am. Closed Mon.

Green Mill, 2626 Hennepin Ave, Mpls, 374-2131. Excellent burgers, good pizza. Mon-Thur 11am-11pm, Fri-Sat 'til midnight. Bar open 'til 1am.

It's Greek to Me, 626 W Lake St, Mpls, 825-9922. Gyros are cheap and even mous-saka is reasonably priced. Tues.-Sun 11am-11pm.

Key's Restaurant, 1007 Nicollet Mall, Mpls, 339-6399. 'Small and friendly café which serves good food at reasonable prices. All day bfast and daily specials are a good deal.'

Lotus, 313 SE Oak St, Mpls, 331-1781, and 3037 Hennepin Ave, near Calhoun

Square, 825-2263. Vietnamese food in a stylish setting. Open 11am-9pm daily.
Mickey's Diner, 36 West Seventh St, St Paul, 222-5633. Living-history museum of this American eating tradition. Meal for two costs about $15. Open 24 hrs.
Mudpie, 2549 Lyndale Ave, Mpls, 872-9435. Natural food— a vegetarian's paradise. Mon-Fri 11am-10pm, Sat 10am-11pm, Sun 10am-10pm.
North Country Co-op, 1929 S 5th St, 338-3110. Full grocery with fresh produce and bread—even pickled Japanese vegetables. Mon-Sat 9am-9pm, Sun 9am-8pm.
Origami, 30 N First St, Mpls, 333-8430. The best sushi in Minneapolis. Open Mon-Fri 11am-2pm for lunch, dinner Mon-Thur 5pm-9:30pm, Fri-Sat 'til 10:30.
Sawatdee, 607 Washington Ave, S Mpls, 338-6451, and 285 E 5th, St Paul, 222-5859. The one in St Paul is the older and better restaurant. Some of the best Thai food. 11am-10pm daily.
Seward Community Cafe, 2129 Franklin Ave, Mpls, 332-1011. 'The Sunday bfast is very cheap and filling.' Mon-Fri 6:30am-2pm, Sat-Sun 8am-4pm.

OF INTEREST: MINNEAPOLIS
Besides being the longest pedestrian walkway in the US, the **downtown mall** along Nicollet Ave is one of the most agreeable and attractive. It's full of flowers, fountains, friendly conversation, strollers, sandwich-eaters, bus stop shelters, wafting classical music and tempting boutiques. Overhead an enclosed **Skyway system** (designed for Minnesota winters) lets pedestrians cross in comfort from building to building across 45 downtown blocks.
    The focal point of the Mall and Skyway complex is the 57-storey **IDS Center** at Nicollet and 8th St. The **Crystal Court**, a 3-level arcade within the IDS complex, has a 'ceiling' of crystal pyramids and shapes which nicely diffuse the sunlight, creating a dappled effect as though one were strolling beneath trees. Both the lighting and the vibrant cafe/meeting-place ambience are best absorbed in the morning. Cafe has reasonably-priced lunch specials, and there's an info centre in the Crystal Court. Suggestions of scenic walks around the Twin Cities can be found in free leaflets from the info centre in the IDS Complex and Minnesota Convention and Visitor Commission, 1219 Marquette Ave, Suite 300, Mpls, MN 55403; 348-4313.
Recommended: cross the Hennepin Ave bridge to the far side of the Mississippi and then return to downtown via the 3rd Ave/Central Ave bridge. The area immediately across the river is called **Riverplace** & **St Anthony Main**, restored warehouses on the original cobblestone Main Street of Minneapolis. The 3rd Ave bridge takes you across to St Anthony Falls; the Minneapolis side is lined with fine old warehouses and flour mills (walk along S 1st St to Portland Ave), eg. the Crown Roller Mill built in 1879. Between these mills and S Washington Ave is the **Milwaukee Road Station**, a handsome complex which the city has decided to preserve. A favourite walk or bike ride is along the Mississippi on either side. Others are around Lake of the Isles, Cedar Lake, Lake Harriet or Lake Calhoun, all in south Minneapolis. This is a city with 153parks and 45 continuous miles of bike paths.
American-Swedish Institute, 2600 Park Ave, 871-4907. Shops, fine art, 33-room mansion with exhibits on Minnesota's Scandinavian heritage. Tue, Thur , Fri, Sat noon-4pm, Wed 'til 8pm, Sun 1pm-5pm; $4.
Historic Fort Snelling, junction of Hwys 5and 55 near airport, 726-1171. Daily May-Oct Mon-Sat 9:30am-5pm, Sun 11:30am-5pm. Reconstruction and preservation of 1827-era fort. Film, exhibits, fort tours; $4.
Historic Orpheum Theater, 910 Hennepin Ave South, Mpls, 339-7007. Pop, jazz and rock events. Also shows such as *42nd St* and *Riverdance*. 2,200-seat facility. Located in the LaSalle Plaza. Call (651)989-5151 for tkts.
MC Gallery, 400 1st Ave N, 339-1480. One of 9 galleries located in the Wyman Building. Features good contemporary American arts. By appointment only.
Minneapolis Institute of Arts, 2400 3rd Ave S, 870-3046. Tue-Sat 10am-5pm, Thur 10am-9pm, Sun 12-5pm; free, special shows. Donations requested.

Minnehaha Falls and Park, south of city. 144-acre woodland with 53-foot cataract popularised (though never seen) by Longfellow in his *Song of Hiawatha*.

University Theater, 120 Rarig Center, 330 21st Ave South, 625-4001. Musicals, comedies and dramas (Shakespeare /Classics/ Contemporary), featuring student and professional actors, designers and directors.

Walker Art Center, 725 Vineland Pl, 375-7622, a modern collection, Tue-Sat 10am-5pm, Thur 'til 8pm, Sun 11am-5pm; $4. Free on Thurs. On the grounds is the **Sculpture Garden**, including the enormous Spoonbridge and Cherry.

OF INTEREST: ST PAUL

Alexander Ramsey House, 265 S Exchange St, 296-0100. Victorian home of early Minnesota governor, run by Minnesota Historical Society. 1 hr tours Tue-Sat 10am-3pm, Sun 1-3pm, $5.

Indian Mounds State Park, Dayton's Bluff, east of downtown. A pleasant picnic spot overlooking the Mississippi, believed to be a Sioux burial site.

James J Hill House, 240 Summit Ave, 297-2555. 45-room Romanesque mansion and private art gallery that once belonged to the builder of the Great Northern Railway. ^{1}/2 hr tours Wed-Sat 10am-3:30pm, rsvs recommended; $5.

Jonathan Padelford Packet Boat Co, 227-1100, Harriet Island, downtown St Paul. Paddlewheel boat tours of Mississippi River. 2 daily 1^1/2 hr cruises in summer (noon and 2pm), less often in May & Sept, $10.

Landmark Center, 75 W 5th St, 292-3225. The old Federal building, now an art gallery. Worth going for the architecture alone. Mon-Fri 8am-5pm, Sat 10am-5pm, Sun 1pm-5pm; free.

Science Museum, 30 E 10th St (corner of Wabasha Ave), 221-9488/44. Mon-Sat 9.30am-9pm, Sun 10.30am-7pm. Omnitheatre, a huge, domed screen, 221-9400. Buy ticket for $7and enter the museum for $2.

State Capitol, near the Science Museum, 296-2881. 45 min tour of building, governor's quarters, golden horses on top and base of dome for panoramic view. Tours Mon-Fri 9am-4pm, Sat 10am-3pm, Sun 1pm-3pm; free; go to info desk.

Summit Avenue District. The Victorian mansions get grander as you work your way up Laurel, Holly, Portland and Summit Aves—just the way the family of F Scott Fitzgerald did. Born at 294 Laurel, FSF and family lived in 4 successively posher homes before ending up at 599 Summit, where he wrote his first novel in 1919. On the **University of Minnesota campus** is the **Goldstein Gallery**, MacNeal Hall; displays on fashion, housing, and interior design.

Nearby: Lake Pepin, 1hr S of the Twin Cities on Hwy 61. Good swimming beaches.

Mall of America, 60 E Broadway, Bloomington, 883-8800, about 15 mins from St Paul; take MTC bus #54. The largest shopping mall in the States with the usual feast for shopping gastronomes and also for added piquancy: a seven acre indoor theme park with a roller coaster and Golf Mountain—a two level 18 hole 'golf course'! Also worth checking out is Underwater World, 300 feet of underwater tunnels showcasing regional aquatic life. The 4th level is home to happening night life, starring Planet Hollywood.

Minnesota Zoo, in Apple Valley south of St Paul, 431-9200. Buses from Twin Cities' downtowns via the Mall of America. 5 zones, from tropics to oceanic, with Siberian tigers, wolves and caribou. May-Sept daily 9am-6pm. Other months, daily 10am-4pm, $8.

Sauk Center. Sinclair Lewis' hometown and the setting for his book, *Main Street*. Located 2 hrs NW of St Paul on 94 West, (320) 352-5201. Interpretative Center and museum; Mon-Fri 8.30am-5pm, Sat-Sun 9am-5pm, free. Lewis' boyhood home open May-Sept only; Mon-Fri, 9.30am-5pm, Sun 10:30am-5pm, $3.

Taylor's Falls, located on the St Croix River near Wisconsin border. Spectacular falls and great rock climbing. On your drive up, stop in Stillwater.

ENTERTAINMENT: MINNEAPOLIS

Pick up a free copy of the *City Pages* (comes out on Wed) at news-stands and coffee shops for the latest word on what's going on or go to *www.citypages.com*.

First Avenue and **7th St Entry**, 701 1st Ave N, 338-8388. First Avenue was made famous by Prince in the movie *Purple Rain* . You probably won't see Prince, but you can see good rock groups. 7th St Entry is around the corner: cheaper, lesser-known groups.

Festivals: summertime noon concerts throughout downtown Mpls, esp Nicollet Mall. Peavea Plaza has Thur night jazz in June, 5pm-7pm; 338-3807 for more information, or go to *www.downtownmpls.com*. Activities of the lakes are featured in the **Aquatennial** in July, and the **Minnesota State Fair** is held in Aug at Snelling Ace, St Paul; (651) 642-2200.

Guthrie Theater, 725 Vineland Pl, 377-2224, was founded in the 1960's by Sir Tyrone Guthrie and has one of the finest repertory companies in the US. Excellent discounts for students week nights and Sunday. Low cost previews; enquire.

Orchestra Hall, 1111 Nicollet Mall, 371-5656. Home of Minneapolis Orchestra. Cabaret in summer; jazz, pop and other concerts.

The Quest Club, 110 N 5th St, 338-6169. $5-$8 cover. 'Great night-club. Thursday night is all ages (18+) $7 entry.'

U of Minnesota Film Society, 17th and University Ave SE, 627-4430. The **Dinkytown** area near campus on the east side of the river is liveliest at night. On campus: 'the Film Society often has free or cheap screenings of recent flicks. See notice board in Student Union'. Good country rock groups perform at many bars in the metropolitan area.

ENTERTAINMENT: ST PAUL

Minnesota History Center, 345 West Kellogg Blvd, (800) 657-3773. Mon-Sat 10am-5pm, Tue 'til 8pm, Sun noon-5pm, free. Winter Adventure Family Festival held in late January offers family activities, music, hands-on crafts and outdoor activities (cross-country skiing).

Ordway, 345 Washington St, near Landmark Center, 224-4222. The St Paul Chamber Orchestra and Minnesota Opera perform here.

Winter Carnival, Rice Park, btwn 4th & 5th Sts and Market & Washington. 10 days of parades, parties, sporting events and fireworks; $3 button, available throughout Twin Cities, entitles holder to participate in most activities. Check out Grande Day Parade, torchlight parade and ice-carving competitions. Call (800) 488-4023 for info.

World Theater, 10 E Exchange St, 290-1221. Once home of *A Prairie Home Companion*, now hosts a Saturday night radio show featuring some of the finest in American folk music. Box Office Mon-Fri 11am-4pm.

INFORMATION

Check the free newspapers (available from street boxes and stores downtown), *Skyway News*, *Twin Cities Reader* and *City Pages* for events, accommodation and job tips.

Minnesota Tourism Bureau, 121 7th Place E, #300, Metro Square, St Paul, (800) 657-3700.

Travelers Assistance, 726-5500. Located at airport, inside security area.

INTERNET ACCESS

CyberX, 3001 Lyndale Ave, Mpls, 824-3558, $6-7 hr.

Internet Cafe's Europe@n Grind, 815 Washington Ave SE, Stadium Village. An essential stop for backpackers— hostelling cards, passport photos, etc. Of course, coffee and Internet, too. $3/hr.

TRAVEL
Amtrak, 730 Transfer Rd, St Paul, 644-6012 or (800) 872-7245. On the 'Empire Builder' route that connects Chicago and Seattle/Portland. 'Located on an industrial estate, no accommodation nearby.'
Greyhound, in Mpls: 29 N 9th St; (800) 231-2222.
Metropolitan Transit Commission (MTC), 349-7000, runs the two cities integrated bus systems. Basic fare $1, $1.50 during rush hour.
Minneapolis/St Paul International Airport, about 9 mi from both downtowns. Take the #7 C,D,E, or F bus from 6th St, Mpls, basic fares on boarding and then 25¢ on disembarking; Airport Express, (612) 827-7777, runs a limousine service to downtown hotels, $9 o/w, $14 rtn to St Paul; $11 o/w, $18 r/t to Mpls.

DULUTH   Situated on a steep hillside overlooking Lake Superior, Duluth is the world's largest fresh-water port and is known for its unbelievably cold winters. The mines that used to provide the city with much of its income have all but disappeared. Now it's you, the happy tourist, who helps keep the place moving. It's access to the lake that attracts most visitors; there is a beautiful 1 mile walkway that traces the shore of the lake and carries you across the harbour. Accommodation can be a problem in the summer when it's busier and the motels bump up their prices, but try **Best Western Downtown Motel**, 131 W 2nd St, (218) 727-6851, S or D-$63 (Sun-Thur), S or D-$85 (Fri and Sat), XP-$5. Visit the **Convention and Visitors Bureau**, 100 Lake Place Dr, 722-4011/(800) 4-DULUTH, for information on the best current deals. For special events, pictures, lodging, attractions, dining and shopping, check out *www.visitduluth.com/*
The telephone area code is 218.

HIBBING   Famous for its Mesabi Range iron ore, Hibbing is also home of the original Greyhound buses and the birthplace of Bob Dylan. For those interested in digging up more knowledge about mining, the Minnesota Museum of Mining in Chisholm and the Iron Range Interpretative Center may be worth visiting. Hwy 73 takes you through a multicoloured mini-Grand Canyon, the mined-out maw of the Pillsbury open pit. Along the way are several vista points for viewing other gaping holes, some as much as four miles long and two miles wide.

GRAND RAPIDS   There's no place like Grand Rapids; it was home to Judy Garland, born there in 1922. Today it's the site of the **Judy Garland Birthplace Historic House**, (800) 664-JUDY. The annual Judy Garland festival is held at the end of June, featuring cameo appearances by some of the surviving Munchkins from her most famous movie, *The Wizard of Oz*. Opened in 1995, the house attracts some 10,000 Judy Garland fans a year. A yellow brick road leads up to the home on which visitors can write messages to Judy. Before Garland's death in 1969 she told an interviewer: 'If we had stayed in Minnesota, my life might have been much happier.' Open daily 9am-5pm, Sun 'til 9pm, $3. *www.judygarland.com*.

NORTHERN MINNESOTA   is known for the beauty of its wild areas. Among the best: **Chippewa National Forest**, a 650,000acre wilderness that contains nearly 500 lakes and rivers with broad vistas of beautiful large and small lakes. Hiking trails have been developed and maintained for visitors. Bald eagles are the star attractions. For information call (218) 335-8600. Try *www.paulbunyan.net/users/blawler/chipp.htm* for recreation opportunities and a complete list of campgrounds.

North Shore, Lake Superior, (218) 626-4300. If you have about a week, you can drive all the way around Lake Superior into Canada and Wisconsin. Otherwise, go to Duluth to see this beautiful shore line.

There is a plethora of campgrounds scattered throughout the area. The best include **Grand Marais Municipal Campground**, 387-1712. Camp sites run $20-26a night, depending on amenities and location. Right on Lake Superior. Near pool; and **Lamb's Campground**, 663-7292. 60 wooded acres and 1 ¹/₂ miles of beach. Fishing, hiking, boat facilities. $21, $25 w/hook-up. On lake sites-$25/29.

Superior National Forest stretches across Minnesota's north-eastern area from the Canadian border to the north shore of Lake Superior. It is especially known for the **Boundary Waters Canoe Area**, a million-acre protected wilderness area honey-combed with rivers. There are bugs, bears and a lot of portaging, but, if you come prepared, this adventure is well worthwhile. For information write to the Forest Supervisor, PO Box 338, Duluth, MN 55801, or call the **Minnesota Tourism Bureau** in St Paul, 296-5029.

VOYAGEURS NATIONAL PARK On the Minnesota-Canadian border, this 219,000acre expanse of forested lake country is just beginning to be developed for public use. The park takes its name from the French Canadians who plied this network of lakes and streams in canoes, transporting explorers (some seeking the Northwest Passage), missionaries and soldiers to the West. They later returned by way of Montreal, carting vast quantities of furs with them. You can reach the park by car, but inside there are only waterways— you'll need to rent a boat. Free primitive camping in designated area. Other lodgings at nearby private resorts. No park entrance fee. A new visitors centre is located 11 miles E of International Falls on Black Bay off County Road 96. Houseboats can be rented on **Rainy Lake, Crane Lake** or the **Ash River**. For more information write **Voyageurs National Park**, 3131 Hwy 53, International Falls, MN 56649 or call (218) 283-9821. **Voyagaire Lodge and Houseboats**, Crane Lake, has a website at *www.voyagaire.com* and its hosts Bill and Deena Congdon can direct you to the places where decades ago Native Americans etched their stones into the granite walls along the park's bluffs.

MISSOURI *The Show-Me State*

Mix equal parts of the Old South, the Wild West and the modern Midwest and you've got the flavour of the Missourian: shrewd, salt of the earth, slightly cantankerous—nobody here believes anything unless they see it with their own eyes. The flat landscape is dominated and divided by the Big Muddy, the Missouri River, a wilful, sediment-laden powerhouse. Missouri produces more tents, lead, Missouri mules, corncob pipes and space vehicles than anyone else. Missouri has also produced Harry S Truman, Mark Twain, TS Eliot, Jesse James and Generals Pershing and Bradley, as well as actors Brad Pitt, Don Johnson, and Kathleen Turner.

In the south-west begins the Ozark Plateau, wooded, full of springs, unspoilt rivers and caverns like Fantastic near Springfield, which has seen service as a speakeasy and a KKK meeting place. Other interesting caves include Meramec (55 miles SW of St Louis), a five-storey cave variously used as a Civil War gunpowder mill, an underground railway station, and a hideout for Jesse James' gang. A portion of the Cherokee Trail of Tears runs through SE Missouri and has been made into a scenic camping and recreational area. *www.yahoo.com/Regional/U_S__States/Missouri/*

ST LOUIS St Louis is associated with several great American traditions. It's here where St Louis Browns baseball fans first gobbled up hot dogs in 1893 and where 1904 World's Fair goers first contended with drippy ice cream cones and sampled hamburgers on buns. St Louis is where WC Handy wrote and sang the blues, where slave Dred Scott sued for freedom, where one-time resident Tennessee Williams set his *Glass Menagerie* and where Charles Lindbergh got the bucks for his trans-Atlantic venture. In 1998, St Louis captured the attention of baseball fans everywhere as Cardinals slugger Mark McGwire shattered Roger Maris' record for single season home runs.

Huge, humid, full of unsavoury slums and heavy industry from meat-packing to beer-brewing, the city nevertheless has a vital cultural life, lots of free attractions and the elegant Gateway to the West arch. St Louis Convention & Visitors Commission has a website, *www.St-Louis-CVC.com* with links to a calendar of events, attractions and nightlife.
The telephone area code is 314.

ACCOMMODATION
Huckleberry Finn Youth Hostel, 1904-1906 S 12th St, 241-0076. $15. 'Oldest facilities but good place to stay.' Get there by downtown #30 bus then #73 bus from Locust St/Tucker Blvd Market/4th St. Alternatively take taxi from Amtrak/Greyhound for safety.
St Louis University, 221 N Grand, 977-3729, offers on-campus housing from mid-May-Aug 1. From $13-47, depending on location and amenities.
To reserve a **B&B** place write: B&B of St Louis, River Country, MO & IL, 1900 Wyoming, St Louis, MO 63118, 771-1993. Over 40 B&Bs. Willing to work within budget restraints and they'll also pick you up at the rail and bus stations.

FOOD
Berkshire Grill, St Charles Road and Natural Bridge Rd, 298-1260. Excellent American classics. Open Sun-Thur 11am-10pm, Fri-Sat 'til 11pm.
Blueberry Hill, 6504 Delmar Blvd, 727-0880. Live bands, outdoor seating in trendy University City Loop. Open Mon-Sat 11am-1.30am, Sun 11am-midnight
Brandt's, 6525 Delmar Blvd, 727-3663. Also in UCity Loop, a good place to go for dessert and coffee. Open Mon-Sat 11am-1am, Sun 10:30am-midnight.
Coffee Cartel, 2 Maryland Plaza, 454-0000, 24 hour coffee shop located in lively Central West End.
Conetto's, 5453 Magnolia, 781-1135. Great Italian food. Open for lunch Mon-Sat 11am-2pm, for dinner Mon-Thur 5pm-10pm, Fri-Sat 'til 11pm.

Crown Candy Kitchen, 1401 St Louis Ave, 621-9650. A 1913 ice cream parlor with a blend of shakes and sundaes. Drink 5 malts in 30 mins and pay nothing! Open daily, 10.30am-10pm.

Culpeppers, 300 N Euclid Ave, 361-2828. Serves great food with outside seating in Central West End. Open 11am-1am daily.

John D McGurks Irish Pub, 1200 Russell Blvd, 776-8309, Open Mon-Fri 11am-1am, Sat from 11:30am, Sun 5pm-midnight.

King Louie's, 3800 Chateau Ave, 865-3662. A fun place to eat. Open 11am-10pm Mon-Thur, 'til 11pm Fri-Sat.

McDonald's, 322 S Leonor K Sullivan Blvd, 231-6725, on a riverboat along the Mississippi. Built along lines of a riverboat, complete with Mark Twain at the helm! Open daily, 7am-9pm.

Morgan St Brewery, 721 N 2nd St, 231-9970. Not only a restaurant and brewery, but also a dance club! In Laclede's Landing.

Old Spaghetti Factory, 727 N 1st St, 621-0276. 'Massive helpings, good atmosphere, spaghetti dinners with dessert, coffee from $4-$8.' Open Mon-Fri 4-10pm, Sat noon-11pm, Sun noon-10pm.

Remy's Kitchen, 222 S Bemiston Ave, 726-5757. One of St Louis' most popular restaurants. Make a reservation or you'll wait for hours. **Rigazzi's,** 4945 Daggett Ave, 772-4900. Another good choice for Italian. Open Mon-Sat 10am-10:30pm.

St Louis Bread Company, 10 S Central, 725-9666, and several other locations. Phenomenal sandwiches, bagels, soups and salads! Hours vary by location.

Ted Drewes, 6726 Chippewa St, 481-2652, and 4224 Grand, 352-7376. 'Naughty-but-nice frozen custard desserts. Take-away/'drive-up' only. Always draws a crowd—be prepared for large queues esp in eves and w/ends'. Open daily, 11am-midnight.

There are also many inexpensive ethnic restaurants around **Laclede's Landing** and on the 4th flr of **St Louis Center**, Locust & 6th St.

OF INTEREST

Gateway Arch, 655-1700. A unique 40-person tram ('don't go if you get seasick') mounts the core of each leg of this 630-ft stainless steel arch designed by Eero Saarinen, in response to a competition in which the architect would best represent St Louis as 'The Gateway to the West'. Once there, you overlook the city and the Mississippi. 'Awesome.' Get there before 11am to avoid long lines. Daily 8am-10pm during summer; 9am-6pm, winter. $6 for tram ride; $2 to enter the grounds of the arch and the **Museum of Westward Expansion** complex beneath the arch. 'The museum is very atmospheric, giving vivid impressions of frontier life.' $4 for film depicting the construction of the arch. **The Old Court House**, west of Arch at 11 N 4th St, 655-1600, was scene of slavery auctions and the unsuccessful attempt by slave Dred Scott to win his freedom in court; the ramifications of his case helped ignite the Civil War. Open 8am-4.30pm, free. Trial room no longer exists, but you may see **Dred Scott's** grave in Section 1, Calvary Cemetery, 4947 W Florissant, 381-0750.

Forest Park, midtown, 5 miles W of Gateway Arch. A large and well laid-out park with numerous attractions; in 1904 the site of the centennial Louisiana Purchase Exposition and World's Fair. An electric signal from the White House simultaneously unfurled 10,000 flags, while fountains flowed, bands played, 62 foreign nations exhibited, and 19 million people visited, there to sample iced tea and ice cream cones for the first time. Of the 1576 buildings erected for the fair, only one was permanent; it's now the **St Louis Art Museum**, 1 Fine Arts Drive, 721-0072; one of the most impressive in the US. Open Tue 1.30pm-8.30pm, Wed-Sun 10am-5pm, free. **The Jewel Box** is a floral conservancy located within Forest Park—a lovely place for a stroll.

Nearby: Anheuser-Busch Brewery, 12th and Lynch St, 577-2626. World's largest brewery gives free 1¹/₂ hr tours (every 15 mins) with free beer and pretzels. Mon-Sat 9am-5pm, also Sun 11.30pm-5pm in summer months, free.

Grant's Farm, Gravois Rd at Grant Rd (outskirts), 843-1700. Ancestral home of the Busch family, formerly owned by Ulysses S. Grant. Free look at the largest group of lovably huge Clydesdale horses anywhere, with a few deer, buffalo & birds thrown in. Tue-Sat 9am-5pm, Sun 10am-6pm June-Aug; Wed-Sun, spring and fall.

The Magic House, 516 S Kirkwood Rd, 822-8900. Mon-Thur; Sat 9.30am-5.30pm, Sun 11am-5.30pm. $4.50. 'Illusions, tests and games meant for children. Just as many adults go.'

Missouri Botanical Gardens, Tower Grove & Shaw Ave, 577-9400. 479acres. See the Climatron, first geodesic-domed greenhouse with computer-controlled climates maintained within. Also home of the largest Japanese garden in North America. Summer hrs: 9am-8pm daily; closes at 5pm in winter. $5.

Outdoor Municipal Opera (1500 free seats at the back of the 12,000-seat amphitheatre) holds operettas, ballets, musical comedies and concerts most nights in summer. Call 361-1900 for schedule.

Six Flags Theme Park, St Louis, PO Box 60, Eureka, 938-5300. 30 miles NW of downtown St Louis on I-44. $35 includes all rides and attractions. Daily April-October, Mon-Sat 10am-9pm, Sun 10am-6pm. 'The inverted looping thrill ride Batman is totally awesome!' Tip: go in evening; less humid and possibility of discount. Also check out **Hurricane Harbor**, a huge new waterpark. Admission free with Six Flags admission.

St Louis Science Center, south-east corner of Forest Park, 289-4444. Daily Mon/Wed/Thur 9am-6pm, Tue-Fri 'til 9pm, Sat 10am-9pm, Sun 10am-6pm; free.

Union Station, Market St, btwn 18th and 20th, recently completed restoration of 19th century Gothic train station (it was once the world's largest train station!) Now full of shops, restaurants and old railroad cars.

Just across the river from St. Louis lies the historic town of **St Charles**. Founded in 1769, St Charles whisks visitors back to the days when riverboats ruled the Midwest and 'prairie schooners' cruised the newly-settled western lands. Today the red-brick streets of Missouri's largest historic district are flanked with shops and restaurants. Visit the **Lewis and Clark Center**, 701 Riverside Dr, 947-3199, for historical background and hands-on activities about their incredible journey. St Charles is also home to the **First Missouri State Capitol**, 200 S Main, 946-9282, the seat of state government from 1821-1826. While in St Charles, eat at the **Trailhead Brewing Co**, 921 Riverside Dr, 946-2739. Open Mon-Thur 11am-10pm, Fri-Sat 'til 11pm. In the nearby town of **Defiance** is the **Daniel Boone Home**, 987-2221, built by the famous pioneer and his son. The elder Boone lived there until his 1820 death.

ENTERTAINMENT

Gateway Riverboat Cruises, below Gateway Arch, 621-4040. The oldest excursion company on the Mississippi offers sightseeing trips of varying duration and price on one of its three boats, *Huck Finn, Tom Sawyer* and the *Belle of St Louis*; 1 hr sightseeing tour $8.50; $32.50 for the cruise, including prime-rib dinner and band.

Paddlewheel steamboat trips are easy to find in St Louis, most of the boats dock in front of the arch.

St Louis nightlife unfolds on three different stages: **University City Loop**, the **Central West End**, and **Laclede's Landing.** U-City Loop draws a lot of college students. Twenty-somethings head to the Central West End (also popular with gay crowds), and the Landing draws an older crowd. **Have a Nice Day Cafe**, 20th and Market Sts, crosses some of the age boundaries for spring break-style fun.

St Louis' best efforts at recreating the European disco scene can be found along **Washington Street** in the Landing. One to try: **The Cheetah.** Also in the Landing is a massive **Blues Festival** held each September. Call **St. Louis Blues Society** on 241-2583 for details.

INFORMATION
Fun Phone, 421-2100. Gives a roundup of events and entertainment.
Missouri Tourism Bureau, 869-7100/ (800) 877-1234.
St Louis Convention and Visitors Commission, 10 S Broadway, Suite 300, 421-1023 or (800) 247-9791.
Travelers Aid, 702 N Tucker Blvd, 241-5820.
Visitors Center at Gateway Arch, 655-1700.

INTERNET ACCESS
The Grind, 56 Maryland Plaza, 454-0202. Free access at cybercafe in hip Central West End, 20 min limit.

TRAVEL
Amtrak, 550 S 16th St, (800) 872-7245. Service to Chicago, New Orleans, Dallas, Denver and Kansas City; station closes at midnight.
Bi-State Transit, 231-2345, runs the city buses with basic fare of $1.25.
Greyhound, 1450 N 31st St, (800) 231-2222. Open 24 hrs.
Metrolink, also run by Bi-State, is the new light railway that can take you to most of the major sights. $1.25 basic fare, 10¢ transfer; day pass valid for both bus and Metro, $4.
Lambert/St Louis International Airport, 426-8000. About 10 miles from downtown and serviced by Bi-State buses and Metrolink: the easiest way is to take the Metro to the new airport station or catch the 'Natural Bridge'
#4 bus on Broadway and Locust, journey time of about 1¹/₂ hr, $1.25 for both. Greyhound also runs buses from their terminal, $9, approx 20 mins.

HANNIBAL   Mark Twain (*ne* Samuel Clemens) spent his boyhood in Hannibal; his adopted hometown flogs Twainiana for all it's worth. Though flagrantly commercial, it's good-natured hucksterism for the most part. The old rogue would no doubt approve, being no stranger to exaggeration himself: 'Recently someone sent me a picture of the house I was born in. Heretofore I have always stated that it was a palace but I shall be more guarded now.'

Twain's mother was a descendant of the Earls of Durham, who occupied Lambton Castle; his father's ancestors included one of the judges who delivered Charles I to the hands of an executioners. Nevertheless, the Clemens family settled in modest Hannibal, where 'everybody was poor but didn't know it, and everyone was comfortable and did know it.'

Hannibal teems with classic Americana; as Twain writes, it's 'a little democracy which was full of liberty, equality and the Fourth of July'. Tom, Huck and Becky's old stomping grounds recall pleasant memories of white-washed fences and frog races. Visit the Becky Thatcher House and Judge Clemens' law office. Eschew Tom Sawyer's cave (2 miles out of town and decidedly unspooky) and take a 1hr boat trip on the Mississippi: departures at 11am, 1.30pm and 4pm (boards ¹/₂ hr before), $8.50; (573)221-3222. 2 hr dinner cruise tours are also available for $26 (inc. band). Bar extra.
Mark Twain's Boyhood Home and Museum, 206 Hill Street, (573)221-9010, is worth a look-in. The $6 ticket includes admission to the boyhood home and museum, plus Judge Clemens' law office, Grant's Drug Store and the new Mark Twain Museum, featuring 15 original Norman Rockwell paint-

ings. 8am-6pm daily.

Twilight Zone time: MT's birth coincided with the appearance of Halley's Comet. Throughout his life, Twain predicted he would go out as he had come in. In 1910, right on cue, the comet reappeared and Twain snuffed it. *www.webcom.com/twainweb/* provides historical and current city info as well as in-depth details and guides. Hannibal Convention and Visitors Bureau, 221-2477.

The telephone area code is 573.

KANSAS CITY   Kansas City is the heart of America. Located within 250 mi of both the population and geographic centres of the US, Kansas City is less than 1900 miles (half the distance from the east coast to the west coast) from every US city. The Missouri River divides the city providing a neighbour with the same name, Kansas City, KS. The spirit of America plays heavily on the Missouri side—suburbs have names like Liberty and Independence. Envelope-maker for the world, international headquarters for Hallmark, and home base of the baseballers, the Kansas City Royals, it's also an important cattle market. No trip to the Midwest is complete without a pilgrimage to Arthur Bryant's, the Holy Grail of barbequedom and a sufficient reason for visiting the city. In fact, *www.rbjb.com/rbjb/ab2.htm* takes you to Bryant's personal homepage, with an amusing read of the history behind the restaurant and even photos of the renowned Arthur Bryant's barbecue sauce!

Once part of a great blues and jazz triangle with New Orleans and Chicago, KC nurtured the careers of Count Basie, Duke Ellington, Charlie 'Bird' Parker. KC's sister city is Seville, Spain, which explains the preponderance of Moorish arches, Spanish tiles and ornamental fountains around the Country Club Plaza. Try as they might, the Spanish architectural additions are unable to stifle the all-American spirit of the city.

The telephone area code is 816.

ACCOMMODATION
Motel 6, 6400 E 87th St, 333-4468. From S-$40, D-$46. XP-$3.
Super 8 Motel, 6900 NW 83 Terrace, NW Kansas City, 587-0808. From S-$53, D-$59. 5 miles from airport. One of several Super 8s in the area. Another is **Super 8 Motel**, 4032 S Lynn Court Drive, Independence, 833-1888. From S-$50, D-$54.

FOOD
Annie's Santa Fe, 100 W Ward Pkwy on the Country Club Plaza, 753-1621. Huge portions of Tex-Mex cuisine. Order the Macho Nachos. Open Sun noon-5pm, Mon 11am-7pm, Tues.-Thur 11am-9pm, Fri-Sat 'til 10pm.
Arthur Bryant Barbecue, 1727 Brooklyn Ave at 17th, 231-1123. A sensational place to eat barbecue. Hot, grainy opaque sauce (which you'll see ageing in the window). Get lots of sauce and take time to look at the memorabilia on the walls. A cartoon depicts Arthur entering heaven, with St. Peter asking him if he brought any sauce with him. 'World class BBQ ribs, swooning beef brisket sandwiches. Go on, stuff yourself!' Open Mon-Thur 10am-9:30pm, Fri-Sat 'til 10pm, Sun 11am-8pm. *www.rbjb.com/rbjb/ab2.htm*
Dixon's Chilli, 9105 E 40 Hwy, 861-7308. Many locales in KC. Harry Truman loved KC chilli—cheap and savoury. Open Mon-Sat 10am-10pm.
Fric and Frac, 1700 W 39th St, 753-6102. Special deals each night; tacos, shrimp dinners, 2-for-1 burger meals, bfast. 'Ideal place for mixing with the locals.' Open Mon-Thur 11am-midnight, Fri-Sat 'til 1.30am.

LC's Barbecue, 5800 Ward Pkwy, 923-4484. When all the tourists hit Arthur Bryant's, true barbecue aficionados head to LC's. A hole in the wall, but exquisite barbecue! Open Mon-Sat 11:30am-9:30pm.

KC Masterpiece, 4747 Wyandotte on the Country Club Plaza, 531-3332. Another great choice for BBQ, its sauce is mass-marketed throughout the US. Open Mon-Thur 11am-10pm, Fri-Sat 'til 11pm, Sun 'til 9:30pm.

Kansas Machine Shed, 12080 S Strang Line Rd in Olathe, KS, (913)780-2697. Authentic farm favourites served in a farm-like setting. Open Mon-Sat 6am-10pm, Sun 7am-9pm.

Leona Yarbrough Restaurant, 2800 W 53rd St, Shawnee Mission, (913) 722-4800. 'Has been a long time bastion of heartland cooking with a feminine touch.' From homey chicken noodle soup and fresh-baked bread to old-fashioned lattice-top apple pie, dinners of braised lamb shank, turkey divan and excellent fried chicken. Menu printed daily.

Otto's Malt Shop, 3903 Wyoming, 756-1010. Built in a vintage 1930's gas station with 50's and 60's decor and music. The definitive milk shake/malt/pancake shop in KC. Cheap food, bfast, lunch and dinner specials. 'With a good atmosphere, make this the perfect place to hang out.' Open daily, 10am-10pm.

River Market Brewing Company, 500 Walnut, 471-6300. Kitchen open daily 11am-10pm, bar closes around 3am.

OF INTEREST

Country Club Plaza, btwn Main St & SW Expressway. Oldest shopping mall in the US. Huge Spanish-style plaza with fountains, genuine Iberian art, beautiful night lighting, interesting food and shops (200 of 'em). At **47th & Nicholas**, a copy of the Giralda Tower in Seville. **47th and Central:** Spanish murals, exquisite sevillano tilework depicting the bullfight. Splendid display of lights at Christmas. *www.countryclubplaza.com*.

Crown Center, Main and Pershing Rd. 'City within a city,' built by those friendly people at Hallmark Cards. Hotel, shops, 5-storey waterfall, indoor gardens, restaurants, etc. In December, it features the nation's tallest Christmas tree. 'Go Sat mornings when woodcarvers, artists, etc are at work.' Attached to it is the **Hallmark Visitors Center**, 274-5672. Mon-Fri 9am-5pm, Sat 9.30am-4.30pm. Lots of exhibits showing how the company grew big, peddling sentiment and gushing rhymes.

Independence, a few miles east of KC and one-time home of that well-known haberdasher Harry Truman. The library and museum contain presidential papers; his grave is in the courtyard. 30 min slide and sound show, *The Man From Missouri*, hourly at the Jackson County Courthouse, 795-8200, $1. The Harry S Truman Home is located at 223 N Main, 254-2720, $2. Round out your Truman experience by visiting the Harry S Truman Library and Museum, 24 Hwy and Delaware St, 833-1400, $5.

Museum of History and Science, 3218 Gladstone Blvd, 483-8300. Tue-Sat, 9.30am-4.30pm, Sun noon-4.30pm; $2.50, $2 w/ student ID. Housed in the 72-room mansion of lumber king RA Long, are exhibits on natural, regional history, and anthropology. Crawl-through igloo, other good native American stuff.

Nelson Atkins Museum of Fine Art, 45th Terrace & Oak Sts, 561-4000. Huge variety, especially of oriental art and crafts. Outdoor sculpture garden is great with its fine Henry Moore collection. Tues.-Thur 10am-4pm, Fri 10am-9pm, Sat 10am-5pm, Sun 1pm-5pm; $5, $2 w/student ID. Free on Sat.

The Livestock Exchange and Stockyards are at 12th & Genessee. If the smell doesn't remove your appetite, the **Golden Ox** next door has good if somewhat pricey steaks.

ENTERTAINMENT

Catch the casino craze! KC's location along the Missouri river make it a prime spot for riverboat casino-hopping. Some to try: **The Argosy Riverside,** 746-3100, **Harrah's North,** 472-7777, **Sam's Town,** 414-7777, and **Station,** 414-7000.

Westport, original city heart btwn 39th & 45th Sts, is famous for good taverns and nightlife. Or try **Grand Emporium**, 3832 Main St, 531-1504; good bands. With luck, you may catch the **Jazz Pub Crawl** in May or Sept, a night of hopping in and out of 30 clubs with hot live jazz. Shuttle buses transport you safely from one to the next at your leisure.

Kelly's Irish Pub, 500 Westport Rd, 561-0635. Cheap drink and a friendly atmosphere.
Stanford and Sons, 504 Westport Rd, 756-1450. Great music, and 2-for-1 drinks.

INFORMATION/TRAVEL
Amtrak, 2200 Main St, 421-3622/(800) 872-7245. For trains to St Louis, Chicago, and even LA.
Convention and Visitors Bureau, 1100 Main, Suite #2550, 221-5242.
Greyhound, 1101 Troost St, 221-2835/(800) 231-2222.
Kansas City Area Transportation Authority (Metro), 221-0660.
Kansas City International Airport, 243-5237, about 18 miles from the city. Take the #29 Metro bus from downtown (90c), about 1hr. The KCI Shuttle, 243-5000, picks up from major downtown hotels and costs $12 o/w; a taxi will cost you about $30.
Kansas City Trolley, 221-3399, $9 will get you a day of unlimited rides. 'Drivers are very friendly and give an interesting commentary.'
KC Funline, 691-3800.

INTERNET ACCESS
The Net @afe, 13344 College Blvd, Lenexa, KS (913)339-9310. Open 1pm-midnight Mon-Fri, 10am-1am Sat, noon-8pm Sun. $4/ 30 min, $6/hr.

ST JOSEPH   Over 100 young masochists applied to a less-than-appealing ad that read: 'Wanted: young skinny wiry fellows, not over 18. Must be expert riders willing to risk death daily. Orphans preferred. Wages $25/week. Apply Central Overland Express.' Thus, on 3 April 1860, the Pony Express was born. Composed of 80 riders, 500 horses, 190 stations and 400 station hands, the Pony Express decreased the average delivery time of a letter from the east to California from 8 weeks to 10 days and played a crucial role in aligning California with the Union during the Civil War. Although the 2000 mile Missouri to California mail delivery system was only in operation for 18 months, it left a lasting impression on the world. **Pony Express Museum** at 914 Penn Street, (816) 279-5059, preserves the original stables and other interesting memorabilia, well worth a visit; Mon-Sat 9am-5pm, Sun 1pm-5pm, $3. Same day, different year in St Joe, Bob Ford shot Jesse James for a $10,000 reward. The house where the shot was fired is now the **Jesse James Home Museum**, 12th & Penn, (816) 232-8206, which is full of original Jamesabilia and even has the hole left by the bullet in the wall. It's also the site of the Pony Express headquarters in 1860; Mon-Sat 10am-5pm, Sun 1pm-5pm, $3.
The telephone area code is 816.

BRANSON   A postcard from Branson jokingly quips, 'Would the last one leaving Nashville for Branson please turn off the light?' Much of Branson (like this postcard) is a little bit corny, but it's dead-on right. Branson proclaims itself the live entertainment capital of America. With over 30 theatres hosting over 60 shows, Branson has more theatre seats than Broadway.

While Branson was originally touted as a country music mecca, the entertainers also dazzle you with comedy, dance and magic. Branson is proud of its image as a source of wholesome family entertainment; its location in the heart of the beautiful Ozark Mountain region supports this claim with camping and outdoors activities for all ages. The shows are many and varied, but perennial favourites include the **Andy Williams Moon River Theatre**, 2500 W 76 Hwy, 334-4500, the **Jim Stafford Theatre**, 3440 W 76 Hwy, 335-8080, and the **Shoji Tabuchi Theatre**, 3260 Shepherd of the Hills Expy, 334-7469. Stop at Shoji's to use the bathrooms! They're like nothing you've ever seen. Show tickets can be pricey— look for discounts at the tourist information centres and ticket outlets scattered throughout town.

In addition to live entertainment, Branson is a great place for outlet shopping. Leading names such as Ralph Lauren, the Gap, and J Crew have set up shop in Branson's 3 outlet malls, each located conveniently off Hwy 76. (Beware the main drag during the summer months, though— viscous traffic clogs the strip, making it impossible to get anywhere).

Branson has made a point of capitalising on the natural splendour of the Ozarks and the lively history of its pioneer past. Branson's hottest attraction, **Silver Dollar City**, Hwy 76 at Indian Point Rd, (800)952-6626, a theme park staged in pioneer days, was honoured as the 1998-99 top theme park in the world by the International Association of Amusement Parks and Attractions. Located just outside of Branson, Silver Dollar City provides the perfect balance of live entertainment, thrill rides, shopping and country cooking in jumbo proportions, $31 (look for discount coupons and promotions at ticket outlets)Also included in the admission price to Silver Dollar City is an hour-long tour of **Marvel Cave**, a geological wonder upon which the theme park was built. Journeying down into the cave is not for the weak— you'll have to climb about 600 stairs!

One of the Ozarks' most popular attractions is **Lambert's**, 1800 W Hwy J, Ozark, 581-7655, a spunky restaurant located north of Branson on Hwy 65, about 10 miles south of Springfield. Lambert's is the home of the 'throwed rolls'; as you're munching on mammoth-sized portions of country favourites, waiters toss soft, piping hot rolls to hungry diners. *Area code is 417.*

CAVES Missouri is blessed with more known caves than any other state, many with guided tours to keep you from getting lost and driving up the owners' insurance premiums. For more information, write Missouri Division of Tourism, PO Box 1055, Jefferson City, MO 65102, or call (573) 751-4133. Some examples: **Bluff Dwellers' Cave**, 2 miles S of Noel, (417) 475-3666. A 45 min tour includes stalactite curtains, corals, 10-ton balanced rock, as well as a 54-foot rimstone dam; $7, open daily 8am-6pm. **Fantastic Caverns**, 4 miles N of Springfield, (417) 833-2010. They are as good as their name implies, and you don't even have to walk! Propane-run jeeps transport visitors through the caves in modern comfort; $14. Open daily 8am-8pm. **Meramec Caverns**, Stanton, (573) 468-3166; '1½ hr tour, lots of stunning formations in calcite and onyx including a very large botryoidal formation and 70 ft high stalactite; $12, well worth it!' Open daily 8:30am-7:30pm. For more in-depth details about each state park, check out the official state parks listing at *www.mostateparks.com*.

NEBRASKA   *The Cornhusker State*

A huge, tilting plate of a state, Nebraska rises from 840 ft at its Missouri River eastern border to nearly 5000 ft as it approaches the Rockies. Through it runs the feeble Platte River, 'a mile wide, a foot deep, too thick to swim and too thin to plow', along which countless buffalo roamed until done in by kill-crazy Buffalo Bills. As shallow as 6 inches in places, the Platte nonetheless made an excellent 'highway' and water supply for the 2.5 million folks who crossed Nebraska in Conestoga wagons, 1840-66. Even today, the most worthwhile things to see in the state are those connected with the pioneer trails west.

There's poetry in these plains, though. Willa Cather, one of the most skilful wordsmiths of the pioneer days used south central Nebraska as the backdrop for her many of her works. Six of her twelve novels and many of her short stories are staged in Red Cloud and Webster County, where she spent the formative years of her life. Cather recognised the beauty in the land around her: 'As I looked about me I felt that the grass was the country, as the water is the sea. The red grass made all the great prairie the colour of wine stains...And there was so much motion in it; the whole country seemed, somehow, to be running.'

Like the other plains states, Nebraska has perfectly miserable weather in the summer and winter. Its speciality is hailstones, which occasionally reach the size of golf balls. A leading producer of beef cattle, TV dinners and popcorn, Nebraska specialises in silos of both the grain and ICBM missile variety. *www.yahoo.com/Regional/U_S__States/Nebraska/*

OMAHA   Once a jumping-off place for pioneers, Omaha is the Union Pacific train headquarters and has taken over the noisome title of 'meat packer for the world' from Chicago. Friendly, yes, but about as lively at night as a hog carcass, except around Old Market.

Hometown of Fred Astaire, Malcolm X and Warren Buffett (the second-richest man in the US, behind Bill Gates), Omaha is the place where Father Flanagan started Boys Town, a home for troubled youth later immortalised by a Spencer Tracy movie of the same name. On a not-so-philanthropic note, it's also the underground Strategic Air Command (SAC) headquarters. A collection of aerial photos of Omaha, Omaha links and a photo map can be accessed thru *www.novia.net/~sadams/Omaha_Pages/ OMA_Pics.html*. Well worth it! *The telephone area code is 402.*

ACCOMMODATION
Ak-sar-ben Super 8, 7111 Spring St, (800)800-8000. The astute reader will notice that the name spells 'Nebraska' backwards. From D-$55.

The Bellevue Campground, Haworth Park, 291-3379, on the Missouri River 10 miles N of downtown at Rt 370. Use the infrequent 'Bellevue' bus from 17th and Dodge to Mission and Franklin, and walk down Mission. Right next to the Missouri. Camp sites-$5 tent, $10 RV w/hook-up.

Economy Inn, 2211 Douglas St, 345-9565. Not the best of areas, but very convenient to downtown. From S/D-$42. Stay 5 nights and next 2 nights are free. Weekly rate S-$175.

Motel 6, 10708 M St, 331-3161. From S-$38, D-$44.
Satellite Motel, 6006 L St, 733-7373. S-$38, D-$42.
YMCA, 430 S 20th, 341-1600. S-$12 (+ $10 key deposit). Weekly rate of $88 (+ $10 key deposit). Pool, 5 mins from Greyhound. 'New, clean, pleasant.'

FOOD/ENTERTAINMENT
Try the cobbled streets of the Old Market, on Howard St, btwn 10th & 13th Sts, for shops, restaurants and bars that maintain the ambience of 19th century Omaha.
Bohemian Cafe, 1406 S 13th St, 342-9838. 'Czech food and atmosphere—the duck is superb.' Lunches for $4, dinners $6-$8.
Delice European Bakery, 1206 Howard, 342-2276, a great place for dessert! Open Mon-Thur 8am-10pm, Fri-Sat 'til midnight, Sun 'til 7pm.
The Diner, 409 S 12th St, 341-9870. For a true diner experience for under $3 for lunch. Open 6pm-4am.
Dubliner Pub, 1205 Harney St, 342-5887. A good place to shoot darts. 150 imported beers. Open 11am-1am.
Garden Cafe, 1212 Harney St, 422-1603. 'Wholesome breakfast' for $3, dinners for $6. Sun-Thur 6am-9pm, Fri-Sat 'til 10.
The Great Wall, 1013 Farnam St, 346-2161, has good Chinese food. Weekday lunch buffet ($6), w/end dinner buffet ($7). Mon-Sat 11am-10pm, Sun 5pm-10pm.
Johnny's, 4702 S 27th St, 731-4774. Omaha's Stockyard's steak house for three-quarters of a century. Every cut of steak available. Open Mon-Sat for lunch, 11am-2pm, for dinner Mon-Thur 5pm-10pm, Fri-Sat 'til 10:30pm.
Spaghetti Works, 502 S 11th St in Old Market, 422-0770. $4.50 lunch, $6 dinner buys pasta, garlic bread and salad bar. Also one in suburban Ralston, off I-80at 84th St and Park Drive. Open Sun-Thur 11am-10pm, Fri-Sat 'til 11pm.
Stella's Hamburgers, 106 Galvin Rd, Bellevue, 291-6088, one of the last of a dying breed of roadside American diners. Open Tues.-Sun 11am-8pm, Mon 'til 3pm.

OF INTEREST
Boys Town, 137th St and W Dodge Rd, 498-1140. Founded in 1917 by Father Flanagan, this home for troubled youth is now a historic landmark. Includes Hall of History, featuring Spencer Tracy's Oscar from 1938portrayal of Flanagan, as well as stamp and coin museum. May-August. Tours daily 8am-5.30pm; free. 'Very interesting.'
General Crook House, 30th & Fort, 455-9990, Italianate brick mansion, with beautiful Victorian gardens stands on the site of Fort Omaha; built in 1879 by the outpost's first commander, General George Crook. Mon-Sat 10am-4pm, Sun 1pm-4pm, $3.50.
Henry Doorly Zoo, 10th and Dear Park Blvd, 733-8400. Contains rare white Bengal tigers and a $4^1/_2$acre aviary, the world's second largest, and 'Lied Jungle', a simulated tropical rain forest with the accompanying wildlife. 9.30am-5pm daily summers; 'til 6pm Sun/hol. Visitors can remain in the park for two hrs after the park has closed; $7.25.
Joslyn Art Museum, 2200 Dodge St, 342-3300. Housed in Art Deco building, Indian and other art; pictures painted during the Maximillian Expedition up the Missouri River in 1833-4are worth seeing. Free jazz Thur eves in July/August. Tue-Sun 10am-4pm, Thur 'til 8pm; $9, $7.50 w/ student ID.
Old Market, 10th & Howard. Cobbled streets, warehouses recycled into smart shops, galleries, restaurants. 'Most interesting place in Omaha.' See where oft eulogised and misrepresented black leader **Malcolm X**—ne Malcolm Little—was born, 3448 Pinkey St. Then see the wider picture, **Great Plains Black Museum**, 2213 Lake St, 345-2212, has extensive exhibits on the black experience, including profiles of black cowboys, athletes and soldiers; Mon-Fri 8.30am-5pm, $2.
Orpheum Theater, 409 S 16th St, 444-4750. An ornate theatre featuring concerts, ballet, plays.

Strategic Air Command Museum, Exit 426 off of I-80, Ashland (between Omaha and Lincoln), 827-3100. Opened in 1998, the museum houses bombers, missiles, a *red phone* (hear the end of the world!) and the SR-71 Blackbird, the world's fastest plane. 'Nuclear nightmare at its *finest*! A must-see!' 9am-5pm daily; $6.

Western Heritage Museum, 801 S 10th St, 444-5071. Housed in the wonderful Art Deco old Union Station, worth a look in itself, this museum has displays on Omaha and Nebraska history. Also home to the **Union Pacific Historical Museum.** Lots of Lincoln memorabilia including replica of his funeral car with original furnishings, plus oddments. Mon-Fri 9am-3pm, Sat 9am-noon; free. Tues.-Sat 10am-5pm, Sun 1am-5pm, $3. Closed Mon.

INFORMATION/TRAVEL
Amtrak, 1003 S 9th St, (800) 872-7245.
Events Hotline, 444-6800.
Greyhound, 16th & Jackson, (800) 231-2222.
Nebraska Tourist Information, (800) 228-4307.
Student Center, U of Nebraska, 60th and Dodge Sts, 554-2383. Helpful with accommodation, rides, general info.
Visitors Bureau, 6800 Mercy Road, #202, (800) 332-1819.

INTERNET ACCESS
Omaha Public Library, 2918 N 60th St, 444-4846. Free.

LINCOLN The Nebraska State Capitol Building dominates this cow town and its many miles of surrounding plains. This is home of the Unicameral, Nebraska's unique one-house, non-partisan legislative body—an improvisation made during the Depression to save money.

The capitol, 'Tower on the Plains', was not blown in by tornado, despite what its incongruent appearance may suggest, but architect Bertram Goodhue did come all the way from New York City in 1920 to design this early 'skyscraper'. The broad base of the building represents the plains; the tower the aspirations of the pioneers.

Lincoln was home to William Jennings Bryan, a turn-of-the-century populist who three times was the Democratic Party's presidential candidate and finally made a monkey of himself at the notorious Scopes Trial in Tennessee. His house stands at 4900 Summer Street. For a virtual tour of downtown Lincoln, click on *http://db.4w.com/lincolntour/*
The telephone area code is 402.

ACCOMMODATION
Visit the Nebraska Association of B&Bs at *www.bbonline.com/ne/nabb* or call (402) 843-2287.
Cornerstone Youth Hostel, 640 N 16th St, on U of Nebraska campus, 476-0926. $10 member, $13 non-member. 11pm curfew.
The Great Plains Budget Host Inn, 2732 O St, 476-3253; large rooms w/small fridges. S-$38/40, D-$46.
The Town House Motel, 1744 M St at 18th, 475-3000. Super-suites with full kitchen, bath, living room and TV. S-$45, D-$50.
Camping: Nebraska State Fair Park Campground, Exit #399, 1402 N 14th St, 473-4287. April-October. Sites $15 for two w/hook-up; **Camp-A-Way**, 1st & W Superior, Exits #401 & #401-A, 200 Ogden Rd, (402) 476-2282. Open year round. Sites $10.
Cheap motels abound on **Cornhusker Hwy**, around the 5600 block (E of downtown).

FOOD
The Coffee House, 1324 P St, 477-6611, is a favourite hangout for locals. Muffin

mania for $1, and a great 'capalpacino' ($1.50)! Mon-Sat 7am-midnight, Sun 11am-midnight.

PO Pears, 322 S 9th St, 476-8551. A college hangout with cheap beer, good burgers, and live music. Open 11.30am-1am.

Rock 'n' Roll Runza, 210 W 14th St, 474-2030. Roller-skating waitresses, and their infamous foot-long chilli cheese dogs ($5). Sun-Thur 10.30am-9pm; Fri/Sat 'til 10:30; serving brunch 10am 'til 2pm.

OF INTEREST

Roller-Skating National Museum, 4730 South St, 483-7551. See the world's largest collection of roller skates, including skates on stilts. Free; Mon-Fri 9am-5pm.

Sheldon Memorial Art Gallery, 12th and R Sts, 472-2461. Houses a fine collection of 20th century American art and sculpture garden. Tues.-Sat 10am-5pm; Thur-Sat also 7pm-9pm; Sun, 2pm-9pm; free.

State Capitol, located btwn 14th & K Sts, 471-0448. In Art Deco style with a bit of everything inside. Mon-Fri 8am-4pm, Sat 10am-4pm, Sun 1pm-4pm; guided tours on the hour (every $1/2$hr w/days in summer).

ENTERTAINMENT

Stroll around the restored 19th century commercial buildings in historic **Haymarket Square District,** between 7th and 9th Sts, from O to R Sts, 435-7496. Today they're home to galleries, restaurants, unique shops, and antiques.

There are several night-spots in Lincoln, among them the notorious **Barry's Bar and Grill**, 235 N 9th St, 476-6511. Mon-Sat 11am-1am. For good music try **The Zoo Bar**, 136 N 14th St, 435-8754, with a cover charge of $4-8. Mon-Fri 3pm-1am, Sat noon-1am. **The Panic**, 2005 18th St, 435-8764, at N, is a great gay dance/video/patio bar. Daily 4pm-1am.

Check out some of these annual events: **Annual Boat, Sport, Travel Show**, Nebraska State Fair Park. Displays of outdoor fun-boats, fishing, camping and other sporting activities. Admission charged. Call (402) 466-8102; **Chocolate Lover's Fantasy**, Ramada, 9th & P St. This festive event features Lincoln celebrities, chefs, and fabulous chocolate in every form with a live and silent auction. Begins 5pm. Call (402) 434-6900; **Jazz in June**, Sheldon Sculpture Garden. Free outdoor concerts featuring well known jazz vocalists and musicians each Tue in June, 7pm-9pm. Call (402) 434-6900.

INFORMATION/TRAVEL

Amtrak, 201 N 7th, (800) 872-7245.

Chamber of Commerce, 1135 M St, #200, 436-2350.

Greyhound, 940 P St, (800) 231-2222.

Lincoln Convention and Visitors Bureau, 1135 M St, #300, 434-5335.

Tourist Information Center, 700 S 16th St, 471-3796.

INTERNET ACCESS

Bennett Martin Public Library, 136 S 14th St, 441-8500. Free.

ALONG THE PIONEER AND PONY EXPRESS TRAILS   The Oregon, Mormon and other pioneer trails plus the Pony Express routes followed the Platte River, which today is paralleled in large part by I-80and by Hwys 30 E and 26 W.

The land outside of Omaha lies flat and covered with farms. If you like corn, you'll be in heaven here. Two and a half hours west from Omaha, in the town of **Grand Island** on Hwy 34, is the **Stuhr Museum of the Prairie Pioneer**, (308) 385-5316, an 1890s frontier village often used in Hollywood western sets. $7.25. Picnic area.

Sixty miles south of Grand Island and 6 miles north of the Kansas border is the town of **Red Cloud,** home of Pulitzer prize-winning author Willa Cather, who deftly chronicled frontier life in her books, *O Pioneers!* and *My Antonia*, among others. The small town of 1200 people boasts 26 sites in the National Registry of Historic Places. The western half of Webster County, 14 miles north of Red Cloud, was dubbed 'Catherland' by the Nebraska State Legislature in 1965. It's one of the largest historical districts dedicated to an author in the United States. An inscription at the **Willa Cather Pioneer Memorial** quotes the author: 'The history of every country begins in the heart of a man or a woman.' Guided tours explore 5 restored buildings, including Cather's childhood home. $1; Call (402)746-2653. *www.willa-cather.org.*

Going east to west: at **Gothenburg** in midstate, you can see two original Pony Express stations (one at 96 Ranch St) and an old stagecoach stop with bullet holes still in the walls. At **Lafayette City Park**, free camping. **North Platte**, long-time home of scout and show biz personality Buffalo Bill Cody, offers a free look at his ranch house—a pretty but prissy-looking Victorian affair, $2.50 per vehicle entrance fee, (308) 535-8035. Open daily, 10am-8pm. B Bill got his nickname for killing 4280 buffalo in 17 months while employed by the railroad to supply meat for its crews.

As you push westward to **Bayard**, the Oregon Trail Wagon Train company offers 1-and 4-day treks that circle **Chimney Rock**. Meals (including pioneer items like vinegar pie and hoecakes), wagon driving or riding, and other activities from an Indian 'attack' to prairie square-dancing for about $150 a day. They also do 3 hr covered wagon tours to Chimney Rock and back, for $8pp (min 5people); leaving at 8am, returning noon. Evening dinner tours are also available, $18. Book through Oregon Trail Wagon Train, Rt 2, PO Box 502, Bayard, NE 69334 or call (308) 586-1850.

Scotts Bluff and **Chimney Rock**, off US 26 in western Nebraska, are two rock formations that served as landmarks for the frontier families. Both are climbable with poignant pioneer graves and clearly defined wagon ruts. The park rangers at Scotts Bluff give daily lectures in summer and the pioneer campsite can be visited. Spectacular views from the bluff.

Box Butte County in the Nebraska panhandle offers one of the most unique sights you'll see on your trek across America. It's home to **Carhenge,** in which stones are represented by 1950s and 60s automobiles, planted in the ground trunk down. The result: a circle of cars with almost the same dimensions as the 4000 year old British model. Jim Reinders, the genius behind this attraction that draws 80,000 visitors annually, used cars because there aren't any stones in the area. Open daily (free). If you journey out to Box Butte County for a taste of synthetic Britain, take time for a taste of real America. The **Mato Yamni Village,** 128 Potash, (308)762-3242, in Alliance was created to preserve and celebrate the old ways of the Lakota Indians. Learn about tepee building, cooking, hunting, deerskin tanning and bead making, then complete your experience by staying overnight in a tepee.

NORTH DAKOTA *The Rough Rider State*

Virtually border to border farmland, interspersed with missile sites, North Dakota grows lots of wheat, sugar beets and cattle. Its superlatives aren't exactly the kind to make you rush up here; although it has no notable national monuments, it does have the world's largest concrete buffalo (in Jamestown), concrete Holstein (in New Salem) and steel turtle with movable head (40,000 lbs in Dunseith). Not to mention the longest road without a curve—110 miles of tedium on Rte 46.

The fertile east is more densely populated than the west, first settled by land-hungry Europeans who capitalised on the Homestead Act of 1862. It's also the east that bore the brunt of the damage of the horrific 1997 flood: 1.7 million acres of farmland were devastated, and the whole state was declared a disaster area.

The Badlands of North Dakota aren't as well-known as their counterparts in South Dakota, but they are strikingly beautiful, with hills and valleys interspersed amongst the dusty rocks. Teddy Roosevelt owned a ranch out here before he entered political life, sparking his lifelong interest and commitment to environmental issues. 'I never would have been president,' he said, 'if it had not been for my experiences in North Dakota.'
www.yahoo.com/Regional/U_S__States/north_dakota/
The telephone area code for the state is 701.

BISMARCK The capital city's name was originally Edwinton, later changed to Bismarck by the secretary of the Northern Pacific Railroad who had a plan to secure Deutschmarks from Otto von B to finance railroad construction and attract Teutonic settlers. The first part was successful, the latter was not, and the name stuck. Bismarck overcame an early period of lawlessness and a major fire to become the state capital.

ACCOMMODATION
AmericInn, 3235 State St, 250-1000. From D-$50.
Hillside Motel, 1601 N 12th St, 223-7986. From D-$37.

OF INTEREST
State Capitol Building, 328-2480. Famous sons and daughters in the Rough-rider gallery: Eric Sevareid, Peggy Lee, Lawrence Welk, Roger Maris. Take the elevator to the 19th floor to the observation deck and see for miles and miles over the prairies. Mon-Fri 8am-4pm, Sat 9am-4pm, Sun 1-4pm; free.
North Dakota Heritage Center (on Capitol grounds), 328-2666, has an Indian collection called one of the finest in the world. Many personal effects of Sitting Bull. Not to be missed: the Indian crafts store—outstanding and authentic artefacts for sale. Mon-Fri 8am-5pm, Sat 9am-5pm, Sun 11am-5pm; free. United Tribes International performs a **pow-wow** in early Sept, where you can see native Americans dance, play drums and chant in full costume. Others take place sporadically at Indian reservations, check with tribal offices at Ft Totten, Turtle Mountain and others.

INFORMATION/TRAVEL
Amtrak, 400 1st Ave SW, Minot, (800) 872-7245. The nearest station to Bismarck; lies

on the 'Empire Builder' Chicago-Seattle route.

Bismarck Visitors Bureau, 107 West Main St, 222-4308; Open Mon-Fri 8am-5pm.
Greyhound, 3453 Franklin Ave, (800) 231-2222.
North Dakota Tourism Dept, Liberty Memorial Building, near State Capitol, (800) 435-5663.

LEWIS AND CLARK TRAIL   By auto or on foot, you can retrace the explorers' route of 1804-05 south along the Missouri River from Wood River, Illinois. Points of interest include: **Ft Yates** (Sioux national headquarters), **Ft Lincoln** (from which Custer and the 7th Cavalry rode out to defeat), **Ft Mandan** (where the French Canadian trader Touissant Charbonneau and his 15-year old Shoshone wife Sacagawea were hired by Lewis and Clark in the winter of 1804-05), buffalo wallows, **Knife River Indian Village**, and **Sitting Bull Historic Site**, where the leader was originally buried. Great hunters, 600 Sioux braves once killed over 6000 buffalo in three days in 1882. An excellent Indian campground one mile W of Ft Yates at **Long Soldier Coulee Park**, open year-round. *www.lewisandclarktrail.com* takes you through the landmarks in their journey, with further suggestions of what to see along the way. Before taking the trail, be sure to read 'Undaunted Courage' by Stephen E Ambrose, for a breathtaking account of the momentous expedition.

BADLANDS AND ROOSEVELT NATIONAL PARK   Called 'mako sica' (land bad) by the Sioux and 'les mauvais terres a traverser' by French settlers, the Badlands have been forming for over 600,000 years, largely due to erosion by the Little Missouri River. Described as 'grand, dismal and majestic', the Badlands formations are best seen early morning and late afternoon. The south unit near Medora has a 36-mile loop with scenic overlooks. You can catch a glimpse of wild ponies, descendants of those who galloped about the rough terrain in the days of Sitting Bull. You'll also see herds of buffalo and families of prairie dogs scurrying around, oblivious to the tourist's eye. Spend the night in the campground at Cottonwood. The **Roosevelt National Park** honours the President's commitment to wildlife preservation. Concerned by the effects of development on the environment, he started the US Forest Service to monitor the destruction of grasslands and big game species. Compared to the other western National Parks, it's refreshingly low in tourists. Teddy's **Elkhorn Ranch** is very remote; the ranch ultimately showed a net loss of $21,000 but he loved the area, saying: 'I owe more than I can ever express to the men and women of the cow country'. Sully Creek Campground, two miles from Medora: 'Primitive, can get cold but very convenient to Roosevelt if one has a car.'

INTERNATIONAL PEACE GARDENS   On the US/Canadian border—the world's longest non-fortified border. The formal gardens commemorate years of peace between the countries. Enter via **Dunseith**. Daily 8am-10pm; $7per vehicle. Tel: (701) 263-4390. For details on the newest and most scenic route to the Peace Gardens, surf the *www.tradecorridor.com/stjohn* website.

OHIO   *The Buckeye State*

Ohio makes everything and more of it than anybody else: comic books, coffins, Liederkranz cheese, bank vaults, vacuums, false teeth, playing cards, rubber, jet turbine engines, soap, glassware—you name it. Small wonder that Ohio also produced America's first billionaire: John D Rockefeller. They're always tinkering in Ohio, birthplace of the cash register, the fly swatter, the menthol cigarette and the beer can, not to mention one of the Wright brothers, Thomas Edison, John Glenn and Neil Armstrong.

Get out of its highly industrialised cities and you'll discover a surprising amount of green and gentle countryside, full of lakes, wineries (50 of them), farms with roadside produce and local colour from Amish villages. Ohio also houses a fair share of oddities like Hinckley, buzzard capital of the world (where you can satisfy that craving for a buzzard cookie). Sinclair Lewis used Ohio as his model setting for small-town America in *Babbitt*, a novel written in 1922 about a businessman whose individuality is eliminated by Republican pressures to conform.

The state also has some of America's best roller coasters and amusement parks, the largest state fair in the US, over 1000 festivals (including Twinsday at Twinsburg) and is birthplace of eight presidents. No wonder Ohio ranks third in tourism, behind New York and California. *www.yahoo.com/Regional/U_S__States/Ohio/*

CINCINNATI   Unique in being a village that grew to cityhood on steamboat traffic, the Queen City of the West is also unique in having formerly elected Jerry Springer mayor. (True to form, Springer thought the town was too polite). The dual nature of Cincinnati— one of utility and burlesque— is part of its history as a port town. As many as 8000 boats a year docked at Cincinnati to take on passengers, lightning rods and lacy 'French' ironwork destined for New Orleans bordellos. Valued for their transportation capacity, steamboats also provided a few less practical thrills. They were raced incessantly, causing huge sums of money to change hands and equally astonishing losses of life; in one five-year period, 2268 people died in steamboat explosions. Settled by Germans, the 'City of Seven Hills' became a leading producer of machine tools, Ivory soap, beer, gin and a variety of ham favoured by Queen Victoria, all without losing its liveable, likeable essence. Check out Cincinnati events such as the Oktoberfest Zinzinnati (Sept) and the Queen City Blues Festival (July) under *www.gccc.com*
The telephone area code is 513.

ACCOMMODATION
Anna Louise Residence for Women, 300 Lytle St, near the Taft Museum, 421-5211. S-$25.

Calhoun Residence Hall, University of Cincinnati, Calhoun St, 556-5250. Near Clifton Ave, south side of campus, 23 miles N of downtown. Take buses #17, #18, #19, from downtown. AC rooms available; call ahead. $15 per room (bring your own linens and pay only $12), discounts for longer stays. Mention BUNAC.

College of Mount St Joseph, 5701 Delhi Road, 244-4327, 8 miles W of downtown off Rt. 50 on Fairbanks St (it turns into Delhi Pike). Clean rooms in quiet location.

S-$25, D-$30. Call for rsvs.

Denizen Hotel, 716 Main St, 241-7035. Rooms begin at $31.

Evendale Motel, 10165 Reading Road, 563-1570. Take a ride on the Reading bus 43 North to Reading and Columbia; then walk ¹/₂ hr north on Reading. Dark, but clean rooms. S-$30 for two.

Camping: Camp Shore Campgrounds, Rt 56 Aurora, (812) 438-2135, 20 miles W of Cincinnati on the Ohio River. $16/site, includes swimming and tennis. **Cedarbrook,** 760 Franklin Rd, btwn Cincinnati and Dayton in Lebanon, 932-7717, sites $18-20. **King's Island Campgrounds**, I-71 exit 24 at Mason, (800) 832-1133. Close to King's Island. Camp site $30 for four w/hook-up, cabins $58, XP-$5.

Also, **Rose Gardens Resort—KOA Campgrounds**, I-75 exit 166, (606) 428-2000; 30 miles N of Cincinnati. Tent sites $20 w/hook-up and cabins $34 w/hook-up.

FOOD

Cincinnati's Germanic tradition means it has a number of beer gardens. It's also noted for chilli, served '3-, 4-or 5-way'; eg with spaghetti, beans, meat, onions, Cheddar cheese. Chilli parlours abound, each with a secret recipe. It's accepted that they all contain cinnamon; rumour has it that **Skyline Chilli** adds chocolate, too. Here are just a few suggestions (meal approx $4 with soft drink):

Camp Washington Chilli, Hopple and Colerain, 541-0061. 'Prime source of 5-way Cincinnati-style chilli: thick, spicy meat sauce atop a bed of plump spaghetti, garnished with beans, shredded cheese and chopped onions.'

Gold Star, 8467 Beachmont Ave, 474-4916, several other locations. Open Mon-Sat 10am-11pm, Sun 11am-10pm.

Graeter's, 41 E 4th St, 381-0653, and several other locations, is the locals' ice cream of choice.

Empress Chilli, 8340 Vine St, 20 min N of downtown, 761-5599. Open 10am-10pm Mon-Sat.

Izzy's, Elm & 8th, 721-4241. A Cincinnati tradition. Open daily 8am-8pm.

The Precinct, 311 Delta Ave, 321-5454. A great place to go for steak. Dinner nightly from 5pm.

Skyline Chilli, 643 Vine St, 241-2020, and several other locations. Open Mon-Fri 11am-7pm, Sat 'til 3:30pm.

Also: Findlay Market, 117 E Elder St, 591-6000. Produce and picnic items. Mon-Wed 7am-1.30pm, Fri-Sat 7am-6pm.

OF INTEREST

The Beach, 2590 Waterpark Dr in Mason, 20 miles N of Cincinnati on I-71, 398-7946. One of the ten largest water parks in the US, with a 25,000 sq ft wave pool, as well as speed, giant inner-tube and body slides, $20. Open Mon-Thur 10am-8pm, Fri-Sun 'til 9pm.

Carew Tower, 5th and Vine Sts. From the 49th floor, take a gander at Cincinnati, the Ohio River and Kentucky opposite.

Cincinnati Art Museum, 920 Eden Park Dr, 721-5204. Tue-Sat 10am-5pm, Sun noon-6pm; $5, $4 w/student ID.

Cincinnati Zoo, 3400 Vine St, 281-4701. Called 'the sexiest zoo in the US' for its successful breeding programme: lots of gorillas, rare white Bengal tigers, an insectarium. Celebrating its 150th anniversary. Daily 9am-6pm, grounds close at 8pm; $10.

Contemporary Arts Center, 115 E 5th St, 721-0390. Mon-Sat 10am-6pm; Sun noon-5pm, $3.50, $2 w/student ID.

Krohn Conservatory, Eden Park, 421-4086. One of the largest public greenhouses in the world. Seasonal floral displays. Daily 10am-5pm, Wed 'til 6pm; donation encouraged.

Meier's Winesellers, 6955 Plainfield Pike, 891-2900. Ohio's oldest and largest winery. Free hourly tours of wine making and wine ageing, ending with wine tasting. Mon-Sat 10am-3pm; bar and garden open 'til 4pm.

Newport Aquarium, just over the bridge in Newport, KY, (606)491-3467. Opened May 1999. View 11,000 exotic creatures from around the world. $13.75, Open daily 10am-9pm (last tkts sold at 7:30pm).

Paramount's Kings Island, in Mason, off I-71, 754-5700. The Midwest's largest and often busiest theme park, the world's longest wooden coaster, 'The Beast' and the inverted, face-to-face roller coaster, 'Face/Off'. Over 100 rides and live shows, including 12 roller coasters— it ties the world record for number of coasters in a theme park! Admission to **WaterWorks,** the adjoining waterpark, is included with regular park admission ticket. Fireworks nightly. Open Sun-Fri, 9am-10pm, Sat 'til 11pm (Memorial Day-Labor Day); $36. WaterWorks open daily 11am-8pm. 'Need a car to get there.' *www.pki.com*

Taft Museum, 316 Pike, 241-0343. Federal 1820 mansion houses collection of paintings (including Rembrandt and Whistler), Chinese porcelains, French enamel, portraits. Mon-Sat 10am-5pm, Sun 1-5pm; $4, $2 w/student ID. 'Exquisite. Marred only by poor taste in carpets.'

Tyler Davidson Fountain Square. The centre of downtown activity is around here. Lunch-time concerts, pre and post-ballgame celebrations; shops and businesses.

Union Terminal, 1301 Western Ave, 287-7000. The newly renovated building, an Art Deco gem with the world's highest unsupported dome, now houses 'Museum Center', which includes a realistic walk-thru replica of King Tut's tomb, the **Museum of Natural History** where a cavern full of bats and the Ice Age (simulated) awaits; the **Cincinnati Historical Society** has a mock-up of a 1860s street to wander in; finally, pop over to the **Omnimax** to see those films on the big screen; $6. Museums open Mon-Sat 10am-5pm, Sun 11am-6pm; to one museum $5.50, to two $9and for everything $15 (inc. Omnimax). Call to check Omnimax show times.

Riverboats breeze past the public landing at the foot of Broadway. The revitalised riverfront area invites you to watch the boats from the Serpentine Wall. Cruises are generally heavily booked and rather pricey, but you can take in arrivals, departures and attendant hoopla and steam calliope-playing for free.

Cincinnati is home base of the *Delta Queen*, a genuine relic on the National Register of Historic Landmarks. This is an authentic paddlewheeler, not merely one of the ignoble beasties that ply the waters in hundreds of US cities and towns. *Showboat Majestic*, (513) 241-6550, also docks here, with live theatre nightly; $12, $11 w/student ID. On the Covington, KY, side is the *Mike Fink*, Greenup St, (606)261-4212, a riverboat restaurant with a delectable New Orleans-style seafood bar. Not cheap but you may feel like splurging on catfish, crab legs and chocolate chip pecan pie. For information about year-round cruising, sightseeing, lunches and dinners aboard boats here contact BB Riverboats, at the foot of Greenup St, (800) 261-8586. 1hr sight-seeing cruises at $9. Located at **Covington Landing**.

ENTERTAINMENT

Mt Adams, Cincinnati's answer to Greenwich Village, is where the yuppies are. The students hang out in the **Clifton area**, where the University of Cincinnati is. The place to go in this college town is **Calhoun St** or **Short Vine** (1 block off Vine St). Many bars and clubs, ranging in musical style, dress code, and price in the U district. Many of the most popular places to eat and hang out are on the Kentucky side of the riverfront.

Cincy's always up for a festival— try to time your visit accordingly. Live music and top bands take the stage during **Pepsi Jamming on Main St** in Apr-May; **Oktoberfest** in mid-Sept and the **Tall Stacks** riverboat expo in Sept-Oct provide lots of opportunities for dancing, eating and beer drinking in downtown area. Check out *www.gccc.com* for a calendar of events.

Arnold's, 210 E 8th St, 421-6234, btwn Main & Sycamore Sts downtown. Has jazz, ragtime and swing music along with sandwiches and dinners. Cincinnati's oldest bar. Open Sun-Fri 11am-1am, Sat from 4pm.

Blind Lemon, 936 Hatch St, Mt Adams, 241-3885. Old-fashioned decor. Pop, acoustic guitar music at 9.30pm, no cover.

Music Hall, 1243 Elm St by Lincoln Park Dr, 721-8222. Classical music; discount w/student ID 10 min before performances.

Playhouse in the Park, 962 Mt Adams Circle, 421-3888. Two theatres with plays Oct-June, cabaret in the summer. Student rush tkts on sale 15 mins before performances.

SPORT

Cincinnati Reds games, 421-REDS, at Cinergy Field (the arena formerly know as Riverfront Stadium). America's first professional baseball team. Tickets are $4-17. The Bengals football team also play at Riverfront Stadium, 621-3550.

INFORMATION/TRAVEL

Amtrak, 1301 Western Ave, (800) 872-7245.

Cincinnati Convention and Visitors Bureau, 300 W 6th St, (513) 621-2142.

The Greater Cincinnati International Airport is actually in Kentucky, about 13 miles away. Jetport Express, (606) 767-3702, runs shuttle buses there from downtown hotels for $12 o/w every 1/2 hr, $15 r/t.

Greyhound, 1005 Gilbert, (800) 231-2222. A long walk from city centre.

Queen City Metro Buses, 6 E 4th, 621-4455 for info and schedules. Basic fare: 50c.

State Information, (800)-BUCKEYE.

INTERNET ACCESS

Laptop Lane, in the Cincinnati/ Northern Kentucky International Airport, Gate B20. Open Sun-Fri 6:30am-9pm, Sat 'til 8pm. $2/5 min.

COLUMBUS   The capital city of Ohio, Columbus sits in the middle of the state, a centre of growth that preserves the state's historical heritage. The home of Ohio State University, Columbus has played host to several notable names. The writer O Henry produced some of his best stories while confined in a Columbus cell for embezzlement. Local humorist James Thurber attended Ohio State University briefly and set his play, *The Male Animal*, there.

Columbus sits in a region of the Buckeye state intriguingly called 'Leatherlips,' named after a Wyandot Indian chief who was executed by his people for siding with palefaces. Discover Columbus, Ohio, with Columbus InfoPages at *www.surpriseitscolumbus.com.*

The telephone area code is 614.

ACCOMMODATION

German Village offers the best value motel accommodation. Student-style accommodation is also available close to the State University.

Heart of Ohio Hostel, 95 E 12th Ave, 294-7157. $14. 'Superb. Highly recommended.' Take #2 bus.

Village Inn Motel, 920 South High St, 443-6506. D-$54. 1mile from downtown.

YMCA, 40 W Long St, 224-1131. Men only; weekly rates depending on income.

FOOD/ENTERTAINMENT

Try the **Short North Area,** between downtown and the Ohio State Campus, for real bohemian atmosphere. The hippest shops, galleries, restaurants and night clubs are to be found here.

Blue Danube, 2439 N High St, 261-9308. Good, cheap restaurant with generous portions. Open daily 11am-2:30am.

The French Market/ Continent, 6076 Busch Blvd. All kinds of European restaurants and food-stalls. Good eating places in the German Village, bus from High St. Also at North Market, 29 Spruce, a century-old centre for produce. For nightlife, try North High St, 2 miles N of downtown. This is where the Ohio State University students go.

Some of the better restaurants are to be found in the Brewery District/German Village, Busch Blvd, and in rather off-beat places like Grand Ave (NW of downtown). Bar bands are Columbus' speciality. Almost all have live music on w/ends. Grand Avenue in the NW is a hidden treasure with it's 'bijou' cinema, open air coffee houses and bookstores. Try

OF INTEREST
Center of Science and Industry (COSI), 280 E Broad St, 228-2674. 4 flrs of science, health, industry and history exhibits. Mon-Sat 10am-5pm, Sun noon-5.30pm; $8. 'Worth it.'
Columbus Zoo, 9990 Riverside Dr, 645-3550. Exit 20, Sawmill Rd, off I-270 outer belt. 100-acre zoo. Impressive collection of great apes, including the first gorilla ever born in captivity; only zoo in the world housing four generations of gorillas. Also features 'Manatee Coast,' one of four manatee exhibits outside of Florida. Daily 9am-6pm, Wed 'til 8pm. $7. Some activities involve additional charges.
Dodge Skatepark: Concrete snake run, three bowls, pyramid and other obstacles suitable for skateboarding and inlining; free.
Easton Town Center, Easton Way, off of I-270. Newly opened mega-shopping and entertainment complex in north-east Columbus. Features shopping, dancing, dining, pottery-making, comedy clubs, and GameWorks, a virtual reality video arcade.
German Village, 624 S Third St, 221-8888. Open daily. Restored 19th century community containing private homes, shops, restaurants.
Ohio State University library: largest collection of Thurber's works, drawings. Thurber is not easy to get to—held under tight security and not generally accessible.
Ohio Theatre, 55 E State St, 469-0939. A 1930s cinema with wonderful Titian red, gold-spangled baroque interior. Show classic movies all year round. 'Amazing decor; organist rises through the floor.'
Topiary Garden, 408 E Town St at Washington Ave, 645-3300. Topiary depiction of Georges Seurat 'A Sunday Afternoon ...' complete with 52 topiary people, 8 boats, 3 dogs, and a monkey!
Wyandot Lake Amusement Park, adjacent to the zoo, 889-9283, has 43 rides. Mon-Thur 10am-8pm, Fri-Sun 10am-9pm, $18 ($11.50 after 4pm).

INFORMATION/TRAVEL
Central Ohio Transit Authority (COTA), 1775 High St, 228-1776, runs the local buses; $1.50 express routes, $1.10 basic fare.
Chamber of Commerce, 221-1321.
Greyhound, 111 E Town St, (800) 231-2222.
Port Columbus International Airport, E of downtown. Take the COTA bus #16 'Long St' from Broad & High, approx 30 mins, $1.10.
Visitors Bureau, 10 W Broad St, Suite 1300, 221-6623 and Visitors Center, 3rd floor of the City Mall, (800) 345-4386.

CLEVELAND   Superman was born in Cleveland in 1933, the brainchild of 2 teenagers who in 1938 sold all rights for $130 and commenced upon a lifetime of generally fruitless litigation. This earthly urban version of Krypton is an entirely suitable birthplace for the 'Man of Steel.' Once an industrial powerhouse, it features an incredible array of bridges yet still looks something like

Dresden after the war. But iron and steel weren't the only things that brought money to Cleveland; its prime location on Lake Erie made it a natural centre for shipbuilding. John D Rockefeller watched his oil business here grow into one of the largest personal fortunes the world has ever known. Downtown Cleveland is thick with corporate headquarters, but industry isn't the only thing that flourishes here. The symphony orchestra, municipal art museum and other cultural endeavours rank amongst the finest in the US—a testament to the second renaissance the city has undergone.

Cleveland is perhaps best known as the site of the Rock 'n Roll Hall of Fame, opened in 1995. The building, designed by IM Pei, was anchored in Cleveland after a lengthy custody battle with Philadelphia and San Francisco. The choice of Cleveland was appropriate, considering the city's musical credentials: one of its ancestral disc jockeys coined the phrase 'rock & roll' and the city hosted the very first rock concert in 1952. The Hall graphically catalogues the decline of Rock 'n Roll from its passionate roots to its later greedy mediocrity. Perhaps that's why attendance has been dropping. Check out the Cleveland web site, *www.cleveland.oh.us/* to find out what's going on now.

The telephone area code is 216.

ACCOMMODATION
There is no downtown hotel accommodation for less than $80. Better to stay at one of the many motels near the airport. The airport is connected to Tower City (downtown) by the 'Rapid' ($1.50 o/w fare).

Brooklyn YMCA, 3881 Pearl Rd (W 25th St), 749-2355; $34, $96 weekly, $85 three weekly, $75 four or more weeks. Men only.

Cleveland Private Lodgings, 321-3213, finds accommodation in private homes around the city. From $55 for B&B; from $175 weekly; from $350 monthly.

Days Inn—Lakewood Manor Hotel, 12020 Plympton Ave, 226-4800. 3 miles W of downtown in Lakewood. Take bus 55 CX. TV, AC. Free coffee daily, and donuts on w/ends. S/D $69.

Knights Inn, 22115 Brookpark Rd, (440)734-4500. S-$55; D-$65.

Ramada Inn-Cleveland Airport, I-480 Exit 12, 13930 Brookpark Rd, (800) 2-RAMADA. From D-$71. Complimentary bfast/airport shuttle, coin laundry.

Red Roof Inn, I-90 & Crocker Rd, exit 156, Westlake, (440) 892-7920. From $66-$76.

Camping: Woodside Lake Park, 2256 Frost Rd, (330) 626-4251. 35 miles E of downtown, off I-480, in Streetsboro. Sites $25 for two w/hook-up.

FOOD
The Arcade, Euclid Ave, east of Public Square. 5-level mall, filled with a wide variety of ethnic restaurants.

Balaton, 13133 Shaker Square, 921-9691, Cleveland prides itself on delicious Hungarian food. Balaton is the best. Open Tue-Thur 11:30am-9pm, Fri 'til 10pm, Sat 12:30pm-10pm, Sun 12:30pm-8pm.

Captain Tony's Pizza and Pasta Emporium, 13208 Shaker Square, 561-8669. Some of the best gourmet pizza in Cleveland. Open daily 11am-11pm.

Geppetto's, 3314 Warren Rd, 941-1120. Winner of the '**National Rib Burn-off**,' held in Cleveland Memorial Day weekend— Geppetto's defeated some of the best ribs from all over the world. In spite of the prestige, the prices are reasonable. Open Mon-Thur 11:30am-11pm, Fri-Sat 'til midnight, Sun noon-10pm.

Lucy's on the Square, 13209 Shaker Square, 283-5647. A specialist in decadent pastries. Open Mon-Sat 8am-7pm.

Mama Santa, 12305 Mayfield Rd (in Little Italy), 231-9567. There are several wonderful Italian restaurants in Little Italy. This one is quite reasonably priced. Open Sun-Thur 11am-11pm, Fri-Sat 'til midnight.

Rock Bottom Brewery, 2000 Sycamore, 623-1555. Great beer and sandwiches. Open Sun-Thur 11:30am-10:30pm, Fri-Sat 'til 1:30am.

Watermark, 1250 Old River Rd (on the east bank), 241-1600. If you're going to splurge in Cleveland, this is the place to do it. Lovely riverside location. Fri night seafood buffet; $18. Sun brunch; $16. Open Mon-Thur 11:30am-10pm, Fri-Sat 'til 11pm, Sun 10am-2pm and 5pm-10pm.

West Side Market, 25th and Lorain Ave, 781-3663. Head to the gastronomic cross-section for mouth-watering old world selections at low prices. Open Mon & Wed 7am-4pm, Fri-Sat, 7am-6pm.

OF INTEREST

Cleveland Indoor Skatepark, close to Ohio turnpike. Approx 32,000 sq ft area for skateboarding/inlining/BMX. Heated and dry with a smooth tile floor. Spine ramp, 8 ft decks, hip ramp on one deck, jumpbox w/dual rail slides, 16 ft wide wallride ramp, assorted funboxes, launches and railslides. Helmets req. Large stage for an assortment of fun shows. Sml shop inside with vital bike/skate parts;

Great Lakes Science Center, 601 Erieside Ave, 694-2000. Hands-on science museum; also features an IMAX theatre. Open daily 9:30am-5pm, $7.75 for the museum or the IMAX, $11 for combo ticket.

Lorain Skatepark, Lorain near Cleveland, has a concrete vert ramp.

Museum of Art, 11150 East Blvd at University Circle, 421-7340. Free and first-rate, second only to the NY Metropolitan. Tue/Thur/Sat/Sun 10am-5pm; Wed/Fri 10am-9pm.

Museum of Natural History, Wade Oval University Circle, 231-4600. Visit the new Planet E—an expedition in time and space. Mon-Sat 10am-5pm, Sun noon-5pm; $6.50, $4.50 w/student ID.

NASA-Lewis Research Center, 21000 Brookpark Rd, adjacent to Cleveland Hopkins Airport, 433-4000. Exhibits of NASA work. Mon-Fri 9am-4pm, Sat 10am-3pm, Sun 1pm-5pm; free.

Rock and Roll Hall of Fame and Museum, 1 Key Plaza, North Coast Harbor, 781-7625. The world's greatest repository of R'n'R memorabilia, incl Lennon's Sgt Pepper outfit, Madonna costumes, Michael Jackson's glove, a comprehensive tribute to Elvis, a myriad selection of lyric sheets and guitars, and other entertaining historical artefacts/exhibitions. Daily 10am-5.30pm, Wed, Fri, Sat 'til 9pm; $15. Takes 3-4 hrs to tour. Check out web site *www.rockhall.com.*

Sea World, (330)995-2121, take Solon Exit off I-480 E from downtown. A 90-acre marine life park with the only Tsunami wave pool in Midwest, 20 miles NE of Cleveland. $31; $20 after 6pm in summers. $6 parking. Busiest July/Aug. Open 10am 'til 7pm/11pm depending on season.

Shaker Historical Museum, 16740 S Park Blvd, Shaker Heights, 921-1201. Tue-Fri 2pm-5pm, Sun 2pm-5pm. By donation. Once the site of a rural commune begun by the Shakers, a religious sect who turned their backs on industrialisation for 10 mins—and along came Cleveland! Today's Shaker Heights is a ritzy suburb with good (and not always expensive) restaurants. It's also home of the nation's second-oldest shopping centre.

Terminal Tower Observation Deck, Tower City Center, 621-7981. A $2 ticket gets you a spectacular view of downtown. Open Sat-Sun, 11am-4:30pm.

ENTERTAINMENT

Pick up a free copy of the *Cleveland Free Times* or *Cleveland Scene* for the latest in entertainment news.

Cleveland Ballet, 1375 Euclid Ave, 1 Playhouse Sq, 426-2500. Professional repertory ballet, featuring modern and classical work. Tkts $15-$55 (30% off w/ID).

Cleveland Orchestra, Severance Hall, 11001 Euclid Ave, 231-7300. World-famous symphony orchestra established in 1918, presenting a variety of concerts. Tkts $31, $24, $17 ($12 w/student ID)

Cleveland Playhouse, 8500 Euclid Ave, 795-7000. 3-theater complex. The season runs Jan-June, Oct-Dec.

The Flats, NW of Public Square, where the Cuyahoga River meets Lake Erie. The centre of Cleveland's nightlife. Many rock bars and good eating establishments including **Fagan's**, 996 Old River, 241-6116 ('live music and excellent food') and **Panini Bar and Grille**, 241-2700, famous for its ample sandwiches and late hours; **The Nautica Stage** at the Flats plays host to a number of outdoor summer concerts (rock, jazz, classical etc). Call 732-5100 for details. Also of interest is the **Powerhouse**, a National Historic Site-turned dining and shopping complex. Take a lunch or sunset dinner cruise down the **Nautica Queen**, 696-8888, for a breathtaking view of downtown; from $22-$45.

INFORMATION/TRAVEL

Amtrak, Lakefront Station, 200 Cleveland Memorial Shoreway, 696-5115/(800) 872-7245. Like the Greyhound Station, this is not a safe part of town. Most trains arrive in the early hours, so use caution when leaving the station. Either take a taxi or wait until daylight before venturing out.

Chamber of Commerce, 621-3300.

Cleveland Convention and Visitors Bureau, 621-6000.

Cleveland Hopkins International Airport, 265-6000. About 11 miles from downtown, the easiest, cheapest and quickest way to get there is to take the #66X—Red Line train; $1.50 o/w.

Greyhound, 1465 Chester Ave, (800) 231-2222. 'High crime area—take extreme care, especially at night, even in restrooms.'

Regional Transit Authority, 566-5124, runs buses and the rapid rail system. Basic fare on buses, $1.25; express buses/rail, $1.50, $4 all day pass.

Visitors Information Center, 50 Public Square, Tower City Center, Suite #3100, 621-7981.

INTERNET ACCESS

Coffeehouse Phoenix, 3750 Pearl Rd, 741-6010. Open 24 hrs. Surf the net for $5/hr.

TOLEDO AND NORTHWEST OHIO A must-see in Ohio is the **Toledo Museum of Art**, 2445 Monroe Street at Scottwood Ave, Toledo, (419) 255-8000. Houses the finest collection of glass in the US; founded by Edward Libbey, who brought the glass industry to Toledo in 1888. Tue-Thur 10am-4pm, Fri 'til 10pm, Sat 'til 5pm, Sun 1pm-5pm, closed Mon; free. A good day trip from Cleveland or Detroit. Toledo's past, preserved through time in magnificent photographs, drawings and documents dating back to the 1860s, comes alive in the Local History and Genealogy Department's collection of over 150,000 images.

Further east lies the town of Port Clinton; from there, sail over to **South Bass Island**, a historical island-turned raging bar scene. The island's principal city, Put-in-Bay, is home to the world's longest bar. Its famous watering hole, the **Beer Barrel Saloon,** 1618 Delaware Ave, (419)285-7281, boasts a 405 ft counter, 160 bar stools, 56 beer taps and holds up to 1200 people!

In **Sandusky**, spend a day or two at **Cedar Point**, 1 Causeway Drive, (419)627-2350. Known as 'America's Rollercoast', the park features 60 rides— more than any other amusement park on the planet. It was recently named the 'Best Amusement Park in the World' by *Amusement Today*; $33.

Toft Dairy, 3717 Venice Rd, (419)625-4376, is famous for serving up phenomenal ice cream. Open daily, 8am-11pm. After a hot, gruelling day at Cedar Point, head just south-west of Sandusky to **Bellevue,** where you can dig into a thick, juicy steak at **McClain's,** 137 E Main, (419)483-2727. Open daily 11am-9pm.

SERPENT MOUND STATE MEMORIAL and MOUND CITY NATIONAL MONUMENT These two Indian sites are located south of Chillicothe, near Locust Grove and 3 miles N of Chillicothe, respectively. The Serpent Mound State Memorial, (937)587-2796, is the largest Indian effigy mound in the US, built by the Adena culture circa 1000 BC. 'Unforgettable, majestic and truly amazing that it's still around at all.' In summer, green grass covers the enormous coils that the mound builders formed out of stone and clay. Open Wed-Sun, 9:30am-8pm, $3/vehicle. **The Mound City Group**, Hopewell Culture, 16062 State Rte 104, Chillicothe, (740) 774-1125, dates back 2000 years; the 23 burial mounds are described as 'the city of the dead'. One contains a window through which you can view a mica grave, four cremation burials and numerous artefacts. Daily in summer 8.30am-6pm; $2, $4 per car load.

SOUTH DAKOTA   *The Mount Rushmore State*

South Dakota is living proof that bad weather (from 40 below zero to a blazing 116 degrees) can't be all bad. To look at its tourist brochures, you'd think the place was full of nothing but jolly Anglo hunters, ranchers and fishermen. It has, however, a large (mostly Sioux) Indian population on nine reservations, regarded as 'uppity Injuns' (and worse) for their quixotic determination to win back more of their traditional lands. It was the discovery of gold in the Black Hills (verified by that catalytic figure, General Custer, in 1874) that further exacerbated relations with the Sioux. The land in question had been granted to the Sioux by an 1868 treaty, and they were not willing to concede it. Settlers came by the wagonload anyway to extract the mineral. In spite of their fervent mining, gold continues to be South Dakota's most abundant mineral today.

Concentrate on the scenic western section: Mt Rushmore, the Black Hills, the Badlands. Because of distances and lack of public transit, it's difficult to sight-see without a car. Wyoming's Devil's Tower is only 35 miles from the South Dakota border, but you'll need a car to reach it as well.

One of the state's most popular tourist attractions is what Kevin Costner left behind— the sets from his highly acclaimed epic, *Dances With Wolves*. A visit to Ft Hays, 394-9653, 4 miles S of Rapid City on Hwy 16, enables you to walk through some of the buildings used in the film production and pick up souvenirs at a number of gift shops; the Sioux winter camp that ends the film is in Little Spearfish Canyon in the Black Hills National Forest.
For info: *www.yahoo.com/Regional/U_S__States/ south_dakota/*
The telephone area code is 605.

RAPID CITY   A strategic spot for exploring the Black Hills and Badlands, the city itself is a hodgepodge of tourist claptrapery. Visit the city guide compiled by the Rapid City Convention & Visitors Bureau at *www.rapidcitycvb.com/*

ACCOMMODATION/FOOD
College Inn Motel, 123 Kansas City St (part of National College), 394-4800/(800) 752-8942 within the state. Rooms begin at $45. 6 blocks from bus depot. 'Clean, well furnished.' Pool, laundry, cafeteria.
Lamplighter Inn, 27 St. Joseph, 342-3385. Rooms $39-65. Book early— it fills up.
Tally's, 530 6th St, 342-7621. Downtown; good food for not much money. 'Nice food and good locale.' Open Mon-Sat 7am-2:30am.

OF INTEREST
The Journey Museum, 222 New York St, 394-6923. Interactive exhibits that explore the history of the region and that of the Great Sioux Nation. The museum is composed of 5 collections: the Museum of Geology, Sioux Indian Museum, State Archaeological Research Center, Minnilusa Pioneer Museum and Dumahel Plains Indians Artefacts Collection. Open daily 8am-7pm; $5, $3 w/ student ID.
Caves in the Rapid City region: Sitting Bull Crystal Caverns, 342-2777, 9 miles N on Hwy 16 (heading toward Mt. Rushmore), has calcite dog-spar crystals. Daily 7am-7pm, $7. **Crystal Cave**, 342-8008, 2 miles W on Hwy 44, is closest and offers complete tours that aren't very strenuous: 'Quite long but very pleasant walk.' Open May-Oct, 8am-7:30pm, $7.50.

INFORMATION
Chamber of Commerce, Rushmore Plaza Civic Center, 343-1744. Useful maps. Ask for the South Dakota Vacation Guide, with a dandy section on panning for gold and rockhounding. 'Very helpful people.'
South Dakota Tourism, Capitol Lake Plaza, Pierre, (800) 487-3223.

TRAVEL
Gray Line Tours, (800) 456-4461. Different itineraries of Black Hills, Rushmore, Devil's Tower, Custer Game Refuge: June 'til mid-Oct. Leaves daily at 9am, returns 5pm, pickup from various hotels. $34 and up for the day. The fully narrated 9hr Black Hills tour is 'quite extensive; well worth the money.'
Stagecoach West, 343-3113. An alternative to Gray Line for tours to the Black Hills and Mount Rushmore. Tours $32-$42.

DEADWOOD   Twenty-eight miles NW of Rapid City via I-90, Deadwood calls itself 'where the West is fun!' but 'where the West is wax' might be more like it. Once the lively stomping ground for Calamity Jane, Wild Bill Hickok and Deadwood Dick, it's amazingly dead today. For links to Deadwood and other Old West sites, click on *www.deadwood.net/*

ACCOMMODATION
HI- Black Hills at the Penny Motel, 818 Upper Main St, 578-1842. Opened in 1999, features dorm-style rooms with common kitchens, bike rentals also available. $12/AYH member, $15/non-member.
Super 8 Motel, 196 Cliff St, 578-2535. Reasonable for groups of 4 or 5; around $80 nightly. Jacuzzi suite Q-$130. From S-$65 (summer), S-$40 (Oct onwards). 'Pool, sauna, friendly, very clean.'

OF INTEREST
Adams Memorial Museum, 54 Sherman St downtown, 578-1714. Gold-mining train, Wild Bill's marriage certificate and a sea of other nonsense. Open summer

Mon-Sat 9am-6pm, Sun noon-5pm; free. 'Interesting.'

Ghosts of Deadwood Gulch, corner of Lee and Sherman St in the Old Towne Hall, 578-3583. A wax museum where a play called *The Trial of Jack McCall* is performed Mon-Sat at 8pm in summer; $7. Starts with dramatic capture of Hickock's killer, continues with trial in town hall. 'A laugh.' Daily 9am-6:30pm, tours every 15 mins; $5.

Mt Moriah 'Boot Hill' cemetery. Good place to do gravestone rubbings: Calamity, Wild Bill are here.

Number 10 Saloon, Main St. See the chair where Wild Bill Hickok was gunned down while holding a poker hand of 2 aces and a pair of eights—still called 'a dead man's hand'. Hickok was never punished for any of his killings, several of which were clearly murders; *his* killer, however, was hanged.

Nearby: Lead (pronounced 'Leed'), is a steep little mining town with the largest gold mine in the western hemisphere, the **Homestake**, 584-3110. Surface tours May-Sept, $5.25, $4.25 w/student ID. Half a million ounces of gold are mined each year; about 13 million tons remain. 'Free ore sample.' Open 8:30am-4:30pm in summer (Mon-Fri 8am-4pm only in May, Sept 10am-5pm w/ends)

Spearfish, (800) 457-0160, for 56 years home of the *Black Hills Passion Play*. June-Aug, at 8.15pm on Tue, Thur & Sun; $14, $12, $9, $7. Huge cast in outdoor setting.

THE BLACK HILLS The Black Hills are neither black nor hills; they are actually ancient mountains cloaked with spectacular pine forests. The impressive result— a green citadel above the expansive tawny plains— was considered sacred ground by the Sioux. For links to everything in the Black Hills and South Dakota, search thru *www.blackhills.org*.

OF INTEREST

Custer State Park, 255-4515. Free if you drive through on Hwy 16A, otherwise $8 for a 7-day vehicle permit; $13 per camp-site. Rsvs recommended. The State Game Lodge, 255-4541, will take you on a **Buffalo Jeep Safari**, where you can see some of the park's 1600 buffalo during a 1½ hr jeep ride for $18. If you prefer horseback riding, call the **Blue Bell Lodge,** 255-4571. They'll arrange it for you for $14/hr. Any tour through the Black Hills should include **Needles Hwy**, past spectacular volcanic pinnacles. Someone once wanted to carve these pillars into Wild West heroes, the genesis of the Rushmore idea. Hike to the top of **Harney Peak**; at 7,242 ft, it's the highest point in the US east of the Rockies.

Crazy Horse Monument, 6 mi N of Custer on Rte 385, 673-4681. A great Oglala Sioux leader, Crazy Horse resisted white encroachment on Indian lands and at 33 was stabbed in the back by an American soldier under a flag of truce. If ever finished, this completely 3-dimensional monument to him will dwarf Rushmore, ultimately standing 563 ft high and 641 ft long— the world's largest mountain carving. Korczak Ziolkoski logged 36 yrs and blasted away some 7 million tons of rock before dying in 1982. His family has carried on and you can see work in progress 7am-8.30pm, daily. Check with Gray Line tours or drive through, $7pp, $17per car.

Jewel Cave National Monument, 673-2288. Dog-tooth crystals of calcite sparkle from its walls in the 2nd longest cave system in the US. Bring a jacket—it gets quite chilly, even in the summer, it gets quite chilly. Park hours and tours are decided each season depending on available federal funds; take the historic tour for $6, more strenuous but fun, if it's offered. Go early to avoid a long wait. Open Mon-Sat 8am-6pm, Sun 9am-5pm.

Mt Rushmore, 574-2523. Free, includes a 12 min film, evening amphitheatre programmes at 8pm. It took 14 yrs to create the 60-ft-high granite faces of Washington, Jefferson, Teddy Roosevelt and Lincoln, carved by Gutzon Borglum and partly paid for with South Dakota school kids' pennies and it is still not finished. Most beautiful in morning light and when floodlit, summer eves. Visitors Center, 8am-10pm. Sculptor Studio, where models and tools are displayed, 9am-6pm, summer only.

HOT SPRINGS   Long before white settlers discovered these waters, they were a point of contention between Sioux and Cheyenne Indian tribes. The warm, mineral-laden waters were also a popular watering hole for mammoths 26,000 years ago. The sides of the sinkhole were quite slippery, however, and some 100 mammoths are believed to have drowned. Today you can follow in the footsteps of the Indians and mammoths alike by bathing in the 87 degree, spring-fed swimming pools at **Evans Plunge**, 1145 N River St, 745-5165, the world's largest natural warm water pool. Open daily, 5:30am-9:45pm, $8.

The first of the star-crossed mammoths was uncovered in 1974; the **Mammoth Site of Hot Springs**, 1800 Hwy 18, 745-6017, was built on top of the original excavation site. It has the largest concentration of Columbian and woolly mammoth bones discovered in the place in which they died in the world. It's also the only in-situ (bones left as found) display of fossil mammoths in the US. Open daily 8am-8pm, $5.

The Black Hills' newest attraction, the **Black Hills Wild Horse Sanctuary**, (800)252-6652, is located 14 miles W of Hot Springs. See hundreds of wild mustangs, displaced from other ranges in the west, running free. Guided tours available Mon-Sat, $15.

If you haven't had your fill of caves yet, take time to visit **Wind Cave National Park**, 11 miles N of Hot Springs, 745-4600. Discovered in 1881, the 10-mile deep cave is named for the winds (caused by changes in barometric pressure) that whistle in and out of it. Open 8:30am-6:30pm daily, 60 mins-90 mins scenic tours; $4-$6. The 2hr candlelight tour ($7) is recommended, as is the 4hr caving tour ($18). Dress warmly. Above ground, take advantage of superb animal watching and photographing: deer, buffalo, antelope and prairie dog towns. Dawn and dusk are the best times. 'The candlelight tour is great.'

BADLANDS NATIONAL PARK   Locals used to say that it looks like hell with the fires put out, but there's something quite heavenly about the 207 square miles of weird and beautiful buttes, canyons and brilliantly coloured rock formations. At sunset, the sandstone slopes blush with shades of pink and purple. Bones of sabre-toothed tigers, three-toed horses and Tyrannosaurus Rex have been found in this dried-up swampland. 'Absolutely amazing—the surprise package of our tour. Come into it at dawn with the sun at your back—it'll blow your mind, it's that good.' 'Well worth the 10 mile hike along rough track to watch the sunset and spend the night at Sage Creek primitive campground. No water on site.'

OF INTEREST
Kadoka, an authentic Western backwater town east of the Badlands on I-90, is the best place to stay overnight to make the favoured dawn drive through the Badlands, emerging at **Wall** . Excellent visitor centre at the **Cedar Pass Badlands entrance**, includes video. To stay, **West Motel**, Hwy 16and I-90 Business Loop, 837-2427; D-$35. 'Clean rooms, friendly staff.'
Wall, notorious for **Wall Drug**, 510 Main St, 279-2175, a drug store that mutated

into a kitschy tourist-trap. Roads leading to and from Wall are peppered with some 3000 billboards hawking the place; other signs can be found at the North and South Poles, a Kenyan rail station and in the Paris Metro, informing potential customers of the number of miles it is to Wall Drug. Sip free ice water and nickel coffee, buy a rattlesnake ashtray and puzzle over a jackalope, a cross between a jackrabbit and an antelope. Open daily, 6am-10pm.

MITCHELL   If passing through, take time to see the **Corn Palace**, 601 N Main St, 996-7311, a vaguely Russian fantasy of onion domes and dazzling pointillist murals, formed from 3000 bushels of coloured corn cobs. Watch artists construct new murals each summer on the outer wall of the civic auditorium. (Find details of the Corn Palace Stampede Rodeo and a link to Corn Palace's own website at *www.mitchell.net/rodeo/*). Open 8am-10pm daily; free. Also in Mitchell, the **Oscar Howe Art Center**, 119 W 3rd Ave, 996-4111, housing work by the most noted Sioux artist of present times. Mon-Sat 9am-5pm; donation. Area lodging: **Skoglund Farm** near Canova off I-90, 247-3445. $30 includes two full meals plus coffee at a friendly family operation. Horses to ride, animals to pet on a working cattle ranch.

WOUNDED KNEE   'I did not know then how much was ended. When I look back from this high hill of my old age, I can still see the butchered women and children lying heaped and scattered all along the crooked gulch as plain as when I saw them with eyes still young. And I can see that something else died there in the bloody mud, and was buried in the blizzard. A people's dream died there. It was a beautiful dream. The nation's hoop is broken and scattered. There is no centre any longer, and the sacred tree is dead.'—Black Elk.

The symbolic end of Indian freedom came at Christmas-time, 1890, at the so-called Battle of Wounded Knee when the US Cavalry opened fire with rifles and field guns on 120 Indian men and 230 Indian women and children. Most were murdered instantly; some wounded crawled away through a terrible blizzard. Torn and bleeding, many did not crawl far: a returning army burial party found numerous bodies frozen into grotesque shapes against the snow.

A shabby monument marks the spot 100 miles SE of Rapid City, a few miles off Rte 18 near Pine Ridge. Movements for a larger memorial have met resistance from the Lakota, who bristle at the thought of surrendering more of their land to the US government for any reason.

Their unquiet mass grave nearby continues to serve as a rallying point for this century's Indians. In 1973, at the second battle of Wounded Knee, two Indians died in the 71-day siege of the American Indian Movement, and the chapter is far from over.

NB: although the reservation has a motel, museum and other tourist facilities, don't expect uniformly friendly attitudes toward white faces. The Wounded Knee homepage is located at *www.dickshovel.netgate.net/WKmasscre.html#* with excellent links to related Native American sites and images.

MOBRIDGE   On a high hill across the Missouri from Mobridge in north-central South Dakota is Sitting Bull's grave. One of the events preceding the massacre at Wounded Knee was the murder of Sitting Bull, the great Sioux leader, organiser and victor at Little Bighorn. It was carried out by Indian policemen under the eye of the US Cavalry.

The authorities always felt uncomfortable with Sitting Bull alive, regarding him as a subversive figure. In death, however, he became something of a commodity. Originally buried in North Dakota, Sitting Bull's body was snatched by South Dakotans, who planted him in Mobridge. A large stone bust was placed over the grave, just to be sure Sitting Bull stays put. Mobridge has a sculpture of Sitting Bull by Korczak Ziolkowski and ten fine murals by Sioux artist Oscar Howe in the municipal auditorium. Mobridge Chamber of Commerce has a fantastic city guide at *www.mobridge.org* detailing events, campgrounds, fishing, parks and maps.

WISCONSIN   *The Badger State*

Wisconsin is known for its liquids: beer, milk and water of all sorts. Like its neighbour, Minnesota, Wisconsin has more inland lakes than it knows what to do with. Wisconsinites gave names to 14,949 of their inland lakes before giving up in despair. On Lakes Michigan and Superior, the state sports no less than 14 ocean-going ports. In addition to the surplus of fresh water, the world's largest waterpark is also located within the state boundaries. Wisconsin is also rich in mineral deposits; while other places had gold rushes, Wisconsin had a 'lead rush'.

Politically, it has swung from the rapacious capitalism of early lumber barons to the progressive decades of the 'fighting LaFollettes', from Commie witch-hunter Joseph McCarthy to present-day liberal Gaylord Nelson, the founder of Earth Day.

The cities here are clean, amiable and altogether charming. Of course, so is the countryside, but watch out for mosquitoes the size of aircraft carriers (it's the price you pay for all those lakes).

Many of the old railroads that used to cross the state have been converted into trails for bicycling, running, hiking and skiing. *www.yahoo.com/Regional/U_S__States/Wisconsin/*

MILWAUKEE   There's a comfortable, old-shoe feeling about Milwaukee, enhanced by its reputation for good beer, 'brats' and baseball. Remarkably short on grime and slums and long on restaurants and festivals, the city is a good-natured mix of ethnic groups, especially Germans, Poles and Serbs. In quantity of beer produced, Milwaukee has now been aced out by Los Angeles. For quality, however, this is still Der Platz. Despite the dominant old world spirit of the city, evidence of a modern renaissance abounds. The new millennium has been ushered in by a new addition to the Milwaukee Art Museum and a brand new stadium for the Milwaukee Brewers. The Riverwalk along the Milwaukee River will also be getting a facelift, with new restaurants, live music and stores slated to open.
The telephone area code is 414.

TAKE ME OUT TO THE BALLGAME

Baseball may be more American than apple pie. First played in modern form, it's said, by Abner Doubleday in Cooperstown, New York, in 1839, America's national sport is an inexpensive (from $1!) treat not to be missed. The pleasure of watching a game on a warm summer evening, beer and hot dogs in hand, cannot be beaten. Along the way, brush up on your ballgame terms, such as steal, chopper, pop-up, fly, walk, bunt, line-drive, slider, RBI, ERA, ball four, bottom-of-the-ninth, check-swing, strikeout, etc. Catch the action now, before every baseball team sells out to a corporate underwriter and commercialises their stadium names. There are two major leagues, each divided into three divisions and each including a Canadian team. The league champions meet in the end-of-season World Series in October: For a complete run-down on each team, go to *www.majorleaguebaseball.com*.

NATIONAL LEAGUE (est 1876): **East**—Atlanta *Braves*, Florida *Marlins*, Montreal *Expos*, New York *Mets*, Philadelphia *Phillies*.
Central—Chicago *Cubs*, Cincinnati *Reds*, Houston *Astros*, Pittsburgh *Pirates*, St Louis *Cardinals*.
West—Arizona *Diamond Backs*, Colorado *Rockies*, LA *Dodgers*, San Diego *Padres*, San Francisco *Giants*.

AMERICAN LEAGUE (est 1900): **East**—Baltimore *Orioles*, Boston *Red Sox*, New York *Yankees*, Tampa Bay *Devil Rays*, Toronto *Blue Jays*
Central—Chicago *White Sox*, Cleveland *Indians*, Detroit *Tigers*, Kansas City *Royals*, Milwaukee *Brewers*, Minnesota *Twins*.
West—Anaheim *Angels*, Oakland *Athletics*, Texas *Rangers*, Seattle *Mariners*.

BALLPARKS: The Ballpark in Arlington/ Texas Rangers, (817) 273-5222. Opened in 1994, the Ballpark has the feel of an old, inner city park situated amongst the mini-vans of a suburban parking lot. In summer, there are only night games played here—it's too hot during the day.
Bank One Ballpark/ Arizona Diamond Backs, (602) 514-8400. The ultra-posh stadium beats the Arizona heat with poolside seats and an air-conditioning unit equivalent to that of 2,500 Arizona homes put together. It's the only sports facility in the world with a retractable roof, air-conditioning and natural turf.
Busch Stadium/ St Louis Cardinals, (314) 421-3060. The first downtown major league ball park of the 20th century is known to be particularly home-run friendly (it wasn't just the creatine that helped Mark McGwire break Roger Maris' home run record)!
Cinergy Field/ Cincinnati Reds, (513) 421-4510. Present home of the first professional baseball team, the Cincinnatti Red Stockings, who made their debut in 1869. Construction is underway for a new stadium in Cincinnati, slated to open in time for the 2002 season.
Comerica Park/ Detroit Tigers, (313) 962-4000. Brand new for the 2000 season, Comerica will replace Tiger Stadium, one of the second-oldest parks in the league, as home of the Detroit Tigers.
Comiskey Park/Chicago Whitesox, (312) 674-1000. Has craziest fans who staged 'Disco Sucks Night' in 1979 and craziest organist Nancy, a jokester who cranks out an appropriate song for every situation and player. As host to the 'Black Sox Scandal', this is where the World Series was fixed in 1919. 'Say it ain't so, Joe,' they asked of Joe Jackson, one of the eight players involved. See the movie *Eight Men Out*.
Coors Field/ Colorado Rockies, (303) 292-0200. In the mile-high city, a horizontal row of upper deck seats marks the point where the ballpark elevation passes the mile-high mark.
Dodger Stadium/Los Angeles Dodgers, (213) 224-1500. Most palatial of the stadia, and probably the only one with as many celebrities in the bleachers as on the field. 1988 World Series opened here, during which Kirk Gibson of LA hit a 2-run homer in the final inning with two outs, giving the Dodgers a 54 victory over the Oakland Athletics.
Edison International Field/ Anaheim Angels, (714) 940-2000. Renovated for the 1998 season, the left-center fence opens to a natural-looking venue, with geysers erupting and a stream trickling down a tree-covered mountainside.
Enron Field/ Houston Astros, (713) 799-9500. Inaugurated for the 2000 season, Enron replaces Houston's legendary Astrodome, called the eighth wonder of the world when it opened in 1965.
Fenway Park/Boston Red Sox, (617) 267-9400. Home of the 'Green Monster' in left field, intimate atmosphere lets you be a part of the game like in the good ol' days. The Red Sox were the first team to win the World Series when it was established in 1903.
Jacobs Field/ Cleveland Indians, (216) 420-4200. Opened in 1994, Jacobs Field is part of the same downtown revival efforts that produced the Rock 'n' Roll Hall of Fame. You can broadcast an inning of Indians baseball from the FanCast booth.

Kauffman Stadium/Kansas City Royals, (816) 921-8000. More than one baseball player has conceded that this is their favourite away stadium. KC barbecue, baked beans and baseball make for a great game. The outfield is particularly beautiful, with waterfalls just beyond the home run barrier.

Miller Park/ Milwaukee Brewers, (414) 933-4114. Opened in 2000 to replace County Stadium, it maintains Milwaukee's reputation for having the best stadium food and beverages, including bratwurst, barbecued chicken and steak with secret sauce. Hank Aaron wound up his career in the old stadium here in 1976 with the major league lifetime home run record of 755. The new stadium features a state-of-the-art, fan-shaped retractable roof.

Oakland Coliseum/Oakland Athletics, (510) 638-4900. Here baseball combines with the finest sound and video system in the league to create baseball-rock. The aesthetics of the stadium leave something to be desired; its drab appearance earned it the nickname, 'The Oakland Mausoleum.'

Olympic Stadium/ Montreal Expos, (514) 253-3434. Built for the 1976 Summer Olympics, the Stadium was the site of baseball's first retractable roof. Adjacent to the stadium is a 552ft observation tower, the world's largest inclined structure.

Oriole Park at Camden Yards/**Baltimore Orioles**, (410) 685-9800. The $105 million, 48,000-seat ballpark downtown opened in 1992. Only 4 blocks from Baltimore's inner harbour, it has a wonderful barbecue-soaked atmosphere.

Pacific Bell Park/ San Francisco Giants, (415) 468-3700. Replaced 3 Com Park in 2000 as home of the Giants. The short wall in right field allows some home run balls to fall into the bay.

Pro-Player Stadium/Florida Marlins (305) 626-7400. In North Miami off the Florida Turnpike, and where the Marlins beat the Cleveland Indians in the World Series in 1997 in only the 5th year of their existence.

Qualcomm Stadium/San Diego Padres, (619) 881-6500. Baseball a la California, complete with sunny skies, warm temperatures, and fans in their bathing suits tossing giant beach balls. A new park is currently scheduled to open in 2002, complete with garden terraces, picturesque views and palm trees luring spectators into the ballpark.

Safeco Field/ Seattle Mariners, (206) 346-4000. When Safeco opened in 1999, Seattle became the first team to move from an indoor facility to an outdoor facility.

Shea Stadium/ New York Mets, (718) 507-METS. Home of the largest scoreboard in the majors. In centerfield, a large apple rises out of a top hat after every Mets home run. It doesn't happen very often.

Three Rivers Stadium / Pittsburgh Pirates, (412) 323-5000. The site of the first World Series night game in 1971.

Toronto Skydome/Blue Jays, (416) 341-1000. Opened in 1989 with the largest retractable roof in the world, the popularity of Toronto's park caused it to break attendance records in its maiden season. The Blue Jays were also the first non-US world champions. They won in 1992 and again in 1993.

Tropicana Field/ Tampa Bay Devil Rays, (813) 825-3137. The stadium was built ten years before professional baseball came to Tampa, with the long-unfulfilled promise that it would one day do so.

Turner Field/ Atlanta Braves, (404) 249-6400. Owned by TV and entertainment mogul Ted Turner, this is the only ballpark in the majors where the concessionaires sell bison— perhaps a tribute to the Indians?

Veterans Stadium/ Philadelphia Phillies, (215) 463-6000. Currently the largest ballpark in the National League, seating 62,382, but plans are on tap for a smaller, more intimate setting.

Wrigley Field/Chicago Cubs, (773) 404-2827. Oldest in league, and most traditional with ivy-covered walls and hand-turned scoreboard. In 1988, Wrigley became the last ballpark to install lights. The decision to do so followed a lengthy debate between traditionalists and modernists. Yet no such debate was necessary; lights had been purchased in 1941 and were slated for installation that same year. Plans changed, however, when the Japanese bombed Pearl Harbor and the lights were donated to the war effort instead. Join legendary Ronnie in shouting 'Go Cubs, Go Cubs.'

Yankee Stadium/New York Yankees (718) 293-4300; 25-time World Champions—so-called 'team of the century'—most recently in 1999 and wellspring of many baseball legends, including Yogi Berra who, once when a game was poorly attended, is reported to have said, 'if the people don't want to come out to the park, nobody's gonna stop them'. Fans voted unfriendliest by baseball players. The 1927 'Murderers' Row Team' included Lou Gehrig, Bob Meusel, Tony Lazzeri, and Babe Ruth who hit a home run every nine trips to the plate that year. Catch Yankees fans at their most partisan during a game with arch-rivals Boston Red Sox.

ACCOMMODATION
The **Wisconsin B&B Assoc**, 108 South Cleveland St, Merrill, W 54452, (877) ENJOY-WI, will assist with info on motels, B&Bs and country inns. Also, **The Wisconsin Innkeepers Assoc** has an interactive website at *www.lodging-wi.com*.
Excel Inn, 115 North Mayfair Rd, Wauwatosa, 257-0140. Rooms from $47-60.
Red Barn Youth Hostel, 6750 W Loomis Rd, 10 miles NW of downtown, 529-3299. Check in 5pm-10pm; $11 AYH.
Red Roof Inn, 6360 S 13th St, Oak Creek. Call 764-3500; rates fluctuate often.
Camping: For a free copy of the **WACO Campground Directory**/info on campgrounds across the state, call (800) 432-TRIP.

FOOD
Besides Wisconsin's famous cheeses, Milwaukee is noted for 'beer and brats', the latter a particularly succulent variety of German bratwurst, boiled in beer and served with a tangy sauce. If you don't go to a Brewers baseball game and gorge in the sun on beer'n'brats, you've blown it. Also try local frozen custard at places like **Kopp's Frozen Custard**, 5373 N Port Washington Rd, Glendale, 961-2006. Other locations include 18880 W Bluemound Rd, Brookfield, 789-1393; and 7631 W Layton Ave, Greenfield 282-4080. All open 10.30am-11.30pm. No matter when you come, it's always mobbed. Sundaes are the speciality of the house—each comes with its own blueprint detailing the exact ingredients and their placement! Call 282-4080 for your 3-day flavour forecast!

German and Serb restaurants are your best ethnic bets, but also check to see if Milwaukee is celebrating one of its famous summer festivals at the lakefront.
Crocus, 3577 S 13th St, 643-6383, Mon-Wed 11:30am-2pm, Tue 4:30pm-8pm, Fri 11:30am-9pm, Sat 4:30pm-9pm. This neighbourhood Polish restaurant offers the strange brew Czarnia—'a sweet brown syrup, thick with little dumplings, beans, shreds of duck, and plump raisins'. One full meal under $10.
Jessica's, 524 E Layton Ave, 744-1119. 1950's-theme burger-and-malt shop. 'Gorgeous creamy shakes and malts. Turtle sundaes recommended!' Open daily 10am-10:30pm, Sun from 2pm.
Karl Ratzsch's, 320 E Mason St, 276-2720. An early dining menu, 4pm-6pm, is under $15pp. Famous for its German food, there are five German beers on tap, but also a whole array of liquors and a non-German food menu, too. Mon-Fri 4:30pm-9:30pm, Sat 10pm.
Real Chilli, 419 E Wells, Milwaukee, 271-4042. Green Bay-style chilli for under $10. Lunch and dinner served. Open daily 11am-midnight.

OF INTEREST
America's Black Holocaust Museum, 2233 N 4th St, 264-2500. A sombre memorial to slavery in America. Open Mon-Sat 9am-7pm, $5, $3 w/ student ID.
The **DASL (Door County Amateur Skateboarding League) Skatepark**, Sturgeon Bay. Across the street from the Palmer Johnson building (the big one where they build the ships). Indoor 2 half pipes, a big one (about 6-7 ft) and a little one (2-3 ft), 3 quarter pipes, a fun box and other fun street obstacles. Free to get in! Helmets must be worn at all times and knee pads rec when skating the big halfpipe. Inliners must wear helmet, kneepads and wristguards.
Discovery World Museum, 815 N James Lovell St, 765-9966. Daily 9am-5pm; $5. free. Science and interactive technology exhibits.
Harley-Davidson, Inc, 11700 W Capitol Dr, Wauwatosa, 535-3666. Free 1hr tours let you see how a motorcycle is born. Mon-Fri 9:30-1pm.
Miller Brewery Tour, 4251 W State, 931-2337. Mon-Sat 10am-3.30pm. Free indoor/outdoor tour, ending with courtesy suds. Take umbrella!
Milwaukee Art Museum, 750 N Lincoln Memorial Dr, 224-3200. Tue/Wed/Fri/Sat 10am-5pm, Thur noon-9pm, Sun noon-5pm; closed Mon; $5, $3 w/student ID.

Strong in Haitian primitives, 19th century German and American contemporary works/pop art such as some Warhol soup cans.

Milwaukee County Zoo, 10001 W Bluemound Rd, 771-3040. Mon-Sat 9am-5pm, Sun 'til 6pm; $8.

Mitchell Park Conservatory, 524 S Layton Blvd, 649-9800. Three 7-storey glass domes with different luxuriant botanical gardens: arid, tropical and a seasonal display. Daily 9am-5pm; $4.

Pettit National Ice Center, 500 S 84th St, 266-0100. The nation's largest ice centre, open daily for public skating. Also an Olympic training complex. Mon-Thur 11am-1pm and 7pm-9:30pm, Fri 11am-1pm and 7pm-10pm, Sat 1pm-3pm and 7pm-10pm; $5, $2 skate rental.

Public Museum, 800 W Wells St, 278-2700. Walk-through European village of Milwaukee's 33 ethnic groups—charming. The Polish and Serbian houses are beautiful. Also a huge hand-made Costa-Rican rain forest, constructed with wood and other natural materials. Remarkable effect. Daily 9am-5pm; $5.50, $3.50 w/student ID.

Washington Park, NW from downtown. Open air concerts every Sat eve in July & Aug; free. Call 342-0215 for details.

Nearby: Germantown is the essence of old world Milwaukee. The town features restored German buildings, shops and restaurants in the **Dheinsville Historical Park**. Just outside of Germantown is **Holy Hill**, atop which is perched the **National Shrine of Mary**. For information, call 255-1812. **Old World Wisconsin**, Hwy 67, Eagle, 594-6300, is a 600-acre living history museum that features 65 historical buildings fashioned into an 1870s village. Costumed guides lead you through authentic farmhouses and barns of the pioneer days. Open daily 10am-5pm; $11.

ENTERTAINMENT

African World Festival: Held in August, this ethnic event showcases the best in African garb, jewellery, authentic foods, heritage, gospel, blues, R&B. Held at Henry Marer Festival Park, noon-midnight. Call 372-4567 for more info.

Bombay Bicycle Club, 509 W Wisconsin Ave, 271-7250. Bar and music videos; open 4:30pm 'til 2am.

Downtown Milwaukee is well-known for its line-up of **summer festivals**. **Summerfest**, two week festival June & July, by lakefront. 'Groups, beer, funfair, massive.' **Festa Italiana** in July, one of the biggest pastafazools anywhere: 'delicious'. Jul-Aug: **German, Irish, Polish Feasts**. **The Great Circus Parade** rolls out in full grandeur in July, downtown.

Marcus Center for the Performing Arts, 929 W Water St, 273-7121. Home of the Milwaukee Symphony.

Milwaukee Repertory Theater, 108 E Wells St, 224-9490. First-class plays; from $12. Season runs Sept-May.

Red Dog Saloon, 3530 W National Ave, 645-5261. Where the Milwaukee's Red Dog beer got its start. Sun-Thur 11am-2am, w/ends 'til 2:30am.

INFORMATION/TRAVEL

Amtrak, 433 W St Paul Ave, (800) 872-7245.

General Mitchell International Airport, 5300 S Howell Ave, 747-5300. Take the #80 bus from 6th & Wisconsin, $1.35. Takes about 30 mins.

Greyhound, 606 N 7th St, (800) 231-2222.

Milwaukee County Transit System, 344-6711. Runs the metro area buses, $1.35 basic fare (or pass allowing 10 rides for $10.50).

Visitors Bureau, 510 W Kilborn, 273-7222/747-4808at airport.

INTERNET ACCESS

Bear Brew Cafe, 708 N Milwaukee St, 224-8877. Open Mon-Fri 6:30am-6:30pm, Sat 8am-2pm.

MADISON Madison, wrapped picturesquely around two lakes, is the bastion of enlightened civilisation. More famous for being a college town than a state capital, its history of radical activism mirrors that of Ann Arbor and Berkeley. It probably has the highest under-employment anywhere; your taxi driver no doubt has a PhD in Medieval Philosophy and your waiter one in Set Theory Topology. The east side houses the alternative community, while the liberal west side is overrun with card-carrying members of the ACLU and the Women's Political Caucus. There's a lot packed into this pretty town, and cheap eats abound. Try both of the open-air farmers' markets for picnic fare. Rent a bike to get around. The City of Madison city guide can be found at *www.ci.madison.wi.us/* including the entertaining 'MAD about MADison' site.
The telephone area code is 608.

ACCOMMODATION
Abendrun B&B Swisstyle, 7019 Gehin Rd 53508, 424-3808. D-$70. TV/movies, non-smoking rooms.
Excel Inn, 4202 E Towne Blvd, 241-3861. S-$40 (more at w/ends), D-$52.
Wisconsin Center Guest House, 610 Langdon, 256-2621. S-$52, Q-$62. On fraternity row. Great frat parties in the vicinity. In **Dodgeville**, 40 miles W of Madison on Hwy 18: **Folklore Village Farm**, Rt 3, 924-4000. $10 AYH, $3 one-time membership fee.

FOOD
Best eateries are on or near campus.
Amy's Cafe, 414 W Gilman St, 255-8172. Good salads and sandwiches. Open 11am-11pm daily.
Babcock Ice Cream, in the Student Union on the University campus, 262-3045. UW's own ice cream—delicious!!
Brat Und Brau, 234 E Towne Mall, 249-1011. Good, cheap burgers, brats and salad bars. Open Mon-Sat 10am-9pm, Sun 11am-6pm.
Ella's Kosher Deli, 2902 E Washington, 241-5291. A real deli, standby of natives; sit and shmooze for hours. There's even a carousel to play on. Open Sun-Thur 10am-11pm, Fri-Sat 'til midnight.
Gino's, 540 State St, 257-9022. Known for its stuffed pizza. Open daily noon-midnight.
Dane County Farmers Market, Capitol Sq, 6.30am-noon. There's no shortage of fresh fruit and veg at this market, held every Sat, April-Nov. 'Beautiful local produce with a festival atmosphere.'
Library Mall, UW campus. A good choice for a pleasant day— food vendors gather en masse, offering a variety of choices.
Monty's Blue Plate Diner, 2089 Atwood, 244-8505. All-American food and fabulous desserts.
Sunprint Cafe and Gallery, 704 S Whitney Way, 274-7374. Original photographs in cafe setting. Specialities are coffee, soups, sandwiches and pastries. An especially good place to have breakfast. Open Mon-Fri 7am-9pm, Sat 'til 10pm, Sun from 8am.
Willy St Co-op, 1202 Williamson St, 251-6776. A well-run co-op on Madison's east side. You'll be at the heart of Madison's alternative culture while you buy veggies. Daily 8am-9pm.

OF INTEREST
It all revolves around the campus—a must for briefing yourself on social action, people, and activities throughout the town. Pick up a copy of *Isthmus*, be sure to read 'Dear Ursula'.

American Players Theater, in Spring Green, 45 miles W of Madison, 588-7401 (Box office: 588-2361). Quality Shakespearean and classical drama performed in the open air. Bring a picnic and enjoy the beautiful countryside. Performances on Tues.-Sun evenings mid-June-Oct; from $18.

Lake Shore path, start behind the Union terrace and walk out to Picnic Point. You'll meet many joggers and Madisonians talking over their problems.

Monona Terrace Community Center, 1 John Nolan Dr, 261-4000. Designed by Frank Lloyd Wright, the Center opens out to a beautiful view of the lake.

Olbrich Botanical Gardens, 3330 Atwood Ave, 246-4551. Especially beautiful in summer, when the roses are in bloom. Open daily, 8am-8pm.

State Capitol, 266-0382. The story goes that it is just a foot shorter than the one in Washington, DC. Mon-Sat 9am-4pm, Sun 1pm-4pm.

Vilas Park Zoo, 702 S Randall, 266-4732. This is not the world's greatest zoo, but Vilas Park has lovely beaches and is a nice place to take a walk. Daily 9.30am-8pm; free.

Nearby: Wisconsin Dells, 53 miles N of Madison. 'Magnificent rock and river scenery but terribly commercialised. Only visible by boat.' All-you-can-eat ($11.95) for breakfast, lunch and dinner at the **Paul Bunyan Lumberjack** restaurant, 254-8717. Also home of **Noah's Ark,** 1410 Wisconsin Dells Pkwy, 254-6351, America's largest waterpark, with 70 acres of rides and attractions. Open Memorial Day-Labor Day, 9am-8pm; $24.

Baraboo, about 40 miles N of Madison. In May 1884, the five Ringling Brothers began their world-renowned circus in a modest way, behind the Baraboo jail. Their former winter quarters is now the site of the excellent **Circus World Museum**, 426 Water St, 356-8341. Daily 1-ring performances, 152 rococo circus wagons, 19th century side-show, calliope. Daily 9am-9pm; $12. While in Baraboo, visit the **International Crane Foundation**, 356-9462. It's the only facility in the world that raises cranes for breeding and release into the wild.

Taliesin, near Spring Green, 45 mins W of Madison. A walk through Frank Lloyd Wright's Wisconsin estate is a journey through his evolution as an architect. Seven different tours, through Hillside Studio (designed as a school in 1902) and Theater, the grounds or through the House. Seasonal tours run May 1-October 31 (April/November Tours, Off-season Tours and Group Tours available). From $8, discount on House Tour every Tues. and Thur w/student ID. Call 588-7900 to reserve tkts. Also, **Riverview Terrace Café,** 588-7937, looking out over Wisconsin River at **The Frank Lloyd Wright Visitor Center**.

FLW may have been more famous, but the prize for sheer originality has to go to Alex Jordan for his spectacular **House on the Rock**, south of Taliesin in Rt. 23, 935-3639. Described by *Roadside America* as 'the Palace of Versailles converted into a Tussaud wax museum by a Kuwaiti sheikh,' House on the Rock is a mind-boggling conglomeration of mermaids, angels, antiques, enormous things (fireplace, steam locomotive, carousel, theatre, organs), catwalks, bisque dolls, and the heart-stopping 'Infinity Room', a horizontal glass-enclosed needle stretching 140 ft out into the clear Wisconsin air with no visible means of support. *See it!* Daily 9am-8pm (tkt office closes at 7pm) for tkts; $16.

ENTERTAINMENT

The liveliest nightlife is, of course, near campus. Head to **State St**— it connects the campus and the Capitol; no cars are allowed. Bars to try near campus: **State St Brats,** 603 State St, 255-5544, and **Brothers Bar,** 704 University Ave, 251-9550. Both are crowded on w/ends. **Concerts on the Square:** Capitol Square, every Wed eve, June-July. Madison also hosts some fun summer festivals. The **Art Show on the Square**, mid-July, colours the area around Capitol Square, and **Taste of Madison,** early Sept, is a wonderful opportunity to sample the cuisine of the best local restaurants.

LAKE SUPERIOR REGION In north-western Wisconsin, two areas to explore: **Indian Head Country,** (800) 826-6966, extending from the shore of Lake Superior to the Mississippi River. Tourist information is also available online at *www.wisconsinindianhead.org*. The **Apostle Islands,** (715) 779-3397, offer another chance to relax and unwind with a national lake shore known for its peaceful beauty. Also look online at *www.nps.gov/apis*. The **Turtle Flambeau Flowage** alone offers 19,000 acres of angling and wildlife watching opportunity.

In these parts, fishing has become a sort of pagan religion. See a testimonial to Wisconsin fish-worship at the **National Fresh Water Fishing Hall of Fame**, on Hwy 27 in **Hayward**, (715) 634-4440. Icons include gigantic fibreglass statues of beloved sports fish, including a muskie the size of a blue whale (in which you can be Jonah—observation deck inside the muskie's mouth). Daily 15 April-1 Nov, 10am-5pm; $4.50. The museum also has a website at *http://Freshwater-fishing.org/museum.html* with the opening greeting, 'A kid hooked on fishing won't get hooked on drugs'!

THE MOUNTAIN STATES

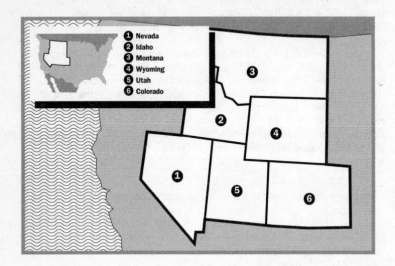

1 Nevada
2 Idaho
3 Montana
4 Wyoming
5 Utah
6 Colorado

After the endless horizontality of the Midwest, with its carefully manicured patterns of fences, townships and agriculture, the landscape of the Mountain States bursts upon you, young, rangy and wild as a colt. The Rockies, the San Juans and the Grand Tetons are intimidating, yet seductive. Crossing them is a pilgrimage; just imagine how their sharp white beauty must have made pioneers' hearts sink into their boots.

The topography doesn't limit itself to mountains, either. In this six-state cluster, you are treated to geysers, glaciers, buttes, vast river chasms, vivid canyons in paintbrush colours. The greater portion of this beauty is protected in National Parks and Monuments, among them: Rocky Mountain, Yellowstone, Craters of the Moon, Glacier, Devil's Tower, Zion and Bryce Canyon. In stark contrast to all this natural grandeur is the flagrant plasticity of Las Vegas, Reno and Hoover Dam/Lake Mead, without a doubt the most wondrously artificial trio of spots on earth.

Organized outdoor adventures are one way to explore the area. Llama trips, white-water rafting and trekking can be booked at no extra cost through American Wilderness Experience (AWE). Write PO Box 1486, Boulder, CO 80306 or call (800) 444-0099 for a catalogue, which lists various outfitter agencies and trips in the Mountain States, Arizona, New Mexico, California, Oregon, Hawaii, Alaska, Canada, Mexico, Minnesota and West Virginia.

Weather throughout the region tends to be dry and hot in summer and, with the exception of Las Vegas, cold and snowy in winter. Even summer evenings can be cold, and violent thunderstorms are common. Plan accordingly.

COLORADO *The Centennial State*

Horace Greeley, the newspaper editor famous for his advice 'Go West, young man', actually found the West a bit raw for his tastes. In 1860, he described what he saw on the frontier: 'They had a careless way of firing revolvers, sometimes at each other, at other times quite miscellaneous—so I left'.

Like other mountain states, Colorado had a lusty, shoot-em-up past filled with gold seekers, gold diggers, cattlemen and con men. Many former mining towns remain, some recycled into ski resorts, others spruced up for tourism but still in settings of unparalleled grandeur.

Modern day Colorado gold has been discovered by the technologically-inclined and politically-aware. Components for the Hubble telescope were manufactured here, and the state is the second-largest employer of federal government workers, Given its natural beauty, colorful history and highly-acclaimed skiing, Colorado is a prime tourist destination. Known as the nation's backbone, the state has 54 peaks over 14,000 feet. Over 75 percent of US land over 10,000 feet is concentrated in Colorado.

The eastern section, a monotony of rangeland cluttered with dun-coloured tumbleweeds and fenced 'hog-tight, horse-high and bull-strong', has little to offer. Concentrate instead on the western half, where you find two national parks, awesome scenery and an extraordinary display of summer wildflowers (some 5000 species).

Colorado's many youth hostels, among the best in the US, include ranches, historic hotels and ski lodges.
www.colorado.com
National Parks: Rocky Mountains, Mesa Verde
There are three telephone area codes for Colorado: 303, 719 and 970.

DENVER Impressively situated against a backdrop of snowy peaks, Denver is a welcome end to a grueling, 'are we there yet?' journey across the Great Plains. In spite of its picturesque setting, much of the unpleasant urban sprawl, crime and pollution that plague other American cities has arrived in Denver. After a painfully awkward decade of rapid development, Denver now sports a modern, well-finished look, befitting its role as banking, government, and industrial capital for the Rocky Mountains.

Perched at the confluence of Cherry Creek and the South Platte River, Denver began as a mining outpost. Its convenient foothills location nicely met the needs of Rocky Mountain miners, who rushed westward in the 1860s to find gold. The city didn't ascend to real prominence, however, until it linked up to the transcontinental railroad in 1869. Growth was further catalysed by a silver rush in the following decade. Denver—complete with Colorado's first saloon—became the state's capital. Today, people pour into Denver by the million, many at Denver International Airport, the first major new airport in the US for 20 years (opened in February 1995). The largest in the world (53 acres), the airport looks like a tented Bedouin city but has the capacity to handle around 32 million passengers a year.

With a median age of 30, over 200 parks and more days of sunshine (300) than San Diego or Miami Beach, the 'Mile High' city is a welcome place for sports and outdoors enthusiasts. Its undying love of the Broncos football team has reached saturation point, erupting into euphoria with the team's 1998 and 1999 Superbowl victories. Games from Sept-Dec are sold out for an undetermined number of years; plans are afoot to find a stadium to hold in excess of 76,000. Coors Field, built in 1995, packs crowds of 50,000 Colorado Rockies baseball fans from March-Sept, while the McNichols Arena hosts the Nuggets (basketball) from Nov-Apr and the Avalanche (ice-hockey) from Sept-Apr. Denver also boasts possibly the world's largest sporting goods store, Gart Sports, where you can shop from a golf cart.

Denver was also once a centre of counter-culture, a mecca for spiritualists, faith healers and radical thought. Though the politicized coffeehouses that appeared in Jack Kerouac's *On the Road* are gone, a lively cultural life still throbs in Denver when the sun goes down. Most likely you'll find the nation's most educated downtown workforce at the movies— the city leads the nation in attendance.

Downtown Denver revolves around 16th St Mall, a mile-long promenade lined with up-market shops. With so many office blocks around the city centre, the Mall is very lively around lunch time and virtually devoid of activity after 6pm. 'Denver is dead after 7pm. Not the sort of place to walk alone at night.'

The telephone area code is 303.
www.denveronline.com/ & www.downtown-denver.com

ACCOMMODATION

Denver International Youth Hostel, 630 E 16th Ave at Washington St, 832-9996. Houseparents are good guides to the area. No curfew. $8.50 per night. Laundry, TV, sundecks. Also serves as a general travel and hostel information centre with discounts on many activities.

Franklin House B&B, 1620 Franklin St, 331-9106. S-$30, D-$40 shared bath, D-$50 private bath. Incls bfast.

Hostel of the Rocky Mtns, 1530 Downing St, 861-7777. $12/night, $77/wk dorm, D-$30-$45 shared bath. 'Clean, comfortable and well equipped.' 'Owners very knowledgeable about sights and attractions.'

Motel 6, 3050 W 49th Ave, 455-8888. S-$45-$54, D-$51-$60. AC, pool, TV, phones. Bus stop 1 blk away. 'Friendly staff, good service.' Also on Wadsworth Blvd, 232-4924.

Melbourne Hotel and Hostel, 607 22nd St, 292-6386. $12 AYH, $15 non-AYH, private rms D-$21 AYH, $24 non-AYH. 6 blocks from bus stn. If arriving at airport call for directions. 'Brilliant.' 'Good, clean rooms. Staff very helpful.' 'Reservations strongly recommended.'

Standish Hotel, 1530 California St, 534-3231. S-$35 private bath, D-$32 shared bath. XP-$6. TV, laundry. 'Quiet, pleasant, simply furnished. Staff and clientele obviously regarded young people as quite a curiosity.' 'Not for a woman alone.'

YMCA, 25 E 16th Ave, Denver, CO 80202, 861-8300. Coed. Across from city bus stn. Write to make rsvs. S-$36 shared bath, S-$42 private bath, D-$60 private bath, $12 key deposit. Full use of sports centre incl. gym and pool. 'Very limited bathroom facilities.'

FOOD

Try Rocky Mountain trout, the local speciality. This is also the home of 'Rocky Mt oysters' or 'swinging steaks', an indelicate dish made of French-fried bull testicles. *The Official Visitor's Guide* (avail. at Visitors Bureau) lists dozens of places to eat in

Denver, and includes an extensive ethnic restaurant guide. 'Larimer & 17th Sts, variety of quite cheap places to eat—Turkish, Greek, Chinese, French, pizza.'

Casa Bonita, 6715 W Colfax, 232-5115. The all-you-can-eat Mexican platter for $8.69 is not the half of it. This isn't a restaurant, it's a Mexican carnival—with gun fights, cliff divers, mariachi bands. Watch out, Casa Bonita in Tulsa! 'Disappointing.' Open Sun-Thur 11am-9:30pm, Sat 'til 10pm.

Cherry Cricket, 2641 E Second Ave, 322-7666. Famous for hamburgers. Open daily 11am-2am.

Duffy's Shamrock, 1635 Court Place near YMCA, 534-4935. 'Good service, excellent value.' 'A godsend for the traditional boozer. Longest bar west of Mississippi - 78ft. $6 specials, home-made red and green chili.' 'All-American food.' Open daily, 6:30am-2am.

The Market, 1445 Larimer St, 534-5140. 'A trendy place to sit and drink coffee, buy health foods, watch people.' $5.50-$6, self-service deli. Open Sun-Thur, 6.30am-11pm, w/ end 'til midnight.

The Old Spaghetti Factory, 18th & Lawrence St, 295-1864, dinners with drink and dessert, $5-$8 with antique surroundings incl. tables made out of beds. Mon-Fri 11.30am-2pm, Mon-Thur 5pm-9:30pm, Fri-Sat 5pm-10.30pm, Sun 4pm-9.30pm.

20th St Cafe, just behind Greyhound bus station at 1123 20th St, 295-9041. $2-$4; chicken-fried steak a speciality. 'Good cheap breakfast and lunch in clean and friendly surroundings.' Open Mon-Fri 6am-6:45pm, Sat 7am-1:30pm.

OF INTEREST

Art Museum, 100 W 14th Ave Pkwy, 640-4433, $4.50, $2.50 w/student ID, free on Saturdays. Striking, fortresslike building covered with a million sparkling tiles. Seven floors of well-displayed art from totem poles to Picasso, incl. Native American and European collections. 'Exhibits on Indians more interesting and paintings better than in many small US galleries.' Tue-Sat 10am-5pm, Wed 'til 9pm, Sun noon-5pm.

Black American West Museum, 3091 California St, 292-2566. Black pioneer history. Founded by Paul Stewart, now in his 70s, who as a child was told he could only play the Indian -'there are no black cowboys'. Wrong again, as his museum proves. Also pays homage to western black women. Winter Wed-Fri 10am-2pm, w/end 12pm-5pm; summer Mon-Fri 10am- 5pm, w/end 12pm-5pm. $4, $3 w/student ID.

Colorado History Museum, 13th and Broadway, 866-3681. The 112-ft time line spans 150 years of Colorado history, with documents, maps, photos, and artifacts. Library and Native American exhibits. Open Mon-Sat 10am-4.30pm, Sun noon-4.30pm; $3. $2.50 w/student ID.

Governor's Residence Tours, 400 E 8th Avenue, 866-3682. Free tours 12pm-2pm, every Tues in June, July and August. No need to book.

Larimer Square, 14th to 16th Sts. Denver's restored Victorian and highly commercial 'heart', with gaslit lamps and horse-drawn carriages. Bring brass or take a pass. Larimer Square runs into **16th Street Mall**, Denver's $76 million pedestrian path with more shops and eateries and free shuttle buses. Nearby is the glittering **Tabor Center** , a completely glass-enclosed shopping complex, named after an 1890s gold rush bonanza king.

Denver Center for Performing Arts, 125 Champa St, 2 blks southeast of Larimer Square, 893-4000. Call to arrange free tour of scene shops, theatres and Metro Concert Hall where high-tech sound is controlled by dozens of 'floating' discs suspended from the ceiling.

Denver Zoo City Park, 2300 Steele St, 331-4100. Tropical Discovery features waterfalls, a mountain cave, tropical streams, temple ruins and a jungle river. Open daily 9am-6pm, $8.

Museum of Natural History, 2001 Colorado Blvd in City Park, 322-7009. Recommended for its detailed dioramas, meteorite and mineral collections, dinosaur displays. Laser and rock shows at planetarium, $6. Admission w/ IMAX giant screen cinema, $9. 'Exhilarating experience.' Open 9am-5pm.

The Molly Brown House Museum, 1340 Pennsylvania St, 832-4092. If you're intrigued by the story of the ill-fated Titanic but sick of seeing Leonardo di Caprio, this might be of interest. When the Titanic sunk, Molly didn't, earning her fame & the name 'the unsinkable Molly Brown'. 'Interesting story, uninteresting museum.' $6. In summers, open Mon-Sat 10am-3.30pm & Sun noon-3:30pm; in winter, closed Mon and at 4pm other days.

State Capitol, 14th St and Broadway, 866-2604. This dome has been gold-leafed 3 times since 1907, but of true value is the Colorado onyx (the world's entire supply) used in the interior of the Capitol. As you ascend to the top, pause at step 15—it's exactly 5280 feet above sea level. On the deck, a brass marker identifies surrounding peaks. Free 30-min tours Mon- Fri 9am-3.30pm, Sat 9.30pm-2.30pm. Closed Sun.

US Mint, 320 W Colfax Ave, entrance on Cherokee St, 405-4761. Free 20-min tours Mon-Fri 8am-3pm (9am on last Wed of month). Production stops at the end of the fiscal year; there are no tours from 25th Aug-2nd Sept. Long queues, get there early. Stamps out 35 million coins a day.

Nearby: Coors Brewery, 13th and Ford, Golden, 277-2337. Free 30-min tours and suds, Mon-Sat 10am-4pm. Bring proper ID. 'Very nice people.' Overlooking Coors, high above on Lookout Mt, is **Buffalo Bill Grave and Museum**, 526-0747. Open daily 9am-5pm. Lots of Wild West show and Pony Express artifacts of this flamboyant figure who symbolised the make-believe West. Among other things, you learn here that scalping was unknown to most Plains Indians until introduced by white scalp hunters. $3.

ENTERTAINMENT

Pick up a copy of *Westword*, a free weekly, for info about the arts in Denver.

Buckhorn Exchange, 1000 Osage St, 534-9505. Pricey downstairs restaurant ($30-$40) with buffalo and elk entrees. Stick to upstairs, Denver's oldest western bar. Outdoor covered patio Wed-Sat, live music in cocktail lounge (incl folk music and 'old ballads'). Open from 11am daily.

El Chapultepec, 20th and Market, 295-9126. 57-year-old jazz bar. $4-$6. 'A real dive, but good jazz.' Open 7am-2am daily.

Glendale is Denver's 'singles scene' with over a dozen discos, saloons and restaurants crammed into a small area. Bars with discos, outdoor volleyball courts, saddles for bar stools ... you name it.

Mercury Cafe, 2199 California, 294-9281. Charismatic and bohemian entertainment; open stage on Wed for poetry, song and acrobatics, swing bands on Sun and Thurs at 7.30pm, dance classes, jazz nights Fri-Sat. Open daily 5.30pm-11pm, night club stays open 'til 2am. 'Laid back and popular with locals.'

Red Rocks Amphitheater, SW edge of Greater Denver in Morrison. Listen to summer rock, country & western, pop and classical concerts surrounded by 440-ft red sandstone bluffs. 'Any concert here is a must—the most beautiful setting in the world with spectacular views over the prairies and Denver.' For tckts, phone 640-7300. Park admission is free; shows up to $30.

Six Flags Elitch Gardens, 2000 Elitch Circle, 595-4386. More than 100 attractions and rides, including the Boomerang, a forward and backwards-looping roller coaster. Open weekends April-May and daily from Memorial Day to Labor Day, 10am-10pm. $29; seasonal discounts available. 'Not for the faint-hearted.'

Wazee Supper Club, 1600 15th St, 623-9518. Great pizza and downtown neighbourhood bar. Live music Sat nights, no cover. 17 beers on tap, $2-$3.50 per glass. Open 11am-2am Mon-Fri, Sat from noon.

Wyncoop Brewing Company, 1634 18th St, 297-2700. Colorado's oldest brewery. Eleven beers on tap at all times, all brewed on premises. Stout, porter, light and medium ales, bitter beers. Tours of brewery Sat 1pm-4pm. Open Sun-Thur 11am-11pm, w/end 'til 2am.

SHOPPING
Tattered Cover, 2955 East 1st Ave, 322-7727. Reputedly one of the nation's most outstanding bookshops (so says the *NY Times*). Four storeys with reading lamps and comfy chairs to aid browsers. Will mail books anywhere in the world. Open Mon- Sat 9am-11pm, Sun 10am-6pm.

INFORMATION
Visitors Bureau, 225 W Colfax Ave, 892-1112. Internet: www.denver.org. Also at airport. Summer, Mon-Fri 8am-5pm, Sat 10am-4pm, Sun 10am-2pm; winters, Mon-Fri 8am-5pm, Sat 9am-1pm.
State Tourism Dept, 1625 Broadway, (800) 433-2656.

INTERNET ACCESS
Cafe @ Netherworld, 1278 Pennsylvania, 861-8NET. Open daily, 11am-2am. $4/hr. Free use of Internet 11am-2pm w/ $5 purchase.
Hole in the Wall, 1402 S Parker Rd, 337-4499. Open daily, 10am-6pm. $9/hr.
Majordomo's Net Cafe, 1401 Ogden, 830-0442. Open Mon-Fri, 7:30am-9pm. 20c/min, 15c/min w/ student ID.

TRAVEL
Greyhound, (800) 231-2222, 1055 19th St & Curtis. Bus service to Salt Lake City is one of the most scenic routes in America. 'The best part is the first 3 hours out of Denver.' 'Do not do it at night, fantastic scenery, too great to sleep through.'
City Bus, RTD, 299-6000, $1.25 during rush hours, 75c mid-day and evenings. $3 to Boulder.
Amtrak, Union Station, 17th and Wyncoop Sts, (800) 872-7245. The 'California Zephyr', Chicago-Oakland,CA route runs through Denver and the stretch to Salt Lake City is one of the best in the US, with the train running slowly up into the mountains, through one of the longest tunnels in the US, into beautiful gorges otherwise inaccessible to humanity. 'Get off at Glenwood Springs to see natural steam rising behind the station.'
Car rental: Rent-A-Heap-Cheap, 4205 Colorado Blvd, 393-0028.
Auto Driveaway, 5777 E Evans, 757-1211.
Interstate Transportation Inc, 9485 W Colfax, Lakewood, 232-1522.

HIKING
The 500-mile Colorado Trail begins at **Chatfield Reservoir,** 10 mi S of Denver. As the trail winds across the state to Durango, it crosses 8 mountain ranges, 7 national forests, 6 wilderness areas, and 5 river systems. For a more feasible day's hike, try **Devil's Head Lookout** in **Rampart Range**, 30 mi SW of Denver. A mile-long climb carries you 1000 ft in the air, where a fantastic view of the Spanish Peaks to the South, Mt Evans to the North, South Park to the West and the plains to the East awaits. For more hiking ideas, check out **Mike's Hikes** online at *www.mtnds.com/hikes.*

HEADING NORTH TO THE ROCKIES Leaving Denver on I-70 west one of the most scenic routes north—the Peak-to-Peak Highway—begins near **Central City**, a well-preserved Victorian town with honky-tonk saloons. The discovery of gold in Central City in 1859 turned fledgling Denver into little more than a revolving door. Everyone cleared out overnight to strike it rich. You can still pan for gold in what was 'the richest square mile on earth'.

The final leg of this road, Highway 7, leads to the east entrance of the Rocky Mountain National Park. An alternate route to this entrance at Estes Park, Highway 36, passes through Boulder.

BOULDER Although it's become too popular for its own good, Boulder still makes a scenic and lively alternative to Denver for explorations in northern Colorado. The anti-smoking laws are fiercely debated by the middle-class professionals and hippy spiritualists who live here. It's largely a laid-back student mecca (25% of the population are university students) at its grooviest along the Pearl Street Mall: 'fun on Sundays, clowns, magic shows, good eats, lots of young people'. 'Quite a magical place and altogether more interesting than Denver.' 'One of my favorite places in the whole USA. A medium-sized university town, full of life and young people.' *visitor.boulder.net*
The telephone area code is 303.

ACCOMMODATION
Boulder International Youth Hostel, 1107 12th St, 442-9304. Dorm $15 with $5 deposit. S-$35, D-$40, $10 deposit, both shared bath. Kitchen, laundry; deposit for fans, phones, refrigerators. 20 mins to mountains. 'Friendly, relaxed.' 'Ill-equipped kitchen.' 'Rather cramped.'

FOOD
Boulder is the only city in the US to own its own glacier, which once served as a delicious water supply. **Alfred Packer Memorial Grill**, U of Colorado, University Memorial Bldg, 16th and Broadway, 492-6578. Named after the only man ever convicted of cannibalism in the US. Alf's orgy took place in 1886, when he and 5 others were trapped by blizzards at Slumgullion Pass for 60 days. Alf got 17 years from the judge, who said: 'There were only 6 Democrats in Hinsdale County and you, you son-of-a-bitch, ate 5 of them!' Postscript: Packer became a vegetarian after his release from prison.
Boulder Dushanbe Teahouse, 1770 13th St, 442-4993. Like nothing you've ever seen. The teahouse was a gift from Boulder's sister city of Dushanbe, Tajikistan, handcrafted and reassembled over the course of 8 years. Open 8am-10pm daily.
Buchanan's Coffee Pub, 1301 Pennsylvania on The Hill, 440-0222. Pastries, sandwiches and flavoured coffees from $1.15. Mon-Fri 7am-11pm, Sat-Sun from 8am.
Colacci's, 816 Main St, 673-9400. Excellent Italian food, huge portions $6—shared. Open 11am-9pm daily.
Old Chicago Pizza Parlour, 1102 Pearl, 443-5031. Huge selection (110) of beers. Beer monsters can try the 'World Tour of Beers Special' in the bar: drink 25 or more and become a member of the *Foamers* club. Prizes! But don't forget the food: 'Best pizza I've ever tasted.' Open Sun-Thur 11am-midnight, Fri-Sat 'til 1am.
Tra Ling's Oriental Cafe, 1305 Broadway, 449-0400. Cheap and cheerful Chinese dishes from $1. Hip with students. Open 11:30am-9:30pm daily.
Trident Cafe, 940 Pearl, 443 3133. Voted 'Best Coffeehouse' by Boulderites in 1997. Browse in the adjoining bookstore, then sip gourmet coffee from $1 with free refill. 'All it lacks is 'Ellen.' Open 10am-11am daily.

OF INTEREST
Arapaho Glacier, 28 miles west. 1 mile long and 100-500 ft thick, the Arapaho moves at a sedate 11 to 27 inches per year. Nothing to worry about.
Celestial Seasonings Tea Co, 4600 Sleepytime Dr, 581-1202, offers free tasting tours of their Boulder factory, including a stroll through their herb garden and a stopover in the refreshing 'mint room'. Call ahead for times.
Colorado Chautauqua, 9th and Baseline, 440-7666. Founded to provide recreation, education and the arts, the centre hosts music festivals and other events in its 100 yr old dining hall and auditorium. Call for events list. A variety of hiking trails start

near here at Flatirons. 'Great views over Boulder—but take plenty of water!'
Eldorado Springs, just off I-70, 499-1316. Fresh water pool, slide and towering mountains above, $5. 'Scenic place to cool off or rock-climb but you need transport.'
U of Colorado, 492-1411, ersatz Spanish architecture, big party place. **Fiske Planetarium**, 492-5002, on campus, Regent Drive: 'Worth a visit, especially the laser show'. Opening times and shows vary, esp during summer. Call to check. Laser show $4.

ENTERTAINMENT
The Mall, 449-3774, along Pearl St. 'Superb spectacles any summer evening—all free.'
Catacombs Bar, 2115 13th St, 443-0486, has good bands, pool tables.
Sundown Saloon, 1136 Pearl, 449-4987 has a wide selection of microbrews. 'Plenty of pool tables downstairs. '
The Walrus, 1911 11th St, 443-9902. Located near the mall. Good mix of students and locals. 'Cozy, friendly atmosphere.'
Colorado Shakespeare Festival, at U of Colorado. Rates 3rd in nation. Call 492-0554 for tickets, $12-$32.
Rockies Brewing Company, 2880 Wilderness Pl, 444-4796. Pub open Mon-Sat from 11am. Free tasting tours of handcrafted Boulder beers at 2pm daily (exc. Sun).

INFORMATION
Boulder Convention and Visitors Bureau,2440 Pearl St, (800) 444- 0447/442-2911.

ESTES PARK A hairbreadth away from the park entrance to Rocky Mountain National Park, Estes may be the most convenient place to lodge if you're without wheels. Commercial campgrounds here have showers and are nearer to everything. The **Estes Park Welcome Center** website, *www.estes-park.com*, is a comprehensive guide with helpful links for lodging and recreation info in Estes Park and Rocky Mountain National Park.
The area code is 970.

ACCOMMODATION
H-Bar-G Ranch Hostel (AYH), 6 miles from Estes Park at the head of Devil's Gulch, 586-3688. $10 per night. Memberships for sale at hostel for $18 to foreign nationals. Former dude ranch with splendid views. 'Lou, the warden, takes hostellers into town every morning at 7.30am and picks people up from the Chamber of Commerce at Estes Park at 5pm.' 'Lou will rent out cars.' 'Best hostel I stayed at.' 'My favourite hostel of the summer.' Open 25 May to 12 September.

FOOD/ENTERTAINMENT
Estes Park Brewery, 470 Prospect Village Drive, 586-5421. Open daily 11am-midnight. 'Pool tables, pinball, basic food and free tasting tours anytime.'
MacDonald Coffee and Paper House, 150 East Elkhorn, 586-3451. Enjoy a relaxed coffee on the patio or, on Fridays, a 30 min massage for $9. Mon-Sat 8am-10pm, Sun 8am-6pm.
Poppie's Pizza and Grill, 342 E Elkhorn, 586-8282. Pizzas from $3. 'Nice cheap restaurant with big patio, frequented by locals.' Open daily, 11am-11pm.
The Stanley Hotel, 333 Wonder View Avenue, (800) 976-1377. A must-see if you're in Estes; this striking 1909 building is where *The Shining* was filmed. 'Creepy.'
The Wheel Bar, 132 E Elkhorn, 586-9381. Cheap liquor, steaks under $11.50. Open daily 10am-2am.

ROCKY MOUNTAIN NATIONAL PARK To the Indians and early trappers, these were the Shining Mountains, gleaming with silvery lakes, golden sunrises, blue-white glaciers and snowpacks. Later settlers prosaically dubbed them 'Rocky', but there is nothing prosaic about this wildlife-rich range of mountains and valleys crowned by a cross-section of the Continental Divide. Over 70 peaks in the park are 12,000 feet or more. Even the untrained eye can see the clear traces of glacial action in the five active glaciers that remain. **Longs Peak** is the highest, at 14,255 ft.

Be sure to take the **Trail Ridge Road** (Hwy 34), which follows an old Ute and Arapaho trail along the very crest of a ridge. Along its 50 miles, you actually overlook 10,000 ft peaks, alpine lakes, spruce forests and wild-flower-spangled meadows. The trail is particularly delightful when the flowers are at their peak, in June and July; indeed, snow keeps this and other park roads impassable until the end of May and from late October on. Look out for elk, moose, hawks, coyote, bighorn sheep and mountain lions.

Other routes lead hikers to a variety of long and short trails. One excellent trail is the 5.6 mile hike from **Glacier Gorge Junction** to **Bear Lake** and **Lake Haiyaha**. At the end of the hike, catch the free park bus back to Glacier Gorge (runs mid-June to Labor Day). For more hiking suggestions and photos, go to Mike's Hikes, at *www.mtnds.com/hikes*. Horseback riding is also popular; horses can be rented at Estes Park and Grand Lake. (Also at Glacier Creek and Moraine stables in the National Park.) The entrance fee is $10 per car for seven days, $20 for one full year. The park has hundreds of trails; for good maps visit the main visitors' centre 2 miles west of Estes Park on Highway 36. Open daily summers, 8am-9pm. Other centres are scattered throughout the park. For info, call Rocky Mountain National Park Office: 586-1206.
www.nps.gov/romo/
The telephone area code is 970.

ACCOMMODATION/ FOOD
Campgrounds near east entrance cost $16 per night: **Moraine Park, Glacier Basin** require booking (through DESTINET, call (800) 365-2267). **Aspen Glen, Longs Peak** and **Timber Creek** are first-come, first-serve and also cost $16. $15 back country camping permits for the entire park are available at Back Country Office, Rocky Mtn National Park, Estes Park, CO 80517, 586-1242. 'Glacier Basin has a free bus to the main hiking area. Campsites have no shops or showers so it is difficult without a car'.
Near southwest entrance. Excellent lodging at **Shadowcliff AYH, Grand Lake**, 627-9220. $10 AYH, $12 non-members. S/D-$25 plus XP $5, up to six per room with shared bath. 'Brilliant Scandinavian-style hostel on cliff overlooking lake.' For pastries, homemade bread and more, go to the British-owned **Carver's Bakery,** 93 Cooper Creek Way, 726-8202. **Moffat Bagel,** behind Conoco gas station in Winter Park, 726-5530, does great bites for very little money.

TRAVEL
The best way to get to the park is by car; see car rentals under Denver. **Gray Line** offers daily 10-hr tour of the park for $50, leaving from Denver, (303)289-2841. Hitching to the park is described as 'very easy'.

COLORADO SPRINGS Founded by bonanza kings and intended as a resort and retirement centre, the Springs grew to become the second largest city in Colorado and site of the US Air Force Academy. Trash features like motel sprawl cannot dim the glory of its setting at the base of Pike's Peak. Constant winds at the Peak blow the snow like a banner— an exhilarating sight to behold. The city makes a good base to explore Garden of the Gods, Cripple Creek and Royal Gorge.
The telephone area code is 719.

ACCOMMODATION
Buffalo Lodge, 3700 W Colorado Ave, 634-2851. S/D-$55, D-$68 for 4. AC, pool, TV, telephones, laundry facilities, continental bfast, bus stop 2 blks. Trolley to Colorado Springs every hour.
Garden of the Gods Campground (AYH), 3704 W Colorado Ave, 475-9450. Summers only; pool. Cabins $35 for 2. Camping $25 for 2. XP-$2.
Golden Eagle Ranch Campground and May Museum Centre, 710 Rock Creek Canyon Road, 576-0450. 5 mls south on Hwy 115. Camping: $15.50; $17.50 for 2 w/hook-up. Museum houses large insect displays, space wing, NASA movies; $4.50 ($1 disc for campers).
Motel 6, 3228 N Chestnut St, 520-5400. S-$56-$70, D-$62-$76. AC, pool. View of Pike's Peak from rooms.

ENTERTAINMENT/FOOD
Barney's Diner, 1403 South Tejon St, 632-1756. Open Mon-Fri 6.30am-3pm, Sat 7.30am-2pm; special roast dinners and hearty breakfasts from $3.30.
Poor Richard's Feed & Read, 324 N Tejon St, 632-7721. Part of an entertainment complex with restaurant, toy and bookstore as neighbours. Poor Richard's has an art gallery and excellent vegetarian dishes for $6. Open daily 11am-10pm.

OF INTEREST
Cave of the Winds, off Hwy 24, 685-5444. Year round horseback riding and nightly laser show during summer; $12.
The Cheyenne Mountain Complex incorporates the North American Aerospace Defence Command (NORAD) and Airforce Space Command; it sits 1800 ft below Cheyenne Mountain in its own cavern, designed to withstand even a direct nuclear hit. Although tours of the base have been suspended for security reasons, you can still catch a free slide presentation in the technical support facility, Mon 10:30am and 2pm, Fri 10:30am only. Call 474-2238/9 to speak to tour scheduler or make resv. Cancellation places are available; passport number needed.
Garden of the Gods, NW of Colorado Springs off Hwy 24, 385-5940. 940 acres of stunning red sandstone formations, especially striking at sunrise or sunset. Free. 'Outstanding scenic beauty—next thing to Grand Canyon.' 'Well worth a visit.'
Pike's Peak, Lon Chaney of horror movie fame was once a guide to this 14,255-ft peak. Hike the Barr National Recreation Trail or take the 18-mile auto highway that climbs 7039 ft—nearly to the top of the mountain, $6 all yr. For experienced mountain drivers only. This is the course of one of the most harrowing and oldest car races in the world, held in July. At the top is the view that inspired Katherine Lee Bates to write *America the Beautiful* in 1893. Pike's Peak **cog railway**, 685-1045, open May-Oct is $23.50 to the summit. Call 685-5401 to make a rsv. Follow one of the trails for as long as you like and then walk down. 'The view is breathtaking.' 'Take a sweater.'
Rock Ledge Ranch Historic Site, across from Garden of the Gods Visitors Center, 578-6777. The living history exhibit chronicles 3 distinct periods of settlement with the 1860s Galloway Homestead, the 1880s Chambers Farm and the 1907 Palmer Estate. Open Wed-Sun, 10am-5pm; $3.
US Olympic Complex, 1750 E Boulder St, 578-4618. Home of the US Olympic

Committee HQ, 15,000 potential Olympians come and train here every year. Free 1 hr tours from the Visitor Center (includes a film). The velodrome is in Memorial Park, 4 blks from main complex. Open Mon-Sat 9am-5pm, Sun 10am-5pm.

World Figure Skating Museum, 20 First St, 635-5200. If you haven't had your fill of the Olympic experience, this is a must-see. Open Mon-Sat, 10am-4pm; $3.

Nearby: Bishop's Castle, 11 mi S of Canon City in Beulah. Every man wants his own castle; Jim Bishop took that dream a little further. For the past 30 years, he has been building a castle on a mountainside in central Colorado, all by himself. He touts the castle as "a monument to hard-working people." Some are amazed by his feat, others think he's just crazy. Decide for yourself. Eventually he hopes to add a moat and drawbridge, as well as a roller coaster on the castle's outer wall.

Canon City, the town from which Tom Mix launched his cowboy career. It may also look familiar to movie-goers as the shooting site of *Cat Ballou* and *True Grit.* If you're bored by the natural beauty of the area, visit **Buckskin Joe's Frontier Town and Railway,** 275-5149, where you can relive the wild, wild west, complete with live hangings! Open daily, 9am-6.30pm, $12. Keeping with the rampant theme of lawlessness, there's also the **Prison Museum,** 201 N First St, 269-3015. Get inside an actual gas chamber or pose for souvenir photo behind bars in black and white-striped overalls. Free admission. Little else of interest except the art shop at the Colorado State Penitentiary and **Royal Gorge,** 275-7505, site of the highest suspension bridge in the world—an acrophobe's nightmare. Lousy with tourist claptrap of all sorts (including the sickening aerial tram), but the view is stupendous. $12.50 for either tram ride or train ride to bottom of the gorge, open daily.

Cripple Creek, on the opposite side of Pike's Peak. The picturesque, but difficult route is via Gold Camp Road (follow Old Stage Road then join up with Gold Camp to avoid the tunnel cave-in) - 3 to 4 hrs of gravel and curves (Teddy Roosevelt called it 'the trip that bankrupts the English language'). Far easier is the route by Hwys 50 and 9 (about an hr). In its heyday, Cripple Creek yielded more than $25 million in gold in one year and had the honour of being called a 'foul cesspool' by Carry Nation for its brothels and 5 opera houses. Today the gold comes in a different form. As a tourism website suggests, "In 1898, Cripple Creek mines paid $190 million in gold. In 1998, Cripple Creek casinos paid $2 billion in 'gold.'"

Despite the overabundance of casinos and tourist traps, the place has considerable charm. Don't miss the salty cemetery (wry epitaphs, heart-shaped madame's tombstone, wooden headstones, etc) . Take part in a **Ghost Walk Tour,** 689-3234, conducted by the mayor, who dons a hat and cape and leads you on a 1.5 hr walking tour of Cripple Creek. Stay overnight at the Victorian relic **Imperial Hotel,** 689-2922, D-$50-$100, to partake of the excellent buffet dinners. The **Mollie Kathleen Gold Mine,** 689-2465. $10—'very worthwhile—free gold ore' and takes you 1000ft down. Open daily 9am-5pm.

Seven Falls, 10 min from downtown Colorado Springs on Cheyenne Blvd, 632-0765. Called "the grandest mile of scenery in Colorado," seven separate falls splash off a sheer granite cliff from a height of 181 ft. Stunning!

INFORMATION
Colorado Springs Convention and Visitors Bureau, (800) 888-4748; Internet: *www.coloradosprings-travel.com.*
Cripple Creek Chamber of Commerce, 689-2169.
Greyhound, 120 S Weber St, Colorado Springs, 635-1608. $12 o/w to Denver.

ASPEN 210 miles west of Denver on Highway 82, Aspen is a tasteful, beautiful ski resort and classical music festival site, set amid National Forests and more recently the multi-million dollar spreads of Jack Nicholson, Don Johnson, Melanie Griffith and Cher, among others. Most

SKI-ING IN THE USA

In 1935 there were no ski resorts in the USA. When Sun Valley, Idaho, introduced the world's first chairlift in 1936, Hollywood stars such as Clark Gable thronged to the slopes and the glamour tag has stuck ever since. Winter sports still have a reputation for being expensive but it's quite possible to ski 2,000 ft verticals, snowboard plow or enjoy a quiet schuss through deserted back-country at over 300 resorts on a budget - and sometimes for free.

TRIP TIPS

Lift passes eat into any budget so avoid peak times such as holidays and weekends; lowest prices are usually from Oct to mid-Dec and in April, with some free skiing between Thanksgiving and Christmas. Look out for multiple-area discount cards and reduced-rate mid-week or evening lift passes w/student ID. If you have time, volunteering for community programs such as working with handicapped skiers or helping out at ski competitions will often earn you a valuable free season pass. Some resorts allow you to 'try before you buy' - just return your lift pass within 1 hr of purchase for a full refund or credit voucher for another day. Cross-country skiing is less expensive than downhill and is free in areas such as **Ski Sunlight**, **Aspen** and **Telluride, Colorado** and **Schweitzer Mountain Resort, Idaho.**

If you don't have your own equipment, check out unlimited all-season rentals, often as low as $130. If you're planning on skiing for a short time, daily equipment rentals (around $15-$20) are your best bet. Look out for pre-season sales in late Oct and 'swaps' in major cities for discounted and nearly-new gear. Clip coupons in local papers for discount meals and drinks; weekly resort entertainment nights are also great for free beer and snacks.

EAST COAST: **Sugarloaf USA, Maine**, RR1 Box 5000, Carrabassett Valley, ME 04947, (207) 237-2000. *www.sugarloaf.com*. Close to the Canadian border with 2,800ft of skiable vertical, snowboarding, cross-country and ice-skating; popular with advanced skiers, discounts w/student ID. **Killington, Vermont**, Killington Rd, VT 05751, (800) 422-3333 boasts the highest vertical in the east at 3,150 ft and the longest ski season. 3 hrs from Boston, it's a pricey resort with buzzing apres-ski. Nearby **Suicide Six**, (800) 448-7900, is much cheaper mid-week and quite challenging. It holds a special place in American skiing history; it's here where, in 1934, a Model T Ford was rigged up to power America's first ski tow. **Mount Jay**, Rte 242, **Jay, VT** 05859, (802) 988-2611, 8 miles from the Canadian border, offers spectacular scenery and excellent snowboarding - also cheaper than **Mount Snow/Haystack**, 105 Mountain Rd, **Mount Snow, VT** 05356, (800) 245-7669, the closest major Vermont resort to New York and Boston. **Mt. Washington Valley, New Hampshire**, Chamber of Commerce, PO Box 2300, N Conway, NH 03860, (800) 367-3364, comprises several resorts including **Wildcat**, good for strong skiers and snowboarders and **Attitash Bear Peak** which has economical tickets for skiing by the vertical foot. **Waterville Valley**, One Ski Area Rd, **Waterville Valley, NH** 03215, (800) 468-2553, *www.waterville.com*, has an exclusive snowboard park called the 'Wicked Ditch of the East' and some of the best cross-country trails in New England. **Ski Windham**, New York, PO Box 459, **Windham NY** 12496, (518) 734-4300 and **Hunter Mountain**, PO Box 295, **Hunter, NY** 12442, (518) 263-4223 (just 2 hrs N of New York City), offer strong intermediate slopes, packed at weekends. Lots of pocket ski areas in the "NE Kingdom" area of Vermont/New Hampshire. Best areas for apres-ski: **Mt Washington Valley, NH** and **Killington, VT**. Best areas for vertical: **Killington** and **Cannon**. For a rundown on all of the major ski resorts in the Northeast, visit *www.nemountainreview.com*.

MOUNTAIN STATES: Colorado offers extensive skiing for all levels with 300 days of sunshine per year. **Aspen**, (970) 925-1220 and **Vail**, (970) 476-5601 are noted for celebrities and astronomical prices; head instead for **Silver Creek**, (970) 887-3384, and **Arapahoe Basin**, (970) 468-0718, which are also cheaper than nearby Winter Park and Keystone. **Purgatory**, One Skier Place, Durango, CO 81301, (800) 982-6103 is an active student haunt with rollercoaster runs and a snowboard park. About 25 miles away, **Durango** is the place for cheap lodging and wild night life during Spring Break. Ski 'Baldy' at **Sun Valley Resort, Idaho**, (800) 786-8259; 3,400 ft of vertical and back country trails through impressive wilderness. For apres-ski, catch world-class bands from $25 at Bruce Willis' nightclub, **The Mint**, 116 Main St (in Hailey), (208) 788-6468. For budget skiing try **Silver Mountain Resort**, (208) 783-1111. Host to the 2002 Winter Olympics, **Salt Lake City, Utah**, has 7 ski areas less than 1 hr from the centre. Call the Visitors Centre, (801) 521-2868, for discount coupons. **Alta**, PO Box 21350, UT 84092-8007, (801) 359-1078 has low-price passes; great for powder-hounds but no snowboarding. **Solitude**, PO Box 21350, UT 84121-0350, (800) 748-4SKI and **Brighton**, Star Rte, UT 84121, (801) 532-4731 are equally good value with intermediate and beginner slopes, challenging canyon walls for experts. **Wolf Mountain**, (435) 649-5400 has ski-jumping and extreme chutes plus free bus service from Park City, 30 miles east of Salt Lake City. **Big Mountain, Montana**, PO Box 1400, Whitefish, MT 59937, (406) 862-1900 is low-key; long on powder, short on sun. **Taos Ski Valley, New Mexico**, Box 90, NM 87525, (505) 776-2291 will challenge experts. 18 miles from the city of Taos and 2,000 ft higher, at the fringe of Carson National Forest; telemark and monoskis but no snowboarding. **Jackson Hole, Wyoming**, Box 290 Teton Village, WY 83025, (307) 733-2292 is laid back with cheap lodging. For deep powder go to **Grand Targhee**, PO Box Ski, Alta, WY 83422, (307) 353-2300. Best apres-ski: **Aspen** (pricey) and **Durango**. Highest verticals: **Big Sky, Montana** (4,180 ft), **Jackson Hole** (4,139 ft). Best night-skiing: **Mt Hood Skibowl**.

WEST COAST: CALIFORNIA. The **Lake Tahoe** area, 200 miles east of San Francisco has world-class ski areas and casino-based nightlife. Avoid the larger, pricer resorts; head out to **Diamond Peak**, 1210 Ski Way, Incline Village, NV 89451, (775) 832-1177, and **Ski Homewood**, (530) 525-2992, for outstanding lake views and great slopes. **Kirkwood**, Box 1, Kirkwood, CA 95646, (209) 258-6000 has the best terrain for all abilities but quiet apres-ski. Don't miss **Badger Pass**, Yosemite National Park, CA, (209) 372-1000; noted for its stunning location and cross-country tracks. OREGON. **Mount Hood Ski Bowl, Oregon,** PO Box 280, Government Camp, OR 97028, (503) 272-3206 has cheap passes, challenging runs, a snowboard obstacle course and halfpipe. ALASKA. Catch the northern lights at **Alyeska, Alaska**, PO Box 249, Girdwood, AK 99587, (907) 754-1111, 40 miles southeast of Anchorage.

For detailed info on the best spots to ski and snowboard, check out www.gowest.com, *www.travelbase.com*/skiareas and www.goski.com, all excellent on-line resources incl. maps, prices, accommodation, events, weather and the latest gear. Also useful: *Skiing on a Budget*, Claire Walter, Better Way Books, $15.99.

SKI JOBS
There are thousands of seasonal jobs in ski resorts - from casual bartending to certified instruction. Job fairs are held throughout the country in the autumn but check *www.coolworks.com* for a head start; it's a huge directory of current opportunities, addresses and details of benefits such as free lift passes and accommodation. "I worked at Sun Valley and got in over 100 days of skiing on the mountain as 'bowl patrol' - cleaning bathrooms. Best ski-bum job in the universe! Assuming it snows . . .

things cost the earth in Aspen but reasonable accommodation can be found here, unlike the case with its patrician sister resort, Vail.
The telephone area code is 970.

ACCOMMODATION
NB: rates are highest in winter, lowest in spring and autumn.
Alpen Hutte, 471 Rainbow Dr, PO Box 919, Silverthorne, (on I-70; get off bus at Silverthorne), 468-6336. $17, $15 AYH ($27, Dec-March). Nr Breckenridge ski area. Strict midnight curfew, laundry, TV lounge, smoking room, kitchen, no spirits. 'Really nice, clean kitchen.'
St Moritz Lodge, 334 W Hyman, (800) 817-2069/925-3220, fax 920-4032. Dorms $34 summer, $55 winter, shared bath. Incls linen, coffee and tea in the summer, bfast in winter. Partial kitchen. Sauna, pool, off- street parking.
In nearby Breckenridge:
Fireside Inn, Wellington & French Sts, 453-6456; fax: (970)453-9577. Email: *fireside@breknet.com*. Summer dorms: $19 AYH, $22 non-members; winter dorms $28/$31. Hot tub, cable TV.
Camping, free wilderness camping w/running water in **White River National Forest**, which covers nearly all of Pitkin County. Closest: E Maroon, 1 mile NW of Aspen on Hwy 32.

FOOD
Rusty's Hickory House on W Main, 925-2313. 'Good breakfast, lunch, reasonably priced.' $5.95 specials. Open daily 6am-2:30pm, 5pm-10pm.
Little Annie's Eating House, 517 East Hymen, 925-1098. Lunchtime specials from $6.95. Open daily, 11:30am-10:30pm.

OF INTEREST
Aspen Music Festival, 9 weeks late June-Aug. Rivals Tanglewood's Berkshire Festival in prestige. 'The combination of setting, fresh air and music blew my mind.' Many open rehearsals and other free events. Call 925-9042 for tickets.
Gondola up Aspen Mt to 11,000 ft, 925-1220; $12.

INFORMATION
Aspen Central Reservations and Visitors Center, 425 Rio Grande Place, (800) 262-7736. The airport lies 5 miles from town; take the county bus from the highway that runs outside the airport, 75c; it will take you downtown.

ACROSS WESTERN COLORADO The northernmost route will take you through **Steamboat Springs**, an expensive ski resort ('fun and friendly—great skiing'), and ultimately to **Dinosaur National Monument**, which overlaps into Utah. The monument presents striking and lonely canyon vistas (used by Butch Cassidy and Co as a hideout) and the fossil remains of stegosaurus, brontosaurus and other big guys, exposed in bas relief on the quarry face, with more being excavated before your eyes. 'Not at all gimmicky; fascinating to anyone even vaguely interested in paleontology or geology.' NB: quarry, visitor centre is in Utah; see that section.

The major route west is the Interstate 70, which passes through the Eisenhower Tunnel, Eagle and **Glenwood Springs**, an invigorating place to pause for a dip in the world's largest open-air thermal pool. Wyatt Earp's sidekick, Doc Holliday, lies buried here; his headstone reads: 'He died in bed.' The scenic interstate follows the Colorado River all the way to Grand Junction, the last town of any size in Colorado. Grand Junction is also the gateway to the towering spires and canyon wilderness of **Colorado National Monument,** which is on the eastern edge of the **Colorado Plateau**. Call 858-3617; $4 per car for 2 weeks, $2 on foot, camping available, $10 a site.

Further south is the **Black Canyon** of the **Gunnison National Monument** ('a very special place—deer wander regularly through campsites') near Montrose, and the high adventure of the journey through Ouray and Telluride to Silverton and well south to Durango. **Ouray**, the 'Switzerland of America', is noted for the Camp Bird Mine, which produced $24 million for the Walsh family and remains productive today. With some of the loot, papa Walsh bought his daughter the Hope Diamond.

'Try getting a ride in the back of a pickup truck between Ouray and **Telluride**. The views are spectacular, the road, hair-raising.' Dizzy Gillespie once said, 'If Telluride ain't paradise, then heaven can wait.' Wait it did for Butch Cassidy, who pulled his first bank job here. Interesting buildings from the mining era have earned Telluride national historic landmark status. Telluride is also well-known as a ski resort (inexpensive, too) and festival centre, featuring the remarkable Labor Day Film Festival (now ranked second only to Cannes) and summer music events from bluegrass and jazz concerts.

The telephone area code is 970.

ACCOMMODATION
Camping at **Dinosaur National Monument**, 374-3000, $10 entrance fee, $12/site with bath and running water; motels at nearby Dinosaur, CO and Vernal, UT. See also *Utah*.

Glenwood Springs Hostel, 1021 Grand Ave, Glenwood Springs, CO 81601, 945-8545. Dorm style, $12, $39/ 4 nights. Large record collection and taping facilities. Will pick up from bus or train with advance notice. Kitchen, laundry, free bedding. 'Comfortable'. Organises half-day white-water rafting trips $25; caving $22; disc for ski areas and Vapour Caves; mountain bike rentals $12 and free transport to 'No Name' for hiking. Local bus to Aspen, $6 return.

At Grand Junction: Hotel Melrose, 337 Colorado Ave, 242-9636. With shared bath, S-$48, D-$54, dorms $16 (AYH only). Walking distance to bus and rail stns. Also have 3 hiking tours, incl Colorado National Mounument. $25-$35 each tour, $75 all three.

At Telluride: New Sheridan Hotel, 231 W Colorado Ave, 728-4351. S/D-$80-$125. Incls bfast, complimentary glass of wine and refreshments. Restored hotel with a bar that appeared in *Butch Cassidy and the Sundance Kid* (but not the version which starred Robert Redford).

At Silverton: French Baker Teller House, 1250 Greene St, 387-5423. S/D-$52 shared bath, S/D-$79, private bath, incls bfast. 'Town worth visiting, price incl. b'fast.'

OF INTEREST
Glenwood Springs Hot Pool, Glenwood Lodge, 945-6571. 'Exhilarating.' 'Especially superb at night.' $8 for all-day pass, 7.30am-10pm.

Million-dollar highway, between Ouray and Silverton. A 6-mile stretch, numbered among the most spectacular roads in the US.

INTERNET ACCESS
CyberSpot Cafe, 820 North Ave in Grand Junction, 257-9032. Open daily, 10am-6pm; $7/hr.

TRAVEL/INFORMATION
Amtrak: Glenwood Springs, 413 7th St, (800)872-7245; Grand Junction, 337 S 1st St,

(800) 872-7245. Both stops on the beautiful 'California Zephyr' route.

Greyhound: Glenwood Springs, 118 W 6th Ave, 945-8501; Grand Junction, 230 5th St, 242-6012, (800) 231-2222.

Grand Junction Visitors Bureau, 740 Horizon Dr, 244-1480.

Glenwood Springs Chamber Resort Association, 1102 Grand Ave, 945-6589. Visitor information centre open Mon-Fri 9am-5pm; w/ends 9am-3pm in summer.

Dinosaur National Monument. No direct transit, but take bus to Vernal, Utah, where you can rent a car or hitch.

Glenwood Springs: 'Day trip from Denver; take 8.25am bus service to Glenwood Springs. Glorious Rocky Mt scenery along the way. If the bus is not late, you arrive at lunchtime. Swim, eat strawberry waffles at Rosie's Bavarian Restaurant behind bus station and catch 4.05pm bus back to Denver, arriving at 7.55pm. A long day, but worth it.'

Ouray and south: bus route from Grand Junction to Durango passes through Montrose, Ouray and Silverton. 'Unparalleled scenery; exceeds the Denver-Salt Lake City run. Canyons through 11,000 ft red rock mountains. Best from mid-Sept when aspens have changed to gold.' 'Wrecked cars 500 ft below, left as warning to other motorists.'

Telluride: jeep trail to Ouray over 13,000-ft Imogen Pass. 'Astounding' in a jeep, a truly remarkable accomplishment when covered on foot-as many people do each summer in a 19-mile race.

DURANGO   Located in the southwestern corner of the state, Durango is as authentically western as a Stetson hat. Billy the Kid and other outlaw types used to make Durango their headquarters; before that, the Spaniards came looking for gold, found it and lost it again when local Ute Indians got fed up with them.

Western hospitality is common currency here, markedly so at the local youth hostel. Durango's location 40 miles east of Mesa Verde makes it a natural base for sightseeing.

ACCOMMODATION

Youth Hostel, 543 E 2nd Ave, 247-9905. $13 AYH and non-AYH $15. 2nd oldest hostel in Colorado, good base for hiking and mountain biking. 'Olsons' very friendly, willing to help.' 'Without a doubt the best hostel I've seen—clean, well-equipped, nice garden and BBQ.'

OF INTEREST

The main local attraction is the circa 1882 **narrow-gauge railway to Silverton**, 479 Main Ave, 247-2733. The coal-fired train runs 45 miles one way and climbs 3000 ft through the sawtoothed San Juan Mts. Round trip takes 9 hours, costs $53 (more if you reserve seat in the elegant parlour car). Runs 4 times daily, early May through mid-Oct. It is recommended that you book 'at least 6 weeks in advance'. Others say arriving at 6.30am the day before suffices, but the odds are against you. Alternatively, take the am bus to Silverton and then catch the train back to Durango (but the price is still the same). 'Plenty of seats on south-bound journey.' 'Beautiful scenery, worth every dollar.'

Toh-Atin Galleries, 145 W 9th and Main Ave, 247-8277. Native American and Southwestern art gallery with fine Navajo weavings, jewellery, sculptures and origninal paintings. Free admission; Mon-Sat 9am-9pm, Sun 9am-6pm.

FOOD/ENTERTAINMENT

'If you're feeling flush, try fresh trout at the **Palace Restaurant**,' 1 Depot Place, 247-2018. Open daily 11am-10pm.

Diamond Belle Saloon, in the Strater Hotel, 699 Main Ave, 247- 4431. 'Authentic saloon atmosphere with ragtime piano.' Open daily, 11am-11:30pm. Also in hotel: **Diamond Circle Theater** has melodramas in the summer every night but Sun at 8pm, $15.
Capers, 150 E College Dr, 247-1510. Cheap and cheerful; Wed night pizza specials, Thurs all-you-can-eat spaghetti from $5.25. Open nightly, 5pm-10pm.

INFORMATION
Durango Area Chamber Resort Association, PO Box 2587, CO 81302, 247-0312. Free visitor's guide and information.

MESA VERDE NATIONAL PARK   'Far above me, set in a great cavern in the face of the cliff, I saw a little city of stone, asleep.'—Willa Cather.

No matter how limited your tourist plans for the West might be, a visit to Mesa Verde, the finest of the prehistoric Indian culture preserves, is a must. The 80-square-mile area sits at an altitude of 6,200ft and rises another 2000 ft above the surrounding plain, gashed by many deep canyons. The tableland you see today bears little to resemblance to the land of the past. Junipers and pion trees grow where the Indians once tilled their squash, beans and corn. From the depths of the canyon they drew their drinking water from springs. Originally they built their pueblos on the flat surface, but later for security dug their homes into the sheer canyon walls.

There are two loops to the park: one leads to **Cliff Palace.** Built by the Anasazi tribe in 1100-1275AD, the palace is a large medieval-looking town, containing 200 living rooms, 23 kivas and eight floor levels, all within a single cave. You can climb on parts of it. The other loop, to **Mesa Wetherill**, provides good vantage points for viewing the ruins scattered throughout the canyons. The dwellings were occupied for about a century beginning in 1200 and were vacated for unknown reasons (probably due to drought).

To really enjoy the park, give yourself at least a day and read the park service pamphlet on the history of human habitation here. A visit to the museum, with its extensive exhibits of tools, clothing, pottery and dioramas depicting the Anasazi way of life is also a must for understanding the culture. Admission to park, $10; tour of Cliff Palace and a balcony house $1.75 each.
www.nps.gov/meve/

ACCOMMODATION
In Cortez: El Capri Motel, 2110 S Broadway, 565-3764. S/D$45. Cheaper in winter. AC, TV.
In Mesa Verde Park: Morefield Campgrounds, 529-4465, $16, $23 w/hook-up. Showers, store, snack bar, laundry. 'Gets very cold at night; need warm sleeping bag as well as tent.' Call (800) 449-2288 for information on alternative accommodation.

TRAVEL
ARA Tours from Far View Lodge in the park save non-drivers the 6-mile hike to Cliff Palace. Buses leave at 9.30am for a full day tour, $35; half-day tours of the Mesa-top dwellings leave at 9am and 1pm, $29. Call 529-4313. Hitching is not allowed in the park, though you can discreetly ask for rides in parking lots.

OF INTEREST
Four Corners. The meeting of Colorado, Utah, Arizona and New Mexico is com-

memorated with a slab of inscribed concrete. You can sprawl to have your picture taken as you perform the amazing feat of being in 4 states at once! In summer, Indians from Navajo and other tribes come in their pickups and sell their hand-crafted wares, often at much better prices than you'll find in the tourist centres or trading posts.

IDAHO *The Gem State*

Rugged with mountains (50 peaks over 10,000 feet), slashed with wild rivers and deep chasms (including the Snake River and Hell's Canyon, deepest in North America), dappled with fishing lakes and hot springs, Idaho is like Colorado without the people or the public transit.

Appropriately called the Gem State, Idaho produces 72 different precious and semi-precious stones, some of which are unique to the area. The state was settled by French trappers, later by a mix of Basques, Mormons and WASPS who came to raise livestock, mine silver, log timber and grow lots of delicious Idaho spuds. Idahoans are a taciturn lot; interesting, then, that the most famous figures associated with the state were noted for eloquence. One was Chief Joseph of the Nez Perce Indians, who surrendered to the US Army by saying: 'From where the sun now stands, I will fight no more forever'. The other, writer Ernest Hemingway, was an adoptive Idahoan who chose to live, write (parts of *For Whom the Bell Tolls*), commit suicide and be buried in Idaho.

The most scenic section is the panhandle, crowned by the shattering beauty of Lake Coeur d'Alene. Located along the northern route taken by Greyhound, it's well worth a stop. The southerly route takes you within 80 miles of the Craters of the Moon and near Sun Valley, but isn't nearly as interesting. *www.visitid.org.*

National Park, Yellowstone (though this is mostly in Wyoming). For main entrances to park, see Montana.

The telephone area code for Idaho is 208.

CRATERS OF THE MOON NATIONAL MONUMENT Located at the northern end of the Great Rift system, this grotesque grey landscape of extinct cones, gaping fissures and cave-like lava tubes is the largest basaltic lava field in the lower 48 states. Since it was only formed a relatively short time ago—within the last 10,000 years—no vegetation has yet grown. The area erupted 2000 years ago. Another eruption is expected at the end of the next millennium, but that fact shouldn't trouble visitors for a few generations!

The most extravagant formations can be seen from one 7-mile loop road in the 83-square-mile preserve; $4 per car, good for 24 hrs. US moon astronauts spent a day in training here, rockhounding; free guided walks explore the extensive caves here about six times/day. **Camping**: $10/night on loose rock, mid-April to mid-October only recommended, 527-3257. No public transport to park; Salmon River Stages runs to **Arco**, 19 miles outside the park. If you have a car, pitching a tent on BLM (Bureau Land Management) tracks outside the park is free. **Mt Borah,** the highest peak in Idaho at 12,662 ft, towers over the wasteland. At the base of the peak lies a fault, created by a 1983 earthquake that rocked central Idaho. As a result of this quake, the mountain grew 2 ft, while the surrounding valley fell 5 ft.

This chilling region, which looks like the day after an atomic attack, is appropriately the home for much nuclear testing and tinkering. 30 miles east is the Idaho National Engineering Laboratory. Nearby **Arco** was the first town lit by atomic power. The area has more nuclear reactors per citizen than anywhere else in the world, and Atomic City needs no introduction. Fifty nuclear reactors were built in this area, home to only 25 daring residents these days. Keep within park limits!

TWIN FALLS Set on a pretty stretch of the Snake River, Twin Falls is a good starting point for a journey into Sun Valley and Sawtooth National Forest. West off US 30, the 40 ft-tall **Balanced Rock** rests on a base only a few feet in diameter. No sneezing. Five miles northeast of town are thundering **Shoshone Falls**, 52 feet higher than Niagara Falls. Most spectacular in winter. If you haven't had your fill of falls yet, venture east to **Idaho's Thousand Springs.** Natural springs pour forth from canyon walls. Legend has it that the Lost River in central Idaho drops into the ground at the base of the Lost River Mountains and comes out here. As you head north to Sun Valley on Rte 75, cool off at **Shoshone Ice Caves**, a lava tube spanning three blks, with naturally frigid temperatures and fascinating ice formations. Open daily 8am-8pm from May-end Sept; $5, 886-2058. 'Bring your coat.'

ACCOMMODATION
Gooding Hotel, 112 Main St, Gooding, 934-4374. Head west from Twin Falls, 10 mls from exit Hwy 46. From S-$25, breakfast included. Full kitchen and lounge. Located near Snake River—rafting, boating, waterskiing, rock-climbing.

OF INTEREST
City of Rocks National Reserve, S of Burley on Hwy 77, 824-5519. Granite columns climb 60 storeys in this eerie, dreamlike landscape. **Hagerman**, 35 miles north of Twin Falls on Hwy 84, was the site of discovery for 3-toed horse fossil in the early 1990s, quite similar to the modern-day zebra. The original fossil is now housed in the Smithsonian, but you'll find a replica in the museum on Main Street. Take a day to enjoy the natural hot springs and beautiful trout-fishing.
Jerry Lee Young's Idaho Heritage Museum, 2390 Hwy 93 S, 655-4444. Jerry has collected over 40,000 artifacts which chronicle the natural and man-made history of Idaho, ranging from pre-historic fossils, to ancient Indian peace pipes and the 'guns that tamed the West.' Open Tues-Sun 10am-4pm, $4.
Malad Gorge, 30 mi NW of Twin Falls, east of Bliss on I-84, 847-4505. This spectacular gorge dips down 250 ft, where the river tumbles over a 60 ft waterfall, emptying into 'Devil's Washbowl' below. A footbridge spans the canyon, offering spectacular views.
Perrine Bridge, (800)255-8946, spans the Snake River Canyon. It's the site of Evil Knievel's failed attempt to jump across the canyon in a rocket-powered motorcycle. Don't get any ideas—take the bridge instead.

INTERNET ACCESS
Metropolis B@kery C@fe, 125 Main Ave, 734-4457. Open Mon-Fri 7:30am-6pm, Sat 8am-1pm; $6/hr.

SUN VALLEY/KETCHUM   In the 1930s, railroad mogul Averell Harriman asked Count Felix Schaffgotsch of Austria to search America for a site "of the same character as the Swiss and Austrian Alps." The Count selected Sun Valley, and thus, the first ski resort destination was born. World-class skiing on ol' Baldy has attracted world-class spenders, with their thirst for ultra-resort fare in tow. Go to nearby Ketchum; it's more congenial and much less ostentatious—but still expensive.

ACCOMMODATION
Ski View Lodge, 409 S Hwy 75, 726-3441. 8 individual cabins, w/2 double beds, kitchens, showers, TV, gas heating. $46-$76 for 1-4 people. Cheap camping by the creek. Pitch a tent for free in designated areas in **Sawtooth National Recreation Area**, north on Rt 75. $5 user fee (for hiking, white-water rafting etc.). Camping outside designated areas from $6-$10. Call (800) 280 2267.

FOOD/ ENTERTAINMENT
Desperado's, 4th & Washington, 726-3068. Tacos for $2.95 and a selection of 15 Mexican beers. Open Mon-Sat 11:30am-10pm.
Pioneer Saloon, 308 N Main, 726-3139. Prime ribs, fresh fish and prices from $6.50. Cheap beer and *the* place to go in town. Open nightly, 4pm-2am.

OF INTEREST
You're in one of the best kept secrets of the West. Spend some time hiking in **Sawtooth**, then relax in one of the many hot springs in the area. The closest is **Warm Springs** near Baldy Mt ski lift, but go three miles further to **Frenchmen's** for a free dip. The ski lift is open in summer; $12, but trip down is free if you hike up (you can even take a mountain bike).
Ice shows at the **Outdoor Resort Ice Rink**, off Sun Valley Road, 622-2194, feature Olympic athletes on Fri-Sat eves, mid- June to mid-Sept. The rink is open to the public all year; $8 plus $3.25 for skates. July 4th and Labour Day are big events here; catch the arts and crafts shows, Sun Valley Symphony, motorised parades, rodeos and bull riding. 24 **jazz bands** from the US, Canada and Europe arrive in mid October for a huge festival; tickets from $15.
The Chamber of Commerce Visitor Centre, 4th & Main St, 726-3423, (800) 634-3347, has maps, info and details of events as does **Redfish Visitors Center,** 774-3376, at the northern end of Stanley Lake, Wed-Sun 9am-5pm.

BOISE   If travelling past an endless trail of small farmhouses has left you comatose, you'll probably be delighted to arrive in Boise, the largest metropolitan area for 300 miles around. The capital of Idaho, Boise is a very pleasant and liveable town, and a good place to plan a white-water rafting trip on the Salmon River, which Lewis and Clark called 'The River of No Return'.

ACCOMMODATION
Budget Inn, 2600 Fairview, 344-8617. S-$35, D-$42. Outdoor spa.
Cabana Inn, 1600 Main St, 343-6000. S-$39, D-$44. Free ice, cable TV.

FOOD
Noodles, 8th and Idaho, 342-9300. Lunchtime slice of pizza and salad for $3.50; $4.95-$7.95 pasta dishes w/salad and garlic bread. Open daily 11:30am-9pm.
At **8th Street Marketplace** are several small cafes and shops, such as **Cafe Ole**, 404 S 8th St, 344-3222, with $5.95 Mexican lunch specials. Open Mon-Thur, 11am-10pm, Fri-Sat 'til 11pm, Sun 3pm-9pm.

OF INTEREST

Basque Museum and Cultural Center, 611 Grove St, 343-2671. The museum explores the surprisingly rich history of the Basques in Idaho, as well as the Basque culture itself. Open Tue-Fri, 10am-4pm, Sat 11am-3pm; $3 adult, $1 w/ student ID.

Boise Art Museum, 670 Julia Davis Dr, 345-2247. Idaho's only public art museum. Open Tue-Fri 10am-5pm, Sat-Sun noon-5pm. $4, $2 w/ student ID.

Discovery Center of Idaho, 131 Myrtle St, 343-9895. Interactive science museum. Open Tue-Sat 10am-5pm, Sun noon-5pm; $4.

Idaho Black History Museum, 508 Julia Davis Dr, 433-0017. Features historical photos, crafts and other articles reflecting black culture. Open Tue-Sat 10am-5pm, Sun 1pm-5pm; donation requested.

Idaho Botanical Gardens, 2355 Old Penitentiary Rd, 343-8649. A lovely place to spend the afternoon. Open Apr-Oct only. Open Mon-Thur 9am-5pm, Fri 'til 8pm, Sat-Sun 10am-6pm; $3, $2 w/ student ID.

Idaho Historical Museum, 610 Julia Davis Dr, 334-2120. Relates the Idaho history from prehistoric times through pioneer selttlement, including Indian, Basque and Chinese influences. Open Mon-Sat 9am-5pm, Sun 1pm-5pm; donation requested.

Idaho Museum of Military History, 4040 W Guard St, 422-6128. Idaho's newest museum, housing an impressive display of firearms and US Military uniforms from post-Civil War to the present. Open Fri-Wed noon-4pm.

Idaho State Capitol Building, Capitol Blvd and Jefferson, 334-2470. A miniature version of the nation's capitol, it's the only capitol building in the country that's heated by geothermal water. Open Mon-Fri 8am-5pm, Sat 9am-5pm; free.

Old Idaho Penitentiary, 2445 Old Penitentiary Rd, 368-6080. The penitentiary was built in 1870 and in use until 1973. There are only 2 others like it in the United States. Open daily, noon-5pm (Sept-May), 10am-6pm (summer); $3.

World Center Birds of Prey, 566 W Flying Hawk Ln, 362-8687. You can see the Harpy Eagle (the world's largest eagle), plus observe a pair of California Condors. Everything you ever wanted to know about birds of prey. Open daily 9am-5pm (10am-4pm Nov-Feb); $4.

Zoo Boise, 355 N Julia Davis Dr, 384-4260. See exotic animals as well as Idaho's native wildlife. Open daily 10am-5pm; $4.

Nearby: Bruneau Dunes State Park, 18 mi SW of Mountain Home on Hwy 51, 366-7919. The Bruneau Dunes are the tallest sand dunes in North America, rising to a height of 470 ft; $2/ vehicle. Camping is also available on a first-come, first-serve basis; $12 per site, $16 w/ hook-up.

Idaho City, 38 mi N of Boise on Hwy 21, a mining town that captures the all-too-wild spirit of the West. Once the largest town in the Pacific Northwest, only 28 of the men, women and children buried here are believed to have died of natural causes. Idaho City has been rebuilt since its gold mining days, with some of the original buildings still in use. Duck into the local museum and arts and crafts to explore the gold rush history, 392-4290.

TRAVEL/INFORMATION

Amtrak, (800) 872-7245 and **Greyhound**, 343-3681/(800) 231-2222 are both at 1212 W Bannock. Amtrak no longer operate trains out of Boise but contracts Greyhound buses to get passengers to Portland train station (9 hrs), $40 o/w.

Idaho Travel Council, 700 W State St, (800) 635-7820.

Boise Convention and Visitors Bureau, (800) 635-5240. There is a visitor centre at 2739 Airport Way; Mon-Fri 8.30-5am.

INTERNET ACCESS

Cyber Playce Cafe, 7079 Overland Rd, 377-8701. Open Mon-Thur 7am-midnight, Fri 'til 2am, Sat 8am-2am, Sun 8am-midnight; $6/ hr.

COEUR D'ALENE The depth and fire of this utterly lovely lake remind one of sapphires. In the keeping of such glamorous company, the city of Coeur d'Alene inevitably went for a facelift, in 1988 tastefully revamping downtown and building a huge resort and the world's largest floating boardwalk.

ACCOMMODATION
Down motel row (Sherman Ave) are several similarly-priced rooms, such as the **Bates Motel**, 2018 E Sherman Ave, 667-1411, S/D-$35.

FOOD
Idaho Rubys, 206 N 4th St, 664-8522. Homemade muffins, soups, salads and fresh bread. 'Half' sandwiches are filling enough in themselves - $2.95. Specials (sandwich and soup) - $5. Open Mon-Fri 9am-4pm.
Rustlers Roost, 819 Sherman, 772-6613. Good food all day long. Serves the city's only barbeque at dinner. Sandwiches w/fries from $4.25. Open daily 6am-9pm, Sun 'til 8pm.

OF INTEREST
Be sure to take the 1¹/₂ hr **lake excursion**, $14, leaving from Independence Point near the resort. Call Lake Cruisers, (800)688-5253, for departure schedules.
Fishing permits are $7.50 per day, available at any marina or tackle shops. **Digging for rare star garnets** at Emerald Creek south of St Maries ranks somewhere between gardening and an Indiana Jones adventure. (Follow Hwy 3 south 25 miles to Rd 447; SE 8 miles to Parking Area, then 1/2 mile hike to 81 Gulch.) All-day digging permits are issued at the campground for $10; call 245-2531. They have very limited equipment, bring a container and shovel if possible! Guides will show you what to do. These black and blue garnets are found only in Idaho and India. Wear old shoes and clothes—it's wet and muddy.
Coeur d'Alene Visitors Information, 105 Sherman, 9am-5pm daily—walk-in centre only.
Coeur d'Alene Convention and Visitor Bureau, 202 Sherman Ave, (800)292-2553.
Chamber of Commerce, PO Box 850, Coeur D'Alene, ID 83816, 664-3194.

NORTH CENTRAL IDAHO hosts a trove of geological treasures. It's no wonder that Lewis and Clark called this region 'paradise'. Among the most famous is **Hells Canyon**, on the Snake River. It stretches 50 miles and is the deepest chasm in North America (up to 7,900ft deep). To see it by car, Rim View Drive (Rd 241 out of Riggins) is one of the rough roads cut through Hells Canyon Nat. Recreation Area. NB: Some areas are restricted by the Forest Service. White Water tours are available, but are generally expensive. Contact Idaho Outfitters and Guides Association, PO Box 95, T- 9, Boise ID 83701, (208) 342-1919 for information 8am-4pm Mon-Thurs or (800) VISIT-ID for a brochure. Near Hells Canyon are the **Seven Devils Peaks**, (509)758-0616, one of Idaho's highest and most spectacular mountain ranges. The peaks tower a mile and a half above the Snake River below. From Heaven's Gate Lookout on the peaks, you can see into four states!
North Central Idaho is also home of the **Nez Perce National Historic Park and Museum**, 843-2261, which chronicles the sad history of Chief Joseph's people. Refusing to sign a treaty with the US government, the Nez Perce fled Idaho to seek safety with their Crow allies to the east. When this

failed, an escape into Canada became their only hope. The Nez Perce National Historic Trail, which winds from Idaho into Oregon, marks the path they followed prior to their 1877 surrender. The park is open 8am-5:30pm in summer ('til 4:30pm in winter).

EASTERN IDAHO   Though not as scenic as the west, there are a few reasons to visit. The **Grand Tetons**, the youngest mountains in the Rockies, flank the eastern portion of the state. The town of **Blackfoot** is the site of the **Idaho Potato Exposition**, 130 NW Main, 785-2517. Featured in the Exposition are the world's largest concrete potato and the world's largest potato chip— a 25-in Pringle donated by Proctor and Gamble. There is also a simulated potato cellar, complete with authentic smells. By the time you've seen the museum, you're bound to be craving some spuds of your own. Not to worry— the Expo offers "Free Taters for Out-of-Staters". Open daily, 10am-5pm; $3.

MONTANA   *Big Sky Country*

Touted as the 'Big Sky' country, Montana is an immense, Western-feeling state, rich in coal, sapphires and chrome, a grower of wheat and cattle, and a major centre for tourism. A regular record-breaker when it comes to the hottest, coldest, windiest and snowiest weather in the lower 48 states, Montana achieved a mind-numbing 76°F below in the early 1980s. And wouldn't you know it—Gary Cooper was born here.

Its only sizeable minority are the Indians—about 30,000 Crows, Northern Cheyennes, Blackfeet, Flatheads, Grox Ventres, Chippewas and Crees. And Montana's the place where the Indians put paid to the whites, not only at the Little Bighorn but at the Battles of Big Hole and Rosebud as well. Indians on the seven reservations offer numerous events and facilities to non-Indians and are generally very friendly.

While in Montana, try to catch a rodeo, and don't overlook the work of artist Charles M Russell. His cowboy days are brilliantly depicted in oils and bronze in the museum in Great Falls and in Helena's Capitol Building. Helena is also the starting point for the **Gates to the Mountains** boat trip, 458-5241, which retraces Lewis and Clark's 1804-05 expedition along the wild and scenic Missouri River; $8.50.

One of America's great train journeys is the *Empire Builder* route across northern Montana— especially the portion that loops around Glacier National Park. Both east and westbound trips are in daylight or at dusk.
National Parks: Glacier, Yellowstone (mostly in Wyoming). For information on volunteer-guided walks in the parks, and maps of designated wilderness areas and National Forests, contact the Montana Wilderness Association, Box 635, Helena, MT 59624, or call 443-7350. For a recreation guide and accommodation listings, contact **Montana Travel** at the Dept of Commerce, Helena, MT 59620, or call (800) 541-1447.

Important note: while most of Yellowstone lies in Wyoming, three of the main entrances and the gateway towns of West Yellowstone and Gardiner are in Montana and are best reached via Greyhound from Montana cities or

from Idaho Falls, Idaho. Read *both* Montana and Wyoming sections when trip planning for the park. *http://visitmt.com.*
Telephone area code for the whole state is 406.

BUTTE Dominated by a giant, ecologically-threatening copper mining company, Butte boasts the dubious distinction of being the largest environmental clean-up site in America. Butte's location, a mile above sea level in southwestern Montana, makes it a good base for exploring the ghost towns and Indian battlefields roundabout. 'Road from Butte to Helena is great—lots of cliffs, narrow canyons, etc.' America's largest madonna figure, 'Our Lady of the Rockies,' stretches 90 feet upward, peacefully observing the city from atop the Continental Divide.

ACCOMMODATION
Capri Motel, 220 N Wyoming St, 723-4391. S-$37, D-$42, incls bfast.
Finlen Motor Inn, Broadway & Wyoming, downtown, 723-5461. S- $37, D-$50.
Kings, 307 S Main, Twin Bridges, (Hwy 41 S from Butte), 684-5639. S/D$45, $50 w/kitchenette.

OF INTEREST
Visit the **mining museum at Montana Tech** or the **World Museum of Mining**, on a shaft-mining site, Park St. Plenty of antique mining equipment. At the same location, **Hell's Roaring Gulch** is a replica of pioneer village including a sauerkraut factory, Chinese laundry and general store at same location; both museums and village are free.
Copper King Mansion, 219 W Granite, 782-7580. 34-room mansion of copper baron W A Clark. Open daily 9am-5pm (last tour 4pm); $5. Or visit his son's home, **Arts Chateau**, 723-7600, at 321 Broadway, for more art and antiques, $3. Tues-Sat 10am-5pm, Sun noon-5pm. **The Dumas**, 45 E Mercury St, 723-6128. The Dumas, Montana's longest running house of ill repute, operated from 1890-1982. Tours are now given of the old brothel, 9am-5pm daily; $3.50.
Ghost Towns. About 60 miles SE of Butte is **Nevada City**, a restored village of 50 buildings and a museum. 'Don't miss the deafening collection of organs, pianolas, etc, and the old RR carriages.' To pan for gold and garnets in nearby streams, visit the **River of Gold** in Nevada City, 843-5526; share a $12 bucket of 'dirt' to pan for gold with. 'Takes lots of patience to pan for gold outside RR station to end up with a few tiny specks of the yellow stuff.' Open daily, 10am-6pm. Restored in 1997, the **Alder Gulch Short Line train** covers a two-mile stretch to Virginia City, a 'working ghost town,' more restored buildings, shops, restaurants, daily Western shootouts, etc.
Our Lady of the Rockies, (800) 800-LADY, a 90ft statue on East Ridge overlooking Butte, only 20ft shorter than the Statue of Liberty. Finished in 1985, it was built by volunteers from many religious sects with donated materials. To get to the statue, take a bus from Butte Plaza Mall, rsvs required; $10. Between Virginia City and **Bannack** (Montana's first boom town and territorial capital) was the 'Vigilante Trail'. In 6 months, 190 murders were committed here and gang activity got so notorious that miners secretly formed a vigilante committee. When they caught up with the gang leader, it turned out to be their sheriff, who was duly hanged on his very own gallows. 'Bannack: the best old Western town I've seen. Still has gallows, jail. View from top of Boot Hill unbelieveable.' **Castle** (Calamity Jane's home town) and **Elkhorn** (300 old buildings still standing) are other interesting destinations.
Anaconda, 27 mi W off I-90, is home to the country's tallest smokestack. At 585 ft, it's tall enough for the Washington Monument to fit inside.
Big Hole National Battlefield. Site of the Nez Perce victory over US troops in 1877. Chief Joseph and his band were in flight to Canada, having refused to accept reser-

vation life. Pursued by troops, they fought courageously and intelligently under Joseph's masterful military leadership. Despite their win, they were pursued and ultimately beaten at Bear Paw, less than 30 miles from the Canadian border. Visitors Centre open daily, 8:30am-6pm. For info, call the National Parks Service in Wisdom, 689-3155.

TRAVEL/INFORMATION
Greyhound, 101 E Front, 723-3287, 8am-8pm daily; (800) 231-2222, 24hrs.
Chamber of Commerce, 1000 George St, 723-3177. 8am-8pm daily.

BILLINGS   Montana's largest and most sophisticated city, Billings is on the Yellowstone River— an ideal stopover point for travellers from North or South Dakota en route to Yellowstone. This is a good route to the park, via the scenic Cook City, Hwy 212. 'A spectacular mountain view— pass 10,000 feet up & lots of elk & buffalo along the way! Don't go before mid-June, though—otherwise, snowed in.'

ACCOMMODATION
Billings Inn, 880 N 29th St, 252-6800. S-$49, D-$53, incls bfast and free popcorn.

FOOD
King's Table, 12th St and 10th Ave S, 454-0302. Take exit 446 off I-90. Enormous buffet of salad, homemade soups, roast beef, ham, breads and much more; $8 dinners, $6 lunches. Open daily 11am-8pm. There are several Chinese and Mexican restaurants in town, some with reasonable lunch specials.

OF INTEREST
Foucault Pendulum, First Citizen's Bank Building, 1st Ave N and Broadway. Two storeys tall, this pendulum is modelled on the same principles that account for the earth's rotation. Free.
Western Heritage Center, 2822 Montana Ave, 256-6809. Exhibits change twice a year, but the theme in general is an 'Interpretive program reflecting on the history of the Yellowstone Valley River region'. Open Tue-Sat 10am-5pm; donations suggested.
Yellowstone Art Center, 401 N 27th, 256-6804. Museum of modern and Western art housed in 1916-vintage jail; 2 new wings added 1997. Tue-Sat 10am-5pm, Thurs 'til 8pm, Sun noon-5pm in summer; free.
Chief Black Otter Trail. N of the city: spectacular views, Indian scout grave, and a monument to settlers. Distraught Indian braves who lost their families to smallpox are said to have ridden their ponies and themselves over **Sacrifice Cliff**, which lies along the trail.
In **Pictograph Cave State Park**, 247-2940, you can see 4,500-year old Indian drawings whose origins are still a mystery. $4 per vehicle or $1 pp. Open daily 8am-8pm.
Pompeys Pillar, 30 miles east of Billings. A National Landmark along the Lewis and Clark trail. 150ft tall sandstone formation 'signed' by Capt William Clark in 1806 and named by him in honour of Sacajawea's son Pompey. Renovated 1996 to include staircase to top!

TRAVEL/INFORMATION
Greyhound, 2502 1st Ave N, 245-5116, (800) 231-2222. 24 hrs.
Chamber of Commerce, 815 S 27th St, 252-4016. Daily 8.30am-6pm (summer).

INTERNET ACCESS
Your Place or Mine Cybercafe, 414 Grand Ave, 254-9874. Open Mon-Fri 9am-9pm, Sat noon-9pm; $4.95/ hr.

CUSTER BATTLEFIELD NATIONAL MONUMENT Here on the Little Big Horn River, just under 60 miles east of Billings, General George Custer imprudently attacked the main camp of the Sioux, Hunkpapas and others. The date was 25 June 1876. 'I did not think it possible that any white man would attack us, so strong as we were,' said one Oglala chief. A Cheyenne recalled that after he had taken a swim in the river he 'looked up the Little Big Horn toward Sitting Bull's camp. I saw a great dust rising. It looked like a whirlwind. Soon a Sioux horseman came rushing into camp shouting: 'Soldiers come! Plenty white soldiers!'

Before they could be moved to safety downstream, several women and children were killed, including the family of warrior Gall. 'It made my heart bad. After that I killed all my enemies with the hatchet.' Brilliantly led by Sitting Bull and Crazy Horse, the Indians routed the soldiers and surrounded Custer's column, killing all 263 of them. Who killed Custer is not known. Sitting Bull described his last moments: His hair 'was the colour of the grass when the frost comes. Where the last stand was made, the Long Hair stood like a sheaf of corn with all the ears fallen around him.' The visitors centre is open daily during the summer, 8am-7:30pm, the trail and cemetery stay open later; $6/ vehicle, $3 pp. Call 638-2621 for info.

GREAT FALLS Home base for Charles M Russell and an outstanding collection of his work; also home base for a fearsome array of Minuteman missiles at Malmstrom AFB. This is a likeable town, the second-largest city in Montana and home of the state fair in August. Lewis and Clark spent a month foraging around these parts in June 1805. It's a useful stopover if heading north towards Canada or Glacier National Park (Kalispell, the western gateway, is actually a better way to the Glacier).

ACCOMMODATION
Super 8 Motel, 1214 13th S, 727-7600. S-$53, D-$65.

OF INTEREST
C M Russell Museum, 400 13th St N, 727-8787. Outstanding collection of his Western paintings, bronzes and wax models. Other famous painters on show include Remington and George Montgomery. Mon-Sat 9am-6pm, Sun 12pm-5pm, $4, $2 w/student ID. Russell's **house and studio** are at 1300 4th Ave N, open in summer, free with museum ticket.

Giant Springs Heritage State Park, NE of town, 454-5840. Site of the Roe River, one of the largest natural cold water springs in the world. It's also the shortest river in the world. Park open dusk 'til dawn; $4/ vehicle.

Lewis and Clark National Historical Trail Interpretive Center, next to Giant Springs, 727-8733. The newest Lewis and Clark interpretive site, perched on the banks of the Missouri. The center focuses on the relations between the expedition and the Indian tribes they encountered along the way. Open daily 9am-8pm; $5.

Malmstrom Air Force Base Museum, 228 75th St, 731-2705. Impressive collection of aircraft and missiles. Open Mon-Fri, 10am-4pm; free.

INTERNET ACCESS
Great Falls Public Library, 301 2nd Ave N, 453-0349. Free, but rsvs recommended.

TRAVEL
Greyhound, 326 1st Ave S, 453-1541, (800) 231-2222.

GLACIER/WATERTON NATIONAL PARK 'Nothing that I can write can possibly exaggerate the grandeur and beauty of their work.' So wrote naturalist John Muir about glaciers. Nowhere are his words truer than here, surely one of the top contenders for the title of 'most beautiful place on earth.' The joining of Glacier in Montana and Waterton in Alberta created this 'International Peace Park', the first in the world to cross national boundaries.

The Glacier section is traversed east to west by the **Going-to-the-Sun Highway**. Open mid-June to mid-Oct (snowed in the rest of the year), these 50 miles of remarkable beauty are most impressive coming from the West: hugging the side of a cliff for dear life, the road grinds its way up a dizzy precipice along a fantastic hanging valley backed by angry peaks to **Logan Pass**. From the visitors centre at the pass, there are day hikes—either along the **Garden Wall** to the north, or up **Mt Oberlin**— an easy peak (by Glacier standards) that pays off with an eagle's eyrie-view of the park. Nearly 1000 miles of trails wind among rugged mountains and cirque glaciers, leading to wildflower-scattered alpine meadows, trout-splashed lakes and quizzical mountain goats. Glacier's dangerous and unpredictable grizzlies are *not* one of the tourist attractions; wear bells on your toes (or boots) to avoid surprising a browsing bear. Park naturalists lead parties to **Grinnell** and **Sperry Glaciers**; one trail goes over the **Triple Divide**, a unique point from which water trickling through tiny streams must choose its ultimate destination: west to the Pacific; south-east to the Gulf of Mexico; or north-east to Hudson Bay.

When it comes to scenery, the Canadian side is no slouch, either. To reach **Waterton**, you must leave Glacier Park at the east entrance (**St Mary**), and re-enter just at the US-Canada border. The Canadian park, much smaller than its sister to the south, centres on Waterton Lake. The cruise from the north shore to the south is wonderful, and the hike around the lake's east side has been called Canada's best.

It's generally warm in summer, with occasional storms and invariably cold nights; by Oct, some of the park is liable to be snowed in. Excellent trout fishing; if you don't fancy catching your own, **Eddy's**, in **Apgar**, 888-5361, (at the foot of Lake McDonald), is famous locally for good $12 trout dinners; 7am-9.30pm (summer). *www.nps.gov/glac/*.

ACCOMMODATION
Glacier Park makes reservations at the 4 hotels and 3 motels within the park. They recommend rsvs 6 months in advance, (602) 207-6000. Last minute cancellations may make space available. Rooms start at $40 for a basic wood cabin, $90 w/bath.
Backpackers Inn, 29 Dawson Ave, East Glacier, 226-9392. Hostel accommodation in cabins $11; bring a sleeping bag—it gets cold at night! Outdoor BBQ grill. 'Good bulletin board.'
Brownie's Grocery and AYH Hostel, 1020 Montana Hwy 49, 226-4426. (800) 662-7625 rsvs. 6 blks from Amtrak station—will pick up. $13 AYH, $17 non-AYH, rooms $17-$23 AYH, $20-$26 non-AYH. Check-in 7.30am-9pm. Kitchen, linen and info provided. Park is 8 miles away.
Many lodges at **East and West Glacier**, just outside park. Best prices for doubles, triples or quads, so it pays to bunch up.
Super 8 Motel,1441 1st Ave E, (800) 800-8000 or 755-1888, D- $60-$77.
Park Campsites cost $10-$15. If you are in a car, $10 buys you a 7-day pass ($5 for pedestrians). Back country camping free with permit from park office; $20 extra if you want to book in advance. Watch out for bears. Call the park office, 888-7800, for information.

TRAVEL
In summer Amtrak, (800) 872-7245, stops at Glacier Park. Since the railtracks through the park have no joints, the ride is silent, except for the park ranger who gives a commentary about the sights and history of the park. **Greyhound** only goes as far as Great Falls. There is no bus service to the park, but the hitchhiking is easy and safe. Horses can be rented in East and West Glacier. If you enjoy exotica, the **Great Northern Llama Company** offers 4-day llama pack trips. Cost is $165 pp per day, incls meals. Call 755-9044 or write 1795 Middle Rd, Columbia Falls, MT 59912. River rafting trips by **Glacier Raft Co** and others, 888-5454, (800) 332-9995, all equipment provided; $38 half-day, $71 whole day—incls BBQ steak lunch. Blackfoot Indians will take you on a cultural tour of the park, incl short hikes, for $45; call Sun Tours, 226-9220, (800) 786-9220.

HELENA Montana's pretty little capital city was crowned "Queen City of the Rockies" following an 1864 gold strike. Today it's listed as one of the top 100 artistic and cultural small towns in America. Situated along the Lewis and Clark Trail, it's also a good place from which to launch your own Corps of Discovery. Stroll down **Last Chance Gulch** (today's Main Street) to see historic buildings and mansions dating back to the 1870s. The **Montana State Capitol,** 6th St and Montana St, 444-4789, is decorated with interior murals featuring themes of Montana's history. The **St Helena Cathedral,** 530 N Ewing, 442-5825, nicely complements its lovely mountain setting. It's a replica of another well-known alpine church, the Votive Church in Vienna. The **Kleffner Ranch,** located just E of town, 227-6645, is one of the most unique ranch properties in the state. The octagonal stone house and enormous 3-storey barn were both built in the 1800s. Tours available by appointment.

There are a half-dozen defunct gold and uranium mines in the mountainous country south of Helena, near the towns of **Boulder** and **Basin**. Despite what some health authorities may warn you, people flock here to bask in the unconfirmed healing properties of radioactive radon gas and drink the radioactive water. Many people claim to have experienced remarkable recoveries after sitting in the mines, whose radon levels run as high as 175 times the federal safety standard for houses. The mines were first opened in the 1950s, before the scary properties of radioactive substances had been explored.

GATEWAY CITIES TO YELLOWSTONE: BOZEMAN, GARDINER, WEST YELLOWSTONE Of *Zen and the Art of Motorcycle Maintenance* fame, Bozeman is a college town and agricultural centre. It lies on the Butte to Billings Greyhound route; south from Bozeman, Hwy 191 dips in and out of Yellowstone Park, coming at length (90 miles) to West Yellowstone. It's also here that you'll find the **Museum of the Rockies**, 600 W Kagy Ave, 994-2251, which has become famous worldwide through the work of its chief paleontologist, dinosaur hunter Jack Horner. Dr. Alan Grant, the protagonist of Michael Crichton's *Jurassic Park*, was fashioned after Horner. Open daily, 8am-8pm; $6.

Gardiner, a small village on Yellowstone's central north border, has the only approach open year-round. West Yellowstone, a few blocks from the western entrance to Yellowstone has numerous lodgings, bike rentals, car rentals and other amenities for exploring the park. Hitching is also good and relatively safe. $20 entrance fee for 7 days.

ACCOMMODATION
In Bozeman: Rainbow Motel, 510 N 7th Ave, 587-4201, S-$45, D- $55, pool.
Royal 7 Motel, 310 N 7th Ave, 587-3103, S/D$41-$51, 4 people $58.
Bozeman International Backpackers Hostel, 405 W Olive St, 586-4659. $12.
In West Yellowstone: Madison Motel, 139 Yellowstone Ave, 646- 7745. $18 AYH, non-AYH $19, private rooms from S-$27. Hotel part circa 1912, reflects early, pre-auto days of Yellowstone. 'Romantic old loghouse.' 'Very friendly.'
Wagon Wheels RV Campground, Gibbon and Faithful Sts, 4 blks from Greyhound, 646-7872. $22 per camping site, XP-$3. 'Very generous host. Shower block is palatial.' 5-min walk to **Running Bear Pancake House**.

TRAVEL
Gray Line bus tours, 646-9374, of the park leave from West Yellowstone; Upper/Lower Loop tours cost $38, plus $10 first time park entry. 'A fascinating day tour. Lots of chances to get out and view the sights.' Tetons tour $49 all day.
Car rental: 'If traveling from Bozeman and returning, try hiring a car for a round trip in 24 hours. Four of us did and it worked out cheaper than busing.'
NB: Chamber of Commerce operates as a **Greyhound** stop.
Park Information, (307) 344-7381.

NEVADA *The Silver State*

'Stark' describes the Silver State. It's a flat and monochrome universe of sagebrush, raked with north-south mountain ranges that rise like angry cat scratches from the dry desert floor.

Nevada's the place for misanthropes. About 800,000 people rattle around in a state that measures 110,000 square miles, and 50 percent of them live in and around Las Vegas. Despite its small population, Nevada became a state in 1864 on the strength of gold and silver from the Comstock Lode, which helped finance the Union side of the Civil War. After several boom-and-bust cycles, Nevada got on a permanent roll when three things happened: the Hoover Dam was built in 1931, drawing thousands of workers into the state; gambling was legalised, also in 1931, which would grow to become the largest single source of revenue; and the government commenced with nuclear testing in the 1950s, providing good jobs and generous amounts of irradiation. Today Nevada produces 60 percent of the gold mined in the US and 10 percent of the world's supply.

Nevada's trademarks may be glitter, fallout and quickie marriages, but it's also a land of ranches, Indian PowWows, Basque and Mormon communities and natural wonders like the Valley of Fire, weirdly beautiful Pyramid Lake, and (unofficially) the oldest tree in the world, in Great Basin National Park. The past and the future also meet here; there are ghost towns—such as Belmont, built in 1865—and a newly designated *Extraterrestrial Highway*, so-named because of its proximity to the top-secret Area 51 Air Force Base. Legend has it that more UFOs have been spotted here than anywhere else in the world. Keep your eyes peeled. *www.travelnevada.com.*
The telephone area codes for the state are 702 and 775.

LAS VEGAS There is a point at which overwhelming vulgarity achieves a certain grandeur, and Las Vegas is living proof. Just remember to see it at night. In the blue velvet hours, it's an opulent oasis of neon jewels, endless breakfasts and raucous jackpots, a snug, clockless world that throbs with totally unwarranted promise and specious glamour. As daylight approaches, the mirage wavers and melts away and the oasis becomes a banal forest of overweight signs, tacky and oppressive.

Best approaches for nighttime views: coming from Boulder City, through Railroad Pass gives you a brilliant view of the entire city, as does the *Desert Wind* train from Los Angeles.

The splashiest casino-hotels are along The Strip, where it all began in 1941 with El Rancho Vegas. It didn't all start with gangster Bugsy Siegel and *The Pink Flamingo* as Hollywood said in the movie *Bugsy*. Like the movies, the scenery is ever- changing. Some of the latest mega-resorts are kitschy reflections of Europe, including a 55-storey replica of the Eiffel Tower at the **Paris Casino Resort,** an upscale Tuscan-village-meets-shopping mall at the **Bellaggio** and a canal-lined shopping place complete with serenading gondoliers at the **Venetian**. The **Aladdin** is a casino experience that promises to outshine the city of lights itself, boasting "the best that Las Vegas has to offer, all in one location." That one location features 130 shops and exotic marketplaces, 21 restaurants and the most innovative casino in the world.

Three miles from The Strip lies 'Glitter Gulch', the downtown area, a high-wattage cluster of 15 casino-hotels where Dustin Hoffman played his special trick in *Rainman*. The Gulch tries harder with looser slots, cheaper eats and a more tolerant and friendly attitude towards newcomers and low-rollers. But there are lots of cheap lodging and food deals on The Strip—it's a toss-up. A word of warning for those under the magic State-side age of 21, the casinos will let you in, will let you gamble, will let you lose but if you win they'll dispatch the security guards to 'card' you. So if you're under 21, say adieu to that money. Finally, a little advice from *Fear and Loathing in Las Vegas* and the Doctor, Hunter S. Thompson: '... this is not a good town for psychedelic drugs. Reality itself is too twisted'. *The area code is 702.* *www.lvol.com, www.unlv.edu/Tourism/lvmisc.html.*

ACCOMMODATION

Since the casino owners want to encourage visits by unwary tourists, cheap lodging is the rule in Las Vegas. Lodgings are cheaper in winter than summer, cheaper midweek than on weekends. Avoid public holidays if you can. Sometimes there are some astonishing bargains, even at big flashy hotels on The Strip on Las Vegas Blvd. 'Don't be afraid of bargaining.' If you find it difficult to get a room on a summer weekend, try one of the big places—more likely to have vacancies and it can still work out cheaply for 2 or more people. Beware of booking agents, 'they tell you the city is fully booked, just one free room. They then charge you $20 to book it. Don't be fooled by the free fun books they offer—you can get them anywhere'. Also, compare freebies (eg coupons for gambling, shows, meals) between hotels—they can make a big difference to your overall expenses. Local radio and giveaway papers advertise the latest bargains, as do the *LA Times'* classified ads.

Downtown (close to bus, train stations):
Budget Inn, 301 S Main St, 385-5560. Across the street from Greyhound. 'Spotless.' From S-$29.
Howard Johnson Airport Inn, 5100 Paradise Rd, 798-2777. S/D-$59, $89 w/ends. 2

pools, 24 hr shuttle service to the strip.

Las Vegas International Hostel, 1208 S Las Vegas Blvd, 385-9955. $12 AYH, $14 non-AYH, $5 key deposit. TV, video, free coffee and tea. 'Real friendly.' 'Ants a problem in summer.'

Lee Motel, 200 S 8th St, 382-1297. S/D-$23, $25 w/ends, incls key deposit. 'Clean.'

Victory Hotel, 307 S Main St, 384-0260. 12 blocks from Greyhound. S-$24, $35 w/ends, D-$28, $45 w/ends. 'Cheap, helpful.'

On the Strip:

The Aztec Inn Casino, 2220 Las Vegas Blvd S, 385-4566. S/D-$22- $30, $40-$45 w/ends, $5 deposit. Prices go up sharply certain w/ends, call to check. 2 pools, slot machines. 'In easy reach of all casinos, safe, with brilliant rooms.'

Circus Circus, 2880 Las Vegas Blvd S, 734-0410. Hundreds of AC rooms, TV, pool, amazing themed amenities including acrobatics. S/D-$39-59, $89-119 w/ends. Payment of first night req in advance; phone (800) 634-3450 for reservations. 'Excellent.'

King Albert, 165 Albert Ave, 732-1555. Behind Maxim Hotel. S/D- $39, $59 w/ends.

Sahara Hotel, 2535 Las Vegas Blvd S, 737-2111. From S/D-$49. Moroccan themed resort. 'First class. Amazing pool.'

Stardust Hotel, 3000 Las Vegas Blvd, 732-6111, (800) 634-6757. Possibly the most garish on The Strip, with 1,034 AC rooms and a motel annex, S/D$50-$125 weekdays, $85-$175 w/ends, with frequent specials advertised in newspapers and elsewhere. 2 pools. 'Sparkling room.'

FOOD

As a ploy to keep you gambling, many casinos dish up cheap and/or free meals to keep your strength up. You don't have to gamble to take advantage, either. Do read the fine print, though; some of the largesse has strings attached. Free or cheap breakfasts are commonplace. Many of the cheapie 'lunches' and 'dinners' actually serve breakfast food, so be prepared to like eggs and toast. The local paper prints a list of the all-you-can-eat buffets and other cheap deals at all hotels and casinos. You shouldn't spend more than $5 at breakfast, $5-$10 at lunch/dinner. Don't expect quality (some of it is barely edible), just quantity. Most frequently mentioned: **Freemont Hotel; Circus Circus**, the Strip, 734-0410, with all-you-can-eat buffets, bfast for $4.99, brunch for $5.99, dinner for $7.49. 'Best you could want.' Free or cheap drinks are another casino attraction. If you are gambling, waitresses are glad to serve all manner of libation. 'To get free drinks, go to casinos where they are playing 'Keno'. Sit down and pretend to play by marking sheets provided. The waitresses then come and take your drink order for free!'

OF INTEREST

You can't leave Las Vegas without ducking into the garish casino properties on The Strip, the prime sight-seeing attraction. Stroll through New York, Paris, medieval Europe, ancient Rome, you name it. Inside the Bellaggio, (888) 488-7111, you'll find a small gallery with art by Monet, Renoir, Picasso, among others. Open daily, 9am-11.30pm, $12.

For a change of scene, try the **Barrick Museum of Natural History**, Uni of Nevada, 4505 S Maryland Parkway, 895-3381. Local archaeology, anthropology and natural history of Mojave Desert and Southwest. Mon-Fri 8am-4.45pm, Sat 10am-2pm. Free.

Binion's Horseshoe, 128 Freemont, 382-1600, has glass elevator to Skye Rm, worth a ride for the views of Glitter Gulch, The Strip, the desert and mountains beyond.

Cranberry World West, 1301 American Pacific Dr in Henderson, (800) 289-0917. Everything you ever wanted to know about cranberries, courtesy of America's largest purveyor, Ocean Spray. Free admission and free samples. Open daily, 9am-5pm.

Ethel M Chocolate Factory, 1 Sunset Way in Henderson, 458-8864. Free tours of chocolate factory, complete with samples! Open daily, 8.30am-7pm.

If nothing else, visit the **Liberace Museum**, 1775 E Tropicana Ave, 798-5595, a memorial to an entertainer who personified the Las Vegas way of life. Open Mon-Sat 10am-5pm, Sun 1pm-5pm, $6.95, $4.95 w/student ID, to look at all 3 bldgs full of glitz (the world's largest rhinestone is here as well).

Fashion Outlet at Las Vegas, a 35 min shuttle ride from New York, New York, 874-1400. If you win big, don't blow your money on the pricey boutiques of the strip, come here instead. Shuttle is $10, r/t.

M&M's World, 3799 Las Vegas Blvd (on the strip next to MGM Grand), 891-1111. Four-storeys of memorabilia dedicated to the little candies. Choose from over 21 colours to make your own custom mix and browse through enough M&M's-decorated items to furnish your entire home. The third floor features an interactive M&M's Academy with a 3-D film, "I Lost my 'M' in Las Vegas.'" Open 10am-midnight Sun-Thur, w/end 'til 1am.

Red Rock Canyon, about 12 miles west of Vegas. Casino Travel and Tours, 798-3020, operates daily tours from the Luxor, leaves at 10:30am, returns at 2:30pm; $40—look out for discount coupons. 'Very beautiful.' **Cowboy Trail Rides**, 387-2457 at Red Rock Canyon stables offer horse-back riding, mustang viewing and cowboy poetry; 8am-9pm daily; $25.

ENTERTAINMENT

Las Vegas is famous for big-name superstar shows featuring comedians such as Bill Cosby, George Carlin and Joan Rivers, as well as entertainers such as George Burns, Diana Ross and Frank Sinatra. Championship boxing matches, golf tournaments and other sporting events also take place here. Paris-style revues, soft-core sex shows and lounge singers are all Las Vegas standards. Few shows are free, but like the restaurants and lodgings, they are less expensive here than most places, and the drinks are usually cheap. **The Luxor Hotel**, 3900 Las Vegas Blvd, has the city's first IMAX 3-D theatre; call (800)288-1000 for listings. **Wet 'N Wild Water Park**, 2601 Las Vegas Blvd, 734-0088. $25.95; opens 10am, closing time varies. For a simple, free way to relax in Las Vegas, hop into any of the fancy pools in the hotels along the strip. Several readers have written to say that no one asked if they were guests at the hotel. The key is to look like you belong there.

INFORMATION

Las Vegas Convention and Visitors Bureau, 3150 Paradise Rd, in the Convention Center, one blk from the Strip, 892-0711.

Las Vegas Entertainment Guide: 225-5554.

What's On guide lists weekly entertainment: 891-8811.

INTERNET ACCESS

Jitters East Tropicana, 2457 E Tropicana Ave, 898-0056. Open Mon-Sat 6am-11pm, Sun 6am-9pm; $1/ 5 min.

Las Vegas Library, 833 Las Vegas Blvd N, 382-3493. Free, but call ahead to reserve time.

TRAVEL

Greyhound, 200 S Main St, downtown, (800) 231-2222. Also at the Tropicana and Rivieria Hotels.

Amtrak, Union Plaza, 1 Main St, (800) 872-7245. Catch the **California Zephyr** from Oakland to Reno, then bus it to Vegas.

Auto Driveaway, 658-8500, 4410 North Rancho.

McCarran International Airport, 5 miles south of downtown. Lavish, carpeted. 'Large couches, ideal for dossing.' Don't play slots here. Take the CATRIDE #108 'Maryland Pkwy' bus from 300 N Casino Ctr, $1, takes about 45 minute (CATRIDE:

228-7433). Many of the big hotels also have free airport shuttles.

Scenic Airlines, 739-1900 or (800) 634-6801, does 15 different trips from Las Vegas to the Grand Canyon. Best value probably the 7-hr air-ground tour over Hoover Dam and all along the Canyon in a small plane. Expensive at $218, but well worth it for a unique experience. Shorter flight-only tours cost between $110-$162. Book in advance. Las Vegas, according to one traveller, is 'hell to hitch out of'.

HOOVER DAM and LAKE MEAD   Proof that engineering can be elegant as well as massive, Hoover's 726-foot vaguely Art Deco wall holds back mirage-like Lake Mead, irrigates over one million acres, and keeps the lights on in LA and elsewhere. 'You can see the best of it by just driving past.' 'Fantastic value. Don't just drive past!' Tours 8.30am-5.15pm, $8; (702) 294-3523. Exhibits only, $4. 'Tour goes right inside the workings of the dam.' 'Probably absorbing for the student engineer but not for the artistically inclined.' An oasis of trees and shade by the shore of Lake Mead is the **Boulder Beach Campground**, (702) 293-8906, $10 a night for a tent space. NB: do *not* stay here in summer, when the temperature is 100°F at 4am and the air is wall-to-wall insects! 'You'd have to camp in the lake to get a decent night's sleep.'

www.hooverdam.com/service/index.html

RENO   Although it tries hard to peddle greed, instant gratification (eg quickie marriages/divorces) and fantasy like its Big Brother, Las Vegas, Reno doesn't quite make it. Despite the worst of intentions, little glimpses of culture, humanity and scenic beauty keep peaking through: its treelined parkway along the Truckee River; its friendly university; its jazz festivals; its good Basque restaurants. Close to enchanting Lake Tahoe and only a day's drive from San Francisco, 'the Biggest Little City' makes a pleasant base to explore Virginia and Carson Cities. For an outstanding view of the lake take the Mt Rose Hwy, south of Reno on Rte 431; it climbs 8,911ft up the highest pass in the state before descending into the Tahoe Basin.

The area code is 775. www.reno.net

ACCOMMODATION/FOOD

El Cortez Hotel, 239 W 2nd St, 322-9161. S/D-$29, $38 w/ends.

Motel 6, 866 N Wells Ave, 786-9852, (800) 466-8356, S/D$ 40-$48.

OF INTEREST

National Automobile Museum, 333-9300. 10 S Lake St in downtown. $7.50. Mon-Sat 9.30am-5.30pm, Sun 10am-4pm. Mind-boggling collection of over 200 classic autos: Bugattis, an 1938 Phantom Corsair Coupe, entertainers' custom vehicles, plus rail cars, boats.

Nevada Historical Museum, 1650 N Virginia St, near campus, 688-1190. Washoe Indian Dat-So-La-Lee was one of the finest weavers of Native American baskets in the country. Her work, as well as mining history and the development of casino industry, is on display here—the state's oldest museum. Mon-Sat 10am-5pm. $2.

Nearby: Virginia City. A $25/week reporter for the local *Territorial Enterprise*, Mark Twain wrote of this semi-ghost town in its boisterous prime: 'It was no place for a Presbyterian, and I did not remain one for very long'. The **Mark Twain Bookstore**, 111 S C St, 847-0454, displays some Mark Twain memorabilia. **The Sundance Saloon**, now a T-shirt shop, still houses the city's oldest bar. The city also has a melting pot of **cemeteries**, from Masonic and Catholic to Chinese and Mexican. Explore also the museums on C St—one of the best being **The Way It Was**,

847-0766, full of mining and local history. Don't miss the annual camel, ostrich and water-buffalo races, held on the weekend following Labor Day. The Chamber of Commerce can tell you more, 847-0311.

Carson City. Loaded with Victorian gingerbread and refreshingly situated in the green Sierra foothills, this is the smallest capital city in the lower 48. Mark Twain lived at 502 N Division St with his brother, who was the first territorial secretary of state. Free sights include a rare collection of natural gold formation at the **Carson Nugget**; the former mint (now the **State Museum**); and the **Nevada State RR Museum** on 600 N Carson St, 687-4810. $3. 9am-5.30pm daily in summer, 8.30am-4.30pm daily in winter. Call the **Carson City Chamber of Commerce** for local events, 882-1565.

TRAVEL/ INFORMATION
Amtrak, E Commercial Row & Lake St, 329-8638, (800) 872-7245.
Greyhound, 155 Stevenson St, 322-2970, (800) 231-2222.
Nevada Visitors Bureau, 5151 S Carson, Capital Complex, Carson City, 687-3636, gives info on state attractions.

GREAT BASIN NATIONAL PARK   Opened in 1986, Great Basin was the first new national park in the lower 48 in 15 years. The youngest of the parks is also the least-visited, due mainly to its location near Route 50, the 'loneliest road in the country' (287 mls through nine mountain ranges, mostly over 10,000ft); Reno is 400 miles west, with Salt Lake City a further 250 miles to the east. The nearest town to the 77,100-acre Great Basin is the miniscule **Baker** whose population of 50 boasts half a dozen houses, a gas station, a two-room school, post office, two bars and a convenience store.

Scenery within the park varies from spectacular mountains topped by the 13,063ft **Wheeler Peak**, to sagebush-studded desert, alpine lakes, deep limestone caves, lush meadows and groves of gnarled bristlecone pines, the oldest living trees. The vistas are said to be 'unbelievable, absolutely outstanding'. Explorer John C. Fremont, who travelled through the area in the early 1800s is credited with naming the region Great Basin. The idea for a national park here is more recent, however, having been under consideration for a mere 50 years.

Park headquarters and visitor centre is at **Lehman Caves**; 90 min ranger-guided tours of the caves run from 8.30am-4.30pm, $6. To camp free, go to Upper or Lower Lehman, Wheeler or Baker Parks; other campgrounds with drinkable water cost $7/site. For park information phone (775) 234-7331.

EXTRATERRESTRIAL HIGHWAY The remote desert area that E.T. Highway snakes its way through probably wouldn't be visited by tourists if it wasn't believed to be frequented by aliens. After the success of the film, *Independence Day*, 100 miles of Hwy 375 were dubbed the Extraterrestrial Highway, attracting thousands of UFO-hungry tourists to an otherwise desolate area. The government's infamous research center, **Area 51,** is located just outside of **Rachel**. Don't expect to sneak inside— security is tight and fines for sneaking in are stiff. Every Wednesday night, people flock to the highway for a weekly UFO watch. No extraterrestrial activity has been verified, though. The only aliens you're likely to see are those depicted in the combination restaurant/ bar/ museum/ gift shop in **Alamo**, the **Little A'Le'Inn**, (702)729-2515.

UTAH   *The Beehive State*

Although the US government owns 70 percent of Utah's land, the Beehive state is, for all intents and purposes, under Mormon control— a unique situation indeed considering the American insistence on separation of church and state.

The Church of Jesus Christ of the Latter-Day Saints (LDS) began in 1827 when New Yorker Joseph Smith was led by an angel named Moroni to some gold tablets. Translated (with the help of Moroni and two seer stones called Urim and Tummim) into English, the writings became the scriptures of the *Book of Mormon*. The fledgling sect was pushed westward from New York but didn't encounter any significant antagonism until Smith introduced polygamy at Nauvoo, Illinois. A hostile mob promptly killed Smith and his brother. The mantle fell to Brigham Young, who ably led his band west to the bleak wilds of northern Utah in 1847, in which no one, not even the local Ute Indians, seemed terribly interested.

The industrious Mormons established their new state of Deseret and applied repeatedly to the US government for admission to the Union but were turned down over the issue of polygamy, which was still going strong. (Brigham himself ultimately had 27 wives and 56 children.) After years of wrangling, in 1890 the Mormons gave in and banned polygamy among themselves. A number of dissenters left and their descendents can be found living quietly and polygamously in Mexico, Arizona and elsewhere.

The importance of Mormonism makes Utah—especially Salt Lake City and environs—sharply different and in many ways better than other states. Hardworking Mormons have built clean, prosperous, humanistic cities and settlements. From early settlement days, Utah has supported the arts; it is home not only to the world-famous Tabernacle Choir but galleries, museums, opera, theatre and the Sundance Film Festival. On the negative side, it's hard to find a drinkable cup of coffee anywhere. Mormons discourage the use of coffee and stimulants and apparently feel the same way about seasonings. Liquor laws, once extremely stringent, have eased somewhat but getting a drink in a restaurant can still be a baroque procedure.

All of Utah's five National Parks are in the south, an area studded with magnificent monuments of the greatest historical, geological and scenic importance. Take a tour or rent a car, allowing yourself ample time for exploration and reflection. Explore the natural attractions on the Utah/Arizona border and further south, such as Monument Valley, the Navajo reservation and the north rim of the Grand Canyon (via Kanab). A boat trip through the flooded canyons of the Glen Canyon National Recreation Area is also an unforgettable (albeit pricey) experience. *www.utah.com*

National Parks: Zion , Bryce Canyon, Canyonlands, Capitol, Reef Arches. *The telephone area codes are 801 and 435.*

SALT LAKE CITY Not just a state capital but the Mecca/ Vatican/Jerusalem for Mormons worldwide, Salt Lake City has a joyful, almost noble air about it. Founder Brigham Young knew how to design a city; Salt Lake City is cradled by the snowy Wasatch Mountains in a setting of remarkable grace. Add to that streets broad enough for a four-oxen cart to turn in, a tree for every citizen, clean air and ecclesiastical architecture that succeeds in being impressive without being dull, and you have quite a place.

In 1995, Salt Lake's 30-year quest to host the winter Olympics ended in triumph. Salt Lake City was selected unanimously by the International Olympic Committee during the first round of voting—a first in Olympic history. The elation soured in 1998, however, when charges of bribery surfaced. The Salt Lake Olympic Committee maintained that by establishing scholarship funds in developing countries it was merely showing a generous spirit. The IOC ruled differently, ousting 6 of its members for accepting bribes. But in the end it was the IOC, not the host city, that ended up taking the fall.

'The beauty of this city is that nearly everything worth seeing is within ten minutes walk of the Greyhound terminal. I managed to see a great deal in the four hours' break I had between buses. I found Mormonism really interesting but it's easier to stomach if taken with a pinch of salt.'

Not hard to do, since the Great Salt Lake lies just 18 miles west of the city. The lake is a mere remnant of Lake Bonneville, a vast prehistoric sea that covered much of Utah and parts of Nevada and Idaho. The outline of the ancient sea is still visible from the air.

The area code is 435.

ACCOMMODATION
The Avenues Hostel, 107 F St, 359-3855, (888) 884-4752. AYH $12. non-AYH $14 dorm; S-$25, D-$30. No telephone rsvs. 1 night's cash in advance req (at least 3 days notice). 'Spacious, well-equipped, kitchen, launderette.'

Carlton Hotel, 140 East South Temple St, 355-3418. S-$69, D- $74. Nr bus depot. 'Super place with lovely bathrooms, restaurant.'

Deseret Inn, 50 W 500 South, 532-2900. S/D-$30, D/Q-$33.

Ute Hostel, 21 E Kelsey Ave, 595-1645. Opened 1994, friendly hostel; dorm $15, D-$35, shared bath.

FOOD/SHOPPING
Lotsa Hotsa Pizza, 50 South Main (basement of Crossroads Plaza Mall), 363-0353. 'Succulent pizza slices $2.15, other specials around $3-$4.' Open Mon-Sat 10am-9pm, Sun noon-6pm.

Union Cafeteria, 581-4741, on the university campus is about the cheapest place in town with good choice.

OF INTEREST
Visitors Centers in Temple Square, in the north and south parts of the square, 240-2534. Run by the Mormon Church, the visitor centers offer a number of free tours on Temple Square. Excellent walking tour maps are also available. 'Guided tour conducted by Mormons who must have been trained to sell insurance. Intimidating.' Open daily, 9am-9pm.

LDS Church office building, 50 East North Temple, 240-2190. Free guided tours Mon-Sat 9am-8:15pm, Sun 'til 4:30pm, plus 'fantastic view from 26th floor'.

Genealogical Library, 35 NW Temple, 240-2331. Because Mormon doctrine recommends the baptism of adherents' long-dead ancestors, the church has been accumulating and organizing genealogical records from all ages and all corners of the earth. With more than 2 billion on record, the library has become a major world centre for genealogical research. If you know the birthdate and birthplace of an ancestor before 1900, the library can probably help you trace your family tree back for generations (they have a separate section for British ancestry). Open Mon 7.30am-5pm, Tue- Sat till 10pm. Free tour and help.

Mormon Temple on Temple Square. This monumental structure in Mormon Gothic took exactly 40 years and $4 million to build. Notice the golden statue of the angel Moroni on one of the towers; according to LDS doctrine, this was the being who appeared to church founder Joseph Smith. 'Even if you're only passing through, go to see the temple. Fantastic the way it's lit up.' Not open to non-church members.

Mormon Tabernacle, home of the Mormon Tabernacle Choir. To witness the weekly radio and TV broadcasts, be in your seat by 9.15am Sun morning to be sure of a place. 'An acoustic wonder.' This is one place where if you stand in the back you can still hear a pin drop in the centre. Call Visitor's Centre, 240-2190, for more information.

Additional Mormonabilia: 'This is the Place' monument at Pioneer Trail State Park, Emigration Canyon, at east edge of city. Also restored pioneer settlement, etc. 'Mormons are obsessed with the pioneers but they don't try to convert you—in fact, I found Mormonism quite fascinating.'

Brigham Young's grave in the cemetery on 1st Ave between State and A Sts.

Beehive House, 67 E South Temple, 240-2671. BY's first residence. Free 30 min tours Mon-Fri 9.30am-6.30pm, Sat 9.30am-4.30pm, Sun 10am-1pm. The tiny dorm rooms in the upper hall and main floor of the adjoining **Lion's House** was home for 19 of BY's wives. Legend has it that after supper the great man would climb the stairs and chalk an X on the door of his lady for the night. Sometimes a rival would erase the X and chalk another on her door before the absent-minded stud came back upstairs. In this fashion, BY brought 56 new Mormons into the world.

Abravanel Hall, at 123 W South Temple, 533-5626; a glorious glass wedge of a place which houses the Symphony. Close by is the **Salt Palace** which houses the **Capitol Theater** and the **Delta Centre**, home to the Utah Jazz (NBA basketball) and Salt Lake Golden Eagles (hockey) teams. 128,000 crowd capacity—free self-guiding tours of both the Palace and Abravanel Hall are available.

Utah Museum of Fine Arts (free) **and Utah Museum of Natural History**, $5, are both at 1530 E South Campus Drive, University of Utah, 581-7049. The Museum of Natural History is open Mon-Sat 9:30am-5:30pm, noon-5pm on Sun, the Museum of Fine Arts is open Mon- Fri 10am-5pm, Sat-Sun noon-5pm.

Shopping: Brigham Young established the first department store in the US, the Zion Cooperative Mercantile Institution (ZCMI). At one time it was the biggest covered mall in the country. Also good browsing at Trolley Square and Crossroads Plaza.

Great Salt Lake, 18 miles west. 1500 square miles and 10 percent saline, the Mormons used to put joints of beef in the water overnight, retrieving them tolerably well pickled. Then the lake was saltier; more fresh water is added each year when the snow melts off the mountains.

Sundance, 328-3456. Established by Robert Redford in 1981, the Sundance Institute sponsors the annual Sundance Film Festival in Park City each January. Over 10,000 people attend the film festival to catch rising stars, emerging screen writers and directors.

ENTERTAINMENT

Days of '47 Festival, 3rd week in July. Rodeo, parades, free concerts, dances, and a sunrise service by the Mormon Tabernacle Choir. 'Fun.'

Raging Waters, 1200 W 1700 S, 977-8300. Utah's largest water theme park. Open Mon-Sat 10.30am- 7.30pm, Sun from 12:30pm. $15.95.

Utah Winter Games, 1760 Fremont Dr, 973-8824; try a bobsled run with the professionals or watch luge and ski-jumping events. 'Hairy but exhilarating!'

NATIONAL PARKS—SOME TOP CHOICES

It can take a lifetime to visit all of North America's National Parks. If you're planning to go to several, think about buying a *Golden Eagle Pass* ($50, valid for a year) from any one of the parks charging entrance fees. Before you go check the National Park Service homepage at *www.nps.gov/parklists/byname.htm*. If you only have time to see a few, here are some of the best:

Acadia/Maine, (207) 288-3338. America miniaturized with beaches, forests, lakes, and Mt Cadillac, the highest point on the Eastern seaboard.

Banff and Jasper/Alberta, (403) 762-1550. Banff, Canada's oldest park, offers mountain grandeur and hot mineral springs. Alongside is Jasper with more mountains, glaciers and lakes. Colombia Icefields, between the two, is the place to spot various big-horned sheep, moose, bears and wapiti (elk). Breathtaking.

Everglades/Florida, (305) 242-7700; $10/vehicle. 2nd largest in US, with panthers, bobcats and alligators; a 50-mile wide river that's only 6 inches deep. Bug spray essential.

Fundy/New Brunswick, (506) 887-6000. Has the highest tides in the world.

Glacier National Park/ Waterton Lakes/Montana and **Alberta**, together making the **International Peace Park**, (406) 888-7800. 10,000 years ago glaciers carved peaks, valleys, ripples here. 50 glacier crumbs remain.

Grand Canyon/Arizona, (520) 638-7888. Deeper, wider and more colourful than thought possible; you cannot prepare yourself for this one.

Great Smoky Mountains/Tennessee, (423) 436-1200. Highly accessible. Home of Clingman's Dome, highest point in the Smokies. Try any of the 900 miles of trails along the Appalachian Trail.

Olympic/Washington, (360) 452-4501. Boasts rain forest, Mt Olympus at 7,965 ft and grey whales along the coast; best seen in Sept-Oct or Mar-Apr. Isolated from the mainland for so long, the park has several unique species of plant and animal, eg. Roosevelt elk and Olympian chipmunk.

Yellowstone/Wyoming, (307) 344-7381. World's 1st national park and largest in Lower 48. Its myriad attractions include Old Faithful and other geysers, wildlife, mudpots and much more.

Yosemite/California, (209) 372-0200. Home of the superlative El Capitan, Half Dome, Bridal Veil Falls, Glacier Point, redwoods you can drive through and more.

To avoid the crowds and high prices that have plagued the National Parks in recent years, consider visiting in the off-season. Or consider visiting one of the less touristy but equally beautiful parks, such as Washington's **North Cascades**, Alaska's **Glacier Bay**, Oregon's **Crater Lake,** North Dakota's **Theodore Roosevelt** or Minnesota's **Voyageurs**.

INFORMATION
Salt Lake Convention and Visitors Bureau, 90 South West Temple, 521-2822; website: *www.saltlake.org*.

INTERNET ACCESS
Salt Lake City Public Library, 209 E 500 S, 524-8200. Free.

TRAVEL
Amtrak, 320 S Rio Grande, 531-0188, (800)872-7245. Catch the **California Zephyr** between Oakland, CA and Chicago; the desert scenery between Salt Lake City and LA is stunning.

Greyhound, 160 W South Temple, (800) 231-2222. Not a good area.
Gray Line Tours, trip to Bingham Canyon and the Great Salt Lake, $32. Leave 2pm, about 4 hrs. Departs from Shilo Hotel, 206 SW Temple, or call 521-7060. 'Bus to San Francisco drives along the lake anyway.'
Utah Transport Authority (UTA), 287-4636, runs the buses; $1 basic fare, $2 all-day pass.
Salt Lake City International Airport, 776 N Terminal Dr, about 4 miles west of downtown. Catch the #50 bus from Main St outside the ZMCI Center, $1; goes straight there.

PROMONTORY   About 80 miles north of Salt Lake City is the **Golden Spike National Historic Site**, (435) 471-2209, which marks the spot where North America's first transcontinental railroad was supposedly completed in 1869. After a symbolic gold-spike ceremony, Leland Stanford and Thomas Durant, the heads of the railroads thus joined, were slated to pound in the final iron stake. Stanford missed and Durant was too woozy from the previous night's revelry to even try; a professional spike-pounder standing nearby was called on to do the job. Or so the story goes—it's more historical myth than fact. The actual Golden Spike (which was only 73% gold) is found in the Art and History Museum at Stanford University in Palo Alto, California. It was purchased by Stanford, the Governor of California, and he took it home with him. An alternate account insists that the junction of the two railroad lines did not, in fact, take place at Promontory Point, but rather 15 months later near Strasburg, Colorado. Nevertheless, the gold-spike ceremony is reenacted each 10 May, the 2nd Sat of August and on w/ends at 1pm and 3pm during the summer.

DINOSAUR NATIONAL MONUMENT   This park overlaps two states (see also Colorado) but the major attractions lie mostly in Utah. **Vernal** has a superb **Field House of Natural History**, 235 E Main St, (435) 789-3799; nearby is dinosaur quarry, where you are on eye level with half-exposed brontosaurus and other remains. See Indian Petroglyphs as you look down into the gorge beside the quarry. The road from Vernal to Daggett is called 'the Drive through the Ages' for the billion years of earth's history that lie exposed on either side. There are numerous campgrounds in and around the Dinosaur National Monument (emphasis on RVs, though). **Dinosaur Gardens**, also at 235 E Main, 789-7894. Mineral hall, educational explanations of ancient fossils plus 14 life-sized dinosaurs including a Raptor recently unveiled in 1997. Open summer 8am-9pm, winter 8am-5pm; $2. $5 per carload (up to 8 people).

ZION NATIONAL PARK   Though not as famous as Yosemite or the Grand Canyon, tiny Zion's outstanding landscapes rank up there with the best. Zion has a huge, painted gorge of magnificent and constantly changing colours; its floor is an oasis of green. At one point the North Fork of the Virgin River pours over the 2000 ft drop of the **Narrows Abyss**, whose walls are just 20 ft apart. Cottonwoods grow on the lush canyon floor, where you can camp. So delightful was the sight that the first Mormons called it Zion. They were later corrected by Brigham Young, who proclaimed 'It is not Zion', and 'Not Zion' it remained for some years.

The 6-mile drive into the canyon passes the *Great White Throne*, *Weeping Rock* and the trail to the *Emerald Pools*, but for a better look you are advised to walk. There are numerous short trails, some dotted with guide boxes containing leaflets on local flora and geological features. You can do any of these on your own, or follow a ranger along the **Gateway** to the **Narrows Trail** in summer. Before setting off on any trail, long or short, check with rangers for advice on availability of drinking water in certain areas, sudden summer cloud-bursts with flash flooding and falling rock.

'We liked the **Emerald Pools footpath**, a gentle stroll for a hot day—beautiful waterfall, a cool and welcome swim.' 'Try walking up to **Angels' Landing**, 5-mile round trip rising 1488 feet. Incredible views.' 'Angels' Landing walk—strenuous but very rewarding.' (NB: sheer drops along path - *not* for acrophobes.) The best view of the **Great White Throne**, a colossal multicoloured butte, is from the **Temple of Sinawava**. Also worth seeing is the **Kolob Arch**. With a 310ft span, it's the world's largest. $5 park entry fee, good for 7 days; back country passes are required prior to hiking. For further info call the Parks Office, 772-3256, 8.30am-7pm.

The area code is 435. www.nps.gov/zion/

ACCOMMODATION
Park HQ: 772-3256. **Camping**: 375 sites, unreserved; arrive by noon to snag one, $10 each. Fuel, running water, toilets. No showers. Motels, groceries, and gas station at **Springdale**, 2 miles from south entrance. **Cedar City**, 40 miles north of Zion, 16 miles from Cedar Breaks National Monument (called 'Little Bryce' for its spires, perhaps more intensely coloured than anywhere else—good camping) makes a good base.
Astro Budget Inn, 323 S Main in Cedar City, 586-6557. S-$39, D-$48. AC, cable TV.
Dixie Hostel, 73 S Main St, Hurricane, 635-8202. Very central—2 hrs from Bryce, Vegas and the north rim of the Grand Canyon, 20 mins from Zion. Dorm $15, D-$35, shared bath. Incls linen and bfast. 'The best place we stayed.'
Economy Motel, 443 S Main St, Cedar City, 586-4461. S-$25, D-$35. AC, TV.
At Kanab: Canyonlands International Hostel, 143 E 100 South, 644-5554. $10, kitchen, TV, launderette. Also good for Grand Canyon, AZ.

TRAVEL
Greyhound, 1355 Main St, Cedar City, 586-9465, (800) 231-2222, from Salt Lake City and Las Vegas.
Within Zion: 45 mins tram rides into main canyon from Zion Lodge, 772-3213. $3.25, daily 9am-5pm. Hitching between Cedar City and Zion is slow.
Car rental: National Car Rental, 189 N Main St, Cedar City, 586-4004. Must be over 25.

BRYCE CANYON NATIONAL PARK Bryce's landscape belongs to God's Gothic period—delicately chiselled spires, colonnades and crenellated ridges in vivid to pastel pinks, madders, oranges, violets. Most stunning when seen against the sun: west rim in morning, east rim in afternoon. Named for Ebenezer Bryce, an unpoetic soul who described the canyon as 'a hell of a place to lose a cow'. From the pine-covered clifftops (site of the visitors centre and other facilities), the horseshoe-shaped amphitheatres reveal surreal formations that have been likened to houses, sunburned people and pertrified sunsets. For hiking, descend the canyon to the **Peekaboo Trail** or take a short trip along the **Navajo** and **Queen's Garden trails,** which link at the bottom. About $1^1/_2$ hours for a quick trot. There is a 16-mile auto road but the views are less spectacular. On full-moon nights, take the free 'moon walks' down Navajo Trail or try a star walk on w/ends of dark-moon nights at 8.30pm. 'Wall Street is more spectacular than Queen's Garden.' In order to alleviate the traffic snarls that have plagued Bryce Canyon (one parking space available for every four cars that enter the park during high season!) The park has instituted a shuttle service to transport people to the major sites. The shuttle fee is $5, in addition to the park entrance fee. Visitors who wish to bring their cars into park will also be subject to the $5 fee, in addition to the $5 vehicle access fee. Park HQ: 834-5322. Entrance fee $10, good for 10 days. *www.nps.gov/brca. Area code is 435.*

ACCOMMODATION
Most accommodation is in Panguich, 24 miles southwest of Bryce.
Bryce Canyon Pines Motel, outside Panguitch on Rt 12, 6 miles from Bryce entrance, 834-5441. S-$65, D-$75; lower in winter. AC, pool, cafe, homey dining room with good home cooking. Horseback riding $8; $85 full day.
Rocking Horse Inn, 2762 N Hwy 89, 676-2287. Free miniature golf, kitchenettes. S-$25, D-$30.
Camping in park, $10/night for up to 6 people per site. 'Arrive by noon to be sure of a place.'

MOAB   A former uranium mining town on US 163 in east-central Utah, Moab makes a convenient centre from which to visit Canyonlands, Arches and Capitol Reef National Parks.

It's also a place to book a tour to one of these parks. **Lin Ottinger's** land tours are recommended: 600 N Main, Moab, 259-7312. Mining/fossil tours, $50-$70. Other operators in town offer bike rentals and tours, horseback riding and white-water rafting. The Visitors Center at Center and Main can help you sort out options. Open daily 8am-9pm summers, (800) 635-6622. For rafting ($44 per day) contact Tag-A-Long Tours, 452 N Main St, Moab, 259-8946. *The area code is 435.*

ACCOMMODATION
Inca Inn Motel, 570 N Main, 259-7261. S/D-$43 private bath, T-$46. Cable TV, AC, pool.
Lazy Lizard Hostel, 1213 S Hwy 191, 259-6057. Dorm-$9, S/D$24. Separate bath/shower room and hot tub in the back; kitchen and laundry facs. Not affiliated w/AYH, same prices for all. 'Nice atmosphere.'
The Virginian, 70 E 200 St S, 259-5951. S-$59, D-$64, XP-$5. Fridges, cable TV, AC, rsvs essential.
Camping in Arches National Park, a mere 2mi from town, 259- 8161. $10 Mar-Oct; $5 otherwise.

ARCHES, CANYONLANDS, CAPITOL REEF   The 76,500 acres of Arches National Park contain waterhewn natural bridges and over 2000 arches of smoky red sandstone carved by the tireless wind. 'Our most memorable national park.' $5 entrance on foot, $10/vehicle for 7 days. **Natural Bridges** is noted for three rock bridges, the foremost a 268-foot span—the 2nd largest in the world. Less well-known features are the hundreds of Anasazi cliff ruins and the world's largest photovoltaic solar generating plant (free viewing), which runs the park's electrical system. For more information, call

(435)259-8161 or visit *www.nps.gov/arch.*

Canyonlands is invitingly rich in colour and landforms: towering spires, bold mesas, needles, arches, intricate canyons, roaring rapids, bottomlands and sandbars. The park is full of petroglyphs, pictographs and ruins: the Maze district with its Harvest Scene and the Needles district south of Squaw Springs campground are particularly good. Call 259-4711 for Needles info or check out the Canyonlands web page: *www.nps.gov/cany.* If you enter Canyonland Park at the **Maze** Visitors Center, 259-2652, there is no entrance charge but you will need a back country camping pass, $25, good for 14 days. There is a $10 admission fee for backpackers, $25 for vehicles, if you enter in the south-eastern corner; camping permits cost $10 for 14 days. 'Superb view from **Dead Horse Pt**, just outside park.'

Capitol Reef, rising 1000 feet above the Fremont River and extending for 20 miles, is the most spectacular monocline (tilted cliff) in the US. The bands of rock exposed along its length are luminous, rich and varied in their colour, and often cut with petroglyphs of unusual size and style. Its formations were named 'sleeping rainbows' by the Navajos.

GLEN CANYON, MONUMENT VALLEY The soaring pink sandstone arch of Rainbow Bridge and the beauties of boating in Glen Canyon can be undertaken from Moab, but closer bases would be **Page**, Arizona, and **Kanab**, Utah.

On Navajo land, **Monument Valley's** landscape of richly-coloured outcroppings was the scene of many a John Ford western. Two campsites: 'the best is in the Tribal Park among the mesas—quiet, hot showers'. $10-$15/night. Call (520) 608-6404 for info. Near Monument Valley, **San Juan State Park**, 678-2238, boasts its famous land formations, the Goosenecks. The San Juan River snakes back and forth, covering a distance of five miles while progressing only one linear mile towards the Colorado River and Lake Powell.

WYOMING *The Equality State*

When Buffalo Bill first saw this land in 1870, he called it 'the foothills of heaven.' The name 'Wyoming' itself has much more mundane origins— it's an Algonquin Indian word that means 'wide prairie place.' The name first belonged to a valley in Pennsylvania—easy to swallow, since the Algonquin-speaking tribes lived thousands of miles away from modern-day Wyoming, on the East Coast. In deference to semantics, however, however, the name is a perfect fit.

Cowboy machismo and women's rights might seem an odd mixture, but Wyoming is nicknamed the Equality State for good reason: it had the first women's suffrage act, the first female governor, juror, justice of the peace and director of the US Mint. (Buffalo Bill was among the early feminists of Wyoming, declaring 'if a woman can do the same work that a man can do and do it just as well, she should have the same pay'.)

A horsy, folksy, gun-totin' state, home of the notorious Hole-in-the-Wall Gang in the 1890s, Wyoming has ranches so huge they're measured in sections instead of acres. Everyone knows about the twin treasures of Yellowstone and Grand Teton National Parks, but Wyoming also keeps a few tourism secrets. Devils Tower is now imprinted on the world's retina as an extra-terrestrial landing pad and Salt Creek, the world's largest light oil field, was the site of the infamous Teapot Dome scandal in 1927. *www.wyomingvisitor.com*

National Parks: Grand Teton, Yellowstone (largely in Wyoming but slivers of the park are in Montana and Idaho; see Montana section for additional information). *The telephone area code for the whole of Wyoming is 307.*

CHEYENNE   Formed in 1867 when Union Pacific Railroad tracks were laid and named after the Indian people who inhabited the area, Cheyenne was once fondly called 'hell on wheels' for its volatile mix of cowpokes, cattle rustlers and con men. Capital city Cheyenne now contents itself with having the purest air and the most frequent hailstorms in the US. A little of the old buckaroo flavour returns each July during the week-long Frontier Days rodeo, largest in the US.

ACCOMMODATION
Big Horn Motel, 2004 E Lincolnway, 632-3122. S-$22, D-$26, TV, AC.
Home Ranch Motel, 2414 E Lincolnway, 634-3575. S-$28, D-$34 summers.
Motel 6, 1735 Westland Rd, 635-6806. S-$46, D-$52, less in summer.
Super 8 Motel, 1900 W Lincolnway, Hwy 30 West, 635-8741. S-$47, D-$52.

FOOD
Albany Cafe and Restaurant, 1506 Capitol Ave, 638-3507. Open 11am-9pm Mon-Sat, dinner from 4.30-9pm, meals from $4.55. Bar is good for meeting people. 'Not a pickup bar, not gay, not expensive, good music. Can this be true?'

OF INTEREST
Frontier Days, 'Daddy of 'em All' rodeo, last full week in July. 778-7200. 4 parades, chuckwagon race, free pancake breakfasts, and perhaps the best rodeo in the US. Tickets are pricey: $8-$20. 'During rodeo, the whole town goes wild on Saturday night but forget it at other times'; 'Cheyenne is dead as a doorpost on Saturday night'. However, there are planned entertainments every evening, eg. country music, Indian dancing at an Indian village. Livestock auctions on first w/end following Frontier Days events.
Holiday Park is home to the world's largest steam locomotive, Old Number 4004. The "Big Boy" was retired by the Union Pacific Railroad in 1956. Now it's on display in downtown Cheyenne.
State Museum, Central Ave & 23rd St, 777-7022. Worthwhile cowboy, Indian and pioneer museum. Free tours available on request (48 hrs notice req). Open Tues-Sat 9am-4:30pm, free. Also the **Old West Museum**, Frontier Park, 778-7290 has splendid collection of horse-drawn vehicles, Oglala Sioux beadwork. Open Mon-Fri 9am-5pm, Sat-Sun 10am-5pm; $4.
Wyoming State Capitol, 200 W 24th St, 777-7220. The building is classical in design, with a sparkling gold leaf dome that can be seen for miles around. Tours available Mon-Fri, 8:30am-4:30pm; free.

TRAVEL/INFORMATION
Amtrak, 1600 Central Ave, 778-3912, (800) 872-7245.
Greyhound, 120 N Greeley Hwy, 634-7744, (800) 231-2222.
Cheyenne Area Convention and Visitors Bureau, 309 Lincoln Way, 778-3133.

INTERNET ACCESS
Laramie County Library, 2800 Central Ave, 634-3561. Free, on a first come, first serve basis.

DEVILS TOWER NATIONAL MONUMENT

Accorded inter-galactic notoriety in *Close Encounters of the Third Kind*, Devils Tower was declared the nation's first national monument by Theodore Roosevelt in 1906 in recognition of the special part it played in Indian legend. A landmark also for early terrestrial explorers and travellers, the monolith is a fluted pillar of sombre igneous rock rising 865 feet above its wooded base and 1270 feet above the Belle Fourche River. Open year-round, $8 entrance fee per vehicle.

NB: 'Tower can be climbed safely *only* by experienced rock-climbers and takes about 4 hours. Descent 1 hour.' In 1998, about 4,000 people made the climb.

The scene is 'creepily impressive, much more so than the movie.' In the park are prairie-dog villages, an outdoor amphitheatre and ranger programmes in summer (talks, demos and guided walks on the subject of wildlife, rockclimbing or the monument, 9.30am-4.30pm). Park Visitors' Center: 467-5283; open 8am-7.45pm in summer, shorter hours in winter. *www.nps.gov/deto.*

ACCOMMODATION
Campsites at the monument open year- round; $12 per night.
Arrowhead Motel, 214 Cleveland St in **Sundance**, 283-3307. S/D$55, T-$60. 'Most clean and attractive. Friendly, helpful and bright.'

YELLOWSTONE NATIONAL PARK

The oldest and perhaps the most well-loved of the national parks, Yellowstone comprises 2.2 million acres; it's larger than Delaware and Rhode Island combined. The land area designated a national park in 1872 covers the northwest corner of Wyoming before dribbling over into Idaho and Montana. Three of the five entrances are in Montana; they and the gateway cities of Gardiner, Bozeman and West Yellowstone are discussed in the Montana section. Wyoming park entrances are from the east via Cody, from the south via Jackson/Grand Teton National Park.

Drought and 40- to 70-mile-per-hour winds set the stage for the uncontrollable forest fires of 1988. The fires burned a mosaic pattern throughout nearly 800,000 acres. Fortunately, only half of this acreage was blackened and much of this is quickly rejuvenating. None of the major attractions were disturbed.

Yellowstone is one of the world's most impressive thermal regions. There are more geysers and hot springs here than in the rest of the world combined. Besides Old Faithful (which blows over 130-foot, dispelling 5,000-8,000 gallons of water every 79 minutes or so), there are some 10,000 thermal features including geysers, hot springs, colourful paint pots and gooey mud pools—an uncanny array of colours, temperatures, smells, disquieting sounds and eruptions. Old Faithful is the most famous geyser, but there are many others nearby that erupt more frequently. Also worth visiting is the

Norris Junction area. There you can see hundreds of geysers and pools on a walk of less than two miles.

Another priority should be the **Grand Canyon** of the **Yellowstone River**, whose 1,540 foot gorge is 'one wild welter of colour', as Rudyard Kipling put it. 'Breath-taking—even better than the Arizona one.' The river tumbles into the canyon through the **Lower Falls**, twice the height of Niagara Falls. **Artist Point** gives possibly the most scenic view of Yellowstone—look over the sheer drop of 700 feet to the canyon below. Don't miss the 110 miles of shoreline and sublime scenery along **Yellowstone Lake**, also famous for its trout. Leave yourself enough time to also visit '**Morning Glory**', a deep turquoise lake rimmed with gold along the Firehole River.

A wildlife sanctuary, the park is home to over 200 species of birds and over 60 species of mammals including deer, moose, bison, and bear. Because so many people fed the bears (often being hurt in the process by these naturally wild, 3ft tall, 300-400 pound animals), the park has removed many of them to remote areas. Human meddling has turned a number of these bears into serious menaces, and over 100 of them have had to be shot. If you do sight bears, do not feed them, get close to them, or come between an adult and cubs. The bears are wild and meant to stay that way.

Cars were not admitted to the park until 1915; today, about 800,000 of them enter, with attendant traffic jams, accidents, pollution and parking problems. But as in other parks, visitors tend to congregate in the same places, leaving the rest of the park refreshingly empty.

Challenging hikes include the 3½-mile walk to the summit of **Mt Washburn** (stay on trails, don't take shortcuts). If you have more time, rent a canoe at West Yellowstone and canoe/camp the **Lewis River** to the **Shoshone Lakes** - a pristine, wildlife-filled journey. Many campsites (free permit required) along the route and at the lake. 'Don't forget Canyon and Upper Falls—on par with Grand Canyon!'

The park is open year-round ($20 per car or $10 on foot, good for 7 days), but the official season runs May to September. During the fall and winter, bus service and other facilities cease and you run the risk of getting caught in a heavy snowstorm. In the off season, the only roads and entrance open are via Gardiner. You can, however, take a snow coach from West Yellowstone. Yellowstone in winter is enchanting: the animals move in close to the warmth of the geysers and thermal springs—awesome to see them in the swirling mists. You can actually ski or snowshoe close to bison and elk. *www.nps.gov/yell/*. Park Information: 344-7381.

ACCOMMODATION

Lodging outside the park is discussed under West Yellowstone and Gardiner, Montana. See also Cody.

Within the Park: 9 different lodges and cabin clusters are available for individuals and small groups. Prices range from $26 a night for a cabin without linens or running water up to $88 for fully equipped lodges. Roosevelt Lodge is the cheapest, $43-$83, 'only place worth the money'. Other bargains are **Old Faithful Snowlodge**, $107-$128, and **Old Faithful Lodge and Cabins**, $34-$62. 'Beds are very comfy.' Lodges open and close at different times in spring and fall. Call 344-7311 to reserve space.

Camping: 12 campgrounds with more than 2300 sites are available for $10-$27 a night. Usually filled before noon in summer, first-come first-served. 'If you are prepared to sleep in the car, you can use the high bear-risk campsites.' 'Arrive before

8pm if you want a shower—or use hotel as we did.' Camping can be very cold, even in July, so bring a warm sleeping bag. To camp outside the developed sites and away from all the RVs, obtain a free permit at one of the park's visitor centres, where you can also buy a necessary hiking map. Do not sleep with food near you. At night some bears can't distinguish between bags of crisps and bags of people! Winter camping at Mammoth Campground only. Call 344-7311 for more information.

FOOD
Six concessions in the park, none of which are particularly cheap. If you can manage, bring in groceries from West Yellowstone.

TRAVEL
AmFac Parks and Resorts, 344-7901, tours Lower and Upper Loops of the park, $30-$32. 'Clerks at West Yellowstone very helpful with advice.' 'You can make your own combinations.' 'If you're on foot, hitch to Old Faithful and do a lower loop tour. You get to see a lot during the day.' Hitching within the park is rated 'very easy'. Greyhound: see W Yellowstone, MT.

GRAND TETON NATIONAL PARK Twenty miles due south of Yellowstone and 15 mins from Jackson lies the totally different world of the Grand Teton Mountains. As awe-inspiring as Yellowstone, this 500 sq mi park reminds one of Alpine Europe rather than the American West. The Tetons rise without preliminaries from a level valley to sharp pinnacles more than 13,000 feet high, separated by deep glaciated clefts. On their crags and flanks, you see remnants of the last great glaciation that once covered North America, 10,000 years ago. Although these are the youngest mountains in the Rockies, you'll see some of the oldest rock formations in North America. Besides peaks, valleys like Jackson Hole, the lakes and the winding Snake River all complement the stunning environment. Jackson Hole, Jenny Spring and Solitude Lakes make for good if icy swimming.

Warm clothes and sturdy shoes are essential here for tackling the many excellent hiking trails. This is mountaineering country; several schools have their headquarters in the area. Free permits for climbing must be obtained from a park ranger. Be careful, though—it's not for novices.

One of the best ways to absorb the Tetons is to float down the Snake River on a large rubber raft steered by boatmen. In the forests at river's edge, look for some of the wapiti (elk). The largest herd in North America is found here in the Grand Tetons. Commercial river rafting tours abound, but depending on your karma you may meet up with a group of locals who are already going. Join in—but remember Snake River rapids require skillful handling.

Admission to the park is combined with Yellowstone: a $20 vehicle pass ($10 if you're on foot) is good for 7 days in both areas. Visitor centres are located in Colter Bay and Moose, 739-3399. *www.nps.gov/grte/*

ACCOMMODATION
Lodging both in the park and in nearby Jackson tends to be more costly than at Yellowstone and vicinity. Call 543-2811 or go to *www.gtlc.com* for details of **Colter Bay Village Cabins** in the park, and **Jackson Lake Lodge.** Both very reasonable. At Colter Bay, one room (8 people) in a tent cabin w/shared bath is $30pp; $64-$91 for two people in a log cabin. The tent cabins are cheaper and more 'adventurous', constructed of canvas and logs, with outdoor grill and woodburning stoves. Bring own bedding for bunks. Rooms at Jackson Lodge are from $110 for two people. Try also **Signal Mountain** cabins in Moran, 543-2831, D-$80.

JACKSON John Colter first stumbled upon this area in 1807. A former member of the Lewis and Clark Expedition, Colter arrived here by himself, later to lure other settlers to the lovely area he'd found. Modern Jackson, pretty and gentrified, is a cross between Aspen and Boulder, drawing crowds of boisterous tourists in summer. In winter, on the other hand, the tiny village entices gentler, nobler visitors when 10,000 elk come to graze at the edge of town. Capture some of this magic on a sleigh ride through the elk refuge, 733-9212, $12. In the spring, local boy scouts collect and sell antlers, some of which end up as aphrodisiacs in the Far East. Look out for the nose, mouth and folded arms of the 'Sleeping Indian' on the horizon.

ACCOMMODATION
Bunkhouse, 733-3668, 2 blks N of town square, 215 N Cache Dr. $22 dorm. The hostel has lounge with TV, kitchen.

The Hostel 'X', Box 546, Teton Village, 12 miles north of Jackson, 733-3415. S/D-$45, T/Q-$55. Game room, lounge with fireplace.

Grand Teton Lodge Co. has tent cabins, with canvas-covered patio, double-deck bunks, outdoor grill, picnic table, woodburning stove, $30 for two, XP-$3. 45 miles N of Jackson on Hwy 89. Write to reserve: PO 240, Moran, WY 83013; or call 543-2811.

FOOD
Bubba's, 515 W Broadway, 733-2288. Good home cooking; breakfast and sandwiches for around $4. Open daily 7am-10pm.

Mountain High Pizza Pie, 120 W Broadway, 733-3646. Traditional, deep-dish and whole wheat crusts, $6.50-$11.75. Outdoor seating; plays Dead music. Open daily, 11am-midnight.

ENTERTAINMENT
For good reading, pick up a copy of *Jackson Hole News* or *Jackson Hole Guide*. Both have been awarded 'best weekly in the nation' over the years, and the competition continues. Try **JJ's Silver-Dollar Bar**, 733-2190, with 2,000 silver coins embedded in the counter; or the **The Rancher**, 733-3886, facing the town square. Large pool hall, open 11am-2am, bar food from $2-$6. The **Mangy Moose**, in Teton Village, 739-2166 has live bands, $1-$5 cover. The **Jackson Hole Brew Pub**, 265 S Millward, 739-2337 has 12 beers incl stout, porter and largers; free tours daily at 3pm. For good music, try **Stagecoach**, 733-3451; disco on Thurs nights, bluegrass on Sun.

Jackson Hole Llamas, 739-9582, (800) 830-7316, *www.jhllamas.com* 5-hr trek with llamas (by group request only) includes lunch and a spectacular view of the Tetons, $540 an outing (ie. 10 people - $54 each). Also available: longer guided trips in Teton, Yellowstone, and Wind River areas, but they're expensive.

Teton Mystery, 10 min S on Hwy 89, 733-4285. Maybe you can solve the mystery—no one else seems to be able to. A whirlpool of gravitational force flowing in a northerly direction will make you lean at a sharp angle in order to stay comfortably balanced. Water seems to flow uphill; you will be able to walk up a wall. Bring a camera! Open May-Sept, 10am-6pm daily; $5.

Teton Village, 12 mls northwest of Jackson offers skiers the largest vertical rise in the USA—4139 ft to **Rendevous Peak**. A 63-passenger aerial tram services the peak year round.

TRAVEL/INFORMATION
Start Buses, 733-4521, runs a service between Jackson and Teton Village several times a day, $2.

Jackson Hole Airport, 733-7682, about 8 miles from town. **Alltrans**, (800) 443-6133, runs a shuttle service from the town's hotels to the airport, $12, or a taxi for $16. Phone ahead to request service.

Jackson Hole Chamber of Commerce, 990 Broadway, 733-3316. For all local information and help. Hitching is described as 'very easy'.

INTERNET ACCESS
Cyber City Cyber Cafe, 265 W Broadway, 734-2582.

CODY It may look like an endless stretch of motels, but be not dismayed. Cody possesses a superlative, four-in-one museum complex and an Old Trail Town that are well worth your attention. About 60 miles east of Yellowstone, Cody is the namesake of William F, also known as Buffalo Bill—a bison hunter/army scout/Pony Express rider-turned-showman. His Wild West show players earned a living by touring the US, Canada and Europe with a mawkish morality play of brave cowboys and savage redskins—very popular at the time. Royalty loved it; Queen Victoria gave Cody a diamond brooch, saying his show was so exciting she found it 'almost impossible to sit.' Annie Oakley and Sitting Bull were among Buffalo Bill's prize 'exhibits;' the mythology created thereby was later recycled by Hollywood.

East of Cody, the vividly coloured strata of **Shell Canyon** along the winding stretch of Highway 14 between Shell and Sheridan is highly scenic; to reach Custer's Last Stand in Montana, turn north at Sheridan.

ACCOMMODATION
Irma Hotel, 1192 Sheridan Ave, 587-4221. Luxurious and expensive, S/D-$102 (annex rooms-$75), but a grandly historic place built by Buffalo Bill and named after his daughter. If you don't stay, at least stop by for a drink at the incredible French cherrywood bar, a gift from Queen Victoria after BB's command performance in England. Lunches ($4.95-$6) and even dinners are very good value at the Irma Grill.
Pawnee Hotel, 1032 12th, 587-2239. S/D-$32-$38.
Rainbow Park Motel, 1136 17th St, 587-6251. S/D-$34, T-$43.

OF INTEREST
Buffalo Bill Historical Center, 720 Sheridan, 587-4771. Daily 7am-8pm, June through August, 8am-5pm Apr-May and Sept-Nov, 10am-3pm Dec-Mar; $10 ($6 w/student ID). Contains 4 museums: The **Buffalo Bill Museum** holds Cody memorabilia, BB's boyhood home. The **Plains Indian Musuem** is huge, imaginative and head and shoulders above most Indian collections. The **Whitney Gallery of Western Art** has bluechip Western painters: Remington, Catlin, Russell and Bierstadt's work on Yellowstone. Recently opened in a new gallery is the **Cody Firearms Museum** (formerly the Winchester Gun Museum), with over 5,000 firearms from America and Europe.
Old Trail Town, 587-5302, 2 miles west in Shoshone Canyon. A well-conceived collection of historic buildings and relics from all over Wyoming from Cassidy and Sundance's hideout to Jeremiah Johnson's grave. 'Non-gimmicky.' Open mid-May to mid-Sept, $4. Open 8am-8pm.
Buffalo Bill Dam Visitors Centre, 13 mls west of Cody on Hwy 14, 16-20 miles from Yellowstone, 527-6076. Exhibits, natural history; interactive displays show how this beautiful dam was built. Open daily 8am-8pm, free.
Rodeos early June-Aug, nightly on the west side of town. Enquire locally. The **Cody Stampede** is held annually from 1st-4th July.

INFORMATION
Cody Chamber of Commerce, 836 Sheridan Ave, 587-2297. Mon-Sat 8am-7pm, Sun 10am-3pm.

THE PACIFIC STATES

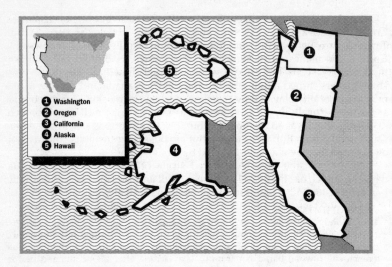

1 Washington
2 Oregon
3 California
4 Alaska
5 Hawaii

The Pacific states have everything and more. From ancient redwoods to modern cities, from lumbermen to film stars, from Polynesian huts to Arctic igloos, and in every state much of the most exciting scenery in America. The Russians, British, French, Spanish and Mexicans have all had claims here, and though Americans swept west under the conquering banner of Manifest Destiny, some of the old influences survive.

But the Pacific is also where the rainbow ends, where expectations must finally prove themselves. Enthusiasm reigns, and that is probably the region's most enjoyable quality—though the final results are still awaited.

ALASKA *The Last Frontier*

Aleut for 'great land,' Alaska has a penchant for superlatives: biggest, coldest, costliest, highest peak, longest coastline, richest animal life, longest *and* shortest days.

Alaskans are proud people who are Alaskans first, and, by the way, Americans. The contiguous states, known as the 'lower 48' are far, far away, and Alaskans seem quite glad about that.

The state was jeered at as 'Seward's Folly' when President Lincoln's Secretary of State bought it from the Russians for 2¢ an acre in 1867. But no one laughed for very long, for gold was discovered only a few years later, inspiring a deluge of opportunists and virtually creating such towns as Skagway, Fairbanks and Juneau.

After becoming the USA's 49th state in 1959, Alaska proved fruitful again when one of the world's richest caches of petroleum was discovered in Prudhoe Bay in 1968. To tap its potential a consortium of oil companies financed the 800-mile Trans-Alaska Pipeline, which now brings 1.5 million barrels daily to Valdez, on Prince William Sound.

In an attempt to spread the oil profits equitably among native people and other Alaskans, the 1971 Alaska Native Claims Settlement Act puts emphasis on money and land ownership, concepts foreign to the state's native peoples. The Act has consequently had a devastating impact: you'll see many downtrodden and misplaced Indians, particularly in Fairbanks and Anchorage.

Alaska is breathtakingly beautiful and well worth visiting, particularly in summer when daytime temperatures are surprisingly warm and there's plenty of daylight. Campers and hikers be forewarned however: the unofficial state bird here is the mosquito. And watch out for the wildlife: humans are expected to give way to bears on trails and pathways. According to travel writer Erik Sandberg-Diment of the *Washington Post*, 'that part is easy. The part about doing it slowly, without running, is more difficult.'

The land route of the Alaska Highway from British Columbia to Fairbanks and Anchorage is an adventure, but the finest approach is by boat from Seattle or Prince Rupert. State-run, inexpensive ferries ply the Inside Passage year-round, allowing closeup looks at glaciers, islands, fjords, whales and stopover privileges at the various ports of call.

Prices in Alaska range from 'tolerable' in the SE panhandle to double those in Seattle, San Francisco and elsewhere. 'Some things are not much more than the lower 48, but be prepared for some nasty shocks.' Bus passes aren't valid in Alaska, but various tours are available. Gasoline prices are on par with or slightly higher than California. Conventional lodging is very costly, but spartan youth hostels do exist, and there are campgrounds everywhere. (Come prepared for plummeting temperatures at night, although one reader notes that the American tourists simply wear their shorts over thermal underwear during the day.) Stick to locally grown produce and seafood to keep food costs down. A note on the sheer size of Alaska—extreme by even American standards. More than twice the size of Texas, superimposed on the Lower 48, Alaska would stretch from Atlantic to Pacific. For unlimited travel on participating ferries, trains and buses, consider the **Alaska Pass**, from $499 for eight consecutive days to $999 for 21 days travel out of 45 days. Call (800) 248-7598 / (206) 463-6550.

National Park: Denali (formerly Mt McKinley).

www.AlaskaOne.com/travel/alaska.htm. The telephone area code for the state is 907.

THE INSIDE PASSAGE and THE PANHANDLE Warmed by the Japanese Current and protected from the open sea by a necklace of islands, this south-eastern waterway enjoys the state's mildest weather (a relative term meaning it rarely gets below zero in winter). Besides access by cruise ships, the state operates an extensive ferry system called the Alaska Marine Highway, an appropriate name since five of the seven ports in the Panhandle have no overland highway access to the outside world. 'Just the sight of a humpback whale breaching is enough to make the journey a memorable one.' 'Good vessels, interesting places to stop over, many opportunities to meet people.' 'In summer, Tongass Forest interpreters give free talks, film shows, on board. An imaginative and interesting service.'

First port of call is **Ketchikan**, still a salmon centre, now more dependent on cruise ship traffic. Weatherbeaten houses on stilts and the harbour give it a New England flavour, but it never rained like this in Massachusetts. The record here is 223.8" a year.

Sitka, once capital of Russian America and beautifully situated at the foot of Fuji-like Mt Edgecumbe, has a reconstructed Russian cathedral full of icons, plus interesting gravestones from this period. There is also a large and well-preserved collection of totems. James Michener spent much time here researching his book, *Alaska*.

Capital city, **Juneau**, climbs steep wooded hillsides with wooden stairways and a kaleidoscope of architectural styles. It's a great irony and a bone of contention among many Alaskans that the capital city is not reachable by highway, only by air or water. The once impassioned-campaign to move the capital city is on hold because of the expense involved. **Mendenhall Glacier**, 14 miles away (and accessible by car) has camping. From Haines, the old Dalton Trail leads off to the **Klondike**, several ghost towns and the amazing overhang of Rainbow Glacier.

In its sourdough heyday, **Skagway** was big-city size. Now down to a population of 767, it's reaping a new gold rush of tourists to photograph its well-preserved wooden sidewalks, false-front buildings and memorials to Soapy Smith, the local bad guy. 'On his birthday, locals urinate on his grave.' Best during the oldtime fervour of Sourdough Days, celebrated in September. *www.alaskainfo.org* specifically focuses on Alaska's Inside Passage and provides useful links to Inside Passage communities.

ACCOMMODATION

Alaska B&B Assoc., Juneau, 586-2959. Can help find you a room downtown from $65.

Alaskan Hotel, 167 Franklin, **Juneau**, (800) 327-9347. $68 w/shared bath. $84 w/private bath. Sauna, jacuzzi, some kitchenettes. On National Register of Historic Places, built 1913. Good bar!

Bear Creek Camp & Hostel, PO Box 908, 1.5 Small Track Road, **Haines**, 766-2259. 1½ miles from Haines; located in pristine wooded area 1 mile from beach, hiking, fishing. Small store on premises. $3 pickup/drop off from ferry. Summer: $14pp, wood-heated cabins. Private cabins, $38 for two, XP-$4. Hot showers, kitchen. Camping from $8p/p.

Eagles Nest Motel, 1183 Haines Hwy, **Haines**, 766-2891. S-$75, D-$85. TV, private bath.

Gilmore Hotel, 326 Front St, **Ketchikan**, 225-9423. Rooms from $76. Next door to **Annabel's Keg and Chowder House**, 7am-10pm (lunch $5-$10; dinner $20-$50).

HI-Juneau Hostel, 614 Harris St, **Juneau**, 586-9559. 3 blocks from downtown; $7 AYH. Kitchen, showers, large common room with fireplace. Year round, daily 7am-9 am, 5pm-11pm. Rsvs req by mail, with $7 deposit included. 'A beautiful facility in a prime location.'

HI-Ketchikan Hostel, First United Methodist Church, Grant and Main Sts, **Ketchikan**, 225-3319. June 1-Sept 1. $8 AYH. 4-night limit, extendible by manager. Clean kitchen, common area, piano, hot showers, open for late-arriving ferries if call beforehand. Sleeping bag recommended.

HI-Sitka Hostel, United Methodist Church, 303 Kimsham St, **Sitka,** 747-8775. PO

Box 2645, **Sitka**, AK 99835. 1 June-31 Aug. $9 AYH. Bring sleeping bag.
Inn at the Waterfront, 455 S Franklin, **Juneau**, 586-2050. Once a Gold Rush brothel!
S-$58. Bfast included.
Ketchikan Reservation Service, 225-3273, provides info on B&Bs (S-$55-85).
Skagway Inn, 7th and Broadway, **Skagway**, 983-2289. B&B, 'delicious breakfast'.
Rooms begin $103, prices are reduced in winter. Shared bath, restaurant open May-
Sept.
Camping: SEAVC, 228-6214, provides info and rsvs for Forest Service camp-
grounds, including **Signal Creek Campground**, 6 miles N of Ketchikan ferry ter-
minal on Tongass Hwy, featuring attractive views and pleasant nature trails. Call
direct for reservations on (877) 444-6777. Approx. $10 at all state parks. In
Ketchikan, 225-2148, US Forest Service manages **Ward Lake** area campgrounds,
$20; 2-week limit June-Aug.
Also: First come first served camping at **Mendenhall Lake Campground** near
Juneau on Montana Creek Road. $8-$16: beautiful views of glacier; no reservations.
Free camping on steep **Chilkoot Trail** from Skagway. Reserve up to 6 mths in
advance. Permits required $35 + $10 p/p booking fee. Call (800) 661-0486 or (867)
667-3910 outside N America. Free permit for overnight in US, not needed for day
hikes. Historic and breathtaking route—one of the most beautiful passes in
Alaska—worth lingering.

FOOD
Channel Bowl Café, 608 W Willoughby Ave (across from Juneau A&P) **Juneau**,
586-6139. Get your $5.50 pancake bfast feast here! Daily 7am-2pm.
Tatsuda's, 633 Stedman at Deermount St, 225-4125. The most convenient supermarket to downtown. Daily 7am-11pm.

OF INTEREST
Ketchikan: Salmon Capital of the World: see **Deer Mountain Fish Hatchery**, 1158
Salmon Road, 225-6760, next to the Totem Heritage Center (see below). A guided
tour explains artificial sex, salmon style. Daily 8.30am-4.30pm. $6.95.
Historic Creek Street is the old red-light district with renovated stores and
galleries and a colourful stretch of houses.
Dolly's House, 24 Creek St, 225-6329. A brothel turned museum. Antiques are set
amid secret hideaways where Dolly kept money, bootleg liquor, and respectable
customers during police raids. $4. Tues-Sat 9am-4.15pm, Sun/Mon 9am-1pm.
Tlingit (pronounced Klinkit!) **Totems** at Saxman Native Village (2 miles south by
bus) have a woodcarver on site, 9am-5pm; Totem Bight State Park (10 miles north),
and **Totem Heritage Center**, 601 Deermount St, 225-5900. It is the largest collection
of authentic, pre-commercial totem poles in the US. Daily 8am-5pm, $4. Go see
Totems 160 yrs old as well as more contemporary ones.
Ketchikan Museum, 225-5600, 629 Dock St, downtown, with displays on local
history, art, native heritage and fishing. Mon-Sun 8am-5pm; $2.
Sitka: Sitka National Historical Park, Lincoln St, at the other end of which is **Castle
Hill**, the actual spot where the sale of Alaska from Russia to US occurred. Daily
8am-6pm, free.
Russian Bishops' House, 501 Lincoln St, 747-6281. Largest and last remaining
Russian-built home in Alaska. Daily guided tours in summer 9am-4.30pm ; other-
wise by appointment only, $4, free w/student ID.
Sheldon Jackson State Museum, 104 College Dr, 747-8981. Impressive collection of
artefacts, representing all four native groups of Alaska: Eskimos, Aleutians,
Athabaskans and NW Indians. Jackson began the Indian Trading School, a boarding school for natives in Alaska. Building itself is a National Historical Site, the first
concrete building in Alaska. Daily in summer, 9am-5pm; Tue-Sat 10am-4pm after
Sept 15, $3.

Southeastern Alaska Indian Cultural Center, 106 Metlakatla St (in park), 747-8061. Tlingit Indian craftsmen and artists at work. Daily 8am-5pm in summer, varies in winter.

St. Michael's Cathedral, 747-8120, Russian Orthodox, in middle of street in centre of town. Stunning, built during Russian period, burned in 1966 and since restored. Mon-Sat 11am-3pm.

Juneau: Alaska State Museum, 465-2907, 395 Whittier St for good artefacts; $3, free w/student ID. In summer, nightly salmon bakes, self-guided walking tours of historic Juneau, through the Division of Tourism at 33 Willoughby St, 9th floor, 465-2010.

Alaskan Brewing Co., 5429 Shaune Dr (in Lemon Creek), 780-5866. The beer has been awarded prizes galore and been featured in *Northern Exposure*. $1/2$ hr tours of the brewery: Mon -Sat 11am-4.30pm summer; Thurs-Sat winter.

The slopes of the **Eaglecrest Ski Area**, 155 S Seward St, Juneau 99801, 586-5284 on Douglas Isl., offer alpine skiing in winter. Call for prices. **Glacier Bay National Park**, 50 miles NW of Juneau, 697-2225. Beautiful and untouched wilderness of seals, whales, bears and 20 glaciers. Access by boat or plane only; expensive. 'Awesome.'

Hiking in Juneau: If you're looking for the best view of Juneau, go to the end of 6th St and head up the steep, 4 mile trail to the summit of **Mt Roberts** (3576ft).

Haines: Old Ft Seward, 766-2202, now a centre for the Chilkat dancers. Don't miss Indian artists at work on totems, masks, and soapstone, Mon-Fri 9am-5pm, Memorial Day-Labor Day. Near Haines is the world's largest concentration of **bald eagles**; best months Oct & Nov.

Skagway: Chilkoot Trail, Dyea (9 miles from Skagway) to Bennett in Canada. 3-5 day hike, must reserve place,(800) 661-0486.

Klondike Gold Rush National Park, 983-2921. The 7-block historic Broadway Street contains many restored structures, leftovers from the Gold Rush days. Daily 8am-6pm.

Trail of '98 Museum, 983-2420, Arctic Brotherhood Hall, btwn 2nd and 3rd Ave on Broadway. Gold Rush and Native artefacts on display. Fascinating stuff. 9am-5pm daily. $2, $1 w/student ID.

INFORMATION

Ketchikan: Southeastern Alaska Visitors Center (SEAVC), on waterfront, 228-6214. Provides info on Ketchikan and entire Panhandle, esp. good on outdoors. May-Sept daily 8.30am-4.30pm; Oct-April Tues-Sat same hrs.

Visitors Bureau, at the City Dock, 131 Front St, (800) 770-3300. May-Sept daily 8am-5pm, limited winter hrs.

Sitka: Visitors Bureau, 303 Lincoln, 747-5940.

Juneau: Davis Log Cabin, 134 3rd St at Seward St, 586-2201/586-2284. Visitors Centre Mon-Fri 8.30am-5pm.

Division of Tourism, 33 Willoughby St, 9th Flr, 465-2010. Mon-Fri, 8am-5pm and Sat & Sun in summer.

National Forest and National Park Services, in Centennial Hall, 101 Egan Dr at Willoughby, 586-8751. Mon -Fri 8am-5pm. Provides info on/rsvs for Forest Service cabins in **Tongass National Forest. Skagway: Visitors Bureau**, 2nd & 3rd at Broadway, 983-2854. 8am-6pm daily.

TRAVEL

Alaska Marine Highway, PO Box R, Juneau, AK 99802-5535, (800) 642-0066. Contact for rsvs, schedules and other info. Alternatively, place a rsvs by filling out an online form via *www.alaska.alaskan.com/~ams/ferry/*. Bellingham, WA — Skagway, $252 walk on, $508 for car; Juneau-Haines $24. Meals, staterooms cost extra, run at or below hotel prices. 'Tolerates camping out and sleeping bags on top-deck solarium for those who have the gear and can't sleep on reclining seats.' 'Board early if you want a place on the solarium.' 'Boat deck is heated, has camping beds, showers, lockers provided free.' 'Cafeteria good value, but taking your own food definitely advisable.' Only one ferry makes the complete Bellingham-Skagway run, once a week in summer. 'Very crowded.' 3 ferries work Prince Rupert-Skagway, runs Sun, Tues, Thurs & Sat, $130. Rsvs necessary on all services.

Allstar Rent-a-Car, 9104 Menden Hall Mall Rd, 790-2414. Provides shuttle from airport or ferry terminal to their office.

Gray Line, (800) 544-2206. Runs buses from Haines to Anchorage, Sun, Tues, Thurs, takes two days, $195 o/w. Also Skagway-Whitehorse daily at 7.30 am, $45 o/w. Both services only run 'til mid-September.

THE ALASKA HIGHWAY
For years nearly all gravel or dirt-surfaced, the highway nowadays is paved from top to bottom. Beginning at Dawson Creek, British Columbia, it's 915 miles to Whitehorse in the Yukon and a total of 1,420 to its official end in Delta Junction. To reach Fairbanks, take the Richardson Hwy, a continuation of the Alaska Highway. The Glenn Highway out of Tok leads to Anchorage.

ACCOMMODATION
Plenty of expensive motels along the way. Also numerous campgrounds; bring a tent. In and near Tok:

HI-TOK Hostel, Mile 1322 $^1/_2$ Alaska Highway, PO Box 532, Tok, AK 99780, 883-3745. Hrs away from any large city, offers clean air, solitude and starry skies. Clean and comfortable, kitchen, beds, all in a big tent. Fishing in the Tanana River; Eagle Trail is 3 miles from hostel. Summer only; $10.

TRAVEL
'Make sure your car is in good running order and carry a few of the more essential spare parts. Garages charge what they like for spares.' Gas stations are every 20-50 miles, occasionally as far apart as 100 miles. Hitching: long waits. Don't get let off at Tok Junction (which gets below-zero temps in Sept): 'horror stories abound of people getting stuck.' Alaskan law requires motorists to pick up hitchhikers when it is very cold out, but we don't recommend you put this to the test. As always, be careful.

Alaska Direct Bus Line (800) 770 6652, operates from Anchorage, Fairbanks, Tok, various other cities. Tok to Anchorage, Sun, Wed, Fri, 6 hrs, $65 o/w.

INFORMATION
Tok Information Center, Alaska Public Lands Info Center, PO Box 359, Tok, AK 99780, 883-5667. 'Friendly, helpful.' Before setting out on your journey, pick up a copy of the free pamphlet *Help Along the Way* at a visitors bureau, or contact the **Department of Health and Social Services**, PO Box 110601, Juneau, AK 99811, 465-3030. Includes exhaustive listing of emergency medical services and emergency phone numbers throughout Alaska, the Yukon, and British Columbia, plus tips on preparation and driving. Also: *Milepost* ($19.95 + $4.50 shipping in US, more for UK), is an essential mile-by-mile guide to the Hwy, both Alaska and Canada portions. To order: Vernon Publishing, 300 Northrup Way #200, Bellevue, WA 98004 or call (800) 726-4707 in Seattle.

ANCHORAGE
Largest city (254 000) in Alaska and unremarkably modern since its rebuilding after the 1964 earthquake, Anchorage makes a good excursion base for Mt McKinley, the peninsula and the islands of southwestern Alaska. The quake sunk some of the land around here below

sea level, inundating the ground with salt water. The result is an eerie vista of sodden, sterile land and skeletal trees.

Besides its transportation links and a fairly rambunctious nightlife, Anchorage also dabbles in the business of love: its *Alaskamen*, published every two months, provides profiles and photos of eligibles for women in the lower 48, and boasts 3-5 matches per month. *Alaska scenes* at *www.alaska.net/~design/scenes/* provides scenery and events in Anchorage, including photo essays about the Fur Rondy, State Fair, wildlife and seasons.

ACCOMMODATION
Alaska Private Lodgings / Stay With A Friend, 704 W 2nd Ave, 278-8800, can refer you to B&Bs from $65 p/n.

HI-Anchorage Hostel, 700 H St at 7th, 276-3635. 8am-11pm. $16 AYH. Laundry, kitchen. 'Good place, easy to meet people.' 'Very crowded July-Aug.' Rsvs rec 1 day before.

Home Hostel, PO Box 104099, Anchorage, AK 99510, 783-2099. $10. Wood-burning stove; 6 bunks, no laundry or bathing facilities. Rsvs req.

North of Anchorage on Hwy 1 (btwn Palmer and Glennallen): **Sheep Mountain Lodge**, HC03 Box 8490, **Palmer**, AK 99645, 745-5121. Summer only; $12 AYH, $15 non-AYH. Cabins also available, D-$130, including sauna. Free showers with both. Hot-tub, jacuzzi extra. Restaurant with home-cooked meals. Hiking.

Inlet Inn, 539 H St, downtown, 277-5541. No-frills budget chain; D-$75, cheaper in winter.

South of Anchorage on the New Seward Hwy, in **Girdwood**, *the* place for mountain biking in the summer, skiing in the winter: **Alyeska Camping: Chugach State Park**, 354-5014, two of the best areas are **Eagle River**, $15, and **Eklutna**, $10, respectively 12½ miles and 26½ miles NE of Anchorage along Glenn Hwy. First come, first served, no reservations taken.

FOOD/ENTERTAINMENT
Blondie's Café, at corner of 4th and D St, 279-0698. All-day bfast includes 3 hot-cakes, $4.25. Daily 5am-11pm.

Chilkoot Charlies, 2435 Spenard Rd, 272-1010, the city's busiest bar, huge sawdust-on-the-floor venue, live music, bar food. Cover around $4.

Mr Whiteky's Fly-by-Night Club, 3300 Spenard Rd, 279-SPAM. Even in darkest Alaska, you can satisfy that unquenchable craving for Spam! This 'sleazy' place has Spam entrees in every imaginable configuration, as well as great nightly entertainment ('adult' musical show 'Whale Fat Follies,' from $10, pokes fun at Alaska and its tourists, 8-10.30pm). Menu has now been 'expanded' to include desserts, sandwiches and seafood. Also serves fine champagnes, the rec accompaniment to spam. (Your spam is free when you order Don Perignon.) Tue-Sat, 4pm-2.30 am.

Twin Dragon, 612 E 15th Ave (near Gambell), 276-7535. Lunch buffet of marinated meats and vegetables, $6.25. A favourite among Anchorage's knowledgeable diners. Daily 11am-midnight.

OF INTEREST
Alaska Experience Theater, 705 W 6th Ave, 276-3730. 40 mins of Alaskan adventures on the inner surface of a hemispherical dome. Every hr, 9am-9pm; $7.

Earthquake Park, close to town off Northern Lights Blvd. Recalls the 1964 Good Friday earthquake. The quake was the strongest ever recorded in North America; 9.2 on the Richter scale.

Imaginarium, 725 5th Ave, Mon-Sat 11am-5pm, $5. Hands-on displays about glaciers, the Northern Lights and Alaskan wildlife, including the Polar Bear.

Museum of History and Art, 121 W 7th Ave, 343-4326. Historic and ethnographic art from all over Alaska, as well as national and international art exhibits. A summer film series shows at no extra cost. Daily 9am-9pm, except Sat 9am-6pm, in summer. $5.

Walk, bike or skate along the **Tony Knowles Coastal Trail**, an 11 mile paved track that skirts **Cook Inlet** on one side and the backyards of Anchorage's upper crust on the other.

Nearby: Ekoutna Burial Grounds, 26 miles N on Glenn Hwy. Indian cemetery with spirit houses that look like doll houses, interesting gravesites. Get info from visitors bureau. 'Fascinating.' There are still regular earth tremors—'one of 5.5 while we were here'—but nothing to compare with the 1964 monster quake—yet.

Portage Glacier, 53 miles S of Anchorage. Gray Line, 277-5581, offers several tours: 1 hr cruise leaving from dock on Portage Lake, $25; 7^{1}/$_{2}$-hr tour includes transport to Portage Glacier and 1 hr cruise, $60. Gray Line and other tours available from Anchorage call at Alyeska Ski Resort, 40 miles S, on the way. Award winning film *Voices of the Ice* shown at Portage Glacier Visitors Information Center (end of Portage Hwy), 783-2326, 9am-6pm daily, $1. 'Superb.' 'A must.'

INFORMATION

Log Cabin Visitor Information Center, W 4th Ave at F St, 274-3531. Dispenses lots of maps, including **Bike Trails** guide. Daily 7am-7.30pm (summer); 9am-5pm (winter).

Alaska Public Lands Information Center, 605 W 4th Ave, 271-2737. Daily 9am-5.30pm. (Camping and shuttle rsvs for Denali National Park stop at 6pm.) Info on state and federal recreational lands. 'Helpful; friendly people.'

INTERNET ACCESS

Get connected at **Surf City**, 415 L St, 279-7877, *www.surfcafe.com* Open till midnight, charges apply.

TRAVEL

Anchorage International Airport, 266-2525. Serviced by 8 international and 15 domestic carriers: **Delta**, (800) 221-1212; **Northwest Airlines**, (800) 225-2525; **United**, (800) 241-6522, and **Alaska Airlines**, (800) 252-7522. Nearly every airport in Alaska can be reached from Anchorage, either directly or through a connecting flight in Fairbanks.

The 80-yr-old **Alaska Railroad**, (800) 544-0552 runs btwn Anchorage and Fairbanks via Denali National Park ($154 one-way). One train daily each way. Anchorage to Seward train ($86 r/t) passes within 800 ft of a glacier. In winter, 1 p/wk to Fairbanks; no service to Seward.

Also daily bus from Anchorage to Portage, **Gray Line of Alaska**, (800) 544-2206. Tip: take train to Whittier, then bus to Portage; several times weekly to Seward. 'Not a good town to be without a car.'

Affordable Car Rental, 4707 Spenard Rd, 243-3370. Charges $35 daily with unlimited mileage. You must be at least 21 w/major credit card.

DENALI NATIONAL PARK Mount McKinley has twin peaks, the south being higher at 20,320 ft. Although native Indians originally named the mountain (and the park) Denali, meaning 'the tall one,' it was renamed for US president William McKinley while he was campaigning. A later president, Jimmy Carter, had the mountain officially renamed Denali in 1979.

This giant, tallest in North America, surveys a vast kingdom of tundra, mountain wilderness and unusual wildlife (caribou, Dall sheep, moose, grizzlies). The highway over **Polychrome Pass** into the valley of Denali is astonishing: a huge bowl, rimmed with frozen Niagaras of clouds tumbling over the encircling cliffs, spreads out before you. And in the distance, Denali itself, shrouded in cloud cover 75 per cent of the time in summer.

Eighty-six miles of gravel road allow you to see much of the park by bus (you can go into the park only 12 miles by car, unless you have a campsite reserved), but hiking one of the trails radiating from McKinley Park Hotel is the best way to enter into the spirit of the place. Best views of the mountain-top at **Wonder Lake**—'have to go at least 8 miles into the park to see the mountain.' Visitors Center ¹/₂ mile up Park Rd, 683-1266/1267, daily 8am-8pm 'til late September, then 7am-6pm. Pick up info on shuttle buses to Wonder Lake here. 'Fantastically situated; caribou come right up to the centre.' No food or gas in the park except at Park entrance. Don't overlook a trip to **Yentana**, the 'Galloping Glacier'—most beautifully coloured on earth. $10 entrance fee good for 7 days. Denali's National Park's website is at *www.nps.gov/dena/* or call on 683-2294.

ACCOMMODATION

Denali Hostel, PO Box 801, Denali Pk, 683-1295, about 9¹/₂ miles N of park entrance. Friendly hosts will pick up from park (Visitor Centre) if you call ahead. Offer bunks, showers, kitchen and free morning shuttles in/out park; $24.

Seven **campgrounds** within the park line Denali Park Rd. Sites $6-12. Must have permit to camp inside park. For rsvs, call (800) 622-7275/272-7272; arrive early! Hikers waiting for a backcountry permit or a campsite can find space in **Morino Campground**, $6, next to hotel.

Grizzly Bear Cabins, 6 miles S of main entrance, 683-2696. Tent cabins, D-$23, T-$25, bath with showers with hot water nearby. Other cabins $49-$125 (subject to change). Rsvs rec (by VISA only), closed by Sep 10th.

TRAVEL

Frequent **shuttle bus** service to all 7 campgrounds in park 'til Labor Day, reduced after that. Booked up quickly but stand-bys available from 5.30 am. From $12.50. Shuttle buses leave **Denali Visitor Center**, daily, 5.30am-2.30pm. Reservations- (800) 622-PARK. **Wildlife coach tours** from the hotel rec; $45 with box lunch; lasts approx. 7 hrs. Mid-May to mid-Sept. 'Interesting—*the* way to see wildlife and the park.' Rail, bus and air service from Anchorage and Fairbanks.

Camper buses, $15, move faster, transporting *only* people with campground permits/backcountry permits. Leave visitors centre 5 times daily. The final bus stays overnight at Wonder Lake, returns 7 am. You can get on/off bus anywhere along the road; flag the next one down. Good strategy for dayhiking/convenient for Park explorers.

FAIRBANKS   Warmest place in Alaska in summer and one of the coldest in the winter, Fairbanks was once a frontier town with 93 saloons in one three-block stretch. Today the second largest city, a direct result of the Pipeline and oil boom, it is 150 miles S of the Arctic Circle. Try to time your visit for one of its many festivals: the Eskimo/Indian Olympics (dancing, blanket toss, etc.) each July and the Solstice Festival, 19-21 June, are among the wildest. Play or watch midnight baseball at the latter. 'Definitely the rough frontier town—drunken Indians everywhere.' 'Surprisingly nice—lots of trees.'

ACCOMMODATION

For info on B&Bs, go to Visitors' Bureau, or call/write **Fairbanks B&B**, 902 Kellum St, Anchorage, 452-4967.

Ah! Rose Marie, 302 Cowles St, 456-2040. From D-$70. 'Loves students.' Close to bus line, centrally located.

Alaska's 7 Gables Inn, 4312 Birch Lane, 479-0751. From D-$90-130. Up-market, special-treat inn with such delights as VCRs in every room and mouth-watering bfasts (peachy pecan crepes and raisin bran muffins.) Inclusive: 'gourmet' bfasts, bikes, canoes, jacuzzis, TV, phones.

Alaska Heritage Inn Youth Hostel, 1018 22nd Ave, (907) 451-6587. Outfitted canoe and raft trips, wildlife viewing, horseback riding. $15 AYH, $16 non-AYH dorm; $44 private room.

Backpackers Hostel, 2895 Mack Rd, 479-2034, near Uni of Alaska. $18 a night; linen charge 50c. Shuttle $7 from train station/airport.

Ester Gold Camp. S-$52, D-$63. Ester City, 6 miles from Uni of Alaska, 479-2500. June—Labor Day. Transport available from downtown hotels. Former mining camp with traditional, family-style meals, saloon, nightly entertainment. Unusual and popular. Home to the Malemute Saloon, notorious in Alaska. 'Awesome Northern Lights show here.'

Grandma Shirley's Hostel, 510 Dunbar St, 451-9816. Beats all other hostels to earn the title of uberhostel of Fairbanks! Showers, free towels, common room, free bike use; co-ed room with 9 beds; $16.25.

Camping: Tanana Valley Campground, 1800 College Rd, 456-7956. Grassy and secluded for its in-town location, sites $8, $15 w/hook-up. **Chena River Campground**, off Airport Way on University Ave, tent sites $15 for two.

FOOD / ENTERTAINMENT

Hot Licks, 3549 College Rd, 479-7813. Ice Cream and espresso bar that stays open until midnight and features live jazz several nights a week.

Howling Dog Saloon, junction of Elliot and Steese highways, 457-8780. Out of town, but good fun. Live bands and midnight volleyball.

Pikes Landing, Mile 4.5 Airport Rd, 479-7113. Bar/restaurant serving good food on a deck overlooking the Chena river.

OF INTEREST

Alaskaland, Airport Way and Peger Road, 2 miles outside city near airport, 459-1087. The 44-acre site, developed to commemorate the Alaska Centennial in 1967, portrays state history with gold rush cabins, a sternwheeler, Indian and Eskimo villages and a mining valley. Free, closes Labor Day. Food pricey, but gets praise: 'Alaska Salmon Bake—all you can eat; salmon, halibut, ribs, etc.—lovely!' New 36-hole miniature golf course—the farthest north in the world! Old-fashioned carousel and train; various nightly shows. Also: **Fairbanks Summer Folk Fest** is held here in July. The **Large Animal Research Station**, is also worth a visit, and its tours offer a chance to see baby musk ox and other animals up close. Tours Tue/Sat 11 am and 1.30pm; Thur 1.30pm. $4 w/student ID. You can also grab your binoculars and view the big beasts from the viewing stand on Yankovitch Rd.

Uni of Alaska Museum, 907 Yukon Drive, 4½ miles NW of city, 474-7505. Features exhibits ranging from displays on the aurora borealis to a 36,000 yr old bison recovered from the permafrost; Eskimo arts and crafts. Daily 9am-7pm summer; 9am-5pm winter. $5. 'Superb, don't miss it.' 'Definitely one of Alaska's highlights.'

Eagle Summit, 108 miles along the Steese Hwy, from where you can watch the sun fail to set on 21 and 22 June.

INFORMATION

Alaska Public Lands Information Center (APLIC), 250 Cushman St #1A, Fairbanks 99707, 456-0527. Has exhibits and info on different parks and protected areas of Alaska. Daily 9am-6pm (summer); Tues-Sat 10am-6pm (winter).

Convention and Visitors Bureau Log Cabin, 550 1st Ave, next to Golden Heart Park, 456-5774. Distributes the free Visitor's Guide. Daily 8am-8pm (summer), 8am-5pm (winter).

Uni of Alaska Student Union: info board for digs, rides, etc.

TRAVEL
Air (see Anchorage)
Alaska Railroad, 280 N Cushman St, 456-4155/1 (800) 544-0552. Runs one train daily from mid-May to mid-Sept to Anchorage and Denali National Park.
Municipal Commuter Area Service (MACS), 6th and Cushman St, 459-1011. Runs 2 rtes thru downtown and surrounding area. 'Very limited, most journeys $1.50.' Day pass $3. Transfers good within 1 hr of stamped time. Daily 6.45am-7.45pm weekdays, more limited at weekends. Night bus on Fri/Sat. 'Fairbanks very difficult without a car.'
Parks Hwy Express, 479-3065, runs daily to Denali ($35 r/t) and Anchorage ($55 o/w, free stop off at Denali).

CALIFORNIA   *The Golden State*

California. The word beckons, like an incantation: the Far West inspires images of sun, sand, surfing, Hollywood, adventure, healthy foods, healthy people, new age mysticism and an easy life. But California is much more complex than its popular image implies. You could spend a lifetime in the Golden State and still not see it all. It has the natural beauty of several states combined: rich redwood groves containing the tallest trees on earth; the stark superlatives of Death Valley; and the dizzying glacier-carved heights of Yosemite Valley. Like Shangri-La, California is cut off from the rest of the world by uninviting terrain: the volatile Trinity Alps in the north and the Sierras in the east; the Mojave Desert in the south; and to the west, over 100 miles of sunny beaches and rocky precipices on the Pacific Ocean coast.

When pioneers crossed the prairie to California, they found a land with potential for riches beyond mere gold, a promise that has since been fulfilled. There's more of everything in California—more people (over 30 million) more money (it's the world's 6th largest economic power), and more science activity (a disproportionate share of the US's pure science research and more Nobel laureates than the former Soviet Union). A key partner in the emerging Pacific Basin economy, California leads in both agricultural and industrial output, from avocados to animation, from Silicon Valley to Sunset Strip.

Over the last decade, however, the golden image has become a little tarnished. As unemployment figures rise, crime rates climb, LA riots and burns and is then hit by a killer earthquake. All the while the state gets more and more crowded, a certain disillusionment is apparent. The result: a *reverse* immigration trend, as Californians head *east* to seek the wide open spaces of states like Montana and Wyoming.

The major regions and cities of California are listed below, roughly from north to south. *www.yahoo.com/Regional/U_S__States/California/*

National Parks: Kings Canyon, Lassen Volcanic, Redwood, Sequoia, Yosemite

ACCOMMODATION OVERVIEW
Perhaps in response to its popularity, California offers a great variety of lodging options, many of them dead cheap. This is but a brief summary to supplement specific information listed under *ACCOMMODATION* for each region or city.
Youth Hostels: number about 40, with new ones opening all the time. Others are in

a state of flux because of precarious funding. Always enquire locally—even the AYH handbook cannot keep pace with developments. There are also independent hostels—with private ownership, each hostel manager and houseparent has a great deal of interest in the hostel being operated to your satisfaction; however expect standards to vary.

Motel 6: The chain began here, in the state that invented the motel. This mega-chain offers basic rooms at very reasonable rates. Call (800) 4-MOTEL-6 to reserve a room anywhere in California. No pampering: their 6pm 'show up or lose your rsvs' policy is extremely firm; if you book ahead, be sure you'll be able to arrive on time. If you pre-paid and can't get there, you need to cancel the rsvs before 6pm or no money back. If you're stuck, **E-Z Motels**, have been recommended as a similar budget alternative. Call (800) 32-MOTEL

B&B Inns: A new comprehensive directory of Golden State B&B Inns is available on the Net or in printed form, produced by the **California Association of B&B Inns**. From San Diego to the Oregon border, the directory showcases more than 268 California inns. Contact (831) 462-9191, or *www.innaccess.com*.

University lodgings: Many universities throw their dorms open to travelling students in the summer; also, most have housing offices that may list information on temporary housing. Accommodation in university towns is often easy to get in the summer, when all the students are gone; it may be more difficult if the university town is also a resort town (e.g. Santa Barbara, Santa Cruz, San Diego).

Camping: National Park and monument fees are from $6-$20 (in addition to an entrance fee of around $5 per vehicle.) Primitive campsites are often much less, sometimes free; most require permits for back country use. 'State campsites are a good deal if you have a carload of people. Very good facilities. ''Police will allow sleeping on Southern Cal beaches (for foreign tourists anyway) but be careful—many are hangouts for gays with attendant queer-bashers.' Also, be advised that some coastal communities respond with hostility to car-or beach-sleepers—even those who are just passing through. Some local ordinances actually prohibit sleeping in any sort of vehicle within the city limits. To reserve campsites: For rsvs and campsite availability in CA state parks: call (800) 444-7275, cost varies btwn sites plus $6.75 service charge, sites can accommodate up to 8 people. For national forests throughout the West Coast, call (800) 280-CAMP, $5-$20 per site plus another ghastly $6 service charge. Most campsites at national parks are first come, first served; however, sites at Yosemite and Sequoia can be reserved 8 weeks in advance in person through MISTIX, call (800) 436-7275 or (800) 365-2267 for info, but be patient, the line is always busy.

NORTHERN COAST The Northern Coast region is a land of rugged shoreline and pounding surf, of towering redwood forests and rushing rivers, of verdant hills and bountiful vineyards. Time spent here is time spent in Paradise.

Redwoods were plentiful on the American continent around the age of the dinosaurs. During the Ice Age, these trees barely escaped the fate of their old contemporaries. A narrow strip, stretching nearly 400 miles N of San Francisco to the Oregon border, was all that survived of the coastal species of *sequoia sempervirens*, this remnant was further repleted by logging early in this century.

You can see these majestic survivors in the very northwesternmost corner of the state along two stretches of Hwy 101: **Humboldt Redwoods State Park**, *www.humboldtredwoods.org/* (take a detour off the hwy north of Garberville to see the **Avenue of the Giants**); and **Redwood National Park**, which stretches from Orick to Crescent City and encompasses three state parks. In this park—a 'UNESCO World Heritage Site'—are the world's tallest trees, two over 367 ft tall. The *North Coast Redwoods* brochure gives an idea of what each park has to offer; available from Humboldt Redwoods State Park and other hostels.

The telephone area code is 707.

ACCOMMODATION

This area is saturated with pricey bed and bfast inns, however, a variety of inexpensive local motels and interesting hostels means affordable accommodation should not be difficult to find.

HI-Redwood Hostel, 14480 US 101, Klamath at Wilson Creek, 482-8265. The northernmost link in the California coastal chain of hostels, this one is located in mist-shrouded Redwood National Park, a World Heritage Site and International Biosphere Reserve. The hostel promotes sustainable living concepts through recycling and conservation of natural resources. $12-14. Private rooms available. Linen $1. Dining room, laundry, kitchen, 2 sundecks overlooking ocean, staple foods for sale. Curfew 11pm, out by 9.30 am. Rsvs recommended by mail 3 weeks in advance.

Humboldt Redwoods State Park, 946-2409. 3 campgrounds, $16 for up to 8 people, extra vehicle $5.

Prairie Creek Motel, PO Box 265, Orick CA 9555, 488-3841, 2 miles N of **Orick** on Hwy 101, at the entrance to the Park. 1pp-$36, 2pp-$49.50. 'Friendly Swiss and German couple. Can't recommend highly enough.' Restaurant next door.

Camping: Redwood National Park, 464-6101, encompasses 3 state parks that offer campsites with showers, $12-14 p/night, reservations required in summer, (800) 444-7275.

FOOD

Eureka's Seafood Grotto, 605 Broadway, Eureka, 443-2075. Choose your own seafood at reasonable prices. 'We ketch 'em, cook 'em, serve 'em!' Daily 11am-9pm.

Mousse Cafe, corner of Alban and Kasten 937-4323, in **Mendocino**, has excellent black-out cake with layer upon layer of chocolate for $5.50. Daily for lunch 11.30 'til 4pm, dinner and brunch on Sundays, closed 4pm-5.30pm.

Orick Market, 488-3225, daily 8am-7pm to stock up on supplies.

Palm Café, Rte 101 in Orick, 488-3381. A locals' joint with delicious homemade fruit pies. Daily 9am-8pm.

Prairie Creek Park Cafe, 2 miles N of **Orick** on Hwy 101 (take Fern Canyon exit), 488-3841. Chow down on elk, buffalo and boar as well as traditional American food for bfast, lunch or dinner, at the only gourmet restaurant in the area; $7-$16 dinners. Daily 8am-9pm. Close Nov-Mar.

OF INTEREST

The Northern Coast offers dozens of parks and beaches strung like pearls along the way; here you can experience nature at its most diverse and best. Take a leisurely cycle through vineyard country, hike in primeval forests, or ramble along clifftops for spectacular views of the ocean. Raft down racing rivers, soak in hot mineral springs or luxuriate in the ultimate mud-bath! In Eureka: **Carson House Mansion**, 2nd & M Sts, said to be the most photographed residence in America, you can only look at the exterior of this quintessential Victorian-Gothic style mansion. Many other examples of Victorian architecture can be found both here and in nearby Arcata. The town's old bank is home to the **Clarke Memorial Museum**, E St, **Arcata**, 443-1947; a local history museum with an interesting collection of Victoriana and Indian baskets. Tue-Sat noon-4pm, donations accepted. Heading south: The **Pacific Lumber Company**, 125 Main St, Scotia, 764-2222. A working Redwood sawmill and historic logging museum. Hear how a sawmill *can* be environmentally friendly; tours Mon-Fri 8am-2pm, free. 'Fascinating.'

Rockefeller Forest in **Humboldt Redwoods State Park** contains the largest grove of old-growth trees, some over 200 yrs old; nearby, in **Founder's Grove**, is the Tree World Hall of Fame, home to the tallest, widest and oldest trees in the world.

Not to be missed is the **Avenue of the Giants**, just north of **Garberville** off US 101. A 33 mile scenic hwy winds its way through majestic redwoods. 16 miles S of Garberville, in Leggett, is the **Drive-Thru-Tree**, 925-6363, where for a $3 park entrance fee, you can do just that (as many times as you wish!)

Skunk Train, 964-6371, Laurel St, **Ft Bragg**. Steam engine (diesel in winter) takes you 40 miles through tunnels and trees on an old logging run btwn Ft Bragg and Willits. $35 for full day, $27 for half, daily, June-Sept. Rsvs rec.

Pygmy Forest, btwn Navarro and Noyo Rivers on Hwy 1; particularly visible around Jug Handle Creek, south of Ft Bragg. A 3 hr hike will take you back five hundred thousand years in time to see how the ocean has shaped this countryside. The 5 mile (r/t) trail dubbed **The Ecological Staircase** meanders through terraces carved by the Pacific. The fifth terrace is the Pygmy Forest, a land of stunted cypress and Bolander pine unique to this area. A 50 yr old tree may grow to no more than an inch in diameter and two to five feet in height. The town of **Mendocino** on Hwy 1, an artists' colony by the sea, is a wonderful place to stop, stretch and stroll. Artisans show & sell at Gallery Faire (crafts) and Studio 2 (jewellery), among others. The town appears as Cabot Cove in the TV series *Murder, She Wrote*. Be sure to visit **Mendocino Headlands State Park** while you're there. When they shot the movie, *The Russians are Coming* along the Mendocino coast, they were wrong: the Russians have been here and gone. See the well-restored proof at **Ft Ross**, a 19th century seal-hunting outpost, and the only genuine Russian military installation in the lower 48 states.

TRAVEL/INFORMATION

Crescent City Area Visitors Center (in Chamber of Commerce), at 1001 Front St, 464-3174. Daily 9am-6pm.

Gaberville Chamber of Commerce, 733 Redwood Dr, 923-2613. Daily 10am-5pm.

Greyhound, 1125 Northcrest Dr, 464-2807/(800) 231-2222, in Crescent City passes through the park, stopping near park entrance. Two buses daily going north and two going south. **Tall Trees Shuttle** from ranger station to grove is a 40 min ride each way with 3 miles of walking through the trees; count on 4-5 hrs total. 'Superb walks through the redwood forest.'

Orick Visitors Center, 464-6101, 1 mile W of Orick on US 101, ext 5265. Daily 10am-2pm.

Prairie Creek Visitors Center, 464-6101 ext 5300. Daily 10am-2pm.

Redwood Information Center at Orick Ranger Station, PO Box 7, Orick, CA 95555, 488-3461. 9am-6pm daily in summer, otherwise 9am-5pm.

MOUNT SHASTA and LASSEN VOLCANIC NATIONAL PARK   Some 160 miles NW of Sacramento lies one of the country's most beautiful and unspoiled regions—the Shasta Cascade; towering mountains, stunning waterfalls, dense forests and glistening lakes create a dramatic landscape, itself dominated by the 14,162-ft **Mt Shasta**, the white-haired patriarch of Northern California. Sharing the crest of the mountain is Shasta's slightly smaller mate, **Shastina**. Nearly overwhelmed by the massive pair is baby **Black Butte**, a pile of volcanic ash that attests to its parents' vigour.

Younger, shorter, hotter-headed sister to Mt Shasta is **Lassen Peak**, which last erupted in 1917—a wink of the geologic eye. Brilliantly bizarre moonscape, nasty mudpots, pools of turquoise and gold, sulphurous steam vents reveal volcanic activity, especially in the **Bumpass Hell** area. You are free to climb the 2¹/₂ miles to the three craters of Lassen: main road takes you near, trail is easy, fine views of Shasta and the devastation to the northeast. Excellent summer programmes: Ishi, the last Stone Age man in America, was found near Lassen, and the Manzanita Lake info centre has photo displays of him. Open year-round but snows keep most sectors inaccessible from late Oct to early June. Passes are valid for 7 days, $10 per car, $5 on foot. 'Yosemite is tame by comparison.' Park Info, 595-4444, 8am-4.30pm. **Cool Mountain Nights** in Mount Shasta at the end of August, features an outdoor concert, street fair, classic car show, blackberry bluegrass festival, Tin Man Triathlon and community bfast. Call (800) 926-4865. In **Yreka** there are several interesting museums, showing exhibits of native Americans, gold mining and local history. Call **Yreka Chamber of Commerce**, 842-1649, or (800) ON-YREKA, for details, Mon-Fri 9am-5pm, wknds 11am-4pm.

The telephone area code is 530.

ACCOMMODATION
Alpenrose Cottage Hostel, 204 E Hinkley Street, **Mount Shasta**, 926-5724, $15 dorm.

Pine Needles Motel, 1340 S Mt Shasta Blvd, **Mount Shasta**, 926-4811. S-$49, D-$59.

Swiss Holiday Lodge, 2400 S Mt Shasta Blvd, **Mount Shasta**, 926-3446. Pretty chalet, Tremendous view of Mt Shasta. S-$46.95, includes continental breakfast. Pool, jacuzzi, communal kitchen.

Camping: Lake Siskiyou, 4239 WA Barr Rd, **Mt Shasta**. CA 96067, 926-2618. A popular recreational lake featuring boating, swimming, fishing, sailing. Campground, RV park, grocery/deli. $16.50 per tent and 2 people, $2.50 for each extra person.

Lassen Volcanic National Park, PO Box 100, **Mineral**, CA 96063, 595-4444. Volcanic lava flows, hot springs, mud pots and old emigrant trails. Season is June 7 until October 6.

Trinity Lake, USDA Forest Service, PO Box 1190, **Weaverville** 96093, 623-2121. Officially known as Clair Eagle lake, includes secluded bays and coves ideal for camping, fishing, houseboating, swimming and other water sports.

TRAVEL
Amtrak, serves Redding and Dunsmuir, (800) 872-7245.

Greyhound, 1321 Butte St, (800) 231-2222, serves Redding.

SACRAMENTO   In 1839 Swiss immigrant John Augustus Sutter landed on the banks of the American River intending to create a trading post and haven for European immigrants, and was granted land by the Mexicans, within a decade a sawmill was built in nearby foothills. A foreman inspecting the mill one morning made a discovery that was to change history—a gold nugget glinting in the sun.

Sacramento mushroomed into prominence as a supply dump for Gold Rush miners. Today, the state's capital, at the confluence of the Sacramento and American Rivers, the city has a pleasant, midwestern feel. If the Gold Rush is your thing, then this is the place for you! All its sights are downtown; the best way to see them is on foot.

The telephone area code is 916 except Nevada County—530. For listings of places to go, things to see and restaurants to dine at, look up *www.worldofweb.com/sacsite.html*

ACCOMMODATION
Berry Hotel, 729 L St, 930-0628. Rooms from $55. 'Threadbare but friendly.' Weekly & monthly rates available. $5 key deposit.
Gold Rush Home Hostel, 1421 Tiverton Ave, 421-5954. $10.
HI-Sacramento Hostel, 900 H St, 443-1691. 1885 Victorian mansion within easy walk Amtrak, Greyhound and public transportation. Patio, gardens, veranda, recreation rm, videos, library, info centre, kitchen, laundry, linen rental, bike storage. $12-14. Private rooms available. 'Fabulous hostel.'
Motel 6, 1415 30th St, 457-0777. Close to Sutter's Ft, accessible by bus. S-$45, D-$52, XP-$3. Pool, AC, noisy (freeway nearby).

FOOD
Delta King Restaurant, Hotel and Saloon. 1000 Front St, Old Sacramento, 441-4440. Located right on river, providing food and entertainment. *www.deltaking.com/*
Fanny Ann's Saloon, 1023 2nd St, 441-0505. Philly, turkey sandwiches, salads. 'A pleasant change from burgers.' Daily 11.30am-2 am.
Fox and Goose, 1001 R St, 443-8825. Real British pub fare, meals under $10. Daily 7am-12 am, Fri & Sat 'til 2 am.

OF INTEREST
California State Railroad Museum, 111 I St, Old Sacramento, 445-7387. Steam train excursions along the scenic Sacramento river depart from the Central Pacific Freight Depot on Front & K Sts, summer w/ends, 9am-8pm, $5.
Crocker Art Museum, 216 O St, 264-5423. Stately old mansion with staid old paintings; catch the sometimes-wild modern art exhibits upstairs. Tues-Sun 10am-5pm, Thurs 'til 9pm, closed Mon. $4.50.
Old Governor's Mansion, 16th & H Sts, 323-3047. Charming wedding-cake Victorian building, now a state museum with furnishings donated by 13 former state governors, including Ronald Reagan. Tours daily 10am-4pm, $3. 'Best sight in city,' 'good tour and stories.'
Old Sacramento, 28-acre historic district on Sacramento River. The riverfront encompasses 26 acres of shops and restaurants in 1849 to 1870-vintage buildings, of which over 100 have been renovated and 41 of them are actual 19th century originals. Especially evocative at night. Includes **Sacramento History Center, Old Eagle Theatre, Pony Express Monument** and **California State Railroad Museum**.
Old Sacramento Riverboat Cruises, 110 L St Landing, (800) 433-0263. Sightseeing cruises, 1hr from $10.
Self guided walking tours of historical Sacramento, free maps available from Visitors Centre.
State Capitol, 10th St at Capitol Mall. Magnificently restored to its ornate, domed 19th century grandeur. Eat lunch in the reasonably-priced basement cafeteria (a pleasant enough dungeon) or picnic on the lawn under massive deodar cedars (the species originated in the Himalayas). Mon-Fri 9am-5pm; Sat/Sun 10am-4pm; hourly tours. Stroll the surrounding **Capitol Park** filled with thousands of varieties of plants.
Sutter's Ft, 2701 L St, 445-4422, the bane of Sacramento schoolchildren, should fascinate anyone interested in history; self-guided tours through exhibit rooms which include a blacksmith's shop, a bakery and prison. **State Indian Museum**, on the same park-like grounds, displays examples of an Indian sweathouse and a teepee. Both daily 10am-5pm; $6, in summer, $3 after Labor Day.
Thursday Night Market, on K, btwn 7th & 13th Sts. Featuring street theatre, arts and crafts and food, 5pm-9pm, May-Sept.
Festivals: California Railroad Festival, End of June. Colourful railroad circus cars, model train displays, performers, circus lore, games, exhibits, activities and entertainment. Call 264-5181 for advance ticket purchases. It is held at the **California**

State Railroad Museum, 2nd I St, 445-7387, $6 admission. **Living History Days** are held on various Saturdays during the summer, which include reenactment of frontier life in 1846 with militia drills, open hearth cooking, spinning, hand sewing and carpentry. Call 445-4422.

Nearby: You can trace the path of the '49er miners on their way through **Gold Country** by following Hwy 49 which links many of the 19th century mining communities in the Mother Lode. The flavour of the Gold Rush still lingers in rustic ghost towns, especially **Coloma**, where James Marshall found the nugget that set off the Rush.

Nevada County is dotted with historic landmarks. Nevada City claims to be the most complete gold town left in California. Victorian houses and flat-topped 'false front' buildings, popular in western frontier towns, line the streets, lending the town a feeling of a living museum. Head north on Hwy 49 to **Empire Mine State Historic Park**, in **Grass Valley**, this was the largest and deepest of California's mines; restored buildings, exhibits and an illuminated mine shaft are included on park tours, call (530) 273-8522. Head south on 49 to **Coloma** and the **Gold Discovery Site State Park**. Nearby is **Placerville**, where Studebaker began making wheel-barrows for miners in 1848 and home to a typical Mother Lode mine, in Gold Bug Park, which remains untouched by the cave-ins and flooding that destroyed others. 10am-4pm, daily in summer, $1 admission, audio tour tape $1. While in this area, read up on the amazing Lola Montez, sample the wonderful gold rush tales of Bret Harte and read Mark Twains story, *The Celebrated Jumping Frog Of Calaveras County*.

To summarise: Huge tracts of thick forests invite hikers, state parks offer meandering streams in which to pan for gold, white-water rivers to raft and breathtaking Sierra mountains to conquer!

INFORMATION
Nevada County Chamber of Commerce, 248 Mill St, Grass Valley, (530) 273-4667.
Sacramento Convention & Visitors Bureau, 1303 J St, Suite 600, Sacramento, 264-7777, 8am -5pm daily.
Visitors Bureau, 1101 2nd Street, Sacramento, 442-7644. 10am-5pm daily.

TRAVEL
Amtrak, 4th & I St, (800) 872-7245.
Greyhound, 715 L St, (800) 231-2222. 'Gambler's buses to Tahoe, Reno—if you can afford to lay out the fare. On arrival several casinos give you money in chips and food vouchers. Details in local papers—a great day out.' To main terminal in Reno $20 o/w.
Regional transit: buses and a new light rail system, 321-2877. $1.25 basic fare, valid for 90 mins from purchase, $3 day pass. You can walk from 6th and K to Old Sacramento (3 blocks).
Sacramento Airport, 8 miles NW of town, is served by numerous shuttle bus companies who pick up from downtown areas. The journey takes 20-30 mins, $10-$18 o/w, XP-$5-$9.

LAKE TAHOE For two adjacent states, California and Nevada seem worlds apart: one is verdant, varied and mellow; the other, desiccated, monotonous and frantically on the make. Nowhere is the contrast greater than on the shores of the lake the states share, Lake Tahoe, a sapphire in a mountain setting two hrs east of Sacramento. On the California side, South Lake Tahoe is a ski-bum village in winter, a granola filling station for hikers in summer. Across the border in Stateline, Nevada, casino-dwellers pump the one-armed bandits year-round, rarely venturing out into the light of day. Both sides have natural beauty to spare, although the area gets ridiculously crowded in mid-summer and during the ski season.

Lake Tahoe's homepage can be found at *www.yaws.com/LakeTahoe/tahoe.shtml* and includes a Lake Tahoe winter guide.

The telephone area code is 530 in California and 775 in Nevada.

ACCOMMODATION

For a guide to ski areas and accommodation, look up *www.highsierra.com*. All listings are for South Lake Tahoe.

Alpine Rose Motel, 4074 Pine Blvd, 544-2985. Summer rates: S/D-$40-$50 weekdays, XP-$5. Colour TV, 4 blocks from Nevada casinos.

Dave's Lake Tahoe Hostel, 3787 Forest, no phone. Skiing, boating, hiking, casinos. Small hostel with friendly ambience. $12.

Econolodge, 3536 S Lake Tahoe Blvd, 544-2036. Rates start at $69 during the week. More expensive at w-ends and during the ski-season.

Tahoe Mountain Lodge, 3868 Hwy 50, 541-6380. W/days: From S/D-$25; 'variable' on w/ends, which means they stick it to you.

Value Inn Motel, 2659 S Lake Tahoe Blvd, 544-3959. D-$68 and upwards during the week, 2 nights min.

Camping: Bayview is the only free campground, 544-5994; June-Sept, 2 night max stay. For up-to-date info on other camping in state parks and forests around Lake Tahoe, contact the Forest Service or **National Park Reservations**, (800) 365-2267.

OF INTEREST

Go to *www.yaws.com/101/index.shtml* for 101 fun things to do.

Take a **sunset cruise** on Lake Tahoe any night during summer on the trimarran boat, by calling MS DIXIE2 on (775) 588-3508. Meal and unlimited wine for $42! Discounts available through Visitors Bureau. At the beginning of March in Tahoe City, **Snowfest** is the largest winter carnival in the West showcasing downhill and cross-country skiing, skating, street dancing, a polar bear swim and zany contests! Call 832-7625.

Truckee near Donner Pass on Hwy 80: wooden buildings and a frontier atmosphere. 2 miles W of Truckee is **Donner State Park**, where in the winter of 1846-47, the 89-member Donner party was trapped by 22-ft snows (memorial statue there is as tall as the snow was deep that year). Only 47 survived the ordeal, many of them resorting to cannibalism.

INFORMATION

South Lake Tahoe Visitors Center, 3066 Lake Tahoe Blvd, 541-5255. Mon-Fri 8.30am-5pm, Sat 9am-4pm. For lodging info call (800) 288-2463.

TRAVEL

Anderson's Bike Rental, 645 Emerald Bay Rd, 541-0500. Deposit (ID) req. Daily 9am-6pm. $20 half a day, $1 each additional hour.

Enterprise Rent-a-Car, 99 Highway 50, Nevada (775) 586-1077.

Greyhound, 1000 Emerald Bay Road, South Lake Tahoe, (800) 231-2222.

Tahoe Area Regional Transport (TART) public buses, 581-6365. Connects the west and north shores from Tahoma to Incline Village. 12 buses daily 6.10am-6.30pm, $1.25.

WINE COUNTRY Both **Napa Valley** and its neighbour **Sonoma Valley** are noted for superlative viticulture; these areas produce everything from world-class cabernets to sassy jug wines. Just two hrs by car from San Francisco, the scenery alone is worth the trip. Bus service to both valleys is good, but renting a car is a capital way to tour. That way, you can alternate wine-tasting with stops at farms, roadside stands, cheese factories, delis and other tasty locales.

Besides wine, you can taste the sparkling mineral water that bubbles out of the ground at **Calistoga** and visit the spas there; watch gliders and hot air balloons over the vineyards; visit Jack London's Beauty Ranch near old-worldly **Glen Ellen**; and maybe even pause a moment at the Tucolay Cemetery near Napa, where Mammy Pleasant is buried. A 19th century black civil rights advocate who owned a string of San Francisco brothels, Mammy Pleasant gave more than $40,000 to finance John Brown's raid on Harper's Ferry and travelled around the South to raise sentiment for Brown among the blacks. Her headstone reads: 'Mother of civil rights in California, friend of John Brown.'

Travel on a virtual visit to Napa Valley for the latest on wineries, lodging, events, and local attractions, *www.napavalley.com/cgi-bin/home.o.*

The area code here is 707.

ACCOMMODATION

Budget accommodation in the wine country is hard to find; B&B prices hover around $60-$225, tending towards the high end of the scale! Best to stay in Santa Rosa, Sonoma or Petaluma for budget accommodation, otherwise you are advised to camp.

Calistoga Spa Hot Springs, 1006 Washington St, Calistoga, 942-6269. Rates start at $91, w/days. Discounts for 4 days (10%), 7 days (15%). Rsvs advised.

Triple-S Ranch, 4600 Mountain Home Ranch Rd, Calistoga, 942-6730. These all-wood cabins are a good deal: 2 pp-$54. Rsvs recommended on w/ends.

Camping: Bothe-Napa Valley State Park, 3801 St Helena Hwy, 942-4575. For rsvs call Destinet at (800) 444-7275. Sites $15, $20 wknds, $5 each additional vehicle or day entry. Hot showers and pool, $3. Daily 8am-dusk.

Napa County Fairgrounds, 1435 Oak St, Calistoga. Dry grass in a parking lot with showers and elec. $18 for 2pp. Closed late June-early July.

FOOD

Restaurant fare tends to be dauntingly expensive in most instances, but there are numerous delis and stores with picnic makings (i.e. numerous Safeways!), and many wineries have pleasant picnic areas. Get suggestions for good grocery stores and bakeries from the locals. Some good ones are the Sonoma and Vella Cheese Factories; the Sonoma French Bakery (San Franciscans come *here* for sourdough bread); the Twin Hill Ranch near Sebastopol (applesauce bread); and the Oakville Grocery in Oakville. Calistoga has at least 7 all-different bfast places. Affordable restaurants with good food include:

Curb Side Cafe, 1245 1st St, **Napa**, 253-2307. Sandwich place, serving up delicious bfasts and tasty pancakes. $5-$7 sandwiches. Mon-Sat 8am-3pm, Sun 9.30am-3pm.

The Diner, 6476 Washington St, **Yountville**, 944-2626. Heavenly wine country hash house serving good bfasts (served all day) and fine Mexican food. Try the flautas and sample a Mimosa. Open 8am-3pm Bfast / lunch, 5.30pm-9pm dinner. Closed Mon.

OF INTEREST

Wineries: Over 250 in Napa Valley alone. The tiny ones tucked away on side roads are informal and fun, but you need a car to get to them. The big 7 wineries, from north to south, are: **Christian Brothers**, housed in a castle with catacomb-like cellars where the wine ages in gargantuan barrels; **Mondavi**, Cliff May building, 'technical tour,' picnics on the lawn; **Inglenook**, mix of old and new buildings (the winery in back is owned by Francis Ford Coppola); **Beaulieu**, good tours; **Martini**; **Beringer**, whose Gothic Rhine House is a landmark; and **Krug**, the oldest in the valley. Other good wineries: **Sterling**, 1111 Dunaweal Ln, 942-3300, near Calistoga. 10.30am-4.30pm daily, $6 includes tasting and aerial-tram to 'spectacular view.' **Stag's Leap** , 5766 Silverado Tr, Napa, has superb wine that measures up to the Continent's best; call 944-2020 to arrange a free tour and tasting—by appointment only. For champagne, hit **Kornell Brothers** in Calistoga. Around Sonoma are 4 more standouts, from **Sebastiani** to **Buena Vista**. The latter is the original winery of Agoston Haraszthy, the Hungarian 'count' who brought European vinestock to the US. Green Hungarian is good; Mozart Festival here in summer. Most wineries have tasting at the end of tours, 10am-4pm or so. 'Christian Brothers' last tour of the day is more like party-night than wine tasting-you get half glasses to taste!' '**Christian**—one of the best—lets you try as many wines as you like.'

Jack London State Historic Park, off Hwy 12 in **Glen Ellen**, 938-5216. Contains ruins of Wolf House, built by author of *Call of the Wild*. Museum 10am-5pm; Park 9.30am-7pm, $6 p/vehicle. Check out **Napa Skatepark**. Lots of concrete banks; free. The annual **Napa Valley Wine Festival**, 252-0872 takes place in November. In August, **Napa Valley Fairgrounds** hosts a summer fair that includes wine-tasting, rock music, juggling, a rodeo and rides. Call Napa Parks and Recreation office, 253-4900 for more info.

Robert Louis Stevenson Park, in **St Helena**, 7 miles NE of Calistoga on Hwy 29, 942-4575. Free, day use only, wonderful picnicking and hiking (new trail leading to former site of RLS house). Bring your own water or wine.

Sonoma is still centred around its lush plaza, where in 1846 Yankee rebels raised a grizzly-bear flag and established the short-lived Republic of California. The republic gave way 40 days later to US control, but the flag, and its symbol, stuck. Remnants of Spanish control still exist here, including the **Mission** and **Lachryma Montis**, home of General Vallejo, who once governed much of California. If you have the chance, take the hwy from Sonoma to Hwy 80; it's a beautiful drive any time of year.

INFORMATION

The local **Napa Visitor Center** is helpful. Be sure to pick up their farm trails brochures, including *Inside Napa Valley* for maps, winery listings and a weekly events guide. Also, **Chambers of Commerce** in:

St Helena, 1010A Main St, , 963-4456. Daily 10am-noon; and **Calistoga**, 1458 Lincoln Ave, 942-6333. Daily 10am-3pm.

Wine Institute, 425 Market St, Suite #1000 (1½ blocks E of Union Sq in San Francisco), (415) 512-0151. Offers information leaflets to Napa Valley. Mon-Fri 9am-5pm.

TRAVEL

Golden Gate Transport, 322-6600, to Santa Rosa ($4.50) and then #80 bus to the vineyards, or call **Sonoma County Transit** 576-RIDE.

Greyhound, (800) 231-2222 serves Napa to St Helena, Calistoga twice daily; but the trip requires an overnight stay. If you get off at St Helena, it's an easy walk to 3 wineries immediately north of town. Service also to Sonoma.

St Helena Cyclery, 1156 Main St, 255-3377. Mon-Sat 9.30am-5.30pm, Sun 10am-5pm.

Gray Line (415) 558 9400 offer guided tours from $43 from the San Francisco Transbay Terminal.

Napa Valley Balloons (253 2224) in Yountville offer the ultimate view for around $160 each.

MARIN COUNTY   Linked to San Francisco by the slender scarlet bracelet of the Golden Gate Bridge is Marin County, whose predominant hues are two shades of Green—green hills and green money. The western edge, facing the Pacific, is wild, windblown, solitary and beautiful. Among its treasures is the 70,000-acre **Pt Reyes National Seashore**, which has an earthquake trail along the San Andreas Fault. At the very point of Pt Reyes is a lighthouse; from December to February, migrating gray whales can sometimes be seen from here. Further up the peninsula is **Tomales Bay State Park. Drake's Beach** is another gem, where Sir Francis may have landed when he claimed all of Nova Albion for Elizabeth I.

Near Pt Reyes are other public wilderness sanctuaries, among them popular **Stinson Beach** (closest swimming beach to San Francisco, enquire locally about the sea serpent) and **Muir Woods**, 6 miles of cool trails through a hushed and fragrant cathedral of *sequoia sempervivens*, some as tall as 240 ft. **Mt Tamalpais**, favourite of hikers and bicyclers, commands fantastic views; its trails link up with Stinson's, Muir Wood's and others.

Inner Marin is stuffed with plush communities that line the northwest shore of San Francisco Bay. From **Tiburon** you can take a ferry to nearby **Angel Island**, which has seen several incarnations as a duelling field, military staging ground for three wars, quarantine station for Asian immigrants and a missile site. The island is now a state park with campsites, friendly deer, bicycling trails and the ghostly ruins of Civil War officers' houses to explore. Former whalers' harbour **Sausalito** has the best view of San Francisco, lots of costly, cutesie bars and boutiques, and a houseboat colony, the last vestige of its bohemian past. 'A fantastic way to get a feel for the area is to take a ferry to Sausalito and walk back across the Golden Gate Bridge. Once across, you can catch a bus back to downtown.'

The telephone area code for Marin County is 415. Check out info on the web at *www.marin.org/*

ACCOMMODATION
The hostel and camping situation in Marin:

Angel Island camping, $10 per site (8 people max). To stay in one of the island's 9 camps, call (800) 444-7275 for rsvs, or write to MISTIX, PO Box 85705, San Diego, CA 92138-5705. Rsvs are accepted up to 8 wks in adv. by phone, 9 wks by mail, which is just about how far ahead you'll have to reserve a place if you want to stay on Sat night. Fireplaces, water, chemical toilets.

HI-Marin Headlands, 941 Fort Barry, **Sausalito**, CA 94965, 331-2777. Hostel sits on a hillside in the serene Marin headlands, just across the Golden Gate Bridge from San Francisco in the Golden Gate National Recreation Area. Surrounded by beaches, forests and rolling hills, wildlife, native plant life and scenic trails. Rec room, well-equipped kitchen, laundry, bicycle storage. 'Very spacious hostel. You'll need a car to get into the city 12 miles away, no public transport. 'Popular but far from centre of town, or anywhere else.' Large common room and well-equipped kitchen, laundry. Sumptuous location. Open year-round; $12-14.

HI-Point Reyes Hostel, Box 247, Point Reyes Station, CA 94956, 663-8811. Hostel is spread btwn 2 cabins on a spectacular site. Hiking, wildlife and Limantour beach all within walking distance. $10-12. Write to rsv beds.

FOOD/ENTERTAINMENT
This area has many organic groceries where you should buy supplies then picnic in one of Marin's countless parks. For one of the best people-watching places, try **The**

Depot Bookstore and Café, 87 Throckmorton Ave, **Mill Valley**, 383-2665. Food and drink at reasonable prices. Daily 7am-10pm.

Gray Whale Pizza, 669-1244, off Hwy 1 in **Inverness**, en route to Pt Reyes. 'Huge, excellent pizzas.' $5-20! Weekdays 10.30am-8pm, Weekends 11.30am-9pm.

Greater Gatsby's, 39 Caledonia, **Sausalito**, 332-4500. Come see Marin mellow out in this restaurant/bar. Open for lunch 11.30am-2.30pm, and dinner 5pm-10pm.

Marin County Fair, San Rafael, July 2-6th. This annual fair includes pig races, pie competitions, fireworks, high-tech exhibits, music and carnival rides! Call 499-6400 for info.

Mayflower Inn, 1533 4th, near Shaver, **San Rafael**, 456-1011. Genuine British pub with darts and raucous singing. Bangers, pasties, fish & chips, and pints of Guinness in front of a blazing fire. Guaranteed to cure any case of homesickness. Lunch Sun-Fri, dinner daily, all meals around $7. Open 11.30am-2 am.

no name bar, 757 Bridgeway, **Sausalito**, (332-1392) genuine beat hangout, great atmosphere.

OF INTEREST/INFORMATION

Ferries from Tiburon to Angel Island, 21 Main St, Tiburon, 435-2131, leave four times daily on weekdays, more frequently on summer weekends. $7, $1 for transporting bikes. Sunset cruises $8 from 6.30pm on Fri & Sat. Call Angel Island State Park direct on (415) 435-1915 for more info on Angel Island.

Marin County Civic Center, 3501 Civic Center Dr, 472-3500, San Rafael. Reminiscent of a Roman aqueduct, the civic center is a riot of pink and turquoise against emerald hills and azure California sky. Some people love this Frank Lloyd Wright structure; some call it the Bay Area's biggest sore thumb. Whatever your opinion, you shouldn't miss seeing it—and if you travel through Marin County on Hwy 101, you won't. Tours on request.

Rainbow Tunnel, Hwy 1 northbound from Golden Gate Bridge to Marin County. A monument to a Cal Trans engineer's whimsy. You'll know it when you see it.

San Francisco Bay Model, 2100 Bridgeway, 332-3871. Constructed by the Army Corps of Engineers, the hydraulic model simulates tides, oil spills, etc. Tue-Fri 9am-4pm, Sat & Sun 10am-5pm.

SAN FRANCISCO   Big, beautiful Baghdad-by-the-Bay, San Francisco is a city that flows like a magic carpet of images: hills, bridges, cable cars, fog, ferryboats, gays, painted Victorians, earthquakes, movie car chases. Known to all simply as 'the City' ('Frisco' warrants the death sentence), San Francisco occupies a peerless setting on the tip of a green and hilly thumb separating ocean from bay. A narrow strait, fraught with dangerous undertows, is spanned with a sense of drama by a shimmering Golden Gate Bridge. Seen from afar, the city is by turns a citadel shining in the sun, a bank of diamonds glittering in the night, a coquette peeking over a ruff of fog, heartbreakingly lovely. Closer examination reveals imperfections: slums, cold corporate canyons, porno districts and boxy tract homes and, with memories of the 1989 earthquake still fresh, the ever-present fear of the 'big one.' Never mind; even with its flaws, San Francisco is still way ahead of whoever's in second place.

History and geography have conspired to make San Francisco a city of neighbourhoods in the European manner. Ethnic differences are not assimilated but encouraged, imparting a cosmopolitan flavour that comes as a welcome relief after the monotony of much of urban America. This western most of Western cities, paradoxically, is America's door to the East—to

China, Hong Kong, Japan, and the rest of Asia—with which California does more business than with Europe.

It's hard to have a bad time here. The wealth of things to see and do, the diverse and delicious foods, and most of all, the San Franciscans themselves, make visiting a delight. People migrate here not to be successful but to be (or learn to be) happy and human. Their efforts make San Francisco a city of good manners, full of little kindnesses and occasional gallant acts, whether saving whales or cable cars, that speak of altruism and love.

Temperatures are mild year-round. Spring and autumn offer the most sunshine, but come prepared for brisk winds and chilly weather at any time. Unexpectedly, summer is when the city's famous fog crosses the line into infamy. Mark Twain, it is said, once complained that the 'coldest winter I ever spent was a summer in San Francisco.'

San Francisco's central location is perfect for daytrips to nearby attractions. Berkeley, Santa Cruz, Marin County and the Napa and Sonoma wine country can be reached within two hrs by public transport. It's more likely that, when it comes time to leave, you'll have to tear yourself away. When in San Francisco, remember three things: wear strong shoes, watch for seagulls and keep an eye on your heart at all times; otherwise as the song says, you'll probably leave it here.

The web is as up to date as you can get at *www.citysearch7.com/*
The telephone area code is 415.

SURVIVAL
San Francisco's Greyhound depot is located in a scruffy-to-rotten district, bearable during the day but predictably worse at night. When seeking accommodation, bear in mind that the large triangle formed by Market, Divisadero and Geary is a high crime area which spills over to the other side of Market, where the Greyhound depot is. The worst section is the Western Addition, bounded by Geary, Hayes, Steiner and Gough. Stay out, day or night (no reason to visit, anyway). Other dicey streets at night are the first four blocks of Turk, Eddy and Ellis. That doesn't mean you shouldn't stay here—just be aware and exercise caution, particularly after dark.

ACCOMMODATION
NB: The best accommodation goes quickly, especially in youth hostels, so check in early. If arriving late, phone ahead. Accommodation info also available at Greyhound. See also hostel listings for Marin County.

Adelaide Inn, 5 Isadora Duncan, 441-2261. From S-$42, D-$58, w/shared bath, XP-$6. Continental bfast included.

Alexander Hotel, corner of O'Farrell/Taylor, (800) 843-8709. Own shower, TV, A/C. Easy access to China Town/Market St. 'Friendly staff, clean.' Rooms from $85.

Allison Hotel, 417 Stockton St, 2 blocks N of Union Square, 986-8737. From $75 up with shared bath, $125 with en-suite, XP-$10. Rsvs req. 'Very friendly, ideal for Chinatown and Fisherman's Wharf.' 'Excellent, safe, clean if dull.'

Ansonia Hotel and Residence Club, 711 Post St, 673-2670. S/D-$56 w/shared bath, $69 w/private bath. XP-$15. Bfast included. International clientele. 'Very clean.'

AYH Travel Services, 308 Mason St, Powell BART Stn, 701-1320, provides hostel info, travel services, books, supplies and all membership facilities. Mon-Sat 10am-6pm in summer.

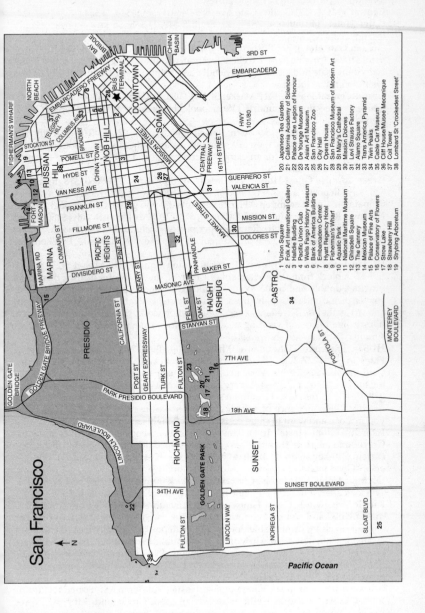

San Francisco

←N

North Beach
Fisherman's Wharf
Bay Bridge
China Basin
3RD ST
EMBARCADERO
EMBARCADERO FREEWAY
BUS TERMINAL
DOWNTOWN
SOMA
HWY 101/80
CENTRAL FREEWAY
16TH STREET
GUERRERO ST
VALENCIA ST
MISSION ST
DOLORES ST
BAKER ST
MARKET STREET
TELEGRAPH HILL
COLUMBUS AVE
BROADWAY
NOB HILL
CHINA TOWN
STOCKTON ST
POWELL ST
HYDE ST
CHINA TOWN
VAN NESS AVE
FRANKLIN ST
FILLMORE ST
DIVISIDERO ST
PINE ST
RUSSIAN HILL
FORT MASON
MARINA RD
MARINA
LOMBARD ST
PACIFIC HEIGHTS
GEARY ST
PANHANDLE
MASONIC AVE
FELL ST
OAK ST
HAIGHT ASHBUG
STANYAN ST
CASTRO
PORTOLA ST
MONTEREY BOULEVARD
GOLDEN GATE BRIDGE
GOLDEN GATE BRIDGE FREEWAY
LINCOLN BOULEVARD
CALIFORNIA ST
PRESIDIO
POST ST
TURK ST
FULTON ST
GEARY EXPRESSWAY
PARK PRESIDIO BOULEVARD
7TH AVE
19TH AVE
RICHMOND
34TH AVE
FULTON ST
LINCOLN WAY
GOLDEN GATE PARK
SUNSET
SUNSET BOULEVARD
NORIEGA ST
SLOAT BLVD
Pacific Ocean

1 Union Square
2 Folk Art International Gallery
3 Haliidie Building
4 Pacific Union Club
5 Wells Fargo History Museum
6 Bank of America Building
7 Embarcadero Center
8 Hyatt Regency Hotel
9 Fisherman's Wharf
10 Aquatic Park
11 National Maritime Museum
12 Ghiradelli Square
13 The Cannery
14 Mexican Museum
15 Palace of Fine Arts
16 Conservatory of Flowers
17 Strow Lake
18 Strawberry Hill
19 Strybing Arboretum
20 Japanese Tea Garden
21 California Academy of Sciences
22 Palace of the Legion of Honour
23 De Young Museum
24 Asian Art Museum
25 San Francisco Zoo
26 City Hall
27 Opera House
28 San Francisco Museum of Modern Art
29 St Mary's Cathedral
30 Mission Dolores
31 Levi Strauss Factory
32 Alamo Square
33 Trans America Pyramid
34 Twin Peaks
35 Cable Car Museum
36 Cliff House/Musée Mecanique
37 Coit Tower
38 Lombard St 'Crookedest Street'

Castor Hotel, 705 Vallejo St, 788-9709. S-$20 pp, mention BUNAC. 'Central location. Given outside key so no curfew.'

Central YMCA, 220 Golden Gate Ave, 885-0460. From S-$46, D-$54.

Gates Hotel, 140 Ellis St, 781-0430. From S-$47, D-$68, $5 key deposit. 'Handy location. Always has beds.'

Golden Gate Hotel, 775 Bush, btwn Powell and Mason, 392-3702. S/D-$72, shared bath, $109 w/private bath. Excellent location, within walking distance to just about everything; safe and clean. 'Very friendly and helpful staff.' Continental bfast and afternoon tea included.

Grand Central Hostel, 1412 Market St, 703-9988, S-$28.50, D-$40, 4-bed dorm $15, free tea, coffee, linens, laundry, TV rm, pool table, jukeboxes. 'Mixed reports.' 'Not a good area.'

Grant Hotel, 753 Bush St, btwn Powell and Mason, 421-7540/rsvs (800) 522-0979.D-$60 'Excellent location in a safe central part of the city. "Our double rm was $65 p/night; we asked for an extra bed and fridge and got them. Large common room. Very comfortable hotel!'

Green Tortoise Guest House, 494 Broadway, off Kearny, 834-9060. $18 dorm plus $20 key deposit, $5 sheet deposit. 'Very friendly, clean hostel on edge of Chinatown. "A bit cramped. "Free tea and bfast if you get up early enough!'

Harcourt Residence Club, 1105 Larkin St, 673-7720. Weekly rates only; $150 shared bath, $175 w/private bath. Rates are per person. Includes bfast and dinner, maid service. Sundeck, lounge with 40" colour TV, $20 key deposit. 'Excellent for meeting friends.'

HI-San Francisco Downtown Hostel at Union Square, 312 Mason St, 788-5604. $19-22. A block from the excitement of Union Sq, in the theatre district, this hostel provides double and triple rooms. Union Sq is a great place to people-watch or enjoy a picnic under the palm trees. Outside hostel is a variety of restaurants, shops and art galleries. 'Excellent on-site information desk, central location.' Kitchen, library, free linen and vending machines. 24hrs, 14 nights max stay. Rsvs req for summer. 'Not enough showers!'

HI-San Francisco Fisherman's Wharf Hostel, Bldg 240, Ft Mason, on Bay & Franklin, 771-7277. Take # 42, # 47 or # 49 bus from Van Ness. Located in the Golden Gate National Recreation Area, an urban national park on the Bay. Dorm overlooking the bay. 'Arrive early—fills very quickly.' Fort Mason is also home to museums, galleries and theatres. Fisherman's Wharf, Chinatown and Ghirardelli Sq all nearby. 'The abundance of British students makes it a good place to head for if you're alone and want to share costs.' $14-16, 3 nights max.

Interclub Globe Hostel, 10 Hallam Pl, 431-0540, on Folsom btwn 7th & 8th. From Greyhound take bus #14 or 15 min walk. $16 shared dorms, in nightclub district, no curfew. $10 key deposit. 'Brilliant atmosphere—best hostel I stayed in.' 'Druggy area.' 'Good food from cafeteria. Mostly "alternative" crowd.'

Olympic Hotel, 140 Mason St, 982-5010. '1 block from AYH, rec for hostel overspill. Will look after your bags for a few hrs after checkout.' 'Friendly, helpful.' D-$60.

Pacific Tradewinds Guest House, 680 Sacramento St, 433-7970. Converted apartment owned and run by two former backpackers. $18 per night ($20 in July and August) in clean, comfortable dorms ($5 key deposit). Centrally and conveniently located in Chinatown, close to Market St and public transport. For $4 *they* will wash your laundry! No curfews. Rsvs recommended in summer. 'Very friendly and homely atmosphere.' 'Best accommodation I stayed in. 'Mattresses and bunks and mixed dorms.' 'Not very clean.'

San Francisco European Guest House Hostel, 761 Minna St, 861-6634. Run by former Greyhound driver and 15 mins walk from Greyhound. Kitchen, TV rm, lockers. No curfew, 24hrs. 'Very friendly; totally mixed.' 'Don't seem to turn anyone away so very hot and crowded.' 'Not a safe area at night.' 'Excellent staff.'

'We arrived at 7.15 am and it was already full (for males).' 'Shared a bathroom with 20 others.' Meals available. Roof garden. Tours to Napa wine country. Dorms from $18, private rooms available.

The Original San Francisco Roommate Referral Service, 610A Cole St, 558-9191. A $35 fee gets you lists of rooms to rent—shared housing only. 'Very helpful, found somewhere straight away.' Mon-Fri 10am-6pm, Sat 11 am, Sun 11am-4pm.

FOOD

Food is one of the things San Francisco does best; sampling the amazing variety of local cuisines is a top priority. The city grew as a seaport, so eat like a sailor: Dungeness crab and sourdough bread, Irish coffee and Anchor Steam, the local beer. Move on to other cultures in one of the many excellent and cheap ethnic Restaurants—Persian and Basque, Salvadorean and Greek, Sichuan and Russian, Italian and Vietnamese. The Bay Area Restaurant Guide, *www.sfbay.com/food* contains almost 14, 000 SF Bay Area restaurants with 10, 000 reviews, including several photographs!

Atmosphere: **Buena Vista Cafe**, 2765 Hyde St, 474-5044. Go on a foggy night and listen to foghorns moan and cable cars clang while you nurse an Irish coffee (introduced to the US in 1953 by SF newspaperman Stanton Delaplane). 'Extremely crowded.'

Hamburger Mary's, 1582 Folsom, 626-5767. 11.30am-1am weekdays, 10am-2am weekends. 'Best hamburgers, good live music, friendly atmosphere.' Closed Mon.

Seattle St Coffee, 456 Geary St, 922-4566. 'Exceptionally friendly and welcoming coffee shop in an area with very few affordable options.' Bagels, scones, muffins $1-2. Sandwiches from $3-6. Great selection of coffees. Daily 6am-9.30pm, 10pm at weekends.

Specs' 12 Adler Museum Cafe, 12 Adler St, off Columbus, 421-4112. Finding this seedy and wonderfully authentic North Beach bar can be a challenge, but its location (down an obscure alley called Saroyan) keeps it safe from the hordes of conventioneers swarming along Columbus. Don't bring your little dog, Dorothy.

Tommy's Joynt, Van Ness and Geary, 775-4216. 'Great decor, huge buffalo stew ($5.75).' Daily 11am-1.45 am.

Breakfast: **Doidges**, 2217 Union, at Filmore, 921-2149, serves brunch 'til 1.45pm w/days, 2.45pm w/ends. Need rsvs.

Economy Restaurant, 18 7th St, 552-8830. '2 eggs, 3 sausage, hash browns, toast—$4.' Bfast all day. Daily 6.30am-8pm.

Pinecrest Restaurant, 401 Geary (at Mason St) 885-6407. 'Dinner and bfast served, all day. 24 hrs.

Sears Fine Foods, 439 Powell, 986-1160. Try French toast made from sourdough bread. 'Excellent bfast, go extra early.' Open 6.30am-2.30pm.

Burritos: La Cumbre, 515 Valencia, near 16th, 863-8205. Mon-Sat 11am-10pm, Sun noon-9pm. Mouth-watering at $2.75.

Greek: **Athens Greek Restaurant**, 39 Mason, 567-6639. Daily, 11am-midnight, Sat 'til 1 am.

Hamburgers: Hayes Street Grill, 320 Hayes St, 863-5545. Intimate, small-restaurant cooking up the finest modern California cuisine. **Hot 'N Hunky**, 4039 18th, 621-6365. Just like it sounds. **Original Joe's**, 144 Taylor, btwn Turk & Eddy, 775-4877, serves 12-ounce burgers—regular or charbroiled (after 5pm)—for around $7. 'Only Brits can finish them,' so they've invented a 'junior' for wimps. (European soccer teams eat here). Mon-Fri, 10.30am-12.30 am.

Italian: **Little Joe's**, 523 Broadway, 982-7639. Spectacular chefs, huge portions—ask to split spaghetti con pesto or roast chicken. Lunch $6-$11, dinner $8-$14. Daily 11am-10.30pm. **Tommasso** 1042 Kearny, 398-9696, for pizza. Daily 5pm-10.45pm.

Oriental: Best tempura at **Sanppo**, 1702 Post, 346-3486, open 11.30am-midnight; best Szechuan at **Tsing Tao**, 3107 Clement, btwn 32nd & 33rd, 387-2344, open 11am-10pm.

Sourdough bread: **Boudin Bakery**. Several locations (Pier 39, Fisherman's Wharf, Ghiradelli Square), 928-1849. Best sourdough (from $2.25) outside Sonoma, CA.

Steaks: **Tad's Steak House**, 120 Powell, 982-1718. Steak, salad and bread for $6. 'Excellent food.' Daily 7am-11pm.

Sweet tooth: **Gelato Classico**, 576 Union, 391-6667. The standard of excellence in Italian ices. **Just Desserts**, locations on Buchanan, Church St and Embarcadero. 'Best cheesecake, chocolate cake in the city.'

Vegetarian: **Green's at**, Bldg A Fort Mason, Laguna St at Marina Blvd, 771-6222. 'Culinary experience for vegetarians.' Lunch $7-$10, dinner $10-$13. 'View of the bay very beautiful.'

OF INTEREST

Don't go looking for 'sights' and miss the best one: San Francisco itself. The best way to take it all in is to alternate walking with cable car or bus riding. Spend a half day at most in the tourist ghetto of Fisherman's Wharf, The Cannery, Pier 39, Ghiradelli Square, etc., all of which are aimed squarely at your wallet. You've missed an essential part of the city's heart if you don't do one or more of the following: take a ferry to Sausalito past Alcatraz, the infamous prison; inch up and down the near-cliffs locally known as 'hills' while dangling from the downslope end of a cable car; hop on a MUNI tram for a tour of the peninsula; or stand on the Marin headlands north of the Golden Gate Bridge in the evening, watching the lights of the city come on. Unlike LA, San Francisco is fairly compact, easy to comprehend and well equipped with public transport to give your legs a much-needed break on its 43-plus hills.

Alcatraz, Pier 41, 705-5555 ferry is $11 (including audio tour). Day trip to 'the Rock,' where the likes of Al Capone, Machine Gun Kelley and the 'Birdman' were incarcerated from Civil War times to 1963. 'Dress warmly.' Tours year-round, 9am-5pm, every $1/2$ hr. 'Must pre-book tkts but well worth it.' 'Long queues—get there early.' 'Best tour I went on in whole of US.'

Alamo Square Take a walk to this green square for the best view of the Painted Ladies, the coloured Victorian houses that epitomise SF living.

Bank of America Building. This building, the second tallest in the city, is pretty obvious, but for the record it's at 555 California St. The Carnelian Room, 433-7500, a posh restaurant on the 52nd floor, offers an excellent view along with prices you can't afford. Cocktails are served between 3pm-11pm if you don't want to splash out on dinner, but don't wear shorts. Restricted viewing is also possible from the 27th floor of the **Transamerica Pyramid**, at Montgomery St, a $34 million corporate symbol that has, amazingly, given the Golden Gate Bridge a run for its money as the City's symbol as well. The view of the Bay and hills beyond is nice, but it's more fun to go right up to the edge of the plate glass window—a plate glass wall, really—and just look down.

Chinatown: more Chinese live here than in any other Chinatown in the states. Inhabiting Grant and Stockton btwn Bush and Broadway, SF's Chinatown can be a crowded confusion of sights, smells and sounds. 'Do yourself a favour and spend a couple of hrs just wandering around taking it all in, especially the seafood shops.' All the tourists go to Grant; you should explore Stockton, Washington and little side streets to see: herbal shops at 837 and 857 Washington; fortune cookies being made at Mee Mee, 1328 Stockton; and T'ai-Chi practiced in the morning at Portsmouth Sq, RL Stevenson's old hang-out btwn Clay and Washington, where the City began.

Civic Center: Btwn Franklin, Larkin, McAllister and Hayes. Its centre is **City Hall**, unhappy scene in 1978 of the dual murder of the mayor and gay supervisor by a former supervisor; both the crime and minimal punishment provoked rioting, outrage, and jolted SF's image as a tolerant mecca for gays.

Cow Hollow also known as Union Street—upwardly mobile locals shop and drink coffee away from the downtown bustle.

Cruises around **the Bay:** from Piers 39 and 41, the Red and White fleets, 447-0597, and the Blue and Gold fleet, 705-5555. Frequent departures. Dress warmly and wait for clear weather. Both offer tours to Alcatraz, Angel Island or Bay cruises ($17), Sausalito ($6 o/w). Blue & Gold has a $2.25 per ticket phone reservation fee, but it's worth it especially for Alcatraz; Golden Gate ferries, 923-2000 to Sausalito ($5 o/w) and Larkspur ($2.85 weekdays, $4.80 weekends o/w), departing from the Ferry Building on Embarcadero, at the foot of Market Street.

Embarcadero: **Vaillancourt walk-through fountain**, a 710-ton assemblage of 101 concrete boxes, unveiled in 1971 to cries of 'loathsome monstrosity,' 'idiotic rubble,' etc. A must-see. Also, overlooking one of the most famous and photogenic skylines in the world is the **Skydeck**, 772-0566, the *only* outdoor observation deck in San Francisco. It offers a show-stopping 360-degree view of the City by the Bay. Located on the 41st floor, the indoor/outdoor observatory also offers multimedia presentations of San Francisco history and culture, and original artwork. 'A visual delight for photographers and visitors. 'Open 9.30am-9pm, daily, $7, $4 student ID.

Financial District: **Montgomery St** is the 'Wall Street of the West.' **Wells Fargo History Museum**, 420 Montgomery, 396-2619. The bank whose symbol is a stagecoach pays homage to its worst enemy, Black Bart, who robbed Wells Fargo 28 times in 7 years (successfully all but once). Also includes other mementoes of the Old West. Free, Mon-Fri 9am-5pm.

Fisherman's Wharf/Pier 39: Minuscule amount of wharf, surrounded by a frightening quantity of souvenir rubbish, overpriced seafood, dreary wax museums and bad restaurants. The working wharf is a series of 3 finger piers, just past Johnson and Joseph Chandlery. **Pier 39** is a carefully hokey construct of carnival and commerce. Dive among other types of sharks under San Francisco Bay at **UnderWater World**, 623-5300, America's first 'diver's-eye view' aquarium. A 30 min headphone narrated dive journey guides visitors along moving walkways through a 400ft long, 16ft deep transparent tunnel. Inches away is a spectacular array of 10,000 rays, salmon, crabs, jellyfish, and other underwater wildlife. Highlights include 'Rocky Surge Pool' exhibit, an octopus and more than 150 sharks. Open 9am-9pm daily, $12.95.

Aquatic Park, 3 blocks left of Fisherman's Wharf. The 6 vessels moored here as well as the nearby **National Maritime Museum** (Free, daily 10am-5pm), 561-6662, are charming, 'especially the restored ferry.' $4 to enter **Hyde Street Pier**, or free the first Tuesday of the month, where you can board 3 of the ships, including the 1886 *Balclutha*. Elsewhere is docked the liberty ship *Jeremiah O'Brien* and the WWII sub *Pompanito*, all with boarding fees. Also at the Aquatic: free swimming beach, cold but fairly clean, with free showers. Nearby is open-air seating where wonderful conga and jam sessions take place on fine Sat-Sun afternoons. Btwn Aquatic and the Wharf are **Ghiradelli Square** and **The Cannery**, both mazes of specialty shops, restaurants and contrived street colour with a thin veneer of history overall.

Golden Gate Bridge: It's painted orange-red but glows gold in the afternoon sun. Perhaps the most famous suspension bridge in the world, the 1 1/2 mile Golden Gate links SF with the green Marin headlands (honeycombed with war fortifications). You can walk or bike across for free (dress warmly); pedestrian walk closes at sunset. At midpoint, you'll be 260 ft above the water, a drop that has drawn over 1000 suicides. By car, the bridge is free northbound, $4 southbound. 'Take Golden Gate Transit bus #20 from Civic Center to bridge, then walk down through wooded area with lovely plants, stroll along beach all the way back to Fisherman's Wharf. Lovely way to spend a day.' Other ways to do the bridge: walk from SF to Marin on the Bay side, and once across, keep going down Alexander Dr to Sausalito (about a mile, downhill all the way) and catch the ferry back to SF—the best of both worlds.

Golden Gate Park and West SF: An exceptional park of 1017 acres, filled with a vast array of plantings, foot and bridle paths. Lots of free events and admissions, especially on first Wed of every month; Sunday concerts on music concourse; lovely **Conservatory of flowers; Stow Lake** and **Strawberry Hill**; scruffy buffalo in the west end; occasional outstanding Sunday jugglers in the park near Conservatory; **Strybing Arboretum**. Get to the enchanting **Japanese tea garden** early or late to miss tour bus hordes. For info on places and events within the park, call the San Francisco Recreation and Parks Department, 666-7200. Within the park: The **California Academy of Sciences**, info line 750-7415, $8.50, $5.50 w/student ID, includes admission to the **Aquarium**, 221-5100, which has huge, open tanks, and the **Natural History Museum**, with the Earthquake Exhibit. Also part of the Academy is the **Morrison Planetarium** and laserium, an additional $2.50, regular show times. Free 1st Wed of every month except Planetarium. Daily opening 10am-5pm winter, 9am-6pm summer.

The **de Young Museum** and **Asian Art Museum**, 668-8921, both located in the Park, are part of the **Fine Arts Museums of San Francisco**. (750-3600). $7 ($5 with MUNI ticket) includes the **Palace of the Legion of Honour**, in Lincoln Park, at 34th St and Clement, including Rodin sculptures and impressionist works. Both open daily except Mon, 9.30am-5pm. The deYoung is free 1st Wed of the month, the Palace on the 2nd Wed, both have extended opening till 8pm on these days. 'deYoung—not worth the price or time'

'Don't walk to the park from the bus station unless you want to find out what it is like to be mugged or raped (local police advice).'

Haight-Ashbury, south of the Golden Gate panhandle, was famous in flower-power days, now spiffed up in what is sometimes called the 'creeping gentrification' of the City, typified by the Gap store at the intersection of Haight/Ashbury. Take a stroll down Hashbury Lane: **Janis Joplin's pad at** 112 Lyon, now home of a charitable organization, and **Jefferson Airplane's hangar** at 2400 Fulton. SE of Haight is **Noe Valley**, a sunny version of Greenwich Village, whose main drag, **Castro St** is synonymous with gaydom. **Twin Peak** provides (on clear days) a fine view of San Francisco. Take bus #37 from Market Street.

Hyatt Regency Hotel, Embarcadero Plaza, 788-1234. Glittering seven-sided pyramid, its lobby filled with trees, birds, flowers and fountains. Ride the twinkly elevators to the 18th floor for costly drinks in Equinox, a restaurant that revolves, with a magnificent view of the Bay Bridge. 'Romantic, delightful—$10 cocktails.' 'Req to buy drink.'

Japantown covers approx. 12 sq blocks with Japancenter Mall at the core. Between Fillmore and Octavia, Geary and Bush. Plenty of authentic Japanese restaurants, and a street fair 1st wknd in Aug.

Marina Safeway, 15 Marina Blvd, 563-4946. Locally infamous pick-up joint and grocery store, nicknamed "the body shop". Visit the produce department for proof that San Franciscans love their fog so much that they create it artificially indoors, too.

Mexican Museum, Bldg D, Ft Mason, 441-0404. $4, $3 w/student ID. Don't pass up this rich panorama of folk, colonial and Mexican-American works, from masks to pottery to Siquieros lithos. Outstanding special exhibits. Get in free 1st Wed of every month. Wed-Sun 11am-5pm.

The Mission District: w/end eves, Chicano youth strut their mechanical stuff with their highly customised vehicles in the phenomenon known as low riding. On Mission btwn 16th and 24th or so; enquire locally. The area is rich in **murals**. See for yourself at the mini-park btwn York and Bryan on 24th; in Balmy Alley btwn 24th and 25th; and on Folsom at 26th. **Mission Dolores** at 16th and Dolores (621-8203) is a simple, restored structure with an ornate basilica peering over its shoulder. May-Sept, daily 9am-4.30pm, $2 donation. Interesting cemetery; drop in any time for free. The first **Levi Strauss Factory**, 250 Valencia, 565-9159, gives good tours every Tues and Weds. Reservations required, or check for trips through one of the AYH hostels.

Nob Hill: Cable car lines criss-cross here; transfer point. **Cable Car Museum**, Washington & Mason, 474-1887: 'The cable cars are powered from here, see how they work, very interesting.' Daily 10am-6pm; free. North of Union Square is the grande dame of SF hills; prior to the quake it was crowded with mansions, of which only the **Pacific Union Club** was left standing. If you're dressed for it, take the elevators to the view bars atop the **Fairmont** and **Mark Hopkins Hotels**. (The Fairmont features in the TV soap *Hotel*.)

North Beach: This, the birthplace of the beat movement, fends off Greenwich Village's claim to the same by maintaining even now a certain junkyard style. Once the centre of the rip-roaring Barbary Coast, the area now hosts topless, bottomless, seemingly endless clubs along Broadway's 'mammary lane.' Clashing crazily with this gaudy neon fleshpot are clubs, coffeehouses and bookstores that reek of intellectual prestige or pretention, depending on your point of view. Among the greatest (if not the latest), is **City Lights Bookstore**, 261 Columbus, 362-8193. Open till midnight. Still owned by Lawrence Ferlinghetti, still stocked with Alan Ginsberg. Original mecca for the Beat writers. The alley next to the store is named in honour of Jack Kerouac. Look for **29 Russell St**, where he wrote *On the Road*. Get *triste* at **Cafe Trieste**, 609 Vallejo, at Grant, 392-6739, to the tune of an aria from a tragic Italian opera performed by the owner (Sat 1pm), and drown your sorrows in a cafe latte; 'the highlight of my trip'! Pay your respects at **Vesuvio Bar**, 255 Columbus, 362-3370. When the beat movement bit the dust, the detritus gravitated here. Once, Kerouac and Dylan Thomas bent elbows at Vesuvio; the drinks are still cheap.

Pacific Heights, with its surpassing collection of **Victorian mansions**, many of them colourfully painted. Webster, Pine and the 1900 to 3300 blocks of Sacramento contain many charming examples.

Palace of Fine Arts, 3601 Lyon St, 563-7337. Built for the 1916 Panama-Pacific Exposition out of plaster of Paris, the palace was not expected to hold up, as it did, for fifty years. It was restored with cement in 1967 and now houses the **Exploratorium**, a carnival of science and art that explains principles of physics and human perception through hands-on exhibits. To see the super-popular Tactile Dome: rsvs are essential, 1 week ahead for w/days, 4-6 weeks for w/ends. Admission to the rest of the Exploratorium is free the first Wed of every month, otherwise $9, $7 w/student ID, $12 will get you into both. Daily 10am-6pm, Wed 'til 9.30pm. 'Don't miss it!'

San Francisco Museum of Modern Art, 151 3rd St btwn Mission and Howard, 357-4000. All the bluechips: Miro, Klee, Jasper, Pollock, etc. Free 1st Tue of every month, otherwise $9, $5 w/student ID. Daily except Weds 11am-6pm, Thur 11am-9pm (half price from 6pm). Worth a visit for the building itself.

San Francisco Zoo, Sloat and 45th, 753-7061. $9, 10am-5pm daily.

Seal Rocks area: **Cliff House**, a spooky, Gothic-style reconstruction of a seaside resort on a cliff above the crashing sea. It offers a panorama from a walk-in *camera obscura*, and on the lower level, the **Musee Mechanique**, 386-1170, a droll collection of vintage arcade machines, from Fatty Arbuckle to zee French flasher! Free, but bring dimes and quarters. Daily 10am-8pm.

SoMA (South of Market): **Anchor Brewing Company**, 1705 Mariposa, 863-8350. See how SF's own Anchor Steam Beer is created. Tasting follows 30-40 min tour, Mon-Fri early afternoons. Rsvs 1 wk in advance, free.

St Mary's Cathedral, Geary & Gough. Almost extra-terrestrial in feeling, with a free-hanging meteor shower over the altar. 'Well worth seeing.' Free.

Telegraph Hill/Russian Hill: Romantic **Telegraph Hill** is topped by **Coit Tower**. Does it look like the nozzle of a firehose to you? $3 for the elevator to the top. **Russian Hill** was the gathering place for bohemian writers, artists and poets, from Ambrose Bierce to George ('cool grey city of love') Sterling. It boasts not 1 but 3 steep streets that make it the most vertical district in SF: most famous; **Lombard**, with its 8 switchbacks and 90-degree angles (almost impossible to photograph but featured in movies such as *What's Up Doc?* and *Foul Play*); also **Filbert** btwn Hyde and Leavenworth; and **Union** btwn Polk and Hyde.

Union Square: City centre, named on the eve of the Civil War. In 1906, the square served as emergency camp for earthquake refugees. Nearby is **Maiden Lane**, once a red-hot red-light district, now a charming cul-de-sac with the only Frank Lloyd Wright building in the city housing the **Folk Art International Gallery**. A striking tunnel entrance and interior ramp leads to the entrance, the prototype for the Guggenheim Museum in New York City. The Gallery is at 140 Maiden Lane, 392-9999, Mon-Sat 10am-6pm, free. North at 130 Sutter is the progenitor of the modern glass skyscraper, the 1917 **Hallidie Building**. Superb stores abound; even Woolworth's is nice, although **Gump's** is the local landmark among them. You'll also find **theatres** on Geary and **cinemas** on Market. At Market and New Montgomery is the **Sheraton-Palace Hotel** , whose lacy skylighted garden court was the sole remnant in this luxurious structure after the 1907 earthquake. Singer Enrico Caruso was staying in the Palace when the quake hit; he rushed out, said 'Give me Vesuvius!' and left SF in haste.

ENTERTAINMENT

Whatever your sexual proclivities, it takes quite a bit of cash (and often a smart appearance) to explore the singles bars, meat-rack taverns and gay watering holes of SF. Some tips: go at happy hour, when drinks are cheaper and hors d'oeuvres available; Union St is hetero, Castro-Polk is gay. A better tip: SF has a high VD and herpes rate, and the action has calmed down considerably since the advent of AIDS. Emphasis is now on 'safe sex,' but sex that's safe hasn't been invented. In unfamiliar environs, your best tip is to relax, enjoy the atmosphere and music, and save your hunting for your home turf. The City's 'happening' nightlife scene is constantly changing due to fashion and nightclubs changing names or going bust (as in any city). The area south of Market is usually quite lively. The best sources of info for events, clubs, music are the BAM monthly, the free *Bay Guardian* (comes out Weds) and the *Pink Datebook* section of the Sunday *Chronicle Examiner*.

330 Ritch Street, 522-9558, in the heart of fashionable Mission district. Alternative, dance or swing, cover around $5.

Club Fugazi, 678 Green Street, 421-4222, Beach Blanket Babylon revue; book in advance.

DNA Lounge, 375 11th St, 626-2532. Subterranean disco-club open for all-night dancing. $10 cover at weekends.

Edinburgh Castle, 950 Geary Street, 885-4074, a little bit of Scotland in SF; not the nicest part of town though.

Pier 23 Cafe, The Embarcadero, 362-5125. Newly remodeled cafe/nightclub, has Bay view, funky atmosphere. Cover $10 after 9pm on Fri & Sat. Tues-Sat 11.30am-2 am.

Rasselas Jazz Club and Ethiopian Restaurant, 2801 California St, 567-5010. Jazz, blues and cabaret-style evenings. Restaurant opens at 5pm, live music 8pm-midnight Sun-Thur, 9pm-1 am Fri & Sat.

Slim's, 373 11th St, 255-0333. No age limit, over 21's get a stamp entitling them to a drink. 'Good for local bands.' Cover and opening times depend on band.

Sigmund Stern Grove Concert Series, 19th Ave and Sloat Blvd, 252-6252. Bring a picnic and listen to opera/jazz/classical in a bower of eucalyptus and redwood trees. Free, Sun 2pm, mid-June-mid-Aug. Serious music, dance, theatre offerings are abundant; see the *Datebook*. The **San Francisco Symphony**, Davies Symphony Hall, Grove St, 864-6000, has occasional inexpensive (around $15) open rehearsal seats; call for details, otherwise normal prices start at $12. Also: 'You can usually get a standing ticket for $8 at the **San Francisco Opera House,** 199 Grove Street, at corner with Van Ness, 864-3330; after 1st act, grab a free seat. Productions of a high standard.'

Festivals: International Film Festival, April/May. More than 100 feature and short films from throughout the world. Check out the website for more information *sfiff.org*. The Festival of Culinary Arts is held on Polk Street at the beginning of September, free food and wine tasting, farmers market etc. Call 249-4640 for further info.

SHOPPING
Tower Records, Columbus and Bay, 885-0500. Vast selection, daily 'til midnight. For deeply discounted records and rare stuff, go to **Rasputin's** in Berkeley; for second-hand records try **Reckless Records**, 1401 Haight St. Try along **Clement**, at the Thrift Town on Mission, and in Haight-Ashbury for **vintage clothing** and factory overruns: many marvellous shops.

SPORT
For professional baseball lovers, the **SF Giants** are based in **3-Com Park**, Gilman Ave. Later in the year, football action takes over, with the **SF 49ers** at **3-Com**. Try looking under *Sports and Recreation* at *www.sfbay.yahoo.com* to find a wealth of online information on amusement/theme parks, baseball, basketball, outdoors, skating, skiing and snowboarding.

INFORMATION
General: SF is a Moonies mecca; they are friendly, may invite you to their camp, 120 miles N, or to dinner. Nip their overtures in the bud with a forthright, 'piss off.' 'Very convincing, hard to get away from.' 'Also watch out for hit artists around North Beach.'
Redwood Empire Association, 2801 Leavenworth, 2nd floor of Cannery at Fisherman's Wharf, 543-8334. Free Guide book available (also at airport). Helpful organisation, friendly staff with info on all 'Redwood' counties—SF and north. Mon-Sat, 10am-5pm.
San Francisco Convention and Visitors Bureau, 201 3rd St, 974-6900. Weekdays 9am-5.30pm, Weekends 9am-3pm.
Visitors Information Center, 900 Market at Powell in Hallidie Plaza, 391-2000. Multilingual, helpful, Mon-Fri 9am-5.30pm, Sat 'til 3pm, Sun 10am-2pm. Events message on 391-2001.
Travelers Aid, (650) 877-0118, general information booth at the airport.

INTERNET ACCESS
At **Royal Ground**, 2060 Fillmore, 567-8822, *www.cafenet.net*, $2.50 / 30 mins. Free access can be found at the **Main Library**, Larkin & Grove Sts, across from the Civic Center, 557-4400. Open till 8pm Tue-Thu.

TRAVEL
'Parking can be very expensive, rely on local public transport.' Pick up BART or Golden Gate Transit maps for free, or a MUNI map for a fee. 'Wonderful but incomprehensible, even with regional transport guide; e.g. trains become street cars. Transfers and cheap deals exist. Ask. Even the natives kept asking us questions in BART stations.'
A/C Transit services East Bay from Transbay Terminal, (510) 839-2882. Often faster than BART in rush hours.
Amtrak, (800) USA-RAIL. Free shuttle from Ferry Building to Emeryville and from Transbay to Oakland depot where you get daily service on *Coast Starlight* and *San Joaquins* (to Merced, Fresno, near National Parks).
BART, 788-BART in SF, (510) 465-BART in East Bay. Sleek, carpeted, comfortable 'Bullet-Beneath-the-Bay,' connecting SF with Oakland, Berkeley, etc. Fares 90¢—$3.45. Long waits during rush hours and on Sun. Transfers valid btwn BART and MUNI for $1 return trip—pick up transfer as exiting BART. 'Worth it just for the experience.' Mon-Sat 6am-midnight, Sun 9am-midnight.

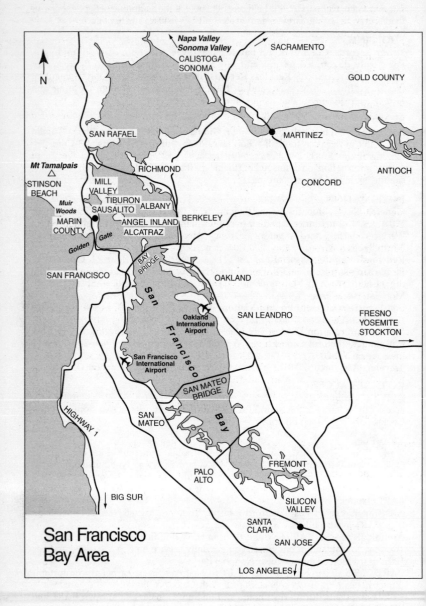

N

Napa Valley
Sonoma Valley
CALISTOGA
SONOMA

SACRAMENTO

GOLD COUNTY

SAN RAFAEL

Martinez

RICHMOND

CONCORD

ANTIOCH

Mt Tamalpais

STINSON
BEACH

MILL
VALLEY

Muir
Woods

TIBURON
SAUSALITO

ALBANY

MARIN
COUNTY

ANGEL INLAND
ALCATRAZ

BERKELEY

Golden   Gate

SAN FRANCISCO

BAY
BRIDGE

OAKLAND

San

Oakland
International
Airport

SAN LEANDRO

FRESNO
YOSEMITE
STOCKTON

San Francisco International
Airport

Francisco

SAN MATEO
BRIDGE

HIGHWAY 1

SAN
MATEO

Bay

BIG SUR

FREMONT

PALO
ALTO

SILICON
VALLEY

San Francisco
Bay Area

SANTA
CLARA

SAN JOSE

LOS ANGELES

Caltrain, 700 4th St at Townsend, 495-4546. Frequent trains, SF-San Jose only. Open 5am-8pm.

Golden Gate Transit, 257-4563. Operates bridge, ferries to Sausalito and Larkspur from Ferry Bldg, about $5 o/w, and buses to Marin and Sonoma counties from Transbay Terminal, at 1st & Mission.

Green Tortoise Bus, 285-2441 or from outside CA, toll-free (800) TORTOISE. Counterculture service to East Coast, Baja, Alaska, Seattle, New Orleans, the Grand Canyon, Yosemite and just about anywhere, in diesels with sleeping platforms. To everything there is a season—and the Tortoises migrate accordingly: Mexico in winter, Alaska in summer, California anytime.

Greyhound, 425 Mission St, (800) 231-2222. Daily 5am-12.30 am.

MUNI local transit, 673-MUNI. 700 mile network of buses and trains with frequent service, friendly drivers and good transfer system; $1 allows travel for 1¹/₂hrs anywhere on system, part of which is underground, a free transfer allows two more journeys. MUNI also runs the fabled cable cars; $2. MUNI "passports" $6 all day, $10 for 3 days, $15 for 7 days, available at Visitors Information Center at Fisherman's Wharf and the cable car ticket booths at Pier 39, Powell & Market or Hyde & Beach, or the Visitors Information Center in Hallidie Plaza. Alternatively, the MUNI Weekly Pass is $9 allowing unlimited travel, except on cable cars, where an additional $1 must be paid. With the "Passports", discounts are available at museums and other attractions. MUNI map available and advisable, $2. 'Make sure you get the front seat on the cable car for the best experience'.

San Francisco Airporter Bus 495-8404, departs the airport for Union Square and hotels every 15-30mins, $10 o/w.

San Francisco International Airport, 12 miles S, 761-0800; customs information (is downtown), 744-7742. Moonie-infested. For airport bus service see above.

San Mateo Transit (Samtrans) , (800) 660-4287. SF to Palo Alto, San Mateo. To complicate matters some routes do not accept luggage—to get you and your luggage **to the airport** take bus #7B (local service which stops everywhere and takes 1hr—leave plenty of time!) from 5th and Mission, $2.20. The express bus, #7F, *will not under any circumstances* allow luggage, it takes ¹/₂ an hour, $3.

Thrifty car rental: 1-800-FOR-CARS, seems to offer the best value. There are massive daily surcharges for insurance, and under 25s must pay an extra $20 per day, rsvs at least 1 week in advance during summer.

For tours: **Gray Line**, 558-9400. City tours, Muir Woods, Sausalito, cruises. From 3¹/₂ hrs to all day; from $26, Alcatraz tour $10, daily 7.30am-11pm. **San Francisco Helicopter Tours**, (800) 400-2404, $80-$130 per person.

BERKELEY and OAKLAND Like Siamese twins, these two neighbour cities blend imperceptibly into one another physically, while each demonstrates a personality of its own. Easily reached by BART or bus, this area—the East Bay—offers good day trips; Berkeley for its university and accompanying cultural and social dividends, Oakland for its Jack London Square, excellent lakeside museum, blues clubs and baseball team known as the 'Athletics.' Both cities are short on cheap lodgings and long on streets that are unsafe to walk at night.

Berkeley: Concentrate on the area in and around the university, the closest you'll come to the fabled Berzerkley of free speech, anti-war, radical fame. 'Rather bohemian atmosphere, good for buying secondhand rare books, homemade trinkets or discussing Marxist ideology with a stranger in a coffeehouse.' *The telephone area code is 510. www.berkeleystyle.com/* is a guide to movies, dining out, community resources and everything else in Berkeley.

ACCOMMODATION

Easily the greatest challenge to visitors is trying to find somewhere cheap to sleep in the East Bay. One source is housing advertised in the *Daily Californian*, the newspaper of the University of California, Berkeley. Also, try UC Berkeley fraternities—easy access to city and inexpensive if not free. 'Filthy but at the price who cares?' Each fraternity determines for itself whether or not to accept guests, and policies are subject to change. If the frats turn you down (or vice versa), here are some more possibilities:

Berkeley Hotel, 2001 Bancroft, Berkeley, 843-4043, S-$32, D-$43.

Motel 6, 8484 Edes, at Oakland airport, 638-1180, S-$49, D-$55.

YMCA, 2001 Allston Way, Berkeley, 848-6800. $33-40 includes use of facilities. $2 key deposit, 14-day max stay.

FOOD

Berkeley: Blondie's Pizza, 2340 Telegraph, 548-1129. Delicious slices for $2.50.

Brennan's, 720 University Ave, 841-0960. Downtown bar with Guinness, cheap and simple foods—a local hangout. Daily 11am-9.30pm (food), bar 'til 12.30 am. Fri and Sat 'til 2 am.

Cafe Milano, 2522 Bancroft, 644-3100. Nicknamed 'Cafe Pretentious.' 'This is a must if you're going to sample the atmosphere of Berkeley properly.' Daily 7am-midnight.

Pasand, 2286 Shattuck, 549-2559. Indian food, excellent and cheap.

Spenger's, 1919 4th, 845-7771. Forget Fisherman's Wharf, this is *the* Bay Area institution for seafood. Sun-Thur 7am-11pm, Fri & Sat 'til midnight; $10-$15.

University cafeterias on campus ('except the main one—expensive'), 'til 3pm in summer. **International House** is also recommended.

OF INTEREST

Berkeley: On campus: Black Oak Books, 1491 Shattuck, 486-0698. 10am-10pm daily. New and used books on all subjects. Readings most evenings at 7.30pm, often given by some very well-known authors and poets. 'A gem. Go!' **Lawrence Hall of Science**, Centennial Dr, 642-5132, sits above campus in the Berkeley hills, take buses #8/65 from downtown. Daily 10am-5pm, $6.50, $4 w/student ID. 'Top of the mountain, excellent view, amazing museum, spent whole afternoon playing computer games.' The football stadium sits directly on the Hayward fault, a branch of the San Andreas; a large vertical crack may be seen through the upper tier. Both the **Campanile (Sather Tower)** in the centre of campus and the **Lawrence Hall of Science** on the hill above, have excellent views of Berkeley and the Bay. **Main Library** (where Mario Savio and Joan Baez addressed the first major student demonstration against the Vietnam War in 1964) has world's largest collection of Mark Twain materials. 'Try the browsing room (Morrison Room)—British newspapers, headphones to listen to records.'

Phoebe Hearst Museum, corner of Bancroft and College, 643-7648. Excellent Indian costumes and crafts, $2. Wed- Sun 10am-4.30pm, open till 9pm and free on Thur. Closed Mon/Tues. **University Art Museum**, 2626 Bancroft Way, 642-0808. Video, performance art, modern works, $6, $4 w/student ID. Wed-Sun, 11am-5pm; Thur 11am-9pm, closed Mon/Tues. 'Not worth it.' Located in the museum building is **Pacific Film Archives**, 2621 Durant, 642-1124. Nightly showing, more at term time. $6 for the first show, $1.50 for additional features. Runs gamut from Japanese samurai flicks to vintage 1930s classics.

Off campus: Tilden Park, above city in the Berkeley Hills.

Moe's Bookstore, 2476 Telegraph, 849-2087. Huge and politically hip—4 floors of books. Daily 10am-11pm.

Sake Takara USA Inc., 708 Addison at 4th, 540-8250. Museum, video and free tastings of wine and sake, noon-6pm daily.

Oakland: Jack London Sq, 10 mins from BART City Center station. Visit Jack London's cabin from his Klondike days, have a drink at the First and Last Chance Saloon, where London and RL Stevenson used to tipple. 'Village is excellent reconstruction of the wharf area.'

Lake Merritt, downtown Oakland, is the largest saltwater lake within a US city; overlooking it is the **Oakland Museum** at 1000 Oak St (Lake Merritt BART Stn), 238-2200. Art, history and natural science of California—interesting. $6, $4 w/student ID. Wed-Sat 10am-5pm, Sun noon-7pm, first Fri of the month open till 9pm.

ENTERTAINMENT / SPORT

Berkeley: Ashkenaz, 1317 San Pablo, 525-5054. Multi-ethnic folk dancing. 'Cheap fun.'

Freight and Salvage Coffeehouse, 1111 Addison St , 548-1761. Mixed bag of country, bluegrass, ethnic groups and comedy. No alcohol or smoking! Daily 7.30pm-midnight.

Larry Blake's, 2367 Telegraph, 848-0886. Big-name blues, funk and rock bands. 'Lively restaurant/bar with good local bands.' 'Lively part is downstairs.' Daily 11am-2 am. Food served 'til 1 am; $4-10 a dish. Cover $2-8, free Sun.

Triple Rock, 1920 Shattuck, 843-2739. Great bar with a redwood deck. Beer brewed on premises. For punk, go to Berkeley Square. Daily 11.30am-12.30 am/1.30 am.

See the **Oakland A's** baseball team at the **Colliseum**, 568-5600

SURVIVAL

Berkeley Free Clinic, 2339 Durant, 548-2570. Mon-Thur from 7pm, call at 6.45pm.

Berkeley Support Services,1931 Center Street, 848-3378. Has info, plus rough and ready crash pad (emphasis on rough!). Not rec for women. 'This is designed for the truly homeless, so use only in emergency.' Donations.

INFORMATION/TRAVEL

A/C Transit 839-2931 serves the campus, take buses #7, 8, 40, 51, 52.

Oakland International Airport. Take the Freemont bus to the Colosseum station ($2.15), AirBART bus from there ($2). Leaves every 10 mins from 6 am 'til midnight, $2. Call 465-BART.

UC/Berkeley Shuttle, 643-5708. From Berkeley BART stations to campus, Botanical Gardens, Hall of Science, etc. 25¢ o/w, 7am-6pm w/days only.

SANTA CRUZ-MONTEREY   This stretch of coast rivals the section north of San Francisco in its scenic beauty. Not nearly so unpopulated, though—tiny hamlets and larger towns line Hwy 1 (also known in this area as the Cabrillo Hwy). The first major city, **Santa Cruz**, is 90 miles S of SF and similarly suffered considerable damage in the October '89 earthquake. Jumping nightlife, lots of movies and bookstores, surfers aplenty and a rowdy beach and boardwalk scene earn the town its name, as pronounced by natives: 'Sanna Cruize.' The **University of California campus**, home of the 'Battling Banana Slugs,' is a special jewel. Eight colleges, independent of one another are hidden in the redwoods on a hill above the town; can you find them all?

Nearby is **Capitola-by-the-Sea**, a doll's village of Victorian houses and beach bungalows; its name comes from the days when this sleepy seaside resort was California's capital. Catch the Begonia Festival if you're here in September. Further south are the towns of **Soquel/Aptos**. Around the curve of the **Monterey Bay**, the towns of **Pacific Grove**, **Monterey**, **Pebble Beach** and **Carmel-by-the-Sea** cluster on a knob of land jutting out into the Pacific. Here, the cheap glitz of the Santa Cruz boardwalk gives way to much more expensive glitz, and the soft warm beauty of the coast turns angular, dramatic and cold. You don't need to shell out $5 for the **17-Mile Drive** to see it, though—bike it for free, or just north of the drive is an even more beautiful stretch, beginning at Ocean View Blvd and 3rd St in Pacific Grove: **Sunset Drive**, which also happens to be the best time to see it. And it's also free. *The telephone area code is 831, except San Jose, 408. www.santacruz-ca.com/* has links to restaurants, clubs and more.

SURVIVAL

This is a resort area, which means the necessities of life—food and shelter—tend to be treated as luxuries here: you can spend exorbitant amounts on either. Fortunately, Santa Cruz has a culture that generally welcomes students, transients or people who combine both qualities at once; the Monterey and Carmel area can be hostile to the same.

ACCOMMODATION

HI-Pigeon Point Lighthouse Hostel, 210 Pigeon Point Rd, **Pescadero** (Hwy 1, 50 miles S of San Francisco), (650) 879-0633. Perched on a cliff on the central California coast, the 115 ft Pigeon Point Lighthouse, one of the tallest lighthouses in America, has been guiding mariners since 1872. From the boardwalk behind the fog signal building, watch for gray whales on their annual migration. Walk through the tidepool area or through the amazing 1,000 yr old redwoods nearby. $12-14. Outdoor hot tub, kitchen; rsvs essential.

HI-Point Montara Lighthouse Hostel, 16th St at Hwy 1, 25 miles S of San Francisco, (650) 728-7177. Restored lighthouse in an exceptionally beautiful place; including an outdoor hot tub. Explore the coastline and watch the annual migration of gray whales btwn Nov and April. There are several great beaches for swimming, surfing, jogging, horseback riding and windsurfing. $12-14.

HI-San Jose Sanborn Park Hostel, 15808 Sanborn Rd, **Saratoga**, (408) 741-0166. This log house hostel is tucked away in a forest of redwoods and madrones in Sanborn County Park. Excellent starting point for hiking in the Santa Cruz Mountains as is nearby Winchester Mystery House, Rosicrucian Egyptian Museum and Technology Center Museum. $8.50.

HI-Santa Cruz Hostel, 321 Main St, **Santa Cruz**, 423-8304. 15 min walk from Greyhound. Hostel is located at the Carmelita Cottages (restored 1870's cottages), on Beach Hill. Only 2 blocks from beach, boardwalk, amusement park, and wharf; 5 blocks from downtown. Extensive bus system makes this a great starting point to state parks in the nearby mountains. Outside lockers store bags of early arrivals, garden, fireplace, barbecue, free evening snack. $13-15. 3 night minimum stay. 11pm curfew. Reservations essential in summer. *www.cse.ucsc.edu/~peter/yh/schs.html.*

Townhouse Motel, 1106 Fremont Blvd, Seaside, 394-3113. 1 block from Monterey, close to beach. From S-$79-109 summer, less in winter. 'Good accommodation.'

Camping: Big Sur Campground and Cabins, 667-2322. $26 for two , XP-$3. Tent cabins $48 for two. Log cabins $88-$230, numbers vary. Rsvs essential in summer. 2 miles N of Pfeiffer-Big Sur State Park on Hwy 1, 26 miles S of Carmel.

FOOD

Generally, be wary of any restaurant that caters too obviously to the tourist trade. Plenty of places, particularly in Santa Cruz, have a reputation with the locals for serving overpriced, mediocre food; the restaurants in Monterey and Carmel are merely overpriced. Here some eateries that are more in line with a hungry budget traveller's needs:

Georgiana's, behind Bookshop Santa Cruz, 1522 Pacific Ave, 427-9900, **Santa Cruz**. In a Mediterranean-style courtyard that becomes the town square on Sunday afternoons.

AMERICAN BEACHES

From the rugged and lonely north Pacific shoreline to the crowded, hedonistic playgrounds of Florida's coasts, America's beaches have something for everyone. Even to the landlocked, the scent of coconut oil strikes a deeper chord than that of traditional apple pie. For a truly American experience, try these beaches:

WEST COAST—The best: Redondo Beach, south of Los Angeles. Hawaiian George Freeth introduced the Polynesian art of surfing to the mainland here. **Most beautiful:** 17 miles of seals and sea lions, pink and purple ice plants between **Pacific Grove** and **Carmel**

See the surfers at sunset. **Most fashionable: Malibu**, with its bleached sandy beaches, celebs' homes dotting the hills above. A close second is **La Jolla**, near San Diego, CA, a ritzy, cove-lined beach frequented by upscale beachcombers, divers and surfers. **Strangest: Venice Beach**, near LA, has rollerskating grannies, graffiti, and a lot of muscle. **Snorkelling: Hanauma Bay**, Oahu, Hawaii. The best. **Surfing: Maui Island** in Hawaii boasts incredible surfing. NB: all the beaches in Hawaii are public. Try the local sport of 'Boogie-boarding', so-called because participants 'boogie' down the beach on rectangular boards, riding on the tail end of the surf. **Windsurfing: Hookipa Beach Park, Maui**—unrivalled as the world's No. 1 location due to constant trade winds and exceptional wave conditions. 'Fun just to watch.' 'If everybody had an ocean, across the USA, then everybody'd be surfing, Californ-I-A,' sang the Beach Boys, most likely with **Long Beach, CA** in mind, *the* place for surfing and site of Howard Hughes' *Spruce Goose*. **Most forgotten: Santa Catalina Island**, 26mi off of Long Beach. Accessible by ferry. No cars, just scuba diving and swimming. **Most peaceful: Long Beach**, on Vancouver Island's west coast, BC 12 miles of sea, sand and solitude.

THE EAST COAST—Hampton Beach, New Hampshire, has boardwalk, arcades, and waterslides. **Virginia Beach**, Virginia, fast growing resort with 28m beach. **Brunswick**, Maine, hosts excellent Beach Bluegrass Festival over Labor Day weekend. **Ocean City**, Maryland, crowded with Washingtonians, wild. **Myrtle Beach**, South Carolina, 3rd most-visited spot on East Coast behind Disneyworld and Atlantic City. Nearby **North Myrtle** becomes a student mecca in early mid-May. **Atlantic City**, New Jersey, birthplace of salt water taffy and showplace of Miss America. **Asbury Park**, decaying but still can lay claim to Bruce Springsteen. **Brighton Beach**, Brooklyn, New York, the only American beach where Russian is the native language!

FLORIDA—Sanibel Island, for the best seashells, starfish; **Cocoa Beach** has cosmic surfing and the added attraction of being the blast-off site for Space Shuttle flights. **Fort Lauderdale**, midway between Palm Beach and Miami is a glut of beer, raw lust and sports cars.

For a rundown on the best beaches go to *www.petrix.com/beaches/best.html*

Each of the 8 colleges of the university has its own coffee house, where you can mix and mingle with students; the best is **Banana Joe's** at Crown College. Closed in summer.
Mike's Seafood Restaurant, 25 Fisherman's Wharf, **Monterey**, 372-6153. 'Cheap

for the area, good seafood.' Delicious deep-fried calimari and linguine Alfredo with shrimp, $8.50. Daily 9am-10pm.

Mr Toots, 221A Esplanade, **Capitola**, 475-3679. Grab a bran muffin ($1.95) and watch the seagulls from the outside deck. Everything under $4. 'A bargain!' Daily 7.30am-11pm weekdays, midnight Fri-Sat.

Village Corner, Dolores & 6th, **Carmel**, 624-3588. Greek food from $8, good bfasts around $7, 'try the eggs Benedict,' informal setting. Daily 7.30am-10pm.

Whole Earth Restaurant, UC Santa Cruz campus, 426-8255. An oversized tree-house with politically-conscious cuisine. Closed w/ends in summer. Mon-Fri 7.30am-4pm. 'World food.' African specialities, from $5.

Zachary's, 819 Pacific, **Santa Cruz**, 427-0646. Huge, good bfasts for cheap; under $10. Try Mike's Mess (if you dare!) $6.50. Go early unless you're keen on queues! Tue-Sun, 7am-2.30pm.

OF INTEREST

Coming down Hwy 1 from SF, you get to **Pt Ano Nuevo** (pronounced 'An-yo Noo-ey-vo') **State Beach** before Santa Cruz. If it's winter, you may be able to see breeding elephant seals lazing in the rookery there. Critters of another sort romp on the area's nude beaches; best known is the 'red, white and blue' beach, marked by a mailbox sporting stripes of those colours 4 miles S of Davenport on Hwy 1. Coming into town, glimpse **UC Santa Cruz** on the swelling green hills to your left; from roads leading to its colleges nestled in the trees, you can get spectacular views of Monterey Bay. The vista from **Cowell College** is particularly good. Of the Coney Island-type boardwalks that once lined California's coast, only one remains, and here it is: the Santa Cruz **beach and boardwalk** . The municipal wharf is also worth a stroll. If you get weary of squishing discarded hot dogs btwn your toes, wander over to the **Pacific Garden Mall**, which has organic restaurants, organic clothing stores and organic people roaming the streets. Just north of the boardwalk is **West Cliff Drive**, which leads to **Natural Bridges State Beach**, 423-4609, ($6 car); though only one of the sandstone bridges still stands. **Roaring Camp & Big Trees Narrow gauge railroad**, 335-4484. $15 round trip from Santa Cruz to Felton, or Felton to Bear Mountain through redwoods, $14 return, on original 19th century steam trains. Call for times. If you have time and transportation, take Hwy 17 (drive carefully) to San Jose to see the **Winchester Mystery House**, 525 S Winchester Blvd, San Jose (408) 247-2101. Tours $13.95, 65 mins. Sara Winchester, the story goes, was directed by the ghosts of people killed by Winchester Rifles to build additions onto her home haphazardly and continuously. The resulting jumble of 160 skewed rooms, staircases that go up and down, and doors leading to nowhere is seen by some as the architectural analogue to development in the surrounding Silicon Valley. Daily 9am-8pm. Also, stick around for a number of festivals around the beginning of July. July 5-6th features the annual **Tahiti Fete** in San Jose, a Polynesian dance competition with arts & crafts, music and dancing. Call 486-9177.

Cannery Row, Monterey. Rows of defunct sardine canneries immortalized by John Steinbeck make wonderful homes for little shoppes. Daily 8am-7pm.

Kalisa's Coffee House, 851 Cannery Row, **Monterey**, 644-9316, is a former brothel, with belly dancing on 2nd Sat of the month; across the street, the more cerebral **Monterey Bay Aquarium**, 648-4888, displays species native to the Monterey Bay in huge tank settings so natural that visitors get the impression that they are the ones behind glass. Daily, 9.30am-6pm in summer; $15.95, $12.95 w/ student ID. 'Great value for money. Fantastic for biologists and non-biologists alike.'

Carmel is an acquired taste. The town draws hordes of curiosity seekers, all of whom want to catch a glimpse of actor and one-time mayor, Clint Eastwood at his **Hog's Breath Inn**, at San Carlos and 5th. You won't, but stop by anyway for a look, maybe a drink—in a setting that would make Bilbo Baggins feel right at home.

Carmel has been accused of calculated cuteness but is worth seeing, if only for the experience of wandering down an alley and discovering a greenhouse in a hidden courtyard.

Derby Skatepark, near Natural Bridges. Concrete snakerun built in the mid-70s, bowls at either end. Roll-out deck added in late 80s; suitable for skateboarding/inlining. Also, **Monterey Bay**, 1855 E Ave, and **The Skate Station**, Sand City (right next door to Monterey Indoor Park) has an 11½ ft vertical ramp, street course includes trannies to wall, a corner bowl, a 6 ft mini ramp/spine. Small but fun, also has a board shop. Daily. *www.TeamAdventures.com*

The Mission, Rio Rd & Lausen Way, **Carmel**, 624-1271, ½ mile from downtown, has a star-shaped window framed by vines, fountains and flowers. It's free (donations are 'nice', recommended $2). The white sand beach nearby is great for running barefoot on; don't attempt to swim in the cold and treacherous surf, though.

Point Lobos State Reserve, 624-4909, 2 miles S of Carmel. Monterey-Salinas Transit stops here several times a day, on its way to Big Sur. $6 p/car, walkers get in free. (You can park your car on the hwy and walk in to avoid the fee!) 450 acres of natural beauty: coves, islands, fearless animals and birds. Best of all are China Cove and the beach beyond (take lunch). Daily 9am-7pm.

Pfeiffer-Big Sur State Park, 667-2315, is only one tiny part of the 90 mile stretch of scissored coastline btwn Carmel and San Simeon known as 'Big Sur.' The stretch is almost pristine and wholly soul satisfying. Free with ticket from Point Lobos, otherwise $6. Do stop on Hwy 1 for the obligatory open-air quaff and sea-gazing at **Nepenthe**, 667-2345, an ambrosia burger perhaps? This was originally the home of Rita Hayworth and Orson Welles; Cafe Amphora on the lower deck actually has the better view. Big Sur was home to the beats and Henry Miller and today continues to be inhabited (sparsely) by rugged individualists. More info at *jrabold.net/bigsur/*

INFORMATION
Carmel Tourist Information Center, on Mission btwn 5th and 6th Sts, 626-3714. Mon-Fri 8am-4pm.
Monterey Convention and Visitors Bureau, 380 Alvarado St, 649-1770, has a self-guiding walk brochure for the city's old buildings. Mon-Fri 9am-5pm.
Santa Cruz Convention and Visitors Center, 701 Front St, 425-1234. Mon-Fri 9am-5pm, w/ends 10am-4pm. Also open at w/ends 9am-6pm is the **Visitors Centre** at 401 Camino El Estero by the Lake.

TRAVEL
Greyhound, 425 Front St (downtown Santa Cruz), (800) 231-2222 has service from SF to Monterey. Daily 7am-6.45pm.
Monterey-Salinas Transit, 899-2555/424-7695. $1.50 per zone, free transfers. All downtown routes stop at Munras/Tyler/Pearl St triangle. Serves Monterey, Pacific Grove and Carmel; spring and summer service to Big and Little Sur as far as Nepenthe ($2.50 o/w).
Santa Cruz Metro, 425-8600. Lots of routes, runs late. $1 or $3 day pass, for bus or summer shuttle to Santa Cruz beach.

SAN LUIS OBISPO and SANTA BARBARA COUNTIES Called the central coast, this region stretches from Big Sur south to Santa Barbara. Among its highlights are **San Simeon**, site of **Hearst Castle**, built by William Randolph Hearst, newspaper magnate and the *Citizen Kane* of Orson Welles' film. This Spanish-style castle houses Hearst's $75 million art collection, which includes now-priceless tapestries, rugs, jade, statuary,

even entire antique ceilings and fireplaces and assorted loot from all over Europe, including Cardinal de Richelieu's bed. 'A two-hour trip into paradise.'

Further down the coast, **Morro Rock** makes a monolithic landmark at water's edge, the first in a series of volcanic peaks that march picturesquely through San Luis Obispo County. You can follow them along Hwy 1 (also the bus route). Beaches and camping opportunities abound; the amiable character of the inland town of **San Luis Obispo** adds to the area's appeal.

90 miles S of Morro Bay on Hwy 101 is **Solvang**, a charming coastal replica of a Danish town, 'worth a visit with its reasonably priced accommodation and restaurants.' Further south, **Santa Barbara** beckons. Far and away the loveliest of coastal cities, from its setting against the Santa Ynez Mountains to its beautiful Spanish adobe architecture. Despite its wealth, Santa Barbara is a non-stuffy, youthful city, with a big UC campus, sophisticated nightlife and the best sidewalk cafe idling anywhere in the US. 'Beautiful unspoilt beaches.' 'Elegant little town with a lot happening.'
The telephone area code is 805.

ACCOMMODATION

Farm Hostel, PO Box 723, Ojai, CA 93024, 646-0311. An independent backpackers lodge located in the beautiful Ojai Valley, gateway to the Southern California outback. 50 miles N of LA; 40 mins drive from Santa Barbara; 20 mins from Ventura beach and ocean. Cable, video, music, A/C, hot showers, near hot springs, 12 beds and a teepee! Free pick up from Ventura Greyhound. Non-smoking, passport and rsvs required $12.

HI-San Luis Obispo SLO Hostel, 1617 Santa Rosa St, 544-4678. Perfect stopover for travellers along California's spectacular Central Coast. Serving as gateway to Big Sur, the hostel is within walking distance of downtown shops, restaurants and theatres. Don't miss the downtown Farmer's Market every Thur night! With its ideal year-round climate, San Luis Obispo is a mecca for bicyclists, hikers and other outdoor enthusiasts. From $16.50, $14.25 for cyclists. Hot tub, laundry, patio and barbecue, sports equipment, garden.

Hotel State St, 121 State St, **Santa Barbara**, 966-6586. 'Excellent; staff very nice and helpful.' From S/D/T-$52, includes bfast.

Santa Barbara Banana Bungalow, 210 E Ortega St, 963-0154. Excellent bars and shopping. Mountain hiking, organised yacht trips to Channel Island and 3 day winery bike rides. $15-22.

Camping: Morro Bay State Park info line: 772-7434 and (800) 444-7275 for all parks in the area. $17 ($18 at wknds) w/out hook-up, up to 8 persons. For Hearst Castle, **camping** at San Simeon and Atascadero Beach.

OF INTEREST

Farmers Market on Higuera Street, San Luis Obispo, every Thurs afternoon—stalls, music, food.

Giant Chessboard, Embarcadero at Front, Morro Bay. The local chess club plays each Sat noon-5pm, on a 16'16' board with redwood pieces that weigh as much as a small child! Possible to rent other days. $17 all day.

Hearst Castle, State Hwy 1, 927-2000. Incredible palatial over-indulgence of 1930s. The influence for Xanadu in *Citizen Kane*, and where William Randolph Hearst entertained presidents, kings and Hollywood stars. 'Absolutely fascinating.' Book at least a day in advance through *Destinet*, (800) 444-4445. $14 for one of four tours covering different aspects of the castle; $25 for evening tours. 'Take Tour 2 or 3—smaller groups, more personal and informative.' Each tour lasts about 1¹/₂ hrs, daily 8.20am-3.20pm.

Morro Bay State Park, Hwy 1, 772-7434. Bird sanctuary, heron rookery. Daily 8.30am-10.45pm.

Old Mission Santa Barbara, upper end of Laguna St, Santa Barbara, 682-4713. Noble facade with columns and towers, many unusual touches, from Moorish fountain to Mexican skulls in the 1786 'Queen of the Missions.' Daily 9am-5pm, self-guided tours $3. More beautiful still is the **County Courthouse**, 1120 Anacapa St: a 1929 Hispano-Moorish treasure, inside and out. Check out **San Luis Obispo SLO Skatepark** on the corner of Oak St and Santa Rosa St where there is a street course and mini ramp for all avid skateboarders, inliners and BMXers.

Festivals: Robert Burns Night in San Luis Obispo, January 25th. Celebration features Scottish foods, music and dancing! Also in January is the **Annual Garden Festival**, San Luis Obispo. Colourful displays of flowers and exotic plants, contests, and demonstrations. Call 781-2777 for the local Chamber of Commerce.

In Santa Barbara, the International Film festival, March 2-12th has premieres and screenings of international and American films with city-wide festivities. Call 963-0023. Later on in the year in July, the **Santa Barbara County Fair** in Santa Maria is a 6 day celebration including nightly performances by nationally-known musicians, arts & crafts, carnival and food. Contact (800) 549-0036. Don't miss the **Santa Barbara PowWow** in early Aug, where more than 300 dancers represent 40 tribes in a Native American dance competition. Also, traditional arts & crafts.

The **Ojai Music Festival**, June 2-5th, is an outdoor classical music festival featuring world-renowned musicians and arts and crafts show. Call 646-2094.

FOOD

In Santa Barbara: Joe's Cafe, 536 State, 966-4638: 'bustling atmosphere, lashings of food at low prices; a favourite student meeting place.' Mon-Thurs 11am-11.30pm, Fri and Sat 'til 12.30 am, Sun noon-9pm.

McConnell's Ice Cream, 835 E Canon Perdido St, 963-8813. 'Best ice cream in America—and we sampled quite a few!' 17% butterfat. 8am-5pm daily.

The Natural Café, 508 State St, 962-9494. Healthy sandwiches and delicious smoothies. Sun-Thurs 11am-10pm, Fri-Sat 11am-11pm.

RG's Giant hamburgers, 922 State St, 963-1654. Voted for the best burgers in Santa Barbara 7 yrs running! Daily 7am-9pm.

In SLO: Your best bet for food is to head for Higuera St. Try **Big Sky Café**, 1121 Broad St, 545-5401; and **Woodstock's Pizza Parlor**, 1000 Higuera St, 541-4420, for good chow.

YOSEMITE An Oxford don once said, 'Think in centuries.' In Yosemite, it's inescapable. Cut in jewel facets by a glacial knife, the park encompasses nearly 1,200 square miles of incredible beauty—luminous lakes and dashing streams; groves of redwood elder statesmen and aged incense cedar; salt-and pepper boulders comically abandoned in boggy alpine meadows by the retreating glaciers of past millennia.

People bemoan the popularity of Yosemite, but not even 3 million visitors per year can ruin it. One-third of them choose to jam the park between July and August, and 80% of those content themselves with a stay in Yosemite Valley (just call it 'nature's parking lot'), leaving vast areas untrampled. Despite its congestion, you shouldn't miss Yosemite Valley's supreme vistas of **Bridalveil Falls** and **Glacier Point**, as well as the steel-blue shoulders of **Half Dome** and **El Capitan**. A mountaineers' mecca, Half Dome is the sheerest cliff in America, just 7% off vertical, and a full days hike (summer only) for those who are certain not to suffer from vertigo. El Capitan is the biggest block of exposed granite in the world, so vast you need binoculars to see the climbers taking a week to scale it.

A fine way to see the park is to travel up Hwy 41 from Fresno to the south entrance near **Mariposa Grove of Giant Sequoias**; the exit from Wawona Tunnel into the valley is absolutely spine-tingling, and you can walk through the Tunnel Tree. If you have the time, don't leave the park right after seeing the valley; instead, take the high road, Hwy 120, over **Tioga Pass** to shimmering, endangered **Mono Lake**. Continue south on Hwy 395 through **Owens Valley**, a neglected gem in a dusty corner of the state; **Mt Whitney** is visible from the highway.

Open year-round, Yosemite Valley is at its best in spring and early autumn; in summer visitors pay for the balmy weather by watching the spectacular waterfalls fade to a trickle. But winter is the time hardy souls and true Yosemite afficionados love best. With the season's first dusting of snow, the valley becomes a stark, eerie, white-on-black tableau—a living Ansel Adams photograph.

A 7-day pass to the park is $20 per vehicle or $10 each for hikers. 'Keep your ticket—checked on exit'. More info at *www.nps.gov/yose/*

The telephone area code is 209.

ACCOMMODATION

Within the park: More than any other spot in California, you must book cabin, lodge or camping accommodation in advance to avoid disappointment. 'Urbanised' campsites can be reserved through MISTIX, (800) 365-2267. Book on the internet at *reservations.nps.gov/*

Outside Park: Motel 6, 1215 R St, **Merced**, 722-2737. S from $38, D $44 X-P $5.

HI-Midpines—Yosemite Bug Hostel, 6979 Hwy 140, Midpines, (209) 966-6666. So-called because of the owner's collection of various mounted insects, this hostel is 20 miles E from Yosemite in several forested acres. The area is great for cycling and mountain biking, skiing, rafting and hiking (organises snowboard/hiking/biking treks). 'Clean, comfortable and set in a beautiful location.' At the end of the day, relax in front of the fireplace or at the hostel's café and coffee house on the deck. 'Fantastic! Can't recommend this place enough!' $15. Also campsites available $17 per tent. *www.yosemitebug.com*

HI-Yosemite Merced Home Hostel, 725-0407. Experience a typical American home. Shop at Farmer's Market every Thurs eve (May-Sept), visit the nearby Applegate Park and zoo or just relax at Lake Yosemite. Breathtaking views of mountains and large, old sequoia trees of Yosemite national Park, 80 miles (2 hrs) from Merced. Sleepsack provided. $12. Rsvs essential. Will pick up from Greyhound and Amtrak.

Campsites: Sunnyside: $3 for a walk-in, and your only hope if you haven't booked in advance. Also possible to take the shuttle to **Backpacker's Camp**, if you have a wilderness permit only, a quiet retreat behind **North Pine's campground**, $15 drive in site.

Other cabins: Reservations call (559) 252 4848. Curry Village, Yosemite Lodge and White Wolf Lodge. Tent cabins at **Curry Village**, $44 for 2 pp, wood cabins $65, XP-$5. 'Pay for 2, fit 6 in!' 'Was too cold to get undressed when I was there in Sept.' Showers nearby, often overtaxed. For rsvs call 252-4848. Housekeeping units have a stove (sometimes outside), cost a little more. No bedding. Also at **Housekeeping Camp**, 1 mile S of Yosemite Village, $48 for 4 pp, mattress beds provided in three-wall concrete shelter. Summer only.

FOOD

Food is costly and often poor in the park. Readers recommend Yosemite Valley's burger shop and pizza house. **The Recovery Café** at The Yosemite Bug Hostel offers bfast, pack lunches, dinners, espresso drinks, beer and wine on tap, pool table and games in the rustic Main Lodge with view decks. Grocery stores, restaurants, cafeterias are located at Yosemite Valley, Curry Village, Wawona, Tioga Lake, White Wolf, Fish Camp, El Portal and Tuolumne Meadows.

OF INTEREST
Everything! If you're adventurous, climb Half Dome by hiking around to the *back* via a 17-mile round-trip trail and hauling yourself up a cable-and-slats 'stairway' to the top. The payoff is the view: the panorama of Yosemite Valley and beyond, and the dizzying drop-off from the cliff. 'Hike Yosemite Valley, Glacier Pt, Illilouette Falls, Panorama Trail, Nevada Falls, Vernal Falls, Happy Isles for best photos. 14 miles, 3200-ft ascents and descents. Walk up to Nevada Falls via John Muir Trail and then down by Mist Trail. Take a swimsuit—icy mountain pools. (Do not swim above waterfalls.) Good for those with less time. Met a bear—terrifying.' Hike or drive to Glacier Point for views of the whole valley.

INFORMATION
Park Information, (559) 454-2088 has info on lodging in the park.
Visitors Center, 372-0299 at village mall in Yosemite Valley. Shuttle bus stop 6 & 9. 8am-8pm daily.

TRAVEL
Round-trip service to Yosemite from Merced: Via Bus Line, from the **Greyhound** Depot, 384-1215 , $38 r/t.
Greyhound, 710 W 16th St, (800) 231-2222, serves all cities along Hwy 99. **Hitching**: 'a bit slow btwn Merced and Yosemite.' Yosemite is 67 miles E of Merced.
Tours: Yosemite Park Tour Co., 372-1240. Various tours 2-8 hrs, $18-$46. Rsvs a day in advance. Picks up from the Lodge in Yosemite Village.
Incredible Adventures, 770 Treat Avenue, San Francisco, CA 94110, (800) 777-8464. Run one and three day tours to Yosemite from San Francisco. $85/$185. Also contact The Ant Bus (800) 336-6049, or the Us Bus (877) 843 8728.
Driving: Park open year-round except Hwy 120 at Tioga Pass. Fill up on gas before you enter the Park!

SEQUOIA-KINGS CANYON NATIONAL PARKS These two parks, established around 1890 and administered jointly since WWII, straddle a magnificent cross-section of the high Sierras, including 14,495-ft **Mt Whitney**, highest peak in the lower 48 states. Here you'll find the beautiful and impetuous **Kings River**, remnants of Indian camps, and wildlife that may venture into view in early morning or at dusk. Here, too, stand giant sequoia; like their redwood cousins along the coast, these trees are survivors of the Ice Age and lumber companies both. One of their number, the 2500-year-old **General Sherman**, is the world's most massive living thing, in all his 275-foot-high, 2145-ton glory. The two-mile **Congress Trail** into the heart of the **Great Forest** begins at the Sherman tree.

Access to the parks is by road from the west and southwest or by foot from the east. Bus service is available from Visalia to trailheads on both sides of the Sierras. 'Road to Owens Valley gives very pretty views and climbs to about 4000 ft above sea level.'
The homepage is located at *www.nps.gov/seki* which has its own virtual visitor centre.
The telephone area code is 559.

ACCOMMODATION
Dow Villa Hotel, 310 S Main, **Lone Pine**, (760) 876-5521. Hospitable place, good

rooms, from $38-105 for two. Use of jacuzzi, pool. 'Centrally located.'
Budget Inn, 138 Willow St, **Lone Pine**, (760) 876-5655. S-$69, D-$89.
Camping: Buckeye Flat 'Campground—pleasant, rustic. We saw a bear in camp.'
Rustic cabins without baths from $35 for 2pp, XP-$7, at **Giant Forest**, in Sequoia,
and at **Grant Grove**, in Kings. Book ahead by calling 561-3314; rsvs for camping,
cabins and cottages recommended.
In Parks: $16 per site, no rsvs required as getting a site 'shouldn't be a problem,'
according to rangers, or call (800) 365 2267. Free backcountry camping with permit.
Also free camping on Sequoia National Forest lands near park.

INFORMATION/TRAVEL
Sequoia and Kings Canyon National Park Information, 565-3134, gives general
information for both parks. For **backpacking** info call 565-3708. 'Helpful and informative.' Parks open year-round, 24 hours. $10 p/vehicle for 7 day access. Access in
winter via hwys 198 and 180. In summer: park bus tours; horse rentals available.

DEATH VALLEY NATIONAL PARK   Covering two million acres, most of
them about a million miles from nowhere, Death Valley has cornered the
market on hottest, driest and lowest (282 ft below sea level) place in the US
(ironically, less than 100 miles from Mt Whitney, highest point in the lower
48 states). High peaks ringing the valley prohibit moisture, and white sand
and hills reflect light in a blinding glare. But the definition of Death Valley is
heat: one July day in 1972, Furnace Creek lived up to its name with a ground
reading of 201 degrees (that's not a typo), while the air was a balmy 128
degrees.

Late October to early May is the sanest time to gaze at the tortured land-
scapes of **Zabriskie Point** and **Dante's View**, climb the **Ubehebe Crater**,
explore **Scotty's Castle**, and slide on the sensuous sand dunes at **Stove Pipe
Wells**. Scotty's Castle is no prospector's shack but a $2 million, 18-room
Spanish fortress with an 1100-pipe organ, a large waterfall in the living
room and other astonishing features built by colourful con-man Walter
Scott. Tours 9am-5pm last 1 hr and cost $8; call 786-2392, 60 miles from
Furnace Creek. Always dramatic, the desert can bring forth storms of wild-
flowers in March and April as suddenly as it does storms of water or sand.

Visitor Information at Park headquarters, **Furnace Creek**, 786-2331, has a
museum of geological interest mainly, descriptive literature, food and a cool
oasis of date palms. Free rangers' hikes and programmes daily, less often in
summer. Daily 8am-6pm. Visitor Information also located at Scotty's Castle.
The telephone area code is 760.

ACCOMMODATION
Death Valley lies 300 miles NE of Los Angeles and 135 miles NW of Las Vegas; the
only bus is from Las Vegas. Park lodging boils down to **camping** for $5 per site
(western campsites are free in summer to escapees from mental institutions), the
costly **Furnace Creek Ranch**, 786-2345 (from $94 for two, XP-$15) and the **Stove
Pipe Wells Motel**, 786-2387 (not much better; from D- $63, XP-$10). 'During
summer, arrive by 6pm. Otherwise no key.' Both located on Highway 190. A better
bet is the gas station/motel at **Panamint Springs**, 10 miles W of the park. 'A
welcome relief in the middle of nowhere.' Also try:
HI-Desertaire Death Valley Hostel, 2000 Old Spanish Trail Hwy, PO Box 306,
Tepoca, CA 92389, 852-4580. Only 1 hr drive from Death Valley National
Monument, the hostel is an excellent base to explore desert peaks and canyons.
Don't miss the free Tecopa Hot Springs Baths—107 F natural mineral water located

just 3 miles from hostel. Also, hiking, biking, patio, watch tower deck, laundry, volleyball. $12.

HI-Johannesburg Death Valley Hostel, 301 Highway 395, PO Box 277, Johannesburg, CA 93528, 374-2323. Situated in the Mojave desert country, 1½ hrs NE of LA, 1½ hrs from Death Valley and 3 hrs from Yosemite. Gold mining and ghost towns are nearby. Native American petroglyphs, Fossil Falls, Red Rock Canyon State Park and Sequoia National Forest are within an easy drive from hostel. Hiking, biking, kitchen, 2 covered patios, free bfast, $12.

PALM SPRINGS A flat desert town hugging snow-capped mountains, Palm Springs is a class act—from artfully weathered New Mexican adobes to its view of 10,831-foot Mt San Jacinto. Even the Indians are millionaires here, but don't let that put you off. During the hot, dry summer, prices melt like ice cubes and swimming pools can be reached within microseconds from air conditioned rooms.

Palm Springs homepage, *www.palmsprings.com/*
The telephone area code is 760.

ACCOMMODATION

Each hotel seems to set its own dates for low season, approximately June through Sept. Rates always lowest Sun-Thurs. To find the best deal, check newspaper specials, ask the Visitors Bureau, call around and don't be afraid to haggle. Except for Motel 6, winter rates are generally shocking.

Carlton Hotel, 1333 N Indian Ave, 325-5416. S-$24, D-$34, XP-$10 in summer. Weekly rates available, from $100.

Motel 6, 595 E Palm Canyon Dr, 325-6129 and 660 S Palm Canyon Dr, 327-4200. Lush setting, pools, book ages ahead. Rates range from S - $38 - quad $52.

Colibri Inn, 312 Camino Monte Vista, 323-3812. Summer rates from S/D-$49. 'Cheerful, small, with pool.'

FOOD

In summer, they practically give the food away; check local paper, giveaway tabloids for 'early bird' brunch and other specials.

Las Casuelas, 222 S Palm Canyon, 325-2794. 'Great Mexican food.' Daily 11 am 'til whenever they feel like it! $5-$13.

Nate's Deli, 100 S Indian Ave, 325-3506. 'Dinner specials good if you're hungry. A local institution.' Early-bird specials 4pm-6.30pm—attempt the 9 course meal for $10! Gulp! You'll be stuffed for days! Daily 8am-8pm.

OF INTEREST

Aerial Tramway, off Hwy 111, 325-1391. 18 mins, 8516 ft, and 5 climatic zones later, you're on **Mt San Jacinto** and it's 30-40 degrees cooler (in summer); you may even need a jacket. At the top: restaurant ('ride and dine' for $22), mule rides, backpacking, events and free camping. 'Can see part of San Andreas fault from top.' Mon-Fri 10am-9pm, 8am-9pm w/ends, $17.50

Cabot's Indian Pueblo Museum, 67616 Desert View Ave, in Desert Hot Springs (N of I-10 on Palm Drive), 329-7610. Eccentric 5-storey pueblo, built of found objects by Cabot Yerxa. Inside are the prospector/packrat's mementos of the Battle of Little Bighorn and Eskimo and Indian relics. Open w/ends only in July & Aug; otherwise daily Wed-Sun 10am-4pm; $2.50.

Desert Museum, 101 Museum Dr, 325-0189. Impressive modern art, Indian basketry. Tues- Sat 10am-5pm, Sun 12am-5pm. July-Sept open Fri-Sun only, 10am-5pm, $7.50.

Living Desert Reserve, 47900 Portola Ave, Palm Desert (E of Palm Springs off Hwy 111), 346-5694. 1200 acres of native plants, gazelles, Bighorn sheep and other desert denizens. 'After sundown' room displays with nocturnal beasties. Summer 8am-1pm, winter 9am-4pm, $6.

Palm Springs International Film Festival, January 13-24. More than 150 films; awards gala honours film makers' careers. Call 322-2930 for more info.

INFORMATION
Chamber of Commerce, 190 W Amado Rd, 325-1577; Mon-Fri 8.30am-4.30pm.
Palm Springs Visitors Bureau, off Hwy 111 in the Atrium Design Center, # 201, 770-9000. Mon-Fri 8.30am-5pm. Pick up the *Palm Springs Desert Guide*, the *Desert Weekly* and the **Calendar of Events** put out by the city: all are free and packed with info, special offers.

TRAVEL
Greyhound, 311 N Indian Ave, (800) 231-2222. On the Phoenix-LA route. Daily 6am-5pm.
Sun Bus Transit, 343-3451. Local buses; also has cheap shuttle around town, transfers 25¢. Daily 7am-5pm.

JOSHUA TREE NATIONAL PARK   In the high desert 54 miles east of Palm Springs is this 870-square-mile sanctuary of startling rock formations, mountain lions and kangaroo rats, colourful cacti and giant 50-foot agave trees with manlike arms and twisted bodies. These odd plants were named in the 1850s by Mormon pioneers, who recalled a line from *The Book of Joshua*: 'Thou shalt follow the way pointed for Thee by the trees.'

Entrance to the Park is $10 per vehicle for a 7 day pass. Campsites charges range from zero to $10—call (800) 365-2267. No shower and you need to bring food, water and firewood. Good exhibits, museum and ranger-guided tours (in autumn/winter only) from park headquarters at **Twentynine Palms**, and the visitor centre at **Cottonwood Springs**, 8am-5pm daily. From 5185-foot **Salton View**, you get a splendid panorama of the Coachella Valley, the Salton Sea and Palm Springs. On a clear day you can see Signal Mountain in Mexico. Also, don't miss the annual **Village Street Fair**, held in the Park itself , the first weeks of May and September, featuring food, beer garden, games and entertainment. Call the Chamber of Commerce on 366-3723 for details.

LOS ANGELES   Everything you have ever heard about LA is true. The place is so large and diverse that it will become whatever you wish to make it. There is urban angst and alienation downtown, and sun-seeking hedonism at Zuma beach. There is Greek sculpture in Malibu and a Cadillac stuck into a Beverly Hills roof. There is the film director sipping Perrier in Venice and the Vietnamese fisherman angling for dinner off the Santa Monica Pier. Remember that this city specializes in creating fantasy. The only way to find your own LA is to jump in with both feet.

Whatever you find, you'll be in good company. Thirteen million Angelenos speak 100 languages, and it's true—most do say 'have a nice day,' some even mean it. Its part climate, and part culture—LA has always drawn more from the Far East and Latin America than from New York and the grimy East Coast. The pace is a bit slower here, and the attitudes more tolerant. Easterners may deride LA as shallow and vain, but there is little doubt among Angelenos that theirs is a city struggling with social, economic and artistic questions difficult for outsiders to appreciate.

Most difficult to grasp is the great fear that one day the California Dream may be over. The place where people came to live a dream is slowly becoming less than that. The freeways are clogged, the air is smoggy and there is a constant worry about water. When in May 1992 four white police officers were acquitted of beating black motorist Rodney King, the riot that ensued did not just leave more than 50 people dead but left the city with a profound sense of identity crisis. Then came the massive earthquake on the 17th January, 1994. More than 50 died and many people were left homeless and stranded. The dream had become a nightmare.

Despite the growing congestion, the youthful LA sense of unlimited possibilities is easily restored with a trip along Mulholland Drive. Named for the engineer of LA's first aqueduct, Mulholland twists along the spine of mountains separating LA from the San Fernando Valley. A drive here offers sweeping vistas out over the enormous possibilities of the LA basin. At night the city lights stretch down to the sea, covering a seemingly limitless expanse. Clearly this was a city meant to dream dreams.

If you haven't acquired a car, it is surely now or never. You will no doubt get lost, spend countless hours looking for parking, but there's a sly exhilaration to driving LA freeways. It's like urban surfing. Once you've experienced the silken pull of seamless traffic, conquered a complex exchange as cars confidently curl on and off into new trajectories, and got a taste of life in the fast lane, you'll probably agree.

Area code for downtown LA is 213, for Hollywood is 323, for Santa Monica and Venice 310, for the San Fernando Valley 818, for Long Beach 562, Orange County 714, Pasadena 626.

Check out LA Yahoo! Metro at.*la.yahoo.com/*. The *LA Times* has a good visitors guide, especially for the low-down on beaches, at *www.latimes.com/home/destla/*. Up-to-date and stylish site at *www.losangeles.com/*, similarly the Visitors Bureau makes pleasant viewing, logically addressing the city by area; *www.lacvb.com/*

GEOGRAPHY

LA is immense and the first thing you need to do is get a sense of how to find your way round. For convenience sake, we'll assume that you have landed at the airport, and you're looking at a map. The airport is on the coast, in the middle of the **Santa Monica Bay**. Moving south along the coast you come to **Long Beach** (the *Queen Mary* is moored here, and Disneyland is about 10 miles inland from here in Anaheim) and then the resort areas of **Huntington Beach**, **Newport Beach**, **Laguna Beach** and finally **San Diego** about 125 miles S of LA.

Moving north along the coast from the airport, you first come to **Marina Del Rey**, the largest man-made marina in the world, and then to the beach community of **Venice**, a bohemian hang-out on the beach. When LA people let it all hang out, this is where it hangs. Moving along, you come to **Santa Monica**, also called Soviet Monica for its liberal leanings. This area is a pleasant beach community with a large British population.

Malibu Beach is about a 25 min drive N from here along the Pacific Coast Hwy. Moving inland from Santa Monica along **Sunset Blvd** you come to **Westwood**, home of UCLA. Further along Sunset, in **Beverly Hills**, the feeling is decidedly posh, and anything but collegiate.

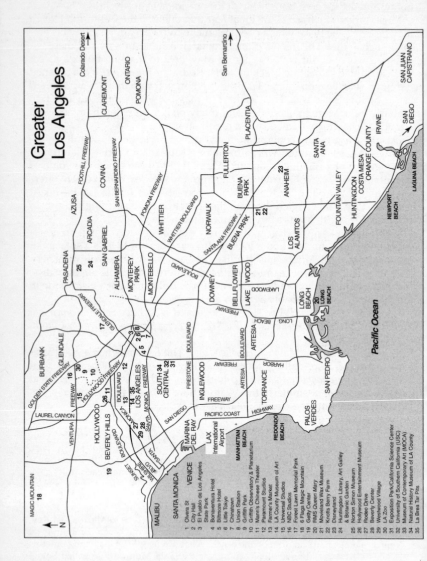

Greater Los Angeles

1 Olvera St
2 City Hall
3 El Pueblo de Los Angeles State Park
4 Bonaventure Hotel
5 Biltmore Hotel
6 Little Tokyo
7 Chinatown
8 Union Station
9 Griffith Park
10 Griffith Observatory & Planetarium
11 Mann's Chinese Theater
12 Paramount Studios
13 Farmer's Market
14 LA County Museum of Art
15 Universal Studios
16 NBC Studios
17 Forest Lawn Memorial Park
18 6 Flags Magic Mountain
19 Getty Center
20 RMS Queen Mary
21 Movieland Wax Museum
22 Knotts Berry Farm
23 Disneyland
24 Huntington Library, Art Gallery & Botanic Garden
25 Norton Simon Museum
26 Hollywood Entertainment Museum
27 Rodeo Drive
28 Beverly Center
29 Westwood Village
30 LA Zoo
31 Exposition Park/California Science Center
32 University of Southern California (USC)
33 Museum of Contemporary Art (MOCA)
34 Natural History Museum of LA County
35 La Brea Tar Pits

Sunset passes through Beverly Hills and **Hollywood** and into **Downtown**. Below Hollywood is the **Melrose/West Hollywood** area, the cutting edge of LA chic. Hopping over the Hollywood Hills to the north, you enter **North Hollywood** and the **San Fernando Valley**. The TV and movie studios are located in Burbank and the North Hollywood area.

If you arrive by train or bus you will come into downtown. By bus it is possible to arrive at Santa Monica, Hollywood, Pasadena, Glendale and North Hollywood stations, but by train you have no other choice. Of course, LA is a tough city in places, particularly Downtown and East LA—'Never go near, especially at night.' Sticking to the West Side—Beverly Hills, Westwood and parts of Hollywood—is generally safe.

ACCOMMODATION

Getting around LA can be a battle, so you should choose lodging near where you will want to spend the most time. Beverly Hills, Westwood, and the West Side are centrally located to many sights. Do not stay downtown just because it sounds as though all the sites are there. They're not. Downtown has many cheap lodgings, but unless you want a concentrated urban and ethnic mix with some artistic trappings, you'll be better off elsewhere.

Downtown: (close to Union Train Station/bus station):

Motel de Ville, 1123 W 7th St, (213) 624-8474. S-$42, D-$47, $2 daily discount w/student ID if you stay 4 nights or longer. TV, AC, pool. Busy street. 'Good value.' 'Terrible area.' 'Don't hesitate to bargain.'

Orchid Hotel, 819 S Flower St, (213) 624-5855. In the heart of downtown. S-$38, D-$43, T-$45. 'Gave us a student discount (15%). Bargain breakfast at the Gaslighter Restaurant.' 'Not a good area at night.'

Beverly Hills/Hollywood/West Side: (close to entertainment, shopping, movie sites):

Banana Bungalow, 2775 Cahuenga Blvd, W Hollywood, 1-800-4-HOSTEL. Resort-style facility. TV, bath, gym, pool, store, restaurant. Theatre w/free nightly videos. $38 LA city tour arranged from hostel/other trips including Hollywood, Universal Studios etc. 'Quite hard to find.' $16 shuttle to airport. 'Fantastic.' $20 mixed dorm, D-$55-75.

Hollywood International Hostel, 6820 Hollywood Blvd (across from Chinese Theater), (800) 750-6561. TV room, kitchen, linen, free coffee, arcade, pool table. 3-4 bed dorms, $16. $98 weekly. Private rooms D-$35-37. No curfew, organised parties. Call for free rides from LAX airport/Amtrak/Greyhound. Tours offered to Disneyland, Magic Mountain and Universal Studios. 'Dubious rsvs system.' 'Most modern, clean and airy hostel we stayed in. Easy access to sights, bus routes etc.'

Hollywood Vine Motel, 1133 Vine St, near Santa Monica Blvd, (323) 466-7501. From $35. 'Friendly and near to Hollywood Greyhound.'

Student Inn International Hostel, 7038 Hollywood Blvd, (800) 557-7038. All rooms en suite, hot showers, complete kitchen, BBQ parties, free pickup. Call for rsvs. $15 in 2/4 bedded rm. Kitchen and free bfast. Free tkts and tours.

The Valley : El Patio Motel, 11466 Ventura Blvd, corner of Tujunga, near studios, (818) 760-9602. S/D-$59-74.

Airport and South Coast: Hostel California, 2221 Lincoln Blvd, (310) 305-0250. Closest hostel to the airport. $14-17 plus $5 deposit, private rooms $40, passport req. 24 hrs. Free pick-up from LAX.

Backpackers Paradise at Adventurers Hotel, 4200 West Century Blvd, Inglewood, (800) 852-0012. Dorms $14, D-$45, $32 for BUNAC members, includes free morning bfast java and muffin. Shuttle to and from airport, Greyhound and Amtrak and organised trips to places of interest. 'Excellent.' 'Mixed area, fun place.' Pool.

Colonial Inn Hostel, 421 8th St, Huntington Beach, about 20 miles S of airport, (714) 536-3315. From airport take the #232 bus to the Long Beach Transit Center, board the #1/1A to 8th St. Not far from the Huntington Beach Pier, Laguna Beach Art Colony, Sawdust art festival and barbecue and beach parties! Run by a self-described 'funky old lady having a good time.' TV, nice garden and porch, kitchen etc. $16.50 dorm, D-$18.70 pp. 'Telephone rsvs made but we were disappointed on arrival.' 'Full of Aussie surfers. Bit awkward to get to on public transport.'

Hacienda Hotel, 525 N Sepulveda Blvd, El Segundo 90245, (800) 262-1314. 'Expensive but safe, excellent facilities—ensuite bathrooms, TV, swimming pool. Most important factor is the free shuttle to LA Airport. S- $75, D-$81.'

HI-Hostel LA South Bay, 3601 S Gaffey St, # 613, San Pedro, (310) 831-8109. Take # 446 bus to Korean Bell from 6th and Los Angeles Sts. Last bus leaves downtown at 2.45pm. This seaside hostel has a panoramic view of the Pacific Ocean and Catalina Island, and features spectacular sunsets. Prime location for whale watching cruises to observe gray whales on their annual Alaska-Baja journey (Christmas to April). 'Clean and friendly.' $11-13.

Santa Monica: HI-Hostel Santa Monica, 1436 2nd St, Santa Monica, CA 90401, (310) 393-9913. Library, kitchen, TV room, open courtyard, laundry, travel store. 2 blocks from beach. Dorms $18-20, D-$59, extra $3 for non-AYH members per night 'Fantastic facilities, but too many rules.' Call hostel upon arrival for shuttle pick-up from airport (first two people free, others $10) or take Parking lot C free airport bus to the Santa Monica Big Blue Bus stand, Blue Bus is 50c. MTA bus #33 from downtown. Reservations advised during summer.

Venice Beach : Cadillac Hotel, 401 Ocean Front Walk, Venice Beach, (310) 399-8876. S/D-$69, w/private bath, dorm $25. Gym, sauna, laundry and sun deck. Will pickup from airport. 'Really friendly.'

Share-Tel International Hostel, 20 Brooks Ave, (310) 392-0325. $17 p/night, $110 p/wk, includes free breakfast, and dinner Mon-Fri. Show passport or student ID. Kitchen, linen, no curfew, safe area, 'a bit dirty'.

Venice Beach Cotel, 25 Windward Ave, Venice, (310) 399-7649. Private rooms from $35, dorm from $13, $5 key deposit, lockers, trips and tours available. On the beach, own bar. 'Great. Very clean and super friendly/helpful staff.' Airport shuttle $7.

Venice Beach Hostel, 701 Washington Blvd, cross with Oxford, (310) 306-5180. Take bus #33 from Spring St near Greyhound terminal as well as Bus Plaza at Union Station, $1.50. Dorms $14, D-36, includes breakfast, a relaxed atmosphere. Kitchen, lounge, sundeck. 'Very sociable hostel but not for those who need privacy.' 'Staff have lots of info on what to do in LA, just ask.' 'Sharing bathroom with at least 14 people!' Walking distance to beach, bars, restaurants and nightclubs. Bike rental.

Venice Marina Hostel, 2915 Yale Ave, Marina Del Rey, (310) 301-3983. Dorms- $14, $91 weekly, D-$36, includes breakfast. Kitchen, lockers, laundry, internet, pool tables, rollerblade / bike rental, near beach. Free pick up from airport. 'Best place I stayed!'

Near Disneyland: Anaheim Inn, 1630 S Harbour Blvd (1 block S of Hwy 5), (714) 774-1050. 'Good location, just across Disneyland Theme park. Free transportation to and from hotel.' $65-$105, up to 5 people.

HI-Hostel Fullerton, 1700 North Harbour Blvd, Fullerton, (714) 738-3721. Closest hostel to Disneyland (5 miles N; 15 min drive). Hostel is situated in Brea Dam Park with a picnic area and golf driving range. Quiet, restful place to relax while in LA area. Kitchen, linen rental $1, tours available. Dorms $12.50.Take the 'Golden Star' or 'Airway' super-shuttles from airport to the door, $18.

FOOD

The greater LA area has over 25,000 eating establishments. Does this city love to eat out, or what? In fact, during the 1982 recession, people in Los Angeles ate out more often than they had before the downturn. One reason for this obsession may be the mobile lifestyle, and the rich mix of ethnic cultures. Don't be surprised to find kosher burritos, Thai Tacos and more. Share the scoop on the best (and worst!) eats and drinks by searching **Bars and Clubs Message Boards** online at *la.yahoo.com/Entertainment_and_Arts/Restaurants/*

Downtown: Cassell's, 3266 W 6th St, (213) 480-8668. Beautiful hamburgers but too crowded any time after noon, cafeteria-style dining. Closed Sun.

Cole's PE Buffet, 118 E 6th St, (213) 622-4090. Oldest restaurant and saloon in LA since 1908. 'Atmosphere hole-in-the-wall cafeteria.' Try the house speciality French dip, a west coast sandwich. Closed Sun.

Clifton's Cafeterias, 648 S Broadway, (213) 627-1673; 515 W 7th St, (213) 485-1726. Vast array of cheap dishes ($6-7), soothing decor from a redwood forest with real waterfall to the Art Deco touches at 7th St. Daily 7am-7pm.

Dupar's, 6333 W 3rd St at the Farmer's Market (also at 12036 Ventura Blvd), (323) 933-8446. Old-style coffee shop specialising in savory pot pies and desert pies, legend bfast pancakes, with the option of buying batter ready to take home!

El Tepayac, 812 N Evergreen, (323) 268-1960, is home to the *Manuel Special*, an enormous burrito requiring two people to finish. This barrio hang-out draws an unusual mix of police, locals and Mexico food junkies. 6am-9.45pm. Closed Tues. Meals around $8 'til 11pm Fri & Sat.

Kosher Burrito, 110 E 1st St, (213) 626-0998, cleanest burritos in town, $3! Daily 7am-4pm.

La Luz Del Dia, 107 Pasedo de la Plaza (next to the Bank of America Building, 600 N Main St), (213) 628-7495. Mexican food mecca. Cheapest deal going ($8.50 and under). Tues Fri 11am-9pm, later at w/ends.

Mandarin Deli, 727 N Broadway in Chinatown (in the food center), (213) 623-6054. You know its authentic because no-one here speaks English! Try the *jiao tzi* (fried dumplings), $5 for eight pieces. Daily 11am-9pm.

Maurice's Snack N Chat, 5549 Pico Blvd, (213) 931-3877. Friendly, unpretentious soul-food landmark where Hollywood celebrities rub elbows with ordinary Angelenos. Fried chicken and pan-fried fish meals vary btwn $10 and $25. Rsvs req.

Pantry Cafe, 877 S Figueroa, (213) 972-9279. Huge helpings of basic meat and potatoes fare for less than $12. The Pantry is famous, not for its food, but because it is so unassuming and has been here forever. An anomaly in trendy LA. 24hrs.

Pho Hoa, 640 N Broadway, (213) 626-5530. 'Good Vietnamese restaurant. Large portions, reasonably priced, average $6.' Daily 7am-7pm.

Pink's Chili Dogs, 709 N La Brea Ave, (213) 931-4223. Bfast, lunch and dinner served. Experiment with the Guadalajara dog, cheese dogs, dogs wrapped in tortillas and chopped dogs in a cup of baked beans. Daily 9.30am-2am, Fri/Sat 3am.

West Side: Apple Pan, 10801 W Pico Blvd, (310) 475-3585. Unassuming burger $5 and apple pie $2.50. Great food with the locals lining up behind the counter stools (no tables) waiting for a spot at the trough! Tues-Sun 11am-12 am.

Barney's Beanery, 8447 Santa Monica Blvd, (323) 654-2287. Things haven't changed too much since Janis Joplin used to hang out here. The pool tables still need new felt, the vinyl in the booths is still bright, and the action at the bar is still pretty fierce. Excellent chili $6. A great place to meet locals, daily 10am-2 am.

Canter's Deli, 419 N Fairfax, (323) 651-2030, 24hrs. In LA's old Jewish section close to CBS Television City. There is no better deli or bakery in town, especially at 3 am; recently awarded 'Best Pastrami in Town' by *LA Times*. 24 hours.

CC Brown's Hot Fudge Shop, on Hollywood Blvd near Mann's Chinese Theater, (213) 464-7062. Pressed tin roof, dark-wood booths, this ice cream store takes you back to the days when ice cream was still made by hand. Claims to be the originator of the hot fudge sundae $5.50. Daily 1pm-10pm; closed Sun.

Dolores' West Restaurant, 11407 Santa Monica Blvd at Purdue, (310) 477-1061. 24 hr old-fashioned burger joint. Bottomless coke and the renowned JJ Burger, $4.50

Ed Debevic's, 134 N La Cienega at Wilshire, (310) 659-1952. '50s-dressed staff dance on tables—totally wild.' Daily 11.30-10pm, Fri & Sat 'til midnight, Sun 'til 10pm. Everything under $8, meatloaf $7.

Musso And Franks, 6667 Hollywood Blvd, (323) 467-5123. This old bar and grill dates from 1919 and is the oldest restaurant in Hollywood. Once a haunt of

Fitzgerald, Hemingway and Faulkner it is now a regular for film industry types. It offers a touch of the golden era of Hollywood elegance at prices that match ($20-$30). Closed Sun & Mon.

Nate 'n' Al's, 414 N Beverly Dr, (310) 274-0101. The Beverly Hills power schmooze takes place here early in the am. $5-$15. Daily 7.30am-9pm.

Tail O' the Pup, 329 N San Vicente at Beverly, (310) 652-4517. A hot-dog shaped stand complete with bright yellow mustard oozing out of the sides! $2-$3. Daily.

The Valley: Dupar's, 12036 Ventura Blvd (also at 6333 W 3rd St), (818) 766-4437, great pies and one of the best coffee shops in town. Coffee $1, pies $2.50. 'This is a real hang-out late on a Friday or Saturday.' Open 'til 1 am.

Along the Beach: Alice's Restaurant, Malibu Pier, 23000 Pacific Coast Hwy, (310) 392-1660. Right on the beach. Good place to stop for brunch or dinner on a trip up the coast to Malibu. Seafood under $20. Daily 11.30am-11pm.

Patrick's Roadhouse, 106 Entrada just off Corner of Pac Coast Hwy and Entrada Dr (across the street from Will Rogers State Beach), (310) 459-4544. Mon-Fri 8am-3pm; 'til 4pm w/ends. Make rsvs for w/ends. Where Arnie had his bachelor party, and where everybody who's anybody comes to feed. 'Good homemade fish and chips.'

Venice: Rose Cafe and Deli, 220 Rose Ave in Venice, (310) 399-0711. Pretty place serving healthy food to beautiful people. Visitors are greeted by a mural of a bright red rose. Daily 7.30am-10pm, Sunday brunch 8am-3pm $7. Reasonable prices.

Santa Monica: Many good places to eat along the 3rd Street Promenade, outdoor tables etc. One of the best is **Broadway Deli**, 1547 3rd Street Promenade, (310) 451-0616, entrees around $15.

La Sirena 101 Broadway (corner with Ocean, overlooking the Pacific) (310) 260-1100. Happy hour with tons of nachos , cheap drinks, 5-7 Mon-Fri.

Wildflour Pizza, 2807 Main St in Santa Monica, (310) 392-3300. *LA Times* says its the best pie in town. Daily 11am-10.30pm, Sun from noon.

Ye Olde King's Head Pub, 116 Santa Monica Blvd, (310) 451-1402, a real ghetto for expatriate Brits, complete with darts, chips, everything!

OF INTEREST

For convenience, sites have been grouped geographically. It would be wise to plan day trips around one important site, rather than, say, attempt to get from Universal Studios to Disneyland, 2 hrs away by car, in one day. The MTA has an excellent self-guided tour booklet for people using the bus. *La Weekly*, the weekly events calendar, is the online source to check for cafes, clubs and comedy, *la.yahoo.com/external/laweekly/index.html/*

Downtown: Despite rumours to the contrary, downtown LA does exist. In fact, film producers use it as a double for Manhattan. Old and graceful structures survive, especially around the beautiful **Pershing Square Park**, but the area is dominated by soaring skyscrapers. To get oriented take DASH, (800) COMMUTE or (213) 626-4455, a bus system which covers all of downtown, 25c each time you board.

City Hall, 200 Spring St was 'til quite recently the tallest building in LA. It features an eclectic style of Babylonian and Byzantine architecture, and has an observation deck on the 27th floor. The **Los Angeles Times Building** (213) 237-5757 is across the street and offers free tours at 11.15 am on w/days. You can see the editorial offices, press and production rooms of this major newspaper. You'll also get a free replica of the first edition in 1881. Just a few blocks from City Hall around First and San Pedro Sts, is **Little Tokyo**, a bustling area which has grown like mad in the last few years. LA has had an important Japanese community since the 1880s, although they were unconstitutionally rounded up during WWII and herded into camps. The community has rebuilt since that shattering experience. This is a good place to walk around. Be sure to visit the **Japanese American Cultural And Community Center gardens**, 244 S San Pedro, the koi pool at the **New Otani Hotel** and the many Japanese speciality shops. Walking along Broadway away from Little Tokyo towards **Pershing Square**, you would think you were in Mexico. This bustling Hispanic area becomes the garment and diamond districts near 7th St. If you turn west on 5th St off Broadway you come to Pershing Square—a graceful park in the middle of downtown. On the site of an Indian (later Spanish) trail, the **Biltmore Hotel**, 506 S Grand, is the square's most charming and sumptuous hotel complete with a fountain and wood-beamed ceiling in the Spanish-style entrance. JFK stayed in the $2400-a-day suite when he won the Democratic presidential nomination in 1960. A graceful architectural counterbalance to the skyscrapers is the Byzantine style **Los Angeles Central Library**, 630 W 5th St btwn Flores and Grand Ave, (213) 612-3200. Mon, Thur, Fri, Sat 10am-5.30pm, Tues & Wed noon-8pm, Sun 'til 5pm.

Each of the enormous skyscrapers surrounding the Library—the **Arco Towers**, the **Citicorp Center**, and the **Bonaventure Hotel**—are small cities in themselves. They house underground shopping, parking and restaurants and are connected to one another by skywalks and underground passages. LA was the first city in the country to develop the concept of such skyscrapers, that function as self-contained shopping, entertainment and office complexes. The idea fits LA well, for it provides a centralized environment in a very decentralized city. The Bonaventure in particular offers a stunning atrium and impressive glass elevators that whisk you along the outside of the building to a restaurant at the top. On clear days the view is remarkable.

Hop on the DASH bus, or walk north along Broadway to get to **Chinatown and Olvera St**. Just off Main St, in the preserved Olvera St area, is the original Spanish settlement of Los Angeles, now the **El Pueblo de Los Angeles State Historic Park**, (213) 628-7164. The small original Mexican settlement lead by Felipe de Neve adopted that big name of El Pueblo de La Reina de Los Angeles de Porciuncula. Olvera St, and the **Iglesia de Nuestra Senora** across the street are the oldest and most colourful reminders of LA's Spanish roots. This is a good area to have a Mexican lunch (try **La Luz Del Dia**) and to shop among the colourful Mexican and Central American stalls. Since the Spanish-style **Union Train Station** is nearby on Alameda St, you may want to save Olvera St 'til your last day in LA. Walk up Main St to Ord and head left to Broadway, and Mexico gives way to China, and **Chinatown**—not as classy as Little Tokyo, but full of good places to eat. The street life is a bit more old-fashioned here. Between crates of live chickens stacked helter skelter on the sidewalk, merchants still hold live birds upside down while old Chinese women poke the breast bones to check for tenderness. Your best orientation to the rest of LA is to take **Sunset Blvd** west away from Downtown (RTD #2). Beginning in El Pueblo Park, Sunset shoots out towards Hollywood, banks in to the **Sunset Strip**, wends through the posh areas of **Beverly Hills** and **Bel Air**, and finally dips down to the Ocean. Sunset Blvd cuts a grand path through LA's many attractions. It is central to the city, and indeed, people measure their success in life by whether or not they have managed to acquire a home on the fashionable 'North Side' of 'The Boulevard.'

Hollywood: At Sunset and Los Feliz Blvd, head north to **Griffith Park**. The largest city park in America, Griffith offers trails, bridle paths, a zoo, the Greek Theater, three golf courses, and an observatory and planetarium. Performances in the Greek Theater from June through September; for info call *Ticketmaster* (213) 480-3232. The park observatory is free, and the 65' long, 12' wide refractor telescope is open to the public, from sundown 'til 9.50pm. The ocean breeze generally blows the smog away, and visibility is good. There is also a free **Hall of Science**, a **Planetarium**, $4, (323) 664-1191, featuring shows about different topics in astronomy, and **Laserium**, $7-8, (818) 901 9405, lasers set to rock music. For astronomical info dial Sky Report, (323) 663-8171. From the Planetarium you will not need a telescope to see the famous Hollywood Sign. The 50 foot letters were built by a real estate developer, and originally spelled out *Hollywoodland*, the name of his development. Not far from the observatory you'll find the stars are on the street along **Hollywood Blvd**. Over 2500 names of stars are laid into the terrazzo sidewalk above bronze symbols of microphones, cameras, television sets or records denoting the craft which brought them fame. Do not expect Hollywood to glitter as brightly as her sidewalks. The area has been a somewhat shabby, red-light district since the 50's. Children who run away from home for the glamour of Hollywood are often suckered into prostitution and worse. The Art Deco **Pantages Theater**, recalls the glamour of by-gone days. Built in 1929, the Pantages for many years housed the Academy Awards, and today draws many Broadway musicals. **Fredericks of Hollywood**, 6608 Hollywood Blvd, (323) 466-8506, is LA's original, and uninhibited, sexual image-maker. Mon-Thur 10am-8pm, Fri 'til 9pm, Sat 'til 6pm, Sun noon-6pm. Free museum.

The most popular Hollywood attraction is **Mann's Chinese Theater**, 6925 Hollywood Blvd, (323) 464-8111. The theatre opened in 1927 with the premiere of DeMille's *King of Kings*, and was christened by Norma Talmage who accidentally stepped in wet cement that night, the birth of a Hollywood tradition. Some of the world's most famous anatomy is imprinted here, including Michael Jackson, Donald Duck, R2-D2, Trigger and Marilyn Monroe. The building itself is a strange blend of Polynesian and Chinese Imperial architecture. Mann's offers one of the best sound systems, and largest screens in LA. Mon-Fri from 11 am, $8.50, $5.50 w/student ID. Just steps from Mann's is **Hollywood Entertainment Museum**, 7021 Hollywood Blvd, (323) 465-7900, daily 11am-6pm except Weds, $7.50, $5.50 w/student ID. A state-of-the-art museum featuring original sets and a collection of famous Hollywood memorabilia. Experience behind-the-scenes 'magic' as you create sound effects, record in the recording studio and edit film in the editing suite. Hollywood offers several other architectural styles than the bizarre Chinese at Mann's. Frank Lloyd Wright designed two homes near here—**Hollyhock House**, (323) 662-7272, open to the public, and **Sowden House**. **Hollywood Bowl**, 2301 N Highland Ave, a large ampitheatre with near-perfect acoustics. The bowl hosts major jazz, classical and rock concerts. Call *Ticketmaster* on (213) 480-3232 for tkts. Mon-Fri 8am-9pm, Sat-Sun 9am-7pm.

Off Hollywood, on Vine St is the **Capitol Records** office, designed to look like a stack of 45s with a huge 92' needle on top. The red beacon on the needle spells out Hollywood in morse code. After leaving Hollywood, but just before Beverly Hills, Sunset Blvd banks into the famous **Sunset Strip**—an exciting night spot lined with inventive, hand-painted billboards, and the best rock clubs in LA. At the other end of the frenzied Sunset Strip, Beverly Hills is as calm as a bank vault on Sunday. Everyone who has seen *Beverly Hills Cop* knows how rich and bizarre the residents are here. Actually, there are more attorneys and businessmen than Arabs, movie stars and drug lords. **Rodeo Drive** (pronounced Row-DAY-o) near Wilshire Blvd is the most expensive retail strip in the world. The Gucci side is the most fashionable. If you want to see the nearby homes of the stars—Gene Kelly lived at 725 Rodeo, Carl Reiner at 714—you'll need to rent a car, take the bus or a mainstream coach tour. Don't bother buying a 'Map of the Star's Homes' from the street vendors— many are inaccurate and out of date, and you rarely can get close to the properties anyway.

For a more affordable shopping experience head to the massive **Beverly Center**, corner 3rd and La Cienega. Next to the center, the Cadillac sticking out of the roof marks the spot of the **Hard Rock Cafe**. Be sure and stop in at the **Beverly Hills Hotel**. The bright pink decor is hard to miss. The film industry does its business at the Hotel bar called the Polo Lounge. Bring your wallet and don't forget to have yourself paged. Sunset continues on past the Polo Lounge along the northern edge of **Westwood Village** and **UCLA**. Tucked in with the campus, Westwood Village is a huge and handsome mall, one of LA's few walking districts, and chockful of cinemas, shops, street buskers and socialising places. 'Fri and Sat nights are like a circus with sword-swallowers, dancers, musicians, and even fortune-telling cats!' Celebs also frequent Westwood. The campus area is a live party spot. 'Frat parties along Gayley from 21 Sept on. Free beer, spirits, food, entertainment and the best-looking women in the world.' 'On a quieter note, **Westwood Village Cemetery**, 1218 Glendon, has the most visited grave in LA, that of Marilyn Monroe; Natalie Wood is also buried here. Continuing past Westwood, Sunset winds through miles of exclusive **Pacific Palisades** real estate (Ronald Reagan lived here) finally reaching Pacific Coast Hwy just above Santa Monica.

The Valley: Made famous by the song *Valley Girl*, (sung by Frank and Moon Zappa) the **San Fernando Valley** is really like a totally coooool bedroom community for like kids who drive really bitchen Camaros. The shopping is like totally excellent at the **Sherman Oaks Galleria**, just er... over the hill from Westwood. The most totally kickin' part of the valley fer shur is near the studios in the North Hollywood area. Other than like, those, the major sites are like the **LA Zoo** in **Glendale**, and the famous **Forest Lawn Memorial Park**, 1712 S Glendale Ave, Glendale, (323) 254-7251, (its like totally freakin' an' fulla dead folks!). Also friendly branches in the Hollywood Hills, near Artesia and in West Covina, each with its own artwork, patriotic themes and style. This is the American way of death as depicted in Evelyn Waugh's *The Loved One*: odourless, spotless, artistically uplifting, almost fun, at least for the survivors. It's hard to keep from giggling at the crass wonder of it all, from repros of the Greatest Hits of Michelangelo and Leonardo da Vinci to the comic-book approach on the 'Life of Jesus' mosaics. Take a copy of Ken Schessler's *This is Hollywood* along (but keep it out of sight—park officials won't allow the book on the grounds) to find where the notables are planted. Free, daily 8am-5pm.

Museums and art galleries:
Downtown: **Exposition Park**, corner of Exposition & Figueroa Blvds. Built in the early 1900s and houses LA's oldest museums and a beautiful rose garden.
LACE, Los Angeles Contemporary Exhibitions, 6522 Hollywood Blvd, (323) 957-1777, is devoted to artists who are still alive. The primary alternative space to the burgeoning traditional museum scene, LACE offers everything from performance art to video art, for free. If there is an avant-garde in LA, it stays one step ahead by coming here.
California Science Center, 700 State Drive, Exposition Park (323) SCIENCE, contains Creative World, World of Life, and Science Plaza exhibitions, many hands-on exhibits. Daily 10am-5pm. Admission is free, except for the IMAX theatre, call for show times. (213) 744-2014. Last film usually around 8pm. $7.50 3D , $6.50 2D films.
Natural History Museum of LA County, 900 Exposition Blvd (213) 763-DINO. Main exhibits include 'battling dinosaurs,' habitat halls with stuffed animals placed in natural settings, and the American History Halls covering the Revolutionary War to 1914. Also impressive are the California and Southwest History Halls and the Pre-Columbian—Meso American Hall covering Maya, Inca, and other civilisations. The Hall of Gems and Minerals includes the 102-karat Ashberg Diamond, thought to have been a part of the Russian crown jewels. 10am-5pm Tue-Sun. $8, $5.50 w/student ID. Nearby is the **Coliseum**, site of the 1932 and 1984 Olympics, and **USC**. Best known for its football team, USC is affectionately called the University of Spoiled Children, although its real name is the University of Southern California.
MOCA, Museum of Contemporary Art, 250 S Grand Ave btwn 2nd and 4th, (213) 62-MOCA-2. Famous Japanese architect Arata Isozaki designed this newest museum on the LA scene. The building itself is a work of art, integrating primary shapes into abstract patterns. The prime materials are rough finished red sandstone, gray granite and green panelling with a pink diamond pattern. The trim is in

polished granite. Most impressive is the large polished onyx gable window above the ticket booth. The collection includes many modern artists from the 1940s to the present—Louise Nevelson, Robert Rauschenberg, David Hockney and others. Thur 11am-8pm; 'til 5pm other days. $6, $4 w/student ID. Thurs after 5pm is free. Closed Mon. MOCA's second building is the **Temporary Contemporary**, 152 N Central Ave. Tkts can be used for both buildings on the same day.

West Side: Los Angeles County Museum of Art, mercifully abbreviated to **LACMA**, 5905 Wilshire Blvd, (323) 857-6111. LACMA has grown impressively in the last few years. A recent building houses the collection of 20th century works by Picasso, Braque and Matisse. The older Armand Hammer Building houses an impressive collection of Far Eastern works. Every day noon- 8pm except Fri till 9pm and Wed closed. LA has been developing the good sense to look west, to Japan and Asia for its artistic inspiration. The proof is found in the new **Pavilion for Japanese Art** which opened in mid-1988. The pavilion houses the Shin'enkan collection of Edo period screens and scrolls. Widely regarded as the most outstanding collection of its kind, the 32,100-square-foot pavilion instantly became a world-class centre for Japanese art. $7, $5 w/student ID, free first Tues of the month.

La Brea Tar Pits are nearby. An ancient source of natural tar, the pits were often covered with a light layer of dust and water. Ice Age animals seeking water became ensnared in the tar and their bones were preserved for history, making the Tar Pits the single richest fossil find in the world. The **George C. Page Museum of La Brea Discoveries**, 5801 Wilshire Blvd, (323) 934-PAGE, exhibits of fossils in atrium. Open pit to watch excavating in summer months. Still millions of fossils. 9.30am-5pm Wkdys, 10-5 wknds, $6, $3.50 w/student ID.

Santa Monica: The Getty Center, 1200 Getty Center Drive, (310) 440-7300. The museum is free, but if you're driving there is a $5 parking fee, and you should reserve your space in advance. Metro bus #561 and Santa Monica Big Blue Bus #14 stop at the entrance. Tues/Wed 11am-7pm, Thu/Fri 11am-9pm, Sat/Sun 10am-6pm, closed Mon. Collection of high quality art, from Greek and Roman sculpture, impressionists and photography, housed in a fantastic new building and with spectacular views of the city. The **Getty Villa**, Malibu, is due to reopen in 2001.

Pasadena: Huntington Library, Art Gallery and Botanical Gardens, 1151 Oxford Rd in San Marino, (626) 405-2275. An impressive and well-housed collection of Gainsborough and Guttenburgs. Summer—Tues-Sun 10.30am-4.40pm, winter—Tues-Fri 12am-4.30pm, Sat/Sun 10.30am-4.30pm, closed Mon. $8.50, $5 w/ student ID. Free 1st Thu of the month. English tea is offered Tues-Fri 12am-4pm in the Rose Garden, $11 for limitless buffet, call (626) 683-8131 for rsvs. 'The gardens are mind-blowing.'

The Norton Simon Museum of Art, 411 W Colorado Blvd, corner with Orange,(626) 449 6840. The worst day in the history of the LACMA was the day that Norton Simon got mad and decided to take his ball and go and start his own game. Simon had been on the museum's board, but decided to open his own museum in Pasadena. Simon's extensive collection includes Degas and Rodin (the *Burgers of Calais*) and a garden graced by Henry Moore's sculptures arranged along a fountain. $4, w/student ID $2. Thur-Sun noon-6pm.

Amusement Parks (plus tips):
Best to go in **off-season** (as it is cheaper and less crowded), or on a **school day**, or when everyone else is somewhere else, e.g. watching the Superbowl, shopping. **Arrive early** before gates open. Check for **discounts**.

Disneyland, 1313 S Harbor Blvd, Anaheim, (714) 781-4560. Call for opening hours. This is the original **Magic Kingdom** and the culmination of Walt Disney's dream. Disney designed the 57 attractions to provide wholesome entertainment for adults & children in this flawlessly clean park. Attractions are grouped into 7 theme parks: you enter the park through Main Street, a re-creation of an old American town. New Orleans Square houses one of the most elaborate rides, the *Pirates of the Caribbean*. Adventureland is devoted to the explorer spirit of African safaris. Fantasyland recreates the magic of the animation classics; the entrance is through Sleeping Beauty's castle, right next to the Matterhorn roller coaster. In Frontierland, you can journey through the old west on an incredible mining train roller coaster. A visionary himself, Disney took special interest in the future. You can do this at Tomorrowland, which includes the legendary Space Mountain roller coaster, the 3-D *Captain EO*, starring Michael Jackson; Star Tours, the original motion simulator set to a *Star Wars* theme; and newer delights such as *Indiana Jones Adventure: The Temple of the Forbidden Eye*. Aboard jeeps, fearless wannabes can revisit the perils of the Indiana Jones movies, evading serpents, spiders and explosions! Finally, Critter Country features the popular *Splash Mountain*, a water flume attraction themed around *Song of the South* adventures.

There is year-round entertainment (e.g. Big bands, the Videopolis Dance Club) but the Electric Light Parade (9pm) with hundreds of light-bedecked floats and fireworks, is only available summer evenings. Since all this is available for the $39 admission fee ($73 for 2-day pass, $99 for 3-day), you really have to ask yourself why you should see any of the other parks in town. 'Get there as early as possible. Lines for good rides become enormous by noon.' 'Avoid Saturday!' 'Take a full day.' 'Don't miss the parade of Disney Characters.' 'Don't leave luggage at Greyhound—station closes at 9pm, Disneyland at midnight.' 'Tomorrowland is best—see it first.' 'Don't miss *America the Beautiful* 360-degree film.' For transport, try MTA, (213) 626-4455, from downtown (2hrs): take #460 E on 6th—$3.35 (runs as late as 1.20 am in summer); local Orange County Transit (OCTD), (714) 636-7433 from Greyhound terminal at corner of Harbor and Orange Wood, #43 on Harbor, every 15 min, and various other routes; and Greyhound—Anaheim, 999-1256/(800) 231-2222, $7 o/w weekdays, $8 wknds, $14/15 rtn.

Knott's Berry Farm, 8039 Beach Blvd, Buena Park, (714) 220-5200. Call for opening hours. The gift shops outnumber the rides and attractions 10 to 1 but its Montezooma's Revenge (with 360-degree upside-down loops) is nauseatingly effective, allowing you to meet yourself (and possibly your lunch) coming back. 'Hurts, but must be tried.' Rides include The Boomerang, a 54 second reverse looping roller coaster; XK-1, where you are launched as from an aircraft-carrier and you do the steering in a cockpit seven stories up; the Whirlpool, an indoor ride with sound and light show; the Ghostrider, and the Bigfoot Rapids. Great waterworks show at lake. Lots of special celebrations, rock concerts, discount promotions. Check the papers. $36, or $16.95 after 4pm. Only 20 mins to Disneyland.

Movieland Wax Museum, 7711 Beach Blvd, Buena Park, 1 block N of Knott's, (714) 522-1154. Go see 200-plus movie and TV stars captured (not always successfully) in wax. The big event is the Chamber of Horrors, based on 13 scary movies, including *American Werewolf in London*, *Dracula*, *The Exorcist* and *Psycho*. Here you can also be fooled by moviestar look-alikes of Clint Eastwood, Michael Jackson, Marilyn Monroe, Bette Davis. Box office Mon-Fri 10am-6pm, wknds 9am-7pm, $12.95.

RMS Queen Mary, (562) 435-3511. On Pier J, Long Beach, #7 at south end of Long Beach Freeway. Daily 10am-6pm; $15.

Six Flags Magic Mountain, Valencia, N of LA, (805) 255-4111. $36, open 10am-10pm. Alton Towers has nothing on this place. Experience some of the biggest rollercoaster rides in the world: The Viper, Collossus, The Revolution and the Ninja are all here. 'Thrilling to the extreme. Also, extreme adventure is in store for those who experience the *Dive Devil*, a 60mph 50ft skydive/bungee jump freefall! 'Arrive early, by the afternoon 2 hr queues are not uncommon.' No outside food or drink allowed.

Universal Studios and Tour, 100 Universal City Plaza, (818) 508-9600. $39 for a 2½ hr tour taken by tram through the 420 acre lot, plus all the usual rides and attractions.

Shows include *Conan the Barbarian*, a *Star Trek* adventure (you'll be in the show), *Jaws* and a 30' King Kong attempting to derail the tram. Tours leave from 9am-7pm summers; varying hours in off-season. Get there early to avoid crowds. 'Get right-hand seat on tram—most scenes, Jaws, etc., to the right.' Catch a tidal wave of action and an ocean of thrills in the more recent attraction *Waterworld*. Or journey deep into the Jurassic Jungle on a turbulent water ride to face a towering T-Rex in *Jurassic Park—The Ride*, where you are thrust into the living, breathing, 3-dimensional world of Jurassic Park. 'Not on a par with Disneyland.' 'Better than Disneyland.' Take MTA # 424 from downtown heading north on Broadway. Near Universal is the 18-theater **Cineplex Odeon Universal City Cinema**, (818) 508-0588. If a movie isn't playing there, it isn't playing. Hardcore movie fans will head to **Eddie Brandt's Saturday Matinee**, 5006 Vineland Avenue, North Hollywood, (818) 506-4242 home to 4 million movie stills from $8. Tue-Fri 1pm-6pm, Sat 8.30am-5pm.

The Industry:
What the cognoscente call the movie business. To get a feel for it, read the trade magazines *Hollywood Reporter* and *Variety*. More hands on experience can be gained by hanging out at the Polo Lounge, or Ma Maison Restaurant, but for those without the necessary wallets, TV shows are free, and you can watch them being taped at any of the major studios. Tkts are available from the Visitors Center ('We got tkts to Jay Leno') ; from the TV reps in front of Mann's Chinese Theater in Hollywood; or try calling LA Film and Video Permit Office on (323) 957-1000 for more information about studio tours and location film shooting. For most sitcoms, the best bet is Audiences Unlimited, (818) 506-0043, although beware it can take up to 4 hrs to get one 22 min episode wrapped up.
NBC Studio Tour, 3000 W Alameda, (818) 840-4444. To see a show taped, arrive early at the ticket office on the west side of the NBC complex off California St. Mon-Fri 8am-5pm, 9.30am-4pm on w/ends. For a more low-key, history-oriented walk around the only studio still active in the heart of old Hollywood, there is the **Paramount Studios** tour. Paramount is the last of a string of studios that once lined the corridor along Gower St and Melrose Ave and is a big part of where the industry began. 'A visit to Paramount is an appealing step into both past and present.' $15 walking tour; 2 hr tours leave w/days every half hour 9am-2pm from the studio's pedestrian gate at **5555 Melrose Ave**, (323) 956-1777. Depending on production schedules, you may get a peek at tapings of shows.

Other Attractions
Beverly Hot Springs, 308 North Oxford Ave (north of Beverly Blvd), (323) 734-7000. Separate spas for males and females, each featuring a giant tiled pool filled with piping hot water, a cool pool to calm down in, a steam room perfumed with fresh-cut eucalyptus branches and a dry sauna. The main spa treatment is a 45 min shiatsu massage ($60), the quintessential Japanese acupressure technique; there's a good deal of stretching, tweaking, twisting and even pounding! Daily 9am-9pm.
Descanso Gardens, 1418 Descanso Dr (off Angeles Crest Hwy exit off the 210 Foothill Freeway), (818) 952-4400, $5, $3 w/student ID. Park nestled in 165 acres in the San Rafael Hills in La Canada-Flintridge. 100,000 camelias in 600 varieties fill winding walkways under a grove of ancient Cal live oaks, five-acre rosarium and a canyon filled with ferns, a lake, a bird observation station and a blue-tiled Japanese teahouse, tucked away in a garden of arched bridges and ponds, which serves tea and cookies on w/ends. Daily 9am-4.30pm.

ENTERTAINMENT
The **Sunset Strip**, with new clubs and restaurants opening in the past few years, is once again becoming LA's cultural epicenter and a destination of choice for both visitors and the truly hip residents. The Strip is divided into three loosely defined zones. **Laurel Canyon West** to **La Cienega Blvd** is a largely pedestrian-free stretch

that includes some of the Strip's newer clubs such as the **Bar Marmont, Roxbury, The House of Blues** and Dublin's **Irish Whisky Pub**, a sports bar. West of La Cienega is one of the few enclaves tailored for pedestrian traffic, **Sunset Plaza**; two blocks of upscale open-air cafes. From here, the Strip winds toward **Doheny** where there is an abundancy of commercial take-away eateries. The six blocks here are also home to the last of the area's clubs, the **Viper Room, Roxy, Whiskey** and **Billboard Live.** *BAM*, free monthly paper, lists gigs up and down the West Coast. Also pick up *The Reader* and *LA Weekly*, free, full of entertainment listings. All available at record/bookstores, newstands. New issues on Thursdays.

Anti-Club, 4658 Melrose, (323) 661-3913. Everything from cow-punk, video poetry and South African. Cheap beer.

The World Famous Baked Potato, 3787 Cahuenga Blvd (near Universal), (818) 980-1615. Oldest major contemporary jazz watering hole. Tiny, but Lee Ritenour, Larry Carlton, among others established themselves here. Get there early for enormous spuds stuffed with whatever you want (served 'til 1 am). Showtimes 9.30pm & 11.30pm.

The Palace, 1735 N Vine St, Hollywood (323) 467-4571. Rock out in a restored old theatre; cover under $15.

The Troubadour, 9081 Santa Monica Blvd, (310) 276-1158. Ageing but legendary launching pad for top rock acts; small and smoky. Cover plus 1 drink min, cheaper on Mon hoot nights. Cover from $5 Sun-Thur; Fri-Sat $10.

Whiskey a Go Go, 8901 Sunset Blvd, (310) 652-4202. Cream of rock triumvirate and hang-out of the stars. Cover, naturally, $3-$15. Legendary Sunset Strip club where Jim Morrison and Van Halen have played.

Theatre/Comedy: LA comedy clubs not only feature some of the hottest up-and-coming comedians, they also enjoy routine surprise visits from comedy legends and almost always have entertainment industry types in the audience seeking the next superstar. Cover charges tend to range from $8 -$10, with a two-drink minimum. Besides **The Improv**, 8162 Melrose Ave, (323) 651-2583 and **The Comedy Store**, 8433 Sunset, (323) 656-6225, here are some of the other hot spots:

The Laugh Factory, 8001 Sunset, (323) 656-1336. Hosts industry showcases and special benefits. Legends such as Rodney Dangerfield pop up from time to time.

The Ice House, 24 N Mentor Ave, Pasadena, (626) 577 1894. This place books star-powered headliners who do full, hour-long shows in comparison to the Hollywood-based clubs' 10 min specials.

LA has an enormous number of larger theatres, including the **Mark Taper Forum**, the **Shubert** and **Ahmanson**. The best theatre is often at the small equity-waiver houses where struggling actors hone their skills while waiting for the big break. Check the *Reader* and *Weekly* for listings. Best bets are usually the **Group Repertory** or **Odyssey**.

Los Angeles Theater Center, 514 S Spring, (213) 485-1681. LA's major regional theatre for new playwrights. $14-$23 w/student ID. Tkts (213) 660-TKTS.

Cinema: As you would expect from the world's film capital, there are a lot of movies around town. Westwood is the place where most films premiere. Dial 777-FILM in the 213 and 310 area codes, to find the location and schedule of current movies, and purchase tkts in advance.

The Beverly Cineplex, in Beverly Center, Beverly and La Cienega, (310) 652-7760. 13 theatres featuring popular first-runs as well as art films.

The Nuart, 11272 Santa Monica Blvd, (310) 478-6379. Revival/art house par excellence.

Pacific Cinerama Dome, 6360 Sunset Blvd, (323) 466-3401. This large-screen geodesic dome-shaped theatre housed the premiere of *Apocalypse Now*, among others. Daily 12.30pm. $8.50 admission, $5.00 matinees.

OUT OF DOORS

Catalina Island, 26 miles off Long Beach. A romantic green hideaway, 85% in its natural state. Well worth a trip to see the perfect harbour of Avalon and its delightful vernacular architecture, plus the natural beauties of the place. Snorkelling is best at Lovers Cove, but look out for sharks. 'Beautiful.' Ships cost $36 r/t, depart (daily at 9 am, return 4.30 pm) from Balbon Pavilion. Call Catalina Passenger Service, (949) 673-5245 (Newport). Rsvs req.

Malibu Canyon, just north of Malibu offers one of the most stunning day trips in Los Angeles. Take this canyon road to the Malibu State Creek Park for trails into the rugged Santa Monica Mountains. Campground with hot showers, bathroom, biking/hiking trails. First come, first served, $11-18 per site. Call (800) 444-PARK for hiking and camping information/park info (310) 457-1324.

800-4-JETTIN, 13477 Fiji Way, Marina Del Rey. Rents waverunners in the harbour, from $65/hr. Ring for reservations.

SPORT

Southern California is a paradise for sports lovers. In professional sport you can catch the **Dodgers** baseball team at Dodger Stadium, 1000 Elysian Park Ave (213) 224-1400. **The Raiders** American Football team play at The Coliseum, 3939 S Figueroa, (213) 748-6131. **The Coliseum** hosted the Olympic Games in 1932 and 1984. For tkts (from $15) to the famous **LA Lakers** basketball at the Forum, Inglewood, call (310) 419-3131.

INFORMATION

Bus and train info, (800) COMMUTE. 6am-10pm daily.

Human Services Hotline, 24 hr, 686-0950, locates doctors, emergency medical help.

Travelers Aid, 1720 N Gower St, Hollywood, (323) 468-2500. Also information at airport. Mon-Fri 8.30am-4pm.

Visitors Information, Greater LA Visitors Bureau, 685 S Figueroa St, by the Hilton Hotel, (take DASH Bus A), (213) 624-7300. Mon-Fri 8am-5pm, from 8.30am-5pm Sat. Very helpful multilingual staff. Offers free maps, bus and rail information, TV taping tkts, and run-downs of special events. Also has a small branch in Hollywood in Jane's House Sq, 6541 Hollywood Blvd, (323) 689-8822. Mon-Sat 9am-5pm.

INTERNET ACCESS

Free internet access is available at the LA **Public Library**, 630 W 5th St downtown, (213) 228-7000, open till 8pm Mon-Thu. One of the best of the many internet cafes springing up all over town is the **World Cafe's** T-1 Tiki Kiosk, 2820 Main St, Santa Monica, (310) 392-8440. Polynesian setting and free access for customers, Tue-Sun, 6pm-11pm.

TRAVEL

Amtrak, 800 N Alameda, (800) 875-7245. Also stations in Fullerton, Santa Ana, San Juan Capistrano, San Clemente and San Diego. The *Coast Starlight* to Seattle is highly recommended for socialising and scenery.

Auto Driveaway, 3407 W 6th St, #525, (323) 666-6100. Mon-Fri 9am-5pm. Ride board, Floor B, Ackerman Union, UCLA.

Car Rentals: Costless Car Rental (800) 770-0606,4831 W Century Blvd, from $17.95 a day. **Fox** (310) 641-3838. **Thrifty**, (800) 367-2277. Call for rates. Rsvs required 1 week in advance; **Midway**, 4900 W Blvd, (323) 292-1239, 'Can bargain with them over rates and mileage.'

Greyhound-Trailways Information Center, 1716 E 7th St (downtown), (800) 231-2222. Call for fares, schedules and local ticket info. Inside, a huge, clean but cheerless terminal with no cafe; outside, the meanest streets anywhere—a zoo. Don't plan any overnights here. 'Friends twice approached by vicious druggies and tramps outside station—be careful.' 'Stay on the upper level.' If you want to avoid the dodgy downtown terminal, Santa Monica is accessed by Greyhound—picks up / drops off at the back of the Santa Monica Plaza—no signposts though!

Guideline Tours (800) 604-8433. Mainstream tours, only really worth doing if you are strapped for time—City tour $41, Disneyland (including entrance) $71.

Hollywood Fantasy Tours, (213) 469-8184. 2 hr Beverly Hills tour ($31), 1 hr Hollywood tour ($16) , or combo ($41) by trolley. Runs Mon-Sun 9am-4pm.

Los Angeles International Airport (LAX), is located on the west side of town, just south of Venice. Transportation to and from downtown is fastest and least complicated using one of the numerous shuttle companies. Many accommodations offer free airport pick-ups so check beforehand. In general, shuttle companies will pick-up/drop-off from any major hotel, 24 hrs, req 1-day notice and cost $10-15. Super Shuttle, (310) 782-6600;. Venice Beach is a $15 cab ride from LAX. Airport information (310) 646-5252. Santa Monica Big Blue Bus #3 goes from Broadway Santa Monica to Parking lot C at LAX, 50c, then free shuttle to your terminal. Metrorail (213) 626-4455 goes closest to LAX on the Green Line $1.35 + 25c transfer, *Aviation* station, 5am-11.25pm. Takes approx. 50 mins from downtown. Then get the free Latzi shuttle to your terminal, 24 hrs.

L.V. International Tours, (888) 800-7878, (310) 581-0718; *www.lvint.com/*. Local LA tours—night club tour, city tour, Disney etc., plus further afield to Mexico, Las Vegas, Grand Canyon, etc. Specialise in small groups and gives discounts to BUNAC members.

MTA Buses and Metrorail: (213) 626-4455 or (800) COMMUTE, or check them out on the Net before you go: *www.mta.net/* $1.35 base fare, 25c transfers. Weekly pass $11, Monthly $42. Can be purchased at MTA (used to be RTD) centres; try 6249 Hollywood Blvd, Mon-Fri 10am-6pm. **Buses**: Bottom level of Greyhound terminal. 'Excellent value.' 'From the airport, change buses at Broadway.' **Metrorail**: 20 mile Blue Line light rail south from 7th & Figueroa downtown to Long Beach, 22 stations, $1.10; 16-station Red Line E-W subway from Union Station/Civic Center downtown to the Wilshire Center and Hollywood. Green Line Norwalk to Redondo Beach. Much of the rail system is still under construction and is not of great help to tourists as there is no beach access. The Red Line does, however, take 15 mins from downtown to Hollywood, with new stations at North Hollywood and Universal City due to open in 2000.

Orange County Transit District, (714) 636-7433.

Santa Monica City 'Big Blue' Bus, (310) 451-5444. Mon-Fri 8am-5pm. Basic fare 50¢, free transfers, #10 Express bus downtown $1.25.

Taxis: Checker Cab, (213) 482-3456; **Independent**, (213) 385-8294; and **United Independent**, (323) 653-5050. Best to call when you need a cab. Bear in mind LA covers huge distances—may be expensive.

THE COAST TO SAN DIEGO: Huntington Beach. Surfer capital, a famed party beach. 'The local surfers love to take a complete novice in hand so don't hesitate to ask how it's done.' Also, check out **Huntington Beach Skatepark #2**: a little bigger and a little wider than its big brother it features concrete banks, ledges, rails and a curb. Located next to Huntington Beach High School on Main St near Yorktown. Absolutely free.

Laguna Beach, 30 miles S of LA, buffered against urban sprawl by the San Joaquin Hills, has a decided Mediterranean look, from its indented coves to its trees and greenery right down to the waterline. The long white sand beach has superb snorkelling, surfing (for experts) and safe swimming at **Aliso Beach Park**. In winter, whale watching and tidepooling are likewise excellent. Long a haven for artists, Laguna is famous for its 7-wk Pageant of the Masters each July-Aug, but the accompanying Sawdust Festival (crafts, live music, jugglers, food) is more accessible and more fun. While here, plan to eat at **The Cottage**, 308 N Coast Hwy (949) 494-3023, or **The Stand** on Thalia St, (949) 494-8101 recommended by a Lagunian for its 'great Mexican food, smoothies and tofu cheeseless cake.' 'Laguna has excellent atmosphere, very picturesque.' Both open daily.

Newport Beach. Terribly yachty and formal except on **Balboa Island**, a mecca for boy/girl-watching. 'Try the Balboa bars and the frozen bananas at the icecream kiosks.' Also, **T-K Burgers** at 2119 W Balboa Blvd (949) 673-3438 is the most popular hangout for the non-deckshoe set.

Orange County/Anaheim: San Juan Capistrano, 12 miles inland from Laguna and 22 miles S of Santa Ana. This Mission town is well served by Greyhound, Orange County buses and Amtrak, so you have little excuse for passing up its Mission, easily the best in California. The chapel, oldest building still standing in the state, is almost Minoan in proportions, feeling and colour. Also on the grounds are the romantic ruins of the great church tumbled by an 1812 earthquake and now a favoured nesting place for the famous swallows. Indian graveyard, jail, various interesting buildings. Well worth your dollar. Take a lunch.

SAN DIEGO   One glimpse of San Diego, and it's hard to believe that when Juan Cabrillo first landed here in 1542, he found not a single tree or blade of grass. Today, this desert-defying city is green, green, green by a blue, blue sea. Developed as a naval port, San Diego is strategically (for the tourist) located 100 miles S of Los Angeles and as close to Tijuana as any sane person should want to get.

The town is breezy and casual, famous for top-notch Mexican and seafood restaurants, monstrous 'happy hour' spreads, a historic old town, and great beaches accessible by bus from downtown. Lavish sunshine and its citizens' personal wealth haven't entirely eliminated the small-town flavour of San Diego and it is one of America's nicest and fastest growing cities.

Local Guy's Guide to San Diego, www.k-online.com/~davemail.LGG is a witty see-and-do guide, authored by an opinionated native. Places, entertainment, roadtrips and dining from a local's point of view.

The telephone area code is 619.

ACCOMMODATION

Capri Hotel, 319 West E St, 232-3369. S-$20, D-$34 or weekly S-$120, D-$158: $25 deposit (show ID and they might reduce deposit). 'Clean, friendly, TV, kitchen, washing facilities.'

Golden West Hotel, 720 4th Ave, 233-7596 (near Horton Plaza). S-$20, D-$32, weekly S-$107, D-$140, all shared bath. Also have some en-suites. $5 refundable key deposit.

Grand Pacific Hostel, 726 5th Ave, 232-3100. In the heart of San Diego's Gaslamp District, this gateway-to-Mexico hostel is close to pubs, clubs and shops. Staff are experienced backpackers. Tons of info on travel, cheap fares and Mexico. 'If we don't have the info, we'll get it for you!' Day tours to Tijuana, beach shuttle, free bfast, dinner available usually around $4, no curfew. Dorms (summer) $18, private rooms $40; weekly rates available. $1 BUNAC discount.

Maryland Hotel, 630 F St, 239-9243. Near Gaslamp District. S-$36.95, D-$46.95. $5 key deposit.

Ocean Beach International Backpacker Hostel, 4961 Newport Ave, (800) 339-7263. Free pick-ups from bus/train/airport. Free muffins at 8 am. Free BBQ Tue & Fri. Laundry, TV & videos, lockers, free use of surf boards, no curfew, alcohol allowed. $17 dorm; private D-$38 'Clean and well-kept.' 'Brilliant! Friendly, laidback, hostel located right on beach—easy bus route to downtown.' 'Well recommended!' Seaworld a 15 min walk, San Diego Zoo a 30 min bus ride.

INLINE HEAVENS—WHERE TO PARK YOUR SKATES IN THE US

Skateboarding, in-line skating and BMX biking are currently three of the fastest growing sports in the world, but most skateparks are not listed in the yellow pages. These are some of the best, most likeable and renowned skateparks in the USA, so dig deep and pull out your best tricks.

EAST COAST & MIDWEST: Riverside Skate Park, NYC, 108th St & Riverside Park, Manhattan, (212) 408-0264. Built by Andy Kessler, one of the original *Zoo York* skateboard company crew, the park has an 11 ft vert ramp, a bank, rail, little grindbox, 2 quarter pipes and a vert wall. Helmet and pads must be worn and it's a mere $3 to get in and shred it all up!

Skatepark of Tampa, FL: 4215 E Columbus Dr, Tampa, (813) 621-6793. This skatepark welcomes skateboarders, rollerbladers and BMXers from wherever. The facility includes 8,000 sq ft street course, hips, pyramids, quarterpipes, corners, banks, a 5ft x 24ft mini-ramp, and an 11ft x 32ft vert ramp; 'the best built ramps in the business!' No pads are required on the street course for boarders, only on vert. However, bladers are required to wear full pads hemlet/elbow/knee) at all times. There is also a pro shop in the park for your skateboarding necessities. Hours of opening vary, so do yourself a favour and call ahead. Membership may be purchased or alternatively, pay-as-you-skate; Mon-Fri $6, $8 w/ends for a full day's worth of blood and sweat!

K-Zoo Skate Zoo, MI: 1502 Ravine Rd, Kalamazoo, (616) 345-9550. Take I-94 N to US 131, exit on Westmain M43 eastbound to Nichols Rd. Turn left on Nichols, then right on Ravine and Skate Zoo is 1 mile up on left side. The K-Zoo, Michigan's oldest indoor skateboard park, open for over 8 years, brag they have 'the best spine ramp and a great street course' which incorporates 6,800 sq ft of skating area! The latest addition is a new bank-to-wall ramp. Daily 3pm-9pm Mon-Fri; Sat noon-9pm and Sun 'til 6pm. Helmet, elbow and knee pads are required, and skateboards, in-line skates and bikes are all permitted (no bikes at w/end). A two day membership pass is $5, $5 per session after this initial payment.

Rhodes Park (aka Boise Skatepark), Boise, ID: This public park is built under an overpass which makes it ideal for skating all seasons. A 2 ft high ledge borders the perimeter of this football-field sized facility. Fun objects to skate include a 6 ft steel halfpipe (situated directly underneath the overpass—watch you don't get too ambitious!), several jump ramps and quarter ramps. There are also 2 8ftx8ft dirt patches to ollie over with a 1 ft high bar running through the middle, suitable for boardslides, feeble-grinds and whatever else you can pull out of your bag.

WEST COAST: Burnside Skatepark, Portland, Oregon: Burnside is regarded as the cornerstone of skateboarding in the Pacific Northwest—broad, solid and permanent. Established in 1990 on public land beneath the eastern side of the Burnside Bridge, just across the river from downtown Portland. From I-5 take the Burnside exit. Pass the turn onto the bridge and turn right on Ankeny, 1 block south of the bridge. After 2-blks turn right and the park is on the right. Burnside is an ever expanding skater-built (unmalleable) concrete haven that initially began as a shoddily built bowl, which still stands as the centrepiece. Today there are new banks, spines, structures ranging from 3ft-9ft in height incl a 6ft sq bowl, a 9ft vert wall, 'and more hips, bumps, and lines than Liz Taylor' all connected and interwoven. The lines there are endless. Free.

Huntington Beach #1/#2, California: Next to Burnside, probably one of the most talked-about, skate parks and nr Los Angeles. The first skatepark, located nr the corner of Golden West and Warner Ave, was a runt first attempt at providing a place to skate, featuring concrete undersized banks, ledges and little room to push…Huntington Beach Skatepark #2, ah-ha now we're getting somewhere. A little bigger, a little wider, the big brother features concrete banks, ledges, rails and a curb. It is located next to Huntington Beach High School, on Main St near Yorktown. Both are free.

Encinitas (aka Magdalena Ecke Family YMCA Skatepark), nr San Diego, California: 200 Saxony RD, Encinitas, (760) 738-5425. From I-5, exit at Encinitas Blvd, go east to first traffic signal, turn left on Saxony Rd and park is at the top of the hill. This 23,000 sq ft street course has an array of quarterpipes, bank ramps, pyramids and manual/slider obstacles. The park also features a 70ft wide by 6ft high double-bowled, double-hipped L-shaped miniramp (gulp) as well as an 11ft high vert bowl ramp. Plenty to keep yourself and your wee wooden toy having fun, but only for the first lucky 75 or so before others are turned away. All of the ramps are surfaced with smooooooth masonite except the vert ramp which is covered in hard steel. Bring your own pads or loan them here (free of charge with valid ID). $10 p/session daily if not an annual member.

For a comprehensive roster of all skateparks in the States and relevant hot links, check out the following on-line Net sites: *www.skateboard.com* and *www.boardpark.com*.

Pickwick Hotel, 132 W Broadway, 234-0141. Next to Greyhound. From S-$53, D-$64. Clean.' 'Dangerous area.'

HI-Point Loma Hostel, 3790 Udall St, 223-4778. 6¹/₂ miles from downtown; take #35 bus to Ocean Beach. San Diego Zoo, Mission Bay Park, Sea World, Balboa Park and Old Town are close by. 'Well equipped, nr cheap markets, 20 min walk from beach.' '2 am curfew but $1 late pass available.' Staff plan activities such as barbecues and beach bonfires. $13-15.

HI-San Diego Downtown Hostel, 521 Market, 525-1531. Second gateway hostel to Mexico, it is located in the soul of the city's historic Gaslamp Quarter. Close by trolley, city bus. Few miles from Balboa Park, the Zoo, Sea World and beaches. Laundry, kitchen, bike rental. $16-18, private rooms available.

FOOD

It's here that you're likely to find some of the best Mexican food in the US, and plenty of places to choose from. Some of the best are:

Big Kitchen, 3003 Grape St, 234-5789. A bfast-and-lunch place with characters. Bfast from $4, lunch from $5. Look for comedienne Whoopi Goldberg's graffiti contribution on the kitchen wall. Mon-Fri 7am-2pm, Sat-Sun 'til 3pm.

Chicken Pie Shop, 2633 Oklahoma Blvd, 295-0156. Scrumptious chicken & turkey pies for $2 to go, $3 to sit down with side dish, $4 pie-dinner. Daily 10am-8pm.

Chuey's Cafe, 1894 Main St, 234-6937. String beef tacos, other outstanding Mexican dishes under $11. Nearby murals at Chicano Park on the Coronado Bay Bridge make a fitting post-comida stroll. Sat 'til midnight.

El Indio Tortilla Shop, 3695 India St, 299-0333. Situated in an artists' district. 'Heavenly chicken burritos ($4.75), 50 takeout items so park across the way and pop in!' Dishes under $8, daily 7am-9pm.

Filipe's Pizza, 4 locations in San Diego. 'Best Italian food in San Diego. Try the lasagne; really superb.'

Non-Mexican: Boll Weevil Restaurants, 17 locations around San Diego. Excellent, inexpensive burgers. 'More flavour than any other burger I had in three months.'

Old Spaghetti Factory, 275 5th St, 233-4323. 'Eat in a train, a change from Greyhound.' Dishes for under $10. Daily 11.30am-2pm & 5pm-10pm, Sat & Sun noon-11pm.

Roberto's, 1555 Palm Ave, 575-9977. Wonderful greasy-spoon dives, popular with the locals; among the best for Mexican food. 'Great place. Try the rolled tacos.' Many locations in and around the city.

OF INTEREST

Old Town, a snippet of the city's original heart, along San Diego Ave. Free walking tours from the Plaza at 2pm make the few historical remnants come to life. Visitor Centre at 4002 Wallace Street, 220-5422. Up the hill is **Presidio Park**; its **Serra Museum**, 2727 Presidio, houses documents, maps, archaelogical finds from the nearby dig, $3.

Balboa Park. Take the bus (#7,16,25) or bike to this superlative 1074-acre park, whose pink-icing Mexican Churrigueresque buildings were designed by Bertram Goodhue for the 1915-16 Panama-California International Exposition. 'Beautiful. Worth going to just for the architecture.' The park has 12 museums and galleries. Purchase a Balboa Park Passport—all 12 museums for $21, valid for 1 wk, from the Visitors Centre or one of the museums. Rotating "free Tuesdays" system, three museums free each Tues—check with the Visitor Centre. All closed Mon. Also houses the world-class zoo, a carousel complete with brass ring, pipe organ and other concerts, free sidewalk entertainment, free facilities for everything from volleyball to frisbee golf. Visitor Center: House of Hospitality, 1549 El Prado, 239-0512, 9am-4pm daily.

Inside the park: Museum of Art, 232-7931. Tue-Sun 10am-4.30pm. $8, $6 under 24; **Natural History Museum**, 232-3821. Daily 9.30am-5.30pm, $12, $10 w/student ID;

Aerospace Museum, 2001 Pan American Plaza, 234-8291. Daily 10am-5pm, $6; **Museum of Man**, 1350 El Prado, 239-2001. Daily 10am-4.30pm, $5; **Reuben H Fleet Science Center**, 1875 El Prado, 238-1233, IMAX films, laser shows, simulator ride and galleries, $6.50 - $11. Open from 9.30 am. 'Science portion is smallish, no great shakes, but the 360-degree films are exhilarating.'

Also at Balboa: summer light opera at the **Starlight Bowl Theatre**, box office 544-STAR, free Sun afternoon music at the **organ pavilion**.

Cabrillo National Monument, Pt Loma, 557-5450. Take a #6 bus from downtown San Diego. Splendiferous view of the site where Juan Cabrillo first touched land at San Miguel Bay. Excellent tidepools, nature walks, films on whales, exhibit hall. Open summer 9am-sunset, winter 'til 5.15pm. Fee $4.

Coronado / Hotel Del Coronado. The hotel is where Edward VIII first met Mrs Simpson, then a Coronado housewife, and where "Some Like it Hot" was filmed. Catch the San Diego Bay Ferry, $2 each way from the Broadway Pier 234-4111, or take the **Trolley Tour** (see below).

Gaslamp District south of Broadway. Sixteen blocks of restored frontier San Diego, filled with smart shops and cafes.

Gondola Cruise in San Diego Bay: Gondola di Venezia offers a relaxing and romantic way to view the San Diego skyline and the beauty of Shelter Island's tranquil waters. A 1hr cruise includes Italian music, hors d'oeuvres, ice and wine glasses. Contact 1551 Shelter Isl Drive, 221-2999.

La Jolla, (pronounced "La Hoya") the jewel of San Diego, from sculptured rocks at Windansea to the St Tropez-like La Jolla Shores and limpid La Jolla Cove. On La Jolla Bvld, rent snorkels and roam in this fabulous underwater park and wildlife preserve. The beach is trying to lose its' stuffy image, especially compared with Mission Beach. Also houses the **Museum of Contemporary Art**, 700 Prospect Street, 234-1001, Tues-Sat 10am-5pm, Wed 10am-8pm, Sun 12am-5pm $4, $2 w/ student ID, free 1st Tues & Sun of the month. Also has a location downtown at 1001 Kettner Blvd, sharing with the **Museum of Photographic Art** till Spring 2000. $2, $1 w/ student ID.

Mission Bay Park, 2581 Quivira Ct, 221-8900. 4600-acre marine park, the largest facility of its kind in the world. Sailing, fishing, water skiing, wind surfing on 27 miles of beaches. **Mission Beach** has a reputation for hedonism, fun, sun and beautiful bodies to rival "Baywatch".

San Diego Wild Animal Park, 30 miles N of San Diego off Hwy I-15 near **Escondido**, (760) 747-8702. 1800 acres of animals freely roaming in their natural habitats; view from a 50 min ride in a monorail. Spanish architecture. 'Lots to see—don't miss bird shows. Best monorail run is 4.30pm for most animal activity.' 'Amazing.' Also, *Mombasa Lagoon* is an interactive attraction where you can climb inside a giant stork eggshell, hop across the water on extra large lily pads, or explore an oversized spider's web. $19.95 includes entrance, monorail, hidden jungle and all live shows. Two park ticket combined with the Zoo—$35.15. Daily 9am-8pm.

San Diego Zoo, off Park Blvd in Balboa Park, 234-3153, is one of the world's best—a luxurious setting for the 3200 animals. General admission $16—$24 includes bus tour, the aerial tram ride, and zoo. Daily 9am-9pm ('til 4pm after Labor Day); gates close at 4pm. Don't miss the walk-through hummingbird aviary, the koalas and the primates. 'Good zoo but not quite as good as expected.' 'Need 5 hours to see it all.'

Sea World, 1720 South Shores Rd, 222-6363, on Mission Bay north of downtown. Expensive at $38 ($42 2-day package), so you'd better like performing whales, dolphins, seals! Best part is the **Penguin Encounter**, with 300 penguins in their beloved refrigerated setting. 'Don't miss the seal and otter shows.' **Shamu Backstage**, a 1.7 million gallon killer whale habitat allows visitors to touch, train and feed the killer whales, even wading with them in their 55 degree water. 'An all-day affair.' Daily—hours vary.

Southern California Exposition, Del Mar Fairgrounds, north of San Diego, 755-1161. Some of everything: outdoor flower and garden show, arts, gems, minerals, hobbies, crafts, jams, jellies, 4600 animals and a carnival June 15-July 4. $7. Horse-racing takes place in summer months.

ENTERTAINMENT

Beachcomber, 539-9902, 2901 Mission Blvd. '2 min walk to Pacific Ocean.' Frequented by Brits and Aussies. Daily 7am-2 am. Margaritas $2.50.

Blarney Stone Pub, 5617 Balboa Ave, Clairemont, 279-2033. Happy hour Mon-Fri, 4pm-6pm. Traditional Irish music Tues thru Sat.

In Cahoots, 5373 Mission Center Rd, Mission Valley, 291-8635. Popular Country and Western bar, 'Always a party! Something cookin' every day of the week.' $2.50 drinks 'til 9pm. 5pm-2 am daily.

Humphrey's, 2241 Shelter Island Dr, 224-3577. Great happy hours Mon-Sat 4.30pm-7.30pm, Sun 6pm-7pm. Live entertainment every day.

Princess Pub and Grille, 1665 India St, downtown, 702-3021. Saturday hosts live bands. '*Real* beers on tap. Biggest surprise is when you walk out of the door and back into California.' Daily 11am-1 am, food served 'til 11pm.

Schooner's, 959 Hornblend St, Pacific Beach, 272-2780. Cheap food, $7 dishes and under. 'Good atmosphere, worth the queue to get in.'

Festivals: National Whale-Watching Weekend, mid-January. Special speakers and presentations at the Cabrillo whale-watching station at Point Loma. Call 557-5450 for more details. Also, **Street Scene** is an annual food and music festival held beginning Sept, featuring more than 100 blues, Cajun, zydeco, rock, jazz, and reggae bands. Telephone 557-8490.

SPORT

San Diego's Padres baseball team plays at Qualcomm Stadium, Friars Rd and Mission Village, 283-4494; **National Football League** here also with the **Chargers**, 280-2121.

Mission Valley YMCA Skatepark, 9115 Clairmont Mesa Blvd, located in Missile Park (just off Missile Rd at General Dynamics). 14,000 sq-ft course which includes 11 ft vert ramp, mini ramp, fun box with two rail slides, pyramid, bank walls, quarter pipes, manual pads and more. Good for boarders, in-liners and bikers. All safety gear req. $10 'one-day' skate fee (includes pad rental) or $6 session (3 hrs).

SHOPPING

Bazaar del Mundo International Marketplace in Old Town, open 10am-10pm.

Horton Plaza, btwn Broadway & G and 1st & 4th Aves. Pseudo-Mediterranean colourful, lively, shopping, eating, cinema complex. Opens 10 am.

San Diego Factory Outlet Center, 4498 Camino de la Plaza. 35 factory outlets. Mon-Fri 10am-8pm, Sat 'til 7pm, Sun 'til 6pm.

Seaport Village, 14-acre shopping complex at West Harbor Dr and Kettner Blvd; 75 shops and restaurants. Opens 10 am.

INFORMATION

Balboa Park Info Center, House of Hospitality, 1549 El Prado, Balboa Park, 239-0512. Small info centres also in Old Town, at airport, and along the hwy. Daily 9am-4pm.

Council of American Youth Hostels, 437 J St, San Diego, CA 92101, 338-9981. Publishes a budget traveller's guide to San Diego. Write, phone or call in for a copy.

Travelers Aid, 1765 4th Ave, #100, 295-8393. Mon-Fri 9am-5pm. Also information booth at airport, 231-7361. 8am-11pm.

Visitor Information Center, 11 Horton Plaza (downtown), 236-1212. Multilingual staff on-hand. Mon-Sat 8.30am-5pm, Sun from 11 am summer only.

INTERNET ACCESS
Many internet cafes including **Espresso Net**, 7700 Regent Rd, #109 Gold Triangle—UTC, 453-5896. Open 7am-11pm, $6/hr, *www.espressonet.com/*. Free access is available at the **Public Library**, 829 E St, 236-5800.

TRAVEL
Auto Driveaway, 7902 Dagget St, 505-0200. Must be over 21yrs. $300 cash deposit, $290 refund when car is returned in same condition, must see passport and credit card. You pay all gas except first tank. Mon-Fri, 8.30am-4.30pm.
Amtrak, 1050 Kettner Blvd at Broadway, 239-9021/(800) 872-7245. Romantic 1915 depot with twin Moorish towers. Around 8 runs a day to LA, takes about 2 hrs 45 mins.
Bargain Auto Rentals car rental, 3860 Rosecans St, 299-0009. Must be one of the only places to rent to 18 year olds, although there is a $6 surcharge for drivers under 25-yrs. Credit card essential. Daily 8am-6pm.
Greyhound, 120 W Broadway, (800) 231-2222. 24 hrs.
San Diego International Airport (Lindbergh Field) lies at northwestern edge of downtown. Take #2 bus from Broadway downtown to reach it, $1.50. Last bus into downtown, 1 am. Cab fare to downtown, $7.50.
San Diego Regional Transit, 233-3004. Runs a 'very efficient and easy-to-understand' bus system. Basic fare $1.50; 'Daytripper' one-day pass, $5. Also operates **San Diego Trolley**, 233-3004, making breaks for the US border near El Cajon and Tijuana every 15 mins from Amtrak; $3.50 r/t. 'Buy a r/t ticket to Tijuana, you won't want to stay long.' 'Quick, comfortable' and cheaper than Mexicoach and Greyhound.
Trolley Tour, 298-8687. Get on/off where you like; city tours and Coronado are worthwhile.

ANZA-BORREGO DESERT and EASTERN SAN DIEGO COUNTY   The 600,000-acre state park is in San Diego's back yard, at the end of a scenic 90-mile climb through forests, mountains and the charming gold mining village of **Julian**, ultimately spiraling down 3000 ft to the **Sonoran Desert** floor.

The route can be traversed by bicycle (tough) or car, but there's also a cheap bus service via the Northeast County Bus Service, 767-4287, several times weekly from **El Cajon**, east of San Diego, to Julian, Borrego Springs and other points. Mon-Fri 7am-noon and 2pm-5pm. $5 per vehicle. Park open only at w/ends during summer.

At once desolate and grand, the Anza-Borrego Desert embraces sandstone canyons, rare elephant trees, pine-rimmed canyons, oases and wadis. Springtime brings wildflowers, which you can see year-round at the excellent sound and light presentation at the visitors center, 767-5311, 9am-5pm. For rsvs: (800) 444-7275. Camping in the park is free at primitive sites, $21/22 w/hook-up $15/16 without, at developed campgrounds in winter, less in summer. Best months are Nov-May; it's terribly hot thereafter. If you don't want to camp, stay in Julian at one of the B&Bs or cottages rather than in expensive Borrego Springs. Either way, don't miss out on the spectacular apple pie ($3) at the **Julian Cafe**, 765-2712. Around beginning of February, the **Native American Days Celebration** in Borrego Springs is an annual Cahuilla and Kumeyaay cultural celebration featuring demonstrations, lectures and nature walks. Call the Visitors Centre 767-4205.
The telephone area code is 760.

HAWAII *Aloha State*

When your plane touches down, congratulate yourself—you've made it to paradise. But, as the song says, they've 'paved paradise and put up a parking lot'—particularly in Oahu, likely to be the first place you see. Japanese investors have fuelled real estate price increases, and prices in general are quite high. Hawaii has its poor and its homeless, but paradise still exists in this tourist-trampled state, if you know where to look.

For the real Hawaiians, this is actually Paradise Lost. Hawaii is the northern tip of the 'Polynesian Triangle'—a four-cornered triangle(!) with Fiji in the west, Easter Island in the east and New Zealand in the south. The spread of the Polynesian peoples (polynesia = many islands) can be charted, by archaeologists and philologists, from Malayan and Indonesian roots. It is believed that Hawaii was first inhabited sixteen hundred years ago by Polynesians setting out in their canoes from the Marquesas Islands in what is now French Polynesia. For centuries they grew their taro, hunted their pigs, and occasionally had each other over for dinner (one-way tkts only), undisturbed by 'civilisation.' Captain Cook, when he arrived at Kona in 1778, inadvertently brought an end to that, but the Hawaiians brought an end to him, which was irony, if not justice. Not for nothing did he name Hawaii the 'Sandwich Islands'; he had inside knowledge!

Polynesian-blooded Hawaiians now number about 250,000, and are well outnumbered by the descendants of the immigrants brought in to expand the sugar industry in the late 19th century: Europeans/Americans, Chinese, Japanese, Koreans, and, lately, Filipinos, Samoans and Vietnamese. The indigenous Hawaiians were powerless when American missionaries-turned-opportunists stole their lands and then their kingdom during the last century, just as they were when the US Government completed the process in 1959.

Just west of Kauai lies Niihau, the 'forbidden isle.' The family that owns Niihau, the western-most island of the archipelago, has prohibited outsiders in an attempt to preserve the culture of old Hawaii. Elsewhere in Hawaii the pure Hawaiian is almost, as Mark Twain put it, 'a curiosity in his own land'. The 'missionaries' also banned the teaching of the Hawaiian language (as well as removing some letters from the alphabet!), so that by 1987 fewer than 2000 people spoke the native tongue. Now, though, children can be taught in Hawaiian if they wish. There is a small but committed movement of Hawaiians still trying to regain their stolen sovereignty.

Hawaii's eight island chain has been formed (and is still being formed) by volcanic activity (mythically, Pele, the goddess of fire). The islands are actually the tips of the tallest volcanic mountains on earth (Mauna Kea on the Big Island is 13,796' above sea level, and over 19,000' below!). The oldest sizeable island (Kauai) is to the west, but the newest island (Hawaii itself, the Big Island) is still growing in the east as tectonic plate movement pushes the islands westward from the faultline. As of 1997, lava bubbling and sizzling into the sea sometimes adds metres per day to the eastern coastline. The Big Island is becoming the Even Bigger Island, and you can stand and watch it happen beneath your feet.

The main islands (from left to right: Kauai, Oahu, Maui and Hawaii) are readily accessible by air and are all worth visiting for their differing flavours, scenery and beaches. All beaches in Hawaii are public and most are excellent. They are home to obsessive hordes of young, tanned hedonists with sun-bleached hair, whose life is the surf, the board they ride on, and the beaten up old campervans they live in. Hippie-dom with a sporting purpose. (Many of those who 'dropped out' in the '60's found their way to Hawaii. The hair is still long, but it's turned grey.) The Big Island is not noted for its beaches, but it has its own spectacular volcanic scenery and '13 different climates'.

From **Oahu**, with its cosmopolitan capital, Honolulu, you can island-hop via the reasonably-priced local airlines to **Hawaii**, the Big Island, for its rural and volcanic scenery, and **Maui** or **Kauai** for beaches and tranquillity. Don't be discouraged by the astronomical prices of the big resort hotels. Good, cheap motels and bed & breakfasts abound. (Pacific-Hawaii B&B, 1312 Oulepe St, Kailua, HI 96734, offers rooms on the four main islands starting from $55: call (800) 999-6026 from mainland; and B&B Honolulu, 3242 Kaohinani Dr, Honolulu 96817, (800) 288-4666, operates throughout the state, rooms also from $55, include bfast). County, state and national campsites are available for overnight stays for a minimal fee; most popular state parks (with the exception of Maui and the Big Island) require an advance (free) permit. Camping is limited to five nights per 30 days. Sites open Fri-Wed on Oahu, daily on other islands. Rustic cabins are available as well, but book way ahead.

National Park: Haleakala Hawaii Volcanoes

The telephone area code is 808. dir.yahoo.com/Regional/U_S__States/Hawaii/

OAHU Most urbanized and brutalised of the islands, but don't write Oahu off entirely. It absorbs the brunt of approx 4.5 million visitors a year. In doing so, it's won a few battles (billboards are banned, flowers are planted everywhere) and lost a few (high-rise forests in Waikiki, plastic leis for tour groups).

Honolulu is the state capital, legally and touristically. But don't come looking for miles of beaches, Hawaiian village charm or quiet. You'll find Waikiki a postage-stamp sized beach covered with bodies in various shades of red. Honolulu's pace, while not quite the gallop of hypertensive Los Angeles, is nonetheless brisk. Crowded with traffic on foot and wheel both, Honolulu is a place to act the tourist, to shop at the International Market, or Hilo Hatties for muu-muu's (traditional Hawaiian costume), to sip maitais and eat puupuus (Hawaii's hors d'oeuvres) and have a good time when the sun goes down.

For cheap food, the city offers huge and colourful produce and seafood markets as well as Japanese box lunch takeouts and noodle stands. If you like, join in the on-going debate over the merits of *poi*, a Hawaiian staple made of taro root. Packaged in plastic bags and sold in local stores, the squishy grey stuff looks remarkably like wallpaper paste. Some people say it tastes like it too, but be open-minded and decide for yourself. Although they are somewhat buried in the barrage of tourist ballyhoo, Honolulu's cultural attractions (from museums to Chinatown) are worth finding, and the city's historical sites, Pearl Harbor and Punchbowl Crater in particular, are tasteful and moving. Get a fantastic view of Honolulu from old war for-tifications atop **Diamond Head**, a volcanic crater overshadowing the city.

Local teens hang out in the smelly bunkers; note an eerie inscription memorialising a murder committed there. Go early—the hike up is as tiring as the view is rewarding, and the parking lot closes at dusk.

Good bus transit on the islands allows you easy access to the beautiful country outside Honolulu. Following Hwy 72 E, you come to **Koko Head State Park**; here, **Hanauma Bay** is snorkeling heaven. Coral reefs form tunnels and pools through which you can chase elusive, colourful fish and sea turtles. To the northeast of Honolulu on Hwy 61 lies the **Koolau Range**, which, like most Hawaiian ranges, is formed by steep, grooved ridges dripping with lush foliage. Cutting through the mountain, **Nuuanu Pali Pass** offers splendid views of the ocean. It was here that King Kamehameha the Great defeated the Oahuans in 1795, literally forcing them over the cliffs; the victorious king became the first ruler of the united Hawaiian Islands.

Near Hauula on the northeast coast, a tough one-mile climb along a rough mountain ravine brings you to the **Sacred Falls**, one of the loveliest sights on the island: 2500-foot cliffs form a splendid backdrop to the falls, dropping 87 ft into the gorge. Oahu's northern side boasts incredible beaches—**Sunset** and **Waimea Bay** among them—as well as some of the best surfing on earth (the infamous **Banzai Pipeline** is here). Further on is the **Puu O Mahuka Heiau**, where humans were once sacrificed to the gods (the practice has since been discontinued). Kick back, relax and explore Oahu by browsing *www.hshawaii.com/ovp/index.html*

ACCOMMODATION

Waikiki, a couple of miles east of downtown, is crowded with low-cost digs, many with kitchens, most a couple of blocks from the beach. Rsvs advised year-round. NB: city buses take backpacks 'at the discretion of the driver.' Anything you can hold on your lap or load under your seat is fine. Otherwise, be prepared to take a cab to your hostel or hotel.

B&B Pacific Hawaii, 19 Kai Nani Place, 262-6026. Books rooms anywhere across island from $55 per couple.

Big Surf Hotel, 1690 Ala Moana Blvd (near boat harbour), 946-6525. From S-$42, suites $60.

Central YMCA, 401 Atkinson Dr, across from Ala Moana Shopping Center, 941-3344. First come, first served; pool, weight room, 4 racquet ball courts. S-$29 male, $36.50 women, 18+only, $10 key deposit. 'Convenient for all buses.'

Edmunds Hotel Apartments, 2411 Ala Wai Blvd, 923-8381. From S/D-$38. TV; homely, recommended.

HI-Honolulu Hostel, 2323A Sea View Ave, 946-0591. Across the street from Uni of Hawaii; take #19 or #20; transfer to bus #6 to University. Small and peaceful. Kitchen, TV room, patio under coconut trees, laundry, clean single-sex facilities. 3 night guaranteed stay. $12.50. Check-out 10 am, lights out 11pm. 'Very busy.' Rsvs essential.

HI-Waikiki Hostel, 2417 Prince Edward St (2 blocks off beach), 926-8313. 3 night guaranteed stay. Dorm $16 AYH, $19 non-AYH, D-$40-46. Kitchen. Free use of snorkelling gear! No lockout or curfew. Rsvs advised.

Interclub Hostel 'Waikiki', 2426 Kuhio Ave, 924-2636. Laundry, BBQs, TV, a/c & fridge in all rooms. Female or mixed dorms, $15 (stay 7 nights, pay for 6), or private D-45, XP-$10. *www.interclubwaikiki.com*

Kim's Island Hostel, 1946 Ala Moana Blvd, Suite #130, 942-8748. Each room has A/C, bathrm, sink, fridge, TV. Cooking facilities available. 4 people per room. $16.75p/n or $105 p/wk. Call for S/D rates.

NB: Camping is not recommended on Oahu; locals like to gather at campsites and may feel you are encroaching on their turf. Check out the grounds; if they are obviously being used by tourists, camping probably OK, particularly if the site seems to be patrolled regularly.

FOOD
In the local parlance, Hawaiians don't eat, they 'grind.' If it's a luau or all-you can eat smorgy, they 'grind to da max!' Grinding episodes usually start with puupuus (Hawaiian munchies), which reflect the state's ethnic diversity, from egg rolls to falafel. This is the home of the maitai, a nobly-proportioned ration of rum, pineapple juice, chunks of fruit and a baby orchid. Another local poison is the blue Hawaii, a toxic-looking concoction made from blue curacao and who knows what else? Good ethnic eating at Japanese delis, Chinese takeaway counters and noodle shops, especially on **Hotel Street**. If you're still not stuffed, tap into Honolulu's lavish happy hour spreads, or better still, a luau. When it comes to luaus, choices are plenty, but prices are high. Read the free *Waikiki Beach Press* and other local papers for Church luaus, generally cheaper and friendlier, with better food and entertainment, than those at the big hotels. Be sure to sample shave ice, Hawaii's better answer to the snowcone. And before you leave Oahu, don't miss the **McDonald's** in **Laie**. Regular old fast food, but the restaurant was constructed to resemble a Hawaiian longhouse, complete with tropical flowers and an indoor grotto. Try the variety of ethnic restaurants located btwn the 500 and 1000 blocks of **Kapahulu Ave. Kaimuki, Moili'ili** and **downtown** districts are thriving with good food and nightlife also.
Hamburger Mary's, 2201 Kalakaua Avenue #8305, 922-6722. Restaurant with w/end barbecues (av. plate $2). Lunch daily except Sun 11.30am-2pm, dinner 5pm-10pm.
Helena's, 1364 N King, Honolulu, 845-8044. Inexpensive Hawaiian specialties—butterfish, laulau, poi. Tues-Fri only.
Queen Kapiolani, 150 Kapahulu Ave, Honolulu, 922-1941. Buffet lunch Fri-Sun 11am-2pm.
Rainbow Drive-In, 3308 Kanaina Ave, 737-0177. Tasty cuisine at rock-bottom prices. Daily 7.30 am 'til 9pm.

OF INTEREST
In Honolulu: Academy of Arts, 900 S Beretania, at Ward (take #2 bus from Waikiki), 532-8701. Tue-Sat 10am-4.30pm, Sun 1pm-5pm; closed Mon. $7, $4 w/student ID. 30 galleries surrounding six garden courts. From Polynesian to avant-garde, including one of the finest collections of Asian Art in America. James Michener collection of Ukiyo-e woodblock prints is one of world's best. Academy also shows 'alternative' and foreign films, and has concert and theatre programmes; call 532-8768.
Bishop Museum and Planetarium, 1525 Bernice St, 847-3511. $14.95 includes gallery tours, dance performances, craft demonstrations and planetarium shows. Incredible feather cloaks (treasured as booty by the ancient kings), Hawaiian and Polynesian artifacts. Daily 9am-5pm. Check free tourist magazines for discounted entry.
Capitol District Walking Tour gives extensive coverage of Honolulu's historic district and may be picked up from the Hawaii Visitor Bureau.
Foster Botanical Garden, 50 N Vineyard Blvd, 522-7065. Cool oasis of rare trees, orchids and flowers. Wear insect repellent! Guided tours weekdays 1pm. Take #4 bus from Waikiki to corner of Vineyard Blvd. Daily 9am-4pm. $5.
Hilo Hatties, 700 N Nimitz Hwy, 544-3500, free shuttle from Waikiki, and complimentary refreshments. Huge selection of Hawaiian clothes and gifts, open daily, 7am-6pm. Six stores throughout the islands.

Honolulu Zoo, 151 Kapahulu Ave, 971-7171. Daily 9am-4.30pm. $6. World's finest group of tropical birds.

Iolani Palace, King and Richards St, 538-1471, 9am-2.30pm, Tues-Sat. Closed Sun/Mon. $10. Only royal palace on American soil, used just 11-yrs by the Hawaiian monarchs. 45 min tours begin every 15 min. Queen Liliuokalani wrote *Aloha Oe*, easily the most famous Hawaiian song, while imprisoned here. $10. 9am-2.30pm Tue-Sat. Very popular; rsvs necessary.

Hawaii's post-modern **State Capitol** stands at the corner of Beretania and Richard St. Mon-Fri 9am-4pm; free.

Outside Honolulu: USS Arizona National Memorial at **Pearl Harbor**, 422-0561. Departures from Halawa Gate. 20 min film on Japanese attack on Pearl Harbor at the Visitors Center, followed by free Navy boat tours of the harbour and memorial. You can look down through the limpid water to see the ghostly outline of the Arizona, wherein lie 1000 of the sailors (some have been removed) who died on 7 Dec, 1941. Shivery. Take #20 bus from Waikiki, 1-hr bus ride, or shuttle bus (see TRAVEL). Daily 7.30am-5pm; tours 8am-3pm. Free; arrive early, queue forms at 7 am for same-day tkts. The **Visitors Center** is open Mon-Sun 7.30am-5pm.

USS Bowfin, nxt to Arizona Memorial, 423-1341. Self-guided tour (w/hand-held receiver) of this WW2 submarine. Daily 8am-5pm (last tour 4.30pm), $8.

Sea Life Park, Makapuu Point (16 miles E of Waikiki on Hwy 72), 259-7933. The huge reef tank gives you skindiver's view of brilliant fish, coral, sharks. Various shows. Daily 9.30am-5pm; $25, cheaper than mainland aquatic parks and better, too.

Beaches: Queen's Surf Beach is close to downtown and attracts swimmers, skateboarders and in-line skaters. Also, try the **Sans Souci Beach**. If you seek more secluded beaches, head east on Diamond Head Rd until you reach **Kahala Ave. Hanauma Bay** is recommended for snorkelling, #22 Bus from Waikiki. Closed Wed am. Daily fee of $3 well worth it to see the coral, turtles and numerous brightly-coloured fish that inhabit the waters. Equipment can be rented for $6, bring your passport as deposit. Tour parties were banned in 1991 to cut down on damage to the fragile ecology. Other snorkelling beaches include **Magic Island, Kahe Point State Park** and **Waimea Bay**. *Aloha!* is a guide to Oahu's popular beaches, *www.aloha.com/~lifeguards/*.

ENTERTAINMENT

Kodak Hula Show, Waikiki Shell by Kapiolani Park, 627-3379. Array of Hawaiian, Tahitian dancing, costumes to blow colour film on; get there early for seats (sometimes already filled by 9.30 am). Tue-Thur 10am-11.15 am. Free. More free shows at the **King Jubilee** at the Hilton Hawaiian Village, Fri at sunset, 949-4321.

The Wave, 1877 Kalakaua, Honolulu, 941-0424. Live rock music every night, 8.30pm-4 am; free entry 'til 10pm, then $5 cover. Mondays , DJ only. 21-yrs +.

World Café, 500 Ala Moana Blvd, 599-4450, has the best tunes and drink specials. Mon-Thurs 4pm-3 am, Fri 'til 4 am, Sat 7pm-4 am and Sun 8pm-2 am.

Festivals: May 1st is **Lei Day** crowning of the Lei Queen, various concerts: give a lei, always accompanied with a kiss! 597-1888. One of the best parades is held June 11-12th in Honolulu, from downtown Iolani Palace through Waikiki, to honor **Kamehameha the Great**, the warrior king who unified the island chain in the early 19th century. See floats festooned with countless tropical blossoms and *pa'u* riders. 586-0333.

INFORMATION/TRAVEL

Camping and Parks, 1151 Punchbowl St, Rm #131, 587-0300. Info and permits for camping in state parks and trail maps. Mon-Fri 9am-3.30pm.

Honolulu Intl. Airport, 836-6413

The Bus, 848-5555, offers good bus service around the island; $1 gets you anywhere; free transfers, $4 day pass. Runs airport bus also.

National Park Service, Prince Kuhio Federal Bldg #6305, 300 Ala Moana Blvd, 541-

2693. Permits are given at individual park HQs. Mon-Fri 7.30am-4pm.

Visitors Bureau , 2270 Kalakaua, 7th flr, Waikiki Business Plaza, 923-1811, or (800) GO-HAWAII. Mon-Fri, 8am-4.30pm.

Waikiki Trolley, 596-2199 and **Aloha Tower Express Trolley**, 528-5700, link Waikiki and downtown Honolulu.

Weather Report, 973-4380

INTERNET ACCESS

The award-winning 24 hr **Internet Cafe**, 559 Kapahula Ave, 735-JAVA also serves great coffee whilst you're surfing. For free access, try down the road at **Waikiki-Kapahula Public Library**, 400 Kapahula Ave, 733-8488.

MAUI Twenty-five flying minutes southeast of Honolulu is Maui, trendiest of the islands and famous for sweet onions, potato chips, humpback whales and Maui wowie, a potent variety of local marijuana. Formed by two volcanic masses linked by a wasp-waisted isthmus, Maui is marked by an extraordinary variety of terrain and climate, from the cold dryness of 10,023-foot **Haleakala volcanic crater** to the lush wetness of **Hana** (to describe it would require a new vocabulary for hues of green). The former whaling port of **Lahaina** is touristy and social; the upcountry eucalyptus land around **Makawao** is rural and mellow. Once past the endless condos of Kihei and Wailea, there are superb beaches and camping opportunities at **Makena** and further south.

At **Haleakala National Park**, 572-9306, $10 per car, the 'House of the Sun' has the largest dormant (for the last 200 years, anyway) volcano in the world, 21 miles in circumference. If you go there, you will be told repeatedly that the crater is big enough to swallow all of Manhattan (you might as well hear it here first). The terrain is magnificent: graceful cones and curves of deep red and purple punctuated by ethereal silversword plants. Huge cumulus clouds sometimes pour over the crater lip and pile up like whipped cream. At dawn and dusk you may see the Spectre of Brocken effect, where your shadow is projected gigantically against the clouds and encircled by rainbow light. Sunrise at Haleakala is like a slow-motion fireworks display, best seen near the Puu Ulaula observation centre. NB: Dress warmly! **Hookipa Beach Park**, on Maui's north shore, is the Mecca of the windsurfing world—a sport that is taking over the island and as much fun to watch as it is to do—well, almost. For an all-photo tour of Maui, get connected to *www.makena.com/lahaina/home.htm*.

ACCOMMODATION/FOOD

Flown-in food is costly on Maui, so stick to local products: seafood, pineapple, lettuce, tomatoes, fabulous sweet onions like nowhere else on earth (it's the soil), potato chips ('Maui Kitch'n Cook'd Potato Chips' is the one you want, accept no substitutes), and 'Maui blanc' (pineapple wine). While on the west side of Maui, seek out cheap hotels; on the east side, try the campgrounds.

Banana Bungalow, 310 N Market St, **Wailuku**, 244-5090/ (800) 8-HOSTEL. Uncrowded rooms and numerous facilities including TV rm, laundry, hot tub, hammocks, kitchen and free internet access! Dorm $17, S-$32, D-$39. Cheap meals, free island tours and beach shuttle, free dropoff at airport. *home1.gte.net/bungalow* or email at *bungalow@gte.net*

Camp Keanae, on East side of Maui (36 miles E of airport), 242-9007. Isolated, beautiful setting (bring food). 12 people $10 pp, (no linens). Kitchen, usual facilities. Check-in 4pm-6pm; out by 9 am. Rsvs in advance. Mailing address and rsvs through YMCA: 250 Kanaloa Ave, Kahuluihi, 96732.

Northshore Inn, 2080 Vineyard St, **Wailuku**, 242-8999. Relaxed place with kitchen, TV, laundry and fridges in every room, free internet! Movies daily at 9pm. Dorm $16, S-$32, D-$43.

Camping: In Haleakala, 572-9306, a small amount of free **tent camping** plus 3 **hiker cabins**, $40 for two; cabins are so popular they're booked by lottery. Access by foot or on horseback only. Worth enquiring about cancellations when you get there. Rsvs attempts at PO Box 369, Makwao, 96768, but don't bother for 'lottery' cabins unless you can write 2 months ahead. Other **camping cabins**, and free tent camping available at various locations. Call the park on for options.

OF INTEREST/TRAVEL

Top 10 things to do in Maui!—www.maui.net/~bikemaui/top10.html is guaranteed to give you some great adventure ideas! **Blue Hawaiian Helicopter Tours**, 871-8844, from $150 p/p. Haleakala crater, rainforests and rugged shores of NE Maui. Also on Big Island -call 961-5600, or from mainland (800) 745-BLUE.

In Hana: 54 miles of bad but beautiful road keep Hana private, let someone else do the driving, try a tour, $75 for a full day, Ekahki Tours (888) 292-2422 / 877-9775, *www.ekahi.com* ; Charles Lindbergh loved it, lived and is buried here. Lodging is expensive, so day trips or camping near Seven Pools is just about it. 'Don't miss the **Oheo Gulch and Stream**; crystal clear, just like paradise.' The Shuttle runs btwn Lahaina and Kaanapali every 25 min, with stops at Royal Lahaina, Sheraton, Marriott, Kaanapali Beach and Hyatt, free.

Lahaina viewing for **humpback whales** who mate and calve in the channel Dec-Mar; lots of whale-watching tours from the harbour. Also see the **whaling museum** on the brig *Carthaginian*, 661-3262, at the harbour. Its A/V show has whale songs and birth of a whale. $4. Daily 10am-4.15pm. 'Not wildy interesting'.

In Kaanapali: Whalers Museum, Village on the Beach, 661-5992. Whaling artifacts, photographs, and antiques from 19th C. 'Small but stunning and poignant.' Daily 9.30am-10pm, free.

INFORMATION / TRAVEL

Regency Rent-a-Car, Kahului Airport, 871-6147. Daily 8am-8pm.
Visitors Bureau, 1727 Pa Loop, Wailuku, 244-3530. Mon-Fri 8am-4.30pm.
Visitor Information Kiosk, 872-3893, at the Kahului Airport terminal. Daily 6.30am-9pm.

HAWAII Called the Big Island for its size (and to distinguish it from Hawaii, the state, which encompasses all of the islands). Also known as the Orchid Island for the 22,000 varieties that grow wild and in nurseries, this is the youngest and firiest of the archipelago. Unlike its sister isles, which draw crowds to their beaches, Hawaii's main attraction is inland—**Hawaii Volcanoes National Park**, a cracked and crumpled moonscape created by the living volcano Mauna Loa. Each day the volcano adds to the island's real estate, dumping 650,000 cubic yards of red-hot lava into the ocean, enough to pave a thin sidewalk from here to New York. Nearby **Mauno Kea** recently earned new fame. From its peak scientists discovered a galaxy 12 billion light years away, that began forming much sooner than was thought possible after the 'Big Bang.' This and **Kilauea** are two of the world's most active volcanoes. Mark Twain (when it was fashionable for 19th century writers, such as Somerset Maugham, Jack London and Robert Louis Stevenson, to visit the islands) wrote of Kilauea, 'The smell of sulphur is strong, but not unpleasant to a sinner.'

But there are other facets to the Big Island: the jungley mystery of the east side; the desert bleakness of the south; the commercialised carnival of the Kona Coast to the west, wafted with coffee-laden breezes; and the rolling hills of the north, Hawaiian cowboy country. Best of all is the comparative lack of crowding; the Big Island is big enough to comfortably accommodate all comers. This is a place where the aloha spirit hasn't frayed too much, and people still get together to 'talk story' and watch the sun set. 'Twenty years behind the times!' Search the Big Island online, *www.bigisland.com/*.

ACCOMMODATION

The **Kona Coast** on the western side is where the high-priced hotels are; **Hilo** on the east retains an unspoiled, if dilapidated charm. Cheap rooms can be found on either side of the island, however.

Arnott's Lodge, 98 Apapane Rd, **Hilo**, 969-7097. $17 bunk, S-$31, D- $42, ensuite $40-55, tents $9. Right on the beach, daily tours & eco-expeditions, free shuttle to / from airport, bikes, snorkels to rent, internet access, laundry, kitchen & TV lounge.

Dolphin Bay Hotel, 333 Iliahi, **Hilo**, 935-1466. From S74, XP-$10 all rms have kitchens. Wonderful garden with pick-your-own bfast (not incl.)

HI-Holo Holo In, 19-4036 Kalani Holua Rd, **Volcano**, 967-7950. Large, clean rooms, dorm $15. Rsvs in advance after 4.30pm.

Hotel Honokaa, PO Box 247,Mammane St, **Honokaa**, 775-0678. Dorm $17, from S-$28, D-$39, 'luxury' D-$65. Bathroom outside. Rsvs required. 'Very simple.' Has been going over 80 years.

Kona Tiki Hotel, 75-5968 Alii Dr, 329-1425, on the **Kona Coast**. Fridge, ocean view, freshwater swimming pool. D-$60 or $72 w/full kitchen, XP-$8.

My Island B&B Inn, 19-3896 Old Volcano Rd, **Volcano Village**, 967-7216. Beautiful rooms in a historic mission-style home. From S-$45, D-$67, XP $20. *www.stay-hawaii.com/myisland/myisld.html myisland@ilhawaii.net*

Camping: The county runs beach parks where you can **camp** for $5 pp; permits required, from one of the four County Parks offices on the island. Call 961-8311 for info. In **Volcanoes National Park**, find free campsites at **Kipuka Nene, Namakani Paio** and **Kamoamoa**-each with shelters and fireplaces but no wood. Register with the visitors centre by 4.30pm. Call 985-6001 for more info. Also, try the **Namakani Paio** cabins, in an *ohia* forest. From S/D-$40, with key deposit. Call the Park on 967-7321.

FOOD

Kona coffee and macadamia nuts are the indigenous items on the menu; restaurants seem to put the nuts in everything. Free samples and self-guided tours at, among others:

Hawaiian Holiday Macadamia Nut Company in Haina off Hwy 19 near Honokaa, 775-7743, daily 9am-5.30pm.

Royal Kona Coffee Mill and Museum, Hwy 160 on the way to Captain Cook's Monument, 328-2511, daily 7.45am-5pm.

OF INTEREST

Only in America—drive-in-volcanoes at **Hawaii Volcanoes National Park**, 967-7311, $10 per car, good for 7 days, via Hwy 11 from Hilo, Crater Rim Drive takes you through the **Kilauea Caldera**, almost into the gaping maw of the **Halemaumau Firepit**. Here lives Pele, the notoriously bad-tempered Hawaiian fire goddess. If you're lucky, you may see a sacrifice to appease Pele at the edge of the firepit. Nowadays, cookies, pineapples and even whole dressed chickens get tossed over the edge (park regulations prohibit virgins), with the result being something of a rubbish bin, as plastic bags and bottles are chucked in with the food. Pele makes her presence known at nearby **Mauna Loa** as well. Being a shield volcano (so-called because of its characteristic shape), Mauna Loa erupts in a relatively controlled manner, allowing the curious to get a closer look. Going south on Hwy 11, the magnificent vista of the island's desert south comes into view.

You can visit the legendary **black sand beaches** at Kaimu and Punaluu, but be warned, the 'sand' is really volcanic rubble. Walking on it is a little like walking on broken glass, so bring shoes. The sand is green at **Ka Lae** (that is, if you can find any sand among the huge boulders that cover most of the shore). This is the most southerly point in the US, and the Hawaiian Plymouth Rock; here, Polynesian explorers first beached their canoes and established Hawaii's oldest known settlement, *circa* AD 750. Ka Lae is not developed for tourists and most car rental agencies prohibit customers from travelling this road. Further north on the island's western side is **Captain Cook's Monument**, accessible only by sea. Here the European discoverer of the Hawaiian Islands, once regarded by natives as a god, suffered a massive drop in popularity in 1779. The marker showing where he was killed (while intervening in a dispute) is under water.

Kahaluu Park Beach, south of **Disappearing Sands Beach** on Alii Drive. Amazing snorkeling among flashy fish, none of which is bigger than you are. It's like swimming through an aquarium. If you've forgotten your mask and fins, rent them from the park or at Jack's Diving Locker, just down the road from the Kona Inn Shopping Village in Kailua-Kona, at 75-5819 Alii Drive, 329-7585.

Manta Ray watching, Kona Surf Hotel. Nightly, the hotel spotlights the ocean where huge rays come to feed; free and thrilling. Taking Hwy 19 from Kailua-Kona, you pass through the verdant hills of northern Hawaii. Turn onto Hwy 24 at Honokaa to see the dreamlike **Waipi'o Valley**, a little green world captured by steep cliffs. The road goes all the way down to the valley, but the last part is too steep for cars. Jeep transport is available for a fee. Spare yourself the expense and the gear-grinding heart-attack ride down by hoofing it; if you're in reasonably good shape, you'll make it back up, too. Your reward: playing in the surf at the wonderful beach. The **Waipi'o Lookout**, offers one of the most striking panoramas in the islands. NB: A road to avoid is Hwy 200, the 50-mile **Saddle Road** with a high fatality rate btwn the twin behemoths Mauna Kea and Mauna Loa. Once you're on it, there's no turning back: attempting a U-turn on the narrow road lined with lava rock guarantees a flat tire or worse. Not to mention the debilitating fog. If you choose to traverse this or other questionable roads in a rented car, you must do so at your own risk. Check the contract for the company's policy.

INFORMATION/TRAVEL
Dollar Rent-a-Car , 961-6059 and **Avis Rent-a-Car**, 935-1290, in main terminal at Hilo Airport. Credit card essential. Cab from airport to Kona approx. $30.

Shuttle bus in **Kona** runs length of Alii Dr. 7.45am-9.15pm, $2.

Hilo Mass Transit, 961-8744, from Mooheau Bus Terminal on Kamehameha Ave. Operates one service a day, Mon-Fri only from Hilo to Volcano NP, return next day. Also other routes on the island.

Visitors Bureau, 250 Keawe St, Hilo, 967-5797. Mon-Fri 8am-4.30pm.

Waipi'o Valley Jeep Shuttle, 775-7121. Catch it at the top of the valley; purchase tkts at the **Waipi'o Woodworks Art Gallery**, $41, 8am-4pm. Rsvs rec.

For **Helicopter Tours** see Maui.

KAUAI   Once the 'Garden Island' was known as the 'undiscovered isle,' but no more. Now Kauai has its share of supermarkets, condos, huge resorts and canned tours. A constant stream of rent-a-cars flows along the highway that almost-girdles the island; crossing the street can be an adventure in itself. The landscape that lent the backdrop for the filming of *South Pacific* in the 1950s still endures: **Lumahai and Haena beaches** on postcard-perfect **Hanalei Bay**. But other patches of paradise are gone: the heavenly waterfall where France Nuygen cavorted with her GI beau has been closed due to tourist overload. Learn how you can experience Kauai on an exciting helicopter tour, an exhilarating boat trip and by driving past some of the most scenic spots imaginable, *www.jans-journeys.com/kauai*.

ACCOMMODATION
Garden Island Inn, 3445 Wilcox Rd, **Nawiliwili** (2 miles from Lihue), (800) 648-0154. Ocean views. From S/D-$84.
Hotel Coral Reef, 1516 Kuhio Hwy, **Kapaa**, 822-4481. Some rooms with ocean view (pay extra), rsvs advised. Fruit in morning, car rentals available. Rooms from S/D-$66.
Kauai International Hostel, 4532 Lehua St, **Kapaa** (800) 858-2295. Located opposite beach and several restaurants, a great base for exploring island. Friendly backpacker crowd and staff. Full kitchen, TV, pool table, laundry, daytrips. Dorm $16, private rooms from $40.
Camping: Kauai County Parks Office, 4444 Rice St. Moikeha Bldg, Lihu'e, 241-6670, has permits for camping in county parks. Permits also available from rangers on-site.

FOOD/OF INTEREST
Kauai is the proud birthplace of **Lappert's ice cream**, available at not one but six Lappert's locations including the Coconut Marketplace, the Coco Palms Hotel and the Princeville Shopping Center. Now you know you're in paradise.
Korean BBQ 4-3561 Kuhio Hwy, **Wailua**, 823-6744. "Best bet for a bargain meal',
National Tropical Botanical Gardens, have two locations on Kauai—**Lawai Kai** on the south shore and **Limahuli Gardens** on the north. Both have expensive tours—call for details, 332-7361. Research centre and various collections of tropical, native and international plants, including award-winning Allerton Estate Garden, leading up to Ocean (palms, gingers, lilies and bamboo grove). Their Native Hawaiian Plant Project protects endangered species.
North from Lihue on Hwy 56: Turn off the road for a panoramic ocean view from **Kilauea Lighthouse**. Further north is the aforementioned Hanalei Bay; don't let its beauty distract you from the oriental splendour of **Hanalei Valley**, inland from the hwy. Wet and dry caves are right on the road; pull off and explore! Hwy 56 ends at **Ke'e Beach**, where the cliffhanging trail along the gorgeous **Na Pali Coast** begins. An easy hike takes you through some of the best scenery in the Hawaiian Islands: as you round one crucial corner, you get your first breathtaking view of a series of precipices plunging into the sea. The beach at the end of the hike is not for swimming, but that will be obvious. Breakers pound continually onto the boulder-strewn shore, sucking back with vacuum force.
South from Lihue on Hwy 50: Two historic sites of European contact with Hawaii: the **Old Russian Fort** (Ft Elizabeth), now a brush-covered rocky ruin; and **Captain Cook's Landing** (Jan 1778) at Waimea Bay. Take a side trip to see the **Menehune Ditch**, an ancient aqueduct built, some say, in a single night by Menehunes—Hawaiian leprechauns! All archaeologists know is that *someone* built the aqueduct years before the first Polynesian explorers arrived in Kauai. Inland on Hwy 550, **Kokee State Park** has the "Grand Canyon of the Pacific', **Waimea Canyon**—'breathtaking'.

INFORMATION
Division of State Parks, 3060 Eiwa St (in State Office Bldg), **Lihue**, 274-3444. Has an abundancy of info on camping in state parks. Permits issued Mon-Fri 8am-4pm.
Hawaii Visitors Bureau, Lihue Plaza Bldg, 3016 Umi St, **Lihue**, 245-3971. Has the fun and informative Kauai Illustrated Pocket map. Mon-Fri, 8am-4pm.

OREGON *Beaver State*

In 1805-1806, Lewis and Clark explored this region, following the mighty Columbia River to its mouth. Their favourable reports brought pioneers along the 2000-mile trail—at first a trickle, swelling by the 1840s into a flood. A remarkably homogeneous bunch they were, too: farmers from the Midwest and South running from the economic depression of 1837-1840, looking for good soil, rainfall and an environment with neither malaria nor snow. Later, Astoria was founded near the mouth of the Columbia River to promote trade with China.

Oregon became a US territory the year of the California gold rush and promptly lost two-thirds of its males to the gold fever. A few struck it rich; more returned home and started selling wheat and lumber to the miners. At one point, Oregon wheat was actually made legal tender at $1 a bushel.

The heavily-forested Beaver State has suffered in recent years from a decline in the demand for lumber but still produces half the plywood in the US, the process having been invented here. Tourism is now the third-largest industry. Fortunately Oregonians work hard to preserve the state's natural beauty and like Vermonters, they have banned the construction of new billboards and kept crass tourist traps to a minimum (with noticeable exceptions along the coast). In 1991, Oregon was judged 'Greenest state in the US' by environmentalists.

The biggest magnet for visitors is the 400-mile coastline, protected as an almost-continuous series of state beaches. At times cold, foggy and windy, this region offers a kaleidoscope of magnificent sights: offshore rocks, driftwood-piled sands, cliffs, caves, twisted pines and acres of rhododendrons. Coastal villages seem to specialise in weather-beaten charm.

Picturesque barns, covered bridges and historic villages make the area from the coast to the east Willamette valley fun to explore. Unless you're bent on speed, avoid the dull ribbon of interstate freeway that unseams the valley north to south.

Both the youth hostel and the bed and bfast networks are alive and well in Oregon. Biking is extremely popular here; just remember that it, like other outdoor activities can be rained out at any moment. Most of the time, it's a slow mournful drizzle, the kind that drove Lewis and Clark nearly crazy during their winter sojourn at Fort Clatsop.

Though many east coasters have drifted west to this state and find it much more beautiful that its more-popular neighbour to the south, Oregon has not drawn nearly the number of converts as California has. This makes Oregonians happy: while there you may spot one of the bumper stickers that define the 'Oregon attitude': 'Don't Californicate Oregon.' Furthering the wry underselling of the state, another slogan warns: 'In Oregon, you don't tan; you rust.' Travellers are welcome, however, as long as they're passing through. The most popular bumper sticker reads, 'Welcome to Oregon. Now go home.'

dir.yahoo.com/Regional/U_S__States/Oregon/.
National Park: Crater Lake

PORTLAND In 1843, a couple of canoeists en route to Oregon City liked what they saw here and staked a 'tomahawk claim' by slashing trees in a 320-acre rectangle. The naming of the town was similarly impromptu: settlers flipped a coin (the losing name was Boston).

Portland modestly revels in its sparkling mountain and riverside setting, its luxuriant rose gardens (two-week Festival of Roses in June) and its low-key neighbourliness. Opportunities abound for good eating and social action in this city of booklovers, art lovers and ardent joggers.

Portland makes an ideal base to explore the Columbia River Gorge: take Hwy 84 E along the river to Troutdale and turn off onto the Columbia River Scenic Hwy. The old highway stops south of Bonneville Dam (its fish hatcheries are nice), but the scenic beauty doesn't. Further east on Hwy 84, the surrounding land dries up. Towns and farms line the river like oases, in stark contrast to the surrounding high desert cliffs. This is a drive that shows the state at its best. The Portland low-budget guide is an alternative offering to what the local Chamber of Commerce may typically offer. For a fun and very informative read, go to *www.levanet.com/chezxx/low-rent/index.html. The telephone area code for the city is 503.*

ACCOMMODATION
McMenamins Edgefield Hostel, 2126 SW Halsey St, (800) 669-8610. Converted farm, this lodge shares estate with a winery, brewery, movie theatre and two restaurants. Two single-sex dorms, showers, tubs. $22.
HI-North West Portland, 1818 NE Glisan St, 241-2783. New hostel close to cafes, shops, brew-pubs and nightlife. Van tours available to Oregon Coast, Mt. Hood etc.; Kitchen, laundry, bike storage, espresso bar. Res rec. $14-15.
HI-Portland Hostel, 3031 SE Hawthorne Blvd, 236-3380. Catch #14 bus from bus / rail terminals. Homey hostel with yard, BBQ, garden and covered porch. All-day van tours run year-round to Mt St. Helen's Volcano, Oregon Coast and Mt. Hood. Women's rooms fill up quickly in summer; rsvs or arrive at 5pm for walk-ins. Coffee-houses, live music clubs and a $1 cinema-pub are within walking distance. No curfew. All-you-can-eat pancakes, $1. Baggage storage available if arriving before 10 am. Dorms $14-$15. AYH-members only July-Aug.
Camping: Ainsworth State Park, 37 miles E of Portland at Exit 35 off I-84. Close to noisy expressway but the drive through gorge is well worth it. Hot showers, flush toilets, hiking trails. $12 / $18 w/hook-up. Also, **Champoeg State Park**, 8239 NE Champoeg Rd, off Hwy 99W. Tent sites $15 /$19 w/ hook-up, 2-day advance rsvs required. Call State Park Reservations on (800) 551-6949 or 731-3493.

FOOD
The tastiest thing in Oregon is free—the drinking water. Grocery prices are high in town, even for local produce. You'll do better at the roadside produce stands, particularly along the Columbia River, where the peaches are huge and drip all over your shirt when you bite into them. Don't miss local specialities: blackberry and boysenberry pie, razor clams (hideously expensive, but with a licence you can dig your own), scallops, smelt and Dungeness crab.
Bijou Cafe, 132 SW 3rd, 222-3187. 'A must for visitors. Great value for money with a friendly and relaxed atmosphere.' Daily for bfast and lunch.
Bread & Ink, 3610 SE Hawthorne, 239-4756. Local favourite for lunch. 'Best burgers.' Also pasta, fish specials, Vietnamese, Italian, Mexican and Jewish! Open daily. 'Nicest restaurant in town.'
Dan and Louis Oyster Bar, 208 SW Ankeny, 227-5906. Outstanding oysters, stew,

marine atmosphere. Daily 11am-10pm, 11pm w/ends.

Fuller's Coffee Shop, 136 NW 9th Ave, 222-5608. Bfast at this old-fashioned lun-cheonette on freshly made cinnamon rolls, four-star French toast, and omelettes accompanied by classic hash browns. Try fried razor clams for lunch. Mon-Sat.

Jake's Famous Crawfish, 401 SW 12th Ave, 226-1419. A daily blackboard of sea creatures, hauled in fresh, choice includes salmon, crab and sole.

Old Wives' Tales, 1300 E Burnside, 238-0470. Multi-ethnic vegetarian, vegan, chicken and seafood; also soup and salad bar. 'New Age, classical and jazz music round out the eclectic atmosphere.' Daily for bfast, lunch and dinner, 8am-10pm, 'til 11pm w/ends.

Papa Haydn's at two locations, 5829 SE Milwaukee, 232-9440 and 701 NW 23rd St, 228-7317. A Viennese coffee-house with dynamite pastries. 'Milwaukee location hard to find.' Tues-Thur 11.30am-11pm, Fri & Sat 'til midnight, Sun 10am-3pm.

OF INTEREST

24-Hour Church of Elvis, 720 SW Ankeny St, 226-3671. 'Most hours', donation. Camp Elvis heaven; marriages can be arranged!

The **Oregon Museum of Science and Industry (OMSI)**, 1945 SE Water Ave (at the corner of Clay St), 797-4537, is open daily 9.30am-7pm, Thu till 8pm, summer, (call for winter) $6.50, extra charges for OMNIMAX Theatre, planetarium etc. Cheap planetarium shows. Don't miss 'state of the heart,' a human heart preserved through plastination; software that checks your cardio-vascular health; and a biofeedback train that goes faster as you get warmer.

Pioneer Courthouse Square, 701 SW 6th Ave, is an open-air city centre square paid for by the sale of 65,000 bricks used to build the square. The benefactors' names are inscribed on each one. Free performances and activities year-round. See the 'weather ball,' a meteorological glockenspiel. 'Silly noon-time fanfare.' In the summer the **Peanut Butter and Jam Sessions** attract huge amounts of jazz and folk music lovers, Tues & Thurs noon-1pm.

Portland Art Museum, 1219 SW Park Ave, at the South Park Blocks, 226-2811. European, 19th and 20th century American, pre-Columbian, West African, Asian and Pacific Northwest Indian art. $7.50, $6 w/student ID. Tue-Sat 10am-5pm, Sun 12pm-5pm. The **Public Art Walking Tour** leaves from here too.

Portland Building, btwn Main and Madison, 4th and 5th. Architect Michael Graves, knowingly or not, has taken a page from Frank Lloyd Wright's notebook by designing a controversial pink and blue public building for a mid-sized American city (cf. 'Marin County' in *California* section). Outside on the 5th Ave side is the *Portlandia* sculpture, a giant lady with hammered copper skin like the Statue of Liberty; she holds a trident instead of a torch.

Skidmore Old Town Historic District, New Market Block, SW 1st and Ankeny. Interconnected townhouses with open plaza, colonnade, outdoor stands. Old Town also marks the end of **Waterfront Park**, an excellent place to picnic, fish, stroll and enjoy community events.

The **Grotto**, NE 85th & Sandy Blvd, 254-7371. Natural grotto in huge cliff, resem-bling grotto at Lourdes. Lower grounds are free, but it's worth $2 to see the monastery above (take elevator) for rose gardens, Marian art and one of the best views you can get of Portland, the Columbia River and Washington State beyond. 9am-8pm daily in summer, 'til 5pm from mid-September.

Some of Portland's most pleasant features are its **fountains**: the **Lovejoy**, SW 3rd & Harrison; the **Rose Fountain**, at O'Bryant Sq, 408 SW Park; **Ira Kellar Fountain**, SW 4th Ave btwn Market & Clay Sts, and the **Skidmore Fountain**, 1888 SW 1st & Ankeny.

Washington Park, west of town, has **Japanese Gardens**, 611 SW Kingston Ave, 223-1321, with 5 traditional styles, especially lovely with the white cone of Mt Hood framed by maple leaves and pagodas. $$6, $3.50 w/student ID. Daily 10am-8pm 'til Sept; 10am-4pm after Oct. Daily tours. Also in the park is the **Rose Test Garden**, 400 SW Kingston Ave, free, with over 8000 rosebushes. From here you can take 'the world's smallest railroad,' $2.75, through the forest to the **Zoo-OMSI** complex. The Zoo, 4001 SW Canyon Rd, 226-1561, daily 9.30am-7pm (last admission 6pm), $6.50, has a huge chimp collection and large elephant herd.

Outside Portland: The Columbia River Gorge, stretches east from Portland to The Dalles and offers truly magnificent scenery. Sailboard enthusiasts will know this place to be the most 'radical' location outside Hawaii due to the constant wind funnelled btwn the high cliffs. Take a car up and along the Historic River Hwy which parts with I-84 at Troutdale to enjoy spectacular views of the Gorge and see some of the numerous waterfalls en route (**Multnomah** is the biggest and most impressive). For real escapism, go up to the tranquil setting of **Lost Lake** and a close-up of **Mt Hood**, the state's tallest mountain. 'Spectacular, picture-book scenery.' Greyhound and Amtrak both serve the area; 'Amtrak is best for views.' **Bonneville Dam**, with its salmon farms and fish ladders is also worth a look.

Hwy 30, west. A beautiful 100-mile drive to **Astoria** that romps up hill, down dale, beside the Columbia and its wooded islands, and past roadside stands, houseboats, picturesque backwaters, juicy blackberries—there's even a pulloff to see **Mt St Helens**. **Westport**, with its Wahkiakum ferry across the river, makes a good lunch stop.

SHOPPING
Oregon has no **sales tax** so make the most of your dollars!

Lloyd Center 282-2511, has 200 shops around an indoor ice-rink.

Niketown store, 930 SW 6th, 221-6453. TVs in the floor, sculptures of famous sports stars and various artefacts such as jerseys and shoes. Mon-Thurs & Sat 10am-7pm, Fri 'til 8pm, Sun 11.30am-6.30pm.

Powells City of Books, 1005 W Burnside, 228-4651, *www.powells.com*. Allegedly the world's biggest bookstore—takes up one whole block and visitors are given a map on entry!

Saturday Market, under west end of Burnside Bridge, in Skidmore, SW 1st and Ankeny, 222-6072. 'Original buyers market.' Stalls with home-made everything. 'Wonderful.' Sat 10am-5pm, Sun 11am-4.30pm.

ENTERTAINMENT
The best entertainment listings are in Friday's *Oregonian* and various free handouts. Check the *Willamette Weekly* (put out each evening on street corners and in restaurants) for listings of good local blues and rock bands. There are 16 **microbreweries** in the state, many in Portland. A favourite, **Bridgeport Brew Pub**, 1313 NW Marshal, 241-7179, offers several cask-conditioned ales. Or watch free movies at **Mission Theatre and Pub**, 17th & Gleason NW, 223-4031, or **Baghdad Pub**, 3702 SE Hawthorne, 236-9234, as you sample seasonal brews. Great pizza, beer and movies.

Key Largo, 223-9919, 31 1st Ave, btwn Couch & Burnside, has rhythm & blues, rock & roll, jazz. Under $10 cover.

Festivals: Portland hosts excellent festivals: the **Blues Fest** in July, 282-0555 *www.waterfrontbluesfest.org*, **The Bite** in mid-August, 248-0600, and others. 'Saw excellent African ballet for $2.'

INFORMATION
Chamber of Commerce , 221 NW 2nd Ave, 228-9411.

Portland/Oregon Visitors Association, 26 SW Salmon, (800) 345-3214. Mon-Fri 9am-5pm, Sat 9am-4pm, Sun 10am-2pm. 'Maps and a bounty of info.' Pick up the *Portland Book*.

INTERNET ACCESS
Internet Arena, 1016 SW Taylor, 224-2718. *interarena.com* Open 10am-12pm, $5 /hr.

Free access at the **Central Library** 801 SW 10th St, 248-5123, open daily, till 9pm Mon-Thu.

TRAVEL
Amtrak, 800 NW 6th Ave, 273-4865/(800) 872-7245.
Broadway Cab, 227-1234; and **Radio Cab**, 227-1212. Cabs won't stop for you on the streets.
Gray Line, 4320 N Suttle Rd, 285-9845. Lots of tours: Mt Hood, the Columbia River, coast, around town. Pickup at local hotels.
Greyhound, 550 NW 6th Ave, next to Union Station, (800) 231-2222.
NW Auto Rental, 9785 SW Shady Lane, 624-1804. Over 21 only, need drivers licence and major credit card.
Tri-Met city bus and MAX rail, 231-3198 for rates and info. Free downtown zone, $1.10-$1.40 to other areas or $3.50 all-day pass.
Portland International Airport is located about 13 miles E of the city. To get there take bus #12 labelled 'Sandy Blvd to Airport' from SW 6th and Main. This will take around 20 mins and costs $1.35. Alternatively take the RAZ Express bus, 684-3322, $9 o/w.
Tours: Green Tortoise, (800) 867-8647/(800) 227-4766. Approx $15 to Seattle, $39 to San Francisco, $59 to LA. Departs from SW 6th and College, outside the university deli.

THE OREGON COAST   Hwy 101 runs along the Pacific coast from the southernmost tip of California to the Canadian border, but the Oregon stretch, especially the pristine 225-mile section from the California boundary to **Newport**, is surely the loveliest. It's also the driest part of the Oregon coast (it gets about half the amount of rain as the stretch north of Newport), a definite attraction for those camping out. 'Best way to see this is by camping, buy a tube tent; light, compact, about $12.' The coast offers driftwood hunting, whale watching, clamdigging and rockhounding, from agates to jasper. While you're on the beach, nose-to-sand, look for glass floats, the ultimate beach-combing prize. The powerful combo of the Japanese Current and westerly winds wash these green, amber and turquoise buoyancy balls from Japanese fishing nets all the way across the Pacific. December through March is the best time to search; look for non-rocky beaches with moderate slope and go early to beat other float-hunters. Swimming is dangerous in many areas and cold everywhere; enquire locally.

Going north-to-south, the Oregon Coast starts at **Astoria**, a miniature San Francisco at the mouth of the Columbia River. Founded in 1811 by John Jacob Astor as a base for the Pacific Fur Company, the town survived as the first permanent US settlement on the Pacific Coast due to successful trading with China. While there, check out the rococo Flavel House and Shallon Winery; try scallops at Pier 11 and Finnish limpa bread at local bakeries. Also of interest is **Ft Clatsop**, a few miles SW of town (8am-6pm, $2 in summer) where Lewis and Clark spent the stormy winter of 1805. If you're in a car, cross the Megler Bridge to Washington, spanning 4.6 miles and barely skimming the surface of the water. Back on Hwy 101, turn west to **Ft Stevens**, a historic park with a picturesque shipwreck. **Seaside**, with its boardwalk, arcades and popular swimming beach, is a candyfloss sort of town, noted for cheap seafood at Norma's. **Cannon Beach** merits a pause: monolithic Haystack Rock, a charming art-village, and great windy walking at Ecola State Park are some of its pluses. Its annual **Sand Sculpture Derby** in spring is one of the most inventive anywhere.

Near **Tillamook**, take the **Three Capes Rd**, a 39-mile loop through a succession of scenic vistas, villages and lighthouses to **Three Arch Rocks National Wildlife Refuge**, with its herd of Steller sea lions. Tillamook provides tasting of its namesake cheese and others, along with wine, at the Blue Heron and Tillamook Cheese Factories. The lively little fishing and beach town **Newport**, on a sheltered and beautiful bay, is a good place to eat Dungeness crab and browse with other holiday makers. 'A friendly young community on NW cliff, where there are quaint wooden summer cottages facing the ocean.' Of interest here is the **Oregon Coast Aquarium**, 2820 SE Ferry Slip Rd, 867-3474, next to the Science Center. The aquarium offers various exhibit galleries of Oregon marine-life, including an outdoor animal park and sea-bird aviary. Open daily summer 9am-6pm (10am-5pm in winter), $8.75. Neighbouring **Depoe Bay** is noted as an excellent whale-watching spot, Nov-March; along its seawall, geyser-like sprays of ocean water often arch over the highway. **Beverly Beach** to the south is the nearest campground and has hiker/biker spots. South of Newport is a likeable tourist trap called **Sea Gulch**, a village of carved lifesize figures. The carving is done freehand—with a chainsaw!—and you can watch. **Yachats** (that's *Yah*-hots) is worth a stop, especially in smelt season May-Sept, or better yet, during the annual Smelt Fry in early July. It's nothing to eat a dozen of the silvery mini-fish and fun to watch the catch, too. Good non-fish offerings at the Adobe Hotel and others. Between rhododendron-happy Florence and Yachats are the **Sea Lion Caves**, 547-3111, *www.sealioncaves.com*, reached via elevator and reeking of perennial, fishy sea lion halitosis. Open daily 9 am 'til dusk, $6.50; you can also see the huge creatures more distantly from various points near the caves.

Oregon Dunes, some as high as 600ft, stretch for 40 miles to Florence; duneside camping is possible but crowded at **Honeyman State Park**; the **Umpqua Lighthouse State Park** (hiker/biker section), 6 miles south of Reedsport, is better. Biggest town in SW Oregon, **Coos Bay** is a fishing and lumber port good for a night's stopover, with a grimy bar, good meals at the Blue Heron Bistro, and myrtlewood factories.

Hwy 101 turns inland at Coos Bay, but you can follow secondary roads nearer the coast to spectacular scenery at **Sunset Bay** (camping) and **Shore Acres State Park**. At cranberry-growing **Bandon** you have a cheese factory, the makings of an art colony, a youth hostel, and natural beauty all around. Further along, the panorama of **Humbug Mountain** and the rock-strewn coast are a worthwhile stop; 3-mile hike to the top. Excellent campground with low-cost hiker/biker section. **Gold Beach** is on the banks of the Rogue, an officially-designated wild river and prime spot for rafting and fishing. Good smoked salmon here. Explore the Oregon Coast from Astoria to Brookings Harbor through *The Wave; www.oregoncoast.com/. The telephone code for the area is 541.*

ACCOMMODATION
Adobe Motel, 1555 Hwy 101 N, **Yachats**, 547-3141. Fireplace, sauna, excellent bfasts and dinners, agate hunting and smelt fishing on their beach. D-$82 with ocean view, $60 without.

City Center Motel, 538 SW Coast Hwy, **Newport**, 265-7381. Rooms from $50.

HI-Sea Star Hostel, 375 2nd St, **Bandon**, 347-9632. Located in the historic 'Old Town Waterfront District,' halfway btwn San Francisco and Seattle on the Oregon Coast Bicycle Route, see some of Oregon's most scenic coastlines: dunes, cliffs, rock formations and white sandy beaches. Hostel has bistro with everything made on premises from organic ingredients (they make their own pasta dough, smoke their own meats—even roll their own sausages). Lots of vegetarian options, open to non-residents. Skylights, wood stove, deck and courtyard overlooking harbour, day use, equipment storage area, information desk, kitchen, laundry facilities, linen. Dorms $13, private rooms available.

HI-Seaside Hostel, 930 N Holladay Dr, **Seaside**, 738-7911. European style hostel on river, 4 blocks from beach; the town hosts festivals and events. Explore neighbouring Cannon Beach, an artists' town, and the historic maritime community of Astoria. Canoes available for use. Outdoor decks with river view and on-site espresso and pastry bar. Movies shown every evening; nature programs too. 5 night max stay, 10 min daily chore, bedding provided $1.50. Dorms $13-15 and private rooms from D-$30. Greyhound stops at hostel.

Camping: There are over 50 campgrounds in Oregon's state park system; approx $18-22 for a tent site. Many sites have hiker/biker sections, set away from vehicles, from $2. Call (800) 452-5687 for rsvs or (800) 551-6949 for general info. State park website has more information: *www.ohwy.com/or/o/prd.htm*.

Tugman State Park: near Lakeside, 759-3604, open mid-April-Labor Day, comes highly praised: 'Best campsites in the US.' Greyhound will drop you where you like. Warm sleeping bag and tent advised, also food as parks are usually distant from shops. Tent sites from $15. **Free camping: near Florence** in the dunes—or try **Siuslaw National Forest**, 750-7000, from $8; and **Sunset Bay State Park**, from $16.

CRATER LAKE NATIONAL PARK   Mt St Helens was a minor firecracker

compared with **Mt Mazama**, which exploded some 6800 years ago to form **Crater Lake**. This inky blue well, in a densely forested part of southern Oregon's Cascade Range, cannot be bettered for dramatic settings: approached through a moonlike landscape and rimmed by 500 to 2000-ft cliffs (all that is left of 12,000-ft Mazama), Crater Lake descends to depths of 1932 ft, making it one of the deepest lakes in the world. Poking through the surface are **Phantom Ship Island** and **Wizard Island**, itself an extinct volcanic cone. Boat excursions visit Wizard, where you can hike to its 760-ft summit and down into its 90-ft-deep crater. The 33 mile **Rim Drive** is open mid-July to October; also recommended are the 1 mile hike down to the lake from Cleetwood Cove and the 1¹/₂ miles **Discovery Pt Trail**

From high points in the park, you can see Mt Shasta, 100 miles to the south. Wonderful bird-watching, wildflowers and nature programmes. Crater Lake is even more beautiful in winter, when snow-capped conifers are reflected in the deep blue iris of the lake. *The telephone code for the Area is 541.*

ACCOMMODATION

Ft Klamath Lodge, Ft Klamath, Hwy 62 (about 22 miles S of Crater Lake), 381-2234. Restaurant and grocery nearby. From S-$33, D-$43.

Lodging also at Klamath Falls and **Medford**; try **Motel 6's**—884-2110 in Klamath Falls, and 773-4290 in Medford, rooms from $50.

Oregon Motel 8 and RV Park, Hwy 97 N, 3¹/₂ miles N of Klamath Falls, 882-0482. Tent sites $10.

Camping: Mazama Campground, 594-2511, at the junction of West and South Entrance Roads. Open mid-June to Oct, depending on snow conditions: sites from

$15; and **Lost Creek Campground**, 594-2211 ext 402, at the SW corner of park has camping sites for $15. The Nature Trail begins here. Grocery store at Rim Village; also excellent fishing.
Backcountry campsites are free.

FOOD
Best to buy food at the **Old Fort Store**, Ft Klamath, 381-2265. Open summer daily 9am-7pm. Also, try **Safeway**, Pine & 8th St; **Hobo Junction**, 636 Main St; and **Cattle Crossing Café**, 381-9801, on Hwy 62 in Ft Klamath for burgers and a filling bfast. Open daily.

INFORMATION/TRAVEL
Amtrak, South Spring depot, (800) 872-7245.
Greyhound, 1200 Klamath Ave, Klamath Falls, 882-4616/(800) 231-2222.
National Park information, 594-2211, ext.402. $10 entrance fee p/car, $3 cyclists/hikers. Rim Drive is closed in winter; enter the park via Hwy 62 south or west.
William G Steel Center, nxt to park HQs, 594-2211 ext 402. Provides free backcountry camping permits. Daily 9am-5pm.

SOUTHERN OREGON   South and west of Crater Lake are a cluster of worthwhile destinations, made more appealing by well-placed hostels and other good lodging. **Ashland**, America's answer to the Old Vic, has three theatres (including a pleasant one outdoors) and an 8-month play schedule that specialises in Shakespeare but draws on other sources as well. Not far away is **Jacksonville**, an intelligently-restored gold mining town. Stagecoach rides are offered to the cemetery and 80-odd homes there. Nearby also are the **Rogue River** and **Oregon Caves National Monument**, 592-3400, $7 tours; the latter are set deep in the marble heart of **Mt Elijah** and full of stalagmites & stalactites, flowstone formations and strenuous hikes. Near **Cave Junction** is **Takilma**, a former hippy mecca which still has a hippy hospital. Nowadays the area is populated with 'survivalists'; apparently the natural convection of the land would eliminate the danger of radiation in the event of nuclear attack. *Telephone code for the area is 541.*

ACCOMMODATION
Ashland Hostel, 150 N Main St, **Ashland**, 482-9217. 3 blocks to Shakespeare Festival. Large kitchen, laundry; located in historic home. Open year round $15.
Cave Junction Fordson Home Hostel , 250 Robinson Rd, **Cave Junction**, 592-3203. Set on 20-acres of woodland with streams and garden. Large private room in addition to dorm rooms ($12 AYH, $15 non-AYH, $2 discount for students w/ID). Solar showers (great fun), baths, kitchen, free use of bicycles, camping, river swimming and free berries in season. 13 miles to Oregon Caves and discounted entrance fee, close to wineries (one is being built next door), bikes for use. Owner Jack Heald is a mine of information about the area and gives his guests 40 min tours covering sights from antique tractors to Douglas Firs. If you stay on a weekend he'll even take you rock' n' roll' dancing! Rsvs essential.
Manor Motel, 476 N Main St, **Ashland**, 482-2246. Downtown. From S/D-$60, TV, AC. Rooms with kitchen also available. Advance rsvs and deposit required.

CENTRAL AND EASTERN OREGON   The much less visited interior of the State does not have the scenic drama of the coastal region, however there are a number of sights and pleasant towns in which to while away a few hours if such is your want. **Eugene** is the state's second city, situated between the Cascade mountains and Coastal ranges, and as the home to the University of Oregon, has a youthful feel to it. Sports enthusiasts will not be disappointed with many trails for running and cycling—this was the place where the *Nike* running shoe was tried and tested. Finally, the area has numerous covered bridges to be explored (and photographed). Contact the Visitor's Centre, 115 W 8th Ave, suite 190, (800) 547-5445 / 484-5307.

On the eastern side of the Cascades, **Bend** is a good base for visiting central Oregon. The Greyhound runs daily from Eugene and Portland. The town centre, set on the Deschutes river, has a laid-back feel, with several lovely cafes with a Californian ambiance—try the **Cup of Magic**, 1304 NW Galveston. The climate here also, is less extreme than on the coast; Bend is said to receive 250 days of sunshine a year. The Visitor's Centre is located at 63085 N Hwy 97, (800) 949-6086.

Further inland still, **Baker City** is an old gold-rush town and commemo-rates the Oregon Trail at the **National Historic Trail Interpretative Centre**, Flagstaff Hill, (800)523-1235 / 523-1843, 5 miles out of town. 150 years ago, thousands of Americans made the 2000 mile trail west to the 'Promised Land', over treacherous rivers and rugged mountains. ten percent of them didn't make it. The Centre also has exhibits on the Native Americans who first settled the land. Open daily, 9am-6pm (summer), 9am-4pm (winter); free. Far in the north-eastern corner of the state, the Snake River has gouged **Hell's Canyon**, a National Recreation Area, and the deepest canyon on the continent. Unlike the Grand Canyon, you can't just go to the edge and peer in, but there are numerous look-out points, or take a boat tour along the river. Contact the HQ at (503) 426-4978.

WASHINGTON   *The Evergreen State*

Unofficially known as *The State of Nirvana*, there is a persistent legend has it that the original name proposed for Washington was 'Columbia'; the idea was dropped to avoid confusion with the nation's capital. True or not, Washington has always been haunted by its name, to the extent that the state once advertised itself to tourists as 'The *Other* Washington,' thereby selling itself short.

Like neighbouring Oregon, Washington is mountainous, rainy and green in the west, and flat, dry and tawny in the east. Likewise, it has but one pre-eminent city, Seattle, which enjoys a pugnacious rivalry with Portland. Once a stronghold of the radical labour movement (the Wobblies were here in the 1930s), Washington now builds more Boeings, raises more apples, processes more seafood, stores more nuclear waste than just about anyone else and is the home of the world's most successful software company, Microsoft.

This is also David Lynch country. *Blue Velvet* and *Twin Peaks* were both filmed here, and there does seem to be a strange atmosphere invoked by the countryside that just might explain the bizarre nature of his work.

A large share of the state's scenic beauty is within reach of Seattle: **Puget Sound** and its hundreds of islands; the still, dark **Olympic rain forest**;

omnipresent **Mt Rainier**; and the obtrusive upstart, **Mt St Helens**, 75 miles south. Other sights are further flung. **North Cascades National Park**, an expanse of alpine loveliness, with canyons, glaciers, peaks and grizzlies, lies along the British Columbia border. In the eastern part of Washington are **Grand Coulee Dam**, the Palouse River Canyon and the 'Scablands,' a weird, scarred landscape left thousands of years ago by a glacial flood that inundated much of the Columbia Plateau. The Long Beach peninsula, though part of SW Washington is more conveniently reached from Astoria, Oregon.

Rain is endemic to the Northwest, but Seattle gets most of its 34 inches per year between October and May; the Olympic rain forest gets up to 150 inches annually. *dir.yahoo.com/Regional/U_S_States/Washington/.*
National Parks: Olympic, Mount Rainier, North Cascades.
The telephone area code for Seattle is 206, for all other places listed is 360.

SEATTLE Long before the advent of 'grunge,' before Nirvana, Soundgarden *et al*, the 'Emerald City' was a place to be. With becoming arrangements of hills, houses, water and mountains Seattle has long been a mecca for those who like life with a more laid-back attitude.

To the SW, the skyline is dominated by snowy Mt Rainier. To the west, the city's great deepwater harbour opens onto island-studded Puget Sound and the Olympic Mountains. Urbanisation is further subdivided by lakes and parks, from tiny to massive, girding the downtown district into a compact and pleasing shape. The look is an idiosyncratic mix of sleek and traditional, of contemporary ranch houses and bohemian houseboats. All this adds up to a city that feels similar to another great Pacific metropolis whose initials are 'SF.' Don't tell Seattlites that; they defend their city's individuality. And rightly so, Seattle does have a certain flair. It's not every city that would make a Wagnerian opera cycle (sung in German and English) its major cultural event, or outfit its waterfront with vintage 1927 Australian streetcars and its airport with a meditation room?

Considering that it's a major gateway to, and trade partner with, the Orient, Seattle shows few Asian influences of non-gustatory kind. Rather, at its core the city is boisterous, adventurous and optimistic, no doubt a legacy of its logging and Klondike gold rush past. America's richest man, Bill Gates, currently assessed at $103 billion, lives in nearby Bellevue near Redmond where his company (Microsoft) is based.

If coffee is your amour then Seattle is the place to get in some serious drinking. The city seems to run on caffeine, supplied by some of the strongest espressos you will ever taste. There are coffee bars and cafes everywhere all serving 'damn fine cups of jo,' as Agent Cooper would say. You'll be wired for weeks. *seattle.yahoo.com/.*

ACCOMMODATION
B&B's: lots of options including **B&B International** and **Northwest B&B**; details in *Accommodation Background*. Also: **Pacific B&B**, 701 NW 60th, Seattle, WA 98107 or call 784-0539; **Traveller's Reservations Service**, Box 492, Mercer Island, WA 98040 or call 232-2345, specialises in B&B's. Rates from S-$40, D-$48 (luxurious accommodations command the higher rates from $75). Covers Seattle and most of the Northwest, including Puget Sound, Tacoma, Olympia, Spokane, Victoria and Vancouver Island, BC.

American Backpackers Hostel, 126 Broadway E, Seattle, (800) 600-2965, $16. 'Helpful, cheap, excellent location…a must!' No curfew; free pick-up from Amtrak, Greyhound and downtown. Airport pick-up for 2+. Free bfast. Pool table. 'Clean and safe.'

College Inn Guest House, 4000 University Way NE, 633-4441. Continental bfast plus all-day coffee, tea. Antique; registered as a historical landmark. From S-$65, D-$75, also has quads, all shared bath.

Green Tortoise Backpacker's Hostel, 1525 2nd Ave, or 888-4AHOSTEL. 1 block from Pike Place Market, within the free bus ride zone, close to Pioneer Sq, art museum and waterfront. All rooms have own wash basin. Kitchen, free bfast, laundry and discount cards. Call hostel for pick-up. $16 dorm ($17 credit card), private rooms, D-$40, T-$60. Also, **Green Tortoise Garden Apartments**, 715 2nd Ave North, 340-0387. Long-term accommodations suitable for travellers. Charming building with a fantastic view of the Space Needle, 2 blocks from Seattle Center and convenient access to stores and bus lines. Lovely backyard and deck, barbecue, herb & veg garden, laundry, free bfast and friendly communal atmosphere. Dorms with 4 beds, $85/wk, $220/month.

Moore Hotel, 1926 2nd Ave, 448-4851. 'Clean, modern, spacious—offered us the best deal.' 'Excellent hotel, warm and friendly.' From S-$55, D-$64.

HI-Seattle Hostel, 84 Union St (near Pike Place Market), 622-5443. A former US immigration station, modern interior. The Seattle Art Museum And Pike Place Market-full of farmers' stalls, eateries and shops-are both only 1 block away. Walk down the waterfront, take a scenic ride on a Washington State Ferry, or stroll into Myrtle Edwards Park for a panoramic view of the Olympic Mountains across Puget Sound. Laundry, info desk, evening programs. Take bus #174 from bus station to Union & 4th Sts. $18 (AYH)/ $21 (non-AYH). Private rooms D-$41/47. Rsvs essential.

St Regis Hotel, 116 Stewart at 2nd, 448-6366. Situated in large gay community. 'Basic but comfortable.' Laundry and restaurant. 'Only hotel with vacancies just before Labor Day.' From S-$35, D-$68.

HI-Vashon Island Ranch Hostel, 12119 SW Cove Rd, Rt 5, Box 349, **Vashon Island**, WA 98070, 463-2592. A ferry ride from downtown, this hostel offers a getaway from the city in a unique setting. Five Sioux Indian tepees offer couple and family rooms, or sleep in covered wagons surrounding a campfire. Get up early for free pancakes, then enjoy beautiful, rural Vashon Island by bikes provided free at hostel. (Non-refundable deposit for obligatory safety gear though—needed as bikes have no brakes!) $10. Rsvs req. 'Check ferry timings carefully—few and far between at weekend. Will pick up from ferry terminal on island; on return , take bus from Vashon to ferry.'

FOOD

Washington is famous for superb fruit (especially peaches, apples and berries), Dungeness crab, Olympia oysters, razor and littleneck clams, and the indigenous candy, 'Aplets' and 'Cotlets,' a sort of jellied fruit bar covered with powdered sugar and guaranteed to be addictive. Seattle is a prime place to sample them all. Excellent Chinese, Thai, Japanese and Vietnamese restaurants, too.

Bakeman's, 122 Cherry St, 622-3375. Turkey or meat loaf; white or wheat; mayo or mustard. Make your mind up and move down the line! Open Mon-Fri only.

Café D'Arte, 2nd Ave and Stewart, 728-4468 (2 blocks from Commodore Hotel). The best coffee shop in Seattle! T-shirts, mugs etc., good to buy as souvenirs. Mon-Sat 8am-5pm.

Cafe Loc, Seattle Center, 728-9292. 'Good Vietnamese food.'

China First Restaurant. 7 branches within city, but try 4237 University Way NE, 634-3553. Lunch 3-course special only $3.50; 'huge and delicious portions'. Also excellent service.

Elliott Bay Book Company, 1st and Main, 624-6600. Cafe and literary gathering place, with over 100,000 titles. Cafe Mon-Fri 7am-10.30pm, Sat from 9.30 am, Sun 11am-5pm.

Emmet Watson's Oyster Bar, 1916 Pike Place, behind the Soames-Dunn Bldg, 448-7721. Best oysters anywhere, three dozen kinds of bottled and draft beer, good ceviche (marinated fish). Savour hangtown fry (oyster omelette) for bfast. Inexpensive, under $10.

Gravity Bar, 415 Broadway E, 325-7186. A trendy, stainless steel decked juice bar serving things like 'Ginger Rogers,' a fruit and vegetable drink containing carrots, apple and ginger, $4.50. Drinks from $2.

Hi-Spot Café, 1410 34th St, 325-7905. Bfast is a must-eat Seattle meal here! Open daily.

Iron Horse, 311 3rd Ave S, ½ block from King St Station, 223-9506. 'Burgers delivered by model trains! Great railroading atmosphere.' Mon-Sun 11am-9pm.

Ivar's Acres of Clams Restaurant, Pier 54, 624-6852. Seattle seafood tradition since 1938. Great old photos and waterfront view. Daily 11am-11pm.

Pike Place Market is *the* place to purchase fresh produce, meat, fish and takeaway items; it's a warren of ethnic treats from Filipino lumpia to Spanish tapas. Check out the **Rainbow Cafe** (if you can find it!) for views of the Sound and super-salads.

Old Spaghetti Factory, Elliot and Broad, near Pier 70, 441-7724. Meals $6-10, daily specials. Open daily.

Streamliner Diner, 397 Winslow Way, Bainbridge Island, 842-8595.Daily; bfast and lunch only; American and Mexican food $6-10; reach the island via ferry from Seattle, Pier 51.

OF INTEREST
Mt St Helens. The Indians called it 'Loowelit-klah,' or 'smoking mountain,' and they knew what they were talking about. On 18 May, 1980, the mountain erupted, blowing away a cubic mile of earth, killing 57 people and 2 million mammals, birds and fish, and exhaling smoke and ash to 72,000 ft to circle the globe. Since then, Mt St Helens has erupted sporadically but on a smaller scale; quakes and ominous rumblings are commonplace. Plan on spending all day on your trip, whether from Seattle or Portland. 'A beautiful place.' To experience the mountain, options include: **air flyovers** from nearby Toledo, Cougar or Randle, which give the best views of flattened trees, debris-choked rivers and devastated landscape slowly regenerating itself; **bus tours** run from Seattle through a loop road leading to the mountain, also accessible by **car**. Check in with the Forest Service info centre (turn W off I-5 on exit 49) to enter the volcano zone. **Hikers** can make a difficult but worthwhile trek from **Meta Lake** to **Independence Pass**, which overlooks ruined **Spirit Lake**, chilling views of desolation and crumpled human artefacts. The Norway Pass trail is also excellent. If you'd like to keep a respectful distance, you can take in the eruption and aftermath on the 100-ft screen of the **Omnidome**, Pier 59, in Seattle, 622-1868. $7. 'It's as if you're flying round the mountain during its eruption.' 'Do not on any account miss this extraordinary 30 min film.' Next to **Seattle Aquarium** at Pier 59, 386-4320, a fishbowl where you are in the bowl, and the fish swim overhead. 'Marvellous.' Daily 10am-7pm ('til 5pm after Labour day); $8.25. Watch out for the 'Coconut Crab' exhibit.

Bainbridge Island Harbour ferries: Pier 51, 464-6400, $4.50 without car, rtn. Pubs and art galleries on the island, even a winery: **Bainbridge Island Winery**, 682 State Hwy 305 NE, 842-WINE. Free informal tours in Washington's second smallest winery, every Sun at 2pm. Otherwise open Wed-Sun noon-5pm for wine-tasting and self-guided tour around vineyards. $1 p/p unless you make a purchase. 'Dirt! Corruption! Sewers! Scandal!' Sound good? Then take an **underground** tour, 610 1st Ave at **Doc Maynard's Public House**, (888) 608-6337 /682-4646. When Seattle burned down in 1889, the city simply built the new on top of the old. What's left below is an odd warren of storefronts, brothels, speakeasies and tunnels where sailors are popularly supposed to have been shanghaied. Tour ends (naturally) at a gift shop. 'Highly amusing account of Seattle's early sewage system. Never thought crap could be so funny.' 'Interesting rip-off.' Tours last 1½ hrs; $8, $7 w/student ID. Rsvs req.

Experience Music Project Following on from Sheffield's National Centre for Popular Music in England, the world has another bizarrely-shaped interactive 'museum' where you can listen, learn, and perhaps be a rock-star for the day. Designed by the architect of the Guggenheim in Bilbao, Frank Gehry, it is set to open in May 2000. It is located just below the Space Needle and a monorail station is being designed to stop within the centre. Funded by one of the Microsoft co-founders, Jimi Hendrix seems to have been a personal favourite, and memorabilia abounds, however much more is also on offer; from the ubiquitous grunge icons to the more technical aspects of production and recording. Check the website for details; as to be expected from the software king, it is informative and innovative; *www.experience.org*

Government Locks, connecting Puget Sound, Lake Union and Lake Washington, were built in 1916 and at that time second only to the Panama locks in size. 'Best free sight in Seattle. Boats and leaping salmon passing through all day.' 'Some salmon nearly jump onto the footpath!' 'Interesting historical/ecological display in building.'

International District, btwn Main & Lane, 4th & 8th. Culturally-neutral official name for Seattle's Chinatown, bright with Buddhist temples, restaurants, herbal shops and the Bon Odori Festival in Aug.

Klondike Gold Rush National Historical Park, 117 S Main, 553-7220. Exhibits, free films and gold panning demos. 'Watch Chaplin's *The Gold Rush* free on 1st Sun every month.' Daily 9am-5pm; free. **Lake View Cemetery**, next to **Volunteer Park**, at 14th Ave & E Prospect. Divided by nationality—Chinese, Japanese, Polish, etc. Also **Bruce Lee's grave**, covered with letters to him, martial arts trophies, mementoes, flowers, etc., left by devotees. NB: For those with a gruesome frame of mind, Kurt Cobain's residence has been torn down, and he isn't even buried in Seattle—sorry.

Museum of Flight, 9404 E Marginal Way S, 764-5720. Over 40 aircraft from the beginnings of aviation to an Apollo command module. Newest exhibit is a full-scale F-18 mock-up where you can sit in the cockpit. Daily 10am-5pm, Thur 'til 9pm. $8.

Pacific Science Center, distinguished by five white arches, nxt to Space Needle, 443-2001, includes 6 buildings: spacerium, planetarium, computer rooms, seismograph, Indian longhouse, lots of science toys. Daily 10am-6pm. $7.50 entrance fee; $12/13 includes IMAX or laser shows. IMAX info line: 443-IMAX. 'Laserium *Rock It* is an exciting presentation.' The Center also has many shops, eateries and entertainment from opera to rock to folk festivals.

Pike Place Market, Pike & 1st, 682-7453. Begun in 1907, this multi-level maze of regional colour boasts over 250 permanent businesses (and a reserve of 200 arts and crafts and 100 farmers), includes dozens of restaurants, stand-up bars and take-away places, plus local produce and seafood. Also bookshops, coffee-houses, bars, second-hand shops, crafts and 'excellent free entertainment by buskers and street musicians.' Daily Mon-Sat 9am-6pm, Sun 11am-5pm.

Pioneer Square, around 1st & Yesler, heart of old downtown. The original 'skid road,' so-named because logs were 'skidded' along the road in lumberjack days, gave rise to 'Skid Row,' a term widely imitated in several cities from LA to NYC. Nicely restored, but still a gathering place for bums and blots-on-the town; good walking tour map available.

Seattle Art Museum, 100 University St, 654-3100. Newly-designed museum designed by Robert Venturi (the man who gave us the National Gallery extension in London) and it is his usual post-modern joke of differing styles from Egyptian to neo-classical. The building is better than its contents. Tue-Sun 10am-5pm, Thu till 9pm; $7, $5 w/student ID. First Thu of every month, free. Also houses the **Seattle Asian Museum**, $3.

The Space Needle, 443-2111, a 605-ft relic of the 1962 Seattle World's Fair, has stunning views, best at night when the city is lit up. $9 for glass elevator ride to the top and info-tour. Find out where *Frasier's* apartment would have to be for *that* view! 'Kitsch-est souvenir shop in Seattle on top.' Revolving restaurant at 500 ft. On the grounds of **Seattle Center**, where various fairs take place over the summer; **Fun Forest** amusement park is there, too.

University of Washington, 15th Ave NE. 'Beautiful, like Berkeley.' On campus, an arboretum and Japanese tea garden, gift of Seattle's sister city, Kobe. Info centre on NE 40th.

The waterfront is the soul of any port town, and Seattle is no exception. The working piers for the Alaska halibut and salmon fleet and the large freighters are remote, but the tourist's waterfront is front and centre. Piers 48 through 70 have steamships to Victoria and also the Victoria Clipper Catamaran, a **waterfront park** and a **fire-fighting museum**.

Nearby: Boeing Aircraft Factory, 3303 Casino Rd S, **Everett**, 30 miles N of Seattle, exit 189 W off I-5. Call 554-1264 for tour info. See jumbo jets in the making in the building where the world's largest jetliners are manufactured. Very heavily booked in summer; $5 90 min tours Mon-Fri 9am-4pm. Tkts available beginning at 8.30am for the day but beware—can be sold out by 9 am.

ENTERTAINMENT
The 5th Ave Theatre, 1308 5th Ave, *circa* 1926 vaudeville house patterned after Imperial Chinese architecture of the Forbidden City, renovated in 1980 for $2.6 million, now hosts Broadway shows. Free tours for groups of 6 or more; call 625-1468. 'Absolutely smashing place.'

Gasworks Park: See beautiful kites being flown high up in the sky, or go get your own from **Gasworks Kite Shop**, 3333 Wallingford Ave N, 633-4780. On the other hand, if you feel inspired to go sailing on Lake Union, **Urban Surf**, 2100 N Northlake Way, 545-WIND, rents windsurfing boards for $35 daily, and in-line skates, $5 p/h or $16 p/day. During lunch hours in the summer, the free **Out to Lunch** series brings music and dancing to all parks, squares and offices downtown Seattle. Call 623-0340 for more info.

Pioneer Square, **Volunteer Park** and the **campuses of University of Washington and Seattle University** (downtown at E Cherry & Broadway) are all nuclei for daylight and after-dark activities. Plenty of good beer, live music and psyched crowds! For a joint cover ($10) you may wander from bar to bar and club to club within the Pioneer Square area; **Color Box** is recommended for typical Seattle bands and good old grunge. Read the *Post-Intelligencer* and the *Seattle Times' Tempo* mag for listings and the 'Hot Tix' column with discount and free stuff.

Seattle Opera, 321 Mercer St, 389-7676, at the Seattle Center. Get there 20 mins before curtain up for 'student rush': leftover tkts sold at half-price, as low as $15. Occasionally, on selected performances, any leftover tkts are sold for $15, regardless of original price. Also performing at the Center, the **Seattle Symphony**, 215-4747. Rock and pop acts as well as legitimate theatre at the **Paramount Theater**, 911 Pine, 682-1414. Not cheap but good acoustics.

The Seattle Arts Festival, Bumbershoot, annually at the Seattle Center over Labor Day w/end. Bands, food, art, etc. 'Amazing, very popular.' Hotline 684-7200.

INFORMATION /SHOPPING
Park Service, Pacific Northwest Region, (ORCI), 220-7450. Mon-Fri 10.30am-7pm,

Sat 9am-7pm, Sun 11am-6pm. Situated within the **REI** store, 222 Yale Ave N, 223-1944. The biggest and best outdoors shop in the west; has its own climbing wall and bike track for testing out that equipment!

Travelers Aid,1100 Virginia St, suite 210, 461-3888. Open Mon-Fri 9am-4pm, 3pm on Weds.

Seattle-King County Visitors Bureau, 520 Pike St, 461-5840. Mon-Fri 8.30am-5pm, Sat-Sun 10am-4pm in summer.

INTERNET ACCESS
The home of good coffee has discovered that web-browsing is a complementary activity, and there are many cyber-cafes—try **Capitol Hill Internet Lounge & Cafe**, 219 Broadway Ave E #23, 860-6858, charges run at $6/hr. The **Central Library** has free access at 1000 4th Ave, 386-4636.

TRAVEL
Alaska Marine Highway System Ferries: to Alaska and the Inside Passage. Departs approx 7pm Fri from port in Bellingham, 89 miles N of Seattle. Call 676-8445 for info; rates vary (cheapest: $164 to Ketchikan). To islands, Olympic Peninsula, Bremerton, Vashon Island and other points: **Washington State Ferries**, Pier 52, 464-6400. 'Excellent way to see the Sound and the islands around Seattle.' Ferries for the **San Juan Islands** and **Sidney, British Columbia** depart from Anacortes (north of Seattle). See 'San Juan' section.

Amtrak, King St Station, 3rd Ave & Jackson, (800) 872-7245. The *Pioneer* goes to Ogden/Salt Lake City; the *Coast Starlight* to Oakland/SF and LA, a beautiful ride down the coast; and the *Empire Builder*, a mammoth 42 hr trip to Chicago via Minneapolis.

Gray Line, 624-5813, from the Westin Hotel, Space Needle and other points.

Green Tortoise Bus Service, (800) 227-4766. Buses leave from 9th Ave & Stewart St, Thurs/Sun at 8 am, to Oregon, San Francisco and LA. Rsvs recommended 5 days in advance.

Greyhound, 8th & Stewart, (800) 231-2222. Serves Bellingham for ferry services north, daily to Sea-Tac Airport, Spokane, Portland, Tacoma and Vancouver, BC.

Metro Transit local public buses, 201 S Jackson, 553-300 / (800) 542-7876. Within the 'Magic Carpet' downtown area all buses free; $1-$1.75, depending on zone and rush-hour restrictions. All-day unlimited passes available only at w/ends and holidays, $2. *www.metrokc.gov.*

Seattle-Tacoma International Airport (Sea-Tac), about 12 miles S of the city. From downtown take #194 from the Metro Tunnel, Mon-Sat, $1.75 peak times, $1.25 off-peak.

Victoria Clipper, 448-5000 / (800) 888-2535, offers a passenger only ferry to Victoria, British Columbia from Pier 69, 3 times daily. $79-109 rtn. The **Princess Marguerite**, 448-5000 / (800) 888-2535, also operates daily, May- Sept, from Pier 48, and takes 4 1/2 hrs to Victoria. $54 per vehicle, $29 foot passenger, o/w.

OLYMPIC NATIONAL PARK Sparkling mountains and lush forests occupying 1400 sq miles in the centre and along the coastline of the Olympic peninsula, making this a crown jewel of US national parks. Hwy 101 circles the park, but only a few roads penetrate inward; its wilderness is further fortified by vast tracts of national forest around it. A hikers' park indeed.

Massive glacier-cut peaks are the park's signature. The highest at 7965 ft, was named **Mt Olympus** by an English sea captain in 1788. Use the **Port Angeles** entrance to get here. 'Don't miss the 18 mile drive from sea level to one mile high at Hurricane Ridge—what views of Mount Olympus and its glaciers!'

The park proves that rain forests are not solely a tropical phenomenon.

West of Olympus in the Bogachiel, Hoh, Quinault and Queets river valleys is the great **Olympic rain forest**. Jewelled with moisture, tree limbs cloaked in clubmoss, this cool Amazon suffused by primordial light gets 150 inches of rain in an average year. Best access is via the 20 mile drive up the Hoh River. Don't overlook the intelligent displays at the visitor centre and the views along Quilcene River. Follow the **Hoh Rainforest Trail** which begins at the **Hoh Rainforest Visitor Center**.

Dense forest runs almost into the sea along the pristine, rocky coastal strip. The best view is at the southern end where Hwy 101 passes close to shore, but the best part is **Lake Ozette**, reached only by trails. Here the undergrowth is extravagant and the ground is boggy; much of the trail is bolstered by boards. Bears sometimes lumber down to the water in search of a meal. About 4 miles from the lake is beautiful **Cape Alava**, especially when silhouetted at sunset. 'Make every effort to see this park—fantastic.'

Admission to the park is $10 per vehicle (at the more built-up entrances), good for 7 days, and $5 per hiker/biker. **Campgrounds** in the park offer tent sites from $8-$12. No food stores in the park, so purchase beforehand in Port Angeles. The unofficial guide to Olympic National Park, *www.halcyon.com/rdpayne/ onp.html*, includes highlights, maps and info on hiking, camping, fishing, scenic drives, biking and hot springs.

INFORMATION/TRAVEL

Greyhound, 612 S Lincoln St, Port Angeles, (800) 231-2222.
Olympic Bus Lines, (800) 550-3858 / 452-3858 operates a shuttle from Port Angeles and downtown Seattle, airport, Amtrak and Greyhound.
Olympic National Park Headquarters, 600 E Park Ave, Port Angeles, and **Visitors Center**, 3002 Mt Angeles Rd, both 452-0300. Information on self-guided trails, camping, backcountry hiking, fishing and generally fields questions about whole park. Displays a map of locations of other park ranger stations. **NB: Backcountry camping** reqs a $5 backcountry permit, available at ranger stations. Daily 9am-4pm. NB: This is bear country—food should be stored appropriately.

PORT TOWNSEND and THE SAN JUAN ISLANDS

Port Townsend shows you that western Washington isn't uniformly soggy; it lies in the 'rain shadow' of the great Olympic Mountains, and gets a mere 18 inches a year. Sunny weather, a vital cultural life, ebullient Victorian architecture and two nearby hostels make Port Townsend an excellent place to base for exploration. Seek out good food and friendly faces at the Lighthouse Cafe and occasional music at the Town Tavern.

In 1859 the US gained the 192-island chain of the **San Juans** in the great 'Pig War,' precipitated when a British pig recklessly invaded an American garden and was shot. The resulting squeal of outrage had US and British troops snout to snout on island soil, but diplomacy won out. With Kaiser Wilhelm the unlikely mediator, the US got the San Juans and the British got bangers, one supposes.

Connected by bridges to the mainland and each other are the islands of **Whidbey, Fidalgo** and **Camano**. The city of **Anacortes** on Fidalgo is a major ferry terminus. Despite their accessibility, these islands are quite rural. Further north and well served by ferry are **Orcas, Lopez** and **San Juan**. All have excellent camping, unsurpassable shorelines and scenery with good clamming and some fine beaches. Lopez is best for bicycling and has a good swimming beach at Spencer Spit, though water temperatures average a chilly 55 degrees. Call island information, 468-3663. The local Chamber of Commerce's Port Townsend net site is at *www.porttownsend.org/*

ACCOMMODATION

Nordland: Fort Flagler HI-Hostel, Ft Flagler State Park (on Marrowstone Island), 20 miles from Port Townsend, 385-1288. With 800 acres of forest and 7 miles of pristine beaches, the park is a wonderful place to enjoy hiking, biking, clamming, sea kayaking, fishing and deer grazing. Olympic National Park is only an hour's drive. Lrge common rm with wood stove, crab pots, info desk. Bikes to borrow. Not very well insulated, rural, and only 14 beds. 'The place to ebb out for a while.' May-Sept, otherwise by rsvs only. $11+ $3 linen. Rsvs recommended thru Sept.

Port Townsend: HI-Olympic Hostel, Ft Worden State Park, 385-0655. The hostel affords outstanding views of the Cascade and Olympic mountain ranges and the Strait of Juan de Fuca. The 450-acre state park is host to music festivals (country, jazz, blues), kite flying and kayak gatherings, the Marine Science Center, and has miles of trails and beaches to explore. Near the town and a sandy beach, in the place where they filmed *An Officer and a Gentleman*. $12, private rooms available.

Palace Hotel, 1002 Water St, 385-0755. From S-$54, D-$58. TV, brass beds, antique decor. Bus stops 1 block up street.

On the San Juans: Doe Bay Village Hostel, Star Rte 86, Olga, **Orcas Island**, 376-2291. 'Used to be a '70s love-camp and is still like one in many ways. Not recommended.' Showers, fully-equipped kitchen, hot tubs $3/24hrs. 'Wonderful view over Otter coast.' $15.50 dorm / $32 private room. $18-22 camping.

Palmer's Chart House, PO Box 51, Upper Road, Deer Harbor, **Orcas Island**, WA 98243, 376-4231. Open year-round, warm place with private baths and entrances, decks, lots of amenities and pampering. Overlooks Deer Harbor. 1 hr ferry ride to Orcas from Anacortes; from Orcas 1 hr to Sidney. Morning or afternoon sailing for $35 pp on the Palmer's 33-ft yacht, *Amante*, weather permitting; rsvs essential. Highly rec for an unusual American experience. S-$65, D-$87, homecooked bfast included.

San Juan Island Camping: Snug Harbour Resort, 4 pp-$25 per site, call 378-4762 to reserve; **Lakedale Campground**, $24 per site, call 378-2350. NB: a reader warns that San Juan island camping is crowded and full of American tourists, whereas the other islands are booked up in August. Rsvs early.

State Park Camping: Star Rte Box 22, Eastsound, WA 98245, 376-2326. $13 + $5 for rsvs for **Moran** on **Orcas**. Rsvs before Labor Day, in writing 2 weeks in advance only.

OF INTEREST

Two excellent guides to the area are *The San Juan Islands Afoot and Afloat* and *Emily's Guide*, with detailed descriptions of each island, both available at bookstores/outfitting stores on the islands and in Seattle.

San Juan Island: Jazz Festival. *www.centrum.org/jazzfest.html* gives more details on the annual jazz and music festival held at the end of July.

Whale Museum, 62 First St N, Friday Harbor, 378-4710. Exhibits of whale skeletons, brains; reading materials. Includes videos on Orcas and other whaling subjects. $5, $3.50 w/student ID. 'Small but very good.' Daily 10am-5pm in summer.

Whale watching at Lime Kiln Point, no entrance fee. From the cliff above the water you can see both Orcas and Minke whales come close to the rocks to feed on salmon. 'Usually arrive in afternoon.'

Wildlife: *www.karuna.com/san-juan-wildlife* is a wildlife guide with discovery maps and animal checklists.

Orcas Island: Moran State Park in Eastsound, 376-2326, has over 21 miles of hiking trails ranging from a light 1 hr stroll to a full day's adventure climbing Mt Constitution. Trail guides available from the registration station.

INFORMATION/TRAVEL

Greyhound, (800) 231-2222. Take Greyhound from Seattle to Port Angeles and connect with Clallam Transit (800) 858-3747 #30 Hwy 101 Commuter Bus to Sequim. Change to Jefferson County Transit (800) 436-3950, #8 to Port Townsend. Each journey 75c, limited service at weekends.

Ferries from Anacortes daily to Shaw, Lopez, Orcas, San Juan and Sidney, BC. Westward journey to any island $4.95/foot passenger, then inter-island travel free. Orcas island to Sidney, BC. Ferry and land combinations are extremely numerous; you'll do best to study the free ferry schedules and maps: call (206) 464-6400 or (800) 542-7052 (in Washington).

Orcas Island Chamber of Commerce, 376-2273.

Port Townsend Visitor Information, (888) 365-6978 / 385-2722, 2437 E Sims Way.

MOUNT RAINIER NATIONAL PARK It was the enterprising 18th century British Admiral Rainier who got this 14,410-foot mountain named after himself. Today Mt Rainier, 80 miles south of Seattle and clearly visible from there, is surrounded by a national park that should interest the most jaded peak peeker. With 575 inches of snow piling up in an average year, little of the mountain shows beneath the glittering whiteness. More than 40 glaciers crown Mt Rainier, and lush conifer forests line its lower slopes, interrupted by meadows bright with wildflowers in July and August.

The **Wonderland Trail** wanders for 90 miles around the mountain, passing through snowfields, meadows and forests, with shelter cabins at convenient intervals. The full walk can take 10 days, but there are lesser trails for those with lesser ambitions. Near the park's SE corner is the **Trail of the Patriarchs**, leading through groves of massive red cedar and Douglas fir. The best place for seeing wildflowers is to march up from **Paradise Valley**. In the northeast, excellent hiking trails branch out from **Sunrise**, the highest point in the park that can be reached by road.

July through Sept are often warm and clear, sunsets and sunrises over the mountain are unforgettable. It rains even in summer, and cloudy, rainy or foggy weather is the rule the rest of the year, always bring raingear! Entrance is $10 per car, $5 for hikers/bikers, or by bus.

The **Cascade foothills**, north of Rainier, are a closer alternative: 'Drive 30 miles E to North Bend, then follow south fork of the Snoqualmie River for 15 miles. Take dirt track marked Lake Talapus to car park. From there, a 2 mile hike to the lake. Gorge yourself on blueberries, swim and dive off rocks, kill bugs—on a sunny day, this beats any city tour. This is the real America.' The unofficial guide to Mount Rainier National Park is at *www.halcyon.com/rdpayne/mrnp.html. Telephone Code 360.*

ACCOMMODATION

Backcountry camping is free: with a permit hikers can use any of the free trailside camps scattered in the park's backcountry. Access to toilets and water.

Campgrounds (best option—that's what you're here for!): **Ohanapecosh** $10; **Cougar Rock and White River**, $8; **Sunshine Point** Ipsut Creek, $5. Open summers only except for Sunshine Point. Come equipped for cold. At higher altitudes, there will be snow on the ground, maybe some from the sky even in the dead of summer.

Mt Haven Campground & Cabins at Cedar Park, 569-2594. $12.50 per site with shower, laundry. Cabins: From D-$50 w/kitchen, bath, shower, fireplace.
Paradise Inn, 569-2413, at 5400 ft. Open mid-June to early Oct. From S/D-$80 ($120 w/bath). Suite for six $158. For rsvs write to Mt Rainier Guest Services, Attn: Reservations, PO Box 108, Ashford, WA 98304 or call 569-2275.

INFORMATION/TRAVEL
Henry M Jackson Memorial Visitors Center (largest centre in the park), ¹/₂ block from Paradise Inn, daily 8am-7pm.
Greyhound, 1319 Pacific Ave, Tacoma, (800) 231-2222.
Longmire Hiker Information Center, 569-2211 ext 3317. Distributes backcountry permits. Daily Sun-Thurs 8am-6pm, Fri-Sat 7am-7pm; closed in winter.
Mount Rainier National Park Headquarters, call 569-2211 for recording on weather and road conditions, food, lodging, camping, hiking, visitors centres and more. Mon-Fri 8am-4.30pm.
Ohanapecosh Visitors Center. Offers info and wildlife displays. Daily 9am-6pm.
Paradise Visitors Center, 569-2211 ext 2328. Offers food, pay showers and guided hikes. Daily Sun-Fri 9am-6pm.
Sunrise Visitors Center. Contains exhibits, snacks and a gift shop. June 25-mid Sept Sun-Fri 9am-6pm, Sat 9am-7pm.

NORTH CASCADES NATIONAL PARK Spectacular scenery in the Cascade Mountains: razor-backed peaks, plunging waterfalls, high snow-fields and deep lakes. From Seattle, take Hwy 5 N to Hwy 20 E. No entrance fee to park; most areas are wilderness, inaccessible by road. You can, however, drive to three **campgrounds** in the park: **Colonial Creek, Newhalen**, and **Goodell Creek**, $7-12. Forest Service info 856-5700. **Visitors Center** on left side of Hwy 20. The unofficial guide to North Cascades National Park is at *www.halcyon.com/rdpayne/ncnp.html*.

LONG BEACH PENINSULA On its long sandy finger of land in extreme SW Washington, the Long Beach peninsula harbours an immense clam and driftwood-filled beach, covered with huge dunes (great for escaping the wind) and backed by pines hiding hundreds of old-fashioned beach cottages. Besides the windswept beauty of the area, visit the free **Lewis and Clark Interpretative Center**, 642-3029, 10am-5pm daily, near **Cape Disappointment Lighthouse**, a superb audio-visual evocation of the extra-ordinary hardships and wonders of the explorers' epic journey. The display ramps lead you to the same magnificent ocean overlook that climaxed Lewis and Clark's trip in 1805. Read Stephen E Ambrose's account of their journey in *Undaunted Courage. www.funbeach.com* includes directions by car, lodging options and a link to the visitors bureau.

ACCOMMODATION
HI-Ft Columbia Hostel, Box 224, **Chinook**, 777-8755. 7 miles from Astoria, Oregon, across a toll bridge (cars $2 o/w, 50¢ bicycles, hitchhikers free). April-Sept; at other times of year, send rsvs 1 month in adv. $10. The hostel is in an old army hospital in a lovely, isolated site in Ft Columbia State Park overlooking the mighty Columbia River in park with museum, and Pacific Ocean. Near Chinook Indian village. Good bathing. Convenient access to Washington's longest beach (26 miles), the site of many festivals and recreational activities. The Long Beach Peninsula, a short bike ride/drive away, is a great place to whale watch and hosts summer festivals for kite flyers, garlic and cranberry lovers and seafood connoisseurs.

THE SOUTHWEST

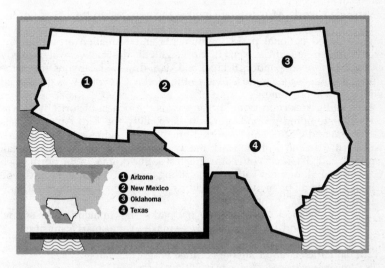

1 Arizona
2 New Mexico
3 Oklahoma
4 Texas

Much of this area is exactly as you would expect from seeing Westerns—whether shot in Spain or elsewhere. Purple mountains, searing deserts, cactus, cowboys and Indians all inhabit Arizona, New Mexico and west Texas. Contrasting with this region are the lush farmlands of east Texas and Oklahoma and the parks and ski resorts of northern Arizona and New Mexico on the tailbone of the Rocky Mountains.

Hardly passing through an intervening industrial stage, the Southwest since World War II has leapt from a simple economy into the nuclear-industrial-aerospace age and is now the bright buckle of the Sun Belt. But the past has not been lost—old Indian and Spanish influences remain.

For several decades after it was blazed in 1822, the Sante Fe Trail served emigrants and traders between Missouri and the Southwest. Now the major thoroughfares is the I-40 (the legendary 'Route 66') to the north and the cross-country I-10 to the south. To enjoy the natural splendour of the region and get a sample of day-to-day life here, stay off I-40 as much as possible.

ARIZONA *Grand Canyon State*

Once called the 'Baby State' (the words of one of the state's first senators) because it is the youngest of the lower 48, Arizona has slid comfortably into its mature role as a mecca for retirees and families on vacation. The low cost of living and unique quality of life are now also drawing younger residents in large numbers. A land of vast silences and arid beauty, the Grand Canyon

State (its new moniker) also contains sharp and sometimes troubling contrasts. One-quarter of Arizona is Indian land, containing the incredibly ancient and artistically advanced cultures of the Hopis, Navajos and others, and one in twenty inhabitants is a Native American. Yet Indians in this state were not allowed to vote until 1948.

Arizona's works of nature are among the grandest in the US, if not the world, beginning with the Grand Canyon and continuing through 21 other highly varied national parks, monuments and recreation areas. But the works of man range from banal to short-sightedly destructive: water-greedy cities, a borrowed London Bridge, and dam-drowned canyons (even the upper portion of the Grand Canyon—the Marble Canyon—was threatened with a dam at one time!).

The southern section from Tucson east is the richest historically. It was once the stomping ground of Wyatt Earp, Billy the Kid, Apache chiefs Geronimo and Cochise and assorted prospectors, padres and gunslingers. Northern Arizona, with its stark mesas and richly coloured canyons (all could be called 'Grand') offers the greatest scenic drama. In the north, Glen Canyon and Monument Valley, both spilling over into Utah, and Canyon de Chelly should all be high on the visitor's list, after the mandatory pilgrimage to the Grand Canyon, of course.

The vast distances between cities and parks—not to mention the sprawl within Phoenix and Tucson themselves—make a car a smart acquisition. *dir.yahoo.com/Regional/U_S__States/Arizona/.*
National Parks: Grand Canyon, Petrified Forest, Saguaro.
The telephone area code for the state is 520, for Phoenix 602.

PHOENIX Huge, hot and horizontal, Phoenix is quite possibly the world's worst city for pedestrians. The city isn't a convenient gateway to anywhere—although at the rate it's sprawling, Phoenix may one day ooze right up to the lip of the Grand Canyon.

Actually the suburbs can be more interesting than the metropolis itself. **Tempe** is home to Arizona State U, with the largest student body in the west. **Scottsdale**, the destination for the moneyed traveller and the rich, boasts some decadent resorts. Go to *Phoenix At Your Fingertips* at *www.ci.phoenix.az.us/* which includes a calendar of events; arts, cultural and sports activities and programmes.

ACCOMMODATION
NB: In general, expect much higher rates Oct-May in large Arizona cities like Phoenix and Tucson. In summer, check rates at the posh resorts—opulence can be had for less than $50 nightly. Check out the ranch-style motels on **Van Buren St** and **Main St** (aka **Apache Trail**).
In Phoenix: Budget Lodge Motel, 402 W Van Buren St, 254-7247, S-$35, D-$38.
HI-Metcalf House, 1026 N 9th St btwn Roosevelt & Portland, 2 blocks E of 7th St, 254-9803. $12. 'Good for help and info. Common room (day use), no curfew, scheduled activities, kitchen, laundry. Glad to provide free sound advice when purchasing a car esp if planning to resell. 'Very family style atmosphere promoted—liked everyone to have dinner together, etc.' 'Clean and quiet, the cheapest place to stay in Phoenix.' $5 taxi to Amtrak.

YMCA, 350 N 1st Ave, 253-6181. Co-ed, 1 floor for women. S-$28; $10 key deposit. Pool, athletic facilities. 'Clean.'

In Mesa: Motel 6, 1511 S Country Club, 834-0066, S-$42, D-$48.

In Scottsdale: Days Inn Scottsdale Fashion Square Resort, 4710 N Scottsdale Rd, 947-5411, Summer specials—D-$49. Excellent location and facilities.

In Tempe: Mi Casa-Su Casa, PO Box 950, Tempe, AZ 85281, 990-0682, (800) 456-0682. Rooms in 135 homes statewide, and also in Utah and New Mexico. From D-$60 incl. bfast. Loves foreign travellers.

Tempe University Travelodge, 1005 E Apache Blvd, 968-7871. From S/D-$48, bfast included.

Camping: Destiny Phoenix, 11 miles W of Phoenix on Citrus Rd, 853-0537. 285 sites, heated pool, jacuzzi. $23 full hook-up.

FOOD

Essentially an expensive gringo resort area, with fast food and a 24 hr convenience store seemingly on every corner. In **Tempe**, near the university, are low-cost bars and nosheries where students congregate. Most are along Mill Ave at University Ave.

Club Rio, 430 N Scottsdale Rd, Tempe, 894-0533. 'Huge burgers.' (Thurs burgers $3.75). For a splurge, try steaks cooked Indian-style, over mesquite, a technique that originated here. Restaurant open during the day Mon-Fri 11am-4pm, club nights Fri/Sat open from 7pm.

Jack's Original Barbecue, 5250 E 22nd St, 750-1280. Try the 'glorious' sloppy joe, a Thursday special. 'Super sweet potato pie. Taste the Wisdom!' Closed Mon.

Pinnacle Peak Patio, 10426 E Jomax Rd in Scottsdale, 585-1599, is where locals go for cheap and excellent mesquite-broiled fare. Mon-Thu 4pm-10pm, Fri/Sat till 11pm, Sun from noon.

Los Dos Molinos, 8646 S Central Ave, 243-9113. Features live music at lunch and dinner. Huge menu offering enchiladas and burritos. Tue-Sat 11am-9pm.

OF INTEREST

Always phone first or check with visitors bureau; sights are far apart and the summer heat will make you believe that Phoenix has, like its namesake, risen from the ashes of some still-smouldering inferno.

In Phoenix: Camelback Mountain, 256-3220, take Echo Canyon Park Rd, Scottsdale. Tallest peak in the Phoenix Mountains, 2 700 ft. Phoenix's most visible landmark offers scenic views, picnicking, good trails, including Summit Trail, just over 1 mile.

Desert Botanical Gardens, 1201 N Galvin Pkwy, 941-1225. On the border of Phoenix and Scottsdale in Papago Park, by the zoo. Carefully maintained colourful collection of cacti, some twice as high as a human being, and 10,000 desert plants that shows how desert ecosystem works. Daily 7am-8pm (summer), 8am-8pm (winter). $7.50. Half a miles west is the **Phoenix Zoo**, 455 N Galvin Parkway, 273-1341. Specialising in Arizona wildlife; recently refurbished Arizona Trail is a 'zoo within a zoo,' covering indigenous species from the state. Walk around or take a guided tour via tram. Daily 7.30am-4pm, after Labor Day 9am-5pm; $8.50. *www.phoenixzoo.org*. The zoo is located within **Papago Park**, Galvin Parkway and Van Buren St, 256-3220; 1200 acres of desert hills and volcanic rock. Museums, picnic areas and the **Hole in the Rock.**

Heard Museum, 22 E Monte Vista Rd, 252-8848. Outstanding collections of Navajo handicrafts, silverwork, weavings, basketry, plus most of former Sen Barry Goldwater's collection of 450 Hopi Kachina dolls. Museum also promotes the work of contemporary Native American artists, and sponsors occasional lectures and Native American dances. Mon-Sat 9.30am-5pm, Sun noon-5pm. $7. Also **Heard**

Museum North, El Pedregal Festival Marketplace, Scottsdale Rd & Carefree Highway, North Scottsdale, 252-8840. Single gallery and shop, $2. *www.heard.org*

Mystery Castle, 800 E Mineral Rd, 268-1581. Bizarre pueblo mansion built by a man who felt guilty about deserting his wife and child. Tour the 18-rooms (none on the same level or in the same shape) for $5. Thu-Sun 11am-4pm Oct-June, closed June-Sept.

Paolo Soleri's gallery/studio, 6433 Doubletree Ranch Rd, Scottsdale, 948-6145. Now houses the Cosanti Foundation. Open to walk around daily 9am-5pm. **Arcosanti**, (520) 632-7135, Soleri's futuristic vertical city in the making, is 65 miles N of the studio, exit 262 off I-17. Free Visitors Centre open daily 9am-5pm, tours 10am-4pm, $5 donation. Must have a car.

Phoenix Art Museum, 1625 N Central, 257-1880. Exhibits art from medieval to Western and Latin American. Tue-Sun 10am-5pm, Thu/Fri till 9pm. $6, $4 w/student ID. Free Thu. Closed Mon.

Pueblo Grande Museum and Cultural Park, 4619 E Washington St, 495-0900. The Hohokam people—the ancestors of modern-day Pimas and Papagos—are thought to have built this irrigated city about 200 BC and disappeared about AD 1450. Visit both museum and dig site here. Mon-Sat 9am-4.45pm, Sun 1pm-4.45pm. $2. Free Sun.

South Mountain Park, 10919 S Central Ave, 495-0222. Largest municipal park in the world; dramatic rock formations and cacti; hiking trails, spectacular lookouts.

In Scottsdale: Rawhide's 1880s Western Town, Scottsdale Rd (4 miles N of Bell Rd), 563-1880. Includes Old West shoot-outs, saloon, a steam powered locomotive *c.* 1880, a steakhouse (with deep-fried rattlesnake on the menu), rodeo country music and stage coach rides. Daily5pm-10pm; free.

Taliesin West, 114th St and Frank Lloyd Wright Blvd, Scottsdale, 860-8810. Frank Lloyd Wright's winter home and workshop. 5 guided tours available June-Sep. Daily 1hr tours, $10, $8 w/student ID, 5 hr $25 tour includes refreshments Mon/Thu only. Fri night tour, $20, also includes refreshments and the chance to see the fire-breathing dragon! Call for exact timings and winter tours. Take a virtual tour and find out about the man himself at *www.franklloydwright.org*

In Tempe:, the **Nelson Fine Arts Center**, 10th and Mill Ave, 1 block S of Uni, 965-2787, built in 1989, is an avant-garde showcase housing a dance lab, playhouse and ASU Art Museum. The museum has 4 galleries of changing exhibits, Tue-Sat 11am-5pm, Sun 1pm-5pm. Free. **Gammage Center for Performing Arts**, cnr of Mill and Apache Sts, 965-4050, designed by Frank Lloyd Wright, is also here. Free 1/2 hr tours, Mon-Fri, Sep-May; to rsvs tkts (discount w/student ID) call box office: 965-8721. Elsewhere on **Arizona State University** campus, most open only Sep-May: the **Matthews Center** (off Forest Mall) houses permanent collections including African and Latin American art, American crockery and ceramics, and a sculpture zoo and aviary. Tue-Fri 9am-5pm Sun 1pm-5pm, free. **Matthews Hall**, 965-6517 (next door), is a museum of photography with changing exhibitions. Mon-Thu 10am-5pm, Sun noon-4.30pm. **Anthropology Museum**, 965-6213, **Planetarium** (Tue/Thu, rsvs required), 965-6891, and **Memorial Union** (SU) Art Gallery, 965-6822, are also free.

About 55 miles SE of Phoenix lies **Casa Grande Ruins National Monument,** 1100 Ruins Drive, Coolidge, (520) 723-3172, $2p/p. $4 p/car; a 4-storey structure built by the Pueblo Indians AD 1300 and protected from further erosion by a hilarious 'umbrella,' courtesy of the US government AD 1936. Far more spectacular are the ruins at **Tonto National Monument**, nr Roosevelt, (520) 467-2241, 60 miles E; $2p/p, $4 p/car. 700 yr old cliff dwellings of the Salado people. 'The **Apache Trail** follows Rte 88 to Tortilla Flats and Roosevelt Lake through superb desert scenery with views of Superstition Mountains and Weavers Needle. Make a day trip of it.'

ENTERTAINMENT
Mesa Golf-land & Sun Splash (plus **Adventure Island** for kids), Mesa, 834-8319. The surf reaches 5ft on this 2^1/$_2$-acre, 450,000 gallon wave pool; no surfing any more but swimming still permitted. 10 giant water slides and waving palms complete the oasis illusion. Open mid-March through Sept, Mon-Thu 10am-8pm, Fri/Sat till 9pm, Sun 11am-7pm. $14.95 ($10.95 after 4pm) plus $4-8 for raft rental. Lockers available, $4. Discount coupons at 'Smithy's.' 'Most indulgent moment of my holiday.' For the after-hours scene, grab the free *New Times Weekly* and the *Cultural Calendar of Events* guide.

Check out **Char's Has The Blues**, 4631 N 7th Ave, 230-0205. Sports dozens of junior John Lee Hookers! Doors 7pm nightly; around $3 cover w/ends.

Mr Luckys, 3660 NW Grand Ave, 246-0686, original cowboy hangout, features bull riding and 25c drinks; call for nightly entertainment.

INFORMATION
Arizona Office of Tourism, (800) 842-8257. *www.arizonaguide.com*

Casa Grande Chamber of Commerce, 575 N Marshall, (520) 836-2125. Mon-Fri 9am-5pm, Sat 10am-4pm. *www.casagrandechamber.org*

Phoenix & Valley of the Sun Convention & Visitors Bureau, 400 E Van Buren St, 254-6500. Mon-Fri 8am-5pm. Also at 2nd St and Adams and at airport.

Scottsdale Chamber of Commerce, Civic Center Mall, 945-8481. Mon-Fri 8.30am-5pm, Sat 10am-5pm, Sun 11am-5pm.

Tempe Convention & Visitors Bureau, 51 W 3rd St, 894-8158. Mon-Fri 8.30am-5pm.

Weekly Events Hotline, 252-5588.

INTERNET ACCESS
Burton Barr Central Library, 1222 N Central Ave, 262-4636, open daily.

Gypsy Java Cyber Cafe, 3321 E Bell Rd, Ste B3, 404-9779. $9 p/hr, open Mon-Fri 8am-8pm, Fri/Sat till 11pm, Sun 1pm-8pm.

TRAVEL
A Advantage Auto Driveaway, 8920 S Hardy, Tempe, 468-1733. 'Good availability of driveaways both east and west. Cheap way to travel.' Mon-Fri 7am-5pm, Sat 9am-noon.

Ace Taxis, 254-1999.

Amtrak, Union Station, 401 W Harrison St, (800) 872-7245. Also at Phoenix North, 8101 Black Canyon Fwy, and at Phoenix Sky Harbor Airport, for departures to Flagstaff.

Greyhound, 2115 E Buckeye Rd, 1 mile w of airport, (800) 231-2222/389-4200, 24 hrs. Also picks up from Terminal 4 at airport. In **Tempe**; 502 S College Ave.

Horseback trail rides into the Superstition Mt Wilderness: **Gold Canyon stables**, Kings Ranch Rd, of E Hwy 60, nr Apache Junction, 982-7822. 2 hr $32, 4 hr $53.

Rent-a-Wreck, 345 N 7th Ave, 254-1000. Mon-Fri 7am-4pm, Sat-Sun 8am-3pm.

Sky Harbor International Airport, SE of downtown, 273-3300. Allow time to see the abundance of contemporary art exhibits depicting Arizona's cultural life. Showers and lockers available. From downtown; Mon-Sat take the 'Red Line' bus from Central Station at Central & Van Buren, $1.25; on Sun and public holidays only, call Dial-a-Ride, 271-4545, trip about $4.

Valley Metro public transport, 253-5000. $3.60 all day pass, basic fare $1.25, free transfers. Most routes operate Mon-Fri 5am-8pm; no Sun service. DASH only 30c between State Capital / downtown / Arizona Center till 6pm.

TUCSON Once capital of the Arizona territory, Tucson (pronounced *Too-sawn*) is now part university town, part giant retirement home. The city is also capitalising on its new age background, and is a burgeoning arts and crafts centre, with over 35 galleries open to the public. Folksiness notwithstanding, Tucson is, like Phoenix, a big, tough town with its share of crime, poverty and drugs. Watch your step in downtown, particularly at night and especially if you are female.

Most worthwhile sights are well away from downtown: the Desert Museum, Mission San Xavier del Bac, Saguaro National Park, Old Tucson and the interesting Yaqui Indian tribe. The Yaquis have been immortalised in the books of Carlos Castaneda, a renegade anthropologist who claims that members of this tribe possess ancient knowledge of true sorcery. Whether or not you buy this view, the Yaquis are a highly spiritual and musical people, whose rites combine native and Catholic traditions. Their public performances (around Pascua, a village south of Tucson) are especially magnificent during Holy Week and at Christmas.

Both Tucson and Phoenix are in the Sonora Desert, surrounded by giant saguaro forests, cacti and mountains—all within driving (not walking) distance. Tucson is 65 miles north of Nogales, an agreeable town on the Arizona/Mexico border. *www.ci.tucson.az.us/* takes you on a whirlwind adventure to the most popular city locations, even providing hot links for city job listings.

ACCOMMODATION
Motel row runs along **South Freeway**, the frontage road along I-10.
Best Western Ghost Ranch Lodge, 801 W Miracle Mile, 791-7565, S/D-$42. Old fashioned, south of the border resort, cactus garden.
Hotel Congress & Tucson International Hostel, 311 E Congress St, 622-8848. Historic railroad hotel built in 1919, conveniently located across from the Greyhound and Amtrak stations. Dorm $15, private rooms: S-$33, D-$35. 'Best value in USA.' 'Wild progressive nightclub in lobby. Great fun.' 'Only 40 miles to Mexico!'
Camping: Travel via the **Catalina Hwy. Mount Lemmon Recreation Area** in the **Coronado National Forest** offers beautiful campgrounds, $6-12, and free off-site camping in certain areas. For more info contact the **National Forest Service HQ**, 300 W Congress Ave, 670-4552. 7 blocks W of Greyhound. Mon-Fri 8am-4.30pm.

FOOD
Tucson is the place to get great Mexican food, especially *chimichangas*, reportedly invented here. *Chimichangas* are essentially fried pastry stuffed with beef, chilies, onion, cheese and salsa. Follow your nose, or pick up a free *Tucson Weekly*.
Caruso's, 434 N 4th Ave, 624-5765. Entrees $6-$9. 'Great lasagna, $7.'Closed Mon.
El Charro, 311 N Court, 622-1922, and 6310 E Broadway, 745-1922. A fortress of Mexican-American food since 1922. Tasty carne seca (air-dried beef), a speciality of Mexican cattle country. Noisy and sociable, packed with tourists, Tucsonians, healthnuts and burrito hounds spooning it all up!
Food Conspiracy Co-op, 412 N 4th Ave, 624-4821. Mon-Sat 9am-8pm, Sun 9am-7pm.
Jacks Steakhouse, 5250 E 22nd St, 750-1280. BBQ and grill.
Little Café Poca Casa, 20 South Scott Ave, no phone. Closet-size café, chili colorado and chili verde. Horchata cooler drink made from rice; try!
Mamas, 831 N Park, 882-3993. Pizza, subs, beer and jazz. 'Very popular student joint.' Open 'til midnight wknds.

Saguaro Corners Restaurant, 3750 South Old Spanish Trail, 886-5424. Unique experience—view wild animals while you dine. Closed Mon.

OF INTEREST
Arizona-Sonora Desert Museum, 2021 N Kinney Rd (14 miles W of the city), 883-2702. A museum, zoo and nature preserve rolled into one. Detailed look at Sonoran desert, from tunnels that let you peer into snake and prairie-dog households to outdoor habitats of Gila monsters and mountain lions. Plants and rock of the desert are represented as well, in a museum that has been called 'the most distinctive in the US.' 'Don't miss this place.' Visit early am or late afternoon to see maximum animal activity; Summer 7.30am-6pm daily, 'til 10pm Sat in Jul/Aug, Winter 8.30am-5pm. $8.95. Entrance fee includes the **Earth Sciences Center** with a manmade limestone cave showing subterranean rock and life forms, and explanations of volcanic activity.

North of the museum, **Saguaro National Park**, 733-5153; 2 sections, one east and one west of Tucson, both open sunrise-sunset. Found naturally only in southern Arizona and Sonora, Mexico (although pirated plants may be seen as far away as LA), giant saguaro cacti grow to 50ft tall and live for as much as 200 yrs. In late May, waxy white flowers sprout from the tips of cacti arms—a charming and improbable sight. **East Park**, 3693 S Old Spanish Trail, has the oldest stands. $4 to drive the loop; $2 p/pedestrian. 128 miles of trails and an 8 miles scenic drive lead through the cactus forest. Get a free permit from the visitors center for backcountry camping (before noon) if you are prepared to brave the summer temperatures of 115F. **West Park** 2700 N Kinney Rd, 883-6366, is free. Hiking trails, auto loop, and paved nature walk near visitors centre (daily 8am-5pm). **Gates Pass** is an excellent spot for watching the sun as it rises and sets.

Biosphere 2 Center, Hwy 77, mile 96.5, **Oracle**, (800)828-2462; 8.30am-5pm, hourly tours, $13.70. Part of the Columbia University, this science project comprises 5 huge self-contained ecosystems inside a giant bubble. Intended as a step towards life on Mars, in the early 90's people lived in them as part of the experiment.

Kitt Peak National Observatory, 56 miles SW of Tucson, on Rte 86, 318-8200. Centre for astronomical research. Daily 9am-4pm. Tours at 10.00am, 11.30am and 1.30pm. Free. 'Fascinating.' Res req for night-time viewing. *www.noao.edu/noao.html*

Mission San Xavier del Bac, 9 miles SW on Tohono O'odham reservation, 294-2624. Completed in 1797 and called 'the white dove of the desert' for its cool beauty, the mission has weathered 3 political jurisdictions, 2 explosions and 1 large earthquake and still serves as church and school for the Indians for which it was originally intended. Mon-Fri 8am-6pm, donation.

Old Tucson Studios, 201 S Kinney Rd, 883-0100, 12 m w of Tucson, next to Saguaro NP West. Daily 10am-4pm, $14.95. Setting for some of Hollywood's finest western movies, incl. *Tombstone, Rio Bravo.* Daily shoot-outs, saloon entertainment and rides.

Pima Air and Space Museum, 6000 E Valencia Rd near airport, 574-0462. Huge aeroplane cemetery. Tour plane used by Presidents Kennedy and Johnson. Daily 9am-5pm, $7.50, $13 combined with Titan Missile Base.

Sabino Canyon, 5700 N Sabino Park Rd, 749-8700 and **Seven Falls**, two of the area's most popular and breathtaking hiking, picnicking and biking areas (bikes before 9am/after 5pm only, except Weds/Sat). Call Canyon folk for best directions. Either take a tram up the canyon ($5) or walk. The falls can be reached only by a 4¹/₂-mile hike. No overnight camping. **Visitors Centre** Mon-Fri 8am-4.30pm, Sat/Sun 8.30am-4.30pm.

Titan Missile Museum, exit 69 on I-19 nr Green Valley, 574-0462. Don a hardhat and see the only ICBM (cruise missiles to the uninitiated!) silo in the world open to the public. Nov-April daily 9am-5pm, May-Oct, closed Mon-Tues. $7.50. 'A chilling, frightening and all-powerful must see.'

Tucson Museum of Art, 140 N Main Ave, 624-2333. Outstanding collection of Pre-Columbian artefacts. Tue-Sat 10am-4pm, Sun noon-4pm. $2, $1 w/student ID, free Tues.

Worthwhile museums on UA campus: **Center for Creative Photography**, 1030 N Olive Rd, Bldg 103, 621-7968, magnificent museum that houses 50,000 fine art photos, including the Ansel Adams and Richard Avedon archives. Three galleries (Mon-Fri 9am-5pm, Sat/Sun from noon) with changing exhibits and a photo library; make appointment to view archives. **Arizona State Museum**, Park Ave at Uni gates, 621-6302. Archaeology, Navajo, Apache, Pueblo artefacts. Mon-Sat 10am-5pm, Sun 1pm-5pm. Free. The **Historical Society**, Park and 2nd, 628-5774. 'Free; excellent displays of Southwest history.' Mon-Sat 10am-4pm, Sun from noon. Donations appreciated. **Flandrau Planetarium**, 1601 E University Blvd, 621-STAR; exhibits on space and astronomy. 'Part of tracking system for Voyager mission and space shuttle. Daily 9am-5pm, eves Wed-Sat 7pm-9pm. $3. Also houses the **Mineral museum**; daily, 9am-5pm; Laser shows with Nirvana vs. Pearl Jam, Pink Floyd and others, $5, $4.50 w/student ID.

Nogales; An hour's drive S from Tucson brings you to this border town, the largest crossing between Arizona and Mexico. It is actually two towns, either side of the border, and it is worth crossing just to see the contrast between the tumbling white-washed Mexican houses clinging to the slopes, and the ordered streets on the American side.

ENTERTAINMENT

UA students are renowned for rocking and rolling on **Speedway Blvd**. Pick up a copy of the free *Tucson Weekly* or the w/end sections of *The Star* or *The Citizen* for current entertainment listings. Head up 4th Ave to **O'Malley's**, 623-8600, which has food, pool tables, and pinball. During **Downtown Saturday Night**, Congress St is blockaded for a celebration of the arts with outdoor singers, crafts, and galleries, and on Thursday evening there is often a free docent-led **Artwalk.**

Bum Steer, 1910 N Stone, 884-7377. Good lunch specials for around $4. 'A must. Good luck lads and don't forget Happy Hour.' Daily 'til 1am. 'Try the house special "Jiffy Burger"'.

The Maverick; King of Clubs, 4702 E 22nd St, 748-0456; honky-tonk cowboy hoe-down.

Near UA Campus: The Shanty Cafe, 401 E 9th, 623-2664. 'Good friendly pub and student watering hole'; 'til 1am daily.

Gentle Ben's Brewing Company, 865 E University Blvd, 624-4177. Closed Sun.

INFORMATION

Metropolitan Tucson Convention and Visitors Bureau, 130 S Scott Ave, (800) 638-8350. Ask for a bus map, the *Official Visitor's Guide*, and an Arizona campground directory. Mon-Fri 8am-5pm, w/ends 9am-4pm.

INTERNET ACCESS

Library of Congress, Hotel Congress, 311 E Congress St, 622-2708, $3 30 mins, open till 1am.

Main Library, 101 N Stone St, 791-4393. Open till 9pm Mon-Wed, otherwise 10am-5pm.

TRAVEL

Amtrak, 400 E Toole Ave (1 block N of Greyhound), (800) 872-7245. On the *Sunset Ltd* LA-Miami route. Open limited hours.

The Bike Shack bike rental, 940 E University, 624-3663. Mon-Fri 9am-7pm, Sat 10am-5pm, Sun from noon. $20 per day.

Budget Car Rental, 3085 E Valencia Rd, 889-8800; **Enterprise car Rental**, 6667 S Tucson Blvd, 294-4100; and **Care Free**, 1615 S Alvernon, 790-2655.

Greyhound, 2 S 4th Ave, (800) 231-2222. 'Girls near depot should stay on the move. This is the local prostitutes' pitch—clients are very persistent and extremely unpleasant.'

Sun-Tran public buses, 792-9222, basic fare 85¢ exact change. Service runs Mon-Fri 5.30am-10pm, Sat-Sun 8am-7pm.

Tucson International Airport, 573-8000; south of downtown on Valencia Rd. Take the #8 bus east on Broadway as far as Alvernon, transfer to #11 'Tucson Airport' and go south, 85¢ (exact change) and free transfer. Mon-Fri till 7pm only, earlier at wknds. After bus hours, call Arizona Stagecoach, 889-1000, pick-up/drop-off at downtown hotels, $13. Rsvs rec.

Yellow Cab taxis, 624-6611. Open 24 hrs.

TOMBSTONE, BISBEE and APACHE COUNTRY

This rugged terrain, once subject to the raids of Mexican revolutionary Pancho Villa, was originally Apache territory. Cochise, who fought the US Cavalry until 1886, was never captured and lies buried somewhere in the **Coronado National Forest**, about 60 miles east of Tucson. (Fellow Apache chief Geronimo was imprisoned in Oklahoma and died there in 1900.)

Tombstone, was named as a bit of death-defying bravado by the prospector who founded the town. Told that in this wild Apache country, he would find 'only his own tombstone', he struck silver instead. The silver was short-lived (1877-90), but the tombstones survive, in this city that lives off the tourists it traps. **Boot Hill Cemetery** (closes at dusk), one of the few sights in town that is free, displays the epitaph of the Clanton Gang, 'Murdered on the Street of Tombstone'—by Marshal Wyatt Earp, Earp's brothers and Doc Holliday at the shootout at **OK Corrall**, 457-3456. Open daily, 9am-5pm, $2.50, $4.50 includes shoot-out daily at 2pm, $6.50 includes shoot-out and museum. *www.tombstone-epitaph.com*. There are various other shoot-outs, entrance fees all apply, check out the **Helldorado Amphitheatre** and **Six Gun City**, both on Toughnut St. 'Whole place is a little false but great fun.' Call Lou at the Legends of the West Saloon, 457-3055, to arrange with one of these groups to treat a friend or relative to a **public mock hanging**! The **Bird Cage Theater**, 457-3421, where the legendary Lola Montez danced—the Madonna of the Gold Rush era—is still standing and houses a museum.

South of Tombstone by 25 miles, **Bisbee** clings to the sides of steep hills—a mining town of great character and considerable charm. Over $2 billion in silver, gold and copper came from these hills, but today Bisbee is famous for a special variety of turquoise, on display at Bisbee Blue Jewelry. Don't miss the delightful Art Deco courthouse or the nearby 'Lavender Pit Queen Mine.' If you're here in the summer, take heart: Bisbee is 5500 ft above sea level, making it much cooler than Tombstone.

ACCOMMODATION

In Cochise, on Route 191: **Cochise Hotel and Waterworks**, Cochise, 384-3156. S-$37, D-$53. Booking mandatory for this authentic relic of the Old West: brass beds, quilts, chamberpots (plus modern plumbing) and chicken ($7) or steak ($12) dinners homecooked by the irascible proprietress. No A/C, bring your own booze.

In Tombstone; Larian Motel, 457-2272, 410 Fremont St. Clean and close to downtown. From S-$35, D-$42.

In Bisbee: Bisbee Grand Hotel, 61 Main St, (800) 421-1909/432-5900. Full bfast included from $55. Try **Jonquil Motel**, 317 Tombstone Canyon, 432-7371. Call ahead especially in winter. From S/D-$35-45.

Copper Queen Hotel, 11 Howell Ave, 432-2216. From S/D-$70. Beautiful, regal, once the headquarters for everyone from Teddy Roosevelt to 'Black Jack' Pershing, hot on Pancho Villa's trail. Good sidewalk cafe, pool, saloon. 'Many rooms with antique furniture—a trip back in time when this was a bustling mining town.'
Camping: free in **Coronado National Forest**, 826-3593.

OF INTEREST/INFORMATION

Copper Queen Mine in Bisbee, 118 Arizona St, 432-2071. Daily tours, 1 hr, $10.75 at 9am, 10.30am, noon, 2pm and 3.30pm. 'Cold, so dress warmly.' 'Extensive, informative, good value.' *Tombstone Epitaph*, the town local newspaper. Saved from bankruptcy by U of Arizona, now published by students.
Visitors Center, 4th & Allen Sts, Tombstone, 457-3929. Daily 10am-4pm.

FLAGSTAFF　Gateway to the Grand Canyon, a college town with character, Flagstaff is home of 'NAU' (Northern Arizona University, or otherwise, 'Not A University'). Other scenic splendours nearby are Oak Creek Canyon and Montezuma Castle to the south; Meteor Crater, Petrified Forest and Canyon de Chelly to the east; and Sunset Crater and Wupatki to the north. Santa Fe Ave, the main drag, used to be part of the infamous Route 66, with the Santa Fe railroad right alongside. Somewhat closer to the Grand Canyon is **Williams**, which has some lodgings and good camping. *www.virtualflagstaff.com/* is a community based system which provides current info on events in the city.

ACCOMMODATION

'Worth getting into a casual conversation with a Northern Arizona University student. Tell them of your exploits and ask for a bed for the night. It worked for me and some others.' Alternatively, cruise historic Rte 66 to find cheap motels. *The Flagstaff Accommodations Guide* available at Visitors Centre, prices all area hotels, motels, hostels and B&Bs. Tip: If seeing the Grand Canyon, check the noticeboard in your hotel/hostel; some travellers leave their still-valid passes behind. Rates begin falling after Labor Day and are cheapest Nov-May. Summer rates given below.
Chalet Lodge, 1919 E Santa Fe, 774-2779. From S-39 /D-$45.
Grand Canyon International Hostel, 19 S San Francisco St, (888) 442-2696. 1 block from Amtrak. Dorm-$15, private rooms D-$32, $35 with shower; all include bfast. Free pickup/drop-off from airport/train/bus stations. No curfew. 'Day trips to Sedona, Grand Canyon and the best staff anywhere in America!' 'Helpful staff.' 'Nice clean rooms; kept bags for us while we saw Canyon.'
Hotel du Beau Hostel, 19 W Phoenix, (800) 332-1944, directly behind Amtrak. $13 dorm, D-$30. A once famous hostel, this friendly and fun hostel has free coffee, fruit and doughnuts for bfast. Runs an all-day tour to the Canyon, $38 incl. lunch and entrance. Free use of bikes, free pick up from airport. Camper area out back $6 pp. Rsvs. 'Cheap, clean, friendly, but not the place for a good night's sleep—don't go if you're a light sleeper!' 'The best hostel I stayed in.' 'Looked after our rucksacks as we visited the Canyon.' 'Best night in America.' 'A real travellers' haven.'
Weatherford Hotel and Hostel, 23 N Leroux, 774-2731. Spacious rooms, bunk beds and funky furniture. Dorm beds $16, D-$35-60. Near Amtrak, buses. 'Lively area at night.' 'Excellent bar with good entertainment, English beer on draught.' Rsvs advisable.
Western Hills, 1580 E Santa Fe Ave, 774-6633. D-$40-$50, higher at wknds. Pool.
In Williams: try the **Red Lake Hostel**, Hwy 64, 635-9122. Dorm $11, D-$33.
Camping: KOA Campground, 5803 N US 89, 526-9926, 6 miles NE of Flagstaff. Local buses stop nearby. Showers, free nightly movies. Tent sites 2 pp $20, $24 w/hook-up, cabins $34. XP-$4. For info on **campgrounds** and **backcountry**

camping in the surrounding **Coconino National Forest**, call the **Coconino Forest Service**, 527-3600, Mon-Fri 7.30am-4.30pm. 'You'll need a car to reach the designated camping areas. Pick up a forest map ($6) at the **Flagstaff Visitors Center**.

FOOD / ENTERTAINMENT

Alpine Pizza, 7 N Leroux, 779-4109, and 2400 E Rte 66. Praised for its Italian food. Popular spot for beer, pool and pizza. Daily 11am-11pm, Fri & Sat 'til midnight. Sun from noon.

Beaver St Brewery:, 11 S Beaver St, 779-0079. Fantastic menu and great beer. Dips and fondues and huge sandwiches. Daily 11.30am 'til late!

Downtown Diner, 7 E Aspen, 774-3492. 'Excellent,' 'best value.' Daily 6am-3pm, Sun 8am-2pm, Fri-Sat till 2am.

Macy's, 14 S Beaver St, 774-2243 (behind Hotel Du Beau). Hippy student hangout serves fresh pasta, veggie food, sandwiches, pastries and coffee. Mon-Wed 6am-8pm, Thu-Sat 6am-9pm; Sun till 7pm.

Mary's Cafe, 7136 N Hwy 89, 526-9739. Open 24 hrs Thu-Sat, till 11pm Sun-Wed. 'Huge homemade cinnamon rolls.'

The Museum Club 3403 E Rte 66, 526-9434; log cabin roadhouse which began life housing a collection of stuffed animals, now hosts country music entertainment.

OF INTEREST

Museum of N Arizona, 3101 N Fort Valley Rd, 774-5213; 3 miles N of Flagstaff; excellent exhibits on native American life; Indian Craft Shows in summer with original items for sale; also find out as much as is known about how the Grand Canyon was created. Daily 9am-5pm, $5, $3 w/student ID. *www.musnaz.org*

Near Flagstaff: Lowell Observatory, 1400 W Mars Hill Rd, 774-3358. Includes telescope through which Percivall Lowell 'discovered' canals on Mars; here also where Pluto was first sighted in 1930. Hands-on astronomy exhibits. 'Worth it if only for view over Flagstaff.' Daily 9am-5pm, 12pm-5pm Nov-Mch; Call for evening times (depends on sunset). $3.50.

Nearby **Mt Agassiz** has the area's best skiing. The **Arizona Snow Bowl**, 779-1951, daily 8am-5pm, operates its 30 trails from Dec to April.

Walnut Canyon, 10 miles E. Lush canyon filled with cliff-hanging ruins. The day-use trail is strenuous in places (involving 240 steps over 185ft). Visitors' Centre 7am-6pm daily, 526-3367. 'Wildlife and Indian relics, very worthwhile and not crowded.' Trail closes at 5pm.

INTERNET ACCESS

Cyber Cafe, 1520 S Riordan Ranch Rd, 774-0005, $6 p/h, open till 10pm Mon-Sat, 9pm on Sun.

Cococino County Public Library, 300 W Aspen, 779-7670.

INFO/TRAVEL

Amtrak, 1 E Rte 66, (800) 872-7245. *Southwest Limited* btwn LA and Chicago stops here. USA Rail Pass holders can use shuttle bus to Canyon, free, otherwise $12.50 o/w, $25 rtn. Leaves at 7.30am / 2.30pm but get there earlier. (Get a rtn ticket; no ticket office in Canyon.)

Greyhound, 399 S Malpais Lane (across from NAU campus), (800) 231-2222. Open 24 hrs.

Peace Surplus camping equipment rental, 14 W Rte 66, 779-4521, 1 block from Grand Canyon Hostel. Daily tent, packs and stoves rental, plus a good stock of cheap outdoor gear. Mon-Fri 8am-9pm, Sat 8am-8pm, Sun 8am-6pm.

Pine Country Transit buses, 970 W Rte 66, 779-6624. Routes cover most of town; buses once every hour.

To get to Grand Canyon: NB: Entry fee $20 p/vehicle, $10 p/pedestrian;

Air; 'If using a Delta pass, we suggest you fly to Flagstaff rather than Canyon airport. Difficult to get on the small commuter planes. Hire a car from Flagstaff, or hitch!' Hitching: reported as 'easy' to and from the Canyon. 'Just as quick as the bus trip.' Elsewhere, best to rent a car.

Gray Line/Nava-Hopi Tours, 114 W Rte 66, (800) 892-8687. *www.navahopitours.com* Use caution in this area at night. Shuttle buses to the Grand Canyon (2 daily, $25 r/t) and Phoenix (3 daily, $43 r/t). Call for exact times.

Lloyd Taylor Tours, 526-2501. Full-day tours with very knowledgeable driver offering flexible day-trips with plenty of freedom at destinations! Tours to various points in Arizona: $31 basic transportation, $45 full tour. Also Lake Powell, Petrified Forest, Indian Reservation and Sunset Crater. Free pick-up from accommodation downtown.

Budget Car Rentals, 175 W Aspen, 779-5255. Daily 7am-9pm. 'Push for a BUNAC student discount.' 'Probably the best way to see the Canyon, if you can round up three other people to split the cost.'

OAK CREEK CANYON and SEDONA Going down Hwy 89A from Flagstaff, the road makes a switchback descent into this brilliantly tinted canyon carved by Oak Creek. From the **Oak Creek Natural Area**, a footpath takes you along the floor, through a dense growth of pines, cypresses and junipers, crossing repeatedly the swift-running brook. After the 16-mile descent you come to **Sedona**, a pretty artists' colony and setting for many of Zane Grey's Western novels. Take Hwy 179, south of Sedona, and the landscape opens up into striking vistas punctuated by mesas and serrated sandstone cliffs of red, pink, ochre and buff. You can visit the Frank Lloyd Wright **Church of the Holy Cross**, 3 miles south of the 'Y'—the intersection of Hwys 179 & 89A, 282-4069, a stunning concrete shadowbox set against rust-coloured cliffs. The view from inside is nearly as moving, often accompanied by Gregorian chants.

ACCOMMODATION
The **Sedona Chamber of Commerce**, 331 Forest Rd at Rte 89A, 282-7722. Mon-Sat 8.30am-5pm, Sun noon-3pm.
Distributes listings for accommodations and private campgrounds in the area. Mon-Sat 8.30am-5pm, Sun 9am-3pm. Both the **Star Motel**, 295 Jordan Rd (282-3641) and **La Vista Motel**, 500 N Rte 89A (282-0000), can lodge you in comfy rooms with TV, S-$55-$60, D-$59-65.
Camping: There are a number of campgrounds within **Coconino National Forest**, 527-3600, along Oak Creek Canyon on US 89A (sites $8-12 p/vehicle). The largest, **Cave Springs** (877) 444-6777 , 20 miles N of Sedona is a busy campground, administering 78 sites. $12 for unreserved sites so get there early. Reservation fee applies. Free **backcountry camping** is allowed in the forest, anywhere outside of Oak Creek and more than 1 mile from any official campground.

OF INTEREST
Sedona Arts Center, N on US 89A at Art Barn Rd, 282-3809. Free. Centre of the performing arts as well as visual arts. Touring exhibitions which change every 5 weeks; very diverse media and subject matter. Daily 10am-4.30pm, except Sun 11am-4pm. NB: Sedona is itself a centre for contemporary and traditional arts; galleries located throughout the city.
Slide Rock Park, 282-3034. 10 miles N of Sedona on US 89A. Takes its name from a natural stone slide into the waters of Oak Creek. Daily in summer 8am-7pm; closes earlier off season. $5 p/car.
Red Rock State Park, 282-6907, 15 miles SW of town on US 89A. Rangers lead day-hikers into the nearby red rocks, including nature and bird walks. Park open daily 8am-5pm. $5 p/car.

MONTEZUMA CASTLE NATIONAL MONUMENT Further south on I-17 is **Tuzigoot National Monument,** 634-5364, $2 p/p, a pueblo ruin atop a mesa overlooking the Verde River. But for a better example, cut across to Hwy 279 for **Montezuma Castle, 567-3322** (AD100-1400), far more picturesque and intact. Neither a castle nor connected with Montezuma, this was a cliff dwelling inhabited by Sinagua farmers. Visitors view the 'castle' from a paved path below. Daily 8am-7pm summer, 8am-5pm winter; $2p/p. 'Ask at visitors centre for directions to **Clear Creek** campground. Friendly owners. You can swim in the nine-foot pool formed by the stream nearby.'

PETRIFIED FOREST NATIONAL PARK This 94,000-acre park actually contains the varicoloured buttes and badlands of the **Painted Desert** as well as Indian petroglyphs at **Newspaper Rock,** pueblo ruins, two museums and a large 'forest' of felled and petrified logs. The trees date back to the Triassic period and were probably brought here by a flood, covered with mud and volcanic ash, preserved by silica quartz and laid bare once again by erosion. Most of the fossilised remains are jasper, agate, a few of clear quartz and amethyst. Like the red, yellow, blue and umber tones of the Painted Desert, these vivid colours are caused by mineral impurities. The only other petrified forest in the world is on the Greek island of Lesvos. An excellent road bisects the park north to south. The park is open daily; $10 p/vehicle, $5 p/pedestrian. **The Painted Desert Oasis Visitors Centre/**restaurant, 524-3756, at the north entrance, I40, contains murals by noted Hopi artists, and shows an info-film about the Park. Open daily 8am-7pm, off-season 8am-5pm. At the South Entrance, US 180, **Rainbow Forest Museum** has further information and a snackbar.

ACCOMMODATION
No lodging in the park. However, lodging is available in **Holbrook**, 27 miles away, or **Gallup, New Mexico** but prices are not always cheap. Budget travellers should return to Flagstaff. **Also: Brad's Motel**, 301 W Hopi Dr, **Holbrook** (3 blocks from Greyhound), 524-6929. S-$18, D-$35.
Camping: There are no established campgrounds in the park, but free **backcountry camping** is allowed in several areas (hikers only) with a permit from the museum.

TRAVEL
There is no public transportation to either part of the park. **Nava-Hopi Bus Lines,** and **Gray Line Tours** offer services from Flagstaff. **Also: Greyhound** operates along I-40 to Holbrook; Terminal at 101 Mission Lane. $36 rtn to Flagstaff.

NAVAJO and HOPI RESERVATIONS The **Navajo** nation occupies the northeast corner of Arizona (plus parts of Utah and New Mexico), an area the size of West Virginia. On it dwell a shy, dignified, beauty-loving people, the largest and most cohesive of all Native American groups. Nearly all Navajos are fluent in their native tongue, a language of such complexity that Japanese cryptographers were unable to decipher it during the Second World War, when the US military used Navajos to send secret information. Originally a nomadic culture, the flexible Navajos adopted sheepherding and horses from the Spanish, weaving and sandpainting from the Pueblo Indians, and more recently such things as pickup trucks from the whites. The reservation, while poor, is a fascinating mix of traditional hogans and wooden frame houses, uranium mines and trading posts, all in a setting of agriculturally marginal but scenically rich terrain, anchored by the four sacred peaks of Mounts Blanca, Taylor, Humphrey and Hesperus.

Amidst the 150,000 Navajos is an arrowhead-shaped nugget of land upon which sit the three mesas of the **Hopis**, a strenuously peaceful and traditional tribe of farmers and villagers. The 6500 Hopis have planted corn and ignored Spaniards, Navajos and Anglos alike for nearly a thousand years, their religion and culture still poetically and distinctly non-Western.

Rte 264 crosses both reservations, allowing you access to the Hopi mesa villages and the Navajo settlements and capital at **Window Rock** on the Arizona-New Mexico border. Neither group is particularly forthcoming with non-Natives, but you can bridge their suspicion by respecting their strong feelings about photographs, alcohol, tape recorders and local customs. Always ask permission to take pictures; if you are allowed, expect to pay for it and live up to your bargain. If you are lucky enough to witness dancing or healing ceremonies, behave as the Indians do to avoid giving offence.

Oraibi on the Third Mesa vies with the Pueblo Indians' Acoma as the oldest continuously inhabited settlement in the US. To enter the village, you must ask permission of the chief and pay a fee—absolutely no cameras, however. One of the most intriguing Hopi villages is **Walpi**, high atop the narrow tip of the Second Mesa. Dating from the 17th century, this classic adobe village of kivas and sculptured houses remains startlingly alien. 'Hire a four-wheel drive to get up very steep roads, dirt tracks.'

Besides looking at the masterful rugs, pottery, jewellery and other crafts, be sure to sample Indian food. Navajo specialties include fried bread, mutton stew and roast prairie dog. Interesting Hopi dishes are *nakquivi* or hominy stew and the beautiful blue cornmeal bread served with canteloupe for breakfast. The Hopi Cultural Center has accommodation, D-$85-90, XP-$5 (rsvs recommended), and also a restaurant serving traditional Hopi food, 734-2401, on Rte 264 at the 2nd Mesa; 7am-9pm daily. More info from the Navajo Tourism Dept, 871-6434.

Navajo National Monument in the north of the reservation, off State Hwy 564, has impressive Anasazi ruins. No entrance fee, Visitors Centre open daily 8am-5pm, has information and a gift shop. One of the highlights includes **Betatakin**, a 135-room structure nestling half way up a 700 ft sandstone cliff. There are ranger led hikes daily in summer to the ruins, takes around 6 hrs. Phone Park Information 672-2345 for details.

MONUMENT VALLEY   The scene of countless John Ford films and full of Navajo sacred places, this sprawls across Arizona-Utah state lines and can be reached via Hwys 160 and 163 from the south. The views here epitomise just about everyone's perception of the wild west; towering rock pinnacles and sandy mesas; a day's visit should be almost obligatory. It is possible to get a hint of the landscape from Hwy 163, but it is well worth paying the $2.50 admission to the **Monument Valley Tribal Park** to get a close-up. The most distinctive formations are **The Mittens**—you will know them when you see them. If you're lucky, you'll be able to spend the night at the Mittens **Campground**, around $10 a night, close by the Visitors Centre. It won't be the most comfortable night you've ever spent—

only a thin layer of sand covers the rocky mesa—but you will be well rewarded by the unforgettable sunrise and sunset, as the mighty rocks and wide sky directly ahead of you change colour by the minute.

Venture onto the valley floor with either a **jeep tour** or on **horseback**—both led by Navajo Indians, and who will tell you some of the legends and history of the sites as you travel around. You may even get to hear some of their traditional songs, complete with tom-toms. 'A truly spiritual experience'. Other highlights include the **Eagle's Eye Rock** and the **Totem Pole**, a giant needle jutting out of the desert floor. Various stalls outside the Visitors Centre will offer to take you for around \$15-30 p/p. There is also the chance to experience life in an Indian Hogan, the traditional six-sided desert home, where crafts are still practised and on sale. An early ride / tour is recommended to beat the glare of the midday sun.

A car is almost a necessity, both here and elsewhere on the reservations. There is some bus service via Nava-Hopi from Window Rock to Tuba City, which stops at Kearns Canyon in Hopiland.

ACCOMMODATION
Discover Navajoland, available from the **Navajoland Tourism Department**, PO Box 663, Window Rock 86515, 871-6434. Has a full list of accommodations, and jeep and horseback tours. Also, *The Visitors' Guide to the Navajo Nation*, \$3, includes a detailed map. Mon-Fri 8am-5pm. Plan to camp at the national monuments or the Navajo campgrounds. Alternatively, you can make your visit a hard-driving day trip from Flagstaff or Gallup.

Greyhills Inn, 160 Warrior Dv, Tuba City, 283-6271. On a Navajo reservation; near Pature Canyon and several dinosaur tracks. 'Easy access' to Grand Canyon. D-\$53, shared bath. Check-in 24 hrs. Tennis courts. Rsvs advisable.

CANYON DE CHELLY NATIONAL MONUMENT Surrounded by
Navajo land, Canyon de Chelly (about 30 miles N of Hwy 264 and pronounced 'Canyon de *Shay*') has the powerful beauty of a bygone Garden of Eden. Occupied successively by the Basket Makers, the Hopis and the Navajos, the canyon was just one of the targets in the 1863 US Army campaign to subdue or annihilate the Navajos. Kit Carson and his men eventually overwhelmed the stronghold at Canyon de Chelly, killing livestock and Indians, destroying hogans and gardens, even cutting down the treasured peach trees, a move which shattered the Navajos. Canyon de Chelly is again inhabited by Navajos, who live among 800-year-old pueblo buildings. Both are upstaged by the fantastic walls of the canyon itself, 1000 ft of sheer orange verticality.

A road runs along the rim with several lookouts to view **White House Ruin** and **Spider Rock**. The only descent you're allowed to navigate solo is the White House Trail; all others require a Navajo guide. The 1¼ mile trail to **White House Ruin** winds down a 400-ft face through an orchard and across a stream. Take an organised jeep tour or—if you happen to have your own 4 wheel drive—get a free permit from the Visitors Centre and pay a guide to show you around.

ACCOMMODATION
There is no budget accommodation anywhere in Navajo territory. **Farmington, NM**, and **Cortez, CO**, are the closest major cities with cheap lodging. **Free camping**: in the park's **Cottonwood Campground**, 1½ miles from visitors center,

674-5500. Facilities include restrooms, picnic tables, water and dump station. First come-first serve, no res.

INFORMATION
Visitors Center, near Chinle, 674-5500. Daily 8am-6pm ('til 5pm, winter). Although a National Monument, Canyon de Chelly is on Navajo land and is therefore subject to certain restrictions designed to limit intrusion into Navajo privacy.

TRAVEL
No public transport to either the Monument or Chinle. Inside the Monument, jeeps tour (six or more passengers) the canyon floor for a good look at ruins and pictographs, $35 p/p half day, $55 p/p full day (includes lunch), through Thunderbird Lodge, 674-5841 (rsvs recommended in summer).
Justin's Horse Rental, on South Rim Dr at mouth of the Canyon, 674-5678. $10 p/hr ride along the canyon floor; $10 for obligatory guide. 'My best experience in America—just like in the movies!' Res 2 days in adv.

SUNSET CRATER and WUPATKI NATIONAL MONUMENTS   Hwy 180, the most direct route from Flagstaff to the Grand Canyon, is also the dullest. A better choice is to travel US 89 past Sunset Crater and Wupatki, turning off for the Canyon at Cameron.

Long a volcanic region, **Sunset Crater** erupted most recently about AD 1066, leaving a colourful cone on a jet black lava field. The crater rim makes an interesting hike although trips into the crater are no longer allowed. From the rim, over 50 volcanic peaks, including the San Franciscos, can be seen. Also: lava tubes to explore, although lava tube tours have been permanently discontinued due to falling lava as well. The self-guided **Lava Flow Nature Trail** wanders 1 mile through the surreal landscape surrounding the cone, 1½ miles E of visitors center. The volcanic ash from Sunset made good fertiliser, and a number of Indian groups built pueblos nearby at **Wupatk**i. There are over 800 ruins on mesa tops, a ball court, dance arena, and a museum to interpret the finds at this long since abandoned settlement. $3 per person, includes entry to both monuments, 8am-5pm, later in summer.

Before travelling, check out some amazing aerial views of Sunset Crater and useful links for further research, by clicking on *www.geo.arizona.edu/Geo256/azgeology/sunsetcrater.html*.
Sunset Crater Volcano National Monument's Visitors Center, 15 miles N of Flagstaff on Hwy 89, 526-0502. Daily 8am-5pm. **Wuptaki National Monument Visitors Centre**, 679-2365, 8am-5pm.
Camping: Bonito Campground, in the Coconino National Forest at the entrance to Sunset Crater, provides the nearest camping. Rents 44 sites, $10. Call 526-0866.

FOUR CORNERS   The only point on the United States map where four states meet can be reached from the Northeast of Arizona; one leg in Arizona, one in New Mexico; an arm in Colorado and another one in Utah. A quadrangle housing the flags of each state marks the spot. Reached by I-160 from Arizona.

THE GRAND CANYON According to legend a Texas cowboy riding across the Arizona desert came to the edge of the Grand Canyon unprepared for what he would see, 'Good God,' he exclaimed, 'something happened here.' This astonishment is probably repeated daily. Approached from a flat, sloping plain on all sides, the Grand Canyon is a startlingly abrupt gash. The Colorado River traverses a magnificent, 277-mile-long canyon through a landscape filled with 270 animal species and containing four of the seven known life zones. To the visitor on the rim, the colourful buttes amid early-morning mist appear as a dreamlike valley of palaces. The proportions of the 1-mile-deep canyon are deceptive; most people find it difficult to believe that it is never less than 4 times wider than it is deep. The cross-sectional prospect from **Grandview Point** helps set matters straight. No-one is quite sure how the canyon was created. The spectacular sandstone and limestone formations were not literally carved out by the river, but are a result of erosion by the wind and extreme cycles of heat and cold. The river helped; when the Colorado Plateau began uplift, the river gnawed through it as it rose. An analogy commonly used by Park Rangers compares the Colorado River cutting the Grand Canyon to cutting a cake by holding the knife still and having someone lift the cake. The rock on the canyon floor is some of the oldest exposed land on earth.

The Grand Canyon has 3 parts: the **South Rim**, open year-round, access via Hwy 64/180 from Williams and Flagstaff; the **North Rim**, open mid-May to mid-Oct, access via Hwy 67 from Jacob Lake; and the **Inner Canyon**, open year-round, access to the rim by foot, mule or boat only. To get from the North to the South Rim or vice-versa is 215 miles by car or an arduous 20-mile hike down and up. If you're not able to take your time in the park, you should choose early on which rim you want to visit.

The South Rim is easy to reach and has the best views as well as the lion's share of the lodgings and amenities. The North Rim boasts cooler temperatures, special autumn colours, an abundance of animal life and uncrowded serenity (a quarter-million tourists per year here versus 3 million on the south side).

If you're at all fit, you'll want to hike to the **canyon floor**, or at least part of the way. If you make it to the bottom, don't forget to touch an outcropping of black Vishnu Schist; this metamorphic rock, the lowest layer in the canyon, was formed when the Earth was half the age it is now. 'Hard work, but an awesome and breath-taking spectacle.' 'Do read the hiking tips under *Of Interest* before setting out; the heat, the stiff 4500 foot climb, the high altitude of the entire area and the need to carry large amounts of water are all factors you must prepare for.' 'No 2-D picture could ever do justice to this scene of nature at her most imposing form. Even if you have to go to great lengths to get here, that first sight of the canyon ... you'll have no regrets.' The scenery is often enhanced or spoiled, depending on your point of view, by the haze coming over from Los Angeles and Las Vegas, which can give the whole place an even more magical aura.

Park entrance fee is $20 per car. It's $10 for someone on foot or on a bus. You will come across a wealth of info through any browser, but *www.kaibab.org* is a worthwhile site to explore for its virtual photo footage.

ACCOMMODATION

Most accommodation on the South Rim is very expensive. You are recommended to make reservations for lodging, campsites or mules well in advance—prepare to battle the crowds! Some accommodation, for example Phantom Ranch, the only lodge on the canyon floor, gets booked up by hikers a year in advance—plan carefully. Brisk weather and fewer tourists in winter, but some hotels and facilities close. The North Rim campgrounds are only open May to October. Check exact dates if you plan to travel at this time. All but the (800) numbers can be called from outside North America, and some campgrounds can also be booked up to 5 months in advance over the internet—*www.nps.gov/grca/* A comprehensive summary of the accommodation options can also be found at *www.thecanyon.com/nps/tripplanner/index.htm* TIP: Check at the visitors centre and the Bright Angel transportation desk after 4pm for vacancies.

South Rim

Inside Park; Grand Canyon Lodges. AmFac Parks & Resorts handles accommodation for all 6 lodges and hotels within the park. Call (303) 297-3175, or write to Amfac at 14001 E Iliff, Aurora, Colorado 80014, fax (303) 297-3175. Book 6-9 months in advance. Prices start at $44 room, $60 full bath. **Bright Angel Lodge and Cabins** is usually the least expensive. **Maswik** and **New Yavapai** are also reasonable. 'Book well ahead, even after Labor Day'.

Outside Park: There are numerous hotels and motels in **Tusayan**, 7 miles south of the South Rim; **Quality Inn**, Hwy 64, (800) 221-2222, 638-2673; S/D $118 approx. Or try further out in **Williams**; **Quality Inn Mountain Ranch Resort**, 6701 E Mountain Ranch Rd, 6 m E of Williams on I-40, (800)228-5151 / 635-2693. $55-108, pool and spa. **Red Lake Hostel**, Hwy 64, Williams, (520) 635-9122. $12 dorm. 'Simple but adequate.'

Camping: Inside the Park there are 3 established campgrounds;

Mather Campground, National Park Reservations (800) 365-2267, Grand Canyon Village. International reservations can be made through **Biospherics** (301) 722-1257, or by mail to National Park Reservations Service, PO Box 1600, Cumberland, MD 21501, up to 5 months in advance. Open year-round, $10-15 a site, depending on season; 7-day max stay. 'Always places reserved for people without own transport.' NB: Tent not needed in June and early July; later in summer, monsoons deluge the area. Campsites fill quickly June through Sept, so get there *very* early (i.e. before 9am).

Trailer Village adjacent to Mather Campground, 638-2631/(303) 297-2757, 2 pp $20 w/hook up; mainly RV site.

Desert View Campground, 26 m E of Grand Canyon Village, no res, first-come first served, May-Oct only. $12 per site, no hook-ups.

Outside Park; Camper Village, 1 m S of South Rim entrance on Hwy 64, 638-2887, opposite IMAX theatre. 2pp $15, XP-$2. Massive campground, 'always have a site'.

Kaibab National Forest; Campground overflow generally also winds up in the National Forest, along the south border of the Park, where you can pull off a dirt road and camp for free, but not within 1/4 m of Hwy 64. 'OK as long as you remain within ¹/₂ mile of public telephone.' For more info, contact the **Tusayan Ranger District**, Kaibab National Forest, PO Box 3088, Grand Canyon, AZ 86023, 638-2443. They also operate the **Ten-X Campground**, 2 m S of Tusayan, May-Sep, $10.

Backcountry camping; Any overnight hiking (or camping away from designated campgrounds) within the park requires a **Backcountry Use Permit**, $20, plus an impact fee of $4 per night. This applies whether you are within the canyon or on the rim. Demand again exceeds supply. Applications in writing only, up to 4 mths in advance, to Backcountry Office, PO Box 129, Grand Canyon, AZ 86023, fax 638-2125. There are a very limited number of permits available 24 hrs beforehand; put your name on the waiting list at the **Backcountry Office**, 638-7875, ¹/₂ mile S of the

Visitors Centre. Daily 8am-noon, 1pm-5pm. Phone queries in the afternoon only. 'As soon as you arrive, go to the Backcountry Office by 7am for a chance at unclaimed permits.' Keep in mind that there's a heavy fine for those caught camping without a permit.

Inner Canyon
Phantom Ranch, on canyon floor, 638-2401. Rustic cabins: D-$67,XP-$11; dorms $23. Booked up *long* in advance, rec res 12 mths. 'Air conditioned, very comfortable.' NB: Anything you buy down here is bound to be expensive, and that includes food. Leave excess luggage on the rim for a fee. Must book any meals in advance.

North Rim
Inside Park; Grand Canyon Lodge. Call **AmFac** (above) or direct on 638-2611. Late May to mid-Oct only. Cheapest are **Pioneer Cabins**, Q-$93. **Western Cabins** are D-$100, but have more comfort and unbelievable views. Campsite rsvs and trail info at Lodge, but no place to check luggage.
Outside park; Jacob Lake Inn, 44 miles N, 643-7232. Open year-round: cabins: S/D-$69. See also under 'Utah' for hostel accommodation at **Kanab**.
Camping; North Rim Campground is the only National Parks operated ground inside the Park; $15 per site. Rsvs through **Biospherics** (800) 365-2267. Outside North America call (301) 722-1257, or write to Reservation Service address, above, up to 5 mths in advance.
Outside Park; Camper Village, 1/4 m S of lake Jacob on Hwy 67, 643-7804 (summer), 526-0924 (winter).
Part of the **Kaibab National Forest** is also located north of the canyon, and it is possible to camp, free of charge, here. Call the **North Kaibab Ranger District**, Kaibab National Forest, PO Box 248, Fredonia, AZ 86022, 643-7395. 'Often necessary to camp outside park on National Forest land the night before, arriving in Park early am to nab site'.

FOOD
Expensive and generally poor everywhere in the park, even at cafeterias, although it is possible to find meals for fast-food prices. **Best bets: South Rim: Delaware North General Store**, 638-2262, (across from Visitors Centre, also at Desert View, East Rim). Has a deli counter and reasonably priced super market. Stock up on trail mix, water and gear. Daily 8am-8pm; deli 8am-7pm.
Bright Angel Dining Room, in Bright Angel Lodge, 638-2631. Check out their hot sandwiches and specials. Daily 6.30am-10pm. Also! The soda fountain here chills 16 flavours of ice cream, daily 6am-8pm.
North Rim: The Grand Canyon Lodge, 638-2611. The restaurant serves bfast $3-7 and dinners from $8 (rsvs only). Sandwiches at buffeteria $2.50. There is also a bar and a jukebox at **The Coffee Shop / Saloon** within the lodge, daily 11am-10pm. Dining room, daily 6.30am-10am, 11.30am-2.30pm, 5pm-9.30pm.

OF INTEREST
Hiking Tips: Whether you descend the canyon or not, guard against heat exhaustion and dehydration by drinking the park-recommended juice mixture. Water alone will not satisfy your body's requirements, as the rangers will tell you. Other hiking tips: wear a hat, don't wear sandals, always check beforehand to make sure your trail is open. For hiking into the Canyon, plan to carry 4 litres of water per person per day. Also carry permit, pocket knife, signal mirror, torch, maps, matches first-aid kit, and importantly, food. Buy energy food at the Visitors Centre—rangers say people make the mistake of drinking too much water without any food which can be just as dangerous as no water. Calculate 2 hrs up for every hr going down. (If you do get lost or injured, stay on the trail so they can find you. Rangers threaten

the cost of an air rescue runs in to the $1000's). The park service warns against hiking to the Colorado River and back in one day. Readers add: 'Do take notice of time estimates.' BUT, 'be aware of what you personally can do—Rangers will try and dissuade you from hiking to the bottom and back in one day precisely because so many idiots try and do it without proper planning—we saw people hiking wearing sandals, carrying tiny 500ml bottles of water and with small children. Those who are fit, and used to the heat and above all act sensibly should not have problems, and the times estimates can be wildly pessimistic.' 'If you plan to camp at the bottom, you need a minimum of equipment—it reaches 100 degrees in summer.' Hardly worth the effort to carry tent.' A final recommendation: 'When camping at the bottom, start the ascent at 3am, escaping the midday heat, seeing sunrise over the Canyon, and catching the 9am bus back to Flagstaff.' 'Start at 5am to go down and up in one day. No shade all day.'

Along the South Rim: The most remarkable views are from Hopi, Yaki, Grand View and Desert View points. Yaki Point is especially recommended for viewing the changing colour of the rocks at sunset. A 9 mile trail from Yavapai Museum to Hermit's Rest follows the very edge of the Canyon. Pick up relevant leaflets from the visitors centres before setting out. The South Rim is also the starting point for the South Kaibab and Bright Angel Trails to descend into the canyon.

Bright Angel Trail, trailhead at the Bright Angel Campground, usually has water at 3 points (May-Sept only) and is 8 miles to the river, 9 m to Phantom Ranch. 'A good one-day hike—Bright Angel to Plateau Point via Indian Gardens and back, 12 miles. Great scenery.' 'Gives you time to sit and take in the scenery'.

South Kaibab Trail, trailhead at Yaki Point, is 6 miles down, no campgrounds, no water and little shade: don't attempt in summer. A nice couple of hours walk is just down to Cedar Ridge and back, at least gives you the experience of being in the Canyon, 3 m round-trip. 'Colorado River is nice to paddle in—too strong for anything else.'

Recommended route **into the Canyon** is down via the South Kaibab and up the Bright Angel—more shade, water available.

From the North Rim: The North Kaibab Trail is 14 miles with water at 4 points. This is the only maintained trail from the North Rim. 'NOT recommended for a day hike—this is from an experienced hiker, and not a Ranger who's job it is to be over-cautious.' It is a 28 mile round-trip to Phantom Ranch. A good day hike would be to Roaring Springs and back, 9 miles. The entire Kaibab Trail is 21 miles and connects North and South Rims.

Views from the North Rim include Cape Royal (nature talks in summer), Angel's Window, overlooking the Colorado River, and the much-photographed Shiva's Temple, a ruddy promontory of great beauty.

Air tours depart from LA, Las Vegas, Phoenix, Flagstaff, Williams and the Grand Canyon National Park airfield. Dozens of small companies offer tours; by day the sky above the canyon is filled with buzzing planes (much to the disgust of environmental groups and visitors who value serenity). For a lot of visitors, this is the most memorable aspect to their trip. Not quite everybody is impressed though;-'Not worth the $94 helicopter ride—just as good views from the viewpoints'. Check Chambers of Commerce and *Yellow Pages* in those cities under Airline Tours. **Grand Canyon Airlines** 638-2407 operate a 45 min tour for $75. **Papillion Helicopter Tours**, (800) 528-2418/638-2419, costs $90 for 30 mins, higher for longer tours. Copters and planes once flew below canyon rim, but this practice was banned after a 1986 crash in the canyon.

Grand Canyon Caverns, on Rte 66 in **Seligman**, 422-3223. Descend 21 storeys into the welcome 56-degree caves of coloured minerals, by elevator. 45 min tours, daily 8am-6pm, $8.50.

Grand Canyon Railway, 1201 W Route 66, Suite 200, Flagstaff, (800) 843-8274. Train leaves from Williams to Grand Canyon for the 2 1/4 hr journey, by steam in Sep, vintage 50's diesel locomotive the rest of the year, from $39.95 one way, $49.95 round-trip. Williams depot includes museum and Old West shoot-out.

For a special experience that few park visitors get to enjoy, hike in to **Havasupai Falls** from the Havasupai Indian Reservation adjacent to the park on the southwest side. The heavy calcium content of Havasu Creek has resulted in coral-like circular deposits that form a stairstep sequence of turquoise pools. Bathers can catch impromptu rides where the water bubbles over the top (watch out—the 'coral' is sharp!). A trail follows the creek downstream to the Colorado River. Ask around for directions, or call the Havasupai Tourist Enterprise (whose land the creek is on) at 448-2121.

IMAX Theater, just before the South entrance to the Park, Hwy 64, 638-2203. For $8 you can almost experience what it must have been like to be one of the first to come across the Canyon, before its existence was generally known. Nearly as good as the real air trip into the Canyon.

Mule Rides into the Canyon: from South and North Rims (summer only). Outrageously popular and booked up for 6 months in advance, but many no-shows so try anyway. On the South Rim they are operated by **Amfac;** to reserve, write to PO Box 699, Reservation Dept, South Rim, Grand Canyon National Park, AZ 86023, or call (303) 297 2757. 7 hr trips $106 pp includes lunch, and overnight trips, $261 with 3 meals, cabin accommodation. The following restrictions apply: you can't be pregnant or handicapped or weigh more than 200 pounds, and you must be at least 4'7" tall, speak fluent English (the mules don't like people who talk funny), and not be afraid of heights. Guaranteed rsvs require prepayment. For the North Rim call **Canyon Trailways** (435) 679-8665, $40 half day, $90 full day.

Ranger programmes are highly recommended; they conduct guided hikes, do evening slide shows, etc. In winter, programmes are inside the Shrine of Ages building. Also recommended: the sunrise and sunset photo walks by the Kodak rep. Check at visitor centre for current topic or look in *The Guide.*

Whitewater boat trips down the Colorado; the park office has list of companies. If you're in two minds about it, see the IMAX presentation which shows the rapids ranging from mild 3's to the toughest of all, level 10's. Minimum duration for most rafting adventures is 3 days, up to about 2 weeks, camping, hiking and braving the rapids. Try **Grand Canyon Expeditions,** (800) 544-2691 / (435) 644-2691, *www.gcex.com.* 7-14 nt packages, operating for over 30 yrs. **Tour West** (800)453-9107 / (435) 225-0755 *www.twriver.com* also offers shorter packages.

INFORMATION
The Guide is the Parks weekly free newspaper; check for ranger programmes, bus timings, and any other park info.

South Rim: Equipment Rental from **Delaware North General Store,** 638-2262, in Grand Canyon Village Visitors Centre. Rents hiking boots (socks included), sleeping bags, tents etc. Deposits required on all items. Daily 8am-8pm.

Visitors Center, 6 miles N of the South entrance station. Daily 8am-6pm, off season 'til 5pm.

Info Line 638-7888. Ask for the free and informative *Trip Planner* to be sent to you. Details of weather / river conditions, lodging, shuttle buses etc.

North Rim: Visitors Centre, 100m from Grand Canyon Lodge, 638-7864. Info on North Rim viewpoints, facilities and some trails. Daily 8am-6pm.

TRAVEL
Transportation Information Desk, Bright Angel Lodge, 638-2631. Rsvs for mule rides, bus tours, Phantom Ranch, taxis, backcountry camping etc. Daily 6am-8pm.
Gray Line in Phoenix, 1245 S 7th St, (800) 732-0327 / (602) 495-9100. From $99 full

day—\$254 3 day trip. Also operates from Las Vegas and other large cities. 'Surprisingly reasonable tours'.

Nava-Hopi Bus Lines, (800) 892-8687, operate out of Flagstaff. Times vary by season, so call ahead.

Hitching: 'Save your money by walking 3 miles out of Flagstaff and hitching. Will get a ride easily.' 'Hitching to North Rim is OK—we did it in less than 24 hrs from Zion in Sept.'

Within the Canyon: **Shuttle Bus service** rides the West Rim Loop (daily 7.30am-sunset) and the Village Loop (daily 6.30am-10.30pm) every 15 mins; from Grand Canyon Village; various stops. 'Very crowded in summer'. A **hiker's shuttle** runs every 15 mins btwn Grand Canyon Village and South Kaibab Trailhead at Yaki Point. Free in summer, \$3 in winter, when the road is open to private vehicles.

Trans-Canyon, 638-2820, run buses between North and South Rim, specifically with hikers in mind. Leaves from Bright Angel Lodge in the South and North Rim Lodge. Res req, \$100 rtn, \$60 o/w. Open late May-Oct.

Bus tours from **Bright Angel Lodge** called 'a waste of money'.

LAKE POWELL and GLEN CANYON   North of the Grand Canyon, on the border with Utah, Glen Canyon is another natural wonder, combined with the monumentally ambitious Glen Canyon Dam, begun in 1956 to provide hydro-electricity. The flooding of the vast canyon, when the dam was completed, took 14 years to fill. The whole of the **Glen Canyon** is now a National Recreation Area, covering hundreds of square miles, and with plenty of opportunities for lakeside relaxation. Beaches and rocky outcrops abound, perfect for swimming and diving, and five marinas supply all your watersports needs. The **Carl Hayden Visitors Centre** in **Page** provides an orientation film, 3D model of the area and information on the dam and lake. Open summer 7am-7pm, winter 8am-5pm, the **dam** itself is open for free tours.

The Canyon was 'discovered' by John Wesley Powell in 1869, who described it as; 'a curious ensemble of wonderful features-carved walls, royal arches, glens, alcove gulches, mounds and monuments. From which of these features shall we select a name? We decide to call it Glen Canyon.' It is ironic that so much of the Canyon he named should now be submerged by a lake named after him. Some of the highlights include the fantastic **Antelope Canyon**, some-times known as 'Corkscrew Canyon' for the twists and turns the rocks take. Much of the steep-sided canyon is almost cavern-like with rock above, as well on all sides; shafts of light filtering through add to the effect. Situated on Navajo land, only authorised tours are allowed into the canyon; try **Eki's Antelope Canyon Tours**, 645-9102, *www.antelopecanyon.com* who organise a number of trips, including a specialist photographers tour which takes best advantage of the changing light. Just as spectacular is **Rainbow Bridge**, the world's largest natural rock bridge, rising 290 ft. It can be reached by a rather arduous hike, or the much more pleasant leisurely boat tour from one of the marinas. **Aramak**, 645-4004, offer a number of options, including a full day tour from Wahweap, 6 miles from the town of Page; \$92, or half day \$69. Res rec. The admission charge to the Recreation Area is \$5 p/car, \$3 for pedestrians.

ACCOMMODATION

There are numerous hotels / motels in **Page**, and camping is allowed inside the Park. A National Parks Service-run campground at **Lee's Ferry** charges \$12 per site.

There are a couple of lodges at **Wahweap** and **Bullfrog.** Call (800) 528-6154 for reservations in the recreation area.
Eastons, Pariah Canyon, Milepost 22, Hwy 89, (435) 689-0938, 30 m W of Page, has a lively campground, often full of *Trek America* vans—the owner used to be a trek leader and loves travellers. Camping $7.50 p/p, or dorm rooms $12 p/p. Besides a lively games room and the chance to meet people from all over, there is a restaurant and climbing wall. Jet-ski's can also be rented out here for $125 a day.

INFORMATION
www.desertusa.com gives a good overview of the area with some excellent photos to give you a taster.
Glen Canyon National Recreation Area general info line is 608-6404.
Page-Lake Powell Chamber of Commerce and **Visitors Centre**, 106 S Lake Powell Blvd, Page, 645-9496. Mon-Sat 8am-6pm.

LAKE HAVASU CITY   If you wanted to hide London Bridge where no one would ever think of looking for it, where would you put it? That's right—in the middle of a big, fat desert! Specifically, at Lake Havasu City, spanning the Colorado River (at least the bridge isn't going to waste). Apparently, the buyer thought it was Tower Bridge. A charmingly ersatz Tudor Village and double-decker bus make this a must for the discerning British visitor. Hwy 95 south to Parker traverses a beautiful stretch of scenery; if you continue all the way to **Quartsite**, you can visit the **Hi Jolly Monument**, a tribute to the Middle Easterner who tried to introduce camels to *this* desert, too. **Lake Havasu Tourism Bureau**, 314 London Bridge Rd, (800) 2HAVASU / 453-3444, can direct you. Mon-Fri 8am-5pm. **Outback Off-Road Adventures** offer 4-wheel drives out into the desert for the day or half a day; 680-6151. Recreationally, the city's lake is described as 'a lake to rent,' as all types of **water sports** are available here from paddle boats to jet-skiing.

NEW MEXICO   *Land of Enchantment*

Travel industry hyperbole aside, New Mexico *does* enchant. It possesses a dramatic landscape heightened by the scalpel-sharp clarity of the desert air; natural wonders like the Navajo's and the Carlsbad Caverns; and the finest array of Indian cultures, past and present, in the country. In human terms, New Mexico is incredibly ancient, having been inhabited for over 25,000 years. More significantly, it is the only state that has succeeded in fusing its venerable Spanish, Indian and Anglo influences into a harmonious and singular pattern. You will notice the benign borrowings everywhere, from sensuous adobes tastefully outfitted with solar heating to the distinctive New Mexican cuisine, currently very chic.

New Mexico inspires awe for more than its beauty. On 16 July 1945, at the appropriately named Jornada del Muerto (Journey of the Dead) Desert, the world's first atomic bomb belched its radioactive mushroom into the air. (Physicist Enrico Fermi reportedly took bets on the chances that the test would blow up the state.) Today, the state is a leader in atomic research, testing, uranium mining and related fields. Blithe as locals may be about nuclear materials (the Alamogordo Chamber of Commerce still sponsors a twice-annual outing to Ground Zero the 1st Saturdays in April and October), think twice before visiting the Alamogordo-White Sands region. Your genes may thank you some day. Instead, concentrate on the fascinating and diverse Indian populations: the 19 pueblo villages, each with its own pottery, dance, arts and style; the Navajos, whose capital is at Window Rock; and the Jicarilla and Mescalero Apaches, noted for dancing and coming of age ceremonies. Celebrations open to the public are so numerous that you could plan an itinerary around them. *Viva New Mexico!* at *www.vivanewmex-ico.com/* provides interesting information about New Mexico's writers and artists and how to buy Indian jewelry and pottery, etc.

National Park: Carlsbad Caverns.

The telephone area code for the entire state is 505.

ALBUQUERQUE Named for a ducal viceroy of Mexico, and where Bugs Bunny didn't turn left, Albuquerque is not as pleasing as its euphonious name would lead you to believe. The state's largest city, Albuquerque contains one-quarter of the state's 1.7 million residents and although it has rather more of the state's trash features, from tacky motels to urban sprawl, it has a youthful feeling due in part to the large student population. Although hot dogs abound, jumping frogs are a little more difficult to spot!

However, the setting and the scenery are spectacular and Albuquerque does make a good base for day trips to the Indian pueblos and to the Sandia Mountains. The best times to visit are during the June Arts and Crafts Fair, the September State Fair (the largest in the US), the October Hot-Air Balloon Fiesta and at Christmas, when city dwellings are outlined with thousands of *luminarias* (candles imbedded in sand, their light diffused by paper). For hints on what to see and do, go to *www.usacitylink.com//albuquer/default.html*

ACCOMMODATION

Central Ave—formerly Route 66—is the north-south divider; railroad tracks divide east-west. 'Cheap hotels on Central SE. Walk to the other side of railroad, right side of Greyhound terminal to Central SE, then straight ahead.' 'Use caution; many are dangerous.'

Grand Western Motor Hotel, 918 Central SW, downtown, 243-1773. S-$33, D-$40. 'Very friendly and clean, but not in good side of town.'

Monterey Non-smokers Motel, 2402 Central SW, 243-3554. S-$42, D-$49, XP-$6. 'Small; friendly, helpful people.' Pool, 2 blocks from Old Town.

Route 66 Hostel, 1012 Central Ave SW, 247-1813. Beautiful, newly renovated private rooms. Dorm $14, S-$18, D-$24, T-$28; $5 key deposit, $1 linen. 'Friendly, no curfew.' Full kitchen. Free coffee, tea, snacks and cereal. Must help out with chores!

Sandia Mountain Hostel, 12234 Hwy 14 N in **Cedar Crest**, 10 miles E of Albuquerque (3$^{1}/_{2}$ miles N of I-40 on New Mexico Hwy N), 281-4117. $10. Kitchen, laundry and ping-pong!

Stardust Inn, 817 Central NE, 243-1321. S-$36, D-$44, XP-$3.

University Lodge, 3711 Central Ave NE, 266-7663. Has basic motel rooms and motel pool. S-$36, D-$41.

Camping: Albuquerque North KOA (off I-25), 867-5227. Tent sites $22. Rsvs required beginning of Oct (hot air balloon festival).

FOOD

Check out the inexpensive eateries around the University of New Mexico.

Capo's Ristorante Italiano, 722 Lomas NW, 242-2007. Inexpensive, attractive place with good Italian food for $10 and less. Mon-Thurs 11am-8.45pm, Fri & Sat 'til 9.45pm. Closed Sun.

M & J Sanitary Tortilla Factory, 403 2nd SW, 242-4890. Neighbourhood chili parlour; excellent Mexican food, written up in the *New Yorker*; interesting art by locals on walls. Mon-Fri 9am-4pm.

Double Rainbow, 3416 Central SE, 255-6633, is a bakery, coffee shop and ice cream store. Salads and sandwiches under $7. Daily 6.30am till midnight.

OF INTEREST

Old Town, 1 block N of Central NW, bounded by Rio Grande Blvd and Mountain Rd. Shops, restaurants and occasional live entertainment. The only nugget of Spanish-ness left in the city. 'Well worth a visit.' On the plaza is the **1706 Church of San Felipe de Neri**.

Indian Pueblos all over the state are particularly accessible from Alberquerque. Religious and other dances are held throughout the year. Dances, fiestas and ceremonials are sacred and special to the Pueblo Indians. Tape recording, photography, sketching or painting may not be permissible. Please call ahead to verify dates and to obtain permission to visit the various pueblos. A list of phone numbers and dates of dances open to the public is available from the **Visitors Centre**. More info is also available at *www.abqcvb.org/natamer/natamer3.html*

Albuquerque Museum, 2000 Mountain Rd NW, 243-7255. Permanent and changing exhibits on history of Albuquerque and southwest US. Tue-Sun 9am-5pm; free. Tours of sculpture garden, daily 9.45am. Entrance includes **Walking Tour of Historic Old Town**. Tue-Sun, 11am.

Hot Air Balloon Fiesta, International Balloon Fiesta Field, off I-25, 821-1000. About 850 balloons from around the world assemble for 9 days in early Oct. High points are the mass ascensions on opening and closing w/ends: get there 6am-7am.

Indian Pueblo Cultural Center, 2401 12th St near I-40, 1 mile E of Old Town, 843-7270. Excellent exhibit and sales rooms by the 19 Pueblo Indian groups allow comparison of techniques and styles. High quality, prices to match. 'Only thing of interest in this town.' Daily 9am-5.30pm, $4, $1 w/student ID. Also **Indian Pueblo dance performances**, Sat & Sun, 11am and 2pm, May early Oct; free, cameras allowed. Restaurant on premises serves traditional pueblo food—give it a try; 7.30am-3.30pm.

National Atomic Museum, Building 358, Wyoming Blvd SE at Kirtland AFB (1 mile inside base), 285-3243. $2, daily 9am-5pm. Disquieting look at selection of nuclear weapons casings, plus 'oops' items like the A-Bomb the US accidentally dropped on Palomares, Spain, in 1966. Regular screenings of *Ten Seconds that Shook the World*. If driving to the museum, you need to show a driving licence, proof of car ownership, and insurance papers in order to gain a visitor's pass. *www.atomicmuseum.com*

New Mexico Museum of Natural History and Science, 1801 Mountain Rd NW, 841-2800. Evolutionary history of New Mexico presented through new hi-tec Dynamax Theatre showing 3D movies, and an 'Evolator time machine,' unique to the museum, taking you millions of years back through time. 'Fantastic. Don't miss your chance to stand inside an "active" volcano.' Daily 10am-5pm, $5, $4 w/student ID each for museum entry and Dynamax Cinema, $8/$6 for combination ticket.

Petroglyph National Monument, 6001 Unser Blvd NW, 899-0205. Open daily, Los Imagines Visitors Centre 8am-5pm. Free entry but parking $1, $2 at w/ends. Call for times of Ranger-led hikes.

Rattlesnake Museum, 202 San Felipe, 242-6569. Daily 10am-6pm. $2 for everyone over 3ft tall! Living and artefact snakes from all over America. Gift shop includes such delights as *Snakebite Salsa* and *Poison Perfume*!

Sandia Peak Aerial Tramway, NE of town, take Tramway Rd off I-25, 856-7325. At 2.7 miles, the world's longest aerial tramway, climbing to 10,378ft. Fantastic panorama which sometimes includes hot air balloons and hang gliders in the area. Daily 9am-9pm. 1½ hr ride, $14. *www.sandiapeak.com*. Mountain biking is also available—take the ski-lift to the top and bike down; 24 miles of trails. $35 bike hire per day, plus $350 deposit.

University of New Mexico, Central NE & University, 277-0111. Pioneer in pueblo revival architecture, has free exhibits, often on Indians, in the **Maxwell Museum**, west end of campus btwn Grand & Las Lomas, 277-4405. Tue-Fri 9am-4pm; Sat 10am-4pm. Closed Sun/Mon. Free. **Fine Arts Museum** in Fine Arts Centre, 277-4001, has sculptures, photography and paintings. Tue-Fri 9am-4pm (Tue also 5pm-8pm), Sun 1pm-4pm.

Christmas: Convention and Visitors Bureau does free night time bus tours of the outstanding *luminaria* displays, a medieval Spanish custom which began as small bonfires lighting the way to the church for the Christ Child.

INFORMATION
Visitors Information Centers: Albuquerque Convention and Visitors Bureau, 20 First Plaza, (800) 284-2282 / 843-9918 (main office), Mon-Fri 8am-5pm; Old Town Plaza, 303 Romero NW, 243-3215, 9am-5pm (summer), 9.30am-4.30pm (winter); Albuquerque International Airport. Daily 9am-9pm.

INTERNET ACCESS
Main Library, 501 Copper Ave NW, 768-5141, Mon-Thu 10am-8pm, Fri/Sat 10am-6pm, no charge.

TRAVEL
Albuquerque International Airport, south of downtown, next to the airforce base. Take Route 50 bus from downtown, 50c, 7am-6pm weekdays, less frequent at weekends.
Amtrak, 214 1st St SW, (800) 872-7245. Daily 9.30am-6pm.
Greyhound, 300 2nd SW, (800) 231-2222. Clean, safe depot with all-night cafe. $11.55 o/w to Santa Fe.
Sandia Shuttle Express, 243-3244. Shuttle vans daily to Santa Fe, $20.
Sun-Tran Transit, 601 Yale Blvd SE, 843-9200. The local city buses, basic fare 75¢, includes two free transfers, $3 for a 3-day pass. After bus hours or on Sun, call **Albuquerque Cab Co.**, 883-4888.

CARLSBAD CAVERNS   Eighth deepest and very possibly the most beautiful caves in the world, the Carlsbad Caverns began their stalactite-spinning activities about 250 million years ago. In contrast, the famous Mexican freetail bat colony has been in residence a mere 17,000 years. Once numbering seven million, give or take a bat, the colony reduced to 250,000, due in part to increased use of insecticides, but is now back to the 1 million mark. It was the eerie sight of bats pouring like smoke from the cave openings that led to Carlsbad's discovery in 1901.

The caves became a National Park in 1930, but the big bucks locally came from the sale of 100,000 tons of prime bat shit ('guano' to the genteel) to California citrus growers. No, the bats don't drink blood—and few harbour rabies, but the superstitious *should* keep the throat and other parts covered while the little boogers are zooming overhead.

Oh yes, the caves. The cross-shaped **Big Room** is 1800 ft by 1100 ft; nearby you'll see a formation called **The Iceberg**, which takes half an hour to circle. The cave's sheer size is not as impressive as the variety of colours and formations and the intricate filigrees (8 percent of which are still living and growing) these caverns house. Don't touch the formations, much as you might like to; a number of them have been turned black by ignorant handling. Carlsbad Caverns National Park homepage, *www.nps.gov/cave/* is a helpful resource for info on facilities and opportunities, recommended activities and adjacent visitor attractions.

ACCOMMODATION
Advised to drive to Carlsbad for cheap motels.
White's City Resort & Best Western Inns, 17 Carlsbad Cavern Hwy, White's City, 785-2291. Pool. 7 miles from the caverns. Mixed reports. S/D-$79.
La Caverna Motel, 223 S Canal, 885-4151. S-$22, D-$24; $2 key deposit.
Motel 6, 3824 National Parks Hwy, Carlsbad, 885-0011. S/D-$40. 22 miles from caves.
Oscuro Hostel, call 648-4007, located on a ranch, on Rt 54, 15 m S of Carizozo. $14 dorm, D-$27.
Camping: AAA Campground, at White's City Resort, above, 785-2291, provides water, restrooms, and pool. Tent sites $18 full hook-up, up to six people. **Carlsbad RV & Campground**, 1430 National Parks Hwy, Carlsbad, 885-6333, indoor pool, shop, games room, $14.50.

OF INTEREST
Carlsbad Caverns National Park, 785-2233, is open all year. **Self-Guided Cave tours: Natural Entrance Tour**, walk in through natural entrance, elevator out; 1m, very steep. Open winter, 8.30am-2pm, summer till 3.30pm. **Big Room Tour**, elevator in and out: 1 mile, about 1 hr. Open winter, 8.30am-3.30pm, till 5pm summer. Both tours have plaques to guide you along. $6, $9 w/ audio, includes both tours **Guided Tours** are an additional $8. There are many other Canyons to visit on guided tours, cost up to $20 p/p. **Slaughter Canyon Cave**, more rugged and only for those in good shape. Advance rsvs and a torch required. Tours available twice daily, $15. Temperature inside the cave is 56 degrees, refreshing in summer but bring a jacket. 'Rangers will not let you descend into the caverns unless you are wearing sensible shoes; i.e. not thongs, sandals, or anything with heels.' 'Free nature walks around cavern entrance at 5pm, something to do while waiting for bats.' (Try to plan your visit to the caves for the late afternoon in order to see the nightly bat flight). Reservations for all guided tours on (800) 967-2283.
Bat facts: bats are in residence Spring through mid-Oct only and are at busiest May-Sept, just before sunset. They leave the cave at dusk to fly up to 120 miles, consume an aggregate five tons of insects, return at dawn to spend the day sleeping in cosy bat-fashion, 300 per sq. ft. Call Visitors Center, 785-2233, (open 8am-7pm summer) for more bat-data. 'No one should miss the incredible sight of a million bats flying a few feet over one's head. Just like Dracula, in fact.' No flash photography allowed.
Bataan Recreational Area, below Lake Carlsbad is for sail boating, canoeing, picnicking and fishing.
Lake Carlsbad & Beach, a three-mile spring-fed water playground with free swimming, boat ramp and docks, water skiing, picnic area, tables, fireplaces, fishing and amusement parks.

TRAVEL
Texas, New Mexico and Oklahoma Coaches (TNM&O), 887-1108, runs two buses daily to White's City from El Paso, $30 o/w, stops at the Park.
Hitching: 'There's about a 15 min wait 7 miles from Caverns while changing bus. Try hitching. If successful, get ticket refund in El Paso.' 'If you hitchhike to Cavern, get in free with whomever gave you a lift.' 'For girls, not worth the risk.'

ROSWELL   A mecca for UFO freaks, this is the spot where an alien space-craft was said to have landed on the night of July 4th 1947. The rapid cover-up and denials exacerbated the rumours, and as is to be imagined, many theories propound as to the real nature of the 'incident'. For sci-fi drama (or tacky tat to the non-nerd population) head to the **International UFO museum,** 400-4-2 N Main St, daily 11am-5pm, free, or **UFO Enigma Museum**, 6108 S Main St, Mon-Sat 9am-5pm, Sun noon-5pm, $1. *www.roswell-online.com/* has lots of UFO links as well as information about the town and its annual **UFO Encounter festival** in July.

SANTA FE   That rarity of rarities, Santa Fe is a city for walkers, full of narrow, adobe-lined streets that meander round its Spanish heart, the old plaza where the Santa Fe trail ends. Long a crossroads for trade routes and the oldest seat of government in the US, Santa Fe has witnessed a remark-able amount of history. But the age of the place doesn't prepare you for its beauty, the friendliness of its locals and the vitality of its artistic and cultural life. The town has a strict architecture policy that requires that all the build-ings must be in 17th century pueblo style and painted in one of 23 varying shades of brown, all of which gives the place a pleasing unity. On the other hand;- 'Disappointing—caters too much to rich American tourists.' While here visit **Los Alamos**, where the first A-Bomb was built, and the ghost town of **Madrid**. *Santa Fe Online*, can be reached at *www.sfol.com/sfol/sfol.html* or for good resources on lodging etc., try *www.santafe.org/*

ACCOMMODATION
For the low-down on budget accommodations, call the **Santa Fe Detours Accommodations Hotline**, 986-0038.
Motel 6 North, 3007 Cerrillos Rd, 473-1380. From S/D-$60, more at wknds, XP-$4. Far from downtown on 'motel row'; other cheapies along Cerrillos, including another **Motel 6** a mile S.
Santa Fe International Hostel, 1412 Cerrillos Rd, 988-1153. $14 AYH, $15 non-AYH; S-$33 for private room, XP-$10. 'Excellent hostel; no curfew; friendly people, full of information.' 'More than adequate facilities: cooking, showers, library.' Organises occasional tours in summer. Linen $2. Rsvs required in Aug, in writing and with full payment.
Camping: Santa Fe KOA, 466-1419. Full hook-up $17.95 for 2 people, Mar-Oct.
Chimayo Campground, Hwy 76, Chimayo, 351-4566, $12 open year-round.
Santa Fe National Forest, 438-7860, has campsites from $4 and free backcountry camping in the beautiful Sangre de Cristo Mountains.

FOOD
Santa Fe is the home of southwestern cooking, a current favourite of American palates, and is based on humble indigenous ingredients—beans, corn and chilies, in imaginative combinations with other foods. Sample a bowl of *posole*, the hominy-based stew served with spicy pork that New Mexicans love. If you have a strong stomach and Teflon tastebuds, try the green chili stew. Prepare your mouth for a re-run of the Mt St Helens explosion.
Burrito Company, 123 Washington Ave, 982-4453. 'Tasty; not too chili-infested Mexican food at cheap prices. Varied clientele—many artists.' Mon-Sat 7.30am-7pm, Sun 10am-5pm. Nothing over $5! Cheap!
Josie's, 225 E Marcy, 983-5311. 'Very generous helpings of well-cooked Mexican food, $4-10, popular with locals.' Mouth-watering desserts. Mon-Fri 11am-3pm.

The Shed, 113¹/₂ E Palace in *circa* 1692 adobe, 982-9030. Good New Mexican lunches, crowded. Order their blue corn enchiladas and lemon souffle. Lunch Mon-Sat 11am-2.30pm; dinner Wed-Sat 5.30pm-9pm. Lunch under $10, dinner under $15.

Tia Sophia's, 210 W San Francisco St, 983-9880. A locals' hangout, the food is exceptional. Try the Atrisco ($6)—chile stew, cheese enchilada, beans, posole and a sopapilla! Mon-Sat for bfast 7am-11am, lunch 11am-2pm. Closed Sun.

OF INTEREST

NB: Despite its compact size, Santa Fe can wear you out—its altitude is 7000ft. Pace yourself.

The Plaza de Santa Fe: city heart, popular gathering place since 1610, and terminus of both the Santa Fe and El Camino Real trails, the Plaza has seen bullfights, military manoeuvres and fiestas. Billy the Kid was exhibited here in chains after causing much trouble in the area. When the Kid vowed to kill territorial governor Lew Wallace, the intended victim hid out in the **Palace of the Governors**, fronting the north side of the Plaza (while cloistered, Wallace began writing *Ben-Hur*).

The oldest public building in America (1610) and seat of 6 regimes, the **Palace of Governors**, 100 Palace Ave, 476-5100, is one of five museums of **The Museum of New Mexico**. Each museum can be visited separately for $5, or $10 gets a 4-day ticket allowing entry to all. Tue-Sun 10am-5pm. Houses historical exhibits and has Indian craft and jewellery for sale under its portal (better quality than elsewhere in town). Nearby is the **Museum of Fine Arts**, 107 W Palace Ave, 827-4468. Incls an amazing collection of 20th century Native American art and temporary exhibitions of more recent works. The **Georgia O'Keeffe Museum**, 217 Johnson St, 995-0785, is also in the area, and has the largest collection of work by the famous adopted-local. *www.okeefemuseum.org*. Further out is the **Museum of International Folk Art**, 706 Camino Lejo, 827-6350. See the Girard Collection, miniature displays of cultures from around the world. 'Well worth the walk.' Call for special performing arts events. A gallery handout will help you appreciate the fascinating, though jumbled exhibit. Finally, museum number five is the **Museum of American Indian Arts and Culture**, 710 Camino Lejo, 827-6344. First state museum devoted to Pueblo, Navajo, Apache Indians, with exhibits on history and ethnology from the Laboratory of Anthropology.

Santa Fe is a city of **churches**. Among them: **El Cristo Rey**, noted for its size and stone reredos; the **San Miguel Chapel**, Old Santa Fe Trail and De Vargas Sts, probably the oldest church in the US; the French Romanesque **St Francis Cathedral**, 13 Cathedral Place, 982-5619, built by Archbishop Lamy (subject of Willa Cather's *Death Comes for the Archbishop*) to house La Conquistadora, a 17th century shrine to the Virgin Mary; the **Loretto Chapel**, Old Santa Fe Trail and Paseo de Peralta, 986-4589, a Gothic structure whose so-called 'miraculous' spiral staircase is of mild interest; and the charming **Sanctuario de Guadalupe**, 100 Guadalupe St, 988-2027, where 18th century travellers stopped to give thanks after their hazardous journeys from Mexico City to Sante Fe.

Bandelier National Monument, 35m NW of Santa Fe, 672-0343, has ruins of Indian settlement and 70 miles of backcountry trails. Open daily, 8am-6pm summer, till 4pm in winter, $10 per vehicle. Camping on a first-come first served basis, $10. 'Need a car to get to, but well worth seeing.' Ask for directions in Santa Fe; easy to get to.

Fiesta de Santa Fe, 988-7575, early to mid-Sept, begun in 1692, the oldest non-Indian celebration in the US; great community spirit. 'Zozobra or Old Man Gloom, a 40ft dummy, is burned amidst dancing and fireworks. Most spectacular!' 'Fantastic.'

Indian Market, 983-5220, annually every 3rd or 4th w/end in August. The largest market of Indian arts and crafts in the world, with 1000 Indian artisans selling handmade jewellery, sculpture, pottery, baskets, beadwork, sand-painting, featherwork et al. Open 8am-6pm, but avoid the initial 8-deep crush in front of the stands by going after 11am. Besides artists' wares there are practical demonstrations, Pueblo dance showcases and a fashion show of traditional and modern Indian dress. NB: Beware the non-authentic tourist-trap vendors who set up stalls in hotels, parking lots and side streets. Free, but admission charge to see the dances. Hotels get very booked up at this time—res rec.

Los Alamos, 30 miles N of Santa Fe: **Bradbury Science Center**, First atom bomb was built here. Museum, 15th & Central, 667-4444, has replicas of 'Fat Man' and 'Little Boy' bombs. Tue-Fri 9am-5pm, Sat-Mon 1pm-5pm; free. 'Helpful, friendly staff. Fantastic scenery.'

Santa Fe Opera, (800) 280-4654 / 986-5955, one of America's truly great opera companies. Tkts for performances (July & Aug) run $20-120; standing room for less. You can also take a 1 hr tour of the open-air **opera house**, set amid hills and white petunias 7 miles N of Santa Fe. Tours run daily at 1pm in July & Aug; call the box office. NB: Unless you have a tkt for a performance or are part of a tour, you won't be allowed in.

Wheelwright Museum of the American Indian, 704 Camino Lejo, 982-4636. This is the best museum in the area, and practically the only one that is still 'free' (donation required). Designed to resemble a traditional Navajo hogan, the Wheelwright contains the artistry of many Indian cultures. Rotating displays. The gift shop is designed as a replica of a turn-of-the-century Navajo Trading Post. Mon-Sat 10am-5pm, Sun 1pm-5pm.

Interesting neighbourhoods: **Canyon Rd** for its adobe art galleries, studios and shops; **Barrio de Analco**, across the Sante Fe River and originally settled by Indian labourers; **Sens** and **Prince Plazas**, good shopping areas.

INFORMATION
Chamber of Commerce, 510 N Guadalupe, 983-7317. Very helpful with details of Pueblo Indian dances, ceremonials, etc. Good maps, booklets. Mon-Fri 8am-5pm.
Santa Fe Convention and Visitors Bureau, 201 W Mary St, (800) 777-2489 / 987-6760. Pick up the useful *Santa Fe Visitors Guide*. Mon-Fri 8am-5pm. Also, an **information booth**, located at Lincoln & Palace, is open summer Mon-Sat 9am-4.30pm.

INTERNET ACCESS
Santa Fe Public Library,145 Washington St, 984-6780, Mon-Wed 10am-9pm, Fri/Sat 10am-6pm, Sun 1pm-5pm.

TRAVEL
Amtrak go to nearby Lamy, and provide a shuttle bus into Santa Fe. (800) 872-7245.
Budget Rent-a-Car, 1946 Cerrillos Rd, 984-8028.
Capital City Taxi, 438-0000. Pick up coupons at hostel for Santa Fe discount cards.
Gray Line, 983-9491, picks up people where they are staying: Taos Indian Pueblo tour at 9am, $60, and Bandelier National Monument tour at 1pm, $55.
Greyhound, 858 St Michael's Dr, (800) 231-2222. Mon-Fri 7am-5.30pm, sporadic hours at w/end. NB: bus station is 3 miles outside town. Taxi to downtown around $8, city bus 50¢.

CHACO CULTURE NATIONAL HISTORIC PARK Situated in the North-west of the state, this is a massive 11th-century ruin, its largest pueblo containing 800 rooms and 39 kivas (sacred chambers) contemporary with Mesa Verde, but much less visited. 786-7014. $8 per vehicle, open year-round, but roads can be impassable in inclement weather—check forecast before travelling. **Visitors Centre**, 8am-6pm summer, till 5pm winter. No food, drink or accommodation available. Stay at **Circle A Ranch Hostel**, 510 Los Pinos County Rd, (Box 2142), **Cuba**, NM 87013, 289-3350. 2.5 hrs drive

NW from Santa Fe. Adobe hacienda in Sante Fe National Forest, remote area but near hiking trails and swimming hole. Rsvs strongly advised. Open May-Oct. Bunks: $13, D-$24-$44. 'Lovely adobe ranch, friendly people—felt part of the family.'

TAOS Set against the rich palette of the crisp, white Sangre de Cristo Mountains, the earth tones of soaring Indian pueblos and the turquoise sky of northern New Mexico, Taos (pronounced to rhyme with 'mouse') has long been a haven for artists and writers like Georgia OíKeefe, John Fowles and D H Lawrence. Given its powerful attractions, and its excellent ski-ing opportunities, the town has become a little precious and more than a little expensive. But get to know its traditional Indian and Hispanic communities and you'll glimpse the real Taos still. More information at *taoswebb.com*

ACCOMMODATION
HI-Taos, The Abominable Snowmansion, Arroyo Seco, 10 miles N of Taos, Rte 150, 776-8298. Kitchen, pool table, games in main bldg. Check-in 8am-11am, 5pm-10pm. Dorms, cabins, and Indian teepees, $13 AYH, $16 non-AYH; S-$26, D-$38, summer, more expensive in ski-season. Camping $10.
Rio Grande Hostel, 15 miles S of Taos on Hwy 68, **Pilar**, 758-0090. Plenty of diversions—in nature or in the hostel's cafe. Theatre and live music in summer. Located in Rio Grande Gorge; organised hikes available twice weekly, discounts available for Grand Canyon/whitewater rafting trips. Buses to/from Albuquerque & Santa Fe will stop here. Dorms $13. Private rooms and bungalows available, $28 shared bath, $35 private.
Camping: easy for those with a car. Check out the **Kit Carson National Forest**, 758-6200, which operates 3 campgrounds, $6-8. **Backcountry camping** requires no permit; call for more info. Also, **La Sombra, Capulin** and **Las Petacas.**

OF INTEREST
NB: Although Taos is small, its attractions are scattered, making a car very useful.
Art galleries. Best of local artists at **The Stables**, next to Kit Carson Park. For O'Keeffes, go to the **Gallery of the Southwest**. Navajo paintings of R C Gorman at the **Navajo Gallery** on Ledoux St.
Kit Carson Museums, 758-0505. Three museums: **Kit Carson Home**, $1/2$ block E of Taos Plaza on Kit Carson Rd. Period rooms (1850s), Indian, gun and Mountain Man (how the fur-trappers lived) exhibits, daily 8am-6pm; **Martinez Hacienda**, daily 9am-5pm, 2 miles S of Taos on Ranchitos Rd, Hwy 240. A restored colonial fortress and living museum. Demonstrators show the Spanish way of life in New Mexico over the past 300 yrs; **Blumenschein Home**, daily 9am-5pm, 2 blocks S of Taos Plaza on Ledoux St. Built circa 1780, the pioneer artist moved here in 1898 where he started Taos' art colony. Furnishings and collectibles from around the world; Indian and Taos artists' work. Entry $5 for one museum, $7.50 for two, $10 for all three.
Millicent Rogers Museum, 1504 Museum Rd, 4 miles N, 758-2462. $6, $5 w/student ID, daily 10am-5pm, May-Nov, closed Mon other months. Fascinating collection of death carts and *santos* (carved saints) of the Penitentes, New Mexico's fanatical religious brotherhood. Still active, the Penitentes once practised flagellation and other mortifications during Holy Week.
Mission of St Francis of Assisi, 4 miles S. A masterpiece of the Spanish Colonial period, the mission has a sculptural quality beloved by painters from O'Keeffe on down. The interior suffers from over-restoration but do see the reredos and Ault's mysterious painting, *The Shadow of the Cross*. Check locally for open hours before setting out.

Taos Plaza is the heart of the town; galleries and restaurants housed in pleasant pueblo adobes.

Taos Pueblo, 1½ miles north, Tourist Information on 758-1028. Best access via Hwy 64,. This eye-satisfying 5-storey pueblo, punctuated with beehive ovens and bright *riatas* of curing corn and chillies, preserves an 1000-year-old architectural tradition. Its 150 residents are equally traditional, having banned electricity, piped water, TV and other contrivances. Noted almost solely for their dancing and devotion to ceremonials, the Taos Indians celebrate numerous fiestas, the biggest being the Sept Fiesta of San Geronimo (races, dancing). 'Craft market also with good prices.' Also of interest are the ruins of the old **Spanish Mission church**, burned by the Spanish in 1680 and again by the US army in 1847. Guided tours by request (tips).

Today visitors are usually tolerated 8am-4.30pm (but call before you go to check); private quarters not open to viewing. $10 admission. Photography permit is $10 and you must also ask permission to take individuals' portraits. No cameras at ceremonial dances. **Faust's Transportation**, 758-3410, sends taxis from Taos to the pueblo for $8 o/w from downtown. 'A spiritual experience—well worth it.' Feast days highlight beautiful tribal dances; **San Geronimo's Feast Days** (end Sept) also feature a fair and races.

Taos Ski Valley, 15 m N of Taos. Offers powder conditions in bowl sections and short, steep downhill runs. Ski lift working in summer too, and the area has excellent hiking opportunities. **Visitors Bureau** and lodging reservations, (800) 776-1111, ski conditions on 776-2916. Online Net site at *www.taoswebb.com/nmusa/skitaos*

INFORMATION / TRAVEL

Chamber of Commerce, 1139 Paseo del Pueblo Sur (Rte 68), (800) 732-8267. Distributes maps and tourist literature. Make sure you ask for a guide to Northern New Mexican Indian pueblos. Daily 9am-6pm. *taoschamber.org*

Eight Northern Indian Pueblos Council, 852-4265, Main Church St, San Juan Pueblo, lies btwn Taos and Santa Fe on Rte 68; for info on all Pueblo activities and regulations.

Greyhound, at Neon-R-Us, 1006 Paseo del Pueblo Sur, (800) 231-2222/758-1144. Two buses daily to Albuquerque, $22 o/w, Santa Fe, $16.50 o/w and Denver, $50 o/w.

Historic Taos Trolley Tours, 751-0366, offer tours at 10.30am and 2pm.

SILVER CITY Located in the southwest mining country, Silver City is an attractive town, also a haven for artists. The **San Vincente Artists of Silver City** sponsors free self-guided artwalks on the 3rd Sat of the month, 11am-5pm, 538-5232. A couple of free museums show the history of the pioneers and the native Americans before them; **Silver City Museum**, 312 W Broadway, 538-5921,9am-4.30pm Tue-Fri, 10am-4pm wknds, closed Mon; **Western New Mexico University Museum**, Alabama St, 538-6386, 9am-4.30pm, 10am-4pm wknds. The town is also close to the **Gila National Forest**, a wild and lovely terrain of blood-red gorges, ghost towns and Indian ruins. Main office 388-2801, Visitors Centre at the **Gila Cliff Dwellings National Monument**, 536-9461, open daily 8am-4.30pm. $3 p/p entry to cliff dwellings. In this region, Geronimo eluded 8000 US Cavalry troops for eight years. Amtrak and Greyhound go to Deming; from there take the **Silver Stage Lines** shuttle bus to city centre, runs twice a day (rsvs essential a day in advance: (800) 522-0162), $10 (they also go to El Paso airport). *Silver Web, www.zianet.com/silverweb/* is the unofficial homepage of Silver City, the Land of Enchantment!

ACCOMMODATION
HI-Carter House Hostel, 101 N Cooper St, (505) 388-5485. A spacious home with a wonderful front porch with views of the nearby mountains and Silver City's historic district. Experience great hiking and biking as well as the area's natural hot springs, diverse terrain and great Mexican food. $12.50. Rsvs essential. Check-in 8am-10am, 4pm-9pm. Min 2 nts if paying by credit card.
Palace Hotel, 106 W Broadway, 388-1811, an 1881 historic hotel, rooms $35-53.
Camping; Gila National Forest, 388-8201. Sites free, first come first served, others $5-10. Free also in the **Gila Cliff Dwellings National Monument**.

INDIAN GROUPS ELSEWHERE IN NEW MEXICO   There are 19 Tewa-speaking Native American groups in all, called collectively the Rio Grande Pueblos. *www.indianpubelos.org* has links to each of the pueblos, or contact the **Pueblo Cultural Center** in Albuquerque, (800) 7666-4405, 843-7270. Among the most interesting of the Pueblos' cities is **Acoma**, 552-6604; the 'Sky City,' 60 miles west of Albuquerque, occupies a huge and spectacular mesa, the ground so stony that the Indians had to haul soil 430 ft for their graveyard. Inhabited since AD 1075, the pueblo vies with Oraibi in Hopiland as oldest settlement in the US. Noted for high quality pottery with intricate linear designs. Photo fee and restrictions, but the dollar is embraced readily enough at the pueblo **Casino**. Buses leave from the bottom of the mesa daily, 8.30am-3pm, from $8. Call the pueblo for further information. **Santa Clara**, 753-7330 between Santa Fe and Taos, is famous for its black polished pottery. More outgoing and open to visitors than other Pueblos, the Santa Clarans have fewer restrictions on photography. This is an excellent place to take in the dancing at the late August festival.

The **Jicarilla Apaches**, 759-3242 in the northwest and the **Mescalero Apaches**, 671-4495 in the southeast have numerous tourist facilities, including camping on their lands. Their ceremonies are very striking, especially the female puberty rites which take place during Fourth of July week. Non-Indians may respectfully watch the principal activities. As with Pueblo Indians, call ahead to ensure the reservations will be open when you plan to travel.

OKLAHOMA   *The Sooner State*

Originally set aside as an Indian Territory, in 1889 Oklahoma was thrown open to settlers in one of the most fantastic landgrabs ever. Thousands of homesteaders impatiently lined up on its borders, and at the crack of a gun at noon, 22 April, raced across the prairie in buckboards, buggies, wagons and carts, on bicycles, horseback and afoot to lay claim to the 2 million acres drawn up by the federal government. Some crossed the line ahead of time, giving Oklahoma its nickname, the Sooner State. The territory was admitted to the Union in 1907. Oklahoma has suffered, from broken promises over Indian lands in the nineteenth century and the flight of the 'Okies' in the 1940's, immortalised in John Steinbeck's book, *The Grapes of Wrath*.

Apart from prairies, the state has generous forests and low rolling mountains in the east. Agriculture, oil and the aviation and aerospace industries bring in most of Oklahoma's revenue. Oklahoma City installed the world's first parking meters way back in 1935.

dir.yahoo.com/ Regional/U_S__States/Oklahoma/. or *www.travelok.com*
The area code for Oklahoma City and western Oklahoma is 405; for eastern Oklahoma and Tulsa it is 918.

OKLAHOMA CITY   Oklahoma City was established in a single day when 10,000 landgrabbers showed up at the only well for miles around in what had till then been scorched prairie-land. The city has become an insurance centre for farming and other enterprises in the area, and like other parts of the state, got rich on oil. Six oil wells slurp away in the grounds of the Capitol Building. The city is also the scene of the biggest domestic terrorist action to take place on American soil; the Oklahoma Bomb of April 19th 1995 took 168 lives and was felt up to 40 miles away. Visit Oklahoma City on a virtual tour, *www.okconline.com.*

ACCOMMODATION
Accommodation in downtown OKC is scarce.
The Economy Inn, 501 NW 5th St, 235-7455. Downtown, near bus station. TV, S-$38, D-$42. 4 blocks from Greyhound.
Motel 6 Airport, 820 S Meridian Ave, 946-6662. D-$46, XP-$3. **Also located at** 4200 W I-40, in Meridian, 947-6550. Palatial rooms come with access to a pool and a spa, D-$50. 'Positively luxurious!'
Camping: RCA, 12115 NE Expressway (next to Frontier City Amusement Park), 478-0278. Has a pool, laundry room, showers, and fast-food restaurants nearby. Sites $12. A state-run campground is located on **Lake Thunderbird**, 30 miles S of OKC at **Little River State Park**, 360-3572. Swim or fish in the lake or hike the cliffs for a view. Showers available. Tent sites $7.

FOOD
Steaks and cafeterias, that's what Oklahoma City is famous for. Most places downtown close early in the afternoon. The best and cheapest steaks can be had near the stockyards at **Cattlemen's Cafe**, 1309 S Agnew, 236-0416, Mon-Fri 6am-10pm; Sat & Sun 'til midnight. Good **cafeterias** in the State Capitol building, the **Furr's** chain, and **Luby's** chain.
Flip's, 5801 N Western, 843-1527. An Italian restaurant and wine bar, food is served in an artsy atmosphere ($5-19). Daily 11am-2am.
The Spaghetti Warehouse, 101 E. Sheridan Ave. 235-0402. Good-value Bricktown place (20 meals under $7), proves that there's more to Oklahoma City dining than steaks.

OF INTEREST
The **Crystal Bridge** is part of the **Myriad Botanical Gardens**, 100 Myriad Gardens, Reno & Robinson, 297-3995. The gardens are a 17 acre oasis in downtown Oklahoma, but the highlight is undoubtedly the Crystal Bridge, a glass-enclosed cylinder 70ft in diameter containing both a desert and a rainforest. Daily 9am-6pm; Gardens are free, but the Crystal Bridge has an admission charge of $4, or $3 w/student ID.
Enterprise Square USA, on the campus of Oklahoma Christian College, 2501 E Memorial Rd, 425-5030. A sort of Disneyland-for-capitalists extolling the virtues of good old fashioned Adam Smith-ism. See the 'World's Largest Functioning Cash Register' with its singing dollar bills, the 'Hall of Achievers' (yay!), the 'Great Talking Face of Government' (boo!) and the 'Time Tunnel' and 'Economic Arcade Game Room,' where you'll find out whether you have the stuff it takes to survive

in an open-market economy. Wed-Sat 9am-5pm; $4, $2.50 w/ student ID. Tours every 15 mins. *www.esusa.org*

National Cowboy Hall of Fame and Western Heritage Center, 1700 NE 63rd, 6 miles N of downtown along I-44, 478-2250. $6.50, daily 8.30am-6pm summer, 9am-5pm winter. Sitting right on the Old Chisholm Trail, this complex, a joint venture by the 17 Western states, is magnificent. The art gallery includes many works by famous painters of the west as it was being opened up in the last century, including Russell, Remington, Schreyrogel, Bierstadt. 'Boring, and not worth it.'

Oklahoma City National Memorial, NW 5th Street and Harvey, 325-3313, due to open in 2000. Memorial to the bombing of the Alfred P. Murrah Building, including the Survivor Tree, interactive learning Museum and the Institute for the Prevention of Terrorism and Violence. On the site of the bomb blast.

Oklahoma City Zoo, 2101 NE 50th St, 424-3344. Daily 9am-6pm summer, till 5pm winter, $6. Rated one of the top zoos in the nation with over 2000 animals from 500 species.

Omniplex, 2100 NE 52nd St, 602-OMNI / (800) 522-7652, *www.omniplex.org*, houses 8 museums and galleries: **Air Space Museum** has exhibits on the state's contribution to aviation and space; the **International Photography Hall of Fame** holds examples of work by leading photographers around the world. There is also the **Red Earth Indian Center**, **the Hands-on Science Museum**, **Planetarium, Kirkpatrick Galleries, Kirkpatrick Gardens and Greenhouse**, and finally the **Omnidome**, Oklahoma's first large format movie screen. Admission to all 8 is $7, plus $1.65 for the Planetarium. Mon-Sat 9am-6pm, Sun 11am-6pm.

State Capitol, 2300 N Lincoln Blvd, 521-3356. Six derricks make politics pay; one of them is 'whipstocked' (drilled at an angle) to get at the oil beneath the Capitol, itself an unimpressive structure, one of the few state capitols without a dome. Daily, 8am-4.30pm; guided tours 9am-3pm. Free.

State Museum of History, just south of the capitol at 2100 N Lincoln Blvd, 522-5244. Displays of Oklahoma history, from prehistoric Indians to the present. 'Interesting Indian relics.' Mon-Sat, 8am-5pm. Free.

Nearby: Indian City USA, near **Anadarko**, 65 miles SW of Oklahoma City on Hwy 62, 247-5661/ (800) 433-5661. Authentic re-creation of Plains Indian villages, done with help of Uni of Oklahoma's Anthropology Dept. Dancing, demonstrations, ceremonies, camping, swimming. $7.50 entry, open daily 9am-5pm. Also **Indian Hall of Fame**, 247-5555, and **Southern Plains Indian Museum** on the same site.

Norman, home of **University of Oklahoma** (20,000 students), 30 mins from Oklahoma City. Student life dominates the town, so there's usually plenty to do. The university's housing dept is helpful in finding accommodation during the summer. The University of Oklahoma **Museum of Art**, 410 W Boyd, 325-3272, is worth a visit. Permanent collections of American, European, Oriental and African art. Tue-Sun noon-4.30pm, free.

Festivals: Festival of the Arts, 270-4848, held annually every April at Myriad gardens, highlights visual, culinary and performing arts. **The Red Earth** festival, 427-5228, held annually every June, is the country's largest celebration of Native America, includes intense dance competitions in which dancers from different tribes perform for prize money.

ENTERTAINMENT

For nightlife ideas, pick up a copy of the *Oklahoma Gazette* or try the Bricktown district on Sheridan Ave, especially the **Bricktown Brewery**, 1 N Oklahoma St, 232-BREW. Dine on chicken dishes ($5-9) and watch the beer brew. The second floor houses live music. Cover $3-10, 21yrs+. Live music Tue and Fri-Sat 8pm. Or try **In Cahoots**, 2301 S. Meridian Ave. 686-1191. Popular dance hall and saloon with nightly live music ranging from country to indie. Quite a way south of downtown.

INFORMATION

Oklahoma City Convention and Visitors Bureau, 189 W Sheridan, 297-8912, (800) 255-5652. Mon-Fri 8.30am-5pm. *www.okccvb.org*

Norman Chamber of Commerce, 115 E Gray St, 321-7260. Mon-Fri, 8am-5pm.

Oklahoma City Tourist Information Centers, Downtown; Colcord Building, 15 N Robinson, 521-2409, Mon-Fri, 8.30am-5pm.; and at Frontier City—12229 N I-35 Service Rd, 478-4637, open daily, 8.30am-5pm.

Travelers Aid, 412 NW 5th, 232-5507; Mon-Fri 8am-4.30pm. Also booth at airport.

TRAVEL

Dub Richardson Ford Rent-a-Car, 2930 NW 39th Expressway, (800) 456-9288.

Greyhound, Union Bus Stn, 427 W Sheridan & Walker St, (800) 231-2222 / 235-6425. 24 hrs; crummy area, but station has security guards (until midnight).

Miller's Bicycle Distribution, 215 W Boyd, 321-8296. Bike rental $10 day. Mon-Sat 9am-8pm, Sun 1-6pm. Credit card essential.

Oklahoma Metro Area Transit, 200 N Shartel, 235-7433. Bus service Mon-Sat approx. 6am-6pm. No service Sunday. $1 basic fare.

Royal Coach, 3800 S Meridian, 685-2638, has 24 hr van service to downtown.

Yellow Cabs, 232-6161 in OKC; 329-3333 in Norman.

Will Rogers International Airport, 7100 Terminal Dr, 681-5311. No buses run directly there. Take the #11 from 10th & Robinson to 29th & Meridian, about 40 mins, from there take a cab, $5-$6; or take a cab from downtown, $15.

TULSA   In its art-deco heyday, Tulsa was once known as the 'oil capital of the world'; now Tulsa has slid technologically sideways to 'aerospace capital of ... Oklahoma.' Its setting among rolling green hills on the Arkansas River is prettier than OKC but it's just as windy. (The whole state is notorious for wild weather). Check out Bret's Slightly Warped Tour o' Tulsa, *www.ionet.net/~bretp/index.html* where a lifetime resident takes a look at some of the things that make the city unique.

ACCOMMODATION

Try the budget motels on I-44 and I-244.

The Baymont, 4530 E Skelly Dr off I-44, (800) 428-3438. Free bfast delivered to your room, free *USA Today* and local calls; S/D -$63.

Georgetown Plaza Motel, 8502 E 27th, 622-6616. TV, S/D-$32-45, some have microwave and fridge.

Motel 6 West, 5828 Skelly Dr, 445-0223. S/D—$35.

Tulsa Inn, 5554 S 48th W Ave, 446-1600. Take exit 222. From D-$28.

Camping: KOA Kampground, 193 East Ave, 266-4227. Pool, laundry, showers, game room. Sites for two $18 (full hook-up). Also, **Heyburn State Park** on Heyburn Lake, 247-6601. Fishing, swimming, bike rentals. Tent sites $6 (full hook-up).

FOOD

Black-Eyed Pea, family style chain; 3 locations but none are downtown, 665-7435. $5-$8 dinner.

Both OKC and Tulsa have **Casa Bonitas**, 21st and Sheridan, 836-6464. A crazed mixture of Mexican village and dining area with waterfall, mariachis, puppets, dancers, etc. Sun-Thurs 11am-9pm, Fri & Sat 'til 10pm. Good value, all-you-can-eat Mexican dinners; deluxe, $8.29.

Harvest Buffet, 3637 S Memorial, 663-9410. All-you-can-eat smorgies, b/fast $4, lunch $4.50, dinner $6. 7am-9pm daily, Sun 'til 8pm.

McDonalds, Vinita, 40m NE of Tulsa on I-44, the old Route 66, memorable as this is the biggest one in the whole wide world.

Metro Diner, 3001 E 11th St, 592-2616. Salads, sandwiches, burgers, and pasta

dishes, under $10. Daily 8am-10pm.
Williams Center, 2 blocks from Greyhound. 'Amazing shopping Centre overlooking ice rink. Cheap bfasts, better value than Greyhound'.

OF INTEREST
Creek Council Oak Tree, 1750 S and Cheyenne. Known as 'Tulsa's First City Hall,' the tree was a meeting place for the first group of Creeks to come from Alabama to Oklahoma in 1828.

Oklahoma in general and Tulsa in particular are in Bible Belt country; here you'll find **Oral Roberts University**, 7777 S Lewis, (800) 678-8876. Founded by the evangelist after a vision from God so specific that he was told what style to build the place in, ORU looks like a fifties version of the future, as seen in those classic B movies. Campus tours, 495-6807. Visitors centre, daily 10.30am-3pm.

Thomas Gilcrease Institute of American History and Art, 1400 Gilcrease Museum Rd, 596-2700. The treasurehouse of Western American art, plus 250,000 Native American-Indian artefacts, interesting maps and documents like the original instructions for Paul Revere's ride, the first letter written from the North American continent by Chris Columbus' son, Aztec codex, etc. $3 donation requested; summer Mon-Sat 9am-5pm, Sun 11am-5pm.

Nearby: Cherokee Heritage Centre, Willis Rd **Tahlequah**, 70 m from Tulsa, 456-6007. Summer performance of the **Trail of Tears** performed June through August, 8.30pm in a lovely amphitheatre, telling the story of the tragic march 1838-39 from eastern Tennessee, in which 4000 of 16,000 Cherokees died of hunger, disease and cold, and were forced to begin life anew in the territory that would become the state of Oklahoma. Haunting music and dance. To understand the full gravity of the march, read John Ehle's *Trail of Tears*. For more info, contact Trail of Tears National Historic Trail, Southwest Region National Park Service, PO Box 728, Santa Fe, NM 87504, (505) 988-6888. Also houses the **Cherokee National Museum**, $3, Mon-Sat 10am-5pm, Sun 1pm-5pm, and the **Tsa-La-Gi Village**, a replica of a 17th century Cherokee village staffed by Cherokee who portray the life of their ancestors, including braves, kids and villagers; 45 min tour $6. Open mid-May through late Aug; Mon-Sat 10am-5pm, Sun 1pm-5pm.

When you are leaving Oklahoma, go by way of **Quapaw**, in the north-east corner of the state where Oklahoma cuts a corner with Kansas and Missouri. In this area, which some call the 'Bermuda Triangle of the prairie,' is the **Tri-State Spooklight**, described as a 'weird, bobbing light' along State Line Road. Scientific explanations (light refraction from an unknown source, underground quartz crystals) have been given for this phenomenon. But everyone knows the spooklight is really caused by UFOs on their way to North Dakota.

ENTERTAINMENT
Pick up a free copy of *Urban Tulsa* at local restaurants.
Bars on Cherry St (15th St, E of Peoria) and S Peoria. The intersection of 18th and Boston caters to the young adult crowd.
Performing Arts Center, 110 E 2nd St, events line 596-2525, houses the ballet, opera etc. Box office (800) 364-7111 / 596-7111.
Steamroller Blues Barbecue, 18th & Boston, 583-9520 is a popular blues venue, with the best performances at weekends.

TRAVEL/INFORMATION
Chamber of Commerce / Convention and Visitors Division, 616 S Boston, 585-1201. Mon-Fri 8am-5pm.
Greyhound, 317 S Detroit, (800) 231-2222 / 584-4428.
Metropolitan Tulsa Transit Authority, 582-2100. Basic fare 75¢, transfer 5¢, runs 5am-7pm. Has 'ozone alert' days in summer when all buses are free.
River Trail Bicycles bike rental, 6861 S Peoria, 481-1818, $3-10 /hr. Inline skates

rental $5/ hr. Mon-Thu 10am-7pm, Fri-Sat 'til 8pm, Sun 11am-7pm. Driver's license/major credit card required.
Thrifty Car Rental, 41st & Memorial Dr, 838-3333. Open 24 hrs.
Tulsa International Airport, 838-5000, just off Hwy 11, about 6 miles NE of downtown.
Yellow Checker Cabs, 582-6161, $12-15 airport to downtown.

TEXAS   *Lone Star State*

Texans may have had to pass the Stetson of 'biggest state' to Alaska but they haven't lost their talent for beer-drinking, braggadocio, BBQ and making Dallas-sized mountains of money. This state has the size, colour and raw energy of a Texas longhorn steer, and it'll wear you out if you try to cover it. As the old jingle has it, 'the sun is riz, the sun is set, and we ain't out of Texas yet'! Better to focus on its two cities of any charm—San Antonio and Austin—and perhaps the tropical coast around Galveston or Corpus Christi.

Always intensely political, Texas has seen six regimes come and five go, from Spanish, French and Mexican, to a brief whirl as the Republic of Texas and finally Confederate. Through it all, Texas remains good ole' boy country, a terrain of hard-bitten little towns and hard-edged cities whose icons are Willie Nelson, the Dallas Cowboys and LBJ. In recent years, with the downturn in oil prices, the state's energy-based economy has been depressed. It may not be wise to argue with a Texan ; there are four guns for every man, woman and child in the state.

The Texan scenery may vary from desert to mountains to vast rolling plains but everywhere in the summer months there is one constant—the heat. Temperatures of 90-100 degrees are the norm and in Houston, especially, there is also high humidity—'Gulf weather' it's called. **National Parks**; Big Bend, Guadalupe Mountains.

dir.yahoo.com/Regional/U_S__States/Texas/.

Texas telephone area codes Corpus Christi & Austin, 512; Dallas, 214; El Paso, 915; Ft Worth, 817; Galveston, 409; Houston, 713; Lubbock, 806; San Antonio, 210.

SAN ANTONIO   About 75 miles south of Austin sits thoroughly Hispanic San Antonio, the only Texas city to possess a proper downtown, much less one with attractions worth walking to. The action centres round the San Antonio River and its pleasant green Riverwalk, where fiestas, music and fun of one sort or another take place year-round.

This city of over a million people began in 1691 as an Indian village with the wacky name of 'drunken old man going home at night,' which the Spaniards bowdlerised to San Antonio. Despite the early Spanish (and later Mexican) presence in Texas, settlement lagged and authorities began admitting Americans. By the 1830s, six of seven inhabitants were Anglo and the resultant friction caused skirmishes and ultimately the Battle of the Alamo. During its 13-day siege, 200 Americans gallantly fought to the last man against the 5000-man Mexican army of Santa Ana. Afterwards, the rallying cry of 'Remember the Alamo' helped Sam Houston and his troops defeat the Mexicans and establish the Republic of Texas, 1836-1845. *At Home in San*

Antonio is a non-commercial view of a local's hometown, located on the web at *www.athomeinsanantonio.com*

ACCOMMODATION

For cheap motels, try **Roosevelt Ave** (an extension of St Mary's), **Fredericksburg Rd** and **Broadway** (btwn downtown and Brackenridge).

B&B Hosts of San Antonio, 8546 Broadway #215, San Antonio, TX 78217, (800) 356-1605. Finds rooms in private homes, From S-$50, D-$60.

Villager Lodge, 1126 E Elmira, (800) 584-0800. Large, well-furnished rooms. TV/AC. 'Very caring management.' S/D-$39. Key deposit $2.

El Tejas Motel, 2727 Roosevelt Ave, 533-7123. Close to missions, 3 miles from downtown. Bus #42 to door. S-$25-$35, D-$40-45. AC, TV.

Motel 6, 5522 N Pan-Am Expressway, I-35 and Rittiman, 661-8791. D-$53, XP-$3; TV, AC, pool. Also, **Motel 6**, downtown at 311 N Pecos, 225-111 (slightly more expensive), and at North WW White Rd off I-10, 333-1850; D-$32-62.

HI-San Antonio International Hostel, 621 Pierce St, 223-9426. Private rooms with AYH discount, S/D-$33. Dorm rooms $14 AYH, $17 non-AYH. Sheets $2, bfast $4. Pool, kitchen. Fills quickly in summer. From bus station take #15 bus E from Houston St to Carson St, walk 2 blocks west or take #11 to Grayson St at Pierce. 'A friendly, ranch-style hostel in a quiet neighbourhood.'

Travelers Hotel, 220 Broadway, 226-4381. Downtown, 1 block from the Alamo. S/D$37 + $2 key deposit.

Camping: Alamo KOA, 602 Gembler Rd, (800) 833-5267. 6 miles from downtown. Each site has a BBQ grill and patio. Showers, laundry, AC, pool, golf course, free movies. Open 'til 10.30pm. $20 for two w/ hook-up, $16 without, XP-$2.50.

FOOD

San Antonio, with its 52 per cent Latin population, has far better Mexican food than most Mexican border towns. A directory of restaurants and other entertainment highlights of SA can be found at *www.food-leisure.com*.

Farmers' Market near Market Sq., 207-8600. Sells Mexican produce and candy. Haggle away with vendors and see prices drop! Daily 10am-8pm summer, 'til 6pm winter.

Henry's Puffy Taco, 815 Bandera, 432-7341. Mon-Sat 10am-9pm, 'til 10pm at w/ends, specials $5.

Hung Fong Chinese Restaurant, 3624 Broadway, 822-9211. The oldest Chinese restaurant in San Antonio, dishes under $10. Open 11am-10.30pm.

Kangaroo Court, 512 S Presa, 224-6821. 'Does Bass ale at $3.25 ¹/₂ pint/$4.75 pint, of very cold beer!' Seafood and sandwiches. Dinners under $15.

Maverick Cafe, 6868 San Pedro, 822-9611. Chinese and Mexican food. $5-$15. 11.30am-9pm, 'til 10pm w/ends. 'One of a kind.'

Mi Tierra, 218 Produce Row in **El Mercado**, 225-1262. Open 24 hrs, dynamite Mexican food. Order the *Chalupa compuesta* and the supercheap *caldo* (soup), $6-$15.

Pig Stand, 1508 Broadway and 801 S Presa (off S Alamo), 227-1691. Diners offer cheap country-style food.

Rio Rio, Riverwalk, 226-8462, open till 10.30 weekdays, 11.30 wknds. Great location, excellent Mexican food.

OF INTEREST

The Alamo: Alamo Plaza near Houston and Alamo St, 225-1391. Texas' most visited tourist attraction, the restored 1718 presidio-mission is free and open daily 9am-5.30pm, Sun from 10am. Mural inside of heroes Bowie, Crockett and Travis. Pass up the slide show across the way—ear-splitting and redundant. 'Boring—don't bother.'

Also in Old San Antonio: **San Fernando Cathedral**, main Plaza, where Alamo heroes are buried. Behind city hall is the beautiful **Spanish Governor's Palace**, 105 Plaza de Armas, 224-0601. Mon-Sat 9am-5pm, Sun 10am-5pm, $1.

Brackenridge Park, 3900 N St Mary's St (3 miles NE of downtown on Hwy 281). Take bus #8. Free Japanese sunken gardens, a skyride, riding stables, and the **San Antonio Zoo**, 3903 St Mary's, 734-7183, includes an extensive African mammal exhibit; $7—'worth the money but packed.' Park open daily 9am-5.30pm, Sat-Sun 'til 6.30pm. Zoo; last admissions at 6pm, open till 8pm.

El Mercado, typical Mexican market with stalls of fresh fruits and meats, cheap clothes and crafts from Mexico. At junction of Santa Rosa and Commerce Sts.

HemisFair Park: The free **Institute of Texan Cultures**, 801 S Bowie at Durango, 485-2300, has displays on 26 ethnic groups; Tue-Sun 9am-5pm, (donation requested), also the **Mexican Cultures Institute**, Tue-Fri 9am-5.30pm, Wknds noon-6pm. The view from the 750ft **Tower of the Americas**, 600 HemisFair Park, 207-8615, 8am-11pm, is worth the $3 fee.

San Antonio has 5 missions, counting the **Alamo**. Unless you're mission-mad, skip the others and see **Mission San Jose**, 6539 San Jose Dr, 932-1001, known as the 'Queen of the Missions'. (Take the hourly S Flores bus marked 'San Jose Mission'). Designated a National Historic Site it has an interesting granary, Indian building, and barracks. Try to time your visit for Sun mass when the mariachis play. Free. Every Sat am, a National Park Ranger leads a 10 mile r/t bike tour from Mission San Jose along the historic corridor. Free; bring your own bike.

La Villita, btwn Nueva & S Alamo Sts, downtown restoration of the city's early nucleus, with cool patios, banana trees, crafts demos and sales. Daily 6am-6pm.

Natural Bridge Caverns, 26495 Natural Bridge Caverns Rd, 651-6101. The caverns' 140-million-year-old phallic rock formations are guaranteed to knock your socks off! $1^1/_2$ hr tours every $^1/_2$ hr. Daily 9am-6pm summer, 'til 4pm winter; $9.

Paseo del Rio or **Riverwalk**. The jade green river is echoed by greenery on both sides, cobblestone walks, intimate bridges at intervals, and lined with restaurants and bars with good Happy Hours and late hours. A civic as well as tourist focal point. 'Free lunch, evening concerts in summer.' 'Free dancing along the Riverwalk.' 'The hub of San Antonio's nightlife.' 'Very pretty but outrageously hyped and a bit fake and plastic—the Mexican Village is a lot more authentic.'

River Boats—pick up across from the Hilton, and for $5.25 will take you on a 35-40 mins tour of the river. Call **Yanaguana Cruises**, (800) 417-4139, who have narrated boat tours along the Paseo del Rio. Tkts available at the **River Center Mall**, 849 E Commerce St, or outside the Hilton Palacio del Rio, 200 S Alamo St.

San Antonio Museum of Art, 200 W Jones Ave, off Broadway, 978-8100. Housed in a restored turn-of-the-century brewery, the museum now exhibits Greek and Roman antiquities, Mexican folk art, 18th-20th century US art and Asian art. $5, $4 w/student ID. Wed-Sat 10am-5pm, Tue 10am-9pm (free entry), Sun noon-5pm. Closed Mon.

Sea World of Texas, 15 miles NW of downtown, at Ray Ellison Dr and Westover Hills Blvd, 523-3611, (800) 722-2762. $170 million park—aquariums, flamingoes, waterfowl, a 12.5 acre lake for water skiers and two water rides (log flume and river raft). Open daily in high summer, otherwise wknds only—call for times. $35.50.

ENTERTAINMENT

For evening fun, any season, stroll down the **River Walk**. Also, the Friday *Express* or weekly *Current* is good for entertainment and what's on.

Arneson Theater, Alamo & Nuevo, 207-8610. Showcases everything from flamenco to jazz to country; river separates you from stage. **Fiesta Noche del Rio** variety show is $8, June-August, Thurs, Fri, Sat at 8.30pm.

Floore Country Store, 14464 Old Bandera Rd, btwn Old & New Hwy 16 in Helotes,

695-8827. One of the oldest Honky-Tonk hangouts and a favourite of Willie Nelson. Open wkdys during the day till 8pm, and Fri-Sun evenings; cover from $5.

Jim Callum's Landing, 123 Losoya (in the Hyatt downtown), 223-7266. Happy Jazz Band Mon-Sat 9pm-1am, and the improv. jazz quintet Small World performs on Sun nights.

For authentic *tejano music* (Mexican-country!) head to **Cadillac Bar**, 212 S Flores, 223-5533. Dancing frenzy heaven. Mon-Thu, 11am-11pm, Fri till midnight, Sat 5pm-2am.

Mexican Festival, 3rd week in Sept, Riverwalk, and **Fiesta San Antonio**, 227-5191, April 22-30. Plenty of Tex-Mex action with concerts and parades, to commemorate the victory at San Jacinto and honor the heroes at the Alamo. Also, numerous fiestas, music events and blowouts (most free) throughout the year; during St Patrick's week, San Antonians dye both their beer and their river green!

INFORMATION
Convention and Visitors Bureau, 121 Alamo Plaza, (800) 447-3372 / 270-8700. Daily 8.30am-6pm.

INTERNET ACCESS
Free at the **San Antonio Public Library**, 600 Soledad, 207-2500, Mon-Thu 9am-9pm, Fri/Sat 9am-5pm, Sun 11am-5pm.

TRAVEL
American Auto Rentals, 3249 SW Military Dr, 922-9464. Mon-Fri 8am-6pm, Sat 9am-6pm, Sun 10am-6pm.

Amtrak, 1174 E Commerce St, (800) 872-7245. For *Sunset Limited* LA-New Orleans-Miami and *Texas Eagle* to Chicago routes.

Greyhound, 500 N St Mary's St, (800) 231-2222 / 270-5824. 24 hrs.

San Antonio International Airport. About 5 miles N of downtown; take #2 'Blanco-Airport' bus from Soledad & Travis Sts, 75¢.

VIA, runs local buses, 362-2020. Basic fare 75¢, transfer 10¢, express $1.50, day-tripper pass $2. Operates daily Sun-10pm, but many routes stop at 5pm. Also runs the El Centro old-fashioned trolleys that circle downtown, 50¢.

Yellow Cab taxis, 226-4242, $15-17 to airport.

AUSTIN Capital city, named after the state's 'founding father,' but Richard Linklater made his film, *Slacker*, here for a reason. With its laid-back attitude it doesn't seem like 'real' Texas but it does seem like the most enjoyable city in the state. Truly an oasis, socially and culturally, in the middle of a desert, it has a huge student population that adds a vigour to the place. Austin is *the* place to go to see bands, hang out, drink too much and party hard. It's also, strangely enough, a centre for bats. In summer, a colony of the little critters roosts under the Congress Ave Bridge. Every evening, at around 8pm, a crowd gathers to see them all leave to feed. *Austin 360* is an online newspaper with info on the Austin music scene, sports and news. *www.Austin360.com/*

ACCOMMODATION
Congress St is cheap hotel/motel row.

HI-Austin International Hostel, 2200 S Lakeshore Blvd (near Barton Springs), (800) 725-2331/ 444-2294. Dorms $14, also has private rooms. Extremely clean, well-kept hostel with a cavernous 24 hr common room overlooking town lake. Waterbeds available! Kitchen, laundry. Located near grocery store.

The Castilian, 2323 San Antonio St, 478-9811. Dorm-style rooms S-$35, D-$50. 3

June-17 Aug only. Private residence hall, coed, overlooking University. Cafe, AC, pool; very nice. Bus stop 1/2 block.

Motel 6, I-35 N Rundberg Ln Exit, (800) 440-6000 / 837-9890. Pool, new AC, TV. S/D-$45, XP-$3. Rsvs required especially at w/ends

Pearl Street Co-op, 2000 Pearl St, 476-9478. Large rooms, laundry, kitchen, courtyard, pool. Friendly atmosphere. 3 square meals, shared bath, access to TV/VCR room. 2 week max stay. S-$13, D-$17.

Taos Hall, 2612 Guadalupe at 27th St, 474-6905. Hallway bathrooms and linoleum floors. 3 meals and a bed, $15.

21st St Co-op, 707 W 21st St, 476-1857. Carpeted suites, AC, common room, co-ed bathroom on each floor. $10 pp, plus $5 for 3 meals and kitchen access. Fills up quickly in summer.

Camping: The Austin Capitol KOA, (800) 284-0206, 6 miles S of city along I-35. Offers a pool, clean bathrooms, game room, laundry, grocery store. Shady tent site, full hook-up $33; XP-$3. Cabins Q-$39, $49 for six. Get 3rd night free. A cheaper option is **McKinney Falls State Park**, 13m SE of downtown, 243-1643, $12, plus $2p/p Park entrance.

FOOD
Great pickings, but you'd better like Texas BBQ, Mexican food and Texas chili. Lots of student hangouts along Guadalupe.

The Filling Station, 801 Barton Springs Rd, 477-1022. Get 12oz ethyl-burgers or a gasket platter ($6). 'Try the high-octane speciality drink, the Tune-up, guaranteed to clean out your spark plugs!' $4. 11am-midnight, Fri & Sat 'til 2am.

Furr's Cafeteria, 4015 S Lamar, 441-7825. Two other branches in Austin. All-U-Can-Eat, $5, Delight plate $6. 11am-9pm.

GM Steakhouse, 626 N Lamar, 472-2172 serves T-bone ($7.95) and sirloin steaks ($8).

Hickory Street Bar and Grille, 800 Congress Ave, 477-8968. Array of speciality food bars (salad, soup, potato, bread and sundae); $1-$5, or All-U-Can-Eat for $5.50. 'Austin's best 1/2 pound hamburgers.' Open till 9.30pm.

Quackenbush's, 43rd St, Hyde Park, 472-4477. A popular café/deli for espresso etc. Daily 8am-11pm.

Richard Jones Pit, 2304 S Congress, 444-2272, serves best BBQ in town. Open till 9.30pm.

Texas Chilli Parlor, 1409 Lavaca St, 472-2828. World class chili joint and saloon, also serves $3 screwdrivers and Bloody Marys on w/ends. Open till midnight wkdys, 2am wknds.

Texas Showdown Saloon, 2610 Guadalupe, 472-2010. Small menu; 'Texas-style' atmosphere; average drinks $2, snacks $2.50. Open till 2am.

Threadgill's, 6416 N Lamar, 451-5440. A stronghold of Texas food, and run by Eddie Wilson, a founding father of Austin's music scene, this soul-food joint has free seconds and was an early stomping ground of the original screamer, Janis Joplin. Eddie plays the place down, 11am-10pm. 'I've got easily the best restaurant in the history of the globe!' Kitchen's motto is 'we don't serve all you can eat, we serve more than you can eat.'

Trudy's Texas Star, 409 W 30th St, 477-2935. Fine Tex-Mex dinner entrees ($5-$8), margaritas and *migas*, a corn tortilla souffle ($4). Outdoor porch bar with picnic tables, open early morn 'til 2am. Food served 'til midnight.

OF INTEREST
Austin Museum of Art, Laguna Gloria, 3809 W 35th St, 458-8191. 8 miles from the State Capitol. Blends art, architecture, and nature, overlooking Lake Austin. Also hosts a yearly arts & crafts festival with concerts and plays in May. $2, $1 w/student ID. Recently opened a new location **downtown**, 823 Congress Ave, 495-9224, quadrupling the museum space. $4, $2 w/student ID, Thu $1. Opening hours

both the same; Tue-Sat 10am-5pm, Thu open till 8pm, Sun noon-5pm
Barton Springs, Zilker Park, 2201 Barton Springs Rd, 476-9044. Open-air swimming hole (not a chlorinated pool) fed by underground springs. 'Reached by lovely 40 min riverside walk, beautiful setting.' $2.50, 'but if you smile and ask for the loan of a swimsuit you might get in free.' Pool's temperature rarely rises above 60F though! Alternatively, walk upstream and swim at any nice-looking spot! Park is open Mon-Fri 5am-10pm, w/ends 10am-6pm, $2. Also **Hamilton Pool**—a favourite with Texan students (on Texas 71 West), 264-2740. 60ft waterfall cascades into a jade green pool. Monitored—closed if bacteria levels are too high. $5 parking fee, $2 walk-ins, 9am-6pm daily.
Capitol Building, Congress Ave & 11th St, 463-0063. 7ft higher than the national one! Free tours leave from Rotunda, unrestricted entry to public areas, including galleries from which you can observe debates. Check out the upside-down rotunda in the new underground Capitol Extension. Tue-Fri 9am-5pm, Sat 10am-5pm.
Museums: O Henry Museum, 409 E 5th St, 397-1465, free. Personal effects of the popular short-story writer who lived in Austin from 1885-1895. Wed-Sun noon-5pm. Also, **Republic of Texas Museum**, 510E Anderson Lane, 339-1997. Indispensable museum for anyone interested in Texas or Civil War history, owned and operated by the Daughters of the Republic of Texas for over 100yrs. $2, $1 w/student ID.
University of Texas, Guadalupe and 24th St, north of Capitol. Huge, rich, highly social school. Has several museums and the **LBJ Library** at 2313 Red River St, 916-5136. Free, daily 9am-5pm. A/V displays, replica of the Oval Office and tapes of LBJ's twang. LBJ's birthplace, home, ranch and grave are west of Austin, in and around Johnson City. Also: **Harry Ransom Center**, 21st & Guadalupe on UT campus, 471-8944. Houses a good art museum, one of the world's four copies of the Gutenburg Bible, lots of Evelyn Waugh and the personal libraries of Virginia Woolf and James Joyce. Mon-Sat 9am-5pm; free.

ENTERTAINMENT
Austin is a major music centre; check *The Daily Texan* and the free *Austin Weekly Chronicle* to see who's playing where. Guadalupe Ave, called The Drag, is a hot spot for student and non-student activity. For nightclubs and fancy bars it has to be 6th St, wall-to-wall music and a great Halloween street party. For a quiet evening, visit **Copper Tank Brewing Company**, 504 Trinity St, 478-8444, the city's best microbrewery. Pop along on a Wed for a freshly brewed pint, $1! Mon-Fri 11am-2am, Sat-Sun 3pm-2am. Lately, much nightlife has also headed to the **Warehouse Area** around 4th St, west of Congress. Also, check out: *Austin City Limits*, an excellent nationwide TV country show broadcast Weekly on public television in the US.
Antone's, 213 W 5th St, 474-5314. Has drawn the likes of BB King and Muddy Waters. $3-8 cover charge admits you to a fine blues club. All ages welcome. Daily 8pm-2am.
Broken Spoke, 3201 S Lamar, 442-6189. Authentic C&W dive with live music, Texas two-step dancing, chicken-fried steaks. Cover, Wed-Thu, $4; Fri/Sat $6.
Liberty Lunch, 405 W 2nd, (cnr w/ Guadalupe) 477-0461. Has all sorts of good touring bands.

INFORMATION
Convention and Visitors Bureau, 201 E 2nd St, (800) 926-2282 / 478-0098. Daily 9am-5pm; 125 pieces of free literature on the area.
University of Texas Info Center, 471-3434.

INTERNET ACCESS
Austin Public Library, 800 Guadalupe, 499-7599. Mon-Thu 9am-9pm, Fri/Sat 9am-6pm, Sun noon-6pm.

TRAVEL
Amtrak, 250 N Lamar Blvd, (800) 872-7245.

Austin Bergstrom International Airport btwn Hwys 183/ 71, S of city, opened in 1999. #100 Buses travel from the Uni / downtown, Mon-Fri 5am-10pm, Sat 7am-9pm, Sun 8am-9pm; 50c.
Capital Metro, (800) 474-1200 /474-1200. Local bus company; basic fare 50¢, free transfers. The **Dillo Bus** serves downtown area to Uni campus; green trolleys run daily (free).
Greyhound, 916 E Koenig Lane, (800) 231-2222 / 458-4463. 24 hrs.
Robert Mueller Municipal Airport, 4600 Manor Rd. About 4 miles NE of downtown; take bus #20 from 6th & Vrazos, 50¢; last bus out midnight in week, Sat 10.50pm, Sun 9.15pm.
Yellow Cab, 472-1111.

DALLAS/FORT WORTH

Big D pushes culture but its finest achievements are Neiman-Marcus, the glittering emporium of the conspicuous consumer, and Tolbert's Chili Parlor, where the serious chiliheads go to eat a bowl of red before they die. 'Dallas is a hard-nosed business environment with entertainment geared to the relaxing businessman.' One of the world's largest permanent trade fairs is located here. The city seems to go on forever and attractions are not centralized. If you are not travelling by car, you may want to visit a city more accommodating to the pedestrian.

An airport larger than Manhattan is the umbilical cord linking Dallas with **Forth Worth**, its cattle-and agriculture-based sister city. Fort Worth, surprisingly, has a lot more of interest to see and do, with a number of top-notch museums and art collections, most free and conveniently clumped in Amon Carter Square. As befits an overgrown cowtown, the honky-tonk country and western scene is alive and well, more cowboy than urban. Forty miles and a heap of freeways separate these two behemoths, so don't plan to lodge in one and visit the other. *Do remember that Dallas (214) and Fort Worth (817) have different telephone area codes. Arlington also uses 817.* Check out the Yahoo! Town Cities online city guide at *dir.dfw.yahoo.com*.

ACCOMMODATION
NB: Budget accommodation in either city does not exist in the downtown areas. We suggest you rent a car and schlepp out to one of the Motel 6s ringing the area, or make your visit a brief one.
Motel 6; seven locations, should be nearby wherever you are. Rates approx. S-$32-52. Call (800) 440-6000.
B&B Texas Style, 4224 W Red Bird Lane, (800) 899-4538. Mon-Fri 8.30am-4.30pm. Rooms in private homes near town, from S-$50, D-$60.
Delux Inn, 4451 South Freeway, **Fort Worth**, (817) 924-5011. Pool, restaurant. From S/D 32-$45. Free bfast.
Market Center Boulevard Inn, 2026 Market Center Blvd, **Dallas**, (214) 748-2243. D-$90, TV, bath, pool.
Red Crown Inn, Hwy 175 E, **Fort Worth,** (817) 557-1571. S-$33, D-$37, $1 key deposit.

FOOD
In Dallas: For the low-down on dining, pick up Friday's *Dallas Morning News*.
Celebration, 4503 W Lovers Lane, 351-5681. 'A real discovery for both its ambience and good food. Magnificent home cooking.'
Farmers' Produce Market, 670-5879, 1010 S Pearl Expressway, Downtown. Daily 5am-6pm. Best places to get fresh produce from local farms; 'veggie oasis.'
Gennie's Bishop Grill, 321 N Bishop Ave, 946-1752. Cafeteria-style, lines are short

and functional. 'Garlic chicken is a must.' Mon-Fri 11am-2pm.

Mecca, 10422 Harry Hines Blvd, 352-0051. A happy-go-lucky roadhouse 'where a squadron of feisty waitresses rules the loose-jointed dining room/joint.' Chicken-fry and cinnamon rolls are specialities.

Norma's Café, 3647 W NW Hwy, 357-7771, also at 3330 Beltline Rd, Farmers Branch (near Dallas). Roadhouse with giant bfasts with everything from catfish to meatloaf on offer.

Sonny Bryan's, 2202 Inwood Rd, 357-7120. 'Best urban barbecue in Texas.' Funky, run-down atmosphere. Other Dallas locations are 302 N Market, 744-1610; 325 N St Paul, 979-0102; 4701 Frankford Rd, 447-0102; Macy's Food Court at the Galleria Mall, 851-5131. And yet more locations around town. Mon-Fri 10am 'til 4pm, Sat 'til 3pm, Sun 11am-2pm. *www.sonnybryans.com*

Tolbert's Chili Parlor, 350 N St Paul St, corner of Bryant St, 953-1353. Mon-Fri 11am-7pm, a primo chili shrine $5-$8.

In Fort Worth: Kincaid's, 4901 Camp Bowie Blvd, 732-2881. Feast your eyes (and mouth) on their world-renowned half-pound hamburger! Mon-Sat, closes 6pm.

Paris Coffee Shop, 704 W Magnolia, 335-2041. Home-baking prepared daily, all under $6. Mon-Fri 6am-2.30pm, Sat 'til 11am. 'The best breakfast and lunches in town.'

Cattlemen's Steak House, 2458 N Main St, 624-3945. A Fort Worth institution thanks to its steaks and margaritas. Dinner is around $15; closed Sun lunch.

OF INTEREST

In Dallas: You have probably seen the Zapruder footage so often that there will be no problem in retracing the route that **John F Kennedy** took to his death on 22 Nov 1963. He was driven on Main to Houston and Elm where Lee Harvey Oswald is alleged to have fired the shot from **The Sixth Floor** of the Texas School Book Depository, 411 Elm St, 747-6660. Now a museum to the Kennedy life and legacy, it is easily reachable from the Greyhound station during a rest stop. Daily 9am-6pm (last entry 5pm), $9, $8 w/student ID, incl. audio tour. 'Very moving and sensitive.' Overlooking the scene is an **obelisk**. A Philip Johnson-designed **Cenotaph** is on Main St at Market. JFK spent his last night on this earth in the **Fort Worth Hyatt Regency**. Just across the street is **The Conspiracy Museum**, 110 S Market St, 741-3040. Exhibits, CD-Roms, maps and photos chronicle the deaths of famous figures including JFK and Lincoln. $7, $6 w/student ID; daily 10am-7pm.

Dallas Museum of Art, 1717 N Harwood at Ross, 922-1200. Anchors the new **Arts District** with its excellent collections of Egyptian, Impressionist, modern and decorative art. Sculpture garden lies adjacent. Some pre-Colombian works. Tue-Fri 11am-4pm, Thu 'til 9pm, wknds 11am-5pm, Closed Mon. Free, except for special exhibits.

Frontiers of Flight Museum, Love Field, 2nd floor, 350-1651. Collection of aviation artefacts including the fur parka as worn by Adm. Richard E Byrd in 1929 on his first flight to the North Pole. Mon-Sat 10am-5pm, Sun 1pm-5pm, $2.

Neiman-Marcus Dept Store, Main and Ervay. Of it, Lucius Beebe said: 'Dallas, for all its oil, banks, insurance wouldn't exist without Neiman-Marcus. It would be Waco or Wichita, which is to say: nothing.'

West End Historic District, Market Street from pacific to McKinney is the restored old town, including the not-so-authentic **West End Marketplace** Mall at the north end of Market St.

Architecture: both the **Hyatt Regency** and **Reunion Tower** at 300 Reunion Blvd, 651-1234, get high marks: 'best things in Dallas,' 'especially beautiful at sunset'. There is an observation deck on the 50th floor of the Tower, $2, a good way to see and get a feel for the whole city before you start walking. Open 10.30am-10.30pm. Also worth a look is the c.1914 **Union Rail Station**, connected to the tower by underground walkway. The **Adolphus Hotel**, Commerce and Field, was built by a brewer and has a 40-ft beer bottle on top, which serves as a closet for a 19th floor suite.

Parks: Fair Park, SE of downtown on 2nd Ave, 670-8400. 277 acres, home to the Annual (Sept-Oct) State Fair, and the Cotton Bowl Football Stadium. Inside park, **African-American Museum**, 3536 Grand Ave., 565-9026, a multimedia collection of folk art and sculpture. Tue-Fri, noon-5pm, Sat 10am-5pm, Sun 1pm-5pm; free. Also the **Science Place**, daily 9.30am-5.50pm, $6, and **IMAX Theater**, Sun-Thu 10am-9pm, Fri/Sat 10am-11pm, $6. Both at the Grand Ave. Park Entrance, 428-5555. The **Planetarium** is an extra $3.

Nearby, **White Rock Lake** provides a haven for walkers, bikers, and inline skaters.

Ft Worth: Amon Carter Square: houses four free museums: the **Amon Carter Museum**, 738-1933, with its splendid Western Art Collection of Russells and Remingtons, Tue-Sat 10am-5pm, Sun 1pm-5pm; the **Kimbell Art Museum**, 332-8451, itself an architectural tour de force by Louis Kahn, housing Oriental, pre-Columbian and late Renaissance works, Tue-Sat 10am-5pm, Fri till 8pm, Sun noon-5pm; the **Modern Art Museum**, 738-9215, Tue-Fri 10am-5pm, Sat 11am-5pm, Sun noon-5pm, includes works by Andy Warhol, and the **Museum of Science and History**, 1501 Montgomery St, 732-1631, Mon 9am-5pm, Tue-Thu 9am-8pm, Fri/Sat 9am-9pm, Sun 9am-8pm, with sophisticated exhibits, and science movies in the Omni Theater, $5, $6 for films, $3 planetarium.*www.fwmuseum.org*

Billy Bob's Texas, 2520 Rodeo Plaza, the Yards, 624-7117, the world's largest honky-tonk bar, a bull ring, a BBQ restaurant, pool tables, video games and 42 bars. Fri-Sat, 9pm & 10pm there is live professional bull riding. Free Texas waltz lessons, Thurs 7-8pm. Cover $1-9. Headliners at w/ends, $5-$25; local bands during week, $1-$3, daily 11am-2am (Sun noon-2am). You can atone for your hangover at the **Cowboy Church** at the **Stockyards Hotel**, corner of Main and Exchange, Sun at 11am.

The **Chisolm Trail Round-Up**, 625-7005, a 3-day jamboree in the stockyards, mid-June, commemorates the heroism of cowhands who led the Civil War-time cattle drive to Kansas, and the **Hog and Armadillo Races** are a must-see.

Fort Worth Stockyard District, along Exchange Ave and N Main St, on North side. Pungent and still active with Mon cattle auctions (free viewing). 'Original stalls and railway exist, storefronts and boardwalks renovated. Gives a feeling of the past.' For info on the Stockyards, obtain a copy of the *Stockyards Gazette* at the **Visitors Information Center**, 130 Exchange Ave., 624-4741, Mon-Fri 9am-6pm. Sat 9am-7pm, Sun noon-6pm. Every Fri pm, Sat and Sun, **Arts and Crafts Market**, Stockyards Market Place, by Coliseum on Plaza. The Stockyards host Weekly rodeos, 625-1025; Sat 8pm, $8. The **Stockyards Collection and Museum**, Livestock Exchange Building, 131 E Exchange Ave., 625-5087 contains photos and memorabilia form the early stockyard days. Mon-Sat 10am-5pm, donations only.

Sundance Square, between 1st & 6th Sts is the heart of downtown. Red-paved blocks filled with shops, cafes and bars.

Tarantula Railroad, steam train runs from stockyards to nearby Grapevine, ticket office at 140 E Exchange Ave., (800) 952-5717 / 625-7245; $22 rtn, $13 o/w. 'OK if you are mad on trains, otherwise, saw lots of dust.'

Nearby; Just outside of Fort Worth in **Plano** is **South Fork Ranch**, from the *Dallas* TV series, (972) 442-7800. Daily tours of the Ewing Mansion and the Dallas Museum—just try to get the theme tune out of your head for days after a visit. Tours 9.30am-4.15pm, every 45 mins, $6.95. Wander round the grounds for free; you can still sit on the patio dinner table from which many a time Sue-Ellen stormed away, and the series wasn't actually filmed inside the house anyway. Miss Ellie's Deli is open 11.30am-4.30pm.

SPORTS/ENTERTAINMENT

The free Weekly *Dallas Observer*, out every Wednesday, can help you assess your entertainment options. Check out **West End Market Place**, off Houston St, where there is a plethora of galleries, eateries, and dance clubs.

Six Flags Hurricane Harbor, I-30 btwn Dallas & Fort Worth, in Arlington, exit Texas 360N, (817) 265-3356. $26.93 plus $5 parking. Open daily in summer, otherwise wknds only—call for details. Includes Sea Wolf, largest water raft ride in the USA. You will also need cash for raft rentals, $6 single, $9 double, and locker rental, $4 plus $2 deposit.

Six Flags Over Texas, 20 miles W of Dallas in Arlington, (817) 640-8900. $38.78 plus a nasty $8 parking, includes all rides and shows. Open daily May-Aug wknds thereafter. The original of this ever expanding chain, the six flags referring to the six regimes that Texas has seen. Especially nauseating is the Texas Chute-Out, a parachute drop of 17 storeys and 'Flashback' a looping rollercoaster with fast forward and reverse. The showpiece is a huge wooden frame coaster, the 'Texas Giant,' voted by those in the know the world's best. Also 5 hrs of air-conditioned shows.

Sport: Football is the main religion in Dallas. **Texas Stadium** on the E Airport Freeway is home to the famous **Dallas Cowboys**. Call (972) 785-5000 for the box office, but they will probably just direct you to *Ticketmaster* (214) 373-3000 for tkt availability (NB: tkts are scarce). The **Texas Rangers** play **baseball** in btwn the two cities in Arlington, off the I-30. Call (817) 273-5100.

INFORMATION

Dallas Convention and Visitors Bureau, Renaissance Tower, 1201 Elm St, suite #2000, 746-6700 / (800) 23-5527 Events hotline. *www.dallascvb.com*

Dallas Visitors Center, 'Old Red' Courthouse, 100 S Houston St, 571-1300, Mon-Fri 8am-5pm, Wknds 9am-5pm.

Fort Worth Convention and Visitors Bureau Information Center, 415 Throckmorton, (800) 433-5747 /624-4741. Mon-Sat 9am-6pm, Sun from 11am.

INTERNET ACCESS

In Dallas; Web Corner Cafe, 3028 N Hall St #179, 303-0869, $5/hr, open till midnight during the week, 2am wknds. Or free at the **J Erik Johnson Central Library**, 1515 Young St, 670-1400, Mon-Thu 9am-9pm, Fri/Sat 9am-5pm, Sun 1pm-5pm. **In Fort Worth, Cyber Rodeo Steakhouse**, 1309 Calhoun St, 332-1288, open till 10pm, or the **Houston Central Library** is located at 300 Taylor St, 871-7701, Mon-Thu 9am-9pm, Fri/Sat 10am-6pm, Sun noon-6pm.

TRAVEL

Dallas: Amtrak, Union Station, 401 S Houston Ave, (800) 872-7245. The bars upstairs in terminal also worth a visit—cheap, and wonderful architecture.' Daily 9am-6.30pm.

Dallas Area Rapid Transit (DART), 979-1111, The local buses and light rail, $1, premium routes $2, day pass $2. Routes radiate from downtown; serves most suburbs. Runs 5am-midnight; to suburbs 5am-8pm. *www.dart.org*

Greyhound, 205 S Lamar St (3 blocks E of Union Station), (800) 231-2222 / 655-7082. 24 hrs.

Dallas-Fort Worth International Airport, btwn the two cities. Take #51 from downtown West Transfer Centre to Peak & Ross; change to #409. Free DFW shuttle will do the rest, and all for just $1 (remember to take a free transfer slip). Or take a **Super Shuttle**, (817) 329-2000, from one of the main downtown hotels for $11 o/w to Dallas, $12 Fort Worth. Rsvs only, 24 hrs in advance from downtown hotels. At airport, in baggage claim area, dial (02) on 'ground transportation' phone.

Dallas LoveField Airport, 670-6080, in the north of the city, take #39 'Lovefield' bus from one of the blue bus stops on Commerce. Has mostly intra-Texas flights.

Fort Worth: Amtrak, 15th and Jones Sts, (800) 872-7245.

Greyhound, 901 Commerce St, (800) 231-2222 / 429-3089, 6am-1am, closed Sun.

Yellow Checker Cab Co, (800) 749-9422, 24 hrs.

HOUSTON   The newer skyscrapers that crowd Houston's skyline have sleek skins of black sun-reflecting glass, the same material used for astronaut helmet visors. Seems appropriate, since this city of 1.8 million, and fourth largest in the US, is inextricably linked with NASA and the first moon landing.

But space money is petty cash compared to Houston's real wealth, which comes from oil refineries and its port activities. A city of scattered satellite nodes, Houston has developed unconstrained by zoning—so it seems to go on for ever. Unless you have an air-conditioned car, ample time and money, skip humid and expensive Houston: 'Houston's wealth has taken a dive as the oil market has gone downhill. It is a huge modern city and has hardly any attractions. It is probably the most boring city I've been to. The tremendous humidity makes it even worse.' 'No car, no skates or bike? Forget Houston!' 'Downtown is dead!' If you are still determined to visit, for an interactive map and guide of Houston, click on *www.houstonet.com/*

ACCOMMODATION

For the most part, hotels are big and expensive in this city. There are, as usual, a number of **Motel 6**'s dotted around the outskirts, and one at the Astrodome, rooms from around $40-50. Call (800) 4MOTEL6.

Houston Downtown YMCA, 1600 Louisiana Ave, 659-8501. S-$20. 'Basic.' Has cafeteria, TV and access to gym/health facilities. 'Usually full by noon.' Rsvs. Co-ed. Another branch, 7903 South Loop, 643-4396 is farther out but less (marginally) expensive, S-$18.45+ $10 deposit.

HI-Houston International Hostel, 5302 Crawford at Oakdale St, 523-1009. $11.40. 'Friendly, clean and efficient with AC.' Laundry. Lock-out 10am-5pm. Within walking distance of museums.

FOOD

Diversity of ethnic restaurants due to city's large Indochinese population. Houston's cuisine mingles Mexican, Greek, Cajun, and Vietnamese food. Reasonably-priced restaurants along **Westheimer** and **Richmond Ave**, intersecting with **Fountainview**.

Bellaine Broiler Burger, 5216 Bellaine Blvd, 668-8171. 'Burgers are delicious, shakes are real!' Open Mon-Sat till 8pm.

Cabo Mix Mex Grill, 419 Travis St, 225-2060, reasonably priced Mexican.

Goode Company Barbeque, 5109 Kirby, 522-2530/523-7154. Pig out on crunch-crusted pork ribs, melt-in-the-mouth brisket, chicken, ham, duck, or turkey with peppery pinto beans and luscious jalapeno cheese bread on the side. Busy at w/ends. Open till 10pm.

J Putty's Pizza, 500 Dallas, 951-9369. Also at 1910 Travis & 500 Jefferson. Closes at 3pm.

Otto's BBQ, 5502 Memorial Dr, 864-8526. Serving best ribs in town since 1963. 11am-7pm Mon-Sat.

OF INTEREST

Astrodome, 799-9544, south of downtown. The first and still one of the largest indoor stadia in the world, modestly called 'Taj Mahal,' 'Eighth Wonder,' etc., in its literature; apparently an 18 storey building could fit inside. Tours $4, 3 times daily (except Sun), obligatory when no event. More worthwhile to combine a visit with a **Houston Astros** baseball game or other happening (from dog shows to dirt-bike races). Cheapest seats in the pavilion ($4, purchased day of game) but also: 'We recommend $6-$9 Upper Reserve seats, seven levels up, behind home base.' Take #15 bus from Main St.

Six Flags Astroworld, opposite A-Dome, 799-8404. Six Flags clone with 100 rides, 11 rollercoasters and a waterpark, $38.96, open daily April-Labor Day, varying hours; thereafter w/ends only.

Take a drive by the **Beer Can House**, 222 Malone. Adorned with 50,000 beer cans, strings of beer-can tops, and a beer-can fence, the house was built by a retired upholsterer from the Southern Pacific Railroad.

Menil Collection, 1515 Sul Ross Ave., 525-9400, Wed-Sun 11am-7pm; free. Large private art exhibition.

For all skateboarding/inline/BMX enthusiasts, there is an abundancy of skateparks, **Baytown Skatepark; Skatepark of Houston;** and **South Side Indoor Skatepark.**

Museum District; home to 11 'museums' in the loosest sense of the word. Includes **Hermann Park, Japanese Gardens,** as well as actual museums or galleries. The **Contemporary Arts Museum**, 5216 Montrose Blvd, 284-8250, has multimedia exhibits. Free; open Tue-Sat10am-5pm, Sun noon-5pm, closed Mon. Across the street is the **Museum of Fine Arts**, 1001 Bissonet, 639-7300. Exhibition wing designed by Mies Van der Rohe. Renaissance art plus renowned Hogg collection of 65 paintings, watercolours by Frederick Remington. Tue-Sat 10am-5pm, Thu 'til 9pm (free all day Thu), Sun 12.15pm-6pm. $3, $1.50 w/student ID. The **Cullen Sculpture Garden**, 5101 Montrose St, includes pieces by artists such as Matisse and Rodin. Daily 10am-10pm, free. **Museum of Natural Science**, 639-4600, $4, has moon-landing equipment, displays of gems and minerals, a planetarium ($4), laserium ($6) and an IMAX theatre, 639-4629 ($6). Inside the museum's **Cockrell Butterfly Centre** in a tropical paradise of 80F, there are more than 2000 butterflies, ($4). An IMAX Plus package allows a film and one or more of the other halls- from $9.50. **Rothko Chapel**, 3900 Yupon, in Montrose area, 524-9839. A multi-faith chapel, its walls bedecked with Rothko's exercises in controlled simplicity. Daily 10am-10pm. **Zoological Gardens**, 525-3300. Gorillas, hippos, reptiles, and rare white tigers. Also hosts a macabre bat colony. You're allowed to see them quaff their daily blood—fascinating, repellent. Entry to zoo $2.50; 525-3300, 10am-6pm daily.

Hundreds of shops and restaurants line the 18 mile **Houston Underground**, which connects all the major buildings in downtown Houston, Civic Center to the Hyatt Regency, 840-9255 for tours. Also, try the **Galleria**, Westhiemer St, an enormous shopping mall with over 300 shops.

NASA-LBJ Space Center, 1601 NASA Rd 1 (20 miles S of downtown via I-45), (800) 972-0369 / 244-2105. *Tour Work*s pick up daily around 9am from downtown hotels, $49, (888) 868-7839. 'Cheaper to rent a car, and take your time.' Also, 'hitching is worst I've ever come across, took us 2 hrs to get a lift.' daily 9am-7pm (summer and wknds), 10am-5pm (winter); $12.95. Or take free guided tour: see spacecraft, shuttle trainer, moon rocks, NASA films. 'No need to book Mission Control tours. First come, first served basis.' 'Very exciting seeing Mission Control in action. We watched a test run for the next shuttle mission.' 'Very informative.' The complex also houses models of Gemini, Apollo and Mercury as well as countless galleries and hands-on exhibits. You too can try to land the space shuttle on a computer simulator!

Port of Houston. Now that a deep channel runs 50 miles S to the Gulf of Mexico, Houston is a major port; 3rd largest in the US, 6th in the world. From the observation platform at Wharf 9 you can watch huge ships in the Turning Basin, open 10am-5.30pm. Free $1^1/_2$ hr boat trips, call *Sam Houston* 670-2416, available Tue-Sun. A free look at the bayou and a stunning perspective of the skyline. Book well ahead in summer. Closed Sept.

Sam Houston Park, downtown at Allen Pkwy and Bagby St, 655-1912. Nice melange of historic Greek Revival, Victorian, log cabin and cottage against a canyon of office buildings. Daily guided tours of the buildings and grounds, 10am-4pm Mon-Sat,

1pm-4pm Sun, on the hour; $6. Not far away is **Tranquillity Park** at Bagby and Walker, named in honour of lunar landings. 'Truly an oasis in the desert.'

ENTERTAINMENT

Houston is trying—in the last couple of years there have been concerted efforts to improve downtown nightlife, especially in the Montrose district. Judge for yourself whether they have succeeded or not. For some chills and thrills, wander down the more established **Richmond Ave.**, btwn Hillcroft & Chimney Rock.

804 Underground Lounge and Disco, 804 Fannin St, 237-1505, music and dancing, usually around $5 cover.

Ale House, 2425 W Alabama at Kirby, 521-2333 has a beer garden to chill in while you experiment some of the 130 brands of beer. Mon-Sat 11am-2am, Sun noon-2am.

Astrodome sometimes features rock shows. Feb sees the Rodeo and Livestock Show, (naturally) the world's largest. Also home of the **Astros** baseball team, for info call 627-8767.

City Streets, 5078 Richmond Ave, 840-8555 has 6 different clubs featuring country, R&B, disco, 80s etc. Tue-Fri 5pm-2am. $2-5 cover good for all 6 clubs.

Spy, 112 Travis St, 228-0007, two levels of dancing, plenty bars, guaranteed to avoid C&W—usual in Houston! Cover $5-10.

Miller Outdoor Theatre, Hermann Park has free symphony, ballet, plays, drama and musicals in the summer. 'Get there 30 mins early for good position.' Tkts required for seats, box office 11am-1pm.

TRAVEL/INFORMATION

Amtrak, 902 Washington Ave, (800) 872-7245, near to main post office. In rough neighbourhood; at night call a cab.

Greater Houston Convention and Visitors Bureau, 801 Congress St across from Market Square, (800) 365-7575 / 627-8767. Mon-Fri 8.30am-5pm. *www.houston-guide.com*

Greyhound, 2121 S Main St, (800) 231-2222. Open 24 hrs—unsafe neighbourhood; call a cab, again!

Houston Intercontinental Airport (HIA), 25 miles N of downtown. Take Metro bus #102 (IAH Express) on Travis going north; last bus out 9.10pm, last into downtown 9.10pm; $1.50. No w/end service. Out of bus hours, catch an **Airport Express** bus, 523-8888, leaving from next door to Hyatt Regency on Louisiana, leaves every 1/2 hr from 7am 'til 11.30pm, $17, rsvs 1 day in advance.

Metro Transit Authority, 739-4000. Local METRO buses, basic fare $1, express $1.50, free transfers. Reliable service within the 'loop' of I-610, anywhere btwn NASA and Katy. Less frequent at w/ends.

Visitor Information Centre, City Hall, 901 Bagby St, 227-3100, daily 9am-4pm.

INTERNET ACCESS

Free at the **Houston Central Library**, 500 McKinney, 247-2222, Mon-Fri 9am-9pm, Sat 9am-6pm, Sun 2pm-6pm. Out of town, there is the **User Friendly Computers and Cyber Cafe**, 12027 Misty Valley, Champin Forest, (281) 397-0161, $9.75 hr.

GALVESTON   History rich, hurricane prone Galveston Island was once headquarters for pirate Jean LaFitte, who liked its 32 miles of sandy beaches (so handy for burying bullion). Houston's ship channel eventually siphoned off the big shipping business, leaving Galveston at its architectural peak: a resplendent little city of scarlet oleanders, nodding palms and fine 19th century mansions. Come here to gorge on bay shrimp, and imbibe the placid, slightly decayed Southern feeling of the place.

Unfortunately, the beach here isn't as fine as those further to the south. Nearby oil wells and refineries pollute the water with annoying globs of tar, and the shore is hard and flat. It reminds you of a parking lot by the seashore. Camping is permitted in the state park. Access via causeway and by free ferry from Port Bolivar to the East. Take a virtual tour of Galveston Island (includes photos), through *www.utmb.edu/galveston*. **Kemah**, meaning 'Wind in the face' to give you an idea of the type of weather to expect, is a 20 min drive from Houston on Galveston Island, and has recently become a getaway for the city slickers, with a cute boardwalk and a few nice seafood restaurants.

ACCOMMODATION / FOOD
To save money, make Galveston a day trip from Houston. However **Galveston Island State Park** on 13 Mile Rd (6 miles SW of Galveston on FM 3005), 737-1222, has sites for $12, plus $3 p/p Park entry. Res rec on wknds. There are hotel rooms to be had, but especially in the summer, there is nothing very close to the 'budget' range—best to try one of the more ordinary looking roadside motels. Along **Seawall Blvd**, check out the bountiful seafood and traditional Texas barbecues. Try **The Original Mexican Café**, 1401 Market, 762-6001, the oldest restaurant on the island. Tex-Mex meals with homemade flour tortillas. Daily lunch specials ($5). Mon-Fri 11am-10pm, Sat-Sun 8am-10pm. **Aquarium Restaurant,** 11 Kemah Waterfront, Kemah (281) 334-2513, expensive—but you can just go in and look at the fish!

OF INTEREST
Texas Seaport Museum, Pier 21 at end of Kempner (22nd) St, 763-1877. Home to *Elissa*, a Scottish-built square-rigged sailing ship restored to its 1877 condition (although occasionally will be out on her travels). Daily 10am-5pm, extd hours in summer, $6, $4 w/student ID.
Some of the **architecture** worth seeing: **Ashton Villa**, 24th and Broadway, 762-3933, an elegantly restored 1859 Italianette mansion. Tour includes slide show about the 1900 hurricane that claimed 5000-7000 lives, $4, 10am-4pm daily, Sun noon-4pm. **The Bishop's Palace**, 762-2475, 1402 Broadway, extravagant 1886 home, $5, 10am-5pm daily, noon-5pm
Sun. **The Strand** contains a fine concentration of over fifty 19th Century iron front buildings, which house a pastiche of cafes, restaurants, gift shops and clothing stores. Audio walking tours available from the Visitors Centre.
'Rollerskate,' bike rental shops on Seawall Blvd. Useful shower/changing facilities on Stewart beach, $5 entry includes use of shower. Has lockers.
Stop by **Moody Gardens**, (800) 582-4673, an area although filled with touristy spas and restaurants, makes room for a l0-story glass pyramid which encloses a tropical rainforest, 2000 exotic species of flora and fauna, a 3D **IMAX Theater** with a six-story-high screen, and the **Bat Cave**. Sun-Thu 9.30am-6pm, Fri-Sat 9.30am-9pm. Each attraction has a separate admission, $6-7 each.

INFORMATION/TRAVEL
Galveston Island Convention and Visitors Bureau, 2106 Seawall Blvd, (800) 425-4753 / 736-4311; daily 8.30am-5pm. Provides info about island activities. *www.galvestontourism.com*
The Strand Visitors Center, 2016 Strand St, 766-1572. Mon-Sat 9.30am-6pm.
Texas Bus Lines (affiliated to Greyhound), 714 25th St, 765-7731. Four buses daily btwn Houston and Galveston, $13 o/w.

CORPUS CHRISTI and THE SOUTH TEXAS COAST A large port city with a leaping population, **Corpus Christi** (translated as 'body of Christ') makes a good gateway to **Padre Island**, a long lean strip of largely unspoilt National Seashore that points toward the Texas toe. Once inhabited by cannibals, the shifting blond sands of Padre have seen five centuries of piracy and shipwrecks and no doubt conceal untold wealth. The natural wonders of the 110-mile-long island are quite sufficient for most people. However, it's a prime area for bird watching, shelling and beachcombing for glass floats. You can camp free at a number of idyllic and primitive spots. All are at the South Padre end, reached only via Hwy 100. Camp on the seaward side of the dunes; the grassy areas may have poisonous rattlesnakes. Besides Galveston and Padre, the South Texas coast has hundreds of miles of coastline and various other islands.

North and east of Padre Island and Corpus Christi is the **Aransas Wildlife Refuge**, (512) 286-3559, $3 p/p or $5 per vehicle, where you can go by boat from Rockport and see (in season and at a distance) the world's remaining 150 whooping cranes, best time to see them is between November and March. Open daylight hours. In **Rockport**, get down to marvellous seafood and gumbo eating at   **Charlotte Plummer's**, 202 N Fulton Beach Rd, (512) 729-1185, open daily 11am-10pm. Corpus Christi, South Padre and the entire area are rich in roadside stands that sell cheap, fresh boiled shrimp and tamales, the local speciality.

South Texas border towns with Mexico are numerous but not particularly appealing. Avoid **Laredo**: 'A dump with rip-off hotels.' **Brownsville/Matamoros** is probably the best and certainly most convenient to South Padre. 'Got free tourist card from Mexican consulate at 10th and Washington Streets in 5 mins.' For links to attractions check out *www.mahpro.com/hometown*

ACCOMMODATION
Cheap accommodation is scarce in downtown Corpus Christi. For the best motel bargains, drive several miles south on Leopard St (bus #27) or I-37 (take #27 express). Campers should head for the **Padre Island National Seashore** (361) 949-8062, $10 Entrance Fee, or **Mustang State Park**, (512) 749-5246. The latter offers elec, water, showers and picnic tables for $7 plus $3 p/p park admission. All must pick up a camping permit from the ranger station at the park entrance.

FOOD
Best to check out the Southside, around **Staples St**, and **S Padre Island Drive**.
Buckets Sports Bar & Grill, 227 N Water St, 883-7776. An eclectic menu of American, Cajun, Italian and Mexican dishes. Daily 11am-2am; sometimes has live music.
Howard's BBQ, 102 N Water St, 882-1200. Ample beef and sausage plate, salad bar buffet and drink ($5). Mon-Fri 11am-3pm.

INFORMATION/TRAVEL
Greyhound, 702 N Chaparral, (800) 231-2222. Daily 7am-3pm.
South Padre Tourist Bureau, 600 Padre Blvd, (800) 7667-2373 / (956) 761-6433 , Mon-Fri 9am-6pm, Wknds 9am-5pm.
Visitors Bureau, 1201 N Shoreline, (800) 678-6232 / (512) 881-1888; *www.cctexas.org*

EL PASO and BIG BEND Biggest Mexican border city, El Paso feels neither Hispanic nor Texan. Backed by mountains, El Paso's main focus is the Rio Grande River, where early Spanish expeditions used to cross. The river also serves as the border and a casual, non-bureaucratic one it is. Other than sampling the sleazy delights of **Ciudad Juarez**, there's little reason to tarry in El Paso. It can serve as a base for Carlsbad Caverns in New Mexico or the Texan National Parks. 'Unless your journey necessitates going via El Paso, take another route.' A one stop information centre is located at *cs.utep.edu/elpaso/main.html* /

ACCOMMODATION
HI-El Paso International Hostel in the **Gardner Hotel**, 311 E Franklin Ave, 532-3661. Small dorms, beautiful, spacious kitchen, common room with pool table, TV and couches for lounging and socialising in basement. $15 AYH, $18 non-AYH. Linen $2. Rsvs. Gardner Hotel has private rooms: S-$20, D-$40. AC, kitchen, laundry, 24 hr check-in.
Gateway Hotel, 104 S Stanton St, 532-2611. Close to San Jacinto Sq. Clean, spacious large beds and closets. Diner downstairs. Check out 4pm. S-$23, D-$35. Few dollars more for TV.

FOOD
Burritos are the undisputed local speciality!
Forti's Mexican Elder Restaurant, 321 Chelsea Dr close to I-10, 772-0066. The fajitas and shrimps are superb. $4-$12. Sun-Thu 11am-10pm, Fri-Sat 11am-11pm.
H&H Coffee Shop, 701 E Yandell, 533-1144. Adjoins H&H car wash; nip in for a quick cuppa! Renowned for its hangover cure of tripe and hominy stew (Sat only). Mon-Sat till 3pm.
Smitty's, 6219 Airport Rd, 772-5876. Tender brisket, lunch and dinner served. Mon-Sat till 8.30pm
Tigua Indian Reservation, 121 Old Pueblo Rd, Ave of America's Exit off I-10, 859-7913. Daily till 4pm Mon-Fri, 5pm wknds. Besides its crafts and rather small restored mission, the reservation has a good eating place in the museum, with excellent red and green chili, and other traditional dishes. Worth a stop, if only for the food.

OF INTEREST
Simply stroll through downtown to see the colourful remnants of El Paso's Wild West history.
Americana Museum, Civic Center Plaza, under Performing Arts Bldg, 542-0394. Explores Native American and pre-Columbian American cultures. Tue-Fri, 10am-5pm, donations.
Hop aboard the **Border Trolleys**, 544-0062, departing every hr from El Paso Civic Center, for a whirlwind exploration of the streets!
Ciudad Juarez, 4th largest city in Mexico, is poor by western standards, though wealthy by Mexican standards. The shopping for leather, rugs and clothing is excellent. Drinking Tecate Beer in the **Kentucky Club**, 629 Avenida Juarez, **Juarez,** an old western bar, you can pretend you're Papa Hemingway as you wait for the bullfights to begin. Three bridges span the Rio Grande between El Paso and Ciudad Juarez. The main bridge is Cordova, which is free. Other bridges charge $1 there, $2 back (cars); on foot, 25¢ there and 50¢ back. 'Mexican immigration didn't even give us a glance.' 'You can also ride the bus over but why bother. If you do, hold on to your passport and don't surrender your IAP-66 to the US authorities.'

El Paso Museum of History, I-10 West and Ave of the Americas, 858-1928. Tells the story of the Indian, Conquistador, Vaquero (Mexican cowboy), cowboy, and the US Cavalryman, all of whom fought and bled to win the Southwest. Tue-Sun 9am-4.50pm, free/donations.

Fort Bliss Replica Museum, in north El Paso, Pleasanton Rd & Sheridan Drive, 568-4518, houses several museums on the base exploring the history of the Civil War, the 3rd Armored Cavalry, and air defence, daily from 9am-4.30pm.

Missions: El Paso has three Missions, older than the more famous ones in California. The jewel is **Nuestra Senora del Carmen (Yseleta Mission)**, 100 block of Old Pueblo Rd, originally built in Mexico, only now in the US because of changes in the flow of the river—the border is said to lie at the deepest channel of the Rio Grande. Open daily.

San Jacinto Plaza, the historic city square plays host to street musicians. In Feb, El Paso hosts the **Southwestern Livestock Show & Rodeo**, 532-1401.

Nearby: 26m outside of El Paso, off Hwy 62/180, visit **Hueco Tanks State Historical Park** for rock climbing and Indian pictographs. 857-1135, $4 p/p entrance fee.

INFORMATION

Convention and Visitors Bureau, 1 Civic Center Plaza (small round building next to Chamber of Commerce), (800) 351-6024 / 544-0653.

Mexican Consulate, 910 E San Antonio St, 533-4082. Mon-Fri 9am-4.30pm.

TRAVEL

Amtrak, Union Station 700 San Francisco St, (800) 872-7245. On *Texas Eagle* route. Mon, Wed and Sat 11am-6.30pm, Tue, Thu and Sun 9am-5pm.

El Paso International Airport, about 5 miles NE of downtown. Take #33 bus from the Plaza, $1; takes about 30 mins.

Greyhound, 111 200 W San Antonio, (800) 231-2222. 24 hrs.

Sun Metro, 533-3333. Local bus service, basic fare $1, departs from San Jacinto Plaza.

Checker Cab Taxis, 533-3433.

BIG BEND NATIONAL PARK is a 329m drive south-east of El Paso and you are recommended to take at least a couple of days to visit this preserved desert environment. The nearest transport links are to **Alpine** 100m away, served by Greyhound and Amtrak. The park, situated on the bend of the Rio Grande, encompasses spectacular deserts, mountains and deep limestone canyons. The river serves as the border with Mexico for a thousand miles in Texas, so this is also where countries and cultures meet. The extreme climate—over 100 degrees in summer, but often freezing in winter, and the isolation of the park mean visits should be carefully planned—you will need to be almost totally self-sufficient for the time you are here.

Recommended sites include **the Ross Maxwell Scenic Drive** which takes you down to the Rio Grande, and is the trailhead for the short hike to **Santa Elena Canyon**. There are over 200 miles of hiking trails in the park. More information can be found at Visitors Centres at **Panther Junction** and **Chisos Basin**. **Park Information** is (915) 477-2251, and the Park Entrance fee is $10 per vehicle, good for 7 days. **Accommodation** is at the **Chisos Mountain Lodge**, (915) 477-2291, or at three developed **campgrounds**, $7; water but no hook-up; no res, first-come, first served. Primitive camping is also available with a permit.

Terlingua, on the western edge of the park, is an old mining ghost town quietly emerging as an alternative tourist centre, and a base for adventurers rafting the Rio Grande. A couple of restaurants and cafes live up to the New Age / South Western traditions with the stunning scenery as a backdrop. Especially recommended is the **Starlight Theatre, Bar and Restaurant,** (915) 371-2305. Stay in nearby **Laquitas;** a reconstructed Old West Resort town; **Lajitas RV Park,** Hwy 170, (915) 424-3467 has tent sites for $10, or **La Placita Motel** has the cheapest accommodation at around D-$60, (800) 944-9907. If you are looking for an excuse to visit his place then pay a visit to the local mayor—a beer-drinking goat who lives outside the **Lajitas Trading Post**.

GUADALUPE MOUNTAINS NATIONAL PARK lies 110 miles east of El Paso. The rocky and rugged terrain includes **El Capitan**, a 8085ft cliff, and 8749ft **Guadalupe Peak**, highest in Texas. Also worth a stop is the **McKittrick Canyon**. For hikers, there are 80 miles of trails some steep, mostly rugged, but there are also chances to view desert wildlife. The park has two main campgrounds, **Pine Springs** and **Dog Canyon**; $7, no rsvs. Nearest lodging is in **White's City**, New Mexico. the **Visitors Centre** is located at **Pine Springs**, and open 8am-4.30 pm, slightly longer in summer. **Park Information** is (915) 828 3251, no entrance fee.

LUBBOCK The link between Texas' heartland and coastal ports and called 'Chrysanthemum Capital of the World,' with over 80,000 plants throughout the city. However, it is perhaps better known as home of the **Red Raiders** (Texas Tech Football Stadium) and site of **Buddy Holly's Memorial and Walk of Fame**, 8th St and Ave A; a collection of plaques commemorating West Texas stars. This was Buddy's birthplace, and also where he is buried. Its status as a 'dry' town thanks to the influence of the Southern Baptists, is somewhat countered by the large student populace.

   Mackenzie Park, off E Broadway and Ave A is home to a population of another kind—wild prairie dogs that used to live all over the state, and also the **Joyland Amusement Park**. BUNACers recommend the **Midnight Rodeo,** S University & Loop 289, 745-2813; closed Mon, a huge dance bar in the middle of town, for the traditional Texan two-step and lots of drinks specials. Open from 5pm. There are plenty of chain motels in the area that offer reasonable **lodging**, and the **Convention and Visitors Bureau** is at 14th St and K Ave., (800) 692-4035 / 763-4666, Mon-Fri 8am-5pm.

THE SOUTH

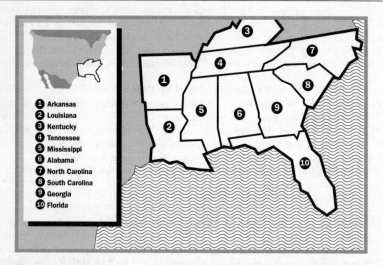

1 Arkansas
2 Louisiana
3 Kentucky
4 Tennessee
5 Mississippi
6 Alabama
7 North Carolina
8 South Carolina
9 Georgia
10 Florida

Although Northerners may hate to admit it, the South has given birth to much of the best American music, architecture and literature. The plaintive call of the blues rose up from the Mississippi Delta, and from the hills of Appalachia came the early strains of country music. Exuberant jazz echoed from the alleys of New Orleans; from Memphis burst rock n' roll. In contrast to the pristine architecture of Puritan New England, Spanish and French sensibilities contributed to the refined antebellum architecture of the deep South. Together, romantic notions of the plantation, the isolation of agricultural life, and rigid social stratification have inspired the works of Southern writers such as Chopin, Faulkner, Welty, Williams and Wright.

From a Southern perspective, the Civil War was a Northern attack upon a different way of life—a planters' aristocracy dependent on slavery. The passions the war unleashed are difficult to appreciate. The fight was to the death, and most of the old South was in fact destroyed. Although the United States had one-sixth the population in 1860 that it had in 1960, six times as many men died in the Civil War as in Vietnam. In spite of their defeat, Virginia General Robert E. Lee and Confederate President Jefferson Davis are still honored with statues and parades in the central square of every Southern city.

Only recently has the South begun to come out from under the economic and racial clouds of the war. The dream of equal rights, deferred since the Civil War, was brought closer to realization by the hard-fought civil rights movement that forced legislative and social change in the 1960s. Today black mayors run many cities, economic success is open to all and schools and businesses are integrated, but growing signs of a 'white backlash' reveal that tensions still run deep. Meanwhile high technology in Alabama, banking in Atlanta, and research in North Carolina testify to the growing economic power of the 'New South.'

While you explore its quirks, the South is bound to treat you well. Being polite counts down here. You won't be travelling long before you are introduced to simple, but gracious 'Southern Hospitality.' Perhaps the sultry weather contributes to a slower, more Mediterranean pace of life. If you travel in the summer, be prepared to sweat it out. It will be hot and humid as you never imagined possible. Do make sure to sample Southern cooking—hearty food, like pecan pie, chicken and catfish fried to crisp, juicy perfection. And don't pass up spicy Cajun cooking in New Orleans!

ALABAMA *The Yellowhammer State*

Thirty years ago the ways of the Old South were dear to the 'Heart of Dixie,' (so called because the old $10 notes issued here before the Civil War bore the word 'dix,' French for ten). Segregation was still the law; Governors stood in the doorways of white schools barring blacks. The world's attention focused on Alabama's racism in 1955 when blacks, led by a young minister named Martin Luther King, Jr, began a peaceful revolt against the Jim Crow laws that walled them in. Today, the civil rights struggle has borne fruit in the form of integrated buses and schools and the first elected black officials since reconstruction.

Economic changes have been as far-reaching. Share-cropping and agrarian poverty still exist, but King Cotton no longer rules Alabama's economy as it did before the Civil War. Medical research in Birmingham, aircraft engines in Mobile, and rockets from Huntsville are major industries. Tourism follows close behind, thanks to the Gulf Coast, the Tennessee Valley lake country in the north, and graceful architectural touches of the Old South in Mobile and Montgomery. The humble peanut provides the base for another booming industry; there are acres of peanut fields in the southern Wiregrass area of the State, and each autumn the town of Dothan hosts the National Peanut Festival.

'The State of Surprises' is home to many of America's most prominent African-Americans, including Joe Louis, the boxer, Hank Aaron, the baseball home run king, W C Handy, father of the blues, George Washington Carver, scientist, Booker T Washington, educator, Jesse Owens, Olympic athlete, and Nat King Cole, singer.

With the scenic Appalachian foothills in the north and beaches in the south, Alabama's diverse geography makes it a perfect destination for those who love the outdoors. More than 26 state parks and 4 national forests (*www.nps.gov*) spread from the rugged wilderness to the Gulf Coast, leaving you with no shortage of places to camp, hike, walk, fish and hunt.
www.yahoo.com/Regional/U_S__States/Alabama.
The area code for Mobile and Montgomery is 334. For Birmingham, use 205. If calling Huntsville, try 256.

MOBILE   The flags of France, Spain, England and the Confederacy have all flown over this attractive port city on the Gulf of Mexico. The town's varied history is best reflected in the architecture of the old quarter, at its loveliest in March and April when the azaleas are in bloom. The people of Mobile have been celebrating Mardi Gras since 1703—longer than anywhere else in the US. Those who have seen it say it is second only to the one in New Orleans, 150 miles west.

The area is not as attractive as it once was. Hurricane Frederick struck in 1979, destroying many charming old buildings that have since been replaced by paper mills and typical highway eyesores. Still, Mobile features some of the most beautiful streets in the South, and some of the most gracious southern hospitality. A 1996 *Wall Street Journal* article listed Mobile as the fifth most hospitable city in America.

ACCOMMODATION
Budget Inn, 555 Government St, Hwy 90, 433-0590. S/D-$35.
Family Inns, 900 S Beltline Rd, 344-5500. I-65 at Airport Blvd. S-$29, D-$36.
Holiday Inn Express, 255 Church St, 433-6923. S/D-$54. 'Right downtown. Rooms of a very good standard. Pool. Bfast included.'
Motel 6, 400 Beltline Rd, I-65 at Airport Blvd, 473-1603. S-$37, D-$43.
Olsson's Motel, 4137 Government Blvd, 661-5331. S-$29, D-$32.

FOOD
Rousso's, 166 S Royal St, 433-3322. Sun-Fri 11am-10pm, Sat 11:30am-10pm. 'Good food, quite reasonably priced.'
Wintzell's Oyster House, 605 Dauphin St, 432-4605. Lunch under $7, dinner from $10. 'Very popular place.' Mon-Thurs, 11am-9pm (Fri-Sat 10pm), Sun 12-8.

OF INTEREST
February is a good time to visit Mobile, when Mardi Gras is in full swing, or in March when the 27-mile Azalea Trail blooms. Enjoy parades, floats, costumes, and the carnival atmosphere. It's nice to wander around the old squares and streets that date back to the 1700s, when the French held sway in Mobile. **Bienville Sq, De Tonti Sq** and **Church Street** have been restored. Check with the Mobile Visitors Center at Fort Conde for walking and driving maps of the neighbourhoods. Among the houses open to the public are: **Condé Charlotte House**, 104 Theatre St, 432-4722. Tues-Sat 10am-4pm, $4.
Richards DAR House, 256 N Joachim St, 434-7320. A $4 charge buys a tour of the 1845 period-furnished home as well as tea and cookies with the house staff. Mon-Sat 10am-4pm, Sun 1pm-4pm.
Oakleigh, 350 Oakleigh Place, 432-1281, 1833 antebellum mansion furnished by the Historic Society. $5, $3 w/student ID. Admission includes tours of the mansion and the nearby **Creole Cottage**. Mon-Sat 10am-4pm.
Museum of the History of Mobile, 355 Government St, 434-7569. 17th, 18th, 19th century artifacts. Tue-Sat 10am-5pm, Sun 1-5. Free.
U.S.S. Alabama Battleship Memorial Park, Mobile Bay, Battleship Pkwy, 433-2703. Roam around the historic WW II battleship moored here on the river along with the submarine U.S.S. Drum. See also the B-52 bomber 'Calamity Jane,' a SR-71 Blackbird spy plane and other military exhibits. The battleship is now a state shrine. 'Can be explored from bow to stern.' $8, flight simulator $3. Tkt office open 8am-6pm, ship closes 7pm. 'Non-drivers must take a taxi to get there—cannot walk through road tunnel—about $4 each way.'
Cathedral of the Immaculate Conception, 4 S Clairbourne St, 434-1565. Designed by Claude Beroujon in 1835 and now named a minor basilica. Open 7am-3pm. 'Worth a look.'

Dauphin Island, 30 miles S of Mobile, is a quiet place where you can camp, swim and wander. Off the hwy just before the island, blooms **Bellingrath Gardens**, 973-2217, designed by the founder of Coca-Cola. Open 8am-5pm.

Mobile's picturesque location on Mobile Bay make it a good place from which to explore the famous Gulf Shores. Relax on the 32 miles of sugar-white sand at **Orange Beach** and **Gulf Coast**. To get there, take I-65 to the Gulf Shores Pkwy. Another tranquil retreat is **Fairhope**, 928-2136, a charming bay town located just outside Mobile on Rte 142.

INFORMATION

Mobile Visitor Center/Fort Condé Welcome Center, 150 S Royal St, (800) 252-3862 or 434-7304. Inside reconstructed 1724 fort complete with canons and costumed guides. Open 8am-5pm.

Chamber of Commerce, 451 Government St, 433-6951.

Alabama Visitors Bureau, 968-7511. For general info call (800) 252-2262.

Also visit *www.mobile.org*

INTERNET ACCESS

Mobile Public Library, 701 Government St, 434-7073, free.

TRAVEL

Amtrak, 11 Government St, 432-4052/(800) 872-7245. Daily 5.30am-midnight.

Greyhound, 2545 Government Blvd, (800) 231-2222.

Mobile Transit Authority, 344-6600. Major depots, Bienville Sq, Royal St parking garage, and Adams Mark Hotel. Runs Mon-Sat, 6am-6pm, $1.25, transfers 50c. NB: There is no service to the airport. For a taxi call 476-7711, around $24 o/w.

BIRMINGHAM   Once known as the steel town of the South, Birmingham is now a major centre for biomedical research, finance, manufacturing, wholesale/retail industries and engineering. A 1997 Cognetics, Inc study named the Birmingham metro area the third hottest place for business growth in the US.

The great civil rights marches of 1963 began here—protests that threw Martin Luther King, Jr. into the city's jail. Sixteen years later, Birmingham elected its first black mayor. The booming steel industry lured immigrants to Birmingham; touches of their ethnic heritages still linger. Birmingham stretches for 15 miles along the Jones Valley—be sure to take in the views from the top of nearby Shades and Red Mountains.

The area code for Birmingham is 205.

ACCOMMODATION

National 9, 2224 5th Ave N, 271-9050, near downtown. TV, pool. S/D-$35-$45.

Oak State Park, 620-2527. 15 miles S of Birmingham, off I-65 in Pelham (exit 246). 10,000 acres of thick forest offer hiking, golf, horse-riding, and an 85 acre lake. Sites $10.55, w/hook-up $16.55.

Tourway Inn, 1101 6th Ave N, 252-3921. S-$33, D-$35. TV, pool. Downtown.

FOOD

Bogues, 3028 Clairmont Ave, 254-9780. Cheap diner serving southern fare. Mon-Fri 6am-2pm, w/end 6am-11:30am.

Ollie's, 1880 S Park Dr, 989-9009. Famous for barbecued dishes. Meals under $6. Mon-Sat 10am-9pm

Milo's, 509 18th St S, 933-5652. Unique hamburgers and fries. Mon-Sun 10am-9pm.

OF INTEREST

Antebellum Arlington—the birthplace of Birmingham, is at 331 Cotton Ave SW, 780-5656. Home features an array of 19th century southern decorative arts. $3. Tue-Sat 10am-4pm, Sun 1pm-4pm. 'Something out of old Dixie.'

The **Vulcan Statue** sits high atop Red Mountain; it's the largest cast iron statue in the world, and, in the US, is second only to the Statue of Liberty in height. Erected to honour the steel industry, Vulcan is 55 ft tall and stands on a 124-foot pedestal; his massive head alone weighs 6 tonnes. He carries a torch in his hand which burns green unless there has been a traffic fatality in the area, in which case the flame turns red: the world's largest traffic safety reminder! Ascents to the Vulcan's observation deck have been suspended indefinitely for repairs, but he's still worth admiring from the ground.

The Red Mountain Museum, 2230 22nd St S, 933-4104. Hands-on science museum with mineral and fossil displays as well as a free self-guided tour of the geology supporting Vulcan's craft. Don't miss the 14 ft mosasaur fossil or the 'discovery' section where you can explore body mechanics and the myths of modern technology. Mon-Fri 9am-5pm, Sat 10am-4pm, Sun 1pm-4pm. $2.

Birmingham Civil Rights Institute, 520 16th St N, in historic civil rights district, 328-9696. Documents the Civil Rights Movement since the 1920s. More than just a museum; it also promotes ongoing research and discourse on human rights issues. Drama performances often held here at night. Tues-Sat 10am-5pm, Sun 1pm-5pm. $5, $1 w/ student ID.

Alabama Sports Hall of Fame, 2150 Civic Center Blvd, 323-6665, pays tribute to all-time greats such as Jesse Owens and Birmingham's own prize hitter, Willie Mays. Mon-Sat 9am-5pm, Sun 1pm-5pm. $5, $3 w/student ID. 'Arrive early.'

Sloss Furnaces, 32nd St by 2nd Ave, 324-1911. Exhibits of iron and steel making. Free. Tue-Sat 10am-4pm, Sun noon-4pm.

Botanical Gardens, 2612 Lane Park Road, 879-1227. Rose Garden, Japanese Garden with tea house and the largest conservatory in the Southeast. Open sunrise to sunset daily. Free. Across the road is **Birmingham Zoo**, 879-0408, the largest zoo in the Southeast which houses nearly 1000 mammals, birds and reptilea over 100 acres. 9am-7pm daily. $5.

Alabama Jazz Hall of Fame, in the historic, art deco Carver theater, 4th Ave and 17th St, 254-2731. Find out how a Birmingham native wrote jazz anthem 'Tuxedo Junction' and browse around this collection of memorabilia paying tribute to the jazz greats of Alabama. Tues-Sat 10am-6pm, Sun 1pm-5pm. Free.

Reynolds Historical Library, on the U of Alabama campus, one of the top historical science libraries in the nation, has original letters from George Washington and Florence Nightingale. Mon-Fri, 9am-5pm.

Birmingham's newest attraction is the **McWane Center,** 200 19th St N, 714-8300. Alabama's newest hands-on science museum features interactive displays and IMAX theatre presentations. $7 admission, $7 for IMAX, $10 for both. Open 9am-6pm Mon-Sat, Sun from noon.

Close to Birmingham, two miles off Hwys 72 and 43 in Colbert County is Tuscumbia, home of **Ivy Green—the Helen Keller Birthplace**, 383-4066, open Mon-Sat 8:30am-4pm, Sun 1pm-4pm.

INTERNET ACCESS

Birmingham Public Library, 1803 11th Ave S, 933-7776, free.

INFORMATION/TRAVEL

Visitors Bureau, 2200 9th Ave N, 252-9825, (800)962-6453. Mon-Fri 8.30am-5pm.

Travelers Aid, 3600 8th Ave S, 322-5426. Mon-Fri 8am-4.30pm.

Chamber of Commerce, 2027 1st Ave N, 323-5461.

Greyhound, 619 N 19th St, (800) 231-2222. 24 hrs.

For a **taxi** to the airport call 788-8294, $8-$11.

MONTGOMERY   The capital of Alabama, Montgomery was once capital of the Confederacy until the honour was transferred to Richmond. The proud confederate tradition lives on in modern Montgomery; the Senate Chamber is kept just as it was the day secession was voted, and the tree-shaded streets lined with ante-bellum homes carry you back a hundred and more years.

It was not until 1955, almost 100 years after the Civil War, that Rosa Parks, a black woman of tremendous courage, dragged Montgomery into the 20th Century; she was arrested after refusing to give up her bus seat to a white passenger. Montgomery blacks voted to stage a bus boycott on Dec 2, 1955, launching a new era in civil rights protest. A young preacher named King helped organize the boycott.
The area code is 334.

ACCOMMODATION
Fort Toulouse Jackson Park, 7 miles N of Montgomery on Rte 6 off US 231, 567-3002. 39 camp sites in woodland w/hook-up. Tents $8.
Motel 6, 1051 East Blvd, I-85 to East Blvd Exit 6, 277-6748. S-$36, D-$42.
The Inn South, 4243 Inn South Ave, 288-7999. S-$29, D-$34.
Town Plaza, 743 Madison Ave, 269-1561, S-$26, D-$32.

FOOD
Chris's Dogs, 138 Dexter Ave, 265-6850. Famous for its chili sauce.
Martha's Place, 548 Sayre St, 263-9135. 'Country lunch,' entree with drink, sides, and dessert, $5.50. Sunday buffet $6.50. Mon-Fri, 11am-3pm.
Montgomery Curb Market, 1004 Madison Ave, 263-6445. Sells home-made pies, fresh produce. Tue, Thur, Sat mornings. Also try **Montgomery State Farmers' Market**, 1655 Federal Dr, 242-5350, a 28-acre complex including cafe serving breakfast and lunch, garden centre and stalls selling farm produce, home baking, and crafts. Daily 7am-5pm.

OF INTEREST
State Capitol, Brainbridge St at Dexter Ave, 242-3935. A gold star marks the spot where Jefferson Davis was inaugurated as president of the Confederacy in February 1861. Note also the impressive murals depicting state history and the graceful hanging spiral staircases. Mon-Fri, 9am-5pm, Sat, 9am-4pm.
First White House of the Confederacy, 644 Washington Ave, across the street from the Capitol, 242-1861, contains memorabilia of Confederate President Jefferson Davis and family. Mon-Fri 8am-4.30pm. Free. 'Worthwhile.'
Designed by the architect of the Vietnam War Memorial in Washington, DC, the **Civil Rights Memorial** was unveiled during the fall of 1989. Visitors can view the outdoor memorial at the corner of Washington Ave and Hull St, 264-0286.
Dexter Ave King Memorial Baptist Church, 454 Dexter Ave. Where Martin Luther King, Jr. was pastor for 6 years. Tours given Mon-Thurs, 10am or 2pm, Fri 10am, Sat 10:30am-1:30pm, walk-thru Sat 1:30-2:00. 263-3970. Donation appreciated.
Montgomery Museum of Fine Arts, 1 Museum Dr, in W M Blount Cultural Park off Woodmere Blvd, 244-5700. Tues-Sat 10am-5pm, Thur 10am-9pm, Sun 12-5pm. Free.
W A Gayle Space Transit Planetarium, 1010 Forest Ave in Oak Park, 241-4799. Simulated space journeys. $3 for shows.
The **Alabama Shakespeare Festival**, 1 Festival Dr, 271-5353. Renaissance-style theatre which flies the flag of Britain's RSC. Performances running from Oct-Sep. Tkts from $15.

Scott and Zelda Fitzgerald Museum, 919 Felder Ave, 264-4222. Home to novelist F Scott and wife Zelda from October 1931 to April 1932, during which time Scott worked on *Tender is the Night*. Works of both writers on display. Wed-Fri 10am-2pm; Sat, Sun 1pm-5pm. Free.

About 40 miles northeast of Montgomery is the noted **Tuskegee University**, a co-ed university founded in 1881 by former slave Booker T Washington. One of the University's alumni was George Washington Carver, who became famous for his research on peanuts. **Grey Columns**, the historical site's visitor center, is open Mon-Fri 9am-5pm with w/end hrs during the summer, 727-3200.

INFORMATION
Montgomery Visitor Information Center, 300 Water St, 262-0013. Mon-Fri 8.30am-5pm, Sat 9am-4pm, Sun 12pm-4pm.
Visit *www.montgomery-al.com*

INTERNET ACCESS
Montgomery Public Library, 245 High St, 240-4999, free.

TRAVEL
Greyhound, 950 W South Blvd, (800) 231-2222. 24 hrs.
Montgomery Area Transit System, 262-7321. Buses run Mon-Fri, 6am-6pm. $1.50, transfers 15¢.
Yellow Cab, 262-5225. $1.75 first mile, $1.20 each additional mile.

HUNTSVILLE Founded by John Hunt in 1805 as the first English settlement in Alabama, this one-time sleepy town has become rather more 'spaced out.' Since 1960, it has been host to one of the state's biggest attractions, the **US Space and Rocket Center**. Thanks to the late German scientist Wernher von Braun and his pioneering work on the Saturn V Moon Rocket, the Center is now the focal point for the research and development of the NASA Space Program. Among its many public attractions is the only full-size model of the space shuttle and a 67ft domed theatre screen showing breathtaking films of space flight. Open 9am-5pm $15 includes the Spacedome Theater and NASA bus tour, 256-837-3400.

For those seeking alternative cultural stimulation back on Earth, Hunstville offers two historic areas: downtown and east of Court House Square. Many of the 19th century houses are inhabited by descendants of the original owners. Located just north of the Tennessee River and its numerous adjoining lakes, the area provides scope for watersport enthusiasts and relaxation for landlubbers in numerous parks such as Big Spring International.

An hour's drive west of Huntsville is **Muscle Shoals**, a town known to few people outside the music business. *Time's better there* according to Deep River Blues. Several recording studios are in and around the town, and musicians ranging from WC Handy to Elton John to Doc Watson have come here to play. Studio tours available free. Call Muscle Shoals Sound, 381-2060, in advance.

ARKANSAS *Land of Opportunity*

Arkansas was named after the native Quapaw Indians, who were called 'Akansea' by other tribes. The name (meaning 'South Wind') was misspelled by early French explorers—hence its present form—which is pronounced 'Ark-an-saw'. The Land of Opportunity was admitted to the Union in 1836 as the 25th state.

Eastern Arkansas, with its long hot summers and rich alluvial soil wellsuited for the cultivation of tobacco, corn and cotton, became prime plantation country. Also known as 'The Natural State,' Arkansas has always drawn its income from agriculture; only in the last two decades has industrial production increased substantially. A predominantly Democratic domain (and home state of President Bill Clinton), Arkansas has only elected 5 Republican governors in its history—against 38 Democrats.

With hills, forests and the colourful Ozarks Mountains to the north, western Arkansas maintains strong frontier undertones. Settler opinion caused the state to hesitate before seceding from the Union. The Ozark and Ouachitas areas retain a strong folksy flavour with a distinct mountain culture which has left its mark on national folk art, legend and music. Although Little Rock is the geographical, legislative and commercial centre of the state, look to Hot Springs National Park and the Ozarks for the truly rustic Arkansas. *www.yahoo.com/Regional/U_S__States/Arkansas.*
The area code for Little Rock and Hot Springs is 501, for the north it's 870.

LITTLE ROCK Named after a local landmark on the bank of the Arkansas River, this one-time hunter and trapper outpost is now the state capital. Known to its residents as the 'City of Roses,' Little Rock came to the world's attention back in 1957 with the attempt to ban nine black children from the segregated Central High School. It came to everyone's attention again in 1992 when former governor Bill Clinton moved to the White House and seemingly took half the town with him. Heady days in Little Rock! Don't neglect the surrounding countryside: west of the town is Hot Springs, and to the northwest lie the Ozarks.

ACCOMMODATION
Motel 6, 7501 I-30, 7 miles outside town, 568-8888, S-$32, D-$38. Pool, AC.
KOA Campground, in North Little Rock on Crystal Hills Road, 758-4598, 7 mile from downtown btwn exit 12 on I-430 & exit 148 on I-48. Sites $25.50, w/hook-up $27.50, cabins $30.50.

FOOD
River Market, btwn Commerce and Rock Sts on E Markham, 375-2552. Fresh crops, food stops and speciality shops by the Arkansas River. Sun 11am-4pm, Mon 10am-3pm, Tues-Sat 7am-6pm.
The Minute Man, 322 Broadway, 375-0392. Cheap hamburgers and Mexican fare 'served up in seconds.' Mon-Fri 10.30am-8pm, Sat 11am-6pm.

OF INTEREST
The only city to have three capitol buildings. The hand-hewn, oak-log territorial capitol is in the **Arkansas Territorial Capitol Restoration**, a collection of 14

restored buildings dating to the 1820s, E 3rd and Scott Sts, 324-9351, hourly tours, 9am-3:45pm, $2. The aristocratic **Old State House**, 300 West Markham St, 324-9685, regarded as one of the most beautiful antebellum structures in the South, was used from 1836 to 1912. Mon-Sat 9am-5pm, Sun 1pm-5pm. Free. The present **State Capitol**, Woodlawn and Capitol Ave, 682-5080, was based on the US Capitol in Washington. Don't miss the beautiful gardens and the brass doors made by Tiffany's of New York. Daily, self-guided tours with audio-headsets, 8am-5pm Mon-Fri, 10am-5pm, Sat and Sun.

The Quapaw Quarter, a 9 sq mile area, is the original Little Rock with many 19th century additions, both business and residential, including the **Governor's Mansion**; the **Pike Fletcher-Terry Mansion**, home of three colourful and famous Arkansans, and now a part of the **Arkansas Arts Center**, 372-4000. Mon-Thur and Sat 10am-5pm, Fri 'til 8:30pm, Sun noon-5pm; free. Also included in the quarter is the Old Arsenal in **MacArthur Park**, birthplace of Gen Douglas MacArthur and now the **Museum of Science and History**, 324-9231. Mon-Sat 9am-4.30pm, Fri til 8:30, Sun 1pm-3.30pm. $3; free on Mon. Of the 49 State Parks in Arkansas, **Burns Park**, N Little Rock is one of the county's largest, over 1,500 acres, offering camping, golf, tennis, hiking, and more.

Riverfront Park btwn the Statehouse Plaza and the Arkansas River has lighted brick walkways, fountains, benches, a pavilion with a pictorial display of the city's history. The park is the site of Riverfest on Memorial Day Weekend, 376-4781, and various concerts throughout the year. The 'Little Rock' from which the city took its name is located here.

INFORMATION/TRAVEL
Little Rock Convention and Visitors Bureau, Markham and Broadway, 376-4781, has maps, info, and helpful staff. Mon-Fri, 8.30am-5pm.
Greyhound, 118 E Washington St in North Little Rock, (800) 231-2222.
Amtrak, 1400 W Markham & Victory Sts, 372-6841/(800) 872-7245.
Local Transit Authority, 375-1163. Basic fare $1, 10¢ transfer. To reach the airport, take the E6 bus from 4th and Louisiana, 6am-6pm. Taxis to the airport cost around $11. Call 374-0333.

INTERNET ACCESS
Little Rock Public Library, 821 N Buchanan St, 663-5457, free.

HOT SPRINGS NATIONAL PARK Pure and bubbling up from the ground at 143 degrees, the waters of the Hot Springs mix with cool water from natural reservoirs to create the ideal 100 degree bath. The hybrid town-national park is cradled between two peaks in the Ouachita Mountains, about an hour south of Little Rock on US 70. From February to April, lodging and bathing costs rise to match the demand of flocking tourists.

Although actual bathing is prohibited in the park, the Visitors Center does offer a free **Thermal Features Tour** during the summer, (mornings only in very hot weather), and information on private bathhouses during the rest of the year. Located at 369 Central, in the middle of Bathhouse Row, the center is open daily 9am-5pm, 623-1433. Elsewhere on the Row, look for baths for about $13-$16 and massages as well as a string of moderately-priced motels. Rooms start at around $25 but the prices double from Feb-April. Cheaper lodging can be had at the motels clustered on Hwys 7 and 88 or at one of several campsites, including two nearby state parks. Contact the **Hot Springs Convention and Visitors Bureau**, 321-4378, (800) 543-2284. *www.nps.gov/hosp/index.htm.*

THE OZARKS   The once-majestic Ozark Mountains have softened into attractive wooded hills and limestone bluffs, refreshed by gushing springs and rivers. It's a good area for white water canoeing, fishing, hiking, cycling and camping, or just getting away from it all. The **Ozark National Forest** is bound on the east by the **White River** and on the west by the **Buffalo National River**. Featured here are **Blanchard Springs Cavern, Cove Lake** and **Mount Magazine**, the highest point in the state. Stop at the **Ozark Folk Center** in **Mountain View**, 870-269-3871, for Ozark music and crafts. Open 10am-5pm daily. Music show 7.30pm-9.30pm.

Summers are very hot, and don't forget to arm yourself with mosquito repellent. Best months to visit are August and September when it's cooler, drier and bugless, or in October, when the trees don their spectacular autumn foliage.

When visiting the area, make the small university town of **Fayetteville** your home base. And don't forget to wear red—the town explodes with pride for its famed Arkansas Razorback athletic teams. Also worth a stop is the Victorian spa town of **Eureka Springs**. Fashioned like a village in the Bavarian Alps, Eureka Springs has its own version of an Oberammergau passion play every year from April to October—just look for the 7 storey tall Christ, weighing in at 2 million pounds. Tkts $14-$16, 253-9200. If you want to leave the natural state with more than just pleasant memories, visit the Crater of Diamonds State Park in **Murfreesboro**, (870) 285-3113. For $4.50, you can scour the park's 36 acres for diamonds and other precious and semi-precious stones—and you get to keep what you find. Over 70,000 diamonds have been found there, including the largest diamond ever uncovered in the US.

FLORIDA   *The Sunshine State*

Beautiful, tacky, over-touristed and overflowing with Miami-sized vices, Florida draws sunseekers young and old from around the world. The climate is warm and gentle, the beaches broad and sandy, the citrus plentiful. Ponce de Leon arrived in 1513 and named this land after the Spanish for Easter—Pascua Florida. It's easy to see why he thought the Fountain of Youth could be found here—students from around the country flock here during Spring Break, while pensioners reclaim their childhood in the Florida sun. High-rise resorts, night clubs and retirement communities abound.

Thanks to its southerly location and plantation-rich panhandle, Florida was one of the hard-core Confederate states. But Florida wasn't entirely plantation country—the southern part of the state remained tropical wilderness. In some areas, such as the swampy Everglades, it's still that way today. During America's revolution, conservative Brits in the northern states fled the conflict by migrating here. Today the state bears few reminders of traditional Dixie culture, but shows its southern hospitality by welcoming tourists from all over the US and Canada. Florida has also become a popular destination for European travellers, competing with Spain for northern Europe's summer holiday-makers.

Florida's youthful draw has caused distinctly middle-aged problems. Rapacious real estate developers have littered the beaches with bland high-rise hotels. The buccaneers who plundered the coasts in the 1700s have given way to the drug lords of the 1980s and 90s. Although authorities have reacted strongly by implementing ultra-strict drug laws, the problem persists. Florida's Spanish heritage lives on in the ethnically rich population. Spanish is as common as English in Dade County, where the hispanic population weighs in at over 50 percent, including a sizable group of Cubans. Most people who call Florida home did not grow up in the state. The tourism-based economy has prevented a developed sense of community. It's great for vacation, but the state is not without its problems.

If you try hard, you may be able to ignore all the bronzed beach babes, the klatches of complaining New York retirees, and rowdy confederates. Once you catch a glimpse of Florida's stunning beauty—primeval Everglades, palms, mangroves, tropical vegetation and miles of sandy beaches groomed by warm seas, plus Cape Kennedy Space Center and the vast empire of Walt Disney World ... well, you'll be hooked.

Note: All hotel prices are for the summer/autumn season. Winter/spring rates are generally double. Shop around for cheap car rental deals, particularly off season, and also good airfares to and from the northern states. *www.yahoo.com/Regional/U_S__States/Florida.*
The Area Code for the Panhandle and the Northern Coast is 904, for the Space Coast and Central Florida it's 407 and 561; Ft Lauderdale 954; Miami and the Keys 305; and for Tampa use 813; for St. Petersburg it's 727.

THE NORTHEAST COAST   The most popular Florida coast begins unimpressively near the Georgia border in the port city of **Jacksonville**. The only site worth seeing is the **Fort Caroline National Monument**, 12713 Fort Caroline Rd, which marks the 1564 demise of the Huguenot Colony. Open daily 9am-5pm, free, 641-7155. Do take time to visit nearby Amelia Island's delightful white sand havens at **Fernandina Beach** and **Fort Clinch State Park**.

St Augustine, 40 miles further south, started as a Spanish colony in 1565 and outlasted a jealous rivalry with the French settlers to the north. Pointedly proud of being the oldest city in the United States, the place works diligently to commercialise its heritage. Try to ignore the billboard signs on the way in ('The Old Jail: Authentic and Educational') and give the historical flavour of the city a chance to soak in. By Florida standards, this is a tranquil town, picturesquely set on a quiet bay.

ACCOMMODATION
The different regions of Florida have different tourist seasons. St Augustine's is the hot and humid summer. Inexpensive hotels are difficult to find anytime—especially in summer. Your best bet here (and throughout Florida) may be camping.
International Haus, 32 Treasury St, 808-1999. Near Greyhound Station. Dorm rooms $15, private rooms $30. Check-in 8-10am, 5-9:30pm. Bike available.
American Inn, 42 San Marco Ave, 829-2292. S-$35, D-$45, more at w/ends.
Monson Motor Lodge, 32 Avenida Menendez, 829-2277. Downtown by historical area and waterfront. D-$75 and up. Pool, TV, AC, 1 mile from Greyhound.
Cooksey's Camping Resort, 2795 State Rd 3, off A1-A south, 471-3171. Sites $25 for

two w/hook-up. Walking distance to beach. Pool, laundry facilities.
North Beach Campground, 824-1806, 4 miles N of town, on west side of A1-A. $29 for two, XP-$2. 'Best campsite in the USA—jungle-type setting.' Rsvs nec at w/ends.

FOOD/ENTERTAINMENT
St. George Street Eatery, 3 St. George St., 824-8914. 10:30am-5pm. Burgers and subs at reasonable prices.
Scarlett O'Hara's, 70 Hipolita St, 824-6535. The place to go for burgers from 12pm-1am. Live R/B Tues-Sat and folk music nightly at 9pm. Karaoke Mon.

OF INTEREST
Among the old Spanish buildings in the town are the **Castillo de San Marcos**, the **Cathedral of St Augustine**, **Mission of Nombre de Dios**, **Old Spanish Inn**, **Oldest House**, **Old Store Museum** and the **Old Slave Market**.
A 208 ft **stainless steel cross** marks the spot where the pioneer Spaniards landed in 1565, although the present mission church dates only from earlier this century.
The Spanish Quarter, 825-6830, is the restored area of the old city. Blacksmiths' shops, crafts shops, and morning cooking demonstrations can be had for the $6.50 admission, $4 w/student ID. 'A lot of it is disappointing, however, since a number of the lovely old buildings are now the home of junk and trash shops. 9am-6pm Sun-Thurs, til 7pm on Fri-Sat. If haven't had enough of Spain yet, you'll want to catch the **Days in Spain Fiesta**, held in the heart of the city every September when St. Augustine celebrates its birthday. Tourist-trap museums—the wax museum, Ripley's Believe it or Not, etc.—abound in St Augustine.
Nearby on Hwy A1-A to the south is **Alligator Farm**, 824-3337. Established 1893, the farm isn't just another man-vs-gator wrestling/souvenir stand but rather a place where people actually learn the difference between a crocodile and alligator. Open daily 9am-5pm, $12.
Marineland Ocean Resort, 9507 Ocean Shore Blvd, 471-1111. The world's first oceanarium, opened in 1938. Dolphin shows, 3-D movie, and some brave divers who risk life (and limb!) to hand-feed dangerous sharks. 9:30am-4.30pm daily. $12.

INFORMATION/TRAVEL ACCOMMODATION
Visitors Information and Preview Center, 10 Castillo Dr, 825-1000, 8am-7.30pm daily. Lots of free information and walking tour maps. Free 30 min movie on St Augustine.
Convention and Visitors Bureau, 88 Riberia St, (800) 653-2489, 8am-5pm Mon-Fri.
Greyhound, 100 Malaga St, 829-6401/(800) 231-2222. St Petersburg, $44.
Visit *www.oldcity.com*.

INTERNET ACCESS
St John's County Public Library, 1960 N Ponce de Leon Blvd, 823-2650, free.

DAYTONA BEACH   Daytona Beach stretches out along the old Buccaneers' Trail, fifty miles south of Saint Augustine. The fast ships of the buccaneers have been replaced by the fastest cars of the NASCAR circuit. The **Daytona International Speedway** draws the best racers in the world, and the warm Feb-Apr temperatures draw thousands of student 'springbreakers.'

ACCOMMODATION
Rates are highest in summer and lowest after Labor Day. After Labor Day—'Haggle.' There are many hotels on the beach, among those recommended:
Beachside Deluxe Inn, 1025 N Atlantic Ave, 252-6213. S-$25, D-$30 (no extra to share). TV, pool, laundry. 'Great location.' Discount for BUNACers staying a week or more. 'Good value motel.'

Candlelight Motel, 1305 S Ridgewood Ave, 252-1142. Rooms $36-$40, XP-$4. 'Loves having Brits.'

Streamline Hotel, 140 S Atlantic, 258-6937. Private rooms $21, $111 weekly. $5 key deposit. 'Two mins from the beach, very friendly.' 'Not very clean.'

Lido Beach Motel, 1217 S Atlantic, 255-2553. D-$50-$60 w/bath, shower, TV. 'Basic, clean rooms. Short walk to main pier and few seconds from beach.'

Majesty's Court, Fiesta Motel, 999 N Atlantic Ave, 252-5396. S-$30, D-$35 up, XP-$5, $50 for 6! w/shower, AC, TV and pool—opposite beach. Offers free phone calls for holders of this guide.

Monte Carlo Beach Motel, 825 S Atlantic Ave, 255-0461. S-$25, D-$35, XP-$10. 'Clean and quiet, friendly atmosphere.' On the oceanfront. Pool.

Ocean Court Motel, 2315 S Atlantic, 253-8185. From $45 (no extra to share), great rates on efficiencies, balconies, ocean view rooms all the time and 10% discount for BUNACers, rates drop in Sept.

Skyway Motel, 906 S Atlantic Ave, 252-7377. S/D-$29, XP-$5, opposite beach.

Surfview Motel, 401 S Atlantic, 253-1626. From $25.

Camping: Daytona Beach Campground, 4601 Clyde Morris Blvd, 761-2663. From I-95, take exit 86A. Sites $22 for two, XP-$5. 5 miles from beach. Also **Tomoka State Park**, 676-4050. Tent site $11, $13 w/hook-up. **Nova Campground**, 1190 Herbert St in Port Orange, 767-0095. Tent site $16, $18 w/hook-up, XP-$3. Various other grounds at **Flagler Beach**.

FOOD/ENTERTAINMENT

Aunt Catfish, west end Port Orange Causeway, 767-4768. Name says it all. Seafood, burgers, BBQ, $7-$17. Sunday brunch $10. Mon-Sat 11.30am-10pm, Sun 9am-10pm.

Ocean Deck, 127 S Ocean Ave, 253-5224. Reasonably priced menu served 11am-2am, live reggae—plus beach volleyball court! Band 9.30pm-2.30am.

Oyster Pub, 555 Seabreeze Blvd, 255-6348. Sandwiches ($5-$7), seafood ($8-$12)—or try the raw oysters: $5.25 p/doz, $3 p/doz happy hr, 4pm-7pm. 11.30am-3am daily.

Sweetwaters, 3633 Halifax Dr in Port Orange, 761-6724. Lunch from $5, dinner from $8, daily 11.30am-10pm.

OF INTEREST

With major automobile and motorcycle races scattered throughout the year, **Daytona International Speedway**, 1801 Volusia Ave is always going at full throttle. The **Daytona 500,** one of the premier races in the US, caps off 'Speed Week' in mid-February. Tkts to any of the races normally start at $45, 3 day pass for D500, $170. Call 253-7223 for race details. **Halifax Historical Society Museum**, 252 S Beach, 255-6976, Tues-Sat 10am-4pm, $3. But it's probably the 23 miles of white sand, not the 500 miles of auto racing, that brought you to the '**World's Most Famous Beach**.' Downtown Daytona is right in the middle. The bulk of the crowds congregate near Main St and Seabreeze Blvd, though quieter spots can be found to the north and south. A variety of shops in the commercial district rent surf boards while shops along the community's western boundary, the Halifax River, rent sail boards and jet skis. Although overnight camping on the beach is illegal, drivers can take cars onto the beach and roam its length from sunrise to sunset; the fee is $5 per car.

Ponce de Leon Inlet Lighthouse, 4931 S Peninsula Dr, 10 miles south of Daytona Beach, offers self-guided tours of the second tallest lighthouse on the eastern US at 175 ft. Call 761-1821 for info. Open 10am-8pm, close at 9pm, $4.

SPORT

Daytona Beach offers a wide variety of sporting activities both on land and in the water. Sailing, surfing, scuba-diving, and jet-skiing are popular off-shore, while everything from skateboarding to karate can be found along the boardwalk and beyond. Baseball fans should head to the **Jackie Robinson Ballpark,** 105 E Orange Ave, 257-3172, home of the **Daytona Cubs,,** the Chicago Cubs Class-A affiliate in the Florida State League. Tkts $4.50 or less. The **Daytona Beach Breakers**, provide non-stop ice-hockey action Nov-Apr, at the **Iceplex**, 304-8400. Public skating all other times.

INFORMATION/TRAVEL
Convention and Visitors Bureau, 126 E Orange Ave, 255-0415 or (800) 854-1234. Mon-Fri 9am-5pm.
Amtrak, 2491 Old New York Ave, (800) 872-7245. Station is in Deland, 24 miles to the west. Taxi to Daytona is $30-$35.
Greyhound, 138 S Ridgewood Ave, (800) 231-2222. A long way from the beach.
Voltran Transit Company, 761-7700, bus service around county and trolley through city. Fare $1.
Water Wheels, 255-2400. Take a historic 1 hr narrated tour aboard the 'Nicholas James,' a 14,000lb amphibious vehicle, taking in historic sites, businesses, and local attractions. Departs daily from the city parking lot at 12:30pm, 2pm and 4:30pm, Beach St and Int Speedway Blvd, $12.75.
Visit *www.daytonabeach.com*.

INTERNET ACCESS
Holly Hill Public Library, 1066 Ridgewood Ave, 239-6454.

SPACE COAST   Space is America's final frontier—the closest you can get to it for now is halfway down the Atlantic side of the Florida peninsula on the Space Coast, the home of the US space program. Because of its close proximity to Orlando and Daytona Beach, the area from Titusville to Melbourne has become a primary stop for anyone travelling through the state. And because it plays second to the other cities' better known attractions, the Space Coast is one of the better values in the state. But be aware of the shuttle launch schedule—lodging prices skyrocket.

Visit **Titusville**, home of the **John F. Kennedy Space Center** and **Cape Canaveral** if you want to catch a shuttle launch. But be prepared—crowds of people clog US 1; some camp out nearly a week in advance to watch lift-off. For an up-to-date launch schedule, call (800) 572-4636 (in state only). *www.kennedyspacecenter.com*.

Spaceport USA, (407) 452-2121, is NASA's tourist centre. Many of the exhibits and attractions are free while a spectacular film on a $5^{1}/_{2}$ storey IMAX movie screen costs $7. An interesting 2hr bus tour of the Space Center, including the world's largest scientific building—the 525-foot VAB (Vehicle Assembly Building) and IMAX screening is $19, specialised VIP Tour is $35. From I-95, take Rte 50 exit from N, 407 exit from S. The Spaceport is open daily from 9am-8pm. Cocoa Beach is the nearest Greyhound stop.

The rockets blast off over spectacular wild-life on **Canaveral National Seashore** and **Merritt Island Wildlife Refugee**. The reserve's visitor center, 861-0667, is located on Rte 406 north of Titusville and is open Mon-Fri 8am-4.30pm, Sat 9am-5pm. *www.nps.gov/cana*. The seashore's southern entrance at **Playalinda Beach** is at the end of Rte 406. Primitive backcountry camping is allowed. On summer evenings, marvel at the flying fish.

Cheap **accommodation** abounds along US 1. Rooms are hard to find in the winter and spring. You'll have an easier go of it in the summer. In **Cocoa**

THE SCOOP ON AMERICAN ICE CREAM

There's nothing nicer than quenching the heat of an American summer day with an ice cream cone or a malted milk shake, a gastronomic experience you're unlikely to forget. America is the ice cream capital of the world, cranking out 1.5 billion gallons a year. It's no wonder Americans eat more ice cream than anyone (15 quarts per person per year). There is even an Ice-Cream University (in Scarsdale, NY). George Washington loved the stuff so much that he once ran up a $200 bill keeping it in stock one hot summer. The flavour choices available in the US are almost bewildering. Genuine, ultra-fattening ice cream has managed to hold its own against the array of sorbets, frozen yoghurts and low-fat/ fat-free ice creams. There has also been an explosion of new-fangled, mouth-watering ice cream bars, and fruit juice bars including **Baskin Robbins'** Jamoca Almond Fudge, Peanut Butter and Chocolate, and Pralines and Cream. **Ben & Jerry's** are more imaginative with their 'Peace pops,' 'S'mores' bars (with chocolate ice cream, marshmallows and graham cracker bits) and Coffee Heath bars. Those holding out for something healthier should savour an **Edy's** mouth-watering frozen raspberry-kiwi bar.

NATIONALLY AVAILABLE: The **Baskin Robbins** franchise, with its trademark 31 flavours, spearheaded the gourmet ice cream trend. Not all of their flavours have been successful; they once tried to market ketchup-flavoured ice cream which (surprise, surprise) was not a big hit. Always new flavours, but standards Rocky Road and Chocolate Fudge are musts.

Ben & Jerry's Ice Cream. The pair of socially-aware Vermonters so famous they were parodied in the film *City Slickers* (remember those two bearded men on the cattle drive?). Recent additions to their family include Phish Food (chocolate with nougat, caramel swirl and fudge fish pieces) and Bovinity Divinity (imagine white chocolate ice cream with dark fudge swirls and fudge cows). There are also classic favourites such as Chubby Hubby, a delicious vanilla malt ice cream rippled with fudge and peanut butter, loaded with fudge covered peanut butter pretzels. Dieters beware! Nut lovers should try Chunky Monkey with its fudge pieces and walnuts, Wavy Gravy for pistachios and brazils, Rainforest Crunch with pecans and brazils or one the newest flavours, Dilbert's World—Totally Nuts (an aptly named buttery ice cream packed with all sorts of nuts). Don't forget the old standbys; World's Best Vanilla truly is, the Chocolate Cookie Dough is supreme, and the Chocolate Fudge Brownie is better than you'll ever taste. Also try their frozen yoghurt and sorbets; Purple Passion Fruit and Doonesberry come highly recommended. *www.ben-jerry.com*.

Haagen-Dazs offers, among other delectables, a decadent, deep, dark Belgian Chocolate flavour, a cool, crisp mint-choc-chip flavour, beautiful Butter Pecan and boozy Baileys Irish Cream flavours. For an obscene treat try the Dulce Split, a melange of Dulce de Leche ice cream, fresh bananas and succulent caramel—worth the calories. Haagen Dazs has also added its name to an innovative line of sorbets. To tantalyse your taste buds, try a Sorbet Sipper, made with any of their refreshing fruit sorbet flavours. Their Vanilla Raspberry Swirl low-fat frozen yoghurt is divine. *www.haagendazs.com*.

Edy's/Dreyer's, offer a wide variety of ice creams, frozen yoghurts, sorbets and sherbets. Now they've teemed up with Godiva Chocolatiers to create ultra-premium, ultra-rich, and surprisingly, not ultra-expensive Godiva Ice Cream. Try classic Edy's flavors such as Cherry Choc-Chip and Chocolate Fudge Sundae ice cream and Strawberry Kiwi or Swiss Orange Chip Sherbet. *www.edys.com*.

Starbucks have recently moved beyond their sumptuous coffee ice creams by introducing rich, 'coffee-free' flavours. In addition to old favourites such as Double Espresso Bean, Café Latté and Biscotti Bliss, sample the sinful Chocolate Almond Chunk and Vanilla Cashew Crunch. Also try juice-sweetened **Gourmet Ice-Cream**, available from health food stores. In Canada, **Laura Secord** is reputed to be the best. For a touch of the bizzarre visit Idaho, famous for producing potatoes and yep! You guessed it, they're making ice cream out of them now! Lobster flavoured ice cream has appeared in Maine, but for the trendiest flavours, such as Avocado, Beer and Rose, you'll have to go to California.

LOCAL PARLOURS: Max's Best Ice Cream, 2416 WisconsinAve NW, **Washington DC**, (202) 333-3111, makes huge sundaes and an Orange Choc Chip ice cream that absolutely must be sampled. Seasonal flavour specialities include a potent Irish Cream and a delicate blackberry sorbet. Also in **DC: Cone E. Island**, 2000 Pennsylvania Ave, (202) 822-8460, a chocolate lover's dream, with tempting possibilities such as 'Moose Tracks' (vanilla laced with peanut butter cups, fudge swirls—heavenly!) and creamy, dreamy Chocolate Eclair. **Thomas Sweet**, on P St and Wisconsin Ave in Georgetown, 337-0616, has a sinful Cinnamon ice cream, a heavenly Black Raspberry and quite possibly the world's best Peppermint. **Uptown Scoop**, 3510 Connecticut NW, (202) 244-4465, will win you over with their exquisite Strawberry Cheesecake and the decadent Death by Chocolate ('Kevorkian in a cup'). **Bob's Famous Ice Cream**, 4706 Bethesda Ave, MD, (301) 657-2963, works magic with Oreo cookies. Try the regular or coffee-flavoured Oreo offerings. **CC Brown's Hot Fudge Shop**, in **Los Angeles, CA**, (323) 464-7062: creators of the hot fudge sundae, they make their ice cream by hand. **Chinatown Ice Cream,** 65 Bayard St, **New York City**, (212) 608-4170, delights the imagination and palate with its intriguing flavours, such as green tea, red bean and ginger flavours. For the best ice cream in the **Boston** Area, try **Emack and Bolio's,** 290 Newbury St in **Cambridge, MA**, (617) 247-8772. Serves Grasshopper, Orange Creamsickle and the patented Original Oreo Cookie. In **San Francisco, CA**, at 576 Union St, (415) 391-6667 and 750 Clement St, (415) 751-1522, **Gelato Classico** is unparalleled for Italian ices (this side of the Atlantic) . They feature a tasty Double Espresso Bean flavour, not to mention a '94% fat-free fresh Banana Walnut and Mocha Chip' which promises to be more of a mouthful than its title! After sampling the frozen treats from **Great Midwestern Ice Cream Co**, 126 E Washington St, Iowa City, IA, (319) 337-7243, Nancy Reagan brought them all the way from Iowa to cater a White House picnic. Try Blueberry and 'Sweet Iowa' (choc-blackberry). **King's Ice Cream**, 1831 SW 8th St, **Miami, FL**, (305) 643-1842, blends the cream of the Caribbean crop: banana, pineapple and coconut straight from the shell. The **University of Maryland** in College Park, the **University of Wisconsin** in Madison, and **Cornell University**, Ithaca, NY, produce award-winning ice cream with milk from their own cows.

Beach, you can stay at **Fawlty Towers**, 100 E Cocoa Beach Causeway, 784-3870. From D-$55 off-season, XP-$6. For camping, try **Jetty Park Campground**, 400 E Jetty Rd, 868-1108. Sites $17 for six, $20 w/hook-up. 'Best location of the campgrounds.' Further south, the **Melbourne Beach HI-AYH Hostel**, 1135 N Hwy AIA, Indianatlantic, 951-0004. $40 for 2-person efficiency, XP-$7, $60 for 4, right on the beach. Check-in 9am-1pm, 3pm-10pm.

Down the coast from **Melbourne** to **Jensen Beach,** 700 pound sea turtles lumber ashore. The **Jensen Beach Turtle Watch** offers late night (**Tue & Thur**) sea turtle egg-laying and hatching tours in June and July, suggested donation $5. Call **Hope Sound Wildlife Refuge** to see if the turtles are up to it, 561-546-2067, rsvs nec.—tours book quickly. Open Mon-Fri 9am-3pm.

More info on the area is available through the **Cocoa Beach Area Chamber of Commerce**, 400 Fortenberry Road in Merritt Island, 459-2200 and the **Titusville Area Chamber of Commerce**, 2000 S Washington Ave, 267-3036.

FORT LAUDERDALE   Fort Lauderdale is something of an anomaly. It's flanked on one side by a six-mile beach (probably the finest on the Gold Coast), while the 250 miles of lagoons, rivers and canals on the other side have earned it the nickname 'The Venice of America.'

A once popular 'Spring Break' destination, students from all over America would flock to Ft Lauderdale for their own 'carnevale'—where artsy masks and costume parades give way to skimpy bikinis and wet t-shirt contests. Local authorities have cracked down on the revellers in recent years, causing somewhat of an exodus to Daytona Beach and Clearwater. Still, March and April can be crazy months in this otherwise fairly sedate vacation place and yachting mecca.

To the north in the little town of **Palm Beach** it is illegal to own a kangaroo, hang a clothesline, and it is impossible to find cheap lodging. A playground for the filthy rich and chronically tacky, Palm Beach is crowded with homes of Kennedys and lesser millionaires. You can look, but if you have to ask the price, you can't afford to shop in the posh stores of **Worth Ave**. For a real taste of the wealth that circulates here, walk through the **Breakers Hotel** and stroll down **Millionaire's Row**. The home of the man who built Palm Beach is now the **Henry Flagler Museum**—an impressive demonstration of what money can buy.

Ft Lauderdale is currently undergoing major re-development. By 2001, $1.5b will have been invested in tourism and recreation related facilities. *Area code is 954.*

ACCOMMODATION

All Ft Lauderdale rates are for the off-season. Expect to pay more during winter and spring. Lodging information: **Broward County Hotel and Motel Association**, 832-9466, 1312 East Broward Blvd, for free directory of budget hotels. **Broward County Parks and Recreation**, camping at Marcom Park, 389-2000. $18 for 4, XP-$2 for full hook-up. State Rd 84 & Weston Rd. CB Smith Park, 437-2650. $17 for full hook-up. 900 N. Flamingo Rd.

Days Inn Hotel, 435 N. Atlantic Blvd, 462-0444. S-$50, room w/kitchen $60. Pool, 2 mins from beach, laundry, kitchen. 'Absolutely gorgeous.'

Floyd's Hostel, 462-0631. Call ahead for address and free pick-up. $13, $99 weekly. Free food and laundry, central location, international students only. 'Excellent reports.'

Lafayette Motel, 2231 N Ocean Blvd, 563-5892, from $39, some w/kitchenette, weekly rates available. 'Bright, simply furnished rooms with very friendly and helpful staff.'

Lamplighter Motel, 2401 N Ocean Blvd, 565-1531. S-$33, D-$39, XP-$10. More at w/end.

Merrimac Hotel, 551 N Atlantic Blvd, 564-2345. Special BUNAC rate of $30 for four or from S/D-$49 room. Pool, right on the beach. Rsvs rec. 'Excellent.'

Ocean Hacienda, 1924 N Ocean Blvd, 566-8261. Efficiencies from $59 for 2, XP-$10. Includes breakfast. 'owner can be haggled with.' Includes bath/shower, fridge, AC, TV; 'Beautiful apts just across the road from the beach; owner very helpful.'

Seagate Apt Motel, 2909 Vistamar St, 566-2491. D-$32, $40 w/kitchen. Pool, close to beach. 'Highly recommended.'

The Seville, 3020 Seville St, 463-7212. S-$39 w/kitchen, XP-$5. 'Very clean, 5 mins from beach; ask for Linda.'

FOOD AND ENTERTAINMENT

Fast food joints and expensive restaurants prey on the students who flock to Fort Lauderdale. Lots of bars and discos along beach-front Atlantic Blvd. Some even have happy hours with free food.

Big Louies has the best pizza, 1990 Sunrise, 467-1166. Open daily 11am 'til 1am. Food $2-$15.

Chili's, 6302 NW 9th Ave at Powerline Rd, 776-6837. Open 11am-11pm. 'The best burgers ever!' Fajitas $9.

Hyde Park, 500 E Las Olas Blvd, 467-7436, best market in the middle of town, daily 7am-10pm.

Southport Raw Bar, 1536 Cordova Road, 525-2526. Cheap seafood and sandwiches. Open daily 'til 2am. Friendly staff: 'Come on down: it's great!'

The Musician's Exchange, 729 W Sunrise, 202-0700, draws national name bands from reggae to blues Thur-Mon. Cover charge ranges from $2-$20. On w/ends cafe serves sandwiches, salads, burgers. It's not the best neighbourhood, though.

OF INTEREST

Tacky tours proliferate along the coast. Choose carefully.

Everglades Park, 21940 Griffin Road West, 434-8111. Free admission to park. 1 hr airboat tour for $13.50. Open 9am-5pm daily. To see the waterways through the city, the *Jungle Queen* sails twice daily (10am & 2pm) for 3 hr tours, $11.50, at the Bahia Mar Yacht Center on A1-A, 462-5596.

Hugh Taylor Birch State Recreation Area, 3109 E Sunrise, 564-4521. One of the few natural sights on the concrete beach, trails, fishing and canoeing. $3.25 per car, pedestrians $1. Open daily 8am-8.15pm.

Museum of Art, 1 East Las Olas Blvd, 525-5500. Largest collection of Cobra Art—post WWII artists from Northern Europe (Karel Appel, Asger Jorn and Joseph Noiret)—in the US. Tues-Thurs 10am-5pm; Fri til 8pm and Sun noon-5pm, $6, $3 w/student ID.

Museum of Discovery and Science, 401 S W 2nd St, 467-6637. The state's most widely visited museum. Hands-on and interactive exhibits, virtual reality, and 5-storey IMAX theatre. Check out 'Speed' and 'Rolling Stones at the MAX,' $9. Mon-Sat 10am-5pm, Sun noon-6pm, $6. Admission+ IMAX ticket, $12.50.

INFORMATION/ TRAVEL

Greater Florida Chamber of Commerce Visitor Information, 462-6000, 200 E Las Olas Blvd, Mon-Fri 8:30am-5pm.

Greyhound, 515 NE 3rd St, 764-6551/(800) 231-2222.

Amtrak, 200 SW 21st Terrace, 587-6692/(800) 872-7245.

Broward County Transit (BCT), 357-8400. $1 basic fare, transfers 15c. This stretch of coast is served by airports at Fort Lauderdale and West Palm Beach. The BCT runs regularly to and from Fort Lauderdale airport (#1) and connects with **Palm Beach County Transit** (233-1111) at the Boca Mall, and Dade County Transit at the Aventura Mall. From West Palm Beach airport, catch the #4 bus to downtown. Call (561) 272-6350 for times.

Tri-Service Commuter Rail, (800) 872-7245. See note under Miami *Travel* section.

INTERNET ACCESS

Cybernation, 2635 E Oakland Park Blvd, 630-0223, Mon-Fri 9:30am-6:30pm, Sat 10-7, Sun 11-5. $7/hr, $5 w/student ID.

Broward County Library, 100 S Andrews Ave, 357-7444, free.

MIAMI Miami's mayor once called his city 'the Beirut of Latin America'. He meant it as a compliment—Beirut used to be the intellectual and economic trade centre for a region, as Miami is for Latin America. Unfortunately, most Americans believed the analogy to Beirut's violence was more appropriate for Miami's legendary crime problems. Boatloads of poor Haitians and Cuban criminals feed the legend. Be cautious while visiting Miami, but don't believe everything you see on television.

Racial tension exists under the surface, but need not be intrusive: for the most part the Anglos, Hispanics and blacks live peaceably alongside one another. Add Nicaraguans to the list of Hispanic transplants in Miami—there is quite a sizeable population. Together with the Cubans, they give the city a very right-wing political flavour.

The city sprawls—as one taxi-driver said, it goes out rather than up. While parts of the city are slums, other parts are very modern and high-tech. The high-speed Metrorail, a people mover and an excellent bus system enable you to easily navigate the city without a car.

ACCOMMODATION/FOOD

Not many motels within Miami that are safe, clean and cheap. Smarter to stay at Miami Beach and commute to Miami attractions by bus or rail.

Kobe Trailer Park, 11900 NE 16th Ave, I-95 exit 14, 893-5121. Sites $20, $28 w/hook-up, XP-$3.

Airport Inn and Suites , 5001 NW 36th St, 883-4700, S-$35, D-$38, pool, movie channel, restaurant. Newly renovated. Pick up at airport.

Canton Too, 2614 Ponce de Leon Blvd, Coral Gables, 448-3736. Reputedly the best Chinese food in Miami. 11:30am-12am daily.

The Versailles, 3555 S W 8th St, 444-0240. Cheap Cuban fare, bfast $2-$4, lunch from $2.50. Open daily 8am-2am.

OF INTEREST

Seaquarium, Rickenbacher Causeway on Key Biscayne, 361-5705. Oldest and best: dolphins, sharks and killer whales; home of TV star Flipper, Lolita the 10,000lb killer whale, Salty the Sea Lion. Also a wildlife sanctuary and rainforest exhibit. Open 9.30am-6pm, $22. Tkt office closes at 4.30pm.

Bayside, Biscayne Blvd and 4th St, 577-3344. $95 million complex of shops, restaurants and night spots highlighting downtown. Mon-Thurs 10am-10pm, Fri and Sat 'til 11pm, Sun 11am-9pm.

Little Havana, lies btwn SW 12th & SW 27th Ave with Calle Ocho (SW 8th St) housing most of the restaurants. Cigar and pinata manufacturers also. **Bay of Pigs Memorial** commemorates the failed US-backed invasion of Cuba in 1961, at SW 13th Ave and SW 8th St.

Vizcaya, 3251 S Miami Ave, 250-9133. An Italian-style mansion created by millionaire James Deering in 1914/16, now the Dade County Art Museum. Open daily 9.30am-5pm, $10. Free tours of the home and formal Italian gardens.

St Bernard de Clarrvaux, the Spanish monastery was imported from Spain and reassembled in North Dade. Self-guided tours of the 'biggest jigsaw puzzle in the world,' Mon-Sat 10am-4pm, Sun noon-4pm. Call 945-1461 for directions.

For wildlife try **Monkey Jungle**, 14805 SW 216 St, 235-1611. Monkeys run wild, you view them from cages: look smart and they might give you a cream bun. $13.50, daily 9.30am-5pm. Tkt office closes at 4pm. $1 discount w/student ID. Also see **Parrot Jungle**, 11000 SW 57th Ave, near US 1, 666-7834. A huge cypress and oak jungle filled with exotic birds, some on roller skates. $13.95, daily 9.30am-6pm. Trained bird shows 10.30am-5pm. Tkt office closes 5pm. $1 discount w/student ID.

Museum of Science and Planetarium, 3280 S Miami Ave, 854-4242. Open daily 10am-5pm (last tkt 5pm); $9. Cosmic Hotline, 854-2222, for recording of everything you ever wanted to know and much more about what's going on in the sky. Rock 'n' Roll laser shows on Fri & Sat nights, $6.

Miami Jai-Alai Fronton, 3500 NW 37th Ave 633-9661, $1 to stand, $2 for rsv seating. Games Mon, Wed-Sat at 12pm, Wed, Fri, Sat at 7pm. Betting on this fast-paced game is a prime Miami attraction.

Coconut Grove, in the southern suburbs, for a look at a 'Florida-style subtropical Chelsea scene'. Galleries, boutiques, boat hiring. Get there via bus 14 going south to Main Hwy. The bulletin boards in Coconut Grove are said to be good for rides going north. South of Miami in Homestead is **Coral Castle**, US 1 at SW 286th St, 248-6344. Designed by a jilted lover who waited for his fiancée by creating a 1,100-ton estate out of coral, the castle stood originally in Florida City; in 1939, it was moved in its entirety to its present location. Open daily 9am-6pm, $7.75 for self-guided tour.

Water Sports: surfing at Haulover Beach Park and South Miami Beach, but beware: the waves are small; good swimming at Cape Florida State Park, Matheson Hammock, Tahiti Beach, Lummus Park, etc. Sailing, jet skiing and windsurfing on Hobie Beach off Rickenbacher Causeway.

On land, 1997 baseball world champs, the **Florida Marlins**, and the occasionally-good **Miami Dolphins** play at Pro-Player Stadium, (800) 255-3094, just north of Miami off the Florida Turnpike. Although they took the crown in only the 5th season of their whole existence, recent seasons have been less spectacular.

INFORMATION

Greater Miami Convention and Visitors Bureau, 701 Brickell Ave #2700, 539-3000, (800) 933-8448, Mon-Fri 8am-6pm.
Go to *www.miami.com*.

INTERNET ACCESS

Cafe and Internet of America, 12536 N Kendall Dr, 412-0100, noon-8pm, Mon-Sat. $3 for 15 min, $5 for 30 min, $9 for 1 hr.
Dade County Library, 1400 NW 37th Ave, 638-5255, free.

TRAVEL

Greyhound, 4111 NW 27th St, (800) 231-2222.
Amtrak, 8303 NW 37th Ave, 835-1221/(800) 872-7245.
Metro Dade Transportation, 770-3131. Extensive network of buses (Metrobus), subway (Metrorail) and downtown people mover (Metromover). Services airport. Bus and rail fare $1.25, 25¢ transfer. Metromover 25¢, 'Best tour of the city for a quarter.'
Tri-County Commuter Rail, 887-4024. Connects West Palm Beach, Ft Lauderdale and Miami. Trains run Mon-Fri 5am-10pm, Sat, 'til midnight. Sun, limited schedule.

MIAMI BEACH

MIAMI BEACH Situated on a long, narrow island, across Biscayne Bay from Miami, Miami Beach would like to think of itself as the ultimate in opulence. True to its reputation, for many it's the dream place for retirement. Seventy years ago this was a steamy mangrove swamp. Now it's a long strip of hotels of varying degrees of grandeur—plus, of course, there's the beach.

While it's still a favourite retirement spot, the really rich have moved further up the coast. Miami Beach is a popular destination for North European package tours, making it harder to get the good hotel rates that used to be available during the summer. It's still worth bargaining, however. The peak season is from late December to April.

ACCOMMODATION

The **Beach Resort Hotel Association**, 407 Lincoln Rd, #10G, 531-3553, will assist you in finding accommodation. Mon-Fri 9am-4.30pm.
Banana Bungalow, 2360 Collino Ave, (800) 7-HOSTEL. $16; $13 with ISIC. Pool, bar, breakfast. 'Rooms cramped but good atmosphere.'
Clay Hotel and International House (HI-AYH), 1438 Washington Ave, 534-2988. $13 AYH, $14 non-AYH, private rooms $38-$52, linen $5, $3 refund, bfast $4 and up. In the heart of the Art Deco district, close to nightlife. Kitchen, laundry, TV. 24 hrs, no curfew. Take Bus C from downtown, Bus L from Amtrak takes you within 3 blocks. 'Outstanding.' 'Clean, safe area.'
Haddon Hall Hotel, 1500 Collins Ave, 531-1251, S-$35.
Palmer House Hotel, 1119 Collins Ave, 538-7725, Art Deco hotel, S/D-$40.

FOOD
La Rumba, 2008 Collins Ave, 534-0522, serves cheap Cuban and Spanish fare. 24 hours.
Puerto Sagua, 700 Collins, 673-1115. Specializes in seafood and Latin food. Try the paella. $5-$15. Open daily, 7:30am-2am.
Wolfie's Restaurant, 2038 Collins Ave, 538-6626, is a New York deli transplanted to Miami Beach. An institution, it is open 24 hrs a day.

OF INTEREST
Whimsical and gaudy, the **Art Deco District** is as close to high art as Miami Beach comes. The art is characterized by a distinct Miami Beach flavour known fondly as 'Tropical Deco'. While considered gaudy by some, it's notable enough to grant the area status as a National Historic District. The most impressive sights can be found along Collins Ave and Ocean Dr. The homes are part of a depression-era development and can be seen on a Preservation League, 672-1836, tour. Only 2 guided tours a week, Thur at 6.30pm and Sat at 10.30am, $7. League office also has maps for self-guided tour, 10th St & Ocean Dr. Different areas of **The Beach** cater to different groups: punks and surfers stick to the area below 5th St, volleyball players hang out at 14th St, gays gather on 21st St and the rich and famous flee to Bal Harbor, near 96th St.
Miccosukee Indian Village, mile marker 20, Hwy 41, 223-8380. Guided tours show Miccosukee craftsmen at work. Museum has Indian artifacts. 9am-5pm daily, $5. Airboat rides $7.

INTERNET ACCESS
Kafka's Cybercafe, 1464 Washington Ave, 673-9669, 9am-11pm daily, $9/hr.

THE KEYS   The only living coral reef in America is draped alongside the Florida Keys—the scimitar-shaped chain of islands curving southwest from Miami to Key West.

You pick up the toll-free Overseas Hwy at Key Largo for the 100-mile run down to Key West. En route, the road hops from island to island; at times you can travel up to 7 miles with only the sea around you. It's worth a brief stop in **Key Largo** to visit the **John Pennekamp Coral Reef State Park** and to pay a brief tribute to Humphrey Bogart. The *African Queen* is permanently docked outside the Holiday Inn and you can visit the rebuilt Caribbean Club Bar, 451-9970, open daily 7am-4am, where the movie *Key Largo* was filmed. Locations along the hwy are designated by milepost markers.

Key West itself is the southernmost and second oldest town in the United States. Hemingway once lived here and it remains a favourite place for gays, writers and artists. Key West is not typical America; it's more like a Caribbean island. Even the food—turtle steak, conch (pronounced 'conk') chowder, Key lime pie—suggests this.

Don't miss sunset over the Gulf of Mexico—the whole town turns out on Mallory Square to watch the show, both in the sky and on the ground. Sundown here is usually accompanied by some kind of performance, such as a waterski display, a magician or a folk singer.

'Key West was virtually deserted when we were there in September and October; very quiet and idyllic.'

ACCOMMODATION

Key Largo: Bahia Honda State Park, mile marker 36.5, 872-2353, $28 site. 'Well worth the stop but be prepared, as it is in the middle of nowhere.' 'White sands and crystal clear water.' Open 8am-sunset, rsvs essential before Aug 20.

John Pennekamp State Park Campsite, mile marker 102.5, 451-1202, Sites $24-$26 w/hook-up. Rsvs rec. 'Take more mosquito spray than you ever believe you'll need. Nice campsite, good swimming, it's just a shame the bugs spoil it.'

Jules Undersea Lodge, world's first underwater hotel, 51 Shoreland Drive, milepost 103.5, 451-2353. A diver's dream; a pinch at $325 inc dinner, unlimited snacking and diving! Worth a peek, if you can scuba!

Key West: Angelina Guest House, 302 Angela St, 294-4480. D/T-$49-$79. 'Clean and simple. Very friendly.'

Boyd's Campground, Stock Island, milepost 5, 294-1465, $31 for two, XP-$8, $6 more for ocean site w/hook-up. Stay 6 nights, 7th night free. 'Worth it if enough people (more than two). Helpful owners, site has washing facilities, pool and TV.' Regular bus service to Key West, 75¢, bus leaves every ½ hr from 6:30am-9pm.

Caribbean House, 226 Petronia St, 296-1600 or (800) 543-4518. D-$49-$59, 4 people, w/bath. 'Excellent.' 'Very friendly and central.' TV & bfast.

El Rancho Motel, 830 Truman St, 294-8700, Rooms from $69, Q-$99. Prices change depending on day/month of arrival. Pool, within walking distance of downtown. 'Excellent, quiet.'

Jabour's Trailer Court, 223 Elizabeth St, 294-5723. $40, 2 in tent. XP-$8. 10% discount if you stay 4 days and pay cash (in the summer).

Key West AYH, 718 South St, 296-5719. $17 AYH, $20 non-AYH. Private rooms available. Bikes for $6 daily. Bfast $2, dinner $2 'Highly recommended.' 'Good friendly atmosphere.' Organises snorkelling trips for $20—'a taste of paradise' and diving trips for $55.

Key West B&B, 415 William St, 296-7274, D-$59, XP-$10. 'Feels like home.' Rates drop in Sept.

FOOD

In Key West, the more expensive restaurants line Duval St while the side streets offer a more eclectic selection. Don't forget to try authentic Key Lime pie.

Sloppy Joe's, 201 Duval, 294-5717. Hemingway was an enthusiastic regular. Live entertainment seven days a week. Conch fritters $5.50. Mon-Sat 9am-4am, Sun noon-4pm. Open 365 days a year! 'Don't miss it.' Nightlife is in abundance in Key West, take a walk along Duval St for some **alternative choices.**

OF INTEREST

Hemingway Museum, 907 Whitehead St, 294-1575. Papa left Paris and moved to Key West in 1928. This became his home in 1931 until he left for Cuba in 1940. He wrote *A Farewell to Arms* and *For Whom the Bell Tolls* among others in this 1851 house. On discovering that the house was as Hemingway left it, when he died the present owners decided to turn it into a museum. 'Full of the overfed descendants of Hemingway's cats.' Open daily 9am-5pm, last tour 4.30pm, $7.50.

Conch Tour Train, 294-5161. Takes you about 14 miles in 1½ hrs and includes 65 points of interest such as Hemingway's house, **Truman's Little White House**, **Audubon House** where the artist stayed while sketching birdlife over the Keys, the **turtle kraals**, the **shrimp fleet**, etc. Tkt Office, 501 Front St or 3840 N Roosevelt,9am-4.30pm, 294-5161, $18 for the whole island.

Tours of the area are also available by **glass-bottomed boat. Fireball**, 296-6293, **Glass Bottom Boat Tour**, $20 for 2 hr trip, $25 at sunset.**Key Largo Princess** leaves 3 times daily, 451-4655, $17. And try snorkelling trips over the coral reefs. 'Well worth splashing out $20 or so—and maybe even buying an underwater camera.' 'Explore the island by foot if you have more than one day in Key West, or rent a bike.' **Moped and Scooter Inc**, 523 Truman Ave, US 1, 294-4556. $4 for day. Mopeds are the most popular mode of transport on the island, $14, 9am-5pm, $23 for 24 hrs. Greyhound runs 3 buses daily from Miami. First bus leaves 7.30am, giving you most of the day at Key West and time for the Conch Train Ride before catching the last bus back at 7pm. R/t, $60, 4¹/₂ hrs.

INFORMATION/TRAVEL
Florida Upper Keys Chamber of Commerce, 451-1414, milepost 103.4 in Key Largo. Open daily 9am-8pm.
Key West Chamber of Commerce, 402 Wall St, 294-2587 open Mon-Fri, 8am-6:30pm.
Key West Visitors Bureau, (800) 352-5397, *www.fla-keys.com*.
Key West Welcome Center, 3840 N Roosevelt Blvd, 296-4444, (800) 284-4482. Mon-Fri 9am-7:30pm, Sun 'til 6pm
Greyhound, 615¹/₂ Duval St in Key West, 296-9072/(800) 231-2222. For a taxi to the airport, call 296-6666, $14-$17.

EVERGLADES and BISCAYNE NATIONAL PARKS   The Everglades lies further south than any other area of the US mainland and is the last remaining subtropical wilderness in the country.

A world-renowned sanctuary for rare and colourful birds, this unique aquatic park is characterised by broad expanses of sawgrass marsh, dense jungle growth, prairies interspersed with stands of cabbage palm and moss-draped cypresses, and mangroves. The level landscape gives the impression of unlimited space. *www.nps.gov/ever/index.htm*.

The western entrance to the park lies near **Everglades City** on Rte 29, but the only auto road leading into the area is Rte 9336. Take it from **Florida City**, 11 miles to the east. The $10 admission will give you up to 7 days access; the Visitors Center, 242-7700, offers a free film and is open 8am-5pm daily. Get out and walk along the paths if you really want to understand the place. Try the **Anhinga Trail**, 2 miles past the entrance. The Royal Palm Visitors Center has great displays on the unique Everglades' ecology. At the northern end of the park off US 41, the **Shark Valley Visitors Center** provides access to the **Tamiami Trail**. The 15-mile trail can be explored by foot, bike or 2hr tram, $9, 221-8455. Shark Valley entrance is $8.

The weather in this southernmost part of Florida is quasi-tropical. Winter temperatures generally range between 60 and 85 degrees F. The rest of the year, the temperature soars past 90 degrees by mid-morning, and the high humidity makes it feel even hotter. Bring sunglasses, suntan oil and gallons of insect repellent. Accommodation, restaurants, sightseeing and charter boats and other services are found in **Flamingo**, at the end of the main park road, about 50 miles from the park entrance. From the Gulf Coast of Florida, you can enter the park at Everglades City.

Biscayne National Park is a jewel for snorkellers and scuba divers and a paradise for those who prefer to stay on dry land. Most of the marine park's treasures are underwater in living coral reefs. Above ground, exotic trees, colourful flowers and unique shrubbery form dense forests. The main entrance is at the western side of the park at the **Convoy Point** Visitor Center, 230-1144, 9 miles E of **Homestead** on North Canal Drive, 8.30am-5pm daily. For snorkelling equipment and canoe rental or info on glass-bottomed boat tours, call the Biscayne Aqua Center in Homestead, 230-1100. *www.nps.gov/bisc/index.htm*.

ACCOMMODATION
Everglades International Hostel, 20 SW 2nd Ave, Florida City, 248-1122 or (800) 372-3874. Newly opened, and 15 min to Everglades National Park and Biscayne National Park. One mile north of Homestead Greyhound Station. Canoe rentals, discounts to local attractions. $10, packages available.
Everglades Motel, 605 S Krome Ave, Homestead, 247-4117. D-$32.50, XP-$5, summer. AC, TV, coin laundry, small pool.
Flamingo Lodge, in Flamingo, 38 miles inside the park, (800) 600-3813. D-$65-95. Higher rates at w/ends.
Camping, $10 a site in winter, at **Lone Pine Key** and **Flamingo**. The Park office, (305) 242-7700, doesn't charge for camping in summer because they feel sorry for anyone who would brave the clouds of mosquitoes to do it. For the truly adventurous, 19 backcountry sites are accessible by motorboat or canoe. Just don't try swimming or paddling in the lakes or ponds—'unless ya' wanna 'gator to getya!' You must have a backcountry permit, if you want to do your own canoe trip overnight. Note: in summer you'll need to bring food if you camp.

TOURS
Gray Line Tours from Miami and Miami Beach, but for a group of people it would be better and cheaper to hire a car for a day.
Everglades National Park Boat Tours, (941) 695-2591 offers boat tours of the park every day, starting at 9am and leaving every half hour until 4:30pm. $13.

ORLANDO Located 35 miles from the east coast in the heart of the Florida lakes area, Orlando is perhaps the most visited place in the state. Tourism has boomed since the opening of Walt Disney World, and the area's easy access to nearby Kennedy Space Center ensures its ongoing popularity. A favourite EU tourist spot, you're likely to meet folks from home. It has the chaotic atmosphere of a boom town, so choose carefully before you set out to see the sights—many of them are waste-of-time, money-grabbing parasitical spinoffs. Cheap car rentals may be the best bet to visit all these attractions. *Area code is 407.*

ACCOMMODATION
A hundred zillion hotels have opened here in the last decade to lure the folks visiting all the nearby worlds. Most are expensive, but a few inexpensive chains like Motel 6 and Days Inn have staked their claim to the action. It may prove cheaper to stay in a more expensive motel nearer to Disney, etc. and get *free* shuttle to the attractions.
Airport Youth Hostel, 7925 Daetwyler Dr, 859-3165. $12, $60 weekly. 'Cheap, but shabby.' Take #11 bus, 75¢.'Clean and friendly.' Shuttle to Disney—$14 r/t.
HI-Orlando/Kissimmee Resort, 4840 W Irlo Bronson Hwy (Rt. 192), (407) 396-8282. $16, $19 non-members. AC, pool, kitchen, laundry.
Quality Inn Plaza, 9000 International Dr, 345-8585/(800) 999-8585. Rates vary but are based on room. $70 for four. Same applies to **Rodeway Inn International,** 6327 International Drive, 996-4444, (800) 999-6327, $60. Both have pools and rsvs are advisable.
Travelodge, 409 Magnolia Ave, 423-1671. Pool, laundry room. Shuttles to Disney $15 r/t. 'Very friendly and helpful.' $65, 2 people, XP-$5. Rsvs rec in June/July.
Camping: Kissimmee Campground, 2643 Alligator Lane (5 miles from Disney World), 396-6851. $18 for two, XP-$3, $108/ week. Call for directions.
KOA Disneyworld, Bronson Memorial Hwy, off US 192 in Kissimmee, 396-2400. Cabins $35-53 for four, XP-$5. 'Basic, no electricity' but 'excellent facilities—pool, store, laundry, showers, free shuttle to Disney. Also has tent sites, $17-24 for two. $30 w/hook-up, XP-$5.

KOA Orlando, 12345 Narcoossee Road SE (Hwy 15, 4¹/₂ miles S of Hwy 528), 277-5075. $20 for two, XP-$3, w/hook-up $30.

FOOD
Church St Exchange offers a collection of shops and cheap places to eat from deli's to Mexican and Chinese. 'Fun atmosphere. Great bar downstairs.'
Fat Boys Bar-B-Q, 1605 W Vine St, Kissimmee, 847-7098. 'Good steak.' Juke Box. Daily 8am-9pm, 10pm Fri. Opens 7am Sun.
Fox and Hounds Pub, 3514 W Vine St, Kissimmee, 847-9927. English/Irish decor and beer. Staffed by British. 'Worth a visit.' Mon-Sat 11.30am-2am, Sun 1pm-2am.

OF INTEREST
Prime your smile, open your wallet because a huge mouse with better name recognition than Bill Clinton is waiting for you at **Walt Disney World**. The huge complex of 4 theme parks, 3 water parks, an entertainment complex and thousands of hotel rooms sits glistening at Lake Buena Vista, about 15 miles S of Orlando on I-4. All this Disney magic comes with a hefty price tag. A day ticket for one of the major theme parks is $47; you're better off purchasing a multi-day pass that you can use to visit any combination of the parks on any given day (4-day $177, 5-day $211). Prices fluctuate greatly, call on day you plan to visit. Arrive early to avoid the long, hot afternoon queues or wait until late afternoon and evening, when crowds thin and early park-goers retire. General info number 824-4321. *www.disney.go.com/Disneyworld/index2.html*.
Magic Kingdom. The park that's the equivalent to Disneyland in Los Angeles and Tokyo, this is the place to sing "It's a Small World," sail along with the Pirates of the Caribbean or to watch all 41 US presidents come to life in one room. When the soft side of Disney gets to be too much, spook yourself with the ExtraTERRORestrial Alien Encounter or zip through Space Mountain. The Magic Kingdom exceeds its older sister, Disneyland, as a magnificent architectural, technological and entertainment achievement. 'You definitely need 2 days.' 'Great! I wish I was a child again.' 'Better than it's hyped up to be.' 'We thought the whole place was very artificial and plastic. Enormous queues for everything.' 'Visit after Labor Day to avoid queuing 1 hr for everything.' 'Buy tickets beforehand to avoid queues.' 'Food expensive, old and pre-packed.' 'Don't miss Space Mountain, but only if you like rollercoasters, Pirates of the Caribbean, and the amazing 3-D movie at the Kodak pavilion.'
Epcot Center (Experimental Prototype of Community of Tomorrow). Billed by some as an 'adult' amusement park and as 'dull' by others, the $1 billion Epcot is the second of the Disney theme parks. Epcot consists of two worlds: Futureworld and the World Showcase. The former has exhibits and rides based on science, nature and society. Don't miss the 3-D film, **'Honey I Shrunk the Audience.'** In the **Wonders of Life** pavilion, **Cranium Command** explores the brain of a love-sick 12yr old boy in a simulator designed by George Lucas, the father of **Star Wars**. 'Hilarious.' The **World of Motion** is home to the newest attraction, a General Motors test track that promotes itself as the longest and fastest attraction in the Disney complex. While some readers describe the pavilions as, 'mind-boggling boredom,' others are applauded as 'wonderful,' eg. the incredible dinosaur ride in the Energy Pavilion. The World Showcase is comprised of pavilions from 11 different countries. All the employees in the showcase come from their host countries and are contracted to work at Disney for one year. Epcot has built a reputation as having the best food of any of the parks; visitors should make lunch and dinner reservations as soon as they enter the park at Spaceship Earth. The best bargain is the all-you-can-eat Norwegian smorgasbord. Be sure to view the park's nightly spectacular laser display, **Illuminations**. 'Not worth the price; very modern and technical, no place to have fun like in Disneyworld.' 'Unique, contemporary—very good.'

Disney/MGM Studios Theme Park. Inspired by the success of Universal Studios Orlando, Disney opened their response to movie madness in 1989 to great reviews and huge crowds. The park, designed as a movie set, is inhabited by various Disney characters as well as 'directors' and 'stars.' In addition to the standard rides and attractions, there is a backstage Studio Tour which offers a behind-the-scenes look at film making. Production for some Disney and Touchstone (its adult subsidiary) releases takes place here, but the main goal of the park is to bring in tourists and their dollars. The Great Movie Ride, Rock and Rollercoaster, Catastrophe Canyon, Star Tours, the Animation studio and the Indiana Jones Stunt Spectacular are the main highlights. The action culminates at the **Twilight Zone Tower of Terror**, where you plunge 13 stories down a darkened elevator shaft—twice! Be sure also to catch the Muppet-Vision 3-D movie.

Disney's Animal Kingdom Park is the latest addition to the Disney family. Land and water habitats radiate outward from the Tree of Life, the park's centerpiece. Animal Kingdom is more than just a glorified zoo—you can go on a Kilimanjaro Safari in Africa, take in one of DinoLand's thrill rides, and catch the live animal performances at the Pocahontas Colors of the Wind theatre. The park is home to countless animals—real, imaginary and extinct. Costume appearances by some of Disney's most famous animal characters remind you that you're still in the Magic Kingdom. **Other Disney Parks.** The scorching Florida sun can be quickly remedied by a stopover at one of the 3 water parks, **Typhoon Lagoon**, **River Country** and **Blizzard Beach**. Typhoon Lagoon is a traditional waterpark, complete with twisting water slides and a wave machine. River Country bills itself as the land of Tom Sawyer, where visitors can spend a lazy day swinging into lakes. The newest water park, Blizzard Beach is the world's only combination ski resort and water adventure park. The artificial snow-and -ice winter landscaping won't do much to beat the Florida heat. Instead, shoot down the Summit Plummet, a 120-ft tower from which you plunge straight down at 60 miles per hour! River Country, $16, Typhoon Lagoon or Blizzard Beach, $27. For a taste of Disney nightlife, venture to **Pleasure Island**. Eight distinct nightclubs, as well as numerous shops and restaurants, inhabit the island. Open 7pm-2am, one admission charge of $19 allows you to visit all of the clubs.

SeaWorld, on I-4 btwn Orlando & Disneyworld, 351-3600. $49. 9am-10pm. Features sharks, killer whales, walruses, multimedia fish and naked dolphins. 'One of the most spectacular aquatic animal displays I've ever seen.'*www.seaworld.com*.

Wet n' Wild Amusement Park, off I-4 10 miles NE of Disney, 351-3200. Water park with slides of all degrees of daring including two 7 storey spectacular slides. 'Brilliant day out.' $27, $17 after 5pm. 9am-11pm daily.

Universal Studios Orlando, near I-4 and the Florida Tnpk, 10 miles SW of downtown, 363-8000. Open since May 1990, the largest movie studios outside Hollywood stretch 444 acres and feature such attractions as *ET Adventure*, King Kong in *Kongfrontation* (no more said), a *Back to the Future* ride with seven-storey high OMNIMAX screens, and the newest attraction, *Twister*—a unique chance to see a tornado from the inside. There is also a tour of famous film sets which include Jaws, and the Bates Motel from *Psycho*. Watch scary creatures come to life at The Gory, Gruesome and Grotesque Horror Make-up Show. Don't miss the **Terminator 2, 'Battle Across Time'** ride or the display of dinosaurs used in the filming of *Jurassic Park*. Open daily 9am-9pm. 1-day pass $44, 2-day pass $80. You might also consider purchasing a Flex Ticket, entitling you to up to 7 days of unlimited admission to SeaWorld, Universal Studios, Wet'n Wild Water Park and the Universal Studios Island of Adventure Water Park

INFORMATION

Orlando-Orange County Visitors and Convention Bureau, 363-5871, several miles SW of downtown in Mercado, 8445 International Dr. Open daily 8am-7pm, tkt office closes 6pm. Pick up *Orlando* for city info and ask for a free **Magic Card**, to receive discounts at various shops, restaurants, hotels and attractions.

INTERNET ACCESS
Orlando Public Library, 101 E Central Blvd, 425-4694, free.

TRAVEL
Orlando International Airport, 825-2001. 'Amazing airport, with fake monorail operated completely automatically.' #11 or 51 bus to town, $1. Taxis or shuttles recommended over public transport.
Amtrak, 1400 Sligh Blvd, 843-7611/(800) 872-7245. Take bus #34 to downtown.
Greyhound, 555 N Magruder St, 292-3422/(800) 231-2222. Take bus #25 to downtown.
Tri-County Transit, 841-8240. Bus system serves downtown, airport and Sea World. Fare $1.
Orlando Airport Limousine, 423-5566, 324 W Gore St, 24 hrs. $21 to airport o/w. Also runs from hotels to Disney for around $25 r/t.

THE GULF COAST   Broad, blindingly white and generally cleaner than those in the East Coast, the beaches of the West Coast are the reason why many people vacation in Florida. Although the area between Fort Myers and St Petersburg (St Pete), (where the best beaches are found) is growing rapidly, areas of relative isolation are fairly easy to come by. The largest concentration of retiree transplants can also be found here.

TAMPA/ST PETERSBURG   Tampa, located 22 miles E of St Pete, best known for its cigars, is the area's business centre. **Clearwater** is the most popular beach destination among the under 25-set. But don't let appearances fool you. Tampa's only real draws are Ybor City, a unique Latin quarter, and Busch Gardens, an amusement park. Clearwater has not-so-pleasant crowds and tall nondescript hotels. The best finds on the Sun Coast, as the area is called, are tucked away and tough to get to. But once there, the beauty and relaxed atmosphere are sublime.
    At the other side of the bay is sedate St Pete, the 'Sunshine City,' whose retirement community reputation—*Cocoon* was filmed here—obscures several interesting attractions as well as miles of excellent beaches. *Area for Tampa and Clearwater is 813. Area code for St. Petersburg is 727.*

ACCOMMODATION
Beach House Motel, 12100 Gulf Blvd, Treasure Island, (727) 360-1153. D-$34, XP-$5.50. Rsvs rec. 'Right on the beach.'
Camping: St Petersburg KOA, 5400 95th St N, (727) 392-2233. $26.95 for two, XP-$6. 'Great.'
Clearwater Beach International Hostel, at the Sands Hotel, 606 Bay Esplanade Ave, Clearwater Beach, 443-1211. $12 AYH, $13 non-AYH, private rooms $33, linen $2. AC, free bikes, pool. Rsvs rec. 'Excellent, friendly & fun.'
Days Inn, 2901 E Busch Blvd, on Rte 580, 1³/₄ miles E of jct I-75, exit 33, (813) 933-6471. Rooms $52-57, up to 4 people, depending on day of arrival. AC, TV, coin laundry, pool. 10 mins from Busch Gardens.
Dunedin Beach Campground, Alt N 19 near Honeymoon Island, (727) 784-3719. Sites $22 w/hook-up. 'Good campsite.'
Fort DeSoto Camp Grounds, (727) 582-2267, near St Pete Beach, follow signs on

Pinellas Bayway. Wildlife sanctuary composed of five islands. Sites $21. Call for availability but must make rsvs in person at camp grounds, or 150 5th St N, #146, in St Pete, or 631 Chestnut St in Clearwater.

Motel 6, I-275 and Fowler Ave Exit, (813) 932-4948. From S/D-$38, XP-$4. AC, Pool.

Pass-A-Grille Beach Motel, 709 Gulf Way in St Petersburg Beach, 367-4726. Efficiency doubles from $45-$70. Hotel overlooks gulf.

St Petersburg AYH Hostel at McCarthy Hotel, 326 1st Ave N, 822-4141. $25 night in hotel room, $15 pp for four in bunk room, w/private bath.

Shirley Ann Hotel, 936 1st Ave N, (813) 894-2759. D-$40, T-$50, Q-$62. 'Clean, comfortable. Owners are lovely people.' Near buses to Orlando.

Spanish Main Travel Parkway, 12110 Spanish Main Resort Trail, (813) 986-2415. Tent sites $19 for two, XP-$1, pool, laundry facilities.

FOOD/ENTERTAINMENT

Cha Cha Coconuts, The Pier in St Petersburg, (727) 822-6655. Mon-Sat 11am-midnight, Sun noon-10pm. Sandwiches and ribs under $5. Live rock daily/evenings.

Gold Coffee Shop, 336 1st Ave N, next to St Pete Hostel, (727) 822-4922. Open 6am-2pm Mon-Sat, Sun at 7am. 'Amazing old-fashioned lunch counter. Really cheap food, full bfast for $3, main meal for $5.

Hurricane Seafood Restaurant, 807 Gulf Way in St Petersburg Beach, (727) 360-9558. Right on Pass-A-Grille beach, famous for its grouper sandwich and other seafood selections from $5. Open daily for bfast, lunch and dinner as well as live jazz, 8am-1am.

Carmine's, 1802 7th Ave in Tampa's Ybor City, (813) 248-3834. Italian and Cuban fare, $7 for lunch, $8 for dinner. Live music on Sat nights.

Cafe Creole, 1330 9th Ave E in Tampa's Ybor City, (813) 247-6283. Delicious Cajun cuisine from $8-$12. Live Cajun music and Dixieland jazz Wed-Sat. Also check the music scene at **El Pasaje Plaza** next door, live Cajun and zydeco played outdoors on the w/ends, Mon-Thurs 11:30am-10pm, Fri 'til 11pm, Sat 5pm-11pm.

OF INTEREST

St Petersburg: Almost everything worth seeing in St Petersburg is located downtown but take caution after dark and stay in well-lit areas. The city's focal point and the centrepiece of the waterfront is **The Pier**, a recently renovated 5 storey upside-down pyramid in the middle of Tampa Bay. The Pier, 2nd Ave NE, 821-6164. Sun-Thurs 12pm-9pm, Fri-Sat til 10pm; houses a variety of shops, restaurants and the **University of South Florida Aquarium**, 895-7437, free. For miles in both directions of The Pier, you can walk through waterfront parks, beaches and marinas.

Salvador Dali Museum, 1000 3rd St S, 823-3767. Largest collection of surrealist works by the Spanish master. $9, $5 w/student ID, Mon-Sat 9:30am-5pm (Thurs til 8pm), Sun noon-5pm. Across the street at 1120 4th St S is **Great Explorations**, 821-8992, one of the better 'hands-on' museums that appeals to adults, $4. Mon-Sat 10am-8pm, Sun 11am-6pm.

Sunken Gardens, 1825 4th St N, 896-3186, is a 5-acre sinkhole filled with tropical flora and fauna, 'gator wrestling and trained macaws. Open 9am-5.30pm (last tkt 5pm); $14. Also has **Biblical Wax Museum** depicting, amongst other things, the life of Christ. Open 10am-4.30pm. Free. 30 miles N of St Petersburg off the hellish Hwy US 19 is **Tarpon Springs**, a small colony of Greek fisherman who have been harvesting sponges for generations. Stroll through the village and dine on Greek fare.

The Museum of Fine Arts, 255 Beach Dr NE, 896-2667, is near the entrance to the Pier and boasts of having one of the largest photography collections in the Southeast. Tues-Sat 10am-5pm, Sun 1pm-5pm. $6, $2 w/student ID.

On the Beaches: Of the group, **Pass-A-Grille Beach** and **Caladesi/Honeymoon Islands** are 'supreme.' **Pass-A-Grille**, at the southern tip of St Petersburg Beach, nicely balances dunes and quaint shops with dolphins and casual sun worshippers. Take I-275 to the Bayway exit, the last exit before leaving the peninsula, then head west to the beach. **Caladesi Island State Park** and **Honeymoon Island State Recreation Area** have preserved the pristine state of the gulf shore while providing miles of white sand for beach goers. Side-by-side, one admission price admits you to both islands, but the only way to get to Caladesi is by ferry, $6 r/t. Call 469-5918 for info. Ferry runs hrly 10am-4pm Mon-Fri, half-hourly 10am-5pm w/ends. When the gate keeper asks if you're from Florida, say yes—it's cheaper (otherwise $4 per car). Located between Tarpon Springs and Clearwater, take US 19 to State Road 586 and head west to the end of the road. Max length of stay on Caladesi, 4 hrs.

Tampa: Watch the **banana boats** dock and unload at Kennedy Blvd and 13th St. A stroll along Bayshore Blvd brings you a string of southern mansions.

Adventure Island, 4500 Bougainvillea Ave, 1 mile northeast of Busch Gardens, 987-5660, is one of the better water parks in Florida complete with water slides, rapids, wave pool, etc. $24. Open daily in summer, Mon-Thur 9am-7pm, Fri, Sat, Sun until 8pm.

Busch Gardens—The Dark Continent, just off Rte 580, 987-5171. $44, open daily in summer although opening hours change monthly, call for details. Take an African safari to view more than 1000 animals, as well as dolphins and belly dancers, roller-coaster rides, shows, etc.

Museum of Art, 600 N Ashley, 274-8130. Ancient and contemporary art from impressionism to photography. Tue-Sat 10am-5pm (Thurs open 'til 8pm), Sun 1pm-5pm. $5, $3 w/student ID.

Museum of Science and Industry, 4801 E Fowler Ave, 987-6100, Features a simulated hurricane. $12 admission includes ticket to IMAX theatre. Open daily 9am-7pm, IMAX open until 12am Fri and Sat.

The Tampa Theater, 274-8286, a genuine old-time movie palace from the 1920s, designed in Rococco, Mediterranean and maybe other styles, the theatre shows old movies and art films at good prices, and when the show starts, watch the stars come out on the ceiling above. Franklin St in downtown Tampa. $6.25, $4 w/student ID. Before 6pm, $4 for everyone.

Ybor City, which was once the 'cigar manufacturing headquarters of the world,' in the process of being gentrified, Ybor retains a stylish Latin influence. Learn of its history and that of the cigar industry at the **Ybor City State Museum**, 1818 9th Ave, 247-6323. Open daily 9am-5pm, tours Sat at 10:30am, $4. Although several restaurants with live music and dance bars are in the area, take precaution when walking through Ybor at night. '97 saw the birth of the **Cigar Festival**, held in November, featuring street shows, dancing and food, call 247-1434 for details.

INFORMATION

St Petersburg Chamber of Commerce, 100 2nd Ave N, 821-4069.
St Pete Beach Chamber of Commerce, 6990 Gulf Blvd, 360-6957.
Clearwater Chamber of Commerce, 1130 Cleveland Street, 461-0011.
Greater Tampa Chamber of Commerce, 401 East Jackson & Florida Sts, 228-7777.

INTERNET ACCESS

Tampa:
Cybercup Internet Cafe, 6914 E Fowler Ave, 980-0860, 3pm-3am daily, $4/hr.
Hillsboro County Library, 3909 W Neptune St, 273-3680, free.
St Pete:
St Petersburg Public Library, 3745 9th Ave, 893-7724, free.

TRAVEL

Tampa: Amtrak, 601 Nebraska Ave, 221-7600/(800) 872-7245. Fort Lauderdale $54, Miami $60.
Greyhound, 610 E Polk St, 229-2112/(800) 231-2222. Kissimmee/Orlando $17.

Hillsborough Area Regional Transit, 254-4278, $1.15, transfers 10-35¢. #30 btwn airport and downtown.

St Petersburg: **Greyhound**, 180 9th St N, (727) 894-4129/ (800) 231-2222. Miami $36, Orlando $17.

Pinellas Suncoast Transit Authority, 530-9911. $1 basic fare, $2.50 for unlimited daily travel.

BATS (bus service through the beaches), 367-3702. $1.50 basic fare.

THE PANHANDLE This strip of land jabbing into Alabama has more in common with the states of the Deep South than it does with sub-tropical South Florida. Winter is distinctly cooler here and the terrain is broken up by an occasional hill.

Hidden away in the hills and forests is **Tallahassee**, the state capital. The town has resisted tour bus invasions much as it avoided capture by the Union forces during the Civil War. This is a city of real Floridians, not transplanted northerners. There's still much of its 19th century architecture to see, and a slower way of life to appreciate.

Moving further west along the Panhandle, you come to **Panama City** and the commercialised resort of **Panama City Beach**. Panama City runs on Central Standard Time and so is one hour behind the rest of Florida. It used to be a peaceful fishing village, but now developers are invading, thanks to their triumphs down the road at Panama City Beach. The beach really is lovely and the sea is clear and warm, but everything is over-priced and overpopulated.

Further west still lies **Pensacola**, the last city in Florida. Since the first successful settlement here in 1698, Pensacola has flown the flags of five nations and has changed hands 13 times. The British used it as a trading post in the 18th century. Business must have been good, for here Scotsman James Panton became America's first recorded millionaire. It's also the place where Andrew Jackson signed the treaty that enabled the United States to purchase Florida from Spain in 1821.

The white sand beaches near Pensacola are among the best in Florida; after a dip you're on your way west to **Gulf Islands National Seashore** (see Biloxi, Mississippi) and to New Orleans. **Information Center** in Gulf Breeze, (850) 932-1500, (800) 635-4803.

GEORGIA *Peach State*

Georgia has seen some rough times. Named after George II, the state began as an English debtor's colony. Many of the original settlers died before the swampy lands could be cleared for planting cotton. Although antebellum Georgia thrived, the Civil War brought destruction. When things were beginning to look up for the weakened Confederate forces, Union General Sherman broke through rebel defenses at Chattanooga and launched his 60 mile march to the sea.

Unlike some other states of the Deep South, the Peach State has chosen to look more to the future than to the past, and since the Second World War has been rising on the crest of an industrial boom. Atlanta is now the unchallenged capital of the 'New South.' Peanut farmer Jimmy Carter marched out of the anonymity of Plains to become president in 1976, and Savannah challenges Charleston's claim to be the most beautiful city in the South. *www.yahoo.com/Regional/U_S__States/Georgia*.

The area code for Atlanta is 404, for Stone Mountain 770, for Savannah and Southern Georgia 912.

ATLANTA Host to the 1996 Olympic Games and home of CNN, Ted Turner, and Coca-Cola, Atlanta's story has been one of fast-growing success. Founded in 1837 as the Southwestern terminal of the Western & Atlantic Railroad, Atlanta was the commercial and industrial centre of the Old South. In 1864, General Sherman 'drove old Dixie down' with his devastating march to the sea, during which Atlanta was bombarded and then burned to the ground, as immortalised in *Gone with the Wind*.

The city rose again to show that progress counts more than prejudice. Atlantans elected their first black mayor in 1973, and it was here that Martin Luther King was raised and first preached.

Its skyscraper skyline, crisscrossing expressway system and ultra-modern airport (one of the 3 busiest in the world) proclaim Atlanta's leadership of the 'New South,' but tend to be boring and charmless. However, Peachtree Street (be careful, there are 32 Peach Tree Streets in Atlanta), financial hub of the ante-bellum South, still retains its dignified presence, and, away from downtown, the city's hills, wooded streets and numerous colleges—Atlanta University, Clark College, Emory University and the Georgia Institute of Technology—create a pleasant atmosphere. The Dogwood Festival here in April is the highlight of the year.

On the debit side, Atlanta has one of the worst murder records of urban America. After working hours, downtown is soulless, even uncomfortable. Tread carefully.

ACCOMMODATION

'Go to the Visitors Bureau. Lots of deals and discount vouchers.'

Atlanta Dream Hostel, 222 E Howard Ave, 370-0380. Located in a safe and fun downtown neighbourhood, 2 blocks from Decatur metro. $15, D-$41. 24 hrs, no curfew, kitchen/laundry, TV. Free linen, coffee, local calls, pick-up service (call for availability) and bike rentals, but surely it is the Elvis shrine, Barbie Doll girls dorm and other theme rooms that set this apart from other hostels! A dream come true, call for directions. 'Funky and friendly.'

B&B Atlanta, 1801 Piedmont Ave NE, 875-0525. Rooms in desirable neighbourhoods in and near Atlanta from S-$55, D-$60. Advance rsvs advisable and free of charge. Mon-Fri 9am-5pm. 'Southern hospitality in the European tradition.'

Hostelling International Atlanta (HI-AYH), 223 Ponce de Leon Ave, 875-2882. 4 blocks E of N Ave MARTA. $15 AYH, $18 non-AYH, student ID may get you the same rate as members depending on availability. 'Clean, safe and friendly.' Check-in 8am-noon, 5pm-midnight. Free coffee and doughnuts.

Villa International, 1749 Clifton Rd NE, 633-6783. 'A ministry of the Christian community.' Situated near Emory U, pleasant, safe suburb, next door to the Center for Disease Control. 'Quiet with a very helpful staff, though a little shabby.' S-$30 w/shower, sm D-$20 pp, lrg D-$23 pp. No TV/tel.

YMCA, 22 Butler St NE, 659-8085. S-$16, $112 weekly, $5 deposit. Men only. No AC, 'stuffy and tatty rooms'.

Numerous budget motels, e.g. **Comfort Inn, Days Inn, Motel 6, Red Roof Inn,** in Atlanta area, but you'll need a car and they usually cost more here than elsewhere, from $34-$85. Look around Myrtle, Piedmont, Peachtree and Ponce De Leon.

FOOD
Atlanta's specialties are fried chicken, black-eyed peas, okra and sweet potato pie.
Aleck's Barbeque, 783 Martin Luther King Dr NW, 525-2062. Pork and beef ribs, chopped pork sandwiches and beef BBQ are bestsellers. Sandwich and sides for less than $6. 'Popular with locals.'
Barkers Red Hots, buy 'Atlanta's Best Hot Dog' from street vendors at various locations around town, from $2.50.
Mary-Macs, 224 Ponce DeLeon Ave NE, 876-1800. Good, cheap food (try the green turnip soup and corn muffins). Open daily 11am-8:30pm. 'Where the natives eat!'
Tortillas, 774 Ponce de Leon Ave, 892-0193. El cheapo Mexican food, popular with local student crowd, upstairs patio for *al fresco* dining. 11am-10pm.
The Varsity, North Ave at I-75, 881-1706. World's largest drive-in, next to Georgia Tech campus. Serves 15,000 people with 8,300 Colas, 18,000 hamburgers, 25,000 hotdogs each day. 'Clean, fast, cheap and good.' Sun-Thurs 9am-11:30pm, Fri-Sat 9am-1:30am. Three large markets with cheap produce, meats, cheeses, etc:
Sweet Auburn Curb Market, 209 Edgewood Ave in downtown, 659-1665, Mon-Thurs 8am-6pm; Fri & Sat 7pm; **DeKalb Farmer's Market**, 3000 E Ponce de Leon Ave outside Decatur, 377-6400, daily 9am-9pm; and **Atlanta State Farmer's Market**, 10 miles S of downtown off I-75, 366-6910, 24 hrs.

OF INTEREST
Atlanta Botanical Garden, Piedmont Ave at The Prado, 876-5859. A tranquil oasis with tropical, desert and endangered plant species. Tues-Sun 9am-7pm, $6.
Memorial & Grave of Martin Luther King Jr, in Ebenezer Baptist Churchyard at 413 Auburn Ave NW, 524-1956. The inscription on the tomb reads: 'Free at last, free at last, thank God Almighty, I'm free at last.' Includes inter-faith Peace Chapel. Mon-Fri 9am-5pm. 'Be careful in this area.' Next door is the **ML King Jr. Center for Non-Violent Social Change**, 449 Auburn Ave, 524-1956. Free tour of his home and exhibits on the slain civil rights leader. Free film of his life. 9am-6pm Mon-Fri, Sat 'til 5pm.*www.nps.gov/malu/*.
State Capitol, Washington at Mitchell, 656-2844. Modelled on the Washington DC capitol building and topped with gold from the Georgia gold field at Dahlonega, brought to Atlanta by special wagon caravan. Houses **State Museum of Science and Industry, Hall of Flags** and **Georgia Hall of Fame**. 8am-5pm Mon-Fri. 10am, 11am, 1pm, 2pm. Free.
Underground Atlanta, in downtown around Upper Alabama St. 12-acre complex housing more than 130 restaurants, shops and nightclubs. Impressive 10-storey light tower at main entrance. Shops open Mon-Sat 10am-9.30pm, Sun 'til 5.30pm; restaurant/club hours vary.
World of Coca-Cola, 55 Martin Luther King Dr, 676-5151. Adjacent to Underground Atlanta; the pavilion includes historic memorabilia, radio and TV retrospective, a futuristic soda fountain and an 18 ft coke bottle! Cool off in the hospitality room with free Coke samples, all you can drink. 'Watch the film and hear how Coca-Cola helped win World War II! ... Brilliant museum, brilliant value.' Mon-Sat 9am-7pm, Sun 11am-6pm; $6.
Science and Technology Museum of Atlanta (SCI Trek), 395 Piedmont Ave, 522-5500. Said to be one of the top ten physical science museums in America; over 100 hands-on science exhibits. Mon-Sat 10am-5pm, Sun noon-5pm, $7.50, $5 w/student ID.
The Atlanta Historical Society, 130 Paces Ferry, 814-4000. 34 acres of landscaped

gardens and trails. Library, archives, exhibitions and films on Atlanta and its history. Mon-Sat 10am-5.30pm, Sun noon-5.30pm. $9, $7 w/student ID, includes admission and guided tour of historic houses and grounds.

Atlanta Preservation Center, 84 Peachtree St NW, 876-2040. 1¹/₂hr guided walking tours of Atlanta's historic districts conducted 3 times weekly. $5, $3 w/student ID.

High Museum of Art, 1280 Peachtree St NE, 733-4200. Tue-Sat 10am-5pm, Fri 'til 9pm, Sun noon-5pm. $6, $4 w/student ID. 'Intriguing design. Excellent and varied temporary exhibitions, plus good American 19th century collection.'

Jimmy Carter Presidential Center, 1 Copenhill, 435 Freedom Parkway, 331-3942. Take bus #16 to Cleburne. Museum on the Carter presidency, also features other US presidents. Mon-Sat 9am-4.45pm, Sun noon-4.45pm, $5. 'Well worth it.' *www.nps.gov/jica/*. Joel Chandler Harris, author of the Uncle Remus stories, lived at **Wren's Nest**, 1050 Abernathy Blvd, 753-7735. See the briar Brer Rabbit lived in, $6. Tue-Sat 10am-4pm, Sun 1pm-4pm.

Cyclorama, in Grant Park, 658-7625. 103-yr-old circular painting (one of the largest in the world) with 3-dimensional diorama complete with lighting and sound effects, depicting the 1864 Battle of Atlanta. Don't miss the *Texas*, of the Great Locomotive Chase of the Civil War (immortalised by Buster Keaton in *The General*). Open daily 9.30am-5.30pm: $5, $4 w/student ID. Further **Civil War memorabilia** in the area include the breastworks erected for the defence of the town—in Grant Park, Cherokee Ave and Boulevard SE—and Fort Walker, Confederate Battery, set up as during the siege.

Stone Mountain, Grant Park. In massive bas-relief the equestrian figures of Generals Robert E Lee, Stonewall Jackson and Confederate President Jefferson Davis have been cut from a 600-ft-high granite dome, the world's largest exposed mass of granite. Astride this mountain, looking down on Lee and Davis you can understand why King, in his 'I have a dream' speech said 'Let freedom ring from Stone Mountain in Georgia.' A cable car runs to the top, or you can climb it. Also in the 3200-acre historical and recreational park is an ante-bellum plantation, an antique auto and music museum, a game ranch, riverboat cruises, a 5-mile steam railroad and more. Park entrance $10 p/car, attractions must be paid for individually, $5 each. Dazzling nightly laser show at 9.30pm at no extra cost (June-Sept only). 'Worth waiting 'til dark: brilliant effects.' 'Take MARTA bus and you don't pay the $6.' 25 miles E of Atlanta off Hwy 78, (770) 498-5690. Gates open 6am-midnight, attractions, 10am-5pm, 8pm in summer.

Stone Mountain Campground, (770) 498-5710. Tents $19, $21 w/hook-up. 'Beautiful sites on the lake.'

Marriott Marquis, 265 Peachtree Center Ave, 521-0000. One of a spectacular genre of hotels featuring a breathtaking atrium. A must-see if you are in Atlanta. Most expensive to construct and largest hotel in the southeast.

CNN Center, Marietta St at Techwood Dr, 827-2400. Tour the studios of this 24 hr all news network. $7. Daily 9am-6pm, every 20 mins. Call for tickets to be a guest on Talk Back Live, CNN's interactive news talk show filmed daily at the CNN Center, 1-800-410-4266. Next door is the **Omni Coliseum**, home of the Atlanta Hawks basketball team. Ticketmaster 249-6400. **Turner Field**, 755 Hank Aaron Blvd, the stadium built especially for the Olympics, is now the home of the **Atlanta Braves** baseball team, current National League champions and World-Series runners-up. Ticketmaster 249-6400. American football is played by the **Falcons** at the **Georgia Dome** which hosted the '94 Superbowl and was also host to some Olympic events in '96.

Centennial Olympic Park, International Blvd and Techwood Dr, 222-7275, commemorates the 1996 Olympic Games. The park was made famous when a bomb exploded here during the Games. Visit the Fountain of Rings—the largest fountain in the world featuring the Olympic symbol. Four 20 min shows daily at 12:30, 3:30,

6:30 and 9pm. Park open 7am-11pm.

Margaret Mitchell House, 990 Peachtree St, 249-7012. Tour the historic home where Mitchell wrote *Gone with the Wind* and relive antebellum Atlanta (unless frankly, my dear, you don't give a damn). Open daily 9am-4pm, $7, $6 w/student ID.

ENTERTAINMENT

Read the free, weekly *Creative Loafing*, *Atlanta Gazette* and *Where Magazine* to find out what goes on. 'Atlanta, especially midtown, is known second only to San Francisco for a large gay community.'

Piedmont Park, free open-air jazz and classical concerts, Atlanta Philharmonic Orchestra, throughout the summer. First week in Sep, Atlanta Jazz Festival. 'Not to be missed. People dance, drink; on a good evening it can be like the last night of the proms. Also watch the fireflies do illuminated mating dances.' Park also has an open-air swimming pool, 892-0117. 'Beautiful; great for a rest and a free shower. Friendly pool attendants.' 1pm-7.15pm daily, 11am-7.15pm w/ends, $2, free btwn 1pm and 4.15pm. Keep eyes open at night; not too friendly neighbourhood.

Six Flags Over Georgia, 12 miles W on I-20, 940-9290. One of the nation's largest theme parks, home to the 'Georgia Cyclone' rollercoaster and such rides as 'Mind Bender' and 'Splashwater Falls.' Sun-Thur 10am-10pm, Fri, Sat 10am-midnight. 1-day pass $33, 2-day pass $40. Take MARTA to Hightower Station, then bus #201. 'Don't go on Saturdays as you will spend the whole day in queues.'

The Fox, 660 Peachtree, 881-2100. Second largest movie theatre in America and now a national landmark. One of the last great movie palaces. Built in 1929; Moorish design. Now a venue for concerts, theatre and special film presentations. Call for listings. Atlanta Preservation Society, 876-2040, operate a history tour of the interior; Mon, Wed, Thurs, at 10am, Sat at 10am and 11am.

INFORMATION

Convention and Visitors Bureau, Harris Tower, 233 Peachtree St NE, Suite 2000, 521-6600. Mon-Fri 8.30am-5.30pm. 'Far more helpful than Chamber of Commerce.' Satellite locations in Lenox Square Mall and Underground Atlanta.

Chamber of Commerce, 235 International Blvd, across from Omni Building, 880-9000. 'Very helpful.'

Tourist information is available online at *www.atlanta.com*.

INTERNET ACCESS

Fulton County Library, 11 Kirkwood Rd NE, 377-6471, free.

TRAVEL

MARTA (Metropolitan Atlanta Rapid Transit Authority), 848-4711, combined bus and rail serves most area attractions and hotels. Free transfers btwn subway and buses. Basic fare $1.50, weekly pass $12, unlimited usage. Subway runs Mon-Fri, 6am-12am Sat-Sun 8am-10pm.

Greyhound, 81 International Blvd NW, (800) 231-2222. Use caution in this area. Savannah $43, Orlando $50.

Amtrak, Peachtree Station, 1688 Peachtree St NW, (800) 872-7245. The NY-New Orleans *Crescent* stops here daily.

Hartsfield International Airport is situated 12 miles S of the city, an impressive, innovative piece of building; 222-6688, general info. MARTA buses can take you downtown, 15 min rides run every 8 mins.

The Atlanta Airport Shuttle (525-2177) runs a van service to over 100 locations in and around the metropolitan area, $8-$30. Taxis downtown $10 o/w (530-6698).

SAVANNAH When Ray Charles sings *Georgia on My Mind*, it's surely Savannah and *not* Atlanta he's mooning over. Laid out in 1733 by English General James Oglethorpe, Savannah was America's first planned city and Georgia's oldest. In one of the earliest evangelical movements, Charles and John Wesley accompanied Oglethorpe as missionaries, later establishing in the city the Wesleyan Methodist Church. After seeing what Sherman had done to Atlanta in 1864, Savannah wisely decided to surrender, protecting her charming gardens, public squares and old homes from certain destruction. What Sherman spared, however, seemed almost doomed by declining cotton prices.

The town was run-down until restoration efforts began on Trustees Garden in the 1950s. Today, the city (which has no less than 21 squares) resonates with reminders of its colonial past. Warehouses that once stored clouds of cotton now house shops and restaurants along the Savannah River. Monthly parades, concerts and other events take place here; St. Patrick's Day celebrations are said to rival those of New York. The first steamship (the *Savannah*, of course) crossed the Atlantic to Liverpool (in 1819) from here, the 10th largest port in the US. And an old seamen's pub referred to in Robert Louis Stevenson's *Treasure Island* still survives as the Pirate's House. *The telephone area code is 912.*

ACCOMMODATION
Bed and Breakfast Inn, 117 W Gordon at Chatham Sq, 233-9481. In the heart of the historic district, an 1853 townhouse. 'Clean and well maintained.' From $85.
Savannah International Youth Hostel (HI-AYH), 304 E Hall St, 236-7744. Renovated victorian mansion in historic district. $15. Check-in 7am-10am and 5pm-11pm. Call ahead for late check-in. Maximum stay 3 nights.
Thunderbird Inn, 611 West Oglethorpe Ave, 232-2661. From S-$35, D-$45. Near bus station.
Camping: Bellaire Woods Campground, GA Hwy 204, 15 miles NW of downtown, 748-4000. $21-27.50 for two, w/hook-up.
Skidway Island State Park, 6 miles SE of downtown on Waters Ave, 598-2300, inaccessible by public transport. $18 1st night, $16 thereafter. Bathrooms and heated showers.

FOOD
Crystal Beer Parlour, 301 W Jones St, 232-1153. Hamburgers, chili dogs, seafood, gumbo. 11am-9pm Mon-Sat.
Piccadilly Cafeteria, 15 Bull St, 232-5264. Good and inexpensive. Sun-Fri 11am-8pm, Sat 'til 6pm.
Shucker's Seafood Restaurant, almost at end of W River St, 443-0054. 'Recommended by the locals, it's casual, with a laid-back atmosphere and good food.' 11.30am-10pm Sun-Thurs, til 11pm Fri-Sat.
Spanky's Pizza Galley and Saloon, 317 East River St, 236-3009. 'River Street's favourite good-time saloon.' Dinner $7-$15. 11am-1am
Toucan Café, 531 Stevenson Ave, 352-2233, serving all kinds of international food, sandwiches and salads, $4-$13. 5-9:30pm Sun-Thurs, 'til 11pm Fri-Sat.
Wally's Sixpence Pub, 245 Bull St, 233-3151. Mon-Thurs 11.30am-midnight, Sun from 12.30pm, Fri-Sat til 2am. 'A haunt of unusual and interesting characters.'

OF INTEREST
Old Savannah offers cobbled streets, charming squares, formal gardens and several beautiful mansions. Among the stately houses of the town is the **Owens-Thomas House**, at 124 Abercorn St, 233-9743, at which Lafayette was a visitor in 1825. Tue-Sat10am-5pm, Sun 2pm-5pm, Mon 12-5pm; $8, $4 w/student ID.
Green-Meldrim House, Madison Sq, 233-3845, is where General Sherman enjoyed his victory, $4, $2 w/student ID. The Green-Meldrim serves as Parish house for the

Gothic Revival style **St John's Episcopal Church**, built 1852. Tue, Thur, Fri, Sat 10am-4pm.

Savannah Waterfront. Pubs, shops, restaurants and night spots housed in old cotton warehouses along cobblestone streets. 'Beware: it's a tourist trap with masses of souvenir shops and over-priced beer.' In the same vein is **City Market**, at St Julian and Jefferson Sts.

Ships of the Sea Maritime Museum, 41 Martin Luther King Blvd, 232-1511. Models and maritime memorabilia. Daily 10am-5pm, $5, $4 w/student ID .

Telfair Academy of Arts and Sciences, 121 Barnard St, 232-1177. The oldest art museum in the southeast and the home of a fine collection of portraits and 18th century masterpieces. Tue-Sat 10am-5pm, Sun 1pm-5pm, Mon 12-5pm. $6, $2 w/student ID; free on Sun.

Christ Episcopal Church, 28 Bull St, 232-8230. First church in Georgia; the present building was erected in 1840. John Wesley preached here in 1736-37, arousing extraordinary emotions in the congregation. He also founded the first Sunday school here. Wed & Fri only 10:30am-3.30pm.

Temple Mickve Israel, 20 E Gordon, 233-1547. Seeking religious freedom, a group of Sephardic Jews from England were among the first to settle here in 1733. The oldest congregation practicing reform Judaism. The synagogue looks like a church, complete with a steeple, choir loft, and gothic design. No one is sure why the Orthodox congregation built it this way. 2 of the Torahs, the oldest in America, are from the original congregation. Tours of museum and archives, Mon-Fri 10am-noon, 2pm-4pm. $2. Services Fri 8.15pm, Sat 11am, all welcome.

ENTERTAINMENT

Kevin Barry's, 117 W River St, 233-9626, Irish pub immortalised in a song, offering good, cheap Irish food, Guinness on draught (not so cheap!) and Irish folk music. Mon-Fri 4pm-3am, 11:30-3am, Sun 12.30-2am. Also check out **Wet Willies,** 101 E River St, 233-5650, for 'irresistible frozen daiquiris.' Mon-Thurs 11am-1am, Fri-Sat til 2am, Sun from 12:30pm.

INFORMATION/TRAVEL

Chamber of Commerce Convention and Visitors Bureau, 101 E. Bay St, 644-6401, Mon-Fri 8:30am-5pm.

Savannah Visitors Center, 301 Martin Luther King Blvd, 944-0460. Literature, maps, a self-guided walking tour leaflet, slide show. Many tours start here. Open daily 8.30am-5pm.

Amtrak, 2611 Seaboard Coastline Dr, 234-2611/(800) 872-7245.

Chatham Area Transit (CAT), 233-5767. Public transportation system serving Savannah and surrounding area. Buses run 6am-midnight, basic fare 75c, 1-day pass $1.50.

Greyhound, 610 W Oglethorpe Ave, 232-2135/(800) 231-2222.

Gray Line Bus Tours, 215 West Boundry St, 236-9604.

For information online, go to *www.savannahgeorgia.com*.

OKEFENOKEE SWAMP   This large swamp area lies in southeast Georgia. 8 miles S of **Waycross** on Hwys US 1 and US 23, is the **Okefenokee Swamp Park**, 283-0583. This is a private park with an observation tower, half-hour boat tour, $14, and walkways that enable you to take in the cypresses, flowers, aquatic birds, bears and alligators without getting your feet wet. There is also a museum telling the story of the 'Land of the Trembling Earth' (the old Indian name for the swamp). Entrance to the park is $10. 8am-8pm daily in summer, off season, 8am-5.30pm. For info on the **Federal Park**, call 496-3331. The park offers 2-5 days canoe trips (reserve in advance), from $14.

KENTUCKY *Bluegrass State*

A land of country pleasures, Kentucky's bluegrass hills have yielded bourbon whiskey, fried chicken, fast horses and even faster bluegrass music. Since Daniel Boone cleared the Wilderness Trail in 1769 to settle the first lands west of the Allegheny Mountains, Kentuckians have quietly elevated country living into an art form. Bluegrass music involves complex guitar-picking, banjo-strumming and fiddle-playing. While sometimes tedious in its traditional forms, it can be exhilarating in its progressive modes. Kentucky is the home state of Merle Travis, whose famous Travis-style picking is a noted method of bluegrass playing today. Kentucky produces 87% of the world's bourbon (from Bourbon county) and bottles almost half of the nation's whiskey. The abundance of fertile bluegrass (which is not actually blue—it's green and blossoms blue in spring) attracted livestock farmers and their horses. The Kentucky equine passion has developed into a refined, multi-million dollar international obsession indulged annually at Louisville's Kentucky Derby.

Hardy country living has bred many proud Kentucky natives, among them Henry Clay, Jefferson Davis, Abraham Lincoln and Mohammed Ali. Kentucky's fighting spirit, important reserves of coal and strategic location made it a decisive factor in the Civil War. The hostility of the Civil War would not condone a state's remaining neutral, but nevertheless, that's what Kentucky tried to be. A worried Lincoln was said to have remarked that he hoped to have God on his side, but he had to have Kentucky. *www.yahoo.com/Regional/ U_S__States/Kentucky.*

The area code for Louisville, Frankfurt and western KY is 502, for Lexington and eastern KY, 606.

LOUISVILLE The most prestigious horse race in the country, the Kentucky Derby, is held here the first week in May amidst a festival atmosphere of parades, concerts and a steamboat race.

Founded by George Rogers Clark as a supply base on the Ohio for his Northwest explorations, Louisville is now a commercial, industrial and educational centre that specializes in things that are supposed to be bad for you. Fast food, bourbon, whiskey and cigarettes are made here in abundance. This is also the hometown of the Louisville Lip, though the boulevard named after him is called Mohammed Ali.

Keep your eyes on the fountain in the Ohio River directly outside downtown. It's the tallest computerized floating fountain in the world, with a series of 41 jets and 102 coloured lights that create some spectacular effects.

En route from here to **Mammoth Caves** are various folksy attractions, including Abraham Lincoln's birthplace at Hodgenville, Stephen Foster's original 'My Old Kentucky Home' and the Lincoln Homestead nearby. Note: Louisville is pronounced Loo-AH-ville.

ACCOMMODATION
Economy Inn, 3304 Bardstown Rd, 456-2861. Exit 16 A off I-264. S-$39, D-$47.
KOA, 900 Marriot Dr, (812) 282-4474. I-65 N across bridge, exit Stansifer Ave. 'Very

handy for downtown.' Free use of pool, mini-golf and fishing lake at motel next door. Sites $20 for two, $27.50 w/hook-up, XP-$4, cabins for two, $34.50.

Thrifty Dutchman Budget Hotel, 3357 Fern Valley Rd, 968-8124. Off I-65. S-$56, D-$58.50. XP-$6.

FOOD

Look along Bardstown Rd for budget cafes serving a wide variety of local and international cuisine.

BBQ's, burgoo stew and cured ham are all Kentucky delicacies, unlike the famed fried chicken (see the Colonel Sanders Museum below).

Check's Cafe, 1101 Burnett, 637-9515. Local favourite where hamburgers start at $2. Oyster specialty. Open Mon-Thurs 11am-9pm, Fri 'til 12am, Sat til 10pm, Sun 1pm-9pm.

The Old Spaghetti Factory, 235 W Market St, 581-1070. Full dinner with pasta, salad, bread and desert $5.50-$8. Mon-Thur 11.30am-2pm and 5pm-10pm. Fri til 11pm, Sat 12pm-11pm, Sun 12:30pm-10pm.

Phoenix Hill Tavern, 644 Baxter Ave, 589-4957. 4 stages offering live blues, rock, and reggae every night 'til 4am. Cover $3-$5. 'Cheap sandwiches.''

The Rudyard Kipling, 422 W Oak St, 636-1311, 7 blocks S of downtown in Old Louisville. 'Hearty food and drink from all around the world.' Here you can eat anything from curry to crepes as well as a variety of national pasties! Try a bowl of Kentucky burgoo (a meat and veg stew) for $3. Mon and Wed nights offer folk and jazz music; theatre is performed on the in-house stage during Sept and Oct. 'If you eat one meal in Louisville, eat it here.' Mon-Fri 11.30am-1.30pm and 5.30pm-midnight, Sat 5:30-midnight.

OF INTEREST

Churchill Downs, home of the **Kentucky Derby**, 700 Central Ave, 636-4400. On the morning of Derby Day, the first Sat in May, arrive around 8am to claim a small piece of the track infield for $30 pp. The big race is in the afternoon, but the partying goes on all day. Potent mint juleps, the drink of the South, are available from vendors. Racing also takes place from late Apr-early Jul and late Oct-late Nov. At gate 1 stands the **Kentucky Derby Museum**, 637-1111, 9am-5pm daily, $6. Shows run twice hourly. Includes exhibits on horse racing and breeding, and an exciting 360 degree movie theatre that puts you in the middle of the race (hourly). Each August Louisville hosts the **Kentucky State Fair** which features the World Championship Horse Show for American saddlebreds—Kentucky's native horse breed.

JB Speed Art Museum, 2035 3rd St, 634-2700. One of the better mid-South galleries. Medieval, Renaissance and French works, a strong Dutch collection and a spacious sculpture court. The museum boasts an elaborately carved, oak-panelled English Renaissance room from 'The Grange,' Devon. Tues-Fri 10:30am-4pm, Thurs til 8pm, Sat til 5pm, Sun noon-5pm, free. Thomas Jefferson was the architect of the **John Speed Mansion**, Farmington, 3033 Bardstown Rd, 452-9920. Tue-Sat 10am-3.45pm, Sun 1.30pm-3.30pm. $4. Shakespeare falls trippingly off the tongue in Louisville's **Central Park**. You will not have to pay a pound of flesh, it's free, 583-8738 for details. Curtain is 8pm, Tue-Sun, early Jun-July.

Col Harland Sanders Museum, 1441 Gardiner Lane, 874-8300. Free museum records the life of the 'finger lickin' good' chicken purveyor who helped start the phenomenon of fast food. Mon-Thur 8am-5pm, Fri 8am-3pm. A pleasant way to spend an afternoon is to take a cruise on the Ohio River on the *Belle of Louisville*, 574-2355, an old sternwheeler. The boat runs from late May-early Sep and departs from the landing at 4th St and River Rd, Tue-Sun at 12pm, $10. 'Sunset cruises,' Tue and Thurs 6pm, $10. 'Nighttime Dance Cruises,' Sat 7pm-11pm, $12.50. The **Corn Island Storytelling Festival**, usually the third w/end in September, 245-0643, uses the *Belle* for a storytelling tour along the river. The most popular festival event is the **Long Run Park** ghost story event. Held near an old graveyard, thousands come out to hear the tales beginning at nightfall. Festival tkts for all the events are $50, $90 for two. Individual event tkts available, $10 pp.

Howard Steamboat Museum, 1101 E Market St, (812) 283-3728, Tue-Sat 10am-4pm, Sun 1pm-3pm, $4, $2 w/student ID. Billed as the 'only museum of its kind in the US,' models of steamboats, tools and pilot wheels are on display. Located across the Ohio River from Louisville in Jeffersonville, Indiana.

Jim Beam's American Outpost, 543-9877. 10 min movie and self-guided tour which shows you the joys of bourbon-making. (Bourbon is made using at least 51% corn and must be aged at least 2 yrs, preferably in a charred white oak container. Anything less is 'just' whiskey.) The tour is free, Mon-Sat 9am-4.30pm, Sun 1pm-4pm. Follow I-65, 22 miles S from Louisville, then E on Rte 245 toward **Clermont**. America hoards her gold at **Fort Knox**, 25 miles SW of Louisville on US 31 W-60. Don't expect to see the metal, but if you're in a military frame of mind, visit the **Gen Patton, KB, OBE, Museum of Cavalry and Armor**, Building 4554, Fayette Ave, in Fort Knox, 624-3812. 200 yrs of military history, from the old frontier fort to displays of weapons, equipment and uniforms dating back to the Revolutionary War. Also see the 'ivory-handled Patton pistols' and war booty that Old Blood and Guts gathered in WW II. Donation appreciated. Mon-Fri 9am-4.30pm, w/end 10am-6pm.

The Coca-Cola Museum, 1201 N Dixie Ave, Elizabethtown, 737-4000. Located 45 miles S of Louisville in the Elizabethtown bottling plant, this museum houses the world's largest collection of Coca-Cola memorabilia. Remnants of forgotten ad campaigns and items dating back to the 1880's, the dawn of the soft-drinks era. Mon-Fri 9am-4pm, $2, 50c w/student ID.

INFORMATION
Kentucky State Dept. Of Tourism, (800) 225-8747.
Visitors Information Center, 400 S 1st St, corner of Liberty, (502) 584-2121/ (800) 792-5595. Mon-Fri 8.30am-5pm, Sat 9am-4pm, Sun 11am-4pm. Later in summer.

INTERNET ACCESS
Louisville Free Public Library, 2762 Frankfort Ave, 574-1793, free.

TRAVEL
TARC, 585-1234, local buses serving most of metro area. Daily 5am-11.30pm. Fare 75¢, $1 peak times. 30 min rides to the airport leave from 1st and Market St throughout the day. Limo service also available from outside the Hyatt and Goldhouse Hotels, $6-$10.
Greyhound, 720 W Mohammed Ali Blvd, (800) 231-2222.
Yellow Tours , 1601 S Preston St, 966-5466.

MAMMOTH CAVES NATIONAL PARK Halfway between Louisville, Kentucky, and Nashville, Tennessee, lies Mammoth Caves National Park. Above ground this is a preserve of forest, flowers and wildlife, while below ground it's several hundred miles of passages, pits, domes, gypsum and travertine formations, archaeological remains and a crystal lake. The caves rival in size the better-known Carlsbad Caverns and may be explored on foot, or afloat during conducted boat trips. Call the park office for details: (502) 758-2328.

Keep to the caves within the park and do not stray into the trashy/commercial/privately-owned/exploited caves nearby. There are several campgrounds within the park. Various tours leave regularly from the Visitors

Center. **Cave City** is the service centre for the Park. Lots of motels here. *www.nps.gov/maca*.

A short drive N from Cave City is **Hodgenville** where you can visit the modest **Lincoln Birthplace and National Historic Site**. Nearby Knob Creek Farm was Abe's boyhood home, 549-3741, 9:30am-6pm in summer, earlier closing rest of year. $1 includes tour.

LEXINGTON Named in honour of its New England counterpart, Lexington was described by one traveller as 'an interesting historical town with a rich economy, not such a 'hillbilly' image as people say.' Sheik Mohammed bin Rashid al-Maktoum would certainly agree. He makes time for the annual horse sales at Keeneland Race Course. He has been known to snatch up prized thoroughbreds for $1 million plus. Lexington horse-traders have a certain shrewdness born of their unique trade. Luckily, the local industry leaves little non-organic pollution to spoil the rolling blue-grass hills of the countryside.

ACCOMMODATION
DIAL-ACCOMMODATIONS, for free assistance. Mon-Fri 8.30am-6pm, Sat 9am-5pm, 233-7299 or (800) 845-3959.
Kimball House, 267 S Limestone, 252-9565. S-$25, D-$32, $5 key deposit. Rsvs rec.
Travelodge, 2250 Elkhorn Dr, Exit 110 off I-75, 299-8481. S-$41, D-$56, XP-$5, more at w/end. Rsvs recommended.
Kentucky Horse Park Campground, 4089 Ironworks Pike, 233-4303. 9 miles N of downtown off Newton Pike. Showers, pool, ball courts, laundry, free shuttle to horse park. Sites $11, $15 w/hook-up.
YMCA, 239 E High St, 254-9622, $20, $85 per week, $40 deposit. Men only. The **University of Kentucky** has rooms and apts available mid-May to Aug. Call the housing office at 257-3721.

FOOD
Alfalfa Restaurant, 557 S Limestone St, 253-0014, across from University Memorial Hall. Wide variety of seafood, meat and vegetarian dishes from $2. Lunch $4-$10, brunch $2-$7, dinner $6-$12. Live music Thur-Sat. No cover.
Central Christian Church Cafeteria, 205 E Short St, 255-3087. Filling Southern food; entrees $3-$4.50. Mon-Fri 11am-2pm.

OF INTEREST
Some of the most magnificent horses in the world have been raised on **Three Chimneys Farm**, 873-7053. Seattle Slew and Affirmed are 2 of the most famous studs hard at work making future Derby winners. Tours 9am and 1:30pm daily by appointment only, with fillies going for up to $10.2 million, many of the farms have decided not to interrupt the horseplay with buses of gawking tourists. **Bluegrass Tours**, 252-5744, provides a twice daily tour of the area which takes you past the paddocks of the famous thoroughbred farms, 3 hrs, $20, Rsvs required. Famous farms include **Calumet**, **Darby Dan** and **King Ranch**. Also visit the **Kentucky Horse Park**, Iron Works Pike, 6 miles N on I-75, exit 120, 233-4303. 'Well worth a visit, especially for horse lovers.' Daily 9pm-5pm, $10. 50 min tour and riding at extra cost, $3.25. **Ashland**, Richmond Rd at Sycamore Rd, 266-8581, was the home of politician Henry Clay, the engineer of the great Missouri compromise on slavery. The compromise allowed slavery below, but not above the 36th parallel. Ultimately proving unworkable, the compromise pushed the war back for years, $6 includes guided tour. Tues-Sat 10am-4pm, Sun 1pm-4pm.
The **Mary Todd Lincoln House**, 578 W Main St, 233-9999, built 1803, is where

Abraham Lincoln's wife lived as a girl; Lincoln himself stayed here several times. Tue-Sat 10am-4pm. $6. The first college west of the Alleghenies was **Transylvania University**. Folklore has it that the old administration building burned down and 10 students suffered nasty deaths because of a curse placed upon the school. Inside the new administration building at Old Morrison Hall lies the crypt of a professor named Rafinesque, which was placed there to remove the curse. Students celebrate the tale each Halloween. Tours of the crypt and the campus, W of Broadway and N of 3rd St, can be arranged by calling 233-8242.

The **University of Kentucky**, 257-3595, gives free campus walking tours; 10am and 2pm, Mon-Sat. **Visitor Center** open daily 9am-4.30pm. Also worth seeing is the **University Art Museum**, 257-5716, featuring over 3000 works including drawings, paintings and sculpture. Tue-Sat noon-5pm; free.

Outside Lexington: Shaker Village, in **Harrodsburg**, 25 miles SW of Lexington on US 68, this community was established by the Shaker sect in 1805 and by the middle of that century numbered 500 inhabitants. The Shakers have departed, but their buildings, with the help of some restoration, still stand. The museum preserves Shaker furnishings, $9.50, $13 includes river boat ride. To relive the Shaker life, you can stay in one of the buildings, furnished in the Shaker style, $66-85. Inexpensive Shaker meals as well (bfast from $7, lunch $5-$10, dinner $12-$19). Call (606) 734-5411 for rsvs. 7 miles from the original Kentucky settlement at Fort Harrod. In the SE corner of the state, the **Cumberland Gap National Historical Park** and the **Daniel Boone National Forest** provide a beautiful retreat into untouched wilderness. The Park Headquarters and Visitors Center, on Hwy 58, 248-2817 (daily 8am-5pm), has info on tours, camping and hiking in the Gap area. No rsvs. For info on hiking and camping in the Daniel Boone National Forest call 745-3100. *www.nps.gov/cuga/index.htm.*

INFORMATION/TRAVEL
Convention and Visitors Bureau, 301 E Vine St, 233-1221, (800) 848-1244. Mon-Fri 8.30am-6pm, Sat 10am-6pm, Sun noon-5pm, in season.
The Visitors Center is in the same building, Suite 363. Mon-Fri 8.30am-5pm.
Greyhound, 477 New Circle Rd NW, 299-8804/(800) 231-2222. There are no buses serving the airport. For a cab, call 231-8294, $12-$15 o/w.
Lex Tran, 253-4636. Buses depart from the Transit Center, 220 W Vine St. Serves university, metro and surrounding area. Daily 5:40am 'til midnight some routes. Fare 80c.

INTERNET ACCESS
Lexington Public Library, 140 E Main, 231-5500, call to reserve time. Free.

LOUISIANA   *The Pelican State*

With its Voodoo, Jazz, Mardi Gras and Cajun cooking, Louisiana is anything but bland. The Creole State has given the United States some of its most exotic cooking, its best party—Mardi Gras, and most flamboyant politicians (depression-era Huey Long vowed to 'Soak the Rich!,' former Governor Edwin Edwards claims that losing $1 million in Vegas was part of his hobby).

Louisiana's cultural heritage is a rich gumbo stew. The original French and Spanish settlers brought old world architecture to the state, while their African and Caribbean slaves laid the musical foundations for what would become jazz music. And, after the British expelled them from Nova Scotia in 1775, the French Acadians, now called Cajuns, brought fur-trapping, Cajun cooking, dialects and their special zydeco music to the bayous.

Caribbean pirates, Mississippi riverboat gamblers and plantation owners have given way to a more respectable economy based upon offshore oil and trade, but Louisiana still beguiles visitors with a care-free, genteel atmosphere unlike anything else in America. *www.yahoo.com/Regional/U_S__States/Louisiana*.
The telephone area code for New Orleans is 504, for Baton Rouge, 225, for Acadiana, 318.

NEW ORLEANS   New Orleans is a party that never ends. First hosted by the French in 1718, followed by the Spanish, and the French again, the party finally passed to the Americans who bought out the last host, Napoleon, for $15 million in the Louisiana Purchase. Each culture has contributed an ingredient to the festivity: Spanish architecture, French joie de vivre, and a Caribbean sense of pace. A limitless supply of alcohol and music have contributed to New Orleans' reputation as the 'city that care forgot.'

Visitors are drawn by the Vieux Carré above Canal Street, where gracious homes, walled gardens, narrow streets overhung by iron-lace balconies, and delicious Creole food struggle to retain a mellow atmosphere against encroaching plastic America. Edgar Degas, the only impressionist to visit North America, captured the atmosphere of the city during his visit here in 1872-73 with some of his paintings, including *The Cotton Exchange of New Orleans*.

And of course there's jazz, though today Bourbon Street comes out with the wrong notes. The street is an over-commercialised strip of bars, drunks, prostitutes, skin shows, rip-off joints and gawking tourists in bermuda shorts. The locals usually avoid it, and the cognoscenti will at once make for the Jazz Museum and Preservation Hall, the place nonpareil for the traditional sound.

The New Orleans police have gained a reputation for brutality towards, and general ill-treatment of, young foreign visitors. Be careful. *www.nawlins.com*.

ACCOMMODATION
Many of the rates given do not apply during Mardi Gras, the Jazz Festival and the Sugar Bowl. Check first. Off season rates prevail Memorial Day to Labor Day.
Campus accommodation available during summer; **Tulane U**, 27 McAlister Dr, 865-5724, on streetcar line. Rooms $42-50 through summer. **Loyola U**, 6363 St Charles St, 865-3735. 25 mins from downtown by streetcar. Jun-Aug. Dorms $25. Includes linen.
Friendly Inn, 4861 Chef Menteur Hwy, (800) 445-3940/283-1531. S-$30, XP-$5. TV, pool, transport to and from Amtrak. 'Excellent.' 'Cheap and comfy but 7 miles out of centre in dodgy area.'
India House , 124 S. Lopez St, 821-1904. $14 during Mardi Gras/Jazz Festival, $5 key deposit. Mid-city area, mins from French quarter. Pool, table tennis, kitchen, laundry, TV room, Internet access. Even an alligator swamp out back.
Hotel LaSalle, 1113 Canal St, 523-5831, (800) 521-9450. S-$30, $59 w/bath, D-$72. 4 blocks from Bourbon St. 'absolutely excellent!' Near Vieux Carre. Clean, large rooms. TV, AC, laundry, safe-deposit boxes.'
Longpré House, 1726 Prytania St, 581-4540. $12 w/student ID or overseas passport. S/D-$35-$40. 1/2 hr walk to French Quarter, 1 block off streetcar route. Free coffee and in the morning. 'Dirty dorms, beautiful private rooms.'

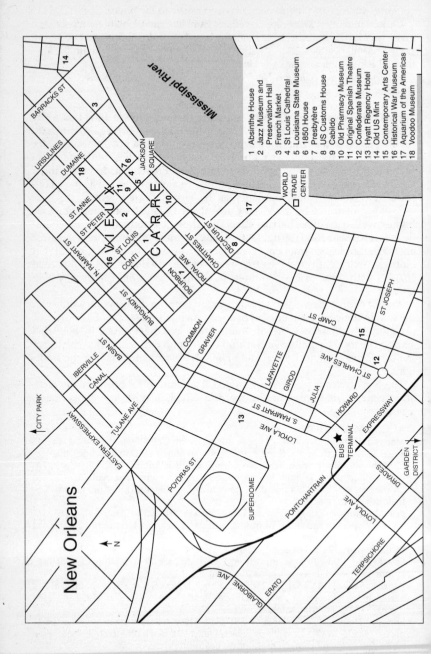

New Orleans

1 Absinthe House
2 Jazz Museum and
  Preservation Hall
3 French Market
4 St Louis Cathedral
5 Louisiana State Museum
6 1850 House
7 Presbytère
8 US Customs House
9 Cabildo
10 Old Pharmacy Museum
11 Original Spanish Theatre
12 Confederate Museum
13 Hyatt Regency Hotel
14 Old US Mint
15 Contemporary Arts Center
16 Historical War Museum
17 Aquarium of the Americas
18 Voodoo Museum

Marquette House Youth Hostel, 2253 Carondelet St, 523-3014. $15.50 AYH, $18.50 non-AYH, private rooms $45-$51.50. More during Mardi Gras/Jazz Festival. Nr Garden District and St Charles streetcar. Rsvs recommended. 'Clean and comfy.' Nr laundry and supermarket. 'Very friendly and helpful.' 'Excellent.'

Prytania Inn, 1415 Prytania St, 566-1515. S-$29-$59. Breakfast included. Rsvs required. Double rates during festivals. 'Excellent; highly recommended.' 1 block from street car.

Prytania Park Hotel, 1525 Prytania St, 524-0427. S/D-$99-$109. AC, TV, includes bfast. Near French Quarter. 'Luxury.' Free parking.

St Charles Guest House, 1748 Prytania St, 523-6556. B&B 10 mins from French Quarter by streetcar, nr Garden District. Backpacker rooms $25-$30, D-$45-$65. Rsvs rec. Pool and sun deck. 'Near small supermarket and laundry. 'Free bfast and newspapers.' 'Owners are very friendly and as kind and generous as anyone could be.'

YMCA, 920 St Charles Ave, 568-9622. Clean, air-conditioned, coed rooms. From $36 for 2. Rsvs recommended. Free use of pool and gym and track. Shared bathrooms only. 'Relatively safe area in French Quarter, helpful travel info in lobby.'

Camping: New Orleans KOA West, 11129 Jefferson Hwy, River Ridge, 467-1792. Site $22, $27 w/hook-up , XP-$3, pool, laundry. Shuttle to French Quarter, leaves 9am, returns 4pm, $3. RTA bus and various tours also pick up from grounds.

Bayou Segnette State Park, 7777 Westbank Expressway, 736-7140. Bus service runs to park. Site $12, cabin up to 8 people (Mon-Fri only), $65. Rsvs essential for cabins.

St Bernard State Park, 682-2101. Follow I-10 to LA 47 S, then left on LA 39, 16 miles from French Quarter. Sites $12. 'Great camping.' Bus service 30 min away. Last bus 6pm.

FOOD

www.neworleansonline.com/food-o.htm

Hot, spicy Cajun food abounds, as does old fashioned stick-to-your-ribs Southern cooking. Gumbo, jambalaya, and crawfish are specialities. Try chocolate pecan pie and beignets—a hot, square doughnut without the hole.

Café du Monde, 800 Decatur, 525-4544, in the French Market. Open 24 hrs. This is the place to get your beignets, 3 for $1.20. 'An experience not to be missed.' Begin and end every day here.

Café Mospero, 601 Decatur, 523-6250. Sandwiches, fried seafood. Open daily 11am-11pm, later at w/end. 'Good food—substantial meal $6.' All meals under $15. 'Expect to queue for a seat.' 'Low prices, big portions.'

Coops Place, 1109 Decatur, 525-9053. Cajun food, dinner around $6. 'The real thing, unpretentious local restaurant.' Open daily, 11am-3am.

Eddie's Restaurant, 2119 Law St, 945-2207. 'Excellent downhome cooking, gumbo recommended.' 'All-you-can-eat' buffet. Mon-Wed 11am-3pm, every Thurs-Sat 5pm-10pm.' 'Great atmosphere.'

Fat Harrys, 4330 St Charles, 895-9582. Student atmosphere, cover $3-$6. Late night spot after the bars, on streetcar line, 11am to 3am. 'Excellent.'

The Fudgery, 1 Poydras St., 522-8030. Delicious homemade fudge. 'Watch them make it right in front of you—yummy!' Open 10am-9pm daily.

Johnny's Po-Boy, 511 St Louis, 524-8129. 'Good sandwiches; excellent gumbo.' 'Friendly staff.' Mon-Fri 8am-4.30pm, Sat-Sun 9am-4pm.

Kaldi's Coffee House and Coffee Museum, 941 Decatur, 586-8989. Escape the tourists at this alternative hang-out. 'Delicious, real, fresh coffee.' 'Very reasonable; a must for coffee lovers.' Open 7am-midnight.

K Paul's Louisiana Kitchen, 416 Chartres St, 524-7394, in the French Quarter, looks like a hole in the wall but is actually world famous, if you're there at dinner time, expect to see a looooong line waiting to get in. Chef Paul Prudhomme has made Cajun cuisine famous worldwide. Excellent, but expensive, $25-$35. Mon-Sat5:30pm-10pm (dinner), Thurs-Sat 11:30pm- 2:30pm (lunch).

Mena's Place, 622 Iberville, 525-0217. Excellent seafood gumbo, $3.50, daily specials around $4. 'Very friendly.' Open 6.45am-6.45pm Mon-Sat.
Seaport Cafe, on Bourbon St, is a combo cafe and bar; not cheap, but has tasty food and a balcony—'fascinating way of viewing the Bourbon St characters.'
Shoney's, 3400 Holiday Dr, 362-5830, and other locations. Bfast special $4, salad bar from $4. 'Superb.' Sun-Thurs 6am-11pm, 'til 2am on w/ends.
You can learn to cook Cajun food from Chef Joe Cahn at the **New Orleans School of Cooking**, 324 St. Louis, 525-2665 for info and rsvs. Crash courses Mon-Sat, 2-4pm $20.

OF INTEREST

French Quarter or **Vieux Carré** (Old Square), the heart and soul of New Orleans, includes about 70 blocks of the old city between the river and Rampart St and Canal and Esplanade Sts. Apart from the pleasure of simply wandering around the streets, and through back alleys, you will find in this area the city's most noteworthy buildings. Caution—do not wander down dark streets at night. As picturesque as they may be, the French Quarter's dark back alleys are good places for the foolish traveller to find trouble.

The Quarter is a National Historic District, within the **Jean LaFitte National Historic Park and Preserve**. Lafitte was a famous New Orleans pirate who also helped defeat the British at the Battle of New Orleans. Legend has it that his most audacious plan was to rescue Napoleon from his British captors. The park service **Folklife and Visitors Center**, 589-2636, 916-918 N Peters St in the French Market (enter through 914 Decatur) offers maps, informed rangers, and different tours throughout the area. A general 90 min **History Tour** covering New Orleans and Louisiana leaves at 10.30am daily. A good starting point in the Quarter is **Jackson Square**. The old Place d'Armes parade ground, Jackson Square has been the central gathering place in the city since it was first laid out in 1721. The square is named after Andrew Jackson, the hero of the battle of New Orleans. The statue honouring 'Old Hickory,' as the scrappy populist was called, was erected in 1856. **St Louis Cathedral**, 525-9585, Jackson Sq's exquisite centrepiece was rebuilt in 1794 after a fire destroyed the original and remodeled in 1850. It is a minor basilica and the oldest active cathedral in the United States. Free guided tours Mon-Sat, 9am-5pm, Sun 1.30pm-5pm. Sun mass 7.30am-6pm.
The Louisiana State Museum, 568-6968, includes several historical buildings in the Quarter which may be toured in combination. Individual museums $5, $4 w/student ID. Purchase tickets to two or more attractions and save 20%. All Museum attractions open Tue-Sun 9am-5pm. Next to the Cathedral is the old Spanish governor's residence, **The Cabildo**, site of the US/French negotiations for the Louisiana Purchase. It was heavily damaged by fire in 1988, but restoration work is now complete. No 2 at the museum is **The Presbytere**, on Chartres St facing the Square. Dates to 1791 and houses portraiture, New Orleans architecture exhibit and changing collections.
The 1850 House, in a portion of the **Pontabla Apartments** (coincidentally also damaged by fire in 1989), facing the Square, offers a glimpse of elegant Southern living. Said to be the oldest apts in the United States, the Pontabla Buildings were built for Baroness Pontabla and are furnished in the traditional antebellum style. Guided tours on the hr.

Finally, the **Old US Mint**, 400 Esplanade, houses historical documents and jazz and carnival exhibits. A working mint from 1838-62 and 1879-1920, it's 'O' mint-mark is a favourite among coin collectors worldwide. Other historic buildings of the French Quarter include:
Absinthe House, 240 Bourbon St, 523-3181. The house where the LaFitte brothers, Pierre and Jean, 'plotted against honest shipping.' Now a bar and literary landmark. Daily 9am-4am.

US Customs House, 423 Canal St, 670-2082. Dates from 1848; used as headquarters during Civil War Union occupation. Mon-Fri 8am-5pm. Free.

The Old French Market, 800, 900, and 1,000 blocks of Decatur St, 522-2621. Has been operating from the same spot since 1791. Many old colonnaded buildings have recently been restored and converted to shops and restaurants. The famous old vegetable market is still in operation 24 hrs. Other attractions open daily 8am-7pm. Flea Market daily. 'Wonderful. Lots of junk and good jazz in the air.'

Contemporary Arts Center, 900 Camp St, 523-1216. 'Visual arts, music theater; stunning interior to building.' $2, some exhibitions are free. Tues-Sun 11am-5pm.

Old Pharmacy Museum, 514 Chartres St, 565-8027. Was first used as a pharmacy in 1823 and is now an interesting museum of old apothecary items, voodoo potions, medical instruments and hand-blown pharmacy bottles and 'show globes'. Tue-Sun 10am-5pm, $2.

Voodoo Museum, 724 Dumaine St, 523-7685. If you are not too squeamish, learn about the magic and history of this ancient religion. Swamp and ritual tours offered for the strong of stomach and spirit. 'Recommended for the entire family', as advertised by the owner. Open daily 10am-8pm. $6, $5.10 w/student ID.

Historical Wax Museum, 917 Conti St, 525-2605, features a recreation of 'Congo Square,' the voodoo center of old New Orleans, as well as the popular Haunted Dungeon. Open 10am-5.30pm Mon-Sat, Sun from 12-5, $6.

Original Spanish Theater, 718 St Peter, built in 1791 was the first Spanish theatre in the US, later a private home, and has housed the well known Pat O'Brien's (of 'hurricane' fame) since 1942. Of note outside the French Quarter:

Confederate Museum, 929 Camp St, 1 block off Lee Circle, 523-4522. Has memorabilia of the Civil War. 'Ten out of ten.' Mon-Sat 10am-4pm. $5, $4 w/student ID. Take the St Charles St streetcar—one of only 2 remaining in the city—through the fashionable **Garden District** ($1, 10¢ transfer). The line is an excellent way to get to know the city. Once you reach the Garden District, get out and wander among the sumptuous houses built by rich antebellum whites to rival the Creole dwellings in the Vieux Carre. The District stretches from Jackson to Louisiana Aves between St Charles and Magazine Sts. Further down the streetcar line, you reach **Audubon Park** and the **Audubon Zoo**, 6500 Magazine, 861-2537. One of the 'top 10 zoos in the US.' Natural habitats for 1800 animals. Open daily 9.30am-5pm, $8.75. Streetcar stop #35. Another prime attraction outside the French Quarter is **City Park**, at Esplanade and Carrollton Sts, 482-4888, site of the famous **Duelling Oaks**, where New Orleans society settled their differences 'under the Oaks at dawn.' The fifth largest park in the USA, 1500 acres. Enjoy its magnificent oaks, statues and fountains, sports and recreational facilities. Botanical gardens, sports stadium, tennis courts, carousel etc. More like a lifestyle than a park. Free, but charges for activities.

The New Orleans Museum of Art , 488-2631, is located in the park. The collection includes works by the Russian jeweller, Fabergé, a local decorative arts exhibit and a large collection of French impressionist paintings. 2 floors of the museum are dedicated to Asian, African and Oceanic art. Tues-Sun 10am-5pm, $10, $9 w/ student ID. More modern sites include the **Hyatt Regency Hotel**, Poydras and Loyola, with a free spectacular view. Not free, but still spectacular is the **Louisiana Superdome**, 1500 Poydras St, 587-3810. Host to the '97 Superbowl. Opened in 1975, and the world's largest indoor stadium with the largest single room in the history of man. 1 hr tours Mon-Fri; 10:30am, noon, 1:30pm, $6. 'The stadium is impressive but the tour is a rip-off; better to pay to see an event. Nothing like it at home.'

Cruises on the Mississippi. A variety of companies offer all kinds of cruises, including buffets and parties, trips to Audubon Zoo, 2 hr port tours ('interesting only if you're into docks and Liberian freighters'), 5 hr explorations of nearby bayous and swamplands, and trips up the Mississippi into the heartland. For bayou, harbour, and zoo cruise info, call 586-8777 for the **New Orleans Steamboat**

Co. The **Creole Queen**, 524-0814, offers a bayou, plantation, and battlefield cruise. Readership consensus is that the boat rides are generally 'boring' and 'not worth it,' but the Bayou trips by bus and boat are highly recommended if you want to see alligators 'au naturel.' Open since late 1989, the **Woldenberg Riverfront Park**, 17 acres of park land down by the Mississippi stretching from Canal Street through the French Quarter to the Moonwalk. You can ride to the top of the **World Trade Center** building, Canal St, for a view of the city and river. The **Old Algiers Ferry** crosses the river from here—and it's free! This is the first time for more than 100 years that residents have had direct access to the river. The **Aquarium of the Americas** on Canal St, 565-3006, recreates the underwater environments of the American continent. Sun-Thurs 9.30am-6pm, Fri-Sat 'til 7pm. $16.25 admission includes ticket to IMAX theatre.

ENTERTAINMENT

New Orleans *is* entertainment. This is a city that knows how to have a good time, and it's not only during Mardi Gras. Here you are likely to find a celebration of some kind at any time of the year. The French Quarter, one of the most European areas in the US, is always full of life. Jazz legends such as Louis Armstrong, Bunk Johnson, Jelly Roll Morton, King Oliver and Kid Ory have all stomped in Storyville. **Bourbon St**, though somewhat sleazy, is a perpetual party, and a visit to this city would not be complete without at least one nightly stroll down this crazy stretch of decadence. Although the jazz revival in New Orleans has brought back many good musicians, there are also, on Bourbon St, scores of over-priced nightclubs, flashy restaurants, endless clip joints, and plenty of bad music. Choose carefully (always check prices before you buy a drink, as you are sometimes paying for the band with them) and carry ID. Check *Gambit* and *Wavelength* newspapers for current listings. New Orleans' temple of jazz is the **Preservation Hall**, 726 St Peter St, 522-2841 (days), 523-8939 (nights), where pioneers of jazz have always performed—and still do, hear jazz in its quintessential form. Doors 8pm, arrive early. 8.30pm-12am nightly, $5 standing. 'An absolute must." 'I'd pay $10 to go and see it again—a magical experience.' 'Whatever you read/hear will never do it justice—Go!' In **Jackson Square**, Saturday jazz concerts are held 2pm-6pm during Oct-Nov, April-Aug. Most shows are free.

Annual Jazz and Heritage Festival. Takes place late Apr-early May, attracting musicians and fans worldwide. Listen to music played on 11 stages, or wander around Cajun food and craft stalls. 'Fantastic day out.' Held at New Orleans Fair Grounds. 522-4786 for info.

Check Point, Decatur St past French Market. Bar, cafe and launderette all in one, plus live music and shelves of books. 'Where the alternative crowd hangs out.'

Pat O'Brien's, 718 St Peter St, 525-4823. Reputed to be the 'busiest and the best' in the French Quarter. Popular with local students. 'Great atmosphere, no cover, closes 4am.' 'Home of the Hurricane Cocktail. Don't miss it.' $5 ($7 w/souvenir glass) Also try **Snug Harbor** and **Storyville** for sweet soulful music. Uptown New Orleans, around Maple, Oak and Willow Sts, down St Charles from Canal. 'Where the locals go. Good bars and clubs. Better music and cheaper.'

Tipitina's, 233 St. Peters St, 895-8477. 'The real thing.' Dixie Cups, good music including zydeco and cheap drinks. Attracts both the best local talent and known artists such as Harry Connick Jr. Learn how to dance Cajun-style on Sun evenings. 'The best part of our stay.'

Top of the Mart, World Trade Center, 2 Canal St, 522-9795. America's largest revolving bar/restaurant is 33 storeys high, seats 500 people and makes one revolution every 1½ hrs (3ft per min). 'Visit in the evening and watch the sunset over the city.' No cover but 1 drink minimum. Mon-Fri 10am-11pm, Sat 11am-1am, Sun 2pm-midnight.

INFORMATION
New Orleans Welcome Center , 529 St Anne Street, 568-5661. In the French Quarter, free city and walking tour maps.
Greater New Orleans Tourist Commission, 1520 Sugar Bowl Drive, 566-5011.

INTERNET ACCESS
Realm of Delirium, 941 Decatur St, 523-CYBER, 20c/min, $7.50/hr. Located inside Kaldi's Coffee Museum.

TRAVEL
New Orleans Regional Transit Authority (RTA), 700 Plaza Dr, 569-2700. City bus and streetcar, major lines run 24 hrs. $1, transfers 10¢. All-day pass $4, 3 days $8.
Louisiana Transit Authority, 737-9611. Bus from airport to downtown, $1.10, 'have exact change'. Last bus leaves airport at 5.40pm.
Amtrak, 1001 Loyola Ave, 528-1610/(800) 872-7245. *Crescent* to NY, *City of New Orleans* to Chicago and *Sunset Limited* to LA originate here. Area not safe after dark.
Greyhound, 1001 Loyola in train station, (800) 231-2222. 'Bad neighbourhood.' Accommodation board here has been recommended. Try Tulane and Loyola for their ride boards.

BATON ROUGE   During the first 150 years of its short history, Louisiana experienced considerable difficulty in deciding on a state capital. Opelousas, Alexandria, Shreveport and New Orleans all enjoyed such status. Finally, in 1849, Baton Rouge was chosen over New Orleans, largely due to concern over the state government being based in such a 'careless' city!

Situated in the heart of plantation country, 60 miles NW of the 'Big Easy' on the Mississippi, Baton Rouge was named after the cypress tree used by the Indians to mark hunting boundaries. Today it is the state's second largest city and one of the nation's largest ports, profiting mainly from petro-chemical and sugarcane production. The abundance of magnolia and cypress trees belies this industrial bias and the city still retains a small-town character. Of special interest are the 34 storey **State Capitol Building** (342-0500); the great white, **Old Governor's Mansion** and the two universities (Louisiana State and Southern). Call (225) 383-1825 for tourist info.

CLOUTIERVILLE   If it weren't for Kate Chopin, no one would probably visit Cloutierville. Chopin herself described the peaceful French settlement as 'two long rows of very old frame houses, facing each other closely across a dusty roadway.' The highly-celebrated author and her husband moved to his family's plantation after falling on hard times in New Orleans. Today the plantation is known as the **Kate Chopin Home**, (318) 379-2233, and is also home to the **Bayou Folk Museum**. The two-storey house is a monument to Bayou life and to the author that chronicled it so well. The museum features an old doctor's office, a blacksmith's shop. Cloutierville lies 20 miles south of Natitoches, off of I-49, about 260 from New Orleans. The house and museum are open Mon-Sat 10am-5pm, Sun 1pm-5pm. $5.

ACADIANA   True bayou country, complete with alligators and Spanish moss hanging from trees, begins in the Cajun area called Acadiana. The original French Acadians came to Louisiana after the British overran their native Nova Scotia. The British insisted that the Acadians swear allegiance to the British crown and renounce Catholicism. The Acadians refused, moving instead to Louisiana where they became known as Cajuns. Using their knowledge of fur-trapping, the Cajuns quickly adapted to the ways of the swamp. (One ingenious adaptation was the use of moths for bedding.)

Today's Cajuns still speak some Creole French, and the bayous of Louisiana continue to account for much of the fur-trapping in the United States. Cajun cooking and music are currently in vogue. Paul Simon's *Graceland* was heavily influenced by Cajun Zydeco music, a version of which makes for wonderful rock and roll. Modern Cajun life centers around **Lafayette**, **New Iberia** and **St Martinville**, about 120 miles NW of New Orleans. **Accommodation** is fairly inexpensive with most lodging centered in Lafayette. Try the **Lafayette Inn**, 2615 Cameron St, 235-9442 (S/D from $30, $2 key deposit) or the **Lafayette Travel Lodge**, 1101 W Pinnhook Rd, 234-7402 (S-$48, D-$52). **Mulate's Cajun Restaurant**, 325 Mills Ave in Breaux Bridge, 332-4648/ (800) 422-2586, is arguably the most famous Cajun restaurant in the world. 'Not to be overlooked. Not cheap but meals can be split—worth it.' Open daily.

OF INTEREST

In Lafayette: Lafayette Museum, 1122 Lafayette St, 234-2208. With Mardi Gras costumes and LA heirlooms. Tues-Sat 9am-5pm, Sun 3pm-5pm, $3, $1 w/student ID. Just outside Lafayette, the **Acadian Village**, 981-2364, is a good place to learn about Cajun culture. Somewhat touristy, with authentic Cajun houses, tools, and furnishings. Open daily 10am-5pm, $6. The **Festival International de Louisiane**, 232-8086, is a 6-day fete celebrating music, art, theatre, dance, cinema, and southern cuisine and takes place in late Apr. 'Don't miss it.' Just N of the city lies the **Academy of the Sacred Heart**, 662-5494, the only known exact spot of a miracle in the US. It was here that St John Berchmans, a Jesuit novice, appeared in response to the prayers of a dying woman. She recovered and Berchman returned to heaven. Mon-Fri 7:30am-4pm. Tours Sun 1pm-4pm; other times call for appointment.

In **Eunice**, about 30 miles N on US-190, every Sat night a live Cajun radio show is staged at the Liberty Center for the Performing Arts featuring Zydeco music, humourists and recipes, $5, 6pm-8pm. Call Eunice Chamber of Commerce for more info 457-2565.

In New Iberia, St Martinville: Shadows on the Teche, 317 E Main St, New Iberia, 369-6446, a famous plantation on the banks of the Bayou Teche. H L Mencken stayed here as did Cecil B DeMille. Open daily 9am-4.30pm, $6.

Evangeline Oak on Port St at Bayou Teche marks the legendary first landing of the Acadians in bayou country. Nearby is statue of **Evangeline** beside **St Martin de Tours Catholic Church**, one of the oldest in Louisiana. Evangeline was one-half of the legendary pair of Acadian lovers immortalised by the Longfellow poem. The reputed home of Evangeline's beau, Gabrielle, is in the **Longfellow-Evangeline Commemorative Area**. A must-see quirk of history is the Roman-era **Statue of Hadrian** standing guard, appropriately, in front of a bank, on the corner of Weeks and Peters Sts.

Jungle Gardens, 369-6243, at end of Hwy 329 about 7 miles S of New Iberia, features a 1000 year old Buddha set in a swamp garden. Daily 8am-5:30, $5.75. If you doubt that Cajuns like hot food, you should know that Tabasco was invented nearby at the **Avery Islands Tabasco Pepper Sauce Factory**, 365-8173, free 20 min tours Mon-Fri 9am-4pm, Sat 9am-noon.

In the bayou: Louisiana swampland is unique, and tours into the swamps abound. Choose carefully, though, as rip-offs exist. Call **Atchafalaya Delta Wildlife Area**, (504) 395-4905, they can refer you to tours. Try **Cajun Jack's Swamp Tours** of the

Atchafalaya, the largest swamp in N America. See first hand how the Cajun people live as their ancestors did hundreds of years ago. If you are heading to Texas, try the drive along Hwys 82 and 27 through the **Creole Nature Trail**.

INFORMATION
Lafayette Convention and Visitors Commission, 1400 NW Evangeline Thruway, 232-3808/(800) 346-1958. Mon-Fri 8.30am-5pm, 9am-5pm at w/end.
Iberia Parish Tourist Commission, 2704 Hwy 14, 365-1540. Open 9am-5pm daily.

MISSISSIPPI *The Magnolia State*

The blues, King Cotton, southern hospitality, southern pride, civil rights, and riverboat rides—Mississippi *is* the Old South—the embodiment of a tarnished American myth of polite Southern gentlemen and elegant plantation life.

Like any myth, parts of it are true—Mississippi folk are more polite than their Yankee neighbours. The graceful plantation homes that survived the Civil War do speak eloquently for the sensibilities of a lost time, before the last stand of the Southern gentleman on the battlefield of Vicksburg. And in the hot, humid Delta backwoods, the rhythms that once consoled the slaves have been pressed gradually into the modern blues by such Mississippi giants as John Lee Hooker, John Hurt, Son House, Elmore James and Muddy Waters.

The Old South begat other legends in the works of Tennessee Williams and William Faulkner, Mississippi's most famous literary sons. From the lazy beat of Williams' long, hot summer to the radical civil rights battles which exposed the ugly, violent underbelly of Southern life in the 1960s, the Magnolia State is the stage upon which an American myth lived and is struggling to survive. Economically, the state has been helped enormously by the casinos that have sprouted up, particularly along the Gulf Coast.

The Natchez Trace Parkway stretches diagonally across Mississippi along the historic highway of bandits, armies and adventurers. You can drive along it or explore the old trails on foot. Along Mississippi's Gulf coastline there runs another old trail. This is the old Spanish Trail that ran from St Augustine, Florida, to the missions in California. US 90 from Pascagoula to Bay St Louis follows the trail through the state. *www.yahoo.com/Regional/U_S_States/Mississippi/*.
The telephone area code for Jackson, Vicksburg, Oxford and Natchez is 601, for Biloxi and the Gulf it's 228.

JACKSON Set on the west bank of the Pearl River, the capital city of the state began as a trading post reputedly established by Canadian Louis LeFleur. General Sherman coined the phrase 'war is hell' here in Jackson, then went on to prove it by commanding his victorious Federal troops to burn the original Jackson to the ground in 1863. Locals renamed their devastated home 'Chimneyville.' It was not until early this century that Jackson recovered to become Mississippi's largest city. The discovery of natural gas in the area saved it from the economic ravages of the Great Depression.

ACCOMMODATION/FOOD

Parkside Inn, 982-1122, 3720 I-55 N at exit 98B, close to downtown. Must be 21 to rent, 18 and under free with adult. TV, pool. S-$29, D-$35.

Sun 'n' Sand Motel, 401 N Lamar St, 354-2501. Central location. From S-$35, D-$40, XP-$5. TV, pool, $5 lunch buffet Mon-Fri, $6.50 Sun.

Timberlake Campgrounds, 100 Timberlake Dr, 992-9100. Popular site with arcade, pool, ball courts. Sites $12, $15 w/hook-up.

Primo's, 4330 N State St, 982-2064. Jazz and southern cooking; Open Mon-Sat 11am-10pm

The Elite Cafe, 141 E Capitol, 352-5606. Homestyle cooking; lunch specials with 2 veg and bread from $5.25. Open Mon-Fri 7am-9:30pm, Sat 5pm-9:30pm.

OF INTEREST

Mississippi Crafts Center, Natchez Trace Parkway at Ridgeland, 856-7546. Traditional and contemporary folk arts and crafts. Open 9am-5pm daily.

Mississippi Museum of Art, 201 E Pascagoula, 960-1515. Jackson's first art museum; opened in 1978. Presents as many as 40 exhibitions each year. Mon-Sat 10am-5pm, Sun 12pm-5pm, Tue 'til 8pm. $5, $3 w/student ID, free Tue and Thur. Closed in Aug.

Russell C Davis Planetarium, 201 E Pascagoula St, 960-1550. The largest in the Southeast, and one of the best in the world. Shows Mon-Fri evenings and w/end afternoons. Call for times. $4-5.

The Oaks, 823 N Jefferson, 353-9339. Jackson's oldest house built 1746, occupied by General Sherman during the Jackson siege in 1863. Period antiques on display including original furniture from Abraham Lincoln's Office. Open Tue-Sat 10am-3pm. $2, $1 w/student ID.

The Old State Capitol, at the intersection of Capitol and State Sts, 359-6920. Houses the **State Historical Museum**. The building has survived 3 torchings and is Mississippi's second state house. Displays artifacts from Native American settlements and documents Mississippi's volatile history both before and after the Civil Rights movement. Open 8am-5pm Mon-Fri, Sat 9:30am-4:30pm, Sun 12:30pm-4:30pm. The 'magnificent' **New State Capitol**, at Mississippi and Congress, 359-3114, is where the state legislature currently gathers. 1 hr guided tours 9am-11am and 1.30pm-3.30pm. Mon-Fri 8am-5pm, free.

INFORMATION/TRAVEL

Jackson Visitor Information Center, 1150 Lakeland Dr, 713-3365. Located inside the Agricultural Museum. Mon-Sat 9am-5pm, Sun 1pm-5pm (Sun in summer only).

Amtrak, 300 W Capitol St, 355-6350/(800) 872-7245.

Greyhound, 201 S Jefferson St, 353-6342/(800) 231-2222. 'This area is best avoided at night.' No buses to/from the airport. For a taxi, call 355-8319, $13-$15 o/w.

INTERNET ACCESS

Jackson-Hinds Library, 300 N State St, 968-5825, free.

OXFORD Literature has blossomed out of this small town, nestled in corn, cotton and cattle country in the north of Mississippi. Pulitzer and Nobel Prize winner William Faulkner based his fictitious Yoknapatowpha County on Oxford as he wrote about the anguish of a decaying South and the plight of the blacks. Today, the mega-selling author of *The Client, The Chamber,* and *The Runaway Jury,* John Grisham, lives in Oxford, alongside some beautiful ante-bellum mansions. The University of Mississippi—*Ole Miss*—is where a courageous student named James Meredith shattered two centuries of white Southern tradition as the first black graduate in 1963.

ACCOMMODATION/FOOD
Ole Miss Motel, 1517 E University Ave, 234-2424, 3 blocks from City Square. S-$32, D-$42.

For mainstream music and tasty bar food, try **The Gin**, 234-0024, just off City Square on Harrison Street. Open 11am-1:30am daily.

Smitty's Cafe, 208 S Lamar, 234-9111, just off the square. Southern cooking means fried chicken and catfish from $4-$8, most entrees under $6. Open daily 7am-4pm.

OF INTEREST
Annual Faulkner Conference in the first week of Aug draws scholars from around the world. 232-5993 for details and tkts. If you go, first read *The Sound and the Fury*, *As I Lay Dying* or *The Reivers*.

William Faulkner's Home, called Rowan Oak, Old Taylor Rd, 234-3284. Tucked back in the woods, unmarked from the street, Faulkner's home until 1962 can be reached by walking down S Lamar Street. Free, Tues-Sat 10am-noon and 2pm-4pm, Sun 2pm-4pm.

Square Books, 160 Courthouse Sq, 236-2262, has impressive collection of Southern writers, and a cafe upstairs. Mon-Thur 9am-9pm, Fri, Sat 9am-10pm, Sun 9am-6pm.

On the way to Vicksburg is the **Delta Blues Museum**, 627-6820, in the Carnegie Public Library at **Clarksdale**, 114 Delta St. Containing archives, books, records and instruments, the free museum is open Mon-Sat 9am-5pm. The museum hosts the **Sunflower River Blues and Gospel Festival** on the first w/end in Aug, with the best contemporary blues and gospel around. Free.

University of Mississippi, 232-7211. Self-guided tours of the 1848 campus, where a handful of the original buildings survive. Also on campus is the **Blues Archive 'N Center for the Study of Southern Culture,** 232-7753, which holds a huge amount of Southern music and literature, including B.B. Kings' personal collection of 10,000 recordings. Mon-Thurs, 8am-8pm, Fri 8am-5pm.

INFORMATION/TRAVEL
Tourist Information Center, in Courthouse Square, 234-4680, 9am-5pm Mon-Fri.
Greyhound, 2612B W Jackson, 234-0094/(800) 231-2222.

INTERNET ACCESS
Oxford Lafayette Library, 401 Bramlett Blvd, 234-5751, free.

VICKSBURG   Lincoln had a simple, but brilliant two-part strategy for winning the Civil War: blockade Southern cotton from reaching European ports, then split the South in two by driving a wedge down the Mississippi river. The wedge fell upon Vicksburg, the stronghold of the South's Mississippi defense. The campaign lasted more than a year and climaxed with 47 days of siege led by Gen. Ulysses S Grant. 'The Gibraltar of the South' finally fell to Union troops on Independence Day, July 4, 1863, giving the Union control of the entire Mississippi River. Not surprisingly, the city has many Civil War sites and antebellum mansions.

ACCOMMODATION/FOOD
Hillcrest Motel, 40 Hwy 80, 638-1491. S-$24.50, D-$30. Pool.
Ramada Hotel, 4216 Washington St, 638-5750. S/D-$46.
Scottish Inn, 3955 Hwy 80 East, ¼ mile from battleground, 638-5511. S/D-$39, includes $5 key deposit.
The Dock, East Clay St, ¼ mile from National Military Park, 634-0450. All-you-can-eat seafood buffet, $11.95.
Walnut Hills Restaurant, 1214 Adams St, 638-4910. Southern cooking, sandwiches,

soup, salads. From $3.50. Mon-Fri 11am-8:30pm. Look along **Washington St**, for cafes, bars and local flavour.

OF INTEREST
Old Courthouse Museum, 1008 Cherry St, 636-0741. Considered by many to be one of the finest Civil War museums in the South. Confederate troops operated from here during the siege of Vicksburg in 1863. Mon-Sat 8.30am-5pm, Sun 1.30pm-5pm, $3. Marble monuments, over 1,600 of them, recreate the fury of the battle at **Vicksburg National Military Park**, 636-0583. The Pantheon-like **Illinois monument** is the largest. Entrance and Visitors centre on Clay St, about 1½ miles E of town on I-20, take exit 4B. Open daily 8am-5pm. A Civil War soldier's life is described by actors who dress in period costume and fire muskets and cannons. Guides provide a 2 hr tour for $20, or you can rent a cassette, $4.50. $4 p/car to enter the park. 'Need a whole day if you plan to walk the park. Bring water.' The *U.S.S Cairo* **Museum**, 636-2199, also on park grounds, houses the Union gunboat of the same name, sunk by the Confederacy in 1862, and raised 100 years later. Open 8:30am-5pm, winter, 9:30am-6pm, summer. A climb up to the **Vicksburg Bluffs** yields a great view of the Mississippi. Among several impressive antebellum mansions to see are: **Cedar Grove**, 2200 Oak St, 636-1605; **McRaven House**, 1445 Harrison, 636-1663; **Balfour House**, 1002 Crawford St, 638-7113; and **Martha Vick House**, 1300 Grove St, 638-7036. Most of the homes are open Mon-Sat 9am-5pm, Sun 1pm-5pm, and cost $5.
Museum of Coca-Cola History and Memorabilia and the **Biedenharn Candy Co**, 1107 Washington, 638-6514. Where Coca-Cola was first bottled in 1894. Open Mon-Sat 9am-5pm, Sun 1:30-4:30, $2.25. In the summer you can get cokes in antique soda fountain. To tour the Mississippi around Vicksburg, call *Mississippi River Adventures* , 638-5443, 3 excursions daily departing from the pier at the end of Clay St, 10am, 2pm and 5pm. $17. S of Vicksburg, beautiful **Port Gibson** was considered by Union General Grant to be 'too beautiful to burn'. A good stop on the way to Natchez.

INFORMATION/TRAVEL
Vicksburg Convention and Visitors Bureau Clay St and Old Hwy 27 (exit 4B off I-20), 636-9421. Open daily 8am-5.30pm in summer.
Greyhound, 1295 S Frontage, 638-8389/(800) 231-2222. Daily 7am-8.30pm.

NATCHEZ Natchez is the Old South. An important cotton trading centre, the port generated some of the great fortunes of the 1850s. Cotton planters, brokers, and bankers settled in the small town named after the Indian tribe that first settled the area. Non-commercialised, Natchez is one of the finest historical towns in the US.

The favoured architectural style of the Old South was Classical Greek and Roman, as promoted by Palladio, Inigo Jones and Thomas Jefferson. Natchez families have carefully preserved their ancestral treasures. For the visitor, a block's walk off Main Street is a retreat to the splendour of the antebellum South.

ACCOMMODATION/FOOD
Days Inn, 109 US Hwy 61 S, 445-8291. S-$46, D-$51, XP-$5.
Natchez Inn, 218 John R Junkin Drive, 442-0221. From S/D-$40.
Camping: Natchez State Park, 230 Wickliff Rd, 442-2658, 10 miles N on US 61. Sites $7, $11 w/hook-up.
Traceway Campground, Hwy 61 North, 101 Log Cabin Ln, 8 miles from Natchez, 445-8278. Sites from $15, XP-$2.
Fat Mama's Tamales, 500 S Canal St, 442-4548. Mild or spicy tamales and other

regional specialities. Mon-Wed 11am-7pm, Thur-Sat 11am-9pm, Sun noon-5pm.
Mammy's Cupboard 555 Hwy 61 S, 445-8957. This unusual restaurant is shaped
like a woman and the dining area lies under her skirt! Soup, sandwiches on home-
made bread, and one hot Dixie lunch special every day. Everything under $10. Tue-
Sat 11am-2pm.

OF INTEREST

There are so many truly stunning homes here, that one can easily see how Natchez
housed one-sixth of America's pre-war millionaires. 30 homes and gardens are
thrown open to visitors during the Pilgrimages each spring and fall while 12 residences are kept open year-round. The most impressive homes are **Dunleith** (Greek
Revival style), **D'Evereaux** (Greek Revival), **Rosalie** (Brick Federal) and **Longwood**
(Moorish style—octagonal with a whimsical cupola). The Pilgrimage Tours
Headquarters, 446-6631, at the Canal St Depot, on the corner of Canal and State St,
sells tkts for tours of individual houses at $6 pp and has maps and literature on the
area. Tkts also available for 35 min horse-drawn carriage tour, $9, and 1hr bus tour,
$10 The once notorious **Natchez-Under-the-Hill**, 446-6345, was the old cotton port
and steamboat landing where gamblers, thieves and good-time girls scandalised
the local residents. More respectable shops and a restored saloon fill the area now,
against a spectacular backdrop of riverboats cruising along the Mississippi.
The Natchez Trace: *www.nps.gov/natc/index.htm*. Natchez is named for the Indian
tribe which lived in the area before the white man came. The Trace was the centre
of Indian activity from 1682-1729. An archeological site inside the city has uncovered the **Grand Village of the Natchez**. The Indians forged the Natchez Trace
which winds its way north to Nashville. A beautiful drive, the trace is also full of
history. **Emerald Mound**, 445-4211, one of the largest Indian Burial mounds is 1
mile off the pkwy, 11 miles NE of Natchez. Built in 1300, the mound covers 8 acres
and is the third largest such site in the US. Free. Davy Crockett travelled the trace,
and the Bowie knife was forged at a campfire along the way. In 1812 Old Hickory
(Andrew Jackson) led his troops against the British at New Orleans using the trace.
The Visitor's Center Museum at the trace, 842-1572, at marker 266, has artifacts
from the site. Open daily 8am-5pm. Free.
Elvis Presley was born along the Trace in the little town of **Tupelo**. Elvis gave a
benefit performance for his home town which raised enough money to create a
park out of the King's first 'shotgun' (read hovel) home. Tours through the home,
205 Elvis Presley Dr on Tupelo's east side, 841-1245 Mon-Sat 9am- 5.30pm, Sun
1pm-5pm. $1, museum, $4. Fans donated for the construction of a chapel in
Presley's honour on the site. (The **Tupelo McDonald's**, 372 S Gloster, is a temple to
the King.) The **Tupelo City Museum**, Hwy 6 W at James A Ball Park, 841-6438,
houses a large collection of Elvis memorabilia, as well as Civil War artifacts. Mon-
Fri 8am-4pm, w/end 1pm-5pm; $1.

INFORMATION/TRAVEL

Mississippi State Welcome Center, 640 S. Canal St, 442-5849, 8:30am-6pm daily.
Provides maps, lists of tours and homes.
Natchez Bus Station, 103 Lower Woodville Rd, 445-5291. Mon-Sat 8am-5.30pm.
Sun 2pm- 5pm. Vicksburg $14, New Orleans $35.
Natchez Chamber of Commerce, 108 S. Commerce, 445-4611. Mon-Fri 8am-5pm.
Natchez Convention and Visitors Bureau, 422 Main St, 446-6345. Mon-Fri 8am-
5pm.
Tupelo Convention and Visitors Bureau, 399 E Main St, 841-6521. Mon-Fri. 8am-
5pm, Sat 9am-5pm, Sun 1pm-5pm.

BILOXI   Although it's situated amongst the scenic white sand beaches of
the Gulf Coast, Biloxi's economic backbone has not been tourism—it's been

a shrimping community since the Civil War. In early June, the fleets are ritually blessed with bountiful shellfish harvests. At the harbour front down the end of Main Street and in the Back Bay area, you can watch the fishermen carry on with their lives, oblivious to the stares and snapshots of curious tourists.

At various times in the town's history, Biloxi has been under the flags of France, Spain, Britain, the West Florida Republic, the Confederacy and the US.

ACCOMMODATION

Beach Manor Motel, 662 Beach Blvd, 436-4361. Near Greyhound. D-$55.
Sea Gull Motel, 2778 Beach Blvd, about 7 miles from town, 896-4211. S/D-$35-$40, AC, TV, pool, near beach.
Camping: Southern Comfort Camping Resort, US 90 at 1766 Beach Blvd, 432-1700, 3 miles from town. Sites $18-24 for two, XP-$2. Across from beach and pier.

FOOD

Mary Mahoney's French House Restaurant, 138 Rue Magnolia, 1 block N of US 90, 374-0163. In a 1737 home, one of the oldest in America, not cheap, but excellent regional cuisine. Open 11am-10pm.
McElroy's Harbour House Restaurant, 695 Beach Blvd, 435-5001. Everything from local seafood to steaks and burgers, $5-$13. Bfast $3. Open daily 7am-10pm.

OF INTEREST

Beauvoir, 2244 Beach Blvd, 388-9074. The last home of Jefferson Davis, President of the Confederacy. See the library where he worked, and the Tomb of the Unknown Soldier of the Confederate States. Open daily 9am-5pm, $7.50. The famous cast iron 65-ft **Biloxi Lighthouse**, built in 1848 and one of the few remaining iron lighthouses, on US 90. Open by appointment only; call 435-6308. $2.
Other than Biloxi's white-sand **beaches**, the most enticing site along the coast is the **Gulf Islands National Seashore**. The seashore stretches into Florida, but there are 4 islands off the Mississippi coast which can be visited—West and East Ship, Petit Bois (pronounced Petty Boy), and **Horn Island**. The islands have a unique ecosystem. They are anchored by sea oats which keep the sand from washing away. The islands are also great places to bird-watch. The *Biloxi* Excursion Boat runs to Ship Island from the Pier four blocks E of the lighthouse. $16r/t, call 432-2197 for details. The main site there is **Fort Massachusetts**, a linchpin of Lincoln's effort to blockade the south.
Four miles from Biloxi, at the Visitors Center in **Ocean Springs**, 3500 Park Rd, 875-9057, shows a movie about the islands. Open 8:30am-5pm daily. Camping is allowed on East Ship, but there is no regular boat service to the island. You can camp out at the grounds near the visitors center in Davis Bayou. *www.nps.gov/guis/*
J L Scott Marine Education Center and Aquarium, 115 Beach Blvd (US Hwy 90), 374-5550. The state's largest public aquarium includes the 42,000 gallon 'Gulf of Mexico' tank which houses sharks, sea turtles and eels. Mon-Sat 9am-4pm. $3.50.

INFORMATION/TRAVEL

Biloxi Visitor Center, 710 Beach Blvd, 374-3105. Mon-Fri 8am-5pm, Sat 9am-5pm, Sun noon-5pm.
Greyhound , 166 Main St, 436-4335/(800) 231-2222.
Also visit *www.biloxi.com*.

INTERNET ACCESS

Digital Den, 2650 Beach Blvd, 594-1999, Mon-Thur 8am-10pm, Fri-Sat 'til 11pm, Sun 12-7. $2 for 15 min.

NORTH CAROLINA   *The Tarheel State*

American writer H L Mencken once described North Carolina as 'a valley of humility between two mountains of conceit.' Wedged between Virginia and South Carolina, this photogenic 'land of beginnings' was the birthplace of English America and powered flight. Its people just don't seem to think it would be polite to boast of all their blessings: a rich heritage, unspoiled beaches, rugged mountains, and a stimulating cultural and intellectual life.

Historically speaking, it's not your typical southern state. Few North Carolinians held slaves and a formidable anti-slavery sentiment reigned until the 1830s, when organised agitation by northerners provoked a defensive reaction. When shots were fired at Ft Sumter, Lincoln rallied troops against the Southern cause. Not until then did North Carolina quietly step out of the Union.

The tarheel state—first in the US in tobacco, textiles and furniture manufacturing—has attracted so many people that some native North Carolinians are now showing their true southern colours, grumbling about an influx of 'Yankees.' Northern companies have flocked into the area around Raleigh-Durham, the so-called 'research triangle,' helping to make it an internationally renowned centre for science and technology.

In just a few years, the triangle has grown to house more PhDs per capita than anywhere else in the country. Outside of the triangle, especially in the Asheville area, the economy has not benefitted from high tech employment. Areas of the Appalachian Mountains are still some of the poorest in the country.

The approachable North Carolinians have welcomed film-makers to their celluloid-friendly state, too. Parts of *Blue Velvet* were filmed here, as was the brutal tale of native Indians and colonists, *Last of the Mohicans*. From Cherokee history to modern folk-art, diversity is one of North Carolina's greatest attractions. Whether you want to enjoy the mountains or the shore, a small town's tranquility or a big town's bustle, you'll find it here. *www.yahoo.com/Regional/U_S__States/North Carolina/.*
The area code for Asheville is 828. For Charlotte it's 704, for Raleigh and Durham, it's 919. For the rest of the Coast, use 252.

THE COAST

THE COAST   The 'Outer Banks' is the name given to the three curving island strips that shelter the North Carolina mainland from the Atlantic surf, **Ocracoke**, **Hatteras** and **Bodie Island**. The sandy beaches are relatively unspoiled and offer some of the best surfcasting in the country.

At the northern end of the Banks, fishing gives way to flying. The first power-driven flight was made near **Kitty Hawk** at **Kill Devil Hills** on 17 December 1903 by brothers Orville and Wilbur Wright. Now in the Smithsonian Institution in Washington, their plane was aloft for 12 seconds and achieved a speed of 35 miles p/hr. Orville later explained that he and his brother had remained bachelors because they hadn't means to 'support a wife as well as an aeroplane.'

From the popular sands of Kitty Hawk, the Banks stretch south past the large dunes at **Jockey's Ridge** towards the primitive wildlife refuge of the country's first National Seashore, **Cape Hatteras**. The deadly currents and frequent hurricanes off the Cape earned this strip of land the nickname 'graveyard of the Atlantic.' A range of ships from tankers to U-Boats lie buried under its waters. Two hundred years ago, pirates used the currents to their advantage and, as legend has it, led unsuspecting ships to their doom by tying a lantern to a horse's neck and then walking up the beach towards Diamond Shoals. Before a navigator realized that the lighthouse he was steering by was moving, he had run aground. Cape Hatteras light-house, the tallest in the US (208 ft), now warns ships away.

Ocracoke Island was home to America's most famous pirate, Edward Teach, better known as Blackbeard. Teach enjoyed the protection of several colonial governors until he was finally done in by the Virginia Militia. Today, the hurricanes and treacherous waters seem to have scared off devel-opers; the Banks' abundant wildlife has largely been left in peace. **Pea Island National Wildlife Refuge**, 987-2394, shelters Great snow geese among others. Open daily 9am-4pm.

Further south along the coast the historical city of **Wilmington** is a good base for exploring the **Cape Fear River** and coastline. Don't let the movie scare you off—the name supposedly originates from sailors' battles with the strong currents at the river mouth.

ACCOMMODATION
Camping: There are 4 National Park Service campgrounds along the 125-mile national seashore. The first three, at Oregon Inlet (south of Nags Head), Cape Point and Frisco (on Cape Hatteras) are filled up on a first-come, first-served basis for $14. The fourth camp is on Ocracoke Island, which can only be reached by ferry. Sites on Ocracoke must be reserved in advance by calling 1-800-365-2267 or going to *www.reservations.nps.gov* and entering the password CAPE. All campgrounds open until Labor Day, Sep 2nd. Private campgrounds are also scattered around the area; for more info contact Hatteras National Seashore, 473-2111.
Kitty Hawk: Outer Banks Youth Hostel (HI-AYH), 1004 Kitty Hawk Rd, 261-2294. All-female dorms $15 AYH, $18 non-AYH. Private rooms $30 AYH, $35 non-AYH.
Ocracoke: The following motels are located off Rte 12. **Blackbeard's Lodge**, 928-3421. From D-$65; **Sand Dollar Motel**, 928-5571. From $60; and the **Pony Island Motel**, 928-4411. From $79 (10% discount for stays of a week or more). **Wilmington: The Glenn Hotel**, 16 Nathan St on Wrightsville Beach, (910) 256-2645. S-$35, D-$45-$50. Basic, shared bath, no AC.

FOOD
Not far from the Wright Brothers Memorial is **Kelly's Outer Banks Restaurant and Tavern**, 2316 S. Croatan Hwy, 441-4116. Seafood, steak, chicken, pasta. Open daily; food served 'til 10pm, bar open 'til midnight. At Nags Head Causeway is **RV's**, 441-4963. Sandwiches, steak, seafood. 4pm-10pm daily.

OF INTEREST
Just on the mainland side of the Banks lies the mysterious small town of **Manteo**. Three hundred Englishmen led by Sir Walter Raleigh built a small fort and settled near here in 1587. When an expedition from Britain set out for the colony three years later, they found that the entire community had disappeared without a trace. The only clue to their fate was the word 'Croatan' scratched onto a tree trunk. Rebuilt **Fort Raleigh**, 473-5772, and **Elizabeth Gardens**, 473-3234, mark the likely site of the lost colony. Both are located at the N end of Roanoke Island on Rte 64. Fort open 9am-dusk; free. Gardens open 9am-7pm, $4. *Lost Colony*, 473-2127, is an outdoor drama which tells the story of the Roanoke Island Colony late Jun-early

NOTES